One-Stop Internet Resources

Log on to twip.glencoe.com

ONLINE STUDY TOOLS

- Chapter Overviews
- Interactive Tutor
- Self-Check Quizzes
- E-Flashcards

ONLINE RESEARCH

- Student Web Activities
- Current Events
- Beyond the Textbook Features
- Web Resources
- State Resources

ONLINE STUDENT EDITION

- Complete Interactive Student Edition
- Textbook Updates

FOR TEACHERS

- Teacher Forum
- Web Activity Lesson Plans
- Literature Connections

5700

Honoring America

Flag Etiquette

Over the years, Americans have developed rules and customs concerning the use and display of the flag. One of the most important things every American should remember is to treat the flag with respect.

- The flag should be raised and lowered by hand and displayed only from sunrise to sunset. On special occasions, the flag may be displayed at night, but it should be illuminated.

- The flag may be displayed on all days, weather permitting, particularly on national and state holidays and on historic and special occasions.

- No flag may be flown above the American flag or to the right of it at the same height.

- The flag should never touch the ground or floor beneath it.

- The flag may be flown at half-staff by order of the president, usually to mourn the death of a public official.

- The flag may be flown upside down only to signal distress.

- The flag should never be carried flat or horizontally, but always carried aloft and free.

- When the flag becomes old and tattered, it should be destroyed by burning. According to an approved custom, the Union (stars on blue field) is first cut from the flag; then the two pieces, which no longer form a flag, are burned.

★ ★ ★ ★ ★ ★ ★ ★

The American's Creed

I believe in the United States of America as a Government of the people, by the people, for the people, whose just powers are derived from the consent of the governed; a democracy in a republic; a sovereign Nation of many sovereign States; a perfect union, one and inseparable; established upon those principles of freedom, equality, justice, and humanity for which American patriots sacrificed their lives and fortunes.

I therefore believe it is my duty to my Country to love it; to support its Constitution; to obey its laws; to respect its flag, and to defend it against all enemies.

The Pledge of Allegiance

I pledge allegiance to the Flag of the United States of America and to the Republic for which it stands, one Nation under God, indivisible, with liberty and justice for all.

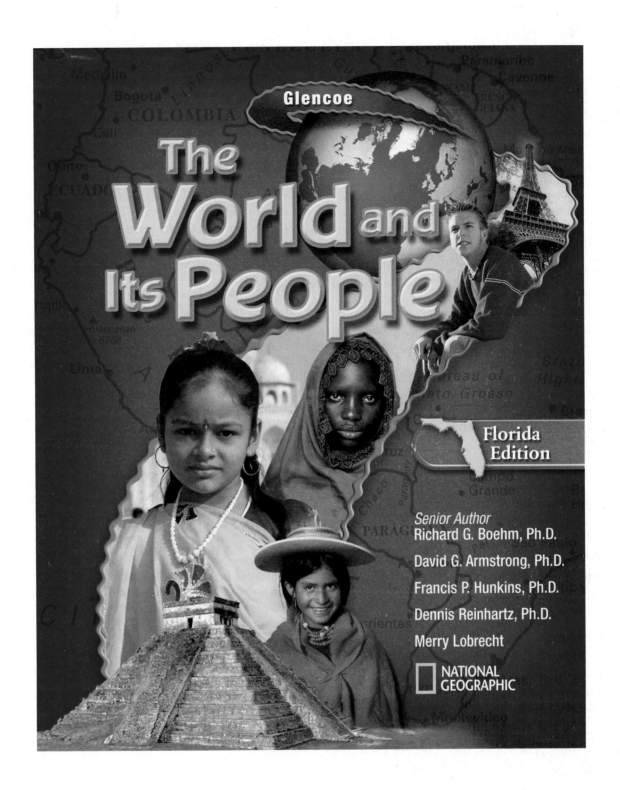

Glencoe

The World and Its People

Florida Edition

Senior Author
Richard G. Boehm, Ph.D.

David G. Armstrong, Ph.D.

Francis P. Hunkins, Ph.D.

Dennis Reinhartz, Ph.D.

Merry Lobrecht

NATIONAL GEOGRAPHIC

McGraw Hill Glencoe

New York, New York   Columbus, Ohio   Chicago, Illinois   Peoria, Illinois   Woodland Hills, California

About the Authors

NATIONAL GEOGRAPHIC

The National Geographic Society, founded in 1888 for the increase and diffusion of geographic knowledge, is the world's largest nonprofit scientific and educational organization. The Society uses sophisticated communication technologies to convey geographic knowledge to a worldwide membership. The School Publishing Division supports the Society's mission by developing innovative educational programs—ranging from traditional print materials to multimedia programs including CD-ROMS, videos, and software.

David G. Armstrong

David G. Armstrong, Ph.D., served as Dean of the School of Education at the University of North Carolina at Greensboro. A social studies education specialist with additional advanced training in geography, Dr. Armstrong was educated at Stanford University, University of Montana, and University of Washington.

Merry Lobrecht

Merry Lobrecht is the Social Studies Curriculum Coordinator for the Humble ISD. She was the recipient of both the 2001 National Council for Geographic Education Distinguished Teacher Achievement Award and the Texas Council of Social Studies Texas Alliance for Geographic Distinguished Teacher Award for 2001.

SENIOR AUTHOR
Richard G. Boehm

Richard G. Boehm, Ph.D., was one of seven authors of *Geography for Life,* national standards in geography, prepared under Goals 2000: Educate America Act. In 1991 he received the George J. Miller award from the National Council for Geographic Education (NCGE) for distinguished service to geographic education. He has twice won the *Journal of Geography* award for best article. He presently holds the Jesse H. Jones Distinguished Chair in Geographic Education at Southwest Texas State University in San Marcos, Texas.

Francis P. Hunkins

Francis P. Hunkins, Ph.D., is Professor of Education at the University of Washington. He began his career as a teacher in Massachusetts. He received his master's degree in education from Boston University and his doctorate from Kent State University with a major in general curriculum and a minor in geography. Dr. Hunkins has written numerous books and articles.

Dennis Reinhartz

Dennis Reinhartz, Ph.D., is Professor of History and Russian at the University of Texas at Arlington. A specialist in Russian and East European history, as well as in the history of cartography and historical geography, Dr. Reinhartz has written numerous books in these fields. He is a consultant to the U.S. State and Justice Departments and to the U.S. Holocaust Memorial Museum in Washington, D.C.

 Glencoe

The McGraw·Hill Companies

Printed in the United States of America

Send all inquiries to:
Glencoe/McGraw-Hill
8787 Orion Place
Columbus, Ohio 43240-4027

ISBN 0-07-865480-7 (Student Edition)   ISBN 0-07-865481-5 (Teacher Wraparound Edition)
2 3 4 5 6 7 8   027/055   09 08 07 06 05

Florida Advisory Board

Consultants and Reviewers

Academic Consultants

Karl Barbir, Ph.D.
Professor of History
Sienna College
Loudonville, New York

Brock Brown, Ph.D.
Associate Professor of Geography
and Planning
Southwest Texas State University
San Marcos, Texas

Thomas H. Buckley, Ph.D.
Professor of History
University of Tulsa
Tulsa, Oklahoma

Frank de Varona
Visiting Associate Professor
Department of Curriculum and Instruction
Florida International University
Miami, Florida

Ramesh Dhussa, Ph.D.
Assistant Professor of Geography
Drake University
Des Moines, Iowa

Charles A. Endress, Ph.D.
Professor of History
Angelo State University
San Angelo, Texas

Dana A. Farnham, Ph.D.
Professor of Anthropology
Lincoln College at Normal
Normal, Illinois

Anne Hardgrove, Ph.D.
Assistant Professor of History
University of Texas at San Antonio
San Antonio, Texas

Ken Hendrickson, Ph.D.
Professor of History
Sam Houston State University
Huntsville, Texas

Terry G. Jordan, Ph.D.
Professor of Geography
University of Texas at Austin
Austin, Texas

Monica Najar, Ph.D.
Assistant Professor of History
Lehigh University
Bethlehem, Pennsylvania

Reverend Marvin O'Dell
Faith Baptist Church
Thousand Oaks, California

Rex Peebles
Dean of Social and Behavioral Sciences
Austin Community College
Austin, Texas

Bernard Reich, Ph.D.
Professor of Political Science and
International Affairs
George Washington University
Washington, D.C.

FOLDABLES **Dinah Zike**
Educational Consultant
Dinah-Might Activities, Inc.
San Antonio, Texas

Reading Consultants

Carol M. Santa, Ph.D.
CRISS: Project Developer
Director of Education
Montana Academy
Kalispell, Montana

Bonnie Valdes
Master CRISS Trainer
Project CRISS
Largo, Florida

Steve Qunell
Social Studies Instructor
Montana Academy
Kalispell, Montana

Teacher Reviewers

Diana Bradford
Scobee Middle School
San Antonio, Texas

Kenneth E. Bridges
Huffines Middle School
Lewisville, Texas

Rosemary Conroy
St. Luke School
Shoreline, Washington

Nancy Eudy
Bammel Middle School
Houston, Texas

Carolyn Grogan
Mesa Elementary School
Somis, California

Pamela Kniffin
Navasota Intermediate School
Navasota, Texas

Sarah L. Matt
Irma Marsh Middle School
Fort Worth, Texas

Karen Muir
George Fox Middle School
Pasadena, Maryland

David Nienkamp
Sandy Creek Junior/Senior High School
Fairfield, Nebraska

Susan Pearson
The Academy For Science and
Foreign Languages
Huntsville, Alabama

Megan Phelps
Moorpark Community College
Moorpark, California

Julie Scott
East Valley Middle School
Spokane, Washington

Michael Yell
Hudson Middle School
Hudson, Wisconsin

Marsha Yoder
Lawton Chiles Middle Academy
Lakeland, Florida

A Note From the Authors

Welcome to World Geography and *The World and Its People*. We have written this text with several goals in mind. First, we want you to succeed in this course. We also want you to succeed on the FCAT, Florida's Comprehensive Assessment Test. To help you, we have noted the major Sunshine State Standards covered by each lesson. We have also provided FCAT Practice symbols and standards throughout the text. As you study world geography, pay attention to this information and be prepared to become a successful student!

This section of your book contains the following:

Sunshine State Standards
    for World Geography **FL8**

How Does *The World and Its People*
    Help Me Learn the Standards? **FL19**

Keys to Succeeding on the FCAT **FL20**

How Does *The World and Its People*
    Help Me Succeed on the FCAT? **FL27**

Sunshine State Standards for World Geography

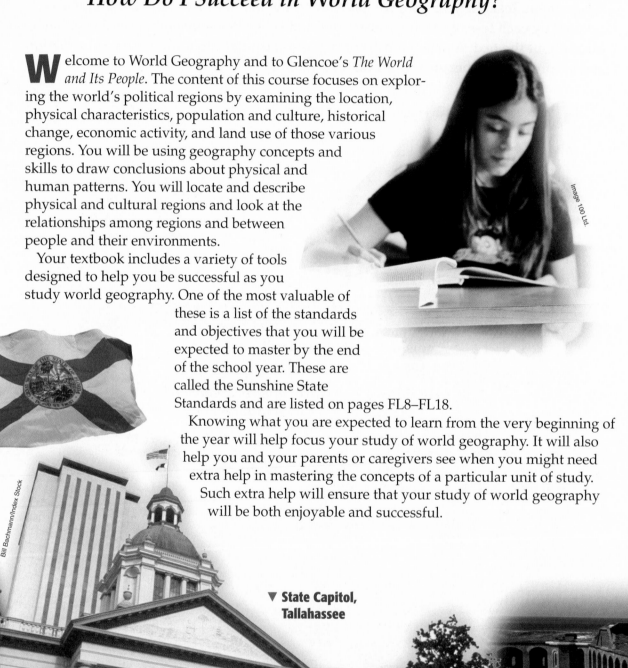

A Guide for Students and Parents

How Do I Succeed in World Geography?

Welcome to World Geography and to Glencoe's *The World and Its People*. The content of this course focuses on exploring the world's political regions by examining the location, physical characteristics, population and culture, historical change, economic activity, and land use of those various regions. You will be using geography concepts and skills to draw conclusions about physical and human patterns. You will locate and describe physical and cultural regions and look at the relationships among regions and between people and their environments.

Your textbook includes a variety of tools designed to help you be successful as you study world geography. One of the most valuable of these is a list of the standards and objectives that you will be expected to master by the end of the school year. These are called the Sunshine State Standards and are listed on pages FL8–FL18.

Knowing what you are expected to learn from the very beginning of the year will help focus your study of world geography. It will also help you and your parents or caregivers see when you might need extra help in mastering the concepts of a particular unit of study. Such extra help will ensure that your study of world geography will be both enjoyable and successful.

▼ **State Capitol, Tallahassee**

Image 100 Ltd.

Bill Bachmann/Index Stock

What Are the Sunshine State Standards?

The Florida State Board of Education approved the Sunshine State Standards in 1996. The purpose of the standards is to provide you, the student, with expectations for achievement in Florida. These standards spell out what you should learn in language arts, mathematics, foreign language, the arts (dance, music, theater, and visual arts), health, and physical education. These standards represent the knowledge and skills you need to achieve success in the world of work or college.

Why Do the Sunshine State Standards Matter to Me?

The Sunshine State Standards are the things you should learn and be able to do as you take the course. The standards are specific for each grade and subject. Your teachers base their lessons and tests on the Sunshine State Standards.

So, to be successful in this course, you may want to read over the standards with your parents or caregivers. (These standards are listed on pages FL8-FL18.) Although some of the names and terms may not be familiar to you at first, you and your family can outline some steps you can take to achieve proficiency. As you take this course, review the standards from time to time to help the things you learn fall into place.

What Is Included on the Following Pages?

Sunshine State Standards for World Geography

- Pages FL8-FL18 include a listing of all of the Sunshine State Standards for this course.

- Turn to page FL19 to see how Glencoe's *The World and Its People* will help you learn the standards and be successful in this course.

Keys to Succeeding on the FCAT

- Page FL20 includes an explanation of the Florida Comprehensive Assessment Test that you will take at the end of the school year.

- Turn to page FL27 to see how Glencoe's *The World and Its People* will help you succeed on the FCAT.

▼ **Fort Jefferson, Dry Tortugas National Park**

Greig Cranna/Index Stock

On the following pages you will find a listing of the Florida Sunshine State Standards. The Sunshine State Standards are the things you should learn and be able to do as you complete this world geography course. Read through these standards with your parents or caregivers to help you become successful in this course. Also review these standards from time to time to help the things you learn fall into place.

History

1. *The student understands historical chronology and the historical perspective.*

SS.A.1.3.1: The student understands how patterns, chronology, sequencing (including cause and effect), and the identification of historical periods are influenced by frames of reference.

Grade 6

1. The student understands that historical events are subject to different interpretations.
2. The student understands chronology (for example, knows how to construct and label a timeline of events).

Grade 7

1. The student extends and refines understanding that historical events are subject to different interpretations (for example, patterns, chronology, sequencing including cause and effect and the identification of historical periods).

SS.A.1.3.2: The student knows the relative value of primary and secondary sources and uses this information to draw conclusions from historical sources such as data in charts, tables, graphs.

Grade 6

1. The student distinguishes between fact and opinion.
2. The student distinguishes between primary and secondary sources of information.
3. The student interprets data from charts, tables, and graphs.

Grade 7

1. The student draws appropriate conclusions based on data from charts, tables, and graphs.
2. The student knows relative value of primary and secondary sources.

SS.A.1.3.3: The student knows how to impose temporal structure on historical narratives.

Grade 6

Content addressed in SS.A.1.3.1.

Grade 7

Content addressed in SS.A.1.3.1.

2. *The student understands the world from its beginning to the time of the Renaissance.*

SS.A.2.3.1: The student understands how language, ideas, and institutions of one culture can influence others (e.g., through trade, exploration, and immigration).

Grade 6

1. The student understands ways language, ideas, and institutions of one culture can influence other cultures (for example, trade, religions in the Eastern Hemisphere).

Grade 7

1. The student extends and refines understanding of ways language, ideas, and institutions of one culture can influence other cultures (for example, exploration, immigration, trade in the Western Hemisphere).

SS.A.2.3.2: The student knows how major historical developments have had an impact on the development of civilizations.

Grade 6

1. The student knows ways major historical developments have influenced selected groups over time (for example, the rise and spread of the Muslim religion).

Grade 7

1. The student extends and refines knowledge of ways major historical developments have influenced selected groups over time (for example, the components essential for the development of civilization, such as division of labor, technology, government, writing, calendar in the Western hemisphere).

SS.A.2.3.3: The student understands important technological developments and how they influenced human society.

Grade 6

1. The student understands ways technological factors have influenced selected groups over time (for example, agriculture in the Eastern hemisphere).

▼ **Boardwalk to beach, Seaside**

Richard Berenholtz/CORBIS

Grade 7

1. The student extends and refines understanding of ways technological factors have influenced selected groups over time (for example, transportation in the Western hemisphere.)

SS.A.2.3.4: The student understands the impact of geographical factors on the historical development of civilizations.

Grade 6

1. The student understands ways geographical factors have influenced selected groups (for example, the development of the Tibetan civilization in the Himalayan Mountains).

Grade 7

1. The student extends and refines understanding of ways geographical factors have influenced selected groups (for example, Native Americans in the Great Plains).

SS.A.2.3.5: The student knows significant historical leaders who shaped the development of early cultures (e.g., military, political, and religious leaders in various civilizations).

Grade 6

1. The student knows significant aspects of the lives and accomplishments of selected men and women in the historical period of ancient civilizations (for example, Confucius, Buddha).

Grade 7

1. The student knows significant aspects of the lives and accomplishments of selected men and women in the historical period of ancient civilizations (for example, Alexander the Great, Hammurabi's development of legal codes, Moses).

SS.A.2.3.6: The student knows the major events that shaped the development of various cultures (e.g., the spread of agrarian societies, population movements, technological and cultural innovation, and the emergence of new population centers).

Grade 6

1. The student knows major events that shaped the development of various cultures (for example, development and spread of major religions).

Grade 7

1. The student refines and extends knowledge of major events that shaped the development of various cultures (for example, development of legal codes).

SS.A.2.3.7: The student knows significant achievements in art and architecture in various urban areas and communities to the time of the Renaissance (e.g., the Hanging Gardens of Babylon, pyramids in Egypt, temples in ancient Greece, bridges and aqueducts in ancient Rome, changes in European art and architecture between the Middle Ages and the High Renaissance).

Grade 6

1. The student knows examples of significant achievements in art and architecture (for example, Chinese and Japanese ink drawing, temple complexes in Southeast Asia).

Grade 7

1. The student knows examples of significant achievements in art and architecture (for example, the Hanging Gardens of Babylon, pyramids in Egypt, bridges and aqueducts in ancient Rome, Gothic cathedrals in Medieval Europe).

SS.A.2.3.8: The student knows the political, social, and economic institutions that characterized the significant aspects of Eastern and Western civilizations.

Grade 6

1. The student knows roles of political, economic, and social institutions in the development of selected civilizations (for example, caste system in India).

Grade 7

1. The student extends and refines knowledge of roles of political, economic, and social institutions in the development of selected civilizations (for example, the Catholic Church in Europe).

3. *The student understands Western and Eastern civilizations since the Renaissance.*

SS.A.3.3.1: The student understands ways in which cultural characteristics have been transmitted from one society to another (e.g., through art, architecture, language, other artifacts, traditions, beliefs, values, and behaviors).

Grade 6

1. The student understands ways in which cultural characteristics have been transmitted from one society to another (for example, through art, architecture, language, other artifacts).

Grade 7

1. The student extends and refines understanding of ways in which cultural characteristics have been transmitted from one society to another (for example, through traditions, beliefs, values, behaviors).

▼ **Florida Marlins baseball team**

SS.A.3.3.2: The student understands the historical events that have shaped the development of cultures throughout the world.

Grade 6

1. The student understands selected historical events that have shaped the development of selected cultures (for example, the spread of Communism in Asia).

Grade 7

1. The student understands selected historical events that have shaped the development of selected cultures throughout the world (for example, the spread of humanism during the Renaissance).

SS.A.3.3.3: The student knows how physical and human geographic factors have influenced major historical events and movements.

Grade 6

1. The student knows ways geographical factors have influenced selected cultures (for example, the Great Wall of China, major river systems in the Eastern hemisphere).

Grade 7

1. The student extends and refines understanding of ways geographical factors have influenced major historical events and movements in selected cultures (for example, mountain ranges in Europe and the Americas).

SS.A.3.3.4: The student knows significant historical leaders who have influenced the course of events in Eastern and Western civilizations since the Renaissance.

Grade 6

1. The student knows aspects of the lives and accomplishments of significant men and women in selected regions since the Renaissance (for example, Ghandi, Mao Zedong, Mother Teresa).

Grade 7

1. The student extends and refines knowledge of aspects of the lives and accomplishments of significant men and women in selected regions since the Renaissance (for example, Christopher Columbus, Simon Bolivar).

SS.A.3.3.5: The student understands the differences between institutions of Eastern and Western civilizations (e.g., differences in governments, social traditions and customs, economic systems and religious institutions).

Grade 6

1. The student understands selected aspects of political, economic, and social institutions in selected cultures in Eastern civilizations (for example, governments, social traditions and customs, economic systems, religious institutions).

▼ **Tomato crop**

Creatas

Grade 7

1. The student understands selected aspects of political, economic, and social institutions in selected cultures in Western civilizations (for example, governments, social traditions and customs, economic systems, religious institutions).

2. The student understands the differences between political, economic, and social institutions of Eastern and Western civilizations.

Geography

1. *The student understands the world in spatial terms.*

SS.B.1.3.1: The student uses various map forms (including thematic maps) and other geographic representations, tools, and technologies to acquire, process, and report geographic information including patterns of land use, connections between places, and patterns and processes of migration and diffusion.

Grade 6

1. The student knows various map forms and other geographic representations (for example, maps, globes, aerial photographs, satellite-produced images).

2. The student uses various map forms to acquire information (for example, location, distance, direction, scale, symbols).

3. The student uses various map forms to process and report geographic information (for example, patterns of land use, connections between places, patterns and processes of migration and diffusion).

Grade 7

1. The student extends and refines knowledge of various map forms and other geographic representations (for example, map projections, Geographic Information Systems technologies).

2. The student extends and refines use of various map forms and other geographic representations to acquire, process, and report geographic information (for example, patterns of population, economics, rainfall, vegetation, landforms).

SS.B.1.3.2: The student uses mental maps to organize information about people, places, and environments.

Grade 6

1. The student develops and uses mental maps of selected regions (for example, from memory the student identifies the continent on which a country is located).

Grade 7

1. The student extends and refines ability to use mental maps of selected regions (for example, mountain chains, bodies of water).

SS.B.1.3.3: The student knows the social, political, and economic divisions on Earth's surface.

Grade 6

1. The student understands that people create social, political, and economic geographic divisions of the Earth's surface (for example, national borders).
2. The student knows selected social, political, and economic divisions in selected regions (for example, national borders in the Eastern hemisphere).

Grade 7

1. The student understands the social, political, and economic divisions in selected regions, (for example, national borders in the Western hemisphere).

SS.B.1.3.4: The student understands ways factors such as culture and technology influence the perception of places and regions.

Grade 6

1. The student understands ways judgments about cultural characteristics and degree of technological development influence perception of places and regions (for example, the designation of "third-world country").

Grade 7

1. The student extends and refines understanding of ways judgments about cultural characteristics and degree of technological development influence perception of places and regions.

SS.B.1.3.5: The student knows ways in which the spatial organization of a society changes over time.

Grade 6

1. The student knows ways in which the spatial organization of a society changes over time (for example, urban sprawl as a result of industrialization).

Grade 7

1. The student extends and refines knowledge of ways in which the spatial organization of a society changes over time (for example, suburbanization in developed countries).

SS.B.1.3.6: The student understands ways in which regional systems are interconnected.

Grade 6

1. The student knows physical and human criteria used to define regions (for example, hemispheres, mountains, deserts, countries, city boundaries, school districts).

Grade 7

1. The student knows ways selected regions are interconnected and interdependent (for example, less-developed regions supplying raw materials and developed regions supplying manufactured goods).

SS.B.1.3.7: The student understands the spatial aspects of communication and transportation systems.

Grade 6

1. The student understands spatial aspects of communication and transportation systems in selected regions (for example, time required to travel and communicate over distances reduced by technological developments).

Grade 7

1. The student extends and refines understanding of spatial aspects of the communication and transportation systems in selected regions (time required to travel and communicate over distances reduced by technological developments).

2. *The student understands the interactions of people and the physical environment.*

SS.B.2.3.1: The student understands the patterns and processes of migration and diffusion throughout the world.

Grade 6

1. The student knows examples of migration patterns and processes in selected regions.

Grade 7

1. The student understands patterns and processes of migration and diffusion in selected regions.

SS.B.2.3.2: The student knows the human and physical characteristics of different places in the world and how these characteristics change over time.

Grade 6

1. The student knows ways physical and human characteristics of selected regions have changed over time (for example, aftereffects of volcanic activity, development of cities).

Grade 7

1. The student extends and refines knowledge of ways physical and human characteristics of selected regions have changed over time (for example, tree clearing in rain forests).

▼ **Valencia orange grove**

SS.B.2.3.3: The student understands ways cultures differ in their use of similar environments and resources.

Grade 6

1. The student understands ways various cultures use similar resources and environments (for example, differing methods of irrigation).

Grade 7

1. The student extends and refines understanding of ways various cultures use similar resources and environments (for example, terracing of mountain sides in the Andes and using mountainous areas for pasture in other areas).

SS.B.2.3.4: The student understands ways the landscape and society change as a consequence of shifting from a dispersed to a concentrated settlement form.

Grade 6

Content addressed in SS.A.4.3.1. [The student knows the factors involved in the development of cities and industries (e.g., religious needs, the need for military protection, the need for a marketplace, changing spatial patterns, and geographical factors for location such as transportation and food supply).]

Grade 7

Content addressed in SS.A.4.3.1. [The student knows the factors involved in the development of cities and industries (e.g., religious needs, the need for military protection, the need for a marketplace, changing spatial patterns, and geographical factors for location such as transportation and food supply).]

SS.B.2.3.5: The student understands the geographical factors that affect the cohesiveness and integration of countries.

Grade 6

1. The student understands the various geographic factors that may divide or unite a country (for example, mountains, rivers, valleys).

Grade 7

1. The student extends and refines understanding of the various geographic factors that may divide or unite a country.

Jerry Driendl Photography /
Panoramic Images

SS.B.2.3.6: The student understands the environmental consequences of people changing the physical environment in various world locations.

Grade 6

1. The student understands environmental consequences of people changing the physical environment in selected regions (effects of deforestation such as reduction in biodiversity).

Grade 7

1. The student extends and refines understanding of environmental consequences of people changing the physical environment in selected regions (for example, effects of ozone depletion, climate change).

SS.B.2.3.7: The student knows how various human systems throughout the world have developed in response to conditions in the physical environment.

Grade 6

1. The student knows examples of human systems that have been developed in response to opportunities afforded by the environment (for example, settlements in valleys, transportation on waterways).

Grade 7

1. The student extends and refines knowledge of examples of ways the environment affects human systems in selected regions (for example, natural barriers that become boundaries).

SS.B.2.3.8: The student knows world patterns of resource distribution and utilization.

Grade 6

1. The student knows patterns of resource distribution and use in selected regions (for example, distribution of arable land).

Grade 7

1. The student knows patterns of resource distribution and use in selected regions (for example, mineral rights).

SS.B.2.3.9: The student understands ways the interaction between physical and human systems affects current conditions on Earth.

Grade 6

Content addressed in SS.B.2.3.6 and SS.B.2.3.7.

Grade 7

Content addressed in SS.B.2.3.6 and SS.B.2.3.7.

Civics

2. *The student understands the role of the citizen in American democracy.*

SS.C.2.3.7: The student understands current issues involving rights that affect local, national, or international political, social, and economic systems.

Grade 6

1. The student understands ways current issues affect political, social, and economic systems in selected regions.

Grade 7

1. The student extends and refines knowledge of ways current issues affect political, social, and economic systems in selected regions.

◀ **Ernest Hemingway House, Key West**

Economics

2. *The student understands the characteristics of different economic systems and institutions.*

SS.D.2.3.1: The student understands ways production and distribution decisions are determined in the United States economy and how these decisions compare to those made in market, tradition-based, command, and mixed economic systems.

Grade 6

1. The student understands elements of basic economic systems commonly found in selected regions (for example, tradition-based and command economies in the Eastern hemisphere).

Grade 7

1. The student extends and refines understanding of basic economic systems commonly found in selected regions (for example, market and mixed economies in the Western hemisphere).

SS.D.2.3.2: The student understands that relative prices and how they affect people's decisions are the means by which a market system provides answers to the three basic economic questions: What goods and services will be produced? How will they be produced? Who will buy them?

Grade 6

Content addressed in seventh and eighth grades.

Grade 7

1. The student applies three basic economic questions to various economic systems in selected regions (What goods and services will be produced? How will they be produced? Who will buy them?).

Anchorage, Dry Tortuga National Park ▶

How Does *The World and Its People* Help Me Learn the Standards?

Every section, or lesson, in Glencoe's *The World and Its People* text has been marked to show the major Sunshine State Standards covered in the lesson. For example, look at page 368, the first section of Chapter 13, shown at right. You will see what looks like a code, **SS.A.3.3.2.** This is actually one of the major standards covered in that section. What does it mean? This reference tells you the subject, category, and level for the Sunshine State Standards covered in the section. For example:

SS.A.3.3.2:

SS   means Social Studies

A   means history (rather than geography, civics and government, or economics)

3   means the category of knowledge, such as world history since the Renaissance

3   means that this is middle-school level

2   means the specific subtopic of the category, in this case the development of world cultures

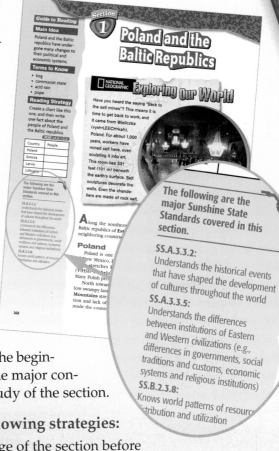

Glencoe has placed these Sunshine State Standards at the beginning of every lesson in this textbook to inform you of the major concepts that you should know after you complete your study of the section.

How should you use these standards? Try the following strategies:

- Read through the standards identified on the first page of the section before you begin your study of the section.
- Become acquainted with the standards so that you will know what information to concentrate on as you study the section.
- Keep these standards in mind as you read the section. Take notes on the key information you find.
- Review these standards after you complete the lesson to see if you have learned what you need to know.

Murry Sill /Index Stock

Keys to Succeeding on the FCAT

What Is the FCAT?

The FCAT is a short way to say Florida's Comprehensive Assessment Test. The FCAT is a series of tests administered by the state of Florida. All Florida students in grades 3 through 10 must take the FCAT. Currently, the subjects that are tested by the FCAT include the Language Arts (Reading and Writing), Mathematics, and Science.

Why Does the FCAT Matter to Me?

As a Florida student, you will be taking the FCAT. Your scores will be delivered to your school district, your school, and your parents or caregivers. All Florida public schools are required to receive a report card on how well you and the other students mastered the Sunshine State Standards that are tested on the FCAT. Your score on the FCAT will be used to determine if you should be promoted to the next grade level or if you should graduate from high school with a standard high school diploma.

▼ Jacksonville riverside area

Glencoe's **The World and Its People** *will help you practice for many of the Sunshine State Standards tested on the FCAT. Those standards are listed below by subject area. Become familiar with these standards as you take this course. This knowledge will help you master the standards and succeed on the FCAT.*

Language Arts

Reading Content Assessed by the FCAT

LA.A.1.3.2: The student uses a variety of strategies to analyze words and text, draw conclusions, use context and word structure clues, and recognize organizational patterns.

Grade 6
1. The student uses context and word structure clues to interpret words and ideas in text.
2. The student makes inferences and generalizations about what is read.
3. The student uses strategies such as graphic organizers and note-making to clarify meaning and to illustrate organizational pattern of texts.

Grade 7
1. The student uses context and word structure clues to interpret words and ideas in text.
2. The student makes inferences and generalizations about what is read.
3. The student uses strategies such as graphic organizers and note-making to illustrate organizational pattern of texts.
4. The student compares and contrasts similar information contained in different text selections.

LA.A.2.2.7: The student recognizes the use of comparison and contrast in a text.

Stuart Westmorland/Index Stock5

LA.A.2.3.1: The student determines the main idea or essential message in a text and identifies relevant details and facts and patterns of organization.

Grade 6

1. The student determines a text's major ideas and how those ideas are supported with details.
2. The student draws inferences and supports them with text evidence and experience (for example, conclusions or generalizations).
3. The student paraphrases and summarizes text to recall, inform, or organize ideas.
4. The student analyzes ways writers organize and present ideas (for example, through chronology, comparison-contrast, cause-effect).

Grade 7

1. The student extends the expectations of the sixth grade with increasingly complex reading texts and assignments and tasks (for example, main ideas, supporting details, inferences, summarizing, analysis of organization and presentation of ideas).

LA.A.2.3.2: The student identifies the author's purpose and/or point of view in a variety of texts and uses the information to construct meaning.

Grade 6

1. The student discusses the meaning and role of point of view in a variety of texts.

2. The student states the author's purpose and relates it to specific details from the text.

Grade 7

1. The student understands ways the author's perspective or point of view affects a text.
2. The student states the author's purpose and relates it to specific details from the text. (Includes LA.A.2.2.3: The student recognizes when a text is primarily intended to persuade.)

LA.A.2.3.5: The student locates, organizes, and interprets written information for a variety of purposes, including classroom research, collaborative decision making, and performing a school or real-world task.

Grade 6

1. The student forms and revises questions for investigations (including but not limited to questions arising from readings).
2. The student uses print and electronic sources to locate books, documents, and articles.
3. The student organizes and interprets information from a variety of sources for a school or real-world task.

Grade 7

1. The student extends previously learned knowledge and skills of the sixth grade with increasingly complex texts and assignments and tasks (for example, forming

▼ **South Beach, Miami**

BEACON

questions for readings, using print and electronic sources to locate information, organizing information from a variety of sources for real-world tasks). (Includes: Benchmark LA.A.2.3.6: The student uses a variety of reference materials, including indexes, magazines, newspapers, and journals, and tools, including card catalogs and computer catalogs, to gather information for research topics. Benchmark LA.A.2.3.7: The student synthesizes and separates collected information into useful components using a variety of techniques, such as source cards, note cards, spreadsheets, and outlines.)

LA.A.2.3.8: The student checks the validity and accuracy of information obtained from research, in such ways as differentiating fact and opinion, identifying strong vs. weak arguments, recognizing that personal values influence the conclusions an author draws.

Grade 6

1. The student distinguishes between fact and opinion.
2. The student examines texts for identification of strong versus weak arguments.
3. The student uses resources, such as expert opinion, to check the validity of information obtained from research.
4. The student identifies and examines the influence of personal values on the conclusions an author draws.

Grade 7

1. The student cites, examines, and discusses the use of and differences between fact and opinion within a text.
2. The student knows differences between strong versus weak arguments and relevant and irrelevant information in reading selections.
3. The student understands the use of comparison and contrast in a text.
4. The student understands the influence of personal values on the conclusions an author draws.

LA.E.2.2.1: The student recognizes cause-and-effect relationships in literary texts.

LA.E.2.3.1: The student understands how character and plot development, point of view, and tone are used in various selections to support a central conflict or story line.

Grade 6

1. The student knows the motives for a character's actions.
2. The student knows the events in the plot related to the central conflict.
3. The student knows the point of view of a literary work and how it affects the story line.
4. The student knows how cause-and-effect relationships affect the development of a plot.

Getty Images

FL23

Grade 7

1. The student knows the reasons for a character's actions.
2. The student knows the events in the plot related to the central conflict.
3. The student knows ways cause-and-effect relationships affect the development of a plot.
4. The student knows ways the tone of a literary work is used to support its story line.
5. The student knows and describes from various characters' points of view a situation related to the central conflict in a literary work. (Includes: Benchmark LA.E.1.3.2: The student recognizes complex elements of plot, including setting, character development, conflicts, and resolutions.)

Writing Content Assessed by the FCAT

LA.B.1.3.2: The student drafts and revises writing that

Grade 6

1. focuses on a central idea or topic (for example, excluding loosely related, extraneous, or repetitious information).
2. uses an appropriate organizational pattern having a beginning, middle, end and transitional devices.
3. demonstrates a commitment to and an involvement with the subject that engages the reader.

4. demonstrates a command of the language including precise word choice and use of appropriate figurative language.
5. uses an effective organizational pattern and substantial support to achieve a sense of completeness or wholeness (for example, considering audience, sequencing events, choosing effective words; using specific details to clarify meaning).
6. proofreads writing to correct convention errors in mechanics, usage, and punctuation, using dictionaries, handbooks, and other resources, including teacher or peers, as appropriate.
7. revises draft to further develop a piece of writing by adding, deleting, and rearranging ideas and details.

Grade 7

1. focuses on a central idea or topic (for example, excluding loosely related, extraneous, or repetitious information).
2. uses devices to develop relationships among ideas (for example, transitional devices; paragraphs that show a change in time, idea, or place; cause-and-effect relationships).
3. uses supporting ideas, details, and facts from a variety of sources to develop and elaborate topics.
4. demonstrates a commitment to and an involvement with the subject that engages the reader.
5. demonstrates a command of the language (including but not limited to precise word choice, appropriate figurative language).
6. uses an effective organizational pattern and substantial support to achieve a sense of completeness or wholeness (for example, considering audience, sequencing events, choosing effective words; using specific details to clarify meaning).

7. proofreads writing to correct convention errors in mechanics, usage, and punctuation, using dictionaries, handbooks, and other resources, including teacher or peers, as appropriate.

8. analyzes and revises draft to further develop a piece of writing by adding or deleting details and explanations; clarifying difficult passages; and rearranging words, sentences, and paragraphs to improve meaning.

▼ Key Biscayne, Florida

Buddy Mays/Words & Pictures/PictureQuest

Mathematics

MA.A.1.3.3: The student understands concrete and symbolic representations of rational numbers and irrational numbers in real-world situations.

MA.B.1.3.4: The student constructs, interprets, and uses scale drawings such as those based on number lines and maps to solve real-world problems.

MA.D.1.3.2: The student creates and interprets tables, graphs, equations, and verbal descriptions to explain cause-and-effect relationships.

MA.E.1.3.1: The student collects, organizes, and displays data in a variety of forms, including tables, line graphs, charts, and bar graphs, to determine how different ways of presenting data can lead to different interpretations.

MA.B.3.3.1: The student formulates hypotheses, designs experiments, collects and interprets data, and evaluates hypotheses by making inferences and drawing conclusions based on statistics (range, mean, median, and mode) and tables, graphs, and charts.

Science

SC.B.1.3.3: The student knows the various forms in which energy comes to Earth from the sun (e.g., visible light, infrared, and microwave).

SC.D.1.3.1: The student knows that mechanical and chemical activities shape and reshape the Earth's land surface by eroding rock and soil in some areas and depositing them in other areas, sometimes in seasonal layers.

SC.D.1.3.3: The student knows how conditions that exist in one system influence the conditions that exist in other systems.

SC.D.1.3.5: The student understands concepts of time and size relating to the interaction of Earth's processes (e.g., lightning striking in a

split second as opposed to the shifting of the Earth's plates altering the landscape, distance between atoms measured in Angstrom units as opposed to distance between stars measured in light-years).

SC.D.2.3.2: The student knows the positive and negative consequences of human action on the Earth's systems.

SC.E.1.3.1: The student understands the vast size of our Solar System and the relationship of the planets and their satellites.

▼ *Discovery* **space shuttle launch, Cape Canaveral**

How Does *The World and Its People* Help Me Succeed on the FCAT?

When you study world geography with Glencoe's *The World and Its People* textbook, you also prepare yourself for the FCAT. This is because the FCAT often uses social studies content. For example, a selection to test your reading comprehension might be on a history topic.

A second reason that studying history helps you prepare for your big exam is that Glencoe's *The World and Its People* gives you practice in many of the same skills tested on the FCAT. For example, each chapter of the textbook ends with questions and activities that reinforce skills such as critical thinking, drawing conclusions, or being able to write a summary of main ideas. Mastering these skills is vital to success on the FCAT.

Throughout this text, you will find many FCAT-related questions and activities such as:

- Section and Chapter Assessments
- Skill lessons
- Primary Sources
- Literature

A list of the FCAT standards found in Glencoe's *The World and Its People* can be found on pages FL21–FL26.

Look at the page shown at left to find an example of an activity that will help you practice for the FCAT. You will see what looks like a code, **FCAT LA.A.1.3.2**. This is actually one of the major standards tested on the FCAT. What does it mean? This reference tells you the subject, category, and level for what is tested.

The subjects are:

LA stands for Language Arts
MA stands for Mathematics
SC stands for Science

So, in **FCAT LA.A.1.3.2**,

LA means Language Arts
A means Reading in the Language Arts
1 means Standard 1
3 means it is middle-school level
2 means it is the second subdivision under Standard 2

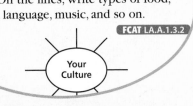

aphic Organizer

. **Organizing Information** Create a diagra. like this one that describes features of your culture. On the lines, write types of food, clothing, language, music, and so on.

FCAT LA.A.1.3.2

Your Culture

Getty Images

How Can I Prepare for the FCAT?

The best way you can prepare for the FCAT is through practice. The more you practice, the more familiar you will become with the content of the FCAT and the types of questions that will appear on the test. The FCAT uses several different question formats, depending on the grade and subject area that is being tested. These formats include:

Multiple Choice questions require you to choose the best answer from four possible choices. You mark your answer by filling in the correct "bubble."

The success of _____ marked the beginning of the modern aircraft industry.

A Henry Ford

B Alexander Graham Bell

C John D. Rockefeller

D Orville and Wilbur Wright

1 Ⓐ Ⓑ Ⓒ Ⓓ

Gridded Response questions require you to solve problems, then mark your numerical answer on answer grids. You must accurately fill in the bubbles below the grids to receive credit for your answer. Examples of the answer grids used on the FCAT include:

60 + 10 =

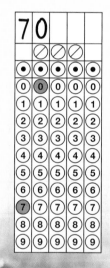

OR

▼ **Everglades National Park**

Short Response questions ask you to respond in your own words or to show solutions in a concise manner.

> **5**
>
> READ
> INQUIRE
> EXPLAIN
>
> How does the author create suspense in relating the story about the animals in the snow? Use details and information from the essay to support your response.
>
> _____
>
> _____
>
> _____
>
> _____

Extended Response questions require you to provide a longer, more detailed, response.

> **11**
>
> READ
> INQUIRE
> EXPLAIN
>
> Why as a child, did the author strongly dislike the saying "If at first you don't succeed, try, try again"? Use details and information from the story to support your answer.
>
> _____
>
> _____
>
> _____
>
> _____
>
> _____
>
> _____

A **Prompt** is an assigned essay topic. The prompt may direct you to write a persuasive essay or an expository essay. Persuasive writing is used to convince someone to believe or agree with your argument or point of view. In an expository essay, you report facts, summarize ideas, explain a process, or define terms.

Getty Images

Contents

Previewing Your Textbook FL44

Scavenger Hunt FL49

Focus On Florida FL50

Florida Data Bank FL50

Florida Special Report FL54

Reading Skills Handbook........RH1

NATIONAL GEOGRAPHIC Reference Atlas

The World: Political RA2

North America: Political RA4

North America: Physical................RA5

United States: Political RA6

United States: Physical..................RA8

Canada: Physical/Political.............RA10

Middle America: Physical/Political......RA12

South America: Political RA14

South America: Physical..................RA15

Europe: Political RA16

Europe: Physical RA18

Africa: Political...............................RA20

Africa: Physical RA21

Asia: Political..................................RA22

Asia: Physical..................................RA24

Middle East: Physical/Political RA26

Pacific Rim: Physical/Political............RA28

Arctic Ocean: Physical RA30

Antarctica: Physical.........................RA30

NATIONAL GEOGRAPHIC Geography Handbook

How Do I Study Geography? 2

How Do I Use Maps and Globes?....................4

Understanding Latitude and Longitude..............5

From Globes to Maps 6

Common Map Projections....................................7

Parts of Maps 8

Types of Maps.................................9

Using Graphs, Charts, and Diagrams................11

Geographic Dictionary..........................14

Be an Active Reader 16

Unit 1 The World 18

Chapter 1 Looking at the Earth 20

1 Thinking Like a Geographer......................22

2 The Earth in Space 29

3 Forces Shaping the Earth 34

4 Landforms and Waterways 39

Chapter 2 Water, Climate, and Vegetation 46

1 The Water Planet 48

2 Climate 52

3 Climate Zones and Vegetation....................61

4 An Environmental Balance 69

Chapter 3 The World's People 78

1 Understanding Culture 80

2 Population Patterns 87

3 Resources and World Trade.......................92

4 Technology "Shrinks" the World..................97

Unit 2 The United States and Canada 112

NATIONAL GEOGRAPHIC Regional Atlas 114

Chapter 4 The United States 124

1 From Sea to Shining Sea 126

2 An Economic Leader 131

3 The Americans 145

Chapter 5 Canada **156**

1 A Resource-Rich Country 158

2 The Canadians 165

Unit 3 **Latin America**..........**174**

NATIONAL GEOGRAPHIC **Regional Atlas** **176**

Chapter 6 Mexico **188**

1 Mexico's Land and Economy....................190

2 Mexico's History...197

3 Mexico Today 202

**Chapter 7 Central America
and the Caribbean Islands** **210**

1 Central America..212

2 Cultures of the Caribbean 219

**Chapter 8 Brazil and Its
Neighbors** **230**

1 Brazil—Emerging Giant 232

2 Argentina to Venezuela 239

Chapter 9 The Andean Countries **252**

1 Colombia's Culture and Challenges 254

2 Land and People of Peru and Ecuador 266

3 The Bolivians and Chileans 271

Unit 4 **Europe**.....................**278**

NATIONAL GEOGRAPHIC **Regional Atlas**..............**280**

Chapter 10 Europe—Early History....**292**

1 Classical Greece and Rome 294

2 Medieval Europe...299

3 From Renaissance to Revolution..............303

**Chapter 11 Europe—
Modern History**.................................**312**

1 The Modern Era Emerges 314

2 A Divided Continent..................................319

3 Moving Toward Unity.................................324

Chapter 12 Western Europe Today....**338**

1 The British Isles..340

2 France and the Benelux Countries............345

3 Germany and the Alpine Countries 350

4 The Nordic Nations 354

5 Southern Europe 358

**Chapter 13 The New
Eastern Europe** **366**

1 Poland and the Baltic Republics................368

2 Hungarians, Czechs, and Slovaks 372

3 Rebuilding the Balkan Countries...............377

4 Ukraine, Belarus, and Moldova..................383

CONTENTS

Unit 5 Russia and the Eurasian Republics 390

NATIONAL GEOGRAPHIC Regional Atlas 392

Chapter 14 Russia's Landscape and History 402

1 A Vast Land.......................404

2 A Troubled History...................................410

Chapter 15 The New Russia and Independent Republics....................422

1 From Communism to Free Enterprise.......424

2 Russia's People and Culture 429

3 The Republics Emerge 436

Unit 6 North Africa and Southwest Asia 452

NATIONAL GEOGRAPHIC Regional Atlas 454

Chapter 16 Birthplace of Civilization 464

1 Mesopotamia and Ancient Egypt 466

2 Three World Religions..............................473

Chapter 17 North Africa Today 482

1 Egypt.................................484

2 Libya and the Maghreb.............................490

Chapter 18 Southwest Asia 500

1 Turkey, Syria, Lebanon, Jordan 502

2 Israel and the Palestinian Territories........508

3 The Arabian Peninsula.............................513

4 Iraq, Iran, and Afghanistan 517

Unit 7 Africa South of the Sahara 532

NATIONAL GEOGRAPHIC Regional Atlas 534

Chapter 19 West Africa 548

1 Nigeria—African Giant 550

2 The Sahel and Coastal West Africa............556

Chapter 20 Central and East Africa...568

1 Central Africa 570

2 People of Kenya and Tanzania....................577

3 Uganda, Rwanda, and Burundi...................582

4 The Horn of Africa 586

Chapter 21 Southern Africa— A Varied Region...................................602

1 The New South Africa.............................604

2 Zambia, Malawi, Zimbabwe, Botswana 609

3 Coastal and Island Countries....................614

Getty Im

Unit 8 Asia 622

NATIONAL GEOGRAPHIC Regional Atlas 624

Chapter 22 South Asia 636
1 India—Past and Present 638
2 Pakistan and Bangladesh 644
3 Mountain Kingdoms, Island Republics 649

Chapter 23 China and Its Neighbors .. 658
1 China's Land and New Economy 660
2 Dynasties to Communism 666
3 China's Neighbors 678

Chapter 24 Japan and the Koreas 688
1 Japan—Past and Present 690
2 The Two Koreas 698

Chapter 25 Southeast Asia 706
1 Life on the Mainland 708
2 Diverse Island Cultures 714

Unit 9 Australia, Oceania, and Antarctica 722

NATIONAL GEOGRAPHIC Regional Atlas 724

Chapter 26 Australia and New Zealand 734
1 Australia—Land Down Under 736
2 New Zealand 741

Chapter 27 Oceania and Antarctica 756
1 Pacific Island Cultures and Economies 758
2 The Frozen Continent 764

Appendix 774
What Is an Appendix? 775
Nations of the World Data Bank 776
Standardized Test Skills Handbook 786
Honoring America 798
Gazetteer 799
Glossary 807
Spanish Glossary 814
Index 823
Acknowledgments 841

One-Stop Internet Resources

This textbook contains one-stop Internet resources for teachers, students, and parents. Log on to twip.glencoe.com for more information. Online study tools include Chapter Overviews, Self-Check Quizzes, an Interactive Tutor, and E-Flashcards. Online research tools include Student Web Activities, Beyond the Textbook Features, Current Events, Web Resources, and State Resources. The interactive online student edition includes the complete Interactive Student Edition along with textbook updates. Especially for teachers, Glencoe offers an online Teacher Forum, Web Activity Lesson Plans, and Literature Connections.

Features

EYE on the Environment

Endangered Spaces.....................................76

Vanishing Rain Forests.............................250

A Water Crisis..498

Ozone: Earth's Natural Sunscreen.............772

GEOGRAPHY & HISTORY

The Columbian Exchange..........................228

Russia's Strategy: Freeze Your Foes...........420

Please Pass the Salt: Africa's Salt Trade.......566

The Silk Road...686

▲ Poison arrow frog

Skills

Social Studies Skills

Using a Map Key.......................................33

Using Latitude and Longitude...................60

Reading a Thematic Map............................86

Mental Mapping.......................................144

Reading a Physical Map.............................196

Interpreting an Elevation Profile..............224

Using B.C. and A.D. 298

Reading a Population Map.........................334

Reading a Vegetation Map.........................349

Reading a Time Zones Map........................613

Reading a Circle Graph.............................648

Reading a Contour Map............................713

Critical Thinking Skills

Sequencing and Categorizing
    Information...238

Understanding Cause and Effect..............416

Drawing Inferences and Conclusions......555

Making Predictions..................................598

Distinguishing Fact From Opinion...........682

Making Comparisons................................702

Technology Skills

Developing Multimedia Presentations.....164

Using a Database......................................258

Using a Spreadsheet.................................494

Evaluating a Web Site...............................528

Study and Writing Skills

Taking Notes...376

Using Primary and Secondary Sources....448

Using Library Resources...........................478

Outlining...752

Writing a Report......................................763

Making Connections

Jeff Schultz/Alaska Stock Images

▲ **Inuit greet with a nose rub.**

Art

Leonardo da Vinci 308

Ukrainian Easter Eggs 382

Carpet Weaving 507

Shadow Puppets.......................................718

Science

Exploring Earth's Water 51

The Aztec Calendar Stone 201

The Galápagos Islands.............................270

Battling Sleeping Sickness 576

Australia's Amazing Animals 740

Antarctica's Environmental Stations.........768

Culture

Americans All 152

Matthews Coon Come:
Man With a Mission.............................170

Poetry on the Pampas 246

The Holocaust 318

Count Leo Tolstoy 435

An Egyptian Folktale 489

Great Mosque of Djenné 562

The Taj Mahal 643

Haiku 697

Technology

Geographic Information Systems 28

Counting Heads..108

The Panama Canal Locks 218

Stonehenge...344

Cooperative Space Ventures....................409

The Egyptian Pyramids............................472

Mining and Cutting Diamonds 608

The Three Gorges Dam 665

EXPLORING CULTURE

Architecture: Quake-Proof Structures........37

Clothing: The Inuit 166

Art: Diego Rivera and His Murals..............203

Sports: Peru...268

Architecture: Leaning Tower of Pisa........361

Food: Slovakia and the Czech Republic 374

Art: Fabergé Eggs.....................................433

Food: Egypt 487

Clothing: The Tuareg...............................557

Sculpture: Shona Artists 611

Clothing: Dyeing Cloth............................640

Customs: Greetings..................................695

Architecture: Angkor Wat 711

Architecture: Sydney Opera House 738

CONTENTS

Exploring GOVERNMENT

Fighting Pollution 428
Stable Democracy 612

teen Scene

Surf's Up! 133
Time to Play 168
What a Catch! 216
Cozy Ballet? 356
Bazaar! 491
Festival Time 504
I Am a Samburu 581
What's for Dinner? 610
School's Out! 646
The Race Is On! 681
Hard Hats to School? 694
Life as a Monk 710
Dreamtime 739

Owen Franken/CORBIS

Teen from Senegal ▶

Believe It or Not!

Solar Eclipse 30
Mt. Pinatubo 55
Saffron—A Valuable Resource 93
San Xavier del Bac 146
Bee Hummingbird 222
Roping a Capybara 242
Islamic Art 359
Transylvania 378
The Aral Sea 439
The Rosetta Stone 470
Petra 505
The Okapi 571
Ship Breakers 647
Clay Warriors 667
The *Endurance* 766

Primary Source

Globalization 99
A Declaration of First Nations 167
Zlata's Diary 380
Alexander Solzhenitsyn 432
Comparing Scripture 475
Nelson Mandela 606

Literature

Botoque 235
The Scarlet Pimpernel 306
Where Are Those Songs? 578
Sadako and the Thousand Paper Cranes ..692
Great Mother Snake 737

Elaine Shay

▼ **This woman is exercising her right to vote.**

TIME PERSPECTIVES — EXPLORING WORLD ISSUES

Our Shrinking World 101
Protecting America's Freedoms
    from Terror 137
Waging War on Drugs 259
The European Union: Good for Everyone? ... 327
The New Russia 441
The Fight for Peace in Southwest Asia 521
Refugees on the Move 591
East Asia: Report Card on Democracy 671
Closing the Gap 745

BUILDING CITIZENSHIP

Public and Private Needs 187
Participation 291
Initiative 401
Religious Tolerance 463
Closing the Door on Racism 546
Women's Rights 634
Voting 733

Exploring Economics

The "Third World" 96
The Quipu 267
Manor Economy 300
Restructuring 321
Centers of Trade 468
Monoculture 558
Labor Costs 664
Exchange of Knowledge 715
East Timor's Challenges 715
The Fate of Nauru 761

▼ **An illustration of the new World Trade Center memorial site, New York City**

Torsten Sedel

Maps

NATIONAL GEOGRAPHIC Reference Atlas

The World: Political RA2
North America: Political RA4
North America: Physical RA5
United States: Political RA6
United States: Physical RA8
Canada: Physical/Political RA10
Middle America: Physical/Political RA12
South America: Political RA14
South America: Physical RA15
Europe: Political....................................RA16
Europe: Physical RA18
Africa: Political.....................................RA20
Africa: Physical RA21
Asia: Political.......................................RA22
Asia: Physical RA24
Middle East: Physical/Political RA26
Pacific Rim: Physical/Political..................RA28
Arctic Ocean: Physical...........................RA30
Antarctica: Physical...............................RA30

NATIONAL GEOGRAPHIC Geography Handbook

Great Circle Route 6
Climate Regions of the United States 8
Spain: Political......................................9
Sri Lanka: Physical.................................9
Sri Lanka: Contour 10
Egypt: Population Density.......................10

Unit 1 The World

Washington, D.C. 33
World Continents and Oceans...................41
Continental Drift...................................45
Prevailing Wind Patterns.........................54
World Ocean Currents 57
Map of the World..................................60
World Climate Regions 63
World Natural Vegetation Regions 64

World Religions.....................................81
World Culture Regions.............................84
Early Civilizations..................................86
World Population Density 89
World Economic Activity 95
A Sweatshirt's Global Journey 102

Unit 2 The United States and Canada

The United States and Canada: Physical 118
The United States and Canada: Political............119
The United States and Canada:
    Food Production.................................120
Contiguous United States and Canada:
    Land Comparison 120
The United States: Physical 127
The United States: Economic Activity...............132
Downtown Chicago, Illinois 144
The United States: Population Density 149
Canada: Economic Activity 161

Unit 3 Latin America

Latin America: Physical 180
Latin America: Political 181
South America: Urban Population Growth 182
Contiguous United States and Latin America:
    Land Comparison 182
Mexico: Political 191
Mexico: Physical..196
Mexico's Native American Civilizations 198
Mexico: Population Density 205
Central America and the Caribbean Islands:
    Political...213
Central America and the Caribbean Islands:
    Economic Activity 214
Contiguous U.S. and Latin America 227
The Spread of Plants and Animals 229
Brazil and Its Neighbors: Physical/Political........233
Brazil and Its Neighbors: Economic Activity 240
The Andean Countries: Political 255
The Drug War in the Andes...........................260
The Andean Countries: Climate 273

Contents

Unit 4 Europe

Europe: Physical 284
Europe: Political 285
Europe: Languages 286
Contiguous United States and Europe:
    Land Comparison 286
Greek and Roman Empires 295
Medieval Europe c. A.D. 1200 301

Western and Eastern Europe (c. 1950) 320
Europe in 2004 328
Spain and Portugal: Population Density............334
Occupation of Germany 1945 337
Western Europe: Political 341
France: Vegetation...................................349
Eastern Europe: Political 369
Eastern Europe: Population Density 384
European Union 2004.....................................389

NATIONAL GEOGRAPHIC

Eastern Europe: Political

Unit 5 — Russia and the Eurasian Republics

Russia and the Eurasian Republics: Physical......396
Russia and the Eurasian Republics: Political......397
The Russian Winter....................................398
Contiguous United States and Russia:
    Land Comparison 398
Russia: Climate 405
Expansion of Russia 412
Average Winter Temperatures 421
Russia: Economic Activity 425
Eurasian Republics: Economic Activity.............437
Russia's 11 Time Zones................................447
Chechnya 451

Unit 6 — North Africa and Southwest Asia

North Africa and Southwest Asia: Physical........458
North Africa and Southwest Asia: Political........459
North Africa and Southwest Asia:
    Oil and Gas Production and Distribution 460
Contiguous United States and North Africa
    and Southwest Asia: Land Comparison 460
Mesopotamia and Ancient Egypt.....................467
Jerusalem 474
Mesopotamian Civilizations, c. 4000 B.C. 481
Ancient Egypt, c. 3100 B.C...............................481
North Africa: Physical/Political 485
Southwest Asia: Physical/Political 503
Southwest Asia: Climate...............................509
Israel and Its Neighbors...............................511
Spread of Islam 518
Where Iraq's Muslims Live............................522

Unit 7 — Africa South of the Sahara

Africa South of the Sahara: Physical...................538
Africa South of the Sahara: Political...................539
Africa South of the Sahara:
    Gems and Minerals.................................540
Contiguous United States and Africa South
    of the Sahara: Land Comparison...................540
West Africa: Political 551
West Africa: Physical 552
West Africa: Population Density.........................560
Salt Trade Routes 567

Central and East Africa: Physical.....................572
Central and East Africa: Political.....................580
East Africa: Economic Activity 583
East Africa: Population Density.........................587
Major African Ethnic Groups 589
Africans on the Move..................................592
Kenya 601
Southern Africa: Political.............................605
World Time Zones 613
African Independence Dates 615
Population Density of Southern African
    Countries..621

Unit 8 — Asia

Asia: Physical...628
Asia: Political...629
Asia: Monsoons 630
Contiguous United States and Asia:
    Land Comparison 630
South Asia: Physical...................................645
South Asia: Economic Activity 650
South Asia: Population Density 653
China and Its Neighbors: Physical/Political 661
China and Its Neighbors: Population Density....668
Who's Free, Who's Not in East Asia 672
China's Defenses 685
Silk Road Routes 687
Japan and the Koreas: Physical/Political 691
Japan and the Koreas: Population Density........700
Asia's Pacific Rim 702
Southeast Asia: Political...............................709
Borneo: Contour Map 713

Unit 9 — Australia, Oceania, and Antarctica

Australia, Oceania, and Antarctica: Physical 728
Australia, Oceania, and Antarctica: Political 729
Australia, Oceania, and Antarctica:
    Endangered Environments 730
Contiguous United States and Australia,
    Oceania, and Antarctica:
    Land Comparison 730
Australia and New Zealand:
    Physical/Political 742
Maori Iwi Lands 746
Oceania and Antarctica: Political 759

Charts and Graphs

NATIONAL GEOGRAPHIC Geography Handbook

Hemispheres 4
Comparing World Languages.......................11
U.S. Farms, 1940–2000 11
World Population 12
Major Automobile-Producing Countries, 2001 12
Climograph: Moscow, Russia 13
Africa: Elevation Profile..............................13
Landforms and Water Bodies 14

Unit 1 The World

The Solar System...30
Seasons...31
Earth's Layers 35
Tectonic Plate Boundaries 36
The Water Cycle 49
El Niño...56
Rain Shadow 58
Number of Hurricanes in a Year.................75
Major World Religions 82
Types of Government 83
World Population: Population Growth 88
World Population: Most Populous Countries.......88
Types of Economic Systems 94
Modern Inventions 98
The Digital Divide.......................................107
Exports by World Region 111

Unit 2 The United States and Canada

Data Bits...117
Population: Urban vs. Rural.........................117
The United States Labor Force 117
Elevation Profile...118
Comparing Population:
    United States and Canada............................121
Ethnic Groups: United States and Canada 121

Country Profiles...122
U.S. State Names: Meaning and Origin..............122
Canadian Province and Territory Names:
    Meaning and Origin 123
Balancing Freedom and Safety...................138
Ground Zero: A Proposal for Renewal..............143
Branches of the United States Government 148
Top 6 Tourist Destinations, 2001 155
St. Lawrence Seaway 159
Native North American Populations by
    Canadian Province in 2001 173

Unit 3 Latin America

Data Bits...179
Population: Urban vs. Rural.........................179
Elevation Profile...180
Comparing Population: United States and
    Selected Countries of Latin America............183
Ethnic Groups: Selected Countries of
    Latin America 183
Country Profiles...184

NATIONAL GEOGRAPHIC Earth's Layers

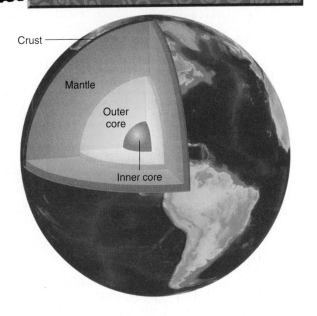

Crust

Mantle

Outer core

Inner core

Contents

CONTENTS

Mexico's Altitude Zones 193
The Panama Canal Locks 218
Jamaica: Elevation Profile 224
Leading Coffee-Producing Countries.................234
What Drug and Alcohol Abuse Cost.................265

Unit 4 Europe

Data Bits...283
Population: Urban vs. Rural..............................283
Elevation Profile...284
Comparing Population: United States and
    Selected Countries of Europe 287
Religions: Selected Countries of Europe............287
Country Profiles..288
Classical Europe...298
It's All About Jobs! 333
Number of Personal Computers per
    1,000 People 365
Language Families of Europe 385

Unit 5 Russia and the Eurasian Republics

Data Bits...395
Ethnic Makeup...395
World Ranking 395
Population: Urban vs. Rural..............................395
Elevation Profile...396
Comparing Population:
    United States and Russia 399
Comparing Area and Population: Russia East
    and West of the Ural Mountains..................399
Country Profiles..400
International Space Station 409
Where Russians Work 443

Unit 6 North Africa and Southwest Asia

Data Bits...457
Population: Urban vs. Rural..............................457

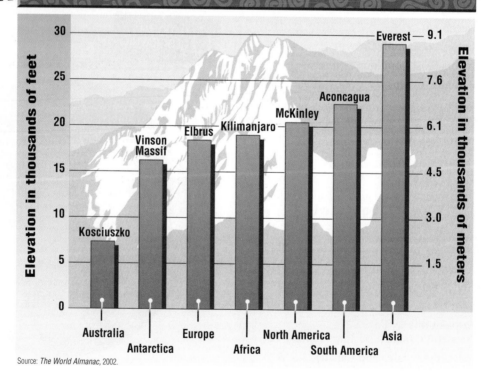

NATIONAL GEOGRAPHIC
Highest Mountain on Each Continent

Source: *The World Almanac*, 2002.

Elevation Profile 458
Comparing Population: United States and
    Selected Countries of North Africa and
    Southwest Asia 461
Urban Populations: Selected Cities of
    North Africa and Southwest Asia 461
Country Profiles 462
Percentage of North Africa's
    People Living in Each Country 497
World Oil Reserves 514
Believers Who Share a Common Ground 527
Countries With the Largest Oil Reserves 531

Unit 7 Africa South of the Sahara

Data Bits 537
Religions 537
Elevation Profile 538
Comparing Population: United States and
    Selected Countries of Africa
    South of the Sahara 541
Selected Rural and Urban Populations:
    Africa South of the Sahara 541
Country Profiles 542
Leading Cacao-Producing Countries 565
Leading Diamond-Producing Countries 571
Where the World's Refugees Come From 597
Tourism in Kenya 598

Unit 8 Asia

Data Bits 627
Ethnic Makeup 627
World Ranking 627
Population: Urban vs. Rural 627
Elevation Profile 628
Comparing Population: United States and
    Selected Countries of Asia 631
World Population: Asia's Share of the
    World's People 631
Country Profiles 632
Religions of South Asia 648

Asia's Pacific Rim: Exports/Imports

Source: *The World Almanac,* 2003.

Highest Mountain on Each Continent 652
Comparing Population 657
Leading Rice-Producing Countries 662
Taiwan: From Dictatorship to Democracy 677
Asia's Pacific Rim: Exports/Imports 702
Top Tin Producers 721

Unit 9 Australia, Oceania, and Antarctica

Data Bits 727
Ethnic Makeup 727
World Ranking 727
Population: Urban vs. Rural 727
Elevation Profile 728
Comparing Population: United States and
    Selected Countries of Australia, Oceania,
    and Antarctica 731
Population Growth: Australia, 1958–2008 731
Country Profiles 732
The Making of a Multicultural Society 751
Leading Wool-Producing Countries 755

Previewing Your Textbook

Your textbook has been organized to help you learn about the many people and places that make up our world. Before you start reading, though, here is a road map to help you understand what you will encounter in the pages of this textbook. Follow this road map before you read so that you can understand how your textbook works.

Units

Your textbook is divided into units. Each unit begins with two pages of photographs and an introduction to the region. These pages will help you begin your study of the geography, culture, and history of that particular region. Next comes a Regional Atlas with a feature that focuses on the region and includes National Geographic maps. You will also find country profiles with facts about each country in the region.

Unit

5

NATIONAL GEOGRAPHIC

Russia and the Eurasian Republics

If you had to describe Russia in one word, that word would be BIG! Russia is the largest country in the world in area. Its almost 6.6 million square miles (17 million sq. km) are spread across two continents—Europe and Asia. As you can imagine, such a large country faces equally large challenges. In 1991 Russia emerged from the Soviet Union as an independent country. Since then it has been struggling to unite its many ethnic groups, set up a democratic government, and build a stable economy.

Workers on the statue *Motherland Calls,* Volgograd

Russians in front of St. Basil's Cathedral, Moscow

▲ Siberian tiger in a forest in eastern Russia

NGS ONLINE
www.nationalgeographic.com/education

390

391

VISUALS

Photographs show you glimpses of landscapes, life, and culture from the region.

INTRODUCTION

An introductory paragraph gives you information and interesting facts about the region you are about to study.

Chapters

Each unit in *The World and Its People* is made up of chapters. Each chapter starts by providing you with background information to help you get the most out of the chapter.

CHAPTER TITLE
The chapter title tells you the main topic you will be reading about.

VISUALS
A photograph shows people or places from the region.

FOLDABLES
Use the Foldables Study Organizer to take notes as you read.

VIDEOS
You can view these National Geographic videos to learn more about the region in the chapter. You will see first-hand the amazing people and places of our world.

WEB SITE
Social Studies Online directs you to the Internet where you can find more information, activities, and quizzes. There are also links to additional resources.

WHY IT MATTERS
Why It Matters tells you how the region you will study is connected to the rest of the world. It also tells you why the region is unique.

Sections

A section is a division, or part, of the chapter. The first page of the section, the section opener, helps you set a purpose for reading.

MAIN IDEA

The *Main Idea* of this section is introduced here. Below it are important terms you will come upon as you read the section.

READING STRATEGY

Completing the *Reading Strategy* activity will help you organize the information as you read the section.

EXPLORING OUR WORLD

This National Geographic feature gives you a unique perspective of the world with a story and photograph about an interesting aspect of the region.

Guide to Reading

Main Idea

Russia is a huge country with a cold climate due to its far northern location.

Terms to Know

- steppe
- tundra
- permafrost
- taiga

Reading Strategy

Create a chart like this one. Give a specific name for each type of physical feature listed.

FCAT L.A.A.1.3.2

Russia	
Plains	
Mountains	
Rivers	

The following are the major Sunshine State Standards covered in this section.

SS.B.2.3.9:
Understands ways the interaction between physical and human systems affects current conditions on Earth

SS.B.2.3.5:
Understands the geographical factors that affect the cohesiveness and integration of countries

Section 1

A Vast Land

NATIONAL GEOGRAPHIC Exploring Our World

Siberian tigers hunt in the eastern forests of Russia—sometimes even climbing trees to find food. Only a few hundred now live in the wild, though. The animals they hunt—elk, deer, and wild boar—are dwindling, and the tigers are hunted by people. Poachers who kill the tigers illegally can sell a skin for $15,000. Russia is trying to enforce laws to save these animals.

Russia is the world's largest country. Nearly twice as big as the United States, Russia is called a Eurasian country because its lands lie on two continents—Europe and Asia. The **Ural Mountains** form the dividing line between the two continents. The European or western part of Russia borders countries such as Finland, Belarus, and Ukraine. The much larger eastern part of Russia stretches across Asia to the Pacific Ocean. The Chukchi Peninsula, on Russia's far eastern border, is separated from Alaska by only about 50 miles (80 km).

Russia is so wide that it shares borders with 14 other countries. It also includes 11 time zones from east to west. When it is 12:00 P.M. (noon) in eastern Russia and people are eating lunch, people in western Russia are still sound asleep at 1:00 A.M.

Russia's Climate

As you can see from the climate map on page 405, Russia's southern border is in the middle latitudes, but the north reaches past the Arctic Circle. Most of the western part of Russia has a humid continental climate. Summers are warm and rainy, while winters are cold

404

Reading Roadmap

You will get more out of your textbook if you recognize the different elements that help you to understand what you read.

MAPS

Easy-to-read maps show you where countries and regions are located in the world. Questions test your understanding of the map's information.

READING CHECKS

Reading Checks help you check your understanding of the main ideas.

OUTLINE

Think of the headings as forming an outline. The red titles are the main headings. The blue titles that follow are the subheadings.

VOCABULARY

The words in blue are the key terms. The definition is also included here.

PHOTOGRAPHS

Photographs show you important people, places, and events from the region. Questions help you interpret the photographs and relate them to what you are learning.

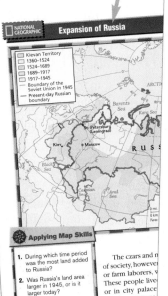

NATIONAL GEOGRAPHIC
Expansion of Russia

Kievan Territory
1360–1524
1524–1689
1689–1917
1917–1945
Boundary of the Soviet Union in 1945
Present-day Russian boundary

Barents Sea
Kara Sea
ARCTIC
St. Petersburg (Leningrad)
Kiev
Moscow
R U S S I A
Black Sea
Caspian Sea
Aral Sea
0 mi.
0 km
Two-

Applying Map Skills

1. During which time period was the most land added to Russia?
2. Was Russia's land area larger in 1945, or is it larger today?

Find NGS online map resources @ www.nationalgeographic.com/maps

The czars and n... of society, however... or farm laborers, v... These people live... or in city palace... Western customs,...

Dramatic Chan...
Bonaparte invade... weather finally f... *1812 Overture,*... and bursts of ca... Tchaikovsky (ch... the Russian vic... about Napoleor...

In the late 1... change. The Ru... Mountains and... Alexander II, k... tied to the lar... though. Russia...

412

boundary. West of the Urals lies the **North European Plain.** This fertile plain has Russia's mildest climate, and about 75 percent of the population live here. This region holds Russia's capital, **Moscow,** and other important cities, such as **St. Petersburg** and **Volgograd.** Much of Russia's agriculture and industry is found on the North European Plain.

Good farmland also lies south of the North European Plain, along the Don and Volga Rivers. This area is part of the **steppe,** the nearly treeless grassy plain that stretches through Ukraine. To the far south of European Russia lay the high, rugged **Caucasus** (KAW•kuh•suhs) **Mountains.** Thickly covered with pines and other trees, the Caucasus are much taller than the Urals.

✓Reading Check What is the steppe?

East of the Urals

The huge Asian part of Russia lies east of the Ural Mountains and is known as **Siberia.** Northern Siberia has one of the coldest climates in the world. Not even hardy evergreens can grow here. Instead, you find **tundra,** a vast and rolling treeless plain in which only the top few inches of the ground thaw during the summer. The permanently frozen lower layers of soil are called **permafrost** and cover 40 percent of Russia.

The few people who live in the tundra make their living by fishing, hunting seals and walruses, or herding reindeer. With so few trees, many of the houses are made of walrus skins. Because the distances are so great and the land is usually covered in ice and snow, people may use helicopters for travel.

The Taiga South of the tundra is the world's largest forest, the **taiga** (TY•guh). Here, evergreen trees stretch about 4,000 miles (6,436 km) across the country in a belt 1,000 to 2,000 miles (1,609 to 3,218 km) wide. As with the tundra, few people live in this area. Those who do support themselves by lumbering or hunting. This area is so sparsely populated that forest fires sometimes burn for weeks before anyone notices.

NATIONAL GEOGRAPHIC On Location

Siberia

This is cold! Boiling water freezes in midair in icy northern Siberia.

Place How do people in the tundra make their living?

SECTION ASSESSMENT

The *Section Assessment* is the last item in every section. Here, you can check your understanding of what you have read.

Section 1 PRACTICE
Assessment

Defining Terms
1. Define steppe, tundra, permafrost, taiga.

Recalling Facts
2. Location What mountain range separates Europe and Asia?
3. Region How many countries does Russia border?
4. Place What is unique about Lake Baikal?

Critical Thinking
5. Analyzing Information Why do you think trains are more important than other kinds of vehicles for moving people and goods across Russia? **FCAT LA.A.2.3.1**
6. Making Comparisons How do the waters of the Caspian Sea and Lake Baikal differ? **FCAT LA.A.1.3.2**

Graphic Organizer
7. Categorizing Information Create a chart like this one. Then place each of the following items into the column in which it is located: Moscow, Lake Baikal, Kamchatka Peninsula, St. Petersburg, Volga River, Volgograd, taiga. **FCAT LA.A.1.3.2**

European Russia	Asian Russia

Applying Social Studies Skills

8. Analyzing Maps Turn to the climate map on page 405. Select a Russian city. Now look at the map of "The Russian Winter" on page 398. On average, how many days of snow cover does your selected city have per year?

Special Features

A variety of special features will help you as you study *The World and Its People.*

MAKING CONNECTIONS

This feature connects you with various art, science, culture, and technology contributions in a particular region.

SKILLS ACTIVITIES

These activities help you learn and practice social studies, critical thinking, technology, and study and writing skills.

EXPLORING CULTURE

Exploring Culture examines art, architecture, clothing, and more in a particular region.

TIME PERSPECTIVES

Time Perspectives: Exploring World Issues takes an in-depth look at issues in the region and helps you understand and analyze those issues.

Making Connections

| ART | SCIENCE | CULTURE | TECHNOLOGY |

FCAT PRACTICE Completing the correlated items below will help you prepare for the **FCAT Reading** test.

Count Leo Tolstoy

Count Leo Tolstoy (1828–1910) was a famous Russian novelist. Two of his epic works are *War and Peace* and *Anna Karenina.* What is not generally known is that Tolstoy also wrote for children. He wrote: "[These writings] will be used to teach generations of all Russian children, from the czar's to the peasant's, and from these readers they will receive their first poetic impressions, and having written these books, I can now die in peace."

Study and Writing Skill

FCAT PRACTICE Completing the correlated items below will help you prepare for the **FCAT Reading** test.

Using Primary and Secondary Sources

So much information comes our way in today's world. How can you analyze it to decide what is truly useful and accurate?

Practicing t...

Read the passage the questions for fo...

I went south t... 4:45 A.M., stumble... ...to the hospi...

EXPLORING Culture

Art

Peter Carl Fabergé was no ordinary Russian jeweler. His successful workshop designed extravagant jeweled flowers, figures, and animals. He is most famous for crafting priceless gold Easter eggs for the czar of Russia and other royalty in Europe and Asia. Each egg was unique and took nearly a year to create. Lifting the lid of the egg revealed a tiny surprise. One egg Fabergé created (shown here) held an intricate ship inside.

Looking Closer Why do you think Fabergé's workshop closed after the Russian Revolution of 1917?

FCAT LA.E.2.2.1

TIME PERSPECTIVES

EXPLO... WOR... ISSUE...

The New Russia

Is Democracy Working?

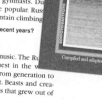

Compiled and adapted from *TIME.*

that at one time lived in Russia have emigrated to other areas. Few... than 1 million Jews live in Russia today.

Celebrations, Foods, and Sports Russians enjoy small family g... togethers as well as national holidays. New Year's Eve is the most f... tive nonreligious holiday. Russian children decorate a fir tree a... exchange presents with others in their families. Russians also celeb... May 1 with parades and speeches. May Day honors Russian worker...

If you were to have dinner with a Russian family, you might begin w... a big bowl of *borscht,* a soup made from beets, or *shchi,* a soup m... from cabbage. Next, you might have meat turnovers called *piroshki....* the main course, you are likely to eat meat, poultry, or fish with bo... potatoes. On special occasions, Russians like to eat caviar. This delic... is made from eggs of the sturgeon, a fish from the Caspian Sea.

Have you ever watched the Olympics? If so, you probably l... seen Russian hockey players, figure skaters, and gymnasts. Du... Russia's cold climate, winter and indoor sports are popular. Russ... also enjoy soccer, tennis, hiking, camping, and mountain climbing...

✓ **Reading Check** How have Russia's cities changed in recent years?

Rich Cultural Traditions

Russia has a rich tradition of literature, art, and music. The Ru... storytelling tradition is one of the oldest and richest in the w... These stories, or *skazki,* were passed down orally from generation to generation, until finally they were recorded in print. Beasts and creatures with magical powers are common in these tales that grew out of a land with dark forests and long, cold winters.

The New Russia and Independent Republics

Scavenger Hunt

The World and Its People contains a wealth of information. The trick is to know where to look to access all the information in the book. If you complete this scavenger hunt exercise with your teachers or parents, you will see how the textbook is organized and how to get the most out of your reading and study time. Let's get started!

1. How many units and how many chapters are in the book?

2. What region does Unit 3 cover?

3. Where can you find facts about each country in a unit?

4. In what four places can you find the key terms for Section 1 of Chapter 10?

5. What does the Foldables Study Organizer at the beginning of Chapter 4 ask you to do?

6. How are the key terms throughout your book highlighted in the narrative?

7. Where do you find graphic organizers in your textbook?

8. You want to quickly find all the maps in the book about Europe. Where do you look?

9. Each Unit's Regional Atlas includes country profile stamps. Where else can you find information about countries in the textbook?

10. Where can you learn the definition of a physical map, a political map, and a special purpose map?

Symbols of Florida

An important part of knowing about Florida is understanding what makes it special. Each of the symbols on this page is associated with Florida. Some of our state symbols were suggested to the House of Representatives by Florida citizens.

Nickname

The "Sunshine State" is the nickname most commonly attached to Florida. It was adopted as the state nickname by the 1970 legislature.

State Tree: Sabal Palm

In 1953, the state legislature named the Sabal Palm as the state tree. The Sabal Palm is also shown on the state seal. This tree grows well in almost any soil and is the most widely distributed tree throughout Florida. The Sabal Palm is also known as the cabbage palm.

Florida's Flag

Many flags have flown over Florida. These included the flags of five nations: Spain, France, Great Britain, the United States, and the Confederate States of America. Many other unofficial flags have flown over Florida in its history. The current flag was approved by the state legislature in 1899 and by the citizens of Florida in 1900.

State Animal: Florida Panther

The panther is the official state animal of Florida. In 1982 Florida students chose the panther over the key deer, the manatee, and the alligator as the state animal. Long ago, panthers were found throughout the southeastern United States, ranging from Texas to the tip of Florida. However, they were hunted and killed because settlers feared them. Now adult panthers remain in national and state parks and on private lands in southwest Florida. Panthers are among the rarest and most endangered animals in the world.

State Seal

The state seal of Florida, revised in 1985, corrected several errors that appeared in the previous seal. The seal shows the sun, a steamboat sailing, a Sabal Palm tree, and a Native American Seminole woman scattering flowers. The seal is encircled by the words: "Great Seal of the State of Florida: In God We Trust." The first seal was designed in 1865.

State Flower: Orange Blossom

Florida's state flower is the orange blossom. These fragrant white flowers grow on the orange tree. At one time, bouquets of orange blossoms were transported to all parts of the United States for brides to carry at their weddings. The orange blossom became the official state flower in 1909.

State Wildflower: Coreopsis

Florida's state wildflower is the coreopsis. The coreopsis blooms in a range of colors from bright lemon yellow to gold to pink. The wildflower is used widely in the state's roadside plantings and highway beautification programs. The state legislature designated the coreopsis as the state wildflower in 1991.

State Day: April 2

In 1953 the state legislature designated April 2 as State Day. Ponce de León first sighted Florida on or about that date in 1513. The idea was suggested by Mary Harrell, a Jacksonville social studies teacher at John Gorrie Junior High School.

Today Is

2

093   273

Friday April

April 2004

S	M	T	W	T	F	S
				1	2	3
4	5	6	7	8	9	10
11	12	13	14	15	16	17
18	19	20	21	22	23	24
25	26	27	28	29	30	

Florida's Counties

0   50   100 miles
0   50   100 kilometers
Albers Conic Equal-Area projection

Gulf of Mexico

ATLANTIC OCEAN

Lake Okeechobee

Tallahassee · Jacksonville · St. Petersburg · Tampa · Orlando · Ft. Lauderdale · Pembroke Pines · Hollywood · Hialeah · Miami

1. Escambia
2. Santa Rosa
3. Okaloosa
4. Walton
5. Holmes
6. Washington
7. Jackson
8. Calhoun
9. Bay
10. Gulf
11. Gadsden
12. Liberty
13. Leon
14. Wakulla
15. Franklin
16. Jefferson
17. Madison
18. Taylor
19. Hamilton
20. Suwannee
21. Lafayette
22. Dixie
23. Columbia
24. Gilchrist
25. Baker
26. Union
27. Bradford
28. Alachua
29. Levy
30. Nassau
31. Duval
32. Clay
33. St. Johns
34. Putnam
35. Flagler
36. Marion
37. Volusia
38. Citrus
39. Hernando
40. Sumter
41. Lake
42. Seminole
43. Orange
44. Brevard
45. Osceola
46. Polk
47. Pasco
48. Pinellas
49. Hillsborough
50. Manatee
51. Sarasota
52. Hardee
53. DeSoto
54. Highlands
55. Okeechobee
56. Indian River
57. St. Lucie
58. Martin
59. Glades
60. Charlotte
61. Lee
62. Hendry
63. Palm Beach
64. Broward
65. Collier
66. Monroe
67. Dade

Florida's 10 Largest Cities in 2000

City	Population
Jacksonville	735,617
Miami	362,470
Tampa	303,447
St. Petersburg	248,232
Hialeah	226,419
Orlando	185,951
Fort Lauderdale	152,397
Tallahassee	150,624
Hollywood	139,357
Pembroke Pines	137,427

Source: Florida Population: Census Summary 2000

Florida's People

Florida and United States: Population, 2000

Comparing the Population of Florida and the United States

	Florida	United States
Population, 2000	15,982,378	281,421,906
Population, percent change, 1990 to 2000	23.5%	13.1%
Persons under 18 years old, percent	22.8%	25.7%
Persons 65 years old and over, percent	17.6%	12.4%
Female persons, percent	51.2%	50.9%
White persons, percent	78.0%	75.1%
African American persons, percent	14.6%	12.3%
Persons of Hispanic or Latino origins, percent	16.8%	12.5%
Native Americans, percent	0.3%	0.9%
Asian Americans, percent	1.7%	3.6%

Source: U.S. Census Bureau.

Florida: Population 1900–2000

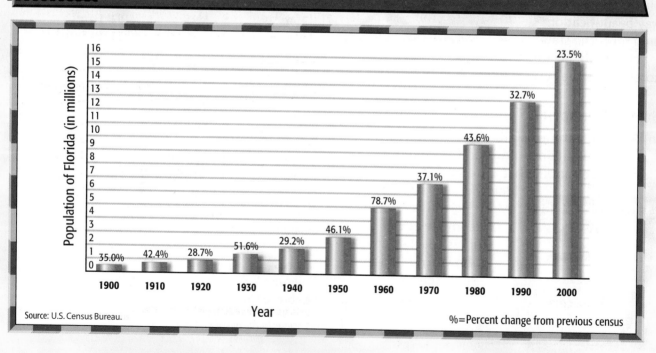

Source: U.S. Census Bureau.

%=Percent change from previous census

Florida's Economy

Florida Employment by Industry in 2000

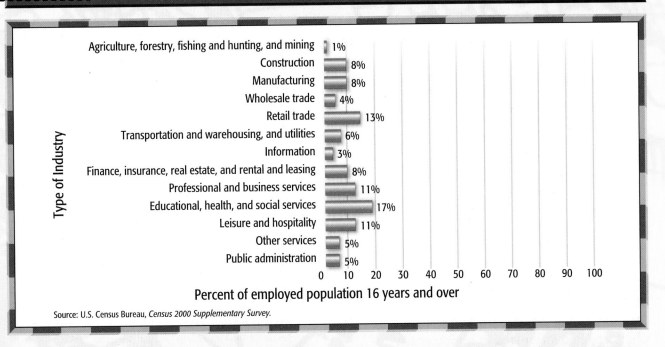

Type of Industry

Industry	Percent
Agriculture, forestry, fishing and hunting, and mining	1%
Construction	8%
Manufacturing	8%
Wholesale trade	4%
Retail trade	13%
Transportation and warehousing, and utilities	6%
Information	3%
Finance, insurance, real estate, and rental and leasing	8%
Professional and business services	11%
Educational, health, and social services	17%
Leisure and hospitality	11%
Other services	5%
Public administration	5%

0 10 20 30 40 50 60 70 80 90 100

Percent of employed population 16 years and over

Source: U.S. Census Bureau, *Census 2000 Supplementary Survey.*

NATIONAL GEOGRAPHIC — Florida's Top 10 Leading Farm Crops in 2000

Crops	Total in millions
Oranges	$1,387
Foliage and Floriculture	$798
Tomatoes	$507
Sugarcane	$442
Milk	$384
Cattle and Calves	$371
Green Peppers	$245
Chickens	$227
Grapefruit	$193
Strawberries	$168

Source: Florida Farm Bureau.

NATIONAL GEOGRAPHIC — Florida's Land Usage

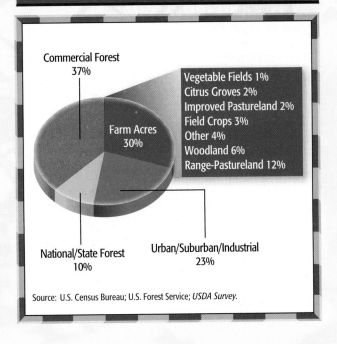

Commercial Forest 37%

Farm Acres 30%

Vegetable Fields 1%
Citrus Groves 2%
Improved Pastureland 2%
Field Crops 3%
Other 4%
Woodland 6%
Range-Pastureland 12%

National/State Forest 10%

Urban/Suburban/Industrial 23%

Source: U.S. Census Bureau; U.S. Forest Service; *USDA Survey.*

Florida's Geography

PROBABLY NO GEOGRAPHICAL FEATURE identifies North America as easily as the peninsula of Florida. Florida is divided into 67 counties. To the north and west, the "panhandle" shares borders with Georgia and Alabama. The bottom two-thirds of the state lie on the distinctive peninsula, surrounded by water on three sides. Florida's location near the Atlantic Ocean, the Gulf of Mexico, and the Caribbean Sea has made it a crossroads of European, North American, and South American history.

When geographers study Florida, they look at its physical conditions—land, water, plants, animals, and climate. Just as important, though, is the study of human geography, the study of people, who they are, where they live, and how they live. Today, more than ever before, geographers are also interested in how humans relate to and interact with their environment.

Physical Geography

Florida ranks twenty-second among the 50 states in total area, with about 58,560 total square miles. Northern Florida is cooler and hillier. Southern Florida is flatter and warmer. All of Florida is rather low, with most of the land less than 100 feet (30 meters) above sea level. Geologists—scientists who study Earth's history through rock formations—think that Florida is one of the youngest parts of the continental United States, the last landform to emerge from the ocean. The Florida landscape is sprinkled with more than 7,000 lakes, and Lake Okeechobee is the second largest freshwater lake in the

United States. Water is important to Florida, and seawater, lakes, rivers, and streams have shaped the land into seven regions.

▼ This map shows Florida's absolute location, the exact spot where it is found. When you say that Florida is located below Georgia and Alabama, you are using relative location.

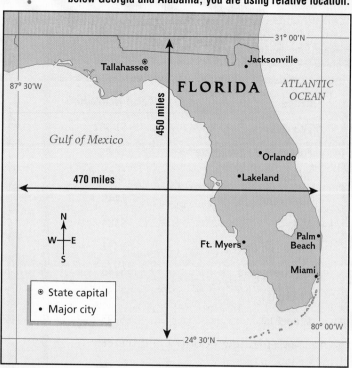

The Coastal Lowlands
The coastal lowlands make up 75 percent of the state's land. These areas border the sea. Most coastal lowlands are very low, less than 25 feet (7.6 meters) above sea level.

The Lake Okeechobee-Everglades Basin
This region is 150 miles long and 50 miles wide. Low and wet, the basin is actually a slow-moving river, sometimes called the "River of Grass." The southern part of the basin contains Everglades National Park and Lake Okeechobee.

The Kissimmee Lowlands
The Kissimmee Lowlands are about the same size as the Okeechobee-Everglades Basin. These flat grasslands provide fine pasture along the Kissimmee River as it flows south toward Lake Okeechobee.

The Marianna Lowlands
The area of the Marianna Lowlands is in the northwest between the Choctawhatchee and Apalachicola Rivers. It is a region of heavy erosion with many sinkholes and caves.

The Tallahassee Hills
The Tallahassee Hills lie east of the Marianna Lowlands. This beautiful rolling area has been an important area for field crops.

The Western Highlands
East of the Marianna Lowlands, extending to the Alabama border, are the Western Highlands. This area, like the Tallahassee Hills, was once part of an ancient upland plain and is now an important agricultural area.

The Central Highlands
The Central Highlands lie east of the Tallahassee Hills and west of the St. John's River, which separate them from the Coastal Lowlands farther east. This region, too, is rolling country and has thousands of lakes.

▲ Key West, Florida

Unique Features of Florida's Geography

Sinkholes Sinkholes are a common geographic phenomenon in Florida. Rainwater filters through the porous limestone of Florida's aquifer beneath the ground's surface. Persistent erosion over time can create underground voids. The collapse of overlying ground into the underground cavities produces sinkholes. Many Florida sinkholes have been converted into lakes, hiking and biking trails, and tourist attractions.

Beaches Florida has over 1,197 miles of coastline, with 663 miles containing sandy beaches. No part of Florida is more than 60 miles (96 km) from its famous beaches. For most people, beaches and palm trees are synonymous with Florida's landscape. Beach erosion is a concern, and measures are underway to protect, preserve, and restore the coastal sandy beach resources of the state.

Coral Reefs Florida is the only state in the continental United States to have extensive shallow coral reef formations near its coasts. The most thriving reef developments are found by the Florida Keys and rival those of many Caribbean areas.

▲ According to legend, oranges became very popular with Spaniards and Native Americans. They unknowingly planted trees across Florida, as they casually dropped seeds during travel.

Climate Sunshine is one of Florida's most important resources. The state's comfortable climate has lured vacationers for more than a century. Other than Hawaii, Florida is closer to the Equator than any other American state, giving it a humid subtropical climate. Heavy rainfall occurs from April to November with hurricane season from June to November. Snow falls occasionally in the north, and valuable crops are sometimes subject to freeze warnings.

Plants and Animals

More than 300 species of trees grow in Florida, including a wide variety of hardwoods and pines in the north. In the south are tropical varieties, such as the Sabal Palm, Florida's state tree. Although citrus trees are not native to Florida, probably no other tree identifies Florida as much as the orange tree. Many historians believe Christopher Columbus first brought citrus fruits to the New World in 1493. Early Spanish explorers planted orange trees around St. Augustine, Florida, in the late 1500s. Florida's unique sandy soil and subtropical climate have proven to be ideal for growing citrus.

In this changing environment live about 100 species of mammals, from the endangered Florida panther to common deer, and more than 400 species and subspecies of birds. Alligators are the largest and most famous reptiles found here, and more than 40 species of snakes have been discovered. Animal life is under pressure from growing cities and suburbs, but steps are in place to protect threatened and endangered species. One example is the Florida Manatee Sanctuary Act, which declares the State of Florida to be a refuge and sanctuary for the manatee, or sea cow.

A Florida alligator

and political and religious systems. They had no written languages.

Two highly organized farming groups, the Apalachee and the Timucua, lived in North Florida. Along the southwest Gulf coast lived the Calusa, who historians think may have originally come from South America. The Calusa dominated South Florida with their advanced fishing and canoeing skills, complex society, and highly structured military.

The lower Atlantic Coast was the home of several small groups who, like the Calusa, fished and hunted rather than farmed. There were the Tekestas of Biscayne Bay, the Ais and Jeagas up the coast, the Keys, and the Mayaimi, builders of large mounded villages near Lake Okeechobee. With a deep understanding and appreciation for their environment, the Native American peoples of Florida made good use of their natural resources. The arrival of Europeans in the early 1500s would soon upset their stable, well-developed communities.

Spanish Exploration

Prehistory ended with the coming of Europeans. Written records about life in Florida began with the arrival of the Spanish explorer Juan Ponce de León in April 1513, on the northeast coast of Florida, possibly near St. Augustine. He called the area *la Florida,* or "the feast of flowers" in Spanish, in honor of Spain's Easter celebration *Pascua Florida.*

Juan Ponce de León

Ponce de León made no attempt to settle the land and clashed with the Calusa as he explored. Eight years later he tried to establish a settlement, but he again fought with the Calusa. Many of his group were killed.

The door had been opened, though, and many expeditions followed. In 1528, Pánfilo Narvaez failed to establish a colony. The Apalachee attacked and only four of his party of 400 survived by escaping to Mexico on rafts

▲ Spanish coin used in Florida, 1600s

made of horsehide. Hernando de Soto arrived in Tampa Bay in 1539, in search of gold and silver. Although his expedition was considered a failure, de Soto explored parts of 10 present-day states over the next four years. Tristán de Luna y Arellano brought 500 soldiers, 1,000 settlers, and 240 horses in 1559, but a hurricane devastated his camp and equipment. After much hardship, he abandoned his attempt.

The French in Florida

The French, too, were interested in Florida for its ideal location for attacking Spanish cargo ships. Jean Ribault landed near present-day Jacksonville and claimed Florida for France in 1562. René Goulainne de Laudonniere founded a colony for French Protestants fleeing religious persecution in 1564. King Felipe II of Spain was angered by this action, and ordered Pedro Menéndez de Avilés to drive out the French. De Avilés founded St. Augustine in

1565, and succeeded completely, although bloodily, in his mission to remove the French.

Over the next century, Spain ruled the territory, sending more missionaries and starting new settlements. The Castillo de San Marcos, built from 1672 to 1695, served as an outpost of the Spanish Empire. It guarded St. Augustine and protected the sea route for treasure ships returning to Spain.

Spain entered the Seven Years' War, known in America as the French and Indian War, on the side of the French against the British. In 1762 the British captured Havana, Cuba, and to get it back at the end of the war, Spain gave up, or ceded, Florida to the British in 1763.

British Rule

With East and West Florida, Great Britain now had 15 colonies in North America. Land was granted to expand colonial settlements. These settlements became large farming communities called plantations. When the American Revolution erupted, the two Florida colonies remained loyal to Britain. Both the French and the Spanish aided the Americans. When the American colonies won their independence, Florida was returned to Spain in 1783.

The Second Spanish Period

The second period of Spanish rule in Florida was marked by the rise of old conflicts between American settlers and the Seminole, a mix of Creek, Timucua, Apalachee, and African Americans. Drawn by Governor Vicente Manuel de Zéspedes' offer of land grants, Spanish colonists, American settlers, and Seminole flocked to the region. Problems soon arose, though. Border agreements were ignored by new settlers. United States slaveholders were also angered when slaves escaped to Florida and were protected by the Seminole. Such conflicts prompted U.S. troops to attack the Seminole in the First Seminole War (1817–1818). General Andrew Jackson, however, led the United States to quick victories in

▼ This time line marks some key events in the history of Florida and the United States.

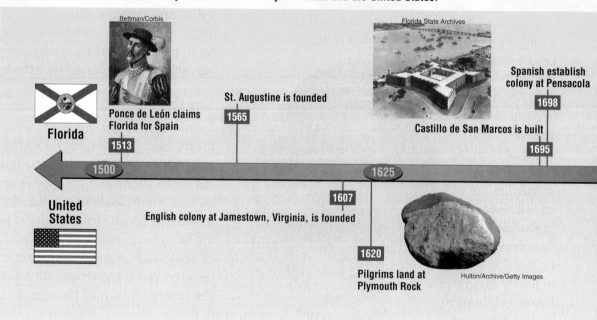

Florida and southern Georgia. Amidst the collapse of other Latin American colonies, and after years of conflict in the region, Spain finally ceded Florida to the United States in 1821.

The United States Takes Over

When Spain ceded the Florida territory with the Adams-Onís Treaty, Andrew Jackson became the territorial governor. During the first war, the Seminole had moved farther south to avoid capture or death. They now were opposed to the settlement of the area, and Jackson considered the 7,000 Seminole, led by Chief Osceola, an obstacle to the development of the region. The Second Seminole War (1835–1842) began over the question of whether the Seminole should be forced to move westward across the Mississippi River into what is now Oklahoma. This war would become the longest of the three conflicts

Florida State Archives

▲ **Chief Osceola**

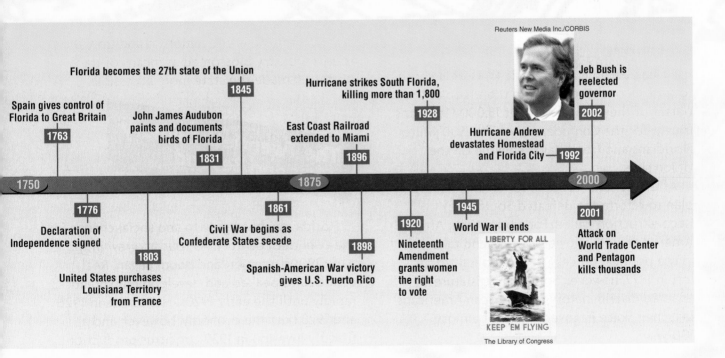

Reuters New Media Inc./CORBIS

Florida becomes the 27th state of the Union
1845

Spain gives control of Florida to Great Britain
1763

John James Audubon paints and documents birds of Florida
1831

Hurricane strikes South Florida, killing more than 1,800
1928

East Coast Railroad extended to Miami
1896

Jeb Bush is reelected governor
2002

Hurricane Andrew devastates Homestead and Florida City — **1992**

1750   **1875**   **2000**

1776
Declaration of Independence signed

1861
Civil War begins as Confederate States secede

1803
United States purchases Louisiana Territory from France

1898
Spanish-American War victory gives U.S. Puerto Rico

1920
Nineteenth Amendment grants women the right to vote

1945
World War II ends

LIBERTY FOR ALL
KEEP 'EM FLYING
The Library of Congress

2001
Attack on World Trade Center and Pentagon kills thousands

Library of Congress

▲ St. Augustine, late 1800s

between Florida's native peoples and the United States. Osceola led the Seminole deep into the Everglades, where they continued to conduct raids on the soldiers and settlers. In 1837, General Zachary Taylor, known as "Old Rough-and-Ready," tricked Osceola into coming out of the Florida Everglades by waving a flag of truce and then arrested him anyway. Osceola died in prison and most of the remaining Seminole surrendered, were killed, or were forced to move to the West.

Statehood

Florida became a state in 1845. Florida chose to secede, or withdraw, from the Union at the outset of the Civil War. About 15,000 Floridians fought for the Confederacy, while 2,500 white Floridians and freed slaves enlisted on the Union side.

After the war, President Abraham Lincoln's plan to reform the defeated South, the Reconstruction, failed. For a brief time, African Americans were allowed to vote and take part in the political process. When federal troops left in 1877, however, Southern legislatures enacted discriminatory laws. African Americans lost their voice in government for almost 100 years.

Growth and Change

In the remaining part of the nineteenth century, Florida continued to grow and change. Not as war torn as some former Confederate states, Florida became an exporter of agricultural products to other states. Henry Flagler developed the Florida East Coast Railroad down the peninsula, into and across the Florida Keys, creating hotels and communities along the way. As railroads expanded in the 1880s, Florida became a source for winter vegetables and fruit for the entire nation. In addition, the tourist industry blossomed as means of transportation made the state more accessible.

The Twentieth Century and Beyond

Florida saw huge growth and social change in the twentieth century. As tourism grew in the early 1900s, a major land boom began. Real estate sales peaked and development spread rapidly until the early 1920s. Hurricanes in 1926 and 1928 hurt the economy, however, and a fruit fly invasion in 1929 cut citrus production

by 40 percent. The onset of the Great Depression brought the economy screeching to a halt in 1929.

During World War II, Florida was an important site for military activities, and after the war, the defense industry continued to be an important part of Florida's economy. In the 1950s, America's space program was established at Cape Canaveral. Industries surrounding this program brought more growth to Florida.

The 1960s brought significant social and population changes to the state. Gradually, Florida reversed centuries of mistreatment of African Americans. Waves of new residents from northern states and the Caribbean Islands changed both the population and the culture. Retirees moved the average age upward, and Florida became the state with the oldest average age. As travel became easier, "the Sunshine State" became a destination for vacationers. People from around the world also moved to Florida, in part due to the sunny weather.

In 1965 Walt Disney secretly purchased 29,900 acres (almost 43 square miles) of land near Orlando, Florida. The creation of his Magic Kingdom became the largest private construction project in the United States. In 1971 Walt Disney World opened and the face of Florida changed forever.

No longer just another southern state, Florida has become an area of global importance in economy, environment, and culture.

FCAT Practice

Answering the questions below will help you prepare for the FCAT Reading, Writing, and Mathematics tests.

1. **How did Henry Flagler's railroad expansion change the course of history in Florida?** FCAT LA.B.1.3.2

2. **Study the map of Native Americans in Florida in the 1500s on page FL58. Of the Pensacola or Apalachee, which people settled the farthest east?** FCAT MA.B.1.3.4

Creating a Time Line **Many different nations attempted to colonize Florida before it became a state in 1845. Use an organizer similar to the one below and write a time line from 1513 to 1821 noting the territorial changes among the different nations.** FCAT LA.A.2.3.5

1513 ⊢——┼——┼——┼——┤ 1821

Florida's Cultural Diversity

Florida is a state with a culturally diverse population. This diversity affects the social, cultural, political, and economic life of the state. In many ways, to be a citizen of Florida is to be a citizen of a global community.

A Unique Cultural Identity

Florida's cultural makeup is unique. History, geography, climate, economy, immigration, and politics have all shaped Florida's population. The state is a meeting place between North, South, and Central America because it lies along the major trade routes of Europe, Africa, and the Caribbean nations. Throughout Florida's rich history, immigrants from many regions have settled here, bringing their own language and traditions. Today Florida continues to grow and change. According to the U.S. Census Bureau, Florida's population grew 23.5 percent between 1990 and 2000.

In Florida, people of African, Hispanic, European, Asian, Caribbean, and many other ethnic groups live and work together. Students from more than 250 different countries, speaking over 200 different languages, attend Florida public schools. About 17 percent of the state's population is new immigrants, not born in the United States. The largest minority group in Florida comes from the Latin American and the Caribbean nations, such as Cuba, Haiti, and Jamaica. Many of these residents are new immigrants. In the metropolis of Miami alone, more than 51 percent of its population of 2.3 million was born outside the United States.

The largest population group in the state, however, is made up of white persons not of Hispanic origin. This group makes up about 78 percent of the population. Even among this large population, there is diversity, as many have come from other states to make their home in Florida.

Because of its pleasing climate, Florida has become a well-known haven for retirees from other parts of the United States. Florida's population of those 65 or older is well above the national average. The beach and

▲ Nearly 10,000 people were sworn in as U.S. citizens at the Orange Bowl Stadium in 1984.

Bettmann/Corbis

tourist culture also draws young and international visitors and residents.

The Impact of Cultural Diversity

When immigrants from different countries moved to Florida, they brought with them their traditions of belief, language, clothing, architecture, art, music, and more. These influences blended with Florida's existing culture, resulting in a rich and colorful community. With cultural diversity came new businesses like restaurants, markets, and clothing stores, which service these groups and boost the economy. Exciting new neighborhood cultures emerged, such as Little Haiti in Miami. A short walk down a Florida street reveals the large Hispanic influence with many signs in Spanish. One can sample Peruvian cuisine, as Cuban salsa music pulses out of shop doorways. Art, clothing, and architecture also reflect the effect of different immigrant traditions.

Cultural diversity is not without its conflicts, however. People from different backgrounds must naturally overcome mistrust. They often compete for economic resources or political control. A long history of social inequality in the United States has also left its mark in Florida, especially with Native American and African American communities.

With a culturally diverse population, Florida mirrors what is happening in the world. Driven by global economies, borders between nations and cultures can become less important. As Americans, Floridians believe that a community is made stronger by the contributions of various ethnic groups. Economic and social exchange between cultures helps people understand each other, and promotes mutual respect, unity, and common goals. Although diversity brings challenges, Florida's cultural diversity also offers the reward of a truly multicultural society in a global community.

▲ Xavier Cortada's "Stepping into the American Dream"

FCAT Practice

Answering the questions below will help you prepare for the FCAT Reading, Writing, and Mathematics tests.

1. **What is the economic impact of cultural diversity?** `FCAT LA.A.1.3.2`

2. **The population of Florida in 2000 was 15,982,378. If 17.6 percent of Florida's population was made up of persons 65 years old and over, what was this group's population in 2000? Round to the nearest 100.** `FCAT MA.A.1.3.1, MA.A.1.3.4, MA.A.3.3.3`

Writing Activity Write a paragraph that explains how a different ethnic group has influenced you. `FCAT LA.B.1.3.2`

Florida Urban Life vs. Environmental Concerns

Florida's rapid development in recent decades has had a price. The balance of nature in some areas has been upset, habitats for wild creatures have been lost, and natural resources are being depleted. These changes threaten humans too, but efforts toward restoring Florida's environment are underway.

Growth and Change

Florida's dramatic growth in the 1970s and 1980s brought hundreds of thousands of people into the state. Population increased 44 percent in the 1970s and then another 33 percent in the 1980s. The completion and expansion of several giant tourist parks in those decades brought hundreds of thousands more visitors.

Jobs rose 24 percent in the 1980s, and more and more of the jobs were in high-tech industries and manufacturing. At first glance, this growth would seem good for the state with the benefits of more jobs, increased population, and economic strength. The trade-off, however, was risk to Florida's natural resources.

The Cost of Development

Increasing population and development were costly to the environment. More homes and recreational facilities required more water and sewage-treatment solutions. Development needed land, too, and some species lost their habitat and became threatened. Drainage systems and canals were built, altering the natural drainage routes, and land was reclaimed, further changing the way the ecosystem worked.

Development and the Environment

To an egret flying over the Everglades, the view on the next page probably looks just like home. An egret flying home a hundred years ago, though, might have had a much longer flight. The Florida Everglades, a unique national treasure, are much smaller than they once were as a result of human activity. The Comprehensive Everglades Restoration Project intends to restore a healthy ecosystem to the Everglades.

The famed Florida Everglades remain the largest subtropical wilderness in the continental United States. Parts of the Everglades look as they have looked for thousands of years, but changes brought on

▶ About 100 years ago, hundreds of thousands of birds lived in the Everglades. In fact, when the birds took to the air, the bright sun would be momentarily blocked and the sky would turn black.

Art Wolfe/Getty Images

Wendell Metzen/Index Stock Imagery

Ben Mangor/Super Stock

▲ Cypress trees

by human activities have shrunk the wilderness to half its original size. Growth and development, while good for Florida's economy, have sometimes caused devastation to natural environments. Unintended consequences of draining swampland, rerouting rivers, building canals, and expanding communities have in places upset the systems of nature. In some places, ecosystems have been damaged almost beyond hope. Unfortunately, repairing the damage is usually not a simple operation.

Why It Matters   Why does it matter if some swampland vanishes and some alligators and birds disappear? Quite apart from the loss of wild places and natural beauty, human beings are part of the ecosystem too. Here are two examples. A canal built to shorten the Kissimmee River dumped excess nutrients into Lake Okeechobee. Algae, a plantlike organism, began to grow, threatening other life-forms living in Lake Okeechobee. In the Everglades, loss of area harmed the natural ability of the land to purify water, putting the aquifer that supplies South Florida's drinking water at risk. Good water became harder to supply, and in some cases, development collapsed.

Achieving a Balance

As Floridians saw the consequences of unrestricted growth, they took steps to balance the desire for growth and the need for preservation. Restoring the Kissimmee River to its original course is scheduled to be complete by 2010. The Comprehensive Everglades Restoration Project will cost billions of dollars, but it is intended to protect this important area.

Federal, state, and local officials, as well as community groups, work together to carefully plan growth. Restrictions on land development and water use are common in many communities. Plans to preserve both scenic and critical ecosystems are now part of development planning. Sometimes parties disagree, but Floridians recognize that careful planning is the only way to preserve both Florida's prosperity and its heritage.

FCAT Practice

Answering the questions below will help you prepare for the FCAT Reading, Writing, and Science tests.

1. **Name three consequences of unrestricted growth.** **FCAT** LA.A.1.3.2, SC.D.2.3.2

2. **Give an example of how Florida is working to restore a damaged ecosystem.** **FCAT** SC.G.2.3.4, LA.A.1.3.2

Writing Activity   Write a paragraph that explains how the opening of a large tourist attraction, such as a theme park, can affect Florida's economy. **FCAT** LA.A.2.3.1, LA.B.1.3.2

"Old Florida" vs. "New Florida"

Huge growth has transformed Florida into an entirely new state. To longtime residents, the "New Florida" has become almost unrecognizable. Everything from the landscape to language has felt the impact of change. As the state enters the twenty-first century, it continues to face the challenges that come with change.

Then and Now

Florida has become a state of contrasts between its past and present. Despite immense development, signs of "Old Florida" show that, in many ways, it is still a place of southern culture and quiet living. In many local areas, agriculture still drives the economies, and rural traditions live on. There are still residents whose families have dwelt in the state for generations, with family histories bathed in Florida's rich past. Visitors to the many historical districts can learn about everything from Florida's Native American heritage and Spanish forts to its southern roots or art deco architecture.

In sharp contrast to the Old Florida, the New Florida is a high-tech player in the global market. In major cities, designer shops, glamorous hotels, and elegant restaurants draw sophisticated patrons and movie stars. The sandy beaches are dotted with international travelers basking in the sun. In addition to English, the New Floridian may speak Jamaican, Spanish, or Haitian Creole. In New Florida's economy, tourism is as important as agriculture, with its amusement parks drawing thousands of visitors every year. The story of New Florida is the story of cultural and economic success.

Immigrants and Residents

From 2000 to 2003, it is estimated that Florida had the nation's highest immigration rate. Population growth has truly shaped Florida's culture today. New immigrants have brought with them new ideas and culture, which affect the economy, education, politics, and all other aspects of life. The majority of Florida's new residents are from two main groups—Latin American and Caribbean immigrants or older persons from other states.

Miami is a boomtown city that is scarcely the same as it was 30 years ago. It is one of many Florida cities with heavy immigration from Latin America and Caribbean nations. In 1970 the population of Miami-Dade County was about 935,000 people. Today the Hispanic population alone numbers almost 1.3 million residents. Miami's many ethnic communities are colorful pockets of Latino culture.

Florida is also famous as the retirement place of choice for many Americans. Retirement communities and homes house tens of thousands of senior citizens from across the United States. Of all the 50 states, Florida has the highest percentage of persons over the age of 65. The increase in the number of seniors has radically altered Florida's landscape and economy as industries try to meet the needs of this ever-growing group of Floridians.

New and Old Industries

As in other states, Florida's economy has changed with the times. While agriculture, heavy manufacturing, and mining are still important, the shift to service and high-tech industries has changed the business environment. Workers

Joseph Sohm/Visions of America, LLC/PictureQuest

▲ Florida's new Capitol looms over the old Capitol. The new high-rise was needed as Florida's growth demanded more government services.

today must acquire new knowledge, skills, and education to seek new opportunities in the shifting job market.

Tourism has become the state's number one industry. In 2002 nearly 70 million tourists visited Florida's sunny beaches and amusement parks, bringing in more than $50 billion to fuel the state's economy.

Since World War II, the United States has become one of the most influential nations in the global economy. Florida, like all other states, strives to participate in global trade to survive today's tough economic climate. In order to meet the needs of the international market, Florida has shifted its local industrial focus to the global market.

Innovation and Heritage

Despite Florida's history of civil rights turmoil, the long shadow of racial discrimination has faded over the last 30 years. In 1979 Bob Martinez was elected the first Hispanic American mayor of Tampa. He went on to become the governor of Florida. Florida has elected many Hispanic and African American legislators and judges to office both locally and nationally. Joe Celestin, a native of Haiti, was the first African American to be elected mayor of North Miami in 2001, and he was reelected in 2003.

Amidst the flurry of new development, Florida tries to preserve its vital past. Florida's Bureau of Historic Preservation manages the nation's largest historical preservation grants program. It successfully protects and maintains Florida's vast architectural heritage.

Florida has successfully survived drastic change and has grown from it. As the old and the new have learned to coexist, the result is a rich combination of culture and connection.

FCAT Practice

Answering the questions below will help you prepare for the FCAT Reading and Writing tests.

1. **How has immigration affected Florida voters in elections for public office?** FCAT LA.A.1.3.2

2. **Create a Venn diagram. List features of "Old Florida" in one circle and features of "New Florida" in the other. In the area where the circles intersect, include the features of Florida that apply to both.** FCAT LA.A.2.2.7, LA.A.2.3.1

Writing Activity Visit the State of Florida's official site for historic preservation at dhr.dos.state.fl.us/. Write a paragraph that provides an example of how Florida is preserving its links to the past. FCAT LA.B.1.3.2, LA.A.2.3.5

Florida's Economy

Florida's economy is diverse and growing. The economic base is changing as the world's economy changes. Florida has a number of advantages as it pursues markets internationally.

On America's coastline, Florida was a natural place for military bases during World War II. At the end of the war, experiments on those bases led to the space program, now located at the Kennedy Space Center at Cape Canaveral. The space program drew high-tech industry to the state, and created a climate of innovation that Florida strives to maintain. High-tech and global industries are an important part of Florida's economy.

Florida's economy is as rich and diverse as its history and population. From its agricultural beginnings to its present-day mix of industries and opportunities, Florida's geographic and cultural advantages have helped its economy grow and change as times required.

▼ **Discovery Space Shuttle Launch, Kennedy Space Center**

Roger Ressmeyer/CORBIS

Agriculture and Natural Resources

Once the backbone of Florida's economy, agriculture still plays an important role. Florida grows about three-quarters of the nation's citrus fruits. After freezes nearly wrecked the citrus industry in the 1890s, Florida farmers began growing vegetables as well. Today Florida ranks second only to California in the amount of vegetables produced. Nearly 30 percent of all of Florida's land is in farm acreage, with another 37 percent in commercial forests. Mining is important too, with a quarter of the world's phosphate, useful for fertilizer, coming from Florida. Fishing is an industry conducted from both Gulf and Atlantic coastal ports and the Florida Keys, with markets on the East Coast and in the Midwest.

Manufacturing

Florida manufacturing grew rapidly in the 1950s and 1960s. Some of the growth was in processing citrus products, but clothing, chemical, and other businesses attracted by the space program developed too. Electrical and electronics employment now lead in the number of manufacturing jobs. The Florida High-Tech Corridor, from coast to coast in the center of the state, produces many of the jobs that rank Florida fourth in the nation in high-tech employment.

Top Five Export Goods

Commodity	Value of Exports (millions of U.S. dollars)
Machinery	$7,168
Electrical Machinery	$5,027
Vehicles, Not Railway	$2,776
Instruments:	
Optical and Medical	$1,658
Aircraft, Spacecraft	$1,526

Source: *Enterprise Florida, Inc., 2002 statistics.*

▲ Florida's top markets include Brazil, the Dominican Republic, Venezuela, and Costa Rica.

Although social services and retail trade employ more workers, tourism is the largest income-producing industry in Florida. Originally a winter destination, Florida now attracts visitors year-round with its theme parks, recreational activities, national parks, golf courses, and coastal cruises. Florida's modern transportation systems, including highways, rail, and air traffic, bring in visitors for business and pleasure from all corners of the nation and world. In addition, 15 ocean ports serve both recreation and commerce.

Florida's Economy in the Future

Florida's economy is changing as it looks to the future. Heavy industry is not as successful as it once was, and service jobs, such as in government, health care, and tourism, are becoming an even more important part of the economy. One reason for these changes is globalization, the linking together of nations through trade. Globalization spreads commerce around the world through common markets, trade agreements, and common standards and money exchange.

Some trade agreements, like the North American Free Trade Agreement (NAFTA), eliminate trade barriers between nations. This was established so that goods could flow freely among the United States, Canada, and Mexico. Florida's people depend on trade for jobs.

Florida has some real advantages in global business. Florida's central location in the Americas is just as important today as it has been throughout history. Florida has workers who are multilingual, or able to speak more than one language. Florida has first-rate airport facilities and deepwater ports. Florida has both national and international banking and financial institutions. The state government and private businesses have formed an organization called Enterprise Florida to encourage high-tech and global business.

As Florida enters the twenty-first century, it looks to both a past and a future of economic growth. Challenges in education, finance, and providing services remain as Florida prepares its workforce for the rest of the century.

FCAT Practice

Answering the questions below will help you prepare for the FCAT Reading, Writing, and Mathematics tests.

1. **Nearly 30 percent of Florida's land is in farm acreage, with another 37 percent in commercial forests, and 10 percent in national/state forests. What percentage of land is urban/suburban/industrial? Show these figures in a circle graph.**
   FCAT LA.A.2.3.5, MA.A.1.3.1, MA.A.3.3.2, MA.E.1.3.1
2. **Review the chart on this page. What is Florida's top commodity to export? What is its value?**
   FCAT MA.E.3.3.1

Writing Activity **Write a paragraph explaining the challenges Florida faces as the state enters the twenty-first century.** FCAT LA.B.1.3.2, LA.A.2.3.1, LA.A.2.3.5

READING TO LEARN

This handbook focuses on skills and strategies that can help you understand the words you read. The strategies you use to understand whole texts depend on the kind of text you are reading. In other words, you do not read a textbook the way you read a novel. You read a textbook mainly for information; you read a novel mainly for fun. To get the most out of your reading, you need to choose the right strategy to fit the reason you're reading.

USE THIS HANDBOOK TO HELP YOU LEARN

- how to identify new words and build your vocabulary;
- how to adjust the way you read to fit your reason for reading;
- how to use specific reading strategies to better understand what you read;
- how to use critical thinking strategies to think more deeply about what you read.

You will also learn about

- text structures;
- reading for research.

TABLE OF CONTENTS

Identifying Words and
  Building Vocabulary RH1

Reading for a Reason RH3

Understanding What You Read RH4

Thinking About Your Reading RH5

Understanding Text Structure RH7

Identifying Words and Building Vocabulary

What do you do when you come across a word you do not know as you read? Do you skip over the word and keep reading? If you are reading for fun or entertainment, you might. But if you are reading for information, an unfamiliar word may get in the way of your understanding. When that happens, try the following strategies to figure out how to say the word and what the word means.

Reading Unfamiliar Words

Sounding out the word One way to figure out how to say a new word is to sound it out, syllable by syllable. Look carefully at the word's beginning, middle, and ending. Inside the word, do you see a word you already know how to pronounce? What vowels are in the syllables? Use the following tips when sounding out new words.

- **Roots and base words** The main part of a word is called its root. When the root is a complete word, it may be called the base word. When you come across a new word, check whether you recognize its root or base word. It can help you pronounce the word and figure out the word's meaning.

ASK YOURSELF

- What letters make up the beginning sound or beginning syllable of the word?

  Example: In the word *coagulate, co* rhymes with *so.*

- What sounds do the letters in the middle part of the word make?

  Example: In the word *coagulate,* the syllable *ag* has the same sound as the

  ag in *bag,* and the syllable *u* is pronounced like the letter *u.*

- What letters make up the ending sound or syllable?

  Example: In the word *coagulate, late* is a familiar word you already know how to pronounce.

- Now try pronouncing the whole word:

  co ag u late.

- **Prefixes** A prefix is a word part that can be added to the beginning of a root or base word. For example, the prefix *pre-* means "before," so *prehistory* means "before history." Prefixes can change, or even reverse, the meaning of a word. For example, *un-* means "not," so *unconstitutional* means "not constitutional."

- **Suffixes** A suffix is a word part that can be added to the end of a root or base word to change the word's meaning. Adding a suffix to a word can also change that word from one part of speech to another. For example, the word *joy,* which is a noun, becomes an adjective when the suffix *-ful* (meaning "full of") is added. *Joyful* means "full of joy."

Determining a Word's Meaning

Using syntax Like all languages, English has rules and patterns for the way words are arranged in sentences. The way a sentence is organized is called the **syntax.**

In a simple sentence in English, someone or something (the *subject*) does something (the *predicate* or *verb*) to or with another person or thing (the *object*): The *soldiers attacked* the *enemy.*

CHECK IT OUT

Knowing about syntax can help you figure out the meaning of an unfamiliar word. Just look at how syntax can help you figure out the following nonsense sentence.

The blizzy kwarkles sminched the flerky fleans.

Your experience with English syntax tells you that the action word, or verb, in this sentence is *sminched*. Who did the *sminching*? The *kwarkles*. What kind of kwarkles were they? *Blizzy*. Whom did they *sminch*? The fleans. What kind of fleans were they? *Flerky*. Even though you don't know the meaning of the words in the nonsense sentence, you can make some sense of the sentence by studying its syntax.

Using context clues You can often figure out the meaning of an unfamiliar word by looking at its context, or the words and sentences that surround it. To learn new words as you read, follow these steps for using context clues.

1. Look before and after the unfamiliar word for:
- a definition or a synonym, another word that means the same as the unfamiliar word.
- a general topic associated with the word.
- a clue to what the word is similar to or different from.
- an action or a description that has something to do with the word.

2. Connect what you already know with what the author has written.

3. Predict a possible meaning.

4. Use the meaning in the sentence.

5. Try again if your guess does not make sense.

Using reference materials Dictionaries and other reference sources can help you learn new words. Check out these reference sources:

- A **dictionary** gives the pronunciation and the meaning or meanings of words. Some dictionaries also give other forms of words, their parts of speech, and synonyms. You might also find the historical background of a word.

- A **glossary** is a word list that appears at the end—or appendix—of a book or other written work. It includes only words that are in that work. Like dictionaries, glossaries have the pronunciation and definitions of words.

- A **thesaurus** lists groups of words that have the same, or almost the same, meaning. Words with similar meanings are called *synonyms.* Seeing the synonyms of words can help you build your vocabulary.

Recognizing Word Meanings Across Subjects

Have you ever learned a new word in one class and then noticed it in your reading for other subjects? The word probably will not mean exactly the same thing in each class. But you can use what you know about the word's meaning to help you understand what it means in a different subject area.

CHECK IT OUT

Look at the following example from three subjects:

Social studies: One major **product** manufactured in southern U.S. states is cotton cloth.

Math: After you multiply those two numbers, explain how you arrived at the **product.**

Science: One **product** of photosynthesis is oxygen.

Reading for a Reason

Why are you reading that paperback mystery? What do you hope to get from your geography textbook? And are you going to read either of these books in the same way that you read a restaurant menu? The point is, you read for different reasons. The reason you are reading something helps you decide on the reading strategies you use. In other words, how you read will depend on **why** you're reading.

Knowing Your Reason for Reading

In school and in life, you will have many reasons for reading, and those reasons will lead you to a wide range of materials. For example,

- **to learn and understand new information,** you might read news magazines, textbooks, news on the Internet, books about your favorite pastime, encyclopedia articles, primary and secondary sources for a school report, instructions on how to use a calling card, or directions for a standardized test.

- **to find specific information,** you might look at a weather report, a bank statement, television listings, the sports section for the score of last night's game, or a notice on where to register for a field trip.

- **to be entertained,** you might read your favorite magazine, e-mails or letters from friends, the Sunday comics, or even novels, short stories, plays, or poems.

Adjusting How Fast You Read

How quickly or how carefully you should read a text depends on your purpose for reading it. Because there are many reasons and ways to read, think about your purpose and choose a strategy that works best. Try out these strategies:

- **Scanning** means quickly running your eyes over the material, looking for *key words or phrases* that point to the information you're looking for. Scan when you need to find a particular piece or type of information. For example, you might scan a newspaper for movie show times.

- **Skimming** means quickly reading a piece of writing *to find its main idea* or to *get a general overview* of it. For example, you might skim the sports section of the daily newspaper to find out how your favorite teams are doing. Or you might skim a chapter in your textbook to prepare for a test.

- **Careful reading** involves *reading slowly and paying attention* with a purpose in mind. Read carefully when you're learning new concepts, following complicated directions, or preparing to explain information to someone else.

Understanding What You Read

Skilled readers adopt a number of strategies before, during, and after reading to make sure they understand what they read.

Previewing

When you preview a piece of writing, you are trying to get an idea about that piece of writing. If you know what to expect before reading, you will have an easier time understanding ideas and relationships.

DO IT!

1. Look at the title and any illustrations that are included.

2. Read the headings, subheadings, and anything in bold letters.

3. Skim over the passage to see how it is organized. Is it divided into many parts? Is it a long poem or short story?

Do not forget to look at the graphics—pictures, maps, or diagrams.

4. Set a purpose for your reading. Are you reading to learn something new? Are you reading to find specific information?

Using What You Know

Believe it or not, you already know quite a bit about what you are going to read. You bring knowledge and personal experience to a selection. Drawing on your own background is called *activating prior knowledge,* and it can help you create meaning in what you read. Ask yourself, *What do I already know about this topic?*

Predicting

You do not need any special knowledge to make *predictions* when you read. The predictions do not even have to be accurate. Take educated guesses before and during your reading about what might happen in the story or article you are reading.

Visualizing

Creating pictures in your mind as you read—called *visualizing*—is a powerful aid to understanding. As you read, set up a movie theater in your imagination. Picture the setting—city streets, the desert, or the surface of the moon. If you can visualize what you read, selections will be more vivid, and you will recall them better later on.

Identifying Sequence

When you discover the logical order of events or ideas, you are identifying *sequence.* Look for clues and signal words that will help you find the way information is organized.

Determining the Main Idea

When you look for the *main idea* of a selection, you look for the most important idea. The examples, reasons, and details that further explain the main idea are called *supporting details.*

Questioning

Keep up a conversation with yourself as you read by *asking questions* about the text. Ask about the importance of the information you are reading. Ask how one event relates to another. Ask yourself if you understand what you just read. As you answer your questions, you are making sure that you understand what is going on.

Clarifying

Clear up, or *clarify,* confusing or difficult passages as you read. Reread the passage using these techniques.

- *Reread* the confusing parts slowly and carefully.
- *Look up* unfamiliar words.
- Simply *"talk out"* the part to yourself.

Reviewing

You probably *review* in school what you learned the day before so that the ideas are firm in your mind. Reviewing when you read does the same thing. Take time now and then to pause and review what you have read. Think about the main ideas and reorganize them for yourself so you can recall them later. Filling in study aids such as graphic organizers can help you review.

Monitoring Your Comprehension

As you read, check your understanding by using the following strategies.

- **Summarize** what you read by pausing from time to time and telling yourself the main ideas of what you have just read. Answer the questions *Who? What? Where? When? Why?* and *How?* Summarizing tests your comprehension by encouraging you to clarify key points in your own words.

- **Paraphrase** Use paraphrasing as a test to see whether you really got the point. *Paraphrasing* is retelling something in your own words. Try putting what you have just read into your own words. If you cannot explain it clearly, you should probably have another look at the text.

Thinking About Your Reading

Sometimes it is important to think more deeply about what you have read so you can get the most out of what the author says. These critical thinking skills will help you go beyond what the words say and understand the important messages of your reading.

Interpreting

To *interpret* a text, first ask yourself, *What is the writer really saying here?* Then use what you know about the world to help answer that question.

Inferring

Writers provide clues and interesting details that suggest certain information. *Inferring* involves thinking and using your own experience to come up with an idea based on what an author implies or suggests. In reading, you *infer* when you use context clues and your own knowledge to figure out the author's meaning.

Drawing Conclusions

Skillful readers are always *drawing conclusions,* or figuring out much more than an author says directly. The process is like a detective solving a mystery. You combine information and evidence that the author provides to come up with a statement about the topic. Drawing conclusions helps you find connections between ideas and events and gives you a better understanding of what you are reading.

Analyzing

Analyzing, or looking at separate parts of something to understand the entire piece, is a way to think critically about written work. In analyzing *informational text,* you might look at how the ideas are organized to see what is most important.

Distinguishing Fact From Opinion

Distinguishing between fact and opinion is one of the most important reading skills you can learn. A *fact* is a statement that can be proved with supporting information. An *opinion,* on the other hand, is what a writer believes, on the basis of his or her personal viewpoint.

FOR EXAMPLE

Look at the following examples of fact and opinion.

Fact: George III was the British king during the American Revolution.

Opinion: King George III was an evil tyrant.

You could prove that George III was king during that period. It is a fact. However, not everyone might see that King George III was a tyrant. That is someone's opinion.

As you examine information, always ask yourself, *Is this a fact or an opinion?* Do not think that opinions are always bad. Very often they are just what you want. You read editorials and essays for their authors' opinions. Reviews of books, movies, plays, and CDs can help you decide whether to spend your time and money on something. It's when opinions are based on faulty reasoning or prejudice or when they are stated as facts that they become troublesome.

Evaluating

When you form an opinion or make a judgment about something you are reading, you are *evaluating.* Ask yourself whether the author seems biased, whether the information is one-sided, and whether the argument that is presented is logical.

Synthesizing

When you *synthesize,* you combine ideas (maybe even from different sources) to come up with something new. For example, you might read a manual on coaching soccer, combine that information with your own experiences playing soccer, and come up with a winning plan for coaching your sister's team this spring.

Understanding Text Structure

Good writers structure each piece of their writing in a specific way for a specific purpose. That pattern of organization is called *text structure.* When you know the text structure of a selection, you will find it easier to locate and recall an author's ideas. Here are four ways that writers organize text.

Comparison and Contrast

Comparison-and-contrast structure shows the similarities and differences among people, things, and ideas. When writers use comparison-and-contrast structure, often they want to show you *how things that seem alike are different,* or *how things that seem different are alike.*

- **Signal words and phrases:** *similarly, on the other hand, in contrast to*

Cause and Effect

Just about everything that happens in life is the cause or the effect of some other event or action. Writers use cause-and-effect structure to explore the reasons for something happening and to examine the results of previous events. This structure helps answer the question that everybody is always asking: *Why?* Cause-and-effect structure is all about explaining things.

- **Signal words and phrases:** *so, because, as a result, therefore*

Problem and Solution

How did scientists overcome the difficulty of getting a person to the moon? How will I brush my teeth when I have forgotten my toothpaste? These questions may be very different in importance, but they have one thing in common: Each identifies a problem and asks how to solve it. *Problems* and *solutions* are part of what makes life interesting. Problems and solutions also occur in fiction and nonfiction writing.

- **Signal words and phrases:** *how, help, problem, obstruction, difficulty, need, attempt, have to, must*

Sequence

Take a look at three common types of sequences, or the order in which thoughts are arranged.

1. **Chronological order** refers to the order in which events take place. First you wake up; next you have breakfast; then you go to school. Those events don't make much sense in any other order.
   - **Signal words:** *first, next, then, later, finally*

2. **Spatial order** tells you the order in which to look at objects. For example, take a look at this description of an ice cream sundae: *At the bottom of the dish are two scoops of vanilla. The scoops are covered with fudge and topped with whipped cream and a cherry.* Your eyes follow the sundae from the bottom to the top. Spatial order is important in descriptive writing because it helps you as a reader to see an image the way the author does.
   - **Signal words:** *above, below, behind, next to*

3. **Order of importance** is going from most important to least important or the other way around. For example, a typical news article has a most-to-least-important structure.
   - **Signal words:** *principal, central, important, fundamental*

REFERENCE ATLAS

World: Political	RA2	Europe: Political	RA16
North America: Political	RA4	Europe: Physical	RA18
North America: Physical	RA5	Africa: Political	RA20
United States: Political	RA6	Africa: Physical	RA21
United States: Physical	RA8	Asia: Political	RA22
Canada: Physical/Political	RA10	Asia: Physical	RA24
Middle America: Physical/Political	RA12	Middle East: Physical/Political	RA26
South America: Political	RA14	Pacific Rim: Physical/Political	RA28
South America: Physical	RA15	Polar Regions	RA30

ATLAS KEY

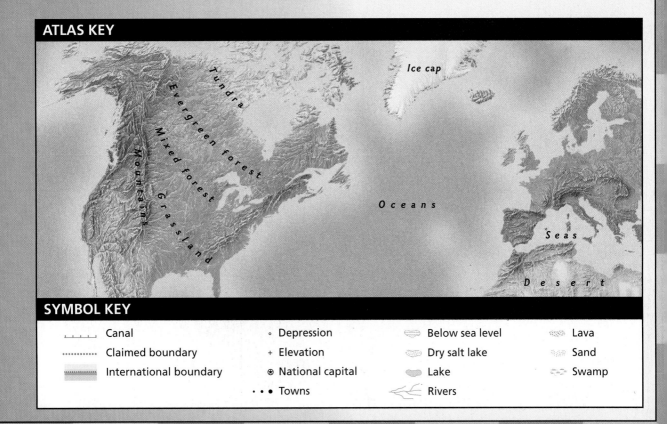

SYMBOL KEY

⊥⊥⊥⊥	Canal	∘	Depression	〰	Below sea level	🗺	Lava
··········	Claimed boundary	+	Elevation	🗺	Dry salt lake	🗺	Sand
▓▓▓▓	International boundary	⊛	National capital	🗺	Lake	⇢	Swamp
· · ●	Towns			⇜	Rivers		

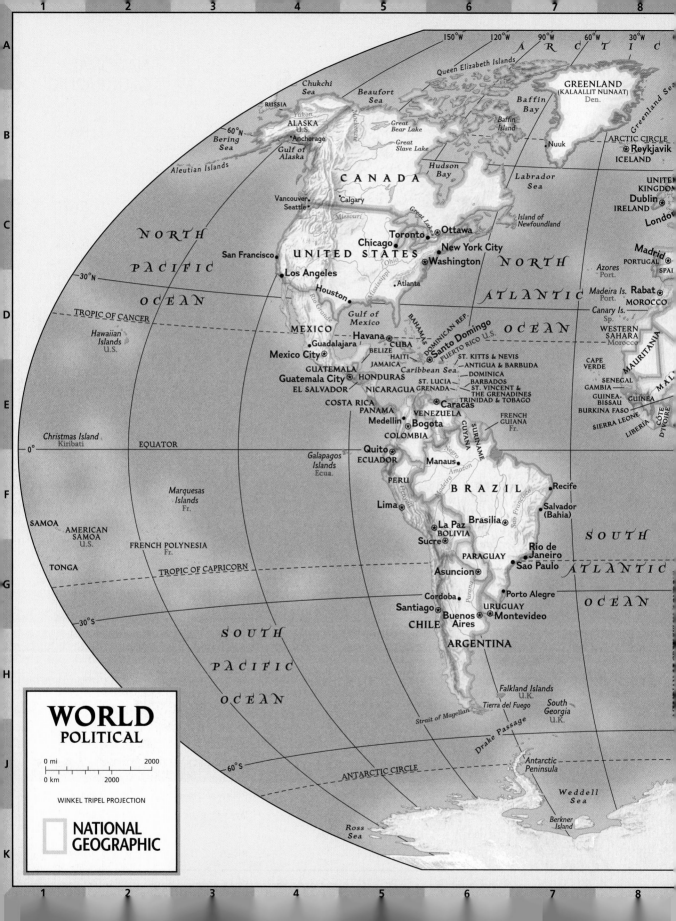

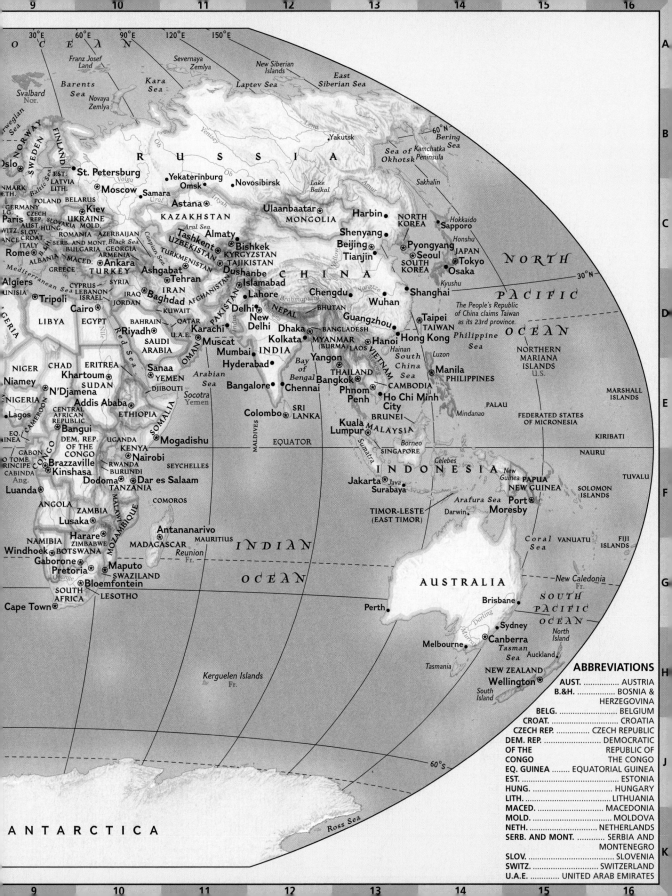

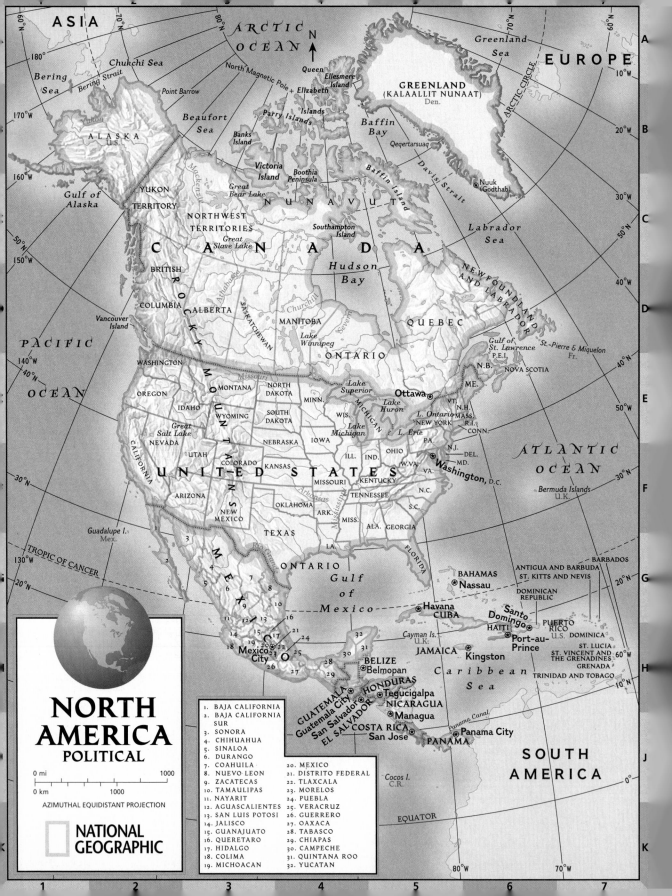

NORTH AMERICA
POLITICAL

0 mi   1000

0 km   1000

AZIMUTHAL EQUIDISTANT PROJECTION

NATIONAL GEOGRAPHIC

1. BAJA CALIFORNIA
2. BAJA CALIFORNIA SUR
3. SONORA
4. CHIHUAHUA
5. SINALOA
6. DURANGO
7. COAHUILA
8. NUEVO LEON
9. ZACATECAS
10. TAMAULIPAS
11. NAYARIT
12. AGUASCALIENTES
13. SAN LUIS POTOSI
14. JALISCO
15. GUANAJUATO
16. QUERETARO
17. HIDALGO
18. COLIMA
19. MICHOACAN
20. MEXICO
21. DISTRITO FEDERAL
22. TLAXCALA
23. MORELOS
24. PUEBLA
25. VERACRUZ
26. GUERRERO
27. OAXACA
28. TABASCO
29. CHIAPAS
30. CAMPECHE
31. QUINTANA ROO
32. YUCATAN

NORTH AMERICA

PHYSICAL

0 mi 1000

0 km 1000

AZIMUTHAL EQUIDISTANT PROJECTION

NATIONAL GEOGRAPHIC

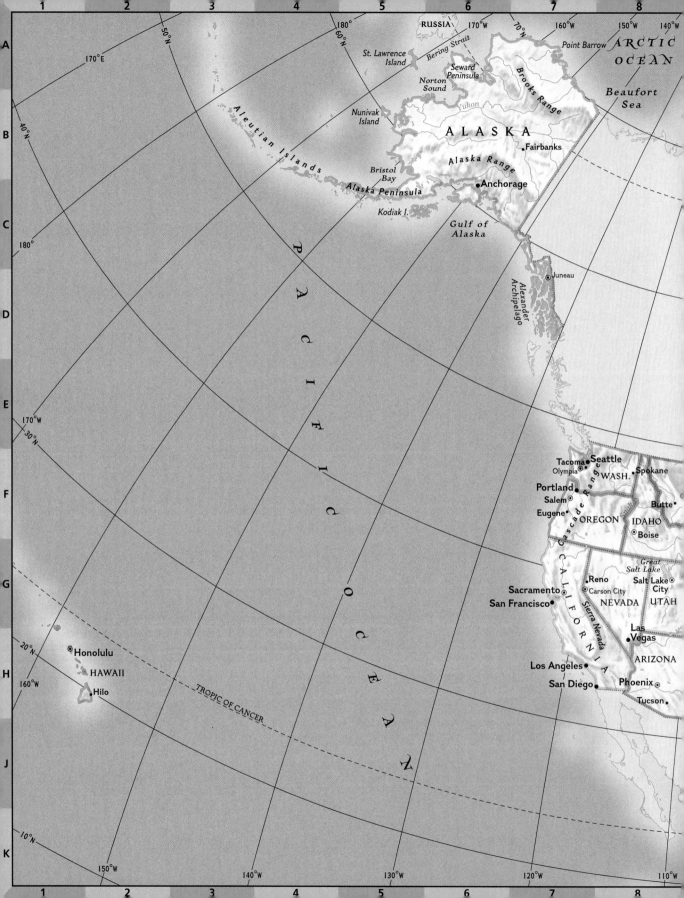

UNITED STATES
POLITICAL

0 mi   600

0 km   600

OBLIQUE AZIMUTHAL EQUIDISTANT PROJECTION

NATIONAL GEOGRAPHIC

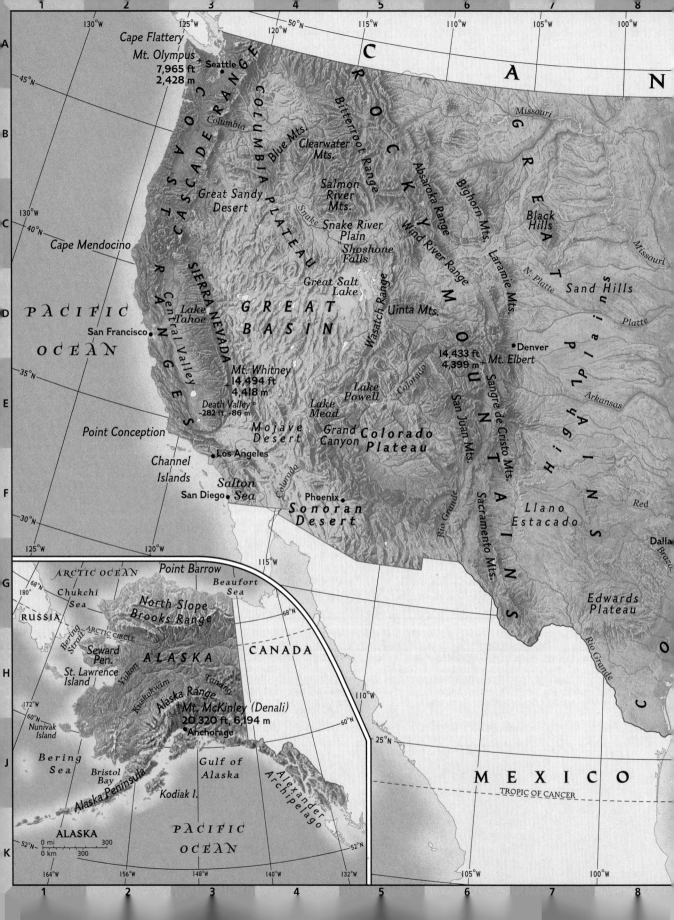

UNITED STATES
PHYSICAL

0 mi   300

0 km   300

ALBERS CONIC EQUAL-AREA PROJECTION

NATIONAL GEOGRAPHIC

Map labels:

Lake of the Woods

C A N A D A

Isle Royale
Lake Superior

Upper Peninsula

Lake Champlain
Adirondack Mts.
Green Mts.
White Mts.
Gulf of Maine

Minneapolis

Lower Peninsula
Lake Michigan
Lake Huron

Lake Ontario
Niagara Falls

Connecticut
Boston
Cape Cod

Mississippi

Milwaukee

Chicago

Detroit
Lake Erie
Cleveland

Hudson

Long Island
New York City

C E N T R A L
L O W L A N D

Pittsburgh

Philadelphia

Appalachian Plateau
Allegheny Mts.
A P P A L A C H I A N   M O U N T A I N S

Baltimore
Washington
Delaware Bay

A T L A N T I C

O C E A N

Indianapolis

Ohio

Chesapeake Bay

Flint Hills

St. Louis

Wabash

Cumberland Plateau
Cumberland Plateau
Blue Ridge

Piedmont

Ozark Plateau

Tennessee

Mt. Mitchell
6,684 ft
2,037 m

Cape Hatteras

Boston Mts.

Memphis

Ouachita Mts.

Black Belt

Atlanta

Savannah

Mississippi

Red

Jacksonville

Houston

New Orleans

Mississippi
River Delta

Cape Canaveral

Lake Okeechobee

G u l f   o f   M e x i c o

The Everglades

Miami

Florida Keys

Straits of Florida

TROPIC OF CANCER

C U B A

Hawaii inset:

Niihau
Kauai
Honolulu
Oahu
Molokai
Maui
Lanai
Kahoolawe

Hawaii

Mauna Kea
13,796 ft
4,205 m

P A C I F I C
O C E A N

PRINCIPAL HAWAIIAN ISLANDS

0 mi   100
0 km   100

CANADA
PHYSICAL/POLITICAL

0 mi   400
0 km   400

AZIMUTHAL EQUIDISTANT PROJECTION

NATIONAL GEOGRAPHIC

Ellesmere Island

Devon Island

ICELAND

GREENLAND
(KALAALLIT NUNAAT)
Den.

Baffin Bay

Melville Peninsula

Foxe Basin

Baffin Island

Davis Strait

A V U T

Southampton Island

○ Iqaluit

Hudson Strait

Labrador Sea

Ungava Bay

Hudson Bay

Belcher Islands

N E W F O U N D L A N D
A N D   L A B R A D O R

Cartwright

Schefferville •
Happy Valley-
Goose Bay •

Smallwood Reservoir
"Churchill Falls"

Island of Newfoundland

James Bay

Q U E B E C

St. John's ⊙
Avalon Peninsula

Manicouagan Reservoir
Sept-Îles •

Anticosti I.

St.-Pierre & Miquelon
Fr.

S   H   I   E   L   D

Gaspé Pen.

Gulf of St. Lawrence

O N T A R I O

Lake Nipigon

Chicoutimi •

PRINCE EDWARD ISLAND

Cape Breton I.

A T L A N T I C

• Rouyn-Noranda

Quebec City ⊙

NEW BRUNSWICK

Charlottetown ⊙
NOVA SCOTIA

Thunder Bay •
Lake Superior

Fredericton ⊙
Saint John •

Halifax •

Sudbury •

Montreal •

St. Lawrence

Bay of Fundy

O C E A N

Ottawa ⊛

Lake Huron

Lake Michigan

Toronto ⊙

Niagara Falls
London •

L. Ontario

L. Erie

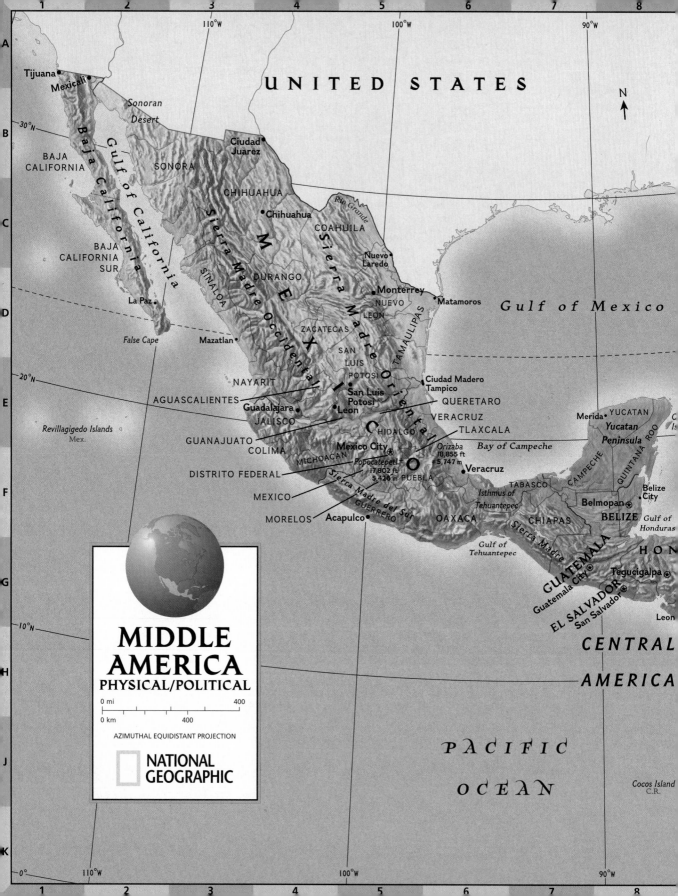

MIDDLE AMERICA

PHYSICAL/POLITICAL

0 mi   400
0 km   400

AZIMUTHAL EQUIDISTANT PROJECTION

NATIONAL GEOGRAPHIC

UNITED STATES

N

Tijuana
Mexicali

*Sonoran
Desert*

BAJA
CALIFORNIA

30°N

Ciudad
Juarez

CHIHUAHUA

Rio Grande

Chihuahua

COAHUILA

Gulf of California

BAJA
CALIFORNIA
SUR

Baja California

Sierra Madre Occidental

M

DURANGO

SINALOA

Nuevo
Laredo

Monterrey

NUEVO
LEON

Matamoros

Gulf of Mexico

La Paz

False Cape

Mazatlan

E

ZACATECAS

Sierra Madre Oriental

X

TAMAULIPAS

Gulf of California

20°N

NAYARIT

AGUASCALIENTES

Guadalajara

JALISCO

SAN
LUIS
POTOSI

San Luis
Potosi

Leon

Ciudad Madero
Tampico

QUERETARO

VERACRUZ

Merida

YUCATAN

*Revillagigedo Islands
Mex.*

GUANAJUATO

COLIMA

I

HIDALGO

TLAXCALA

Bay of Campeche

*Yucatan
Peninsula*

QUINTANA ROO

Is

MICHOACAN

Mexico City

Popocatepetl
17,802 ft
5,426 m

Orizaba
18,855 ft
5,747 m

CAMPECHE

Belize
City

DISTRITO FEDERAL

O

PUEBLA

Veracruz

TABASCO

Belmopan

BELIZE

*Gulf of
Honduras*

MEXICO

MORELOS

Acapulco

Sierra Madre del Sur

GUERRERO

OAXACA

*Isthmus of
Tehuantepec*

CHIAPAS

Sierra Madre

HON

10°N

*Gulf of
Tehuantepec*

GUATEMALA

Guatemala City

Tegucigalpa

EL SALVADOR
San Salvador

Leon

CENTRAL

AMERICA

PACIFIC

OCEAN

*Cocos Island
C.R.*

110°W

100°W

90°W

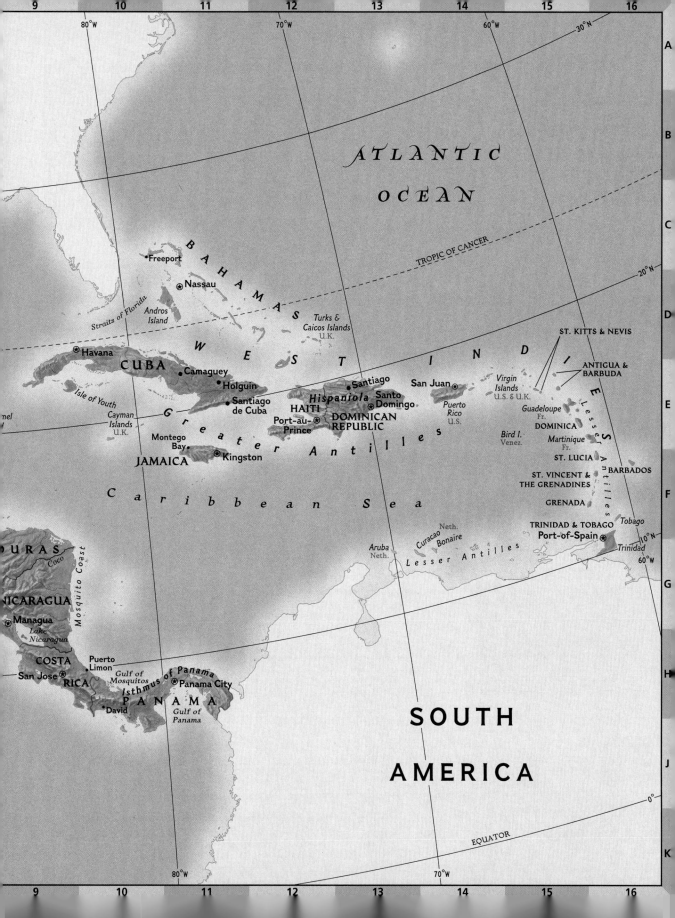

| | 9 | | 10 | | 11 | | 12 | | 13 | | 14 | | 15 | | 16 |

80°W 70°W 60°W 30°N

A

B

ATLANTIC

OCEAN

C

TROPIC OF CANCER

20°N

● Freeport

B A H A M A S

⊛ Nassau

W

E

Straits of Florida

Andros
Island

Turks &
Caicos Islands
U.K.

S

T

I

N

D

I

E

ST. KITTS & NEVIS

D

● Havana

CUBA

● Camaguey

● Holguin

Isle of Youth

Cayman
Islands
U.K.

nel

● Santiago
de Cuba

G

r

e

a

Montego
Bay

JAMAICA

⊛ Kingston

Hispaniola

HAITI

Port-au-
Prince

Santo
⊛ Domingo

DOMINICAN
REPUBLIC

t

● Santiago

San Juan ⊛

Puerto
Rico
U.S.

Virgin
Islands
U.S. & U.K.

e

r

A

n

t

i

l

l

e

s

ANTIGUA &
BARBUDA

Guadeloupe
Fr.

DOMINICA

Bird I.
Venez.

Martinique
Fr.

ST. LUCIA

L
e
s
s
e
r

A
n
t
i
l
l
e
s

BARBADOS

E

ST. VINCENT &
THE GRENADINES

GRENADA

F

C a r i b b e a n   S e a

Neth.

Curacao

Bonaire

Aruba
Neth.

Lesser Antilles

TRINIDAD & TOBAGO
Port-of-Spain ⊛

Tobago

Trinidad

60°W

10°N

G

URAS

Coco

Mosquito Coast

NICARAGUA

⊛ Managua

Lake
Nicaragua

COSTA

San Jose ⊛

RICA

Puerto
Limon

Gulf of
Mosquitos

Isthmus of Panama

PANAMA

David ●

⊛ Panama City

Gulf of
Panama

H

SOUTH

J

AMERICA

0°

K

EQUATOR

80°W 70°W

| | 9 | | 10 | | 11 | | 12 | | 13 | | 14 | | 15 | | 16 |

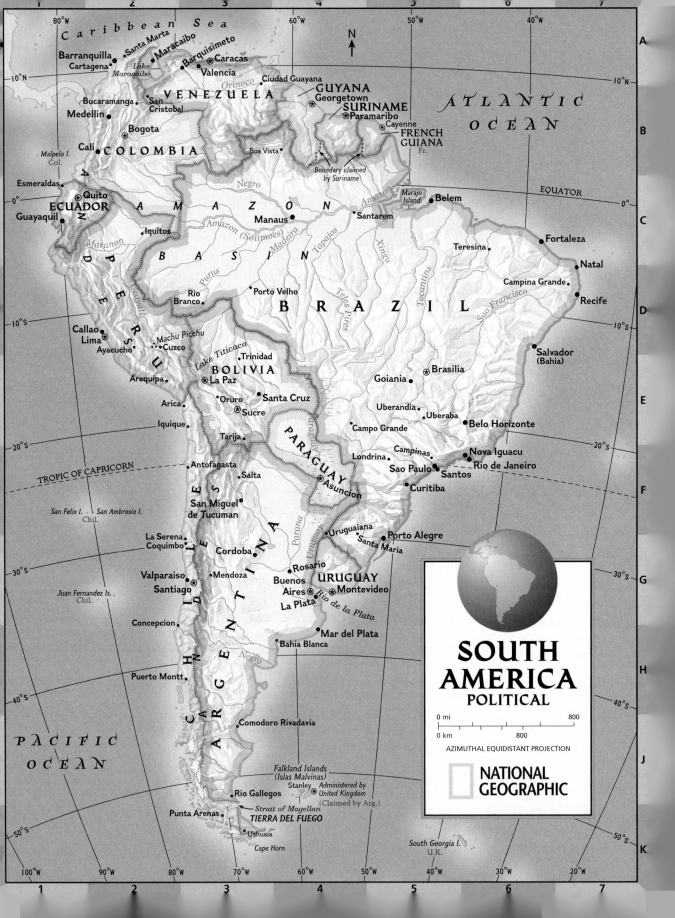

SOUTH AMERICA POLITICAL

0 mi 800
0 km 800

AZIMUTHAL EQUIDISTANT PROJECTION

NATIONAL GEOGRAPHIC

SOUTH AMERICA
PHYSICAL

0 mi   800
0 km   800

AZIMUTHAL EQUIDISTANT PROJECTION

NATIONAL GEOGRAPHIC

Caribbean Sea

ATLANTIC OCEAN

Lake Maracaibo

⊛ Caracas

VENEZUELA

Orinoco

Llanos

GUYANA
Georgetown ⊛

SURINAME
⊛ Paramaribo

Cayenne ◦
FRENCH
GUIANA

◦ Bogota

COLOMBIA

GUIANA HIGHLANDS

Angel Falls
Total drop =
3,212 ft 979 m

Boundary claimed
by Suriname

Malpelo I.

⊛ Quito
ECUADOR

Negro

Amazon

Marajo
Island

EQUATOR

AMAZON

Selva

Amazon

s

Madeira

Tapajos

Xingu

Purus

Tocantins

Sao Francisco

BASIN

BRAZIL

Ucayali

Lima ⊛

Machu Picchu

Teles Pires

BRAZILIAN

Lake Titicaca

MATO GROSSO

HIGHLANDS

BOLIVIA
La Paz

PLATEAU

⊛ Brasilia

Altiplano

⊛ Sucre

Salar
de Uyuni

PARAGUAY

Iguazu
Falls

TROPIC OF CAPRICORN

GRAN CHACO

Paraguay

⊛ Asuncion

San Felix I.   San Ambrosio I.

Parana

Uruguay

Aconcagua   22,834 ft
6,960 m

Santiago ⊛

PAMPAS

Buenos
Aires ⊛

URUGUAY
⊛ Montevideo

Rio de la Plata

Juan Fernandez Is.

Negro

PACIFIC
OCEAN

Chiloe Island

-131 ft
-40 m Valdes Peninsula

Taitao
Peninsula

Gulf of
San Jorge

PATAGONIA

Wellington I.

Falkland Islands
(Islas Malvinas)

Stanley

Strait of Magellan
Tierra del Fuego

Cape Horn

South Georgia I.

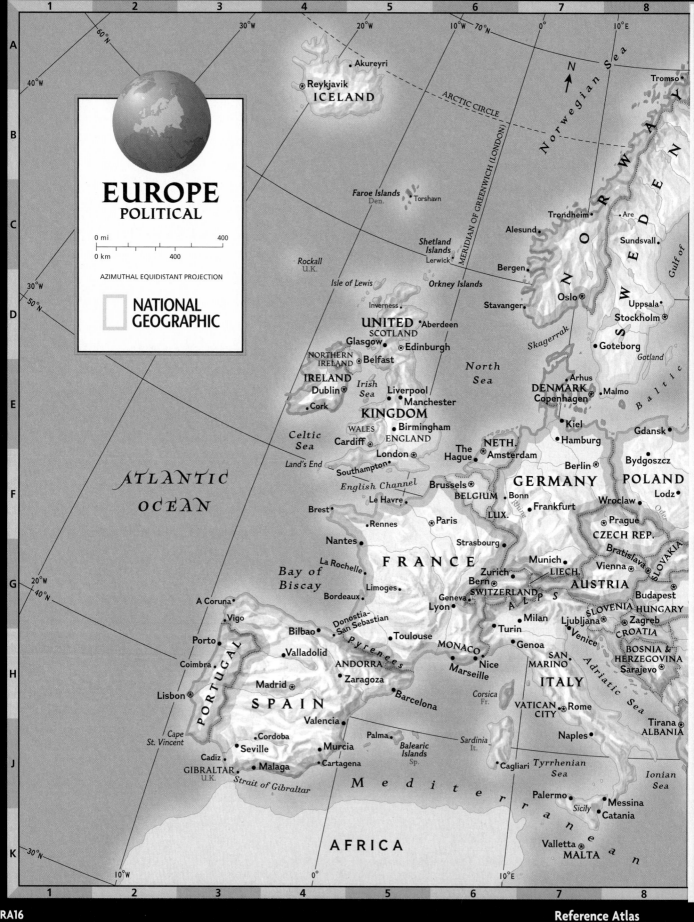

EUROPE
POLITICAL

0 mi 400
0 km 400

AZIMUTHAL EQUIDISTANT PROJECTION

NATIONAL GEOGRAPHIC

ATLANTIC OCEAN

Akureyri
⊛ Reykjavik
ICELAND

ARCTIC CIRCLE

MERIDIAN OF GREENWICH (LONDON)

Norwegian Sea

Tromso

N O R W A Y

Faroe Islands
Den.
Torshavn

Shetland Islands
Lerwick

Trondheim
Are
Alesund
Sundsvall

Rockall
U.K.

Isle of Lewis

Orkney Islands

Bergen
Oslo ⊛
Stavanger

S W E D E N

Uppsala
Stockholm ⊛

Inverness

UNITED
SCOTLAND
Glasgow ⊛ Edinburgh
Aberdeen

Skagerrak

Goteborg
Gotland

NORTHERN IRELAND
Belfast

North Sea

DENMARK
Arhus
Copenhagen Malmo

IRELAND
Dublin ⊛
Cork

Irish Sea

Liverpool
Manchester

KINGDOM
WALES
Cardiff ⊛ ENGLAND

Birmingham

Kiel
Hamburg

Baltic

Gdansk
Bydgoszcz

Celtic Sea

London ⊛

The Hague
⊛ Amsterdam
NETH.

Berlin

POLAND

Land's End
Southampton

English Channel
Le Havre

Brussels ⊛
BELGIUM
Bonn

GERMANY
Frankfurt

Wroclaw
Lodz

Brest

LUX.
Paris ⊛

Rhine

Prague ⊛
CZECH REP.

Rennes

Nantes

Strasbourg

Munich

Bratislava
Vienna ⊛
SLOVAKIA

Bay of Biscay

La Rochelle

Limoges

Bordeaux

F R A N C E

Zurich
Bern ⊛
SWITZERLAND
Geneva
Lyon

LIECH.

A L P S

AUSTRIA
Budapest

Milan
SLOVENIA
HUNGARY
Ljubljana
Venice
Zagreb ⊛
CROATIA

20°W
40°N

A Coruna
Vigo

Porto

Coimbra

Donostia-
San Sebastian
Bilbao

Toulouse

MONACO
Marseille
Nice

Turin

Genoa

SAN MARINO

Adriatic Sea

BOSNIA & HERZEGOVINA
Sarajevo ⊛

PORTUGAL

Lisbon ⊛

Valladolid

Pyrenees

ANDORRA
Zaragoza

ITALY

Madrid ⊛

S P A I N

Barcelona

Corsica
Fr.

VATICAN CITY
Rome ⊛

Tirana ⊛
ALBANIA

Cape
St. Vincent

Cadiz

Cordoba
Seville

Valencia

Murcia
Cartagena

Palma

Balearic Islands
Sp.

Sardinia
It.

Naples

GIBRALTAR
U.K.
Malaga

Strait of Gibraltar

Cagliari

Tyrrhenian Sea

Ionian Sea

M e d i t e r r a n e a n

Palermo
Sicily
Messina
Catania

Valletta ⊛
MALTA

A F R I C A

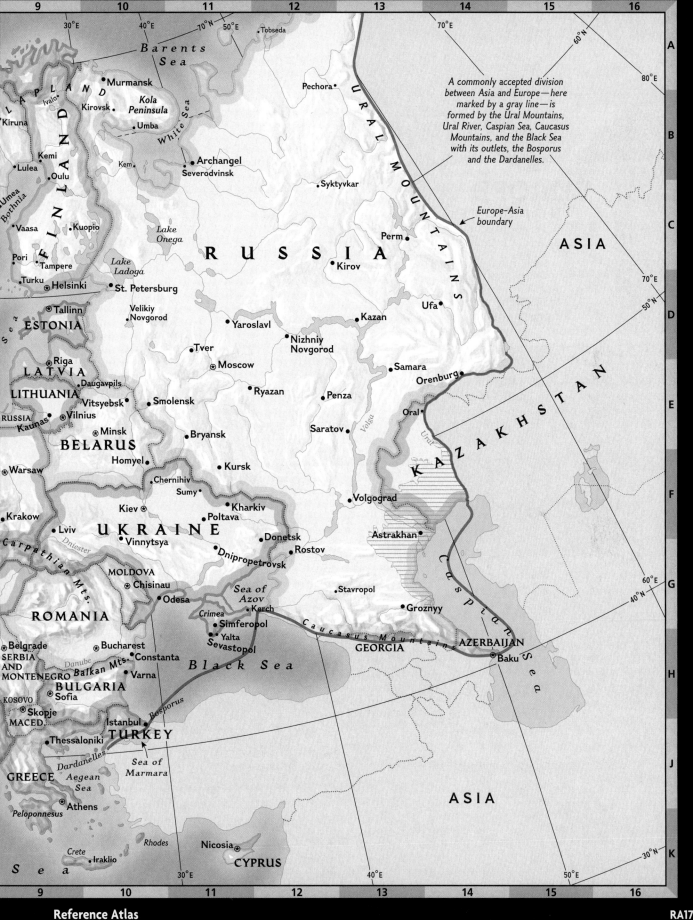

A commonly accepted division between Asia and Europe—here marked by a gray line—is formed by the Ural Mountains, Ural River, Caspian Sea, Caucasus Mountains, and the Black Sea with its outlets, the Bosporus and the Dardanelles.

Europe-Asia boundary

EUROPE
PHYSICAL

0 mi — 400
0 km — 400

AZIMUTHAL EQUIDISTANT PROJECTION

NATIONAL GEOGRAPHIC

Reykjavik
ICELAND

ARCTIC CIRCLE

Faroe Islands

Shetland Islands

Orkney Islands

Outer Hebrides

British Isles

Highlands

Edinburgh

Belfast

UNITED

IRELAND
Dublin

Irish Sea

Great Britain

KINGDOM

Cardiff

London

ATLANTIC OCEAN

English Channel

Brittany

Seine

Paris

Loire

FRANCE

Bay of Biscay

Mont Blanc
15,771 ft
4,807 m

Massif Central

Rhone

MONACO

Riviera

Cantabrian Mountains

Douro

IBERIAN

Madrid

Pyrenees

Ebro

ANDORRA

Corsica

PORTUGAL

Lisbon

Tagus

SPAIN

PENINSULA

GIBRALTAR
Strait of Gibraltar

Baetic Mountains

Balearic Islands

Sardinia

Mediterranean

AFRICA

North Sea

DENMARK
Copenhagen

Jutland

Zealand

NETH.

Amsterdam

BELGIUM
Brussels

LUX.

Berlin

GERMANY

Rhine

Elbe

Prague

CZECH REP.

Danube

Oslo

Stockholm

NORWAY

SCANDINAVIA

SWEDEN

Gulf of

Baltic

POLAND

Oder

NOR

Bratislava
SLOVAKIA

Vienna

LIECH.

Bern
SWITZ.

ALPS

AUSTRIA

Budapest

HUNGARY

Drava

SLOVENIA

Ljubljana

Zagreb

CROATIA

Sava

Po

Danube

APENNINES

SAN MARINO

ITALY

VATICAN CITY
Rome

BOSNIA & HERZEGOVINA
Sarajevo

Adriatic Sea

Tirana
ALBANIA

Tyrrhenian Sea

Ionian Sea

Sicily
Etna
10,902 ft
3,323 m

Valletta
MALTA

Norwegian Sea

MERIDIAN OF GREENWICH (LONDON)

A18

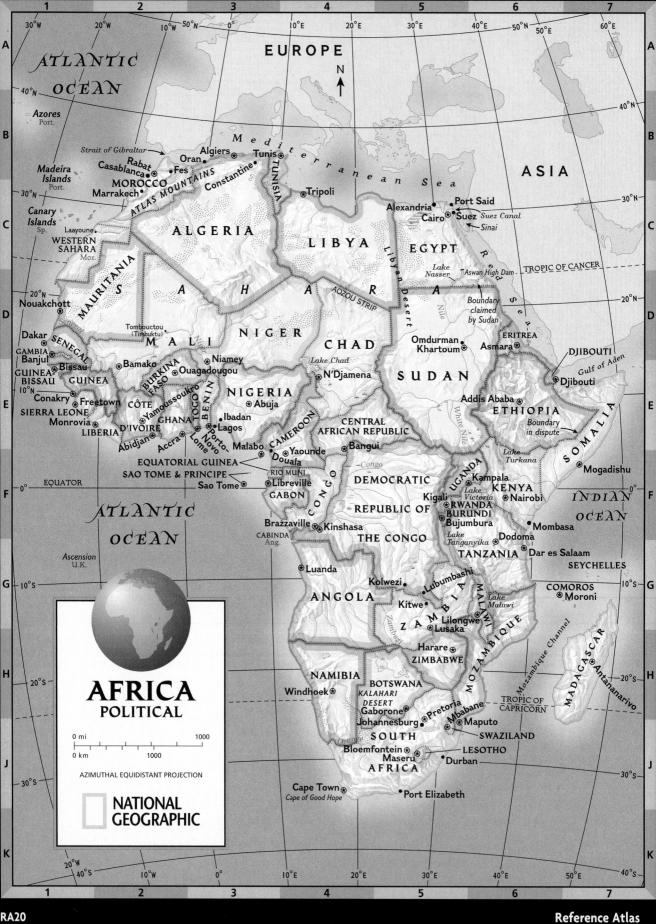

AFRICA
POLITICAL

0 mi 1000
0 km 1000

AZIMUTHAL EQUIDISTANT PROJECTION

NATIONAL GEOGRAPHIC

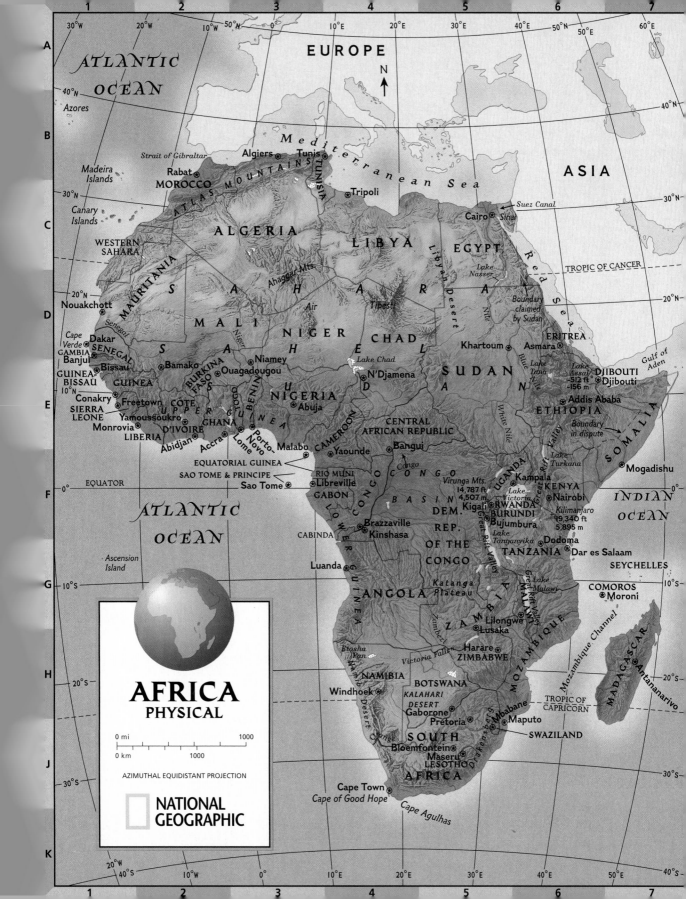

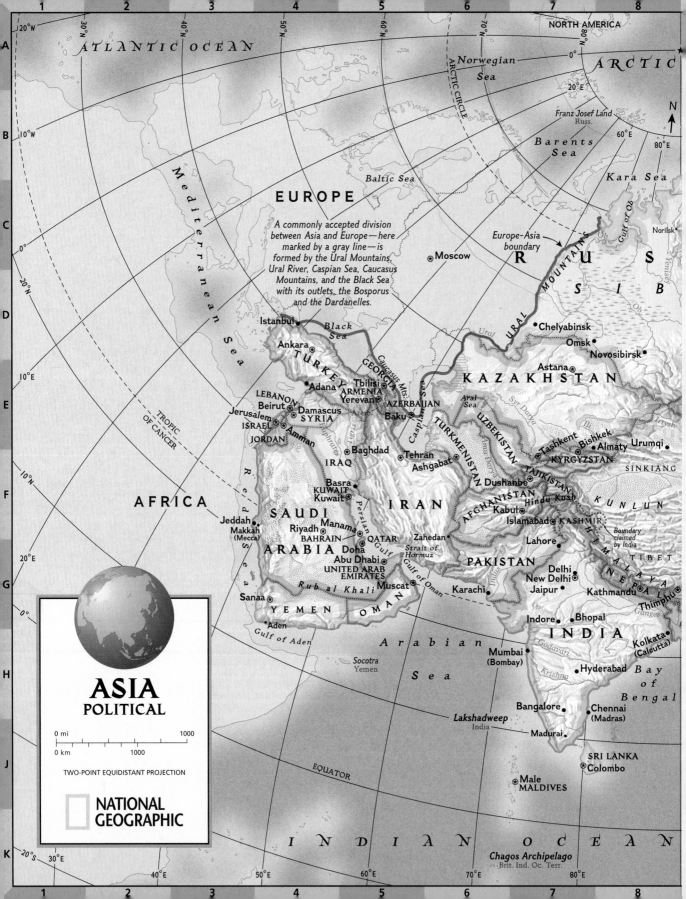

ATLANTIC OCEAN

ARCTIC

NORTH AMERICA

Norwegian Sea

Franz Josef Land
Russ.

Barents Sea

Kara Sea

Norilsk

Baltic Sea

EUROPE

⊛ Moscow

A commonly accepted division
between Asia and Europe—here
marked by a gray line—is
formed by the Ural Mountains,
Ural River, Caspian Sea, Caucasus
Mountains, and the Black Sea
with its outlets, the Bosporus
and the Dardanelles.

Europe-Asia
boundary

R   U   S   S   I   B

• Chelyabinsk
Omsk •
Novosibirsk •

Mediterranean Sea

Istanbul ⊛
Ankara ⊛

Black Sea

TURKEY

Adana •

Caucasus Mts.

GEORGIA
Tbilisi ⊛
ARMENIA
Yerevan ⊛
AZERBAIJAN
Baku ⊛

Astana •

KAZAKHSTAN

Aral Sea

Syr Darya

TROPIC
OF CANCER

LEBANON
Beirut ⊛
Damascus
JERUSALEM ⊛ SYRIA
ISRAEL ⊛
AMMAN ⊛
JORDAN

Caspian Sea

Tehrān ⊛
Ashgabat ⊛

TURKMENISTAN

UZBEKISTAN
Tashkent ⊛
Bishkek ⊛ Almaty •
KYRGYZSTAN

Urumqi •

SINKIANG

AFRICA

Baghdad ⊛

IRAQ

Basra •
KUWAIT
Kuwait ⊛

IRAN

Dushanbe ⊛
TAJIKISTAN

Hindu Kush

KUNLUN

Jeddah ⊛
Makkah
(Mecca)

SAUDI

Riyadh ⊛
Manama ⊛
BAHRAIN

ARABIA

Doha ⊛ QATAR

Abu Dhabi ⊛
UNITED ARAB
EMIRATES

Persian Gulf

Zahedan •

Strait of
Hormuz

AFGHANISTAN
Kabul ⊛
Islamabad ⊛ KASHMIR

PAKISTAN

Lahore •

HIMALAYA

Boundary
claimed
by India

TIBET

Delhi •
New Delhi ⊛
Jaipur •

NEPAL
Kathmandu ⊛

Thimphu ⊛

Rub al Khali

Muscat ⊛

Gulf of Oman

Karachi •

Indus

Indore • Bhopal •

INDIA

Kolkata
(Calcutta) •

Sanaa ⊛

YEMEN

Aden •
Gulf of Aden

OMAN

Arabian Sea

Socotra
Yemen

Mumbai
(Bombay) •

Godavari

Krishna

Hyderabad •

Bay
of
Bengal

Bangalore •

Chennai
(Madras) •

Lakshadweep
India

Madurai •

ASIA
POLITICAL

0 mi   1000

0 km   1000

TWO-POINT EQUIDISTANT PROJECTION

NATIONAL
GEOGRAPHIC

EQUATOR

SRI LANKA
⊛ Colombo

Male
MALDIVES

INDIAN OCEAN

Chagos Archipelago
Brit. Ind. Oc. Terr.

Reference Atlas   RA23

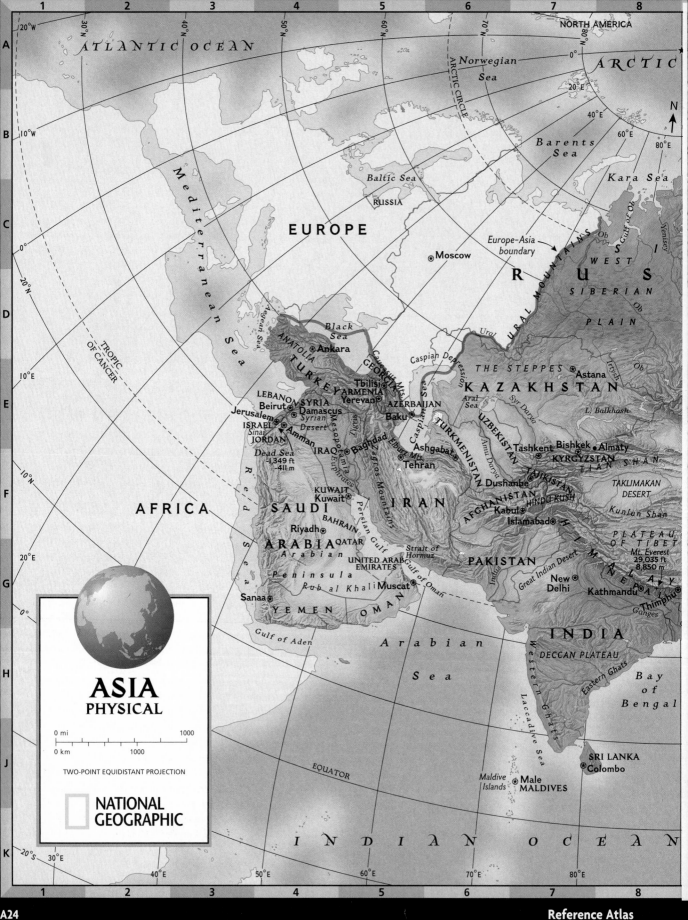

ATLANTIC OCEAN

ARCTIC

NORTH AMERICA

Norwegian
Sea

ARCTIC CIRCLE

Barents
Sea

Kara Sea

Baltic Sea

RUSSIA

EUROPE

Moscow

Europe-Asia
boundary

W E S T
S I B E R I A N
P L A I N

R U S S

Ob

Gulf of Ob

Yenisey

Mediterranean Sea

TROPIC
OF CANCER

Black
Sea

Aegean Sea

ANATOLIA

Ankara

TURKEY

Caucasus Mts.

GEORGIA

ARMENIA

Tbilisi

Yerevan

Caspian Depression

Ural

URAL MOUNTAINS

S I B E R I A N

P L A I N

Ob

Irtysh

Ob

THE STEPPES

Astana

KAZAKHSTAN

L. Balkhash

LEBANON

Beirut

Jerusalem

ISRAEL

JORDAN

Amman

Dead Sea
-1,349 ft
-411 m

SYRIA

Damascus

Syrian
Desert

Mesopotamia

Euphrates

IRAQ

Baghdad

Zagros Mountains

AZERBAIJAN

Baku

Caspian Sea

Elburz Mts.

Tehran

TURKMENISTAN

Ashgabat

UZBEKISTAN

Aral
Sea

Syr Darya

Amu Darya

Tashkent

Bishkek

Almaty

KYRGYZSTAN

TIAN SHAN

TAKLIMAKAN
DESERT

Dushanbe

TAJIKISTAN

AFRICA

Red Sea

SAUDI

Riyadh

ARABIA

Arabian

Peninsula

Rub al Khali

Sanaa

YEMEN

KUWAIT

Kuwait

BAHRAIN

QATAR

Persian Gulf

IRAN

Strait of
Hormuz

UNITED ARAB
EMIRATES

Gulf of Oman

Muscat

OMAN

AFGHANISTAN

Kabul

HINDU KUSH

Islamabad

Kunlun Shan

PLATEAU
OF TIBET

Mt. Everest
29,035 ft
8,850 m

PAKISTAN

Indus

Great Indian Desert

New
Delhi

Kathmandu

Thimphu

Ganges

HIMALAYA

Gulf of Aden

Arabian

Sea

INDIA

DECCAN PLATEAU

Western Ghats

Eastern Ghats

Bay
of
Bengal

Laccadive
Sea

SRI LANKA

Colombo

EQUATOR

Maldive
Islands

Male

MALDIVES

INDIAN OCEAN

N

20°W

30°N

40°N

50°N

60°N

70°N

80°N

0°

20°E

40°E

60°E

80°E

10°W

0°

10°E

20°N

10°N

0°

20°S

30°E

40°E

50°E

60°E

70°E

80°E

ASIA
PHYSICAL

0 mi   1000

0 km   1000

TWO-POINT EQUIDISTANT PROJECTION

NATIONAL
GEOGRAPHIC

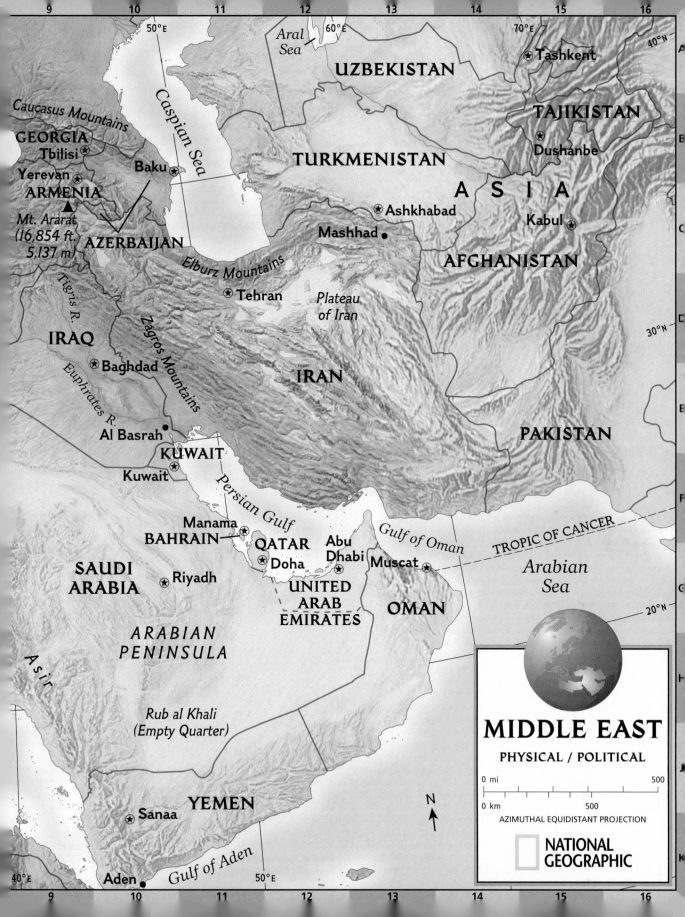

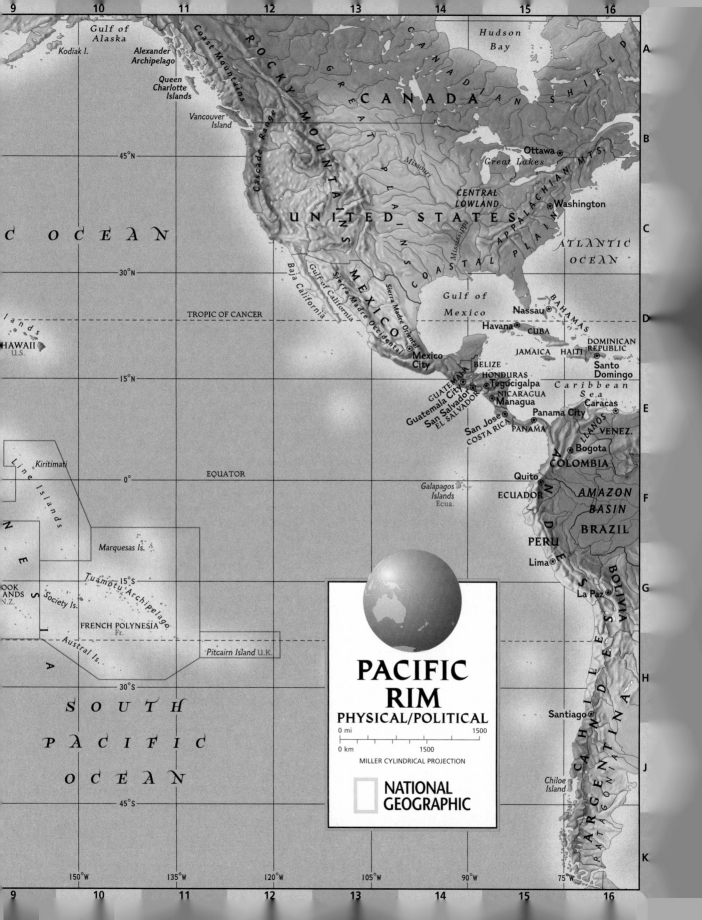

PACIFIC
RIM
PHYSICAL/POLITICAL

0 mi   1500
0 km   1500
MILLER CYLINDRICAL PROJECTION

NATIONAL
GEOGRAPHIC

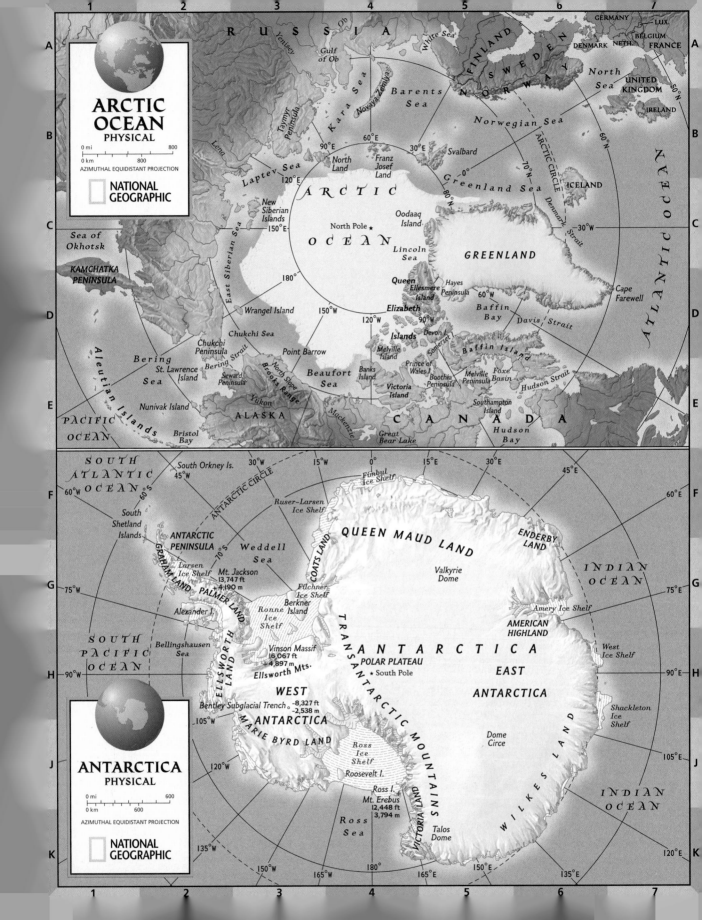

NATIONAL GEOGRAPHIC

Geography Handbook

The story of the world begins with geography—the study of the earth in all of its variety. Geography describes the earth's land, water, and plant and animal life. It is the study of places and the complex relationships between people and their environment.

The resources in this handbook will help you get the most out of your textbook—and provide you with skills you will use for the rest of your life.

The Gui River, Guilin, China ▼

▲ Saharan sand dunes, Morocco

The Amazon, Brazil ▶

How Do I Study Geography?

To understand how our world is connected, some geographers have broken down the study of geography into five themes. The **Five Themes of Geography** are (1) location, (2) place, (3) human/environment interaction, (4) movement, and (5) regions. You will see these themes highlighted in the Section and Chapter Assessments in The World and Its People.

Six Essential Elements

Recently, geographers have broken down the study of geography into **Six Essential Elements,** which are explained here. Being aware of these elements will help you sort out what you are learning about geography.

Element 2

Places and Regions

Place has a special meaning in geography. It is not just a geographic location. It also describes characteristics. It might describe physical characteristics such as landforms, climate, and plant or animal life. Or it might describe human characteristics, including language and way of life.

To help organize their study, geographers often group places into regions. **Regions** are united by one or more common characteristics.

Element 1

The World in Spatial Terms

Geographers first take a look at where a place is located. **Location** serves as a starting point by asking "Where is it?" Knowing the location of places helps you develop an awareness of the world around you.

Alabama Street

Peachtree Street

Element 3

Physical Systems

When studying places and regions, geographers analyze how **physical systems**—such as hurricanes, volcanoes, and glaciers—shape the earth's surface. They also look at communities of plants and animals that depend upon one another and their surroundings for survival.

Geography Handbook

Element 4

Human Systems

Geographers also examine **human systems,** or how people have shaped our world. They look at how boundary lines are determined and analyze why people settle in certain places and not in others. A key theme in geography is the continual **movement** of people, ideas, and goods.

Element 5

Environment and Society

How does the relationship between people and their natural surroundings influence the way people live? Geographers study how people use the **environment** and how their actions affect the environment.

Element 6

The Uses of Geography

Knowledge of geography helps us understand the relationships among people, places, and environments over time. Applying geographic skills helps you understand the past and prepare for the future.

How Do I Use Maps and Globes?

Hemispheres

To locate places on the earth, geographers use a system of imaginary lines that crisscross the globe. One of these lines, the **Equator,** circles the middle of the earth like a belt. It divides the earth into "half spheres," or **hemispheres.** Everything north of the Equator is in the Northern Hemisphere. Everything south of the Equator is in the Southern Hemisphere.

Another imaginary line runs from north to south. It helps divide the earth into half spheres in the other direction. Find this line—called the **Prime Meridian**—on a globe. Everything east of the Prime Meridian for 180 degrees is in the Eastern Hemisphere. Everything west of the Prime Meridian for 180 degrees is in the Western Hemisphere.

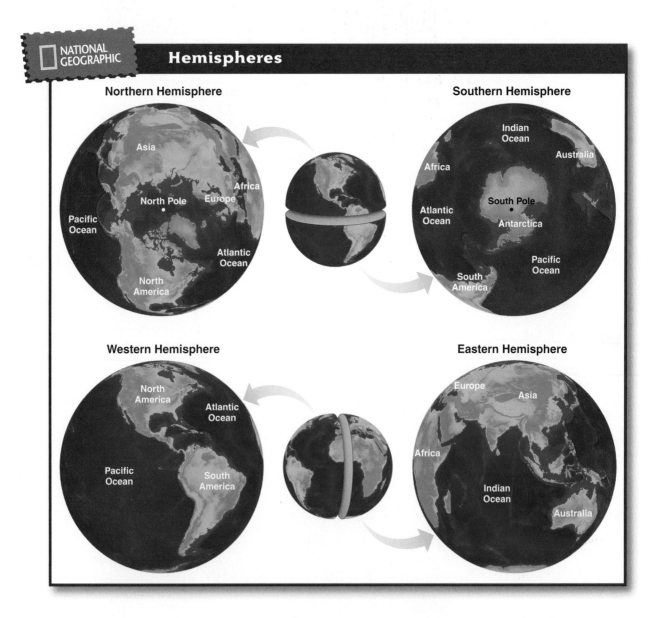

NATIONAL GEOGRAPHIC

Hemispheres

Northern Hemisphere

Asia
Africa
Europe
North Pole
Pacific Ocean
Atlantic Ocean
North America

Southern Hemisphere

Indian Ocean
Australia
Africa
Atlantic Ocean
South Pole
Antarctica
Pacific Ocean
South America

Western Hemisphere

North America
Atlantic Ocean
Pacific Ocean
South America

Eastern Hemisphere

Europe
Asia
Africa
Indian Ocean
Australia

Geography Handbook

Understanding Latitude and Longitude

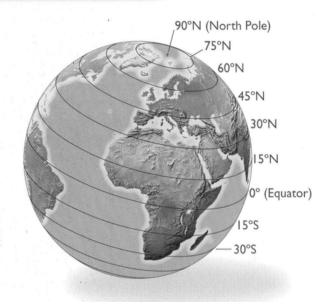

Lines on globes and maps provide information that can help you easily locate places on the earth. These lines—called **latitude** and **longitude**—cross one another, forming a pattern called a grid system.

Latitude

Lines of latitude, or **parallels,** circle the earth parallel to the **Equator** and measure the distance north or south of the Equator in degrees. The Equator is at 0° latitude, while the North Pole lies at latitude 90°N (north).

Longitude

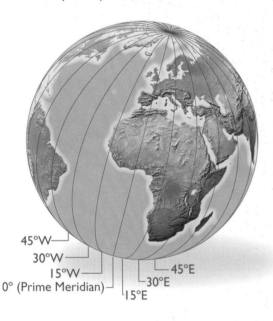

Lines of longitude, or **meridians,** circle the earth from Pole to Pole. These lines measure distances east or west of the starting line, which is at 0° longitude and is called the **Prime Meridian.** The Prime Meridian runs through the Royal Observatory in Greenwich, England.

Absolute Location

The grid system formed by lines of latitude and longitude makes it possible to find the absolute location of a place. Only one place can be found at the point where a specific line of latitude crosses a specific line of longitude. By using degrees (°) and minutes (′) (points between degrees), people can pinpoint the precise spot where one line of latitude crosses one line of longitude—an **absolute location.**

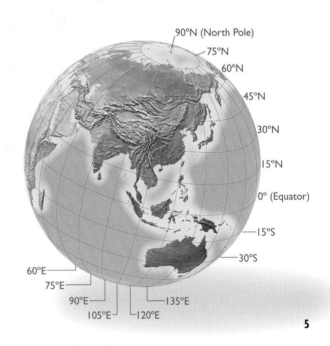

From Globes to Maps

The most accurate way to depict the earth is as a **globe,** a round scale model of the earth. A globe gives a true picture of the continents' relative sizes and the shapes of landmasses and bodies of water. Globes accurately represent distance and direction.

A **map** is a flat drawing of all or part of the earth's surface. Unlike globes, maps can show small areas in great detail. Maps can also display political boundaries, population densities, or even voting returns.

From Globes to Maps

Maps, however, do have their limitations. As you can imagine, drawing a round object on a flat surface is very difficult. **Cartographers,** or mapmakers, use mathematical formulas to transfer information from the round globe to a flat map. However, when the curves of a globe become straight lines on a map, the size, shape, distance, or area can change or be distorted.

Great Circle Routes

Mapmakers have solved some problems of going from a globe to a map. A **great circle** is an imaginary line that follows the curve of the earth. A line drawn along the Equator is an example of a great circle. Traveling along a great circle is called following a **great circle route.** Airplane pilots use great circle routes because they represent the shortest distances from one city to another.

The idea of a great circle shows one important difference between a globe and a map. Because a globe is round, it accurately shows great circles. On a flat map, however, the great circle route between two points may not appear to be the shortest distance. See the maps to the right.

Mapmaking with Technology

Technology has changed the way maps are made. Most cartographers use software programs called **geographic information systems (GIS).** This software layers map data from satellite images, printed text, and statistics. A **Global Positioning System (GPS)** helps mapmakers and consumers locate places based on coordinates broadcast by satellites.

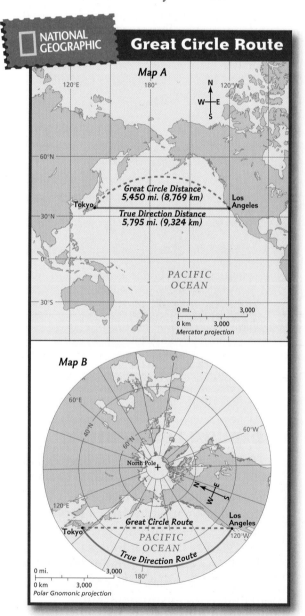

NATIONAL GEOGRAPHIC

Great Circle Route

Map A

Great Circle Distance 5,450 mi. (8,769 km)

True Direction Distance 5,795 mi. (9,324 km)

Tokyo

Los Angeles

PACIFIC OCEAN

0 mi.   3,000
0 km   3,000
Mercator projection

Map B

North Pole

Great Circle Route

Tokyo

Los Angeles

PACIFIC OCEAN

True Direction Route

0 mi.   3,000
0 km   3,000
Polar Gnomonic projection

Geography Handbook

Common Map Projections

Imagine taking the whole peel from an orange and trying to flatten it on a table. You would either have to cut it or stretch parts of it. Mapmakers face a similar problem in showing the surface of the round earth on a flat map. When the earth's surface is flattened, big gaps open up. To fill in the gaps, mapmakers stretch parts of the earth. They choose to show either the correct shapes of places or their correct sizes. It is impossible to show both. As a result, mapmakers have developed different **projections,** or ways of showing the earth on a flat piece of paper.

Goode's Interrupted Equal-Area Projection

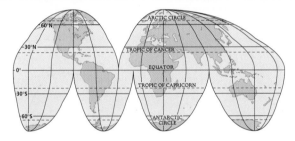

▲ Take a second look at your peeled, flattened orange. You might have something that looks like a map based on **Goode's Interrupted Equal-Area** projection. A map with this projection shows continents close to their true shapes and sizes. This projection is helpful to compare land areas among continents.

Robinson Projection

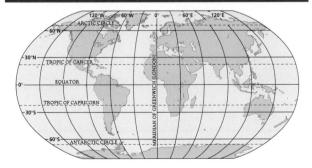

▲ A map using the **Robinson** projection has minor distortions. Land on the western and eastern sides of the Robinson map appears much as it does on a globe. The areas most distorted on this projection are near the North and South Poles.

Winkel Tripel Projection

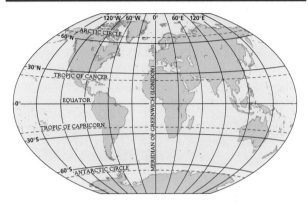

▲ The **Winkel Tripel** projection gives a good overall view of the continents' shapes and sizes. Land areas in a Winkel Tripel projection are not as distorted near the Poles as they are in the Robinson projection.

Mercator Projection

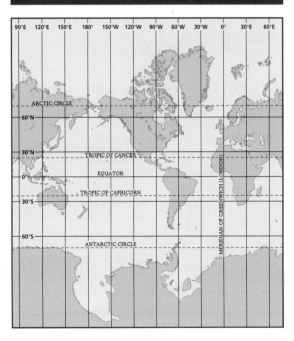

▲ The **Mercator** projection shows true direction and land shapes fairly accurately, but not size or distance. Areas that are located far from the Equator are quite distorted on this projection. Alaska, for example, appears much larger on a Mercator map than it does on a globe.

Parts of Maps

Map Key An important first step in reading a map is to note the map key. The **map key** explains the lines, symbols, and colors used on a map. For example, the map on this page shows the various climate regions of the United States and the different colors representing them. Cities are usually symbolized by a solid circle (•) and capitals by a star (★). On this map, you can see the capital of Texas and the cities of Los Angeles, Seattle, New Orleans, and Chicago.

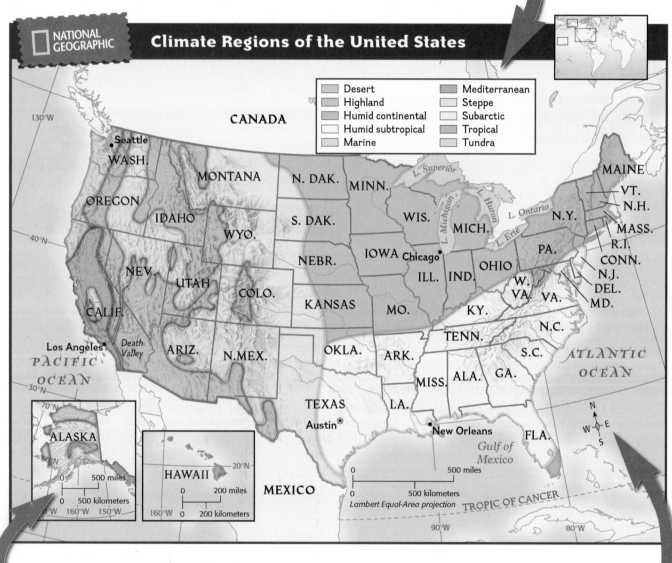

NATIONAL GEOGRAPHIC

Climate Regions of the United States

Desert
Highland
Humid continental
Humid subtropical
Marine
Mediterranean
Steppe
Subarctic
Tropical
Tundra

Scale Bar A measuring line, often called a **scale bar,** helps you figure distance on the map. The map scale tells you what distance on the earth is represented by the measurement on the scale bar.

Compass Rose A map has a symbol that tells you where the **cardinal directions**—north, south, east, and west—are positioned. This symbol is called a compass rose.

Geography Handbook

Types of Maps

General Purpose Maps

Maps are amazingly useful tools. You can use them to preserve information, to display data, and to make connections between seemingly unrelated things. Geographers use many different types of maps. Maps that show a wide range of general information about an area are called **general purpose maps.** Two of the most common general purpose maps are physical and political maps.

Physical Maps ▼

Physical maps call out landforms and water features. The physical map of Sri Lanka below shows rivers and mountains. The colors used on physical maps include brown or green for land, and blue for water. These colors and shadings

may show **relief**—or how flat or rugged the land surface is. In addition, physical maps may use colors to show **elevation**—the height of an area above sea level. A key explains what each color and symbol stands for.

Political Maps ▲

Political maps show the names and boundaries of countries, the location of cities and other human-made features of a place, and often identify major physical features. The political map of Spain above, for example, shows the boundaries between Spain and other countries. It also shows cities and rivers within Spain and bodies of water surrounding Spain.

Contour Maps ▼

One kind of physical map, called a **contour** map, also shows elevation. A contour map has **contour lines**—one line for each major level of elevation. All the land at the same elevation is connected by a line. These lines usually form circles or ovals—one inside the other. If contour lines come very close together, the surface is steep. If the lines are spread apart, the land is flat or rises very gradually. Compare the contour map of Sri Lanka below to its physical map on page 9.

Special Purpose Maps ▶

Some maps are made to present specific kinds of information. These are called **thematic** or **special purpose maps.** They usually show specific topics in detail. Special purpose maps might

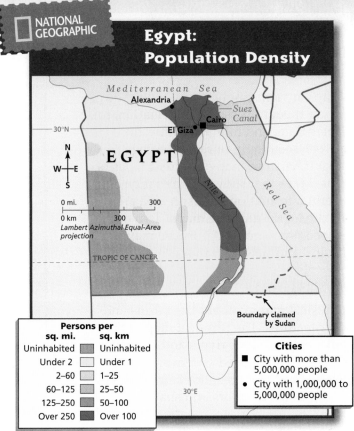

NATIONAL GEOGRAPHIC

Egypt: Population Density

Persons per

sq. mi.		sq. km
Uninhabited		Uninhabited
Under 2		Under 1
2–60		1–25
60–125		25–50
125–250		50–100
Over 250		Over 100

Cities
■ City with more than 5,000,000 people
● City with 1,000,000 to 5,000,000 people

Lambert Azimuthal Equal-Area projection

Boundary claimed by Sudan

present climate, natural resources, or population density. They might also display historical information, such as battle sites or territorial expansions. The map's title tells what kind of special information it shows. Colors and symbols in the map key are especially important on these types of maps.

One type of special purpose map uses colors to show population density, or the average number of people living in a square mile or square kilometer. As with other maps, it is important to first read the title and the key. The population density map of Egypt above shows that the Nile River valley and delta are very densely populated.

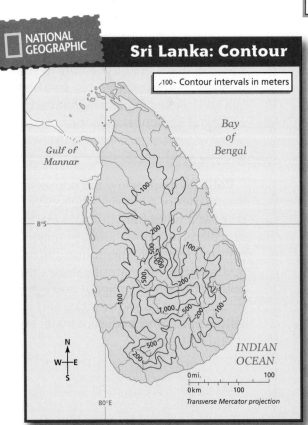

NATIONAL GEOGRAPHIC

Sri Lanka: Contour

/100￣ Contour intervals in meters

Gulf of Mannar

Bay of Bengal

INDIAN OCEAN

Transverse Mercator projection

Using Graphs, Charts, and Diagrams

Graphs

A graph is a way of summarizing and presenting information visually. Each part of a graph gives useful information. First read the graph's title to find out its subject. Then read the labels along the graph's **axes**—the vertical line along the left side of the graph and the horizontal line along the bottom. One axis will tell you what is being measured. The other axis tells what units of measurement are being used.

Bar and Line Graphs

Graphs that use bars or wide lines to compare data visually are called **bar graphs.** Look carefully at the bar graph above, which compares world languages. The vertical axis lists the languages. The horizontal axis measures the number of speakers of the language in millions. By comparing the lengths of the bars, you can quickly tell which language is spoken by the most people. Bar graphs are especially useful for comparing quantities.

A **line graph** is a useful tool for showing changes over a period of time. The amounts being measured are plotted on the grid above each year, and then are connected by a line. Line graphs sometimes have two or more lines plotted on them. The line graph to your left shows that the number of farms in the United States has decreased since 1940.

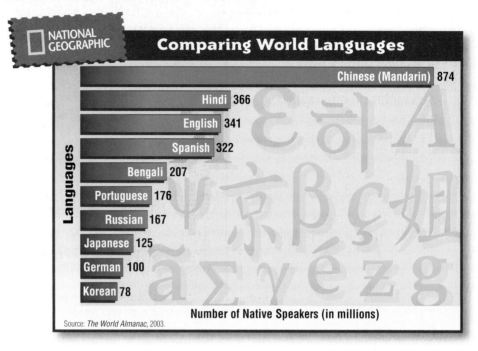

NATIONAL GEOGRAPHIC

Comparing World Languages

Languages — Number of Native Speakers (in millions)

- Chinese (Mandarin) 874
- Hindi 366
- English 341
- Spanish 322
- Bengali 207
- Portuguese 176
- Russian 167
- Japanese 125
- German 100
- Korean 78

Source: *The World Almanac,* 2003.

NATIONAL GEOGRAPHIC

U.S. Farms, 1940–2000

Number of farms (in millions) vs. Year (1940–2000)

Source: *The World Almanac,* 2003.

Circle Graphs ▼

You can use **circle graphs** when you want to show how the *whole* of something is divided into its *parts*. Because of their shape, circle graphs are often called pie graphs. Each "slice" represents a part or percentage of the whole "pie." On the circle graph below, the whole circle (100 percent) represents the world's population in 2002. The slices show how this population is divided among the world's five largest continents.

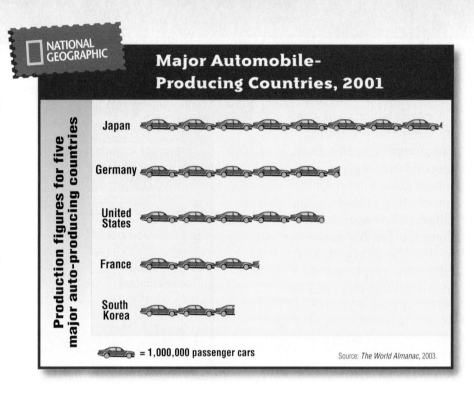

NATIONAL GEOGRAPHIC

Major Automobile-Producing Countries, 2001

Production figures for five major auto-producing countries

Japan

Germany

United States

France

South Korea

= 1,000,000 passenger cars

Source: *The World Almanac*, 2003.

Charts

Charts present facts and numbers in an organized way. They arrange data, especially numbers, in rows and columns for easy reference. Look at the chart called "Population Growth" on page 88. To interpret the chart, first read the title. It tells you what information the chart contains. Next, read the labels at the top of each column and on the left side of the chart. They explain what the numbers or data on the chart are measuring.

Pictographs ▲

Like bar and circle graphs, pictographs are good for making comparisons. **Pictographs** use rows of small pictures or symbols, with each picture or symbol representing an amount. Look at the pictograph showing the number of automobiles produced in the world's five major automobile-producing countries above. The key tells you that one car symbol stands for 1 million automobiles. The total number of car symbols in a row adds up to the auto production in each selected country.

NATIONAL GEOGRAPHIC

World Population*

Latin America 9%

North America 5%

Europe 12%

Africa 13%

Asia 61%

Source: *World Population Data Sheet*, 2003.

*Excluding Australia

Climographs ▶

A **climograph,** or climate graph, combines a line graph and a bar graph. It gives an overall picture of the long-term weather patterns in a specific place. Climographs include several kinds of information. The green vertical bars on the climograph of Moscow to your right show average monthly amounts of precipitation (rain, snow, or sleet). These bars are measured against the axis on the right side of the graph. The red line plotted above the bars represents changes in the average monthly temperature. You measure this line against the axis on the left side.

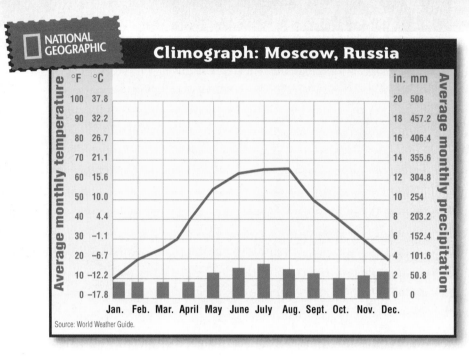
NATIONAL GEOGRAPHIC

Climograph: Moscow, Russia

Source: World Weather Guide.

Diagrams ▼

Diagrams are drawings that show steps in a process, point out the parts of an object, or explain how something works. An **elevation profile** is a type of diagram that can be helpful when comparing the elevations—or heights—of an area. It shows an exaggerated side view of the land as if it were sliced and you were viewing it from the side. The elevation profile of Africa below clearly shows sea level, low areas, and mountains.

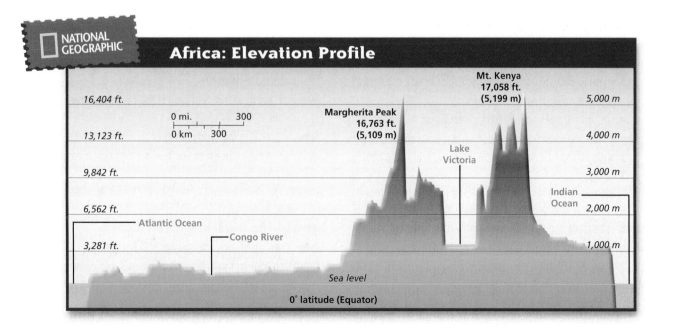
NATIONAL GEOGRAPHIC

Africa: Elevation Profile

NATIONAL GEOGRAPHIC
Geographic Dictionary

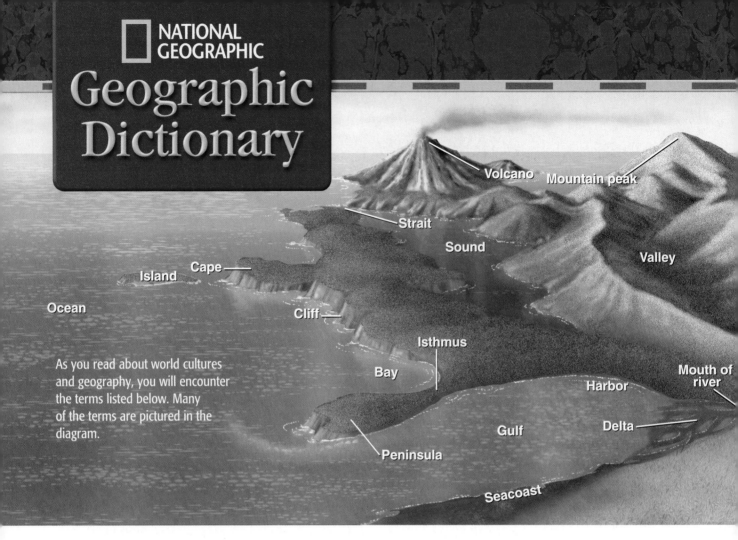

As you read about world cultures and geography, you will encounter the terms listed below. Many of the terms are pictured in the diagram.

Labels in diagram: Volcano, Mountain peak, Strait, Sound, Valley, Island, Cape, Ocean, Cliff, Isthmus, Mouth of river, Bay, Harbor, Gulf, Delta, Peninsula, Seacoast

absolute location exact location of a place on the earth described by global coordinates

basin area of land drained by a given river and its branches; area of land surrounded by lands of higher elevation

bay part of a large body of water that extends into a shoreline, generally smaller than a gulf

canyon deep and narrow valley with steep walls

cape point of land that extends into a river, lake, or ocean

channel wide strait or waterway between two landmasses that lie close to each other; deep part of a river or other waterway

cliff steep, high wall of rock, earth, or ice

continent one of the seven large landmasses on the earth

cultural feature characteristic that humans have created in a place, such as language, religion, housing, and settlement pattern

delta flat, low-lying land built up from soil carried downstream by a river and deposited at its mouth

divide stretch of high land that separates river systems

downstream direction in which a river or stream flows from its source to its mouth

elevation height of land above sea level

Equator imaginary line that runs around the earth halfway between the North and South Poles; used as the starting point to measure degrees of north and south latitude

glacier large, thick body of slowly moving ice

gulf part of a large body of water that extends into a shoreline, generally larger and more deeply indented than a bay

harbor a sheltered place along a shoreline where ships can anchor safely

highland elevated land area such as a hill, mountain, or plateau

hill elevated land with sloping sides and rounded summit; generally smaller than a mountain

island land area, smaller than a continent, completely surrounded by water

isthmus narrow stretch of land connecting two larger land areas

lake a sizable inland body of water

latitude distance north or south of the Equator, measured in degrees

longitude distance east or west of the Prime Meridian, measured in degrees

lowland land, usually level, at a low elevation

map drawing of the earth shown on a flat surface

meridian one of many lines on the global grid running from the North Pole to the South Pole; used to measure degrees of longitude

mesa broad, flat-topped landform with steep sides; smaller than a plateau

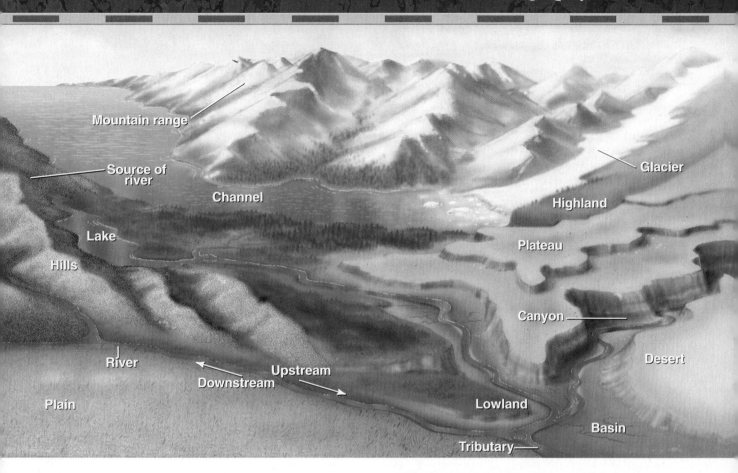

Mountain range
Source of river
Channel
Glacier
Highland
Lake
Plateau
Hills
Canyon
Desert
River
Downstream
Upstream
Lowland
Plain
Basin
Tributary

mountain land with steep sides that rises sharply (1,000 feet [305 m] or more) from surrounding land; generally larger and more rugged than a hill

mountain peak pointed top of a mountain

mountain range a series of connected mountains

mouth (of a river) place where a stream or river flows into a larger body of water

ocean one of the four major bodies of salt water that surround the continents

ocean current stream of either cold or warm water that moves in a definite direction through an ocean

parallel one of many lines on the global grid that circle the earth north or south of the Equator; used to measure degrees of latitude

peninsula body of land jutting into a lake or ocean, surrounded on three sides by water

physical feature characteristic of a place occurring naturally, such as a landform, body of water, climate pattern, or resource

plain area of level land, usually at a low elevation and often covered with grasses

plateau area of flat or rolling land at a high elevation, about 300–3,000 feet (91–914 m) high

Prime Meridian line of the global grid running from the North Pole to the South Pole through Greenwich, England; starting point for measuring degrees of east and west longitude

relief changes in elevation over a given area of land

river large natural stream of water that runs through the land

sea large body of water completely or partly surrounded by land

seacoast land lying next to a sea or ocean

sea level position on land level with the surface of a nearby ocean or sea

sound body of water between a coastline and one or more islands off the coast

source (of a river) place where a river or stream begins, often in highlands

strait narrow stretch of water joining two larger bodies of water

tributary small river or stream that flows into a larger river or stream; a branch of the river

upstream direction opposite the flow of a river; toward the source of a river or stream

valley area of low land between hills or mountains

volcano mountain created as liquid rock or ash erupts from inside the earth

Be an Active Reader

Think about your textbook as a tool that helps you learn more about the world around you. It is an example of nonfiction writing—it describes real-life events, people, ideas, and places. Here is a menu of reading strategies that will help you become a better textbook reader. As you come to passages in your textbook that you don't understand, refer to these reading strategies for help.

✔ Before You Read

Set a purpose
- Why are you reading the textbook?
- How does the subject relate to your life?
- How might you be able to use what you learn in your own life?

Preview
- Read the chapter title to find what the topic will be.
- Read the subtitles to see what you will learn about the topic.
- Skim the photos, charts, graphs, and maps. How do they support the topic?
- Look for vocabulary words that are blue. How are they defined?

Draw From Your Own Background
- What have you read or heard concerning new information on the topic?
- How is the new information different from what you already know?
- How will the information that you already know help you understand the new information?

Question

- What is the main idea?
- How do the photos, charts, graphs, and maps support the main idea?

Connect

- Think about people, places, and events in your own life. Are there any similarities with those discussed in your textbook?
- Can you relate the textbook information to other areas of your life?

Predict

- Predict events or outcomes by using clues and information that you already know.
- Change your predictions as you read and gather new information.

Visualize

- Pay careful attention to details and descriptions.
- Create graphic organizers to show relationships that you find in the information.

Look For Clues As You Read

Comparison and Contrast Sentences

- Look for clue words and phrases that signal comparison, such as *similarly*, *just as*, *both*, *in common*, *also*, and *too*.
- Look for clue words and phrases that signal contrast, such as *on the other hand*, *in contrast to*, *however*, *different*, *instead of*, *rather than*, *but*, and *unlike*.

Cause-and-Effect Sentences

- Look for clue words and phrases such as *because*, *as a result*, *therefore*, *that is why*, *since*, *so*, *for this reason*, and *consequently*.

Chronological Sentences

- Look for clue words and phrases such as *after*, *before*, *first*, *next*, *last*, *during*, *finally*, *earlier*, *later*, *since*, and *then*.

✓ After You Read

Summarize

- Describe the main idea and how the details support it.
- Use your own words to explain what you have read.

Assess

- What was the main idea?
- Did the text clearly support the main idea?
- Did you learn anything new from the material?
- Can you use this new information in other school subjects or at home?
- What other sources could you use to find more information about the topic?

Unit

Young boy from the island of New Guinea

City of Hong Kong, China

NATIONAL GEOGRAPHIC

The World

You are about to journey to dense rain forests, bleak deserts, bustling cities and marketplaces, and remote villages. In your study of the earth, you will learn about different places and different peoples. Imagine that you could visit any place in the world. Where would you want to go? What would you want to see?

▲ Hot air balloon floating over cultivated fields, Egypt

Chapter 1

Looking at the Earth

The World and Its People — NATIONAL GEOGRAPHIC

To learn more about Earth's structure and landforms, view **The World and Its People Chapter 1** video.

Social Studies Online

Chapter Overview Visit **The World and Its People** Web site at <u>twip.glencoe.com</u> and click on **Chapter 1—Chapter Overviews** to preview information about Earth.

Spaceship Earth

A famous inventor once compared the planet Earth to a large spaceship hurtling through the galaxy. The spaceship-planet carries all the resources needed for its journey. As passengers on this "ship," we need to know something about how it works to avoid costly repairs and breakdowns.

◀ Skydiving over Key West, Florida

FOLDABLES™
Study Organizer

FCAT PRACTICE The activity below will help you prepare for the **FCAT Reading** test.

Summarizing Study Foldable To fully understand what you read, you must be able to identify and explain key vocabulary terms. Use this foldable to identify, define, and use important terms in Chapter 1. **FCAT LA.A.1.3.2**

Step 1 Fold a sheet of notebook paper in half from side to side.

Step 2 On one side, cut along every third line.

Tabs will form as you cut.

Step 3 Label your foldable as you read the chapter. The first vocabulary term is labeled on the model below.

You should have 10 tabs.

Reading and Writing As you read the chapter, select and write key vocabulary terms on the front tabs of your foldable. Then write the definition of each term under the tabs. After each definition, write a sentence using each vocabulary term correctly. **FCAT LA.A.1.3.2**

Thinking Like a Geographer

NATIONAL GEOGRAPHIC Exploring Our World

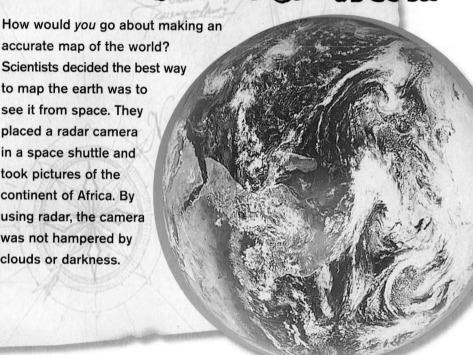

How would *you* go about making an accurate map of the world? Scientists decided the best way to map the earth was to see it from space. They placed a radar camera in a space shuttle and took pictures of the continent of Africa. By using radar, the camera was not hampered by clouds or darkness.

Why do geographers want to know exactly what the earth looks like? Think about the following: Mount Etna in **Italy** is one of the world's most active volcanoes. Two eruptions between 2001 and 2003 were the most explosive in the volcano's history. Scientists who study volcanoes constantly watch Mount Etna. By doing so, they hope to learn enough about the volcano to be able to predict eruptions and warn the people living nearby. Earthquakes, which usually happen before a volcanic eruption, can also give local residents advance warning. In addition, scientists study movements under the surface of the earth to predict volcanic activity.

This is just one example of how people around the world use geographic knowledge collected from various sources. **Geography** is the study of the earth in all its variety. When you study geography, you learn about the earth's land, water, plants, and animals. This is physical geography. You also learn about how the continents were formed and what causes erosion. You also study people—where they live, how they live, how they change and are influenced by their environment, and how different groups compare to one another. This is human geography.

A Geographer's View of Place

Geographers look at major issues—like the eruptions of Mount Etna, which affect many people over a wide area. They also look at local issues—such as where the best place is for a company to build a new store in town. Whether an issue is global, national, or local, geographers try to understand both the physical and human characteristics, or features, of the issue.

Physical Characteristics   Geographers study places. They look at *where* something is located on the earth. They also try to understand what the place is *like*. They ask: What features make a place similar to or different from other places?

To answer this question, geographers identify the landforms of a place. **Landforms** are individual features of the land, such as mountains and valleys. Geographers also look at water. Is the place near the ocean or on a river? Does it have plentiful or very little freshwater? They consider whether the soil will produce crops. They see how much rain the place usually receives and how hot or cold the area is. They find out whether the place has minerals, trees, or other resources.

On Location

Varied Landforms

This mountain valley in France and this desert in Africa have very different physical characteristics.

Place List two physical features shown in each photograph.

Looking at the Earth

Human Characteristics Geographers also look at the social characteristics of the people living in the place. Do many or only a few people live there? Do they live close together or far apart? Why? What kind of government do they have? What religions do they follow? What kinds of work do they do? What languages do they speak? From where did the people's ancestors come?

People and Places Geographers are especially interested in how people interact with their environment, or natural surroundings. People can have a major impact on the environment. In many parts of the world, people have built dams along rivers. As a result, they have changed the ways that rivers behave in flood season.

Where people live often has a strong influence on *how* they live. The earliest settlements were near rivers, which provided water for crops and transportation. Today people near the sea might catch fish and build ships for trade. Those living inland might farm or take up ranching. More and more people are using computers and other technology in their work today. This means people depend less on their physical environment to make a living.

Regions Geographers carefully study individual cities, rivers, and other landforms. They also look at the big picture, or how individual places relate to other places. In other words, geographers look at a region, or an area that shares common characteristics. Regions can be relatively small—like your state, town, or school district. They can also be huge—like the western **United States.** Some regions may even include several countries if they have similar environments or their people follow similar ways of life and speak the same language. The countries of western South America are often discussed as a region. They are called the Andean countries because the **Andes,** a series of mountain ranges, run through all of them.

✓ **Reading Check** What do geographers study to determine the human characteristics of a place?

The Tools of Geography

Geographers need tools to study people and places. Maps and globes are the main tools they use. As you read in the Geography Handbook on page 9, geographers use many different types of maps. Each type gives geographers a particular kind of information about a place.

Collecting Data for Mapping Earth How do geographers gather information so they can make accurate maps? One way is to take photographs from high above the earth. Landsat images are photographs taken by satellites that circle the earth. These images show details such as the shape of the land, what plants cover an area, and how land is being used. Radar cameras can even reveal hidden information. Photos of **Antarctica** taken from radar cameras show rivers of ice 500 miles (805 km) long—all hidden by snow.

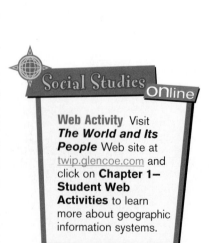

Social Studies Online

Web Activity Visit *The World and Its People* Web site at twip.glencoe.com and click on **Chapter 1– Student Web Activities** to learn more about geographic information systems.

Mt. Everest

GPS satellites measure as well as locate places on the earth. A GPS receiver placed on top of Mt. Everest, the tallest mountain in the world, showed that it is 7 feet (2.1 m) higher than people previously thought.

Location Why is it important for geographers to know exactly where places are located on the earth?

How do geographers accurately label the exact locations of places on a map? Believe it or not, the best way to find a location is from outer space. Another group of satellites traveling around the earth makes up the Global Positioning System (GPS). A GPS receiver is a special device that receives signals from these satellites. When the receiver is placed at a location, the GPS satellite can tell the exact latitude and longitude of that location. As a result, a mapmaker can know where exactly on the earth the particular area is located. GPS devices are even installed in vehicles to help drivers find their way.

Geographic Information Systems Today geographers use another powerful tool in their work—computers. Special computer software called geographic information systems (GIS) helps geographers gather many different kinds of information about the same place. First geographers input all the data they collect. Then they use the software to combine and overlap the information on special maps.

In the early 2000s, scientists developed GIS technology to help conserve the plants and animals that live in the Amazon rain forest. More than 50 million acres of the rain forest are destroyed each year because of logging, mining, and other such activities. Using GIS technology, scientists can compare data gathered from the ground to data taken from satellite pictures. For example, they can see what species live where within the rain forest. Land use planners use this information to help local people make good decisions about how to use the land. These activities help prevent the rain forest from being destroyed.

Reading Check What is the difference between GPS and GIS?

Looking at the Earth

Artifacts

Cave paintings, pottery, arrowheads, and other artifacts provide clues about how ancient people lived.

History What clues can you gather about the society that made this arrowhead?

Uses of Geography

Have you ever gone on a long-distance trip in a car or taken a subway ride? If you used a road map or subway map to figure out where you were going, you were using geography. This is just one of the many uses of geographic information.

Geographic information is used in planning. Government leaders use geographic information to plan new services in their communities. They might plan how to handle disasters or how much new housing to allow in an area. Businesses study population trends to see where people are moving in a region. If people are moving out of an area, for example, a business may decide to close or relocate.

In addition, geographic information helps people make sound decisions. Perhaps a question arises over whether a new building should be constructed. City leaders look at street use to see if the area can handle additional traffic. They make sure the area has the power, water, and sewage systems the building will need.

Finally, geographic information helps people manage resources. Resources such as trees or water can be replaced or renewed. Other natural resources, such as oil or coal, are available only in limited supply. People can use geographic information both to locate more of these limited natural resources and to manage them wisely.

✓**Reading Check** Why do people have to manage resources carefully?

Clues to Our Past

So far, you have learned about the tools geographers use to study the world and how to think like a geographer. You will use these tools as you read about the people and places of today, as well as learn about the past—from ancient civilizations to modern history. Historians, archaeologists, and anthropologists are scientists who try to unravel the mysteries of early times. Like geographers, these scientists also have tools to help them in their work.

Written Records Historians rely mostly on written records to create their stories of the past. For example, they search through diaries, newspapers, and legal documents for information about how people used to live. However, no written records exist for the prehistory of humankind. In fact, *prehistory* means the time before writing was developed. How, then, do we know about ancient times and early humans?

Artifacts and Fossils Much of what is known about ancient people comes from studies by archaeologists and anthropologists. These scientists study past societies by analyzing what people have left behind. They dig up and examine artifacts—tools, pottery, paintings, weapons, and other items. They also study the remains of humans, or human fossils, to determine how ancient people lived. By examining artifacts such as tools and weapons, for example, scientists may learn that an early society was able to farm and had military strength. By analyzing bones, animal skins, and plant seeds, they are able to piece together what early people ate and what animals they hunted.

✓ **Reading Check** How is prehistory different from history?

FCAT PRACTICE You can prepare for the FCAT-assessed standards by completing the correlated item(s) below.

Assessment

Section 1

Defining Terms
1. **Define** geography, landform, environment, Global Positioning System (GPS), geographic information systems (GIS), artifact, fossil.

Recalling Facts
2. **Place** What two kinds of characteristics of a place do geographers study?
3. **Technology** What are the main tools of geography?
4. **Human/Environment Interaction** What are three uses for geography?

Critical Thinking
5. **Understanding Cause and Effect** How have the physical characteristics of your region affected the way people live there?
   FCAT LA.E.2.2.1
6. **Categorizing Information** Give five examples of regions. Begin with an area near you that shares common characteristics, then think of larger and larger regions.

Graphic Organizer
7. **Organizing Information** Draw a diagram like this one. In the center, write the name of a place you would like to visit. In the outer ovals, identify the types of geographic information you would like to learn about this place.
   FCAT LA.A.1.3.2

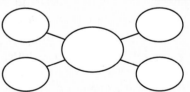

Applying Social Studies Skills

8. **Analyzing Maps** Find Egypt on the map on page RA21 of the **Reference Atlas.** Along what physical feature do you think most Egyptians live? Why? Turn to the population density map of Egypt on page 10 of the **Geography Handbook** to see if you are correct. **FCAT MA.B.1.3.4**

Making Connections

ART | SCIENCE | CULTURE | TECHNOLOGY

Geographic Information Systems

What if a farmer could save money by applying fertilizer only to the crops that needed it? Today, thanks to computer technology called geographic information systems (GIS), farmers can do just that.

The Technology

Geographic information systems (GIS) use computer software to combine and display a wide range of information about an area. GIS programs start with a map showing a specific location on the earth. This map is then linked with other information about that same place, such as satellite photos, amounts of rainfall, or where houses are located.

Think of geographic information systems as a stack of overhead transparencies. Each transparency shows the same general background but highlights different information. The first transparency may show a base map of an area. Only the borders may appear. The second transparency may show only rivers and highways. The third may highlight mountains and other physical features, buildings, or cities.

In a similar way, GIS technology places layers of information onto a base map. It can then switch each layer of information on or off, allowing data to be viewed in many different ways. In the case of the farmer mentioned above, GIS software combines information about soil type, plant needs, and last year's crop to pinpoint exact areas that need fertilizer.

How It Is Used

GIS technology allows users to quickly pull together data from many different sources and construct maps tailored to specific needs. This helps people analyze past events, predict future possibilities, and make sound decisions.

FCAT PRACTICE Answering question 3 below will help you prepare for the **FCAT Reading** test.

A person who is deciding where to build a new store can use GIS technology to help select the best location. The process might begin with a list of possible sites. The store owner gathers information about the areas surrounding each place. This could include shoppers' ages, incomes, and educations; where shoppers live; traffic patterns; and other stores in the area. The GIS software then builds a computerized map composed of these layers of information. The store owner can use the information to decide on a new store location.

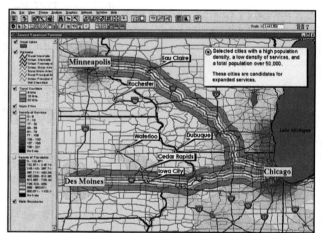

Graphic image created using ArcView® GIS software, and provided courtesy of Environmental Systems Research Institute, Inc.

Making the Connection

1. What is GIS technology?

2. In what ways do GIS programs analyze data?

3. **Asking Questions** What questions would you ask to locate the best place to add a new school to your district? **FCAT LA.A.2.3.5**

The Earth in Space

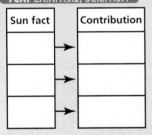

NATIONAL GEOGRAPHIC — Exploring Our World

The sun warms Earth, but the sun's warmth barely reaches Antarctica at the southern tip of our planet. Even in summer, temperatures are often below 0°F (−18°C). Winter temperatures may fall to −100°F (−73°C). Every part of this scientist's body must be protected against the freezing cold as he moves through an enormous ice tunnel in Antarctica.

The sun's heat provides life on our planet. Earth, eight other planets, and thousands of smaller bodies all revolve around the sun. Together with the sun, these bodies form the solar system. Look at the diagram of the solar system on page 30. As you can see, Earth is the third planet from the sun.

The Solar System

Each planet travels along its own path, or orbit, around the sun. The paths they travel are ellipses, which are like stretched-out circles. Each planet takes a different amount of time to complete one full trip around the sun. Earth makes one trip in 365¼ days. Mercury orbits the sun in just 88 days. Far-off Pluto takes almost 250 years!

Planets can be classified into two types—those that are like Earth and those that are like Jupiter. Earthlike planets are Mercury, Venus, Mars, and Pluto. These planets are solid and small. They have few or no moons. They also rotate, or spin, fairly slowly.

The other four planets—Jupiter, Saturn, Neptune, and Uranus—are huge. Uranus, the smallest of the four, is 15 times larger than Earth.

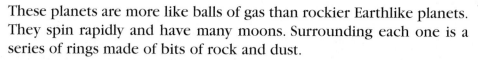

These planets are more like balls of gas than rockier Earthlike planets. They spin rapidly and have many moons. Surrounding each one is a series of rings made of bits of rock and dust.

Sun, Earth, and Moon The sun—about 93 million miles (150 million km) from Earth—is made mostly of intensely hot gases. Reactions that occur inside the sun make it as hot as 27 million degrees Fahrenheit (about 15 million degrees Celsius). As a result, the sun gives off light and warmth. Life on Earth could not exist without the sun.

The layer of air surrounding Earth—the atmosphere—also supports life. This cushion of gases measures about 1,000 miles (1,609 km) thick. Nitrogen and oxygen form about 99 percent of the atmosphere, with other gases making up the rest.

Humans and animals need oxygen to breathe. The atmosphere is important in other ways, too. This protective layer holds in enough of the sun's heat to make life possible, just as a greenhouse keeps in enough heat to protect plants. Without this protection, Earth would be too cold for most living things. At the same time, the atmosphere also reflects some heat back into space. As a result, Earth does not become too warm. Finally, the atmosphere shields living things. It screens out some rays from the sun that are dangerous. You will learn more about the atmosphere in Chapter 2.

Earth's nearest neighbor in the solar system is its moon. The moon orbits Earth, taking about 30 days to complete each trip. A cold, rocky sphere, the moon has no water and no atmosphere. The moon also gives off no light of its own. When you see the moon shining, it is actually reflecting light from the sun.

NATIONAL GEOGRAPHIC

The Solar System

Analyzing the Diagram

Earth and eight other planets in our solar system travel around the sun.

Movement Between which two planets' orbits is Earth's orbit?

FCAT SC.E.1.3.1

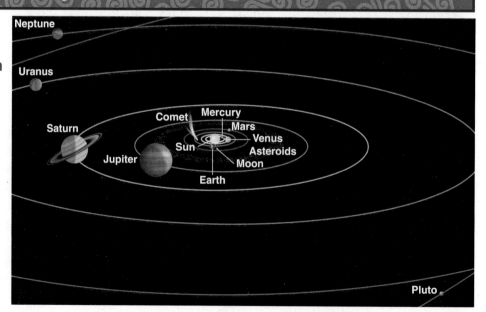

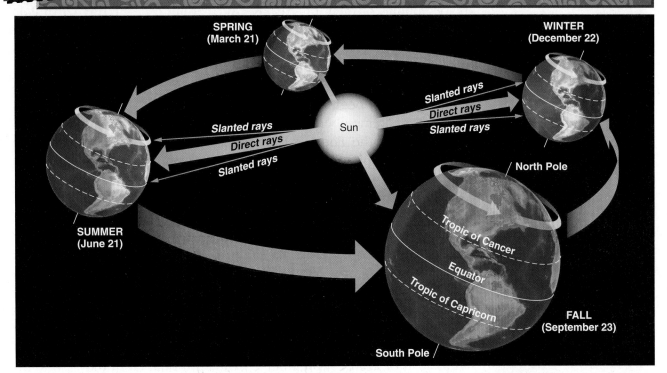

SPRING
(March 21)

WINTER
(December 22)

Slanted rays
Direct rays
Slanted rays

Slanted rays
Direct rays
Slanted rays

Sun

North Pole

SUMMER
(June 21)

Tropic of Cancer

Equator

Tropic of Capricorn

FALL
(September 23)

South Pole

Analyzing the Diagram

Because Earth is tilted, different areas receive direct rays from the sun at different times of the year.

Movement How does this fact cause changes in seasons? **FCAT** SC.E.1.3.1

FCAT PRACTICE

Completing the exercise above will help you prepare for the **FCAT Science** test.

Earth's Movement   Like all the planets, Earth rotates, or spins, on its axis. The axis is an imaginary line that runs through Earth's center between the North and South Poles. Earth takes 24 hours to finish one complete spin on its axis. As a result, one day is 24 hours. As Earth turns, different parts of the planet are in sunlight or in darkness. The part facing the sun has day, and the part facing away has night.

Earth has another motion, too. The planet makes one revolution, or complete orbit around the sun, in 365¼ days. This period is what we define as one year. Every four years, the extra one-fourths of a day are combined and added to the calendar as February 29. A year that contains one of these extra days is called a leap year.

✓ Reading Check How does Earth's orbit affect you?

The Sun and the Seasons

Earth is tilted 23½ degrees on its axis. As a result, seasons change as Earth makes its year-long orbit around the sun. To see why this happens, look at the four globes in the diagram above. Notice how sunlight falls directly on the northern or southern halves of Earth at different times of the year. Direct rays from the sun bring more warmth than the slanted rays. When the people in a hemisphere receive those direct rays from the sun, they enjoy the warmth of summer. When they receive only indirect rays, they experience winter, which is colder.

Solstices and Equinoxes Four days in the year have special names because of the position of the sun in relation to Earth. These days mark the beginnings of the four seasons. On or about June 21, the North Pole is tilted toward the sun. On noon of this day, the sun appears directly overhead at the line of latitude called the Tropic of Cancer (23½°N latitude). In the Northern Hemisphere, this day is the **summer solstice,** the day with the most hours of sunlight and the fewest hours of darkness. It is the beginning of summer—but only in the Northern Hemisphere. Remember that the Northern Hemisphere includes everything north of the Equator. Everything south of the Equator is in the Southern Hemisphere. In the Southern Hemisphere, that same day is the day with the fewest hours of sunlight and marks the beginning of winter.

Six months later—on or about December 22—the North Pole is tilted away from the sun. At noon, the sun's direct rays strike the line of latitude known as the Tropic of Capricorn (23½°S latitude). In the Northern Hemisphere, this day is the **winter solstice**—the day with the fewest hours of sunlight. This same day, though, marks the beginning of summer in the Southern Hemisphere.

Spring and autumn begin midway between the two solstices. These are the **equinoxes,** when day and night are of equal length in both hemispheres. On or about March 21, the vernal equinox (spring) occurs. On or about September 23, the autumnal equinox occurs. On both of these days, the noon sun shines directly over the Equator.

✓ Reading Check **Which seasons begin on the two equinoxes?**

FCAT PRACTICE You can prepare for the FCAT-assessed standards by completing the correlated item(s) below.

Section 2 Assessment

Defining Terms

1. **Define** solar system, orbit, atmosphere, axis, revolution, leap year, summer solstice, winter solstice, equinox.

Recalling Facts

2. **Region** Which bodies make up the solar system? **FCAT SC.E.1.3.1**

3. **Science** List two gases in the atmosphere.

4. **Movement** Which two motions does Earth make in space?

Critical Thinking

5. **Analyzing Information** How does the position of Earth determine whether a day is one of the solstice or equinox days?

6. **Summarizing Information** In a paragraph, describe why the seasons change. **FCAT LA.B.1.3.2**

Graphic Organizer

7. **Organizing Information** Draw two diagrams like those below. First, list the effects of Earth's rotation on human, plant, and animal life. Then list the effects if Earth were to stop rotating.

FCAT LA.E.2.2.1

| Earth rotates | → | | Earth stops rotating | → | |

Applying Social Studies Skills

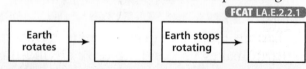

8. **Analyzing Diagrams** Look at the diagram on page 31. When the sun's direct rays hit the Tropic of Capricorn, what season is it in the Northern Hemisphere? **FCAT SC.E.1.3.1**

Social Studies Skill

 FCAT PRACTICE Completing the correlated items below will help you prepare for the **FCAT Mathematics** test.

Using a Map Key

To understand what a map is showing, you must read the **map key,** or legend. The map key explains the meaning of special colors, symbols, and lines on the map.

Learning the Skill

Colors in the map key may represent different elevations or heights of land, climate areas, or languages. Lines may stand for rivers, streets, or boundaries.

Maps also have a compass rose showing directions. The cardinal directions are north, south, east, and west. North and south are the directions of the North and South Poles. If you stand facing north, east is the direction to your right. West is the direction to your left. The compass rose might also show intermediate directions, or those that fall between the cardinal directions. For example, the intermediate direction *northeast* falls between north and east. To use a map key, follow these steps:

- Read the map title.
- Read the map key to find out what special information it gives.
- Find examples of each map key color, line, or symbol on the map.
- Use the compass rose to identify the four cardinal directions.

Practicing the Skill

Look at the map of Washington, D.C., below to answer the following questions.

1. What does the red square represent?
   FCAT MA.B.1.3.4
2. What does the blue square represent?
   FCAT MA.B.1.3.4
3. Does the Washington Monument lie east or west of the Lincoln Memorial?
   FCAT MA.B.1.3.4
4. From the White House, in what direction would you go to get to the Capitol? **FCAT** MA.B.1.3.4

Applying the Skill

Find a map in a newspaper or magazine. Use the map key to explain three things the map is showing. **FCAT** MA.B.1.3.4

GO TO Practice key skills with **Glencoe Skillbuilder Interactive Workbook, Level 1.**

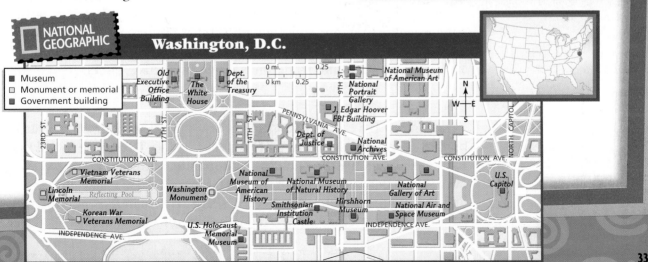

NATIONAL GEOGRAPHIC — Washington, D.C.

- Museum
- Monument or memorial
- Government building

Forces Shaping the Earth

NATIONAL GEOGRAPHIC Exploring Our World

Forces beneath the earth's surface shape the land and the lives of the people who live on it. Here in the Azores, a volcano makes cooking easy. People wrap pots of meat and vegetables in a cloth and bury the bundle in a hole where heat from deep inside the earth rises to the surface. The temperature reaches 200°F (93°C), which is hot enough to steam the food.

Thousands of miles beneath your feet, the earth's heat has turned metal into liquid. You may not feel these forces, but what lies inside the earth affects what lies on top. Mountains, deserts, and other landscapes were formed over millions of years by forces acting below the earth's surface—and they are still changing today. Some forces work slowly and show no results for thousands of years. Others appear suddenly and have dramatic, and sometimes very destructive, effects.

Inside the Earth

Scientists have only been able to study the top layer of the earth, but have developed a picture of what lies inside. They have found that Earth has three layers—the core, the mantle, and the crust. Have you ever seen a cantaloupe cut in half? The earth's core is like the center of a cantaloupe, where you find the seeds. The mantle is like the part of the fruit that you eat, between the center and the rind, or outer layer. The crust is like the melon's rind. Let us look closer at Earth's three layers.

In the center of the earth is a dense core of hot iron mixed with other metals and rock. The inner core is solid, but the outer core is so hot that the metal has melted into liquid. Surrounding the core is the mantle, a layer of rock about 1,800 miles (2,897 km) thick. Like the core, the mantle also has two parts. The section nearest the core remains solid, but the rock in the outer mantle sometimes melts. If you have seen photographs of an active volcano, then you have seen this melted rock, called magma. It flows to the surface during a volcanic eruption.

The uppermost layer of the earth, the crust, is relatively thin. It reaches only 31 to 62 miles (50 to 100 km) deep. The crust includes the ocean floors. It also includes seven massive land areas known as continents. The crust is thinnest on the ocean floor. It is thicker below the continents. Turn to the map on page 41 to see where the earth's seven continents are located.

Reading Check Which layer of the earth is thinnest?

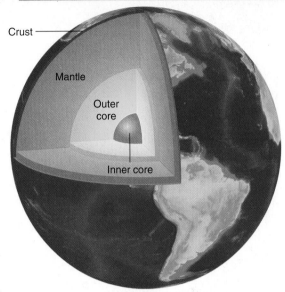

Crust

Mantle

Outer core

Inner core

Analyzing the Diagram

Hot rock and metal—some of it liquid—fill the center of the earth.

Region What is the innermost layer inside the earth called? In which layer do you find the continents?

FCAT SC.D.1.3.5

FCAT PRACTICE

Completing the exercise above will help you prepare for the **FCAT Science** test.

Forces Beneath the Earth's Crust

You have probably watched science shows about earthquakes and volcanoes. You have probably also seen news on television discussing the destruction caused by earthquakes. These events result from forces at work inside the earth.

Plate Movements Scientists have developed a theory called plate tectonics to explain the earth's structure. This theory states that the crust is not an unbroken shell but consists of plates, or huge slabs of rock, that move. The plates float on top of liquid rock just below the earth's crust. They move—but often in different directions. Oceans and continents sit on these gigantic plates, as shown on page 36.

Have you ever noticed that the eastern part of **South America** seems to fit into the western side of **Africa?** That is because these two continents were once joined together in a landmass that scientists call **Pangaea.** Millions of years ago, however, the continents moved apart. Tectonic activity caused them to move. The plates are still moving today, but they move so slowly that you do not feel it. The plate under the Pacific Ocean moves to the west at the rate of about 4 inches (10 cm) per year. That is about the same rate that a man's beard grows. The plate along the western edge of South America moves east at the rate of about 1.8 inches (5 cm) per year. That is a little faster than your fingernails grow. Turn to page 45 to see what Pangaea looked like before and after it experienced this movement, known as continental drift.

Looking at the Earth

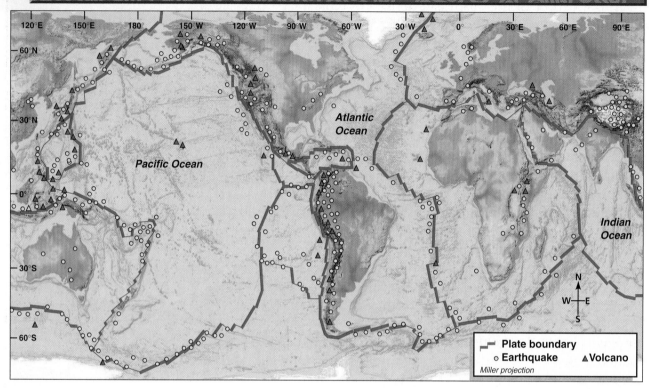

Tectonic Plate Boundaries

Plate boundary
o Earthquake ▲ Volcano
Miller projection

Analyzing the Diagram

Most of North America sits on one plate.

Region What pattern do you see among plate boundaries, earthquakes, and volcanoes?

FCAT SC.D.1.3.5

Completing the exercise above will help you prepare for the **FCAT Science** test.

When Plates Meet The movements of the earth's plates have actually shaped the surface of the earth. Sometimes the plates spread, or pull away from each other. That type of tectonic action separated South America and Africa millions of years ago. Sometimes, though, the plates push against each other. When this happens, one of three events occurs, depending on what kinds of plates are involved.

If two continental plates smash into each other, the collision produces high mountain ranges. This kind of collision produced the **Himalaya** in South Asia.

If a continental plate and an ocean plate move against each other, the thicker continental plate slides over the thinner ocean plate. The downward force of the lower plate causes molten rock to build up. Then, as magma, it erupts to form volcanic mountains. Another result may occur from the pressure that builds up between the two sliding plates. This pressure may cause one plate to move suddenly. The result is an **earthquake**, or a violent and sudden movement of the earth's crust.

Earthquakes can be very damaging to both physical structures and human lives. They can collapse buildings, destroy bridges, and break apart underground water or gas pipes. Undersea earthquakes can cause huge waves called **tsunamis** (tsu•NAH•mees). These waves may reach as high as 98 feet (30 m). Such waves can cause severe flooding of coastal towns.

Sometimes two plates do not meet head-on but move alongside each other. To picture this, put your hands together and then move them in opposite directions. When this action occurs in the earth, the two plates slide against each other. This movement creates **faults,** or cracks in the earth's crust. Violent earthquakes can happen near these faults. In 1988, for example, an earthquake struck the country of Armenia. About 25,000 people were killed, and another 500,000 lost their homes. One of the most famous faults in the United States is the **San Andreas Fault** in California. The earth's movement along this fault caused a severe earthquake in San Francisco in 1906 and another less serious earthquake in 1989.

✓ Reading Check   What happens when two continental plates collide?

Forces Shaping Landforms

The forces under the earth's crust that move tectonic plates cause volcanoes and earthquakes to change the earth's landforms. Once formed, however, these landforms will continue to change because of forces that work on the earth's surface.

Weathering   **Weathering** is the process of breaking surface rock into boulders, gravel, sand, and soil. Water and frost, chemicals, and even plants cause weathering. Water seeps into cracks of rocks and then freezes. As it freezes, the ice expands and splits the rock. Sometimes entire sides of cliffs fall off because frost has wedged the rock apart. Chemicals, too, cause weathering when acids in air pollution mix with rain and fall back to the earth. The chemicals eat away the surfaces of stone structures and natural rocks. Even tiny seeds that fall into cracks can spread out roots, causing huge boulders to eventually break apart.

Architecture

In earthquake-prone parts of the world, engineers design new buildings to stand up to tremors, or shaking of the earth. Flexible structures allow buildings to sway rather than break apart. Placing a building on pads or rollers cushions the structure from the motion of the ground. Some so-called intelligent buildings automatically respond to tremors, shifting their weight or tightening and loosening joints.

Looking Closer   How can studying earthquake-damaged buildings help designers improve future construction?

San Francisco, California, 1989 ▶

Erosion   Erosion is the process of wearing away or moving weathered material. Water, wind, and ice are the greatest factors that erode, or wear away, surface material. Rain and moving water in oceans, rivers, and streams can erode even the hardest stone over time. Rainwater that works its way to streams and rivers picks up and moves soil and sand. These particles make the river water similar to a giant scrub brush that grinds away at riverbanks and any other surface in the water's path.

Wind is also a major cause of erosion as it lifts weathered soil and sand. The areas that lose soil often become unable to grow crops and support life. The areas that receive the windblown soil often benefit from the additional nutrients to the land. When wind carries sand, however, it acts like sandpaper. Rock and other structures are carved into smooth shapes.

The third cause of erosion is ice. Giant, slow-moving sheets of ice are called glaciers. Forming high in mountains, glaciers change the land as they inch over it. Similar to windstorms, glaciers act like sandpaper as they pick up and carry rocks down the mountainside, grinding smooth everything beneath them. Some glaciers are thousands of feet thick. The weight and pressure of thousands of feet of ice also cut deep valleys at the mountain's base.

✓ Reading Check   **List three things that can cause weathering.**

FCAT PRACTICE   You can prepare for the FCAT-assessed standards by completing the correlated item(s) below.

Section 3 Assessment

Defining Terms

1. **Define** core, mantle, magma, crust, continent, plate tectonics, earthquake, tsunami, fault, weathering, erosion, glacier.

Recalling Facts

2. **Region** What are the three layers of the earth?

3. **Movement** In what three ways can tectonic plates move?

4. **Science** What are the three greatest factors that cause erosion?   **FCAT** SC.D.1.3.1

Critical Thinking

5. **Making Comparisons** How does water play a role in the processes of weathering and erosion?   **FCAT** SC.D.1.3.1, LA.A.2.2.7

6. **Understanding Cause and Effect** How does erosion hurt some areas yet benefit others?   **FCAT** SC.D.1.3.1, LA.E.2.2.1

Graphic Organizer

7. **Organizing Information** Draw a diagram like this one, then label the inner arrows with inside forces that shape landforms. Label the outer arrows with surface forces that change the earth's landforms.   **FCAT** SC.D.1.3.1, SC.D.1.3.5

Applying Social Studies Skills

8. **Analyzing Diagrams** Look at the diagram of tectonic plate boundaries on page 36. Why might it be a problem that many of the world's people live along the western edge of the Pacific Ocean?   **FCAT** SC.D.1.3.5

Landforms and Waterways

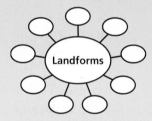

NATIONAL GEOGRAPHIC Exploring Our World

Mountains and other landforms are usually formed by forces under the earth's crust. Yet some landforms are not created by the earth's forces—they are made by animals. Here, off Australia's northeast coast, coral and algae have joined together underwater, creating the Great Barrier Reef. They worked hard—the reef stretches more than 1,250 miles (2,012 km).

The earth's land surface consists of seven continents—North America, South America, Europe, Africa, Asia, Australia, and Antarctica. All have a variety of landforms—even icy Antarctica.

Types of Landforms

Look at the illustration on pages 14–15 of the **Geography Handbook.** Notice the many different forms that the land may take. Which ones are familiar to you? Which ones are new to you?

On Land Mountains are huge towers of rock formed by the collision of the earth's tectonic plates or by volcanoes. Some mountains may be a few thousand feet high. Others can soar higher than 20,000 feet (6,096 m). The world's tallest mountain is **Mt. Everest,** located in South Asia's Himalaya mountain ranges. It towers at 29,035 feet (8,850 m)—nearly 5.5 miles (8.9 km) high.

Valleys vs. Canyons

The Great Rift Valley in Africa is surrounded by mountains (above). Canyons, like the Grand Canyon in Arizona (right), are carved from plateaus.

Place How are valleys and canyons similar?

Mountains often have high peaks and steep, rugged slopes. Hills are lower and more rounded. Some hills form at the foot, or base, of mountains. As a result, these hills are called foothills.

In contrast, plains and plateaus are mostly flat. What makes them different from one another is their elevation, or height above sea level. Plains are low-lying stretches of flat or gently rolling land. Many plains reach from the middle of a continent to the coast, such as the **North European Plain.** Plateaus are also flat but have higher elevation. With some plateaus, a steep cliff forms on one side where the plateau rises above nearby lowlands. With others, such as the **Plateau of Tibet** in Asia, the plateau is surrounded by mountains.

Between mountains and hills lie valleys. A valley is a long stretch of land lower than the land on either side. Rivers are often found at the bottom of valleys. Canyons are steep-sided lowlands that rivers have cut through a plateau. One of the most famous canyons is the **Grand Canyon** in Arizona. For millions of years, the Colorado River flowed over a plateau and carved through rock, forming the Grand Canyon.

Geographers describe some landforms by their relationship to larger land areas or to bodies of water. An isthmus is a narrow piece of land that connects two larger pieces of land. A peninsula is a piece of land with water on three sides. A body of land smaller than a continent and completely surrounded by water is an island.

Under the Oceans If you were to explore the oceans, you would see landforms under the water that are similar to those on land. Off each coast of a continent lies a plateau called a continental shelf that stretches for several miles underwater. At the edge of the shelf, steep cliffs drop down to the ocean floor.

Tall mountains and very deep valleys line the ocean floor. Valleys here are called **trenches,** and they are the lowest spots in the earth's crust. The deepest one, in the western Pacific Ocean, is called the **Mariana Trench.** This trench plunges 35,840 feet (10,924 m) below sea level. How deep is this? If Mt. Everest were placed into this trench, the mountain would have to grow 1.3 miles (2 km) higher just to reach the ocean's surface.

Landforms and People   Humans have settled on all types of landforms. Some people live at high elevations in the Andes mountain ranges of South America. The people of Bangladesh live on a low coastal plain. Farmers in Ethiopia work the land on a plateau called the Ethiopian Highlands.

Why do people decide to live in a particular area? Climate—the average temperature and rainfall of a region—is one reason. You will read more about climate in the next chapter. The availability of resources is another reason. People settle where they can get freshwater and where they can grow food, catch fish, or raise animals. They might settle in an area because it has good supplies of useful items such as trees for building, iron for manufacturing, or petroleum for making energy. You will read more about resources in Chapter 3.

✓**Reading Check**   How are plains and plateaus similar? How are they different?

Applying Map Skills

1. What are the names of the seven large landmasses on the earth?

2. What are the earth's four major oceans?

Find NGS online map resources @ www.nationalgeographic.com/maps

NATIONAL GEOGRAPHIC

World Continents and Oceans

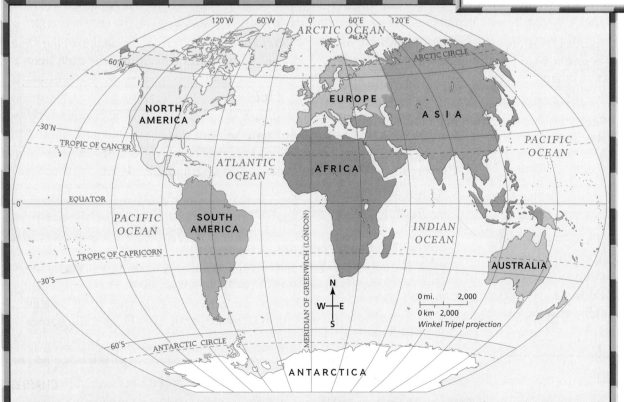

Bodies of Water

About 70 percent of the earth's surface is water. Most of that water is salt water, which people and most animals cannot drink. Only a small percentage is freshwater, which is drinkable. Oceans, consisting of salt water, are the earth's largest bodies of water. Smaller bodies of salt water are connected to oceans but are at least partly enclosed by land. These bodies include seas, gulfs, and bays.

Two other kinds of water form passages that connect two larger bodies of water. A strait is a narrow body of water between two pieces of land. The **Strait of Magellan** flows between the southern tip of South America and an island called Tierra del Fuego (tee•EHR•uh DEHL fu•AY•GOH). This strait connects the Atlantic and the Pacific Oceans. A wider passage is called a channel. The Mozambique Channel separates southeastern Africa from the island of Madagascar.

Bodies of freshwater appear on the world's continents and islands. They include larger bodies like lakes and rivers as well as smaller ones such as ponds and streams. The point at which a river originates—usually high in the mountains—is called its source. The mouth of a river is where it empties into another body of water. As you learned in Section 3, rivers carry soil and sand. They eventually deposit this soil at the mouth, which builds up over time to form a delta.

✓ **Reading Check** What is the difference between the source and the mouth of a river?

FCAT PRACTICE You can prepare for the FCAT-assessed standards by completing the correlated item(s) below.

Assessment

Defining Terms

1. **Define** elevation, plain, plateau, isthmus, peninsula, island, continental shelf, trench, strait, channel, delta.

Recalling Facts

2. **Place** What is the difference between mountains and hills?

3. **Place** How are straits and channels similar? How are they different?

4. **Culture** What are two reasons people decide to settle in a particular area?

Critical Thinking

5. **Analyzing Information** What two landforms are created by rivers?

6. **Making Inferences** Why do people often settle on the edges of rivers?

FCAT LA.A.1.3.2

Graphic Organizer

7. **Organizing Information** Make a chart like this and give three examples for each item.

FCAT LA.A.1.3.2

Landforms			
Landforms Under the Ocean			
Types of Bodies of Water			

Applying Social Studies Skills

8. **Analyzing Maps** Look at the map of Asia on pages RA24–RA25 of the **Reference Atlas.** Find an example of the following: plain, plateau, peninsula, island, strait. List the specific names of each landform.

Reading Review

Section 1 — Thinking Like a Geographer

Terms to Know

geography
landform
environment
Global Positioning System (GPS)
geographic information systems (GIS)
artifact
fossil

Main Idea

Geographers use various tools to understand the world.

✓ **Place** Geographers study the physical and social characteristics of places.

✓ **Human/Environment Interaction** Geographers are especially interested in how people interact with their environment.

✓ **Technology** To study the earth, geographers use maps, globes, photographs, the Global Positioning System, and geographic information systems.

✓ **Economics** People can use information from geography to plan, make decisions, and manage resources.

Section 2 — The Earth in Space

Terms to Know

solar system   leap year
orbit   summer solstice
atmosphere   winter solstice
axis   equinox
revolution

Main Idea

Earth has life because of the sun. Earth has different seasons because of the way it tilts and revolves around the sun.

✓ **Science** The sun's light and warmth allow life to exist on Earth.

✓ **Science** The atmosphere is a cushion of gases that protects Earth and provides air to breathe.

✓ **Movement** Earth spins on its axis causing day and night.

✓ **Movement** The tilt of Earth and its revolution around the sun cause the changes in seasons.

Section 3 — Forces Shaping the Earth

Terms to Know

core   plate tectonics
mantle   tsunami
magma   fault
crust   weathering
continent   erosion
earthquake   glacier

Main Idea

Forces both inside the earth and on its surface affect the shape of the land.

✓ **Region** Earth has an inner and outer core, a mantle, and a crust.

✓ **Movement** The continents are on large plates of rock that move.

✓ **Movement** Earthquakes and volcanoes can reshape the land.

✓ **Science** Wind, water, and ice can change the look of the land.

Section 4 — Landforms and Waterways

Terms to Know

elevation   continental shelf
plain   trench
plateau   strait
isthmus   channel
peninsula   delta
island

Main Idea

Landforms in all their variety affect how people live.

✓ **Location** Mountains, plateaus, valleys, and other landforms are found on land and under the oceans.

✓ **Science** About 70 percent of the earth's surface is water.

✓ **Culture** People have adapted in order to live on various landforms.

Assessment and Activities

 You can prepare for the FCAT-assessed standards by completing the correlated item(s) below.

Using Key Terms

Match the terms in Part A with their definitions in Part B.

A.

1. elevation
2. landform
3. summer solstice
4. plate tectonics
5. geographic information systems
6. Global Positioning System
7. erosion
8. equinox
9. fault
10. weathering

B.

a. height above sea level
b. wearing away of the earth's surface
c. theory that the earth's crust consists of huge slabs of rock that move
d. a group of satellites around the earth
e. special software that helps geographers gather and use information
f. when day and night are of equal length
g. a process that breaks surface rocks into gravel, sand, or soil
h. a crack in the earth's crust
i. the day with the most hours of sunlight
j. particular features of the land

Reviewing the Main Ideas

Section 1 Thinking Like a Geographer

11. **Place** Give three examples of the physical characteristics of a place.
12. **Region** How is a region different from a place?
13. **Human/Environment Interaction** Give an example of how people use geographic knowledge.

Section 2 The Earth in Space

14. **Region** How many planets are in the solar system? **FCAT SC.E.1.3.1**
15. **Movement** What movement of Earth causes day and night? **FCAT SC.D.1.3.5**
16. **Movement** How does Earth's revolution around the sun relate to the seasons? **FCAT SC.D.1.3.5**

Section 3 Forces Shaping the Earth

17. **Movement** How do the plates in the earth's crust move?
18. **Movement** Give an example of erosion. **FCAT SC.D.1.3.1**

Section 4 Landforms and Waterways

19. **Place** Which has a higher elevation—plains or plateaus?
20. **Movement** What are two reasons people settle in a particular region?

 **The World**

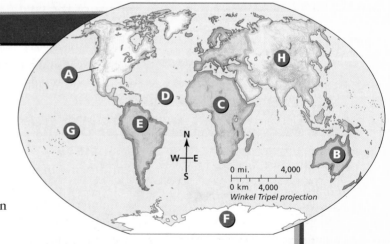

Place Location Activity

On a separate sheet of paper, match the letters on the map with the numbered places listed below.

1. North America
2. Pacific Ocean
3. Africa
4. South America
5. Antarctica
6. Australia
7. Atlantic Ocean
8. Asia

Critical Thinking

21. **Drawing Conclusions** Why do people in Australia snow-ski during the Northern Hemisphere's summer months? **FCAT** LA.A.2.2.7

22. **Understanding Cause and Effect** Create a diagram like this one. In the "Cause" box, write "plate movements." In the "Effect" box, describe the effect that this force has on the earth. Draw four more pairs of boxes and do the same for the other forces that shape the earth: earthquakes, volcanoes, weathering, and erosion. **FCAT** LA.A.2.3.1, SC.D.1.3.1

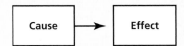

Comparing Regions Activity

23. **Geography** Think about your neighborhood. List the characteristics that make it a region. Organize into pairs and compare the characteristics of your region to your partner's region.

Mental Mapping Activity

24. **Focusing on the Region** Draw a simple outline map of the earth, then label the following:

- core
- crust
- mantle
- atmosphere

Technology Skills Activity

25. **Building a Database** Use a word processing program to make a database like the following. In the first column, list forces inside Earth that have shaped the land. Then write the result of the force in the second column. In the third column, research to find an example of each result. The first row has been filled in for you.

Force	Result	Example
collision of plates	mountains	Himalaya

Standardized Test Practice

Directions: Study the maps below, and then answer the question that follows.

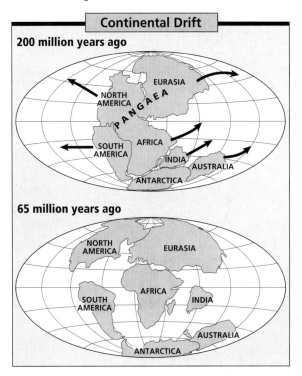

1. **What "supercontinent" do many scientists believe existed 200 million years ago?**

   A Eurasia

   B Pangaea

   C Gondwana

   D Antarctica

Test-Taking Tip: Use information on the maps to answer this question. Read the title above the maps and then the two subtitles. If you reread the question, you see it is asking about a certain time period. Make sure you use the correct map above to answer the question.

Chapter 2

Water, Climate, and Vegetation

The World and Its People

NATIONAL GEOGRAPHIC

To learn more about water, climate, and vegetation, view *The World and Its People* Chapter 2 video.

Social Studies Online

Chapter Overview Visit *The World and Its People* Web site at twip.glencoe.com and click on **Chapter 2—Chapter Overviews** to preview information about water, climate, and vegetation.

Why It Matters

A Balancing Act

Many of the daily decisions you make pertain to the weather and climate. Climate affects where you live, what you wear, what you eat, and what activities you participate in. Climate also affects what types of vegetation will grow in certain areas. Understanding climate—and the human activities that can change it—is the first step in understanding the need to have a balance in the global environment.

◄ Grand Teton National Park, Wyoming, United States

FOLDABLES™ Study Organizer

FCAT PRACTICE The activity below will help you prepare for the **FCAT Reading** test.

Summarizing Make this foldable and use it to organize note cards with information about water, climate, and vegetation. **FCAT LA.A.1.3.2**

Step 1 Fold a two-inch tab along the long edge of a sheet of paper.

Step 2 Fold the paper in thirds so the tab is on the inside.

The tab is inside when the paper is folded.

Step 3 Open the paper pocket foldable, turn it, and glue the edges of the pockets together.

Glue here.

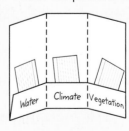

Step 4 Label the pockets as shown.

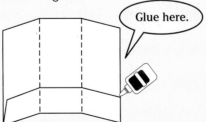

Water | Climate | Vegetation

Reading and Writing As you read each section in the chapter, summarize key facts about water, climate, and vegetation on note cards or on quarter sheets of notebook paper. Organize your notes by placing them in your foldable inside the appropriate pocket. **FCAT LA.A.1.3.2**

The Water Planet

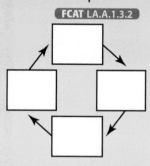
NATIONAL GEOGRAPHIC Exploring Our World

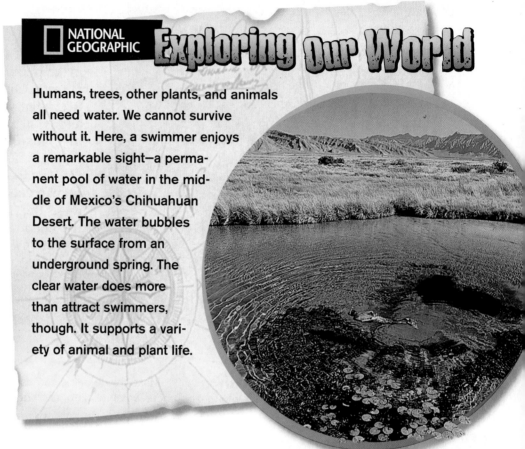

Humans, trees, other plants, and animals all need water. We cannot survive without it. Here, a swimmer enjoys a remarkable sight—a permanent pool of water in the middle of Mexico's Chihuahuan Desert. The water bubbles to the surface from an underground spring. The clear water does more than attract swimmers, though. It supports a variety of animal and plant life.

Some people call Earth "the water planet." Why? Water covers about 70 percent of the earth's surface. Water exists all around you in many different forms. Streams, rivers, lakes, seas, and oceans contain water in liquid form. The atmosphere holds **water vapor,** or water in the form of gas. Glaciers and ice sheets are masses of water that have been frozen solid. As a matter of fact, the human body itself is about 60 percent water.

The Water Cycle

The total amount of water on the earth does not change. It does not stay in one place, either. Instead, the water moves constantly. In a process called the **water cycle,** the water goes from the oceans to the air to the ground and finally back to the oceans.

Look at the diagram on page 49 to see how the water cycle works. The sun drives the cycle by evaporating water mostly from the surface of oceans, but also from lakes and streams. In **evaporation,** the sun's heat turns liquid water into water vapor—also called humidity. The amount of water vapor that the air holds depends on the air temperature. Warm air can hold more humidity than cool air. This explains those warm, muggy summer days.

In addition, warm air tends to rise. As warm air rises higher in the atmosphere, it cools. The cooler air loses its ability to hold as much humidity. As a result, the water vapor changes back into a liquid in a process called condensation. Tiny droplets of water come together to form clouds. Eventually, the water falls back to the earth as some form of precipitation—rain, snow, sleet, or hail—depending on the temperature of the surrounding air.

When this precipitation reaches the earth's surface, it soaks into the ground and collects in streams and lakes. During collection, streams and rivers both above and below the ground carry the water back to the oceans. Then the cycle begins again.

 Reading Check Which kind of air—warm or cold—holds the most water vapor?

Water Resources

It is a hot day, and you rush home for a glass of water. Like all other people, and all plants and animals, you need water to survive. Think about the many ways you use water in a single day. You use it to bathe, to brush your teeth, to cook your food, and to quench your thirst. People and most animals need freshwater to live. Other creatures make their homes in the earth's more plentiful kind of water: salt water.

Freshwater   Only about 2 percent of the water on the earth is freshwater. Eighty percent of that freshwater is frozen in polar ice caps or glaciers, which are giant sheets of ice. Only a tiny fraction of all freshwater—not even four-hundredths of a percent—is found in lakes and rivers.

FCAT PRACTICE

Completing the exercise below will help you prepare for the **FCAT Mathematics** and **Science** tests.

 **NATIONAL GEOGRAPHIC**

The Water Cycle

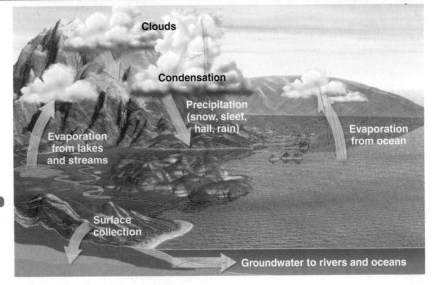

Analyzing the Diagram

The water cycle involves evaporation, condensation, precipitation, and the collection of water above and below the ground.

Movement How does water get from the ground to the oceans? **FCAT** MA.E.3.3.1, SC.D.1.3.3

Clouds

Condensation

Precipitation (snow, sleet, hail, rain)

Evaporation from lakes and streams

Evaporation from ocean

Surface collection

Groundwater to rivers and oceans

Water, Climate, and Vegetation

When you think of freshwater, you probably think of mighty rivers and huge lakes. People can get freshwater from another source, though. Groundwater is water that fills tiny cracks and holes in the rock layers below the surface of the earth. This is a vital source of water because there is 10 times more groundwater than there is water in rivers and lakes. Groundwater can be tapped by wells. Some areas have aquifers, or underground rock layers that water flows through. In regions with little rainfall, both farmers and city dwellers sometimes have to depend on aquifers and other groundwater for most of their water supply.

Salt Water   All the oceans on the earth are part of a huge, continuous body of salt water—almost 98 percent of the planet's water. Look at the map on page 57. You will see that the four major oceans are the **Pacific Ocean,** the **Atlantic Ocean,** the **Indian Ocean,** and the **Arctic Ocean.**

The Pacific Ocean is the largest and deepest of these four oceans. It covers almost 64 million square miles (166 million sq. km)—more than all the land areas of the earth combined. As you learned in Chapter 1, bodies of salt water smaller than the oceans are called seas, gulfs, bays, or straits. Look back at the diagram on pages 14-15 of the **Geography Handbook** to see these features again.

✓ Reading Check **What is the difference between groundwater and aquifers?**

FCAT PRACTICE You can prepare for the FCAT-assessed standards by completing the correlated item(s) below.

Assessment

Defining Terms

1. **Define** water vapor, water cycle, evaporation, condensation, precipitation, collection, glacier, groundwater, aquifer.

Recalling Facts

2. **Region** What percentage of the earth is covered by water?

3. **Movement** In which part of the water cycle does water return to the earth? FCAT SC.D.1.3.3

4. **Region** What are the world's four oceans?

Critical Thinking

5. **Understanding Cause and Effect** How does the temperature of the air affect the amount of humidity that you feel? How does the air's temperature also influence the form of precipitation that falls?
FCAT SC.D.1.3.3, LA.E.2.2.1

6. **Drawing Conclusions** Why do you think it is important to keep groundwater free of dangerous chemicals? FCAT SC.D.1.3.3, SC.D.2.3.2

Graphic Organizer

7. **Organizing Information** Draw a diagram like this one. List at least four sources of freshwater and salt water on the lines under each heading.
FCAT LA.A.1.3.2

Salt Water — Water — Freshwater

Applying Social Studies Skills

8. **Analyzing Diagrams** Look at the diagram of the water cycle on page 49. From where does water evaporate? FCAT MA.E.3.3.1, SC.D.1.3.3

Making Connections

Exploring Earth's Water

More than two-thirds of the earth's surface is covered with water, yet scientists know more about the surface of the moon than they do about the ocean floor. Using an AUV, or autonomous underwater vehicle, called *Autosub*, researchers hope to gain a new understanding about the earth's watery surface.

What It Does

It looks like a giant torpedo, but *Autosub* is really a battery-powered robotic submarine that is 23 feet (7 m) long. Its mission is to explore parts of the ocean that are beyond the reach of other research vessels or are too dangerous for humans. Although it is still being tested, *Autosub* has already conducted hundreds of underwater missions.

Exploring Ice Shelves

One of the most promising areas of research for *Autosub* lies in seawater under the ice shelves near Greenland in the Arctic and near Antarctica at the southern extreme of the globe. Traditional submarines are unable to explore these places safely. Satellite photographs show that the area of the ice shelves is changing. Scientists want to use *Autosub*'s technology to measure changes in the thickness of sea ice. They believe that this information may give important clues about the possible rise in the earth's temperature.

Sea ice plays an important role in keeping the earth's climate stable. It acts as insulation—a kind of protection—between the ocean and the atmosphere. Sea ice reflects light, so it limits the amount of heat absorbed into the water. This keeps the ocean from getting too warm. In winter, sea ice helps prevent heat from escaping the warmer oceans into the atmosphere.

FCAT PRACTICE Answering question 3 below will help you prepare for the **FCAT Reading** and **Science** tests.

What the Future Holds

So far, *Autosub*'s missions have been fairly short. Scientists hope to someday program *Autosub* to make long voyages, sampling seawater and collecting data from ocean floors. The information that *Autosub* provides will help scientists make better predictions about the earth's climate.

▲ *Autosub* can be launched from shore, towed out to sea by a small boat, or lowered by a crane into the water.

▶ Making the Connection

1. What is *Autosub*?
2. Why do scientists want to use *Autosub* to explore under the ice shelves?
3. **Understanding Cause and Effect** How could a loss of sea ice affect the earth's climate?

FCAT SC.D.1.3.3, LA.E.2.2.1

Section 2 — Climate

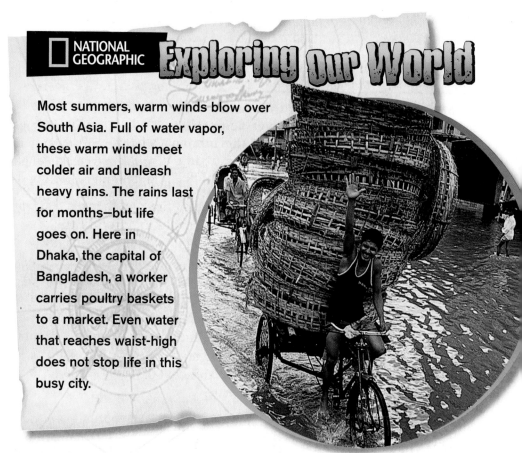

NATIONAL GEOGRAPHIC — Exploring Our World

Most summers, warm winds blow over South Asia. Full of water vapor, these warm winds meet colder air and unleash heavy rains. The rains last for months—but life goes on. Here in Dhaka, the capital of Bangladesh, a worker carries poultry baskets to a market. Even water that reaches waist-high does not stop life in this busy city.

Why are some areas of the world full of lush forests, while others are covered with bone-dry deserts? Why do some people struggle through chilling winters, while others enjoy a day at the beach? To understand these mysteries, you need to unlock the secrets of climate.

Weather and Climate

As you learned in Chapter 1, the earth is surrounded by the atmosphere, which holds a combination of gases we call air. The many layers of the atmosphere protect life on the earth from harmful rays of the sun. The layer of atmosphere closest to the earth is also where you will find weather patterns. Suppose a friend calls you and asks what it is like outside. You might say, "It's a beautiful day—warm and sunny!" You are describing the weather. Weather refers to the unpredictable changes in air that take place over a short period of time.

Suppose that someone from another country asks what summers and winters are like in your area. You might say, "Summers are usually hot and rainy, and winters are cool but dry." This answer describes not the weather but your area's climate. Climate is the usual, predictable pattern of weather in an area over a long period of time. Studies of climate show the highs and lows of temperature and precipitation over the course of 30 years or more.

Reading Check What is the difference between weather and climate?

The Sun and Climate

What causes climate? The original source of climate is the sun. It gives off energy and light that all plants and animals need to survive. The sun's rays warm the air, water, and land on our planet. Warm gases and liquids are lighter than cool gases and liquids. Because they are lighter, the warmer gases and liquids rise. Then wind and water carry this warmth around the globe, spreading the sun's heat.

Latitude and Climate Climate is also affected by the angle at which the sun's rays hit the earth. As you learned in Chapter 1, the sun's rays hit various places at different angles at different times of the year. These changes are caused by the earth's tilt and revolution around the sun. The sun's rays hit places in low latitudes—regions near the **Equator**—more directly than places at higher latitudes. The low latitudes near the Equator, known as the Tropics, lie between the **Tropic of Cancer** (23½°N latitude) and the **Tropic of Capricorn** (23½°S latitude). If you lived in the Tropics, you would almost always experience a hot climate, unless you lived high in the mountains where temperatures are cooler. Find the Tropics on the map on page 54. (To learn how to use latitude and longitude, turn to page 60.)

NATIONAL GEOGRAPHIC On Location

Washington, D.C.

A cross-country skier braves a blizzard in the capital of the United States.

Place When scientists study climate, what two factors do they analyze?

Water, Climate, and Vegetation

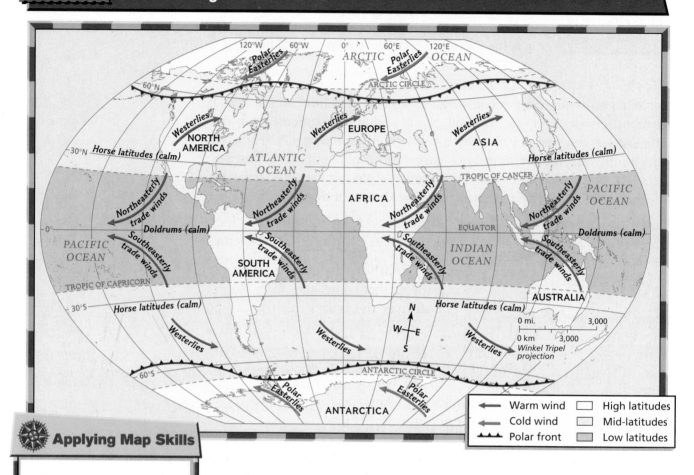

Applying Map Skills

1. In which general direction does the wind blow over North America?

2. What winds did European sailors use to get to South America and the islands north of it?

Find NGS online map resources @ www.nationalgeographic.com/maps

Outside the Tropics, the sun is never directly overhead. The mid-latitudes extend from the Tropics to about 60° both north and south of the Equator. When the North Pole is tilted toward the sun, the sun's rays fall more directly on the Northern Hemisphere. This affects our climate by giving us warm summer days. Six months later, the South Pole is tilted toward the sun, and the seasons are reversed. At the high latitudes near the North and South Poles, the sun's rays hit very indirectly. Climates in these regions are always cool or cold.

✓ Reading Check How does the tilt of the earth affect climate?

The Wind's Effect on Climate

Movements of air are called winds. From year to year, winds follow prevailing, or typical, patterns. These patterns are very complex. One reason is that winds do more than move east and west or north and south. They also go up and down. As you learned earlier, warm air rises and cold air falls. Thus, the warmer winds near the Equator rise and move north and south toward the Poles of the earth. The colder winds from the Poles sink and move toward the Equator. This exchange is complicated by the fact that the earth rotates, which causes the winds to curve. Winds, then, are in constant motion in many directions.

Another important wind pattern is the monsoon. Monsoons are tremendous seasonal winds that blow over continents for months at a time. They are found mainly in Asia and some areas in Africa. Although they often are destructive, the summer monsoons in South Asia bring much-needed heavy rains.

Storms As you read in Section 1, part of the water cycle is rain and other types of precipitation that fall to the earth. A little rain may ruin a picnic or spoil a ball game, but it is not a serious problem. Sometimes, though, people suffer through fierce storms. What causes these destructive events?

When warm, moist air systems meet cold air systems, thunderstorms may develop. These storms include thunder, lightning, and heavy rain. They tend to be short, lasting only about 30 minutes. Some areas are more likely to see thunderstorms than others. In central Florida, as many as 90 days per year may experience thunderstorms.

A thunderstorm can produce another danger—a tornado. Tornadoes are funnel-shaped windstorms that sometimes form during severe thunderstorms. They occur all over the world, but the United States has more tornadoes than any other area. Winds in tornadoes often reach 250 miles (402 km) per hour.

Hurricanes, or violent tropical storm systems, form over the warm Atlantic Ocean in late summer and fall. Hurricanes bring high winds that can reach more than 150 miles (241 km) per hour. They also produce rough seas and carry drenching rain. Hurricanes strike North America and the islands in the Caribbean Sea. They also rip through Asia, although in that region they are called typhoons. These storms can do tremendous damage. Their strong winds destroy buildings and snap power lines. Heavy rains can flood low-lying areas.

El Niño and La Niña In 1998 the world experienced unusual weather. Heavy rains brought floods to Peru, washing away whole villages. Europe, eastern Africa, and most of the southern United States also had severe flooding. In the western Pacific, normally heavy rains never came. Indonesia suffered a drought, a long period of extreme dryness. The land there became so dry that forest fires burned thousands of acres of trees. Thick smoke from the fires forced drivers to put their headlights on at noon!

Why did these disasters take place? They resulted from a combination of temperature, wind, and water effects in the Pacific Ocean called El Niño (ehl NEE•nyoh). The name "El Niño" was coined by early Spanish explorers in the Pacific. They used the phrase—which refers to the Christ child and means "the boy"—because the effect hits South America around Christmas.

El Niños form when cold winds from the east are weak. Without these cold winds, the central Pacific Ocean grows warmer than usual. More water evaporates, and more clouds form. The thick band of clouds changes wind and rain patterns. Some areas receive heavier than normal rains and others have less than normal rainfall.

El Niño

NORMAL CONDITIONS

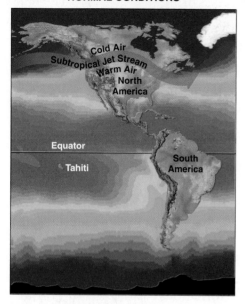

Cold Air
Subtropical Jet Stream
Warm Air
North America
Equator
Tahiti
South America

EL NIÑO CONDITIONS

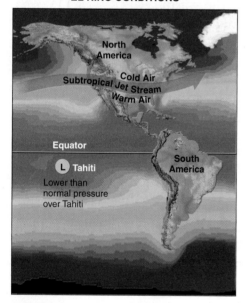

North America
Cold Air
Subtropical Jet Stream
Warm Air
Equator
L Tahiti
Lower than normal pressure over Tahiti
South America

Analyzing the Diagram

The temperature of the oceans varies from warm (dark red) to very cold (dark purple).

Movement What happens to the jet stream during El Niño conditions? **FCAT SC.D.1.3.3**

Does El Niño happen every year? Scientists have found that El Niño occurs about every three years. They also found that in some years, the opposite kind of unusual weather takes place. This event is called **La Niña** (lah NEE•nyah), Spanish for "the girl," because the effects are the opposite of those in El Niño. Winds from the east become very strong, cooling more of the Pacific. When this happens, heavy clouds form in the western Pacific.

✓**Reading Check** Why do El Niños occur?

Ocean Currents

Winds carry large masses of warm and cool air around the earth. At the same time, moving streams of water called **currents** carry warm or cool water through the world's oceans. Look at the map on page 57. As you can see, these currents follow certain patterns. Notice how the warm currents tend to move along the Equator or from the Equator to the Poles. The cold currents carry cold polar water toward the Equator.

These currents affect the climate of land areas. Look at the warm current called the Gulf Stream. It flows from the Gulf of Mexico along the east coast of North America. Then it crosses the Atlantic Ocean toward Europe, where it is called the North Atlantic Current. Winds that blow over these warm waters bring warm air to western Europe. Because these winds blow from west to east, areas in Europe enjoy warmer weather than areas lying west of the Gulf Stream in Canada.

✓**Reading Check** What areas of the world would be affected by a change in the Gulf Stream?

Landforms and Climate

Wind and water affect climate, but the shape of the land has an effect on climate as well. Where the landforms are in relation to one another and to water influences climate too.

Landforms and Local Winds Although geographers study major wind patterns that blow over the earth, they also look at local winds. **Local winds** are patterns of wind caused by landforms in a particular area. Some local winds occur because land warms and cools more quickly than water does. As a result, cool sea breezes keep coastal areas cool during the

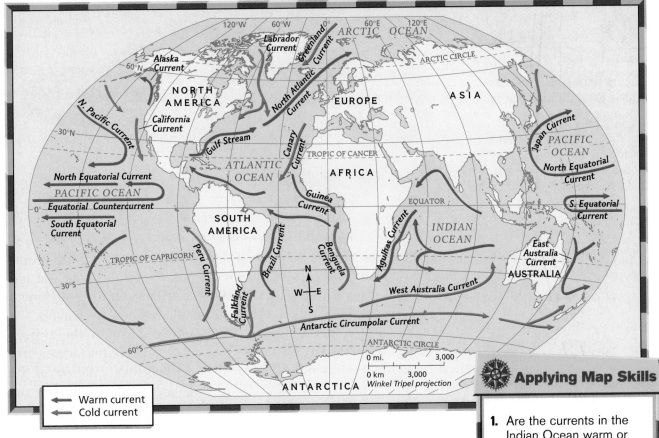

Warm current
Cold current

Applying Map Skills

1. Are the currents in the Indian Ocean warm or cold?

2. Where does the Peru Current flow?

Find NGS online map resources @ www.nationalgeographic.com/maps

day. After the sun sets, the opposite occurs. The air over the land cools more quickly than the air over water does. At night, then, a cool breeze blows from the land out to the sea.

A similar effect occurs near mountains. Air warmed by the sun rises up mountain slopes during the day. At night, cooler air moves down the mountain into the valley below. Have you ever seen fog lying on a valley floor on a cool morning? That fog was caused by the cool air that came down the mountain during the night.

Mountains, Temperature, and Rainfall   The higher the elevation of a particular place, the lower the temperature that place will have. In high mountains, the air becomes thinner and cannot hold as much heat from the sun. The temperature drops. Even in the Tropics, snow covers the peaks of high mountains.

Mountains also have an effect on rainfall. When warm, moist winds blow inland from the ocean toward a coastal mountain range, the winds are forced upward over the mountains. As these warm winds rise, the air cools and loses its moisture. Rain or snow falls on the mountains. The climate on this windward—or wind-facing—side of mountain ranges is moist and often foggy. Trees are thick and green.

Water, Climate, and Vegetation

Analyzing the Diagram

Rain shadows usually occur on the leeward sides of mountain ranges.

Location What is the term for the side of a mountain where the climate is moist and often foggy?

Mountain range

Warm dry air in rain shadow

North

Cool moist air drops moisture

LEEWARD SIDE

Warm moist air

WINDWARD SIDE

Ocean

South

By the time the air moves over the mountain peaks, it is cool and dry. This creates a **rain shadow,** a dry area on the side of the mountains facing away from the wind. Geographers call this side the leeward side. The dry air of a rain shadow warms up again as it moves down the leeward side, giving the region a dry or desert climate.

A rain shadow occurs along the western coast of the United States and Canada. Winds moving east from the Pacific Ocean lose their moisture as they move upward on the windward slopes of the coastal mountains. Great deserts and dry basins are located on the leeward side of these ranges.

✓**Reading Check** Why are areas of higher elevation often cooler?

The Impact of People on Climate

People's actions can affect climate. You may have noticed that temperatures in large cities are generally higher than those in nearby rural areas. Why is that? The city's streets and buildings absorb more of the sun's rays than do the plants and trees of rural areas.

Cities are warmer even in winter. People burn fuels to warm houses, power industry, and move cars and buses along the streets. This burning raises the temperature in the city. The burning also releases a cloud of chemicals into the air. These chemicals blanket the city and hold in more of the sun's heat, creating a so-called heat island.

The Greenhouse Effect In the past two hundred years, people have burned coal, oil, and natural gas as sources of energy. Burning these fuels releases certain gases into the air. Some scientists warn that the buildup of these gases presents dangers. It creates a **greenhouse effect**—like a greenhouse, the gases prevent the warm air from rising and escaping into the atmosphere. As a result, the overall temperature of the earth will increase. Some scientists predict disastrous results from this global warming. They say the ice at the North and South Poles will melt. Then ocean levels will rise and flood coastal cities. Some areas that are now fertile will become unable to grow crops.

Not all scientists agree about the greenhouse effect. Some argue that the world is not warming. Others say that even if it is, the predictions of disaster are extreme. Many scientists are studying world temperature trends closely. They hope to be able to discover whether the greenhouse effect is a real threat.

Clearing the Rain Forests   Along the Equator, dense forests called **rain forests** receive high amounts of rain each year. In some countries, people are clearing large areas of these forests. They want to sell the lumber from the trees. They also want to use the land to grow crops or as pasture for cattle. Clearing the rain forests, though, can hurt the world's climate.

One danger is related to the greenhouse effect. People often clear the forests by burning down the trees. This burning releases more gases into the air, just like burning oil or natural gas does. Another danger of clearing the rain forests is related to rainfall. Remember the water cycle discussed in Section 1? Water on the earth's surface evaporates into the air and then falls as rain. In the rain forests, much of this water evaporates from the leaves of trees. If the trees are cut, less water will evaporate. As a result, less rain will fall. Scientists worry that over time the area that now holds rain forests will actually become dry and unable to grow anything.

✓Reading Check   What are two dangers of clearing the rain forests?

FCAT PRACTICE   You can prepare for the FCAT-assessed standards by completing the correlated item(s) below.

Section **2** **Assessment**

Defining Terms

1. **Define** weather, climate, Tropics, drought, El Niño, La Niña, current, local wind, rain shadow, greenhouse effect, rain forest.

Recalling Facts

2. **Movement** What five elements affect climate?

3. **Location** Between what two lines of latitude are the Tropics?

4. **Place** Provide an example of how landforms influence climate.

Critical Thinking

5. **Making Comparisons** How does the amount of rainfall on the windward side of a mountain differ from that on the leeward side? **FCAT LA.A.2.2.7**

6. **Summarizing Information** What general patterns do wind and currents follow? **FCAT LA.A.2.3.1**

Graphic Organizer

7. **Organizing Information** Draw a diagram as shown. First, list three human actions that lead to the greenhouse effect. In the third box, list four results of the greenhouse effect. **FCAT LA.A.1.3.2, SC.D.2.3.2**

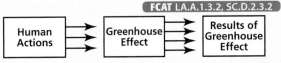

Applying Social Studies Skills

8. **Analyzing Maps** Look at the world ocean currents map on page 57. Which continent lies completely outside the Tropics?

Water, Climate, and Vegetation

Social Studies Skill

FCAT PRACTICE Answering question 1 below will help you prepare for the **FCAT Mathematics** test.

Using Latitude and Longitude

Learning the Skill

To find an exact location, geographers use a set of imaginary lines. One set of lines—**latitude** lines—circles the earth's surface like a stack of rings. The starting point for numbering latitude lines is the Equator, which is 0° latitude. Lines of latitude are numbered from 1° to 90° and are followed by an N or S to show whether they are north or south of the Equator. Latitude lines are also called parallels.

A second set of lines—**longitude** lines—runs vertically from the North Pole to the South Pole. These lines are also called meridians. The starting point—0° longitude—is called the Prime Meridian (or Meridian of Greenwich). Longitude lines are numbered from 1° to 180° followed by an E or W—to show whether they are east or west of the Prime Meridian.

To find latitude and longitude, choose a place on a map. Identify the nearest parallel, or line of latitude. Is it located north or south of the Equator? Now identify the nearest meridian, or line of longitude. Is it located east or west of the Prime Meridian?

Practicing the Skill

1. On the map below, what is the exact location of Washington, D.C.? **FCAT MA.B.1.3.4**
2. Which cities on the map lie south of 0° latitude?
3. Which city is located near 30°N, 30°E?

Applying the Skill

Turn to pages RA2–RA3 of the **Reference Atlas.** Determine the latitude and longitude for one city. Ask a classmate to use the information to find and name the city.

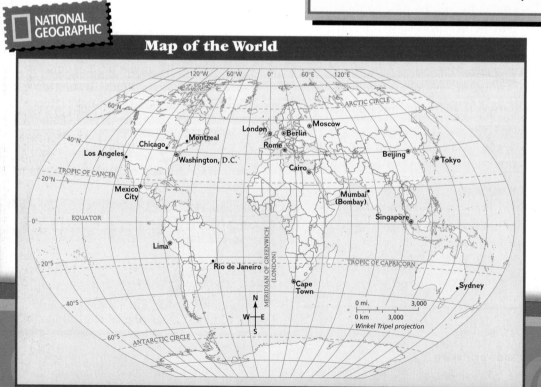

NATIONAL GEOGRAPHIC

Map of the World

Climate Zones and Vegetation

Guide to Reading

Main Idea

Geographers divide the world into different climate zones.

Terms to Know

- savanna
- marine west coast climate
- Mediterranean climate
- humid continental climate
- humid subtropical climate
- subarctic
- tundra
- steppe

Reading Strategy

Create a chart like this one by listing the categories of each type of climate next to the correct headings.

FCAT LA.A.1.3.2

Climate Type	Categories
Tropical	
Mid-Latitude	
High Latitude	
Dry	
Highland	

The following is the major Sunshine State Standard covered in this section.

SS.B.1.3.6:
Understands ways in which regional systems are interconnected

NATIONAL GEOGRAPHIC **Exploring Our World**

The United States is home to a wide variety of plant life—from cacti to cattails and from microscopic mosses to giant trees. The incredible tree shown here is a giant sequoia. Although not the tallest, it is the largest of all trees. A few sequoias tower more than 300 feet (91 m) high and measure 100 feet (30 m) around at their base.

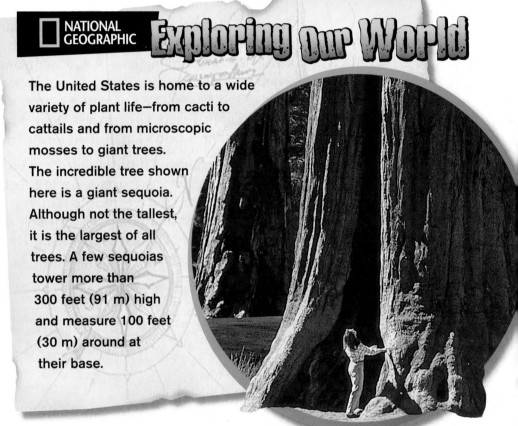

Why do you think a photograph of a giant tree is in a chapter on climate? The reason is that climate and vegetation go together. Consider this: The state of Washington sits next to the state of Idaho. The plant life in western Washington, however, is much more similar to that of the United Kingdom, which is thousands of miles away, than it is to the plant life in eastern Washington and Idaho, which touch each other. Why? The patterns of temperature, wind, and precipitation in western Washington and the United Kingdom are similar.

Scientists use these patterns to group climates into many different types. They have put the world's climates into five major groups: tropical, mid-latitude, high latitude, dry, and highland. Three of these groups—tropical, mid-latitude, and high latitude—are based on an area's latitude, or distance from the Equator. Some of these major groups have subcategories of climate zones within them. In addition, each climate zone has particular kinds of plants that grow in it.

Tropical Climates

The tropical climate gets its name from the Tropics—the areas along the Equator reaching from 23½°N to 23½°S. If you like warm weather, you would love a tropical climate. The tropical climate region can be separated into two types—tropical rain forest and tropical savanna. The tropical rain forest climate receives up to 100 inches (254 cm) of rain a year. As a result, the rain forest climate is wet in most months. The tropical savanna climate has two distinct seasons—one wet and one dry.

Tropical Rain Forest Climate Year-round rains in some parts of the Tropics produce lush vegetation and thick rain forests. These forests are home to millions of kinds of plant and animal life. Tall hardwood trees such as mahogany, teak, and ebony form the canopy, or top layer of the forest. The vegetation at the canopy layer is so thick that little sunlight reaches the forest floor. The Amazon Basin in South America is the world's largest rain forest area.

Tropical Savanna Climate In other parts of the Tropics, such as southern India and eastern Africa, rain falls in just a few months of the year. This is called the wet season. The rest of the year is hot and dry. Savannas, or broad grasslands with few trees, are the main type of vegetation in this climate region. Find the tropical savanna climate areas on the map on page 63.

✓Reading Check **Where are the tropical climate zones found?**

NATIONAL GEOGRAPHIC **On Location**

Tropical Vegetation

The **tropical rain forest** climate remains wet most of the year (far left), whereas the **tropical savanna** climate has distinct wet and dry seasons (below).

Region What is a savanna?

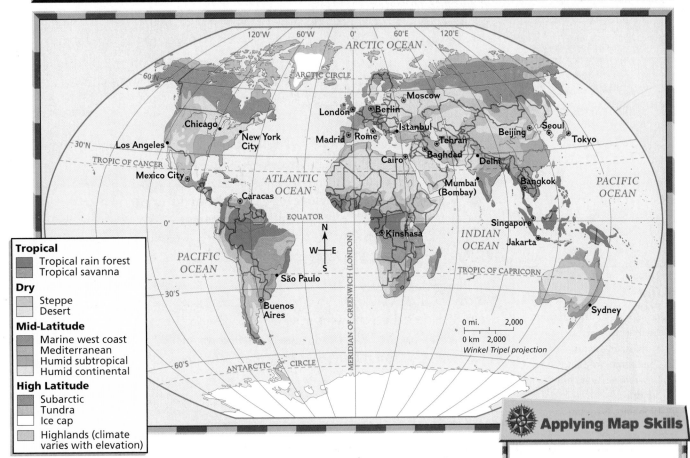

Tropical
- Tropical rain forest
- Tropical savanna

Dry
- Steppe
- Desert

Mid-Latitude
- Marine west coast
- Mediterranean
- Humid subtropical
- Humid continental

High Latitude
- Subarctic
- Tundra
- Ice cap
- Highlands (climate varies with elevation)

Mid-Latitude Climates

Mid-latitude, or moderate, climates are found in the middle latitudes of the Northern and Southern Hemispheres. They extend from about 23½° to 60° both north and south of the Equator. Most of the world's people—probably including you—live within these two bands around the earth. The climate zones found here are called mid-latitude because they are in the middle of both the Northern Hemisphere and the Southern Hemisphere. The mid-latitude climates are neither as close to the Equator as the tropical climates nor as close to the Poles as the high latitude climates.

The mid-latitude region includes more and different climate zones than other regions. This variety results from a mix of air masses. As you remember from Section 2, warm air comes from the Tropics. Cool air comes from the polar regions. In most mid-latitude climates, the temperature changes with the seasons. Sometimes the climate zones in this region are called temperate climates.

Marine West Coast Climate Coastal areas that receive winds from the ocean usually have a mild **marine west coast climate.** If you lived in one of these areas, your winters would be rainy and mild, and your summers would be cool. Most areas with this climate—such as

Applying Map Skills

1. Which climate covers most of the southeastern United States? **FCAT MA.B.1.3.4**

2. Which climate is most common in countries directly on the Equator? **FCAT MA.B.1.3.4**

Find NGS online map resources @ www.nationalgeographic.com/maps

FCAT PRACTICE

Completing the exercise above will help you prepare for the **FCAT Mathematics** test.

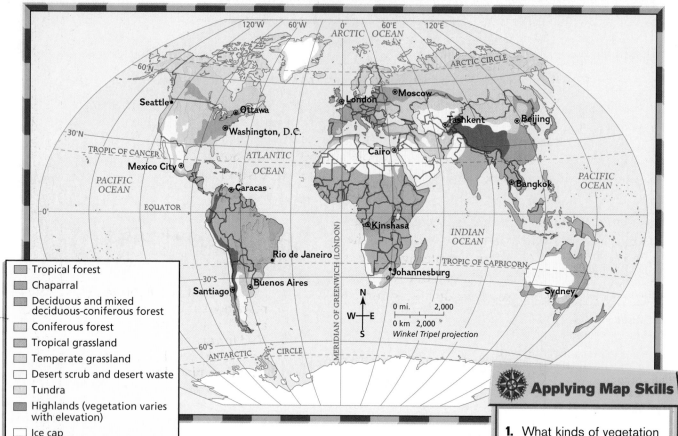

Tropical forest
Chaparral
Deciduous and mixed deciduous-coniferous forest
Coniferous forest
Tropical grassland
Temperate grassland
Desert scrub and desert waste
Tundra
Highlands (vegetation varies with elevation)
Ice cap

FCAT PRACTICE

Completing the map exercise will help you prepare for the **FCAT Mathematics** test.

Applying Map Skills

1. What kinds of vegetation surround Washington, D.C., and Moscow? **FCAT MA.B.1.3.4**

2. What type of vegetation grows around Bangkok? **FCAT MA.B.1.3.4**

Find NGS online map resources @ www.nationalgeographic.com/maps

the northwestern United States—receive heavy rainfall. This supports the growth of deciduous trees, or those that lose their leaves in the fall. Coniferous forests, evergreens with cones and needles, also thrive.

Mediterranean Climate Another mid-latitude coastal climate is called a Mediterranean climate because it is similar to the climate found around the Mediterranean Sea. This climate has mild, rainy winters like the marine west coast climate. Instead of cool summers, however, people living in a Mediterranean climate experience hot, dry summers. The vegetation that grows in this climate includes chaparral, or shrubs and short trees. Some are evergreens, but others lose their leaves in the dry season.

Humid Continental Climate If you live in inland areas of North America, Europe, or Asia, you usually face a harsher humid continental climate. In these areas, winters can be long, cold, and snowy. Summers are short but may be very hot. Deciduous trees grow in forests, and vast grasslands flourish in some areas of this zone.

Humid Subtropical Climate   Mid-latitude regions close to the Tropics have a **humid subtropical climate.** Rain falls throughout the year but is heaviest during the hot and humid summer months. Humid subtropical winters are generally short and mild. Trees like oaks, magnolias, and palms grow in this zone.

✓Reading Check   What causes the mid-latitude region to have more and different climate zones than other regions?

High Latitude Climates

High latitude climate regions lie mostly in the high latitudes of each hemisphere, from 60°N to the North Pole and 60°S to the South Pole. These climates are generally cold, but some are more severely cold than others.

Subarctic Climate   In the high latitudes nearest the mid-latitude zones, you will find the **subarctic** climate. The few people living here face very cold and bitter winters, but temperatures do rise above freezing during summer

Mid-Latitude Vegetation

Fir trees (bottom left) thrive in a **marine west coast** climate. Shrubs and olive trees (top right) grow in a **Mediterranean** climate. Deciduous trees (bottom right) flourish in a **humid continental** climate. Palm trees are common in **humid subtropical** zones.

Place Which type of vegetation is most common in your area?

NATIONAL GEOGRAPHIC **On Location**

Water, Climate, and Vegetation

months. Huge evergreen forests called taiga (TY•guh) grow in the subarctic region, especially in northern Russia.

Tundra Climate   Closer to the Poles than the subarctic zone lie the tundra areas, or vast treeless plains. The climate in this zone is harsh and dry. In the tundra and parts of subarctic regions, the lower layers of soil are called permafrost because they stay permanently frozen. Only the top few inches of the ground thaw during summer months. Because of permafrost, melting snow does not seep into the ground. Instead, the tundra turns marshy during the summer. This provides the moisture that plants need to grow. Trees cannot set up roots, however, so only sturdy grasses and low bushes grow in the tundra.

Ice Cap Climate   On the polar ice caps and the great ice sheets of Antarctica and Greenland, the climate is bitterly cold. Monthly temperatures average below freezing. Temperatures in Antarctica have been measured at −128°F (−89°C)! Although no other vegetation grows here, lichens—or funguslike plants and mosses—can live on rocks.

✓ Reading Check   What are the three types of high latitude climates?

On Location

High Latitude Vegetation

Vegetation in high latitude climates includes **tundra** grasses and bushes (top left), **subarctic** evergreen forests (bottom left), and **ice cap** lichens (background).

Region How does permafrost affect vegetation in the tundra and subarctic regions?

NATIONAL GEOGRAPHIC On Location

Dry Climate Vegetation

The vegetation that survives **desert** and **steppe** climates includes cacti (above) and short grasses (left).

Region Are very dry climates always hot? Explain.

Dry Climates

Dry climates refer to dry or partially dry areas that receive little or no rainfall. Temperatures can be extremely hot during the day and very cold at night. Dry climates can also have severely cold winters. You can find dry climate regions at any latitude.

Desert Climate The driest climates receive less than 10 inches (25 cm) of rainfall per year. Regions with such climates are called deserts. Only scattered plants such as scrub and cacti can survive a desert climate. With roots close to the surface, cacti can collect any rain that falls. Most cacti are found only in North America. In other countries, however, small areas of thick plant life dot the deserts. These arise along rivers or where underground springs reach the surface.

Steppe Climate Many deserts are surrounded by partly dry grasslands and prairies known as **steppes.** The word steppe comes from a Russian word meaning "treeless plain." The steppes receive more rain than deserts, averaging 10 to 20 inches (25 to 51 cm) per year. Bushes and short grasses cover the steppe landscape. The Great Plains of the United States has a steppe climate.

✓ Reading Check Where are steppe climate zones often located?

Water, Climate, and Vegetation

67

Highland Vegetation

The wildflowers and shrubs that grow in meadows above the timberline are often called *alpine* vegetation.

Location How does elevation affect climate?

Highland Climate

As you read in Section 2, the elevation of a place changes its climate dramatically. Mountains tend to have cool climates—and the highest mountains have very cold climates. This is true even for mountains that are on the Equator. A highland, or mountain, climate has cool or cold temperatures year-round.

If you climb a mountain, you will reach an area called the timberline. The timberline is the elevation above which no trees grow. Once you reach the timberline, you will find only small shrubs and wildflowers growing in meadows.

✓ **Reading Check** What is the timberline?

FCAT PRACTICE You can prepare for the FCAT-assessed standards by completing the correlated item(s) below.

Section 3 Assessment

Defining Terms

1. **Define** savanna, marine west coast climate, Mediterranean climate, humid continental climate, humid subtropical climate, subarctic, tundra, steppe.

Recalling Facts

2. **Region** What are the five types of climate regions?

3. **Region** How do the climate zones in the mid-latitude region differ?

4. **Region** What kind of vegetation grows in the tundra climate zone?

Critical Thinking

5. **Making Comparisons** What do the tropical savanna and humid continental climates have in common? **FCAT LA.A.2.2.7**

6. **Drawing Conclusions** How can snow exist in the Tropics along the Equator?
   FCAT LA.A.2.3.1

Graphic Organizer

7. **Organizing Information** Draw a globe like this one. Label the three climate regions that are based on latitude, then identify the lines of latitude that separate the climate regions.

FCAT LA.A.1.3.2

Equator →

Applying Social Studies Skills

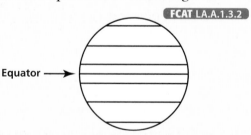

8. **Analyzing Maps** Look at the world natural vegetation regions map on page 64. What type of natural vegetation thrives around Cairo?

An Environmental Balance

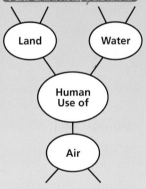
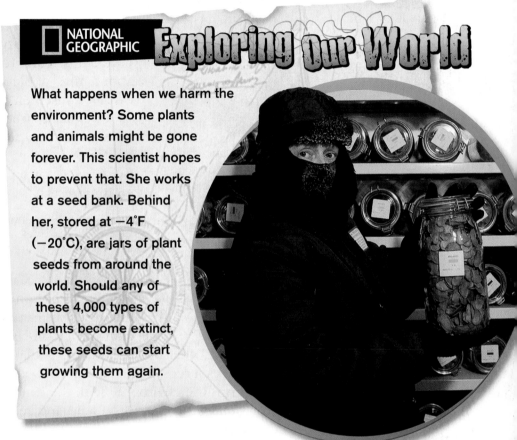

NATIONAL GEOGRAPHIC Exploring Our World

What happens when we harm the environment? Some plants and animals might be gone forever. This scientist hopes to prevent that. She works at a seed bank. Behind her, stored at −4°F (−20°C), are jars of plant seeds from around the world. Should any of these 4,000 types of plants become extinct, these seeds can start growing them again.

Earth's physical geography is made up of four basic parts. The atmosphere, as you read in Chapter 1, is the blanket of gases, or air, surrounding the earth. The lithosphere is the earth's hard outer shell, or what we view as land areas. The hydrosphere includes all the water in the oceans, lakes, rivers, and glaciers, plus all precipitation. Humans are part of the biosphere, which includes all living things and the environments in which they live. A delicate balance exists among these four "spheres." The world's people must act to preserve this balance.

The Atmosphere

Throughout the world, fumes and chemicals from vehicles and industries pollute the air. Air pollution also includes solid particles such as ash and dust. When air pollution is concentrated in urban areas, the air becomes harmful to breathe. Yet air pollution has an even greater effect on the earth as a whole.

Taiwan

Vehicles and factories add harmful chemicals to the air.

Human/Environment Interaction What are some effects of air pollution? **FCAT** SC.D.2.3.2

The global effects of air pollution include global warming, ozone depletion, and acid rain. Some scientists believe that increasing amounts of pollutants in the atmosphere have caused the earth to warm. You learned earlier about this greenhouse effect.

Air pollution also affects the ozone layer in the atmosphere. The ozone layer serves as a protective shield as it filters out harmful rays of the sun. Certain chemicals, when they move into the upper atmosphere, destroy ozone molecules. Turn to page 772 to read more about the depletion—and repair—of the earth's "sunscreen."

Chemicals in air pollution can also combine with precipitation, which then falls as acid rain. Acid rain kills fish and eats away at the surfaces of buildings. It can even destroy entire forests.

✓ **Reading Check** What are two forms of pollutants found in air?

The Lithosphere

The telephone you use, the microwave that heats your snacks, and the food you eat all come from land resources. Copper, iron, aluminum, and other minerals and ores are mined from the earth. To get to these resources, huge amounts of soil and rock must be removed. This harms the environment. In the United States, mining companies are required to restore the land and replant vegetation when their mining operations are finished.

Topsoil Rich topsoil is a vital part of the lithosphere. If people do not carefully manage the soil, it can be carried away by wind or water. In the Tropics, erosion by water presents a problem—especially if farmers plant their crops on sloping land. When heavy rains come, the soil may simply wash down the hillside. Some farmers have solved this problem by terracing their fields, or planting their crops in a stair-step fashion on slopes.

Deforestation, or cutting down forests without replanting, is another way in which topsoil is lost. When the tree roots are no longer there to hold the soil, wind and water can carry it away.

To enrich their topsoil, many farmers use fertilizers. Some also practice crop rotation, or changing what they plant in a field. This avoids using up all the minerals in the soil. Some crops, such as beans, actually restore valuable minerals to the soil. Many farmers now plant bean crops every three years to build up the soil.

✓ **Reading Check** How does deforestation lead to erosion?

The Hydrosphere

People, plants, and most animals need freshwater to live. Remember that only a small fraction of the world's freshwater is unfrozen, however. Since the earth's supply of water is limited, people must learn to manage freshwater carefully.

Water Management   Managing water supplies involves two main steps. The first step is conservation, or the careful use of resources so they are not wasted. Did you know that 6 or 7 gallons (23 to 27 liters) of water go down the drain every minute that you shower? Taking shorter showers is an easy way to prevent wasting water.

Throughout most areas of the world, farmers use irrigation, or the practice of collecting water and distributing it to their crops. In fact, as much as 70 percent of all water used is for farming. Most irrigation methods are wasteful because water often evaporates or seeps into the ground before it reaches crops. Many farmers today, however, are trying to use more efficient practices, such as drip irrigation.

The second step in managing the water supply is to avoid polluting water. Most industrial processes use water. Sometimes those processes result in dangerous chemicals entering the water supply. Farmers who apply fertilizers to their soil may also use pesticides, or powerful chemicals that kill crop-destroying insects. These substances help increase food production, but they also seep into rivers and groundwater supplies, polluting the waterways.

✓ Reading Check How can industry and farming harm the water supply?

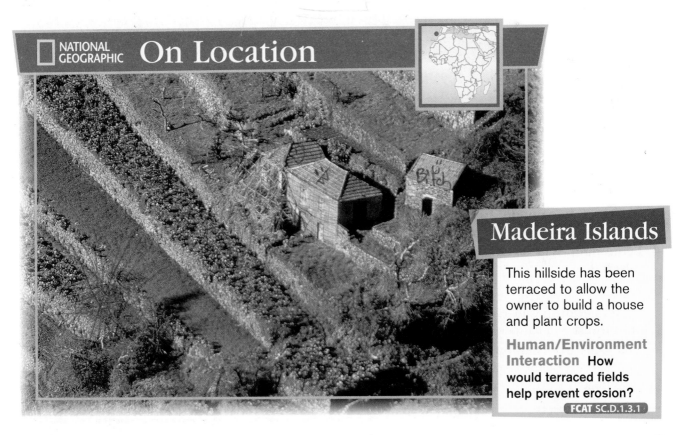

NATIONAL GEOGRAPHIC On Location

Madeira Islands

This hillside has been terraced to allow the owner to build a house and plant crops.

Human/Environment Interaction How would terraced fields help prevent erosion?

FCAT SC.D.1.3.1

Water, Climate, and Vegetation

71

The Biosphere

As the human population increases and people expand their communities, they invade **ecosystems.** These are places where the plants and animals are dependent upon one another and their surroundings for survival. Ecosystems can be found in every climate and vegetation region of the world. For example, some people may want to drain a wetland, or marshy area, to get rid of disease-carrying mosquitoes and to make the soil useful for farming or for building homes. When the area is drained, however, the ecosystem is destroyed. The delicate balance among the wetland's biodiversity—the various insects, reptiles, birds, and water plants—is upset.

People are becoming aware of the need to protect ecosystems, and communities are making increased efforts to do so. Wetlands are now recognized as valuable ecosystems. They are protected from development in the United States. Worldwide concern for rain forest ecosystems also has emerged.

Sometimes, though, protecting the environment for the future seems to clash with feeding people in the present. Remember that people, as well as plants and other animals, are also part of the biosphere. Thus, farmers in the rain forests burn or cut down trees not because they want to, but because they need to feed their families. Before they stop cutting down forests, these farmers will need to find new ways to meet their needs.

✓ Reading Check **How does saving the rain forests clash with current human needs?**

FCAT PRACTICE You can prepare for the FCAT-assessed standards by completing the correlated item(s) below.

Assessment

Defining Terms

1. **Define** acid rain, deforestation, crop rotation, conservation, irrigation, pesticide, ecosystem.

Recalling Facts

2. **Region** What are the four "spheres" of the earth?

3. **Human/Environment Interaction** What are two ways of managing water?

4. **Economics** Why do farmers practice crop rotation?

Critical Thinking

5. **Understanding Cause and Effect** Why are most irrigation methods inefficient?

6. **Analyzing Information** Which ecosystems were affected by the growth of your community? **FCAT** SC.D.1.3.3

Graphic Organizer

7. **Organizing Information** Draw a diagram like this and list three results of air pollution.

FCAT SC.D.2.3.2, LA.A.1.3.2

Air Pollution

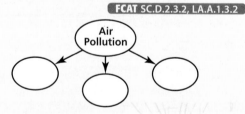

Applying Social Studies Skills

8. **Analyzing Maps** Look at the vegetation map on page 64. In what parts of the world are tropical rain forests located?

Section 1   The Water Planet

Terms to Know
water vapor   collection
water cycle   glacier
evaporation   groundwater
condensation   aquifer
precipitation

Main Idea
Water is one of the earth's most precious resources.
✓ **Region** Water covers about 70 percent of the earth's surface.
✓ **Movement** Water follows a cycle of evaporation, condensation, precipitation, and collection on and beneath the ground.
✓ **Science** Humans and most animals need freshwater to live. Only a small fraction of the world's water is found in rivers and lakes.

Section 2   Climate

Terms to Know
weather   current
climate   local wind
Tropics   rain shadow
drought   greenhouse
El Niño   effect
La Niña   rain forest

Main Idea
Wind and water carry rainfall and the sun's warmth around the world to create different climates.
✓ **Region** Climate is the usual pattern of weather over a long period of time.
✓ **Region** The Tropics, near the Equator, receive more of the sun's warmth than other regions.
✓ **Location** Landforms and position near water affect climate in a local area.
✓ **Culture** Human actions like building cities, burning fuels, and clearing the rain forests can affect climate.

Section 3   Climate Zones and Vegetation

Terms to Know
savanna
marine west coast climate
Mediterranean climate
humid continental climate
humid subtropical climate
subarctic
tundra
steppe

Main Idea
Geographers divide the world into different climate zones.
✓ **Region** The world has five main climate regions that are based on latitude, amount of moisture, and/or elevation. These regions are tropical, mid-latitude, high latitude, dry, and highland.
✓ **Region** Each climate zone has particular kinds of vegetation.

Section 4   An Environmental Balance

Terms to Know
acid rain   irrigation
deforestation   pesticide
crop rotation   ecosystem
conservation

Main Idea
People's actions affect the environment.
✓ **Human/Environment Interaction** A delicate balance exists among the earth's hydrosphere, lithosphere, atmosphere, and biosphere.
✓ **Human/Environment Interaction** People need to carefully manage and conserve water and land resources.

Water, Climate, and Vegetation

Assessment and Activities

FCAT PRACTICE You can prepare for the FCAT-assessed standards by completing the correlated item(s) below.

Using Key Terms

Match the terms in Part A with their definitions in Part B.

A.

1. evaporation
2. savanna
3. crop rotation
4. tundra
5. condensation
6. greenhouse effect
7. rain forest
8. El Niño
9. precipitation
10. current

B.

a. moving streams of water in the oceans
b. treeless plain in which only the top few inches of ground thaw in summer
c. weather pattern in the Pacific Ocean
d. alternating what is planted in a field
e. buildup of certain gases in the atmosphere that holds the sun's warmth
f. water that falls back to the earth
g. dense forest that receives much rain
h. water vapor changes back into a liquid
i. sun's heat turns water into water vapor
j. broad grassland in the Tropics

Reviewing the Main Ideas

Section 1 The Water Planet

11. **Movement** What are the four steps in the water cycle?
12. **Region** What percentage of the world's water is freshwater?
13. **Region** Which has more freshwater—lakes and rivers or groundwater?

Section 2 Climate

14. **Movement** How do wind and water affect climate? **FCAT SC.D.1.3.3**
15. **Location** How do mountains affect rainfall? **FCAT SC.D.1.3.3**
16. **Human/Environment Interaction** Why are cities warmer than nearby rural areas? **FCAT SC.D.2.3.2**

Section 3 Climate Zones and Vegetation

17. **Region** Which climate region has the most climate zones? Why?
18. **Place** What kind of vegetation grows in Mediterranean climates?

Section 4 An Environmental Balance

19. **Human/Environment Interaction** How can farmers restore the minerals in the soil?
20. **Region** What makes up a wetlands biodiversity?

World Oceans and Currents

Place Location Activity

On a separate sheet of paper, match the letters on the map with the numbered places listed below.

1. Arctic Ocean
2. Atlantic Ocean
3. California Current
4. Japan Current
5. Indian Ocean
6. Gulf Stream

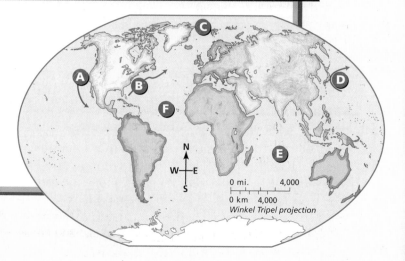

0 mi.   4,000
0 km   4,000
Winkel Tripel projection

Critical Thinking

21. **Analyzing Information** From where does the freshwater in your community come? How can you find out?

22. **Categorizing Information** Create five webs like the one shown here. In each large oval, write the name of a climate region. In the medium-sized ovals, write the name of each climate zone in that region. For each zone, fill in the three small ovals with the usual weather in summer, the usual weather in winter, and the kind of vegetation. **FCAT LA.A.1.3.2**

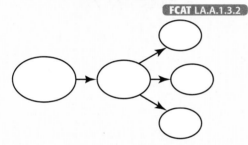

Comparing Regions Activity

23. **Culture** As you have learned, a region's climate helps determine how people live. Flip through your textbook or a geographic magazine to find pictures of people in their environments. What can you infer about their climates? **FCAT LA.A.1.3.2**

Mental Mapping Activity

24. **Focusing on the Region** Draw a freehand map of the world's oceans and continents. Label the following items:

- Equator
- Pacific Ocean
- high latitude climate regions
- tropical climate regions
- North America
- Africa

Technology Skills Activity

25. **Using the Internet** Research a recent hurricane or tornado. Find out when and where it occurred, how much force the storm had, and what damage it caused.

Standardized Test Practice

Directions: Study the graph below, and then answer the question that follows. **FCAT MA.E.3.3.1**

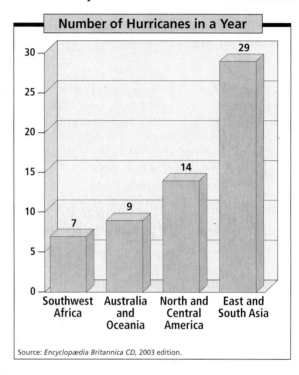

Number of Hurricanes in a Year

Source: *Encyclopædia Britannica CD*, 2003 edition.

1. **How many more hurricanes do East and South Asia experience in a year than North and Central America?**

   F 29

   G 14

   H 9

   J 15

Test-Taking Tip: Make sure you read the question carefully. It is not asking for the total number of hurricanes in East and South Asia. Instead, the question asks how many *more* hurricanes one region has than another.

Endangered Spaces

Shrinking Habitats When you think of Africa, what images come to mind? Roaring lions? Sprinting cheetahs? Lumbering elephants? Unless conditions change, some wild African animals may soon be only memories. Many are endangered, primarily because their habitats—their grassland and forest homes—are being destroyed in many ways.

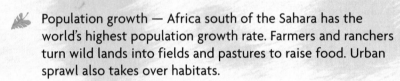

🌿 Population growth — Africa south of the Sahara has the world's highest population growth rate. Farmers and ranchers turn wild lands into fields and pastures to raise food. Urban sprawl also takes over habitats.

🌿 Logging — Logging companies build roads and cut valuable trees, destroying forest habitats.

🌿 Mining — Open pit mines scar the land, pollute waters, and destroy trees.

As habitats shrink, so do populations of African animals.

◰ Cheetahs
▨ Elephants
● Mountain Gorillas

🌿 Cheetahs live in Africa's grasslands. As people move into the cheetahs' home, the big cats struggle to survive. Only about 12,000 cheetahs are left in the wild.

🌿 Mountain gorillas live in the misty mountain forests of Central and East Africa. Logging and mining are destroying these forests. Only about 650 mountain gorillas remain.

These and other endangered African animals will survive only if their habitats are saved.

Loggers destroy a forest in the Democratic Republic of the Congo.

Cheetahs are running out of room in Africa.

Making a Difference

The Cheetah Conservation Fund Cheetahs in Africa are getting a helping hand from the Cheetah Conservation Fund (CCF). This organization is based in Namibia, which is home to about 2,500 cheetahs. Namibian ranchers often trap and shoot cheetahs to protect their livestock. The CCF has donated about 80 special herding dogs to ranchers. The dogs protect the livestock and keep cheetahs out of harm's way at the same time. The CCF also teaches villagers and schoolchildren about cheetahs and about why it is important to save these big cats and their habitats.

Namibian children learn about cheetahs.

Protecting Gorillas For nearly 20 years, Dian Fossey studied mountain gorillas in Rwanda. Through her book, *Gorillas in the Mist*, which was made into a movie, Fossey told others about mountain gorillas and how their survival was threatened by habitat destruction and poaching. Fossey established the Karisoke Research Center and an international fund to support gorilla conservation.

Dian Fossey fought fiercely to end gorilla poaching. Although Fossey was murdered at Karisoke in 1985, the Dian Fossey Gorilla Fund International continues its work protecting mountain gorillas and their habitat.

What Can You Do?

Adopt a Cheetah
You and your classmates can help save cheetahs in the wild by adopting one. To learn more, contact the Cheetah Conservation Fund at www.cheetah.org

Find Out More
What animal habitats are endangered where you live? Work with a partner to investigate endangered spaces in your area. Summarize your findings in a report to the class.

FCAT LA.B.1.3.2

A mountain gorilla

The World's People

To learn more about the world's culture regions, view *The World and Its People* **Chapter 3** video.

Social Studies
Online

Chapter Overview Visit *The World and Its People* Web site at <u>twip.glencoe.com</u> and click on **Chapter 3–Chapter Overviews** to preview information about the world's people.

FCAT PRACTICE 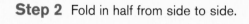 The activity below will help you prepare for the **FCAT Reading** test.

Organizing Information Make this foldable to help you organize what you learn about culture, the world's population, resources, and the effect of technology on the world. **FCAT LA.A.1.3.2**

Step 1 Fold the sides of a piece of paper into the middle to make a shutter fold.

Step 2 Fold in half from side to side.

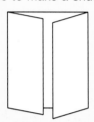

The World's People

Step 3 Open and cut along the inside fold lines to form four tabs.

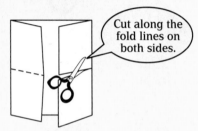

Cut along the fold lines on both sides.

Step 4 Label the tabs as shown.

Under-standing Culture	Population Patterns
Resources & World Trade	Technology "Shrinks" the World

Reading and Writing As you read each section in the chapter, write notes under the correct tab of your foldable. **FCAT LA.A.1.3.2**

Why It Matters

Discovering Other Cultures

A while ago it was common for people to spend most of their lives in the same town or place in which they were born. Today your neighbor may be someone from another state, another country, or another continent. How do people in the rest of the world live? How do we get along with them? This book will help you learn about other people and places and what issues are important to them.

◄ **Painted elephants are part of the Dussehra festival in India.**

Understanding Culture

Guide to Reading

Main Idea

People usually live with others who follow similar beliefs learned from the past.

Terms to Know

- culture
- ethnic group
- dialect
- democracy
- dictatorship
- monarchy
- cultural diffusion
- civilization
- culture region

Reading Strategy

Draw a diagram like this one. In each section, write one of the eight elements of culture and give an example of each from the United States today. **FCAT** LA.A.1.3.2

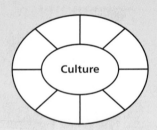

Culture

The following are the major Sunshine State Standards covered in this section.

SS.A.2.3.4:
Understands the impact of geographical factors on the historical development of civilizations

SS.A.3.3.1:
Understands ways in which cultural characteristics have been transmitted from one society to another (e.g., through art, architecture, language, other artifacts, traditions, beliefs, values, and behaviors)

NATIONAL GEOGRAPHIC Exploring Our World

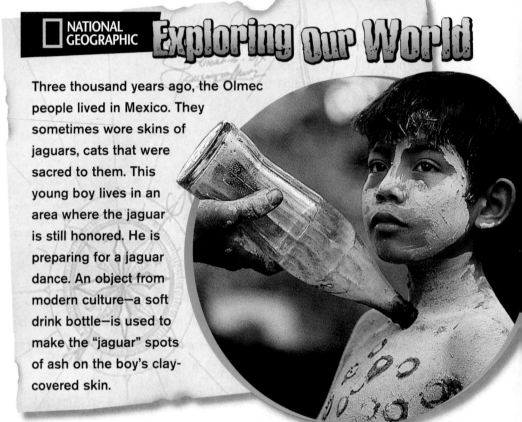

Three thousand years ago, the Olmec people lived in Mexico. They sometimes wore skins of jaguars, cats that were sacred to them. This young boy lives in an area where the jaguar is still honored. He is preparing for a jaguar dance. An object from modern culture—a soft drink bottle—is used to make the "jaguar" spots of ash on the boy's clay-covered skin.

If you wake up to rock music, wear denim jeans, and celebrate the Fourth of July, these things are part of your culture. If you eat tortillas, speak Spanish, and honor the jaguar, these things are part of your culture.

What Is Culture?

Culture is the way of life of people who share similar beliefs and customs. Social scientists look at eight elements called traits. They study what groups a society is divided into, what language the people speak, and what religions they follow. They examine people's daily lives and look at their history and artwork. They also look at how a society is governed and how the people make a living.

Social Groups One way of studying cultures is by looking at the different groups of people in a society. For instance, scientists compare the number of rich, poor, and middle class people. They look at how the young and the old are treated. In addition, they study the differing roles of men and women. Social scientists also examine a country's different ethnic groups. An **ethnic group** is a group of people who share a common history, language, religion, and some physical characteristics. One particular ethnic group in a country may be the majority group. This group in society controls most of the wealth and power. The other ethnic groups in that country are minority groups—people whose race or ethnic origin is different from that of the majority group in the region. The largest ethnic minority groups in the United States are African Americans and Hispanic Americans.

Language   Sharing a language is one of the strongest unifying forces for a culture. Even within a culture, though, there are language differences. Some people may speak a **dialect,** or a local form of a language that differs from the same language in other areas. The differences may include pronunciation and the meaning of words. For example, people in the northeastern United States say "soda," whereas people in the Midwest say "pop." Both groups are referring to soft drinks, however.

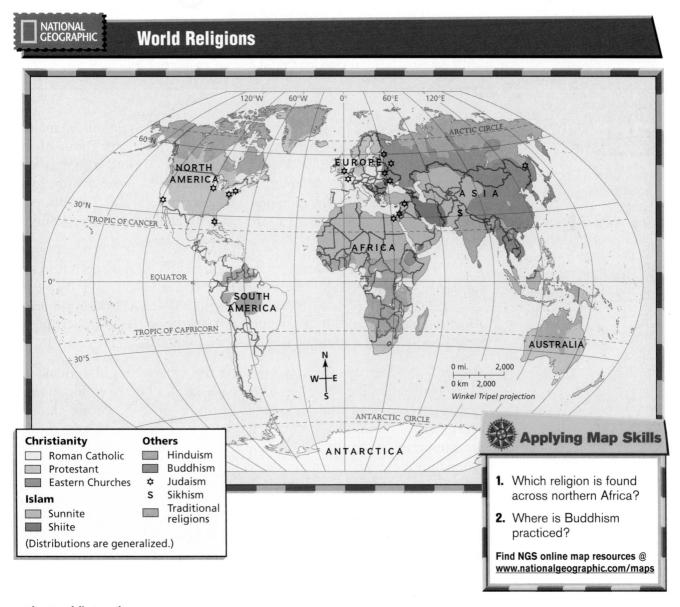

World Religions

NATIONAL GEOGRAPHIC

Christianity
☐ Roman Catholic
☐ Protestant
☐ Eastern Churches

Islam
☐ Sunnite
☐ Shiite

Others
☐ Hinduism
☐ Buddhism
✡ Judaism
S Sikhism
☐ Traditional religions

(Distributions are generalized.)

Applying Map Skills

1. Which religion is found across northern Africa?

2. Where is Buddhism practiced?

Find **NGS** online map resources @ www.nationalgeographic.com/maps

Major World Religions

Religion	Major Leader	Beliefs
Buddhism	Siddhartha Gautama, the Buddha	Buddhists believe that to escape the suffering caused by worldly desires, people must follow the Eightfold Path, or rules that lead to a life of morality, wisdom, and good thought. By following the Eightfold Path, one can achieve nirvana—a state of bliss.
Christianity	Jesus Christ	Christians believe that Jesus, the Son of God, was sent to Earth and died on the cross to save humanity. By having faith in Jesus and through God's grace, believers are saved from God's penalty for sin and receive eternal life with God.
Hinduism	Unknown	Hindus believe in reincarnation—after death, the soul is reborn in another person, animal, or vegetable. Where a soul is reborn depends upon a person's karma, or the spiritual force resulting from actions in past lives. The three main Hindu gods are Brahma, Vishnu, and Siva.
Islam	Muhammad	The followers of Islam, known as Muslims, believe in one God, Allah. Muslims follow the teachings of the Quran, which the prophet Muhammad said were revealed to him by Allah. By following the five pillars of faith—belief, prayer, charity, fasting, and pilgrimage—believers go to an eternal paradise.
Judaism	Abraham	Jews believe in one God, Yahweh. By following God's laws, Jews believe they will have peace with God and with each other. The main laws and practices of Judaism are contained in the Torah, the first five books of the Hebrew Bible.

Analyzing the Chart

How do we become good people? What happens when we die? These are some of the questions that religions attempt to answer.

Culture Who was the founder of Buddhism?

Religion Another important part of culture is religion. In many cultures, religion helps people answer basic questions about life's meaning. Religious beliefs vary significantly around the world. Struggles over religious differences are a challenge in many countries. Some of the major world religions are described in the chart above. The map on page 81 shows you the main areas where these religions are practiced.

Daily Life Do you eat pizza, tacos, yogurt, and egg rolls? All of these foods came from different cultures. What people eat and how they eat it—with their fingers, silverware, or chopsticks—reflect their culture. What people wear also reflects cultural differences. The same is true of how people build traditional homes in their societies.

History History shapes how we view the world. People remember the successes of the past. We often celebrate holidays to honor the heroes and heroines who brought about those successes. Stories about these heroes reveal the personal characteristics that the people think are important. A group also remembers the dark periods of history, when they met with disaster or defeat. These experiences, too, influence how a group of people sees itself.

Arts People express their culture through the arts. Art is not just paintings and sculptures, but also architecture, dance, music, theater, and literature. By viewing the arts of a culture, you can gain insight into what the people of that culture think is beautiful and important.

Government   People need rules in order to live together without conflict. Rules or laws are created by governments. Countries may have limited governments or unlimited governments. In a limited government, all citizens—including the country's leaders—must obey the laws of the land as written in a constitution or statement of rights. A **democracy** is a form of limited government where power rests with the people of the nation. The United States has a representative democracy in which citizens vote to elect representatives who then make and enforce laws.

In unlimited governments, rulers have powers that are *not* limited by laws. One type of unlimited government is a **dictatorship,** where a dictator usually takes power by force. To stay in power, most dictators rely on the police and the military. Dictators are not responsible to the people, and they limit freedom of speech, assembly, and the press. In a **monarchy,** kings or queens are born into a ruling family and inherit their power to rule. Until about the 1600s, such rulers were absolute monarchs with unlimited power. Now, in most countries, absolute monarchy has given way to constitutional monarchy. The United Kingdom, for example, is both a constitutional monarchy and a democracy. The queen is the symbolic head of the country, but elected leaders hold the power to rule. The chart below summarizes forms of government.

The Economy   Culture includes economic activities, or how the people in a society earn a living. Some people farm or manufacture products. Others provide services, such as designing a Web page or preparing food. You will learn more about economic systems in Section 3.

Reading Check   What is culture?

Types of Government

Type of Government	Who Holds Power?	Examples
Direct Democracy	All citizens vote directly on issues.	• Parts of Switzerland • Some New England towns
Representative Democracy	People vote for representatives who lead the country and make laws.	• United States • Russia • France
Constitutional Monarchy	A monarch inherits the right to rule but is limited by laws and a law-making body elected by the people.	• United Kingdom • Japan • Sweden • Jordan
Absolute Monarchy	A monarch inherits the right to rule and has unlimited power.	• Saudi Arabia
Dictatorship	A dictator makes all laws and suppresses any opposition.	• Cuba • Iraq under Saddam Hussein • Germany under Adolf Hitler

Analyzing the Chart

The United States is one of many countries with a democratic type of government.

Government What is the difference between a direct democracy and a representative democracy?

The World's People

83

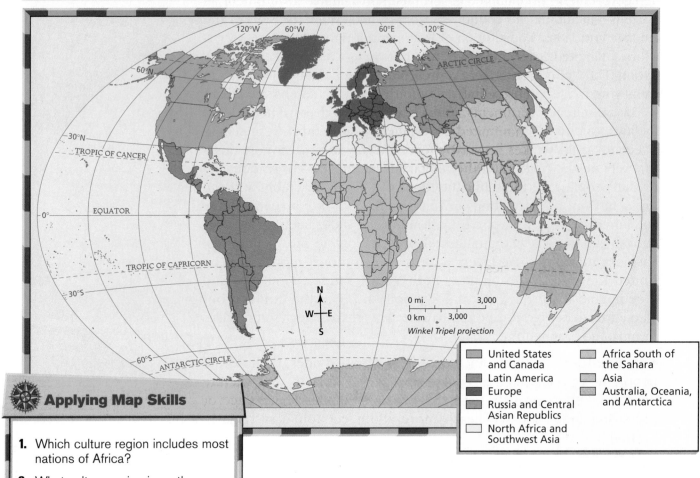

United States and Canada
Latin America
Europe
Russia and Central Asian Republics
North Africa and Southwest Asia
Africa South of the Sahara
Asia
Australia, Oceania, and Antarctica

Winkel Tripel projection

Applying Map Skills

1. Which culture region includes most nations of Africa?

2. What culture region is on the continents of both Africa and Asia?

Find NGS online map resources @ **www.nationalgeographic.com/maps**

Cultural Change

Cultures do not remain the same. Humans constantly invent new ideas and technologies and create new solutions to problems. Trade, the movement of people, and war can spread these changes to other cultures. The process of spreading new knowledge and skills to other cultures is called **cultural diffusion.** Today television and the Internet are making cultural diffusion take place more rapidly than ever before.

Culture Over Time Historians have traced the tremendous changes that humans have made in their cultures. In the first human societies, people lived by hunting animals and gathering fruits and vegetables. They were nomadic, moving from place to place, to follow sources of food.

Starting about 10,000 years ago, people learned to grow food by planting seeds. This change brought about the Agricultural Revolution. Groups stayed in one place and built settlements. Their societies became more complex. As a result, four **civilizations,** or highly developed cultures, arose in river valleys in present-day **Iraq, Egypt, India,** and **China.** These civilizations included cities, complex governments and religions, and systems of writing. The map on page 86 shows you where these civilizations were located.

Thousands of years later—in the 1700s and 1800s—came a new set of changes in the world. Some countries began to industrialize, or use machines and factories to make goods. These machines could work harder, faster, and longer than people or animals. As a result of the Industrial Revolution, people began to live longer, healthier, more comfortable lives.

Recently, the world began a new revolution—the Information Revolution. Computers make it possible to store and process huge amounts of information. They also allow people to instantly send this information all over the world. You will learn more about this revolution and how it connects the cultures of the world in Section 4.

Culture Regions   As you recall, geographers use the term "regions" for areas that share common characteristics. Today geographers often divide the world into areas called culture regions. Each culture region includes different countries that have traits in common. They share similar economic systems, forms of government, and social groups. Their languages are related, and the people may follow the same religion. Their history and art are similar. The food, dress, and housing of the people may have common characteristics as well. In this textbook, you will study the different culture regions of the world.

✓ **Reading Check**   What three revolutions have changed the world?

 FCAT PRACTICE   You can prepare for the FCAT-assessed standards by completing the correlated item(s) below.

 **Section 1**

Assessment

Defining Terms

1. Define culture, ethnic group, dialect, democracy, dictatorship, monarchy, cultural diffusion, civilization, culture region.

Recalling Facts

2. Culture What kinds of social groups do social scientists study?

3. Government What are the different forms of government a society may have?

4. Culture In what ways does cultural diffusion occur?

Critical Thinking

5. Understanding Cause and Effect How does history shape cultures? **FCAT LA.E.2.2.1**

6. Making Comparisons Describe the beliefs of two major religions. **FCAT LA.A.2.2.7**

Graphic Organizer

7. Organizing Information Create a diagram like this one that describes features of your culture. On the lines, write types of food, clothing, language, music, and so on.

FCAT LA.A.1.3.2

Your Culture

 Applying Social Studies Skills

8. Analyzing Maps Look at the map on page 84. In which culture region do you live? In which culture region(s) did your ancestors live?

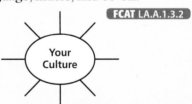

The World's People

Social Studies Skill

 FCAT PRACTICE Completing the activity below will help you prepare for the **FCAT Writing** test.

Reading a Thematic Map

Thematic maps concentrate on a single theme. This theme may be to show the battles of a particular war or habitats of endangered species, for example.

Learning the Skill

To read a thematic map, follow these steps:

- Read the map title. It tells what kind of special information the map shows.
- Find the map's scale to determine the general size of the area.
- Read the key. Colors and symbols in the map key are especially important on this type of map.
- Analyze the areas on the map that are highlighted in the key. Look for patterns.

Practicing the Skill

Look at the map below to answer the following questions.

1. What is the title of the map?
2. Read the key. What four civilizations are shown on this map?
3. Which civilization was farthest west? East?
4. What do the locations of each of these civilizations have in common?

Applying the Skill

Find a thematic map in a newspaper or magazine. Write three questions about the map's purpose, then have a classmate answer the questions. **FCAT LA.B.1.3.2**

GO TO Practice key skills with **Glencoe Skillbuilder Interactive Workbook, Level 1.**

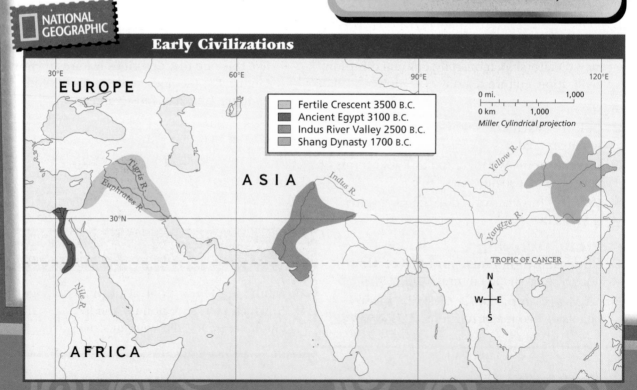

NATIONAL GEOGRAPHIC

Early Civilizations

Key:
- Fertile Crescent 3500 B.C.
- Ancient Egypt 3100 B.C.
- Indus River Valley 2500 B.C.
- Shang Dynasty 1700 B.C.

0 mi. 1,000
0 km 1,000
Miller Cylindrical projection

EUROPE

ASIA

AFRICA

Tigris R. Euphrates R. Nile R. Indus R. Yellow R. Yangtze R.

30°E 60°E 90°E 120°E

30°N

TROPIC OF CANCER

N W E S

Population Patterns

Guide to Reading

Main Idea

The world's population is growing rapidly, and how and where people live are changing too.

Terms to Know

- death rate
- birthrate
- famine
- population density
- urbanization
- emigrate
- refugee

Reading Strategy

Draw a chart like this one. In the "Result" column, write a result of the fact listed in the left column. **FCAT** LA.A.1.3.2

Fact	Result
World population is increasing.	
Population is unevenly distributed.	
People move from place to place.	

The following are the major Sunshine State Standards covered in this section.

SS.A.1.3.1:
Understands how patterns, chronology, sequencing (including cause and effect), and the identification of historical periods are influenced by frames of reference

SS.B.2.3.1:
Understands the patterns and processes of migration and diffusion throughout the world

NATIONAL GEOGRAPHIC Exploring Our World

Imagine that you and your friends are in Berlin, Germany. Can you hear the music? Every summer, hundreds of thousands of young people gather here for a music festival. Although most of these young people are here only to visit, many thousands of others come to find jobs and new lives. Germany faces challenges in finding room for its newcomers.

On October 12, 1999, the world reached a significant point in its history. About 370,000 babies were born around the world that day. One of those babies—no one knows exactly which one—was the world's six billionth human being.

Population Growth

How fast has the earth's population grown? The graph on page 88 shows world population over the years. You will see that for more than fifteen hundred years, the world's population remained about the same. The world did not have 1 billion people until about 1800. It was not until 1930 that the population reached 2 billion. By 1974 the population had doubled to 4 billion. In 1999 it reached 6 billion.

Reasons for Population Growth Why has the world's population grown so fast in the past 200 years? One reason is that the death rate has gone down. The **death rate** is the number of people out of every 1,000 who die in a year. Better health care and living conditions have decreased the death rate.

Another reason for the rapid increase in the world's population is that in some regions of the world the birthrate is high. The **birthrate** is the number of children born each year for every 1,000 people. In Asia, Africa, and Latin America, families traditionally are large because children help with farming. High numbers of births have combined with low death rates to increase population growth in these areas. As a result, population in these areas has doubled every 25 years or so.

Challenges From Population Growth   Rapid population growth presents many challenges. An increase in the number of people means that more food is needed. Fortunately, since 1950 world food production has increased faster than population on all continents except Africa. Because so many people there need food, disaster can result if bad weather or war ruin crops. Millions may suffer from **famine,** or lack of food.

Also, populations that grow rapidly may use resources more quickly than populations that do not grow as fast. Some countries face shortages of water and housing. Population growth also puts a strain on economies. More people means a country must create more jobs. Some experts claim that rapid population growth could harm the planet. Others are optimistic. They predict that as the number of humans rises, the levels of technology and creativity will also rise.

✓ Reading Check **How do the definitions of death rate and birthrate differ?**

Where People Live

Where do all the people live? The world's people actually live on a surprisingly small part of the earth. As you learned in Chapter 2, land covers only about 30 percent of the earth's surface. Half of this land is

FCAT
PRACTICE
Completing the exercise below will help you prepare for the **FCAT Mathematics** test.

World Population

Analyzing the Graph and Chart

The world's population is expected to reach about 9 billion by 2050.

Place Which country has the second-largest number of people?
FCAT MA.D.1.3.2

Visit twip.glencoe.com and click on **Chapter 3– Textbook Updates.**

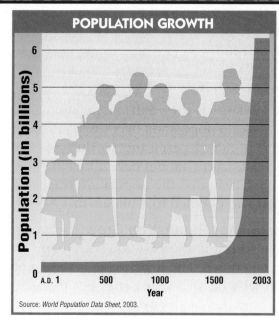

POPULATION GROWTH

Population (in billions) vs. Year (A.D. 1, 500, 1000, 1500, 2003)

Source: *World Population Data Sheet*, 2003.

MOST POPULOUS COUNTRIES

Country	Millions of People
China	1,288.7
India	1,068.6
United States	291.5
Indonesia	220.5
Brazil	176.5
Pakistan	149.1
Russia	145.5

Source: *World Population Data Sheet*, 2003.

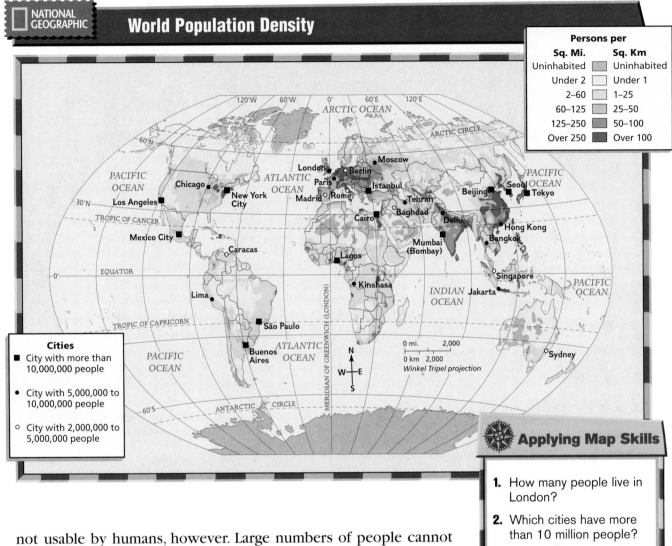

Persons per

Sq. Mi.		Sq. Km
Uninhabited		Uninhabited
Under 2		Under 1
2–60		1–25
60–125		25–50
125–250		50–100
Over 250		Over 100

Cities
- ■ City with more than 10,000,000 people
- ● City with 5,000,000 to 10,000,000 people
- ○ City with 2,000,000 to 5,000,000 people

Applying Map Skills

1. How many people live in London?

2. Which cities have more than 10 million people?

Find NGS online map resources @ www.nationalgeographic.com/maps

not usable by humans, however. Large numbers of people cannot survive on land covered with ice, deserts, or high mountains. The world's people, then, live on a small fraction of the earth's surface.

Population Distribution   Even on the usable land, population is not distributed, or spread, evenly. People naturally prefer to live in places that have plentiful water, good land, and a favorable climate. During the industrial age, people moved to places that had important resources such as coal or iron ore to run or make machines. People gather in other areas because these places hold religious significance or because they are government and transportation centers. The chart on page 88 shows you the most populous countries in the world. Four of these countries are located on the Asian continent.

Population Density   Geographers have a way of determining how crowded a country or region is. They measure population density— the average number of people living in a square mile or square kilometer. To arrive at this figure, the total population is divided by the total land area. For example, the countries of **Afghanistan** and **Nepal** have about the same number of people. They are very different in terms of population density, though. With a smaller land area, Nepal has

Web Activity Visit **The World and Its People** Web site at twip.glencoe.com and click on **Chapter 3— Student Web Activities** to learn more about the world population "clock."

443 people per square mile (171 people per sq. km). Afghanistan has an average of only 114 people per square mile (44 people per sq. km). Nepal, then, is more crowded than Afghanistan.

Remember that population density is an *average.* It assumes that people are distributed evenly throughout a country. Of course, this seldom happens. A country may have several large cities where most of the people actually live. In Egypt, for example, overall population density is 186 people per square mile (72 people per sq. km). In reality, about 99 percent of Egypt's people live within 20 miles (32 km) of the Nile River. The rest of Egypt is desert. Thus, some geographers prefer to figure a country's population density in terms of farmable or usable land rather than total land area. When Egypt's population density is measured this way, it equals about 6,550 people per square mile. The map on page 10 of the **Geography Handbook** shows how population density can vary within a country. The areas with high density in Egypt follow the path of the Nile River.

✓**Reading Check** What is population density?

Population Movement

Throughout the world, people are moving in great numbers from place to place. Some people move from city to city, or suburb to suburb. More and more people are leaving villages and farms and moving to cities. This movement to cities is called **urbanization.**

People move to cities for many reasons. The most common reason is to find jobs. Rural populations have grown. The amount of land that can be farmed, however, has not increased to meet the growing number of people who need to work and eat. As a result, many people find city jobs in manufacturing or in services like tourism.

Nearly half the world's people live in cities—a far higher percentage than ever before. Between 1960 and 2000, the population of **Mexico City** more than tripled. Other cities in Latin America, as well as cities in Asia and Africa, have seen similar growth. Some of these cities hold a large part of a country's entire population. About one-third of Argentina's people, for instance, live in the city of **Buenos Aires.** As more and more people come to cities looking for work, the boundaries of cities and their suburbs keep expanding outward. This situation is called urban sprawl.

Some population movement occurs between countries. Some people *emigrate,* or leave the country where they were born and move to another. They are called emigrants in their homeland and immigrants in their new country. In the past 40 years, millions have left Africa, Asia, and Latin America to find jobs in the richer nations of Europe and North America. Many of these people were forced to flee their countries because of wars, political unrest, food shortages, or other problems. They are *refugees,* or people who flee to another country to escape persecution or disaster.

✓ **Reading Check** **What is urban sprawl?**

FCAT PRACTICE You can prepare for the FCAT-assessed standards by completing the correlated item(s) below.

Section 2 Assessment

Defining Terms

1. Define death rate, birthrate, famine, population density, urbanization, emigrate, refugee.

Recalling Facts

2. Culture What are three problems caused by overpopulation?

3. Human/Environment Interaction Why do people live on only a small fraction of the earth?

4. Economics What is the main reason for growing urbanization?

Critical Thinking

5. Making Comparisons What is the difference between an emigrant and an immigrant? **FCAT LA.A.2.2.7**

6. Understanding Cause and Effect Why have populations in areas of Asia, Africa, and Latin America doubled about every 25 years?

FCAT LA.E.2.2.1

Graphic Organizer

7. Organizing Information Draw a diagram like this one, and list three causes of population growth. **FCAT LA.A.1.3.2**

Causes	
_____	→ Population Growth
_____	
_____	

Applying Social Studies Skills

8. Analyzing Maps Look at the population density map on page 89. How would you describe the population density around Tokyo?

Resources and World Trade

Guide to Reading

Main Idea

Many resources are limited and distributed unevenly, so countries must trade for goods.

Terms to Know

- natural resource
- renewable resource
- nonrenewable resource
- economic system
- export
- import
- tariff
- quota
- free trade
- developed country
- developing country

Reading Strategy

Draw a chart like this one. Write the names of different resources and how they are used.

FCAT LA.A.1.3.2

Resource	Use

The following are the major Sunshine State Standards covered in this section.

SS.B.2.3.8:
Knows world patterns of resource distribution and utilization

SS.B.1.3.6:
Understands ways in which regional systems are interconnected

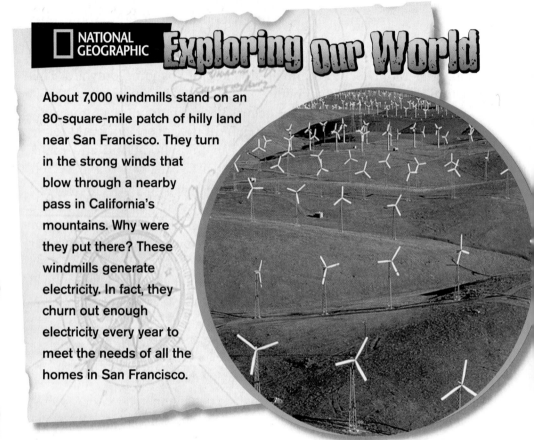

NATIONAL GEOGRAPHIC Exploring Our World

About 7,000 windmills stand on an 80-square-mile patch of hilly land near San Francisco. They turn in the strong winds that blow through a nearby pass in California's mountains. Why were they put there? These windmills generate electricity. In fact, they churn out enough electricity every year to meet the needs of all the homes in San Francisco.

Natural Resources

As you learned in Section 2, people settle in some areas to gain access to resources. Natural resources are products of the earth that people use to meet their needs. Wind, water, and oil are resources that provide energy to power machines. Good soil and fish are resources that people use to produce food. Stones like granite and ores like iron ore are resources people can use for making products.

Renewable Resources People can use some natural resources as much as they want. These renewable resources cannot be used up or can be replaced naturally or grown again. Wind and sun cannot be used up. Forests, grasslands, plants and animals, and soil can be replaced—if people manage them carefully.

Today many countries are trying to find efficient ways of using renewable energy sources. Some produce hydroelectric power, the energy generated by falling water. Do you have a solar-powered calculator? If so, you know that the sun can provide energy to run people's machines. Solar energy is power produced by the heat of the sun. Making use of this energy on a large scale requires huge pieces of equipment. As a result, this energy source is not yet economical to use.

Nonrenewable Resources   Minerals found in the earth's crust are also resources. They are nonrenewable resources because the earth provides limited supplies of them and they cannot be replaced. These resources were formed over millions of years by forces within the earth. Thus, it simply takes too long to generate new supplies.

One major nonrenewable source of energy is fossil fuels—coal, oil, and natural gas. People burn oil and gas to heat homes or run cars. They burn fossil fuels to generate electricity. Oil and coal are also used as raw materials to make plastics and medicines.

Another nonrenewable energy source is nuclear energy. Nuclear energy is power made by creating a controlled atomic reaction. Nuclear energy can be used to produce electricity, but some people fear its use. Nuclear reactions produce dangerous waste products that are difficult to dispose of. Still, some countries rely on nuclear energy to generate electricity. France and Japan are examples.

✓ Reading Check **List three fossil fuels.**

Economic Systems

People and nations use natural resources to produce and exchange goods and services. A country's economic system sets rules for deciding what goods and services to produce, how to produce them, and who will receive them. There are four main types of economic systems: traditional, command, market, and mixed.

Traditional Economies   In a traditional economy, economic decisions are based on customs handed down from generation to generation. For example, if your grandparents and parents fished for a living, you will fish for a living. You will probably use the same fishing tools. To get other products you need, you may barter, or exchange part of your catch, instead of using money.

Command Economies   Under a command economy, the government makes all economic decisions. Individuals have little or no say about what goods and services to produce and how to produce them. The government decides how much something will cost and which people receive training for particular jobs. The term "communism" applies to command economies.

Market Economies   In a market economy, individuals make their own decisions about what to produce, how to produce it, and for whom to produce it. People and businesses make what they think customers want (supply). Consumers have choices about which goods or services to buy (demand). Prices are determined by supply and demand.

Saffron— A Valuable Resource

A resource does not have to produce energy to be valued. The people in the Indian region of Kashmir are picking a resource that is precious to cooks—crocus flowers. Inside each crocus are three tiny orange stalks. When dried, the stalks become a spice called saffron. Cooks use it to add a delicate orange color and flavor to food. Saffron—the world's most expensive spice—is in short supply, though. Producers need nearly 4,700 flowers to produce just 1 ounce (28 g) of saffron!

Types of Economic Systems

Analyzing the Chart

This chart shows economic systems in theory. In reality, most nations have a mixed economy.

Economics Who owns or controls resources in each type of system?

Economic System	WHAT, HOW, and FOR WHOM to produce	Examples (in theory)
Traditional	Customs and traditions determine what and how to produce. Resources are usually shared. Many traditional systems use bartering to exchange goods and services.	• Inuit • Some parts of Africa and South America
Command	Government owns resources and controls production, prices, and wages. Shortages of consumer goods occur because government sets prices low and resources are often used for military goods.	• China • North Korea • Former USSR
Market	Individuals own resources and determine what and how to produce. Prices and wages are determined by producer supply and consumer demand.	• United States
Mixed	Individuals own most resources and determine what and how to produce. Government regulates certain industries.	• Most nations

A market economy is based on "free enterprise." This is the idea that you have the right to own property or businesses and to make a profit without the government interfering. Capitalism is another name for a market or free enterprise economy.

Mixed Economies Most nations have a mixed economy. China, for example, has mostly a command economy, but the government has allowed some free enterprise. In the United States, most decisions are made by individuals, but the government regulates certain areas. Government agencies, for example, inspect meat and other products.

✓Reading Check What is free enterprise?

World Trade

Resources, like people, are not distributed evenly around the world. Some areas have large amounts of one resource. Others have none of that resource but are rich in another one. These differences affect the economies of the world's countries. The competition for scarce resources may also lead to conflict.

Look at the map on page 95. Do you see the centers of manufacturing in the northern and eastern United States? There are large supplies of coal in the region and deposits of iron ore nearby. These areas became industrial centers because the people here took advantage of the resources they had.

In the western United States, you see another picture. People use much of the land for ranching. The soil and climate are well suited to raising livestock. Commercial farming—or growing food for sale in markets—occurs throughout much of the United States.

Countries respond to the unequal distribution of resources by specializing, or focusing on the economic activities best suited to their resources. Parts of **Brazil** have the perfect soil and climate for growing coffee. As a result, Brazil produces more coffee beans than any other country.

Countries often cannot use all that they produce. Therefore, they export what they do not need, trading it to other countries. When they cannot produce as much as they need of a good, they import it, or buy it from another country. The world's countries, then, are connected to one another in a complex web of trade.

Barriers to Trade Governments try to manage trade to benefit their country's economy. Some charge a tariff, or a tax added to the price of goods that are imported. If there is a tariff on cars, for instance, people who buy an imported car pay extra. Governments often create tariffs to persuade their people to buy products made in their own country.

Governments sometimes create other barriers to trade. They might put a strict quota, or number limit, on how many items of a particular product can be imported from a particular country. A government may even stop trading with another country altogether as a way to punish it.

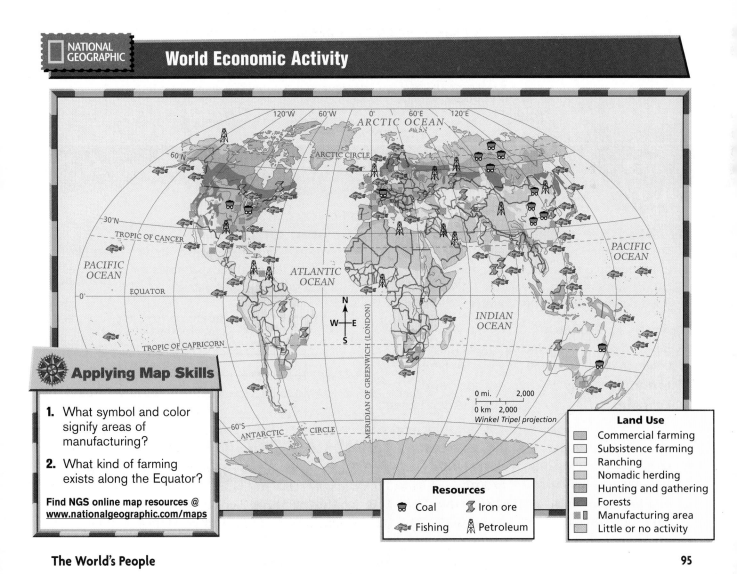

World Economic Activity

NATIONAL GEOGRAPHIC

Applying Map Skills

1. What symbol and color signify areas of manufacturing?

2. What kind of farming exists along the Equator?

Find NGS online map resources @ www.nationalgeographic.com/maps

Resources

🐚 Coal   ⚒ Iron ore

🐟 Fishing   🗼 Petroleum

Land Use

Commercial farming
Subsistence farming
Ranching
Nomadic herding
Hunting and gathering
Forests
Manufacturing area
Little or no activity

0 mi.   2,000
0 km 2,000
Winkel Tripel projection

Exploring Economics

The "Third World"

Until the Soviet Union collapsed in 1991, developed and developing countries were divided into three groups. Developed countries with market economies were known as the "first world." Countries with communist command economies were known as the "second world." Developing countries outside of these two groups were together known as the "third world."

Free Trade Governments around the world are moving toward free trade. Free trade means removing trade barriers so that goods flow freely among countries. Several countries have joined together to create free trade agreements in certain parts of the world. The United States, Mexico, and Canada have agreed to eliminate all trade barriers to one another's goods. These three countries set up the North American Free Trade Agreement (NAFTA). The largest free trade organization—the European Union (EU)—includes many countries of Europe.

✓Reading Check **What are three barriers to trade?**

Differences in Development

Countries that have a great deal of manufacturing are called **developed countries.** Countries in Europe and North America are developed countries. So are Australia and Japan. Other countries have few, or no, manufacturing centers. Many people in these lands practice subsistence farming, which means they grow only enough food for their own families. These countries—mostly in Africa, Asia, and Latin America—are called **developing countries.** They may be rich in natural resources, however, and are working toward industrialization.

Countries want manufacturing centers because industry generally makes more money than agriculture. As a result, industrial countries are richer than agricultural ones. The spread of industry has created booming economies in Singapore, South Korea, China, and Taiwan.

✓Reading Check **Why do developing countries want more industry?**

 **FCAT PRACTICE** You can prepare for the FCAT-assessed standards by completing the correlated item(s) below.

Section 3 Assessment

Defining Terms

1. **Define** natural resource, renewable resource, nonrenewable resource, economic system, export, import, tariff, quota, free trade, developed country, developing country.

Recalling Facts

2. **Economics** What is the difference between commercial farming and subsistence farming?
3. **Economics** Why do countries specialize?
4. **Economics** How do developed and developing countries differ? **FCAT LA.A.2.2.7**

Critical Thinking

5. **Drawing Conclusions** Why are tariffs and quotas called "barriers" to trade?
6. **Making Comparisons** Describe two kinds of economic systems. **FCAT LA.A.2.2.7**

Graphic Organizer

7. **Organizing Information** Draw a chart like this one, listing three examples for each type of resource. **FCAT LA.A.1.3.2**

Renewable resources	Nonrenewable resources

 Applying Social Studies Skills

8. **Analyzing Maps** Look at the economic activity map on page 95. What two types of farming are shown on the map?

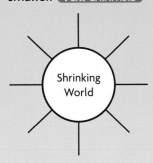

Section 4
Technology "Shrinks" the World

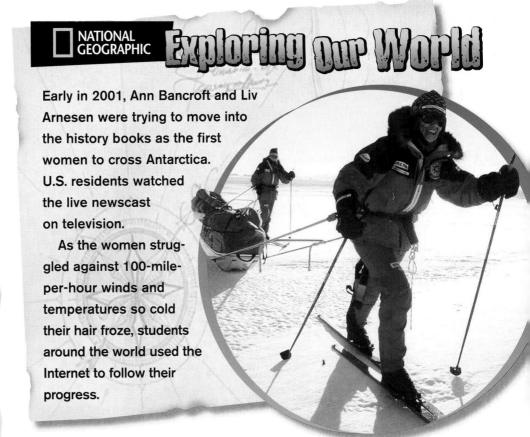

NATIONAL GEOGRAPHIC Exploring Our World

Early in 2001, Ann Bancroft and Liv Arnesen were trying to move into the history books as the first women to cross Antarctica. U.S. residents watched the live newscast on television.

As the women struggled against 100-mile-per-hour winds and temperatures so cold their hair froze, students around the world used the Internet to follow their progress.

People today can talk across an ocean as easily as across a backyard fence. This is what is meant when you hear people say that the world is "shrinking." The technology that has brought about the Information Revolution has enabled people to talk instantly with others practically everywhere on the earth.

Effects of Technology

The word "technology" refers to the ability of human beings to make things that will help them and give them some control over their environment. As you learned in Section 1, the first civilizations arose in about 8000 B.C. when humans learned farming technology—or how to grow crops on a regular basis. In just the past 100 years, new technology has emerged in transportation and communication. This new technology has possibly had an equal—if not greater—effect on human society than the Agricultural Revolution did 10,000 years ago.

Modern Inventions

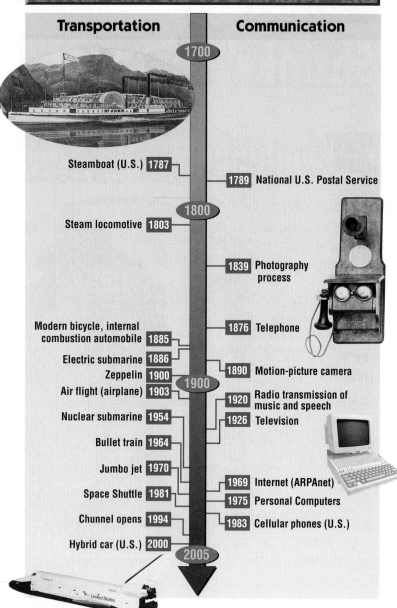

Transportation

- Steamboat (U.S.) **1787**
- Steam locomotive **1803**
- Modern bicycle, internal combustion automobile **1885**
- Electric submarine **1886**
- Zeppelin **1900**
- Air flight (airplane) **1903**
- Nuclear submarine **1954**
- Bullet train **1964**
- Jumbo jet **1970**
- Space Shuttle **1981**
- Chunnel opens **1994**
- Hybrid car (U.S.) **2000**

1700
1800
1900
2005

Communication

- **1789** National U.S. Postal Service
- **1839** Photography process
- **1876** Telephone
- **1890** Motion-picture camera
- **1920** Radio transmission of music and speech
- **1926** Television
- **1969** Internet (ARPAnet)
- **1975** Personal Computers
- **1983** Cellular phones (U.S.)

Analyzing the Time Line

In the last century, communication and transportation technologies have evolved at an amazing rate.

Technology Which nineteenth-century inventions are still used today?

Transportation Technology When steamboats first traveled upstream, people marveled at the technological feat. Settlers in western regions of the United States celebrated when railroad tracks were laid near their towns. Trains could carry passengers from New York City to San Francisco in about 10 days. Imagine their astonishment if early Americans could see how people travel today. Bullet trains speed workers from city to city, often moving well over 300 miles (483 km) per hour. Jet planes cross oceans in several hours, carrying people from one continent to another. The result is a shrinking world.

Communication Technology New inventions also have enabled people to communicate faster. For example, when the first telephone cable was laid along the bottom of the Atlantic Ocean in 1956, it could carry only 36 calls between Europe and North America at a time. Nearly forty years later, glass cables as fine as hairs were carrying 300,000 long-distance calls at once. Communication satellites surrounding the earth in space receive radio, television, and other signals. News can be broadcast live to the entire world so that more people than ever can see what is happening at the same time. Even cellular phones and fax machines have brought the world's cultures closer together.

Because of improved telephone cables and satellites, millions of people today use the **Internet**, a global network of computers. Other inventions made the Internet possible in the first place, however. The most important of these were the computer and the microchip. Today's personal computers have more processing power than the large computers of the 1960s that helped put an American on the moon! Millions of people use the Internet to exchange mail, shop, do research, take classes, play games with friends in other countries, and much more. The Internet helps make the world seem smaller yet.

✓ Reading Check Name two ways in which technology makes the world seem smaller.

Globalization

Because the world seems to be getting smaller, it is likely that you know or will meet people from many other cultures. What is your role in this new, shrinking world?

Civic Participation   First, you must learn civic participation. This means being an involved citizen and being concerned with the public affairs of your community, state, nation, and the world. You need to be aware of your rights and responsibilities. **Rights** are benefits and protections guaranteed to you by law. In a democracy like the United States, for example, you have the right to speak freely and to practice the religion of your choice. **Responsibilities** are duties that you owe to other citizens and your government. You have a responsibility to respect the property and privacy of others. When you turn 18 years old, you will be responsible for electing government leaders by voting.

Second, you can learn about the beliefs and values of other people in the world. By studying other cultures, you will become able to see connections between the United States and the world around us. Learning to understand and respect what makes each culture unique—and recognizing common experiences that link all people—will help you become an informed member of the global village.

FCAT
PRACTICE
Completing the activity below will help you prepare for the **FCAT Reading** and **Writing** tests.

Primary Source

GLOBALIZATION

Kofi Annan, secretary-general of the United Nations, spoke to the General Assembly about globalization.

❝*If one word [describes] the changes we are living through, it is 'globalization.' . . . What are [the] global issues? I have grouped them under three headings, each of which I relate to a fundamental human freedom . . . . First, freedom from want. How can we call human beings free and equal in dignity when over a billion of them are struggling to survive on less than one dollar a day? . . . The second . . . is freedom from fear. . . . We must do more to prevent conflicts from happening at all. . . . The third [is] the freedom of future generations to sustain their lives on this planet. . . . We need to remember the old African wisdom which I learned as a child—that the earth is not ours. It is a treasure we hold in trust for our descendents.*❞

Millennium Report, April 3, 2000.

Analyzing Primary Sources

Do you think these are the only global issues? Do these issues affect you in your daily life? If they do, how? If they don't, do you think you should have to worry about them?   **FCAT** LA.A.2.3.8, LA.B.1.3.2

Interdependence   Why should we be concerned about what happens on the other side of the globe? The world's countries are interdependent. Interdependence exists when countries depend on one another for goods, raw materials to make goods, and markets in which to sell goods. Think of the many ways you use products from other countries. The fruit you put on your breakfast cereal might be from Mexico or South America. Your running shoes may be from China or Taiwan. Your book bag might have been made in India.

Events around the world have a rippling effect because of interdependence. A war or drought in another country, for example, causes instability in that country but also affects the people and economies that are linked to it through trade.

Many people perceive cultures in developing countries as backward because they do not have the same level of technology as developed countries. Others, however, appreciate the diverse cultures that exist in many developing countries. They fear that globalization, or the development of a world culture and an interdependent economy, might erase traditions and customs of smaller groups. Thus, an important issue in the world today is to make products, services, and technology available to developing countries yet still preserve local cultures and values. Read more about this challenge in **TIME Reports: Focus on World Issues** on pages 101–107.

✓ Reading Check **Why is it important to learn about other cultures?**

FCAT PRACTICE   You can prepare for the FCAT-assessed standards by completing the correlated item(s) below.

Section 4 Assessment

Defining Terms
1. **Define** rights, responsibilities, interdependence, globalization.

Recalling Facts
2. **Technology** What are two examples of new transportation technology?
3. **Technology** What are two examples of new communication technology?
4. **Government** What responsibilities do people in democracies have?

Critical Thinking
5. **Synthesizing Information** What products found in your classroom were made in other countries?
6. **Making Comparisons** Which do you think had the greater impact on human

society—the Agricultural Revolution or the Information Revolution? Explain. **FCAT LA.B.1.3.2**

Graphic Organizer
7. **Organizing Information** Draw a diagram like this one. On the outer spokes, write ways that people use the Internet. **FCAT LA.A.1.3.2**

(Internet uses)

Applying Social Studies Skills

8. **Interpreting Time Lines** Look at the time line on page 98. About how many years after the internal combustion engine was invented was air flight invented?

TIME
PERSPECTIVES

ciudadan

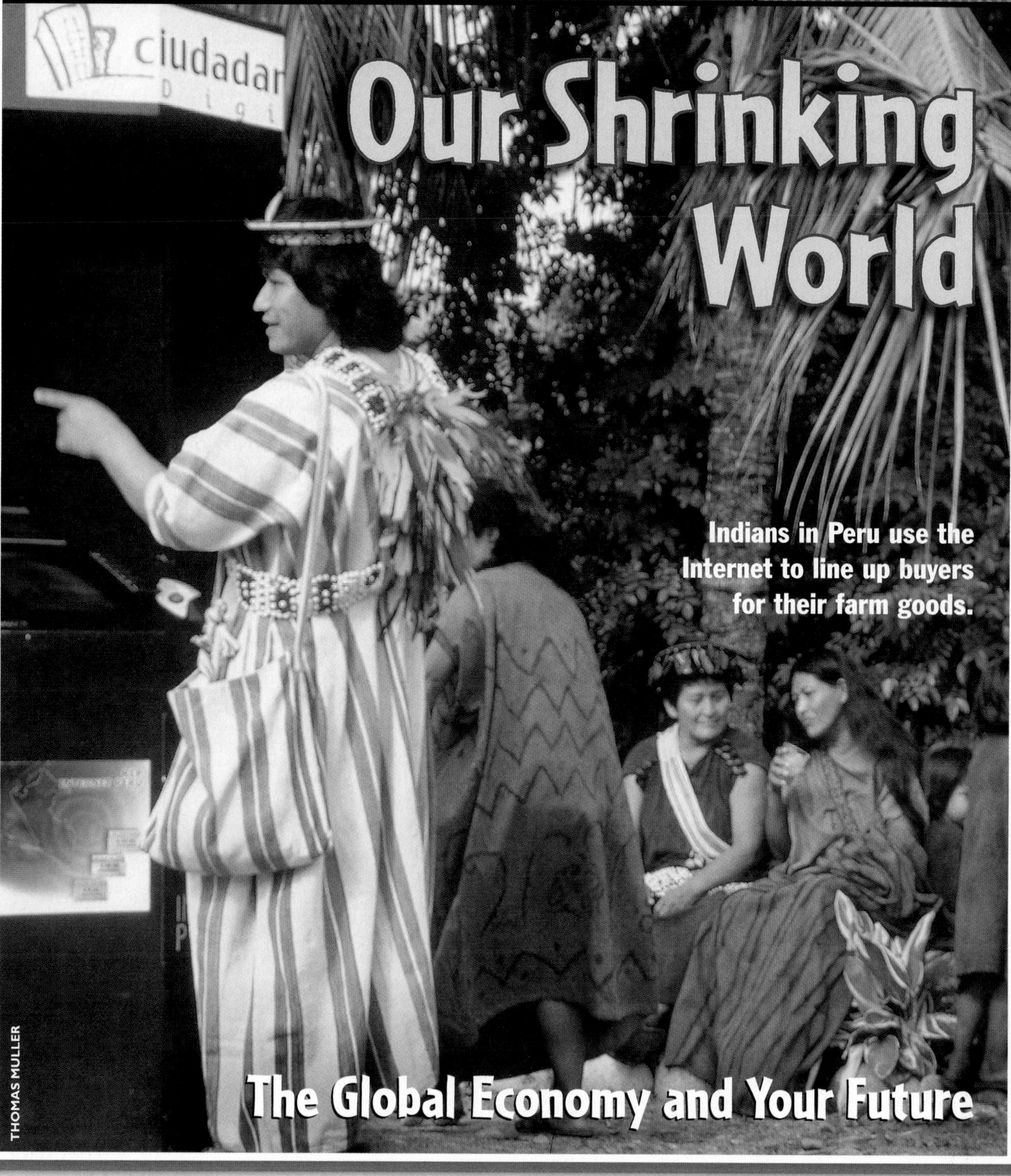

Our Shrinking World

Indians in Peru use the Internet to line up buyers for their farm goods.

The Global Economy and Your Future

THOMAS MULLER

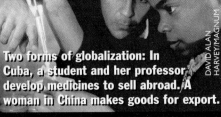

EXPLORING **WORLD ISSUES**

Two forms of globalization: In Cuba, a student and her professor develop medicines to sell abroad. A woman in China makes goods for export.

How Trade Changes Lives

Evaluating Media
LA.A.2.3.6

For Nora Lydia Urias Perez, life has never been easy. A single mother, she lived with her five-year-old daughter in the Mexican state of Veracruz. The only work she could find there was on a farm, earning $5 a day. That just wasn't enough.

In 2000 she moved to Nogales, a city just south of the New Mexico border. She got a job in a stapler factory that had moved to Nogales from New York City. Ms. Urias's job paid her $10 a day. To her, it was a fortune.

Thanks to the North American Free Trade Agreement (NAFTA), hundreds of thousands of Mexicans work in factories like Ms. Urias's. Companies in Mexico, Japan, and Europe hire their workers to assemble products with parts that come from the United States. They send the finished goods—everything from dresses to TVs—back to the United States and Canada.

Global Relationships

This relationship is an example of **globalization**, the linking together of the world's nations through trade. What's driving globalization today is the search for cheap labor. Cheap labor helps manufacturers keep costs low. Low costs can mean lower prices for many things you buy.

A Sweatshirt's Global Journey

This map follows the route cotton has actually taken to a popular store near you.

1. Uzbekistan: Workers harvest cotton.

2. Iran: A freight train moves bales of raw cotton to the Arabian Sea.

3. Indian and Pacific Oceans: A ship carries the cotton 4,000 miles to South Korea.

4. South Korea: Workers spin cotton into thread and weave it into cloth.

5. Sea of Japan: A ship carries finished cloth to Russia's Far East.

6. Russia's Far East: Workers cut and stitch the cloth into sweatshirts.

7. Pacific Ocean: A ship takes the finished sweatshirts to California.

8. The United States: Trucks haul the sweatshirts to stores.

Source: The Nation

INTERPRETING MAPS

Making Inferences How do you think the price of the sweatshirt might be affected if the sweatshirt were made entirely in the United States? **FCAT LA.A.2.3.1**

SERGE ATTAL/GAMMA LIASON NETWORK
ROBIN MOYER

Some fear global companies may neglect the environment.

ITSU INOUYE/AP

Police block a march by globalization's foes.

REUTERS/TIMEPIX

A U.S. resident made this Taiwanese movie in China.

Globalization is changing far more than prices. More people, money, and goods than ever before are crossing national borders.

Pop Goes Global

Popular entertainment is no exception. A movie popular in the United States is likely to be a favorite elsewhere. Asians love basketball as much as Americans do. Kids everywhere listen to Latin pop music and wear jeans and sneakers to school.

This doesn't mean all kids think and act the same way. "It is important to see individual differences from one country to the next," advises a woman who has studied teens in 44 nations.

Culture Clash

Companies that forget that advice can get into trouble. A U.S. company opened a theme park outside Paris, France. But the French stayed away. They hated the fast food the park sold. They didn't even like the park's name. It contained the word "Euro," short for "European." The French see themselves as French first, Europeans second.

When the park's owners figured all this out, they made the park more French. They offered food and drinks that suited French tastes, for example. They even put the word "Paris" in the park's name. Today that theme park is one of the most popular in the world.

Good for Everyone?

As the park's owners learned, globalization isn't **"Americanizing"** the world. Local **cultures,** or ways of life, are too strong for that.

But globalization hasn't been good for everyone. The poorest countries have seen little or no increase in trade. Many Americans' jobs have moved to countries where wages are low. And so far the lives of people like Ms. Urias haven't improved much. It costs more to live in Nogales than in Veracruz. So Ms. Urias is still poor.

Gaining Skills

Experts say these problems are only temporary. In recent years, trade has created millions of jobs. It has enabled people in poorer countries like Mexico to pick up new skills. The more skilled workers are, the more they get paid.

Ms. Urias looks forward to better times. "I am not saying it will be easy to start life [in Nogales]," she said. "But at last there is a chance that things for me will get better. There was no chance of that in Veracruz. I had no hope."

EXPLORING THE ISSUE

1. **Cause and Effect** How might the health of the U.S. economy shape Ms. Urias's life? **FCAT** LA.E.2.2.1

2. **Making Inferences** Why do you think that the poorest countries have seen few gains from globalization? **FCAT** LA.A.2.3.1

Globalization's New Face

Evaluating
Media
LA.A.2.3.6

The Phoenicians were great sailors. They lived in Southwest Asia, on the coast of Lebanon. They set up **trade routes** all around the Mediterranean Sea. Some experts think they may have sailed to England to bring back tin. They did all this as far back as 1200 B.C.

▲ A Yagua (right) takes part in an Internet poll in the rain forests of Peru.

GARWOOD & AINSLIE.
PLANET PROJECT

As the Phoenicians showed, globalization is not new. People have traded in faraway lands, moved around, and mixed cultures for thousands of years.

What is new is the speed at which these exchanges take place. Technology is shrinking the world. Telephones zip our voices around the world. Jet planes carry us great distances in a few hours.

High-speed cargo ships crisscross the oceans, carrying goods from nation to nation.

The Internet

The Internet has changed the way we swap goods, too. Twenty-five years ago, an American importer might have used "snail mail" to order a shipment of French bikes. Today she can check out the manufacturer's stock on his Web page. Then, in seconds, she can e-mail her order halfway around the world.

The deals she makes aren't much different from those the Phoenicians made. They traded timber for horses. She trades money for bicycles.

What's different is that she makes her trades in a flash, and without leaving her seat. She can do more business in less time, and she can do business anywhere. The Phoenicians could do business only where they could sail. ▪

EXPLORING THE ISSUE

1. **Making Inferences** How might trade help people from different cultures understand one another? FCAT LA.A.2.3.1

2. **Analyzing Information** How does the Internet make growing up different for you than it was for your parents?

Sharing Globalization's Gains

Evaluating Media LA.A.2.3.6

A little more than 6 billion people live on Earth. About half of them get by on less than $2 a day. What does globalization mean to them? So far, not much.

Overall, the impact of increased trade has been amazing. The ability of people to make and spend money has grown almost everywhere.

Yet the fruits of globalization haven't been spread evenly. **Industrialized countries** have more to trade than **developing countries**. Foreign companies prefer to build more factories in rich countries than in poor ones.

The result is that countries like Kenya tend to create new jobs slowly. Places like Canada tend to create them more quickly. Some countries in Asia and Africa are barely able to create any new jobs at all.

A Wider Gap

These differences worry many people. If the trend continues, experts say that the gap between rich and poor countries can only get wider.

What can be done to narrow that gap? There are no easy answers. International businesses are certainly part of it. During the 1990s, private companies spent more than $1 trillion to build factories in developing countries.

Rich nations are also part of the answer. They are already helping poorer countries pay for new roads, phone lines, seaports, and airports. And they are encouraging poor nations to

MARIE DORIGNY/TIMEPIX

▲ Nowhere is the gap between rich and poor clearer than in Pakistan. Here a child laborer makes soccer balls for sale around the world.

produce things that people elsewhere want to buy.

China figured out how to do that years ago. Thanks to trade, the ability of the Chinese to earn and spend money now doubles every 10 years. Finding ways to help about 200 other nations equal that success is one of today's biggest challenges. ▪

EXPLORING THE ISSUE

1. Making Inferences Why do you think experts worry about the widening gap between rich and poor countries? **FCAT LA.A.2.3.1**

2. Problem Solving What would you do to help spread the fruits of globalization more evenly around the globe? **FCAT LA.B.1.3.2**

Preparing for a Smaller World: What Can One Person Do?

Evaluating
Media
LA.A.2.3.6

Every day in 2000, half a million airline passengers, 1.4 billion e-mail messages, and $1.5 trillion crossed national borders. All that shifting about of people, ideas, and money would have been unthinkable 10 years earlier. The Internet was a toddler. The World Wide Web had just been born.

What will the world look like 10 years from now? No one can say. But two things are sure. Inventions that create faster ways to communicate will make the world seem a lot smaller than it is today. And more and more Americans will have jobs that require them to deal with people from other nations.

Learning About Other Cultures

You will be able to do that well if you have taken the time to learn about other countries. To really get to know people from other cultures, you need to understand what makes them tick. You can do that best by speaking to them in their own language.

You won't have to leave the United States to need that knowledge. Globalization has enabled more and more people to cross borders to find work. Employers will want to hire people who can work well with people born in other countries.

▲ Which of Pepperdine University's nine teammates was born in the U.S.? It's Anh Nguyen, fourth from left.

They will also want to know if you are committed to a lifetime of learning. As technology changes, your job will, too. Your need to learn new things won't stop when you leave high school or college.

Globalization is shaping tomorrow's job market. Only you can prepare yourself to thrive in it. And there's no time like today to start.

EXPLORING THE ISSUE

1. **Determining Cause and Effect**
   How does the Internet make the world seem smaller? **FCAT** LA.A.2.3.1

2. **Analyzing Information** Modern companies require employees at every level to solve problems they face on the job. Why are lifetime learners better equipped than others to solve problems?
   FCAT LA.B.1.3.2

REVIEW AND ASSESS

UNDERSTANDING THE ISSUE

1. Defining Key Terms Write definitions for the following terms: *globalization, cultures, trade route, industrialized country, Americanizing, developing country.*

2. Writing to Inform Write a short article about how globalization shapes the way people live and what they do. Use as many words as you can from the above list. **FCAT LA.B.1.3.2**

3. Writing to Persuade Overall, is globalization good or bad for the world? Defend your answer in a letter to an imaginary friend who lives in a developing country in Africa. **FCAT LA.B.1.3.2**

INTERNET RESEARCH ACTIVITY

4. With your teacher's help, use Internet resources to contact two classrooms—one in an industrialized country and one in a developing country. Exchange lists on what imported goods kids in your country and theirs own or use. Compare the lists, and discuss what they say about the importance of trade.

5. Use the Internet to find information on the history of the Internet. Write an essay telling how the Internet sped up communication. Create a time line that notes important developments. **FCAT LA.A.2.3.5**

BEYOND THE CLASSROOM

6. Look through your local newspaper for a week. Find articles on topics related to globalization. For example, look for stories about the Internet, imports and exports, immigration, and even crimes like drug-smuggling. In an oral report, tell how the articles suggest that globalization is making the world smaller. **FCAT LA.A.2.3.5, LA.B.1.3.2**

▲ **More and more Americans are crossing the borders for fun.**

PHOTODISC

7. Take an inventory of your room at home. Write down the name of each item made in another country. Count the items imported from the same country. Then make a bar graph to show how many imported items you own. Have each bar stand for one category—clothing, CDs, or sports equipment, for example. Write a caption explaining what the graph says about how important trade is to you. **FCAT MA.D.1.3.2**

The Digital Divide
(Individuals with home access to the Internet in 2001)

Worldwide	7%
Industrialized Nations	
United States	58%
South Korea	54%
United Kingdom	40%
Japan	36%
Germany	34%
Developing Nations	
Mexico	3.4%
South Africa	3.4%
China	2.0%
India	1.3%
Egypt	0.3%

Source: Neilsen//NetRatings, July 2001

Where in the world are people wired to the Internet at home? Almost everywhere. But industrialized nations have a big lead. People with home access make up a big chunk of the populations of these richer nations. It's just the opposite with developing nations. People with home access make up a tiny part of the populations of these poorer nations. Experts call this gap the "digital divide," and it worries them. The Internet is a tool. Nations must use it to participate fully in world trade.

BUILDING GRAPH READING SKILLS

1. Comparing Compare the amount of Internet use in industrialized and developing nations. **FCAT MA.E.3.3.1**

2. Determining Cause and Effect What does a nation need besides Internet access to succeed in world trade? **FCAT LA.A.2.3.1**

FOR UPDATES ON WORLD ISSUES GO TO www.timeclassroom.com/glencoe

Making Connections

ART   SCIENCE   CULTURE   **TECHNOLOGY**

Counting Heads

How did we know there were nearly 292 million people in the United States in 2000? Who counts the people? Every 10 years since 1790, the United States Census Bureau has counted heads in this country. Why and how do they do this?

The First Census

After the American colonies fought the Revolutionary War and won their independence, the new government ordered a census. By knowing how many people were in each state, the government could divide the war expenses fairly. The census would also determine the number of people that each state could send to Congress.

This census began in August 1790, about a year after George Washington became president. The law defined who would be counted and required that every household be visited by census takers. These workers walked or rode on horseback to gather their data. By the time it was completed, the census counted 3.9 million people.

The first census asked for little more than one's name and address. Over time, the census added questions to gather more than just population data. By 1820 there were questions about a person's job. Soon after, questions about crime, education, and wages appeared.

Changing Technology

As the country's population grew and the quantity of data increased, new technology helped census workers. In 1890 clerks began to use a keypunch device, invented by a Census Bureau worker, to add the numbers. The Tabulating Machine, as it was called, used an electric current to sense holes in punched cards and to keep a running total of the data. In 1950 the census used its first computer to process data. Now census data are released over the Internet.

FCAT PRACTICE Answering question 3 below will help you prepare for the **FCAT Reading** test.

Remarkably, one technology slow to change has been the way the government takes the census. Not until 1960 did the U.S. Postal Service become the major means of conducting the census. Even today, census takers go door-to-door to gather information from those who do not return their census forms in the mail.

▲ The Electric Tabulating Machine processed the 1890 census in 2½ years, a job that would have taken nearly 10 years to complete by hand.

→ Making the Connection

1. In what two ways were population data from the first census used?

2. How has technology changed the way census data are collected and processed?

3. **Drawing Conclusions** Why do you think the national and state governments want information about people's education and jobs? **FCAT** LA.A.2.3.1

Reading Review

Section 1 | Understanding Culture

Terms to Know

culture
ethnic group
dialect
democracy
dictatorship
monarchy
cultural diffusion
civilization
culture region

Main Idea

People usually live with others who follow similar beliefs learned from the past.

✓ **Culture** Culture is the way of life of a group of people who share similar beliefs and customs.

✓ **Culture** Culture includes eight elements or traits: social groups, language, religion, daily life, history, arts, a government system, and an economic system.

✓ **Culture** Cultures change over time and influence other regions.

Section 2 | Population Patterns

Terms to Know

death rate
birthrate
famine
population density
urbanization
emigrate
refugee

Main Idea

The world's population is growing rapidly, and how and where people live are changing too.

✓ **History** In the past 200 years, the world's population has grown at a very rapid rate.

✓ **Movement** Some areas are more densely populated than others.

✓ **Culture** About 50 percent of the world's people live in cities.

Section 3 | Resources and World Trade

Terms to Know

natural resource
renewable resource
nonrenewable resource
economic system
export
import
tariff
quota
free trade
developed country
developing country

Main Idea

Many resources are limited and distributed unevenly, so countries must trade for goods.

✓ **Human/Environment Interaction** Renewable resources cannot be used up or can be replaced fairly quickly.

✓ **Human/Environment Interaction** Some resources—such as fossil fuels and minerals—are nonrenewable.

✓ **Economics** Countries specialize by producing what they can produce best with the resources they have.

✓ **Economics** Countries export their specialized products and import what they need.

Section 4 | Technology "Shrinks" the World

Terms to Know

rights
responsibilities
interdependence
globalization

Main Idea

Modern technology has helped to bring the world's diverse peoples closer together.

✓ **Technology** Advancements in transportation and communication technology, including the Internet, have "shrunk" the world.

✓ **Interdependence** The world's countries are linked through trade, and some people fear that globalization will erase traditional cultures.

The World's People

FCAT PRACTICE You can prepare for the FCAT-assessed standards by completing the correlated item(s) below.

Using Key Terms

Match the terms in Part A with their definitions in Part B.

A.

1. culture
2. developed country
3. democracy
4. globalization
5. population density
6. emigrate
7. urbanization
8. quota
9. developing country
10. cultural diffusion

B.

a. power rests with the people of a nation
b. spreading knowledge to other cultures
c. countries working toward industrialization
d. to move to another country
e. a number limit on imports from a country
f. the average number of people living in a square mile
g. country where much manufacturing is carried out
h. the way of life of a group of people who share similar beliefs and customs
i. movement to cities
j. development of a world culture and an interdependent world economy

Reviewing the Main Ideas

Section 1 Understanding Culture

11. **Culture** What are the major religions?
12. **Movement** Give an example of cultural diffusion.

Section 2 Population Patterns

13. **Culture** What has created rapid population growth? **FCAT LA.E.2.2.1**
14. **Culture** How do you calculate population density?
15. **Movement** Why have many people moved to cities? **FCAT LA.A.2.3.1**

Section 3 Resources and World Trade

16. **Human/Environment Interaction** What are three renewable energy sources?
17. **Economics** What is the difference between a traditional and market economy? **FCAT LA.A.2.2.7**
18. **Economics** How do countries respond to the unequal distribution of resources?

Section 4 Technology "Shrinks" the World

19. **Technology** In what ways is the world shrinking?
20. **Culture** How can globalization affect cultures in a negative way? **FCAT LA.E.2.2.1**

NATIONAL GEOGRAPHIC **World Culture Regions**

Place Location Activity

On a separate sheet of paper, match the letters on the map with the numbered places listed below.

1. Latin America
2. North Africa and Southwest Asia
3. Europe
4. Russia and Central Asian Republics
5. East Asia
6. United States and Canada
7. Australia, Oceania, and Antarctica
8. Africa South of the Sahara

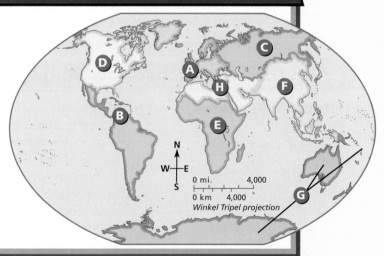

0 mi. 4,000
0 km 4,000
Winkel Tripel projection

Critical Thinking

21. **Making Predictions** In what ways do you think a company investing in a developing country could help the people there? How could that same company harm the culture?

22. **Sequencing Information** Make a chart like the one below, and list the ways you use electricity from the moment you wake up until you go to sleep. In the second column, write how you would perform the same activity if you had no electricity to rely on.

FCAT LA.A.1.3.2

Activities With Electricity	Without Electricity

Comparing Regions Activity

23. **Culture** With your teacher's help, find a service that matches pen pals from different regions. In your first letter, describe your clothing, the sports you play, and what you do for fun. Ask your pal to describe the same. **FCAT LA.B.1.3.2**

Mental Mapping Activity

24. **Focusing on the Region** Draw a simple outline map of the United States. On your map, label the areas where the following activities take place:

- Commercial farming
- Manufacturing
- Raising livestock
- Fishing
- Obtaining oil

Technology Skills Activity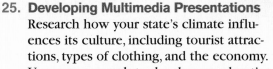

25. **Developing Multimedia Presentations** Research how your state's climate influences its culture, including tourist attractions, types of clothing, and the economy. Use your research to develop an advertisement promoting your state.

Standardized Test Practice

Directions: Study the graph below, and then answer the question that follows. **FCAT MA.E.3.3.1**

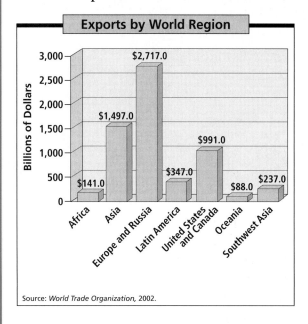

Exports by World Region

Source: *World Trade Organization*, 2002.

1. **According to the graph, how much do the United States and Canada export?**

   A $991,000,000,000

   B $991,000,000

   C $991,000

   D $991

Test-Taking Tip: In order to understand any type of graph, look carefully around the graph for keys that show how it is organized. On this bar graph, the numbers along the left side represent billions of dollars. Therefore, you need to multiply the number on the graph by 1,000,000,000 to get the correct answer.

◀ **Skier in Idaho's stretch of the Rocky Mountains**

Grocer in Chinatown, New York City

Farm on the Manitoba plains

The United States and Canada

Which of the world's culture regions do you call home? It is probably the United States and Canada. If you look at a globe, you will see that the United States and Canada cover most of North America. These two nations share many of the same landforms, including rugged mountains in the west, rounded mountains in the east, and rolling plains in the center.

NGS ONLINE
www.nationalgeographic.com/education

Focus on:

The United States and Canada

SPANNING MORE THAN 7 MILLION square miles (18 million sq. km), the United States and Canada cover much of North America. These huge countries share many of the same landscapes, climates, and natural resources.

The Land

The United States and Canada make up a region bordered by the very cold Arctic Ocean in the north and bathed by the Gulf of Mexico's warm currents in the south. The western coast faces the Pacific Ocean. Eastern shores are edged by the Atlantic.

Landforms Rugged mountains are found in the western part of each country. The Pacific ranges follow the coastline. Farther inland are the massive, jagged peaks of the Rocky Mountains. Relatively young as mountains go, the Rockies stretch more than 3,000 miles (4,828 km) from Alaska to the southwestern United States.

East of the Rockies are the wide and windswept Great Plains. This gently rolling landscape covers the central part of both the United States and Canada.

The Appalachian range, much older than the Rockies, is the dominant landform in the eastern part of the region. East and south of the Appalachians' low, rounded peaks are coastal plains that end at the Atlantic shores.

Waterways The Mississippi River is the largest river system in North America. It flows through the heart of the Great Plains from near the United States–Canadian border in the north to the Gulf of Mexico in the south.

The largest lake system is the Great Lakes—Superior, Huron, Michigan, Erie, and Ontario. The waters of these connected lakes flow into the St. Lawrence River, which empties into the Atlantic Ocean. The St. Lawrence Seaway—built by the United States and Canada—provides large ships with a water route between the Great Lakes and the Atlantic Ocean. The diagram on page 159 shows you that the St. Lawrence Seaway includes a series of canals, rivers, and other inland waterways.

The Climate

This region's vast size and varied landforms help give it great diversity in climate and

Parachutist plunging toward the Appalachian Mountains, West Virginia ▶

◀ Polar bear snoozing in the Canadian Arctic

vegetation. In the far northern parts of Alaska and Canada, amid the treeless tundra and dense evergreen forests, brief summers and bitterly cold winters prevail. The Pacific coast, from southern Alaska to northern California, has a mild, wet climate. Rain clouds blowing in from the ocean are blocked by the Pacific ranges. Robbed of moisture, the land immediately east of these mountains is dry.

Hot, humid summers and cold, snowy winters are the norm in the Great Plains. This humid continental climate extends from the plains across southeastern Canada and the northeastern United States. The southeastern states, however, have much milder winters. The mildest of all are found on Florida's southern tip, the only part of the U.S. mainland that has a tropical climate.

The Economy

The United States and Canada are prosperous countries. Abundant natural resources and plenty of skilled workers have been key ingredients in creating two of the most successful economies in the world. Both countries operate under the free enterprise system, in which individuals and groups—not the government—control businesses and industries.

The region's strong economy was built on agriculture, which remains important today. Fertile soil, numerous waterways, a favorable climate, and high-tech equipment have made the United States and Canada two of the world's top food producers. Livestock, grains, vegetables, and fruits are all raised by the region's farmers.

Rich oil, coal, and natural gas deposits occur in this region. So do deposits of valuable minerals, including copper, iron ore, nickel, silver, and gold. These energy sources and raw materials have made it possible for the United States and Canada to develop large industrial economies. Today, however, people are more likely to work in offices than in factories. Service industries such as banking, communications, entertainment, insurance, and health care employ most people in the region.

The People

The United States and Canada have a rich mix of cultures. Native Americans were the nations' first inhabitants. Centuries later, settlers from Europe arrived. Immigrants from Africa, Asia, Latin America, and almost every other part of the world eventually followed. Some came looking for religious or political freedom. Some came as enslaved laborers. Some came for a fresh start in these immense lands of boundless

◄ **Worker in sterile gown manufacturing computer chips in Texas**

opportunity. Even today large numbers of immigrants continue to make the United States and Canada their new home. Every ethnic group and religion are represented in both countries. In many large cities, several different languages can be heard on the streets.

Today more than 324 million people call this region home. Thirty-two million of them live in Canada, while the remaining 292 million live in the United States. Most people live in urban areas on both sides of the border. Toronto, Vancouver, and Montreal are among Canada's largest cities. In the United States, New York City, Los Angeles, and Chicago are the most populous cities.

Inuit boys examining a Native American sculpture ▼

Data Bits

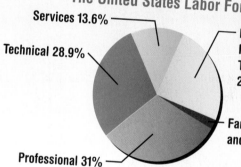

Country	Automobiles per 1,000 people	Television sets per 1,000 people
United States	478	844
Canada	459	709

Population: Urban ▨ vs. Rural ▨

United States	75%	25%
Canada	79%	21%

The United States Labor Force

- Services 13.6%
- Technical 28.9%
- Professional 31%
- Manufacturing, Mining, and Transportation 24.1%
- Farming, Forestry, and Fishing 2.4%

Sources: *World Development Indicators*, 2002; *The World Factbook*, 2003; *The World Almanac*, 2004.

Exploring the Region

1. Which oceans border the region?
2. Why is the climate dry just east of the Pacific ranges?
3. What factors have helped make the region prosperous?
4. In which country do most of the region's people live?

The United States and Canada

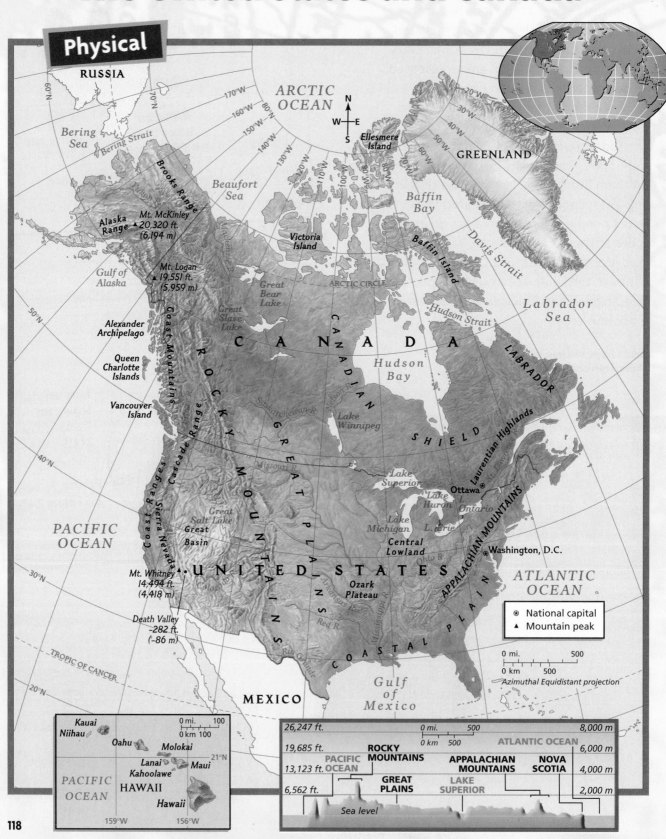

Physical

RUSSIA

ARCTIC OCEAN

Bering Sea

Bering Strait

Brooks Range

Alaska Range

Mt. McKinley ▲ 20,320 ft. (6,194 m)

Gulf of Alaska

Mt. Logan ▲ 19,551 ft. (5,959 m)

Alexander Archipelago

Queen Charlotte Islands

Vancouver Island

Coast Mountains

Coast Ranges

Cascade Range

Sierra Nevada

Mt. Whitney ▲ 14,494 ft. (4,418 m)

Death Valley -282 ft. (-86 m)

PACIFIC OCEAN

Beaufort Sea

Ellesmere Island

GREENLAND

Baffin Bay

Victoria Island

ARCTIC CIRCLE

Great Bear Lake

Great Slave Lake

CANADA

Baffin Island

Davis Strait

Labrador Sea

Hudson Strait

Mackenzie R.

CANADIAN SHIELD

Hudson Bay

LABRADOR

Laurentian Highlands

Saskatchewan R.

Nelson R.

Lake Winnipeg

Missouri R.

ROCKY MOUNTAINS

GREAT PLAINS

Great Salt Lake

Great Basin

UNITED STATES

Colorado R.

Lake Superior

Lake Huron

L. Ontario

Lake Michigan

L. Erie

Ottawa ⊛

Central Lowland

Ohio R.

APPALACHIAN MOUNTAINS

Washington, D.C. ⊛

ATLANTIC OCEAN

Ozark Plateau

Arkansas R.

Red R.

Mississippi R.

Rio Grande

COASTAL PLAIN

TROPIC OF CANCER

MEXICO

Gulf of Mexico

⊛ National capital
▲ Mountain peak

0 mi. 500
0 km 500
Azimuthal Equidistant projection

Kauai
Niihau
Oahu
Molokai
Lanai
Kahoolawe
Maui
HAWAII
Hawaii
PACIFIC OCEAN

0 mi. 100
0 km 100

21°N
159°W 156°W

26,247 ft.
19,685 ft.
13,123 ft.
6,562 ft.

PACIFIC OCEAN

ROCKY MOUNTAINS

GREAT PLAINS

ATLANTIC OCEAN

APPALACHIAN MOUNTAINS

LAKE SUPERIOR

NOVA SCOTIA

8,000 m
6,000 m
4,000 m
2,000 m

Sea level

0 mi. 500
0 km 500

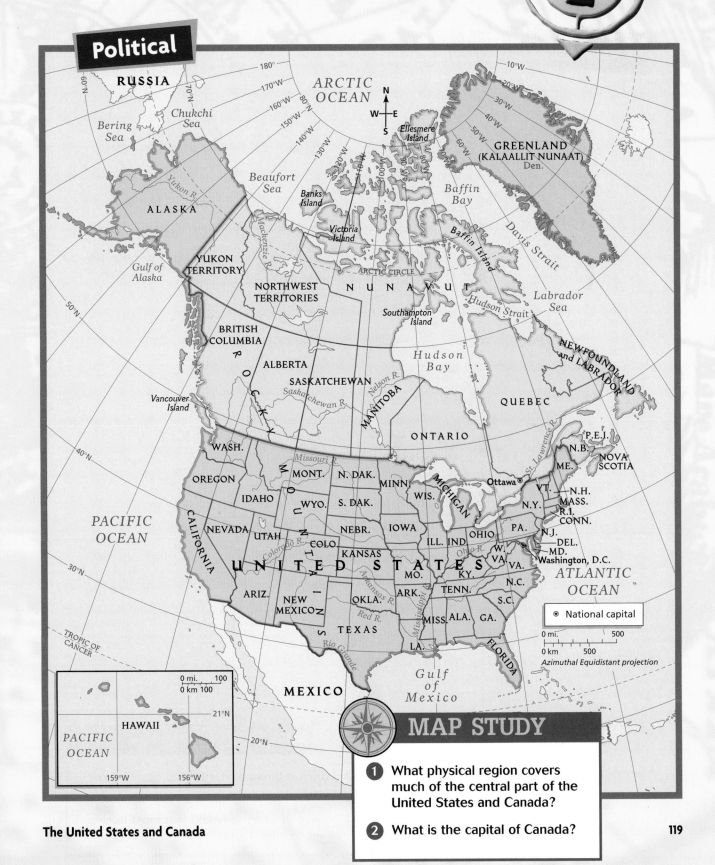

Political

RUSSIA

ARCTIC OCEAN

Chukchi Sea

Bering Sea

Ellesmere Island

GREENLAND (KALAALLIT NUNAAT) Den.

ALASKA

Beaufort Sea

Banks Island

Baffin Bay

Yukon R.

Victoria Island

Baffin Island

Davis Strait

Gulf of Alaska

YUKON TERRITORY

NORTHWEST TERRITORIES

ARCTIC CIRCLE

NUNAVUT

Mackenzie R.

Southampton Island

Hudson Strait

Labrador Sea

BRITISH COLUMBIA

ALBERTA

SASKATCHEWAN

MANITOBA

Nelson R.

Hudson Bay

NEWFOUNDLAND and LABRADOR

Vancouver Island

Saskatchewan R.

QUEBEC

ONTARIO

P.E.I.

N.B.

NOVA SCOTIA

WASH.

Missouri R.

St. Lawrence R.

ME.

PACIFIC OCEAN

OREGON

MONT.

N. DAK.

MINN.

WIS.

MICHIGAN

Ottawa ⊛

VT.

N.H.

MASS.

R.I.

CONN.

IDAHO

WYO.

S. DAK.

N.Y.

PA.

NEVADA

UTAH

COLO.

NEBR.

IOWA

ILL. IND.

OHIO

W. VA.

N.J.

DEL.

MD.

Washington, D.C.

CALIFORNIA

Colorado R.

KANSAS

MO.

KY.

VA.

ATLANTIC OCEAN

UNITED STATES

ARIZ.

NEW MEXICO

OKLA.

Arkansas R.

ARK.

TENN.

N.C.

S.C.

⊛ National capital

Red R.

MISS.

ALA.

GA.

0 mi. 500

TEXAS

Rio Grande

LA.

Mississippi R.

FLORIDA

0 km 500

Azimuthal Equidistant projection

MEXICO

Gulf of Mexico

Inset:

0 mi. 100

0 km 100

21°N

HAWAII

PACIFIC OCEAN

159°W 156°W

TROPIC OF CANCER

20°N

MAP STUDY

1 What physical region covers much of the central part of the United States and Canada?

2 What is the capital of Canada?

The United States and Canada

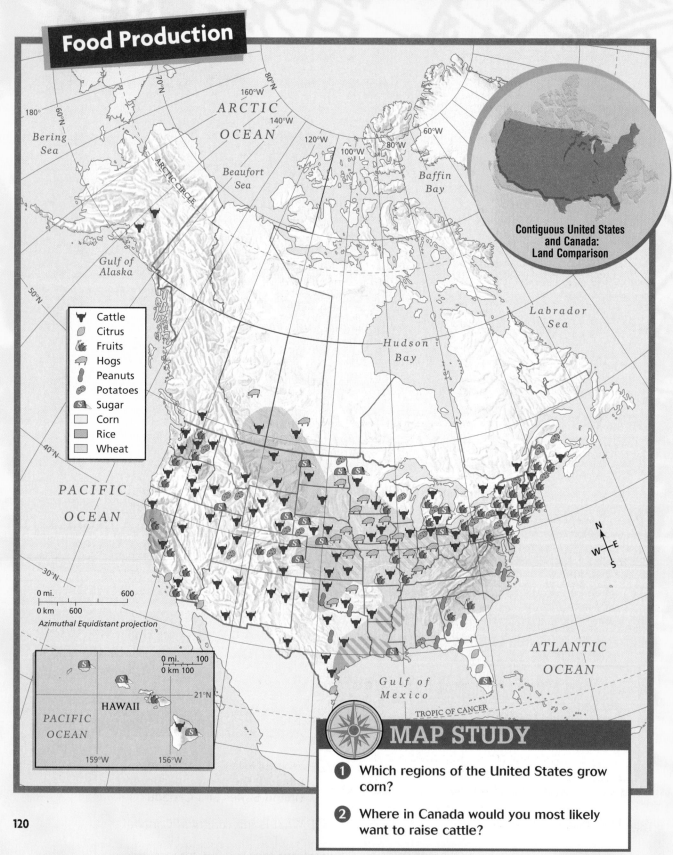

Food Production

Cattle
Citrus
Fruits
Hogs
Peanuts
Potatoes
Sugar
Corn
Rice
Wheat

Contiguous United States and Canada: Land Comparison

ARCTIC OCEAN

Bering Sea

Beaufort Sea

Baffin Bay

Gulf of Alaska

Labrador Sea

Hudson Bay

PACIFIC OCEAN

0 mi. 600
0 km 600
Azimuthal Equidistant projection

HAWAII

PACIFIC OCEAN

0 mi. 100
0 km 100

21°N

159°W   156°W

Gulf of Mexico

TROPIC OF CANCER

ATLANTIC OCEAN

MAP STUDY

❶ Which regions of the United States grow corn?

❷ Where in Canada would you most likely want to raise cattle?

120

Geo Extremes

① **HIGHEST POINT**
Mount McKinley (Alaska)
20,320 ft. (6,194 m) high

② **LOWEST POINT**
Death Valley (California)
282 ft. (86 m)
below sea level

③ **LONGEST RIVER**
Mississippi-Missouri
(United States)
3,710 mi. (5,971 km) long

④ **LARGEST LAKE**
Lake Superior
31,700 sq. mi.
(82,103 sq. km)

⑤ **LARGEST CANYON**
Grand Canyon (Arizona)
277 mi. (446 km) long
1 mi. (1.6 km) deep

⑥ **GREATEST TIDES**
Bay of Fundy (Nova Scotia)
52 ft. (16 m)

COMPARING POPULATION:
United States and Canada

UNITED STATES

CANADA

= 50,000,000

Source: *Population Reference Bureau*, 2003.

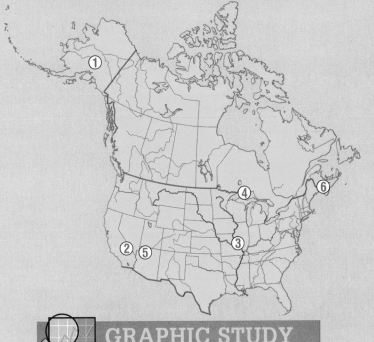

ETHNIC GROUPS:
United States and Canada

UNITED STATES

Native American/Inuit 0.7%
Asian 3.6%
Other 1.9%
Hispanic 12.5%
African American 12.1%
White 69.2%

Source: *U.S. Census Bureau*, 2000.

CANADA

Other (mostly Asian, African, Arab) 6%
Native American/Inuit 2.0%
British Isles 28%
Other European 15%
French 23%
Mixed Background 26%

Source: *CIA World Factbook*, 2000.

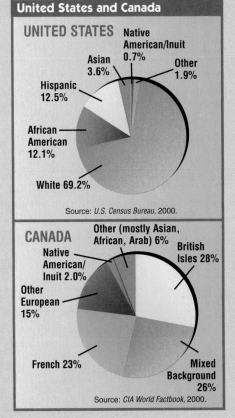

GRAPHIC STUDY

① In what area of the United States do you find both the lowest point and largest canyon?

② How does the percentage of Native American/Inuit population in the United States compare with their percentage of the population in Canada?

Country Profiles

UNITED STATES

POPULATION:
291,500,000
78 per sq. mi.
30 per sq. km

LANGUAGE:
English

MAJOR EXPORT:
Machinery

MAJOR IMPORT:
Crude Oil

Washington, D.C.

CAPITAL:
Washington, D.C.

LANDMASS:
3,717,796 sq. mi.
9,629,091 sq. km

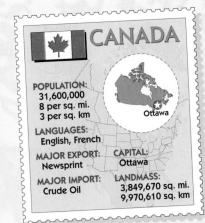

CANADA

POPULATION:
31,600,000
8 per sq. mi.
3 per sq. km

LANGUAGES:
English, French

MAJOR EXPORT:
Newsprint

MAJOR IMPORT:
Crude Oil

Ottawa

CAPITAL:
Ottawa

LANDMASS:
3,849,670 sq. mi.
9,970,610 sq. km

U.S. State Names: Meaning and Origin

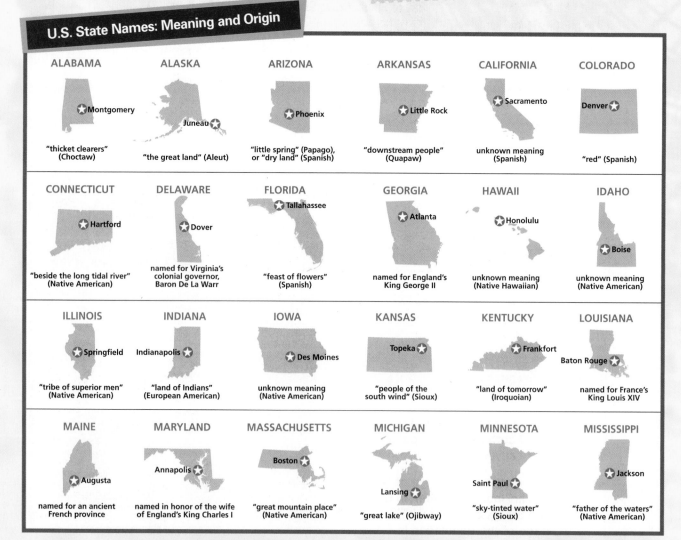

ALABAMA — Montgomery
"thicket clearers"
(Choctaw)

ALASKA — Juneau
"the great land" (Aleut)

ARIZONA — Phoenix
"little spring" (Papago),
or "dry land" (Spanish)

ARKANSAS — Little Rock
"downstream people"
(Quapaw)

CALIFORNIA — Sacramento
unknown meaning
(Spanish)

COLORADO — Denver
"red" (Spanish)

CONNECTICUT — Hartford
"beside the long tidal river"
(Native American)

DELAWARE — Dover
named for Virginia's
colonial governor,
Baron De La Warr

FLORIDA — Tallahassee
"feast of flowers"
(Spanish)

GEORGIA — Atlanta
named for England's
King George II

HAWAII — Honolulu
unknown meaning
(Native Hawaiian)

IDAHO — Boise
unknown meaning
(Native American)

ILLINOIS — Springfield
"tribe of superior men"
(Native American)

INDIANA — Indianapolis
"land of Indians"
(European American)

IOWA — Des Moines
unknown meaning
(Native American)

KANSAS — Topeka
"people of the
south wind" (Sioux)

KENTUCKY — Frankfort
"land of tomorrow"
(Iroquoian)

LOUISIANA — Baton Rouge
named for France's
King Louis XIV

MAINE — Augusta
named for an ancient
French province

MARYLAND — Annapolis
named in honor of the wife
of England's King Charles I

MASSACHUSETTS — Boston
"great mountain place"
(Native American)

MICHIGAN — Lansing
"great lake" (Ojibway)

MINNESOTA — Saint Paul
"sky-tinted water"
(Sioux)

MISSISSIPPI — Jackson
"father of the waters"
(Native American)

Countries, states, provinces, and flags not drawn to scale

For more information on the U.S. and Canada, refer to the Nations of the World Data Bank in the Appendix.

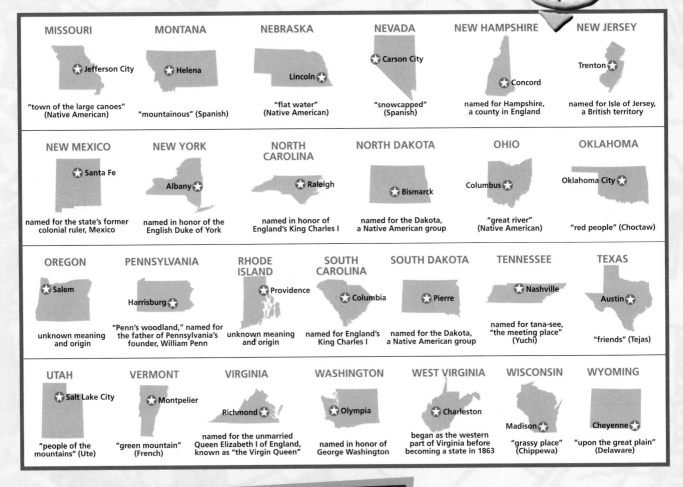

MISSOURI — Jefferson City
"town of the large canoes" (Native American)

MONTANA — Helena
"mountainous" (Spanish)

NEBRASKA — Lincoln
"flat water" (Native American)

NEVADA — Carson City
"snowcapped" (Spanish)

NEW HAMPSHIRE — Concord
named for Hampshire, a county in England

NEW JERSEY — Trenton
named for Isle of Jersey, a British territory

NEW MEXICO — Santa Fe
named for the state's former colonial ruler, Mexico

NEW YORK — Albany
named in honor of the English Duke of York

NORTH CAROLINA — Raleigh
named in honor of England's King Charles I

NORTH DAKOTA — Bismarck
named for the Dakota, a Native American group

OHIO — Columbus
"great river" (Native American)

OKLAHOMA — Oklahoma City
"red people" (Choctaw)

OREGON — Salem
unknown meaning and origin

PENNSYLVANIA — Harrisburg
"Penn's woodland," named for the father of Pennsylvania's founder, William Penn

RHODE ISLAND — Providence
unknown meaning and origin

SOUTH CAROLINA — Columbia
named for England's King Charles I

SOUTH DAKOTA — Pierre
named for the Dakota, a Native American group

TENNESSEE — Nashville
named for tana-see, "the meeting place" (Yuchi)

TEXAS — Austin
"friends" (Tejas)

UTAH — Salt Lake City
"people of the mountains" (Ute)

VERMONT — Montpelier
"green mountain" (French)

VIRGINIA — Richmond
named for the unmarried Queen Elizabeth I of England, known as "the Virgin Queen"

WASHINGTON — Olympia
named in honor of George Washington

WEST VIRGINIA — Charleston
began as the western part of Virginia before becoming a state in 1863

WISCONSIN — Madison
"grassy place" (Chippewa)

WYOMING — Cheyenne
"upon the great plain" (Delaware)

Canadian Province and Territory Names: Meaning and Origin

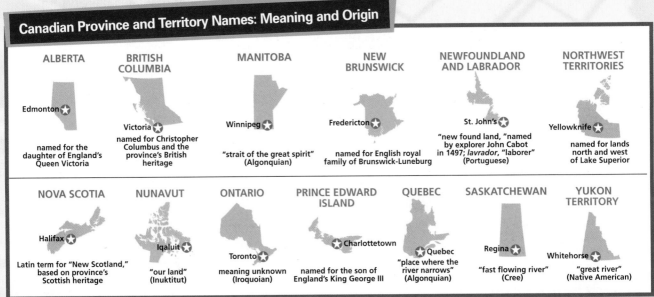

ALBERTA — Edmonton
named for the daughter of England's Queen Victoria

BRITISH COLUMBIA — Victoria
named for Christopher Columbus and the province's British heritage

MANITOBA — Winnipeg
"strait of the great spirit" (Algonquian)

NEW BRUNSWICK — Fredericton
named for English royal family of Brunswick-Luneburg

NEWFOUNDLAND AND LABRADOR — St. John's
"new found land, "named by explorer John Cabot in 1497; *lavrador*, "laborer" (Portuguese)

NORTHWEST TERRITORIES — Yellowknife
named for lands north and west of Lake Superior

NOVA SCOTIA — Halifax
Latin term for "New Scotland," based on province's Scottish heritage

NUNAVUT — Iqaluit
"our land" (Inuktitut)

ONTARIO — Toronto
meaning unknown (Iroquoian)

PRINCE EDWARD ISLAND — Charlottetown
named for the son of England's King George III

QUEBEC — Quebec
"place where the river narrows" (Algonquian)

SASKATCHEWAN — Regina
"fast flowing river" (Cree)

YUKON TERRITORY — Whitehorse
"great river" (Native American)

The United States

The World and Its People

NATIONAL GEOGRAPHIC

To learn more about the people and places of the United States, view *The World and Its People* **Chapter 4** video.

Social Studies online

Chapter Overview Visit *The World and Its People* Web site at twip.glencoe.com and click on **Chapter 4—Chapter Overviews** to preview information about the United States.

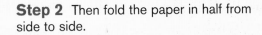

FCAT PRACTICE The activity below will help you prepare for the **FCAT Reading** test.

Identifying Main Ideas Asking yourself questions as you read helps you to focus on main ideas of the material and better understand it. Make this foldable and use it as a journal to record and answer your own questions about the United States. **FCAT LA.A.2.3.5**

Step 1 Fold a sheet of paper in half from top to bottom.

Step 2 Then fold the paper in half from side to side.

Step 3 Label the foldable as shown.

Reading and Writing Before you read the chapter, list questions you have about the land, people, and economy of the United States. Then, as you read the chapter, write down more questions that occur to you on the pages of your journal. Be sure to review your questions and fill in all the correct answers. **FCAT LA.A.2.3.5**

◀ **Statue of Liberty in New York Harbor, New York**

Why It Matters

Leading the Free World

The United States is the most powerful nation in the world. It has the world's largest economy and is a leading representative democracy. Immigrants from nearly every other nation of the world have moved here in order to enjoy the freedom the United States Constitution provides.

From Sea to Shining Sea

Guide to Reading

Main Idea

The United States has a great variety of landforms and climates.

Terms to Know

- contiguous
- megalopolis
- coral reef

Reading Strategy

Create a chart like the one below. Fill in details about each of the seven physical regions of the United States. **FCAT** LA.A.1.3.2

Region	Details

The following are the major Sunshine State Standards covered in this section.

SS.B.1.3.6:
Understands ways in which regional systems are interconnected

SS.B.1.3.3:
Knows the social, political, and economic divisions on Earth's surface

SS.B.1.3.1:
Uses various map forms (including thematic maps) and other geographic representations, tools, and technologies to acquire, process, and report geographic information including patterns of land use, connections between places, and patterns and processes of migration and diffusion

NATIONAL GEOGRAPHIC Exploring Our World

Who in the United States gets to see the sunrise first? The people in Maine are the first. As the earth rotates, the sun shines on an extremely varied land. It warms the valleys in the East, shimmers on the lakes in the North, and bakes the deserts in the Southwest. In the far Pacific, the sun greets Hawaii's tropical beaches. Finally, the sun sets beyond Alaska in the North.

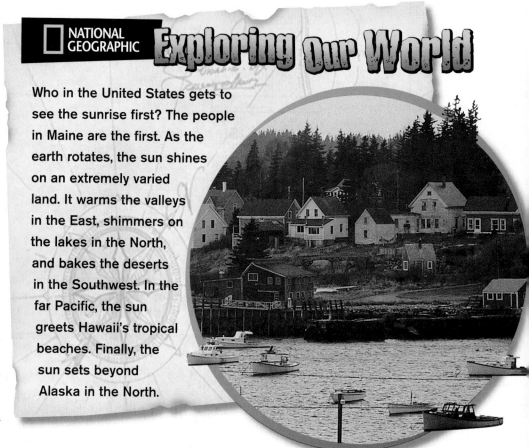

The United States stretches 2,807 miles (4,517 km) across the middle part of North America. The 48 states in this part of the country are **contiguous**, or joined together inside a common boundary. These states touch the Atlantic Ocean, the Gulf of Mexico, and the Pacific Ocean. Two states lie apart from the other 48. Alaska lies in the northwestern portion of North America. Hawaii is in the Pacific Ocean about 2,400 miles (3,862 km) southwest of California. Find Alaska and Hawaii on page RA6 of the **Reference Atlas**.

A Vast, Scenic Land

The United States is the third-largest country in the world. Only Russia and Canada are larger. The contiguous states have five main physical regions: the Coastal Plains, the Appalachian Mountains, the Interior Plains, the Mountains and Plateaus, and the Pacific Coast. Alaska and Hawaii each has its own set of physical landforms.

The Coastal Plains   A broad lowland runs along the eastern and southeastern coasts of the United States. The eastern lowlands are called the **Atlantic Coastal Plain.** The lowlands in the southeast border the Gulf of Mexico and are called the **Gulf Coastal Plain.** Find these coastal plains on the map below. Excellent harbors along the Atlantic Coastal Plain led to the growth of shipping ports. The soil in the northern part of the region tends to be thin and rocky, though.

Boston, New York City, Philadelphia, Baltimore, and Washington, D.C., all lie in the Atlantic Coastal Plain. These cities and their suburbs form an almost continuous line of settlement. Geographers call this kind of huge urban area a **megalopolis.**

The Gulf Coastal Plain is wider than the Atlantic plain. Soils in this region are better than those along the Atlantic coast. Large cities here include Houston and New Orleans, shown on the map on page 149.

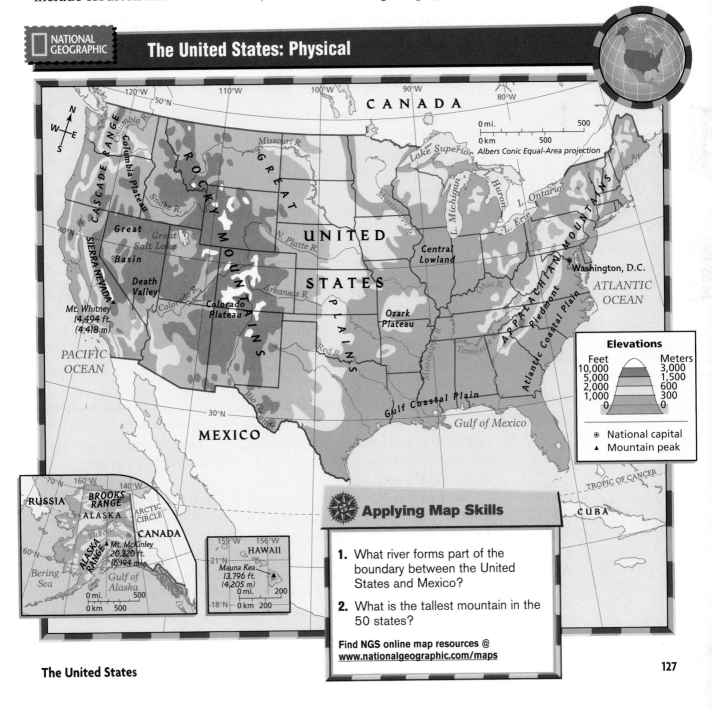

NATIONAL GEOGRAPHIC

The United States: Physical

0 mi. 500
0 km 500
Albers Conic Equal-Area projection

Elevations

Feet	Meters
10,000	3,000
5,000	1,500
2,000	600
1,000	300
0	0

⊛ National capital
▲ Mountain peak

Mt. Whitney 14,494 ft. (4,418 m)

Mt. McKinley 20,320 ft. (6,194 m)

Mauna Kea 13,796 ft. (4,205 m)

Applying Map Skills

1. What river forms part of the boundary between the United States and Mexico?

2. What is the tallest mountain in the 50 states?

Find **NGS** online map resources @ www.nationalgeographic.com/maps

NATIONAL GEOGRAPHIC On Location

City and Country

The Interior Plains of the United States include industrial cities of the North, such as Chicago (above), and the agricultural lands of the Great Plains, like this area in Texas (above right).

Region Which river divides much of the Interior Plains?

The Appalachian Mountains As you move west from the Atlantic Coastal Plain, you run into the hilly—yet very fertile—Piedmont area. These hills eventually turn into the **Appalachian** (A•puh•LAY•chuhn) **Mountains,** which run from eastern Canada to Alabama. The Appalachians are the oldest mountains on the continent. How can you tell? Their rounded peaks show their age. Erosion has worn them down over time. The highest peak, Mount Mitchell in North Carolina, reaches 6,684 feet (2,037 m).

The Interior Plains When you cross the Appalachians heading west, you enter the vast Interior Plains. This region has two parts. East of the **Mississippi River** is the **Central Lowland** area. Here you will find grassy hills, rolling flatlands, and thick forests. The land is fertile, and farms are productive. This area also contains important waterways.

The Great Lakes—the largest group of freshwater lakes in the world—lie in the Central Lowlands. Glaciers formed Lake Superior, Lake Michigan, Lake Huron, Lake Erie, and Lake Ontario in the distant past. The waters of these connected lakes flow into the St. Lawrence River, which empties into the Atlantic Ocean.

West of the Mississippi River stretch the **Great Plains.** The landscape in many places is blanketed with neat fields of grain and grassy pastures and takes on a checkerboard pattern. The Great Plains are about 500 miles (805 km) wide and stretch west to the Rocky Mountains, north into Canada, and south to the Mexican border. The rich grasslands of the Great Plains once provided food for millions of buffalo and the Native Americans who lived there. Today farmers grow grains and ranchers raise cattle on the Great Plains.

Mountains and Plateaus   The **Rocky Mountains** begin in Alaska and run south to Mexico. Along the tops of these mountains is a ridge called the Continental Divide. This ridge separates rivers that flow west—toward the Pacific Ocean—from those that flow east—toward the Mississippi River. Many rivers begin in the high, snowy peaks of the Rockies. The Rio Grande as well as the Missouri, Platte, Arkansas, and Red Rivers flow east. The Colorado, Snake, and Columbia Rivers flow west.

Between the Rockies and the Pacific Coast are plateaus, canyons, and deserts. Plateaus are areas of flat land that rise above the land around them. A canyon is a deep valley with steep sides. The most famous of these is the Grand Canyon in Arizona.

The Pacific Coast   Near the Pacific Coast rise two other mountain ranges. The Cascade Range reaches from Washington State south to California. Volcanoes formed these high peaks—and some of them still erupt. Along California's eastern side runs the Sierra Nevada. The name *Nevada* means "snow covered" in Spanish. Even in a place as far south as California, these high mountains remain covered with snow.

To the west of these Pacific ranges lie fertile valleys. The Willamette Valley in Oregon and the Central Valley in California both produce abundant crops. Many of the fruits and vegetables you eat may come from these valleys.

Alaska   Mountain ranges form a semicircle over the northern, eastern, and southern parts of Alaska. **Mount McKinley**—the tallest mountain in North America—stands 20,320 feet (6,194 m) high in the Alaska Range. The northern part of the state borders on the frigid Arctic Ocean, and you can almost see Russia from Alaska's western shores. Most people in Alaska live along the southern coastal plain or in the central Yukon River valley.

Hawaii   Eight large islands and more than 120 smaller islands make up Hawaii, the island state in the Pacific Ocean. Volcanoes on the ocean floor erupted and formed these islands. Some of the islands have coral reefs, formed by the skeletons of small sea animals. These structures lie just above or submerged just below the surface of the water.

✓Reading Check   What is the Continental Divide?

Mt. McKinley

Fierce winds, high elevation, and location in the high latitudes make McKinley one of the coldest mountains in the world.

Location Why do you think the climate gets colder as elevation increases?

A Variety of Climates

Because the United States is such a large country, you probably expect it to have many different climates. You are right! Most of the country lies squarely in the mid-latitude region—about 23½°N to 60°N latitude. As you recall from Chapter 2, this part of the earth has the greatest variety of climates.

Look at the climate map of the world on page 63. You can see that the northeastern United States has a humid continental climate. Winters here are cold, and summers are hot and long. Winter snows often blanket the region—especially around the Great Lakes. The southeastern states have a humid subtropical climate. Winters are mild, and summers are hot and humid. Nearness to the Gulf of Mexico and the Caribbean Sea often causes violent hurricanes and tornadoes in summer.

The Pacific coast from northern California up to Washington has a marine west coast climate. Temperatures are mild year-round, and Pacific winds bring much rain. Southern California, however, has a Mediterranean climate. People enjoy dry, warm summers and mild, rainy winters.

Much of the western Great Plains has a dry, steppe climate. Why? The Pacific mountain ranges block the humid ocean winds. Therefore, hot, dry air gets trapped in between the Pacific ranges and the Rockies. In the southwest, even less rain falls. This arid region has a hot, desert climate.

Alaska, in the high latitudes, has subarctic and tundra climates. Hawaii and southern Florida have warm, tropical climates with heavy rainfall much of the year.

✓ **Reading Check** Why are dry climates found in the western Great Plains?

FCAT PRACTICE You can prepare for the FCAT-assessed standards by completing the correlated item(s) below.

Section 1 Assessment

Defining Terms

1. **Define** contiguous, megalopolis, coral reef.

Recalling Facts

2. **Place** How does the United States rank in size among all the countries of the world?

3. **History** Which region once supported Native Americans and millions of buffalo?

4. **Place** What is the largest group of freshwater lakes in the world?

Critical Thinking

5. **Understanding Cause and Effect** How were the Hawaiian Islands formed? **FCAT** LA.E.2.2.1

6. **Drawing Conclusions** What challenges do you think result from the distance between Alaska, Hawaii, and the other states?
FCAT LA.A.2.3.1

Graphic Organizer

7. **Organizing Information** Create a diagram like this one to compare the Atlantic and Gulf Coastal Plains. In the separate outer parts of the ovals, write the qualities that make each region different. In the overlapping area, write the characteristics that the two areas share.
FCAT LA.A.1.3.2

Atlantic Coastal Plain ⬭⬭ Gulf Coastal Plain

Applying Social Studies Skills

8. **Analyzing Maps** Look at the physical map on page 127 and the population density map on page 149. At what elevations do the cities with more than 5 million people lie?

An Economic Leader

NATIONAL GEOGRAPHIC Exploring Our World

In the mid-1900s, many Southerners went north to find jobs. By the late 1900s, however, Northerners were flocking to cities in the South. Atlanta, Georgia, is one such growing city. In 1980 Atlanta had a population of 2.2 million. By 2000 it had more than 4 million people. Shown here, Atlanta's mayor Shirley Franklin (center) helps break ground for the city's new aquarium.

The United States has a large, energetic, and growing economy. Fueling all of this economic activity is freedom. As you recall from Chapter 3, the free enterprise system is built on the idea that individual people have the right to run businesses to make a profit. They do so with limited interference from the government. Americans are free to start their own businesses and to keep the profits they earn after paying taxes. They are free to work in whatever jobs they want. Freedom has helped create great economic success.

The World's Economic Leader

The United States is rich in resources and has hardworking, inventive people. As a result, the country has built the world's largest economy—in terms of how much money is made from the sale of its goods and services. In fact, the American economy is larger than the next two largest economies—China's and Japan's—combined.

Farms in the United States produce about one-half of the world's corn and about one-tenth of its wheat. American farmers raise about 20 percent of the world's beef, pork, and lamb. The country exports more food than any other nation. Yet agriculture is only a small part of the American economy. Food makes up about 2 percent of the value of all goods produced in the country.

The United States has rich mineral resources. About one-fifth of the world's coal and copper and one-tenth of the world's petroleum come from the United States. The country also has large amounts of iron ore, zinc, lead, silver, gold, and many other minerals. Mining, though, makes up less than 1 percent of the nation's economy.

American factory workers build cars and airplanes. They make computers and appliances. They process foods and make medicines. Manufacturing accounts for nearly one-fifth of the American economy.

By far, the largest part of the economy is services. A **service industry** is a business that provides services to people instead of producing goods. Banking and finance are services. So is entertainment—and people all over the world buy American movies and CDs. The United States is a leader in tourism, another service industry. Computer-based, online services have also emerged as an important American service industry.

✓ **Reading Check** What is the largest part of the U.S. economy?

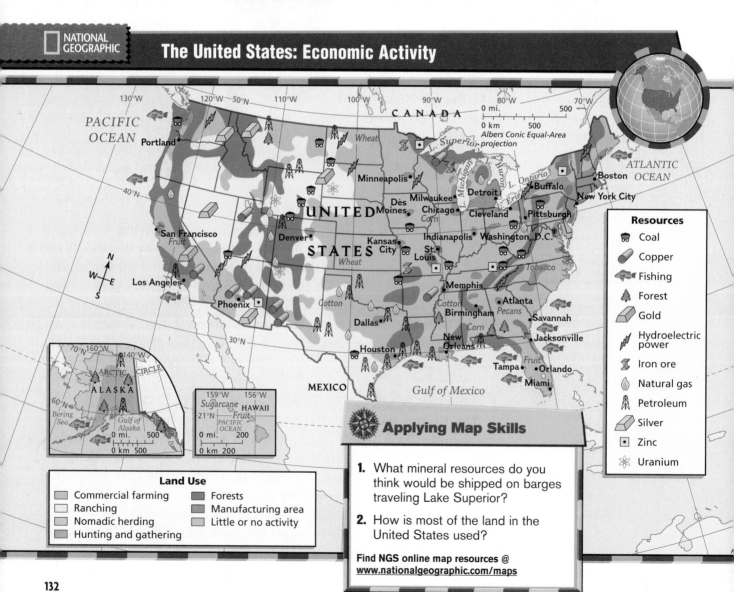

NATIONAL GEOGRAPHIC

The United States: Economic Activity

Resources
- 🪨 Coal
- Copper
- 🐟 Fishing
- 🌲 Forest
- Gold
- ⚡ Hydroelectric power
- Iron ore
- 💧 Natural gas
- Petroleum
- Silver
- ▣ Zinc
- ✳ Uranium

Land Use
- Commercial farming
- Ranching
- Nomadic herding
- Hunting and gathering
- Forests
- Manufacturing area
- Little or no activity

Applying Map Skills

1. What mineral resources do you think would be shipped on barges traveling Lake Superior?

2. How is most of the land in the United States used?

Find NGS online map resources @ www.nationalgeographic.com/maps

America's Economic Regions

Geographers group states together into five economic regions—the Northeast, the South, the Midwest, the Interior West, and the Pacific.

The Northeast Some farmers in central Pennsylvania and western New York grow grains and fruits. Yet as you read in Section 1, the rocky soil and steep hills in this region are a challenge to the farmers. The area has plenty of deep water ports and swiftly moving rivers, though. As a result, manufacturing, trade, and fishing are the heartbeat of this region. In fact, the Northeast was home to the first mills powered by running water and coal. Look at the economic activity map on page 132. As you can see, coal mining takes place in Pennsylvania and West Virginia.

With their deep, natural harbors, Boston, New York City, Philadelphia, and Baltimore are all important ports. Goods are shipped all over the world to and from these ports. These cities are also important centers of banking, insurance, and finance. **New York City** is one of the financial capitals of the world. It is also a world center in the fashion, entertainment, and communications industries. Farther south, the nation's capital—**Washington, D.C.**—employs hundreds of thousands in government and tourism services.

The South With rich soil on most of the Coastal Plains, agriculture flourishes in the Southern states. Because of the region's warm, wet climate, farmers in Louisiana and Arkansas grow rice and sugarcane. Tobacco flourishes in Virginia and the Carolinas. In Florida you can sample the citrus fruits that farmers grow. Peanuts and pecans are found in Georgia. Alabama farmers grow corn and soybeans. You also see cotton growing in several Southern states, including Texas. Texas, in fact, has more farms than any other state. The people of Texas grow cotton, sorghum, and wheat and raise livestock as well.

The traditional image of the South as an agricultural region is changing, however. As you tour the South, you see expanding cities, growing industries, and diverse populations. New manufacturing centers have drawn new businesses and people to the South from the Northeast and elsewhere. Workers make textiles, electrical equipment, and airplane parts. Oil is found in Texas, Louisiana, and Alabama. As a result, these states produce petroleum-based products.

Service industries are important in the South as well. Florida is a major tourist center. People come to enjoy amusement parks in Orlando, the Kennedy Space Center at Cape Canaveral, and the beautiful beaches on both coasts. Millions of people flock to New Orleans each year to taste spicy food and hear lively music. Houston, Dallas, Atlanta, and Miami are just a few of this region's major centers of business and finance.

The Midwest This part of the United States has been called "America's breadbasket." Miles and miles of grain and soybean fields greet you as you travel over flat land and fertile soil. In this farm belt, farmers grow corn, soybeans, oats, and wheat to feed animals and people all over the world. Dairy farms in the upper Midwest produce

Surf's Up!

Fourteen-year-old Shawn Kilgore lives on Florida's Captiva Island, along the Gulf of Mexico. "I really like warm weather," he says. "Who needs snow? My dog Sunny and I couldn't go surfing if we lived in Ohio where my cousins are." Shawn's parents manage a resort for tourists. "My mom and dad are always reminding me that we live in one of the world's richest countries. So my older sister and I volunteer to grocery-shop for people around here who can't do it themselves."

Natural Attractions

Tourists from all over the world visit the United States to see everything from Florida's Everglades (right) to California's surf (above).

Place What other natural and human-made attractions draw tourists to our country?

milk and cheese. However, technology has changed many farms from small, family-owned operations to big businesses. The graph on page 11 of the **Geography Handbook** shows you the decrease in the number of farms over the past few decades.

Many of the region's rivers are **navigable,** or wide and deep enough to allow the passage of ships. As a result, many cities here are major ports—even though they are far from an ocean. Businesses in Cincinnati and Louisville send goods down the Ohio River. St. Louis and Memphis serve as centers of trade along the Mississippi River. Chicago's and Cleveland's industries ship goods through the Great Lakes and St. Lawrence Seaway to ports around the world.

Because of their abundant coal and iron resources, many cities in the Midwest are manufacturing centers. A complex network of railroads also helps the region's many industries. Detroit is called Motown (short for Motor Town) because the country's auto industry started and grew there. Other major industries include steel, heavy machinery, and auto parts.

The Interior West Magnificent landscapes greet visitors to this region. However, this area is short on an important resource—water. With its dry climate, the region discourages farming. Yet grasses thrive in much of the land, and where the land is irrigated, you find agriculture. Large areas are used for raising cattle and sheep. Ranches here may be huge—as large as 4,000 acres (1,619 ha). In the past, cowhands worked the range on horseback. Although they still use horses today, you are just as likely to see them driving a sturdy truck.

Look at the map on page 132. You see rich deposits of minerals and energy resources in the Interior West. The discovery of gold and silver in the mountains and riverbeds drew settlers here more than 150 years ago. Mining still plays an important role in the economy.

Many people work in service industries too. Every year tourists travel to Denver, Salt Lake City, Albuquerque, and Phoenix. They use these cities as starting points for trips to sites such as Yellowstone National Park or the Grand Canyon. Some visit the ruins of ancient Native American settlements, such as those found at Mesa Verde in southwestern Colorado.

The Pacific The Pacific region includes the states on the western coast plus Alaska and Hawaii. The fertile valleys of California, Oregon, and Washington produce large amounts of food. As you learned in Section 1, many of the fruits and vegetables you enjoy every day come from these states. Do you like pineapple? If so, it may have come from Hawaii. This state also grows sugarcane, coffee, and rice because of its tropical climate and rich volcanic soil.

In this region, just like the Atlantic coast, fishing is a major industry. The states of Washington and Oregon draw many people to work in the lumber industry. Mineral resources are important in the Pacific region too. California has gold, lead, and copper. Alaska has vast reserves of oil.

Factory workers in California and Washington make airplanes. The areas around San Francisco and Seattle are world-famous centers of research in computers and software. **Los Angeles** is the world capital of the movie industry. These states in the Pacific region also attract millions of tourists who visit California's redwood forests, Hawaii's tropical beaches, or the stunning glaciers of Alaska.

✓ Reading Check **What goods are manufactured in the Pacific states?**

In the Twenty-First Century

The American economy, although strong, faces challenges in the twenty-first century. One of these challenges is how to clean up pollution and trash. Americans burn **fossil fuels**—coal, oil, and natural gas—to power their factories and run their cars. Burning these fuels pollutes the air, endangering all who breathe it. The pollution also mixes with water vapor in the air to make **acid rain,** or rain containing high amounts of chemical pollutants. Acid rain damages trees and harms rivers and lakes.

Technology

A worker inspects computer components. Along with agriculture, America's economy is strong in technology, science, education, and medicine.

Place What areas in the United States are important software centers?

NATIONAL GEOGRAPHIC **On Location**

The fast-paced American way of life creates another problem. People generate huge amounts of trash. **Landfills,** the areas where trash companies dump the waste they collect, grow higher and higher each year. Many communities now promote **recycling,** or reusing materials instead of throwing them out. Recycling cuts down on the amount of trash.

New Technology   The ability to develop new technology has been a major source of strength for the American economy. Researchers work constantly to find new products to make people's lives easier and healthier. Quality schools that produce educated and creative people have helped the country become a world leader in satellites, computers, medicine, and many other fields. You will need to learn and use new technologies to be productive and successful in your future jobs.

World Trade   The United States leads the world in the value of all its imports and exports. Millions of Americans depend on trade for their jobs. American leaders have worked hard to promote free trade. **Free trade** means taking down trade barriers such as tariffs and quotas so that goods flow freely among countries. In 1993 the United States joined Mexico and Canada in the North American Free Trade Agreement (NAFTA). This agreement promised to remove all barriers to trade among these countries.

✓ **Reading Check** How do factories and cars harm the environment in the United States?

FCAT PRACTICE You can prepare for the FCAT-assessed standards by completing the correlated item(s) below.

Section 2 Assessment

Defining Terms

1. **Define** free enterprise system, service industry, navigable, fossil fuel, acid rain, landfill, recycling, free trade.

Recalling Facts

2. **Economics** Why is the Midwest called "America's breadbasket"?

3. **History** The discovery of which resources first brought settlers to the Interior West?

4. **Economics** What was the goal of NAFTA?

Critical Thinking

5. **Analyzing Information** Describe two characteristics of the United States that have made it a world economic leader.

6. **Understanding Cause and Effect** What reasons can you give for the economic changes taking place in the South?

FCAT LA.A.2.3.1

Graphic Organizer

7. **Organizing Information** Draw a diagram like this one. Name one economic region of the United States in the center oval. In the outer ovals write examples for each subtopic.

FCAT LA.A.1.3.2

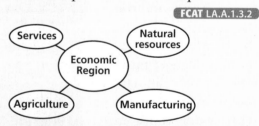

Applying Social Studies Skills

8. **Analyzing Maps** Study the economic activity map on page 132 and the physical map on page 127. What type of resources are found in or near the Rocky Mountains?

TIME PERSPECTIVES

Protecting America's Freedoms from Terror

Keeping Liberty Safe

Compiled and adapted from TIME.

Firefighters douse the flames at Ground Zero.

The Day the Towers Fell

Evaluating
Media
LA.A.2.3.6

September 11, 2001, is a day no one will forget. At 8:46 A.M., a hijacked jumbo jet slammed into the north tower of the World Trade Center in New York City. A second hijacked plane plowed into the south tower at 9:03 A.M. About a half hour later, the south tower collapsed. Outside Washington, D.C., at 9:43 A.M., a third hijacked plane crashed into the Pentagon, the headquarters of the U.S. military. About 30 minutes later, a fourth jumbo jet crashed onto a field in Shanksville, Pennsylvania. Its target, which it never reached, may have been the White House, 124 miles away. Back in New York, the World Trade Center's north tower collapsed. It was 10:28 A.M. In less than two hours, 19 terrorists had murdered 2,976 innocent people.

America Reacts

The attacks stunned the world. They especially jarred the 4,000 students at the U.S. Military Academy at West Point, New York. These students realized they would soon be defending the nation against an entirely new kind of enemy.

"How do you fight this war and still stay true to the values of the United States?" a West Point professor asked her students shortly after the attack. She brought out a poster. It showed two curved lines facing each other. Outside one of the lines was the word *Liberty*. Outside the other line was the word *Security*. "What is the proper balance?" she asked. Americans have been wrestling with that question ever since that day—September 11, 2001.

Balancing Freedom and Safety

Freedom First

In the United States, the government can't take away people's right to...

- be free from unreasonable searches
- worship as they wish
- speak freely
- print and read what they want
- be free from cruel punishments
- protest government actions
- have fair, speedy, and public trials
- keep their personal affairs private

Compromises

To increase their safety, most Americans have seemed willing to accept...

- airport baggage searches
- metal detectors in schools
- court-okayed wiretaps
- concrete barriers in front of government buildings
- state bans on driving without a license
- police searches of people suspected of carrying weapons

Security First

In a country that puts security before freedom, the government might...

- search anyone without warning
- keep lists of members of a particular religion
- ban criticism of the government
- torture suspects
- hold trials in secret
- be free to access anyone's medical and financial records
- keep track of what people download to their computers
- close down newspapers it does not like

Adults without proper I.D.s can't fly.

Blocked: the road to the Idaho Statehouse

National Guardsmen patrol the streets.

Airlines and Patriots

"September 11," or "**9/11,**" as the terrible event is called, made people everywhere more aware of the need for security. Governments reacted to those concerns in different ways. Some countries, like Japan, planned to require their citizens to carry electronic identification cards.

The United States tackled the problem in a different way. Shortly after 9/11, the United States Congress created new tools with which to combat terrorism. One of those tools was a new government agency, the Transportation Security Administration (TSA). The TSA's job is to find ways to make the nation's airlines and other transportation systems, such as railroads and trucking, safer.

The USA **Patriot Act** is another new weapon against terrorism. The law contains strong measures to prevent terrorism, detect it, and take legal action against it.

Most Americans welcomed the TSA and the Patriot Act. But many criticized them too. They worried that some freedoms might be taken away.

No-Fly Lists

The TSA created "no-fly" lists, which contained the names of people suspected of having links to terrorists. This means that airlines are not allowed to let anyone on the lists board an airplane. But many law-abiding Americans have been caught in TSA's web. One man complained that he was stopped every time he tried to fly. He had to prove each time that he was who he was— a 71-year-old, gray-haired, American-born English teacher.

The Patriot Act contained other measures that critics didn't like. One provision made it fairly easy for federal agents to search a citizen's library, business, and medical records.

This provision bothered Lynn Bradley, who works for an organization that represents librarians. She did not like the fact that the government could access private records. "People ask [me], 'Why are you interested in privacy when thousands of people were killed and there are soldiers at risk?'" she said. "We have in the United States a Constitution, a Bill of Rights, and all sorts of laws protecting privacy. One of the reasons we're fighting is to protect **rights** that [the terrorists] attacked us for in the first place."

EXPLORING THE ISSUE

1. **Analyzing Information** Why did the TSA create no-fly lists? FCAT LA.A.2.3.1

2. **Interpreting Points of View** Do you agree with Lynn Bradley that the Patriot Act might threaten individual rights? Why or why not? FCAT LA.A.2.3.2

Protecting the Homeland

On November 25, 2002, President George W. Bush signed a bill that gave birth to the U.S. government's third-largest department—the **Department of Homeland Security.** At its birth, the new department employed 170,000 people who worked for 22 different agencies. Among those agencies are the Coast Guard, the Border Patrol, the Secret Service, and the Customs Service. The president chose Tom Ridge, a former U.S. Congressman and governor of Pennsylvania, to head the department.

Department Responsibilities

The new department has four basic functions:

1. It analyzes information about terrorism provided by the Federal Bureau of Investigation (FBI) and the Central Intelligence Agency (CIA). It also helps state and local governments keep power plants and other possible homeland targets safe from terrorists.

2. It works to keep travelers safe and to protect airports, borders, and seaports.

3. It deals with natural and human-made disasters, ranging from hurricanes to terrorist attacks.

4. It oversees the development of new ways to detect weapons. It is also responsible for creating new medicines to protect Americans against smallpox and other biological agents.

The FBI and the CIA are not part of the new department. Secretary Ridge prefers it this way. "The CIA and the

▲ **At the U.S.–Canadian border, the U.S. Border Patrol has been working overtime since 9/11.**

FBI provide reports and analysis to this department," he said. "We're a customer."

Americans cherish their right to be left alone. Can a government department dedicated to keeping citizens safe respect that right?

Secretary Ridge certainly thinks so. "Everyone from the president on down understands that protecting certain liberties and freedoms is at the very heart of who we are," he said. "[We intend] to make sure that we do everything we can within the law, within the Constitution, to improve our own security. It's a line that we have to walk carefully. There's a balance there, and I'm convinced it can be done."

EXPLORING THE ISSUE

1. Making Inferences Why should the Department of Homeland Security be involved with scientific research?
FCAT LA.A.1.3.2

2. Drawing Conclusions What are some of the reasons people might be concerned about the new department's powers?
FCAT LA.A.2.3.1

A Memorial for Heroes

Evaluating
Media
LA.A.2.3.6

Ancient people used to tell the story of the phoenix (FEE-nix). The phoenix was a sacred bird. When it reached the end of its life, it would burn itself up. Then it would rise from the ashes to begin its life again.

It took hundreds of workers eight months to haul away the smoldering remains of the World Trade Center. Then architects went to work. They drew up plans for a 16-acre city that would rise from the ashes like the phoenix.

A woman who lost her husband on 9/11 was happy to see the plans. "The greatest tribute to the people who died there," she said, "is to see life and rebirth."

A Long Process

It will take at least ten years to see exactly what will rise on the site. City planners, architects, political leaders, and builders will first have to agree on the size and shape of the buildings.

The memorial on the World Trade Center site has been chosen. It consists of two reflecting pools and a large grove of trees. This memorial, named "Reflecting Absence," occupies the towers' two "footprints." The names of all the 9/11 victims will be arranged around the pools to look like a ribbon of names.

The highest structure on the site will be the Freedom Tower. This twisting structure, exactly 1,776 feet (541 m) high, will be the first building to go up. Its height is a reminder of 1776, the year Americans declared their independence from Great Britain.

The Freedom Tower (left), 1,776 feet (541 m) high, will be the first building constructed on the site.

TORSTEN SEDEL

EXPLORING THE ISSUE

1. **Summarizing the Main Idea** Write a new title for this article. Tell your classmates why you think your title is a good one.

   FCAT LA.A.2.3.1

2. **Problem Solving** What sort of memorial would you like to see on the site?

   FCAT LA.B.1.3.2

Defense Against Terror: What Can One Person Do?

Terrorism forces us to make a choice," says Tom Ridge, secretary of the Department of Homeland Security. "We can be afraid. Or we can be ready."

It is very, very unlikely that terrorists will attack your neighborhood. But it can never hurt to prepare for the unexpected.

JOEL MEYEROWITZ

▲ **This New York firefighter survived 9/11. More than 300 did not.**

How can you do that? Prepare the same way you would if you were getting ready for a natural disaster like a hurricane or flood. Put together a kit of needed supplies: medicines, flashlights, batteries, a portable radio, and enough canned food and water to last three days. Add dense cotton cloth to your kit. Held over your mouth and nose, the cloth would filter out tiny airborne materials that could get into your lungs. Decide how family members will keep in touch with each other during a

disaster. Get together with neighbors to figure out how you can help one another during an emergency.

Special Preparations

Terrorists use fear and misunderstanding to reach their goals. Make *understanding* one of your goals! Learn why some groups turn to terrorism. You'll find out that, in most cases, the terrorists cause as much fear and frustration in their own countries as they try to cause in the rest of the world. Promote communication and understanding by becoming pen pals with students in other regions.

As Secretary Ridge suggests, the mere fear of terrorism can leave scars. After 9/11, a West Point cadet knew what she would do to prevent that kind of fear. She recalled the Battle of Britain in 1940, when the Germans bombed English cities. The British "refused to let [the bombing] shut them down," she said. In the end, the British rallied together and won the battle. In the same way, we can prevent terrorists from shutting us down. ■

EXPLORING THE ISSUE

1. **Problem Solving** What suggestions would you give Secretary Ridge to help in the fight against terrorism?
   FCAT LA.B.1.3.2

2. **Making Inferences** What does the West Point cadet believe we should do to protect ourselves against the fear of terrorism? **FCAT** LA.A.1.3.2

REVIEW AND ASSESS

UNDERSTANDING THE ISSUE

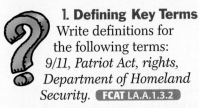

1. Defining Key Terms
Write definitions for the following terms: *9/11, Patriot Act, rights, Department of Homeland Security.* **FCAT LA.A.1.3.2**

2. Writing to Inform In a brief essay, explain how 9/11 changed the nation. Use the words *airport, search, freedom,* and *security* in your essay. **FCAT LA.B.1.3.2**

3. Writing to Persuade
A judge once said, "Your right to swing your arm stops at my nose." How might that statement apply to luggage searches at airports? Do you agree with the statement? Explain your answers in a short essay. **FCAT LA.B.1.3.2**

INTERNET RESEARCH ACTIVITIES

4. With your teacher's help, navigate to **www.ready.gov**. Explore one of the three main items on the page. Write a short essay that explains what you learned about preparing for a terrorist attack. **FCAT LA.B.1.3.2**

5. Navigate to **www.lifeandliberty.gov**, where the United States Department of Justice defends the Patriot Act. Jot down two arguments for the law. Then navigate to **www.epic.org/privacy/terrorism/usapatriot**. EPIC is a group that has some concerns about the law. Jot down two of EPIC's concerns. Explain to your classmates how these arguments shaped your view of the law. **FCAT LA.A.2.3.5**

BEYOND THE CLASSROOM

6. In your local library, research the impact of terrorism on nations such as Sri Lanka and Israel. Why is terrorism more common in those nations than in the

United States? Summarize your conclusions and share them with your classmates. **FCAT LA.A.2.3.1**

7. Working in groups, create posters that explain how to prepare for any disaster, including a terrorist attack. Display your posters where other students in your school can see them.

PHOTODISC

▲ **The American flag is a symbol of freedom.**

Ground Zero: A Proposal for Renewal

This plan for rebuilding Ground Zero is sure to change as time goes by.

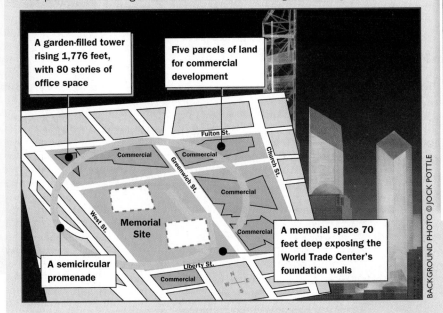

A garden-filled tower rising 1,776 feet, with 80 stories of office space

Five parcels of land for commercial development

A memorial space 70 feet deep exposing the World Trade Center's foundation walls

A semicircular promenade

Memorial Site

BACKGROUND PHOTO © JOCK POTTLE

BUILDING MAP READING SKILLS

1. Explaining Two pools with cascading waterfalls will be placed in the two towers' "footprints." The architect named this memorial "Reflecting Absence." What does this mean to you?

2. Making Generalizations How do you think you would feel if you visited the site and saw the exposed foundation wall? **FCAT LA.A.1.3.2**

FOR UPDATES ON WORLD ISSUES GO TO www.timeclassroom.com/glencoe

Social Studies Skill

FCAT PRACTICE Answering the correlated questions below will help you prepare for the **FCAT Mathematics** test.

Mental Mapping

Think about how you get from place to place each day. In your mind you have a picture—or **mental map**—of your route. If necessary, you could probably create sketch maps like the one below of many familiar places.

Learning the Skill

To develop your mental mapping skills, follow these steps.

- When a country or city name is mentioned, find it on a map to get an idea of where it is and what is near it.
- Create a sketch map of it and include a compass rose to determine the cardinal directions.
- As you read or hear information about the place, try to picture where on your sketch you would fill in this information.
- Compare your sketch to an actual map of the place. Change your sketch if you need to, thus changing your mental map.

Practicing the Skill

Study the sketch map at the right. Picture yourself standing *in* the map, then answer the following questions.

1. If you were facing north, looking at the Chicago Cultural Center, what route would you take to reach the Chicago Harbor? **FCAT MA.B.1.3.4**

2. You are at the Sears Tower, one of the tallest buildings in the world. About how many miles would you have to walk to get to Medinah Temple? **FCAT MA.B.1.3.4**

3. If you met your friend at the cultural center, would it be too far to walk to the Art Institute? Should you take a taxi? Explain. **FCAT MA.B.1.3.4**

Applying the Skill

Think about your own neighborhood. Create a sketch map of it from your mental map. Which neighborhood streets or roads did you include? What are the three most important features on your map?

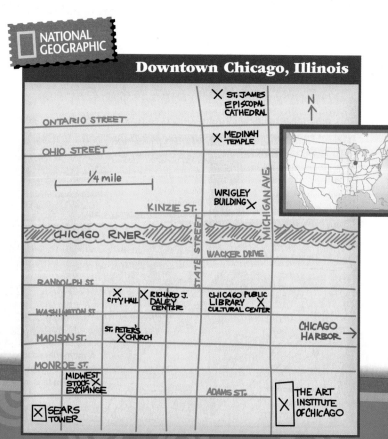

NATIONAL GEOGRAPHIC

Downtown Chicago, Illinois

Guide to Reading

Main Idea

The United States is a land of many cultures.

Terms to Know

- colony
- representative democracy
- federal republic
- secede
- immigrant
- rural
- urban
- suburb

Reading Strategy

Create a diagram like this one. In each outer oval, write one fact about American society as it relates to the topic given.

FCAT LA.A.1.3.2

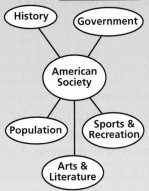

The following are the major Sunshine State Standards covered in this section.

SS.A.3.3.1:
Understands ways in which cultural characteristics have been transmitted from one society to another (e.g., through art, architecture, language, other artifacts, traditions, beliefs, values, and behaviors)

SS.B.2.3.1:
Understands the patterns and processes of migration and diffusion throughout the world

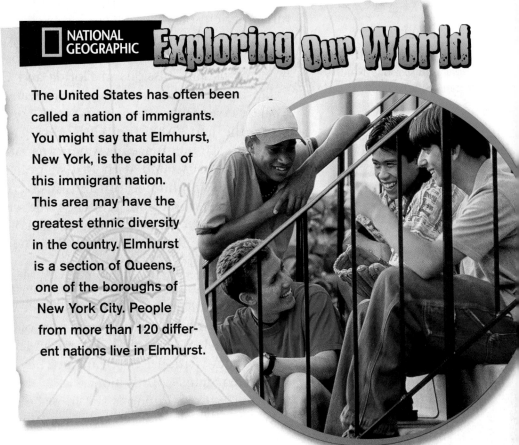

NATIONAL GEOGRAPHIC — Exploring Our World

The United States has often been called a nation of immigrants. You might say that Elmhurst, New York, is the capital of this immigrant nation. This area may have the greatest ethnic diversity in the country. Elmhurst is a section of Queens, one of the boroughs of New York City. People from more than 120 different nations live in Elmhurst.

The United States is a young country compared to many others. It became an independent nation a little more than 225 years ago. American history starts much earlier than this, however.

A Rich History

Experts have long believed that the first people to settle in the Americas came from Asia about 15,000 years ago. At that time, the earth's climate was much colder than it is now. Huge sheets of ice covered much of the Northern Hemisphere. As a result, sea levels were lower, and a land bridge connected Asia and Alaska. Herd animals crossed this bridge—and the people who hunted them followed.

Native Americans The people who crossed the land bridge from Asia slowly fanned out over the Americas. Their descendants today are called Native Americans. Over time, they developed different ways of life using local resources. In the Northeast, the people hunted deer and fished. In the fertile lands of the Southeast and Mississippi Valley, they grew corn and other crops. On the dry, treeless Great Plains, the Native

Americans hunted buffalo, which provided them with food, clothing, and shelter. In the dry Southwest, the people irrigated the land to grow corn and beans. In the Northwest, they fished.

Explorers and Colonists

Around A.D. 1500, Europeans began to explore the Americas. The raw materials they saw—forests, animal furs, and rich soils—soon led them to set up **colonies.** These are overseas settlements tied to a parent country. The French built trading posts around the Great Lakes and interior river valleys. The Spanish built towns and missions in Florida and Georgia and from Texas to California. British and northern European colonists settled along the Atlantic coast from Massachusetts to Georgia.

By the mid-1700s, the people living in the British colonies had started to see themselves as Americans rather than as British citizens. They were frustrated with British policies that disregarded their rights. In 1775, thirteen of the British colonies rebelled. On July 4, 1776, they declared independence and created the United States of America. For the next five long years, colonial troops battled British soldiers in the American Revolution. With the help of France and Spain, the Americans won the war.

The U.S. Constitution

The 13 former British colonies became the first 13 states. Each quickly wrote a state constitution, or plan of government. Developing a *national* plan of government proved harder, however. In 1787 a group of American leaders met in Philadelphia to create a new national government. They wrote the document called the United States Constitution.

The U.S. Constitution is still in place after more than 200 years. It is the basis for all our laws. It also explains how our national or central government is set up and works. Early American leaders' goal was to create a government strong enough to provide for the common good. They also wanted a government with limited powers so that people's rights would be protected from government interference. Because the U.S. Constitution has worked so well in achieving both goals, it has been used as a model by many other countries.

The U.S. Constitution went into effect in 1789, but it has grown and changed over the years. Through a process called amending, Americans have a peaceful way to change the basic laws of their government. A constitutional amendment is a change or addition to the Constitution. The first ten amendments, passed in 1791, are called the Bill of Rights. They list specific freedoms guaranteed to individual Americans, such as freedoms of speech and religion.

A Federal Republic

Our government is based on the principle of democracy, or rule by the people. There are many different types of democracies. We have a **representative democracy,** in which voters choose leaders who make and enforce the laws.

When the Constitution was approved in 1788, each state kept its own government. Voters of each state also chose people to serve in the national government. This system makes the United States a

San Xavier del Bac

Is this Catholic church in Spain? In Mexico? No, this Spanish-style church, called San Xavier del Bac, stands near Tucson, Arizona. Settlers built the church in 1797, when the area was part of Spain's colonial empire. In fact, many Spanish settlements in the American Southwest were founded in the 1500s, long before the English Pilgrims sailed to the Americas on the *Mayflower.*

federal republic. This is a form of government in which power is divided between the federal, or national, government and the state governments. A president serves as the leader of the nation. The Constitution also divided the national government into three branches so that no person or group could gain too much power. The chart on page 148 shows the three branches of the national government.

A Period of Growth From 1800 to 1900, the United States experienced tremendous growth. It expanded from the 13 states along the Atlantic coast to include 45 states that reached to the Pacific Ocean. The population boomed as millions of people settled here from other lands. Surveyors were hired to establish plot boundaries for land sales. In what is today the Midwest, settlers purchased rectangular plots, cleared forests, and grew corn. In the South, huge cotton plantations arose. When gold was discovered in California, miners surged past the Rocky Mountains. In their rush to grab land, settlers often fought with Native Americans who were being pushed out of the way.

The Industrial Revolution, which began in Great Britain, spread to the United States. Water-powered factories sprang up along fast-moving rivers. Roads and canals were built to help farmers move their products to ports. The emergence of steamboats allowed upstream travel.

In the mid-1800s, the nation experienced a crisis. The South had built its economy on slavery. Hundreds of thousands of enslaved Africans had been forced to work on Southern plantations. Over time, the issues of slavery and states' rights divided the country. In 1861 several Southern states **seceded,** or withdrew from the national government. For four years, the North and the South fought the bitter Civil War. In the end, the Southern states were brought back into the Union, and slavery was abolished.

The Civil War did more than end slavery. It also launched the country into a period of great economic and technological growth.

NATIONAL GEOGRAPHIC On Location

The Founders

With very few exceptions, the world knew only monarchies and absolute rulers when courageous leaders such as Thomas Jefferson (left), George Washington (center), and James Madison (right) risked their lives and fortunes to spearhead the drive for an independent United States. Jefferson was the chief author of the Declaration of Independence, which the Continental Congress formally issued on July 4, 1776. Washington led the new nation's army in the Revolution, chaired the Constitutional Convention, and became the first president under the U.S. Constitution. Madison is considered the master builder of the Constitution. He later served as president.

Beliefs Why do you think that the Founders were willing to risk their lives and fortunes to establish the United States?

Branches of the United States Government

Analyzing the Diagram

The United States government has three main branches.

Government Which branch makes the laws?

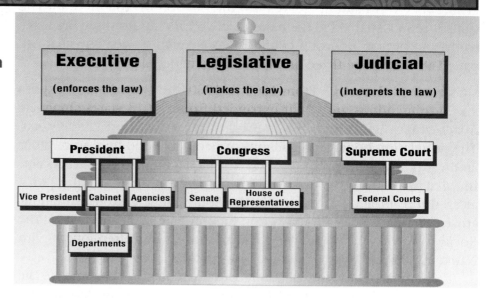

Executive	Legislative	Judicial
(enforces the law)	(makes the law)	(interprets the law)
President	Congress	Supreme Court
Vice President, Cabinet, Agencies	Senate, House of Representatives	Federal Courts
Departments		

Railroads crisscrossed the land, and large factories were built, especially in the Northeast and Midwest. This economic expansion attracted another great wave of **immigrants,** or people who move to a new country to make a permanent home.

A World Leader During the early 1900s, the United States became one of the leading economies in the world. Automobiles rolled off assembly lines and electricity became common. Other technologies, such as the telephone and the radio, entered daily life.

The world plunged into two World Wars in the first half of the twentieth century. The United States took part in these wars. Our country's leaders urged the world's people to fight for freedom against dangerous dictators. American factories produced tanks and airplanes, while American soldiers helped win the wars.

After World War II, the United States enjoyed great influence around the world. American companies shipped their products to all continents. American leaders pushed for democracy and free enterprise in other countries. American culture spread around the globe.

At home, however, tensions existed among groups within American society. Many of the Americans who had fought in the two World Wars or had taken care of the home front were women, African Americans, Hispanic Americans, and Native Americans. After World War II, these groups became more active in seeking equal rights. Many people, including such leaders as Martin Luther King, Jr., developed methods that led to civil change. The poems on page 152 describe two views of Americans struggling to be accepted.

Security Americans have normally felt safe in their own country. After terrorists attacked New York City and Washington, D.C., on September 11, 2001, this feeling of security was tested, however.

President Bush responded by signing the Homeland Security Act into law. This act established a new cabinet department—the Department of Homeland Security—to coordinate government agencies charged with protecting the nation from terrorist attacks.

☑ Reading Check How did a strong economy help spread American culture?

One Out of Many

About 292 million people live in the United States, making it the third most populous country after China and India. Compared with people in most other countries, Americans enjoy a high standard of living. Americans, on the average, can expect to live about 77 years. Medical advances have helped people to live longer than earlier generations.

Almost three-fourths of the people in our country descended from European ethnic groups. African Americans form about 12 percent of the population. Hispanics, who trace their heritages to the countries of Latin America and Spain, are the fastest-growing ethnic group. Today many immigrants to the United States come from China, India, other

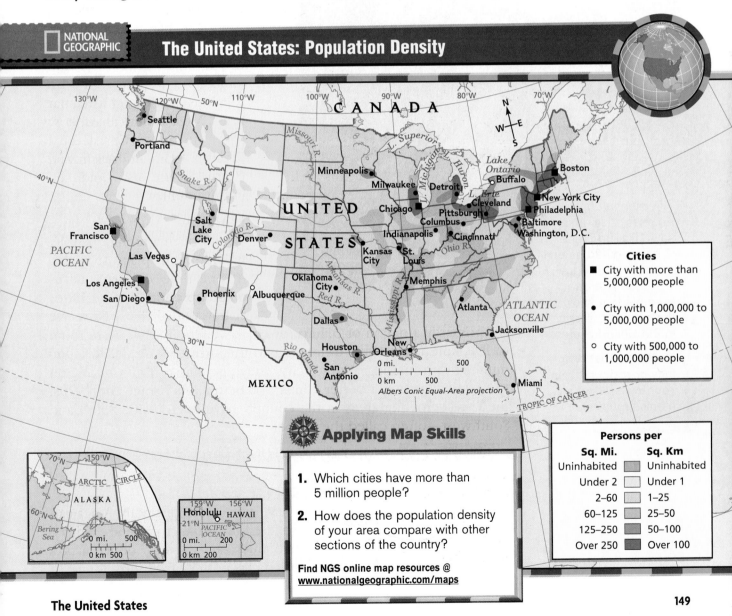

NATIONAL GEOGRAPHIC

The United States: Population Density

Cities
- ■ City with more than 5,000,000 people
- ● City with 1,000,000 to 5,000,000 people
- ○ City with 500,000 to 1,000,000 people

0 mi. 500
0 km 500
Albers Conic Equal-Area projection

⊕ Applying Map Skills

1. Which cities have more than 5 million people?

2. How does the population density of your area compare with other sections of the country?

Find NGS online map resources @ www.nationalgeographic.com/maps

Persons per	
Sq. Mi.	**Sq. Km**
Uninhabited	Uninhabited
Under 2	Under 1
2–60	1–25
60–125	25–50
125–250	50–100
Over 250	Over 100

The United States

POLLING PLACE

投票站 CASILLA ELECTORAL
投票所 LUGAR NG BOTOHAN
투표소 PHÒNG PHIẾU

Language Diversity

This sign in Los Angeles, California, says "Polling Place" in seven different languages. Multilingual signs are just one example that show the cultural diversity in the United States.

Culture What buildings or restaurants in your town reflect an ethnic group?

Asian countries, and the Pacific Islands. The smallest ethnic group—Native American—has lived in the country the longest. A graph on page 121 shows the country's different ethnic groups.

Language and Religion The main language of the United States is English, but you can hear many languages spoken here. Spanish is commonly heard throughout Florida, Texas, and California. In California you can also read signs in Chinese and Korean.

Religion has always been an important influence on American life. About 80 percent of Americans consider themselves religious, and almost 50 percent attend a religious service on a regular basis. Most Americans follow some form of Christianity. Judaism, Islam, Buddhism, and Hinduism are also practiced in our country.

Mobility Americans have always been a mobile people, moving from place to place. At one time, our nation was made up entirely of **rural,** or countryside, areas. Now we are primarily a nation of **urban,** or city, dwellers. To find more room to live, Americans move from cities to the **suburbs,** or smaller communities surrounding a larger city. They also move from one region to another to seek a better climate or better jobs. Since the 1970s, the fastest-growing areas in the country have been in the South and Southwest—often called the Sunbelt.

✓ Reading Check **Which ethnic group is the fastest growing?**

American Culture

American artists and writers have developed distinctly American styles. The earliest American artists used materials from their environments to create works of art. Native Americans carved wooden masks and totems or made beautiful designs on pottery from clay found in their areas. Later artists were attracted to the beauty of the landscape. Winslow Homer painted the stormy waters of the North Atlantic. Georgia O'Keeffe painted the colorful deserts of the Southwest. Thomas Eakins and John Sloan often painted the gritty side of city life.

Two themes are common to American literature. One theme focuses on the rich diversity of the people in the United States. The poetry of Langston Hughes and the novels of Toni Morrison portray the triumphs and sorrows of African Americans. The novels of Amy Tan examine the lives of Chinese Americans. Oscar Hijuelos and Sandra Cisneros write about the country's Hispanics.

A second theme focuses on the landscape and history of particular regions. Mark Twain's books tell about life along the Mississippi River in the mid-1800s. Nathaniel Hawthorne wrote about the people of New England. Willa Cather and Laura Ingalls Wilder portrayed the struggles people faced in settling the Great Plains. William Faulkner wrote stories about life in the South.

Sports and Recreation Many Americans spend their leisure time at home, reading books or using a computer. Many also pursue active lives outdoors. They may bike, ski, shoot baskets, or kick soccer balls. Spectator sports such as baseball and football draw large crowds. Millions each year travel to national parks, or areas set aside to protect wilderness and wildlife.

Social Studies Online

Web Activity Visit *The World and Its People* Web site at twip.glencoe.com and click on **Chapter 4— Student Web Activities** to learn more about the national park system in the United States.

✓ Reading Check What are two common themes in American literature?

FCAT PRACTICE You can prepare for the FCAT-assessed standards by completing the correlated item(s) below.

Section 3 Assessment

Defining Terms

1. Define colony, representative democracy, federal republic, secede, immigrant, rural, urban, suburb.

Recalling Facts

2. History What route do experts think the first Americans took to reach North America?

3. Government What document explains the form of government used in the United States?

4. Culture What theme do the works of Langston Hughes and Toni Morrison share?

Critical Thinking

5. Analyzing Information After World War II, what tensions existed at home?

6. Drawing Conclusions How do climate and culture influence the popularity of sports in your area? **FCAT LA.A.2.3.1**

Graphic Organizer

7. Organizing Information Draw a diagram like the one below. At the tops of the three arrows, list three reasons that Americans today are moving more frequently than ever.

FCAT LA.A.1.3.2

Americans are on the move.

Applying Social Studies Skills

8. Analyzing Maps According to the population density map on page 149, what are the two largest cities in the Pacific Northwest?

Making Connections

Americans All

FCAT PRACTICE Answering the correlated questions below will help you prepare for the **FCAT Reading** test.

Native Americans and African Americans endured many years of injustice. Even so, the pride and determination of these Americans remained strong. Read the poems by Native American poet Simon J. Ortiz and African American poet Langston Hughes to see how they express these feelings.

▲ Picking cotton near Dallas, Texas, 1907

Survival This Way
by Simon J. Ortiz (1941–)

Survival, I know how this way.
This way, I know.
It rains.
Mountains and canyons and plants
grow.
We travelled this way,
gauged our distance by stories
and loved our children.
We taught them
to love their births.
We told ourselves over and over
again, "We shall survive
this way."

"Survival This Way" by Simon J. Ortiz. Reprinted by permission of the author.

I, Too
by Langston Hughes (1902–1967)

I, too, sing America.

I am the darker brother.
They send me to eat in the kitchen
When company comes,
But I laugh,
And eat well,
And grow strong.

Tomorrow,
I'll be at the table
When company comes.
Nobody'll dare
Say to me,
"Eat in the kitchen,"
Then.

Besides,
They'll see how beautiful I am
And be ashamed—

I, too, am America.

"I, Too" from *Collected Poems* by Langston Hughes. Copyright © 1994 by the Estate of Langston Hughes. Reprinted by permission of Alfred A. Knopf, a Division of Random House, Inc.

▲ Native Americans on the Great Plains, 1891

Making the Connection

1. How does the poem "Survival This Way" tell how Native Americans feel about their children? **FCAT** LA.A.2.3.2

2. What does Langston Hughes mean by the phrase "I, too, sing America"? **FCAT** LA.A.2.3.2

3. **Making Comparisons** In what way do both poems convey a message of hope? **FCAT** LA.A.2.3.1

Reading Review

Section 1 | From Sea to Shining Sea

Terms to Know

contiguous
megalopolis
coral reef

Main Idea

The United States has a great variety of landforms and climates.

✓ **Region** The United States has five main physical regions: the Coastal Plains, the Appalachian Mountains, the Interior Plains, the Mountains and Plateaus region, and the Pacific Coast. Alaska and Hawaii make up two additional regions.

✓ **History** Forty-eight of the United States are contiguous, joined together inside a common boundary between the Atlantic and Pacific Oceans.

✓ **Economics** The Central Lowlands area is well suited to agriculture, as are western coastal valleys.

✓ **Place** The high Rocky Mountains have a ridge called the Continental Divide, which separates rivers that flow east from rivers that flow west.

Section 2 | An Economic Leader

Terms to Know

free enterprise system
service industry
navigable
fossil fuel
acid rain
landfill
recycling
free trade

Main Idea

The United States economy runs on abundant resources and the hard work of Americans.

✓ **Economics** Because of many natural resources and an inventive people, the United States has the world's most productive economy.

✓ **Economics** Service industries contribute the most to the American economy, followed by manufacturing, agriculture, and mining.

✓ **Economics** The United States has five economic regions—the Northeast, the South, the Midwest, the Interior West, and the Pacific.

✓ **Economics** Creativity and hard work are needed to continue to develop new technologies and help the American economy grow.

Section 3 | The Americans

Terms to Know

colony
representative democracy
federal republic
secede
immigrant
rural
urban
suburb

Main Idea

The United States is a land of many cultures.

✓ **Culture** The American people are immigrants or the descendants of immigrants who have come from all over the world.

✓ **Government** The United States is a republic. A republic is a type of representative democracy.

✓ **Culture** Ethnic groups in America are descendants of five main peoples: Europeans, Africans, Hispanics, Asians and Pacific Islanders, and Native Americans.

✓ **Culture** American arts celebrate the country's ethnic and regional diversity.

The United States

Chapter 4

Assessment and Activities

FCAT PRACTICE You can prepare for the FCAT-assessed standards by completing the correlated item(s) below.

Using Key Terms

Match the terms in Part A with their definitions in Part B.

A.

1. contiguous
2. megalopolis
3. free enterprise system
4. fossil fuel
5. suburb
6. colony
7. recycling
8. free trade
9. secede
10. representative democracy

B.

a. oil, natural gas, and coal
b. smaller community surrounding a city
c. areas joined inside a common boundary
d. reusing materials
e. limited government control over the economy
f. overseas settlement tied to a parent country
g. huge urban area
h. withdraw from national government
i. goods flow freely between countries
j. voters choose government leaders

Reviewing the Main Ideas

Section 1 From Sea to Shining Sea

11. **Region** What are the five main physical regions of the United States?
12. **Place** What cities make up the huge urban area along the East Coast of the United States?
13. **Region** List nine kinds of climates found in the United States.

Section 2 An Economic Leader

14. **Economics** Name four of the mineral resources found in the United States.
15. **Economics** Name four of the South's agricultural products.
16. **Human/Environment Interaction** What is happening to America's landfills?

Section 3 The Americans

17. **Government** How has the United States Constitution been able to change over the years? **FCAT LA.B.1.3.2**
18. **Science** What has helped lengthen people's lives in the United States?
19. **Place** Which parts of the United States have the fastest-growing populations?

 **The United States**

Place Location Activity

On a separate sheet of paper, match the letters on the map with the numbered places listed below.

1. Rocky Mountains
2. Mississippi River
3. Appalachian Mountains
4. Washington, D.C.
5. Chicago
6. Lake Superior
7. Ohio River
8. Gulf of Mexico
9. Texas
10. Los Angeles

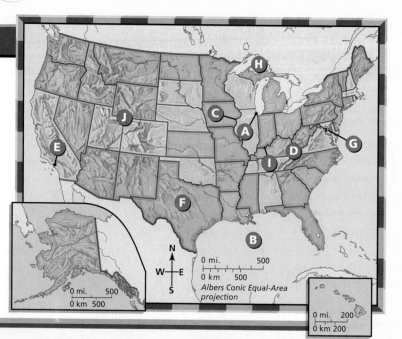

Critical Thinking

20. **Understanding Cause and Effect** What physical features of the Interior Plains have affected the economy of that region? **FCAT LA.A.2.3.5**

21. **Categorizing Information** Create a diagram like the one below. In the outer ovals, write two facts about the United States under each heading. **FCAT LA.A.1.3.2**

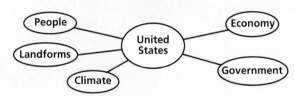

People

Landforms

Climate

United States

Economy

Government

Comparing Regions Activity

22. **Geography** Research to find information on Death Valley in California and the Sahara in Africa. Write a paragraph comparing them. **FCAT LA.B.1.3.2**

Mental Mapping Activity

23. **Focusing on the Region** Create a simple outline map of the United States and then label the following:

- Appalachian Mountains
- Great Lakes
- Alaska
- Rocky Mountains
- Hawaii
- Mississippi River
- Pacific Ocean
- Atlantic Ocean
- Gulf of Mexico
- Great Plains

Technology Skills Activity

24. **Using the Internet** Search the Internet to find out where different ethnic groups have historically settled in your state. Create a state map and label the cities founded by immigrants.

Standardized Test Practice

Directions: Study the graph below, and then answer the questions that follow.

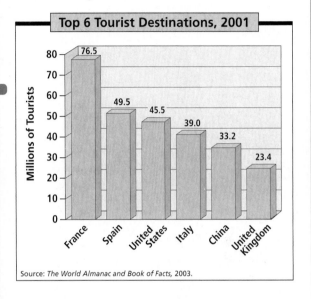

Top 6 Tourist Destinations, 2001

Millions of Tourists

France 76.5
Spain 49.5
United States 45.5
Italy 39.0
China 33.2
United Kingdom 23.4

Source: *The World Almanac and Book of Facts,* 2003.

1. **According to the graph, about how many tourists visited the United States in 2001?**

   A 45.5

   B 76.5

   C 45,500

   D 45,500,000

2. **Which country on the graph had the least number of tourists?**

   F France

   G United Kingdom

   H Spain

   J Italy

Test-Taking Tip: A common error that occurs when you are reading graphs is to overlook the information on the bottom and the side of the graph. Check these areas to see what the numbers mean.

Chapter 5 Canada

The World and Its People — NATIONAL GEOGRAPHIC

To learn more about Canada's people and places, view *The World and Its People* **Chapter 5** video.

Social Studies online

Chapter Overview Visit *The World and Its People* Web site at twip.glencoe.com and click on **Chapter 5—Chapter Overviews** to preview information about Canada.

FOLDABLES™
Study Organizer

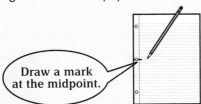 The activity below will help you prepare for the **FCAT Reading** test.

Compare-Contrast Make this foldable to help you analyze the similarities and differences between the landforms, climate, and cultures of northern and southern Canada. **FCAT** LA.A.1.3.2, LA.A.2.2.7

Step 1 Mark the midpoint of the side edge of a sheet of paper.

Draw a mark at the midpoint.

Step 2 Turn the paper and fold the outside edges in to touch at the midpoint.

Step 3 Turn and label your foldable as shown.

Northern Canada

Southern Canada

Reading and Writing As you read the chapter, collect and write information under the appropriate tab that will help you compare and contrast northern and southern Canada. **FCAT** LA.A.1.3.2, LA.A.2.2.7

Why It Matters

Sharing a Border

The boundary line between Canada and the United States forms the longest unprotected border in the world. Citizens of these countries have been allowed to travel freely across the border, which is symbolic of the free trade between these nations.

◀ **Vancouver, British Columbia**

A Resource-Rich Country

Guide to Reading

Main Idea

Canada is a vast country with many landforms and resources.

Terms to Know

- province
- glacier
- tundra
- prairie
- cordillera
- newsprint

Reading Strategy

Create a chart like this one and list Canada's provinces in the left column. In the right column, list the main economic activities in each province. **FCAT** LA.A.1.3.2

Province	Economic Activities

The following are the major Sunshine State Standards covered in this section.

SS.B.2.3.8:
Knows world patterns of resource distribution and utilization

SS.B.2.3.7:
Knows how various human systems throughout the world have developed in response to conditions in the physical environment

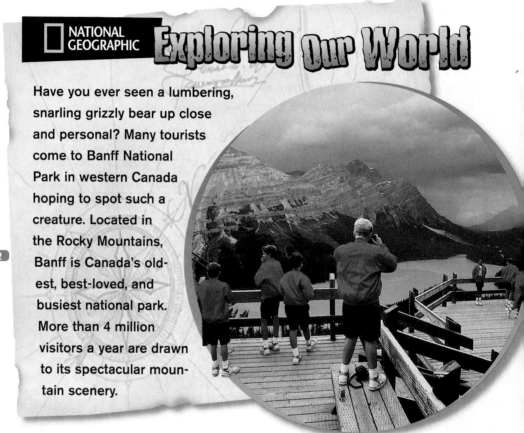

NATIONAL GEOGRAPHIC Exploring Our World

Have you ever seen a lumbering, snarling grizzly bear up close and personal? Many tourists come to Banff National Park in western Canada hoping to spot such a creature. Located in the Rocky Mountains, Banff is Canada's oldest, best-loved, and busiest national park. More than 4 million visitors a year are drawn to its spectacular mountain scenery.

Vikings landed their boats on its eastern coast around A.D. 1000. Niagara Falls thunders in the southeast. Grizzly bears roam its western regions. What country are we describing? It is **Canada.**

Canada's Landscape

Canada, located north of the contiguous United States, is the world's second-largest country in land area. Only Russia is larger. Between Canada and the United States lies the world's longest undefended border. The friendship between the two countries has allowed thousands of people to cross this 5,522-mile (8,887-km) border every day. Like the United States, Canada has the Atlantic Ocean on its eastern coast and the Pacific Ocean on its western coast. The Arctic Ocean lies to the far north.

Unlike the United States, Canada does not have states. Instead, it has 10 **provinces,** or regional political divisions. It also includes three territories. Look at the map on page 119 to find the eastern province of Newfoundland and Labrador. Now locate the Maritime Provinces of Nova Scotia, New Brunswick, and Prince Edward Island. Heading west, you see Quebec and Ontario, followed by the Prairie Provinces of Manitoba, Saskatchewan (suh•SKA•chuh•wuhn), and Alberta. On the far western coast lies British Columbia. Now find the Yukon Territory and the Northwest Territories. In 1999 a third territory—Nunavut (NOO•nuh•vuht)—was carved out of part of the Northwest Territories. This area is the homeland of the Inuit.

The Effect of Glaciers   Thousands of years ago, huge glaciers, or giant sheets of ice, covered most of Canada. The weight of these glaciers pushed much of the land down and created a large, low basin. Highlands rose on the western, eastern, and northern edges of this basin. Water filled the land that was pushed very low. As a result, Canada today has many lakes and inland waterways—more than any other country in the world.

Look at the map on page 118 to see the horseshoe-shaped region known as the **Canadian Shield** that is wrapped around **Hudson Bay.** Rocky hills worn down by erosion along with thousands of lakes dot much of this wilderness region. Deep within the Canadian Shield are iron ore, copper, nickel, gold, and uranium deposits. Because of the region's location and cold climate, few people live here.

To the north lie the Arctic Islands. Much of the landscape here consists of tundra—vast rolling, treeless plains in which only the top few inches of ground thaw in summer. Glaciers blanket the islands that are farthest north.

Southern Canada From Atlantic to Pacific   Many of southern Canada's physical features extend into the United States. Along Canada's southeastern Atlantic coast stretch the Appalachian Highlands

Analyzing the Diagram

The St. Lawrence Seaway provides a water link between the Great Lakes and the Atlantic Ocean.

Geography Which lake is completely above sea level?

St. Lawrence Seaway

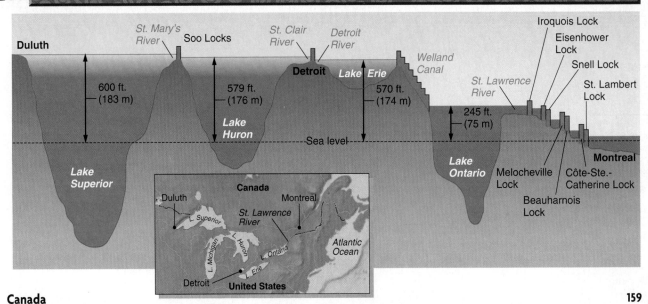

and the Laurentian Highlands. Traveling through this area of Canada, you see rolling hills. The valleys between them are dotted with farms. Forests also blanket much of the landscape. Many deepwater harbors nestle along the jagged, rocky coasts.

Cutting through these highland areas are the fertile lowlands of the **St. Lawrence River** and Great Lakes region. This area experiences a humid continental climate—long, cold winters and short, warm summers. Because of its rich soil and warm summers, this region holds most of Canada's urban centers, industries, and farms. Canada's largest city, **Toronto,** is located in this region. The St. Lawrence River and the Great Lakes form the major waterway linking central Canada with the Atlantic coast. A diagram on page 159 shows the St. Lawrence Seaway's system of locks and canals. Huge, slow-moving barges carry grain, ore, coal, and more through this waterway, which Canada shares with the United States.

Canada also shares the **Great Plains** with its southern neighbor. Look at the physical map on page 118 to locate this region. It is a huge prairie—a rolling, inland grassy area with fertile soil. Herds of buffalo once roamed here. Today large cattle ranches and farms occupy most of the land.

Another landform shared by Canada and the United States is the **Rocky Mountains,** part of an area called the cordillera (KAWR•duhl•YEHR•uh). A cordillera is a group of mountain ranges that run side by side. The Canadian Rockies are known for their scenic beauty and rich mineral resources. Tourists are drawn to this area, particularly to Banff and Jasper National Parks.

West of the Rockies you cross high plateaus until you reach the **Coast Mountains.** These mountains skirt Canada's Pacific shore and

On Location

Toronto

Toronto and its suburbs have well over 4 million people, making the area Canada's largest urban center.

Place In which province is Toronto located?

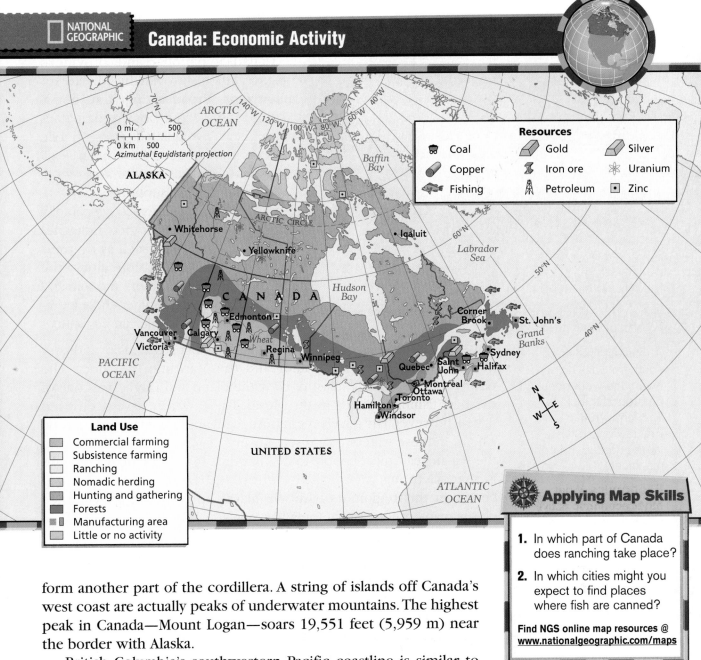

Resources

Coal	Gold	Silver
Copper	Iron ore	Uranium
Fishing	Petroleum	Zinc

Land Use

- Commercial farming
- Subsistence farming
- Ranching
- Nomadic herding
- Hunting and gathering
- Forests
- Manufacturing area
- Little or no activity

Applying Map Skills

1. In which part of Canada does ranching take place?

2. In which cities might you expect to find places where fish are canned?

Find NGS online map resources @ www.nationalgeographic.com/maps

form another part of the cordillera. A string of islands off Canada's west coast are actually peaks of underwater mountains. The highest peak in Canada—Mount Logan—soars 19,551 feet (5,959 m) near the border with Alaska.

British Columbia's southwestern Pacific coastline is similar to the coastlines of Washington and Oregon. With its marine west coast climate, this is the only area in Canada that has wet, mild winters. In fact, British Columbia's capital—Victoria—is known for its well-kept gardens that bloom year-round.

✓ Reading Check What are three landforms that Canada shares with the United States?

Canada's Economic Regions

Canada is known for fertile farmland, rich natural resources, and skilled workers. Manufacturing, farming, and service industries are the country's major economic activities. Like the United States, Canada has a free market economy in which people start and run businesses with limited government involvement. Canada's government, however,

Nighttime Harvest

At harvest time in southern Saskatchewan, the work goes on around the clock. The farms in the Prairie Provinces are large and depend on machinery.

Economics What other economic activities take place in the Prairie Provinces?

plays a more direct role in the Canadian economy. For example, Canada's national and provincial governments provide health care for citizens. Broadcasting, transportation, and electric power companies are heavily regulated. These public services might not have been available in Canada's remote areas without government support.

As you would expect, geography plays a major role in where industries are located. Factors such as nearness to the ocean, location along the U.S.–Canadian border, and oil and coal deposits determine where industries, jobs, and people can be found.

Eastern Canada   Fishing traditionally has been the major industry in Newfoundland and Labrador and the Maritime Provinces. The **Grand Banks,** off the coast of Newfoundland and Labrador, is one of the best fishing grounds in the world. These waters have been overfished, however. The government now regulates how many fish may be caught in these waters. As a result, fewer Canadians make a living from the sea. Instead, most people in the Maritime Provinces today hold jobs in manufacturing, mining, and tourism. **Halifax** is a major shipping center in this region. Its harbor remains open in winter when ice closes many other eastern Canadian ports.

Quebec and Ontario   Manufacturing and service industries are dominant in Canada's largest province, Quebec. Almost one-fourth of Canadians live in Quebec, where agriculture and fishing are also important. **Montreal,** an important port on the St. Lawrence River, is Canada's second-largest city. It is also a major financial and industrial center. The city of **Quebec,** founded by the French in 1608, is the capital of the province of Quebec. Many historic sites and a European charm make it popular with tourists.

Canada's second-largest province is Ontario. It has the most people and greatest wealth, however. It produces more than half of Canada's manufactured goods. Southern Ontario also has fertile land and a growing season long enough for farming. Farmers here grow grains, fruits, and vegetables and raise beef and dairy cattle.

As you know, Toronto is Canada's largest city. It is also the capital of Ontario and the country's chief manufacturing, financial, and communications center. **Ottawa,** the national capital, lies in Ontario near the border with Quebec. Many Canadians work in government offices in Ottawa.

The Prairie Provinces and British Columbia   Farming and ranching are major economic activities in the Prairie Provinces of Manitoba,

Saskatchewan, and Alberta. Canada produces large amounts of wheat, most of which is exported to Europe and Asia. Some of the world's largest reserves of oil and natural gas are found in Alberta and Saskatchewan. Huge pipelines carry the oil and gas to other parts of Canada and the United States. Canada is the fifth-largest energy producer in the world.

Thick forests blanket much of British Columbia. The province helps make Canada the world's leading producer of newsprint, the type of paper used for printing newspapers. Timber and mining industries add to British Columbia's wealth. Fishing and tourism are also strong economic activities. Fishing fleets sail out into the Pacific Ocean to catch salmon and other kinds of fish. **Vancouver** is a bustling trade center and Canada's main Pacific port.

NAFTA About $1 billion worth of trade passes between Canada and the United States each day. In 1994 Canada, the United States, and Mexico entered into the North American Free Trade Agreement (NAFTA) to remove trade barriers among the three countries. Some Canadians fear that their economy is too dependent on the United States. They worry that the American economy is so large that it will dominate the partnership.

✓ Reading Check **Which city is Canada's chief manufacturing and communications center?**

FCAT PRACTICE You can prepare for the FCAT-assessed standards by completing the correlated item(s) below.

Assessment

Defining Terms
1. **Define** province, glacier, tundra, prairie, cordillera, newsprint.

Recalling Facts
2. **History** What is unusual about the border between Canada and the United States?
3. **Place** Name four of the mineral resources found in the Canadian Shield.
4. **Economics** Which province is the world's leading producer of newsprint?

Critical Thinking
5. **Making Inferences** Why is Vancouver a useful port for Canadian trade with Asian countries? **FCAT** LA.A.2.3.1
6. **Drawing Conclusions** Explain why some Canadians worry about NAFTA. **FCAT** LA.A.2.3.1

Graphic Organizer
7. **Organizing Information** Create a chart like this one. Then list each province, the resources found in it, and major cities located there, if any. **FCAT** LA.A.1.3.2

Province	Resources	Cities

Applying Social Studies Skills

8. **Analyzing Maps** Look at the economic activity map on page 161. Name the resources and types of economic activity that can be found near the city of Edmonton.

Technology Skill

Developing Multimedia Presentations

Your homework is to make a presentation about a Canadian province. You want to make your presentation informative but also interesting and fun. One way to do this is to combine several types of media into a **multimedia presentation.**

Learning the Skill

A multimedia presentation involves using several types of media, including photographs, videos, or sound recordings. The equipment can range from cassette players to overhead projectors to VCRs to computers. In your presentation on the Canadian province of Ontario, for example, you might show photographs of Niagara Falls. You could also find a video of people working in a large corporation in Toronto. You can then combine these items on a computer.

Computer multimedia programs allow you to combine text, video, audio, graphics, and animation. The tools you need include computer graphic and drawing programs, animation programs that make certain images move, and systems that tie everything together.

Practicing the Skill

Use the following questions as a guide when planning your presentation:

1. Which forms of media do I want to include? Video? Sound? Animation? Photographs? Graphics?
2. Which of the media forms does my computer support?
3. Which kinds of media equipment are available at my school or local library?
4. What types of media can I create to enhance my presentation?

Applying the Skill

Plan and create a multimedia presentation on a province in Canada. List three ideas you would like to cover. Use as many multimedia materials as possible and share your presentation with the class. **FCAT LA.A.2.3.5**

▼ Various equipment is needed to make multimedia presentations. For example, a photograph of the Ice Palace (left) will make your report on the province of Quebec more interesting.

164

The Canadians

Guide to Reading

Main Idea

Canadians of many different backgrounds live in towns and cities close to the United States border.

Terms to Know

- dominion
- parliamentary democracy
- prime minister
- bilingual
- autonomy

Reading Strategy

Create a chart like this one and give at least two facts about Canada for each topic.

FCAT LA.A.1.3.2

History		
Population		
Culture		

The following are the major Sunshine State Standards covered in this section.

SS.A.3.3.2:
Understands the historical events that have shaped the development of cultures throughout the world

SS.B.1.3.3:
Knows the social, political, and economic divisions on Earth's surface

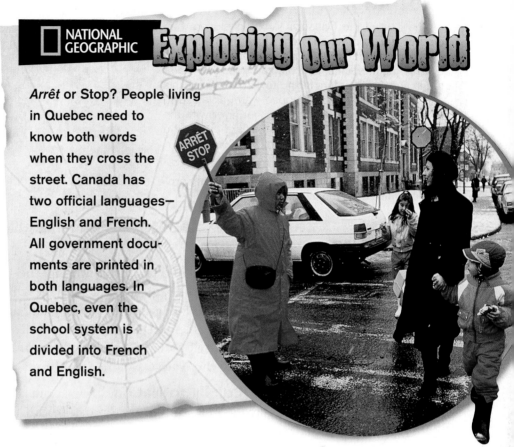

NATIONAL GEOGRAPHIC Exploring Our World

Arrêt or Stop? People living in Quebec need to know both words when they cross the street. Canada has two official languages—English and French. All government documents are printed in both languages. In Quebec, even the school system is divided into French and English.

About 32 million people live in Canada. Like the United States, Canada's population is made up of many different cultures. The largest group of Canadians has a European heritage, but the country is home to people from all countries. Unlike the United States, Canada has had difficulty achieving a strong sense of being one nation. The country's vast distances and separate cultures cause some Canadians to feel more closely attached to their own region than to Canada as a whole.

Canada's History

Inuit and other Native North Americans lived for thousands of years in Canada before European settlers arrived. Some lived in coastal fishing villages. Others were hunters and gatherers constantly on the move. Still others founded permanent settlements. The first Europeans in Canada were Viking explorers who landed in about A.D. 1000. They lived for a while on the Newfoundland coast but eventually left.

In the 1500s and 1600s, both Britain and France claimed areas of Canada. French explorers, settlers, and missionaries founded several cities. The most important were Quebec and Montreal. For almost 230

Exploring Culture

Clothing

The Inuit of the Canadian Arctic designed their clothes for protection from the harsh climate. Traditional clothing was made up of a caribou or sealskin parka, pants, mittens, and boots. In winter the Inuit wore their furs facing toward the skin. This created air pockets that trapped warm air close to the body. On top they wore another layer with the fur facing outward. The clothing flapped as the wearer moved, creating a breeze that kept the person from overheating while running or working.

Looking Closer **How does traditional clothing protect the Inuit from the harsh climate?**

years, France ruled the area around the St. Lawrence River and the Great Lakes. This region was called New France.

During the 1600s and 1700s, England and France fought each other for territory around the globe. Eventually, by 1763, the British gained control of all of Canada. Tragically, European warfare and diseases were destroying the Native American cultures during this time.

From Colony to Nation   For about 100 years, Great Britain held Canada as a colony. As you recall from Chapter 4, a colony is an overseas territory with ties to the parent country. While Canada was ruled by Great Britain, English and French areas were kept separate. Each region had its own colonial government. In 1867 the different colonies of Canada became one nation known as the Dominion of Canada. As a **dominion,** Canada had its own government to run local affairs. Great Britain, however, still controlled Canada's relations with other countries.

The new Canadian government promised continued protection for the French language and culture in Quebec. Yet many English-speaking Canadians did not always keep this promise. French speakers often claimed that they were treated unfairly because of their heritage. Canada was often torn apart by disputes between the two ethnic groups.

During the 1900s, Canadians fought side by side with the British and Americans in the two World Wars. Canada's loyal support in these conflicts gradually led to the nation's full independence. In 1982 Canadians peacefully won the right to change their constitution without British approval. Today only one major link between Canada and Great Britain remains. The British king or queen still reigns as king or queen of Canada, but this is a ceremonial position with no real power.

Canada's Government   The Canadians have a British-style parliamentary democracy. In a **parliamentary democracy,** voters elect representatives to a lawmaking body called Parliament. These representatives then choose an official called the prime minister to head the government. The British king or queen visits Canada only once in a while, so a Canadian official called the governor-general carries out most of the government's ceremonial duties.

Reading Check What was the result of Great Britain keeping the French and British areas separate?

A Bilingual Country

Canada's history of being colonized by both France and Great Britain means that two European languages and cultures exist together today. About one-fourth of the Canadians are descended from French-speaking settlers. (By comparison, in the United States, only 1 person out of 20 claims French ancestry.) Most of these people live in Quebec. There, the French, not the British, are the majority ethnic group.

The people of Quebec have long refused to give up their French language and customs. They did not want to "become English." As a result, Canada today is a bilingual country, with two official languages.

FCAT PRACTICE

Completing the activity below will help you prepare for the **FCAT Reading** test.

Primary Source

A DECLARATION OF FIRST NATIONS

"We the Original Peoples of this land know the Creator put us here. The Creator gave us laws that govern all our relationships to live in harmony with nature and mankind.

The Laws of the Creator defined our rights and responsibilities.

The Creator gave us our spiritual beliefs, our languages, our culture, and a place on Mother Earth, which provided us with all our needs. We have maintained our Freedom, our Languages, and our Traditions from time immemorial.

We continue to exercise the rights and fulfill the responsibilities and obligations given to us by the Creator for the land upon which we were placed.

The Creator has given us the right to govern ourselves and the right to self-determination.

The rights and responsibilities given to us by the Creator cannot be altered or taken away by any other Nation."

Copyright © Assembly of First Nations National Indian Brotherhood 2001

Analyzing Primary Sources

The U.S. Declaration of Independence states that ". . . all men are created equal, that they are endowed by their Creator with certain **unalienable** Rights. . ." Look up the meaning of *unalienable*. Then, identify the line in the Declaration of First Nations that expresses the same idea. **FCAT LA.A.2.3.2**

Time to Play

Fifteen-year-old Natalie Menard has been playing ice hockey since she was five years old. Winters are long in Quebec, so Natalie enjoys plenty of time on the ice. Natalie also enjoys visiting her cousin Angela, who lives in Toronto, Ontario. More than 6 miles (10 km) of covered walkways and underground tunnels in downtown Toronto connect subways with shops, offices, hotels, and restaurants. Natalie and Angela walk from place to place without even thinking of the weather.

An official language is one that is recognized by the government as being a legal language for conducting government business. Government documents and publications in Canada are printed in English and French. Traffic signs are also printed in both languages. School students learn to speak both languages. Of course, some areas of the country favor one language over the other. What language do you think is more popular in Quebec?

For many years, many French-speaking people have wanted Quebec to secede, or withdraw, from Canada. They would like Quebec to become an independent country, apart from the rest of the Canadian provinces. They do not believe that French culture can be protected in a largely English-speaking country. So far, they have been defeated in two very important votes on this issue. However, Canada's future as a united country is still uncertain.

Reading Check What are Canada's two official languages?

Nunavut, A New Territory

As you have already learned, the first peoples of Canada were Inuit and other Native Americans. In recent years, the Canadian government has given these peoples more control over their land. In 1999 the new territory of Nunavut was created for the Inuit. *Nunavut* is an Inuit word that means "our land." The Inuit now control the government and mineral rights in this new territory. In this way, most of the Inuit living in Canada have autonomy, or the right to govern themselves. When issues involve other nations, however, the national government of Canada still makes the decisions.

Nunavut is almost three times the size of the state of Texas. Part of it lies on the North American continent, but more than half of Nunavut is made up of hundreds of islands in the Arctic Ocean. As large as it is, Nunavut does not include all of Canada's Inuit people. Many live in Quebec, Newfoundland and Labrador, and the Northwest Territories.

The population of Nunavut is also different from the rest of Canada because of its age. More than 60 percent of the population is under the age of 25. Finding jobs to take care of the young population is difficult because there is not much industry in this region. The government is the largest employer, but there are not enough jobs. People often must hunt and fish to make sure they have enough food and warm clothes to stay alive. Nunavut must develop an economy that will grow along with its population so that its citizens will not have to depend on government welfare.

Reading Check For whom was Nunavut created?

A Growing Ethnic Diversity

Like the United States, Canada has opened its doors to a great many immigrants. Ukrainians, for example, first settled in the Prairie Provinces about 100 years ago. Many other settlers came from Italy, Hungary, and other European countries.

In the 1960s, Canada welcomed refugees and other people who lost their homes due to war or natural disasters. Many of these people came from Asia, especially China, Southeast Asia, and India. Cities such as Vancouver on the west coast have sizeable Asian populations. Many Africans have also migrated to Canada.

Canada has a long history of religious diversity as well. Most Canadians are Roman Catholic or Protestant. Many also follow Judaism, Buddhism, Hinduism, or Islam.

Food, Sports, and Recreation   Since Canada has such ethnic diversity, people here enjoy a variety of tasty foods. People from many different groups have settled in cities such as Toronto. You can walk down the street and sample the foods of Ukraine, Greece, Italy, the Caribbean, and Asia all in the same day.

Canadians enjoy a variety of activities, especially outdoor sports. You will find local parks and national parks crowded with people exercising and having fun. Many young Canadians enjoy playing ice hockey. They also take part in other winter sports, including skiing, skating, curling, and snowboarding. During the summer, they might go sailing on Lake Ontario. Professional football and hockey are popular spectator sports. Many Canadian sports fans also flock to see the major league baseball games played in Toronto's and Montreal's large indoor stadiums.

Social Studies Online

Web Activity Visit *The World and Its People* Web site at twip.glencoe.com and click on **Chapter 5— Student Web Activities** to learn more about Quebec's French culture.

✓ **Reading Check** What groups make up Canada's diverse population?

FCAT PRACTICE You can prepare for the FCAT-assessed standards by completing the correlated item(s) below.

Section 2 Assessment

Defining Terms

1. **Define** dominion, parliamentary democracy, prime minister, bilingual, autonomy.

Recalling Facts

2. **History** Who were the first peoples to live in Canada?

3. **Government** What is the new territory that was created in 1999, and what does its name mean?

4. **Culture** Name four activities enjoyed by Canadians.

Critical Thinking

5. **Analyzing Information** What is the link between Canada and Great Britain?

6. **Summarizing Information** What are two reasons for Canada's ethnic diversity?

FCAT LA.A.2.3.1

Graphic Organizer

7. **Organizing Information** Create a diagram like this one. List two examples under each heading in the outer ovals. **FCAT LA.A.1.3.2**

Food   Religion
Canada's Diversity
Sports   Language

Applying Social Studies Skills

8. **Analyzing Graphs** Look at the bottom circle graph on page 121. What percentage of Canada's people are French? British? Other European? **FCAT MA.E.3.3.1**

Matthew Coon Come: Man With a Mission

Ne-Ha-Ba-Nus—"the one who wakes up with the sun"—is also known as Matthew Coon Come. A leader of his Cree people and the National Chief of the Assembly of First Nations, Matthew has worked to preserve the rights of Canada's native peoples.

A Proud Chief

In 1990 Matthew Coon Come led a fight against a proposed hydroelectric project, which would have flooded Cree lands in Quebec. He helped organize a canoe trip to get publicity for Cree leaders. The trip was from James Bay, across Lake Erie, down the Hudson River, and finally to New York City. The strategy was brilliantly effective. Coon Come gained much-needed worldwide attention and made his plea directly to New Yorkers, who cancelled their plans to buy power from the proposed project.

As Grand Chief of the Cree of northern Quebec, Coon Come became a foe of industry and politicians who want to separate Quebec from Canada. He stated that even if Quebec secedes from Canada, the Native Americans living there want to stay part of Canada. Coon Come spoke for only 12,000 Cree, Inuit, Nadkapi, and Innu people, but they live on two-thirds of the land area of Quebec.

What if these Native American peoples, who control two-thirds Quebec's land, would elect to rejoin Canada if Quebec seceded? Would this mean a problem for the newly formed Quebec nation? No one is really sure what would happen in that case.

For recognition of his leadership in environmental, human rights, and tribal communities, Matthew Coon Come has received numerous awards.

▲ Matthew Coon Come

Making the Connection

1. Why was Matthew Coon Come so opposed to the proposed hydroelectric project?

2. How will the Native Americans be affected if Quebec is successful in seceding from Canada?

3. **Synthesizing Information** Matthew Coon Come has his Christian name and his Cree name. They represent the two worlds he lives in. Develop a new name for yourself and explain what it represents.

Reading Review

Section 1 | A Resource-Rich Country

Terms to Know
province
glacier
tundra
prairie
cordillera
newsprint

Main Idea

Canada is a vast country with many landforms and resources.

✓**Region** Canada, the second-largest country in the world, is rich in natural resources.

✓**Economics** Canada's economy is rich in fertile farmland, mineral resources, and skilled workers.

✓**Economics** One of the best fishing grounds in the world is found in the Grand Banks off the coast of Newfoundland and Labrador.

✓**Place** Quebec is the largest province.

✓**Culture** Quebec and Ontario have Canada's largest cities and most of its people.

Section 2 | The Canadians

Terms to Know
dominion
parliamentary
  democracy
prime minister
bilingual
autonomy

Main Idea

Canadians of many different backgrounds live in towns and cities close to the United States border.

✓**History** Inuit and other Native Americans were the first Canadians. French and British settlers later built homes in Canada. Large numbers of immigrants have recently come from Asia and eastern Europe.

✓**Government** Canada's government is a parliamentary democracy headed by a prime minister.

✓**Culture** Some people in French-speaking Quebec want to separate from the rest of Canada.

✓**Culture** Canada's native peoples have recently been given more autonomy to govern themselves.

Horseshoe Falls, Canada— one of the two waterfalls that makes up Niagara Falls ▶

Chapter 5 Assessment and Activities

FCAT PRACTICE You can prepare for the FCAT-assessed standards by completing the correlated item(s) below.

Using Key Terms

Match the terms in Part A with their definitions in Part B.

A.

1. province
2. glacier
3. prairie
4. cordillera
5. newsprint
6. dominion
7. autonomy
8. bilingual
9. prime minister
10. parliamentary democracy

B.

a. having or speaking two languages
b. giant sheet of ice
c. right of self-government
d. voters elect representatives to a lawmaking body called Parliament
e. government leader chosen by Parliament
f. inland grassy area with fertile soil
g. type of paper used for newspapers
h. regional political division
i. group of mountain ranges that run side by side
j. nation that has its own government to run local affairs

Reviewing the Main Ideas

Section 1 A Resource-Rich Country

11. **Economics** What kind of economy does Canada have?
12. **Region** Which three provinces are good agricultural areas?
13. **Location** Which province is the most heavily populated?
14. **Government** Describe two ways in which Canada's government plays a role in the nation's economy.
15. **Geography** Which of Canada's landforms are shared with the United States?
16. **Economics** What are three economic activities of British Columbia?
17. **Human/Environment Interaction** Explain why Canada's government must regulate how many fish can be caught in the Grand Banks.

Section 2 The Canadians

18. **Culture** Why do some of Quebec's people want independence from Canada?
19. **Place** What is Canada's national capital, and in which province is it located?
20. **History** Who were the first people of Canada?

 **Canada**

Place Location Activity

On a separate sheet of paper, match the letters on the map with the numbered places listed below.

1. Hudson Bay
2. Nunavut
3. British Columbia
4. Ottawa
5. Quebec (province)
6. St. Lawrence River
7. Rocky Mountains
8. Winnipeg
9. Ontario
10. Nova Scotia

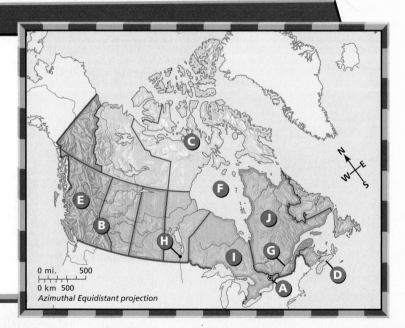

Critical Thinking

21. **Making Comparisons** Compare the climates of western and eastern Canada. **FCAT LA.A.2.2.7**

22. **Analyzing Information** Why do most Canadians live in southern Canada?

23. **Categorizing Information** Choose one of Canada's provinces or territories. Complete a chart like the one below with at least two facts or examples under each heading.

FCAT LA.A.1.3.2

Province or Territory	Landforms	Resources
	Major Cities	Products

Comparing Regions Activity

24. **Culture** As you learned in this chapter, Canada is a bilingual country. India and Belgium are also bilingual nations. Make a chart to list these three countries and research to find the languages spoken there. Then research the histories of these nations to determine why each is bilingual. Compare your findings among nations. **FCAT LA.A.1.3.2**

Mental Mapping Activity

25. **Focusing on the Region** Create a simple outline map of Canada. Refer to the map on page 119, and then label the following:

- Arctic Ocean
- Quebec (province)
- Pacific Ocean
- Ontario
- Atlantic Ocean
- British Columbia
- Rocky Mountains
- Nunavut
- Hudson Bay
- Ottawa

Technology Skills Activity

26. **Using the Internet** Access the Internet and search for information on the Inuit and the new territory of Nunavut. Create an illustrated time line that shows the steps leading to the creation of the new territory.

Standardized Test Practice

Directions: Study the graph below, and then answer the questions that follow. **FCAT MA.E.3.3.1**

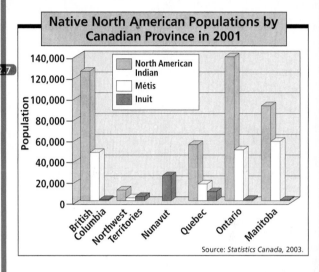

Native North American Populations by Canadian Province in 2001

Source: *Statistics Canada*, 2003.

1. **Which of the following provinces has the largest North American Indian population?**

   A Northwest Territories

   B Manitoba

   C Ontario

   D British Columbia

2. **In what part of Canada does most of the Métis population live?**

   F The northern part of the country

   G The center of Canada

   H Near the Atlantic coast

   J In cities such as Toronto and Ontario

Test-Taking Tip: Sometimes you cannot answer a question directly from the information in a map or a graph. In these cases, you have to make an *inference,* or draw a conclusion, that is supported by information in the map or graph. The clues may also help you get rid of wrong choices.

Unit 3

Peruvian Indian woman and child

Spanish colonial architecture in Guatemala

NATIONAL
GEOGRAPHIC

Latin America

Where can you find steamy tropical forests, frigid mountain peaks, thundering waterfalls, and peaceful island beaches? All of these contrasts can be found in Latin America—a huge part of the world made up of 33 nations on two continents. This region stretches from the Mexico–United States border, in North America, to the southernmost tip of South America.

NGS ONLINE
www.nationalgeographic.com/education

Spider monkey and Mayan ruins, Mexico ▲

Focus on:

Latin America

COMMON THREADS OF LANGUAGE AND RELIGION unite this region. Once claimed as European colonies, most Latin American countries still use either Spanish or Portuguese as the official language. These two languages are based on Latin, which is how the region gets its name. Most Latin Americans are Roman Catholic, another influence from colonial times.

The Land

Latin America stretches from the Rio Grande south to Tierra del Fuego, just 600 miles (966 km) from Antarctica's frozen shores. Three times larger than the continental United States, the region includes Mexico, Central America, the Caribbean islands, and South America.

Mountains   Mountains are prominent features in many parts of Latin America. Some Caribbean islands are actually the exposed tops of ancient, submerged volcanoes. In Mexico, the branches of the Sierra Madre spread like welcoming arms to hug a central highland known as the Mexican Plateau. Mist-covered peaks stretch through the interior of Central America. The Andes, the longest series of mountain ranges in the world, follow the western coast of South America for 4,500 miles (7,242 km). Volcanic activity and earthquakes are common in these mountainous areas of Latin America.

Plains   Narrow coastal plains line the edges of Mexico and Central America. South America has vast inland plains. These include the pam-

pas of Argentina and the llanos of Colombia and Venezuela. The largest lowland area on this continent is the basin of the Amazon River, the longest river in the Western Hemisphere. Other rivers in Latin America are the Rio Grande, the Magdalena, the Orinoco, the Río de la Plata, and the São Francisco River in South America.

The Climate

Most of Latin America has a tropical climate. Daily showers drench the rain forests, which thrive in the lowlands. In Brazil, the Amazon River and its tributaries snake through the largest area of rain forest regions, which covers roughly one-third of South America.

The climate tends to be drier and cooler at higher elevations and farther away from the Equator. Under these conditions, tall grasses and scattered trees flourish. Drier still are parts of northern Mexico and southern Argentina. Here, rainfall is sparse and so is vegetation. Yet even these places are lush compared to the Atacama Desert, along Chile's coast. The barren Atacama is among the world's driest places.

Three-toed sloth in rain forest, Panama ▶

◀ Peaks of the Andes, Chile

The Economy

Latin America is rich in natural resources. Gold drew many of the first European conquerors. Copper, silver, iron ore, tin, and lead also are abundant in the region. Some Latin American countries are among the world's leading producers of oil and natural gas.

Agriculture plays an important role in the region's economy. Coffee, bananas, and sugarcane thrive in the moist, fertile lowlands. On higher ground, farmers grow grains and fruits, while cowhands known as gauchos drive huge herds of cattle across rolling grasslands.

Many countries in the Caribbean islands rely on tourism to support their economies. A warm, sunny climate and beautiful beaches attract millions of tourists a year.

Industrialization is increasing in Latin America. However, some countries are moving along this path more quickly than others. In recent years, Mexico, Brazil, and Chile have become major producers of manufactured goods. Lack of money, skilled labor, and reliable transportation have hindered industrial development in other parts of the region. Geographic barriers such as rugged mountains and thick forests have also been obstacles to development.

The People

Long before Europeans crossed the Atlantic Ocean, great Native American civilizations had developed in Latin America. The Olmec set up an early civilization along the Gulf of Mexico. The Maya later flourished in the Guatemalan lowlands and across Mexico's Yucatán Peninsula. The central highlands of Mexico were the site of the Aztec Empire. In South America, the Inca established an empire that stretched from southern Colombia to central Chile.

From Colonies to Nations
Beginning in the 1500s, Spain and Portugal ruled most of Latin America. Explorers and settlers from these European countries destroyed the Native American civilizations. They also brought enslaved Africans to work alongside Native Americans on large farms called plantations.

Independence came for many Latin American countries in the early 1800s. Wealthy landowners and military officials controlled governments. They often ignored the needs of poor farmers and workers. During the mid-1900s, Latin America experienced dramatic economic, social, and political changes. Today a number of Latin American countries have democratic governments.

◀ **Mexican boy carrying decorated cross for religious celebration**

Latin America Today

Latin America's countries remain a cultural mixture—Native Americans, Europeans, Africans, and others have all left their mark. Yet the region's cultures do maintain common threads. For example, the majority of Latin Americans practice the Roman Catholic faith brought by the Spanish and the Portuguese. In addition, most of them speak either the Spanish or Portuguese languages. Because these languages are based on the ancient Roman language Latin, the region became known as Latin America.

Most Latin Americans today live in urban areas along the coasts of South America or in a band reaching from Mexico into Central America. Some of the largest cities in the world are in Latin America, including Mexico City, Rio de Janeiro, and São Paulo.

Rio de Janeiro, Brazil ▼

Data Bits

Country	Automobiles per 1,000 people	Television sets per 1,000 people
Chile	88	240
Colombia	43	279
Ecuador	41	213
Mexico	102	272
Suriname	123	241
Venezuela	68	185

Population: Urban ■ vs. Rural ■

Country	Urban	Rural
Chile	86%	14%
Colombia	76%	24%
Ecuador	63%	37%
Mexico	75%	25%
Suriname	75%	25%
Venezuela	87%	13%

Sources: *World Development Indicators*, 2002; *The World Almanac*, 2004.

Exploring the Region

1. What is Latin America's longest series of mountain ranges?
2. What type of climate is found across most of the region?
3. Which European countries once ruled Latin America?
4. Which Latin American countries are industrializing most rapidly?

Latin America

Physical

UNITED STATES

Rio Grande

120°W 110°W 100°W 90°W 80°W 70°W 60°W 50°W

30°N

Bermuda Is.

Baja California

Plateau of Mexico

SIERRA MADRE OCCIDENTAL

SIERRA MADRE ORIENTAL

Gulf of Mexico

BAHAMAS

TROPIC OF CANCER

20°N

CUBA

WEST INDIES

Yucatán Peninsula

Greater Antilles

HAITI DOM. REP.

MEXICO

Sierra Madre del Sur

BELIZE JAMAICA

HONDURAS

Puerto Rico

ATLANTIC OCEAN

GUATEMALA NICARAGUA

EL SALVADOR

Caribbean Sea

Lesser Antilles

COSTA RICA Isthmus of Panama

Lake Maracaibo

VENEZUELA

10°N

PANAMA

Llanos

Orinoco R.

GUYANA SURINAME

FRENCH GUIANA

COLOMBIA

Guiana Highlands

Galápagos Islands

ECUADOR

EQUATOR 0°

AMAZON

Negro R.

Amazon R.

BASIN

PERU

BRAZIL

ANDES

Madeira R.

10°S

Mato Grosso Plateau

PACIFIC OCEAN

Lake Titicaca

BOLIVIA

BRAZILIAN

São Francisco R.

HIGHLANDS

Altiplano

PARAGUAY

Atacama Desert

Gran Chaco

Paraná R.

20°S

TROPIC OF CAPRICORN

CHILE

▲ Mountain peak

0 mi. 1,000

0 km 1,000

Lambert Azimuthal Equal-Area projection

Aconcagua 22,834 ft. (6,960 m)

ARGENTINA URUGUAY

30°S

Pampas

Río de la Plata

ATLANTIC OCEAN

ANDES

PATAGONIA

40°S

Strait of Magellan

Falkland Islands

26,247 ft. 0 mi. 500 8,000 m

19,685 ft. 0 km 500 6,000 m

ANDES BRAZILIAN HIGHLANDS 4,000 m

13,123 ft.

AMAZON BASIN MATO GROSSO PLATEAU 2,000 m

6,562 ft.

LIMA Sea level SALVADOR

Tierra del Fuego

Cape Horn South Georgia I.

Political

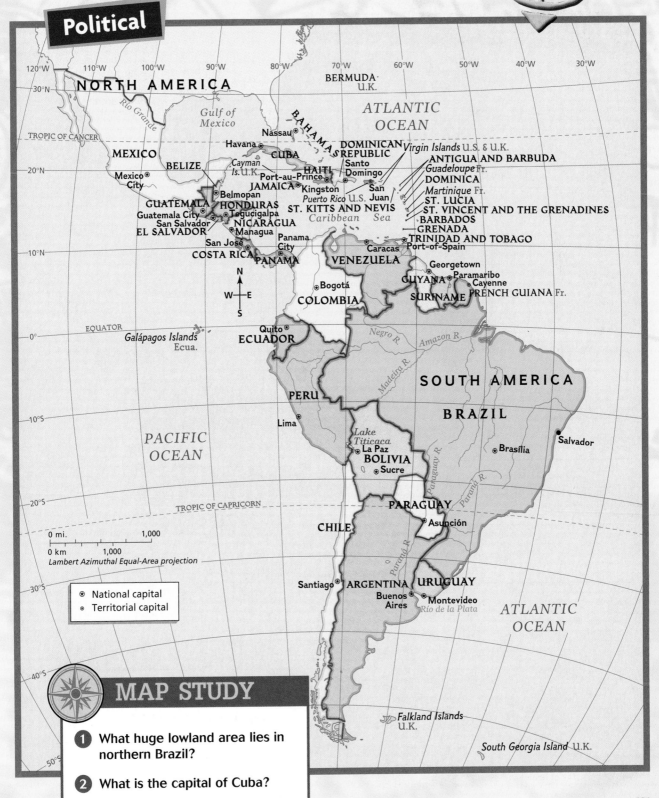

120°W 110°W 100°W 90°W 80°W 70°W 60°W 50°W 40°W 30°W

30°N **NORTH AMERICA** BERMUDA U.K. **ATLANTIC OCEAN**

Río Grande

Gulf of Mexico

TROPIC OF CANCER

Nassau ⊛ **BAHAMAS**

Havana ⊛ **CUBA** **DOMINICAN REPUBLIC** *Virgin Islands* U.S. & U.K.

MEXICO

20°N

BELIZE *Cayman Is.* U.K. **HAITI** Santo Domingo **ANTIGUA AND BARBUDA**

Guadeloupe Fr.

Mexico City ⊛ Port-au-Prince ⊛ **DOMINICA**

Kingston ⊛ **JAMAICA** San Juan *Martinique* Fr.

Belmopan ⊛ *Puerto Rico* U.S. **ST. LUCIA**

GUATEMALA **HONDURAS** **ST. KITTS AND NEVIS** **ST. VINCENT AND THE GRENADINES**

Guatemala City ⊛ Tegucigalpa ⊛ *Caribbean Sea* **BARBADOS**

San Salvador ⊛ **NICARAGUA** **GRENADA**

EL SALVADOR ⊛ Managua **TRINIDAD AND TOBAGO**

San José ⊛ Panama City Caracas ⊛ Port-of-Spain

10°N **COSTA RICA** **PANAMA** **VENEZUELA** Georgetown ⊛ Paramaribo ⊛

N **GUYANA** Cayenne ⊛

W E ⊛ Bogotá **SURINAME** **FRENCH GUIANA** Fr.

S **COLOMBIA**

EQUATOR *Galápagos Islands* Quito ⊛ *Negro R.* *Amazon R.*

0° *Ecua.* **ECUADOR**

Madeira R.

PERU **SOUTH AMERICA**

BRAZIL

10°S Lima ⊛ *Paraguay R.*

PACIFIC OCEAN *Lake Titicaca* • Salvador

La Paz ⊛ • Brasília

BOLIVIA

⊛ Sucre

20°S TROPIC OF CAPRICORN *Paraná R.* **PARAGUAY**

⊛ Asunción

CHILE

ATLANTIC OCEAN

30°S Santiago ⊛ **ARGENTINA** **URUGUAY**

Buenos ⊛ Montevideo

Aires *Río de la Plata*

0 mi. 1,000

0 km 1,000

Lambert Azimuthal Equal-Area projection

⊛ National capital

• Territorial capital

40°S

Falkland Islands U.K.

South Georgia Island U.K.

50°S

MAP STUDY

1 What huge lowland area lies in northern Brazil?

2 What is the capital of Cuba?

South America

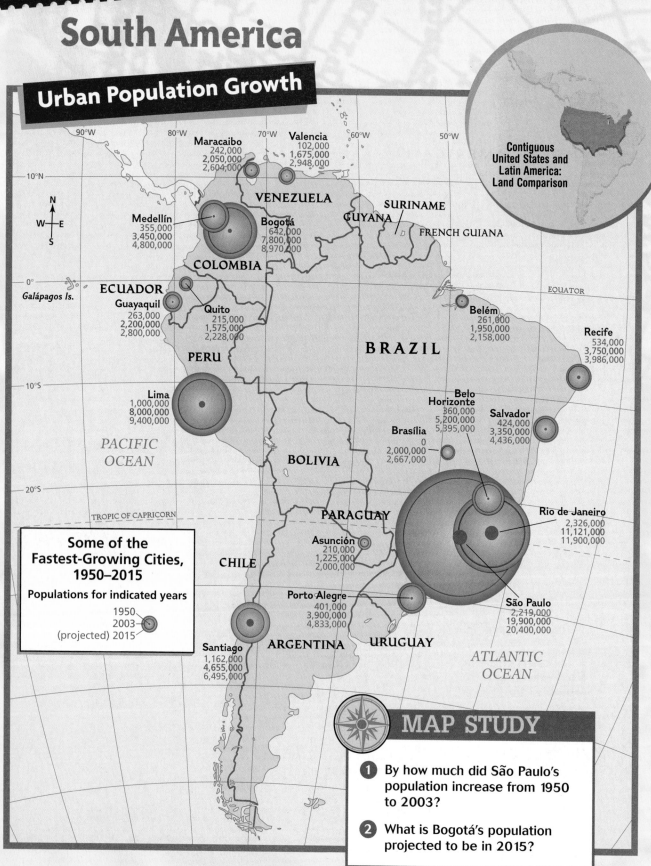

Urban Population Growth

Contiguous United States and Latin America: Land Comparison

Maracaibo
242,000
2,050,000
2,604,000

Valencia
102,000
1,675,000
2,948,000

VENEZUELA

GUYANA

SURINAME

FRENCH GUIANA

Medellín
355,000
3,450,000
4,800,000

Bogotá
642,000
7,800,000
8,970,000

COLOMBIA

ECUADOR

Galápagos Is.

Guayaquil
263,000
2,200,000
2,800,000

Quito
215,000
1,575,000
2,228,000

EQUATOR

Belém
261,000
1,950,000
2,158,000

BRAZIL

Recife
534,000
3,750,000
3,986,000

PERU

Lima
1,000,000
8,000,000
9,400,000

Belo Horizonte
360,000
5,200,000
5,395,000

Salvador
424,000
3,350,000
4,436,000

PACIFIC OCEAN

Brasília
0
2,000,000
2,667,000

BOLIVIA

PARAGUAY

Rio de Janeiro
2,326,000
11,121,000
11,900,000

Some of the Fastest-Growing Cities, 1950–2015

Populations for indicated years

1950
2003
(projected) 2015

Asunción
210,000
1,225,000
2,000,000

CHILE

Porto Alegre
401,000
3,900,000
4,833,000

São Paulo
2,219,000
19,900,000
20,400,000

Santiago
1,162,000
4,655,000
6,495,000

ARGENTINA

URUGUAY

ATLANTIC OCEAN

MAP STUDY

1 By how much did São Paulo's population increase from 1950 to 2003?

2 What is Bogotá's population projected to be in 2015?

Geo Extremes

① **HIGHEST POINT**
Aconcagua (Argentina)
22,834 ft. (6,960 m) high

② **LOWEST POINT**
Valdés Peninsula (Argentina)
131 ft. (40 m) below sea level

③ **LONGEST RIVER**
Amazon River
(Brazil and Peru)
4,000 mi. (6,437 km) long

④ **LARGEST LAKE**
Lake Maracaibo (Venezuela)
5,217 sq. mi. (13,512 sq. km)

⑤ **HIGHEST LARGE NAVIGABLE LAKE**
Lake Titicaca
(Peru and Bolivia)
12,500 ft. (3,810 m) high

⑥ **HIGHEST WATERFALL**
Angel Falls (Venezuela)
3,212 ft. (979 m) high

⑦ **DRIEST PLACE**
Atacama Desert (Chile)
rainfall barely measurable

COMPARING POPULATION:
United States and Selected Countries of Latin America

UNITED STATES

BRAZIL

MEXICO

ARGENTINA

GUATEMALA

 = 25,000,000

BOLIVIA

Source: *Population Reference Bureau*, 2003.

ETHNIC GROUPS:
Selected Countries of Latin America

ARGENTINA
| 97% | 3% |

BOLIVIA
| 55% | 30% | 15% |

BRAZIL
6%
| 55% | 38% | 1% |

GUATEMALA
| 56% | 44% |

MEXICO
9%
| 60% | 30% | 1% |

☐ Black ☐ Indian ☐ African/European
☐ White ☐ Mestizo ☐ Other

Source: *CIA World Factbook*, 2002.

GRAPHIC STUDY

1. What two Latin American "extremes" are found in Venezuela?

2. What countries have a majority of mestizos (people of mixed European and Native American ancestry)? **FCAT** MA.E.3.3.1

Country Profiles

ANTIGUA and BARBUDA

POPULATION:
100,000
436 per sq. mi.
168 per sq. km

LANGUAGE:
English

MAJOR EXPORT:
Petroleum Products

MAJOR IMPORTS:
Foods and Livestock

CAPITAL:
St. John's

LANDMASS:
170 sq. mi.
440 sq. km

St. John's

ARGENTINA

POPULATION:
36,900,000
34 per sq. mi.
13 per sq. km

LANGUAGE:
Spanish

MAJOR EXPORT:
Meat

MAJOR IMPORT:
Machinery

CAPITAL:
Buenos Aires

LANDMASS:
1,073,514 sq. mi.
2,780,401 sq. km

Buenos Aires

BAHAMAS

POPULATION:
301,000
58 per sq. mi.
22 per sq. km

LANGUAGES:
English, Creole

MAJOR EXPORT:
Pharmaceuticals

MAJOR IMPORT:
Foods

CAPITAL:
Nassau

LANDMASS:
5,359 sq. mi.
13,880 sq. km

Nassau

BARBADOS

POPULATION:
300,000
1,524 per sq. mi.
588 per sq. km

LANGUAGES:
English

MAJOR EXPORT:
Sugar

MAJOR IMPORT:
Manufactured Goods

CAPITAL:
Bridgetown

LANDMASS:
166 sq. mi.
430 sq. km

Bridgetown

BELIZE

POPULATION:
300,000
31 per sq. mi.
12 per sq. km

LANGUAGE:
English

MAJOR EXPORT:
Sugar

MAJOR IMPORT:
Machinery

CAPITAL:
Belmopan

LANDMASS:
8,865 sq. mi.
22,960 sq. km

Belmopan

BOLIVIA

POPULATION:
8,600,000
20 per sq. mi.
8 per sq. km

LANGUAGES:
Spanish, Quechua, Aymara

MAJOR EXPORT:
Metals

MAJOR IMPORT:
Machinery

CAPITALS:
La Paz, Sucre

LANDMASS:
424,162 sq. mi.
1,098,580 sq. km

La Paz
Sucre

BRAZIL

POPULATION:
176,500,000
53 per sq. mi.
21 per sq. km

LANGUAGE:
Portuguese

MAJOR EXPORT:
Iron Ore

MAJOR IMPORT:
Crude Oil

CAPITAL:
Brasília

LANDMASS:
3,300,154 sq. mi.
8,547,399 sq. km

Brasília

CHILE

POPULATION:
15,800,000
54 per sq. mi.
21 per sq. km

LANGUAGE:
Spanish

MAJOR EXPORT:
Copper

MAJOR IMPORT:
Machinery

CAPITAL:
Santiago

LANDMASS:
292,135 sq. mi.
756,626 sq. km

Santiago

COLOMBIA

POPULATION:
44,200,000
100 per sq. mi.
39 per sq. km

LANGUAGE:
Spanish

MAJOR EXPORT:
Petroleum

MAJOR IMPORT:
Machinery

CAPITAL:
Bogotá

LANDMASS:
439,734 sq. mi.
1,138,911 sq. km

Bogotá

COSTA RICA

POPULATION:
4,200,000
211 per sq. mi.
81 per sq. km

LANGUAGE:
Spanish

MAJOR EXPORT:
Coffee

MAJOR IMPORT:
Raw Materials

CAPITAL:
San José

LANDMASS:
19,730 sq. mi.
51,100 sq. km

San José

CUBA

POPULATION:
11,300,000
264 per sq. mi.
102 per sq. km

LANGUAGE:
Spanish

MAJOR EXPORT:
Sugar

MAJOR IMPORT:
Petroleum

CAPITAL:
Havana

LANDMASS:
42,803 sq. mi.
110,860 sq. km

Havana

Countries and flags not drawn to scale

For more information on countries in this region, refer to the Nations of the World Data Bank in the Appendix.

DOMINICA

POPULATION:
100,000
242 per sq. mi.
93 per sq. km

LANGUAGES:
English, French

MAJOR EXPORT:
Bananas

MAJOR IMPORT:
Manufactured Goods

CAPITAL:
Roseau

LANDMASS:
290 sq. mi.
751 sq. km

Roseau

DOMINICAN REPUBLIC

POPULATION:
8,700,000
463 per sq. mi.
179 per sq. km

LANGUAGE:
Spanish

MAJOR EXPORT:
Ferronickel

MAJOR IMPORT:
Foods

CAPITAL:
Santo Domingo

LANDMASS:
18,815 sq. mi.
48,731 sq. km

Santo Domingo

ECUADOR

POPULATION:
12,600,000
115 per sq. mi.
44 per sq. km

LANGUAGES:
Spanish, Quechua

MAJOR EXPORT:
Petroleum

MAJOR IMPORT:
Transport Equipment

CAPITAL:
Quito

LANDMASS:
109,483 sq. mi.
283,561 sq. km

Quito

EL SALVADOR

POPULATION:
6,600,000
817 per sq. mi.
315 per sq. km

LANGUAGE:
Spanish

MAJOR EXPORT:
Coffee

MAJOR IMPORT:
Raw Materials

CAPITAL:
San Salvador

LANDMASS:
8,124 sq. mi.
21,041 sq. km

San Salvador

FRENCH GUIANA*

POPULATION:
200,000
5 per sq. mi.
2 per sq. km

LANGUAGE:
French

MAJOR EXPORT:
Shrimp

MAJOR IMPORT:
Foods

CAPITAL:
Cayenne

LANDMASS:
34,749 sq. mi.
89,999 sq. km

Cayenne

* Territory of France

GRENADA

POPULATION:
100,000
800 per sq. mi.
309 per sq. km

LANGUAGES:
English, French

MAJOR EXPORT:
Bananas

MAJOR IMPORT:
Foods

CAPITAL:
St. George's

LANDMASS:
131 sq. mi.
339 sq. km

St. George's

GUATEMALA

POPULATION:
12,400,000
294 per sq. mi.
114 per sq. km

LANGUAGES:
Spanish, Mayan Languages

MAJOR EXPORT:
Coffee

MAJOR IMPORT:
Petroleum

CAPITAL:
Guatemala City

LANDMASS:
42,042 sq. mi.
108,889 sq. km

Guatemala City

GUYANA

POPULATION:
800,000
9 per sq. mi.
4 per sq. km

LANGUAGE:
English

MAJOR EXPORT:
Sugar

MAJOR IMPORT:
Manufactured Goods

CAPITAL:
Georgetown

LANDMASS:
83,000 sq. mi.
214,969 sq. km

Georgetown

HAITI

POPULATION:
7,500,000
703 per sq. mi.
271 per sq. km

LANGUAGES:
French, Creole

MAJOR EXPORT:
Manufactured Goods

MAJOR IMPORT:
Machinery

CAPITAL:
Port-au-Prince

LANDMASS:
10,714 sq. mi.
27,750 sq. km

Port-au-Prince

HONDURAS

POPULATION:
6,900,000
159 per sq. mi.
61 per sq. km

LANGUAGE:
Spanish

MAJOR EXPORT:
Bananas

MAJOR IMPORT:
Machinery

CAPITAL:
Tegucigalpa

LANDMASS:
43,278 sq. mi.
112,090 sq. km

Tegucigalpa

JAMAICA

POPULATION:
2,600,000
624 per sq. mi.
241 per sq. km

LANGUAGES:
English, Creole

MAJOR EXPORT:
Alumina

MAJOR IMPORT:
Machinery

CAPITAL:
Kingston

LANDMASS:
4,243 sq. mi.
10,989 sq. km

Kingston

Latin America

Country Profiles

MEXICO

POPULATION:
104,900,000
139 per sq. mi.
54 per sq. km

LANGUAGES:
Spanish,
Native American
Languages

MAJOR EXPORT:
Crude Oil

MAJOR IMPORT:
Machinery

CAPITAL:
Mexico City

LANDMASS:
756,062 sq. mi.
1,958,201 sq. km

Mexico City

NICARAGUA

POPULATION:
5,500,000
109 per sq. mi.
42 per sq. km

LANGUAGE:
Spanish

MAJOR EXPORT:
Coffee

MAJOR IMPORT:
Manufactured
Goods

CAPITAL:
Managua

LANDMASS:
50,193 sq. mi.
129,999 sq. km

Managua

PANAMA

POPULATION:
3,000,000
102 per sq. mi.
32 per sq. km

LANGUAGE:
Spanish

MAJOR EXPORT:
Bananas

MAJOR IMPORT:
Machinery

CAPITAL:
Panama City

LANDMASS:
29,158 sq. mi.
75,519 sq. km

Panama City

PARAGUAY

POPULATION:
6,200,000
39 per sq. mi.
15 per sq. km

LANGUAGES:
Spanish, Guaraní

MAJOR EXPORT:
Cotton

MAJOR IMPORT:
Machinery

CAPITAL:
Asunción

LANDMASS:
157,046 sq. mi.
406,749 sq. km

Asunción

PERU

POPULATION:
27,100,000
55 per sq. mi.
21 per sq. km

LANGUAGES:
Spanish, Quechua,
Aymara

MAJOR EXPORT:
Copper

MAJOR IMPORT:
Machinery

CAPITAL:
Lima

LANDMASS:
496,224 sq. mi.
1,285,220 sq. km

Lima

PUERTO RICO*

POPULATION:
3,900,000
1,123 per sq. mi.
434 per sq. km

LANGUAGES:
Spanish, English

MAJOR EXPORT:
Pharmaceuticals

MAJOR IMPORT:
Chemical Products

CAPITAL:
San Juan

LANDMASS:
3,456 sq. mi.
8,951 sq. km

San Juan

* U.S. Commonwealth

ST. KITTS and NEVIS

POPULATION:
50,000
339 per sq. mi.
128 per sq. km

LANGUAGE:
English

MAJOR EXPORT:
Machinery

MAJOR IMPORT:
Electronic Goods

CAPITAL:
Basseterre

LANDMASS:
139 sq. mi.
360 sq. km

Basseterre

ST. LUCIA

POPULATION:
200,000
677 per sq. mi.
261 per sq. km

LANGUAGES:
English, French

MAJOR EXPORT:
Bananas

MAJOR IMPORT:
Foods

CAPITAL:
Castries

LANDMASS:
239 sq. mi.
619 sq. km

Castries

ST. VINCENT and the GRENADINES

POPULATION:
100,000
731 per sq. mi.
282 per sq. km

LANGUAGES:
English, French

MAJOR EXPORT:
Bananas

MAJOR IMPORT:
Foods

CAPITAL:
Kingstown

LANDMASS:
151 sq. mi.
391 sq. km

Kingstown

SURINAME

POPULATION:
400,000
6 per sq. mi.
3 per sq. km

LANGUAGE:
Dutch

MAJOR EXPORT:
Bauxite

MAJOR IMPORT:
Machinery

CAPITAL:
Paramaribo

LANDMASS:
63,039 sq. mi.
163,271 sq. km

Paramaribo

TRINIDAD and TOBAGO

POPULATION:
1,300,000
661 per sq. mi.
255 per sq. km

LANGUAGE:
English

MAJOR EXPORT:
Petroleum

MAJOR IMPORT:
Machinery

CAPITAL:
Port-of-Spain

LANDMASS:
1,981 sq. mi.
5,131 sq. km

Port-of-Spain

Countries and flags not drawn to scale

For more information on countries in this region, refer to the Nations of the World Data Bank in the Appendix.

URUGUAY

POPULATION:
3,400,000
49 per sq. mi.
19 per sq. km

LANGUAGE:
Spanish

MAJOR EXPORT:
Wool

MAJOR IMPORT:
Machinery

CAPITAL:
Montevideo

LANDMASS:
68,498 sq. mi.
177,410 sq. km

Montevideo

VENEZUELA

POPULATION:
25,700,000
73 per sq. mi.
28 per sq. km

LANGUAGE:
Spanish

MAJOR EXPORT:
Petroleum

MAJOR IMPORT:
Raw Materials

CAPITAL:
Caracas

LANDMASS:
352,143 sq. mi.
912,050 sq. km

Caracas

VIRGIN ISLANDS*

POPULATION:
123,498
922 per sq. mi.
356 per sq. km

LANGUAGE:
English

MAJOR EXPORT:
Chemical Products

MAJOR IMPORT:
Crude Oil

CAPITAL:
Charlotte Amalie

LANDMASS:
134 sq. mi.
347 sq. km

Charlotte Amalie

* Territory of U.S.

BUILDING CITIZENSHIP

Public and Private Needs

More than one-third of the area of Brazil is covered by a rain forest. This fragile ecosystem is home to millions of plant, animal, and insect species. Some of the plants are important sources of medicines. According to scientists, more than 50 percent of the world's species live in the rain forest.

The rain forest is also a major source of timber, minerals, fruits, and vegetables. Building roads and clearing land to reach these resources has led to major destruction of the rain forest habitat. The government of Brazil has tried to set aside large portions of the rain forest as preserves. The government does allow development of its natural resources as income for its citizens, however.

Because of its effect on climate, the rain forest is important not just to Brazil but to the whole world. Who should have more say about how much of the rain forest is preserved—Brazil or the United Nations?

WRITE ABOUT IT **FCAT PRACTICE** Completing the activity below will help you prepare for the **FCAT Writing** test.

Imagine that a new golf course is being built in your city. The area where it is being built includes natural wetlands where birds and animals live. Write a letter to the city council outlining what steps you think the golf course developers should take to protect the wetlands.

FCAT LA.B.1.3.2

Brazilian rain forest ▲

Chapter 6

Mexico

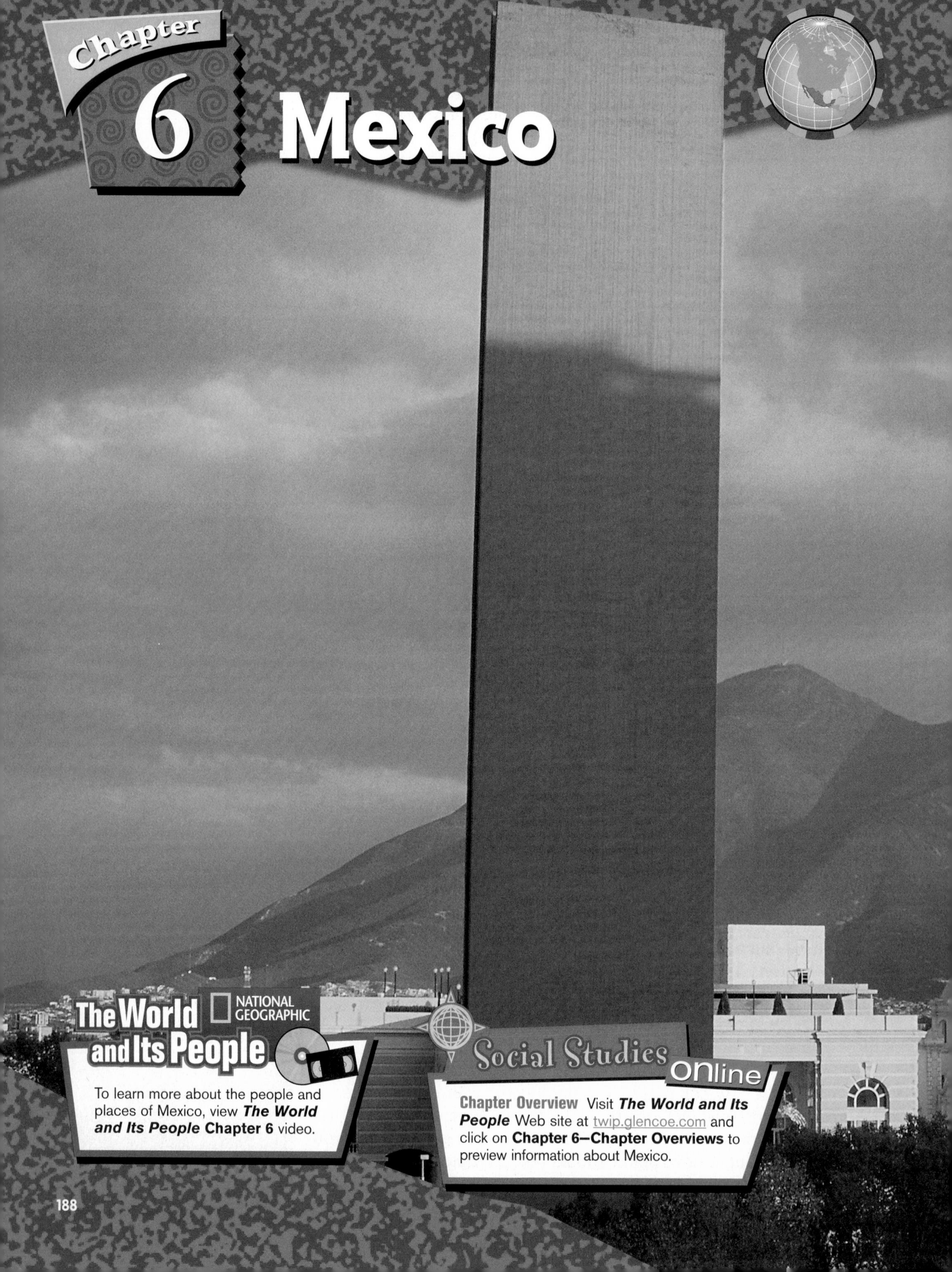

The World and Its People NATIONAL GEOGRAPHIC

To learn more about the people and places of Mexico, view ***The World and Its People*** **Chapter 6** video.

Social Studies Online

Chapter Overview Visit ***The World and Its People*** Web site at twip.glencoe.com and click on **Chapter 6—Chapter Overviews** to preview information about Mexico.

FCAT PRACTICE The activity below will help you prepare for the **FCAT Reading** test.

Categorizing Information When you group information into categories on a table, it is easier to study characteristics of items. Make this foldable to help you describe Mexico's land, economy, and government—past and present. **FCAT LA.A.1.3.2**

Step 1 Fold a sheet of paper into thirds from top to bottom.

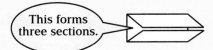
This forms three sections.

Step 2 Open the paper and refold it into fourths from side to side.

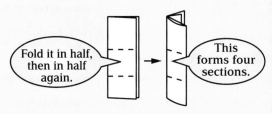
Fold it in half, then in half again.

This forms four sections.

Step 3 Unfold, turn the paper, and draw lines along the folds.

Step 4 Label your table as shown.

	Past	Present
Mexico's Land		
Mexico's Economy		
Mexico's Government		

Reading and Writing As you read the chapter, record key facts about Mexico's land, economy, and government in the appropriate places on your table foldable. **FCAT LA.A.1.3.2**

Why It Matters

Moving Forward

Mexico is a country working hard to catch up with the more industrialized countries of the world. Today Mexico is an important trading partner of the United States. However, a rapidly growing population and a developing economy have made it difficult for Mexico to support all of its people.

◀ **The Lighthouse of Commerce and the Cathedral of Monterrey, Monterrey, Mexico**

Mexico's Land and Economy

Guide to Reading

Main Idea

Mexico's mountainous landscape and varied climate create different economic regions.

Terms to Know

- land bridge
- peninsula
- latitude
- altitude
- hurricane
- vaquero
- maquiladora
- subsistence farm
- plantation
- industrialize
- service industry

Reading Strategy

Create a chart of Mexico's economic regions like this one. List the main economic activity of each region. **FCAT** LA.A.1.3.2

Region of Mexico	Economic Activity
Northern	
Central	
Southern	

The following are the major Sunshine State Standards covered in this section.

SS.B.2.3.9:
Understands ways the interaction between physical and human systems affects current conditions on Earth

SS.B.2.3.7:
Knows how various human systems throughout the world have developed in response to conditions in the physical environment

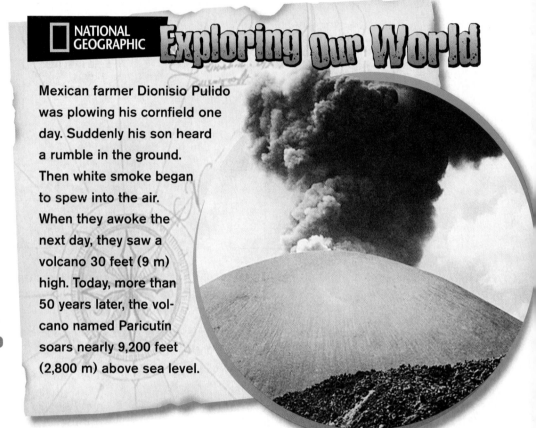

NATIONAL GEOGRAPHIC **Exploring Our World**

Mexican farmer Dionisio Pulido was plowing his cornfield one day. Suddenly his son heard a rumble in the ground. Then white smoke began to spew into the air. When they awoke the next day, they saw a volcano 30 feet (9 m) high. Today, more than 50 years later, the volcano named Paricutín soars nearly 9,200 feet (2,800 m) above sea level.

Paricutín and other volcanoes are part of the rugged landscape of Mexico, which sits where three plates in the earth's crust collide. Sometimes the movement of these plates brings disastrous results. Hot magma, or melted rock, shoots through a volcano. The ground shifts violently in an earthquake. Do you see why Native Americans once called Mexico "the land of the shaking earth"?

Bridging Two Continents

Mexico forms part of a **land bridge,** or narrow strip of land that joins two larger landmasses. This land bridge connects North America and South America. Look at the map on page 191. You can see that Mexico borders the southern United States.

Physical geographers, or people who study continents and landforms, think of Mexico as part of North America. Cultural geographers, however, think of Mexico as being part of Latin America. For cultural geographers, language, customs, religion, and history are important areas of study. Both groups are correct. Mexico is a Latin (Spanish-speaking) country on the continent of North America. Its location in North America makes it an important trading partner to the United States and Canada. Yet Mexico's culture is closely tied to Central and South America. It is a country that bridges two continents.

The Pacific Ocean borders Mexico on the west. Extending south along this western coast is **Baja** (BAH•hah) **California.** It is a long, narrow peninsula, or piece of land with water on three sides. On Mexico's eastern side, the **Gulf of Mexico** and the **Caribbean Sea** border the coasts. Between the Gulf and the Caribbean Sea is another peninsula—the **Yucatán** (YOO•kah•TAHN) **Peninsula.**

Mexico is a rugged land. If you were to see it from space, you might think that the country looked like a crumpled piece of paper with deep folds. Towering mountain ranges and a huge, high plateau occupy the center of the country.

The Sierra Madre   Three different mountain ranges in Mexico make up the **Sierra Madre** (SYEHR•ah MAH•thray), or "mother range." Because of

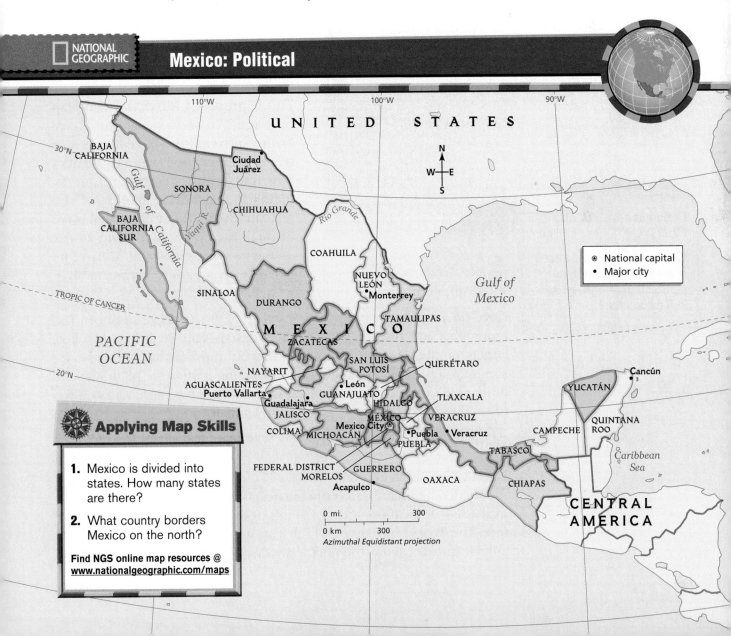

NATIONAL GEOGRAPHIC

Mexico: Political

UNITED STATES

30°N
BAJA CALIFORNIA
Ciudad Juárez
SONORA
Gulf of California
Yaqui R.
CHIHUAHUA
Rio Grande
BAJA CALIFORNIA SUR
COAHUILA
NUEVO LEÓN
Monterrey
SINALOA
DURANGO
TAMAULIPAS
TROPIC OF CANCER
M E X I C O
ZACATECAS
PACIFIC OCEAN
NAYARIT
SAN LUIS POTOSÍ
QUERÉTARO
Gulf of Mexico
20°N
AGUASCALIENTES
Puerto Vallarta
León
GUANAJUATO
HIDALGO
TLAXCALA
Guadalajara
JALISCO
VERACRUZ
Cancún
YUCATÁN
COLIMA
MICHOACÁN
Mexico City
Puebla
Veracruz
QUINTANA ROO
CAMPECHE
PUEBLA
TABASCO
Caribbean Sea
FEDERAL DISTRICT
MORELOS
GUERRERO
Acapulco
OAXACA
CHIAPAS
CENTRAL AMERICA

⊛ National capital
• Major city

0 mi.   300
0 km   300
Azimuthal Equidistant projection

Applying Map Skills

1. Mexico is divided into states. How many states are there?

2. What country borders Mexico on the north?

Find NGS online map resources @ www.nationalgeographic.com/maps

the rugged terrain, few people live in the Sierra Madre. The mountains are rich in resources, though. They hold copper, zinc, silver, and timber.

Many of Mexico's mountains are volcanoes. Popocatepetl (POH•puh•KA•tuh•PEH•tuhl), or "El Popo," as Mexicans call it, erupted violently centuries ago. In December 2000, El Popo erupted again, hurling molten rock into the sky. About 30,000 people from surrounding areas were forced to temporarily leave their homes. Tens of millions of people live 50 miles (80 km) or less from the mountain and could face even worse eruptions in the future.

Mexicans face another danger from the land. Earthquakes can destroy their cities and homes. A 1985 earthquake killed nearly 10,000 people in Mexico's capital, **Mexico City,** even though the earthquake's center was about 185 miles (298 km) away. Mexico experiences many earthquakes because it is one of the countries that border the "Ring of Fire." This name describes the active volcanic zone that forms the western, northern, and eastern edges of the Pacific Ocean. Earthquakes in the zone are common due to movement of the huge Pacific plate deep under the earth's crust.

Mexico City

Popocatepetl rises above Mexico City's hazy skyline.

Human/Environment Interaction What two natural dangers do people in Mexico face?

The Plateau of Mexico   The map on page 196 shows that the Sierra Madre surround the large, flat center of the country, the Plateau of Mexico. You find mostly deserts and grassy plains in the northern part of the plateau. Broad, flat valleys that slice through the center hold many of the country's chief cities and most of its people. To the south, the plateau steadily rises until it meets the high, snowcapped mountains of the Sierra Madre del Sur.

Coastal Lowlands   Mexico's lowland plains squeeze between the mountains and the sea. The Pacific Coastal Plain begins with a hot, largely empty desert in the north. As you move farther south, better soil and rainfall allow ranching and farming along this plain. On the other side of the country, the Gulf Coastal Plain has more rain and fertile soil for growing crops and raising animals.

✓ Reading Check What is the volcanic zone called that affects Mexico?

Land of Many Climates

Mexico has many different climates. Why? As you read in Chapter 2, latitude—or location north or south of the Equator—affects temperature. The Tropic of Cancer, which cuts across the center of Mexico at 23½°N latitude, marks the northern edge of the Tropics. Areas south of

Mexico's Altitude Zones

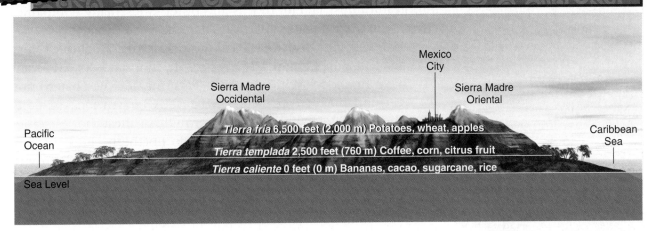

Mexico City

Sierra Madre
Occidental

Sierra Madre
Oriental

Pacific
Ocean

Caribbean
Sea

Tierra fría 6,500 feet (2,000 m) Potatoes, wheat, apples

Tierra templada 2,500 feet (760 m) Coffee, corn, citrus fruit

Tierra caliente 0 feet (0 m) Bananas, cacao, sugarcane, rice

Sea Level

Analyzing the Diagram

Mexico has zones of different climates that result from different altitudes.

Location In which altitude zone is Mexico City located?

this line have warm temperatures throughout the year. Areas north of this line are warm in summer and cooler in winter.

Altitude, or height above sea level, also affects temperatures in Mexico. The higher the altitude, the cooler the temperatures are— even within the Tropics. The diagram above shows that Mexico's mountains and plateau create three altitude zones. You could travel through all of these zones in a day's trip across the Sierra Madre.

Because the coastal lowlands are near sea level, they have high temperatures. Mexicans call this altitude zone the *tierra caliente* (tee•EH• rah kah•lee•EHN•tay), or "hot land." Moving higher in altitude, you find the *tierra templada* (tehm•PLAH•dah), or "temperate land." Here the climate becomes more moderate. In the highest zone, the climate becomes even cooler. Mexicans call this the *tierra fría* (FREE•ah), or "cold land."

Rainfall varies throughout Mexico. Baja California and northern Mexico receive very little precipitation. Other regions receive more, mostly in the summer and early fall. From June to October, Mexico can be hit by **hurricanes.** These fierce tropical storms with high winds and heavy rains form over the warm waters of the Atlantic or Pacific Oceans. They can strike Mexico with fury.

Reading Check What is Mexico's warmest altitude zone?

Mexico's Economic Regions

Mexico's physical geography and climate together give the country three distinct economic regions: the North, Central Mexico, and the South. Large stretches of northern Mexico are too dry and rocky to farm without irrigation. By building canals to carry water to their fields, farmers can grow cotton, fruits, grains, and vegetables.

Northern Mexico Did you know that the skills used by American cowhands originated in Mexico? Mexican cowhands, called **vaqueros** (vah•KEHR•ohs), developed the tools and techniques for herding, roping, and branding cattle. Vaqueros carry on this work today.

▲ A skilled seamstress makes clothing in a maquiladora in northern Mexico.

Northern Mexico has seen an economic boom. **Monterrey,** Mexico's main producer of steel and cement, has long been an important industrial city. In this and other cities, many companies from the United States and elsewhere have built **maquiladoras** (mah•KEEL•ah•DOHR•as), or factories that assemble parts made in other countries. As a result, thousands of Mexicans have flocked to cities such as **Tijuana** (tee•WAH•nah) and **Ciudad Juárez** (see•ooh•DAHD HWAH•rayz), located along the U.S.–Mexico border. The growth in these border cities has raised the standard of living in northern cities through factory work and increased trade. However, this quick growth has also brought concerns about damaging the environment, pollution, and dangers to the health and safety of workers.

Central Mexico More than half of Mexico's people live in the central region, the country's heartland. Why do they call this area home? The climate is one reason. Although central Mexico lies in the Tropics, its high elevation keeps it from being hot and humid. Temperatures are mild, and the climate is pleasant year-round. A second reason is the fertile soil. This soil was created by volcanic eruptions over the centuries and allows for productive farming.

Large industrial cities such as Mexico City and **Guadalajara** (GWAH•duhl•uh•HAHR•uh) also prosper in central Mexico. About 22 million people live in Mexico City and its suburbs, making it one of the largest cities in the world. Mexico City has been the largest city in the Americas since before the Spanish arrived in the early 1500s.

Southern Mexico The South is the poorest economic region of the country. The mountains towering in the center of this region have poor soil. **Subsistence farms,** or small plots where farmers grow only enough food to feed their families, are common here. In contrast, the coastal lowlands of this area have good soil and plentiful rain. Wealthy farmers grow sugarcane or bananas on **plantations,** large farms that raise a single crop for sale.

Both coasts of Mexico also have beautiful beaches and a warm climate. Tourists from all over the world flock to such resort cities as **Acapulco** and **Puerto Vallarta** on the Pacific coast and **Cancún** on the Yucatán Peninsula.

✓ Reading Check How does the economic region of northern Mexico differ from that of southern Mexico?

Mexico's Economy Today

With many resources and workers, Mexico has a growing economy. Did you know that Mexico's economy ranks among the top 15 in the world? As in the past, agriculture is important. Farmers raise food to feed people at home—and also to ship around the world. Corn, beans, wheat, and rice are the main crops grown for food. Exports include coffee, cotton, vegetables, fruits, livestock, and tobacco.

In recent years, Mexico has **industrialized,** or changed its economy to rely less on farming and more on manufacturing. Factories in Mexico now make cars, consumer goods, and steel. The labels on your clothing might even say "Made in Mexico."

Mexico has large deposits of petroleum and natural gas in the Gulf of Mexico and along the southern coast. As a result, Mexico is among the world's major oil-producing nations.

Mexico is also home to important service industries such as banking and tourism. **Service industries** are businesses that provide services to people rather than produce goods.

NAFTA   As you learned in the last unit, Mexico, the United States, and Canada entered into NAFTA, the North American Free Trade Agreement, in 1994. Remember that under this agreement, most goods traded between these countries are free of tariffs, or special taxes. This means a homemaker in Canada would probably choose to buy a tablecloth made in Mexico rather than to pay more for a taxed tablecloth produced in Europe.

Some Americans have been afraid that belonging to NAFTA means American jobs will "go south." They fear that the lower rate of pay for labor in Mexico will encourage many manufacturers to move their businesses to Mexico rather than keep them in the United States. The debate about the overall effect of NAFTA is still going on.

✓ **Reading Check** Why are some Americans afraid jobs will "go south"?

FCAT PRACTICE   You can prepare for the FCAT-assessed standards by completing the correlated item(s) below.

Section 1 Assessment

Defining Terms
1. **Define** land bridge, peninsula, latitude, altitude, hurricane, vaquero, maquiladora, subsistence farm, plantation, industrialize, service industry.

Recalling Facts
2. **History** How did the vaqueros of Mexico influence American ranching?
3. **Location** Why is Mexico a land bridge?
4. **Economics** Why have many Mexicans moved to the cities of the north?

Critical Thinking
5. **Understanding Cause and Effect** How has NAFTA affected the people in Canada and the people in Mexico? Do you think NAFTA has been good or bad for the people in border cities of the United States? Explain.

FCAT LA.A.2.3.1, LA.B.1.3.2

6. **Analyzing Information** Why is Mexico part of both North America and Latin America?

Graphic Organizer
7. **Organizing Information** Create a diagram like this one, and then list two facts that explain the large population of central Mexico.

FCAT LA.A.1.3.2

High Population of Central Mexico

Applying Social Studies Skills

8. **Analyzing Diagrams** Study Mexico's altitude zones on page 193. At which elevation do you think most people live? Why do they live here?

Social Studies Skill

FCAT PRACTICE Completing the correlated items below will help you prepare for the **FCAT Mathematics** test.

Reading a Physical Map

A map that shows the different heights of the land is called a **physical map.** Physical maps use colors and shading to show relief–or how flat or rugged the land surface is. Colors are also used to show the land's elevation–or height above sea level. Green often shows the lowest elevations (closest to sea level). Yellows, oranges, browns, and reds usually mean higher elevations. Sometimes the highest areas, such as mountain peaks, are white.

Learning the Skill

To read a physical map, apply these steps:

- Read the map title to identify the region shown on the map.
- Use the map key to find the meaning of colors and symbols.
- Identify the areas of highest and lowest elevation on the map.
- Find important physical features, including mountains, rivers, and coastlines.
- Mentally map the actual shape of the land.

Practicing the Skill

Look at the map to answer the following:

1. What country is shown on the map?
2. What mountain ranges are labeled?
3. What is the elevation of the green areas on the map (in feet and meters)?

4. What color on the map means 2,000–5,000 feet (600–1,500 m)?
5. Briefly describe the physical landscape of the area shown on the map, moving from west to east. **FCAT MA.B.1.3.4**

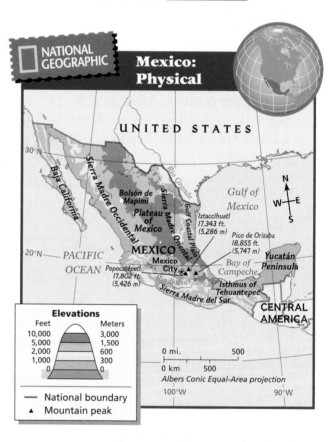

Applying the Skill

Look at the physical map of Latin America on page 180. Describe the physical landscape of the region, moving from east to west.

FCAT MA.B.1.3.4

GO TO Practice key skills with **Glencoe Skillbuilder Interactive Workbook, Level 1.**

Mexico's History

Guide to Reading

Main Idea

Mexico's culture reflects a blend of its Native American and Spanish past.

Terms to Know

- jade
- obsidian
- maize
- hieroglyphics
- mural
- hacienda

Reading Strategy

Create a chart like this one, and then provide one example of how Native Americans and Europeans influenced Mexican culture. **FCAT** LA.A.1.3.2

Ethnic Groups	Influence on Mexican Culture
Native Americans	
Europeans	

The following are the major Sunshine State Standards covered in this section.

SS.A.2.3.2:
Knows how major historical developments have had an impact on the development of civilizations

SS.A.3.3.2:
Understands the historical events that have shaped the development of cultures throughout the world

NATIONAL GEOGRAPHIC Exploring Our World

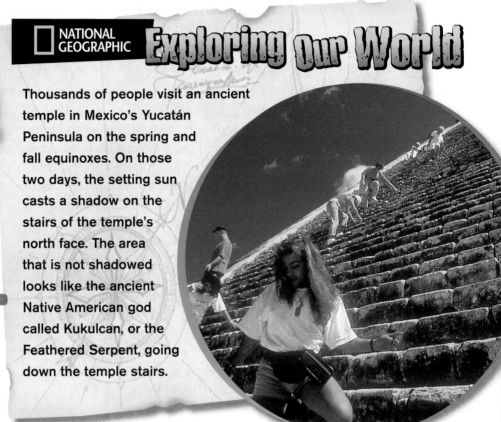

Thousands of people visit an ancient temple in Mexico's Yucatán Peninsula on the spring and fall equinoxes. On those two days, the setting sun casts a shadow on the stairs of the temple's north face. The area that is not shadowed looks like the ancient Native American god called Kukulcan, or the Feathered Serpent, going down the temple stairs.

The first people to arrive in Mexico were the ancestors of today's Native Americans. Mexico's Native American heritage has shaped the country's culture. So has Mexico's European heritage, brought by the Spaniards who conquered the area in the 1500s.

Native American Civilizations

Native Americans came to Mexico thousands of years ago. From about 1200 B.C. to the A.D. 1500s, these people built a series of brilliant, highly advanced civilizations on Mexican soil. Of these, the Olmec, Mayan, and Aztec civilizations are the best-known. Look at the map on page 198 to see where the Olmec, Mayan, and Aztec civilizations thrived.

The Olmecs The Olmecs built the first civilization in the Americas around 1200 B.C. They decorated their cities with large carved stone statues, some standing about 10 feet (3 m) high and weighing over 20 tons (18 t). They also carved smaller and more personal objects like jewelry out of **jade,** a local shiny stone that comes in many shades of green as well as other colors. All these items were carved with **obsidian,** a hard, black glass created by the volcanoes in the area. Obsidian was used because the Olmecs had no metals.

The Olmecs were the first to grow **maize,** or corn, to feed their many people. In addition to cities and ceremonial centers, they built large drainage systems to direct rainwater away from their fields and settlements. The Olmecs lasted longer than any other Native American civilization, finally disappearing about 400 B.C.

The Maya The people called the Maya lived in the rain forests of the Yucatán Peninsula and surrounding areas from about A.D. 250 to 900. Religion held Mayan society together. Mayan priests needed to measure time accurately to hold religious ceremonies at the correct moment. They studied the heavens and developed a calendar of 365 days.

The Maya built huge stone temples in the shape of pyramids with steps. One of these structures, the temple of Kukulcan, showed careful planning. Each side of Kukulcan had 91 steps, totaling 364. The platform at the temple's top made one more step for a grand total of 365—just like the days in the year.

The Maya also developed **hieroglyphics,** a form of writing that uses signs and symbols. They had a complex number system. Artists decorated temples and tombs with elaborate **murals,** or wall paintings.

Around A.D. 900, Mayan civilization declined. Why? Historians do not know. Some suggest that the Maya overused the land and could not grow enough food. Others suggest that warfare or the spread of disease caused their decline. The Maya did not disappear, however. Their descendants still live in the same area and speak the Mayan language.

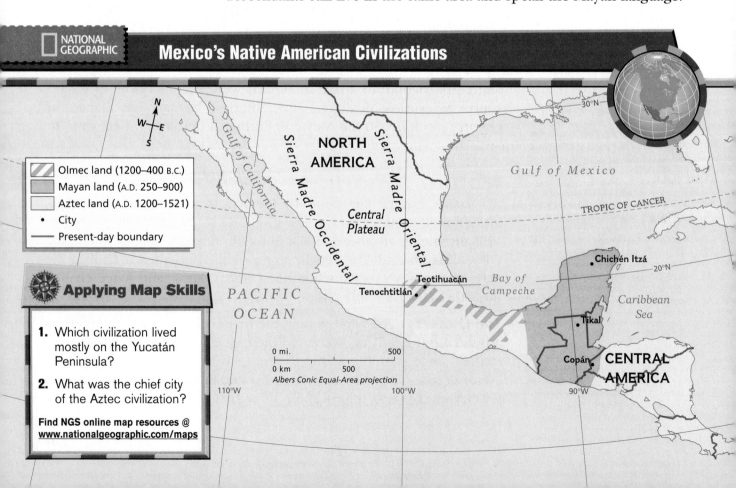

NATIONAL GEOGRAPHIC

Mexico's Native American Civilizations

Olmec land (1200–400 B.C.)
Mayan land (A.D. 250–900)
Aztec land (A.D. 1200–1521)
• City
— Present-day boundary

Applying Map Skills

1. Which civilization lived mostly on the Yucatán Peninsula?

2. What was the chief city of the Aztec civilization?

Find NGS online map resources @ www.nationalgeographic.com/maps

NORTH AMERICA

Gulf of California

Sierra Madre Occidental

Sierra Madre Oriental

Central Plateau

Gulf of Mexico

TROPIC OF CANCER

Chichén Itzá

Teotihuacán

Tenochtitlán

Bay of Campeche

Tikal

Copán

Caribbean Sea

CENTRAL AMERICA

PACIFIC OCEAN

0 mi. 500
0 km 500
Albers Conic Equal-Area projection

30°N
20°N
110°W
100°W
90°W

The Aztec Around A.D. 1200, a people called the Mexica moved into central Mexico from the north. The Spanish later called these people the Aztec. The Aztec conquered a large empire in central Mexico. Their capital, **Tenochtitlán** (tay•NAWCH•teet•LAHN), was magnificent. Mexico City—Mexico's capital—stands on this ancient site today.

Tenochtitlán was originally built on two islands in the middle of Lake Texcoco. Long dikes connected it to land. The city had huge stepped pyramids. Merchants traded gold, silver, and pottery in busy marketplaces. Farmers grew their crops in structures called "floating gardens," or rafts filled with mud. The rafts eventually sank to the lake bottom and piled up, forming fertile islands.

The Aztec people and many of their traditions survive today in Mexico. The food, crafts, and language of Mexico have roots in Aztec culture. Even the name of the country comes from the word the Aztec called themselves—the *Mexica*. The flag of modern Mexico honors this ancient civilization. In the center of the flag is the Aztec symbol of an eagle with a snake in its beak.

✓ **Reading Check** What Native American cultures flourished in Mexico?

Spanish Mexico

In 1519 Mexico's history changed dramatically. A Spanish army led by Hernán Cortés landed on Mexico's Gulf coast. He and about 600 soldiers marched to Tenochtitlán, which they heard was filled with gold. Some Native Americans who opposed the harsh rule of the Aztec signed treaties with the Spanish and joined them. The Spanish had swords, muskets, cannons, and horses. This enabled them to defeat the Aztec Empire, which contained about 6 million people, within two years.

Spain made Mexico a colony, or an overseas territory, because Mexico's rocky land held rich deposits of gold and silver. Many Spanish settlers came to live in Mexico. Some raised cattle on large ranches called **haciendas** (ah•see•EHN•duhs). Others started gold and silver mines. The Spaniards made Native Americans work on the ranches and in the mines. Thousands of Native Americans died from mistreatment. Many thousands more died of diseases such as the common cold and smallpox, which they caught from Europeans. Spanish priests came to Mexico and in their own way tried to improve the lives of Native Americans. Because of their work, many Native Americans accepted the priests' teachings. Today about 90 percent of Mexico's people follow the Roman Catholic religion.

✓ **Reading Check** Why was Mexico a valuable colony for Spain?

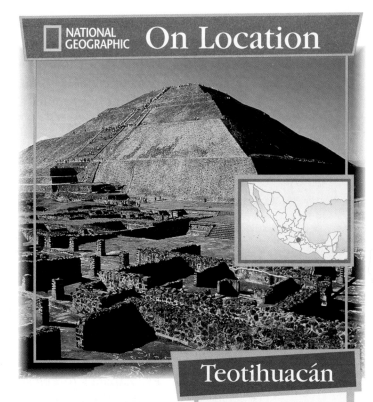

NATIONAL GEOGRAPHIC On Location

Teotihuacán

Hundreds of years before the appearance of the Aztec or the Spanish, Native Americans built monuments, such as the Temple of the Sun in the city of Teotihuacán. Teotihuacán was located near what is now Mexico City.

History How was the small Spanish army able to defeat the Aztec?

Independence and Revolution

The people of Mexico resented Spanish rule. In 1810 they rallied behind a Catholic priest, Miguel Hidalgo. He led an army of peasants in revolt. Spanish officials brought charges against Hidalgo and executed him, but the rebellion did not stop. Mexicans won their independence from Spain in 1821. In 1824 they set up a republic with an elected president.

Soon after independence, Mexico lost some valuable territory. Mexico's northern province of Texas fought for and won its own independence from Mexico and asked to join the United States. In 1846 the United States fought Mexico in a dispute over the southern boundary of Texas. In the treaty ending the war, Mexico gave up its claims to Texas. Mexico lost other valuable territory to the United States that included what are today the states of California, Utah, and Nevada.

For many decades, rich families, army officers, and Catholic Church leaders held most of the power and wealth in Mexico. In 1910 Mexican peasants revolted. Emiliano Zapata, who commanded a rebel army, stated the goals of this revolution. He wanted to give to the poor "the lands, woods, and water that the landlords or bosses have taken from us." Zapata's forces seized many large haciendas and divided the land among the poor. In Mexico's northwest area, Francisco "Pancho" Villa also tried to help the poor, mostly Native American peasants.

✓ **Reading Check** Who led the 1910 revolution in Mexico?

FCAT PRACTICE You can prepare for the FCAT-assessed standards by completing the correlated item(s) below.

Section 2 Assessment

Defining Terms
1. **Define** jade, obsidian, maize, hieroglyphics, mural, hacienda.

Recalling Facts
2. **History** Describe three achievements of the ancient Maya.
3. **History** Which European country conquered and colonized Mexico?
4. **History** What were Emiliano Zapata's goals?

Critical Thinking
5. **Sequencing Information** Put the following events in the correct chronological order: Cortés conquers the Aztec, Mexico wins independence from Spain, the Mexica move into central Mexico, Zapata leads a revolution. **FCAT LA.A.2.3.1**

6. **Understanding Cause and Effect** How did the arrival of Europeans affect the Native Americans in Mexico? **FCAT LA.A.2.3.1**

Graphic Organizer
7. **Organizing Information** Create a chart like this one. In each column, list the major advancements of each civilization. **FCAT LA.A.1.3.2**

Olmec	Maya	Aztec

Applying Social Studies Skills

8. **Analyzing Maps** Refer to the map of Mexico's Native American civilizations on page 198. Which Native American group settled the farthest south?

Making Connections

ART   SCIENCE   CULTURE   TECHNOLOGY

The Aztec Calendar Stone

It is hard to imagine how a huge stone filled with carved figures can serve as a calendar. Known commonly as the Sun Stone, the Aztec calendar is full of both scientific and religious information.

History

In 1790 workers in the heart of the *zócalo*, or main square, of Mexico City uncovered a massive circular stone. Mexico City sits on top of Tenochtitlán, the ancient capital of the Aztec Empire. Some 300 years earlier, the Aztec at Tenochtitlán had carved the 25-ton (23-t) basalt rock calendar. Using stone tools, they created a monument that measured 12 feet (3.6 m) in diameter and 3 feet (0.9 m) thick.

The face of the Aztec sun god appears at the center of the calendar stone. The sun god was thought to be one of the most important Aztec gods. Seven rings surround the sun god. In the closest ring are four squarelike spaces, each with a symbol that represents the four past ages of the world—the time that existed before humans appeared. Circling these symbols is a ring with signs representing the 20 days of the Aztec month.

Meaning of the Calendar

The Aztec calendar stone is actually two calendars in one. One calendar is a religious calendar based on a 260-day cycle. The Aztec believed that their lives depended on fulfilling their gods' demands. The calendar told Aztec priests when to make offerings and hold rituals for each god. It also divided the days among the gods. According to the Aztec view, this kept the universe in balance. An imbalance could lead to a power struggle among the gods and bring about the end of the world.

The second calendar is an agricultural calendar based on a 365-day solar cycle. The Aztec were very efficient farmers. They used this calendar to keep track of the seasons and ceremonies related to agricultural cycles.

Making the Connection

1. What does the Aztec agricultural calendar reveal about the scientific understanding of the Aztec?

2. Why was it important for the Aztec to divide the days among the gods?

3. **Making Comparisons** How do the two calendar systems of the Aztec differ? **FCAT LA.A.2.2.7**

◀ Today the Aztec calendar stone is displayed in the National Museum of Anthropology in Mexico City.

Guide to Reading

Main Idea

Mexicans enjoy a rich and lively culture but face many serious challenges.

Terms to Know

- plaza
- adobe
- federal republic
- migrant worker
- national debt
- smog

Reading Strategy

Create a diagram like this one. In each of the smaller ovals, write a feature of Mexican culture. Add as many smaller ovals as you need. **FCAT** LA.A.1.3.2

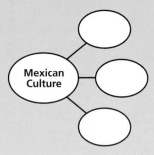

Mexican Culture

The following are the major Sunshine State Standards covered in this section.

SS.A.3.3.5:
Understands the differences between institutions of Eastern and Western civilizations (e.g., differences in governments, social traditions and customs, economic systems and religious institutions)

SS.B.2.3.4:
Understands ways the landscape and society change as a consequence of shifting from a dispersed to a concentrated settlement form

NATIONAL GEOGRAPHIC Exploring Our World

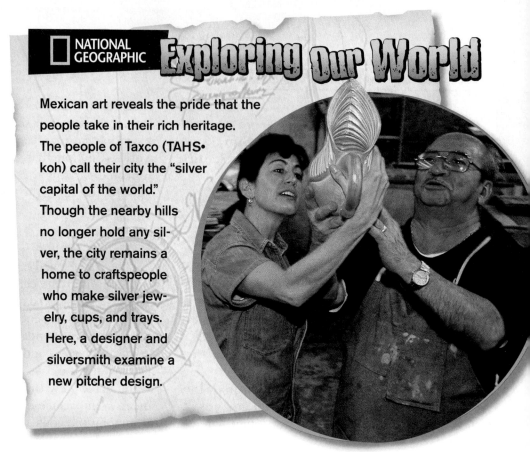

Mexican art reveals the pride that the people take in their rich heritage. The people of Taxco (TAHS•koh) call their city the "silver capital of the world." Though the nearby hills no longer hold any silver, the city remains a home to craftspeople who make silver jewelry, cups, and trays. Here, a designer and silversmith examine a new pitcher design.

Mexico—the third-largest country in area in Latin America, after Brazil and Argentina—has a large and dynamic population. About 75 percent of all Mexicans live in the country's bustling cities.

Mexico's Cities and Villages

In the center of Mexico's cities, you often find large **plazas,** or public squares. Around each city's plaza stand important buildings such as a church and a government center. When you look at the buildings, you can see the architectural style of Spanish colonial times. Newer sections of the cities have a mix of towering glass office buildings and modern houses. In the poorer sections of town, people build small homes out of whatever materials they can find. These materials may include boards, sheet metal, or even cardboard.

Rural villages also have central plazas. Streets lead from the plazas to residential areas. Many homes are made of **adobe** (uh•DOH•bee), or sun-dried clay bricks. The roofs might be made of straw or of colored tile, in the Spanish style.

✓**Reading Check** What do you find in the center of Mexico's cities and villages?

Mexican Culture

Mexican artists and writers have created many national treasures. In the early 1900s, Mexican painters produced beautiful murals—just as Native American painters had done centuries before. Among the most famous of these mural painters were José Clemente Orozco, David Alfero Sequieros, and Diego Rivera. Rivera's wife, Frida Kahlo, became well-known for her paintings, which revealed her inner feelings. Modern writers such as Carlos Fuentes and Octavio Paz have written poems and stories that reflect the values of Mexico's people.

Food   If you have tasted Mexican food, you know that it is a rich blend of flavors. Corn—first grown in Mexico—continues to be an important part of the Mexican diet. Chocolate, tomatoes, beans, squash, and chilies were all Native American foods as well. When the Spanish came, they brought beef, chicken, cheese, and olive oil, which Mexicans added to their cooking.

Today Mexicans use these different cooking traditions in popular foods such as tacos and enchiladas. Both dishes combine a flat bread called a tortilla with meat or beans, vegetables, cheese, and spicy chilies.

Celebrations   Throughout the year, Mexicans enjoy celebrations called fiestas (fee•EHS•tuhs). These special days include parades, fireworks, music, and dancing. Mariachi (MAHR•ee•AH•chee) bands may play such traditional instruments as the violin, guitar, horn, and bass at fiestas. More likely, though, you will hear the fast-paced rhythms and singing of Latino bands, which have influenced the United States.

National holidays include Independence Day (September 16) and Cinco de Mayo (May 5). Cinco de Mayo celebrates the day in 1862 that Mexicans defeated an invading French army in battle. November 2 is a

EXPLORING CULTURE

Art

Mexican artist Diego Rivera is one of the most famous mural painters of the twentieth century. He believed that art belonged to the people. In Mexico City, Rivera's murals line the courtyard of the Ministry of Education building and cover the walls of the National Palace. With their characteristically vivid colors and distinctive style, Rivera's murals tell the story of the work, culture, and history of the Mexican people.

Looking Closer How did Rivera's work support his belief that art belongs to the people?

Mexico Through the Centuries ▶

Fiestas

On September 16, Mexicans have parades to celebrate the women and men who helped win Mexican independence.

Culture What is the purpose of fiestas?

special religious celebration called the "Day of the Dead." On this day, families gather in cemeteries where they honor their departed loved ones by laying down food and flowers.

✓ **Reading Check** What are some important celebrations in Mexico?

Mexico's Government

Mexico, like the United States, is a **federal republic,** where power is divided between national and state governments. A strong president leads the national government. Mexico's national government differs in that it has much more power than the state governments. The president of Mexico is head of the executive branch of government. He or she can serve only one six-year term but has more power than the legislative and judicial branches.

For many decades, one political party, called the Party of Institutional Revolution (PRI), led Mexico. All the presidents and most other elected officials came from this party. In recent years, economic troubles and the people's lack of political power led to growing frustration. In the year 2000, the newly elected president of Mexico, Vicente Fox, came from a different political party—for the first time in more than 70 years.

Mexico's government faces many difficult challenges. People in Mexico are demanding more political freedom to make decisions that affect their everyday lives. Traffic in illegal drugs is of concern to the government as well. Nearly 40 percent of Mexico's 100 million people live below the poverty line. To fight the country's pressing problems, from poverty to drugs, a strong central government is needed. To increase democracy in Mexico, however, Fox must give power back to local and state agencies. Fox will have to help his country find the balance between these two levels of government.

✓ **Reading Check** What form of government does Mexico have?

Mexico's Challenges

Mexico has tried to use its resources to improve the lives of its people. These actions have had strong effects on Mexican life—and have created some challenges for the future.

Population Mexico's population has increased rapidly in recent decades. Because many people have moved to the cities to find jobs, the cities have grown quickly. A large number of people have had to take jobs that pay low wages. As a result, hundreds of thousands of people crowd together in slums, or poor sections of the cities.

Those Mexicans who cannot find any work in their country may become **migrant workers.** These are people who travel from place to place when extra workers are needed to plant or harvest crops. They legally and sometimes illegally cross Mexico's long border to work in the United States. Though the pay is low, the migrant workers can earn more in the United States than in Mexico.

Another challenge concerning Mexico's people involves the descendants of the ancient Maya Indians. The present-day Maya live in the southernmost state of Mexico called **Chiapas.** Turn to the map on page 191 to see where Chiapas is located. This state is one of the poorest states in Mexico. Over 75 percent of the people there live below the poverty level. Most of the wealth in Chiapas is concentrated in a very small number of ranching families who are of Spanish descent. Diseases and illness that result from poverty and lack of health care cause thousands of deaths every year. Many Maya are fighting for independence from the central government because they lost hope in the Mexican government.

Foreign Debt   For decades, the Mexican government refused to let foreign companies build factories in Mexico. Leaders feared that the companies would take their profits to their own country, thus draining

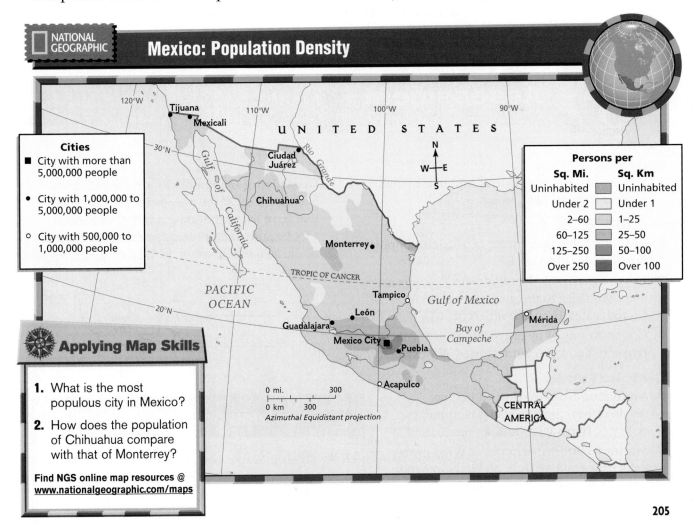

Mexico: Population Density

NATIONAL GEOGRAPHIC

Cities

■ City with more than 5,000,000 people

● City with 1,000,000 to 5,000,000 people

○ City with 500,000 to 1,000,000 people

Persons per

Sq. Mi.	Sq. Km
Uninhabited	Uninhabited
Under 2	Under 1
2–60	1–25
60–125	25–50
125–250	50–100
Over 250	Over 100

UNITED STATES

Tijuana
Mexicali
Ciudad Juárez
Chihuahua
Rio Grande
Gulf of California
Monterrey
TROPIC OF CANCER
PACIFIC OCEAN
Tampico
Gulf of Mexico
León
Mérida
Guadalajara
Bay of Campeche
Mexico City
Puebla
Acapulco
CENTRAL AMERICA

0 mi. 300
0 km 300
Azimuthal Equidistant projection

Applying Map Skills

1. What is the most populous city in Mexico?

2. How does the population of Chihuahua compare with that of Monterrey?

Find NGS online map resources @ www.nationalgeographic.com/maps

money out of Mexico. In the 1990s, the government changed this policy. Mexican officials were still concerned that money would be lost, but hoped that the new factories would create more jobs for Mexicans.

To help its economy grow, Mexico borrowed money from foreign banks. The government then had to use any money it earned in taxes to pay back the loans. As a result, Mexico's leaders did not have enough funds to spend on the Mexican people when the economy began to struggle. Many Mexicans grew angry. Yet, if the government did not make the loan payments, banks would refuse to lend more money for future plans. Because there are still loans to be repaid, Mexicans will face this situation for many years. The problem of repaying a **national debt,** or money owed by the government, is one that is being faced by many countries in the world today.

Pollution As Mexico's population boomed, its cities grew very large. At the same time, the economy industrialized. Both of these changes contributed to rising pollution in Mexico.

The mountains that surround Mexico City trap the exhaust fumes from hundreds of thousands of cars. People in this city wake each day to a thick haze of fog and chemicals called **smog.** Many people wear masks when they leave their homes to go to work or school. In northern Mexico, many factories release dangerous chemicals into the air or water. One environmental group says that the Rio Grande is now one of the most polluted rivers in North America.

✓ Reading Check **What challenges does Mexico face?**

FCAT PRACTICE You can prepare for the FCAT-assessed standards by completing the correlated item(s) below.

Assessment

Defining Terms
1. **Define** plaza, adobe, federal republic, migrant worker, national debt, smog.

Recalling Facts
2. **Culture** What percentage of Mexico's population lives in urban areas?

3. **Government** Explain how Mexico's government is similar to the government of the United States. How is it different? **FCAT LA.A.1.3.2**

4. **Government** Why did Mexico's government refuse to allow foreign factories in Mexico?

Critical Thinking
5. **Analyzing Information** What has resulted from the Mexican government's policy of borrowing from foreign banks?

6. **Summarizing Information** What problems have resulted from Mexico's expanding population? **FCAT LA.A.2.3.1**

Graphic Organizer
7. **Organizing Information** Create a diagram like this one. On the arrows, list three factors that have led to the smog problem of Mexico City. Be sure to consider physical characteristics of the area when listing the factors. **FCAT LA.A.1.3.2**

Smog in Mexico City

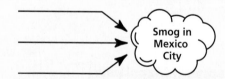

Applying Social Studies Skills

8. **Analyzing Maps** Look at the population density map on page 205. What is the population of Guadalajara? What is the population density of the area surrounding Mérida?

Chapter 6

Reading Review

Section 1 — Mexico's Land and Economy

Terms to Know

land bridge
peninsula
latitude
altitude
hurricane
vaquero
maquiladora
subsistence farm
plantation
industrialize
service industry

Main Idea

Mexico's mountainous landscape and varied climate create different economic regions.

✓ **Location** Mexico is part of a land bridge that connects North and South America.

✓ **Location** Much of Mexico lies in the Tropics, but the climate in some areas is cool because of high elevation.

✓ **Economics** Landforms and climate combine to create three economic zones in Mexico.

✓ **Movement** Mexico's economy is growing, and many people are moving to the northern cities.

Section 2 — Mexico's History

Terms to Know

jade
obsidian
maize
hieroglyphics
mural
hacienda

Main Idea

Mexico's culture reflects a blend of its Native American and Spanish past.

✓ **History** Mexico's Native American civilizations—the Olmec, Maya, and Aztec—made many contributions to Mexico's culture.

✓ **Culture** Mexico's people reflect the country's Native American and Spanish roots.

✓ **History** The Spanish ruled Mexico from the 1500s to 1821, when Mexico won its independence.

✓ **History** The poor people in Mexico revolted against the rich and powerful church and military leaders in 1910.

Section 3 — Mexico Today

Terms to Know

plaza
adobe
federal republic
migrant worker
national debt
smog

Main Idea

Mexicans enjoy a rich and lively culture but face many serious challenges.

✓ **Location** About 75 percent of Mexicans live in cities today.

✓ **Culture** Mexicans enjoy celebrations called fiestas, which can include parades, fireworks, and music.

✓ **Government** Mexico's government is a federal republic.

✓ **Economics** Challenges facing Mexico include problems caused by population growth, foreign investment and debt, and pollution.

Assessment and Activities

 FCAT PRACTICE You can prepare for the FCAT-assessed standards by completing the correlated item(s) below.

Using Key Terms

Match the terms in Part A with their definitions in Part B.

A.

1. altitude
2. hurricane
3. vaquero
4. maquiladora
5. jade
6. adobe
7. plaza
8. smog
9. mural
10. subsistence farm

B.

a. factory that assembles parts from other countries
b. cowhand
c. sun-dried clay bricks
d. wall painting
e. height above sea level
f. fog mixed with smoke
g. produces only enough to support a family's needs
h. fierce tropical storm
i. public square
j. shiny stone that comes in many shades of green

Reviewing the Main Ideas

Section 1 Mexico's Land and Economy

11. **Location** How does Mexico's latitude affect its climate?
12. **Economics** What are Mexico's major exports?
13. **Movement** How have maquiladoras affected northern Mexico's cities?

Section 2 Mexico's History

14. **History** What was the capital city of the Aztec civilization?
15. **History** What effects did Spanish conquest have on Native Americans? **FCAT LA.E.2.2.1**
16. **History** When did Mexico win its independence from Spain?

Section 3 Mexico Today

17. **Government** What are people in Mexico demanding from the Mexican government?
18. **Culture** What does Cinco de Mayo celebrate?

 **Mexico**

Place Location Activity

On a separate sheet of paper, match the letters on the map with the numbered places listed below.

1. Pacific Ocean
2. Mexico City
3. Plateau of Mexico
4. Yucatán Peninsula
5. Baja California
6. Rio Grande
7. Gulf of Mexico
8. Guadalajara
9. Monterrey
10. Caribbean Sea

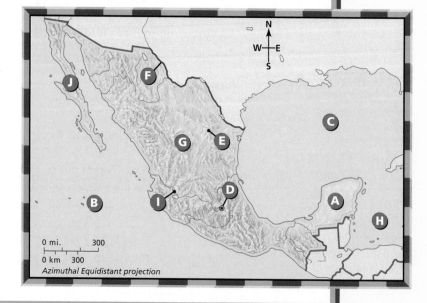

Critical Thinking

19. **Understanding Cause and Effect** Why have Mexico's leaders encouraged free trade agreements with other countries? **FCAT** LA.A.2.3.1

20. **Problem Solving** If you were Mexico's president, what would you do to rid Mexico of the problems of illegal drugs and poverty?

Comparing Regions Activity

21. **Culture** People from different regions may have different ways of measuring time. The Aztec Stone, for example, was both a religious and an agricultural calendar. Compare the Aztec Stone to another region's calendar that is no longer in use, such as the ancient Egyptian or Roman calendar. How are they alike? How are they different? **FCAT** LA.B.1.3.2

Mental Mapping Activity

22. **Focusing on the Region** Create a simple outline map of Mexico. Refer to the physical map on page 196 and then label the following:

   • Pacific Ocean
   • Gulf of Mexico
   • Yucatán Peninsula
   • Baja California
   • Mexico City
   • Rio Grande
   • Sierra Madre Occidental

Technology Skills Activity

23. **Developing a Multimedia Presentation** Imagine that you work for Mexico's Economic Development Office. Create a multimedia presentation to present to a group of foreign investors. Use a software application such as PowerPoint® to showcase positive features like climate, resources, and labor supply. Your goal is to show investors that Mexico is a good place for them to invest their money. **FCAT** LA.A.2.3.5

Standardized Test Practice

Directions: Read the paragraph below, and then answer the question that follows.

   The Aztec civilization was organized into classes. At the top was the emperor. His power came from his control of the army and the religious beliefs of the people. Next came the nobles, followed by commoners. Commoners included priests, merchants, and artists. Below commoners were the serfs, or workers who farmed the nobles' fields. Slaves, the lowest class, included criminals and people in debt, as well as female and child prisoners of war. Male prisoners of war were sacrificed to the Aztec gods. The Aztec believed that live human sacrifices were needed to keep the gods pleased and to prevent floods and other disasters.

1. **Which of the following statements is an opinion about the information given above?** **FCAT** LA.A.2.3.8

   F The Aztec civilization was organized into classes.

   G Male prisoners of war were sacrificed to the Aztec gods.

   H Slaves included children.

   J The Aztec should not have sacrificed people to the gods.

> **Test-Taking Tip:** This question asks you to identify an opinion. An opinion is a person's belief. It is not a proven fact (such as answer F). Opinions often contain subjective words, such as *easier, best,* or *should.*

Central America and the Caribbean Islands

The World and Its People

NATIONAL GEOGRAPHIC

To learn more about the people and places of Central America and the Caribbean, view **The World and Its People Chapter 7** video.

Social Studies online

Chapter Overview Visit **The World and Its People** Web site at <u>twip.glencoe.com</u> and click on **Chapter 7—Chapter Overviews** to preview information about Central America and the Caribbean islands.

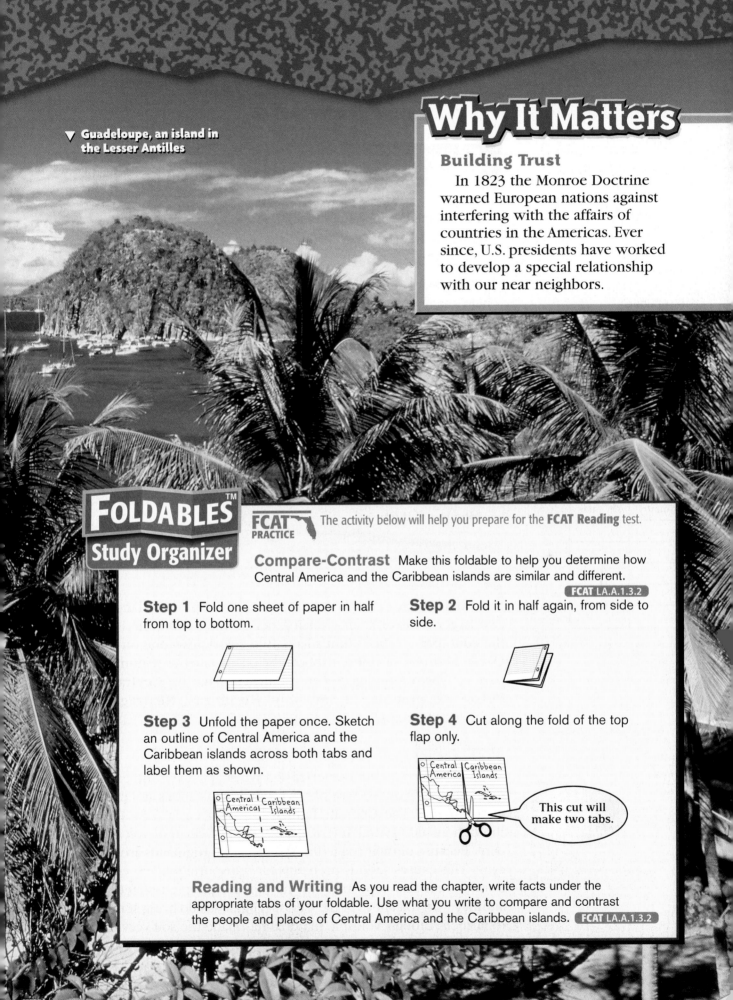

▼ **Guadeloupe, an island in the Lesser Antilles**

Why It Matters

Building Trust

In 1823 the Monroe Doctrine warned European nations against interfering with the affairs of countries in the Americas. Ever since, U.S. presidents have worked to develop a special relationship with our near neighbors.

FOLDABLES™
Study Organizer

FCAT PRACTICE The activity below will help you prepare for the **FCAT Reading** test.

Compare-Contrast Make this foldable to help you determine how Central America and the Caribbean islands are similar and different.

FCAT LA.A.1.3.2

Step 1 Fold one sheet of paper in half from top to bottom.

Step 2 Fold it in half again, from side to side.

Step 3 Unfold the paper once. Sketch an outline of Central America and the Caribbean islands across both tabs and label them as shown.

Central America | Caribbean Islands

Step 4 Cut along the fold of the top flap only.

Central America | Caribbean Islands

This cut will make two tabs.

Reading and Writing As you read the chapter, write facts under the appropriate tabs of your foldable. Use what you write to compare and contrast the people and places of Central America and the Caribbean islands. **FCAT LA.A.1.3.2**

Central America

Guide to Reading

Main Idea

Central America is made up of seven nations that are home to a variety of peoples, exotic animals, and diverse landforms.

Terms to Know

- isthmus
- canopy
- ecotourist
- literacy rate
- republic
- parliamentary democracy

Reading Strategy

Create a chart like this one. List several countries in Central America, and write two key facts about each country. **FCAT** LA.A.1.3.2

Country	Key Facts

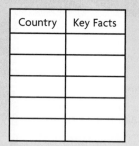

The following are the major Sunshine State Standards covered in this section.

SS.B.2.3.8:
Knows world patterns of resource distribution and utilization

SS.B.1.3.3:
Knows the social, political, and economic divisions on Earth's surface

NATIONAL GEOGRAPHIC Exploring Our World

Unusual animals found nowhere else on the earth roam the floor and canopy of Central America's rain forests. The small frog here seems as if it would be a snack for other, larger animals. Do not be fooled by the enlargement of the photo, however. Many frogs like this one hold a deadly poison in their skin, which would quickly kill anything that tried to eat them.

Central America is an isthmus, or a narrow piece of land that links two larger areas of land—North America and South America. Most of the countries on the isthmus have two coastlines—one on the Pacific Ocean and one on the Caribbean Sea. This narrow region is actually part of North America. Seven countries make up Central America: **Belize, Guatemala, El Salvador, Honduras, Nicaragua, Costa Rica,** and **Panama.**

A Rugged Land

Like Mexico, Central America sits where plates in the earth's crust meet. The collision of these plates produces volcanoes and earthquakes in the region. The Central Highlands, which curve like a backbone through inland Central America, are actually a chain of volcanic mountains. Because of their ruggedness, the Central Highlands are difficult to cross. This causes serious problems for transportation and communication and has also kept many of the region's people isolated from one another. The volcanoes of the Central Highlands do bring some benefits to farmers, though. Volcanic material has made the soil very fertile.

Central America is mostly tropical, although the mountains remain cool. Lowlands along the Caribbean side receive about 100 inches (254 cm) of rain year-round. Lowlands along the Pacific, however, are drier from December through April. Cooling breezes from the Caribbean Sea can become deadly hurricanes during the summer and fall. Remember that hurricanes are fierce storms with heavy rains and high winds of more than 74 miles (119 km) per hour.

✓ **Reading Check** How have the volcanoes in Central America been helpful?

Central American Economies

The economies of the Central American countries depend on farming and harvesting wood from their rain forests. Central America has two kinds of farms. Wealthy people and companies own plantations, which, as you learned in Chapter 6, are commercial farms that grow crops for sale. Major crops include coffee, bananas, cotton, and sugarcane. Plantations export their harvest to the United States and other parts of the world. Farmers in Guatemala and Costa Rica also grow flowers and ornamental plants for export.

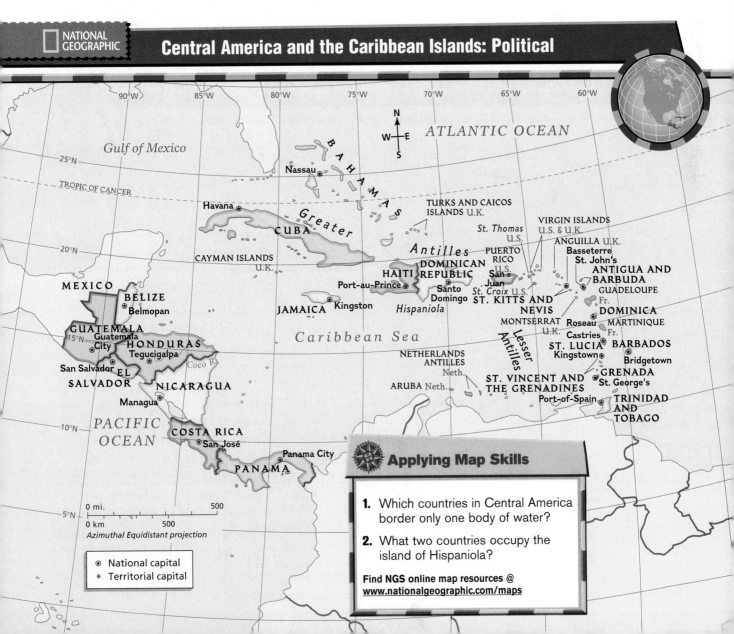

NATIONAL GEOGRAPHIC

Central America and the Caribbean Islands: Political

Applying Map Skills

1. Which countries in Central America border only one body of water?

2. What two countries occupy the island of Hispaniola?

Find **NGS** online map resources @ www.nationalgeographic.com/maps

● National capital
∘ Territorial capital

Many farms in Central America are not plantations but subsistence farms. These are small plots of land where poor farmers grow only enough food to feed their families. Subsistence farmers typically raise livestock and grow corn, beans, and rice.

Rain Forests   Beneath Central America's green canopy, or topmost layer of the rain forest that shades the forest floor, lie many treasures. Ancient ruins of past empires can be found as well as valuable resources. The dense forests offer expensive woods—mahogany and rosewood, for example. Unusual animal and plant species also thrive here. Scientists research the plants to develop new medicines.

Both local and foreign-owned companies have set up large-scale operations in the rain forests. Lumber companies cut down and export the valuable trees. Other companies and local farmers also cut or burn the trees to clear land for farming. Without trees to hold the soil in place, rains wash the soil and its nutrients away. As a result, the land soon becomes poor. The businesses and farmers then move on, clearing trees from another piece of land.

Many Central Americans worry about the rapid destruction of the rain forests. Some countries are responding to this crisis by helping workers replant cleared areas. Costa Rica has set aside one-fourth of its

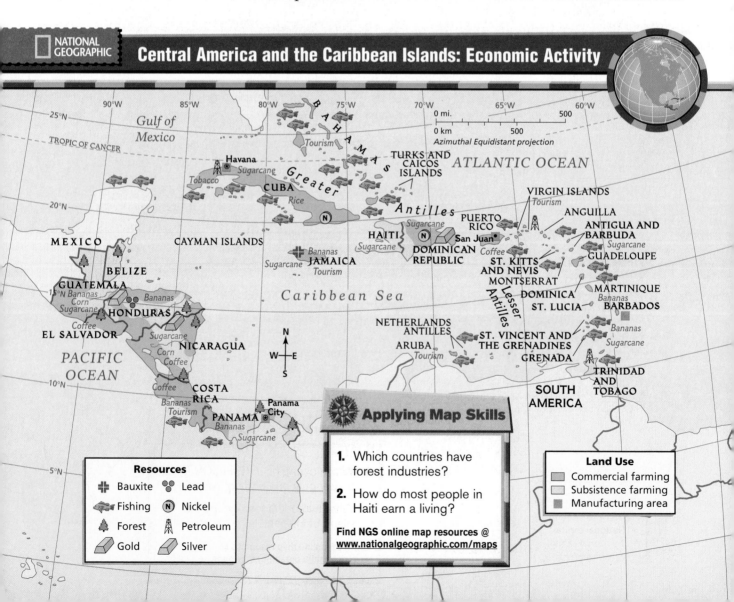

Central America and the Caribbean Islands: Economic Activity

Applying Map Skills

1. Which countries have forest industries?

2. How do most people in Haiti earn a living?

Find NGS online map resources @ www.nationalgeographic.com/maps

Resources
- Bauxite
- Fishing
- Forest
- Gold
- Lead
- Nickel
- Petroleum
- Silver

Land Use
- Commercial farming
- Subsistence farming
- Manufacturing area

forests as national parks. It uses the rain forests to attract **ecotourists,** or people who travel to other countries to enjoy natural wonders.

Industry Missing from the skylines of most major Central American cities are the smokestacks of industry. The few industries that exist generally focus on food processing. In Guatemala, Honduras, and Nicaragua, some factories produce clothing for export.

Guatemala, which has some oil reserves, exports crude oil. Costa Rica produces computer chips, other electronic goods, and medicines. With its varied economy, Costa Rica enjoys one of the highest standards of living in Latin America. It also has one of the highest **literacy rates,** or percentage of people who can read and write.

Tourism is of growing importance in Central America. If you like bird-watching, Costa Rica is the place to visit. The country has about 850 different kinds of birds. Guatemala and Honduras also draw many tourists to the magnificent ruins of their ancient Mayan culture.

The Panama Canal The economy in Panama—just like the other countries of Central America—is based on farming. Panama also earns money from its canal, however. The Panama Canal stretches across the narrow Isthmus of Panama. Ships pay a fee to use the canal to shorten travel time between the Atlantic and Pacific Oceans. Turn to page 218 to see how the canal works.

The United States built the canal and owned it for more than 80 years. Panama was given final control of the canal on December 31, 1999. Panama hopes to use this waterway to build its economy. Nearly half of Panama's 3 million people live and work in the canal area.

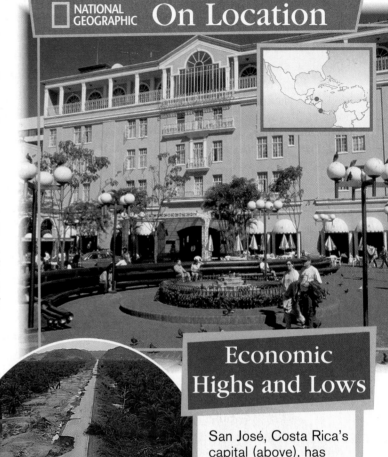

NATIONAL GEOGRAPHIC On Location

Economic Highs and Lows

San José, Costa Rica's capital (above), has shopping malls and fast-food chains like many North American cities. In 1998 Hurricane Mitch caused massive mudslides that buried whole villages and destroyed crops in Honduras (left).

Issues During what seasons do hurricanes strike Central America?

✓**Reading Check** What are the major crops grown on Central America's plantations?

Central Americans—Then and Now

Native Americans settled Central America thousands of years ago. The Olmecs were the first civilization in the area, from about 1200 B.C. to 400 B.C. The Maya flourished in the rain forests of the north from about A.D. 250 to 900. Look at the Native American civilizations map on

What a Catch!

The deep, blue waters of Lake Nicaragua are home to the world's only freshwater sharks and swordfish. Now the lake holds one less swordfish. Amadeo Robelo, who lives in Granada, Nicaragua, just spent three hours battling the powerful fish. Amadeo enjoys fishing with his father on weekends. His father wants Amadeo to become part of Nicaragua's middle class—something new in a region where you are either one of the few with wealth or one of the many who live in poverty.

page 198. In **Tikal** (tee•KAHL), Guatemala, and **Copán** (koh•PAHN), Honduras, the Maya created impressive temples and sculptures. Before Columbus arrived, Tikal was the site of the highest structure in the Americas, a 212-foot (64.6-m) temple rising from the floor of the rain forest. The Maya were a highly developed civilization. Their religion focused on the careful study of time and the stars, astronomy, and mathematics. The Maya developed a calendar and kept records on stone slabs. Then the Maya mysteriously left their cities. Many of their descendants still live in the area today.

In the 1500s, Spaniards established settlements in Central America. For the next 300 years, Spanish landowners forced Native Americans to work on plantations. The two cultures gradually blended. Native Americans started to speak the Spanish language and follow the Roman Catholic faith. Native Americans taught the Spanish about local plants for medicines and how to trap animals for food and hides.

Most Central American countries gained independence from Spain by 1821. The two exceptions are Panama and Belize. Panama was part of the South American country of Colombia for decades. In 1903 the United States helped Panama win its independence in exchange for the right to build the Panama Canal. Belize, a British colony until 1981, was the last Central American country to gain independence.

After Independence Most Central American countries faced constant conflict after they became independent. A small number of people in each country held most of the wealth and power. Rebel movements arose as poor farmers fought for changes that would give them land and better lives. Civil wars raged in Nicaragua, El Salvador, and Guatemala as recently as the 1980s and 1990s.

In Guatemala from 1960 to 1996, government military forces fought rebel groups living in the highlands. About 150,000 people died, and the civil war severely weakened Guatemala's economy. Tens of thousands of Guatemalans left the country to look for work in the United States.

In contrast, Costa Ricans have enjoyed peace. A stable democratic government rules, and the country has avoided conflict for most of its history. As a result of these peaceful relations, the country has no army—only a police force to maintain law and order.

Today each country in Central America has a democratic government, with voters choosing government officials. Six countries are also republics, with elected presidents as head of the government. Belize is a British-style parliamentary democracy, in which an elected legislature chooses a prime minister to head the government.

Daily Life Nearly 40 million people live in Central America. About one-third of this number live in Guatemala, the most heavily populated country in the region. In contrast, only about 300,000 people live in Belize, the region's least populous country. Spanish is the official language throughout the region, except for English-speaking Belize. Many Central Americans also speak Native American languages, such as Mayan. Guatemala's population, for instance, is largely Native American and has more than 20 different Native American languages. Most Central Americans follow the Roman Catholic religion.

About 50 percent of all Central Americans live on farms or in small villages. At least one major city, usually the capital, is densely populated in each country. Guatemala's capital, **Guatemala City,** ranks with **San José,** Costa Rica, as one of the most populous cities in Central America. People living in urban areas hold manufacturing or service industry jobs, or they work on farms outside the cities. Those living in coastal areas may harvest shrimp, lobster, and other seafood to sell in city markets or for export.

Whether rural or urban, most people enjoy a major celebration called Carnival. This festival comes before Lent, a solemn period of prayer and soul-searching before the Christian celebration of Easter. During Carnival—and at other times—bands play salsa, a mixture of Latin American popular music, jazz, and rock. Do you like baseball? It is a national sport in Nicaragua and is very popular in Panama too. Most people throughout the region also enjoy *fútbol,* or soccer.

✓ **Reading Check** Why is the government of Belize different from that of other countries in Central America?

FCAT PRACTICE You can prepare for the FCAT-assessed standards by completing the correlated item(s) below.

Assessment

Defining Terms
1. **Define** isthmus, canopy, ecotourist, literacy rate, republic, parliamentary democracy.

Recalling Facts
2. **Economics** What is the difference between plantation and subsistence farming? **FCAT LA.A.2.2.7**
3. **Culture** What are the major religion and language of Central America?
4. **Place** Which country in Central America is the most heavily populated? The most sparsely populated?

Critical Thinking
5. **Making Comparisons** How have the differences in government stability affected the citizens of Guatemala and Costa Rica in the past and today? **FCAT LA.A.2.3.1**

6. **Analyzing Cause and Effect** Explain why rain forest soil does not keep its nutrients long after trees are cut down. **FCAT LA.A.2.3.1, SC.D.2.3.2**

Graphic Organizer
7. **Organizing Information** Create a diagram like this one. On the lines, list the major products and industries of Central America. **FCAT LA.A.1.3.2**

Major products and industries

Applying Social Studies Skills

8. **Analyzing Maps** Refer to the political map on page 213. Which countries of Central America border Mexico? Which border the Pacific Ocean?

Making Connections

ART   SCIENCE   CULTURE   TECHNOLOGY

The Panama Canal Locks

Before the Panama Canal was built, ships had to sail around the southern tip of South America to go from the Atlantic Ocean to the Pacific Ocean and vice versa. The canal provides a shortcut that reduces that trip by about 7,000 miles (11,270 km).

Digging the Canal

The first attempts to build a canal across Panama were begun in 1881 by a private French company. Huge expenses, poor planning, and the effects of diseases such as malaria and yellow fever stopped construction. In 1904 the United States government took over. Doctors had recently learned that bites from infected mosquitoes caused malaria and yellow fever. Workers drained swamps and cleared brush to remove the mosquitoes' breeding grounds. Then the digging began. The canal's course ran through hills of soft volcanic soil. Massive landslides regularly occurred before the 50-mile (80-km) canal was completed in 1914.

FCAT PRACTICE Answering question 3 below will help you prepare for the **FCAT Reading** test.

An Engineering Masterpiece

To move ships through the canal, engineers designed three sets of locks—the largest concrete structures on the earth. They allow ships to move from one water level to another by changing the amount of water in the locks. Together, the locks can raise or lower ships about 85 feet (26 m)—the height of a seven-story building. The diagram below shows you how these locks work.

Making the Connection

1. Why was a canal through Panama desirable?

2. What function do locks perform?

3. **Understanding Cause and Effect** How did medical advances affect the building of the Panama Canal? **FCAT LA.E.2.2.1**

The Panama Canal Locks

Culebra Cut — Pedro Miguel Locks — Miraflores Lake — Miraflores Locks — Gatun Locks — *Gatun Lake* — Atlantic Ocean — Pacific Ocean — 85 ft. — Level of the Atlantic

1. The downstream gates are opened and the ship moves slowly into the lock.

2. After the ship is secured, the gates close and valves open to fill the lock with water from upstream.

3. As the lock fills, the ship rises to the level of the water upstream.

4. The upstream gates are then opened and the ship passes through.

To move a vessel upstream, where the water level is higher, the water level in the lock is lowered to that of the water just downstream.

To move a vessel downstream, the process is reversed.

Downstream gate open — Downstream water level — Lock chambers — Upstream water level — Upstream gates closed — Control station — Power station

Cultures of the Caribbean

NATIONAL GEOGRAPHIC Exploring Our World

The warm waters of the Caribbean Sea lure millions of tourists to the Caribbean islands every year. Some tourists go scuba diving so they can see the colorful fish, which swim in the islands' clear waters. Others shop at the local stores, buying hand-crafted goods. This diver uses a metal detector to look for objects from a Spanish ship that sank in the 1600s.

Several **archipelagos** (AHR•kuh•PEH•luh•GOHS), or groups of islands, dot the **Caribbean Sea.** East of Florida are the **Bahamas,** an archipelago of nearly 700 islands. South of Florida you find the **Greater Antilles.** This group includes the large islands of **Cuba, Jamaica, Hispaniola,** and **Puerto Rico.** To the southeast are smaller islands called the **Lesser Antilles.**

Mountaintop Islands

Many of the Caribbean islands (also known as the **West Indies**) are the tops of an underwater chain of mountains formed by volcanoes. A typical volcanic island has central highlands ringed by coastal plains. The volcanic soil in the highlands is rich. Other islands are limestone mountains that have been pushed up from the ocean floor by pressures under the earth's crust. Limestone islands are generally flatter than volcanic islands and have sandy soil that is not good for farming.

Climate   Most of the Caribbean islands have a fairly constant tropical savanna climate. Sea and wind, more than elevation, affect the climate here. Northeast breezes sweep across the Caribbean Sea and become the temperature of the cooler water beneath them. When the winds blow onshore, they keep temperatures pleasant. For half the year, however, hurricanes threaten the islands.

✓ Reading Check   What formed the Caribbean islands?

The Caribbean Economy

Tourism and farming are the most important economic activities in the Caribbean. The sunny climate and beautiful beaches attract millions of tourists each year. Tourism is the region's major industry. Airlines and cruise ships make regular stops at different islands.

Wealthy landowners grow sugarcane, bananas, coffee, and tobacco for export. Many laborers work on the plantations that grow these commercial crops. Some areas are used for subsistence farming. People may own or rent small plots of land. They grow rice and beans, which are basic parts of the diet in this region. They also grow fruits and vegetables.

Some countries in the Caribbean islands face an economic danger by depending on one commercial crop. If the crop fails, no income is earned. If too much of the crop is produced worldwide, overall prices fall and the economy is in serious trouble.

Look at the map on page 214. You can see that most of the islands do not have large amounts of minerals. Jamaica, however, mines bauxite, a mineral used to make aluminum. The country of Trinidad and Tobago exports oil products. In Puerto Rico, companies make chemicals and machinery. Haiti and the Dominican Republic have textile factories where workers make cloth. Several islands have banking and financial industries.

✓ Reading Check   What is the major industry in the Caribbean?

Caribbean History and Culture

When Christopher Columbus reached the island of San Salvador—now part of the Bahamas—in 1492, who met him? It was a Native American group—the Taíno. The Taíno and other Native Americans lived on the islands long before the coming of Europeans.

The Spaniards established the first permanent European settlement in the Western Hemisphere in 1496. That settlement is now the city of **Santo Domingo,** capital of the Dominican Republic. During the next 200 years, the Spaniards, the English, the French, and the Dutch also founded colonies, or overseas settlements, on many of the islands. They found the soil and climate perfect for growing sugarcane. During this time, new plants, animals, and other products were traded between the Americas and other parts of the world. Turn to page 228 to learn more about this so-called Columbian Exchange.

By the mid-1600s, most Native Americans had died from European diseases and harsh treatment. The Europeans then brought enslaved Africans to work on sugar plantations. When the slave trade ended in

Schoolgirls on Barbados walk past vast sugar plantations that European countries started in the colonial period (above left). A steel-drum band entertains tourists in Trinidad (above).

Region What attracts so many tourists to the Caribbean islands?

the early 1800s, plantation owners still in need of workers brought them from Asia, particularly India. Asians agreed to work a set number of years in return for free travel to the Caribbean and low wages.

Independence During the 1800s and 1900s, many Caribbean islands won their freedom from European rule. The first to become independent were the larger island countries, such as Haiti, the Dominican Republic, and Cuba. Later, smaller islands such as Barbados and Grenada became independent. Many countries—like Haiti and the Dominican Republic—are republics. Others—like Jamaica and the Bahamas—are British-style parliamentary democracies.

Cuba is the only country in the Western Hemisphere with a government based on communism. In a **communist state,** government leaders have strong control of the economy and society as a whole.

Some Caribbean islands are still not independent. Two large islands—Martinique and Guadeloupe—have ties to France. Puerto Rico and some of the Virgin Islands are linked to the United States. Other small islands are owned by the British or the Dutch.

Daily Life Many people in Central America have Native American ancestors. The peoples of the Caribbean, however, have African or mixed African and European ancestry. Large Asian populations live in Jamaica and Trinidad and Tobago as well.

More than 38 million people live in the Caribbean islands. Cuba, with about 11.3 million people, has the largest population in the region. Saint Kitts and Nevis has only about 50,000 people. Most people speak a European language and follow the Roman Catholic or Protestant religion.

Bee Hummingbird

How small is this bird? The bee hummingbird of Cuba measures only 2 inches (5.1 cm) from head to tail. That is small enough to make it the tiniest bird in the world. The bird's wings move so fast—80 beats per second—that the human eye cannot see them. At two grams, the bee hummingbird weighs less than a penny.

About 60 percent of the people live in cities and villages. The other 40 percent live and work in the countryside. Many islanders have jobs in the hotels or restaurants that serve the tourist industry. If you visit the Caribbean, you are likely to hear lively music. The bell-like tones of the steel drum, developed in Trinidad and Tobago, are part of the rich musical heritage of the region. Jamaica's reggae music combines African rhythms and American popular music. Cuban salsa blends African rhythms, Spanish styles, and jazz.

On several islands, you will hear a different sound—the crack of a baseball bat. People in Puerto Rico, the Dominican Republic, and Cuba have a passion for baseball. Soccer is another popular sport.

✓ Reading Check Where was the first permanent European settlement in the Caribbean islands?

Island Profiles

The Caribbean islands have many similarities, but they also have differences. Some of these differences can be seen in Cuba, Haiti, the Dominican Republic, and Puerto Rico.

Cuba One of the world's top sugar producers, Cuba lies about 90 miles (145 km) south of Florida. Most farmers work on **cooperatives,** or farms owned and operated by the government. In addition to growing sugarcane, they grow coffee, tobacco, rice, and fruits. In **Havana,** Cuba's capital and the largest city in the region, workers make food products, cigars, and household goods.

Cuba won its independence from Spain in 1898. The country had a democratic government, but in 1959 Fidel Castro led a revolution that took control of the government. Almost immediately, he set up a communist state and turned to the Soviet Union for support. When Castro seized property belonging to American companies, the United States government responded. It put in place an **embargo,** or a ban on trade, against Cuba.

Cuba relied on aid from the Soviet Union. When the Soviet Union broke apart in 1989, it stopped giving economic support to the island. The Cuban economy is struggling, and many Cubans live in poverty.

Haiti On the western half of the island of Hispaniola, you will find the country of **Haiti.** Led by a formerly enslaved man, Francois-Dominique Toussaint-Louverture, Haiti fought for and won its independence from France in 1804. It was the second independent republic in the Western Hemisphere (after the United States). It became the first nation in the history of the world to be founded by formerly enslaved persons. About 95 percent of Haiti's 7.5 million people are of African ancestry. Civil war has left Haiti's economy in ruins, and most Haitians are poor. Coffee and sugar, the main export crops, are shipped through **Port-au-Prince,** the country's capital.

Dominican Republic The **Dominican Republic** shares the island of Hispaniola with Haiti. The two countries have different histories and little contact, however. Haiti was a French colony. The Dominican

Republic was settled by Spaniards, who brought enslaved Africans to work on sugar plantations. Sugar is still an important crop. Tourism is growing too, and many Dominicans sell goods in the country's free trade zone. **Free trade zones** are areas where people can buy goods from other countries without paying taxes.

The government of the Dominican Republic hopes to build up the country's electrical power so the economy can grow more quickly. Poverty remains a problem. As a result, many Dominicans have left the country looking for work.

Puerto Rico   To be or not to be a state in the United States? This is the question that Puerto Ricans ask themselves every few years. The last time they voted, they said no. How did Puerto Rico become part of the United States? The island was a Spanish colony from 1508 to 1898. After the Spanish-American War in 1898, the United States won control of Puerto Rico. Since 1952 the island has been a **commonwealth,** or a partly self-governing territory, under U.S. protection. By law, Puerto Ricans are U.S. citizens. They can come and go as they wish from the island to the United States.

Puerto Rico has a high standard of living compared to most other Caribbean islands. It boasts more industry, with factories producing chemicals, machinery, clothing, and more. **San Juan** is the capital and largest city. In rural areas, farmers grow sugarcane and coffee. Puerto Rico makes more money from tourism than any country in the region.

✓ **Reading Check** What is a commonwealth?

FCAT PRACTICE You can prepare for the FCAT-assessed standards by completing the correlated item(s) below.

Assessment

Defining Terms

1. **Define** archipelago, bauxite, communist state, cooperative, embargo, free trade zone, commonwealth.

Recalling Facts

2. **Region** What three archipelagos make up the Caribbean islands?

3. **History** Name four groups who have influenced the culture of the Caribbean region.

4. **Government** How is Cuba different from every other country in the Western Hemisphere? **FCAT LA.A.2.2.7**

Critical Thinking

5. **Drawing Conclusions** Explain why you think Puerto Ricans might be satisfied remaining a commonwealth. **FCAT LA.A.2.3.1**

6. **Making Predictions** What is the danger of a country's dependence on only one crop? **FCAT LA.B.1.3.2**

Graphic Organizer

7. **Organizing Information** Complete a chart like the one below with facts about Haiti and the Dominican Republic. **FCAT LA.A.1.3.2**

Facts	Haiti	Dominican Republic
Colonized by		
Economy		

Applying Social Studies Skills

8. **Analyzing Maps** Refer to the economic activity map on page 214. What resources are found in Cuba?

Social Studies Skill

Interpreting an Elevation Profile

You have learned that differences in land elevation are often shown on physical or relief maps. Another way to show elevation is on **elevation profiles.** When you view a person's profile, you see a side view. An elevation profile is a diagram that shows a side view of the landforms in an area.

Learning the Skill

Suppose you could slice right through a country from top to bottom and could look at the inside, or *cross section.* The cross section, or elevation profile, below pictures the island of Jamaica. It shows how far Jamaica's landforms extend above or below sea level.

Follow these steps to understand an elevation profile:

- Read the title of the profile to find out what country you are viewing.
- Look at the line of latitude written along the bottom of the profile. On a separate map, find the country and where this line of latitude runs through it.
- Look at the measurements along the sides of the profile. Note where sea level is located and the height in feet or meters.
- Now read the labels on the profile to identify the heights of the different landforms shown.
- Compare the highest and lowest points.

Practicing the Skill

Use the elevation profile below to answer the following questions.

1. At what elevation is Kingston?
2. What are the highest mountains, and where are they located?
3. Where are the lowest regions?
4. Along what line of latitude was this cross section taken?

Applying the Skill

Look at the elevation profile on page 118. What are the highest mountains? Where is the lowest point?

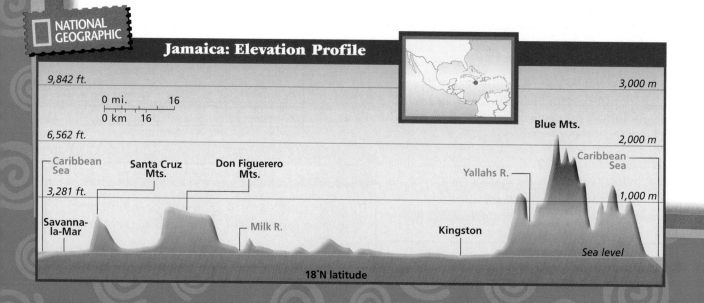

Jamaica: Elevation Profile

9,842 ft.   3,000 m

0 mi.   16
0 km   16

6,562 ft.   2,000 m

Blue Mts.

Caribbean Sea   Santa Cruz Mts.   Don Figuerero Mts.   Yallahs R.   Caribbean Sea

3,281 ft.   1,000 m

Savanna-la-Mar   Milk R.   Kingston

Sea level

18°N latitude

Reading Review

Section 1 | Central America

Terms to Know

isthmus

canopy

ecotourist

literacy rate

republic

parliamentary
democracy

Main Idea

Central America is made up of seven nations that are home to a variety of peoples, exotic animals, and diverse landforms.

✓ **Region** Central America includes seven countries: Belize, Guatemala, Honduras, El Salvador, Nicaragua, Costa Rica, and Panama.

✓ **Region** Volcanic mountains run down the center of Central America with coastal lowlands on either side.

✓ **Economics** Most people in the region farm—either on plantations or on subsistence farms.

✓ **Culture** Most countries in Central America have a blend of Native American and Spanish cultures.

The Panama Canal ▶

Section 2 | Cultures of the Caribbean

Terms to Know

archipelago

bauxite

communist state

cooperative

embargo

free trade zone

commonwealth

Main Idea

The Caribbean islands rely on tourism to support their economies.

✓ **History** Christopher Columbus landed in this region in 1492.

✓ **History** Most of the islands were at one time colonies of European countries.

✓ **Economics** Farming and tourism are the major economic activities in the Caribbean region.

✓ **Culture** The cultures of the Caribbean islands mix Native American, European, African, and Asian influences.

✓ **Government** Most governments in the Caribbean islands are democratic, but a dictator rules Communist Cuba.

Assessment and Activities

FCAT PRACTICE You can prepare for the FCAT-assessed standards by completing the correlated item(s) below.

Using Key Terms

Match the terms in Part A with their definitions in Part B.

A.

1. isthmus
2. literacy rate
3. cooperative
4. ecotourist
5. archipelago
6. bauxite
7. commonwealth
8. embargo
9. free trade zone
10. republic

B.

a. farm owned and operated by the government
b. mineral ore from which aluminum is made
c. ban on trade
d. narrow piece of land connecting two larger pieces of land
e. area where people can buy goods from other countries without paying taxes
f. person who travels to another country to enjoy its natural wonders
g. country with an elected president
h. percentage of adults who can read and write
i. partly self-governing territory
j. a group of islands

Reviewing the Main Ideas

Section 1 Central America

11. **Region** What seven countries make up Central America?
12. **Economics** Why are the Central American rain forests being destroyed? **FCAT SC.D.2.3**
13. **History** In what Central American countries did the Maya live?
14. **Culture** What percentage of Central Americans live on farms or in small villages?

Section 2 Cultures of the Caribbean

15. **Economics** What two activities form the basis of the Caribbean economies?
16. **Region** Which country has the largest population in the Caribbean?
17. **Culture** What types of music can you find in the Caribbean islands?
18. **History** What was the first nation in the world to be founded by formerly enslaved people?
19. **Economics** Why are commercial crops sometimes a risky business?

NATIONAL GEOGRAPHIC **Central America and the Caribbean Islands**

Place Location Activity

On a separate sheet of paper, match the letters on the map with the numbered places listed below.

1. Guatemala
2. Caribbean Sea
3. Cuba
4. Puerto Rico
5. Costa Rica
6. Panama
7. Bahamas
8. Haiti
9. Jamaica
10. Honduras

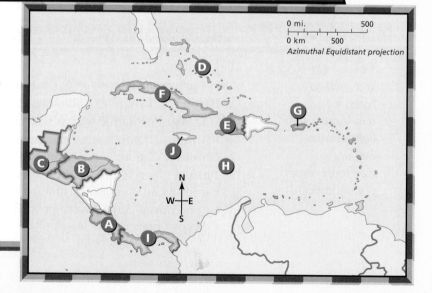

Critical Thinking

20. **Analyzing Information** Explain why Cuba's location is an important factor in the United States's relationship with that nation. **FCAT LA.B.1.3.2**

21. **Categorizing Information** Create a diagram like this with details about the people, history, and economy of a country in this chapter. **FCAT LA.A.1.3.2**

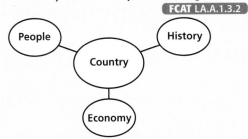

Comparing Regions Activity

22. **History** Compare the early Spanish settlements in Central America to the early British settlements in New Zealand. Use these examples to write a paragraph about what can happen when one country colonizes another. **FCAT LA.B.1.3.2**

Mental Mapping Activity

23. **Focusing on the Region** Create an outline map of Central America and the Caribbean islands, and then label the following:

- Pacific Ocean
- Cuba
- Caribbean Sea
- Puerto Rico
- Guatemala
- Dominican Republic
- Panama
- Bahamas

Technology Skills Activity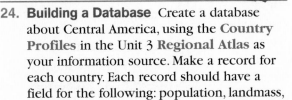

24. **Building a Database** Create a database about Central America, using the **Country Profiles** in the Unit 3 **Regional Atlas** as your information source. Make a record for each country. Each record should have a field for the following: population, landmass, and capital city. Sort the records from largest to smallest for population. What generalizations can you make based on these data? **FCAT LA.A.1.3.2**

Standardized Test Practice

Directions: Study the map below, and then answer the question that follows.

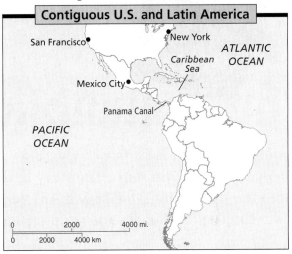

Contiguous U.S. and Latin America

1. **Which of the following was true before the Panama Canal was completed?**

   A A ship sailing from New York to San Francisco had to travel nearly 12,000 additional miles.

   B A ship sailing from New York to San Francisco had to travel nearly 5,000 additional kilometers.

   C The completion of the canal increased trade between Mexico City and San Francisco.

   D Mexico City was extremely far away from New York City.

   Test-Taking Tip: The scale shows you the actual distance between places on a map. Use your finger or a piece of paper to mark off the distance of the scale. Then use your finger or piece of paper to gauge the distance between two places on the map.

Columbus with King Ferdinand and Queen Isabella of Spain

The Columbian Exchange

The next time you eat a french fry, think about the long history of the lowly potato. The story begins high in the Andes mountain ranges of Bolivia and Peru (facing page), where thousands of years ago potatoes grew wild.

By the 1400s, the Inca, an early people who ruled a vast empire in western South America, had developed thousands of varieties of potatoes. The story of how potatoes came from such a faraway time and place is one that began even before the Inca. Now, potatoes are part of our everyday diet.

Two Separate Worlds

Before the 1400s, people living in the world's Eastern Hemisphere were unknown to those living in the Western Hemisphere. This changed on October 12, 1492, when explorer Christopher Columbus, who had sailed from Spain, landed in the Bahamas in the Americas. Believing he had reached the Indies of Asia, Columbus named the people on the islands "Indians" and claimed the land for Spain. Columbus returned to the Americas the following year,

bringing more than a thousand men in 17 ships. With his second trip, Columbus began what became known as "the Columbian Exchange"—an exchange of people, animals, plants, and even diseases between the two hemispheres.

For Better and for Worse

The Europeans brought many new things to the Americas. Columbus brought horses, which helped the Native Americans with labor, hunting, and transportation. European farm animals such as sheep, pigs, and cattle created new sources of income. Explorers brought crops—oats, wheat, rye, and barley—that eventually covered North America's Great Plains. The sugarcane brought by Europeans flourished on plantations in Central and South America.

Some parts of the exchange were disastrous, however.

Europeans brought diseases that killed millions of Native Americans. Plantation owners put enslaved Africans to work in their fields.

From the Americas, explorers returned home with a wide variety of plants. Spanish sailors carried potatoes to Europe. Nutritious and easy to grow, the potato became one of Europe's most important foods. (European immigrants then brought the potato to North America.) Corn from the Americas fed European cattle and pigs. Tobacco grown there became as valuable as gold. Peanuts, tomatoes, hot peppers, and cacao seeds (from which chocolate is made) changed the landscapes, eating habits, and cooking styles in Europe, Asia, and Africa.

QUESTIONS

1 What is "the Columbian Exchange"?

2 Exchanges continue today. What are some present-day exchanges among the world's hemispheres?

Women in Peru tend a potato field. ▶

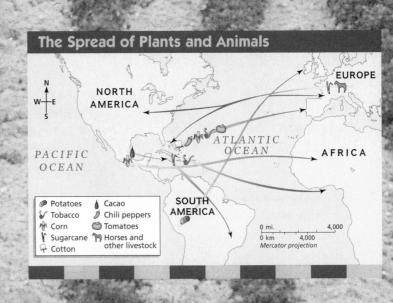

The Spread of Plants and Animals

Potatoes
Tobacco
Corn
Sugarcane
Cotton
Cacao
Chili peppers
Tomatoes
Horses and other livestock

NORTH AMERICA

EUROPE

PACIFIC OCEAN

ATLANTIC OCEAN

AFRICA

SOUTH AMERICA

0 mi. 4,000
0 km 4,000
Mercator projection

Brazil and Its Neighbors

The World and Its People
NATIONAL GEOGRAPHIC

To learn more about the people and places of Brazil and its neighbors, view **The World and Its People Chapter 8** video.

Social Studies online

Chapter Overview Visit **The World and Its People** Web site at twip.glencoe.com and click on **Chapter 8—Chapter Overviews** to preview information about Brazil and its neighbors.

 FCAT PRACTICE The activity below will help you prepare for the **FCAT Reading** test.

Summarizing Information Make this foldable and use it to organize note cards with information about the people and places of Brazil and its neighbors. **FCAT LA.A.1.3.2**

Step 1 Fold a 2-inch tab along the long edge of a sheet of paper.

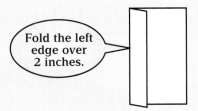

Fold the left edge over 2 inches.

Step 2 Fold the paper in half so the tab is on the inside.

The tab can't be seen when the paper is folded.

Step 3 Open the paper pocket foldable, turn it, and glue the edges of the pockets together.

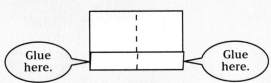

Glue here.

Glue here.

Step 4 Label the pockets as shown.

Brazil | Brazil's Neighbors

Reading and Writing As you read the chapter, summarize key facts about Brazil and its neighbors on note cards or on quarter sheets of notebook paper. Organize your notes by placing them in your pocket foldable inside the appropriate pockets. (Keep your pocket foldable to use with Chapter 9.) **FCAT LA.A.1.3.2**

Why It Matters

Preserving the Environment

The Amazon rain forest—sometimes called the "lungs of the planet" because of the huge amounts of oxygen given off by its trees—is home to up to 30 percent of the animal and plant life on Earth. Destroying these trees may cause the extinction of many wildlife species and damage to the earth's environment—on which we depend for our survival. This is just one of many issues facing the people and government of Brazil.

◄ **The Amazon River, Brazil**

Brazil–Emerging Giant

NATIONAL GEOGRAPHIC Exploring Our World

Some of the world's largest fresh-water fish swim in the mighty Amazon River in Brazil. Called pirarucu (pih•RAHR•uh•KEW), these fish can grow up to 15 feet (4.6 m) long. What a catch! The people who catch these huge fish often make the fish scales into souvenir key chains for tourists.

Like the pirarucu, Brazil is large. It is the fifth-largest country in the world and the largest in South America. In fact, Brazil makes up almost half of South America.

Brazil's Rain Forests and Highlands

Brazil has many different types of landforms and climates. The map on page 233 shows you that Brazil has narrow coastal plains, highland areas, and lowland river valleys. The **Amazon River** is the world's second-longest river, winding almost 4,000 miles (6,437 km) from the **Andes** mountain ranges to the Atlantic Ocean. Its powerful current carries soil 60 miles (97 km) out to sea! On its journey to the Atlantic, the Amazon drains water from a wide, flat basin, or low area surrounded by higher land. In the **Amazon Basin,** rainfall can reach as much as 120 inches (305 cm) per year. These rains support the growth of thick rain forests, which Brazilians call *selvas.*

Brazil has lowlands along the Paraná and the São Francisco Rivers. The **Brazilian Highlands** cover about half of the country, then drop sharply to the Atlantic Ocean. This drop is called the Great Escarpment. An escarpment is a steep cliff between higher and lower land.

✓ **Reading Check** What is significant about the Amazon River?

Brazil's Economy

How do Brazilians earn a living? Agriculture, mining, and forestry have been important for centuries. The Amazon Basin has been a mysterious region with secrets that were guarded by the Native Americans living there. This began to change in the mid-1800s. World demand skyrocketed for the rubber harvested from the basin's trees, and new

NATIONAL GEOGRAPHIC

Brazil and Its Neighbors: Physical/Political

Elevations

Feet	Meters
10,000	3,000
5,000	1,500
2,000	600
1,000	300
0	0

▲ Mountain peak

Mt. Ojos del Salado
22,572 ft.
(6,880 m)

Aconcagua
22,834 ft.
(6,960 m)

Mt. Tupungato
22,310 ft.
(6,800 m)

⊛ National capital
◉ Other capital
• Major city

0 mi.   800
0 km   800
Azimuthal Equidistant projection

Applying Map Skills

1. Which area of Brazil—the north or the south—has the higher elevation?

2. Name two rivers that flow into the Amazon River.

Find NGS online map resources @ www.nationalgeographic.com/maps

Analyzing the Graph

Brazil's highlands have the right soil and climate to grow coffee.

Economics Which leading coffee-producing countries are in South America? **FCAT** MA.E.3.3.1

Visit twip.glencoe.com and click on **Chapter 8— Textbook Updates.**

Completing the exercise above will help you prepare for the **FCAT Mathematics** test.

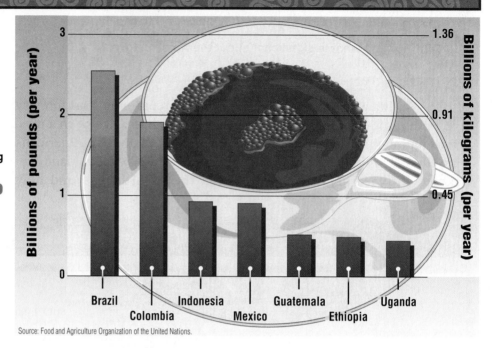

Source: Food and Agriculture Organization of the United Nations.

settlers streamed to Brazil's interior. Today mining companies dig for minerals such as bauxite, tin, and iron ore. Logging companies harvest mahogany and other woods from the rain forest. Farmers use the cleared land to grow soybeans and tobacco and to graze cattle.

South of the Amazon Basin are rich mineral resources and fertile farmland. The southern region of Brazil boasts one of the world's largest iron ore deposits. The highlands are perfect for growing coffee. As the graph above shows, Brazil produces far more coffee than other countries. It also has huge cattle ranches and exports beef all over the world.

Brazil's major cities are located in the south. Tourists flock to coastal **Rio de Janeiro,** which has more than 11.2 million people. **São Paulo,** home to more than 18.5 million people, is one of the fastest-growing urban areas in the world. It is also Brazil's leading trade and industrial center.

Brazil's Economic Challenges Today Brazil's economy is diverse and productive, yet the country still faces serious economic challenges. Brazil's economy has brought wealth to many Brazilians and created a large and strong middle class. Yet as many as one-fifth of Brazil's people live in extreme poverty. Many Brazilian cities are surrounded by favelas, or slum areas. Thousands of poor people move to cities looking for work in the factories. They live in crude shacks with neither running water nor sewage systems. City governments have tried to clean up these areas, but people continue to settle here because they have no money to pay for housing. Many children as young as 10 years old go to work to help earn money for their families.

Although Brazil has the largest area of remaining rain forest in the world, it also has the highest rate of deforestation. **Deforestation** is the destroying of large areas of forest. To increase jobs and products for export, the government has encouraged mining, logging, and farming in the rain forest. However, as you learned in Chapter 2, deforestation leads to soil erosion. It also harms the rain forest ecosystem and biodiversity. As deforestation takes place, roads are built, bringing companies, farmers, and change. Native Americans who live in the Amazon Basin find it difficult to follow their traditional cultures as this occurs. In addition, tropical forests give off huge amounts of oxygen and play a role in regulating the earth's climate. Thus, although the Amazon rain forest belongs to Brazil, the effects of deforestation are felt worldwide. Turn to page 250 to learn more about the vanishing rain forests.

✓ **Reading Check** Why has the Brazilian government encouraged mining, logging, and farming in the rain forest?

Brazil's History and Culture

With 176.5 million people, Brazil has the largest population of all Latin American nations. Brazil's culture is largely Portuguese. The Portuguese were the first and largest European group to colonize

FCAT PRACTICE

Completing the exercise below will help you prepare for the **FCAT Reading** test.

Literature

BOTOQUE
Kayapo Indian Myth
In this myth of central Brazil, the hero brings fire to his people.

❝*Botoque and the animals safely returned to their village with Jaguar's possessions. Everyone was delighted to eat grilled meat. They loved being able to warm themselves by the fire when the nights became cool. And they liked having the village fires provide protection from wild animals.*

As for Jaguar, when he returned home and found that he had been robbed of his special possessions, his heart flooded with fury. 'So this is how Botoque has repaid me for adopting him as my son and teaching him the secret of the bow and arrow!' he exclaimed. 'Why, he did not even leave me fire. Well, no matter. In memory of this theft, from this time forth and evermore, I will eat my catch raw! This will keep the memory of my adopted son before my eyes and hatred for him—and all who walk the earth as he does—alive in my heart!'❞

Source: *"Botoque, Bringer of Fire"* excerpted from *Folklore, Myths, and Legends: A World Perspective.* Edited by Donna Rosenberg. NTC Publishing, 1997.

Analyzing Literature

Do you think the Kayapo Indians feared jaguars? Why or why not? **FCAT LA.A.2.3.2**

Rio de Janeiro

A huge statue of Christ overlooks Rio de Janeiro (above right). Crowds of people in Rio de Janeiro celebrate Carnival wearing brightly colored costumes (above).

Culture What groups make up Brazil's population?

Brazil. Today Brazilians are of European, African, Native American, Asian, or mixed ancestry. Almost all of them speak a Brazilian form of Portuguese, which includes many words from Native American and African languages. Most of the population follow the Roman Catholic religion. Many Brazilians, however, combine Catholicism with beliefs and practices from African and Native American religions.

Influence of History   Native Americans were the first people to live in Brazil. In the 1500s, the Portuguese forced Native Americans to work on large plantations that grew tobacco and, later, sugarcane. Many Native Americans died from disease or overwork. To replace them, early Portuguese settlers brought people from Africa and enslaved them. Slavery finally was banned in 1888, but Africans remained in Brazil, most of them living in the northeastern part of the country. Over the years, African traditions have influenced Brazilian religion, music, dance, and food.

Moving to the Cities   Much of Brazil is sparsely populated. Millions of people have moved from rural areas to coastal cities to find better jobs. Now the government is encouraging people to move back to less populated inland areas to reduce city crowding. Highways now criss-cross the country and reach many formerly remote regions. In 1960 Brazil moved its capital from coastal Rio de Janeiro 600 miles (966 km) inland to the newly built city of **Brasília.** With more than 2 million people, Brasília is a modern and rapidly growing city.

The Government   Brazil declared independence from Portugal in 1822. At first the new nation was an empire, with emperors ruling until 1889. Then, like some other countries in Central and South America, Brazil was ruled by military dictators. Today Brazil is a democratic republic, where people elect a president and other leaders. In Brazil, though, citizens cannot choose whether to vote or not vote. People from ages 18 to 70 are required by law to vote. Brazil has more than a dozen political parties—not just two main ones, as in the United States.

The national government of Brazil is much stronger than its 26 state governments. Brazil's president has more power over the country than an American president does in the United States.

Leisure Time   Brazilians enjoy soccer, which they call *fútbol.* Every village has a soccer field, and the larger cities have stadiums. Maracana Stadium in Rio de Janeiro seats 220,000 fans. Basketball is another popular sport.

Brazil is also famous for Carnival. This festival is celebrated just before the beginning of Lent, the Christian holy season that comes before Easter. The most spectacular Carnival is held each year in Rio de Janeiro. The celebration includes Brazilian music and showy parades.

Brazil has one of the largest television networks in the world. This network produces prime-time soap operas called *telenovelas.* These programs are wildly popular in Brazil—and viewers in more than 60 other nations enjoy them too.

✔ Reading Check   **Why do most Brazilians speak a form of Portuguese?**

 **FCAT PRACTICE**   You can prepare for the FCAT-assessed standards by completing the correlated item(s) below.

Section 1 Assessment

Defining Terms
1. **Define** basin, *selva,* escarpment, favela, deforestation.

Recalling Facts
2. **History** Who was the first and largest group of Europeans to colonize Brazil?

3. **Economics** What resources attract companies to the Amazon Basin?

4. **Culture** What is the major religion of Brazil?

Critical Thinking
5. **Drawing Conclusions** In what way is deforestation threatening the Native Americans who live in the rain forest? **FCAT** LA.A.2.3.1, SC.D.2.3.2

6. **Summarizing Information** What economic challenges face Brazilians? **FCAT** LA.A.2.3.1

Graphic Organizer
7. **Organizing Information** Create a diagram like this one. Beside the left arrow, write the cause of the government action. On the right, list three results of this action. **FCAT** LA.A.1.3.2, SC.D.2.3.2

```
             ┌─────────────────┐
             │ Government action:│ →  _____
_____  →  │ Government        │ →  _____
             │ encouraged mining,│
             │ logging, and farming │ → _____
             │ in the rain forest.│
             └─────────────────┘
```

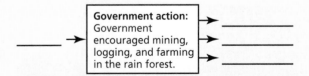 **Applying Social Studies Skills**

8. **Analyzing Maps** Look at the physical map on page 233. What large landform in Brazil surrounds the Amazon River?

Critical Thinking Skill

FCAT PRACTICE Completing the correlated items below will help you prepare for the **FCAT Reading** test.

Sequencing and Categorizing Information

Sequencing means placing facts in the order in which they occurred. *Categorizing* means organizing information into groups of related facts and ideas. Both actions help you deal with large quantities of information in a manageable way.

Learning the Skill

Follow these steps to learn sequencing and categorizing skills:

- Look for dates or clue words that provide you with a chronological order: *in 2004, the late 1990s, first, then, finally, after the Great Depression,* and so on.
- If the sequence of events is not important, you may want to categorize the information instead. Categories might include economic activities or cultural traits.
- List these characteristics, or categories, as the headings on a chart.
- As you read, fill in details under the proper category on the chart.

Practicing the Skill

Read the paragraphs below, and then answer the questions that follow.

After Brazil's independence from Portugal in 1822, a bill was presented to build a new capital named Brasília. More than 100 years later, in 1955, a planning committee chose the site for the new capital. The first streets were paved in 1958. On April 20, 1960, the festivities to officially "open" the new capital started at 4:00 P.M.

Brasília has both positive and negative aspects. The positive include virtually no air pollution, no threat of natural disasters, many green areas, and a pleasant climate. The negative aspects of the capital include very high housing prices, inefficient public transportation, few parking spaces, and long distances between the various government buildings.

1. What information can be organized sequentially?
2. What information can be organized under these categories: "Positive Aspects" and "Negative Aspects"? **FCAT LA.A.2.3.1**

Applying the Skill

Find two newspaper or magazine articles about Brazil or another South American country. Sequence or categorize the information in the articles on note cards or in a chart. **FCAT LA.A.2.3.1**

GO TO Practice key skills with **Glencoe Skillbuilder Interactive Workbook, Level 1.**

Brasília

Argentina to Venezuela

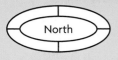
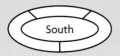

NATIONAL GEOGRAPHIC Exploring Our World

The traditional music of Paraguay seems to be out of place with the rest of its culture. The harp is the country's national instrument, and Paraguayans are famous for their slow, mournful guitar playing. In contrast, the traditional dances are much livelier. Here, a woman performs the bottle dance—a difficult feat even though the bottles are attached to one another.

South of Brazil lie **Argentina, Uruguay,** and **Paraguay.** North of Brazil is Caribbean South America, which includes **Venezuela, Guyana, Suriname,** and **French Guiana.**

Argentina

Argentina is South America's second-largest country, after Brazil. Its southern tip reaches almost to the continent of Antarctica. Argentina is about the size of the United States east of the Mississippi River.

The Andes tower over the western part of Argentina. Snowcapped peaks and clear blue lakes attract tourists for skiing and hiking. **Aconcagua** (AH•kohn•KAH•gwah) soars to a height of 22,834 feet (6,960 m), making it the highest mountain in the Western Hemisphere.

South and east of the Andes lies a dry, windswept plateau called **Patagonia.** Most of Patagonia gets little rain and has poor soil. As a result, sheep raising is the only major economic activity there.

Brazil and Its Neighbors: Economic Activity

Resources

✚	Bauxite		Iron ore
	Coal	◑	Manganese
	Copper	◌	Natural gas
▽	Diamonds		Petroleum
	Fishing		Silver
🌲	Forest	▼	Tin
	Gold	✳	Uranium
		⊡	Zinc

Land Use

- ▢ Commercial farming
- ▢ Subsistence farming
- ▢ Ranching
- ▢ Forests
- ▢ Little or no activity
- ▪ Manufacturing area

Applying Map Skills

1. What agricultural activities take place throughout Argentina?

2. In what countries is gold mined?

Find NGS online map resources @ www.nationalgeographic.com/maps

The center of Argentina has vast treeless plains known as the pampas. Similar to the Great Plains of the United States, the pampas are home to farmers who grow grains and ranchers who raise livestock. More than two-thirds of Argentina's people live in this region.

Argentina's Economy Argentina's economy depends heavily on farming and ranching. The country's major farm products include beef, sugarcane, wheat, soybeans, and corn. Huge *estancias* (ay•STAHN•see•ahs), or ranches, cover the pampas. **Gauchos** (GOW•chohs), or cowhands, take care of the livestock on the ranches. Gauchos are the national symbol of Argentina, admired for their independence and horse-riding skills. The livestock that the gauchos herd and tend are a vital part of the country's economy. Beef and food products are Argentina's chief exports. Turn to page 246 to read more about gauchos.

Argentina is one of the most industrialized countries in South America. Most of the country's factories are in or near **Buenos Aires,** Argentina's capital and largest city. The leading manufactured goods are food products, automobiles, chemicals, textiles, books, and magazines.

Petroleum is Argentina's most valuable mineral resource. The country's major oil fields are in Patagonia and the Andes. Other minerals, such as zinc, iron ore, copper, tin, and uranium, are mined in the Andes as well. Despite these resources, Argentina's economy has struggled during the early years of the twenty-first century.

Argentina's History In the late 1500s, Spaniards settled in the area that is now Buenos Aires. By 1800 the city was a flourishing port. In 1816 a general named José de San Martín led Argentina in its fight for freedom from Spain. After independence, the country was torn apart by civil war. By the mid-1850s, a strong national government had emerged, and Argentina entered a time of prosperity. During the first half of the 1900s, however, Argentina's elected leaders governed poorly. The economy suffered, and the military took over.

One of these military leaders, Juan Perón, became a dictator in the late 1940s. With his popular wife, Eva, at his side, Perón tried to improve the economy and give more help to workers. His crackdown on freedom of speech and the press made people unhappy, however. In 1955 a revolt drove Perón from power, and democracy returned.

Military officers again took control of Argentina in the 1970s. They ruled harshly, and political violence resulted in the deaths of many people. In 1982 Argentina suffered defeat in a war with the United Kingdom for control of the **Falkland Islands.** The Falklands, known in Argentina as the Malvinas, lie in the Atlantic Ocean off the coast of Argentina. The military stepped down, and elected leaders regained control of the government when Argentina lost this war.

Today Argentina is a democratic republic. As in the United States, the national government is much stronger than the 23 provincial, or state, governments. A powerful elected president leads the nation for a four-year term. A legislature with two houses makes the laws.

Argentina's People   About 85 percent of Argentina's people are of European ancestry. During the late 1800s, immigrants in large numbers came to Argentina from Spain and Italy. Their arrival greatly influenced Argentina's society and culture. Many more immigrants arrived from Europe after World War II. European ways of life are stronger in Argentina today than in most other Latin American countries.

The official language of Argentina is Spanish, although the language includes many Italian words. Most people are Roman Catholic. About 90 percent of Argentina's people live in cities and towns. More than 13 million people live in Buenos Aires and its suburbs. Buenos Aires has wide streets and European-style buildings. Its citizens call themselves *porteños* (pohr•TAY•nyohs), which means "people of the port." Many have a passion for the national dance of Argentina, the tango.

✓ Reading Check Why does Argentina have a strong European culture?

Uruguay and Paraguay

Uruguay and Paraguay differ from each other in environment, population, and development. Uruguay has a mild climate, rolling hilly plains and rich grasslands. This nation is a buffer zone between the two powerful nations of Brazil and Argentina. Originally settled by the Portuguese, then taken over by Spain, Uruguay revolted against both countries and eventually became completely independent in 1828.

Immigration from Spain and Italy and the introduction of sheep are keys to Uruguay's development. The country's 3.4 million people, half of whom live in the capital city of **Montevideo,** are mostly of European descent. Uruguay's economy depends on raising sheep and cattle. In fact, sheep and cattle outnumber people by ten to one, and about 70 percent of the country is pasture. Animal products—meat, wool, and hides—top Uruguay's exports. The major industries—textiles, footwear, and leather goods—use the products of the vast animal herds. Large haciendas are complemented by many medium-sized and

Web Activity Visit *The World and Its People* Web site at twip.glencoe.com and click on **Chapter 8— Student Web Activities** to learn about Paraguay.

small farms. The Uruguayans have the highest literacy rate, the lowest population growth rate, the best diet, and one of the highest standards of living of any South American country. Spanish is the official language, and the Roman Catholic faith is the major religion.

Paraguay In Paraguay, the society and economy have followed quite a different course. The eastern third of Paraguay, with its rich soils and fertile grasslands, was settled by the Spanish. The western two-thirds of the country, a great forest area known as the **Gran Chaco,** was brought into the Spanish territory by Roman Catholic missionaries.

In the 1800s and 1900s, a series of wars severely hurt Paraguay, destroying the economy of the country. After the worst of these—the five-year war against Brazil, Argentina, and Uruguay in the 1860s—Paraguay's male population was cut in half. Experts estimate that Paraguay also lost 55,000 square miles of territory.

Forestry and farming are Paraguay's major economic activities. Large cattle ranches cover much of the country. Most farmers, however, grow grains, cotton, soybeans, and cassava on small plots. Cassava roots can be ground up to make tapioca. They can also be sliced and fried just like potatoes.

Paraguay also exports electricity. The country has the world's largest hydroelectric power generator at the Itaipu (ee•TY•poo) Dam, on the Paraná River. **Hydroelectric power** is electricity that is generated by flowing water. Paraguay sells nearly 90 percent of the electricity it produces to neighboring countries.

Paraguayans today are mostly of mixed Guaraní—a Native American group—and Spanish ancestry. Both Spanish and Guaraní are official languages, but more people speak Guaraní. Most people practice the Roman Catholic faith. About one-half of the people live in cities. **Asunción** (ah•SOON•see•OHN) is the capital and largest city.

Paraguayan arts are influenced by Guaraní culture. Guaraní lace is Paraguay's most famous handicraft. Like people in Uruguay, the people of Paraguay enjoy meat dishes and sip *yerba maté,* a tealike drink.

✔ **Reading Check** What important export is generated at the Itaipu Dam?

Venezuela

Venezuela (VEH•nuh•ZWAY•luh) is the westernmost country of Caribbean South America. In the northwest lie the lowland coastal areas surrounding **Lake Maracaibo** (MAH•rah•KY•boh), the largest lake in South America. Swamps fill much of this area, and few people live here. The great number of towering oil wells, however, give you a clue that rich oil fields lie under the lake and along its shores. Venezuela has more oil reserves than any other country in the Americas.

The Andean highlands begin south of the lake and are part of the Andes mountain ranges. This area includes most of the nation's cities, including **Caracas** (kah•RAH•kahs), the capital and largest city. East of the highlands, you see grassy plains known as the **llanos** (LAH•nohs). The llanos have many ranches, farms, and oil fields. Venezuela's most

Roping a Capybara
Capybaras are the world's largest rodents. They can grow to be 2 feet tall and 4 feet long, and weigh more than 100 pounds. Found in Central and South America, capybaras (ka•pih•BAR•uhs) live along rivers and lakes and eat vegetation. Here, a gaucho ropes a dog-sized capybara in Venezuela. Some Venezuelans eat capybara during the Easter season.

important river—the **Orinoco**—flows across the llanos. This river is a valuable source of hydroelectric power for Venezuela's cities.

South and east of the llanos rise the Guiana Highlands, which are deeply cut by rivers. **Angel Falls**—the world's highest waterfall—spills over a bluff in this region.

Because it is close to the Equator, Venezuela has a mostly tropical climate. In the Guiana Highlands to the south, you enter a steamy rain forest. As in Mexico, temperatures in Venezuela differ with altitude, or height above sea level. Higher altitudes have cooler climates.

Venezuela's Economy   Venezuelans once depended on crops such as coffee and cacao to earn a living. Since the 1920s, petroleum has changed the country's economy. Venezuela is a world leader in oil production and one of the chief suppliers of oil to the United States. Because the government owns the oil industry, oil provides nearly half of the government's income. A two-month national oil strike from December 2002 to February 2003 temporarily halted Venezuela's economic activity. This shows how much the country relies on its oil production.

Iron ore, limestone, bauxite, gold, diamonds, and emeralds are also mined. Factories make steel, chemicals, and food products. About 10 percent of the people farm, growing sugarcane and bananas or raising cattle.

History and Government   Originally settled by Native Americans, Venezuela became a Spanish colony in the early 1500s. With its many rivers, the land in South America reminded early Spanish explorers of Venice, Italy, which is full of canals. They named the area *Venezuela,* which means "Little Venice."

In the early 1800s, rebellion swept across the Spanish colonial empire. Simón Bolívar (see•MOHN boh•LEE•VAHR), who was born in Venezuela, became one of the leaders of this revolt. He and his soldiers freed Venezuela and neighboring regions from Spanish rule. In 1830 Venezuela became independent.

During most of the 1800s and 1900s, the country was governed by military rulers called caudillos (kow•THEE•yohz). Their rule was often harsh. Since 1958, Venezuela has been a democracy led by a president and a two-house legislature.

Rising oil prices during the 1970s benefited many Venezuelans. When oil prices fell in the 1990s, the country suffered. In 1998 voters

Angel Falls

Angel Falls—the highest waterfall in the world at 3,212 feet (979 m)—roars over a cliff in Venezuela. It would take 11 football fields stacked end-to-end to reach the top.

Economics What is one of the rivers that provides Venezuela with hydroelectric power?

Celebration

Venezuelan dancers in costumes and playing maracas take part in Corpus Christi, a local Roman Catholic celebration.

Religion What is the major religion in Venezuela?

elected a former military leader, Hugo Chávez, as president. Chávez promised to solve Venezuela's problems, but his growing power split the country into opposing groups. In 2000 the military overthrew Chávez, but street protests put him back in office. Two years later, a nationwide strike also failed to remove Chávez from office. This strike lasted three months and damaged Venezuela's already weak economy.

Venezuela's People Most of the 25.7 million people in Venezuela have a mix of European, African, and Native American backgrounds. Spanish is the major language of the country, and the major religion is Roman Catholicism. About 90 percent of Venezuelans live in cities. Some 2.8 million people live in Caracas, the capital, which has skyscrapers surrounded by mountains.

✓ **Reading Check** What product changed Venezuela's economy?

The Guianas

Caribbean South America also includes the countries of Guyana (gy•AH•nuh) and Suriname (SUR•uh•NAH•muh) and the territory of French Guiana (gee•A•nuh). Guyana was a British colony called British Guiana. Suriname, once a colony of the Netherlands, was called Dutch Guiana. As a result, these three lands are called "the Guianas."

The Guianas have similar landforms. Highlands in the interiors are covered by thick rain forests. Toward the Caribbean coast, the land descends to low coastal plains. The climate is hot and tropical. Most people live on the coastal plains because of the cooling ocean winds. Sugarcane grows in Guyana and French Guiana, while rice and bananas flourish in Suriname. Many people earn their living mining gold and bauxite.

Guyana In the early 1600s, the Dutch were the first Europeans to settle in Guyana. They forced Native Americans and Africans to work on tobacco, coffee, and cotton farms and, later, on sugarcane plantations. The United Kingdom won possession of the Dutch colonies in the early 1800s and ended slavery. Still needing workers, the British paid Indians from Asia to move here. Today people from India make up most of Guyana's population. Another one-third are of African ancestry. Small numbers of Native Americans and Europeans also live here. Christianity and Hinduism are the chief religions. Most people speak English. **Georgetown,** the capital, is the major city.

Guyana won its independence from Britain in 1966. Guyana remains a very poor country, however, and depends on aid from the United Kingdom and other countries.

Suriname   The British were the first Europeans to settle Suriname, but the Dutch gained control in 1667. As in Guyana, the Dutch brought enslaved Africans to work on large sugarcane plantations. Because of harsh treatment, many Africans fled into the isolated interior of the country. Their descendants still live there today. Later the Dutch hired workers from the Asian lands of India and Indonesia.

Asians form a large part of Suriname's population. About half of Suriname's people practice Christianity. The rest follow Hinduism or Islam. The main language is Dutch. **Paramaribo** (PAH•rah•MAH•ree•boh) is the capital and chief port. In 1975 Suriname won its independence from the Dutch. The country is poor, however, so it still relies on aid from the Dutch government.

French Guiana   French Guiana became a colony of France in the 1600s and remains one today. The country is headed by a French official called a *prefect,* who lives in the capital, **Cayenne** (ky•EHN). The French government provides jobs and aid to many of French Guiana's people.

Most people in French Guiana are of African or mixed African and European ancestry. They speak French and are Roman Catholic. In Cayenne, you see sidewalk cafés and police in French uniforms. Shoppers use euros, the French currency—just as they would in Paris, France. You also see local influences, such as Carnival, Native American woodcarving, and Caribbean music and dance.

 **Reading Check**   What European countries influenced the development of Guyana, Suriname, and French Guiana?

FCAT PRACTICE   You can prepare for the FCAT-assessed standards by completing the correlated item(s) below.

Section 2 Assessment

Defining Terms
1. **Define** pampas, *estancia,* gaucho, hydroelectric power, llanos, altitude, caudillo.

Recalling Facts
2. **Region** Describe two ways in which the pampas are similar to the Great Plains of the United States.
3. **Human/Environment Interaction** What is the significance of the Itaipu Dam?   **FCAT SC.D.2.3.2**
4. **History** Who was Simón Bolívar?

Critical Thinking
5. **Analyzing Cause and Effect** Which of Juan Perón's policies led to his removal from office?   **FCAT LA.E.2.2.1**
6. **Drawing Conclusions** Why is Hinduism one of the major religions of Guyana?
   FCAT LA.A.2.3.1

Graphic Organizer
7. **Organizing Information** Create a diagram like this one. In the top box, under the heading, list similarities about the Guianas. In the bottom boxes, under the headings, write facts about each country that show their differences.

   FCAT LA.A.1.3.2

   ```
          The Guianas
      ┌───────┼───────┐
   Guyana  Suriname  French
                     Guiana
   ```

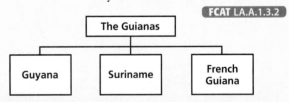 **Applying Social Studies Skills**

8. **Analyzing Maps** Look at the economic activity map on page 240. What agricultural activities take place in Venezuela?

Brazil and Its Neighbors

Making Connections

ART   SCIENCE   CULTURE   TECHNOLOGY

Poetry on the Pampas

As you learned in Section 2, gauchos herd cattle on the pampas. In 1872 José Hernández wrote the epic poem *El Gaucho Martín Fierro*. The poem tells the story of Martín Fierro, who recalls his life as a gaucho on the pampas. The following lines were translated from the poem.

El Gaucho Martín Fierro
by José Hernández (1834–1886)

A son am I of the rolling plain,
  A gaucho born and bred;
    For me the whole great world is small,
    Believe me, my heart can hold it all;
  The snake strikes not at my passing foot,
    The sun burns not my head.

• • • • • • • • •

FCAT PRACTICE Answering question 3 below will help you prepare for the **FCAT Reading** test.

Ah, my mind goes back and I see again
  The gaucho I knew of old;
    He picked his mount, and was ready aye,
    To sing or fight, and for work or play,
And even the poorest one was rich
  In the things not bought with gold.

The neediest gaucho in the land,
  That had least of goods and gear,
    Could show a troop of a single strain,
    And rode with a silver-studded rein,
The plains were brown with the grazing herds,
  And everywhere was cheer.

And when the time of the branding came,
  It did one good to see
    How the hand was quick and the eye
      was true,
    When the steers they threw with the
      long lassoo [lasso],
And the merry band that the years have swept
  Like leaves from the autumn tree.

Excerpt from *The Gaucho Martin Fierro*, adapted from the Spanish and rendered into English verse by Walter Owen. Copyright © 1936 by Farrar & Rinehart. Reprinted by permission of Henry Holt and Company, LLC.

Gauchos on Argentina's pampas ▲

▶ Making the Connection

1. How does the poet describe the land on which the gaucho lives?

2. How can you tell from the poem that a gaucho is often on the move?

3. **Drawing Conclusions** What evidence does the poem give that the gaucho's way of life was a proud and happy one? **FCAT LA.A.2.3.2**

Section 1 Brazil—Emerging Giant

Terms to Know

basin
selva
escarpment
favela
deforestation

Main Idea

Brazil is a large country with many resources, a lively culture, and serious economic challenges.

✓ **History** Brazil declared independence in 1822 after centuries of colonial rule by Portugal.

✓ **Economics** Brazil is trying to reduce its number of poor people and balance the use of resources with the preservation of its rain forests.

✓ **Culture** Most Brazilians are of mixed Portuguese, African, Native American, and Asian ancestry.

Section 2 Argentina to Venezuela

Terms to Know

pampas
estancia
gaucho
hydroelectric power
llanos
altitude
caudillo

Main Idea

Brazil's neighboring countries have a diverse array of landforms, climates, and cultures.

✓ **Region** Few people live in Argentina's Andes region or Patagonia. The most populous area is the vast grassland called the pampas.

✓ **Culture** Argentina's capital, Buenos Aires, is a huge city with European style.

✓ **Economics** Uruguay and Paraguay have large areas of grass-covered plains that support ranching and industries that depend on raising livestock.

✓ **Culture** Most Venezuelans are of mixed European, African, and Native American ancestry. Most live in cities in the central highlands.

✓ **History** Simón Bolívar led a revolt that freed Venezuela from Spain in 1830.

✓ **Culture** Guyana and Suriname have large numbers of people descended from workers who were brought from Africa and Asia.

This broad street in Buenos Aires is the Avenida 9 de Julio—or the Avenue of the Ninth of July. It is named in honor of the day Argentina won independence from Spain. ▶

Brazil and Its Neighbors

Assessment and Activities

FCAT PRACTICE You can prepare for the FCAT-assessed standards by completing the correlated item(s) below.

Using Key Terms

Match the terms in Part A with their definitions in Part B.

A.

1. basin
2. *estancia*
3. escarpment
4. caudillo
5. altitude
6. gaucho
7. *selva*
8. deforestation
9. llanos
10. pampas

B.

a. steep cliff separating two flat land surfaces, one higher than the other
b. cowhand
c. cutting down large areas of forest
d. military ruler
e. large, grassy plains region with many ranches, farms, and oil fields
f. height above sea level
g. broad, flat lowland surrounded by higher land
h. vast treeless plains
i. tropical rain forest in Brazil
j. large ranch

Reviewing the Main Ideas

Section 1 Brazil—Emerging Giant

11. **History** Why are Brazil's inland areas sparsely populated?
12. **Government** What are the voting requirements in Brazil?
13. **History** When and why did Brazil's government move the capital city to Brasília?

Section 2 Argentina to Venezuela

14. **Economics** Why are the pampas an important region of Argentina?
15. **Culture** What are the major language and religion of Uruguay?
16. **Economics** What are the major economic activities of Paraguay?
17. **Economics** Which of Venezuela's resources is its main source of income?
18. **Culture** Where do most of the people of the Guianas live? Why do they live there?
19. **History** Which of Brazil's neighbors has been a colony of France since the 1600s?

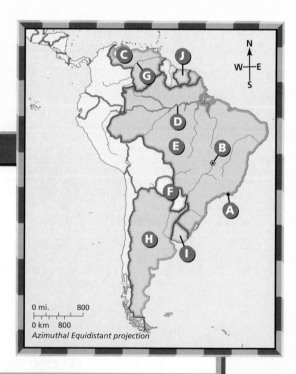

NATIONAL GEOGRAPHIC Brazil and Its Neighbors

Place Location Activity

On a separate sheet of paper, match the letters on the map with the numbered places listed below.

1. Brazil
2. Amazon River
3. Argentina
4. Rio de Janeiro
5. Paraguay
6. Orinoco River
7. Uruguay
8. Venezuela
9. Brasília
10. Suriname

Self-Check Quiz Visit *The World and Its People* Web site at <u>twip.glencoe.com</u> and click on **Chapter 8—Self-Check Quizzes** to prepare for the Chapter Test.

Critical Thinking

20. Analyzing Information What facts support the statement "Argentina is one of the most industrialized countries in South America"? **FCAT LA.A.2.3.1**

21. Identifying Points of View In a chart like the one below, identify arguments for and against the cutting down of the rain forest. **FCAT LA.A.1.3.2**

Cutting Down the Rain Forest	
For	Against

Comparing Regions Activity

22. Geography Rain forests of the Amazon have the highest rate of deforestation. Other regions in the world face similar challenges to their natural resources. Create a chart in your notebook that shows the current deforestation rates of five regions: Africa, Asia, Europe, Latin America, and North America. Find sample pictures of each region's forests to illustrate your chart. **FCAT SC.D.2.3.2**

Mental Mapping Activity

23. Focusing on the Region Create an outline map of South America. Refer to the map on page 233, and then label the following:

- Patagonia
- Brazil
- Atlantic Ocean
- Argentina
- Pacific Ocean
- Brazilian Highlands
- Amazon Basin
- Falkland Islands
- Venezuela
- Guiana Highlands

Technology Skills Activity

24. Using the Internet Conduct a search for information about the Amazon rain forest and create an annotated bibliography of five useful Web sites. Your bibliography should contain the Web address, a brief summary of the information found on the site, and a statement of why you think the site is useful. **FCAT LA.A.2.3.1**

Standardized Test Practice

Directions: Read the passage below, and then answer the question that follows.

The Amazon Basin is a gigantic system of rivers and rain forests, covering half of Brazil and extending into neighboring countries. Much of the Amazon is still unexplored, and the rain forest holds many secrets. Some of the animals found here include the jaguar, tapir, spider monkey, sloth, river dolphin, and boa constrictor. Forest birds include toucans, parrots, hummingbirds, and hawks. More than 1,800 species of butterflies and 200 species of mosquitoes give you an idea about the insect population. In addition, the fish—such as piranha, pirarucu, and electric eel—are very unusual. Biologists cannot identify much of the catch found in markets.

1. On the basis of this passage, which of the following generalizations is most accurate? **FCAT LA.A.2.3.1**

F The Amazon rain forest covers about one-third of the South American continent.

G Native Americans living in the rain forest are losing their old way of life.

H The Amazon Basin is huge, and its rain forests hold thousands of animal species.

J The Amazon Basin is located only in Brazil.

Test-Taking Tip: This question asks you to make a generalization about the Amazon Basin. A *generalization* is a broad statement. Look for facts and the main idea *in the passage* to support your answer. Do not rely only on your memory. The main idea can help you eliminate answers that do not fit. Also, look for the statement that is true and that is covered in the paragraph.

VANISHING
Rain Forests

Rain Forest Riches Imagine never tasting chocolate. Think about never eating a banana, chewing gum, or munching cashews. If there were no rain forests, we would have none of these foods. We also would not have many of the drugs used to treat malaria, multiple sclerosis, and leukemia. In fact, rain forest plants provide one-fourth of the world's medicines.

Millions of kinds of plants and animals live in rain forests—more than half of all species on Earth. Scientists have studied only a fraction of these species. So no one really knows what new foods, medicines, or animals are there, just waiting to be discovered.

Rain Forest Destruction Yet we may never know. Why? Because a chunk of rain forest the size of two football fields vanishes every second! The forests are being destroyed for many reasons.

- Loggers cut trees and sell the lumber worldwide.

- Ranchers and farmers clear land for cattle and crops.

- Miners level acres of forest to get at valuable minerals.

People are trying to find ways to use rain forests without destroying them. Changing farming practices and developing different forest industries are possible solutions. However, time is running out. Can we afford to lose rain forests and all their treasures?

Settlers clear trees for a home in the rain forest.

Male golden toad

Making a Difference

Discovering New Monkeys How would it feel to discover an animal that no one knew existed? Dutch scientist Marc van Roosmalen knows. He recently discovered a new species of monkey (photo, at right) in Brazil.

New species *Callithrix humilis*, a dwarf marmoset

Van Roosmalen runs an orphanage for abandoned monkeys. One day, a man showed up with a tiny monkey van Roosmalen had never seen before. He spent about a year tracking down a wild population of the monkeys deep in the Amazon rain forest. Of some 250 kinds of monkeys known worldwide, about 80 live in Brazil. At least 7 new species have been discovered since 1990.

Rain Forest Field Trip With help from the Children's Environmental Trust Foundation, students from Millbrook, New York, traveled to Peru's Yarapa River region, deep in the Amazon rain forest. Students studied the forest from platforms built in the canopy, and they soared among the tall trees using ropes. The students met rain forest creatures at night, went birdwatching at dawn, and swam in the Yarapa River—home to crocodiles called caimans.

Back in Millbrook, the students educate others about saving rain forests. They also raise money to help support a Peruvian zoo that protects rain forest animals.

A Millbrook student traps insects for study.

What Can You Do?

Write a Note
Write to your government representatives and encourage them to support plans that help save rain forests. **FCAT** LA.B.1.3.2

Check Out Your Community
What environmental problems face your community? What can you do to help solve the problems? For example, does your community have problems with water pollution or water shortages? What steps does your community take to make sure you have clean water to drink? **FCAT** SC.D.2.3.2

The Andean Countries

The World and Its People NATIONAL GEOGRAPHIC

To learn more about the people and places of the Andean countries, view **The World and Its People Chapter 9** video.

Social Studies ONLINE

Chapter Overview Visit **The World and Its People** Web site at twip.glencoe.com and click on **Chapter 9—Chapter Overviews** to preview information about the Andean countries.

FCAT PRACTICE The activity below will help you prepare for the **FCAT Reading** test.

Summarizing Information Make this foldable and use it to organize note cards with information about the people and places of the Andean countries of South America. **FCAT LA.A.1.3.2**

Step 1 Fold a 2-inch tab along the long edge of a sheet of paper.

Fold the left edge over 2 inches.

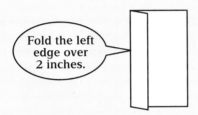

Step 2 Fold the paper in half so the tab is on the inside.

The tab can't be seen when the paper is folded.

Step 3 Open the paper pocket foldable and glue the edges of the pockets together.

Glue here.

Glue here.

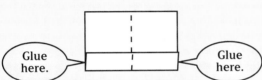

Step 4 Label the pockets as shown.

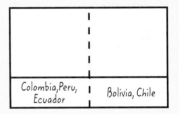

Colombia, Peru, Ecuador

Bolivia, Chile

Reading and Writing As you read the chapter, summarize key facts about the Andean countries on note cards or on quarter sheets of notebook paper. Organize your notes by placing them in your pocket foldable inside the appropriate pockets. (Glue your foldable from Chapter 8 on the front cover of this foldable to form a four-pocket foldable on South America.) **FCAT LA.A.1.3.2**

Why It Matters

Wealth in the Andes

The Andes form the spine of South America and are the longest mountain chain on Earth. These high, rocky peaks are the source of some of the world's most highly desired substances, including oil, emeralds, gold, silver, coffee, and "Colombian Gold"—the illegal drug, cocaine. Worldwide demand for these products has caused corruption and instability in the countries of this region.

◄ **Monastery of San Francisco, Quito, Ecuador**

Colombia's Culture and Challenges

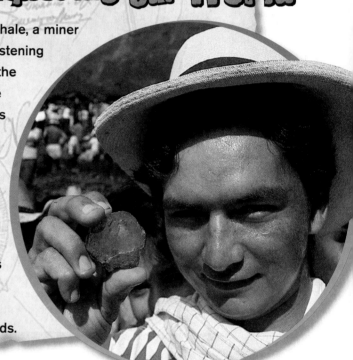

NATIONAL GEOGRAPHIC Exploring Our World

In a thin vein of black shale, a miner in Colombia spots a glistening green stone. He is not the first Colombian to mine the precious gemstones we call emeralds. The Colombian mine called Muzo has been producing top-quality emeralds for a thousand years. Early Native American rulers would offer these gems—more rare than diamonds—to their gods.

Colombia was named after Christopher Columbus. The lofty Andes mountain ranges at the northwestern edge of South America run through Colombia. These mountains continue south through five other countries—**Ecuador, Peru, Bolivia, Chile,** and **Argentina.**

Colombia's Landscape

Colombia—almost three times larger than Montana—has coasts on both the Caribbean Sea and the Pacific Ocean. The Andes rise in the western part of Colombia. Here they become a cordillera—mountain ranges that run side by side. Nearly 80 percent of Colombia's people live in the valleys and highland plateaus of the Andes. Thick forests spread over lowlands along the Pacific coast. Few people live there.

Only a few Native American groups live in the hot, steamy tropical rain forests of the southeast. In the northeast, ranchers drive cattle across the llanos, which, as you recall, are grassy plains.

Colombia lies within the Tropics. Temperatures are very hot, and heavy rains fall along the coasts and in the interior plains. In the high elevations of the Andes, temperatures are very cool for a tropical area. **Bogotá,** Colombia's capital and largest city, lies on an Andean plateau. High temperatures there average only 67°F (19°C).

✓ Reading Check   **Where do most of Colombia's people live?**

Colombia's Economic Resources

Colombia has many natural resources. The mountains hold valuable minerals and precious stones, and Colombia has more coal than any other country in South America. Second only to Brazil in its potential hydroelectric power, Colombia also has large petroleum reserves in

NATIONAL GEOGRAPHIC

The Andean Countries: Political

National capital
Major city

Azimuthal Equidistant projection

Applying Map Skills

1. What bodies of water does Colombia border?

2. What country has a name that sounds like "Equator"?

Find NGS online map resources @ www.nationalgeographic.com/maps

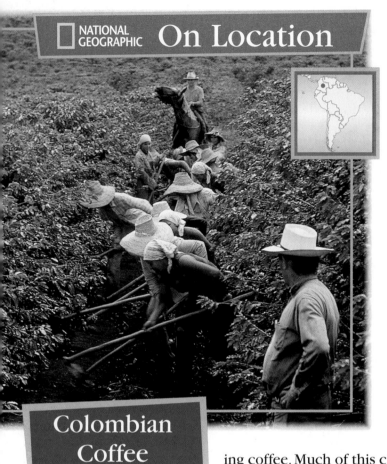

Colombian Coffee

Many historians believe that coffee was "discovered" in Ethiopia, Africa. Eventually, Spanish missionaries brought the first coffee plants to Colombia.

Economics What other crops does Colombia export?

the lowlands. In addition, the country is a major supplier of gold and the world's number one source of emeralds. Factories produce clothing, leather goods, food products, paper, chemicals, and iron and steel products.

Agriculture The coastal regions and the highlands have good soil for growing a variety of crops. Coffee is the country's major **cash crop**—a product sold for export. Colombian coffee is known all over the world for its rich flavor.

Colombia exports bananas as well as cacao, sugarcane, rice, and cotton. Huge herds of cattle roam large *estancias,* or ranches, in the llanos. The rain forests also supply a valuable resource—lumber.

Economic Challenges Despite many natural resources, Colombia faces economic challenges. Since the 1980s, drug dealers have been a major force in Colombia. The dealers pay farmers more to grow coca leaves—which are used to make the illegal drug cocaine—than the farmers earn growing coffee. Much of this cocaine is smuggled into the United States and western Europe. The drug dealers have used their immense profits to build private armies. They have threatened—and even killed—government officials who have tried to stop them.

With U.S. support, the government of Colombia has stepped up its efforts to break the power of the drug dealers. In addition, the government has tried to persuade thousands of farmers to switch back to growing other crops. See **TIME Reports: Focus on World Issues** on pages 259–265 for an in-depth study of the drug problem.

✓ Reading Check What crop has been a problem in Colombia? Why?

Colombia's History and People

About 44.2 million people live in Colombia. Nearly all Colombians are **mestizos** (meh•STEE•zohs). This means they have mixed European and Native American backgrounds. Most speak Spanish and follow the Roman Catholic faith.

In 1810 Colombia was one of the first Spanish colonies in the Americas to declare independence. Simón Bolívar, whom you read about in Chapter 8, led this struggle for independence. In 1819 Colombia became part of New Granada, an independent country that included Venezuela, Ecuador, and Panama. Later, these other regions broke away and became separate countries.

Colombia today is a republic with an elected president. Political violence has scarred the country's history, though. During the late 1800s alone, Colombia suffered through more than 50 revolts and 8 civil wars. Fighting broke out again in 1948. About 250,000 people died in this conflict, which ended in the late 1950s.

To prevent further unrest, the two main political parties agreed to govern the country together. Efforts were made to improve the lives of poor farmers by giving them more land. Factories and industrial jobs opened up. Still, a wide gap between rich and poor remained, causing further disturbances.

In the 1960s, rebels in the countryside began fighting the government. This latest civil war is still being fought. It has left more than 100,000 people dead. In 2003 the United States responded to the Colombian government's call for help. It sent U.S. special forces to Colombia to train Colombian soldiers and to protect an oil pipeline.

A Diverse Culture   Colombia has a rapidly growing urban population. Colombian farmers, or **campesinos,** and their families have journeyed to cities to look for work or to flee the fighting in the countryside. Thirty cities have more than 100,000 people each.

You can see Colombia's Spanish, Native American, and African heritages reflected in its culture. Native American skills in weaving and pottery date back before the arrival of Columbus. Caribbean African rhythms blend with Spanish-influenced music.

Web Activity Visit *The World and Its People* Web site at twip.glencoe.com and click on **Chapter 9— Student Web Activities** to learn more about Colombia.

√ Reading Check   What is a mestizo?

FCAT PRACTICE   You can prepare for the FCAT-assessed standards by completing the correlated item(s) below.

Assessment

Defining Terms
1. **Define** cordillera, cash crop, mestizo, campesino.

Recalling Facts
2. **Economics** Colombia is the world's number one source of what resource?

3. **Culture** What language do most Colombians speak? What religion do they practice?

4. **History** Who led Colombia's struggle for independence from Spain?

Critical Thinking
5. **Analyzing Cause and Effect** Why does Bogotá, which is located in the Tropics, have an average temperature of only 67°F (19°C)? **FCAT** LA.A.2.3.1

6. **Drawing Conclusions** Why do you think it is so difficult for Colombian farmers to stop growing coca? **FCAT** LA.A.2.3.1

Graphic Organizer
7. **Organizing Information** Create a time line like this one. Then put the following events and their dates in the correct order on it: U.S. special forces sent to Colombia, groups of rebels fight the government, Colombia declares independence from Spain, Colombia suffers 50 revolts and 8 civil wars, Colombia becomes part of New Granada.
   FCAT LA.A.1.3.2

Applying Social Studies Skills

8. **Analyzing Maps** Study the political map on page 255. What rivers run through Colombia? What are Colombia's major cities?

Technology Skill

Using a Database

An electronic **database** is a collection of data—names, facts, and statistics—that is stored in a file on the computer. Databases are useful for organizing large amounts of information. The information in a database can be sorted and presented in different ways.

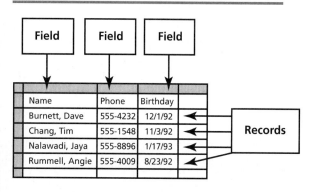

▲ Using a database can help organize statistics, names and addresses, and even baseball card collections.

Learning the Skill

The database organizes information in categories called fields. For example, as shown above, a database of your friends might include the fields **Name, Telephone Number,** and **Birthday.** Each person you enter into the database is called a record. After entering the records, you might create a list sorted by birthdays or use the records to create a personalized phonebook. Together, all the records make up the database.

Scientists use databases for many purposes. They often have large amounts of data that they need to analyze. For example, a sociologist might want to compare and contrast certain information about the people of the Andean countries. A database would be a good place to sort and compare information about the languages, religions, and ethnic groups of these countries.

Practicing the Skill

Follow these steps to build a database about the Andean countries.

1. Determine what facts you want to include in your database and research to collect that information.
2. Follow the instructions in the database that you are using to set up fields. Then enter each item of data in its assigned field.
3. Determine how you want to organize the facts in the database—chronologically by the date, alphabetically, or by some other method.
4. Follow the instructions in your computer program to sort the information.
5. Check that all the information in your database is correct. If necessary, add, delete, or change information or fields.

Applying the Skill

Research and build a database that organizes information about an Andean country of your choice. Explain why the database is organized the way it is. **FCAT** LA.A.2.3.5

TIME
PERSPECTIVES

Waging War on Drugs

Small, hidden cocaine labs are difficult to eliminate.

South America Fights a Global Problem

Compiled and adapted from TIME.

A war on many fronts: U.S. Navy Seals on patrol in Brazil. Police in Peru seize cocaine.

LUKE FRAZZA/AFP

MARIANA BAZO/REUTERS

The Drug Trade's Tragic Effect

Evaluating Media
LA.A.2.3.6

Chris Farley lived every actor's dream. During the 1990s, the comic actor spent five successful years on television's hit series *Saturday Night Live.* Farley became so popular that in 1995 he left *SNL* to start a career in films.

Hollywood quickly became a fan of Farley's and his fame grew. He played roles in movies such as *Tommy Boy* and *Black Sheep.* By 1997, a well-known talk-show host predicted Farley would be "a major motion picture star."

Farley played outrageous characters that battled the world with humor and a big heart. In real life, the actor also battled an addiction to alcohol and drugs like cocaine and heroin. **Cocaine** is a drug that can cause brain injuries if taken only once. In December 1997, Farley used cocaine and other drugs and died.

A Deadly Import

The cocaine that killed Chris Farley came from South America. And so did the 650 tons of cocaine smuggled into the United States in 2000. Every day Americans died as a result of using this drug.

Cocaine is made from the coca plant, which is grown in only three countries. Colombia is by far the biggest producer, followed by Peru and Bolivia.

In all three countries, coca is grown high up in the Andes. Cocaine "factories" there turn coca leaves into a white powder. **Smugglers** use boats and airplanes to slip that powder, cocaine, into countries around the world.

Chris Farley's career was heading to the top.

CORBIS SYGMA

The Drug War in the Andes

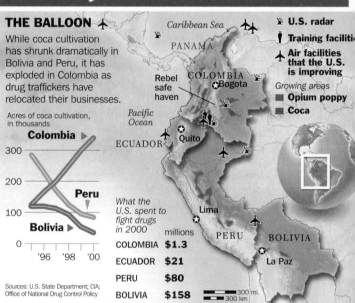

THE BALLOON
While coca cultivation has shrunk dramatically in Bolivia and Peru, it has exploded in Colombia as drug traffickers have relocated their businesses.

Acres of coca cultivation, in thousands

Colombia ▶
Peru ▼
Bolivia ▶

300
200
100
0

'96 '98 '00

Sources: U.S. State Department; CIA; Office of National Drug Control Policy

Caribbean Sea
PANAMA
Rebel safe haven
COLOMBIA ✪Bogota
Pacific Ocean
ECUADOR ✪ Quito
Lima ✪
PERU
BOLIVIA
La Paz ✪

≋ U.S. radar
✦ Training facilitie
✈ Air facilities that the U.S. is improving

Growing areas
■ Opium poppy
■ Coca

What the U.S. spent to fight drugs in 2000 — millions

COLOMBIA	$1.3
ECUADOR	$21
PERU	$80
BOLIVIA	$158

300 mi.
300 km

INTERPRETING MAPS AND CHARTS

1. **Interpreting Data** What does this map tell you about the U.S. role in South America's drug war? FCAT MA.B.1.3.4

2. **Making Inferences** Suppose the war against drugs succeeds in Colombia. How might the lines on the graph change? FCAT MA.D.1.3.2

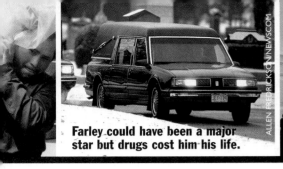

Farley could have been a major star but drugs cost him his life.

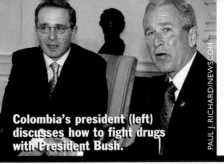

Colombia's president (left) discusses how to fight drugs with President Bush.

44 WAYS TO SAY NO TO WEED & STILL BE COOL

▲ **The beautiful poppy is harvested for deadly heroin.**

Heroin, another deadly drug, is made from the poppy plant. In South America, poppies are turned into heroin only in Colombia.

Rebels' Businesses

Drugs have nearly brought Colombia to its knees. Colombia is a country about the size of Texas and California combined. Rebel armies based in Colombia's jungles have fought government troops for some 40 years. The rebels make and sell cocaine and heroin. Their drug business brings them more than $1 million a day. They spend a lot of that money on weapons.

Paramilitaries add to Colombia's woes. These are armed men that landowners and businesses hire to protect their workers. In 2000, rebels and paramilitaries kidnapped eight innocent civilians every day and murdered 80 more. The chaos has forced some 2 million Colombians to flee their homes.

U.S. money had helped Bolivia and Peru tackle drug problems during the 1990s. But many cocaine producers in those countries moved their operations to Colombia, where cocaine production doubled between 1995 and 2000.

In 2000, the U.S. decided to help Colombia rid itself of the drug trade. It gave Colombia's government $1.3 billion to equip and train its army to fight drugs.

Think, Laugh and Live

If no one bought drugs, no one would produce them. Chris Farley's death helped persuade many people to avoid cocaine. But millions still use it, so the cocaine business remains strong.

Farley's friends and family have created the Chris Farley Foundation to teach kids about the dangers of **drug abuse.** The Foundation encourages young people to "think, laugh and live" when peers try to get them to use drugs. And it does so—as Farley would have—with humor. ▪

EXPLORING THE ISSUE

1. **Explaining** What comment does this article's title make about the trade in illegal drugs? **FCAT** LA.A.2.3.1

2. **Cause and Effect** Describe how Chris Farley's death could have persuaded millions of Americans to avoid cocaine. **FCAT** LA.A.2.3.1

Targeting Drug Supplies

Evaluating
Media
LA.A.2.3.6

Pop works for the U.S. Customs Service in Hidalgo, Texas. He looks for illegal drugs in vehicles that cross into the United States from Mexico.

By any measure, Pop is good at his job. In 1998 he discovered 3,075 pounds of cocaine in a pineapple truck. In 1999 he found 50 pounds of marijuana hidden in an ice chest.

CHRIS USHER

Popsicle's nose earned him a Significant Seizure Medal in 1999.

What makes Pop so successful? His nose. Pop—short for Popsicle—is a pit bull. Like 500 other **customs dogs** in the U.S., he's been trained to sniff out drugs.

Popsicle plays a role in the worldwide effort to stop the flow of drugs. Many thousands of people are also part of that effort. Police officers, for example, arrest people who sell drugs on the street. Members of the U.S. Coast Guard head off smugglers at sea. Soldiers in Colombia destroy coca plants and cocaine factories.

U.S. Help

About 80 percent of the cocaine that reaches the United States comes from Colombia. That's why the U.S. has put more than $1.3 billion behind Colombia's fight against drugs. Colombia's armed forces use most of the money to train soldiers and buy equipment. Planes bought with U.S. dollars drop chemicals that kill growing coca plants. New helicopters rush soldiers to cocaine factories defended by heavily armed rebel troops.

Stopping cocaine at its source isn't just a military job. It's also an effort to change minds. Colombian officials are trying to persuade farmers to stop growing coca and poppies. They pay farmers to grow cocoa, coffee, palm hearts, and other crops instead.

Will those efforts work? Some experts think so. Others aren't so sure. "Those that profit from producing cocaine and heroin are not about to roll over and play dead," said one expert. "There is evidence that drug factories are moving into Brazil and Ecuador."

If she's right, Popsicle has a lot of work ahead of him. ▇

EXPLORING THE ISSUE

1. **Explaining** Why is stopping cocaine at its source important to the war on drugs?
   FCAT LA.A.2.3.1

2. **Analyzing Information** Why might it be more effective to wipe out cocaine in Colombia than to stop it in the United States? **FCAT** LA.A.2.3.2

Dealing With Demand

Evaluating
Media
LA.A.2.3.6

It's tragic but true: Someone somewhere is always going to want to buy illegal drugs. And someone else will be willing to **supply** them. Worldwide, about 14 million people use cocaine today. About 5.3 million of them live in the United States. Nine million people in the world use heroin. More than 650,000 of them are Americans.

Suppose those numbers were cut in half. Heroin and cocaine production would plunge. And illegal drugs would cause far less misery.

Inside Drug Court

Is slashing the **demand** for drugs by 50 percent an impossible dream? Not in Baltimore, Maryland. Baltimore has a Drug Treatment Court. The court's goal is to help people arrested for carrying illegal drugs to stop abusing them. "If you ask for help," a Drug Court judge said in 2001, "you'll get it. If you don't ask, you'll go to jail."

According to the Maryland courts, half the addicts placed in treatment by the Drug Court have stayed away from drugs. Copy that success rate throughout the nation, and the demand in the U.S. for illegal drugs would nose-dive.

Educating Americans

No war on drugs can be successful without such a drop in usage, experts say. U.S. president George W. Bush shares their view. "The main reason drugs are shipped . . . to the United States," he said in 2001, "is because

PAUL F. GERO/SABA

▲ Phoenix, Arizona, has a drug court like Baltimore's. Here a judge rewards a drug offender's good behavior with tickets to Phoenix's science museum.

United States citizens use drugs. Our nation must do a better job of educating our citizenry about the dangers and evils of drug use."

Yes, someone somewhere is always going to want to buy illegal drugs. But proper education and treatment will surely reduce the demand for drugs everywhere. ▪

EXPLORING THE ISSUE

1. **Analyzing Information** Which is more important—reducing the demand for illegal drugs or stopping criminals from producing them? Why? **FCAT** LA.A.2.3.1

2. **Problem Solving** What could schools do to lower the demand for illegal drugs? **FCAT** LA.B.1.3.2

Fighting Drug Abuse: What Can One Person Do?

Andy McDonald is a man with a mission—helping kids stay away from drugs. Andy is a national spokesperson for the Partnership for a Drug-Free America. His message: "Kids don't need drugs to succeed."

Andy should know. He's one of the few top-ranked skateboarders in the world. He's so good, he once jumped over three SUVs and one car—all at the same time. That feat landed him in *The Guinness Book of World Records*. "That right there," he says of skateboarding, "is my idea of getting high."

Speaking Out

You don't have to be a champion athlete to fight drug abuse. Kaelin Weiler proved it. Between 1996 and 1998,

DANIAL BOURQUI

▲ **Andy McDonald: too active to do drugs**

EXPLORING THE ISSUE

1. Making Inferences Experts say that the risk for alcohol and other drug use skyrockets in the sixth grade. Assuming that's true, when—and why—should kids begin learning about the dangers of illegal drugs? **FCAT LA.A.2.3.1**

2. Analyzing Information What makes Andy McDonald an effective promoter of a drug-free life? **FCAT LA.A.2.3.1**

heroin killed 11 teens in her hometown of Plano, Texas. The youngest victim was a seventh-grader.

Kaelin, 17, persuaded other kids to fight back. They tied white ribbons around traffic lights to remind people

of the problem. They created a "memorial wall"—pictures of kids lost to drugs and the families they left behind. And they made videos about the dangers of drugs and showed them at assemblies.

You can work with school officials to start a similar program in your school and town. Learn as much as you can about the dangers of illegal drugs. Then design a program to teach what you learned to young students and their parents. Launch your program. Afterwards, describe the program and its results in a letter to your local newspaper's editor. E-mail a copy to the "In Your Own Words" Web site page of the Partnership for a Drug-Free America (**www.drugfreeamerica.org**). ▨

REVIEW AND ASSESS

UNDERSTANDING THE ISSUE

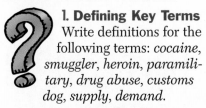

1. Defining Key Terms Write definitions for the following terms: *cocaine, smuggler, heroin, paramilitary, drug abuse, customs dog, supply, demand.*

2. Writing to Inform In a 300-word article, explain why the drug trade needs both buyers and suppliers for its survival. Use at least five of the key terms listed above. FCAT LA.B.1.3.2

3. Writing to Persuade In your view, can the war against drugs ever be won? Support your answer to that question in a brief essay. FCAT LA.B.1.3.2

INTERNET RESEARCH ACTIVITY

4. Since 1998 the U.S. government has funded ads designed to combat drug abuse among young people. How good are the ads? You be the judge. Browse the Internet or use copies of current magazines and newspapers to find ads designed to combat drug abuse. Choose two you think are effective and two you think are not effective. Either print copies off the Internet, or photocopy ads from magazines and newspapers. Attach a comment to each one explaining why it does or doesn't work well. FCAT LA.A.2.3.2

5. The No. 1 drug problem in America isn't cocaine or heroin. It's underage drinking. One organization that works to prevent underage drinking is Mothers Against Drunk Driving (MADD). Use Internet resources to learn more about this organization and report your findings to the class. FCAT LA.A.2.3.5

BEYOND THE CLASSROOM

6. Research the way farmers live in Colombia, Bolivia, or Peru. In a short article, explain why those farmers might

▲ **Venus and Serena Williams are at the top of their game— and far from drugs.**

see growing poppies or coca as a way to improve their lives. FCAT LA.B.1.3.2

7. Research the geography and people of Afghanistan and Myanmar. Most of the world's heroin is produced in those two countries. Make a list of conditions—poverty, climate, and location, for example— that each country shares with Colombia. In class, explain what your list suggests about places in which drug production thrives.

WHAT DRUG AND ALCOHOL ABUSE COST

Annual Cost of Alcohol Abuse in the U.S. $185 billion
- ■ Output[1] lost to alcohol-related illness: **$87.6 billion**
- ■ Output lost to early deaths: **$36.5 billion**
- ■ Healthcare: **$23.6 billion**
- ■ Car-crash damage: **$15.7 billion**
- ■ Alcohol-related crime: **$6.3 billion**
- ■ Other costs: **$15.3 billion**

Annual Cost of Drug Abuse in the U.S. $143 billion
- ■ Output[2] lost by crime victims: **$32.2 billion**
- ■ Property damage, government expenses[3]: **$31.4 billion**
- ■ Output lost to lives of crime: **$24.6 billion**
- ■ Output lost to drug-related illness: **$23.1 billion**
- ■ Output lost to early deaths: **$16.6 billion**
- ■ Healthcare: **$12.8 billion**
- ■ Other costs: **$2.3 billion**

[1]Output is the estimated amount of goods and services that workers would have produced if they had not died or gotten sick, injured, or jailed. [2]Includes output lost by victims of drug-related crimes and criminals jailed for those crimes. [3]Includes the cost of government anti-drug efforts, police, prisons, and other items.
Source: National Institutes of Health

BUILDING GRAPH READING SKILLS

1. Explaining A worker's "output" consists of the goods and services that he or she produces. The abuse of alcohol and other drugs costs the U.S. billions of dollars in lost output. How do these two graphs show that? FCAT MA.D.1.3.2

2. Making Inferences Suppose the U.S. Congress made cocaine and heroin as legal as alcohol. What might happen to the annual cost of drug abuse? FCAT LA.A.2.3.1

FOR UPDATES ON WORLD ISSUES GO TO
www.timeclassroom.com/glencoe

Land and People of Peru and Ecuador

Guide to Reading

Main Idea

Peru and Ecuador share similar landscapes, climates, and history.

Terms to Know

- navigable
- foothills
- empire

Reading Strategy

Create two ovals like these. Under each heading, list facts about Peru and Ecuador in the outer parts of the ovals. Where the ovals overlap, write facts that apply to both countries. **FCAT** LA.A.1.3.2

Peru   Ecuador

The following are the major Sunshine State Standards covered in this section.

SS.B.2.3.3:
Understands ways cultures differ in their use of similar environments and resources

SS.A.2.3.7:
Knows significant achievements in art and architecture in various urban areas and communities to the time of the Renaissance (e.g., the Hanging Gardens of Babylon, pyramids in Egypt, temples in ancient Greece, bridges and aqueducts in ancient Rome, changes in European art and architecture between the Middle Ages and the High Renaissance)

NATIONAL GEOGRAPHIC Exploring Our World

They built thousands of miles of roads. They built a city on mountain peaks and were expert bridge builders. The Inca accomplished these feats in western South America during the 1400s and 1500s. The ruins of their ancient city of Machu Picchu (MAH•choo PEEK•choo), built nearly 8,000 feet (2,438 m) high in the Andes, were not even known to modern people until 1911.

Peru and **Ecuador** lie along the Pacific coast of South America, west of Brazil and south of Colombia. The Andes form the spine of these countries. *Peru*—a Native American word that means "land of abundance"—is rich in mineral resources.

Peru

Dry deserts, the snowcapped Andes, and hot, humid rain forests greet you in Peru. Most of Peru's farms and cities lie on a narrow coastal strip of plains and deserts. The cold **Peru Current** in the Pacific Ocean keeps temperatures here fairly mild even though the area is very near the Equator. Find the Peru Current on the map on page 57.

The Andes, with their highland valleys and plateaus, sweep through the center of Peru. On Peru's border with Bolivia, you can see **Lake Titicaca** (TEE•tee•KAH•kah), the highest navigable lake in the world. Navigable means that a body of water is wide and deep enough to allow ships to travel in it. East of the Andes you descend to the foothills and flat plains of the **Amazon Basin. Foothills** are the low hills at the base of a mountain range. Rainfall is plentiful here, and thick, hot rain forests cover almost all of the plains area.

Mining, Fishing, and Farming   Peru's economy relies on a variety of natural resources. The Andes contain many minerals, including copper, silver, gold, and iron ore. Peru's biggest export is copper. The second-largest export—fish—comes from the Peru Current.

About one-third of Peru's people farm the land. Some grow sugar-cane, cotton, and coffee for export. Like Colombia, Peru grows coca leaves. Most people, however, work on subsistence farms, where they grow only enough food to meet their family's needs. Some of these farms are terraced, or stair-stepped, up the mountainsides of the Andes. The chief crops are rice, plantains (a kind of banana), and corn. Native Americans in the Andes were the first people ever to grow potatoes. Today potatoes are Peru's main food crop, and farmers grow hundreds of varieties in different colors and shapes. Refer back to page 228 to see how the potato was part of the Columbian Exchange.

From Empire to Republic   During the 1400s, a Native American people called the Inca had a powerful civilization in the area that is now Peru. Their empire, or group of lands under one ruler, stretched more than 2,500 miles (4,023 km) along the Andes.

The Incan emperor developed courts, military posts, trade inspections, work rules, and a complex system of record keeping. Work crews built irrigation systems, roads, and suspension bridges that linked the regions of the empire to Cuzco, the capital city of the Inca. You can still see the remains of magnificent fortresses and buildings erected centuries ago by skilled Incan builders. The photograph on page 266 shows the ruins of one of the Inca's most famous cities—Machu Picchu.

In the early 1500s, Spaniards arrived in Peru. They desired the gold and silver found here. The Spaniards defeated the Inca and made Peru a Spanish territory. Peru gained its freedom from Spain in the 1820s. After independence, Peru fought wars with neighboring Chile and Ecuador over land.

Peru is now a republic with an elected president. In recent years, the country's economy has grown very rapidly. Many of Peru's people, however, still live in poverty and cannot find steady jobs.

Peru's Culture   Peru's 27.1 million people live mostly along the Pacific coast. **Lima** (LEE•mah), with more than 7 million people, is the capital and largest city. In recent years, many people from the country-side have moved to Lima in search of work. Because of this sudden rise in population, the city has become overcrowded, noisy, and polluted.

About half of Peru's people are Native American. In fact, Peru has one of the largest Native American populations in the Western Hemisphere. Many live in the Andean highlands or eastern rain forests where they follow a traditional way of life. Most of them blend the Catholic faith, Peru's main religion, with beliefs of their ancestors.

The Quipu

The Inca did not have a written language. To keep records, they used a system of knotted strings called the quipu. The strings were of various lengths and colors, and each knot meant a different item or number. Men in charge of the quipu used the knots to record all the taxes brought each year to the Inca. They recorded the number of men who went to war and how many were born and died every year. In short, it might be said that they recorded on their quipu everything that could be counted.

Sports

Sports have been played in Peru for centuries. Ancient vases show the Inca playing early forms of badminton and basketball. Today soccer, called *fútbol*, is the national sport of Peru. Boys and girls learn the sport at a young age, and every village has a local soccer team. Peruvians also enjoy baseball and basketball. In addition, volleyball has become very popular since 1988. That was the year the women's volleyball team from Peru won an Olympic medal.

Looking Closer How is the game shown here similar to and different from an American soccer game?

Peruvians also include many people of mixed or European ancestry. People of Asian heritage form a small but important part of the population. Although a minority, Peruvians of European ancestry (mainly Spanish) control most of Peru's wealth and political power.

Spanish is Peru's official language, but about 70 Native American languages also are spoken. You can hear Quechua (KEH•chuh•wuh), the ancient language of the Inca, in many Native American villages. Another sound you may hear is the flutelike tones of the panpipe. An ancient instrument, panpipes are made from different lengths of bamboo stalks tied together.

✓ Reading Check Who built a huge empire centered in Peru?

Ecuador

Ecuador is one of the smallest countries in South America. Can you guess how it got its name? *Ecuador* is the Spanish word for "Equator," which runs right through Ecuador. West of Ecuador and also on the Equator are the **Galápagos Islands.** Owned by Ecuador since 1832, these scattered islands are known for their rich plant and animal life. Turn to page 270 to learn more about the unusual Galápagos Islands.

Ecuador's land and climate are similar to Peru's. Swamps and fertile plains stretch along Ecuador's Pacific coast. The Peru Current in the Pacific Ocean keeps coastal temperatures mild. The Andes run through the center of the country. The higher you climb up these mountains, the colder the climate gets. In contrast, hot, humid rain forests cover the lowlands of eastern Ecuador. Few people live in the rain forests.

An Agricultural Economy Agriculture is Ecuador's most important economic activity. Because of the mild climate, bananas, cacao, coffee, rice, sugarcane, and other export crops grow plentifully in the coastal lowlands. Farther inland, farms in the Andean highlands grow coffee, beans, corn, potatoes, and wheat. The eastern lowlands yield petroleum, Ecuador's major mineral export.

Ecuador's People   Mestizos and Native Americans each make up about 40 percent of Ecuador's population. Spanish is the official language, but many Native Americans speak their traditional languages. About half of Ecuador's 12.6 million people live along the coast. The port of **Guayaquil** (GWY•ah•KEEL) is the most populous city. The other half of the population live in the valleys and plateaus of the Andes. **Quito** (KEE•toh), Ecuador's capital, lies more than 9,000 feet (2,743 m) above sea level. From the heart of Quito, you can see several snowcapped volcanoes. The city's historic center has Spanish colonial churches and old whitewashed houses with red-tiled roofs. These houses are built around central courtyards. You will not find flashing neon signs here because the construction of modern buildings has been strictly controlled since 1978. In that year, the United Nations Educational, Scientific, and Cultural Organization (UNESCO) declared the "old town" section of Quito a protected world cultural heritage site. Quito does have a "new town" section, though, in the north. This area has modern offices, embassies, and shopping centers.

✓ Reading Check   **Why are Ecuador's eastern lowlands important economically?**

FCAT PRACTICE   You can prepare for the FCAT-assessed standards by completing the correlated item(s) below.

Assessment

Defining Terms
1. **Define** navigable, foothills, empire.

Recalling Facts
2. **History** Who were the first people to grow potatoes?
3. **Culture** What has been the result of Lima's sudden population growth?   **FCAT LA.A.2.3.1**
4. **Economics** What is Ecuador's major mineral export?

Critical Thinking
5. **Analyzing Information** Why is Peru's name, which means "land of abundance," appropriate? Why is it also inappropriate?
6. **Analyzing Cause and Effect** What effect does the Peru Current have on the coastal areas of Peru?   **FCAT LA.E.2.2.1**

Graphic Organizer
7. **Organizing Information** Create two diagrams like this one, one for Peru and one for Ecuador. Under each heading, list facts about the countries.   **FCAT LA.A.1.3.2**

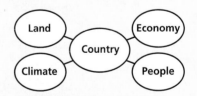

Applying Social Studies Skills

8. **Analyzing Maps** Turn to the political map on page 255. What Andean capital city lies closest to the Equator?

The Andean Countries

269

The Galápagos Islands

The Galápagos Islands are located in the eastern Pacific Ocean about 600 miles (966 km) west of mainland Ecuador. Since 1959 about 95 percent of the islands has been maintained as a national park.

History of Exploration

From the first documented visit to the Galápagos Islands in 1535, people have commented on the islands' unusual wildlife. Sailors, including pirates and whalers, stopped on the islands to collect water and to trap the huge *galápagos*, or tortoises, found on the islands. Sailors valued the tortoises as a source of fresh meat because the giant tortoises could live on ships for months without food or water.

Charles Darwin

The most famous visitor to the Galápagos Islands was Charles Darwin, a scientist from England. He was studying animals all over the

FCAT PRACTICE Answering question 3 below will help you prepare for the **FCAT Science** and **Reading** tests.

world. In 1835 Darwin spent five weeks visiting four of the biggest islands in the Galápagos. He carefully studied the volcanic landscape and the plant and animal life that he saw. He took notes on the differences among animals such as finches, mockingbirds, and iguanas from island to island. Darwin believed that these differences showed how populations of the same species change to fit their environment.

A Fragile Environment

Today the Galápagos Islands are still prized for their amazing variety of animal and plant life. Many of the species found here exist nowhere else on the earth. For instance, the marine iguana that lives here is the only seagoing lizard in the world.

Unfortunately, years of contact between the islands and humans have had serious effects. Three of the 14 types of tortoises are extinct, and others are seriously threatened. Populations of goats, pigs, dogs, rats, and some types of plants, brought by visitors, have grown so large that they threaten the survival of native plants and animals. Demand for exotic marine life, including sharks and sea cucumbers, has led to overfishing. The government of Ecuador, along with environmentalists worldwide, is now working to protect the islands.

▲ Giant Galápagos tortoise

➤ Making the Connection

1. Why did sailors long ago stop at the islands?

2. What did Darwin observe about the islands?

3. **Drawing Conclusions** Why are environmentalists and the government of Ecuador working to protect the Galápagos Islands? **FCAT** SC.D.2.3.2, LA.A.2.3.1

Guide to Reading

Main Idea

Bolivia and Chile share the Andes, but their economies and people are different.

Terms to Know

- landlocked
- altiplano
- sodium nitrate

Reading Strategy

Create a chart like the one below. In each row, write at least one fact about Bolivia and one about Chile. **FCAT LA.A.1.3.2**

	Bolivia	Chile
Land		
Climate		
Economy		
People		

The following are the major Sunshine State Standards covered in this section.

SS.B.2.3.8:
Knows world patterns of resource distribution and utilization

SS.B.2.3.7:
Knows how various human systems throughout the world have developed in response to conditions in the physical environment

The Bolivians and Chileans

NATIONAL GEOGRAPHIC Exploring Our World

The woman hides her face from the gusting wind as she follows her herd of sheep across the plains of Bolivia. She worries about her teenage children, who want to leave their home to find work in the city. The woman is part of a Native American group called the Chipaya, who raise sheep and farm in the dusty altiplano of Bolivia.

At first glance, **Bolivia** and **Chile** seem very different. Bolivia lacks a seacoast, while Chile has a long coastline on the Pacific Ocean. The Andes, however, affect the climate and cultures of both countries.

Bolivia

Bolivia lies near the center of South America. It is a landlocked country, which means it has no sea or ocean that touches its land. Fortunately, in 1993 Peru agreed to give Bolivia a free trade zone in the port city of **Ilo.** This gave Bolivia better access to the free flow of people, goods, and ideas. Bolivia is the highest and most isolated country in South America. Why? The Andes dominate Bolivia's landscape. Look at the map on page 180. You see that in western Bolivia, the Andes surround a high plateau called the altiplano. Over one-third of Bolivia is a mile or more high. Unless you were born in this area, you would find that the cold, thin air makes it difficult to breathe. Few trees grow on

271

Chile's Contrasts

Chile has a wide variety of climates and landforms. The moderate capital city of Santiago in central Chile (above) contrasts sharply with the icy southern region (right).

Location What group of islands lies at the southern tip of Chile?

the altiplano, and most of the land is too dry to farm. Still, the vast majority of Bolivians live on this high plateau. Those areas that have water have been farmed for many centuries.

Bolivia also has lowland plains and tropical rain forests in the east and north. Most of this area has a hot, humid climate. South-central Bolivia, however, has more fertile land, and many farms dot this region.

A Struggling Economy Bolivia is rich in minerals such as tin, silver, and zinc. Miners remove these minerals from high in the Andes. Workers in the eastern lowlands draw out gold, petroleum, and natural gas.

Still, Bolivia is a poor country. About two-thirds of the people live in poverty. Throughout the highlands, many villagers practice subsistence farming. They struggle to grow wheat, potatoes, and barley. At higher elevations, herders raise animals such as alpacas and llamas for wool and for carrying goods. In the south, farmers plant soybeans, a growing export. Timber is another important export. Unfortunately, one crop that can be grown for sale is coca, which is made into cocaine.

Bolivia's People Bolivia was part of the Incan Empire until Spain conquered the Inca. The country won independence in 1825 and was named after Simón Bolívar. What is unusual about Bolivia's capital? There is not just one capital city, but two. The official capital is **Sucre** (SOO•kray). The administrative capital and largest city is **La Paz** (lah PAHZ). Both capital cities are located in the altiplano. La Paz—at 12,000 feet (3,658 m)—is the highest capital city in the world.

Most of Bolivia's 8.6 million people live in the Andean highlands. About half are of Native American ancestry, and another 30 percent are mestizos. In the cities, most people follow modern ways of living. In the countryside, you may hear traditional sounds, such as music played with panpipes and other flutelike instruments.

✓ Reading Check What is the altiplano?

Chile

Chile is almost twice the size of California. Although its average width is only 110 miles (177 km), Chile stretches 2,652 miles (4,267 km) along the Pacific Ocean.

About 80 percent of Chile's land is mountainous. The high Andes run along Chile's border with Bolivia and Argentina. Except in the altiplano area of Chile's north, very few Chileans live in the Andes.

Also in the north is the **Atacama Desert.** It is one of the driest places on the earth. Why? This area is in the rain shadow of the Andes. Winds from the Atlantic Ocean bring precipitation to regions east of the Andes, but they carry no moisture past them. In addition, the cold Peru Current in the Pacific Ocean does not evaporate as much as a warm current does. As a result, only dry air hits the coast.

A steppe climate zone lies just north of **Santiago,** Chile's capital. Most of Chile's people live in a central region called the Central Valley. With a mild Mediterranean climate, the fertile valleys here have the largest concentration of cities, industries, and farms.

The lake region, also known as "the south," has a marine west coast climate that supports thick forests. Chile's far south is a stormy, wind-swept region of snowcapped volcanoes, thick forests, and huge glaciers. The **Strait of Magellan** separates mainland Chile from a group of islands known as **Tierra del Fuego** (FWAY•goh)—or "Land of Fire." This region is shared by both Chile and Argentina. Cold ocean waters batter the rugged coast around **Cape Horn,** the southernmost point of South America.

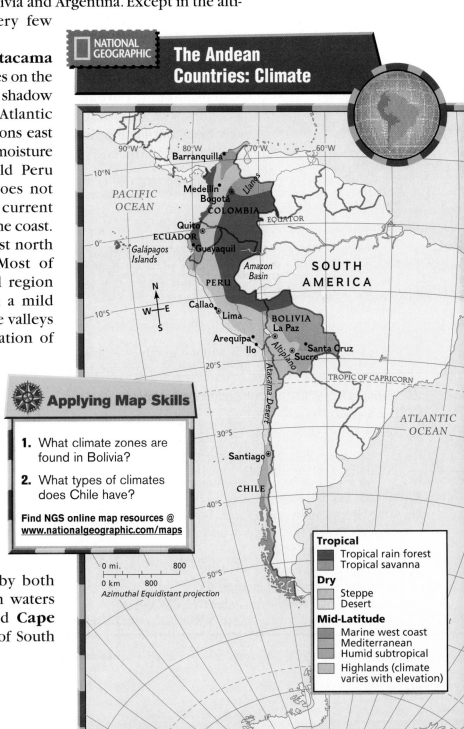

NATIONAL GEOGRAPHIC

The Andean Countries: Climate

Applying Map Skills

1. What climate zones are found in Bolivia?

2. What types of climates does Chile have?

Find NGS online map resources @ www.nationalgeographic.com/maps

0 mi. 800
0 km 800
Azimuthal Equidistant projection

Tropical
Tropical rain forest
Tropical savanna
Dry
Steppe
Desert
Mid-Latitude
Marine west coast
Mediterranean
Humid subtropical
Highlands (climate varies with elevation)

The Andean Countries

Chile's Economy In recent years, Chile has had high economic growth, and the number of people below the poverty line has fallen by half. Mining forms the backbone of Chile's economy. The Atacama region is rich in minerals. Chile ranks as the world's leading copper producer. The country also mines and exports gold, silver, iron ore, and sodium nitrate—a mineral used in fertilizer and explosives.

Agriculture is also a major economic activity. Farmers produce wheat, corn, beans, sugar, and potatoes. The grapes and apples you eat in winter may come from Chile's summer harvest. (Remember that the seasons here in the Southern Hemisphere are opposite of those you experience in the Northern Hemisphere.) Many people also raise cattle, sheep, and other livestock.

Chile has factories that process fish and other foods. Other workers manufacture wood products, iron, steel, vehicles, cement, and textiles. Service industries such as banking and tourism also thrive.

Chile's Culture Of the 15.8 million people in Chile, most are mestizos. A large minority are of European descent, and some Native American groups live in the altiplano and "the south." Nearly all the people speak Spanish, and most are Roman Catholic. Some 80 percent of Chile's population live in urban areas. Chile has been a democratic republic since the end of strict military rule in 1990.

✓ Reading Check What are the three cultural backgrounds of Chile's 15.8 million people?

 FCAT PRACTICE You can prepare for the FCAT-assessed standards by completing the correlated item(s) below.

 **Section 3 Assessment**

Defining Terms
1. **Define** landlocked, altiplano, sodium nitrate.

Recalling Facts
2. **Economics** What part of Bolivia's population lives in poverty?
3. **Geography** What makes La Paz unusual?
4. **Economics** Chile is the world's leading producer of what mineral?

Critical Thinking
5. **Analyzing Cause and Effect** Why is the Atacama Desert one of the world's driest places? **FCAT LA.E.2.2.1**
6. **Making Comparisons** What are differences and similarities between the economies of Bolivia and Chile? **FCAT LA.A.1.3.2**

Graphic Organizer
7. **Organizing Information** Create a diagram like this one. Under each arrow, list supporting facts for the main idea. **FCAT LA.A.1.3.2**

> Main Idea: Bolivia is rich in minerals but is still a poor country.
>
> ↑   ↑   ↑   ↑

 Applying Social Studies Skills

8. **Analyzing Maps** Study the physical map on page 180. The southernmost tip of South America is part of what country? What is the name of the group of islands at the southern tip of South America? What does the name mean?

Reading Review

Section 1 | Colombia's Culture and Challenges

Terms to Know
cordillera
cash crop
mestizo
campesino

Main Idea
Although it has many resources, Colombia faces political and economic unrest.

✓ Economics Colombia is rich in hydroelectric power, gold, and emeralds.

✓ Government The government of Colombia is struggling to combat the power of drug dealers who make huge fortunes from selling cocaine, which comes from the coca plant.

✓ Culture Most Colombians speak Spanish and follow the Roman Catholic religion.

✓ History Civil war in Colombia is still being fought today.

Section 2 | Land and People of Peru and Ecuador

Terms to Know
navigable
foothills
empire

Main Idea
Peru and Ecuador share similar landscapes, climates, and history.

✓ History The Inca had a powerful civilization in the area that is now Peru. They developed a complex system of record keeping.

✓ Economics Peru's main exports are copper and fish. Many people farm. Ecuador's economy is focused on agriculture.

✓ Culture Most people in Peru and Ecuador live along the coast.

▲ Dancers in Peru

Section 3 | The Bolivians and Chileans

Terms to Know
landlocked
altiplano
sodium nitrate

Main Idea
Bolivia and Chile share the Andes, but their economies and people are different.

✓ Human/Environment Interaction Bolivia is a poor country consisting mainly of the towering Andes and a high plateau that is difficult to farm.

✓ Culture Most of Chile's people speak Spanish and follow the Roman Catholic religion.

✓ Economics Chile has a diverse economy that includes mining—especially copper and sodium nitrate—farming, and manufacturing.

Assessment and Activities

FCAT PRACTICE You can prepare for the FCAT-assessed standards by completing the correlated item(s) below.

Using Key Terms

Match the terms in Part A with their definitions in Part B.

A.

1. cordillera
2. campesino
3. cash crop
4. altiplano
5. navigable
6. foothills
7. empire
8. sodium nitrate
9. landlocked
10. mestizo

B.

a. person of mixed Native American and European ancestry
b. crop grown to be sold, often for export
c. mineral used in making fertilizer
d. group of lands under one ruler
e. group of mountain ranges that run side by side
f. when a body of water is wide and deep enough for ships to pass through
g. land that does not have a sea or an ocean touching it
h. low hills at the base of a mountain range
i. farmer in Colombia
j. large highland plateau

Reviewing the Main Ideas

Section 1 Colombia's Culture and Challenges

11. **Economics** List four of Colombia's natural resources.
12. **History** What is the heritage of most of Colombia's people?
13. **History** What type of activities have scarred Colombia's history?

Section 2 Land and People of Peru and Ecuador

14. **Place** What is the highest navigable lake in the world?
15. **History** What ancient Native American civilization of the Andes lived in Peru?
16. **Government** Which country owns the Galápagos Islands?

Section 3 The Bolivians and Chileans

17. **Culture** What is life like for about two-thirds of Bolivia's people?
18. **Government** What type of government does Chile have?
19. **Culture** What is the ethnic background of most Chileans?

NATIONAL GEOGRAPHIC The Andean Countries

Place Location Activity

On a separate sheet of paper, match the letters on the map with the numbered places listed below.

1. Colombia
2. Peru
3. Chile
4. Andes
5. Lake Titicaca
6. Quito
7. Bogotá
8. Strait of Magellan
9. Lima
10. Bolivia

0 mi.   800
0 km   800
Azimuthal Equidistant projection

Social Studies Online

Self-Check Quiz Visit *The World and Its People* Web site at <u>twip.glencoe.com</u> and click on **Chapter 9—Self-Check Quizzes** to prepare for the Chapter Test.

Critical Thinking

20. **Making Inferences** Why are Native Americans who live in the Andean highlands more likely to follow a traditional way of life than those who live in the cities? **FCAT LA.A.1.3.2**

21. **Analyzing Cause and Effect** On a diagram like the one below, list factors that have led to political violence during Colombia's history. **FCAT LA.A.2.3.1**

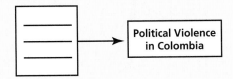

```
┌──────────┐
│          │
│          │  ──▶  ┌─────────────────┐
│          │       │ Political Violence │
│          │       │   in Colombia     │
└──────────┘       └─────────────────┘
```

Comparing Regions Activity

22. **Geography** Compare the features of the Andes to the Himalaya in South Asia. Write a travel article for a mountain climbing magazine to tell potential climbers which region might be best for them to try.
FCAT LA.B.1.3.2

Mental Mapping Activity

23. **Focusing on the Region** Create a simple outline map of South America, and then label the following:

- Pacific Ocean
- Peru
- Andes
- Colombia
- Atacama Desert
- Galápagos Islands
- Strait of Magellan
- Lake Titicaca
- Chile
- Ecuador

Technology Skills Activity

24. **Building a Database** Create a fact sheet about the Andean countries by building a database. Create fields for such categories as physical features, natural resources, capital cities, population, and type of government. When you have entered data for each field, print your fact sheet.

Standardized Test Practice

Directions: Read the paragraphs below, and then answer the question that follows.

Simón Bolívar, an aristocrat from Venezuela, led many of South America's lands to independence. He believed in equality and saw liberty as "the only object worth a man's life." Called "the Liberator," Bolívar devoted his life to freedom for Latin Americans.

Bolívar was the son of a rich family in New Granada, or what is today Colombia, Venezuela, Panama, and Ecuador. In 1805 he went to Europe. There he learned about the French Revolution and its ideas of democracy. He returned home, vowing to free his people from Spanish rule. In 1810 Bolívar started a revolt against the Spaniards in Venezuela. Spanish officials soon crushed the movement, but Bolívar escaped and trained an army. During the next 20 years, Bolívar and his forces won freedom for the present-day countries of Venezuela, Colombia, Panama, Bolivia, and Ecuador.

1. **What is the main idea of the paragraphs above?** **FCAT LA.A.2.3.1**

   A Bolívar was the son of a rich family.

   B Bolívar traveled to Europe and learned about democracy.

   C Simón Bolívar was called "the Liberator."

   D Bolívar devoted his life to freedom for Latin Americans.

Test-Taking Tip: This question asks you to find the main idea, or to make a generalization. Most of the answer choices provide specific details, not a general idea. Which of the answers is more of a general statement?

Unit 4

Woman in Hungary creating folk art

Ancient ruins in Delphi, Greece

Europe

You have learned about the Americas. Now let us spin the globe and travel to Europe. Relatively small as continents go, Europe is rich in history and culture. Like the United States, most nations in Europe are industrialized and have high standards of living. Unlike the United States, however, the people of Europe do not share a common language or government.

▲ The Louvre museum, Paris, France

NGS ONLINE
www.nationalgeographic.com/education

279

Focus on:

Europe

BOTH A CONTINENT and a region, Europe has a wide range of cultures—and a history of conflict among its people. Recently, connections in trade, communication, and transportation have helped to create greater unity among European nations.

The Land

Jutting westward from Asia, Europe is a great peninsula that breaks into smaller peninsulas and is bordered by several large islands. Europe's long, jagged coastline is washed by many bodies of water, including the Arctic and Atlantic Oceans, and the North, Baltic, and Mediterranean Seas. Deep bays and well-protected inlets shelter fine harbors. Closeness to the sea has enabled Europeans to trade with other lands. Many Europeans also depend on the sea for food.

Mountains sweep across much of the continent. Those in the British Isles and large parts of northern Europe are low and rounded. Higher and more rugged are the Pyrenees, between France and Spain, and the Carpathians, in eastern Europe. The snow-capped Alps are Europe's highest mountains, towering over the central and southern parts of the continent.

Curving around these mountain ranges are broad, fertile plains. In the north, the North European Plain stretches from France to Russia. Cities, towns, and farms dot the gently rolling landscape.

Rivers For centuries, Europe's rivers have provided links between coastal ports and inland population centers. In western Europe, the Rhine flows northwest from the Alps until it empties into the North Sea. The Danube winds through eastern Europe on its way to the Black Sea.

The Climate

Despite its northern location, Europe enjoys a relatively mild climate. This is because of the region's closeness to the Atlantic Ocean. An ocean current known as the North Atlantic Current brings warm waters and winds to bathe Europe's western shores. As a result, northwestern Europe enjoys mild temperatures all year, along with plentiful rainfall. Farther south, countries along the Mediterranean Sea have hot, dry summers and mild winters. The region's northernmost countries have longer, colder winters than their southern neighbors. Winters are also cold in Europe's interior, which lies far from the influence of the North Atlantic Current.

Diverse Vegetation The vegetation varies from one climate zone to another.

Village at the foot of the
Alps, Switzerland ▼

◄ Fisherman mending
nets in Malta

In Scandinavia's far north, you would find mostly mosses and small shrubs blanketing a tundra-like landscape. In northwestern and eastern Europe, grasslands and forests cover the rolling land. Farther south, drought-resistant shrubs and small trees cover rugged hills.

The Economy

An abundance of key natural resources, waterways, and ports has helped make Europe a global economic power. Agriculture, manufacturing, and service industries dominate the region's economies.

Rich Farmland Some of the most productive farmland in the world can be found on the European continent. From the fertile black soil, farmers gather bountiful harvests of grains, fruits, and vegetables. Cattle and sheep graze through lush European pastures.

Resources and Industry Vast reserves of oil and natural gas lie offshore. Rich deposits of iron ore, coal, and other minerals have provided the raw materials for heavy industry and manufacturing. Europe was the birthplace of the Industrial Revolution, which transformed the region from an agricultural society into an industrial one. Today countries such as France, Germany, Italy, Poland, and the United Kingdom rank among the world's top manufacturing centers. These industrial countries produce steel, machinery, cars, textiles, electronic equipment, food products, and household goods. Service industries such as banking, insurance, and tourism are also important to Europe's market economies.

The People

After Asia, Europe is the most densely populated continent on the earth. In some European countries, such as Sweden, most people belong to the same ethnic group. The populations of other countries, however, are made up of several ethnic groups. Some ethnic groups live together peacefully. Other groups often face tension and conflict.

Artistic Treasures Europeans enjoy a rich cultural heritage that stretches back thousands of years. In fact, all Western cultures have their roots in the ancient periods of Classical Greece and Rome. If you walk through the heart of any large European city, you might see ancient Roman ruins, Gothic cathedrals built during the Middle Ages, and sculptures created by Renaissance masters, such as Michelangelo and Leonardo da Vinci.

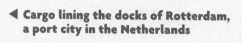

◄ **Cargo lining the docks of Rotterdam, a port city in the Netherlands**

Revolutions After the 1700s, political changes increased freedom for the common people. An interest in science and the invention of machines during the Industrial Revolution changed the economy and raised standards of living. In eastern Europe, once-powerful empires faced growing challenges from ethnic groups that wanted independence.

Global Influence Throughout their history, Europeans have explored and settled other lands. They have spread their culture around the world. Competition among European nations in the past led to two World Wars and a bitter division into communist and non-communist areas. Many European nations have recently joined the European Union to become a united economic force.

Children by road signs in Ireland ▼

Data Bits

Country	Automobiles per 1,000 people	Television sets per 1,000 people
Austria	495	526
Finland	403	643
France	469	620
Greece	254	480
Ireland	272	406

Population: Urban ▨ vs. Rural ▨

Country	Urban	Rural
Austria	67%	33%
Finland	59%	41%
France	76%	24%
Greece	60%	40%
Ireland	59%	41%

Sources: *World Development Indicators*, 2002; *The World Almanac*, 2004.

Exploring the Region

1. What bodies of water border Europe?
2. Why is Europe's climate relatively mild?
3. What has helped make Europe a global economic power?
4. How did European culture spread to other parts of the world?

Europe

Physical

▲ Mountain peak

0 mi.   500
0 km   500
Lambert Azimuthal Equal-Area projection

ICELAND

ARCTIC CIRCLE

60°N

Faroe Is.

Shetland Is.

Orkney Is.

ATLANTIC OCEAN

UNITED KINGDOM

IRELAND

50°N

British Isles

North Sea

Jutland

DENMARK

NETH.

GERMANY

BELG.

LUX.

NORTH EUROPEAN PLAIN

POLAND

Norwegian Sea

NORWAY

SCANDINAVIA

SWEDEN

FINLAND

Baltic Sea

ESTONIA

LATVIA

LITHUANIA

RUSSIA

BELARUS

RUSSIA

CZECH REP.

Carpathian Mountains

UKRAINE

SLOVAKIA

MOLDOVA

FRANCE

LIECH.

SWITZ.

AUSTRIA

Hungarian Plain

HUNGARY

Bay of Biscay

Loire R.

Seine R.

A L P S

Mt. Blanc 15,771 ft. (4,807 m)

Matterhorn 14,690 ft. (4,478 m)

SLOV.

CROATIA

ROMANIA

Dnieper R.

Crimean Peninsula

Black Sea

40°N

ANDORRA

Pyrenees

MONACO

Corsica

SAN MARINO

A p e n n i n e s

ITALY

Adriatic Sea

BOSN. & HERZG.

SERB. & MONT.

Danube R.

Balkan Peninsula

BULGARIA

MACED.

PORTUGAL

SPAIN

IBERIAN PENINSULA

Douro R.

Ebro R.

Tagus R.

Strait of Gibraltar

Sardinia

M e d i t e r r a n e a n

Sicily

MALTA

ALBANIA

GREECE

Aegean Sea

Crete

S e a

CYPRUS

RUSSIA

26,247 ft.	0 mi.	500	8,000 m
19,685 ft.	0 km	500	6,000 m
		ALPS	
13,123 ft.	PYRENEES		4,000 m
6,562 ft.			2,000 m
	LISBON	Sea level WARSAW	

20°W   10°W   0°   10°E   20°E   30°E

MERIDIAN OF GREENWICH (LONDON)

UNIT

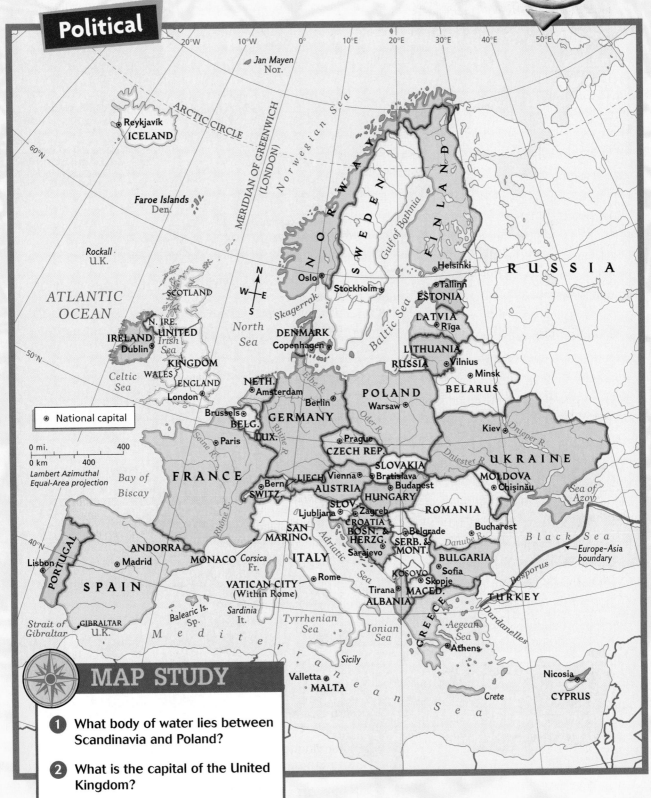

Political

MAP STUDY

1. What body of water lies between Scandinavia and Poland?

2. What is the capital of the United Kingdom?

Map labels:

20°W 10°W 0° 10°E 20°E 30°E 40°E 50°E

Jan Mayen Nor.

ARCTIC CIRCLE

60°N

⊛ Reykjavík
ICELAND

Faroe Islands Den.

Rockall U.K.

Norwegian Sea

ATLANTIC OCEAN

Gulf of Bothnia

N   O   R   W   A   Y

S W E D E N

F I N L A N D

⊛ Helsinki

R U S S I A

⊛ Oslo

Stockholm ⊛

⊛ Tallinn
ESTONIA

LATVIA
Rīga ⊛

Baltic Sea

LITHUANIA
RUSSIA
⊛ Vilnius

⊛ Minsk

SCOTLAND

N. IRE.
UNITED
IRELAND
Dublin ⊛
Irish Sea

Celtic Sea

KINGDOM
WALES

ENGLAND
London ⊛

North Sea

DENMARK
Copenhagen ⊛

Berlin ⊛

Elbe R.

POLAND
Warsaw ⊛

BELARUS

Kiev ⊛
Dnieper R.

50°N

NETH.
⊛ Amsterdam

Brussels ⊛
BELG.
LUX.

GERMANY

⊛ Paris

Seine R.

Rhine R.

⊛ Prague
CZECH REP.

Oder R.

SLOVAKIA
⊛ Bratislava

Dniester R.

UKRAINE

MOLDOVA
⊛ Chişinău

Sea of Azov

⊛ National capital

0 mi. 400
0 km 400
Lambert Azimuthal
Equal-Area projection

Bay of Biscay

FRANCE

Bern ⊛
SWITZ.

LIECH
Vienna ⊛
AUSTRIA

⊛ Budapest
HUNGARY

SLOV.
Ljubljana ⊛
Zagreb ⊛
CROATIA
BOSN. &
HERZG.

ROMANIA

Bucharest ⊛

Black Sea

Europe–Asia boundary

40°N

PORTUGAL
Lisbon ⊛

ANDORRA

⊛ Madrid

SPAIN

MONACO
Corsica Fr.

SAN
MARINO
ITALY

Adriatic Sea

Sarajevo ⊛

⊛ Belgrade
SERB. &
MONT.

Danube R.

BULGARIA
⊛ Sofia

Bosporus

VATICAN CITY
(Within Rome)

⊛ Rome

KOSOVO
Skopje ⊛
MACED.

TURKEY

Strait of Gibraltar

GIBRALTAR U.K.

Balearic Is. Sp.

Sardinia It.

Tyrrhenian Sea

Tirana ⊛
ALBANIA

GREECE

Ionian Sea

Aegean Sea

Dardanelles

Nicosia ⊛
CYPRUS

M   e   d   i   t   e   r   r   a   n   e   a   n   S   e   a

Sicily

Valletta ⊛
MALTA

⊛ Athens

Crete

W — N — E — S (compass)

285

Europe

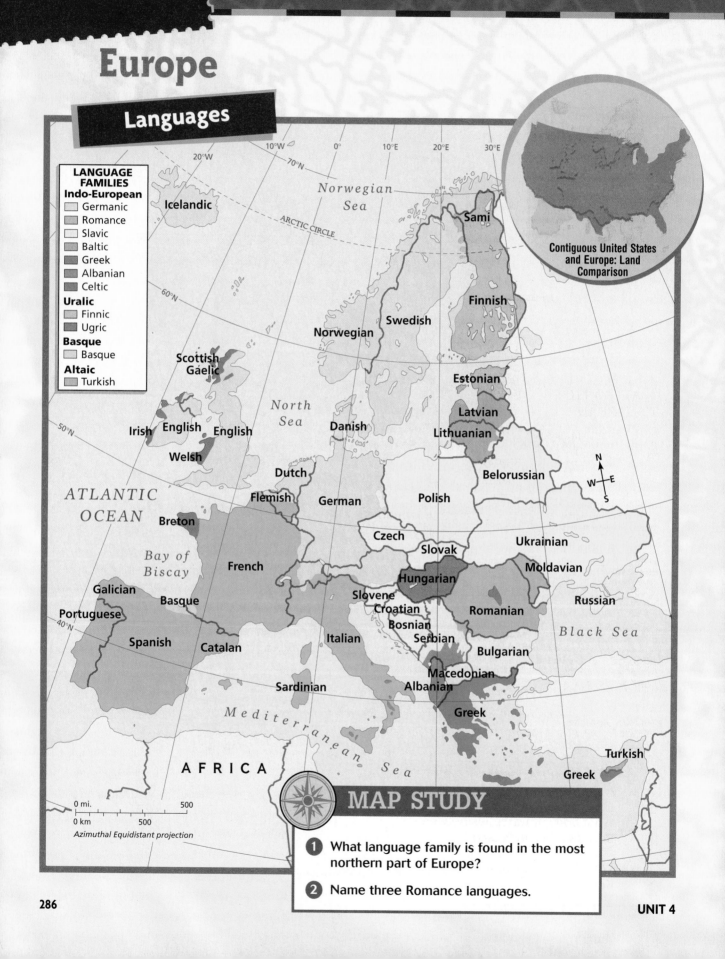

Languages

LANGUAGE FAMILIES

Indo-European
- Germanic
- Romance
- Slavic
- Baltic
- Greek
- Albanian
- Celtic

Uralic
- Finnic
- Ugric

Basque
- Basque

Altaic
- Turkish

Contiguous United States and Europe: Land Comparison

Norwegian Sea

ARCTIC CIRCLE

Icelandic

Sami

Finnish

Swedish

Norwegian

Estonian

Latvian

Lithuanian

Scottish Gaelic

North Sea

Danish

Belorussian

Irish English English

Welsh

Dutch

German Polish

ATLANTIC OCEAN

Flemish

Czech

Ukrainian

Breton

Slovak

Bay of Biscay

French

Hungarian

Moldavian

Galician

Slovene

Russian

Basque

Croatian

Romanian

Portuguese

Bosnian

Serbian

Black Sea

Spanish Catalan

Italian

Bulgarian

Macedonian

Sardinian

Albanian

Greek

Mediterranean Sea

AFRICA

Turkish

Greek

0 mi. 500
0 km 500
Azimuthal Equidistant projection

MAP STUDY

❶ What language family is found in the most northern part of Europe?

❷ Name three Romance languages.

Geo Extremes

① **HIGHEST POINT**
Mont Blanc (France and Italy)
15,771 ft. (4,807 m) high

② **LOWEST POINT**
Nieuwerkerk aan
den IJssel (Netherlands)
22 ft. (7 m) below sea level

③ **LONGEST RIVER**
Danube (central Europe)
1,776 mi. (2,858 km) long

④ **LARGEST LAKE**
Lake Vänern (Sweden)
2,156 sq. mi. (5,584 sq. km)

⑤ **HIGHEST WATERFALL**
Mardalsfossen,
Southern (Norway)
2,149 ft. (655 m) high

⑥ **LARGEST ISLAND**
Great Britain
84,210 sq. mi.
(218,103 sq. km)

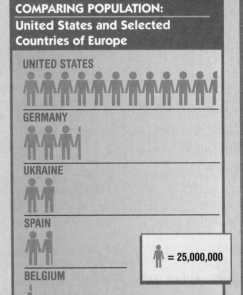

COMPARING POPULATION:
United States and Selected
Countries of Europe

UNITED STATES

GERMANY

UKRAINE

SPAIN

🚹 = 25,000,000

BELGIUM

Source: Population Reference Bureau, 2003.

RELIGIONS:
Selected Countries of
Europe

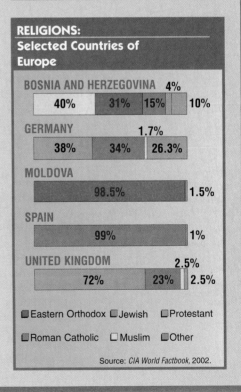

BOSNIA AND HERZEGOVINA **4%**

| 40% | 31% | 15% | 10% |

GERMANY **1.7%**

| 38% | 34% | 26.3% |

MOLDOVA

| 98.5% | 1.5% |

SPAIN

| 99% | 1% |

UNITED KINGDOM **2.5%**

| 72% | 23% | 2.5% |

⬛ Eastern Orthodox ⬛ Jewish ⬜ Protestant

⬜ Roman Catholic ⬜ Muslim ⬜ Other

Source: *CIA World Factbook*, 2002.

GRAPHIC STUDY

❶ Which two countries share the highest point in Europe?

❷ Roughly what is the population of Germany? What percentage of the population is Protestant? **FCAT** MA.E.3.3.1

Country Profiles

ALBANIA

POPULATION:
3,100,000
282 per sq. mi.
109 per sq. km

LANGUAGE:
Albanian

MAJOR EXPORT:
Asphalt

CAPITAL:
Tirana

MAJOR IMPORT:
Machinery

LANDMASS:
11,100 sq. mi.
28,749 sq. km

ANDORRA

POPULATION:
100,000
578 per sq. mi.
222 per sq. km

LANGUAGES:
Catalan, French,
Spanish

MAJOR EXPORT:
Electricity

CAPITAL:
Andorra la Vella

MAJOR IMPORT:
Manufactured
Goods

LANDMASS:
174 sq. mi.
451 sq. km

AUSTRIA

POPULATION:
8,200,000
252 per sq. mi.
97 per sq. km

LANGUAGE:
German

MAJOR EXPORT:
Machinery

CAPITAL:
Vienna

MAJOR IMPORT:
Petroleum

LANDMASS:
32,378 sq. mi.
83,859 sq. km

BELARUS

POPULATION:
9,900,000
123 per sq. mi.
47 per sq. km

LANGUAGES:
Belarussian, Russian

MAJOR EXPORT:
Machinery

CAPITAL:
Minsk

MAJOR IMPORT:
Fuels

LANDMASS:
80,154 sq. mi.
207,599 sq. km

BELGIUM

POPULATION:
10,400,000
881 per sq. mi.
340 per sq. km

LANGUAGES:
Flemish, French

MAJOR EXPORTS:
Iron and Steel

CAPITAL:
Brussels

MAJOR IMPORT:
Fuels

LANDMASS:
11,787 sq. mi.
30,528 sq. km

BOSNIA and HERZEGOVINA

POPULATION:
3,900,000
197 per sq. mi.
76 per sq. km

LANGUAGE:
Serbo-Croatian

MAJOR EXPORT:
N/A

CAPITAL:
Sarajevo

MAJOR IMPORT:
N/A

LANDMASS:
19,741 sq. mi.
51,129 sq. km

BULGARIA

POPULATION:
7,500,000
176 per sq. mi.
68 per sq. km

LANGUAGE:
Bulgarian

MAJOR EXPORT:
Machinery

CAPITAL:
Sofia

MAJOR IMPORT:
Fuels

LANDMASS:
42,822 sq. mi.
110,909 sq. km

CROATIA

POPULATION:
4,300,000
196 per sq. mi.
76 per sq. km

LANGUAGE:
Serbo-Croatian

MAJOR EXPORT:
Transport
Equipment

CAPITAL:
Zagreb

MAJOR IMPORT:
Machinery

LANDMASS:
21,830 sq. mi.
56,540 sq. km

CYPRUS

POPULATION:
900,000
262 per sq. mi.
101 per sq. km

LANGUAGES:
Greek, Turkish

MAJOR EXPORT:
Citrus Fruits

CAPITAL:
Nicosia

MAJOR IMPORT:
Manufactured
Goods

CZECH REPUBLIC

POPULATION:
10,200,000
334 per sq. mi.
129 per sq. km

LANGUAGES:
Czech, Slovak

MAJOR EXPORT:
Machinery

CAPITAL:
Prague

MAJOR IMPORT:
Crude Oil

LANDMASS:
30,448 sq. mi.
78,860 sq. km

DENMARK

POPULATION:
5,400,000
324 per sq. mi.
125 per sq. km

LANGUAGE:
Danish

MAJOR EXPORT:
Machinery

CAPITAL:
Copenhagen

MAJOR IMPORT:
Machinery

LANDMASS:
16,637 sq. mi.
43,090 sq. km

ESTONIA

POPULATION:
1,400,000
78 per sq. mi.
30 per sq. km

LANGUAGE:
Estonian

MAJOR EXPORT:
Textiles

CAPITAL:
Tallinn

MAJOR IMPORT:
Machinery

LANDMASS:
17,413 sq. mi.
45,100 sq. km

Countries and flags not drawn to scale

For more information on countries in this region, refer to the Nations of the World Data Bank in the Appendix.

FINLAND

POPULATION:
5,200,000
40 per sq. mi.
15 per sq. km

LANGUAGES:
Finnish, Swedish

MAJOR EXPORT:
Paper

MAJOR IMPORT:
Foods

CAPITAL:
Helsinki

LANDMASS:
130,560 sq. mi.
338,150 sq. km

FRANCE

POPULATION:
59,800,000
281 per sq. mi.
109 per sq. km

LANGUAGE:
French

MAJOR EXPORT:
Machinery

MAJOR IMPORT:
Crude Oil

CAPITAL:
Paris

LANDMASS:
212,934 sq. mi.
551,499 sq. km

GERMANY

POPULATION:
82,600,000
599 per sq. mi.
231 per sq. km

LANGUAGE:
German

MAJOR EXPORT:
Machinery

MAJOR IMPORT:
Machinery

CAPITAL:
Berlin

LANDMASS:
137,830 sq. mi.
356,980 sq. km

GREECE

POPULATION:
11,000,000
216 per sq. mi.
83 per sq. km

LANGUAGE:
Greek

MAJOR EXPORT:
Foods

MAJOR IMPORT:
Machinery

CAPITAL:
Athens

LANDMASS:
50,950 sq. mi.
131,961 sq. km

HUNGARY

POPULATION:
10,000,000
282 per sq. mi.
109 per sq. km

LANGUAGE:
Hungarian

MAJOR EXPORT:
Machinery

MAJOR IMPORT:
Crude Oil

CAPITAL:
Budapest

LANDMASS:
35,919 sq. mi.
93,030 sq. km

ICELAND

POPULATION:
300,000
7 per sq. mi.
3 per sq. km

LANGUAGE:
Icelandic

MAJOR EXPORT:
Fish

MAJOR IMPORT:
Machinery

CAPITAL:
Reykjavík

LANDMASS:
39,768 sq. mi.
102,999 sq. km

IRELAND

POPULATION:
4,000,000
147 per sq. mi.
57 per sq. km

LANGUAGES:
English, Irish Gaelic

MAJOR EXPORT:
Chemicals

MAJOR IMPORT:
Foods

CAPITAL:
Dublin

LANDMASS:
27,135 sq. mi.
70,280 sq. km

ITALY

POPULATION:
57,200,000
491 per sq. mi.
190 per sq. km

LANGUAGE:
Italian

MAJOR EXPORT:
Metals

MAJOR IMPORT:
Machinery

CAPITAL:
Rome

LANDMASS:
116,320 sq. mi.
301,269 sq. km

LATVIA

POPULATION:
2,300,000
93 per sq. mi.
36 per sq. km

LANGUAGES:
Latvian, Russian

MAJOR EXPORT:
Wood

MAJOR IMPORT:
Fuels

CAPITAL:
Rīga

LANDMASS:
24,942 sq. mi.
64,600 sq. km

LIECHTENSTEIN

POPULATION:
40,000
567 per sq. mi.
219 per sq. km

LANGUAGE:
German

MAJOR EXPORT:
Machinery

MAJOR IMPORT:
Machinery

CAPITAL:
Vaduz

LANDMASS:
62 sq. mi.
161 sq. km

LITHUANIA

POPULATION:
3,500,000
137 per sq. mi.
53 per sq. km

LANGUAGES:
Lithuanian, Polish, Russian

MAJOR EXPORTS:
Foods and Livestock

MAJOR IMPORT:
Minerals

CAPITAL:
Vilnius

LANDMASS:
25,174 sq. mi.
65,201 sq. km

LUXEMBOURG

POPULATION:
500,000
452 per sq. mi.
175 per sq. km

LANGUAGES:
Luxembourgian, German, French

MAJOR EXPORT:
Steel Products

MAJOR IMPORT:
Minerals

CAPITAL:
Luxembourg

LANDMASS:
999 sq. mi.
2,587 sq. km

Country Profiles

MACEDONIA, Former Yugoslav Republic of

POPULATION:
2,100,000
207 per sq. mi.
80 per sq. km

LANGUAGES:
Macedonian, Albanian

MAJOR EXPORT:
Manufactured Goods

CAPITAL:
Skopje

MAJOR IMPORT:
Fuels

LANDMASS:
9,927 sq. mi.
25,711 sq. km

 Skopje

MALTA
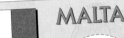

POPULATION:
400,000
3,205 per sq. mi.
1,237 per sq. km

LANGUAGES:
Maltese, English

MAJOR EXPORT:
Machinery

CAPITAL:
Valletta

MAJOR IMPORT:
Foods

LANDMASS:
124 sq. mi.
321 sq. km

Valletta

MOLDOVA

POPULATION:
4,300,000
327 per sq. mi.
128 per sq. km

LANGUAGES:
Moldovan, Russian

MAJOR EXPORT:
Foods

CAPITAL:
Chişinău

MAJOR IMPORT:
Petroleum

LANDMASS:
13,012 sq. mi.
33,701 sq. km

 Chişinău

MONACO

POPULATION:
30,000
45,333 per sq. mi.
11,503 per sq. km

LANGUAGE:
French

MAJOR EXPORT:
N/A

CAPITAL:
Monaco

MAJOR IMPORT:
N/A

LANDMASS:
1.0 sq. mi.
2.6 sq. km

 Monaco

NETHERLANDS

POPULATION:
16,200,000
1,030 per sq. mi.
398 per sq. km

LANGUAGE:
Dutch

MAJOR EXPORT:
Manufactured Goods

CAPITAL:
Amsterdam

MAJOR IMPORT:
Raw Materials

LANDMASS:
15,768 sq. mi.
40,839 sq. km

 Amsterdam

NORWAY

POPULATION:
4,600,000
37 per sq. mi.
14 per sq. km

LANGUAGE:
Norwegian

MAJOR EXPORT:
Petroleum

CAPITAL:
Oslo

MAJOR IMPORT:
Machinery

LANDMASS:
125,050 sq. mi.
323,880 sq. km

 Oslo

POLAND

POPULATION:
38,600,000
309 per sq. mi.
119 per sq. km

LANGUAGE:
Polish

MAJOR EXPORT:
Manufactured Goods

CAPITAL:
Warsaw

MAJOR IMPORT:
Machinery

LANDMASS:
124,807 sq. mi.
323,250 sq. km

 Warsaw

PORTUGAL

POPULATION:
10,400,000
294 per sq. mi.
114 per sq. km

LANGUAGE:
Portuguese

MAJOR EXPORT:
Clothing

CAPITAL:
Lisbon

MAJOR IMPORT:
Machinery

LANDMASS:
35,514 sq. mi.
91,981 sq. km

Lisbon

ROMANIA

POPULATION:
21,600,000
235 per sq. mi.
91 per sq. km

LANGUAGES:
Romanian, Hungarian

MAJOR EXPORT:
Textiles

CAPITAL:
Bucharest

MAJOR IMPORT:
Fuels

LANDMASS:
92,042 sq. mi.
238,389 sq. km

 Bucharest

SAN MARINO

POPULATION:
30,000
1,295 per sq. mi.
500 per sq. km

LANGUAGE:
Italian

MAJOR EXPORT:
Building Stone

CAPITAL:
San Marino

MAJOR IMPORT:
Manufactured Goods

LANDMASS:
23 sq. mi.
60 sq. km

San Marino

SERBIA AND MONTENEGRO

POPULATION:
10,700,000
271 per sq. mi.
105 per sq. km

LANGUAGES:
Serbo-Croatian, Albanian

MAJOR EXPORT:
Manufactured Goods

CAPITAL:
Belgrade

MAJOR IMPORT:
Machinery

LANDMASS:
39,448 sq. mi.
102,170 sq. km

 Belgrade

SLOVAKIA

POPULATION:
5,400,000
283 per sq. mi.
110 per sq. km

LANGUAGES:
Slovak, Hungarian

MAJOR EXPORT:
Transport Equipment

CAPITAL:
Bratislava

MAJOR IMPORT:
Machinery

LANDMASS:
18,923 sq. mi.
49,011 sq. km

Bratislava

Countries and flags not drawn to scale

For more information on countries in this region, refer to the Nations of the World Data Bank in the Appendix.

SLOVENIA

POPULATION:
2,100,000
256 per sq. mi.
99 per sq. km

LANGUAGES:
Slovene,
Serbo-Croatian

MAJOR EXPORT:
Transport
Equipment

CAPITAL:
Ljubljana

MAJOR IMPORT:
Machinery

LANDMASS:
7,819 sq. mi.
20,251 sq. km

Ljubljana

SPAIN

POPULATION:
41,300,000
212 per sq. mi.
82 per sq. km

LANGUAGES:
Spanish, Catalan,
Galician, Basque

MAJOR EXPORTS:
Cars and Trucks

MAJOR IMPORT:
Machinery

CAPITAL:
Madrid

LANDMASS:
195,363 sq. mi.
505,990 sq. km

Madrid

SWEDEN

POPULATION:
9,000,000
52 per sq. mi.
20 per sq. km

LANGUAGE:
Swedish

MAJOR EXPORT:
Paper Products

MAJOR IMPORT:
Crude Oil

CAPITAL:
Stockholm

LANDMASS:
173,730 sq. mi.
449,961 sq. km

Stockholm

SWITZERLAND

POPULATION:
7,300,000
460 per sq. mi.
178 per sq. km

LANGUAGES:
German, French,
Italian

MAJOR EXPORT:
Precision
Instruments

MAJOR IMPORT:
Machinery

CAPITAL:
Bern

LANDMASS:
15,942 sq. mi.
41,290 sq. km

Bern

UKRAINE

POPULATION:
47,810,000
205 per sq. mi.
79 per sq. km

LANGUAGES:
Ukrainian, Russian

MAJOR EXPORT:
Metals

MAJOR IMPORT:
Machinery

CAPITAL:
Kiev

LANDMASS:
233,089 sq. mi.
603,701 sq. km

Kiev

UNITED KINGDOM

POPULATION:
59,200,000
626 per sq. mi.
242 per sq. km

LANGUAGES:
English, Welsh,
Scottish Gaelic

MAJOR EXPORT:
Manufactured
Goods

MAJOR IMPORT:
Foods

CAPITAL:
London

LANDMASS:
94,548 sq. mi.
244,879 sq. km

London

VATICAN CITY

POPULATION:
1,000

LANGUAGES:
Italian, Latin

MAJOR EXPORT:
N/A

MAJOR IMPORT:
N/A

CAPITAL:
N/A

LANDMASS:
0.2 sq. mi.
0.4 sq. km

BUILDING CITIZENSHIP

Should students have to wear uniforms? ▼

Participation   All citizens are expected to obey the laws of their country. Sometimes, however, the right thing to do is not clear. During World War II, many people in Germany broke the law by helping Jews escape Nazi persecution. During Communist rule, many citizens in Eastern Europe bought and sold goods on the black market.

What do you think would have happened to people helping the Jews if they had been caught?

WRITE ABOUT IT   **FCAT PRACTICE**   Completing the exercise below will help you prepare for the **FCAT Writing** Test.

In the United States, we work to change laws we believe are unfair. Trying to influence the decisions of our elected leaders is an important part of being an active citizen. Write a letter to your school board explaining why you think students should or should not wear uniforms.

FCAT LA.B.1.3.2

Europe– Early History

The World and Its People
NATIONAL GEOGRAPHIC

To learn more about Europe and its people, view *The World and Its People* Chapters 10–13 videos.

Social Studies Online

Chapter Overview Visit *The World and Its People* Web site at twip.glencoe.com and click on **Chapter 10–Chapter Overviews** to preview information about the early history of Europe.

Sequencing Events Make this foldable to help you organize information and sequence events into a flowchart about the early history of Europe. **FCAT LA.A.2.3.1**

Step 1 Fold a sheet of paper in half from side to side.

Fold it so the left edge lies about ½ inch from the right edge.

Step 2 Turn the paper and fold it into thirds.

Step 4 Turn the paper and label it as shown.

Classical Greece and Rome

Medieval Europe

From Renaissance to Revolution

Step 3 Unfold and cut the top layer only along both folds.

This will make three tabs.

Reading and Writing As you read the chapter, list events that occurred during these three periods in European history under the appropriate tab of your foldable. **FCAT LA.A.2.3.1**

▲ **Muiderslot Castle in Muiden, Netherlands**

Why It Matters

Roots of Western Culture

Our government, economy, and social systems had their beginnings in Europe. Our laws, family structure, and political ideas are rooted in ancient Greek and Roman traditions. During the Middle Ages, Europe experienced the growth of cities and the beginnings of capitalism. Christianity, Europe's major religion, spread from there to other parts of the world, including the Americas.

Classical Greece and Rome

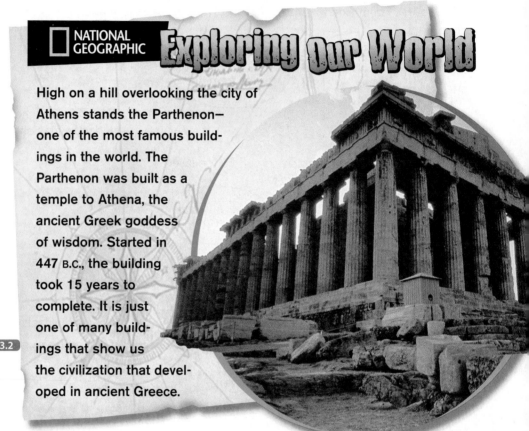

NATIONAL GEOGRAPHIC Exploring Our World

High on a hill overlooking the city of Athens stands the Parthenon—one of the most famous buildings in the world. The Parthenon was built as a temple to Athena, the ancient Greek goddess of wisdom. Started in 447 B.C., the building took 15 years to complete. It is just one of many buildings that show us the civilization that developed in ancient Greece.

When historians talk of **Classical** Europe, they mean ancient Greece and Rome. These civilizations flourished from about 800 B.C. to A.D. 400, and their achievements profoundly influenced Western culture.

The Golden Age of Greece

Greece reached its "Golden Age" in the 400s B.C. Before then, the city-state, or **polis,** had been ruled by a king. The Golden Age brought in direct rule of the people, or **democracy.** Classical Greece has been called the "cradle of democracy" because we trace the beginnings of our political system to this time.

Athens The city-state of **Athens** was the home of the world's first democratic constitution. All free males over the age of 20 had the right to vote and speak freely. Athenians also produced significant works of philosophy, literature, and drama. The word *philosophy* is Greek for "love of wisdom." Two great philosophers, Socrates and his student Plato, sought to understand and explain human nature. Aristotle, a student of Plato's, wrote powerful works dealing with politics, literature, ethics, and philosophy. Greek writers and dramatists dealt with these timeless themes in their poems and plays.

Conflict Between the City-States   During this period, the Greek city-states of Sparta and Athens wanted to expand their boundaries. **Sparta,** ruled by a few nobles, disliked change. Athens, as you learned, was open to democracy and new ideas. These two rivals often fought against each other. Sparta and Athens briefly united during the Persian Wars, when they prevented the Persians from taking over Greece. From 431 B.C. to 404 B.C., however, they fought each other again. Sparta finally defeated Athens in the Peloponnesian War, which further divided and weakened Greece.

Greek Culture Spreads   In the 300s B.C., Philip II of Macedonia and his son Alexander the Great invaded the northern border of Greece. They easily conquered all of Greece. Alexander went on to create an empire that included Persia and Egypt and stretched eastward into India. Locate the extent of Alexander's empire on the map below. Although his empire barely survived his death, Alexander spread Greek culture everywhere he invaded. Over time, Greek customs mixed with Persian and Egyptian culture. The empire's important center was at Alexandria in northern Egypt. There, a great center of learning—a museum-library—was founded. The last traces of Alexander's empire came under Roman rule by about 130 B.C.

▲ Greek theater comedy mask

✓ **Reading Check** Why has Greece been called the "cradle of democracy"?

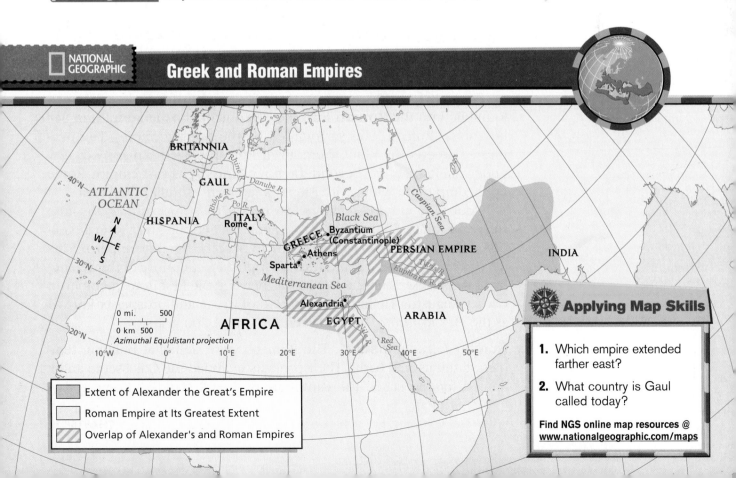

NATIONAL GEOGRAPHIC

Greek and Roman Empires

BRITANNIA

GAUL

ATLANTIC OCEAN

HISPANIA

ITALY
Rome

GREECE
Byzantium (Constantinople)

Athens

Sparta

Mediterranean Sea

AFRICA

Alexandria

EGYPT

Black Sea

Caspian Sea

PERSIAN EMPIRE

INDIA

ARABIA

Red Sea

Rhine R.
Danube R.
Rhône R.
Po R.
Tigris R.
Euphrates R.

0 mi.   500
0 km 500
Azimuthal Equidistant projection

10°W   0°   10°E   20°E   30°E   40°E   50°E

40°N   30°N   20°N

- Extent of Alexander the Great's Empire
- Roman Empire at Its Greatest Extent
- Overlap of Alexander's and Roman Empires

Applying Map Skills

1. Which empire extended farther east?

2. What country is Gaul called today?

Find NGS online map resources @ www.nationalgeographic.com/maps

Ancient Rome

The Colosseum was built as an arena for gladiator fights.

Place Name some arenas where public events take place today.

The Rise of Rome

According to legend, the city of **Rome** was founded by twin brothers Romulus and Remus. As infants, they had been left to die on the banks of the Tiber River. They were rescued by a she-wolf, who raised them as her cubs. When grown, the twins built the city on seven hills in central Italy.

Historical Rome What we know for fact is that Rome was settled sometime around 1000 B.C. By about 700 B.C., it had evolved into a major city-state that began to dominate much of the Italian peninsula. Italy was more easily invaded than mountainous Greece, so the Romans developed a strong army. The Romans borrowed the Latin alphabet from the Greeks, who also influenced Roman art, religion, and mythology.

The Roman Republic Rome started as a monarchy but changed to a republic. In a **republic,** people choose their leaders. Rome was led by two **consuls,** or individuals elected by the people of Rome to represent them. The consuls reported to the Senate. Members of the Senate were landowners who served for life. This was guaranteed by the system of Roman law. The foundation of Roman law was the Twelve Tables. The "tables" were actually bronze tablets on which laws regarding wills, courts, and property were recorded. Along with Greek democracy, republican government and Roman law were important contributions to Western civilization and the Modern Age.

✓ Reading Check How has Rome influenced Western civilization?

From Republic to Empire

From 264 to 146 B.C., a series of wars transformed the Roman Republic into the **Roman Empire.** Eventually, the Mediterranean Sea became a "Roman lake" surrounded by the Roman Empire. The peoples conquered by Rome were given Roman citizenship and equality under the Roman law. Beyond the boundaries of its vast empire, Rome opened up trade with civilizations as far away as India and China.

Under the empire, senators lost power to **emperors,** or absolute rulers, of Rome. Supporters of the Senate killed the great Roman general Julius Caesar in 44 B.C. for trying to become the first emperor. This led to a civil war between Caesar's supporters and those of the Senate. In 31 B.C., Caesar's nephew Octavius became the first Roman emperor, Caesar Augustus. He initiated a period of peace and prosperity known as the *Pax Romana,* which lasted for almost 200 years.

Roman Achievements The Romans were skilled at building temples, stadiums, and baths. Their projects included the Colosseum and a domed temple called the Pantheon. Both still stand in Rome today.

Romans used the arch to build aqueducts, or overhead channels that carried water long distances. They also built roads to bring goods and people into Italy. This led to the growth of Rome's population and wealth.

Christianity and Rome   Jesus of Nazareth was born in Palestine, which was under the rule of Caesar Augustus. Jesus carried out his teaching during the early *Pax Romana.* Two disciples, Peter and Paul, established the new Christian Church in Rome. Even though the early Christians were cruelly persecuted, Christianity spread over the Roman world. In the A.D. 300s, under the emperors Constantine I and Theodosius I, Christianity became the official religion of the Roman Empire.

The Decline of the Empire   After the period of the *Pax Romana,* the Roman Empire began to decline. In A.D. 330, Emperor Constantine I moved the capital from Rome in Italy eastward to the newly built city of **Constantinople,** near the Black Sea. Constantine tried to save the empire by reforming the government, but it was too late. Plagues that came in from Asia over trade routes killed numerous people.

   Finally, in the A.D. 400s, the northern defenses crumbled. Rome was left open to invasion by various groups of Germanic peoples. The Germans came to rule over Rome and much of Italy and Europe. The Eastern Roman Empire, or Byzantine Empire, did not fall to the Germans but continued on for another 1,000 years until its conquest by the Ottoman Turks in 1453.

▲ Roman soldier's breastplate

✓ Reading Check What are aqueducts?

FCAT PRACTICE   You can prepare for the FCAT-assessed standards by completing the correlated item(s) below.

Section 1 Assessment

Defining Terms
1. **Define** Classical, polis, democracy, republic, consul, emperor.

Recalling Facts
2. **Government** In its democratic constitution, what two rights did Athens give all free males over the age of 20?
3. **Culture** Name four influences that Greece had on Roman culture. FCAT LA.A.2.3.1

Critical Thinking
4. **Analyzing Information** Why do you suppose some of Rome's citizens wanted absolute rulers instead of elected senators?
5. **Making Connections** What is one freedom that American democracy has today that was clearly not recognized in the Roman Empire? FCAT LA.A.2.3.1

Graphic Organizer
6. **Creating Time Lines** Create a time line like the one below. Place the letter of the event next to its date. FCAT LA.A.1.3.2
   A. Greek empire comes under Roman rule.
   B. Julius Caesar is killed.
   C. Germans invade Rome.
   D. Rome is settled.
   E. Octavius becomes the first Roman emperor.

| 1000 B.C. | 130 B.C. | 44 B.C. | 31 B.C. | A.D. 400s |

 Applying Social Studies Skills

7. **Making Inferences** Why do you think the story of Romulus and Remus was created? FCAT LA.A.1.3.2

Social Studies Skill

Using B.C. and A.D.

Cultures throughout the world have based their dating systems on significant events in their history. For example, Islamic countries use a dating system that begins with Muhammad's flight from Makkah to Madinah. For most Western cultures, the dating system is based on the birth of Jesus. Christians refer to Jesus as "Christ."

Learning the Skill

About 515, a Christian monk developed a system that begins dating from *anno Domini,* Latin for "the year of the Lord." Although some historians believe that the monk made a small mistake in his figuring of the exact year of Christ's birth, his system of dating has lasted. Events before the birth of Christ, or "B.C.," are figured by counting backward from A.D. 1. There was no year "0." The year before A.D. 1 is 1 B.C. Notice that "A.D." is written before the date, while "B.C." is written following the date.

Practicing the Skill

Study the time line of Classical Europe to answer the following questions.

1. How old was Plato when he became a student of Socrates?
2. For how long did Alexander the Great rule?
3. How old was Julius Caesar when he was assassinated?
4. Who was emperor nearly 500 years after the rule of Alexander the Great?

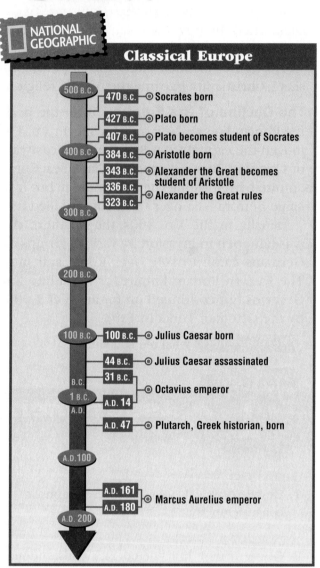

NATIONAL GEOGRAPHIC

Classical Europe

- 500 B.C.
- 470 B.C. — Socrates born
- 427 B.C. — Plato born
- 407 B.C. — Plato becomes student of Socrates
- 400 B.C.
- 384 B.C. — Aristotle born
- 343 B.C. — Alexander the Great becomes student of Aristotle
- 336 B.C. — Alexander the Great rules
- 323 B.C.
- 300 B.C.
- 200 B.C.
- 100 B.C.
- 100 B.C. — Julius Caesar born
- 44 B.C. — Julius Caesar assassinated
- 31 B.C.
- B.C. 1 B.C. — Octavius emperor
- A.D. A.D. 14
- A.D. 47 — Plutarch, Greek historian, born
- A.D. 100
- A.D. 161 — Marcus Aurelius emperor
- A.D. 180
- A.D. 200

Applying the Skill

Create a time line using the terms B.M.B. (before my birth) and A.M.B. (after my birth). Fill in the time line with key events that happened before and after you were born. Illustrate the time line with drawings or cutouts from magazines.

GO TO

Practice key skills with **Glencoe Skillbuilder Interactive Workbook, Level 1.**

Medieval Europe

Guide to Reading

Main Idea

The Middle Ages saw the spread of Christianity, the growth of cities, and the growing powers of kings.

Key Terms

- pope
- missionary
- common law
- feudalism
- vassal
- manor
- serf
- guild
- charter

Reading Strategy

Create a chart like the one below. Fill in the chief duty or role of each of these members of society.

FCAT LA.A.1.3.2

Lord	
Vassal	
Guild member	
Apprentice	
Serf	

The following are the major Sunshine State Standards covered in this section.

SS.A.2.3.8:
Knows the political, social, and economic institutions that characterized the significant aspects of Eastern and Western civilizations

SS.A.2.3.6:
Knows the major events that shaped the development of various cultures (e.g., the spread of agrarian societies, population movements, technological and cultural innovation, and the emergence of new population centers)

NATIONAL GEOGRAPHIC **Exploring Our World**

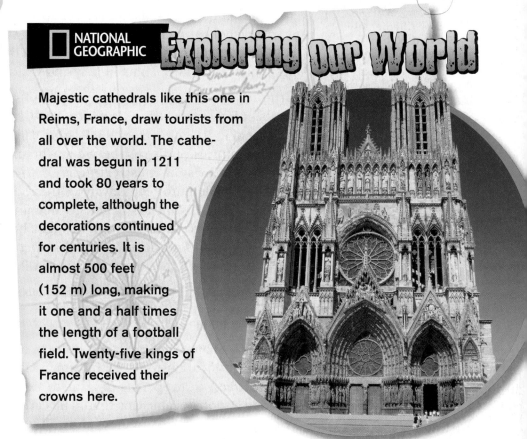

Majestic cathedrals like this one in Reims, France, draw tourists from all over the world. The cathedral was begun in 1211 and took 80 years to complete, although the decorations continued for centuries. It is almost 500 feet (152 m) long, making it one and a half times the length of a football field. Twenty-five kings of France received their crowns here.

With the decline of the Roman Empire, a new age began called the Middle Ages. *Medieval* is derived from a Latin word for "Middle Ages." It is a fitting name for the 1,000-year period that took place between Classical and modern times. Medieval Europe combined characteristics of the Roman Empire with practices of Christianity and other European traditions.

The Rise of Christianity

It was during the Middle Ages that Christianity, in the form of the Roman Catholic Church, became a political power in western Europe. A leader called a bishop headed each major Christian community. By the A.D. 500s, the bishops of Rome, now known as popes, became the leaders of the Catholic Church. The influence of the Church was so strong at this time that the popes also became important political figures.

In eastern Europe, the Byzantine Empire, started by Constantine I, continued. There, Christianity was known as Eastern Orthodoxy. It was not under the leadership of the popes in Rome, but rather under the emperors in Constantinople.

Exploring Economics

Manor Economy

A medieval manor had a traditional economy in which jobs and skills were handed down generation after generation. For example, a tenant farmer's son became a farmer. The children of serfs had no choice but to learn the skills of their parents. Serfs were not always farmers, however. Some were millers who made flour out of grain, or coopers who made barrels and buckets. Some were blacksmiths and made tools, weapons, or horseshoes out of iron and other metals. Young women were usually married by age 14 and worked at home and in the fields.

Spreading the Faith By A.D. 500, the first Christian Bible was completed. The early popes sent **missionaries,** or those who spread their religious views, to every part of Europe. Many were monks and nuns. Monks were men who devoted their lives to prayer, study, and good works. They lived in monasteries. Women who chose a similar life were called nuns and lived in convents. Missionaries helped the poor and needy, and they were teachers as well. Through its schools, the Christian Church greatly advanced learning in Europe. In the 1100s, the Church also founded the first universities at Bologna in Italy and Oxford in England.

Crusades Beginning in the A.D. 1000s, the Church sponsored a series of holy wars called Crusades. The Church sent armies to capture Jerusalem in Palestine from the Islamic caliphs, or rulers. The Crusades led to centuries of distrust between Christians and Muslims. They also increased Christian mistreatment of the Jews in Europe. Yet the Crusades made Europeans aware of the rich cultures of the Byzantines and Muslims. Europeans began to demand more spices and woven cloth that the crusading armies brought home from the east. To meet these demands, European merchants opened up new trade routes. As trade grew, so did the towns of western Europe.

✓ **Reading Check** How did missionaries help spread Christianity?

The Holy Roman Empire

The Germans combined their **common law,** the unwritten laws that come from local customs, with Roman law and founded kingdoms all over Europe—from Spain to England to Germany and Italy. Many of these kingdoms soon became Christian. The early kings, like the German tribal chiefs before them, were elected by all nobles and knights. Over time, however, the kings became more independent and powerful. The crown was passed down to the next generation, usually the king's first-born son.

Charlemagne One of the most important German kingdoms was that of the Franks. By the A.D. 700s, the Franks controlled much of what would become France and Germany. In fact, the name "France" comes from the word *Franks.* In 771 Charlemagne was elected king of the Franks. Through war he added more of Germany and parts of Spain and Italy, including Rome, to the kingdom of the Franks.

On Christmas Day in the year 800, Charlemagne knelt before the pope in the Church of St. Peter in Rome. He was proclaimed the protector of the Christian Church in the West. He was also crowned the head of the Roman Empire in the West. That empire came to be known as the **Holy Roman Empire.**

After Charlemagne's death in 814, his empire was inherited by his son and grandsons and broken up into several kingdoms. These kingdoms were the foundations for modern Germany, Italy, France, and Spain. At about the same time, several Germanic groups like the Angles, Saxons, Jutes, and Danes helped found the first English kingdom. England gets its name from "Angle land."

✓ **Reading Check** What was Charlemagne's role in the spread of Christianity?

Medieval Society

During the Middle Ages, a new political and social system known as **feudalism** emerged. Under this system, kings gave land to their loyal nobles or lords. In exchange for the land or feudal estate, the nobles provided military service and knights for the king's army. These nobles who swore loyalty to the king were known as **vassals.** The king's vassals, great lords themselves, might also have had their own vassals who would owe them military service in return for a grant of land.

The Manor The feudal estate was called the **manor.** At its heart was usually a manor house or a castle. Most of the population of the manor was made up of common people who farmed and performed other tasks. There were two types of farmers. Those who paid rent for their land and then worked the land as they pleased were known as tenants. The other much larger group was the **serfs.**

Serfs were not as free as tenant farmers and were usually poorer. In return for the use of land, seed, tools, and protection, serfs had to work as ordered by the lords of the manors, whether in the fields or elsewhere. Often the serfs worked on roads, walls, fortifications, and other hard jobs. In times of trouble, male serfs also became foot soldiers who served under the direction of the cavalry of knights.

These were often quite violent times, and the common people rarely strayed too far from the safety of the manor. On occasion, the manors might be visited by wanderers with special skills. For example, tinkers made a living by moving from estate to estate, patching pots or fixing other metal objects. Minstrels and other troubadours entertained by playing music, juggling, or acting as comedians or fools.

✓ Reading Check **What did a vassal receive for his service to a king or lord?**

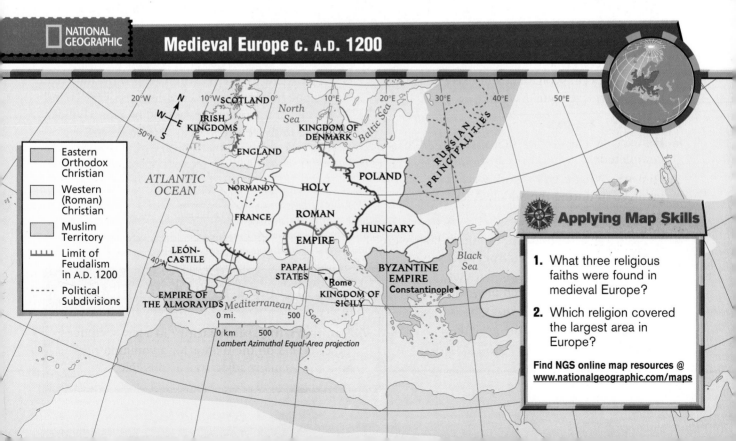

NATIONAL GEOGRAPHIC

Medieval Europe c. A.D. 1200

Legend:
- Eastern Orthodox Christian
- Western (Roman) Christian
- Muslim Territory
- Limit of Feudalism in A.D. 1200
- Political Subdivisions

20°W 10°W 0° 10°E 20°E 30°E 40°E 50°E

SCOTLAND
IRISH KINGDOMS
North Sea
KINGDOM OF DENMARK
Baltic Sea
RUSSIAN PRINCIPALITIES
ENGLAND
POLAND
ATLANTIC OCEAN
NORMANDY
HOLY
FRANCE
ROMAN
HUNGARY
EMPIRE
LEÓN-CASTILE
PAPAL STATES
Rome
BYZANTINE EMPIRE
Constantinople
Black Sea
EMPIRE OF THE ALMORAVIDS
KINGDOM OF SICILY
Mediterranean Sea

0 mi. 500
0 km 500
Lambert Azimuthal Equal-Area projection

Applying Map Skills

1. What three religious faiths were found in medieval Europe?

2. Which religion covered the largest area in Europe?

Find NGS online map resources @ www.nationalgeographic.com/maps

▲ Stained glass showing a craftsman at work

The Growth of Cities

Towns in the Middle Ages were fairly independent and wanted to be free of the feudal lords' control. Towns served as centers of trade and manufacturing. Their importance increased during the Crusades because the Christian armies needed supplies. By the twelfth century, towns hosted great trade fairs, where merchants from far and wide came together to do business.

Manufacturing came under the control of workers' organizations known as **guilds.** Different guilds controlled industries such as brewing, cloth making, boat building, and many others. Young workers, called apprentices, spent years learning a trade so that they could join a guild. With experience, the apprentices became journeymen and eventually master craftsmen.

Over time, some towns grew into cities and became political and religious centers as well. The new, more powerful kings and churchmen understood the importance of cities. They built great cathedrals and granted the residents privileges and freedoms in written documents called **charters.** By doing this, the kings won the support of the townspeople. This support was useful in times of war and for protection against powerful nobles. The kings also raised money by collecting taxes from the towns in return for granting charters. Now, with an economy based on money, kings could pay their soldiers instead of giving them feudal estates. Serfs could buy their freedom. Thus, feudalism and the power of the nobles began to decline.

☑ **Reading Check** Why did kings want the support of large cities?

FCAT PRACTICE You can prepare for the FCAT-assessed standards by completing the correlated item(s) below.

Section 2 Assessment

Defining Terms
1. Define pope, missionary, common law, feudalism, vassal, manor, serf, guild, charter.

Recalling Facts
2. History When was the first Christian Bible completed?

3. History What kind of work were most people involved in during the Middle Ages?

Critical Thinking
4. Evaluating Information Common laws were unwritten laws that came from local customs. What are the possible difficulties that can arise from having such unwritten laws?

5. Understanding Cause and Effect How did the Crusades affect the growth of towns in western Europe? **FCAT LA.E.2.2.1**

Graphic Organizer
6. Organizing Information Create a pyramid like the one below. On the lines, list serfs, vassals, and tenants in the order they would be ranked under a king in the feudal system. **FCAT LA.A.1.3.2**

Kings

Applying Social Studies Skills

7. Summarizing Information In a few sentences, describe life on the manor for a common person. Use as many adjectives as possible.
FCAT LA.B.1.3.2

From Renaissance to Revolution

Guide to Reading

Main Idea

The study of science, art, and education was renewed in the period following the Middle Ages.

Key Terms

- indulgences
- revolution
- divine right of kings

Reading Strategy

Create a time line like the one below. As you read the section, add the following events to the line in the correct order. **FCAT LA.A.1.3.2**

Protestant
  Reformation
Age of Exploration
American Revolution
Renaissance
French Revolution

├──┼──┼──┼──┤

The following are the major Sunshine State Standards covered in this section.

SS.A.3.3.2:
Understands the historical events that have shaped the development of cultures throughout the world
SS.A.2.3.5:
Knows significant historical leaders who shaped the development of early cultures (e.g., military, political, and religious leaders in various civilizations)

NATIONAL GEOGRAPHIC Exploring Our World

From the 1300s to the 1600s, important cultural achievements in the arts and learning spread throughout Europe. Merchant families used their wealth to help artists and scholars explore new ways of thinking. Michelangelo's statue of David, shown here, is one of the many masterpieces from this period we call the Renaissance.

The growth of cities and trade and the gradual breakup of feudalism led to the end of the Middle Ages. Around 1350 interest in education, art, and science peaked in several parts of Europe, especially in the cities and towns. The result was the Renaissance—a French word meaning "rebirth."

The Renaissance

To many people, the Renaissance was the beginning of a new golden age like that of ancient Greece and Rome. The Renaissance began in the cities of northern Italy and spread to other cities of Europe.

Humanism   During the Renaissance, scholars became less concerned about the mysteries of heaven and more interested in the world and humans around them. Because of this, Renaissance scholars

▲ The Sistine Chapel, painted by Michelangelo

were called humanists. Humanist ideas—the right of people to learn and think for themselves—broke with medieval thinking and helped bring about the rise of the modern world.

Renaissance Artists   Like the ancient Greeks and Romans, Renaissance artists appreciated the beauty in human beings and nature. They developed new ways to make their works true to life and full of color and action. They painted and sculpted not only religious images but also people and creatures from myths. Above all, they were more interested in the human qualities than the religious qualities of their subjects. Two of the many outstanding Renaissance artists were Leonardo da Vinci and Michelangelo Buonarotti. (See page 308 to learn more about the achievements of Leonardo da Vinci.)

The painter and sculptor Michelangelo expressed human emotions such as anger, sorrow, and strength in his paintings and sculptures. His most famous work is the mural on the ceiling of the Sistine Chapel in the Vatican Palace in Rome. It is made up of 145 separate paintings and took nearly five years to complete.

Renaissance Writers   Writers were also inspired by the ideas of the Renaissance. Until this time, most literature was written in Medieval Latin. To reach a wider audience, writers began to use the language they spoke every day instead of Latin or French, the languages of the educated. Geoffrey Chaucer wrote *The Canterbury Tales* and William Shakespeare wrote plays such as *Hamlet* and *Romeo and Juliet* in English. Miguel de Cervantes wrote his novel *Don Quixote* in Spanish.

These works were reproduced in many copies for the first time by the printing press, which was invented by Johannes Gutenberg around 1450. Although the Chinese had developed a printing process, Gutenberg developed the idea of movable type. The printing press made books more numerous and less expensive, thereby encouraging more people to learn to read and write.

Rise of Nations   During the Renaissance, western European rulers became more powerful. They used their power to unite their peoples, creating nations based on a common language and culture. England was strengthened by the first Tudor king, Henry VII, and his famous granddaughter Elizabeth I. King Ferdinand and Queen Isabella united Spain by driving out the last of the Muslims and Jews. By the 1450s, the kings of France finally liberated their country from the English.

√ Reading Check   How did the printing press make it easier for people to learn to read and write?

The Protestant Reformation

Many of the new ideas of the Renaissance led to questions about religion. Some people believed that Church leaders were more interested in wealth than religion. Others disagreed with corrupt practices of the Church. One of these practices was the selling of documents called indulgences, which freed their owners of punishment for sins they had committed. The Christians who "protested" corrupt Church practices and wanted to return to basic Christian teachings came to be called Protestants. The movement to reform, or change, the Catholic Church was called the Protestant Reformation.

One of the first Protestant leaders to challenge the Catholic Church was Martin Luther, a German monk and scholar. In 1520 the pope banished Luther from the Catholic Church for his criticism. Luther organized his own new Christian church, which taught in German, not Latin, from a Bible that Luther himself had translated into German. This split between the Catholics and Protestants led to many long years of religious wars in Europe.

Another early Protestant leader was John Calvin. His followers in France were called Huguenots, and in England they were called Puritans. Many came to the Protestant cause seeking not only greater religious freedom, but also political, economic, and intellectual freedom. The Puritans eventually sought freedom in the Americas to practice their own religion.

✓ **Reading Check** What was the Protestant Reformation?

The Age of Exploration

By the mid-1400s, Europe began to reach out beyond its boundaries in a great age of discovery and exploration. The Portuguese began to sail southward in the Atlantic, down the West African coast. They were seeking a route to the profitable spice trade in Asia. In 1488 Bartholomeu Dias reached the Cape of Good Hope at the southern tip of Africa. Ten years later, Vasco da Gama sailed around it to India.

While the Portuguese were searching for a way around Africa, King Ferdinand and Queen Isabella of Spain were trying to find another way to Asia. In 1492 they sent an Italian navigator, Christopher Columbus, with three small ships—the *Niña,* the *Pinta,* and the *Santa María*—westward across the Atlantic. Although he never realized it, Columbus had landed in a part of the world unknown to Europeans at that time. He called its people "Indians" because he believed he was in the East Indies in Asia.

The Dutch, English, and French soon joined the Spanish and Portuguese in exploring and settling and trading with the Americas, Asia, and Africa. Eventually—in addition to trade goods—people, diseases, and ideas were distributed around the world in a process called the Columbian Exchange. You read about this on page 228. Europeans unknowingly brought to the Americas diseases such as measles and smallpox, which infected and killed millions of Native Americans. These natives had been used as laborers on plantations and in mines. In their place, traders eventually transported more than 20 million Africans to the Americas as enslaved persons, until the slave trade was outlawed in the early 1800s.

▲ Luther criticized Catholic Church officials for selling indulgences.

✓ **Reading Check** Which European nation first explored the coast of Africa?

The Age of Revolution

A **revolution** is a great and often violent change. In the Americas, the colonies won freedom from the European countries that ruled them. In Europe, people fought for freedom from their kings, queens, and nobles.

The Rule of the People   The eighteenth century ended with great changes to Europe and many of its American colonies. The belief in the **divine right of kings**—that European kings and queens ruled by the will of God—was fading. In learning about the examples from ancient Greece and Rome, people came to feel that they should play a greater, more direct role in government. Philosophers such as John Locke and Jean Jacques Rousseau looked at the nature of man and government. They believed that government should serve and protect citizens and their freedom. However, this also meant that citizens had to take more responsibility for themselves and their own actions.

British Democracy   Revolutionary changes came more peacefully in some countries than in others. Over many centuries, Great Britain had slowly developed a system of shared power and responsibility. The king ruled with the Parliament, a popular representative body that gradually took power in the name of the people. Eventually, British

FCAT PRACTICE

Completing the exercise below will help you prepare for the **FCAT Reading** test.

Literature

THE SCARLET PIMPERNEL
by Baroness Orczy

During and after the French Revolution, many nobles were executed by the lower classes that had rebelled against them. The number of these executions shocked the people of Europe. *The Scarlet Pimpernel* is a novel about an English nobleman who helps aristocrats escape from France.

❝*It had all occurred in such a miraculous way. She and her husband had understood that they had been placed on the list of 'suspected persons,' which meant that their trial and death was but a matter of days—of hours, perhaps. Then came the hope of salvation: the mysterious [letter], signed with the scarlet device; . . . the flight with her two children; the covered cart; . . . Every moment under that cart she expected recognition, arrest. [These young Englishmen] . . . had risked their lives to save them all, as they had already saved scores of other innocent people. And all only for sport? Impossible!*❞

Analyzing Literature

1. Do you think that the Scarlet Pimpernel's actions were really just for sport? Why or why not?   **FCAT LA.A.2.3.2**
2. Do you think the Englishmen were right to try to save the French nobility? Explain.   **FCAT LA.A.2.3.2**

kings and queens were forced to accept a constitution that shared power but gave most of it to the Parliament.

Democracy in the Americas   In the 1770s, the American colonies, beginning with the thirteen British colonies in North America, revolted against British control. The new United States, with its Declaration of Independence, Constitution, and representative Congress, became a model for many other revolutions. By the 1830s, most of the Spanish, Portuguese, and British colonies in the Americas south of Canada had also gained their independence.

The French Revolution   In the 1780s, revolution erupted in Europe as well, starting with France. The French Revolution began in 1789 and went through several stages. When King Louis XVI and Queen Marie Antoinette opposed the revolution and tried to aid the nobility, they were executed. By 1799, Napoleon Bonaparte, a military hero of the French Revolution, became the dictator of France. He declared himself emperor of a new French Empire in 1804. Eventually, people almost everywhere in Europe reacted against Napoleon and went to war against France. Napoleon was finally defeated in 1815.

The revolution in France stimulated Latin Americans and other European peoples to demand more personal and political control over their lives. Countries such as Greece, Belgium, Italy, and Germany also experienced revolutions.

✔ Reading Check   How was the growth of democracy in Great Britain different from that in France?

FCAT PRACTICE   You can prepare for the FCAT-assessed standards by completing the correlated item(s) below.

Assessment

Defining Terms

1. **Define** indulgences, revolution, divine right of kings.

Recalling Facts

2. **History** What was the movement to reform the Catholic Church called?

3. **People** Why were Renaissance scholars known as humanists?

Critical Thinking

4. **Examining Results** Describe the effects of the Columbian Exchange. **FCAT LA.A.2.3.1**

5. **Making Connections** How might a revolution in one country encourage political changes around the world? **FCAT LA.B.1.3.2**

Graphic Organizer

6. **Identifying People** Create a table like the one below. In the left column, list ten people from this section. Then explain why they are considered significant. **FCAT LA.A.1.3.2**

Person	Significance

Applying Social Studies Skills

7. **Drawing Conclusions** Why do you suppose the period known as the Renaissance was considered a rebirth?

Making Connections

ART   SCIENCE   CULTURE   TECHNOLOGY

Leonardo da Vinci

The Italian Leonardo da Vinci is considered to be one of the greatest artists of the Renaissance. He painted the *Mona Lisa* and the *Last Supper*, two of the world's best-known paintings. He was also a talented architect, engineer, and inventor.

FCAT PRACTICE Answering question 3 below will help you prepare for the **FCAT Reading** test.

The Artist

Leonardo da Vinci was born in 1452 in a small town near Florence, Italy. As the son of a wealthy man, he received the best education that Florence could offer. Leonardo became known for his ability to create sculptures and paintings that looked almost lifelike. Much of his success in this area came from his keen interest in nature. He also studied human anatomy and used this knowledge to make his figures realistic.

The Inventor

As a child, Leonardo was fascinated with machines and began to draw his own inventions. The first successful parachute jump was made from the top of a French tower in 1783—but Leonardo had sketched a parachute in 1485. He designed flying machines, armored tanks, and aircraft landing gear. He even drew a diver's suit that used tubes and air chambers to allow a swimmer to remain underwater for long periods of time.

Leonardo's Notebooks

Much of what we know about Leonardo comes from the thousands of pages of notes and sketches he kept in his notebooks. He used mirror, or reverse, writing, starting at the right side of the page and moving across to the left. No one is sure why Leonardo wrote this way. Some think he was trying to keep people from reading and stealing his ideas. He may also have been trying to hide his thoughts from the Roman Catholic Church, whose teachings sometimes conflicted with his ideas. From a practical standpoint, writing in reverse probably helped him avoid smearing wet ink, since he was left-handed.

▲ Leonardo da Vinci, self-portrait

▲ The *Mona Lisa*

Making the Connection

1. What are two of Leonardo's best-known works?

2. Why might Leonardo have written his notebooks in mirror writing?

3. **Understanding Cause and Effect** In what way did Leonardo's interest in the world around him influence his work? **FCAT LA.E.2.2.1**

Reading Review

Section 1 | Classical Greece and Rome

Terms to Know

Classical
polis
democracy
republic
consul
emperor

Main Idea

Ancient Greece and Rome made important contributions to Western culture and civilization.

✓ **Government** The world's first democratic constitution was written in Athens.

✓ **History** Alexander the Great conquered all of Greece and spread Greek culture everywhere he invaded.

✓ **History** Rome grew from a republic on the Italian Peninsula to an empire that included western Europe, northern Africa, and southwest Asia.

✓ **Religion** Christianity spread throughout the Roman world.

✓ **History** The Roman Empire was invaded by Germanic peoples and declined.

Section 2 | Medieval Europe

Terms to Know

pope   manor
missionary   serf
common law   guild
feudalism   charter
vassal

Main Idea

The Middle Ages saw the spread of Christianity, the growth of cities, and the growing powers of kings.

✓ **Religion** The Roman Catholic Church became a political power in western Europe.

✓ **History** The first Christian Bible was completed by A.D. 500.

✓ **History** Charlemagne was crowned head of the Roman Empire and proclaimed Protector of the Christian Church in the West.

✓ **Government** Feudalism, the medieval political and social system, was an exchange of land from the king to nobles who provided military service.

Section 3 | From Renaissance to Revolution

Terms to Know

indulgences
revolution
divine right of kings

Main Idea

The study of science, art, and education was renewed in the period following the Middle Ages.

✓ **Culture** Important cultural achievements in the arts and learning spread throughout Europe in the period known as the Renaissance.

✓ **History** Johannes Gutenberg invented the printing press.

✓ **Government** Countries formed into nations based on a common language and culture.

✓ **Religion** The Protestant faith emerged in protest to the corrupt practices of the Roman Catholic Church.

✓ **History** Christopher Columbus sailed across the Atlantic.

✓ **Government** Revolution erupted in the Americas and Europe.

Assessment and Activities

10

FCAT PRACTICE You can prepare for the FCAT-assessed standards by completing the correlated item(s) below.

Using Key Terms

Match the terms in Part A with their definitions in Part B.

A.

1. emperor
2. common law
3. feudalism
4. democracy
5. indulgences
6. serf
7. polis
8. charter
9. missionary
10. guild

B.

a. unwritten laws from customs
b. poor people who were controlled by the lords of the manor
c. freed owners from punishment for sins
d. medieval political and social system
e. absolute ruler
f. direct rule of the people
g. person who spreads his or her religious views
h. documents giving townspeople privileges and freedoms
i. workers' organization
j. city-state

Reviewing the Main Ideas

Section 1 Classical Greece and Rome

11. **Government** Where was the first democratic constitution written?
12. **History** Who conquered all of Greece?
13. **Religion** Which religion spread all over the Roman world?
14. **History** Who invaded the Roman Empire?

Section 2 Medieval Europe

15. **Religion** Which religious group became a political power in western Europe?
16. **Economics** Explain the difference between vassals and serfs.
17. **Government** Name the political and social system in medieval Europe.

Section 3 From Renaissance to Revolution

18. **History** What did Johannes Gutenberg invent?
19. **Religion** Which faith emerged out of protest to the Catholic Church?
20. **History** For what is Christopher Columbus historically known?
21. **Government** Where were revolutions taking place in the eighteenth century?

 **NATIONAL GEOGRAPHIC** **Classical Europe**

Place Location Activity

On a separate sheet of paper, match the letters on the map with the numbered places listed below.

1. Alexandria
2. North Africa
3. Mediterranean Sea
4. Constantinople
5. Black Sea
6. Greece
7. Athens
8. Rome
9. Tiber River
10. Sparta

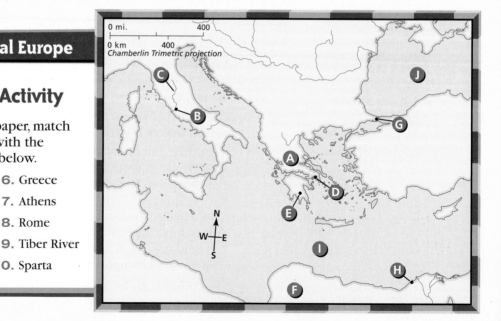

0 mi. 400
0 km 400
Chamberlin Trimetric projection

Self-Check Quiz Visit *The World and Its People* Web site at <u>twip.glencoe.com</u> and click on **Chapter 10—Self-Check Quizzes** to prepare for the Chapter Test.

Critical Thinking

22. Making Connections In what ways have our political and social lives today been influenced by ancient Greek and Roman customs?
FCAT LA.A.2.3.1

23. Drawing Conclusions Eastern Orthodoxy was ruled by emperors rather than by popes. This made the emperors very powerful. What kinds of problems might have occurred because of this? **FCAT** LA.A.2.3.1

Comparing Regions Activity

24. Culture Research to find information on an American artist from the nineteenth century. Write a paragraph with information about the artist's life and contributions. Compare this information to what you learned about Renaissance artists.
FCAT LA.A.1.3.2

Mental Mapping Activity

25. Identifying People and Places Create a simple outline map of Europe that includes Germany, Italy, France, Rome, and Greece. Place the letter of the individual's name next to the place from which he originated.

a. Michelangelo Buonarotti
b. Alexander the Great
c. Julius Caesar
d. Socrates
e. Charlemagne
f. Leonardo da Vinci
g. Christopher Columbus
h. Napoleon Bonaparte
i. Martin Luther
j. Plato

Technology Skills Activity

26. Using the Internet Search the Internet for information on the Twelve Tables of Roman law. After reading about the laws, note the ones that you strongly agree or disagree with and tell why. For example, tablet 10 states that "the women shall not tear their faces nor wail on account of the funeral." In our society, we are not punished for expressing grief.
FCAT LA.A.2.3.5

Standardized Test Practice

Directions: Read the paragraphs below, and then answer the question that follows.

The ancient Greeks held the Olympic Games in Olympia every four years. The games were a religious festival in honor of Zeus, the Greeks' chief god. Trading and wars stopped while the games took place. The first Greek calendar began with the supposed date of the first Olympic Games in 776 B.C.

Athletes came from all over the Greek-speaking world to compete. Only male athletes, however, were allowed to take part, and women were not permitted even as spectators. Olympic events at first consisted only of a footrace. Later the broad jump, the discus throw, boxing, and wrestling were added. The Greeks crowned Olympic winners with wreaths of olive leaves and held parades in their honor.

1. From the paragraphs, which of the following statements about Greek culture is correct? FCAT LA.A.1.3.2

F The Greeks stressed group effort over individual achievement.

G The Greeks believed in one God.

H The Greeks were not religious.

J The Greeks encouraged individual glory.

Test-Taking Tip: Read all the choices carefully before choosing the one that correctly describes Greek culture. Eliminate answers that you know are incorrect. For example, all the Olympic events were performed by individuals, not by teams. Therefore, answer F does not describe Greek culture. The question is asking for the statement that DOES describe Greek culture.

Europe–Modern History

The World and Its People

NATIONAL GEOGRAPHIC

To learn more about Europe and its people, view **The World and Its People Chapters 10–13** videos.

Social Studies **online**

Chapter Overview Visit **The World and Its People** Web site at twip.glencoe.com and click on **Chapter 11–Chapter Overviews** to preview information about the modern history of Europe.

FCAT PRACTICE The activity below will help you prepare for the **FCAT Reading** test.

Summarizing Information Make the following foldable to help you organize and summarize information about historic events and modern events in Europe, and how they are related. **FCAT** LA.A.1.3.2

Step 1 Fold a sheet of paper from side to side, leaving a 2-inch tab uncovered along the side.

Fold it so the left edge lies 2 inches from the right edge.

Step 2 Turn the paper and fold it into thirds.

Step 3 Unfold and cut along the two inside fold lines.

Cut along the two folds on the front flap to make 3 tabs.

Step 4 Label the foldable as shown.

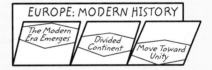

EUROPE: MODERN HISTORY

The Modern Era Emerges | Divided Continent | Move Toward Unity

Reading and Writing As you read about the modern history of Europe, write important facts under each appropriate tab of your foldable.

FCAT LA.A.1.3.2

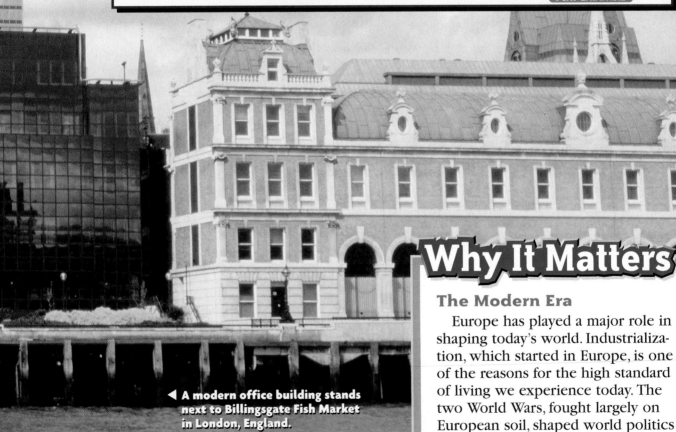

◀ **A modern office building stands next to Billingsgate Fish Market in London, England.**

Why It Matters

The Modern Era

Europe has played a major role in shaping today's world. Industrialization, which started in Europe, is one of the reasons for the high standard of living we experience today. The two World Wars, fought largely on European soil, shaped world politics and preserved democracy.

The Modern Era Emerges

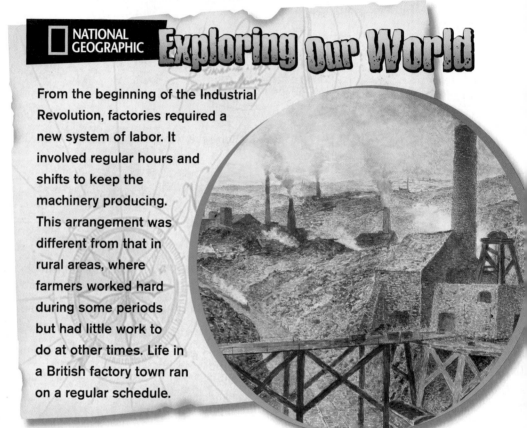
NATIONAL GEOGRAPHIC *Exploring Our World*

From the beginning of the Industrial Revolution, factories required a new system of labor. It involved regular hours and shifts to keep the machinery producing. This arrangement was different from that in rural areas, where farmers worked hard during some periods but had little work to do at other times. Life in a British factory town ran on a regular schedule.

The Industrial Revolution began in Great Britain in the 1700s. It was a time when people used machinery and new methods to increase **productivity**. Productivity is a measure of how much work can be done in a certain length of time. The changes these machines brought led to a revolution in the way work was done and in how people lived.

A Rapidly Changing World

The Industrial Revolution started in Great Britain for several reasons. Great Britain had a ready supply of natural resources such as coal and iron. These were needed to make and run machinery. There was also a plentiful supply of raw materials such as wool and imported cotton, used to make cloth. In addition, there was a supply of people—**human resources**—who could run the machines. As farmers relied more on machines to plant and harvest crops, fewer people were needed in the fields. Many people who used to work on the farms went to the cities to find work in factories and shops.

Major Industries Textiles, or woven cloth, was the first industry to be moved to factories. Before that, spinning and cloth weaving had been a cottage industry, in which family members supplied their own equipment to make goods. With industrialization, huge quantities of cloth could be produced in factories that employed many workers. Textile mills became even more productive when steam replaced waterpower for running the machinery.

The steam engine was invented by Thomas Newcomen in the early 1700s and was first used to pump water out of coal mines. In 1769 James Watt invented a more efficient steam engine, which was used for textile mills, riverboats, and locomotives. Inventions like the railroad improved transportation and stimulated the growth of more industries. By the early 1800s, the Industrial Revolution had spread from Great Britain to much of western Europe and North America.

✔ Reading Check How did machinery affect the textile industry?

Changing Lifestyles

As towns and cities grew, people's lives changed dramatically. At first, industrial workers, including women and children, had to work hard for long hours often under dangerous conditions. Eventually, the workers formed groups called unions. A union spoke for all the workers in a factory or industry and bargained for better working conditions, higher pay, and a shorter working day. If a factory owner refused these demands, union members often went on strike. That is, they refused to work until their demands were met.

Overall, the Industrial Revolution made life more difficult for people in the short term but easier in the long run. For example, because manufactured cotton clothing was better and cheaper, people could afford more. They could change their clothes and wash them more often. This new cleanliness reduced sickness and disease, so people generally lived healthier and longer lives.

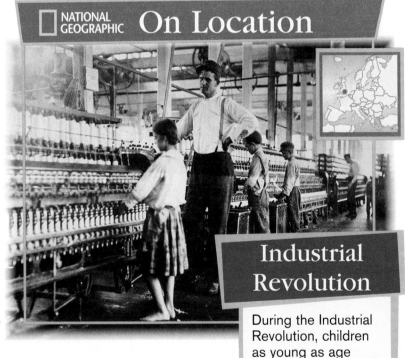

NATIONAL GEOGRAPHIC On Location

Industrial Revolution

During the Industrial Revolution, children as young as age seven worked 12 to 15 hours per day, six days a week.

Economics How did new machinery affect production?

The Industrial Revolution also resulted in strong economies in western Europe. It was because of this economic strength that Europe was able to dominate the world in the 1800s and early 1900s.

✔ Reading Check How did the Industrial Revolution improve people's lives?

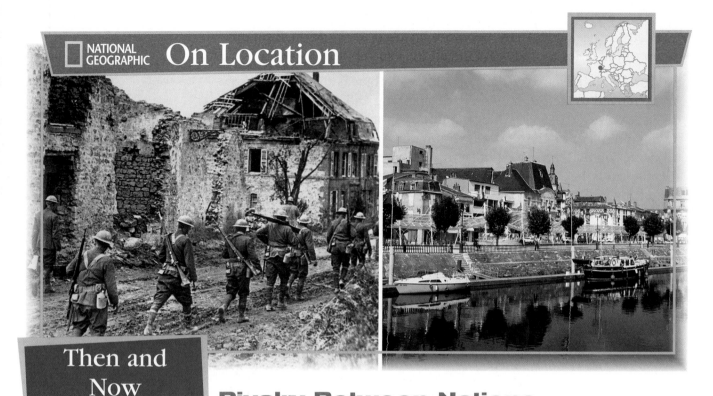

Then and Now

The town of Verdun, France, was nearly destroyed during World War I (above). Today it is a thriving commercial center and tourist attraction (above right).

Place Name another city that has been rebuilt since World War I.

Rivalry Between Nations

Industrialization created new rivalries among the countries of Europe. Great Britain, France, Germany, and other European countries competed around the world for markets and resources for their factories. Under a system called imperialism, European countries claimed colonies in Africa and Asia in the late 1800s. European nations built up armies and navies to protect themselves and their empires. Different alliances were formed, whereby various countries agreed to support one another in times of war.

World War I In 1914 a war broke out in Europe that quickly spread to the European colonies and other areas of the world. It was known as the Great War, and later called World War I. This war was not like any earlier wars. With the techniques learned in the Industrial Revolution, machines designed for war were mass-produced. Tanks, heavy artillery, machine guns, and airplanes helped make the war more violent than any before it. In the four years of the war, millions of people were killed or wounded, and many European cities and villages were destroyed.

New Problems Arise As a result of the war, Europe faced political and social turmoil. Millions were homeless and hungry. Germany was blamed for starting the war and was asked to pay for much of it. The United States and Japan became great powers. A revolution in Russia in 1917 led to a new political, economic, and social system called communism. Communism was based on the teachings of a German philosopher named Karl Marx. Marx believed that industrialization had created two classes of people. One class owned the means of producing goods and the other worked to produce the goods. He wrote that this system was unfair and needed to be overthrown.

World War II In the 1930s, a worldwide depression severely tested the ability of many governments to provide for their citizens. The problems that were not solved after World War I eventually led to new alliances in Europe. Germany became a dictatorship under Adolf Hitler and his National Socialist German Workers' Party. Its members, called Nazis, believed in German superiority. By 1939 Germany, Italy, and Japan (the Axis Powers) were at war with Great Britain, France, and China (the Allies). In 1941 the United States and Soviet Union joined the Allies in the war that became known as World War II.

▲ Hitler at a Nazi rally, Dortmund, Germany

During the war, Hitler and the Nazis carried out the Holocaust, in which over 12 million people were killed. Over 6 million of the victims were Jews. Other persecuted groups included the Roma people (called Gypsies), Poles, individuals with disabilities, and many other groups that were classified as "undesirable" by the Nazi leaders. The Holocaust is an example of the war crime of genocide, or the mass murder of a people because of race, religion, ethnicity, politics, or culture.

Italy surrendered in 1943. Germany was finally defeated in May 1945, but the Japanese continued to fight. In August, the United States—in an effort to end the war in Asia—dropped two atomic bombs on the Japanese cities of Hiroshima and Nagasaki. From this global conflict, the United States and the Soviet Union emerged as superpowers.

✓ Reading Check What was the Holocaust?

FCAT PRACTICE You can prepare for the FCAT-assessed standards by completing the correlated item(s) below.

Assessment

Defining Terms

1. Define productivity, human resources, textiles, cottage industry, union, strike, imperialism, communism, Holocaust, genocide.

Recalling Facts

2. History Where did the Industrial Revolution begin?

3. Government Name the political, economic, and social system that was based on the teachings of Karl Marx.

Critical Thinking

4. Comparing and Contrasting How did people's living habits change after the introduction of factories? Do you think people were generally better off? Explain.
FCAT LA.A.2.2.7

5. Evaluating Information Why did the new military equipment introduced in World War I change the way wars were fought?

Graphic Organizer

6. Organizing Information Create a diagram like the one below. Then fill in the names of the countries that made up the two powers fighting each other in World War II. **FCAT LA.A.1.3.2**

Axis Powers	Allies

Applying Social Studies Skills

7. Analyzing Maps Refer to the **Reference Atlas** map of the world on pages RA2-RA3. Which of the Allies was located nearest to Japan?

Making Connections

The Holocaust

The Holocaust is one of the most horrifying events in human history. *Holocaust* is a word that means complete and total destruction. Learning about the Holocaust is important so that such crimes against humanity can be prevented in the future.

The Final Solution

Adolf Hitler, chancellor of Germany, believed that the Germanic peoples of the world, called Aryans, were a superior race. His goal was to populate Europe with one "master" race of people. In the years before and during World War II, Hitler's government persecuted many racial, religious,

▲ Auschwitz Nazi concentration camp in Oswiecim, Poland

FCAT PRACTICE Answering question 3 below will help you prepare for the **FCAT Reading** test.

and ethnic groups that he considered "undesirable." These groups included the Roma (Gypsies), Jehovah's Witnesses, people with disabilities, and political protesters of all backgrounds.

The chief target of Hitler's plan—which he called his "Final Solution"—was the Jews. Jewish communities throughout Germany and German-controlled territory suffered terribly. Jews, forced to wear identification badges, were blamed for all of Germany's economic and social problems.

Between 1939 and 1945, Hitler's Nazi forces attempted to kill the Jews in every country Germany invaded, as well as in those countries that were Nazi allies. Jews from Germany, Poland, the Soviet Union, France, Belgium, the Netherlands, Greece, and Hungary were among those killed during the Holocaust.

Mass Murder

In the early years of the war, Jewish people in Eastern Europe were rounded up, gathered together, shot by machine guns, and buried in mass graves. Later, millions of Jews were uprooted and forced into concentration camps. Few people survived these. Those who were too young, sick, or elderly for heavy labor were executed in gas chambers. In all, more than 6 million Jews and about 6 million Roma (Gypsies), Poles, Soviet prisoners of war, and others were murdered.

→ Making the Connection

1. What was the Holocaust?
2. Why did Hitler want to rid Europe of its Jewish people?
3. **Understanding Cause and Effect** How can studying about the Holocaust today help prevent another genocide from happening in the future?

FCAT LA.A.2.3.8

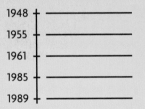
Section 2

A Divided Continent

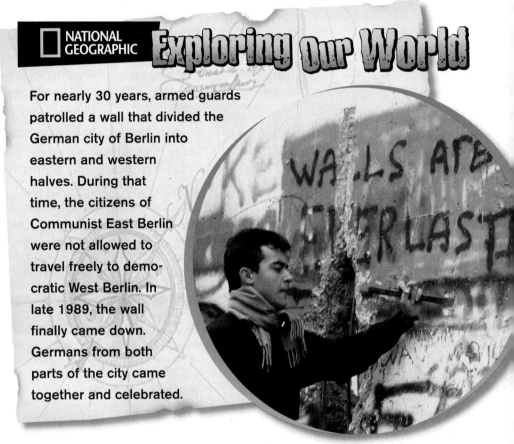

NATIONAL GEOGRAPHIC Exploring Our World

For nearly 30 years, armed guards patrolled a wall that divided the German city of Berlin into eastern and western halves. During that time, the citizens of Communist East Berlin were not allowed to travel freely to democratic West Berlin. In late 1989, the wall finally came down. Germans from both parts of the city came together and celebrated.

After World War II, much of Europe was in ruins. The total defeat of Germany, Italy, and Japan left a power gap that would be filled by two rivals—the United States and the Soviet Union.

The Cold War

The global competition between the democratic United States and its allies and the Communist Soviet Union and its supporters came to be called the **Cold War.** It was a dangerous time because by 1950 both sides had **nuclear weapons.** Nuclear weapons use atomic reactions to release enormous power and can cause mass destruction. It was a "cold" war because countries never mobilized armies in an official war.

The Cold War began in Europe. In 1948 the United States started a loan program called the Marshall Plan. The goals were to help rebuild Europe and try to stop the spread of communism. Under the Marshall Plan, factories were rebuilt, mines were reopened, and roads were repaired and replaced. Western European countries that were liberated by the United States and Great Britain during World War II began to develop prosperous economies.

✓ Reading Check What was the Cold War?

Western Europe Cooperates

In 1948 under the Truman Doctrine, the United States offered military aid to countries such as Greece and Turkey that were fighting communism inside their borders. In 1949 the North Atlantic Treaty Organization (NATO) was formed to respond to possible attacks by the Soviet Union. Each country in NATO agreed to treat an attack on any other member as an attack on itself. The NATO countries believed that the Soviet Union would not attack Western Europe if Soviet leaders thought such an attack would trigger nuclear war with the United States. This policy is known as **deterrence,** because it is designed to deter, or discourage, an attack.

Eventually, Western European countries began to cooperate economically with one another. The small countries of Belgium, the Netherlands, and Luxembourg joined together in 1948 to form the Benelux trade union, an arrangement for the free movement of money, goods, and people among these nations. West Germany, France, and

NATIONAL GEOGRAPHIC

Western and Eastern Europe (c. 1950)

0 mi. 500
0 km 500
Lambert Azimuthal Equal-Area projection

Western Europe
Eastern Europe

Applying Map Skills

1. Were there more countries in Western Europe or Eastern Europe?

2. Which Eastern European countries bordered Western Europe?

**Find NGS online map resources@
www.nationalgeographic.com/maps**

Italy joined with the Benelux countries to form the European Coal and Steel Community. In 1958 this became the European Economic Community, also called the Common Market. The members agreed to free trade amongst themselves. This meant that no tariffs blocked trade and that workers from one country could get jobs in any of the other member countries. Between 1958 and 1986, Denmark, the United Kingdom, Ireland, Spain, Portugal, and Greece also joined the Common Market. Now known as the European Union, its goal is greater cooperation and economic development.

✓ **Reading Check** Why did the countries of Western Europe join NATO?

Soviets Control Eastern Europe

In Eastern Europe, the Soviet Union made **satellite nations** of those countries bordering it. Satellite nations are dependent upon a stronger power. Bulgaria, Romania, Czechoslovakia, Hungary, Poland, and East Germany became communist. They were strictly controlled by the Soviet Union. With these countries, the Soviet Union created the Council for Mutual Economic Assistance, or COMECON, primarily for its own economic benefit.

To counter NATO, the Soviet Union formed its satellites into an anti-Western military alliance known as the Warsaw Pact in 1955. It was named after the Polish capital city of Warsaw, where the treaty of alliance was signed.

Yugoslavia and Albania also became communist but refused to be placed under Soviet control. During the Cold War, Yugoslavia joined a number of Asian and African countries to form the Non-Aligned Community. Its members tried to stay neutral—to not support either side—during the Cold War.

✓ **Reading Check** In what way was the Warsaw Pact like NATO?

A Clash in Berlin

During the Cold War, there were many "hot spots," or areas of tension and conflict. Some of these were China, Korea, Cuba, and Vietnam. The earliest clash, however, took place in Berlin, Germany.

Divided Berlin At the end of World War II, the Allies (the United States, the Soviet Union, Great Britain, and France) occupied Germany. Germany was divided into four occupation zones. The Soviet Union controlled the eastern part of the country, while the other three Allies divided and controlled the western part. Turn to the map on page 337 to see the four occupation zones. The German capital of Berlin, located deep within Soviet-controlled East Germany, was also divided among the four nations. In 1948, to promote peace and German recovery, the United States, Great Britain, and France united their occupation zones. The Soviet Union was against any plan that would strengthen Germany, its historical enemy. In June 1948, the Soviets **blockaded,** or closed off, all land and water traffic into the western part of Berlin. They hoped this would force the other three powers to leave the city.

Exploring Economics

Restructuring

Under Soviet control, the satellite nations had command economies. This meant that the government owned all resources. A communist central planning committee decided what goods and services to produce, and how and for whom they would be produced. When the Soviet Union fell in 1991, the Eastern European satellites tried to restructure to a free market economy. This was not easy. Why? Imagine a family-owned business in which the head of the family makes all the decisions. Then suddenly the head of the family disappears. Family members must now make the business decisions, even though they have had no experience doing so. In a similar way, moving from a command economy to a free market economy has been a difficult change.

Berlin Airlift

People in West Berlin (above right) wave to an American airlift plane. A line of planes (above) waits to be unloaded at a Berlin airfield.

Technology How did airplane technology affect Soviet military plans in Germany?

In response, the United States and Great Britain began an **airlift,** or a system of carrying supplies into West Berlin by airplane. Day and night, the planes flew tons of food, fuel, and raw materials into the city. This heroic effort caused the Soviets to finally end the 11-month blockade of West Berlin. That same year, two separate governments were set up. Bonn became the capital of West Germany, which was democratic. East Berlin, in the Soviet zone, became the capital of East Germany, which was communist. West Berlin remained a democratic stronghold surrounded by communism.

The Berlin Wall Many people in East Germany were unhappy under communist rule. About 3 million people fled to West Berlin in search of political freedom and better living conditions. The East German government wanted to stop this movement. In August 1961, the government built a 103-mile (166-km) wall between East and West Berlin. The wall, with Soviet soldiers guarding it, became a symbol of the split between Eastern and Western Europe. Many East Germans continued to risk their lives trying to escape over or under the wall.

✔Reading Check What did the Berlin Wall symbolize?

Freedom for Eastern Europe

During the Cold War, the Soviet Union spent large sums of money on military and space ventures. In spite of plans to improve consumer housing and agriculture, the economies of the Soviet Union and its satellites kept falling further and further behind the United States and its Western European allies.

In 1985 Mikhail Gorbachev became the leader of the Soviet Union. To encourage economic growth, he introduced reforms that loosened government control over the Soviet people and the satellite nations. These reforms unleashed a powerful desire for independence. Soon, the satellite nations in Eastern Europe began to demand their freedom. The first successful challenge to communist rule came in Poland. In 1989 the Polish communists lost power as a result of a democratic election. In East Germany, massive protests caused the country's communist government to resign. The Berlin Wall came down, and West Germany and East Germany reunited in October 1990. By 1991 all of the Soviet-controlled nations in Eastern Europe had thrown off communist rule in favor of democracy.

The Soviet Union officially broke up on December 25, 1991. It separated into Russia and a number of other independent republics. Yugoslavia and Czechoslovakia also broke up. After much fighting and a number of civil wars, Yugoslavia became the independent republics of Slovenia, Croatia, Bosnia and Herzegovina, Macedonia, and Serbia and Montenegro. Czechoslovakia peacefully became the Czech Republic and Slovakia. All of these countries today struggle with poor economies, ethnic tensions, and a lack of understanding of democracy. You will read more about the countries of Eastern Europe in Chapter 13.

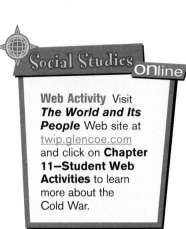

Web Activity Visit **The World and Its People** Web site at twip.glencoe.com and click on **Chapter 11—Student Web Activities** to learn more about the Cold War.

✓ **Reading Check** Which Russian leader moved the Soviet Union and Eastern Europe toward democracy?

FCAT PRACTICE You can prepare for the FCAT-assessed standards by completing the correlated item(s) below.

Section 2 Assessment

Defining Terms

1. Define Cold War, nuclear weapon, deterrence, satellite nation, blockade, airlift.

Recalling Facts

2. History What was the purpose of the Marshall Plan?

3. Place Which countries were considered satellites of the Soviet Union?

Critical Thinking

4. Making Inferences What are the similarities and differences between a "cold" war and a "hot" war? FCAT LA.A.2.2.7

5. Analyzing Information How did the city of Berlin reflect tensions between the United States and the Soviet Union?

Graphic Organizer

6. Organizing Information Create a chart like this. Explain how each of the following events intensified the Cold War. FCAT LA.A.1.3.2

Marshall Plan	
Truman Doctrine	
NATO	
Warsaw Pact	

Applying Social Studies Skills

7. Analyzing Maps Look at the map of Western and Eastern Europe on page 320. Name the Western European countries that shared a border with countries in Eastern Europe.

Moving Toward Unity

Guide to Reading

Main Idea

Although the Cold War is over, many challenges still face the old and new nations of Europe.

Term to Know

• euro

Reading Strategy

Create a chart like the one below and write one key fact about each topic. **FCAT** L.A.A.1.3.2

European Union	
NATO	
Chunnel	
Pollution	

The following are the major Sunshine State Standards covered in this section.

SS.B.1.3.6:
Understands ways in which regional systems are interconnected
SS.B.1.3.7:
Understands the spatial aspects of communication and transportation systems

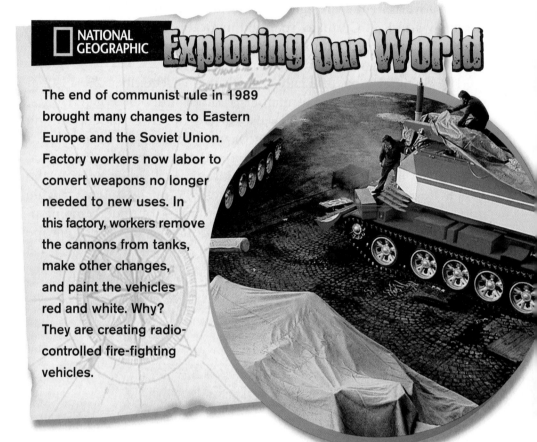

The end of communist rule in 1989 brought many changes to Eastern Europe and the Soviet Union. Factory workers now labor to convert weapons no longer needed to new uses. In this factory, workers remove the cannons from tanks, make other changes, and paint the vehicles red and white. Why? They are creating radio-controlled fire-fighting vehicles.

Since the fall of communism and the Soviet Union, there is no longer a political division between western and eastern Europe. Cultural and economic differences remain, however. As a result of cooperation though, Europe is becoming an economic powerhouse in the world.

The New Europe

As you learned in Section 2, many European countries joined together for economic reasons after World War II. One of the economic alliances was the Common Market, which became the European Union (EU) in 1993. At that time, the twelve members included the United Kingdom, Ireland, France, Luxembourg, Spain, Portugal, Denmark, the Netherlands, Belgium, Germany, Italy, and Greece. Austria, Finland, and Sweden joined in 1995. In 2004, ten additional countries, including many from eastern Europe, joined the EU. Three other nations have begun preparations to join the EU.

The European Union is moving toward even greater unity today. Some Europeans would eventually like to see it become a United States of Europe that would include all European countries. Citizens of EU countries hold common passports and can travel anywhere in the EU to work, shop, save, and invest. In January 2002, most EU members began using a common currency, the euro, to replace their national currencies. This means that citizens of countries in the EU are using the same type of money to buy goods and services. You can read more about the European Union and its significance in **Time Reports: Focus on World Issues** on pages 327–333.

Continued Cooperation European countries have cooperated in science and technology as well as economics. Europe had one of the first treaties on nuclear energy. The European Atomic Energy Community (EURATOM) has wide powers. These include the right to enter into contracts, obtain raw materials, and establish standards to protect workers and the general population from nuclear radiation.

Technology has also brought Europe's countries closer. A high-speed rail system links London in the British Isles with Paris and Brussels on the European mainland. The rail line passes beneath the English Channel through the Chunnel, or Channel Tunnel. In 2000 Denmark and Sweden were connected for the first time when they opened a bridge and tunnel system linking the two countries.

NATO's New Role In recent years, the once-communist eastern European countries have joined NATO. Russia, at first, was opposed to NATO's growth toward its borders. Now it cooperates with NATO as a limited partner. With more members, NATO is moving beyond its original role as Europe's protector from communism. It has taken on

NATIONAL GEOGRAPHIC On Location

The Euro

Ten different national sides of the one euro coin are shown, along with the front image (above) that does not change.

Place How many nations can you identify by the images chosen to represent the country?

peacekeeping tasks in the former Yugoslav republics. Its forces are also now being trained to respond quickly to terrorist threats that may arise in areas far beyond NATO's borders. NATO's success, however, depends on close ties among its members. In 2003 these ties were strained as a result of the United States-led war on Iraq. Several member countries, such as France and Germany, opposed the conflict.

✓ Reading Check **What is the name of the new European Union currency?**

Facing the Region's Challenges

Several challenges face Europe, which Europeans are actively trying to solve. The income gap between the rich and poor nations of Europe needs to be lessened. The increasing food and health needs of the people of these countries must also be met.

Environmental Issues Another important challenge for Europe concerns the environment. In France, rivers like the Seine and the Loire are polluted, as are the major canals. Nowhere is the problem worse than in the Rhine River. As the river flows north, it passes through a continuous bank of cities and industrial regions. By the time it reaches the Netherlands, it is carrying a staggering 25 million tons of industrial waste per year. This is all dumped into the North Sea. Air pollution is another environmental issue in the region. You will learn more about these and other challenges in Chapters 12 and 13.

✓ Reading Check **Why is water pollution a problem in Europe?**

FCAT PRACTICE You can prepare for the FCAT-assessed standards by completing the correlated item(s) below.

 Section 3

Assessment

Defining Terms
1. Define euro.

Recalling Facts
2. **History** List three of the original twelve members of the European Union.

3. **Economics** What is the European Union trying to achieve?

Critical Thinking
4. **Making Inferences** What allowed the construction of the Chunnel? **FCAT LA.E.2.2.1**

5. **Making Predictions** Do you think Russia will join the European Union? Why or why not? **FCAT LA.A.2.3.1**

Graphic Organizer
6. **Organizing Information** Create a diagram like the one below. Then write three of Europe's challenges in the ovals. **FCAT LA.A.1.3.2**

Europe's Challenges

Applying Social Studies Skills

7. **Summarizing** Write a paragraph that summarizes the changing role of NATO. In your summary, be sure to include NATO's original role, why that role has changed, and any issues surrounding its new role. **FCAT LA.B.1.3.2**

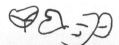

TIME
PERSPECTIVES

The European Union: Good for Everyone?

A Common Currency for a Common Market

Compiled and adapted from TIME.

Europeans began using new currency in January 2002. The impact was gigantic—like this mocked-up coin.

Building a United Europe

Evaluating Media LA.A.2.3.6

Damien Barry had a problem. In 2001 he wanted to work in Paris, France. The trouble was, the French were fussy. French people could work in France. And so could people from 14 other loosely united European nations. All 15 nations belonged to the **European Union**, or the EU. Barry wasn't from an EU nation. He was from Brooklyn, New York.

But that didn't stop him. Ireland is an EU nation. It grants citizenship to anyone with an Irish parent or grandparent. Barry had Irish grandparents. He applied for an Irish passport and got one. Soon after that he had a job in a French bank.

A Big Story for Americans

Barry would never give up his U.S. citizenship. Yet he's not letting go of his Irish passport, either. "It's worth a million dollars to me," he said.

Barry's story suggests how much the EU matters to Americans. The EU nations form the world's largest trading group. That gives them awesome power to control jobs and the price of many things you buy.

That's not all. The EU is expanding. In 2004, ten new countries—including Poland and Estonia—joined the Union. In

the past, the U.S. dealt one-on-one with those countries. Now it has to deal with them through the EU. By 2020, the EU plans to grow to 30 nations.

What's more, the EU is piecing together a small army. That army will change the U.S. military's role in Europe. "In the next 10 years," TIME magazine said in 2001, "there may be no bigger story than the EU."

Europe in 2004

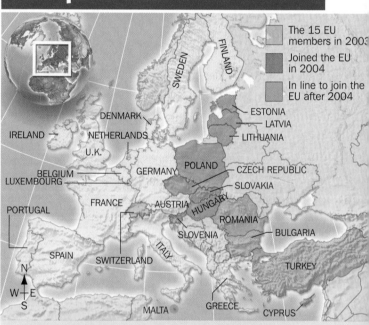

The 15 EU members in 2003

Joined the EU in 2004

In line to join the EU after 2004

INTERPRETING MAPS

1. **Categorizing** In which part of Europe—east or west—are most current EU members? In which part are nations that want to join?

2. **Making Inferences** Why might it be hard for all these nations to agree on important issues?

FCAT LA.A.1.3.2

The new euro is exchanged for bread.

Farm animals' health is a big EU concern.

This Dutchman is one of hundreds of pro soccer players in the EU.

Common Problems

What is the EU? Simply put, it is a group of nations that have joined forces to solve common problems. Finding a safe way to recycle used batteries is one problem. Convincing Europeans to stop smoking is another. Making sure goods flow freely within Europe is still another. The EU is a **free trade zone**. That means EU nations don't tax goods they import from each other.

The EU hopes to help its members prosper. But it has another goal—bringing peace to a continent with a long history of conflict.

A Heavy Load

To get the euro to shoppers by January 2002, the EU sent 56 billion coins to banks in 12 nations. The coins weighed 168,000 tons—24 times more than the Eiffel Tower in Paris, France!

Weak Government

Some people compare the EU with the United States around 1785. The U.S. government had little muscle then. It had no president, no army, no power to raise money. The states had all the money and almost all the power.

In many ways, the EU is like that. Officials at EU offices in Brussels, Belgium, make a lot of decisions, but they have no **authority** to force member nations to give up their armies. They can't even make them stop printing money.

In 1789 America's original 13 states agreed to give up some powers. They did it by approving the U.S. Constitution.

The EU doesn't have a constitution. Its members are joined by treaties, or written agreements. Without a constitution to guide them, it's hard to get all of the nations to agree on anything.

New Money

One thing most EU members have agreed on is a common currency, the **euro**. In January 2002, most EU nations replaced their own money with the euro. Three nations—the United Kingdom, Denmark, and Sweden—chose not to make the switch immediately.

In 2001 Damien Barry got paid in French francs. Now he gets paid in euros. When he goes to Italy and Holland, he no longer carries Italian lira and Dutch guilders. Like his Irish passport, the euro has made his life easier. And it's done the same for the more than 300 million Europeans who use the euro every day.

EXPLORING THE ISSUE

1. **Making Generalizations** Three EU nations refused to replace their currencies with the euro. Why might a nation want to keep its own currency?
   FCAT LA.A.1.3.2

2. **Cause and Effect** How might the EU affect your life—today, and in the future?

From Peace to Prosperity

Evaluating Media
LA.A.2.3.6

World War II ended in 1945. It was the third time in 75 years that Germany and France had fought each other.

Could another war be prevented? A Frenchman named Jean Monnet thought so. He proposed taking coal and steel production out of the hands of individual countries. Without fuel and steel, he said, nations couldn't wage war.

How the EU Grew

1951: France, Germany, Italy, the Netherlands, Belgium, and Luxembourg agree to pool their coal, iron ore, and steel industries.

1973: Denmark, Ireland, and the United Kingdom join.

1981: Greece joins.

1986: Spain and Portugal join.

1995: Austria, Finland, and Sweden join.

2004: Cyprus, the Czech Republic, Estonia, Hungary, Latvia, Lithuania, Malta, Poland, Slovakia, and Slovenia join.

U.S. President John F. Kennedy shares a smile with Jean Monnet.

In 1951 six nations accepted Monnet's proposal. They were Belgium, West Germany, Italy, Luxembourg, the Netherlands, and France. They set up an organization that told each nation how much coal and steel it could produce.

A Free Trade Zone

That was a big step. Next, in 1957, all six nations agreed to stop taxing goods they imported from each other. Those **import taxes** acted like walls, stopping goods from moving between nations. By removing those walls, these nations created a **common market**.

Common markets were nothing new. The United States had had one for more than 150 years. California never taxed beef "imported" from Texas, for instance. Free trade was new for Europe, however. And it helped businesses there grow.

Growing Pains

By 1995, nine nations had joined the original six, and ten countries became new members in 2004. Looking ahead, the EU expects to let other nations join by 2020.

Getting so many nations to work together won't be easy. But no one doubts that the EU's impact on the world is going to grow. ▦

EXPLORING THE ISSUE

1. **Explaining** In what ways might the simple fact of the EU's existence promote peace? FCAT LA.A.2.3.1

2. **Cause and Effect** How might a common market help businesses grow? FCAT LA.A.2.3.1

UPI/CORBIS-BETTMANN

A Model for Change

Hungary had a bumpy 50 years after World War II. This East European nation suffered under Communist rule from 1948 to 1990. Now Hungarians have a democratic government. Individuals there can own their own businesses again. Those changes put Hungary on track to join the EU in 2004.

Qualifying for entry wasn't easy. Hungary's government had to budget its spending. It had to sell factories and land it owned to private citizens. Thousands of workers lost their jobs.

Creating Jobs

Hungarians were willing to make the sacrifices, because they wanted to join the EU. Once in, they would be able to sell what they made to other

▲ **U.S. President George W. Bush confers with an EU official.**

as a model for Hungary and other former Communist nations to follow.

The EU has been especially good for the United States. Every day the U.S. and the EU nations sell each other goods worth $2 billion. In 2000 EU citizens bought nearly $41 billion worth of goods from Texas and California alone. That money paid the salaries of at least 696,000 Texans and Californians.

Democracy

The U.S. and the EU compete with each other. They often disagree on major issues. But they are firm friends, and both advocate democracy and free trade. The prospect of joining their "club" spurred Hungary and other nations to change—and to change quickly.

The Top Two Output of goods and services in 2001, in trillions of dollars

$7.9 — European Union
$10 — United States

Analyzing information One of every 10 people in the world lives in the U.S. or in EU nations. But every year U.S. and EU workers together create more than half the world's goods and services. Why do you think this is so?

FCAT LA.A.1.3.2

EU members. Those sales would create jobs at home and make lives easier for Hungarians.

Would Hungary have changed if the EU didn't exist? Certainly. But chances are it wouldn't have changed so fast— and so completely. The EU has served

EXPLORING THE ISSUE

1. **Comparing** How are the U.S. and the EU alike?
FCAT LA.A.2.3.1

2. **Making Inferences** Why might a Hungarian worker be both for and against change?
FCAT LA.A.1.3.2

Resolving Differences: What Can One Person Do?

Evaluating Media
LA.A.2.3.6

The EU and the United States are good friends. But friends have their differences. Here are four:

1. The U.S. doesn't trade with Libya, Iran, and Cuba. It tried to get EU nations to do the same, but the EU refused. Companies in EU nations want to be free to sell goods to anyone.

2. The EU puts limits on some U.S. companies that do business in Europe. Some Americans don't think the EU should be able to tell U.S. companies how to run their businesses.

3. Another dispute involved food. U.S. food companies wanted to grow **genetically altered crops** that resisted disease. So their scientists invented new types of crops. Many Europeans are afraid that those crops might pose health risks. Some EU countries won't even allow those products inside their borders.

4. Global warming is another sticking point. Scientists fear that gases from factories and automobiles keep the earth's heat from escaping into space. EU nations and the U.S. can't agree on the best way to solve the problem.

Choose one of the four problems. Research each side's argument. Then create a solution to the problem—one you think both sides might accept.

Make your views public. Put them in a letter. Send the letter to your repre-

▲ Genetically altered foods are creating an EU controversy.

sentatives in Congress. You might even want to send a copy to the European Union's ambassador to the United States. Address: Ambassador, Delegation of the European Commission to the United States, 2300 M Street, NW, Washington, D.C., 20037. ▪

EXPLORING THE ISSUE

1. Analyzing Information What might all four disputes have to do with each side's view of its "rights"? **FCAT LA.A.1.3.2**

2. Making Predictions How might these disputes affect parts of the world outside the U.S. and the EU? **FCAT LA.A.1.3.2**

REVIEW AND ASSESS

UNDERSTANDING THE ISSUE

1. Defining Key Terms Write definitions for the following terms: *European Union, free trade zone, authority, euro, import taxes, common market,* and *genetically altered crops.*
FCAT LA.A.1.3.2

2. Writing to Inform Write a short article about the European Union, explaining how it could affect you and other students. Use as many words as you can from the above list. **FCAT** LA.B.1.3.2

3. Writing to Persuade Write a letter to an imaginary friend in Denmark. Convince your friend that all European countries should use the euro.
FCAT LA.B.1.3.2

INTERNET RESEARCH ACTIVITY

4. Use Internet resources to find information about the European Union. Read about the EU's three main governing bodies. Choose one and write a brief description of it in your own words. Then decide, with your classmates, how those bodies work together and which ones have the most power.
FCAT LA.A.2.3.5

5. With your teacher's help, use Internet resources to research the symbols of the European Union: the flag, the anthem, and Europe Day. How is the EU's flag like—and different from—the first U.S. flag? Download the EU anthem. Why do you think the EU chose it? How is Europe Day like Independence Day in the U.S.? Put your answers in a 250-word essay.
FCAT LA.A.2.3.5

BEYOND THE CLASSROOM

6. Research the history of the U.S. dollar. How hard was it to get Americans to accept U.S. currency in 1792? Ask your parents about the U.S.

The EU flag's gold stars represent solidarity and harmony among European peoples.

$2.00 bill. How did they react to its introduction? How is the dollar like the euro? Explain your answers in an article appropriate for a school newspaper.
FCAT LA.B.1.3.2

7. Organize the class into three teams. Debate this resolution: "It is unfair for the EU to let only European citizens work in EU countries." A panel of student judges will decide which team has the most convincing arguments.

It's All About Jobs!

Where U.S. Exports Create Jobs
(Top ten states with jobs supported by exports to Europe)

	State	Number of Jobs
1	California	490,300
2	New York	281,100
3	Washington	221,500
4	Texas	206,200
5	Mass.	141,400
6	Illinois	127,200
7	New Jersey	114,100
8	Michigan	88,800
9	Ohio	88,300
10	Penn.	83,200

Where Europe's Money Creates Jobs
(Top ten states with jobs supported by European companies)

	State	Number of Jobs
1	California	336,300
2	New York	268,500
3	Texas	260,600
4	N. Carolina	200,000
5	Penn.	188,200
6	Illinois	185,000
7	Florida	183,800
8	Michigan	176,900
9	New Jersey	173,400
10	Ohio	162,200

Source: European-American Business Council. Note: "Europe" refers to the 15 EU members in 2003 plus four members of a related group, the European Free Trade Association (Iceland, Liechtenstein, Norway, and Switzerland).

BUILDING SKILLS FOR READING TABLES

1. Analyzing Data Using an almanac, find the 10 states with the largest populations. How many of those states are listed among the top 10 on each graph? What relationships do you see between state populations and jobs supported by exports? How might state populations influence the number of jobs European companies create in the U.S.? Put your answers in a short report.
FCAT MA.E.3.3.1

2. Making Inferences European companies create more jobs in Florida and North Carolina than exports do. How might you explain this?
FCAT LA.A.1.3.2

FOR UPDATES ON WORLD ISSUES GO TO www.timeclassroom.com/glencoe

Social Studies Skill

FCAT PRACTICE Completing the correlated items below will help you prepare for the **FCAT Mathematics** test.

Reading a Population Map

Population density is the number of people living in a square mile or square kilometer. A **population density map** shows you where people live in a given region. Mapmakers use different colors to represent different population densities. The darker the color, the more dense, or crowded, the population is in that particular area. Cities that are shown by dots or squares also represent different population sizes.

Learning the Skill

To read a population density map, follow these steps:

- Read the title of the map.
- Study the map key to determine what the colors mean.
- On the map, find the areas that have the lowest and highest population density.
- Identify what symbols are used to show how heavily populated the cities are.

Practicing the Skill

Look at the map below to answer the following questions.

1. Which color stands for 125–250 people per square mile (50–100 per sq. km)?
2. Which cities have more than 1 million people? **FCAT MA.B.1.3.4**
3. Which areas have the lowest population density? Why? **FCAT MA.B.1.3.4**

Applying the Skill

Obtain a population density map of your state. What is the population density of your area? What is the nearest city with 1 million people? **FCAT MA.B.1.3.4**

GO TO Practice key skills with **Glencoe Skillbuilder Interactive Workbook, Level 1.**

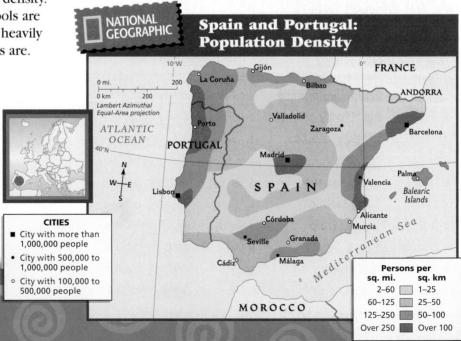

NATIONAL GEOGRAPHIC

Spain and Portugal: Population Density

CITIES
- ■ City with more than 1,000,000 people
- • City with 500,000 to 1,000,000 people
- ◦ City with 100,000 to 500,000 people

Lambert Azimuthal Equal-Area projection

Persons per	
sq. mi.	sq. km
2–60	1–25
60–125	25–50
125–250	50–100
Over 250	Over 100

11 Reading Review

Section 1 | The Modern Era Emerges

Terms to Know
productivity
human resources
textiles
cottage industry
union
strike
imperialism
communism
Holocaust
genocide

Main Idea
Industrialization led not only to a higher standard of living for some, but also to increased tensions in the world.

✓ **Economics** Machinery made it possible to increase productivity, leading to the Industrial Revolution.

✓ **Culture** Industry changed the way people worked and lived.

✓ **Economics** Competition for markets and resources led to imperialism and friction among European countries.

✓ **History** The two World Wars changed the way wars were fought and created new political power for the United States and the Soviet Union.

Section 2 | A Divided Continent

Terms to Know
Cold War
nuclear weapon
deterrence
satellite nation
blockade
airlift

Main Idea
After World War II, the democratic United States and the Communist Soviet Union worked to bring their forms of government to the war-torn nations of Europe.

✓ **History** Competition between the United States and the Soviet Union started the Cold War.

✓ **Economics** Western European countries joined together to form the European Common Market, which moved toward greater cooperation and economic development.

✓ **Government** The Soviet Union made satellites of its surrounding nations.

✓ **History** Berlin became a "hot spot" for conflict between the superpowers, symbolized by the Berlin Wall.

✓ **Government** By 1991 countries in Eastern Europe had thrown off communist rule in favor of democracy.

Section 3 | Moving Toward Unity

Term to Know
euro

Main Idea
Although the Cold War is over, many challenges still face the old and new nations of Europe.

✓ **Economics** The European Union is moving much of Europe toward greater economic and political unity. It has expanded to include many eastern European countries.

✓ **Economics** In 2002 most EU member countries began using a common currency.

✓ **Human/Environment Interaction** Problems still remain in Europe, including poverty and pollution.

Europe–Modern History

FCAT PRACTICE You can prepare for the FCAT-assessed standards by completing the correlated item(s) below.

Using Key Terms

Match the terms in Part A with their definitions in Part B.

A.

1. productivity
2. union
3. imperialism
4. communism
5. genocide
6. Cold War
7. deterrence
8. textiles
9. cottage industry
10. euro

B.

a. group that bargains for better working conditions

b. woven cloth

c. mass murder of a people because of race, religion, ethnicity, politics, or culture

d. European Union common currency

e. work carried out in homes rather than in factories

f. countries claim colonies for their resources and markets

g. how much work can be done in a certain length of time

h. conflict between the United States and the Soviet Union

i. political system that called for the overthrow of the industrialized system

j. designed to discourage a first attack

Reviewing the Main Ideas

Section 1 The Modern Era Emerges

11. **History** How did the Industrial Revolution change working and living conditions? **FCAT LA.E.2.2.1**

12. **Economics** Why did European countries find it necessary to have colonies?

13. **History** What were some of the problems that led to World War II? **FCAT LA.E.2.2.1**

Section 2 A Divided Continent

14. **History** What was the Truman Doctrine, and why was it important?

15. **History** What is the Common Market known as today?

16. **Government** What was the Non-Aligned Community, and which European nation belonged to it?

17. **History** Why did the Soviet Union build the Berlin Wall? **FCAT LA.E.2.2.1**

18. **Government** How did the policies of Mikhail Gorbachev affect Eastern Europe? **FCAT LA.E.2.2.1**

Section 3 Moving Toward Unity

19. **Economics** What are the advantages to citizens of EU member countries?

20. **Economics** What is the euro?

21. **Human/Environment Interaction** What environmental issues does Europe face? **FCAT SC.D.2.3.2**

 **NATIONAL GEOGRAPHIC**   **The Allies and Axis Powers**

Place Location Activity

On a separate sheet of paper, match the letters on the map with the numbered places listed below.

1. Germany
2. Italy
3. United Kingdom
4. France
5. China
6. Soviet Union
7. Japan
8. United States

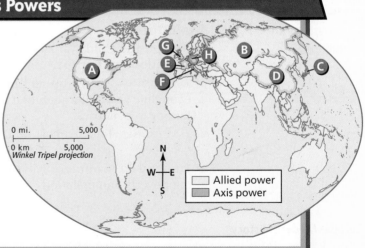

0 mi.   5,000

0 km   5,000
Winkel Tripel projection

N W—E S

☐ Allied power
☐ Axis power

Critical Thinking

22. **Predicting Consequences** What further changes will occur in Europe as a result of the European Union and the collapse of the Soviet Union? **FCAT LA.A.2.3.1**

23. **Sequencing Events** List five events that made the Cold War "colder."

    1. _____
    2. _____
    3. _____
    4. _____
    5. _____

Comparing Regions Activity

24. **History** Like Europe after World War II, the Korean Peninsula was comprised of Communist and non-Communist countries. Eastern Europe had much in common with North Korea during the Cold War. Create a chart and list the similarities between Communist Eastern Europe and North Korea. On another chart, list the similarities between non-Communist Western Europe and South Korea. **FCAT LA.A.1.3.2**

Mental Mapping

25. **Focusing on the Region** Draw a simple outline map of Europe and label the following:

    • United Kingdom   • Russia
    • Germany   • Spain
    • Italy   • Greece
    • France

Technology Skills Activity

26. **Using the Internet** Research the national currencies that are being used in at least three European countries that have not yet adopted the euro. Note what each country's currency is called and when the country plans to phase it out. Research to find how the transition to the euro works. **FCAT LA.A.2.3.5**

Standardized Test Practice

Directions: Study the map, and then answer the question that follows.

Occupation of Germany 1945

1. **In 1945, which country controlled the land surrounding Berlin, Germany's capital?**

    F the United Kingdom

    G the Soviet Union

    H the United States

    J France

Test-Taking Tip: This question asks you to synthesize information on the map with prior knowledge. Notice that the map does not specifically state that the United Kingdom, for example, controlled a portion of Germany. Instead, it refers to this area as "British."

Western Europe Today

The World and Its People

NATIONAL GEOGRAPHIC

To learn more about the people and places of western Europe, view *The World and Its People* Chapters 10–12 videos.

Social Studies online

Chapter Overview Visit *The World and Its People* Web site at twip.glencoe.com and click on **Chapter 12—Chapter Overviews** to preview information about western Europe.

FCAT PRACTICE The activity below will help you prepare for the **FCAT Reading** test.

Categorizing Information Make this foldable to organize information from the chapter and to help you learn more about the people and places of western Europe. **FCAT LA.A.1.3.2**

Step 1 Collect three sheets of paper and place them about 1 inch apart.

Keep the edges straight.

Step 2 Fold up the bottom edges of the paper to form 6 tabs.

This makes all tabs the same size.

Step 3 When all the tabs are the same size, crease the paper to hold the tabs in place and staple the sheets together. Turn the paper and label each tab as shown.

WESTERN EUROPE TODAY
The British Isles
France and Benelux Countries
Germany and Alpine Countries
The Nordic Nations
Southern Europe

Staple together along the fold.

Reading and Writing As you read, use your foldable to write down what you learn about western Europe. Write facts under each appropriate tab.

FCAT LA.A.1.3.2

Why It Matters

Building a Community

Western Europe has been a center of world trade for hundreds of years. In the past, however, the nations of this region often set up trade barriers against one another in order to protect their own industries. Today, as the European Union, these same countries are working together to make their region a stronger, united economic power.

◀ **The Eiffel Tower in Paris, France**

The British Isles

Main Idea

The United Kingdom and Ireland are small in size, but their people have had a great impact on the rest of the world.

Terms to Know

- moor
- parliamentary democracy
- constitutional monarchy
- peat
- bog

Reading Strategy

Create a diagram like this one. Fill in the names of the four regions that make up the United Kingdom and one fact about each. Create a second diagram for Ireland and include one fact about it. **FCAT** LA.A.1.3.2

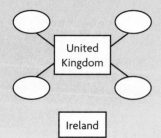

The following are the major Sunshine State Standards covered in this section.

SS.B.1.3.3:
Knows the social, political, and economic divisions on Earth's surface

SS.A.3.3.2:
Understands the historical events that have shaped the development of cultures throughout the world

NATIONAL GEOGRAPHIC Exploring Our World

Every year millions of tourists visit London, England. They come to see the crown jewels or dungeons in the Tower of London. They also visit the Houses of Parliament and the tall clock known as Big Ben. You cannot be afraid of heights if you ride one of London's newest attractions. Known as the London Eye, it is the tallest Ferris wheel in the world.

The countries of the **United Kingdom** and the **Republic of Ireland** are known as the British Isles. They lie in the North Atlantic Ocean, west of the European continent. These two countries share similar physical characteristics but are different culturally.

The United Kingdom

About the size of Oregon, the United Kingdom is made up of four regions. **England** dominates the United Kingdom, in population and economic strength. However, **Scotland** and **Wales** are important parts of the United Kingdom. Both were conquered by England centuries ago. Today, movements for independence have grown in both countries. In 1999 Scotland and Wales set up legislatures to run their local affairs. The people of Scotland and Wales also take pride in their ancient languages—Scottish Gaelic in Scotland and Welsh in Wales. These languages are taught in schools to keep the old cultures and traditions alive.

In northern England, Scotland, and Wales, you find rugged hills and low mountain ranges. You also cross **moors**—treeless, windy highland

areas with damp ground. The United Kingdom's fourth region—
Northern Ireland—shares the island of Ireland with the Republic of
Ireland. In Northern Ireland, you see a landscape of gentle mountains,
valleys, and fertile lowlands.

The Economy Over 250 years ago, inventors and scientists here
sparked the Industrial Revolution. Today, the United Kingdom is still a
major industrial and trading country. Manufactured goods and machinery are the leading exports. New computer and electronic industries,
however, are gradually replacing older industries. Service industries
such as banking, insurance, communications, and health care employ
most of the country's people.

Farming is very efficient here. Still, the United Kingdom must
import about one-third of its food. Why? A lack of farmland and a limited growing season make it impossible to feed the large population.

The Government The United Kingdom is a **parliamentary
democracy.** In this form of government, voters elect representatives
to a lawmaking body called Parliament. It has two houses—the House
of Commons and the House of Lords. The political party that has
the largest number of members in the House of Commons chooses the
government's leader, the prime minister. The House of Lords has little

Western Europe: Political

● National capital

0 mi.   500
0 km   500
*Lambert Azimuthal
Equal-Area projection*

Applying Map Skills

1. What four regions make
   up the United Kingdom?

2. What capital in western
   Europe is farthest north?

**Find NGS online map resources @
www.nationalgeographic.com/maps**

London

People get around London by riding colorful double-decker buses or by using the subway, which the British call "the Tube."

Place What percentage of the United Kingdom's people live in towns and cities, such as London?

power. Most members of the House of Lords are nobles who have inherited their titles or who have been given titles by the queen.

The United Kingdom's government is also a **constitutional monarchy,** in which a queen or king is the official head of state. Although the monarch represents the country at public events, he or she has little power.

The People and Culture
About 60 million people live in the United Kingdom. The British people speak English, although Welsh and Scottish Gaelic are spoken in some areas. Most people are Protestant Christians, although immigrants practice Islam and other religions.

About 90 percent of the United Kingdom's people live in cities and towns. With more than 7 million people, the capital city of **London** is one of Europe's most heavily populated cities.

For centuries, the people of the United Kingdom have left their mark on world culture. Visitors see prehistoric stone monuments, ruins of Roman forts, and medieval churches and castles. Famous writers, such as William Shakespeare, have also made an impact on the world.

✔️**Reading Check** What form of government does the United Kingdom have?

The Republic of Ireland

Surrounded by the blue waters of the Atlantic Ocean and the Irish Sea, Ireland has lush green meadows and tree-covered hills. It is called the Emerald Isle because of its landscape. At Ireland's center lies a wide, rolling plain covered with forests and farmland. The area is rich in **peat,** or plants partly decayed in water which can be dried and used for fuel. Peat is dug from **bogs,** or low swampy lands.

The Economy   Potatoes, barley, wheat, sugar beets, and turnips are Ireland's major crops. Farmers raise sheep, as well as beef and dairy cattle. Manufacturing employs more people than farming and contributes more to the country's economy. Ireland joined the European Union so that it could market its products more widely. The Irish work in many manufacturing industries. These include processing foods and beverages and making textiles, clothing, pharmaceuticals, and computer equipment.

The Northern Ireland Conflict   Ireland has suffered hundreds of years of unrest under British rule. The southern, mostly Catholic, counties of Ireland won independence from Britain in 1921. They later became a republic. The northern counties, where many British Protestants had settled, remained part of the United Kingdom. Peace still did not come to the island. The Nationalists, who are typically Catholic, want the six counties of Northern Ireland to be reunited with the Republic of Ireland. The Loyalists, who are typically Protestant, prefer that Northern Ireland remain under British rule. The fighting between these two groups, which the Irish refer to as "the troubles," has led to many deaths.

In 1998 officials of the United Kingdom and the Republic of Ireland met with leaders of both sides in Northern Ireland. They signed an agreement to end the violence, but disputes have since erupted.

The People   The Irish trace their ancestry to the Celts (KEHLTS) who settled Ireland around 500 B.C. Gaelic, a Celtic language, and English are Ireland's two official languages.

Today, Ireland is an urban nation. About 58 percent of the country's people live in cities or towns. Nearly one-third live in or around **Dublin,** the capital. Life often centers on the neighborhood church.

Irish music and folk dancing are performed around the world. Of all the arts, however, the Irish have had the greatest influence on literature. Playwright George Bernard Shaw, poet William Butler Yeats, and novelist James Joyce are some of the country's best-known writers.

▲ The Irish countryside

 **Reading Check**   How are Northern Ireland and the Republic of Ireland different?

FCAT PRACTICE   You can prepare for the FCAT-assessed standards by completing the correlated item(s) below.

Section 1 Assessment

Defining Terms
1. **Define** moor, parliamentary democracy, constitutional monarchy, peat, bog.

Recalling Facts
2. **Region** What are the four regions of the United Kingdom?
3. **Economics** What are the two leading exports of the United Kingdom?
4. **Economics** Why did Ireland join the European Union?

Critical Thinking
5. **Analyzing Information** Why does the House of Lords have little power in the United Kingdom's Parliament?
6. **Understanding Cause and Effect** What disagreement has led to fighting in Northern Ireland? **FCAT LA.A.2.3.1**

Graphic Organizer
7. **Organizing Information** Create two diagrams like this one, one for the United Kingdom and one for the Republic of Ireland. Under each heading, list as many facts as you can for both countries. **FCAT LA.A.1.3.2**

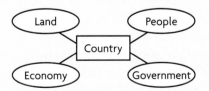

Applying Social Studies Skills
8. **Analyzing Maps** Look at the political map on page 341. What is the capital of the United Kingdom? Of the Republic of Ireland?

Making Connections

Stonehenge

FCAT PRACTICE Answering question 3 below will help you prepare for the **FCAT Reading** test.

Stonehenge, one of the world's best-known and most puzzling ancient monuments, stands in southern England.

History of Stonehenge

The most noticeable part of Stonehenge is its huge stones set up in four circular patterns. A circular ditch and mound form a border around the site. Shallow dirt holes also circle the stones.

Stonehenge was built over a period of more than 2,000 years. The earliest construction, that of the circular ditch and mound, probably began about 3100 B.C. The outer ring of large pillars, topped with horizontal rocks, was built about 2000 B.C. An inner ring of stone pillars also supports horizontal stones.

There was no local source of stone, so workers carried it from an area that was about 20 miles (32 km) north. The stones are huge—up to 30 feet (9 m) long and 50 tons (45 t) in weight. Before setting the stones in place, workers smoothed and shaped them. They carved joints into the stones so that they would fit together perfectly. Then the builders probably used levers and wooden supports to raise the stones into position.

About 500 years later, builders added the third and fourth rings of stones. This time they used bluestone, which an earlier group of people had transported 240 miles (386 km) from the Preseli Mountains of Wales.

What Does It Mean?

Experts do not agree on who built Stonehenge. In 2003, however, archaeologists uncovered the 4,500-year-old remains of seven people near Stonehenge. The people are believed to have lived during the building of the monument.

An even greater mystery is why Stonehenge was built. Most experts agree that Stonehenge was

▲ Stonehenge

probably used as a place of worship. Some believe that the series of holes, stones, and archways were used as a calendar. By lining up particular holes and stones, people could note the summer and winter solstices. They could also keep track of the months. Some scientists think that early people used the site to predict solar and lunar eclipses.

Making the Connection

1. About how old is Stonehenge?

2. From where did the stones used at Stonehenge come?

3. **Sequencing Information** Describe the order in which Stonehenge was built. **FCAT LA.A.2.3.1**

France and the Benelux Countries

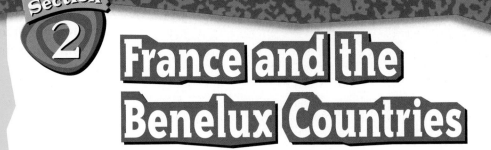

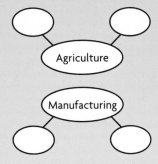
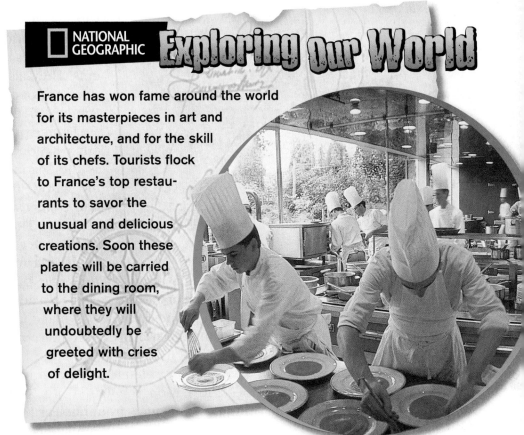

NATIONAL GEOGRAPHIC *Exploring Our World*

France has won fame around the world for its masterpieces in art and architecture, and for the skill of its chefs. Tourists flock to France's top restaurants to savor the unusual and delicious creations. Soon these plates will be carried to the dining room, where they will undoubtedly be greeted with cries of delight.

France and its Benelux neighbors rank as major economic and cultural centers of the world. The word *Benelux* comes from combining the first letters of three countries' names: **Belgium,** the **Netherlands,** and **Luxembourg.**

France

The largest country in western Europe, **France** is slightly smaller than the state of Texas. France's landscape includes high mountain ranges that separate the country from Spain, Italy, and Switzerland. In contrast, most of northern France is part of the vast North European Plain. A network of rivers, including the **Seine** (SAYN) and the **Loire** (LWAHR), connects the different regions of France. Most of these rivers are navigable, or wide and deep enough to allow the passage of ships.

Most of France has a climate that is ideal for agriculture. The rich soil in the North European Plain makes France an important food

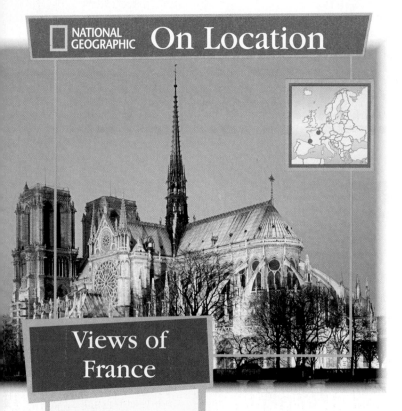

Views of France

Tourists in Paris, France, enjoy the grandeur of Notre Dame, a cathedral built in the 1100s (above). Wine grapes are harvested in one of France's grape-growing valleys (below).

Place What details in the photos suggest that France has a mild climate?

producer. In many French towns, you can find open-air markets displaying an abundance of fresh farm produce.

France's Economy France's well-developed economy relies on agriculture and manufacturing. Most people, however, work in service industries such as banking, commerce, communications, and tourism. Tourists from all over the world visit France's historic and cultural sites, such as palaces and museums. They also come to enjoy the blue skies, rocky cliffs, and lovely beaches of France's Mediterranean coast.

France produces more food than any other nation in western Europe. It ranks as the second-largest food exporter in the world, after the United States. Yet only 5 percent of French workers labor on farms. Their success is partly due to France's fertile soil, mild climate, and modern farming methods.

French farmers grow grains, sugar beets, fruits, and vegetables. They also raise beef and dairy cattle. In addition, vineyards are a common sight. The grapes are used to make famous French wines. Olives are grown along the warm, dry Mediterranean coast.

France's natural resources include bauxite, iron ore, and coal. France has small petroleum reserves and little hydroelectric power. How does the nation power its industries? About 80 percent of France's electricity comes from nuclear power plants.

Workers produce a variety of manufactured goods, including steel, chemicals, textiles, airplanes, cars, and computers. France is a leading center of commerce, with an international reputation in fashion.

The French People "Liberté . . . Egalité . . . Fraternité" (Liberty, Equality, Fraternity)—France's national motto—describes the spirit of the French people. The French share a strong national loyalty. Most French trace their ancestry to the Celts, Romans, and Franks of early Europe. They speak French, and about 90 percent of them are Roman Catholic.

France's government is known as the Fifth Republic. A republic is a strong national government headed by elected leaders. A powerful president, elected for a five-year term, leads the nation. The French president manages the country's foreign affairs. He or she appoints a prime minister to run the day-to-day affairs of government.

About three-fourths of France's 59.8 million people live in cities and towns. **Paris,** the capital and largest city, has a population of more than 10 million people, which includes its suburbs. The city is home to many universities, museums, and other cultural sites. Outstanding cultural figures who lived in Paris include the writer Victor Hugo and the painters Claude Monet and Pierre-Auguste Renoir. Each year, millions of tourists go to the City of Light, as Paris is called. They visit such sites as the Eiffel Tower, the cathedral of Notre Dame, and the Louvre (LOOV), one of the world's most famous art museums.

Reading Check What is the main religion in France?

The Benelux Countries

The small Benelux countries of Belgium, the Netherlands, and Luxembourg have much in common. Their lands are low, flat, and densely populated. Most people live in cities, work in businesses or factories, and enjoy a high standard of living. All three nations are members of the European Union. They are also parliamentary democracies with constitutional monarchies.

Belgium About the size of Maryland, Belgium touches France, Luxembourg, Germany, and the Netherlands. Lying near major industrial regions, Belgium has long been a trade and manufacturing center. Belgian lace, chocolate, and diamond-cutting all have a worldwide reputation for excellence. With few natural resources of their own, the Belgian people import metals, fuels, and raw materials from less-developed countries. They use these materials to make and export vehicles, chemicals, and textiles.

Most Belgians are Roman Catholic. The country has two main cultural and language groups. The Flemings in the north speak Flemish, a language based on Dutch. The south is home to the French-speaking Walloons. Tensions sometimes arise between the two groups, especially because there is more wealth and industry in the north than in the south. Most Belgians live in crowded urban areas. **Brussels,** the capital and largest city, is an international center for trade.

The Netherlands The Netherlands—about half the size of Maine—is one of the most densely populated countries in the world. Sometimes called Holland, its people are known as the Dutch.

Netherlands means "lowlands." Nearly half of this small, flat country lies below sea level. Without defenses against the sea, high tides would flood much of the country twice a day. The Dutch build dikes, or banks of soil, to control and confine the sea. Then they drain and pump the wetlands dry. Once run by windmills, pumps are now driven by steam or electricity. These drained lands, called **polders,** have rich farming soil. The Dutch build factories, airports, and even towns on them. The Delta Plan Project, completed in 1986, consists of huge barriers that keep the North Sea from overflowing the countryside during storms.

High technology makes small farms so productive that the Dutch can export cheese, vegetables, and flowers. The Netherlands ranks third in the world—after the United States and France—in the value of its agricultural exports. Because machines make farming more productive, most people work in service industries, manufacturing, and trade.

▲ A tulip field in the Netherlands

Social Studies Online

Web Activity Visit *The World and Its People* Web site at twip.glencoe.com and click on **Chapter 12— Student Web Activities** to learn more about the Delta Plan Project.

About 90 percent of the Dutch live in cities and towns. **Amsterdam** is the capital and largest city. Living in a densely populated country, the Dutch make good use of their space. Houses are narrow but tall, and apartments are often built on canals and over highways. Some of Amsterdam's most famous people are the painters Rembrandt van Rijn and Vincent van Gogh. You may have read *The Diary of Anne Frank.* This Dutch teenager's autobiography tells how she and her family tried to hide from the German Nazis during World War II.

About two-thirds of the Dutch people are Christian. A small number of immigrants are Muslims. The people of the Netherlands speak Dutch, but most also speak English.

Luxembourg   Southeast of Belgium lies Luxembourg, one of Europe's smallest countries. The entire country is only about 55 miles (89 km) long and about 35 miles (56 km) wide.

Despite its size, Luxembourg is prosperous. Many **multinational companies,** or firms that do business in several countries, have their headquarters here. It is home to the second-largest steel-producing company in Europe and is a major banking center as well.

Why is Luxembourg so attractive to foreign companies? First, the country is centrally located. Second, most people in this tiny land are **multilingual,** or able to speak several languages. They speak Luxembourgian, a blend of old German and French; French, the official language of the law; and German, used in most newspapers.

✓ Reading Check **What industries are important in Luxembourg?**

FCAT PRACTICE   You can prepare for the FCAT-assessed standards by completing the correlated item(s) below.

Section 2 Assessment

Defining Terms

1. Define navigable, polder, multinational company, multilingual.

Recalling Facts

2. Economics Name five of France's agricultural products.

3. Culture What are the two major cultures and languages of Belgium?

4. Human/Environment Interaction How do the Dutch protect their land from the sea?

Critical Thinking

5. Drawing Conclusions France is the second-largest food exporter in the world. Why is that remarkable? **FCAT LA.A.2.3.1**

6. Analyzing Information Why do foreign companies come to Luxembourg?
FCAT LA.E.2.2.1

Graphic Organizer

7. Organizing Information Create a diagram like this one. In the center circle, list three characteristics that are shared by these countries.
FCAT LA.A.1.3.2

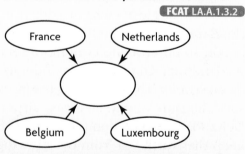

France → Netherlands → ← Belgium ← Luxembourg

Applying Social Studies Skills

8. Analyzing Maps Turn to the political map on page 341. Which country borders France, Belgium, the Netherlands, and Luxembourg?

Social Studies Skill

FCAT PRACTICE Completing the correlated items below will help you prepare for the **FCAT Mathematics** test.

Reading a Vegetation Map

Vegetation maps show the kinds of plants that naturally grow in a given area. Climate largely determines the vegetation of an area. For example, evergreen trees with cones and needle-shaped leaves (also called conifers) such as firs and spruces grow in cool climates. In the year-round warmth of the Tropics, evergreens with broad leaves, such as palm trees and rubber trees, can grow. Between these two extremes, deciduous trees are common. Deciduous trees have broad leaves, but they shed them in autumn. In dry or Mediterranean climates, grasses and shrubs are found because there is not enough water to support tree growth. Highland climates may have alpine vegetation—small shrubs and wildflowers. Extremely cold or dry climates may have little or no vegetation.

NATIONAL GEOGRAPHIC

France: Vegetation

Natural Vegetation
- Deciduous forest
- Coniferous forest
- Mixed forest (coniferous and deciduous)
- Mediterranean vegetation
- Alpine vegetation

0 mi. 200
0 km 200
Lambert Azimuthal Equal-Area projection

Learning the Skill

To read a vegetation map, follow these steps:

- Read the title of the map.
- Study the map key.
- Find examples of each vegetation zone on the map.
- Look at other aspects of the area's geography, such as rivers, oceans, and landforms to explain the vegetation patterns.

Practicing the Skill

Look at the map above to answer the following questions.

1. What vegetation covers most of France?
2. What type of vegetation is found along France's Mediterranean coast?
3. From the map, what conclusions can you draw about the amount of rain the regions of France receive? **FCAT MA.B.1.3.4**

Applying the Skill

Find a vegetation map of your state. What types of vegetation are common in your part of the country? **FCAT MA.B.1.3.4**

Germany and the Alpine Countries

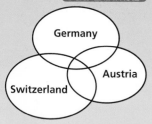
NATIONAL GEOGRAPHIC Exploring Our World

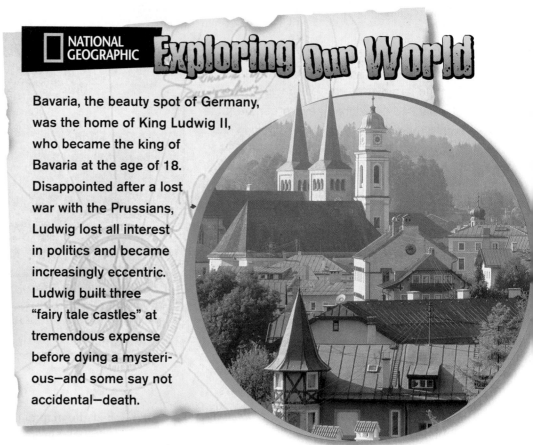

Bavaria, the beauty spot of Germany, was the home of King Ludwig II, who became the king of Bavaria at the age of 18. Disappointed after a lost war with the Prussians, Ludwig lost all interest in politics and became increasingly eccentric. Ludwig built three "fairy tale castles" at tremendous expense before dying a mysterious—and some say not accidental—death.

The people of **Germany** and the Alpine countries—**Switzerland, Austria,** and **Liechtenstein**—are adjusting to the changes sweeping Europe since the fall of communism. Fortunately, these countries have strong market economies, so their people enjoy high standards of living.

Germany

About the size of Montana, Germany lies in the heart of Europe. The North European Plain forms the northern landscape. The Alps rise in the southern German state of **Bavaria.** The lower slopes of these mountains—a favorite destination for skiers—are covered with forests.

One of Europe's most important waterways originates in the Alps. The **Danube River** winds eastward across southern Germany. Rivers are also important in northern Germany, where they are used to transport raw materials and manufactured goods. The **Rhine River,** in the west, forms part of the border with France.

Because of the rivers and fertile land, Germany's northern plain has many cities and towns. **Berlin,** the capital, is the major center of the northeast. To the west lies **Hamburg,** Germany's largest port city, located on the Elbe River.

An Economic and Industrial Power   Germany is a global economic power and a leader in the European Union. An area in western Germany called the Ruhr ranks as one of the world's most important industrial centers. The Ruhr developed around rich deposits of coal and iron ore. Europe's leaders have fought for control of this productive area. Factories here produce high-quality steel, ships, cars, machinery, chemicals, and electrical equipment.

The growth of factories, service industries, and high technology in the last decade has used up the supply of workers. Thus, a growing number of immigrant workers have come from Turkey, Italy, Greece, and the former Yugoslav republics. Sometimes they are the targets of racist attacks. When the economy takes a downturn and jobs are scarce, native-born people sometimes resent foreign laborers.

Germany imports about one-third of its food, although it is a leading producer of beer, wine, and cheese. Farmers raise livestock and grow grains, vegetables, and fruits. Superhighways called autobahns, along with railroads, rivers, and canals, link Germany's cities.

Lying just north of the Alps, Germany's Black Forest is famous for its beautiful scenery and for its wood products. The forest is not really black, but in places the trees grow so close together that it appears this way. The Black Forest has suffered severe damage from acid rain. Much of the pollution comes from industries in other countries. The Germans have to work together with other Europeans to find a solution to this acid rain problem.

Germany's Government   Like the United States, Germany is a federal republic in which a national government and state governments share powers. An elected president serves as Germany's head of state, but he or she carries out only ceremonial duties. The country's chancellor, chosen by one of the two houses of parliament, is the real head of the government.

One of the challenges of the current government has been reunification—bringing together Germany's two parts under one government. Remember that Germany was divided into East and West Germany after World War II. Workers in East Germany had less experience and training in modern technology than workers in West Germany. After reunification, many old and inefficient factories in the east could not compete with the more advanced industries in the west and were forced to close.

The Germans   Most of Germany's 82.6 million people trace their ancestry to groups who settled in Europe from about the A.D. 100s to 400s. The people speak German, a language that is related to English.

In Chapter 10, you learned that a German priest named Martin Luther began a new form of Christianity known as Protestantism.

▲ A cuckoo clock from the Black Forest region of Germany

NATIONAL GEOGRAPHIC On Location

Swiss Chocolate

Switzerland's factories produce some of the best chocolate in the world.

Economics What other products are made in Switzerland?

Today Protestants and Catholics are fairly evenly represented in Germany. Germans have made important contributions to music and culture. Johann Sebastian Bach and Ludwig van Beethoven composed some of the world's greatest classical music. **Munich** (MYOO•nihk), the largest city in southern Germany, is known for its theaters, museums, and concert halls. Berlin has also emerged as a cultural center.

✓ Reading Check What links Germany's cities?

The Alpine Countries

The **Alps** form most of the landscape in Switzerland, Austria, and Liechtenstein. That is why they are called the Alpine countries. Liechtenstein is a tiny country—only 60 square miles (155 sq. km)—sandwiched between Switzerland and Austria. The rugged Swiss Alps prevent easy travel between northern and southern Europe. For centuries, landlocked Switzerland guarded the few routes that cut through this barrier.

Switzerland The Swiss have enjoyed a stable democratic government for more than 700 years. Because of its location in the center of Europe, Switzerland has practiced neutrality—refusing to take sides in disagreements and wars between countries. As a result of this peaceful history, the Swiss city of **Geneva** is today the center of many international organizations. Switzerland's policy of neutrality is likely to be tested in the years ahead. It is building closer ties to the European Union and has joined the United Nations.

The Alps in Switzerland are the continental divide of central Europe. A continental divide is a high place from which rivers flow in different directions. Several rivers, including the **Rhine** and the **Rhône,** begin in the Swiss Alps. Dams built on Switzerland's rivers produce great amounts of hydroelectric power. Most of Switzerland's industries and its richest farmlands are found on a high plateau between two mountain ranges. **Bern,** Switzerland's capital, and **Zurich,** its largest city, are also located on this plateau.

Although it has few natural resources, Switzerland is a thriving industrial nation. Using imported materials, Swiss workers make high-quality goods such as electronic equipment, clocks, and watches. They also produce chemicals and gourmet foods such as chocolate and cheese. Tourism is an important industry, as are banking and insurance. Zurich and Geneva are important centers of international finance.

Given its geographic location, Switzerland has many different ethnic groups and religions. Did you know that the country has four national

352 CHAPTER 12

languages? They are German, French, Italian, and Romansch. Most Swiss speak German, and many speak more than one language.

Austria   Austria is a landlocked country located south of Germany. The Alps cover three-fourths of Austria. In fact, Austria is one of the most mountainous countries in the world. Have you ever seen the movie *The Sound of Music*? It was set in Austria's spectacular mountains. The country's climate is similar to Switzerland's. In winter, lowland areas receive rain, and mountainous regions have snow. Summers are cooler in Austria than they are in Switzerland.

Austria's economy is strong and varied. Its rivers generate hydroelectric power, and the mountains provide valuable timber. Millions of tourists come to enjoy hiking and skiing. Factories produce machinery, chemicals, metals, and vehicles. Farmers raise dairy cattle and other livestock, sugar beets, grains, potatoes, and fruits.

Most of Austria's 8.2 million people live in cities and towns and work in manufacturing or service jobs. The majority of people speak German. About 80 percent of the people are Roman Catholic.

Vienna, on the Danube River, is the capital and largest city. It has a rich history as a center of culture and learning. Some of the world's greatest composers, including Mozart, Schubert, and Haydn, lived or performed in Vienna. The city's concert halls, historic palaces and churches, and grand architecture continue to draw musicians today.

▲ Young people dance in one of Vienna's many ballrooms.

√ Reading Check   **What economic benefits do Austria's mountains provide?**

FCAT PRACTICE   You can prepare for the FCAT-assessed standards by completing the correlated item(s) below.

Section 3 Assessment

Defining Terms
1. **Define** autobahn, federal republic, reunification, neutrality, continental divide.

Recalling Facts
2. **Human/Environment Interaction** What has damaged the Black Forest? **FCAT SC.D.2.3.2**
3. **Culture** Name Switzerland's four languages.
4. **Economics** What types of jobs do most Austrians have?

Critical Thinking
5. **Understanding Cause and Effect** What problems have emerged as a result of German reunification? **FCAT LA.A.2.3.1**
6. **Analyzing Information** Why has Switzerland maintained a policy of neutrality?

Graphic Organizer
7. **Organizing Information** Create a diagram like the one below. On the lines list two facts about Austria's physical features, two facts about Austria's people, and four facts about Austria's economy. **FCAT LA.A.1.3.2**

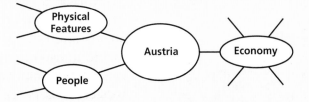

Applying Social Studies Skills

8. **Analyzing Maps** Look at the political map on page 341. The city of Berlin, Germany, is located at what degree of latitude?

The Nordic Nations

NATIONAL GEOGRAPHIC Exploring Our World

Like their Viking ancestors, Scandinavians today have learned to adapt to their cold climates. Here, a footbridge is almost buried in snow, and a hardy Swede seeking adventure explores on his snowmobile. A thousand years ago, a Viking named Leif Eriksson also sought adventure. He became possibly the first European to explore North America's coast.

The northernmost part of Europe—also known as Scandinavia or the Nordic countries—is made up of five nations: **Norway, Sweden, Finland, Denmark,** and **Iceland.** Scandinavians have standards of living that are among the world's highest.

Norway

Norway's far northern location results in a mostly cold climate. About one-third of Norway lies north of the Arctic Circle. This rugged area is often called Land of the Midnight Sun. Here the sun never sets in the midsummer months. In the midwinter months, the sun never rises. A mild climate, however, is found along Norway's southern and western coasts. This is due to warm winds from the North Atlantic Current. Most of Norway's 4.6 million people live near these coasts.

Norway's long, jagged coastline on the Atlantic Ocean includes many **fjords** (fee•AWRDS), or steep-sided valleys that are inlets of the sea. Thousands of years ago, glaciers carved these deep valleys that became flooded when the glacial ice melted. Today the fjords provide sheltered harbors and beautiful scenery that is popular with tourists.

Norway is a wealthy country, partly because of oil and natural gas pumped from beneath the North Sea. It is one of the world's largest oil exporters. The seas themselves provide an important export—fish. Warm ocean currents keep most of Norway's harbors ice-free all year—a great plus for the country's commercial and cruise ships.

Norway is a parliamentary democracy. It has a monarchy but is governed by an elected prime minister. In 1994 Norway voted not to join the European Union (EU) so that it could keep control of its own economy. EU membership is still hotly debated, however.

The people of Norway greatly value their cultural traditions. Elaborate folk dress is often seen at weddings and village festivals. Norwegians are a very modern people, though. Three-fourths of the population live in urban centers like the capital, **Oslo.** About half of the Norwegians own computers. For recreation, they enjoy skiing and riding snowmobiles.

✓ Reading Check **What type of government does Norway have?**

Sweden

Like Norway, Sweden is a wealthy, industrial country. Its prosperity comes from abundant natural resources, including iron ore deposits and extensive pine forests. Exports include machinery, motor vehicles, paper products, wood, and electronic products. Only about 8 percent of Sweden's land can be used for farming. Swedish farmers have developed efficient ways to grow crops, and their farms supply most of the nation's food.

Sweden's wealth enabled it to become a welfare state—a country that uses high rates of taxation to provide services to people who are sick, needy, jobless, or retired. Sweden is a constitutional monarchy and a member of the European Union.

Norway's Economy

A shopper goes from boat to boat looking for bargains in Bergen, Norway's water market (below left). Europe's richest oil and natural gas fields are found in the North Sea (below right).

Human/Environment Interaction What keeps Norway's harbors ice-free all year?

NATIONAL GEOGRAPHIC On Location

Most of Sweden's 9 million people live in cities in the southern lowlands. **Stockholm** is the country's capital and largest city. Sweden's high standard of living has attracted more than 1 million immigrants from nearby Norway and Denmark and distant Turkey and Vietnam.

✓Reading Check What resources have helped make Sweden wealthy?

Finland

Finland holds some of the largest unspoiled wilderness in Europe. Most of Finland's wealth comes from its huge forests of spruce, pine, and birch. Paper and wood products are important exports. In recent years, **heavy industry**—or industry that produces manufactured goods such as machinery—has driven Finland's economy. The Finns are also leaders in the electronic communications industry. In 1995 Finland joined the European Union.

The ancestors of the Finns settled in the region thousands of years ago, probably coming from what is now Siberia in Russia. As a result, Finnish language and culture differ from those of other Nordic countries.

Most of Finland's 5.2 million people live in towns and cities on the southern coast. **Helsinki,** the capital, has more than 1 million people, but the city has still kept a small-town atmosphere. For example, there are no high-rise buildings. With snow on the ground for about half of the year, Finns enjoy cross-country skiing. They also like to relax in **saunas,** or wooden rooms heated by water sizzling on hot stones.

✓Reading Check Where did the ancestors of the Finns come from?

Denmark and Iceland

Denmark and Iceland are countries whose histories are closely tied to the sea. For centuries, Iceland was ruled by Denmark so Danish is still widely spoken and understood in Iceland.

Most of Denmark is made up of a peninsula known as Jutland. Denmark also includes nearly 500 islands, only about 100 of which have people living on them. Denmark also rules the large island of Greenland. Throughout history, Denmark's location has made it a link for people and goods between the Nordic countries and the rest of Europe. Ferries and bridges connect Jutland and the islands. A bridge and tunnel now join Denmark's Zealand Island to Sweden.

Denmark has some of the richest farmland in northern Europe. Danish farm products include butter, cheese, bacon, and ham. Royal Copenhagen porcelain, a famous Danish export, is among the finest in the world. The Danes also invented and export the world-famous LEGO® toy building blocks.

The 5.4 million Danes enjoy a high standard of living. Instead of noisy, traditional festivals, many Danes prefer quiet evenings at home or spending time with friends at small cafés. The country has a parliamentary democracy, with a king or queen as head of state. Elected officials run the government. Denmark joined the European Union in 1993. **Copenhagen,** Denmark's capital, is the largest of the Nordic cities.

Cozy Ballet?

Helle Oelkers (far right) is a member of one of Europe's finest ballet companies—the Royal Danish Ballet. Helle likes to think that her performance encourages audience members to feel *hygge. Hygge* means feeling cozy and snug. She explains, "The greatest compliment a Dane can give is to thank someone for a cozy evening."

In Copenhagen's harbor is a famous attraction: a statue of the Little Mermaid. She is a character from a story by the Danish author Hans Christian Andersen. Andersen, who lived and wrote during the 1800s, is one of Denmark's most famous writers.

Iceland   Iceland, an island in the North Atlantic, is a land of glaciers and **geysers**—springs that shoot hot water and steam into the air. The people of Iceland make the most of this unusual environment. They use **geothermal energy,** or heat produced by natural underground sources, to heat most of their homes, buildings, and swimming pools.

What makes such natural wonders possible? Sitting on top of a fault line, Iceland is at the mercy of constant volcanic activity. Every few years, one of the country's 200 volcanoes erupts. The volcanoes heat hot springs that appear across the length of Iceland.

Iceland's economy depends heavily on fishing. Fish exports provide the money to buy food and consumer goods from other countries. Iceland is concerned that overfishing will reduce the amount of fish available. To reduce its dependence on the fishing industry, Iceland has introduced new manufacturing and service industries.

More than 90 percent of the nearly 300,000 Icelanders live in urban areas. More than half the people live in the capital city of **Reykjavík** (RAY•kyah•VEEK). The people have a passion for books, magazines, and newspapers. In fact, the literacy rate in Iceland is 100 percent.

▲ The Little Mermaid statue in Copenhagen

✓ Reading Check   How do the people of Iceland take advantage of the country's geysers?

FCAT PRACTICE   You can prepare for the FCAT-assessed standards by completing the correlated item(s) below.

Section 4 Assessment

Defining Terms
1. **Define** fjord, welfare state, heavy industry, sauna, geyser, geothermal energy.

Recalling Facts
2. **Location** Name the five Nordic countries.
3. **Economics** What resource produces most of Norway's wealth?
4. **History** Why do some Icelanders speak Danish? **FCAT LA.E.2.2.1**

Critical Thinking
5. **Analyzing Information** How has Denmark's location affected its relationship with the rest of Europe? **FCAT LA.E.2.2.1**
6. **Understanding Cause and Effect** Why is Finnish culture different from the rest of the Nordic countries? **FCAT LA.A.2.3.1**

Graphic Organizer
7. **Organizing Information** Create a diagram like the one below. Explain three effects on Iceland that result because of its location on a fault line. **FCAT LA.A.1.3.2**

| Fault | → → → | Effects on Iceland |

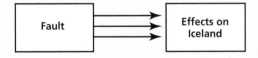

Applying Social Studies Skills

8. **Analyzing Maps** Study the political map on page 341. Which Nordic capital lies the farthest north? Which Nordic capital lies the farthest south?

Southern Europe

Guide to Reading

Main Idea

The sea has played an important role in southern European countries.

Terms to Know

- dry farming
- sirocco
- coalition government

Reading Strategy

Create a chart like this one for each of the following countries: Spain, Portugal, Italy, and Greece. Fill in at least one key fact about each country for each category listed.

FCAT LA.A.1.3.2

Country	
Land	
Economy	
Government	
People	

The following are the major Sunshine State Standards covered in this section.

SS.B.2.3.5:
Understands the geographical factors that affect the cohesiveness and integration of countries

SS.A.3.3.5:
Understands the differences between institutions of Eastern and Western civilizations (e.g., differences in governments, social traditions and customs, economic systems and religious institutions)

NATIONAL GEOGRAPHIC Exploring Our World

The "running of the bulls" is an annual and controversial event in Pamplona, a city in northern Spain. Although animal rights groups object to it, each morning during the weeklong Festival of San Fermín, a half dozen bulls are released to run along the city's narrow streets. People risk their lives by running ahead of the bulls. Their goal is to stay in the race as long as possible.

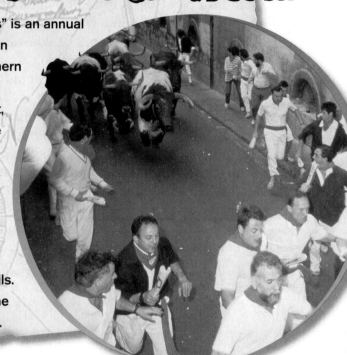

Spain, **Portugal, Italy,** and **Greece**—along with several tiny countries—make up southern Europe. A rich cultural heritage has produced many of the world's greatest writers, artists, and musicians. As you read in Chapter 10, it was the people of ancient Greece and Rome who played an especially important role in the development of Western civilization.

The Iberian Peninsula

Spain and its neighbors, Portugal and **Andorra,** make up the **Iberian Peninsula.** Tiny Andorra, with only 174 square miles (451 sq. km), perches high in the **Pyrenees** mountain range near Spain's border with France.

Portugal and most of Spain have mild winters and hot summers. Much of the interior of the peninsula is a dry plateau. In many areas the reddish-yellow soil is poor, and the land is dry-farmed to grow crops such as wheat and vegetables. In **dry farming,** irrigation is not used. Instead, the land is left unplanted every few years so that it can store moisture.

Growing Economies   Spain and Portugal both belong to the European Union. The two countries were once slow in developing manufacturing. In recent years, however, they have worked hard to catch up economically with other European Union nations.

Spain is one of the world's leading producers of olive oil. Portuguese farmers grow potatoes, grains, fruits, olives, and grapes. Portugal is also the world's leading exporter of cork. The cork comes from the bark of certain oak trees, which grow well in central Portugal.

People travel to the Iberian Peninsula to enjoy the sunny climate, beautiful beaches, and ancient castles and cathedrals. Andorra draws millions of tourists each year to its duty-free shops. Spain and Portugal also depend on the tourist industry.

Manufacturing industries benefit both countries' economies as well. Spanish workers mine rich deposits of iron ore and make processed foods, clothing, footwear, steel, and automobiles.

Democratic Governments   Spain and Portugal are modern democracies. Spain is a constitutional monarchy, in which a king or queen is head of state, but elected officials run the government. Portugal is a parliamentary republic, with a president as head of state. A prime minister, chosen by the legislature, is the head of government. Andorra is a parliamentary democracy that is a semi-independent principality— it is governed by both Spain and France.

Spanish and Portuguese Cultures   Most people in Spain and Portugal are Roman Catholic. Despite similar histories, the people of Spain and Portugal have cultural differences. Portugal developed a unified culture based on the Portuguese language. Spain remained a "country of different countries." The Spanish people do not all speak the same language or even have a single culture.

The Basque people in the Pyrenees see themselves as completely separate from Spain. They speak Basque, a language unlike any other in the world. Having lived in Spain longer than any other group, many Basques want independence in order to preserve their way of life. Some Basque groups have used violence against the Spanish government.

Lisbon is Portugal's busy capital, but Portugal is mostly rural. In contrast, more than three-fourths of Spain's people live in cities and towns. **Madrid,** Spain's capital, has nearly 5 million people and ranks as one of Europe's leading cultural centers. Madrid faces the usual urban challenges of heavy traffic and air pollution. Fast-paced **Barcelona** is Spain's leading seaport and industrial center.

You find some centuries-old traditions even in the modern cities. For example, most Spanish families usually do not eat dinner until 9 or 10 o'clock at night. On special occasions, Spaniards enjoy *paella* (pah•AY•yuh), a traditional dish of shrimp, lobster, chicken, ham, and vegetables mixed with seasoned rice.

Rock and jazz music are popular with young Spaniards and Portuguese. The people of each region have their own traditional songs, dances, and instruments as well. Spanish musicians often

Islamic Art

The Muslims brought scientific knowledge to Spain. They introduced methods of irrigation and new crops. They also brought literature, music, and art.

Islam discourages art that includes human forms. As a result, Muslim artists create complex patterns and elaborate designs. The tile below is an example of the beautiful mosaics seen today throughout the world.

Italy's Economy

The canals of Venice draw thousands of tourists (above). The city of Milan boasts a fashion industry with stylish models (below).

Economics How has Italy's economy changed in the past 50 years?

accompany singers and dancers on guitars, castanets, and tambourines. Spanish dances, such as the *bolero* and *flamenco,* and soulful Portuguese folk songs known as *fado* have spread throughout the world.

✓ Reading Check Portugal leads the world in what export?

Italy

The Italian peninsula sticks out from Europe into the center of the **Mediterranean Sea.** The peninsula looks like a boot about to kick a triangular football. The "football" is **Sicily,** an island that belongs to Italy. Two tiny countries—**San Marino** and **Vatican City**—lie within the Italian "boot."

The Alps tower over northern Italy, while the rumbling of volcanic mountains echoes through the southern part of the peninsula and the island of Sicily. Throughout history, southern Italy has experienced volcanic eruptions and earthquakes.

Most of Italy has a mild climate of sunny summers and rainy winters. In spring and summer, hot dry winds called siroccos blow across Italy from North Africa.

Italy's Economy In the past 50 years, Italy has changed from a mainly agricultural country into one of the world's leading industrial economies. Many products are manufactured by small, family-owned businesses rather than by large corporations. Italian businesses are known for creating new designs and methods for making products. Italy is a member of the European Union.

Most of the country's manufacturing takes place in northern Italy. Tourism is also important in northern and central Italy. Resorts in the Alps attract skiers. **Venice,** to the northeast, is built on 117 islands. You find no cars in this city, which is crisscrossed by canals and relies on boats for transportation. In central Italy lies **Rome,** Italy's capital and largest city. In Classical times, Rome was the seat of the Roman Empire. In Rome, you can still see ancient Roman ruins and magnificent Renaissance churches and palaces.

Southern Italy is poorer and less industrialized than northern and central Italy. Unemployment and poverty are common. Many southern Italians have moved to northern Italy or to other parts of Europe.

Italy's Government After World War II, Italy became a democratic republic. Yet democracy did not bring a stable government. Rivalry between the wealthy north and the poorer south has caused political tensions. In addition, many political parties exist, and no single party has been strong enough to gain control. Instead, Italy has seen many coalition governments, where two or more political parties work together to run the country.

Italy's People   About 70 percent of Italy's 57.2 million people live in towns and cities. More than 90 percent of Italians work in manufacturing and service industries. Most Italians—more than 95 percent—are Roman Catholic. Celebrating the Church's religious festivals is a widely shared part of Italian life. Vatican City, surrounded by Rome, is the headquarters of the Roman Catholic Church. The pope, who is the head of the Church, lives and works here. Vatican City has many art treasures as well as the world's largest church, St. Peter's Basilica.

The people of Italy speak Italian, which developed from Latin, the language of ancient Rome. Italian is closely related to French and Spanish. Pasta, made from flour and water, is the basic dish in Italy. Some pasta dishes are spaghetti, lasagna, and ravioli.

✓ Reading Check Why have coalition governments been necessary in Italy?

Greece

The Greek mainland sits on the southern tip of the **Balkan Peninsula,** which juts out from Europe into the Mediterranean Sea. Greece also includes 2,000 islands around the mainland. Like other Mediterranean areas, Greece is often shaken by earthquakes. Mountain ranges divide Greece into many separate regions. Historically, this has kept people in one region isolated from people in other regions.

Of the 2,000 Greek islands, only about 170 have people living on them. The largest Greek island, covering more than 3,000 square miles (7,770 sq. km), is **Crete.** Farther east in the Mediterranean is the island country of **Cyprus.** Once under Turkish and then British rule, Cyprus became independent in 1960. For centuries Greeks and Turks have lived on Cyprus, but fighting between the two groups has resulted in a divided country.

EXPLORING CULTURE

Architecture

For more than 800 years the Leaning Tower of Pisa in Italy has stood as a monument to construction mistakes. Begun in 1173, the tower began to tilt even before it was finished. Over time the tower moved even more, until by 1990, it leaned 15 feet (4.5 m) to the south. Fearing the tower would fall over, experts closed it. They added 800 tons (726 t) of lead weights to its base. They also removed 30 tons (27 t) of subsoil from underneath the north side of the tower in hopes that it would sink the opposite way. Visitors have again returned to the tower.

Looking Closer Why do you think experts fixed the tower's problem but still left it leaning?

▲ Greek folk dancers

Greece's Economy   Greece belongs to the European Union but has one of the least industrialized economies in Europe. Because of the poor, stony soil, most people living in the highlands must graze sheep and goats. Greece must import food, fuels, and many manufactured goods. Farmers cultivate sugar beets, grains, citrus fruits, and tobacco. The major crops of Greece are olives, used for olive oil, and grapes, used for wine.

No part of Greece is more than 85 miles (137 km) from the sea. Shipping is vital to the economy. Greece has one of the largest shipping fleets in the world, including oil tankers, cargo ships, fishing boats, and passenger vessels.

Tourism is another key industry. Each year millions of visitors come to Greece to visit historic sites, such as the Parthenon in the capital city of **Athens** and the temple of Apollo at Delphi. Others come to relax on beaches and to enjoy the beautiful island scenery.

The Greeks Today   Greece is a parliamentary republic. About 60 percent of Greece's 11 million people live in urban areas. The Greeks today have much in common with their ancestors. They debate political issues with great enthusiasm, and they value the art of storytelling.

More than 95 percent of Greeks are Greek Orthodox Christians. Religion influences much of Greek life, especially in rural areas. Easter is the most important Greek holiday. Traditional holiday foods include lamb, fish, and feta cheese—made from sheep's or goat's milk.

✓ Reading Check   What are two key industries in Greece?

FCAT PRACTICE   You can prepare for the FCAT-assessed standards by completing the correlated item(s) below.

Section 5 Assessment

Defining Terms
1. **Define** dry farming, sirocco, coalition government.

Recalling Facts
2. **Location** What three countries are located on the Iberian Peninsula?
3. **Economics** Which is the more prosperous region in Italy—north or south?
4. **Culture** List four things tourists see in Italy.

Critical Thinking
5. **Analyzing Information** Why is it expected that Greece's economy would be dependent upon the sea?   FCAT LA.A.2.3.1
6. **Understanding Cause and Effect** Why do the Basque people feel separate from the rest of Spain?   FCAT LA.E.2.2.1

Graphic Organizer
7. **Organizing Information** Draw a diagram like this one. Choose two countries from this section and compare them. Write statements that are true of both countries where the ovals overlap. List information unique to each country in the outer parts of the ovals.   FCAT LA.A.1.3.2

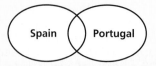

Spain   Portugal

Applying Social Studies Skills

8. **Analyzing Maps** Turn to the political map on page 341. What body of water touches most of the southern countries of Europe?

12 Reading Review

Section 1 | The British Isles

Terms to Know

moor   peat
parliamentary   bog
   democracy
constitutional
   monarchy

Main Idea

The United Kingdom and Ireland are small in size, but their people have had a great impact on the rest of the world.

✓ Geography   Ireland is called the Emerald Isle because of its landscape.

✓ Economics   The United Kingdom is a major industrial and trading country.

✓ History   After years of conflict, a peace plan was adopted in Northern Ireland.

Section 2 | France and the Benelux Countries

Terms to Know

navigable
polder
multinational
   company
multilingual

Main Idea

France and the Benelux countries are important cultural, agricultural, and manufacturing centers of Europe.

✓ Culture   Paris is a world center of art, learning, and culture.

✓ Location   Belgium's location has made it an international center for trade.

✓ Economics   Luxembourg is home to many multinational companies.

Section 3 | Germany and the Alpine Countries

Terms to Know

autobahn
federal republic
reunification
neutrality
continental divide

Main Idea

Germany, Switzerland, and Austria are known for their mountain scenery and prosperous economies.

✓ Economics   The German economy is very strong.

✓ Economics   Switzerland produces high-quality manufactured goods.

✓ Economics   Austria's economy makes use of the mountainous terrain.

Section 4 | The Nordic Nations

Terms to Know

fjord
welfare state
heavy industry
sauna
geyser
geothermal energy

Main Idea

The Nordic countries have developed diverse economies, and their people enjoy a high standard of living.

✓ Region   The Nordic countries include Norway, Sweden, Finland, Denmark, and Iceland.

✓ Culture   Finnish culture differs from other Nordic countries.

✓ Economics   Sweden's prosperity comes from forests and iron ore.

Section 5 | Southern Europe

Terms to Know

dry farming
sirocco
coalition government

Main Idea

The sea has played an important role in southern European countries.

✓ Location   Spain, Portugal, and Andorra occupy the Iberian Peninsula.

✓ Economics   Italy is one of the world's leading industrial economies.

✓ Place   Greece consists of a mountainous mainland and 2,000 islands.

chapter 12

Assessment and Activities

Using Key Terms

Match the terms in Part A with their definitions in Part B.

A.

1. multilingual
2. heavy industry
3. coalition government
4. neutrality
5. dry farming
6. welfare state
7. polder
8. autobahn
9. constitutional monarchy
10. multinational company

B.

a. land reclaimed from the sea
b. leaving land unplanted to store moisture
c. refusing to take sides
d. country that uses tax money to help people in need
e. company that has offices in several countries
f. government that has a king or queen but is run by elected officials
g. superhighway
h. able to speak several languages
i. two or more political parties working together to run a country
j. production of industrial goods

Reviewing the Main Ideas

Section 1 The British Isles

11. **Region** What regions make up the United Kingdom?
12. **Culture** Name the two official languages of the Republic of Ireland.

Section 2 France and the Benelux Countries

13. **Government** What is the Fifth Republic?
14. **Location** Why do the Dutch have to protect their land from the sea? **FCAT SC.D.2.3.2**

Section 3 Germany and the Alpine Countries

15. **Government** What challenges does the reunification of Germany bring? **FCAT LA.E.2.2.1**
16. **Location** Why is Geneva the center of many international organizations? **FCAT LA.E.2.2.1**

Section 4 The Nordic Nations

17. **Economics** What makes Norway wealthy?
18. **Culture** What is Iceland's literacy rate?

Section 5 Southern Europe

19. **Culture** Why do the Basque people want independence from Spain?
20. **Economics** How does the rocky landscape influence Greece's economy? **FCAT LA.E.2.2.1**

Western Europe

Place Location Activity

On a separate sheet of paper, match the letters on the map with the numbered places listed below.

1. Ireland
2. North Sea
3. Belgium
4. Austria
5. Switzerland
6. Spain
7. Norway
8. Portugal
9. Sweden
10. Iceland

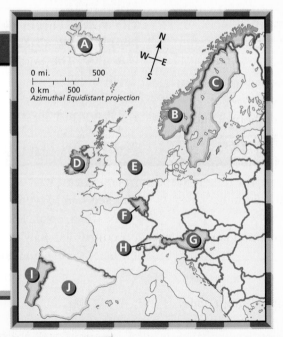

0 mi. 500
0 km 500
Azimuthal Equidistant projection

Critical Thinking

21. **Analyzing Information** Why is the name Land of Fire and Ice appropriate for Iceland?

22. **Organizing Information** Create an outline for each country in Section 5. Use the following guide as your base outline. **FCAT LA.A.1.3.2**
    - **I.** Name of Country
        - **A.** Land
        - **B.** Economy
        - **C.** People

Comparing Regions Activity

23. **Culture** Visit a newsstand or library to find a magazine published for European teens. Does it have the same look and feel as a magazine you read? What common features or advertisements do you see?
    FCAT LA.A.1.3.2

Mental Mapping Activity

24. **Focusing on the Region** Create a simple outline map of western Europe, and then label the following:

    - United Kingdom
    - France
    - Germany
    - Sweden
    - Italy
    - Spain
    - Switzerland
    - Iceland

Technology Skills Activity

25. **Using a Spreadsheet** List the names of the western European countries in a spreadsheet, beginning with cell A2 and continuing down the column. Find each country's population and record the figures in column B. In column C list each country's area in square miles. Title column D "Population Density," then divide column B by column C to find the population density. Print and share your spreadsheet with the class.

Standardized Test Practice

Directions: Study the graph below, and then answer the question that follows.

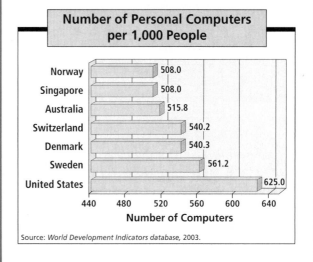

Number of Personal Computers per 1,000 People

Country	Number of Computers
Norway	508.0
Singapore	508.0
Australia	515.8
Switzerland	540.2
Denmark	540.3
Sweden	561.2
United States	625.0

Source: *World Development Indicators database*, 2003.

1. **Which Nordic country has the highest number of personal computers per 1,000 people?** **FCAT MA.E.3.3.1**
    - **A** United States
    - **B** Switzerland
    - **C** Denmark
    - **D** Sweden

Test-Taking Tip: Use the information on the graph to help you answer this question. Look carefully at the information on the bottom and the side of a bar graph to understand what the bars represent. The important word in the question is *Nordic*. Other countries may have more personal computers, but which Nordic country listed on the graph has the most personal computers per 1,000 people?

The New Eastern Europe

The World and Its People
NATIONAL GEOGRAPHIC

To learn more about the people and places of eastern Europe, view *The World and Its People* **Chapter 13** video.

Social Studies Online

Chapter Overview Visit *The World and Its People* Web site at <u>twip.glencoe.com</u> and click on **Chapter 13—Chapter Overviews** to preview information about eastern Europe.

The activity below will help you prepare for the **FCAT Reading** test.

Compare-Contrast Make the following foldable to help you compare and contrast what you learn about western Europe and eastern Europe.

FCAT LA.A.1.3.2

Step 1 Fold a sheet of paper in half from side to side.

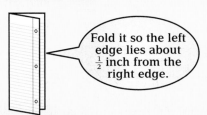

Fold it so the left edge lies about $\frac{1}{2}$ inch from the right edge.

Step 2 Turn the paper and fold it into thirds.

Step 3 Unfold and cut the top layer only along both folds.

This will make three tabs.

Step 4 Label as shown.

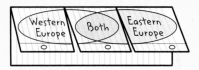

Western Europe — Both — Eastern Europe

Reading and Writing Before you read Chapter 13, record what you learned about western Europe in Chapter 12 under the "Western Europe" tab of your foldable. As you read Chapter 13, write what you learn about eastern Europe under the correct tab. Then list ways these two regions are similar under the middle tab.

FCAT LA.A.1.3.2

Why It Matters

From Communism to Democracy

Since the fall of communism, the countries of eastern Europe have continued to change. The formation of new democratic governments has led to closer ties with other free nations in Europe. The economic influence of eastern Europe grows as the region becomes a new market for western goods. The changes are not occurring smoothly, however, and many challenges have to be met.

◄ **Starometske Namesti and Tyn Church in Prague, Czech Republic**

Poland and the Baltic Republics

NATIONAL GEOGRAPHIC Exploring Our World

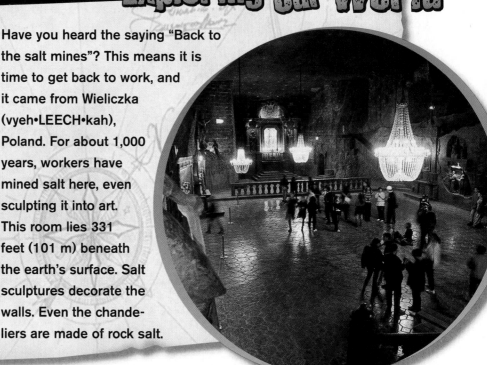

Have you heard the saying "Back to the salt mines"? This means it is time to get back to work, and it came from Wieliczka (vyeh•LEECH•kah), Poland. For about 1,000 years, workers have mined salt here, even sculpting it into art. This room lies 331 feet (101 m) beneath the earth's surface. Salt sculptures decorate the walls. Even the chandeliers are made of rock salt.

Along the southern shores of the Baltic Sea lie **Poland** and the Baltic republics of **Estonia, Latvia,** and **Lithuania.** Although they are neighboring countries, they have distinct histories and cultures.

Poland

Poland is one of the largest countries in Europe. About the size of New Mexico, Poland lies on the huge North European Plain. This plain stretches from France to Russia. Rivers such as the Vistula (VIHSH•chuh•luh) and the Oder flow through Poland's flat lowlands. Many Polish people live in this fertile central region.

North toward the Baltic Sea, you find lakes, forests, and **bogs,** or low swampy lands. In the south, the **Carpathian** (kahr•PAY•thee•uhn) **Mountains** stretch along Poland's border with Slovakia. Poland's location and lack of mountains on its eastern and western borders have made the country an easy target for invading armies.

Warm winds blowing across Europe from the Atlantic Ocean bring year-round mild weather to western Poland. Cooler weather can be found in eastern Poland. It has cool summers and cold winters.

A Changing Economy   In the past, Poland was a communist state, or a country in which the government has strong control over the economy and society. The Polish government decided what, how, and for whom goods would be produced. In 1989 Poland started moving toward a market economy. The change has been difficult. In their communist state, workers had jobs for life, even if business was slow. Today businesses lay off workers if they cannot afford to keep a large staff. Poland is adjusting to meet economic challenges. Many people have started businesses, and Poles no longer suffer from shortages of goods.

Poland is dotted with thousands of small farms, on which about 25 percent of Poles work. Polish farmers grow more potatoes and rye than farmers in any other European country. Other crops include wheat,

NATIONAL GEOGRAPHIC

Eastern Europe: Political

Applying Map Skills

1. What is the capital of Poland?

2. Which eastern European countries border the Adriatic Sea?

Find NGS online map resources @ www.nationalgeographic.com/maps

⊛ National capital
• Major city

Azimuthal Equidistant projection

Poland's Economy

Coal mining is one of Poland's most important industries and is concentrated near the Czech Republic.

Economics What are some products manufactured in Poland?

sugar beets, fruits, and vegetables. Some farmers raise cattle, pigs, and chickens.

Most mining and manufacturing take place in central and southern Poland. Coal mining is one of Poland's major industries. The mountains also hold copper, zinc, and lead. Petroleum and natural gas are found here as well. The country produces hydroelectric power, or electric power produced by moving water.

Polish factories process foods and make machinery, transportation equipment, and chemicals. The city of **Gdańsk** (guh•DAHNSK), a Baltic seaport, is an important shipbuilding center. Under Communist rule, Polish factories caused some of the worst water and air pollution in Europe. Since 1989 there has been a decline in heavy industry and the government is more concerned with the environment. Still, problems continue because Polish factories rely on burning coal. Factory smoke causes acid rain, or rain containing chemicals that pollute water, air, and land.

Struggle for Freedom Founded in the A.D. 900s, Poland was a powerful kingdom during the Middle Ages. By the 1800s, it had fallen victim to stronger neighbors—Germany, Russia, and Austria. In 1939 German troops overran western Poland, starting World War II. Poles suffered greatly during the war. **Warsaw,** the capital, was bombed to ashes. Some 6 million European Jews and 6 million others were murdered in brutal prison camps set up by the Germans in Poland and elsewhere. After the war, the Soviet Union swallowed up lands in eastern Poland. In exchange, the Poles gained western areas belonging to defeated Germany.

In 1947 a communist government came to power in Poland. Resisting its rule, workers and farmers in 1980 formed Solidarity, a labor group that struggled peacefully for democratic change. The communist government finally allowed free elections in 1989, and a new democratic government was formed. A year later, Solidarity leader Lech Walesa (LEHK vah•LEHN•suh) was elected Poland's first democratic president. Today Poland is a democratic republic, or government headed by elected leaders. Drawing closer to western Europe, Poland joined the European Union in 2004.

Daily Life About 38.6 million people live in Poland. Almost all are ethnic Poles who belong to a larger ethnic group called Slavs. They speak Polish, which is a Slavic language. Poland is more rural than nations in other parts of Europe. About one-third of the people live in the countryside. As Poland's economy changes, more people are moving to cities such as Warsaw and Kraków.

Poles feel a deep loyalty to their country. Religion unites Poles as well. Most are Roman Catholic, and religion has a strong influence on daily life. The Polish people were very proud in 1978 when Karol Wojtyla (voy•TEE•wah) was named **pope,** or head of the Roman Catholic Church. Taking the name John Paul II, he was the first Pole to become pope.

✓ Reading Check What two beliefs or attitudes unite the Polish people?

The Baltic Republics

The small Baltic republics of Estonia, Latvia, and Lithuania lie on the shores of the **Baltic Sea.** For much of their history, the Baltic republics were under Russian control. With the fall of the Soviet Union in 1991, Estonia, Latvia, and Lithuania became independent. All three countries still have large Russian minority populations. Most people in Estonia and Latvia are Protestants, while Roman Catholics make up the majority in Lithuania.

The Baltic republics are located on poor, swampy land. Even so, their well-developed economies are based mainly on dairy farming, beef production, fishing, and shipbuilding. In recent years, increased trade and industry have raised standards of living in this region.

✓ Reading Check Which two major religions are practiced in the Baltic republics?

▲ Fish caught in the nearby Baltic Sea are sold in Rīga's Central Market.

FCAT PRACTICE You can prepare for the FCAT-assessed standards by completing the correlated item(s) below.

Section 1 Assessment

Defining Terms
1. Define bog, communist state, acid rain, pope.

Recalling Facts
2. **Human/Environment Interaction** Why does pollution continue to be a problem in Poland?
3. **Economics** Why is Gdańsk important?
4. **Region** Which three countries are considered the Baltic republics?

Graphic Organizer
5. **Organizing Information** On a time line like this one, label five important events and their dates in Poland's history.

FCAT LA.A.1.3.2

Critical Thinking
6. **Understanding Cause and Effect** Which of Poland's physical features has made it an easy target for invading armies? Why? **FCAT LA.A.2.3.1**
7. **Making Comparisons** What is the difference in job security under a communist state and a free market economy? **FCAT LA.A.2.2.7**

Applying Social Studies Skills

8. **Analyzing Maps** Refer to the political map on page 369. The Vistula River empties into what body of water? Now turn to the population density map on page 384. What is the population density of the area surrounding Kraków?

Guide to Reading

Main Idea

Hungary, the Czech Republic, and Slovakia are changing to free market economies.

Terms to Know

- landlocked
- nomad
- spa
- privatize

Reading Strategy

Fill in a chart like the one below with facts about the past and present of Hungary, the Czech Republic, and Slovakia. **FCAT LA.A.1.3.2**

Country	Past	Present
Hungary		
Czech Republic		
Slovakia		

The following are the major Sunshine State Standards covered in this section.

SS.B.2.3.8:
Knows world patterns of resource distribution and utilization

SS.A.2.3.1:
Understands how language, ideas, and institutions of one culture can influence others (e.g., through trade, exploration, and immigration)

SS.A.3.3.2:
Understands the historical events that have shaped the development of cultures throughout the world

Section 2
Hungarians, Czechs, and Slovaks

NATIONAL GEOGRAPHIC
Exploring Our World

Prague, the capital of the Czech Republic, is often called "the city of a hundred spires" because of its many church steeples. You won't hear just religious music here, however. Musical contributions range from classical to punk. More recently, the Czech Republic has become a leading European center of jazz.

In the center of eastern Europe are **Hungary,** the **Czech Republic,** and **Slovakia.** All three countries became communist under Soviet control after World War II. In 1989 they all became independent democracies with free market economies.

Hungary—Land of the Magyars

Hungary, almost the size of Indiana, is landlocked, meaning that its land does not border a sea or an ocean. Hungary depends on the mighty **Danube River** for trade and transportation. Its vast waters flow 1,776 miles (2,858 km) before emptying into the Black Sea.

The Hungarian Plain runs through eastern Hungary. This vast lowland area has excellent soil for farming and grazing animals. The Danube River separates the plain from Transdanubia, a region in western Hungary. Rolling hills, forests, and lakes are found there. Many Hungarians vacation near Lake Balaton—one of Europe's largest lakes.

The Carpathian Mountains rise in northern Hungary. In this scenic area, you can wander through thick forests, find strange rock formations, and explore underground caves.

The Economy   Hungary's farmers grow corn, sugar beets, wheat, and potatoes in the country's rich soil. Grapes, used to make wine, are also grown here. Hungary's natural resources include coal, petroleum, and natural gas. Foods, beverages, and tobacco products are manufactured along with machines, chemicals, and metals. Service industries, such as financial services and tourism, also thrive.

The Hungarians   Magyars came to the Danube area from Central Asia about 1,000 years ago. They were **nomads,** or people who move from place to place, often with herds of animals. The Magyars were skilled horse riders who used the grassy plains to feed their animals. Eventually they set up a large kingdom and adopted Christianity.

Beginning in the 1500s, the Ottoman Turks and later the Austrians ruled most or all of Hungary. In 1867 Hungary and Austria became partners in a large empire. After being defeated in World War I, Hungary lost territory and became the landlocked nation it is today.

About 90 percent of Hungary's 10.1 million people are descended from the Magyars. Almost all speak the Hungarian language. About two-thirds are Roman Catholic, while another one-fourth is Protestant. **Budapest** (BOO•duh•PEHST), the capital and largest city, is called "the Paris of eastern Europe." It is actually two cities divided by the Danube River. On the western bank lies the old city of Buda, full of beautiful churches and palaces. Bridges link this older settlement to the newer city of Pest, which has factories and tall, modern buildings.

✓ Reading Check   What river is important to Hungary, and why?

NATIONAL GEOGRAPHIC On Location

Budapest, Hungary

Hungary's capital extends along both banks of the Danube River.

Place Which two physical regions does the Danube River separate?

Food

In Slovakia and the Czech Republic, lunch is the main meal of the day. It commonly includes roast pork; dumplings, potatoes, or rice covered with a thick sauce; and sauerkraut or another heavily cooked vegetable. Czech dumplings are not like American dumplings, however. They are made with either potatoes or stale bread rolls, mixed with flour and milk, and then boiled. The Slovak national dish is *bryndzové halušky*—sheep's cheese with pasta.

Looking Closer What would you consider the national dish of the United States?

The Czech Republic

The Czech Republic is also a landlocked country. Many areas are known for their natural beauty. In the mountains to the north and south, you can hike trails and visit spas, or health resorts with hot mineral springs. The Czechs enjoy a high standard of living compared to other eastern Europeans. Large fertile areas make the Czech Republic a major agricultural producer. Manufacturing forms the backbone of the country's economy, however. Factories make machinery, vehicles, metals, and textiles. Minerals include limestone, coal, and kaolin, a fine clay used for pottery.

Prague, the capital, is a center of service industries, tourism, and high-tech companies. Although manufacturing provides consumer products, many factories are old, inefficient, and harmful to the environment. The Czechs are trying to modernize their factories and move toward nuclear energy.

The Czechs Slavic groups settled in the Czech region in the A.D. 400s and 500s. By 900 the Czechs had adopted Christianity and formed a kingdom called Bohemia. It became part of the Austrian Empire, which ruled from the 1500s until 1918. In that year, the Czechs and their Slovak neighbors formed Czechoslovakia, which came under Soviet rule. In 1993 the Czechs and Slovaks agreed to split into the Czech Republic and the Republic of Slovakia. Today the Czech Republic is a parliamentary democracy with a president and a prime minister.

Two-thirds of the 10.2 million Czechs live in cities, many in crowded apartment buildings. The country is famous for the splendor of its historic buildings and monuments. The Czechs have also produced great literature, including plays written by the Czech Republic's first president.

✓ Reading Check What country ruled the Czechs from the 1500s to 1918?

Slovakia

The Carpathian Mountains tower over the northern region of Slovakia. They are rich in iron ore, lead, zinc, and copper. Factories use these minerals to produce iron and steel products. Under communist rule, factories were built for heavy industry. Although communism is now gone, the push to develop industries continues. Workers also make cement, plastics, textiles, and processed foods. Rugged peaks, thick forests, and blue lakes make this area a popular vacation spot. Farther south, vineyards and farms spread across fertile lowlands. Farmers grow barley, corn, potatoes, sugar beets, and grapes.

Slovakia has had difficulty changing to a free market economy. After the fall of communism, Slovak leaders set out to privatize businesses. This means that factory ownership transfers from the government to individual citizens. Some government officials acted corruptly, giving advantages to themselves or to their friends. This made few foreign companies willing to start new businesses here. Slovak factories also suffer from outdated technology, which contributes to pollution.

The Slovaks have a language and culture different from the Czechs. Most Slovaks are Roman Catholics. Nearly 60 percent of Slovakia's 5.4 million people live in modern towns and cities. **Bratislava,** a port on the Danube, is Slovakia's capital and largest city. Tourists visit village festivals to see people dress in traditional clothes and to hear musicians play folk music on shepherds' flutes and bagpipes.

✓ **Reading Check** What contributes to pollution in Slovakia?

FCAT PRACTICE You can prepare for the FCAT-assessed standards by completing the correlated item(s) below.

Section 2 Assessment

Defining Terms
1. **Define** landlocked, nomad, spa, privatize.

Recalling Facts
2. **Culture** To what ethnic group do most Hungarians belong?
3. **Geography** What are three of the Czech Republic's natural resources?
4. **Economics** Why has Slovakia had difficulty changing to a free market economy?

Critical Thinking
5. **Analyzing Information** Why do the Czechs have a high standard of living?
6. **Understanding Cause and Effect** Why do you think the Magyars settled in the Danube area? **FCAT LA.A.2.3.1**

Graphic Organizer
7. **Organizing Information** Draw a diagram like the one below. Then add at least two facts under the headings in each outer oval.

FCAT LA.A.1.3.2

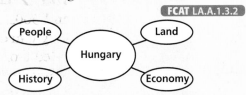

Applying Social Studies Skills

8. **Analyzing Maps** Turn to the political map on page 369. What countries border Hungary to the north? To the east?

Study and Writing Skill

FCAT PRACTICE Completing the activities below will help you prepare for the **FCAT Reading** test.

Taking Notes

Effective note taking involves more than just writing facts in short phrases. It involves breaking up information into meaningful parts so that it can be remembered.

Learning the Skill

To take good notes, follow these steps:

- Write key points and important facts and figures quickly and neatly. Use abbreviations and phrases.
- Copy words, statements, or diagrams from the board or your research.
- Ask the teacher to repeat important points you do not understand.
- When studying textbook material, organize your notes into an outline or a concept map that links important information.
- For a research report, take notes on cards. Note cards should include the title, author, and page number of sources.

Practicing the Skill

Suppose you are writing a research report on eastern Europe. First, identify main idea questions about this topic, such as "Who has ruled Poland?" or "What economic activities are found in the Czech Republic?" Then research each question.

Using this textbook as a source, read the material on pages 369–370 and 374 and prepare notes as shown below. The first few have been started for you. **FCAT LA.A.1.3.2**

Main Idea: What economic activities are found in Poland?
1. Agriculture: potatoes, rye . . .
2. Mining: coal, copper, zinc . . .
3. Manufacturing: foods, machines . . .
Main Idea: What economic activities are found in the Czech Republic?
1.
2.
3.

Applying the Skill

In an encyclopedia or on the Internet, find information about Poland's coal industry and the environmental consequences of burning coal. Take notes by writing the main idea and supporting facts. Then rewrite the article using only your notes. **FCAT LA.A.1.3.2**

◄ A Czech teenager displays Soviet souvenirs for tourists who visit Prague.

Rebuilding the Balkan Countries

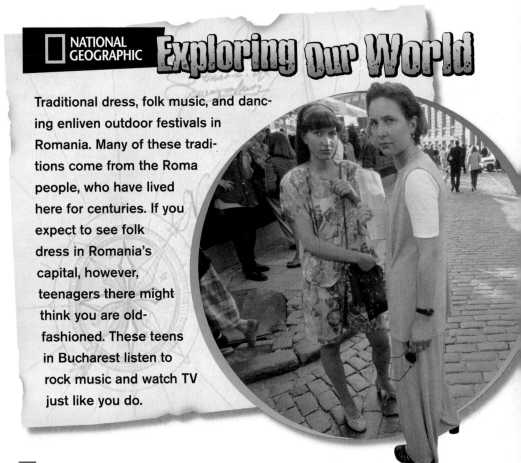

NATIONAL GEOGRAPHIC Exploring Our World

Traditional dress, folk music, and dancing enliven outdoor festivals in Romania. Many of these traditions come from the Roma people, who have lived here for centuries. If you expect to see folk dress in Romania's capital, however, teenagers there might think you are old-fashioned. These teens in Bucharest listen to rock music and watch TV just like you do.

Europe's **Balkan Peninsula** lies between the Adriatic Sea and the Black Sea. The physical map on page 284 shows you that several countries make up this Balkan region. They are **Romania, Bulgaria,** the former **Yugoslav republics,** and **Albania.**

Romania

Romania sits on the northeastern edge of the Balkan Peninsula. The Carpathian Mountains take up about one-third of the country's land area. A vast plateau covers central Romania. A coastal region along the Black Sea includes the mouth of the Danube River. Winters can be very cold and foggy, with much snow. Summers are hot and sunny, but rainfall is abundant.

Romania's economic activities include farming, manufacturing, and mining. The forested mountains and central plateau contain deposits of coal, petroleum, and natural gas. Oil derricks rise in the south. Orchards and vineyards stretch along Romania's western, eastern, and southern borders. Farmers also grow grains, vegetables, and herbs here.

Despite abundant resources, Romania's economy has been held back by the communist policies of the past. Under communism, Romania's factories produced steel, chemicals, and machinery. Few **consumer goods**—clothing, shoes, and other goods that people use—were manufactured. Romania now has a free market economy to supply these goods, but aging factories need to be updated for Romania's economy to grow. In addition, the country needs to heal an environment widely damaged by air and water pollution.

The Romanians   About 56 percent of Romania's 21.6 million people live in towns and cities. **Bucharest,** the capital and largest city, has more than 2 million people. What does Romania's name tell you about its history? If you guessed that the Romans once ruled this region, you are correct. Romania's history and culture were greatly influenced by the Romans. The Romanian language is closer to French, Italian, and Spanish—all based on Latin—than it is to other eastern European languages. In other ways, the Romanians are more like their Slavic neighbors. Many Romanians are Eastern Orthodox Christians.

✓ Reading Check To what other languages is Romanian related?

Bulgaria

Mountainous Bulgaria lies south of Romania. Fertile valleys and plains are tucked among the Balkan Mountains and the Rhodope Mountains, which span most of the country. The coast along the Black Sea has warmer year-round temperatures than the mountainous inland areas.

Bulgaria's economy relies on both agriculture and manufacturing. Wheat, corn, and sugar beets grow in the fertile valleys. Roses are grown in the central Valley of the Roses. Their sweet-smelling oil is used in perfumes. Manufacturing depends on the country's deposits of zinc and coal. Factories produce machinery, metals, textiles, and processed foods. Tourism is growing as visitors seek out Bulgaria's scenic resorts on the Black Sea.

Daily Life   Most of Bulgaria's 7.5 million people trace their ancestry to the Slavs, Turks, and other groups from Central Asia. Most Slavic people use the Cyrillic (suh•RIH•lihk) alphabet, which was first created to write the Slavic language. The Bulgarian language, similar to Russian, is also written in this Cyrillic alphabet. Most Bulgarians are Eastern Orthodox Christians. About 13 percent of the people are Muslims, or followers of the Islamic religion.

Sofia, with over 1 million people, is the capital and largest city. During the summer, Bulgarians join vacationers from other countries at resorts on the Black Sea coast. Here, modern hotels line wide, sandy beaches.

✓ Reading Check What alphabet is used in many Slavic languages?

Transylvania

The region of central Romania known as Transylvania was the setting for English author Bram Stoker's vampire novel *Dracula*. Recently, a doctor noticed that many myths about vampires matched the symptoms of rabies, including pain from bright lights. He found that rabies had spread through the region at the same time that the vampire tales began.

Former Yugoslav Republics

The former Yugoslav republics used to be one large country called **Yugoslavia.** In the early 1990s, long-simmering disputes among ethnic groups boiled to the surface and tore the country apart. Five countries eventually emerged: **Slovenia, Croatia, Bosnia and Herzegovina** (HEHRT•seh•GAW•vee•nah), **Serbia and Montenegro,** and **Macedonia,** also known as the Former Yugoslav Republic of Macedonia (or **F.Y.R.O.M.**).

After the breakup, Serbia and Montenegro kept the name of Yugoslavia. Serbia wanted to control the other former Yugoslav republics and to protect the Serbs living in them. As a result, wars erupted throughout the 1990s. Some countries listed above forced people of other ethnic groups to leave their homes, a policy called ethnic cleansing. Tens of thousands died or were murdered. Thousands more became refugees, or people who flee to another country to escape danger or disaster. These wars left the region badly scarred. By 2002 Serbia's hope of one Yugoslavia had ended. Serbia and Montenegro formed a looser union and dropped the Yugoslav name.

NATIONAL GEOGRAPHIC On Location

Vukovar, Croatia

In 1991 Serbs attacked Vukovar in a revolt against Croatian independence. The revolt became a war, which lasted many years and took many lives.

Place What are some ways the war affected Croatia?
FCAT LA.E.2.2.1

Slovenia   Slovenia is located in the northwest of the Balkans region. It has rugged mountains and fertile, densely populated valleys. Of all the countries of the old Yugoslavia, Slovenia is the most peaceful and prosperous. With many factories and service industries, it also has the region's highest standard of living. About 52 percent of the 2 million Slovenians live in towns and cities. Most are Roman Catholic.

Croatia   Croatia spreads along the island-studded coast of the Adriatic Sea. Inland, Croatia has rugged mountains and a fertile plain. **Zagreb,** the capital and largest city, lies in this inland area. A republic, Croatia supports agriculture as well as industry. Tourists once crowded Croatia's beautiful Adriatic beaches, but war has since damaged many of these places.

The Croats, a Slavic group, make up 78 percent of Croatia's 4.3 million people. Another 12 percent are Serbs. Both Croats and Serbs speak the same Serbo-Croatian language, but they use different alphabets. The Croats use the Latin alphabet, the same one that you use for English. The Serbs write with the Cyrillic alphabet. Religion also divides Croats and Serbs. Croats are mainly Roman Catholic, while Serbs are Eastern Orthodox Christians.

ZLATA'S DIARY
by Zlata Filipović

Young Zlata Filipović kept a diary about her experiences in Sarajevo.

"BOREDOM!!! SHOOTING!!! SHELLING!!! PEOPLE BEING KILLED!!! DESPAIR!!! HUNGER!!! MISERY!!! FEAR!!! That's my life! The life of an innocent eleven-year-old schoolgirl!!! A schoolgirl without a school. A child without games, without friends, without the sun, without birds, without nature, without fruit, without chocolate or sweets, with just a little powdered milk. In short, a child without a childhood. A wartime child. . . . I once heard that childhood is the most wonderful time of your life. And it is. I loved it, and now an ugly war is taking it all away from me. Why? I feel sad. I feel like crying. I am crying."

Taken from *Zlata's Diary: A Child's Life in Sarajevo*, © 1994 by Viking Penguin.
Translation copyright Fixotet editions Robert Laffont, 1994.

Analyzing Primary Sources

Making Inferences What things do you think you would miss the most if war or another tragedy took them from you? **FCAT LA.A.2.3.2**

FCAT PRACTICE

Completing the exercise above will help you prepare for the **FCAT Reading** test.

Bosnia and Herzegovina Mountainous and poor, the country of Bosnia and Herzegovina has an economy based mainly on crops and livestock. **Sarajevo** (SAR•uh•YAY•voh), the capital, has the look of an Asian city, with its marketplaces and mosques, or Muslim houses of worship. Many of the Bosnian people are Muslims. Others are Eastern Orthodox Serbs or Roman Catholic Croats. Serbs in the region began a bitter war after Bosnia's independence in 1992. The Dayton Peace Accords divided Bosnia into two regions under one government in 1995. American soldiers and other troops came as peacekeepers.

Serbia and Montenegro Since 2002 Serbia and its reluctant partner Montenegro have formed a loose union. In 2003 an agreement was reached to vote for independence in each republic in 2006. The economies of these two republics are based on agriculture and industry. The region's largest city is **Belgrade.** Most of the 10.7 million Serbs and Montenegrins practice the Eastern Orthodox faith.

Serbia has faced growing unrest in some of its local provinces. Muslim Albanians living in the province of **Kosovo** want independence from Serbia. Also living in Kosovo is a smaller group of Eastern Orthodox Serbs. For centuries, Albanians and Serbs have felt a deep anger toward each other. In 1999 Serb forces tried to push the Albanians out of Kosovo. The United States and other nations bombed Serbia to force it to withdraw its troops. Even with the help of United Nations peacekeeping troops, peace in Kosovo remains shaky.

Macedonia (F.Y.R.O.M.) Macedonia's 2.1 million people are a mix of different ethnic groups from the Balkans. In **Skopje** (SKAW•pyeh), Macedonia's capital, there is an amazing mix of ancient Christian churches, age-old Turkish markets, and modern shopping centers. Close to Kosovo, Macedonia handled a huge wave of ethnic Albanian refugees from Kosovo who fled Serb forces in 1999.

✓ **Reading Check** What nations were formed from the former Yugoslavia?

Albania

Bordering the Adriatic Sea, Albania is slightly smaller than the state of Maryland. Mountains cover most of Albania, contributing to its isolation from neighboring countries. Albania is a very poor nation. Although the country has valuable mineral resources, it lacks the money to mine them. Most Albanians farm—growing corn, grapes, olives, potatoes, sugar beets, and wheat—in mountain valleys.

Almost two-thirds of Albanians live in the countryside. The capital and largest city, **Tirana,** and its suburbs have a population of about 270,000. Although 3.1 million people live in Albania, another 3.2 million Albanians live in nearby countries. These refugees fled Albania to escape the violence that occurred in the 1990s.

About 70 percent of Albanians are Muslim. The rest are Christian. The Communists that once ruled Albania opposed religion, but Albania's current democratic government has allowed people to practice their faith. A famous Albanian, the Catholic nun Mother Teresa, served the poor in India.

NATIONAL GEOGRAPHIC On Location

Albania

Rugged mountains have isolated Albania from neighboring countries.

Movement Why have many Albanians fled the country in recent years?

✓ **Reading Check** What is the main religion in Albania?

FCAT PRACTICE You can prepare for the FCAT-assessed standards by completing the correlated item(s) below.

Section 3 Assessment

Defining Terms
1. **Define** consumer goods, ethnic cleansing, refugee, mosque.

Recalling Facts
2. **Place** What is the capital of Romania?
3. **Economics** How are roses used in Bulgaria?
4. **Economics** Which of the former Yugoslav republics is most prosperous?

Critical Thinking
5. **Drawing Conclusions** How do you think people in the Balkans feel about the recent changes in their countries? **FCAT LA.A.2.3.1**
6. **Understanding Cause and Effect** What effect did the policy of ethnic cleansing have on the people of Serbia? **FCAT LA.A.2.3.1**

Graphic Organizer
7. **Organizing Information** Create a chart like the one below and complete it by filling in two facts under each country's name. **FCAT LA.A.1.3.2**

Romania	Bulgaria	Slovenia	Croatia
Bosnia and Herzegovina	Serbia and Montenegro	Macedonia	Albania

Applying Social Studies Skills

8. **Analyzing Maps** Study the political map on page 369. What countries are found on the east coast of the Adriatic Sea?

The New Eastern Europe

Making Connections

ART SCIENCE CULTURE TECHNOLOGY

Ukrainian Easter Eggs

Ukrainians have a rich folk art tradition that dates back thousands of years. It includes pottery, textiles, and woodworking. The best-known Ukrainian art form, however, is that of *pysanky,* or decorated eggs.

History

Ukrainian Easter eggs are known worldwide for their beauty and skillful designs. Many of the designs date back to a time when people in the region worshiped a sun god. According to legend, the sun god preferred birds over all other creatures. Birds' eggs became a symbol of birth and new life, and people believed the eggs could ward off evil and bring good luck. Eggs were decorated with sun symbols and used in ceremonies that marked the beginning of spring.

FCAT PRACTICE Answering question 3 below will help you prepare for the **FCAT Reading** test.

When Christianity took hold in Ukraine in A.D. 988, the tradition of making decorative eggs continued. The egg came to represent religious rebirth and new life. People decorated eggs in the days before Easter and then gave them as gifts on Easter morning.

Technique

The word *pysanky* comes from Ukrainian words meaning "things that are written upon." This phrase helps explain the wax process used to decorate the eggs. An artist uses a pin or a tool called a *kistka* to "write" a design in hot wax onto the egg. The egg is then dipped into yellow dye, leaving the wax-covered portion of the eggshell white. After removing the egg from the dye, the artist writes with hot wax over another section of the egg. This portion stays yellow as the egg is dipped into a second dye color. The process continues, with the artist adding wax and dipping the egg into a darker and darker color. At the end, the artist removes the wax layers to reveal the multicolored design.

▶ Making the Connection

1. What is *pysanky,* and when did it originate?

2. What role does placing wax onto the eggshell play in creating a decorative egg?

3. **Drawing Conclusions** What purposes, other than entertainment, might folk art accomplish?

FCAT LA.A.2.3.1

◀ Ukrainian Easter eggs

Ukraine, Belarus, and Moldova

Guide to Reading

Main Idea

Past ties to Russia have had different effects on the economies and societies of Ukraine, Belarus, and Moldova.

Terms to Know

- steppe
- potash

Reading Strategy

Create a diagram like this one. Under the country's name, list at least one fact that shows the Soviet Union's effect on these countries.

FCAT LA.A.1.3.2

Soviet Union's effect on
Ukraine — Moldova
Belarus

The following are the major Sunshine State Standards covered in this section.

SS.A.3.3.2:
Understands the historical events that have shaped the development of cultures throughout the world

SS.B.2.3.8:
Knows world patterns of resource distribution and utilization

NATIONAL GEOGRAPHIC Exploring Our World

On April 26, 1986, Reactor 4 of the Chernobyl (chuhr•NOH•buhl) Nuclear Power Plant in Ukraine exploded. More than 200,000 people were evacuated from surrounding areas to avoid radiation exposure. Millions of acres of good farmland were poisoned. These vehicles have been permanently scrapped after being used to clean up the explosion.

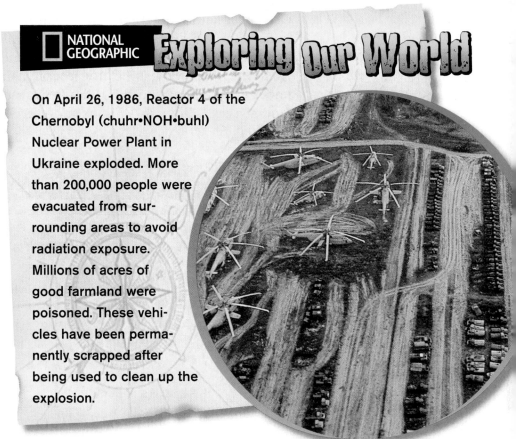

Ukraine, **Belarus** (BEE•luh•ROOS), and **Moldova** (mawl•DAW•vuh) once belonged to the Soviet Union. When the Soviet Union broke apart in late 1991, Ukraine, Belarus, and Moldova became independent. Since then, they have struggled to build new economies.

Ukraine

Slightly smaller than Texas, Ukraine is by far the largest eastern European country (excluding Russia). The Carpathian Mountains rise along its southwestern border. Farther east, a vast **steppe,** or gently rolling, partly wooded plain, makes up the country. Numerous rivers, most of which are too shallow for ships, twist across the steppe. The most important waterway, the **Dnieper** (NEE•puhr) **River,** has been made navigable so that ships can carry goods to distant markets. The **Crimean Peninsula** juts into the Black Sea. Most of Ukraine has cold winters and warm summers.

Rich, dark soil covers nearly two-thirds of Ukraine. Farms are very productive, earning the country the name "breadbasket of Europe." Farmers grow sugar beets, potatoes, and grains and raise cattle and sheep. Factories make machinery, processed foods, and chemicals.

The Ukrainians   Early Slavic groups settled and traded along the rivers of the region. During the A.D. 800s, warriors from Nordic countries united these groups into a large state centered on the city of Kiev (KEE•ihf). A century later, the people of Kiev accepted the Eastern Orthodox faith. They built one of Europe's most prosperous civilizations. After 300 years of freedom, the people of Kiev were conquered by Mongols, then Lithuanians and Poles, and finally the Russians.

In the 1930s, Soviet dictator Joseph Stalin brought Ukraine's farms under government control. Millions were murdered or starved in the famine that followed. Millions more died when Germans invaded

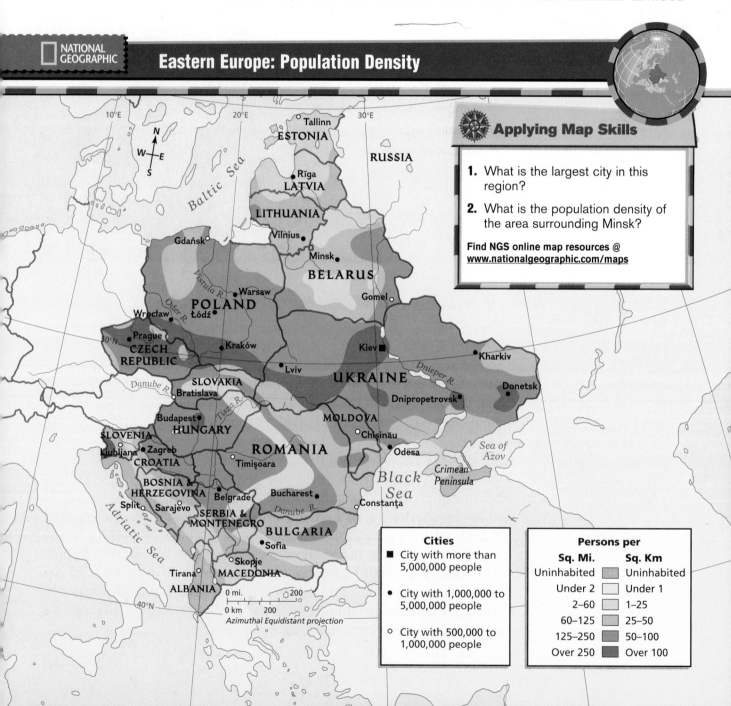

NATIONAL GEOGRAPHIC

Eastern Europe: Population Density

Applying Map Skills

1. What is the largest city in this region?

2. What is the population density of the area surrounding Minsk?

Find NGS online map resources @ www.nationalgeographic.com/maps

Cities

■ City with more than 5,000,000 people

● City with 1,000,000 to 5,000,000 people

○ City with 500,000 to 1,000,000 people

0 mi. 200
0 km 200
Azimuthal Equidistant projection

Persons per	
Sq. Mi.	**Sq. Km**
Uninhabited	Uninhabited
Under 2	Under 1
2–60	1–25
60–125	25–50
125–250	50–100
Over 250	Over 100

Language Families of Europe

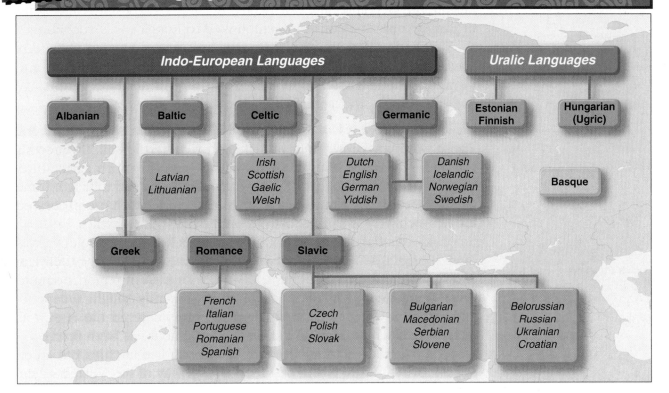

Indo-European Languages

- Albanian
- Baltic
  - Latvian
  - Lithuanian
- Celtic
  - Irish
  - Scottish
  - Gaelic
  - Welsh
- Germanic
  - Dutch
  - English
  - German
  - Yiddish
  - Danish
  - Icelandic
  - Norwegian
  - Swedish
- Greek
- Romance
  - French
  - Italian
  - Portuguese
  - Romanian
  - Spanish
- Slavic
  - Czech
  - Polish
  - Slovak
  - Bulgarian
  - Macedonian
  - Serbian
  - Slovene
  - Belorussian
  - Russian
  - Ukrainian
  - Croatian

Uralic Languages

- Estonian Finnish
- Hungarian (Ugric)
- Basque

Ukraine during World War II. Finally in 1991, with the decline of Soviet power, Ukraine once again became a free nation.

Ukraine has about 48 million people. Nearly 75 percent are ethnic Ukrainians. About 22 percent are Russians, who live mainly in eastern areas. Most of the people follow the Eastern Orthodox religion and speak Ukrainian, a Slavic language closely related to Russian.

More than 70 percent of the people live in cities. **Kiev,** the capital, has more than 2.6 million people. Modern Ukrainians, even teenagers, enjoy listening to folk music played on a stringed instrument called a bandura and watching the acrobatic leaps of the *hopak* dance.

✓ **Reading Check** Why is Ukraine called the "breadbasket of Europe"?

Belarus and Moldova

Belarus, slightly smaller than Kansas, is largely lowlands. If you visited Belarus, you would see wide stretches of birch tree groves, vast forested marshlands, and wooden villages surrounded by fields. Summers are cool and wet, and winters are cold.

Farmers grow potatoes, grains, vegetables, sugar beets, and fruits. Factory workers make equipment, chemicals, and construction materials. Food processing is another important industry. In addition to having petroleum and natural gas, Belarus has **potash,** a mineral used in fertilizer.

Slavic groups first settled the area that is today Belarus in the A.D. 500s. Surrounded by larger countries, Belarus was under foreign rule

Analyzing the Chart

Seven main language families stem from Indo-European origins. Compare this chart with the locations of the languages on the map on page 286. **FCAT MA.E.1.3.1**

History From what language family did Ukrainian develop?

FCAT MA.E.3.3.1

FCAT PRACTICE

Completing the exercise above will help you prepare for the **FCAT Mathematics** test.

for most of its history. Communist Party leaders still control Belarus's government, which is a republic, and have maintained close ties with Russia. Foreign companies have been unwilling to do business in Belarus, in part because the country is still linked to Russia's weak economy.

The 9.9 million people of Belarus are mostly Eastern Orthodox Slavs. Their Belorussian language is closely related to Russian and Ukrainian and is written in Cyrillic. Two-thirds of Belarus's people live in cities. **Minsk,** the largest city, is the capital.

Moldova Moldova is mostly a rolling, hilly plain sliced by rivers. These waterways form valleys that hold rich, fertile soil. Due to this soil and a favorable climate, Moldova can support much agriculture. Farmers grow sugar beets, grains, potatoes, apples, and tobacco. Some grow grapes that are used to make wine. Factories turn out processed foods, machinery, metals, construction materials, and textiles.

Moldova's flag looks similar to Romania's flag. Why? Moldova was once part of Romania. About two-thirds of the people trace their language and culture to that country. Moldova's eastern region, home to many Russians, Ukrainians, and Turks, has recently sought independence. After a violent civil war, Russian troops entered the region as peacekeepers. Despite talks, no lasting settlement has been reached.

Moldova has 4.3 million people. About half live in cities, but much of Moldova's culture is still based on a rural way of life. Villagers celebrate special occasions with lamb, cornmeal pudding, and goat's milk cheese. The main city is the capital, **Chişinău** (KEE•shee•NOW).

✓ **Reading Check** With what nation does Belarus have close ties?

FCAT PRACTICE You can prepare for the FCAT-assessed standards by completing the correlated item(s) below.

Section 4 Assessment

Defining Terms
1. Define steppe, potash.

Recalling Facts
2. **Location** Where is the Crimean Peninsula located?
3. **Government** What type of government does Belarus have?
4. **Economics** Name three of Moldova's agricultural products.

Critical Thinking
5. **Categorizing Information** List four agricultural products and three manufactured products of Ukraine.

6. **Understanding Cause and Effect** Why is the culture of Moldova similar to that of Romania?
FCAT LA.E.2.2.1

Graphic Organizer
7. **Organizing Information** Create a time line like this one. Then label five important periods or events in Ukraine's history. **FCAT LA.A.1.3.2**

|———————|———————|———————|———————|

Applying Social Studies Skills

8. **Analyzing Maps** Compare the political and population maps on pages 369 and 384. What is the population density around Ukraine's Dniester River?

Reading Review

Section 1 — Poland and the Baltic Republics

Terms to Know
bog
communist state
acid rain
pope

Main Idea
Poland and the Baltic republics have undergone many changes to their political and economic systems.
✓ **Place** Poland is a large country with southern mountains and northern plains.
✓ **Economics** The change to a free market economy has brought challenges.
✓ **Culture** The Poles feel deep loyalty to their country and the Catholic Church.
✓ **Place** The countries of Estonia, Latvia, and Lithuania border the Baltic Sea and have recently raised their standards of living.

Section 2 — Hungarians, Czechs, and Slovaks

Terms to Know
landlocked
nomad
spa
privatize

Main Idea
Hungary, the Czech Republic, and Slovakia are changing to free market economies.
✓ **Geography** The Danube River separates the fertile Hungarian Plain from Transdanubia's rolling hills and forests.
✓ **Economics** The Czech Republic is prosperous but must modernize its factories.
✓ **Economics** Slovakia has had difficulty moving to a free market economy.

Section 3 — Rebuilding the Balkan Countries

Terms to Know
consumer goods
ethnic cleansing
refugee
mosque

Main Idea
The Balkan countries have suffered greatly from ethnic conflicts and economic setbacks.
✓ **Culture** The people of Romania are not related to the Slavic peoples who form the populations of most eastern European countries.
✓ **History** Ethnic conflicts have torn apart the former Yugoslav republics.
✓ **Economics** Albania is rich in minerals but is too poor to develop them.

Section 4 — Ukraine, Belarus, and Moldova

Terms to Know
steppe
potash

Main Idea
Past ties to Russia have had different effects on the economies and societies of Ukraine, Belarus, and Moldova.
✓ **Geography** Ukraine's rich soil allows it to grow large amounts of food.
✓ **Economics** Belarus maintains close economic ties to Russia.
✓ **Economics** Moldova's eastern region has tried to seek independence, but even after a civil war, no lasting settlement has been reached.

Chapter 13 Assessment and Activities

FCAT PRACTICE You can prepare for the FCAT-assessed standards by completing the correlated item(s) below.

Using Key Terms

Match the terms in Part A with their definitions in Part B.

A.

1. spa
2. ethnic cleansing
3. acid rain
4. pope
5. steppe
6. landlocked
7. mosque
8. consumer goods
9. refugee
10. potash

B.

a. head of the Roman Catholic Church
b. health resort with hot mineral springs
c. mineral used in fertilizer
d. having no access to the sea
e. products made for people to use themselves
f. Muslim house of worship
g. rain containing chemical pollutants
h. forcing people from other ethnic groups to leave their homes
i. person who must flee to another country to escape danger or disaster
j. gently rolling, partly wooded plain

Reviewing the Main Ideas

Section 1 Poland and the Baltic Republics

11. **Economics** What is one of Poland's most important industries?
12. **History** What has raised standards of living in the Baltic republics?

Section 2 Hungarians, Czechs, and Slovaks

13. **Place** What river divides Hungary?
14. **Place** What is the Czech Republic's capital?

Section 3 Rebuilding The Balkan Countries

15. **Economics** What factors are holding back Romania's economy?
16. **Culture** What is the main religion of Bulgaria?
17. **History** What caused Yugoslavia to fall apart?

Section 4 Ukraine, Belarus, and Moldova

18. **Place** What is the capital of Ukraine?
19. **Culture** To what languages is Belorussian similar?
20. **History** Why does Moldova's flag look similar to Romania's flag?

NATIONAL GEOGRAPHIC — Eastern Europe

Place Location Activity

On a separate sheet of paper, match the letters on the map with the numbered places listed below.

1. Danube River
2. Black Sea
3. Croatia
4. Albania
5. Latvia
6. Hungary
7. Warsaw
8. Carpathian Mountains
9. Baltic Sea
10. Ukraine

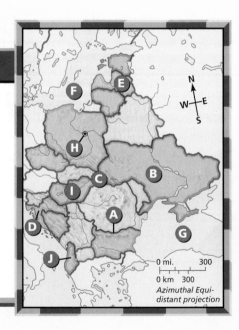

0 mi. 300
0 km 300
Azimuthal Equidistant projection

388

CHAPTER 13

Social Studies ONline

Self-Check Quiz Visit **The World and Its People** Web site at twip.glencoe.com and click on **Chapter 13—Self-Check Quizzes** to prepare for the Chapter Test.

Critical Thinking

21. **Understanding Cause and Effect** What has led to the unrest in parts of Serbia and Montenegro? FCAT LA.A.2.3.1

22. **Categorizing Information** In a chart like the one below, identify eastern European countries that are succeeding economically and ones that continue to struggle. FCAT LA.A.1.3.2

Countries That Are Succeeding	Countries That Are Struggling

Comparing Regions Activity

23. **Culture** People in eastern Europe have experienced much conflict over ethnic identity. This conflict has produced a large number of refugees from countries such as Bosnia and Croatia. There are large numbers of refugees in parts of Africa due to conflict as well. With a partner, research to find information about refugees in eastern European and African countries. Write a conversation that an eastern European refugee and an African refugee might have. FCAT LA.B.1.3.2

Mental Mapping Activity

24. **Focusing on the Region** Create a map of eastern Europe, and then label the following:

- Poland
- Albania
- Czech Republic
- Serbia & Montenegro
- Hungary
- Lithuania
- Black Sea
- Danube River
- Ukraine
- Adriatic Sea

Technology Skills Activity

25. **Building a Database** Create a database of eastern European countries. Include fields for capital, size, population, government, and products. After analyzing your database, predict which countries have a good chance of improving their standard of living.

Standardized Test Practice

Directions: Study the map below, and then answer the question that follows.

European Union 2004

Existing members

Applying for membership

SWEDEN FINLAND

ESTONIA
LATVIA
LITHUANIA

IRELAND DENMARK
THE NETH.
U.K.
BELG. GERMANY POLAND
LUX. CZECH REPUBLIC
FRANCE AUSTRIA SLOVAKIA
HUNGARY
ROMANIA
PORTUGAL SLOVENIA
SPAIN BULGARIA
ITALY
GREECE TURKEY
MALTA
CYPRUS

1. **Which of the following nations in eastern Europe has applied for membership in the European Union?**

   A Bulgaria

   B Spain

   C Ireland

   D Germany

Test-Taking Tip: Notice that the question asks you to base your answer on location. Three of the choices are countries in western Europe. You should use the process of elimination to find the correct answer.

Workers on the statue *Motherland Calls*, Volgograd

Russians in front of St. Basil's Cathedral, Moscow

NATIONAL GEOGRAPHIC

Russia and the Eurasian Republics

If you had to describe Russia in one word, that word would be BIG! Russia is the largest country in the world in area. Its almost 6.6 million square miles (17 million sq. km) are spread across two continents—Europe and Asia. As you can imagine, such a large country faces equally large challenges. In 1991 Russia emerged from the Soviet Union as an independent country. Since then it has been struggling to unite its many ethnic groups, set up a demo-cratic government, and build a stable economy.

▲ Siberian tiger in a forest in eastern Russia

NGS ONLINE
www.nationalgeographic.com/education

Focus on:

Russia and the Eurasian Republics

THIS REGION spans the continents of Europe and Asia. It includes Russia—the world's largest country—and the neighboring independent republics of Armenia, Georgia, Azerbaijan, Kazakhstan, Uzbekistan, Turkmenistan, Kyrgyzstan, and Tajikistan. Russia and the Eurasian republics cover about 8 million square miles (20.7 million sq. km). This is greater than the size of Canada, the United States, and Mexico combined.

The Land

The region of Russia and the Eurasian republics stretches nearly halfway around the globe and includes many different landscapes. The Ural Mountains run north to south, dividing Russia into a European region and a much larger Asian region. West of the Urals is the fertile North European Plain—home to three-fourths of the country's population. East of the Urals lies Siberia, which means "sleeping land." Immense and sparsely populated, Siberia is an area of harsh, forbidding landscapes.

In the southern part of the region, the Caucasus Mountains rise along the borders of Russia, Georgia, and Azerbaijan. Mountains also pass through several republics in Central Asia. The Pamirs in Tajikistan have some of the region's highest peaks. The Tian Shan range in Kyrgyzstan holds some of the world's largest glaciers.

The Caspian Sea is actually a salt lake that lies at the base of the Caucasus Mountains in Russia's southwest. Farther east is Lake Baikal, the world's deepest lake. Many rivers wind through Russia and the Eurasian republics. Some of the rivers flow eastward, like the Amur, which forms Russia's border with China. Others, like the Volga, flow south through plains. The Lena, Yenisey, and Ob Rivers all flow north to the Arctic Ocean.

The Climate

Russia's far north is dominated by tundra, a treeless plain. Winters on the tundra are long, dark, and fiercely cold. During the brief summers, only the top few inches of soil thaw out. Deeper down is permafrost—permanently frozen ground.

South of the tundra are vast evergreen forests. This vast woodland area, known as the

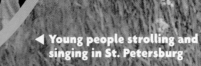

Wildflowers and wooden churches on the North European Plain, in north-western Russia ▼

◄ Young people strolling and singing in St. Petersburg

taiga, is the largest continuous stretch of forest on the earth. Snow blankets the taiga for as many as eight months of the year. Even farther south, the taiga gives way to flat grass-covered plains, or steppes. Here the climate is less harsh, and the soil is quite rich. For centuries, routes across these plains brought invading armies. Today the plains make up Russia's most important farming and industrial area.

The Economy

For many years, Russia and the Eurasian republics formed one state called the Soviet Union. It had an economy planned and run by Communist leaders. Wheat and other crops were grown on huge government-owned farms. The top economic priority was heavy industry, or the manufacturing of goods such as machinery and military equipment. Rich deposits of minerals, coal, and oil supplied the raw materials and energy for many industries. The Soviet push to industrialize, however, led to widespread pollution of the air, soil, and water.

Industrial growth was also more important than the needs of the people. Shortages of consumer goods—clothing and household products, for example—were common.

In the 1990s, when Russia and the other republics of the Soviet Union became independent countries, each took charge of its own economy. Today Russia and the Eurasian republics are struggling to make the change to a free market system, in which people run their own businesses and farms.

The People

About 220 million people live in Russia and the Eurasian republics. Russia has the region's largest population with about 145.5 million people. Climate and landscape affect where people live in Russia and the Eurasian republics. Most people in Russia live west of the Ural Mountains, where the climate is mildest and the land is most fertile.

Ethnic Groups Each of the republics has a major ethnic group, language, and culture. There are also many smaller groups in each republic. More than 100 different ethnic groups live throughout the region. Most Russians are descendants of Slavic peoples, or Slavs. They speak Russian and practice Eastern Orthodox Christianity. Various ethnic groups inhabit Armenia and Georgia. They practice their own forms of Christianity. Turkic ethnic groups (Uzbeks, Kazakhs, Turkmenis, and Azeris) are dominant in Central Asia. They have their own languages and practice the religion of Islam.

◀ **Russian worker inspecting tractors in a factory**

The Arts The arts of Russia and the Eurasian republics include architecture, painting, music, and dance. Each republic has its own rich heritage. You have probably seen pictures of Russia's onion-domed churches and heard the classical music of Peter Tchaikovsky and other Russian composers. Ancient churches with drumlike tops and bells are scattered across the rugged countryside of Armenia and Georgia. In the Central Asian republics, beautiful tiles in swirling patterns decorate Islamic mosques.

▼ **Church of the Resurrection in St. Petersburg, Russia**

Russia
Data Bits

🚗	Automobiles per 1,000 people	120
📺	Television sets per 1,000 people	421
VOTE	Democratic elections	Yes

Ethnic Makeup

Tatar 4%
Chuvash 1%
Ukrainian 3%
Other 10%
Russian 82%

World Ranking

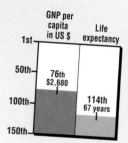

GNP per capita in US $
1st
50th
76th $2,680
100th
150th

Life expectancy
114th 67 years

Population: Urban ▦ vs. Rural ▦

73%   27%

Sources: *World Desk Reference*, 2000; *World Development Indicators*, 2002; *The World Almanac*, 2004.

Exploring the Region

1. Why might Russia's north-flowing rivers be difficult to travel in winter?

2. Why would it be hard to grow crops on the tundra?

3. What was the top economic priority of Communist leaders?

4. To which ethnic group do most Russians belong?

Russia and the Eurasian Republics

Physical

GREENLAND

ICELAND

ATLANTIC OCEAN

ARCTIC CIRCLE

ARCTIC OCEAN

+ North Pole

Wrangel I.

Chukchi Peninsula

East Siberian Sea

EUROPE

Barents Sea

Novaya Zemlya

North Land

New Siberian Islands

Laptev Sea

Klyuchevskaya Sopka 15,584 ft. (4,750 m)

KAMCHATKA PENINSULA

RUSSIA

Baltic Sea

Kola Peninsula

Kara Sea

Verkhoyansk Range

Kolyma R.

Kolyma Range

Sea of Okhotsk

NORTH EUROPEAN PLAIN

⊛ Moscow

Ob R.

WEST SIBERIAN PLAIN

S I B E R I A

CENTRAL SIBERIAN PLATEAU

Lena R.

Stanovoy Range

Sakhalin Island

URAL MOUNTAINS

Don R.

Kama R.

Volga R.

Ural R.

Irtysh R.

Ob R.

Yenisey R.

R U S S I A

Lake Baikal

Yablonovyy Range

Amur R.

Sayan Mts.

Mt. Elbrus 18,510 ft. (5,642 m)

Caucasus Mts.

GEORGIA
T'bilisi

ARMENIA
Yerevan

Baku

AZERBAIJAN

Caspian Sea

KAZAKHSTAN

⊛ Astana

Aral Sea

THE STEPPES

Lake Balkhash

Sea of Japan (East Sea)

UZBEKISTAN

TURKMENISTAN

Garagum

Ashgabat

Tashkent

Bishkek

KYRGYZSTAN

Dushanbe

TAJIKISTAN

A S I A

⊛ National capital
▲ Mountain peak

N
W E
S

0 mi. 1,000
0 km 1,000
Two-Point Equidistant projection

TROPIC OF CANCER

PACIFIC OCEAN

26,247 ft.	8,000 m
19,685 ft.	6,000 m
13,123 ft.	4,000 m
6,562 ft.	2,000 m

NORTH EUROPEAN PLAIN

URAL MOUNTAINS

SAYAN MOUNTAINS

KAMCHATKA PENINSULA

STANOVOY RANGE

MOSCOW

IRTYSH RIVER

LAKE BAIKAL

SEA OF OKHOTSK

Sea level

0 mi. 500
0 km 500

Political

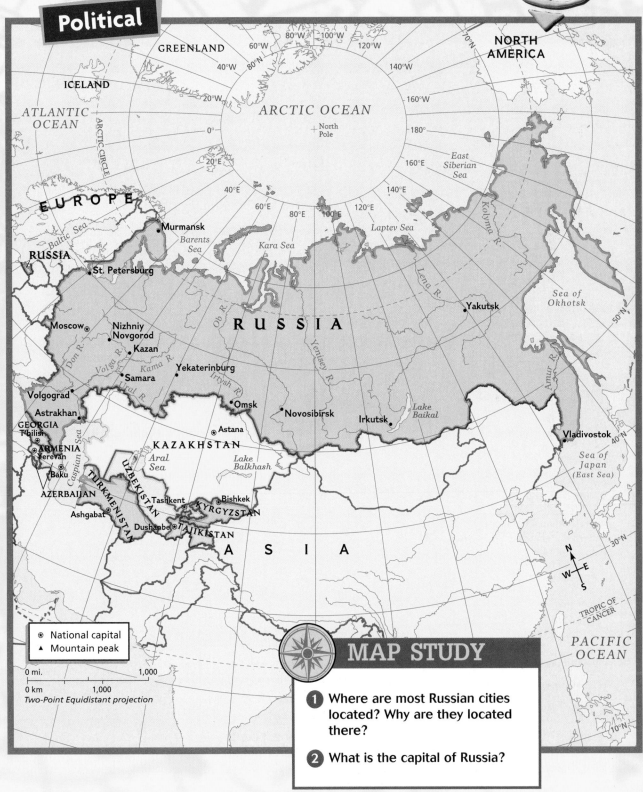

GREENLAND

ICELAND

80°W 100°W

60°W

120°W

40°W 80°N

140°W

NORTH AMERICA

20°W

ARCTIC OCEAN

ATLANTIC OCEAN

160°W

ARCTIC CIRCLE

0°

+ North Pole

180°

70°N

EUROPE

40°E

160°E

East Siberian Sea

60°E

80°E

100°E

120°E

140°E

Baltic Sea

Murmansk

Barents Sea

Laptev Sea

Kolyma R.

RUSSIA

Kara Sea

St. Petersburg

60°N

Sea of Okhotsk

Moscow

Nizhniy Novgorod

Lena R.

Yakutsk

50°N

Kazan

R U S S I A

Don R.

Yekaterinburg

Volga R.

Kama R.

Yenisey R.

Amur R.

Samara

Irtysh R.

Volgograd

Aral R.

Omsk

Lake Baikal

Astrakhan

Novosibirsk

Irkutsk

GEORGIA

Vladivostok

T'bilisi

40°N

ARMENIA

KAZAKHSTAN

Yerevan

Caspian Sea

Aral Sea

Lake Balkhash

Sea of Japan (East Sea)

Baku

Astana

AZERBAIJAN

UZBEKISTAN

30°N

TURKMENISTAN

Tashkent

Bishkek

KYRGYZSTAN

Ashgabat

Dushanbe

TAJIKISTAN

A S I A

N

W E

S

TROPIC OF CANCER

PACIFIC OCEAN

* National capital
▲ Mountain peak

0 mi. 1,000

0 km 1,000

Two-Point Equidistant projection

10°N

MAP STUDY

1 Where are most Russian cities located? Why are they located there?

2 What is the capital of Russia?

Russia and the Eurasian Republics

Russia

The Russian Winter

Average annual number of days with snow cover

- More than 240
- 200 to 240
- 160 to 200
- 120 to 160
- 80 to 120
- 40 to 80
- Less than 40

7 — Daily average hours of sunshine in January

MAP STUDY

1 On average, how many days of snow cover does Moscow have per year?

2 Which city would you expect to have more hours of sunlight in June—Vladivostok or Khatanga?

Contiguous United States and Russia: Land Comparison

Russia's Geo Extremes

① **HIGHEST POINT**
Mount Elbrus
18,510 ft.
(5,642 m) high

② **LOWEST POINT**
Caspian Sea
92 ft. (28 m)
below sea level

③ **LONGEST RIVER**
Ob-Irtysh
3,362 mi.
(5,411 km) long

④ **LARGEST LAKE**
Caspian Sea
143,244 sq. mi.
(371,000 sq. km)

⑤ **DEEPEST LAKE**
Lake Baikal
5,315 ft.
(1,620 m) deep

⑥ **LARGEST ISLAND**
Sakhalin
29,500 sq.mi.
(76,405 sq. km)

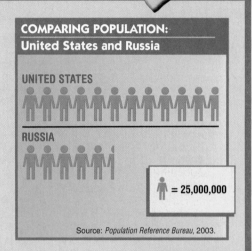

COMPARING POPULATION:
United States and Russia

UNITED STATES

RUSSIA

👤 = 25,000,000

Source: *Population Reference Bureau,* 2003.

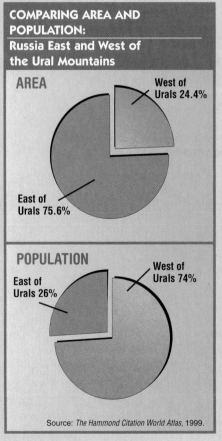

COMPARING AREA AND POPULATION:
Russia East and West of the Ural Mountains

AREA

West of Urals 24.4%

East of Urals 75.6%

POPULATION

East of Urals 26%

West of Urals 74%

Source: *The Hammond Citation World Atlas,* 1999.

GRAPHIC STUDY

❶ What two "extremes" does the Caspian Sea lay claim to?

❷ What percentage of Russia's people live west of the Ural Mountains?

FCAT MA.E.3.3.1

Russia and the Eurasian Republics

REGIONAL ATLAS

Country Profiles

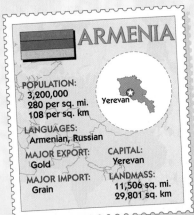

ARMENIA

POPULATION:
3,200,000
280 per sq. mi.
108 per sq. km

LANGUAGES:
Armenian, Russian

MAJOR EXPORT:
Gold

CAPITAL:
Yerevan

MAJOR IMPORT:
Grain

LANDMASS:
11,506 sq. mi.
29,801 sq. km

Yerevan

AZERBAIJAN

POPULATION:
8,200,000
246 per sq. mi.
95 per sq. km

LANGUAGES:
Azeri, Russian,
Armenian

MAJOR EXPORT:
Petroleum

CAPITAL:
Baku

MAJOR IMPORT:
Machinery

LANDMASS:
33,436 sq. mi.
86,599 sq. km

Baku

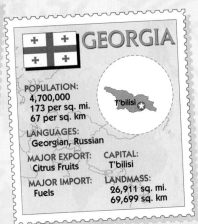

GEORGIA

POPULATION:
4,700,000
173 per sq. mi.
67 per sq. km

LANGUAGES:
Georgian, Russian

MAJOR EXPORT:
Citrus Fruits

CAPITAL:
T'bilisi

MAJOR IMPORT:
Fuels

LANDMASS:
26,911 sq. mi.
69,699 sq. km

T'bilisi

KAZAKHSTAN

POPULATION:
14,800,000
14 per sq. mi.
5 per sq. km

LANGUAGES:
Kazakh, Russian

MAJOR EXPORT:
Petroleum

CAPITAL:
Astana

MAJOR IMPORT:
Machinery

LANDMASS:
1,049,151 sq. mi.
2,717,301 sq. km

Astana

KYRGYZSTAN

POPULATION:
5,000,000
66 per sq. mi.
25 per sq. km

LANGUAGES:
Kirghiz, Russian

MAJOR EXPORT:
Cotton

CAPITAL:
Bishkek

MAJOR IMPORT:
Grain

LANDMASS:
76,641 sq. mi.
198,500 sq. km

Bishkek

▼ **Reindeer pulling sled across
the tundra, Siberia**

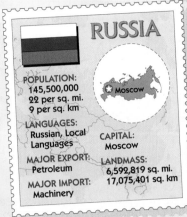

RUSSIA

POPULATION:
145,500,000
22 per sq. mi.
9 per sq. km

LANGUAGES:
Russian, Local
Languages

MAJOR EXPORT:
Petroleum

CAPITAL:
Moscow

MAJOR IMPORT:
Machinery

LANDMASS:
6,592,819 sq. mi.
17,075,401 sq. km

Moscow

Countries and flags not drawn to scale

For more information on countries in this region, refer to the Nations of the World Data Bank in the Appendix.

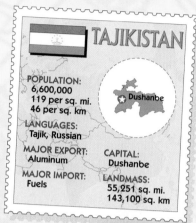

TAJIKISTAN

POPULATION:
6,600,000
119 per sq. mi.
46 per sq. km

LANGUAGES:
Tajik, Russian

MAJOR EXPORT:
Aluminum

MAJOR IMPORT:
Fuels

CAPITAL:
Dushanbe

LANDMASS:
55,251 sq. mi.
143,100 sq. km

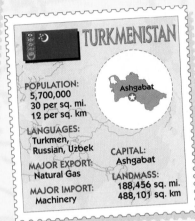

TURKMENISTAN

POPULATION:
5,700,000
30 per sq. mi.
12 per sq. km

LANGUAGES:
Turkmen,
Russian, Uzbek

MAJOR EXPORT:
Natural Gas

MAJOR IMPORT:
Machinery

CAPITAL:
Ashgabat

LANDMASS:
188,456 sq. mi.
488,101 sq. km

UZBEKISTAN

POPULATION:
25,700,000
149 per sq. mi.
58 per sq. km

LANGUAGES:
Uzbek,
Russian, Tajik

MAJOR EXPORT:
Cotton

MAJOR IMPORT:
Machinery

CAPITAL:
Tashkent

LANDMASS:
172,741 sq. mi.
447,399 sq. km

BUILDING CITIZENSHIP

Initiative Under communism, the government is the main employer. Many people no longer had a steady income when the Soviet Union broke apart. The government could no longer take care of them. People had to figure out on their own how to solve the problem of making enough money to feed their families. In other words, they had to show initiative.

Describe a time when you showed initiative to solve a challenge you faced. FCAT LA.B.1.3.2

Teens washing cars to earn money ▼

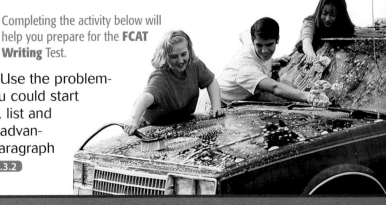

WRITE ABOUT IT

FCAT PRACTICE — Completing the activity below will help you prepare for the **FCAT Writing** Test.

You can develop initiative with practice. Use the problem-solving process to identify a business you could start alone or with friends. Gather information, list and consider your options, and consider the advantages and disadvantages. Then write a paragraph about the business you chose. FCAT LA.B.1.3.2

Russia's Landscape and History

The World and Its People
NATIONAL GEOGRAPHIC

To learn more about Russia's land and history, view *The World and Its People* Chapter 15 video.

Social Studies online

Chapter Overview Visit *The World and Its People* Web site at twip.glencoe.com and click on **Chapter 14—Chapter Overviews** to preview information about Russia.

The activity below will help you prepare for the **FCAT Reading** test.

Categorizing Information When you group information into categories, it is easier to make sense of what you are learning. Make this foldable to help you learn about Russia's past and present. **FCAT** LA.A.1.3.2

Step 1 Fold one sheet of paper in half from top to bottom.

Step 2 Fold it in half again from side to side.

Step 3 Unfold the paper once. Cut up the inside fold of the top flap only.

This cut will make two tabs.

Step 4 Turn the paper and sketch a map of the Soviet Union and Russia on the front tabs. Label your foldable as shown.

Past
Soviet Union

Present
Russia

Reading and Writing As you read the chapter, write under the appropriate flaps of your foldable what you learn about the former Soviet Union and present-day Russia. **FCAT** LA.A.1.3.2

Why It Matters

A New Government

Russia is a land rich in natural resources but has a troubled political history. The various peoples in Russia have had little experience with hands-on government. This experience is needed for a stable democracy to work. On the other hand, a strong central government is needed to create policies to prevent continued air and water pollution and to build up the economy. How will Russia meet both of these aims? The answer is important to us all.

◄ **Statue of Vladimir Lenin at the Exhibition of Economic Achievement, Moscow, Russia**

A Vast Land

Guide to Reading

Main Idea

Russia is a huge country with a cold climate due to its far northern location.

Terms to Know

- steppe
- tundra
- permafrost
- taiga

Reading Strategy

Create a chart like this one. Give a specific name for each type of physical feature listed.

FCAT LA.A.1.3.2

Russia	
Plains	
Mountains	
Rivers	

The following are the major Sunshine State Standards covered in this section.

SS.B.2.3.9:
Understands ways the interaction between physical and human systems affects current conditions on Earth

SS.B.2.3.5:
Understands the geographical factors that affect the cohesiveness and integration of countries

NATIONAL GEOGRAPHIC

Exploring Our World

Siberian tigers hunt in the eastern forests of Russia—sometimes even climbing trees to find food. Only a few hundred now live in the wild, though. The animals they hunt—elk, deer, and wild boar—are dwindling, and the tigers are hunted by people. Poachers who kill the tigers illegally can sell a skin for $15,000. Russia is trying to enforce laws to save these animals.

Russia is the world's largest country. Nearly twice as big as the United States, Russia is called a Eurasian country because its lands lie on two continents—Europe and Asia. The **Ural Mountains** form the dividing line between the two continents. The European or western part of Russia borders countries such as Finland, Belarus, and Ukraine. The much larger eastern part of Russia stretches across Asia to the Pacific Ocean. The Chukchi Peninsula, on Russia's far eastern border, is separated from Alaska by only about 50 miles (80 km).

Russia is so wide that it shares borders with 14 other countries. It also includes 11 time zones from east to west. When it is 12:00 P.M. (noon) in eastern Russia and people are eating lunch, people in western Russia are still sound asleep at 1:00 A.M.

Russia's Climate

As you can see from the climate map on page 405, Russia's southern border is in the middle latitudes, but the north reaches past the Arctic Circle. Most of the western part of Russia has a humid continental climate. Summers are warm and rainy, while winters are cold and snowy. In contrast, eastern Russia experiences short, cool summers and long, snowy winters. Russia has a long coastline along the Arctic Ocean, which is frozen most of the year. Ice makes shipping difficult or impossible. Many of Russia's ports on the Baltic Sea and Pacific Ocean are also closed because of ice part of the year.

Russia's gigantic size and harsh climates make transportation difficult within the country as well. If you visited Russia, you would discover that, unlike in the United States, railroads, rivers, and canals are still important means of getting around. With about 54,000 miles (about 87,000 km) of track, railroads are the leading movers of people and goods in Russia.

✓ **Reading Check** How does Russia's climate affect shipping?

European Russia

Find the Ural Mountains on the physical map on page 396. The ancient Urals, worn by years of erosion, are not very tall. Their length is extensive, though, running from the Arctic Ocean to Russia's southern

NATIONAL GEOGRAPHIC

Russia: Climate

Dry
- Steppe

Mid-Latitude
- Humid continental

High Latitude
- Subarctic
- Tundra

Applying Map Skills

1. What high latitude climate zones cover much of Russia?

2. What type of climate does Moscow have?

Find NGS online map resources @ www.nationalgeographic.com/maps

boundary. West of the Urals lies the **North European Plain.** This fertile plain has Russia's mildest climate, and about 75 percent of the population live here. This region holds Russia's capital, **Moscow,** and other important cities, such as **St. Petersburg** and **Volgograd.** Much of Russia's agriculture and industry is found on the North European Plain.

Good farmland also lies south of the North European Plain, along the Don and Volga Rivers. This area is part of the steppe, the nearly treeless grassy plain that stretches through Ukraine. To the far south of European Russia lay the high, rugged **Caucasus** (KAW•kuh•suhs) **Mountains.** Thickly covered with pines and other trees, the Caucasus are much taller than the Urals.

√ Reading Check What is the steppe?

East of the Urals

The huge Asian part of Russia lies east of the Ural Mountains and is known as **Siberia.** Northern Siberia has one of the coldest climates in the world. Not even hardy evergreens can grow here. Instead, you find tundra, a vast and rolling treeless plain in which only the top few inches of the ground thaw during the summer. The permanently frozen lower layers of soil are called permafrost and cover 40 percent of Russia.

The few people who live in the tundra make their living by fishing, hunting seals and walruses, or herding reindeer. With so few trees, many of the houses are made of walrus skins. Because the distances are so great and the land is usually covered in ice and snow, people may use helicopters for travel.

The Taiga South of the tundra is the world's largest forest, the taiga (TY•guh). Here, evergreen trees stretch about 4,000 miles (6,436 km) across the country in a belt 1,000 to 2,000 miles (1,609 to 3,218 km) wide. As with the tundra, few people live in this area. Those who do support themselves by lumbering or hunting. This area is so sparsely populated that forest fires sometimes burn for weeks before anyone notices.

NATIONAL GEOGRAPHIC On Location

Siberia

This is cold! Boiling water freezes in midair in icy northern Siberia.

Place How do people in the tundra make their living?

hi Bi.

Vegetation in Russia

The tundra (left) is found in northern Russia. South of the tundra is the huge expanse of the taiga (center). The steppes dominate southwest Russia (right).

Place What type of vegetation grows on the taiga?

Southern Siberia Plains, plateaus, and mountain ranges cover the southern part of Siberia. Southeastern Siberia is home to the majestic Siberian tiger, now an endangered species. Other wildlife found here include bear, reindeer, lynx, wolf, wildcat, elk, and wild boar.

The Kamchatka Peninsula Mountains also rise on the far eastern Kamchatka (kam•CHAHT•kuh) Peninsula. Many of these mountains are part of the Ring of Fire. This name is used to describe the active volcanic zone that forms the western, northern, and eastern edges of the Pacific Ocean. Volcanic eruptions and earthquakes sometimes occur on this peninsula.

✔ **Reading Check** What is the Ring of Fire?

Inland Water Areas

Russia touches many inland bodies of water. In the southwest, it borders the **Black Sea.** Through the Black Sea, Russian ships can reach the Mediterranean Sea. Look at the physical map on page 396 to find another large sea in southwestern Russia—the **Caspian Sea.** About the size of California, the Caspian Sea is actually the largest inland body of water in the world. Like the Great Salt Lake in Utah, the Caspian Sea has salt water, not freshwater. Russia shares this sea with four other countries—Azerbaijan, Iran, Turkmenistan, and Kazakhstan.

High in the Central Siberian Plateau is **Lake Baikal**—the world's deepest freshwater lake. In fact, Lake Baikal holds almost 20 percent of the world's supply of unfrozen freshwater. It is also the world's oldest lake, dating back nearly 30 million years. Some of the plant and fish species in the lake can be traced to prehistoric times. Scientists come from all over the world to study its rare and unusual species. Tourists travel by train to see the lake's shimmering blue waters.

Unfortunately, a large paper mill nearby has polluted the Lake Baikal region. The paper mill is a major source of jobs and wealth. An important issue for this region is to try to save both the lake and the badly needed industry.

Russia has several major rivers. The **Volga**—the longest river in Europe—is a vital transportation route. Canals connect it and other rivers of European Russia. Boats use the canals to transport people and goods from one city to another. Many rivers also flow through the Asian side of Russia. Most of these rivers begin in the mountains of southern Siberia and flow north across the marshy lowlands to empty into the frigid Arctic Ocean. The Lena (LEE•nuh), the Yenisey (YIH•nih•SAY), and the Ob (AHB) are among the longest rivers in the world.

✓ **Reading Check** What is an important issue for the Lake Baikal region?

FCAT PRACTICE You can prepare for the FCAT-assessed standards by completing the correlated item(s) below.

Assessment

Section 1

Defining Terms

1. Define steppe, tundra, permafrost, taiga.

Recalling Facts

2. Location What mountain range separates Europe and Asia?

3. Region How many countries does Russia border?

4. Place What is unique about Lake Baikal?

Critical Thinking

5. Analyzing Information Why do you think trains are more important than other kinds of vehicles for moving people and goods across Russia? **FCAT** LA.A.2.3.1

6. Making Comparisons How do the waters of the Caspian Sea and Lake Baikal differ? **FCAT** LA.A.1.3.2

Graphic Organizer

7. Categorizing Information Create a chart like this one. Then place each of the following items into the column in which it is located: Moscow, Lake Baikal, Kamchatka Peninsula, St. Petersburg, Volga River, Volgograd, taiga.

FCAT LA.A.1.3.2

European Russia	Asian Russia
Bonny	cool

Applying Social Studies Skills

8. Analyzing Maps Turn to the climate map on page 405. Select a Russian city. Now look at the map of "The Russian Winter" on page 398. On average, how many days of snow cover does your selected city have per year?

Making Connections

| ART | SCIENCE | CULTURE | TECHNOLOGY |

Cooperative Space Ventures

The space age officially began in 1957 when Russia launched _Sputnik I_. It was the first artificial satellite to orbit the earth.

The Space Race

The Russians sent the first person into space in 1961, when cosmonaut Yuri Gagarin orbited the earth. A few weeks later, Alan Shepard made the United States's first spaceflight. John Glenn was the first astronaut to orbit the earth in 1962. After this, the "space race" between the United States and Russia was of global importance. It was feared that one country could dominate the world if it had the right equipment in space.

Over the years, both Russia and the United States launched many spacecraft. In 1986 the Russian space station _Mir,_ which means "peace," began to orbit the earth. This was the first permanently staffed laboratory in space. Astronauts from more than a dozen countries were invited to

FCAT PRACTICE Answering question 3 below will help you prepare for the **FCAT Writing** test.

participate on the space station _Mir._ The astronauts and Russian cosmonauts performed many experiments on the effects of weightlessness.

In 1993 the United States and Russia decided to work jointly to build the International Space Station. In July 2000, the Russian space module _Zvezda_ ("star") linked up with the rest of the station. Four months later, the International Space Station had its first permanent human inhabitants. The crew was made up of both Russian cosmonauts and American astronauts.

▶ Making the Connection

1. What country launched the space age?

2. How have the United States and Russia cooperated on space ventures?

3. **Making Predictions** What space technology do you think we will see in the future? What social consequences might result from this? **FCAT** LA.B.1.3.2

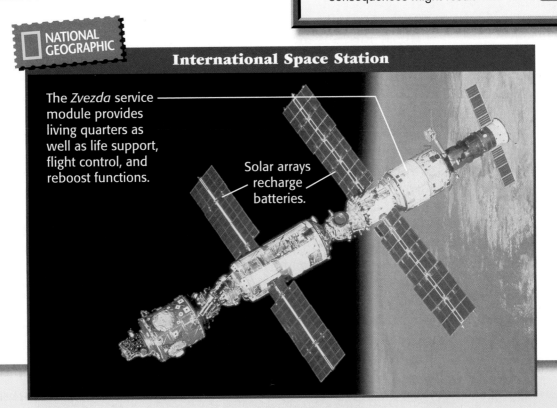

NATIONAL GEOGRAPHIC

International Space Station

The _Zvezda_ service module provides living quarters as well as life support, flight control, and reboost functions.

Solar arrays recharge batteries.

A Troubled History

Guide to Reading

Main Idea

The harsh rule of powerful leaders has often sparked violent uprisings in Russia.

Terms to Know

- czar
- serf
- industrialize
- communist state
- Cold War
- perestroika
- free enterprise system
- glasnost

Reading Strategy

Create a chart like this one. List three main czars and important facts to remember about them. **FCAT** LA.A.1.3.2

Czar	Importance

The following are the major Sunshine State Standards covered in this section.

SS.A.3.3.2:
Understands the historical events that have shaped the development of cultures throughout the world

SS.A.3.3.4:
Knows significant historical leaders who have influenced the course of events in Eastern and Western civilizations since the Renaissance

NATIONAL GEOGRAPHIC Exploring Our World

After becoming czar in 1698, Peter the Great wanted to modernize Russia. He toured parts of Europe to learn about shipyards and factories. After returning home, Peter forced the Russian nobles to adopt western European ways. In fact, those who refused to study math and geometry were not allowed to get married.

Today Russia is the world's largest country. Early in its history, however, it was a small territory on the edge of Europe. Strong rulers gradually expanded Russia's borders. Their harsh rule led to unrest, eventually leading to two major upheavals—one in 1917, the other in 1991.

Early Russia

To understand the challenges facing Russia today, let us go back through Russia's history. Modern Russians descend from early groups of Slavs who settled along the rivers of what are today Ukraine and Russia. During the A.D. 800s, these early Slavs built a civilization around the city of **Kiev,** today the capital of Ukraine. This civilization was called Kievan Rus (KEE•EH•vuhn ROOS). By the A.D. 1000s, the ruler and people of Kievan Rus had accepted Eastern Orthodox Christianity. They prospered from trade with the Mediterranean world and western Europe.

In the 1200s, the Mongols swept in from Central Asia and conquered Kiev. Under their 200-year-rule, Kiev lost much of its wealth and power. Meanwhile, Moscow became the center of a new Slavic territory called Muscovy (muh•SKOH•vee). In 1480 Ivan III, a prince of Muscovy, drove out the Mongols and made Muscovy independent. Ivan III was known as "Ivan the Great."

Rise of the Czars Muscovy slowly developed into the country we know today as Russia. Russian rulers expanded their power, built up armies, and seized land and other resources. They called themselves **czars,** or emperors. They had total control over the government. As a citizen of Muscovy, you would have feared Czar Ivan IV, who ruled during the 1500s. Known as "Ivan the Terrible," he used a secret police force to tighten his iron grip on the people and control their lives.

As the map on page 412 shows, the czars gradually conquered surrounding territories. As a result, many non-Russian peoples became part of the growing Russian Empire. (Russia still suffers from ethnic tensions caused by these early conquests.) Czars such as Peter the Great and Catherine the Great pushed the empire's borders southward and westward. They also tried to make Russia modern and more like Europe. Peter built a new capital—St. Petersburg—in the early 1700s. Built close to Europe near the Baltic coast, St. Petersburg was designed like a European city with elegant palaces, public squares, and canals. If you had been a Russian noble at this time, you would have spoken French as well as Russian. You also would have put aside traditional Russian dress, worn European clothes, and attended fancy balls and parties.

Early Czars

Ivan III, or "Ivan the Great," (left) ruled Muscovy until 1505. His grandson, Ivan IV, also known as "Ivan the Terrible," (right) used a secret police force to control the people of Muscovy.

History Who drove the Mongols out of Kiev?

NATIONAL GEOGRAPHIC On Location

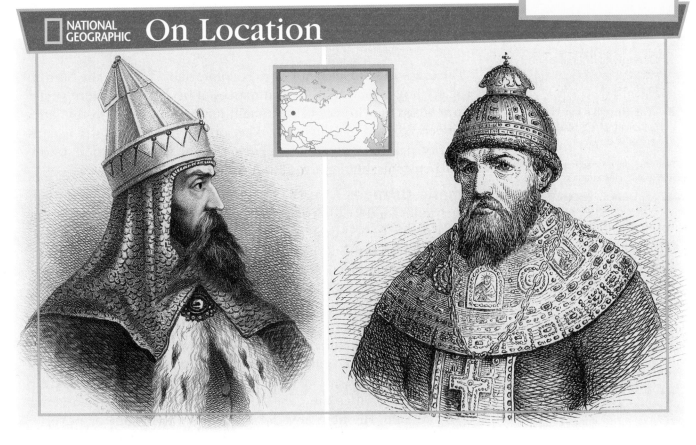

| Kievan Territory |
| 1360–1524 |
| 1524–1689 |
| 1689–1917 |
| 1917–1945 |
| — Boundary of the Soviet Union in 1945 |
| — Present-day Russian boundary |

20°W 0° 20°E 40°E 60°E 80°E 100° 120°E 140°E 160°E 160°W 180°

North Pole

ARCTIC OCEAN

Chukchi Sea

ALASKA (Sold to U.S. in 1867)

East Siberian Sea

Bering Sea

Barents Sea

Kara Sea

Laptev Sea

St. Petersburg (Leningrad)

Kiev

Moscow

ARCTIC CIRCLE

Sea of Okhotsk

R U S S I A

Black Sea

Lake Baikal

Caspian Sea

Aral Sea

0 mi. 1,000
0 km 1,000
Two-Point Equidistant projection

Applying Map Skills

1. During which time period was the most land added to Russia?

2. Was Russia's land area larger in 1945, or is it larger today?

Find NGS online map resources @ www.nationalgeographic.com/maps

The czars and nobles enjoyed rich, comfortable lives. At the bottom of society, however, were the great masses of people. Most were **serfs,** or farm laborers, who could be bought and sold along with the land. These people lived hard lives, working on the nobles' country estates or in city palaces. Few could read or write. They did not follow Western customs, but kept the Russian traditions.

Dramatic Changes In 1812 a French army led by Napoleon Bonaparte invaded Russia. Brave Russian soldiers and the fierce winter weather finally forced the French to retreat. Have you ever heard the *1812 Overture,* with its dramatic ending that includes ringing bells and bursts of cannon fire? Written by the Russian composer Peter Tchaikovsky (chy•KAWF•skee), this musical masterpiece celebrates the Russian victory over Napoleon. Turn to page 420 to read more about Napoleon's defeat.

In the late 1800s, Russia entered a period of economic and social change. The Russian Empire expanded southward into the Caucasus Mountains and eastward toward the Pacific Ocean. In 1861 Czar Alexander II, known as the Czar-Liberator, freed the serfs from being tied to the land. His new law did little to lift them out of poverty, though. Russia began to **industrialize,** or change its economy to rely more on manufacturing and less on farming. Railroads, including the famous Trans-Siberian Railroad, spread across the country. It linked Moscow in the west with Vladivostok on Russia's Pacific coast.

✓ **Reading Check** What civilization did early Slavs build in Ukraine?

The Soviet Era

In 1914 World War I broke out in Europe. Russian and German armies met and fought bloody battles in eastern Europe. Unprepared for war, Russia suffered many defeats and had few victories. As the fighting dragged on, shortages of food in Russian cities caused starvation. The Russian people blamed the czars for their troubles.

The Russian Revolution In 1917 political leaders, soldiers, and factory workers forced Czar Nicholas II to give up the throne. Later that year, a political revolutionary named Vladimir Lenin led a second revolt and seized control. He and his followers set up a **communist state.** This means the country's government has strong control over the economy and society as a whole. Fearing invasion, the Communists moved Russia's capital from coastal St. Petersburg inland to Moscow.

Social Studies Online

Web Activity Visit **The World and Its People** Web site at twip.glencoe.com and click on **Chapter 14— Student Web Activities** to learn more about the Russian Revolution.

Growth of Soviet Power By 1922, after a brutal civil war, Russia's Communist leaders were securely in power. In that year, they formed the Union of Soviet Socialist Republics (USSR), or the Soviet Union. This vast territory included the republic of Russia and 14 other republics—most of the conquered territories of the old Russian Empire. After Lenin died in 1924, Communist Party officials disagreed over who was to lead the country.

Within a few years, Joseph Stalin had won out over the others and became the Soviet Union's leader. Under Stalin's orders, the government took complete control of the economy. Stalin ended private ownership of farms and businesses, and he set up five-year plans to industrialize the country. Under this type of system, called a command economy, factory managers were told what to make and how to make it. Those who opposed Stalin's actions were killed or sent to remote prison camps deep in the vast forests of icy Siberia. Millions of people were brutally murdered or forced into slave labor under Stalin's rule.

In 1941 Nazi Germany invaded the Soviet Union, drawing the country into World War II. During the conflict, the Soviets joined with Great Britain and the United States to defeat the Germans. About 20 million Russian soldiers and civilians died in what Russians call the Great Patriotic Fatherland War.

Superpowers Wage the Cold War When World War II ended, Stalin wanted to protect the Soviet Union from any more invasions. He set up Communist governments in the neighboring Eastern European countries of Poland, East Germany, Czechoslovakia, Hungary, Romania, and Bulgaria. They became satellite nations, or countries controlled by another, more powerful nation. The Soviet government cut off these countries from contact with the rest of the world. As a result, they

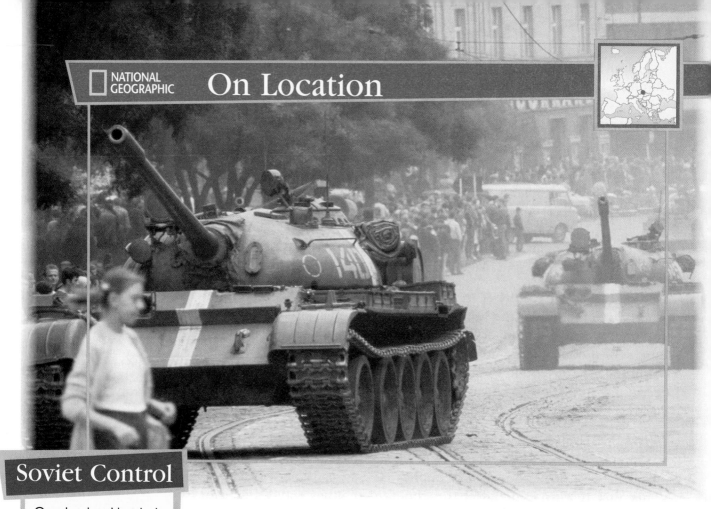

Soviet Control

Czechoslovakia tried to throw off Soviet control in 1968. Soviet tanks and troops poured into Bratislava to crush the revolt.

Movement Why did Stalin set up Communist governments in Eastern European countries?

FCAT LA.E.2.2.1

were said to lie behind an "iron curtain." Any satellite nations that opposed Soviet rule were brutally put down.

Stalin and the leaders who followed him spent large amounts of money on the military and weapons. The Soviet Union became one of the two most powerful nations in the world. The other superpower—the United States—opposed Soviet actions. These two nations engaged in the **Cold War,** competing for world influence without breaking out in actual fighting. They even competed in space. Both the Soviet Union and the United States launched rockets in a bid to be first in outer space. Turn to page 409 to learn more about the space race.

During the Cold War years—from 1940 to the late 1980s—the Soviet economy faced many problems. With no competition, government-owned factories became inefficient and produced poor-quality goods. The government cared more about making tanks and airplanes for military purposes than consumer goods, such as cars and refrigerators. As a result, people had few goods to buy. Food often became scarce, and people waited in long lines to buy bread, milk, and other necessary items.

The Soviet Union had another challenge. This vast empire included not only Russians but also people from many other ethnic groups. Non-Russians in the Soviet republics resented the control of the government in Moscow, which they believed favored ethnic Russians. They wanted to leave the Soviet Union and form their own countries.

Soviet Collapse Despite plans to improve housing and agriculture, the Soviet economy fell even further behind the economy of the United States. In 1985 Mikhail Gorbachev (GAWR•buh•CHAWF) became the leader of the Soviet Union. He introduced changes to get the Soviet economy moving. Under his policy of perestroika, or "restructuring," Gorbachev allowed farmers and factory managers to make many of their own decisions. By loosening government control, Gorbachev moved the economy toward a free enterprise system. In this type of economy, most businesses are privately owned, and there is competition—resulting in better products at lower prices.

Gorbachev also allowed people to speak freely about the government and important issues, a policy called glasnost, or "openness." Instead of strengthening the country, however, Gorbachev's policies made the people doubt communism even more. Some people thought Gorbachev was moving too quickly with reforms. Others thought he was not moving fast enough. People's demands for more and more changes eventually led to the collapse of both communism and the Soviet Union.

In the late 1980s, massive protests against Soviet control erupted in the satellite nations. By 1991, all of the Soviet satellites had thrown off communist rule in favor of democracy. By the end of that year, each of the 15 republics that made up the Soviet Union also declared their independence. The Soviet Union no longer existed. Russia emerged as the largest and most powerful of those republics.

▲ Mikhail Gorbachev tried to lessen the Russian government's control of the economy and society.

Reading Check Who helped move the Soviet Union toward democracy?

FCAT PRACTICE You can prepare for the FCAT-assessed standards by completing the correlated item(s) below.

Section 2 **Assessment**

Defining Terms
1. Define czar, serf, industrialize, communist state, Cold War, perestroika, free enterprise system, glasnost.

Recalling Facts
2. History Why did Peter the Great build a new capital of Russia?
3. History Who led the 1917 revolution in Russia?
4. History What happened to the Soviet Union in 1991?

Critical Thinking
5. Understanding Cause and Effect How did the Soviet economy change under perestroika? **FCAT LA.A.2.3.1**
6. Analyzing Information How did glasnost weaken the communist system? **FCAT LA.E.2.2.1**

Graphic Organizer
7. Organizing Information In a chart like this one, write facts that show the contrast between the nobles and the serfs of Russia. **FCAT LA.A.1.3.2**

Nobles	Serfs

Applying Social Studies Skills

8. Creating Mental Maps Create your own map of early Russian territory. Label where Kievan Rus was located. Then label where Peter the Great moved the capital.

Critical Thinking Skill

FCAT PRACTICE Completing the correlated items below will help you prepare for the **FCAT Reading** test.

Understanding Cause and Effect

Understanding cause and effect involves considering *why* an event occurred. A *cause* is the action or situation that produces an event. What happens as a result of a cause is an *effect*.

▲ Revolutionary leaders and philosophers Lenin, Engels, and Marx

Learning the Skill

To identify cause-and-effect relationships, follow these steps:

- Identify two or more events or developments.
- Decide whether one event caused the other. Look for "clue words" such as *because, led to, brought about, produced, as a result of, so that, since,* and *therefore.*
- Look for logical relationships between events, such as "She overslept, and then she missed her bus."
- Identify the outcomes of events. Remember that some effects have more than one cause, and some causes lead to more than one effect. Also, an effect can become the cause of yet another effect.

Practicing the Skill

For each number below, identify which statement is the cause and which is the effect. **FCAT** LA.A.2.3.1

1. (A) Russia's capital was moved from coastal St. Petersburg to Moscow in the heart of the country.
   (B) The capital of Russia was threatened by an outside invasion.

2. (A) Revolutionary leaders seized control of the Russian government.
   (B) During World War I, shortages of food in Russian cities caused much starvation.
   (C) Discontent grew among the Russian people.

3. (A) The Soviet government kept prices for goods and services very low.
   (B) Many goods and services were in short supply in the Soviet Union.

Applying the Skill

In your local newspaper, read an article describing a current event. Determine at least one cause and one effect of that event. Show the cause-and-effect relationship in a diagram like the one here: **FCAT** LA.A.2.3.1

GO TO

Practice key skills with **Glencoe Skillbuilder Interactive Workbook, Level 1.**

Section 1 — A Vast Land

Terms to Know

steppe
tundra
permafrost
taiga

Main Idea

Russia is a huge country with a cold climate due to its far northern location.

✓ **Location** Spanning two continents—Europe and Asia—Russia is the world's largest country.

✓ **Region** The western part of Russia is mostly plains. The eastern Siberian region is covered with mountains and plateaus.

✓ **Region** European Russia has the mildest climate, while most of Siberia, or Asian Russia, has cold high-latitude climate zones.

✓ **Movement** Inland waterways are important for moving goods through Russia, but many long rivers drain north into the frigid Arctic Ocean and freeze in winter.

Section 2 — A Troubled History

Terms to Know

czar
serf
industrialize
communist state
Cold War
perestroika
free enterprise system
glasnost

Main Idea

The harsh rule of powerful leaders has often sparked violent uprisings in Russia.

✓ **History** Emperors known as czars ruled the Russian Empire from 1480 to 1917.

✓ **History** The czars expanded Russian territory to reach from Europe to the Pacific.

✓ **Government** Under the Communists, Russia became part of the Soviet Union.

✓ **History** In 1991 the Soviet Union broke apart into 15 independent republics.

◄ A train on the Trans-Siberian Railroad runs along Lake Baikal.

417

FCAT PRACTICE You can prepare for the FCAT-assessed standards by completing the correlated item(s) below.

Using Key Terms

Match the terms in Part A with their definitions in Part B.

A.

1. permafrost
2. czar
3. perestroika
4. steppe
5. serf
6. taiga
7. glasnost
8. communist state
9. industrialize
10. tundra

B.

a. huge, subarctic evergreen forests
b. dry, treeless plains in the high latitudes
c. dry, treeless grasslands
d. permanently frozen lower layers of soil
e. farm laborer
f. former emperor of Russia
g. openness
h. rely more on manufacturing and less on farming
i. restructuring
j. government controls the economy

Reviewing the Main Ideas

Section 1 A Vast Land

11. **Human/Environment Interaction** Why is Russia unable to use ports along its Arctic coast for most of the year? **FCAT LA.E.2.2.1**
12. **Location** Which area of Russia has the mildest climate?
13. **Movement** What is an important means of transportation for people in Russia?
14. **Region** Why is the Kamchatka Peninsula considered part of the Ring of Fire?
15. **Place** What is the longest river in Europe?

Section 2 A Troubled History

16. **Location** Where was the earliest center of Russian civilization?
17. **History** Which czar used secret police to maintain strict control over the people?
18. **History** When was the Union of Soviet Socialist Republics formed?
19. **Government** Why did Stalin send people to Siberia?
20. **Economics** How did Gorbachev try to change the Soviet economy? **FCAT LA.E.2.2.1**

 **Russia's Landscape and History**

Place Location Activity

On a separate sheet of paper, match the letters on the map with the numbered places listed below.

1. Ural Mountains
2. Kamchatka Peninsula
3. Lake Baikal
4. Volga River
5. Moscow
6. Don River
7. Siberia
8. Caspian Sea
9. Caucasus Mountains
10. St. Petersburg

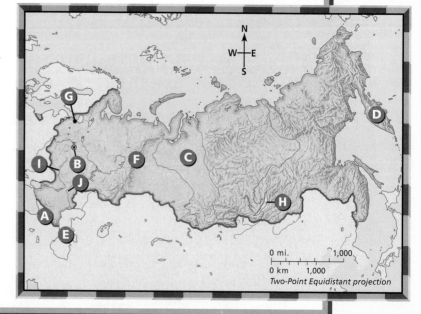

Social Studies online

Self-Check Quiz Visit *The World and Its People* Web site at twip.glencoe.com and click on **Chapter 14—Self-Check Quizzes** to prepare for the Chapter Test.

Critical Thinking

21. Understanding Cause and Effect How did World War I help lead to the Russian Revolution? **FCAT LA.A.2.3.1**

22. Organizing Information Create a diagram like this one. Complete it with four physical features in Siberia. **FCAT LA.A.1.3.2**

Physical Features in Siberia

Comparing Regions Activity

23. History Catherine the Great expanded Russia's territory when she was czar in the eighteenth century. There are many other powerful women who have shaped the world's history. Create a list of five influential women, and include the region where they had influence. What do these women have in common?

Mental Mapping Activity

24. Focusing on the Region Create a simple outline map of Russia and label the following:

- Arctic Ocean
- Pacific Ocean
- Vladivostok
- Moscow
- Ural Mountains
- St. Petersburg
- Siberia
- Baltic Sea

Technology Skills Activity

25. Developing Multimedia Presentations Choose an ethnic or political problem that the Russian people have faced in the last 10 years. Research your choice and create a multimedia presentation on this problem. Include information on when, what, and where. Use pictures, maps, and time lines to make your presentation more visual. **FCAT LA.A.2.3.5**

Standardized Test Practice

Directions: Read the paragraph below, and then answer the question that follows. **FCAT LA.A.2.3.1**

You may be surprised to know that the former Soviet republic of Kazakhstan was—and still is—important to the exploration of outer space. The Russian space center Baikonur (by•kuh•NOOR) lies in south-central Kazakhstan. During the Soviet period, Baikonur was used for many space launches. Several historic "firsts in space" occurred here. For example, the first satellite was launched in 1957. The first crewed flight took place when cosmonaut Yuri Gagarin orbited the earth in 1961. In addition, the flight of the first woman in space, Valentina Tereshkova, was launched in 1963. After the Soviet collapse, the Russian-owned center remained in independent Kazakh territory.

1. The Soviet space program at Baikonur holds great importance, mostly because

F it is located in south-central Kazakhstan.

G it provides jobs for the people who live near the launch site.

H many "firsts in space" flights were launched from it.

J Valentina Tereshkova was the first woman in space.

Test-Taking Tip: When a question uses the word *most* or *mostly*, it means that more than one answer may be correct. Your job is to pick the *best* answer. For example, Baikonur's location in Kazakhstan may be important to the people who live near it, which is answer G. Another answer, however, provides a more general reason for Baikonur's importance.

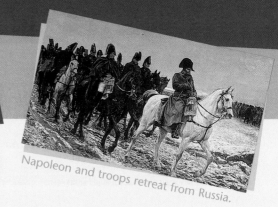

Napoleon and troops retreat from Russia.

RUSSIA'S STRATEGY:
Freeze Your Foes

Winter weather can cancel school and stop traffic. It can even change history. Such was the case when French ruler Napoleon Bonaparte thought he had conquered the Russian Empire.

In fact, Napoleon did not want to conquer Russia. His real enemy was Great Britain. Napoleon wanted Russia and other countries to stop trading with Great Britain. Yet Russia's czar, Alexander I, refused. By 1812, Napoleon was determined to change Alexander's mind. In June, leading an army of more than half a million soldiers, Napoleon invaded Russia. To reach Moscow and the czar, Napoleon had to fight his way across the Russian countryside.

By the time Napoleon's battle-weary forces reached Moscow, supplies were scarce. All along the route, Russians had burned villages as they retreated, leaving no food or shelter. Reaching Moscow, Napoleon found the city in flames and nearly empty of people. The czar had moved to St. Petersburg. Napoleon took Moscow without a fight, but most of the city was in ashes.

Winter Wins a War

With winter approaching, Napoleon waited in Moscow for Alexander I to offer peace. The czar remained silent, however. With dwindling supplies and many of his troops lacking winter clothes, Napoleon was forced to retreat. He tried to take a new way back, but the Russians made Napoleon use the same ruined route he had used before. Armed bands of Russians attacked at every turn. Starving and desperate to escape the bitter cold, several of Napoleon's soldiers threw themselves into burning buildings. Most of Napoleon's troops never made it out of Russia.

History Repeats

More than a century later, during World War II, Russia's winter was again a mighty foe. On June 22, 1941, Adolf Hitler's German army invaded Russia, then part of the Soviet Union. As the German army fought its way to Moscow, Soviet leader Joseph Stalin issued his own "scorched-earth policy." Soviet citizens burned anything of use to the invaders. By December, German troops were within sight of the Kremlin, Moscow's government center, when winter struck.

Snow buried the invaders. Temperatures fell below freezing. Grease in guns and oil in vehicles froze solid. German soldiers suffered frostbite and died. The Soviets were better clothed and had winterized their tanks and trucks. Stalin's troops pushed back the German army. Once again the Russians triumphed with help from "General Winter."

QUESTIONS

1 After Napoleon conquered Moscow in 1812, why did he retreat?

2 How did Russia's winter affect fighting in World War II? **FCAT** LA.E.2.2.1

German prisoners of Russia's winter ▶

Average Winter Temperatures

EUROPE

⊕ Moscow

RUSSIA

ASIA

Napoleon's Advance,
June–October 1812

German Forces Front
Line, December 1941

< -40°F
-40° to -31°F
-30° to -21°F
-20° to -11°F
-10° to 0°F
0° to 10°F
11° to 20°F
21° to 30°F
> 30°F

The New Russia and Independent Republics

The World and Its People | **NATIONAL GEOGRAPHIC**

To learn more about Russia and the Eurasian Republics, view **The World and Its People** **Chapters 14** and **18** videos.

Social Studies Online

Chapter Overview Visit **The World and Its People** Web site at twip.glencoe.com and click on **Chapter 15—Chapter Overviews** to preview information about Russia and its southern neighbors.

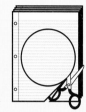

The activity below will help you prepare for the **FCAT Reading** test.

Compare-Contrast Make this foldable and use it to help you organize what you learn about Russia and the independent Eurasian republics. **FCAT LA.A.1.3.2**

Step 1 Stack four sheets of paper, one on top of the other. On the top sheet of paper, trace a large circle.

Step 2 With the papers still stacked, cut along the circle line you traced.

Step 3 Staple the paper circles together at one point around the edge.

Staple here.

This makes a circular booklet.

Step 4 Label the front circle **Russia**. Take notes on the pages that open to the right. Turn the book over and label the back **Eurasian Republics**. Take notes on the pages that open to the right.

Russia

Reading and Writing As you read the chapter, write facts about the people and places of Russia and the Eurasian republics in the appropriate places of your circular foldable booklet. **FCAT LA.A.1.3.2**

Why It Matters

Rebuilding a Country

For nearly half a century, two superpowers—the United States and the Soviet Union—dominated world politics. With the fall of communism, the Soviet Union broke up into 15 independent nations. Russia, which was the heart of the Soviet Union, is now trying to rebuild its government and economy. Russia's efforts to create a democratic government may show whether democracy is a workable system, not just for some, but for all people.

◄ **Cathedral of St. Basil the Blessed, Red Square, Moscow, Russia**

From Communism to Free Enterprise

 NATIONAL GEOGRAPHIC **Exploring Our World**

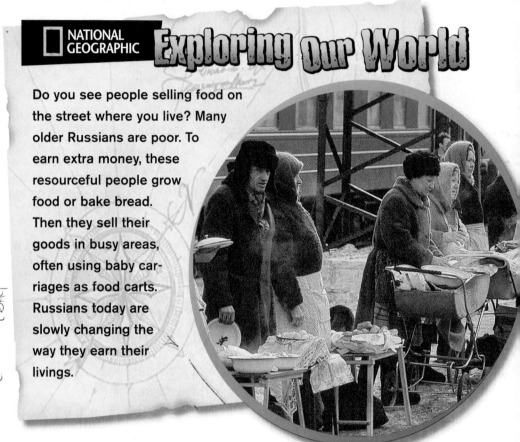

Do you see people selling food on the street where you live? Many older Russians are poor. To earn extra money, these resourceful people grow food or bake bread. Then they sell their goods in busy areas, often using baby carriages as food carts. Russians today are slowly changing the way they earn their livings.

The fall of communism turned the economies of Russia, the other Soviet republics, and the Soviet satellite nations upside down. All of the new governments turned to a free market economy (also called a free enterprise economy or capitalism). In a **free market economy,** the people—not the government—decide what goods and services to produce, how to produce them, and who will buy them.

Difficult Changes in Russia

Changing to a free market economy has not been easy. In Chapter 13, you read about the economic challenges facing many eastern European countries. Most of these nations were either Soviet republics or satellites. Some, such as Ukraine and the Czech Republic, have been able to prosper from capitalism faster than other countries, such as Slovakia or Romania. All, however, have had to learn how to make changes. In this section, we will focus on the changes in the economy of Russia.

The map below shows that Russia has many resources and manufacturing areas. Factory managers can decide what products to make from these resources. People can choose their own careers and open businesses—such as restaurants, stores, or computer companies. People now can make their own decisions, but those decisions do not always lead to success. Businesses can fail. People may become unemployed. Under communism, everybody had jobs. Workers today can lose their jobs if business is poor.

In addition, the government no longer sets prices for food and other goods. When prices were set low, the Russian people could afford the goods, but they often faced shortages. Without government controls, prices have risen. Higher prices make it harder to buy necessities such as food and clothing. Eventually, however, the higher prices and profits will encourage more manufacturers to start producing goods and services. The competition among producers will increase supplies and drive prices down.

In the meantime, though, a large number of Russians remain poor. These people lack the money to buy the consumer goods that are

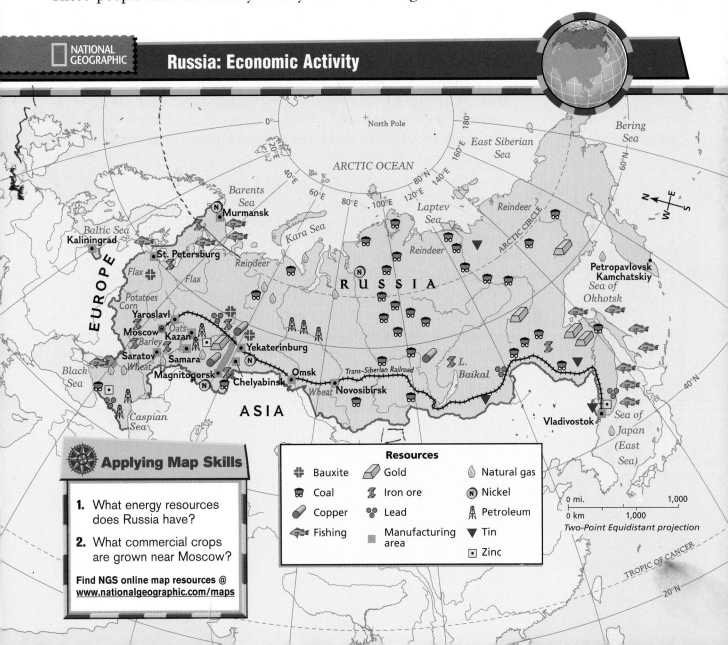

NATIONAL GEOGRAPHIC

Russia: Economic Activity

Applying Map Skills

1. What energy resources does Russia have?

2. What commercial crops are grown near Moscow?

Find NGS online map resources @ www.nationalgeographic.com/maps

Resources

- Bauxite
- Coal
- Copper
- Fishing
- Gold
- Iron ore
- Lead
- Manufacturing area
- Natural gas
- Nickel
- Petroleum
- Tin
- Zinc

0 mi. 1,000
0 km 1,000
Two-Point Equidistant projection

slowly becoming available. Many survive by standing in long lines to receive food given away by government agencies. Turn to the **TIME Reports** on page 441 to learn more about the challenges that Russians are facing in their shift to a free market economy.

✓ Reading Check **How does competition among producers affect supplies and prices?**

Russia's Economic Regions

Russia is rich in resources and depends on them for economic growth. Russia is divided into four different economic regions: the Moscow region, Port Cities, Siberia, and the Volga and Urals region.

The Moscow Region   About 800 years old, **Moscow** is the political and cultural center of Russia. Moscow is also the largest city, the country's economic center, and the largest transportation hub. Many of Russia's manufacturing centers are located in or near Moscow. In the past, most of the country's factories focused on **heavy industry,** or the production of goods such as machinery, mining equipment, and steel. In recent years, more factories have shifted to **light industry,** or the production of consumer goods such as clothing, shoes, furniture, and household products. High-technology services and electronics industries also have emerged in Moscow.

Farming takes place in the Moscow region as well. Farmers raise dairy cattle, barley, oats, potatoes, corn, and sugar beets. Other crops include flax, which is used to make textiles. Railroads and canals that crisscross the Moscow region are used to transport farm products and raw materials.

Port Cities   Russia has two important northwestern ports— **Kaliningrad** and **St. Petersburg.** Look at the economic activity map on page 425. Do you see that Russia owns a small piece of land on the Baltic Sea separated from the rest of the country? The port of Kaliningrad is located on this land. This city is Russia's only Baltic port that remains free of ice year-round. Russian officials, hoping to increase trade here, have eliminated all taxes on foreign goods brought to this city. Companies that deliver goods to Kaliningrad, however, must transport their products another 200 miles (322 km) through other countries to reach the nearest inland part of Russia. In summer, when St. Petersburg's port is not frozen, ships must travel another 500 miles (805 km) north to reach that city.

St. Petersburg, once the capital of Russia, is a vital port and a cultural center. Czar Peter the Great built this city in the early 1700s on a group of more than 100 islands connected by bridges. Large palaces stand gracefully on public squares. Factories in St. Petersburg make light machinery, textiles, and scientific and medical equipment. Located on the Neva River near the Gulf of Finland, the city is also a shipbuilding center.

Murmansk, in Russia's far north, and **Vladivostok,** in the east, are other important port cities. Vladivostok is Russia's largest port on the

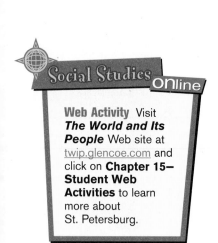

Social Studies Online

Web Activity Visit **The World and Its People** Web site at twip.glencoe.com and click on **Chapter 15— Student Web Activities** to learn more about St. Petersburg.

St. Petersburg

Ice forms on the Neva River in the heart of St. Petersburg. The Hermitage Museum in the background is Russia's best gallery of art and the main tourist attraction in St. Petersburg.

Economics Name an economic activity that takes place in St. Petersburg.

Pacific Ocean. Trade in these port cities brings needed goods to the Russian people. Vladivostok is also a base for Russia's huge fishing industry.

Siberia As you learned in Chapter 14, Siberia is the Asian part of Russia. It has the largest supply of minerals in Russia, including iron ore, uranium, gold, diamonds, and coal. Huge deposits of oil and natural gas lie beneath the frozen ground of northern Siberia. About two-thirds of Siberia is covered with forests that could support a lumber industry.

Tapping all of these resources is very difficult, however. Siberia is mostly undeveloped because of its harsh, cold climate. Another problem is size—it can take eight or more days to travel across all of Russia by train. Finding a way to develop the remote resources of Siberia is very important for Russia's economic future. Many of the minerals and fuels of western Russia have been used up. The industrial centers there need the resources from Siberia.

The Volga and Urals Region Tucked between the Moscow region and Siberia lies the industrial region of the Volga River and Ural Mountains. The **Volga River** carries almost one-half of Russia's river traffic. It provides water for irrigation and for hydroelectric power—the power generated by fast-flowing water. The region is also home to Russia's most productive farmlands.

The Ural Mountains are rich in minerals. Workers here mine copper, gold, lead, nickel, and bauxite, a mineral used to make aluminum. The mountains also have energy resources such as coal, oil, and natural gas.

✓ **Reading Check** Why are Siberia's mineral resources important?

Fighting Pollution

The United States government passes laws to prevent or limit pollution. However, some companies fight the laws because making their factories pollution-free is very expensive. Fortunately, our government is strong and is able to enforce the anti-pollution laws. In Russia, the new government is not strong enough to enforce the anti-pollution laws that it has passed. Many companies are still polluting areas such as Lake Baikal.

Environmental Issues

Although Russians are moving toward a free market economy, they must learn to balance making profits with protecting the environment. Forests have been cut down, and seedlings have not been planted to replace the trees and hold the soil. This is causing soil erosion in some areas. Chemical fertilizers have been heavily used to increase crop production. These chemicals have built up in the soil over time, destroying its ability to grow food. In addition, the Soviet government built power plants to make **nuclear energy,** or energy from controlled atomic reactions. Many of these nuclear power plants are in decay, which can lead to dangerous nuclear waste.

Air Pollution   Smog cloaks many of Russia's large cities. Pollution from heavy industry is particularly bad. Smoke and gases are given off by coal-fired electric plants, vehicles, and other forms of transportation. Many Russians suffer from lung diseases, and rising numbers of people have cancer. Life expectancy, or the number of years that an average person is expected to live, has fallen in Russia.

Water Pollution   Chemicals used in agriculture and industry often end up in rivers and lakes. Poor sewer systems pollute waterways in Russia as well. Water pollution is also caused by the chemical weapons that were developed by the Soviet Union during the Cold War. Many of these weapons are buried in dumps throughout Russia and the former Soviet republics. Containers that hold the chemicals are deteriorating, and some of the chemicals leak into groundwater.

✓ **Reading Check** What are some environmental effects of the Soviet era?

FCAT PRACTICE   You can prepare for the FCAT-assessed standards by completing the correlated item(s) below.

Section 1 Assessment

Defining Terms

1. Define free market economy, heavy industry, light industry, nuclear energy, life expectancy.

Recalling Facts

2. Place What is the political and cultural center of Russia?

3. Location Why is Kaliningrad such an important city in Russia?

4. Economics List five mineral resources found in the Ural Mountains.

Critical Thinking

5. Drawing Conclusions Why would consumers want the Russian economy to change from relying on heavy industry to a greater emphasis on light industry?
FCAT LA.A.2.3.1

6. Understanding Cause and Effect How have economic changes affected the Russian people?
FCAT LA.A.2.3.1

Graphic Organizer

7. Organizing Information Draw a chart like the one below. Fill in at least two causes of soil, air, and water pollution in Russia. **FCAT** LA.A.1.3.2

Soil Pollution	Air Pollution	Water Pollution

Applying Social Studies Skills

8. Analyzing Maps Turn to the economic activity map on page 425. Which manufacturing areas are connected by the Trans-Siberian Railroad?

Russia's People and Culture

NATIONAL GEOGRAPHIC Exploring Our World

Russians have long valued their music, literature, and art. Here, Russian art students enjoy one reminder of Russia's past. In 1764 the empress Catherine the Great enlarged the Russian Academy of Fine Arts to train Russian artists. She hoped they would develop the skills shown by European artists. The school, now known as the Repin Institute, remains open.

Russia is one of the most populous countries in the world, with 145.5 million people. Since the breakup of the Soviet Union in 1991, the Russian people have seen not only their economy change, but also their political structure and daily lives.

Political Challenges

Under communism, members of the Communist Party controlled Russia's government and told people how to vote. Today Russia is a democracy, a government in which people freely elect their leaders. Russia is also a federal republic. This means that power is divided between national and state governments with a president who leads the nation.

A Russian president has stronger powers than an American president. For example, the Russian president can issue orders that become laws even if they are not passed by the legislature. Russia's first two

Standing for Democracy

In 1991 Russia's first president, Boris Yeltsin (holding paper), stood on a tank in defiance of a communist group who wanted to stop Russia's move to democracy.

Government How did Russian government officials deal with criticism in the past?

presidents—Boris Yeltsin and Vladimir Putin—used their powers to help develop and strengthen Russia's economy and democracy.

In adjusting to a new form of government, Russians face important political challenges. They have to learn how to function in a democracy. Democracy is built on the idea of the rule of law. This means that laws govern not just ordinary people but also government officials. In the past, Russian leaders did what they wanted. In the new system, they must learn to follow the law. Also, past governments punished people who criticized their decisions. Now officials have to learn to accept disagreements over government policies.

✓ **Reading Check** What is the rule of law?

Ethnic Challenges

A large challenge facing the new government results from the fact that Russia is home to many different ethnic groups. Russians, along with Ukrainians and Belorussians, are part of a larger group of people called Slavs. Hundreds of years ago, the Slavs migrated from northeastern Europe to western Russia. In Russia today, more than 80 percent of the people are Slavs who speak Russian. Slavs are the **majority group,** or the group that controls most of the wealth and power.

About 100 other ethnic groups also live in Russia. Each group has its own distinctive language and culture. These peoples are known as **minority groups** because they are not the group that controls most of the wealth and power in the society.

When the Soviet Union existed, the central government kept tight control over its majority and minority groups. After the Soviet Union fell apart, many old feuds and remembered wrongs came to the surface. Fighting broke out among many of the ethnic groups who had been enemies in the past and whose differences had never been resolved. The Russian government today faces the task of protecting people in minority groups as well as promoting cooperation among the ethnic groups.

However, some of the minority groups want to form their own countries. Among them are the Chechens (CHEH•chehnz), who live in **Chechnya** (CHEHCH•nee•uh) near the Caspian Sea and Caucasus Mountains in southern Russia. Find Chechnya on the map on page 451. This region has oil reserves, and many oil pipelines crisscross Chechnya transporting fuel to major Russian cities. Russian troops have fought Chechen forces to keep Chechnya a part of Russia.

✓ **Reading Check** What is the largest, most powerful ethnic group in Russia?

Daily Life

As you learned in Chapter 14, the most densely populated area of Russia is the region west of the Ural Mountains—particularly around Moscow. About 75 percent of Russians live clustered in cities.

Urban and Rural Life   Russia's urban, or city, areas are large and modern, with stone and concrete buildings and wide streets. Tall buildings hold apartments for hundreds of families. Many of these apartments are small and cramped, however. A typical Russian apartment has one bedroom, living room, kitchen, and bathroom for a family of four. The living room may also be used as a bedroom.

It is very hard to find housing in the cities. For this reason, many generations may share the same home. This can be helpful because many Russian mothers work outside of the home. The grandmother, or babushka, may cook, clean, shop, and care for young children. Shopping for food can take a long time because it often means waiting in long lines. When people in cities relax, they take walks through parks or attend concerts, movies, and the circus.

Russian cities have changed in recent years. Some people have benefited from the economic changes sweeping the country. Many of

NATIONAL GEOGRAPHIC On Location

Urban vs. Rural

The GUM state department store (left) is very similar to modern malls in the United States. In some rural areas, however, people still live without heat, electricity, or plumbing (below).

Culture How are cities in Russia like urban areas in the United States?

these prosperous people have clustered near Moscow. They are building large houses outside the city limits, where few people lived before. As a result, Russia is developing its first suburbs, or smaller communities that surround a city.

In Russia's rural areas, or countryside, most people live in houses built of wood. As in the United States, the quality of health care and education is often lower in rural areas than in the cities. Over the years, many people have left rural areas to find work in Russia's cities.

Religion in Russia Despite Communist laws in the past forbidding the practice of religion, the Russian Orthodox Church is very popular. Russian Orthodox is a Christian faith. It is headed by a figure called the patriarch—the Greek term for "father." Russian Orthodoxy was responsible for a special alphabet called Cyrillic. According to legend, St. Cyril, an Orthodox priest, developed the Cyrillic alphabet to help the Slavs read and write their own language. He invented new letters for sounds in the Slavic language that were not present in Greek or Latin languages.

Although more than 70 percent of the Russian population is Russian Orthodox, this is by no means the only religion in Russia. Many Muslims (followers of Islam), Roman Catholics, Protestants, and Buddhists live within Russia's boundaries. However, many of the Jews

FCAT PRACTICE

Completing the exercise below will help you prepare for the **FCAT Reading** and **Writing** tests.

Primary Source

ALEXANDER SOLZHENITSYN

(1918–)

For many years, Russian author Alexander Solzhenitsyn was the voice of protest for his people, speaking out through his novels about injustices in the Soviet Union's Communist system. Since the people could not "see" freedom for themselves, he used his great literary talent to bring truth to as many people as possible.

"The sole substitute for an experience which we have not ourselves lived through is art and literature," he wrote. **"Wherever else it fails, art always has won its fight against lies, and it always will."**

Source: *Nobel Lecture, 1972* by Alexander Isayevich Solzhenitsyn.

Analyzing Primary Sources

1. What does Solzhenitsyn mean when he says that literature can substitute for an experience we have not had? Do you agree? **FCAT LA.A.2.3.2, LA.A.2.3.8**

2. Describe an event you "experienced" through art. This might include a scary story or a powerful scene from a film. **FCAT LA.B.1.3.2**

Art

Peter Carl Fabergé was no ordinary Russian jeweler. His successful workshop designed extravagant jeweled flowers, figures, and animals. He is most famous for crafting priceless gold Easter eggs for the czar of Russia and other royalty in Europe and Asia. Each egg was unique and took nearly a year to create. Lifting the lid of the egg revealed a tiny surprise. One egg Fabergé created (shown here) held an intricate ship inside.

Looking Closer Why do you think Fabergé's workshop closed after the Russian Revolution of 1917?

FCAT LA.E.2.2.1

Fabergé egg ▲

that at one time lived in Russia have emigrated to other areas. Fewer than 1 million Jews live in Russia today.

Celebrations, Foods, and Sports Russians enjoy small family get-togethers as well as national holidays. New Year's Eve is the most festive nonreligious holiday. Russian children decorate a fir tree and exchange presents with others in their families. Russians also celebrate May 1 with parades and speeches. May Day honors Russian workers.

If you were to have dinner with a Russian family, you might begin with a big bowl of *borscht,* a soup made from beets, or *shchi,* a soup made from cabbage. Next, you might have meat turnovers called *piroshki.* For the main course, you are likely to eat meat, poultry, or fish with boiled potatoes. On special occasions, Russians like to eat caviar. This delicacy is made from eggs of the sturgeon, a fish from the Caspian Sea.

Have you ever watched the Olympics? If so, you probably have seen Russian hockey players, figure skaters, and gymnasts. Due to Russia's cold climate, winter and indoor sports are popular. Russians also enjoy soccer, tennis, hiking, camping, and mountain climbing.

✓ Reading Check How have Russia's cities changed in recent years?

Rich Cultural Traditions

Russia has a rich tradition of literature, art, and music. The Russian storytelling tradition is one of the oldest and richest in the world. These stories, or *skazki,* were passed down orally from generation to generation, until finally they were recorded in print. Beasts and creatures with magical powers are common in these tales that grew out of a land with dark forests and long, cold winters.

▲ Ballet in Russia dates back to 1738 with the founding of the first dancing school in St. Petersburg.

The great novels and plays of Russia reflect mostly historical political themes. Leo Tolstoy's novel *War and Peace* recounts how Russians rallied to defeat the French emperor Napoleon Bonaparte. Fyodor Dostoyevsky (FEE•uh•dor DAHS•tuh•YEHF•skee) wrote many novels that explored Russian life during the late 1800s. In the 1970s, Alexander Solzhenitsyn (SOHL•zhuh•NEET•suhn) wrote novels that revealed the harsh conditions of Communist society.

Art and Music   St. Petersburg has many beautiful museums and statues. This is why it is called "Venice of the North" after the cultural center of Italy. One of Russia's top ballet companies dances in the Mariinsky (MAH•ree•IHN•skee) Theater in St. Petersburg. Russian ballet dancers are famous around the world. Composer Peter Tchaikovsky (chy•KAWF•skee) wrote some of the world's favorite ballets, including *Sleeping Beauty* and *The Nutcracker.* Nikolay Rimsky-Korsakov used Russian folktales and tunes in his operas and other works. Igor Stravinsky's *Firebird Suite* is based on a Russian legend.

If you enjoy painting, you would definitely want to stroll through St. Petersburg's Hermitage Museum. It was originally built to hold the art collection of the czars, including the famous Fabergé (fa•behr•zhay) eggs. The museum now publicly displays these and other works by Russian and European painters and sculptors.

✓ **Reading Check**   Which Russian author wrote about the harsh conditions of Communist society?

FCAT PRACTICE   You can prepare for the FCAT-assessed standards by completing the correlated item(s) below.

Section 2 Assessment

Defining Terms
1. **Define** democracy, federal republic, majority group, minority group.

Recalling Facts
2. **Government** Why has the Russian government sent troops to Chechnya? **FCAT LA.E.2.2.1**
3. **Culture** What is the major religion of Russia?
4. **Culture** Which Russian composer wrote the world famous ballet *The Nutcracker?*

Critical Thinking
5. **Analyzing Information** Describe the problems Russians face living in a democracy after years of Communist rule. **FCAT LA.A.2.3.1**
6. **Making Predictions** Art ideas are frequently drawn from life. What themes do you think you will see in future Russian arts?

Graphic Organizer
7. **Organizing Information** Create a diagram like this one, and list two facts for each topic in the four outer ovals. **FCAT LA.A.1.3.2**

Food   Cities

Russian Life

Religion   Sports

Applying Social Studies Skills

8. **Synthesizing Information** Write a paragraph describing ways in which Russian and American cultures are different and similar. Then describe how your family's living conditions would change if you lived in a typical Russian apartment. **FCAT LA.B.1.3.2**

Making Connections

Count Leo Tolstoy

FCAT PRACTICE Completing the correlated items below will help you prepare for the **FCAT Reading** test.

Count Leo Tolstoy (1828–1910) was a famous Russian novelist. Two of his epic works are *War and Peace* and *Anna Karenina*. What is not generally known is that Tolstoy also wrote for children. He wrote: "[These writings] will be used to teach generations of all Russian children, from the czar's to the peasant's, and from these readers they will receive their first poetic impressions, and having written these books, I can now die in peace."

Russian literature, even stories for children, contains more suffering and tragedy than American children would appreciate. The stories also celebrate qualities such as helpfulness, compassion, mercy, and justice. These values are needed to survive difficult times. This story is an example of just such literature.

▲ Russian grandfather

The Grandfather and His Little Grandson
by Count Leo Tolstoy (1828–1910)

The grandfather had become very old. His legs would not carry him, his eyes could not see, his ears could not hear, and he was toothless. And when he ate, he was untidy. His son and the son's wife no longer allowed him to eat with them at the table and had him take his meals near the stove. They gave him his food in a cup. Once he tried to move the cup closer to him and it fell to the floor and broke. The daughter-in-law scolded the old man, saying that he damaged everything around the house and broke their cups, and she warned him that from that day on she would give him his food in a wooden dish. The old man sighed and said nothing.

One day the old man's son and his wife were sitting in their hut, resting. Their little son was playing on the floor. He was putting together something out of small bits of wood. His father asked him: "What are you making, Misha?" And Misha said: "I'm making a wooden bucket. When you and Mommie get old, I'll feed you out of this wooden bucket."

The young peasant and his wife looked at each other and tears appeared in their eyes. They were shamed to have treated the old man so unkindly, and from that day they again ate with him at the table and took better care of him.

Source: "The Grandfather and His Little Grandson" from *A Harvest of Russian Children's Literature*, edited by Miriam Morton. Copyright © 1967. University of California Press (Berkeley and Los Angeles, CA)

▶ Making the Connection

1. What reasons did Tolstoy give for writing stories for children? **FCAT LA.A.2.3.2**

2. What do you think the young peasant and his wife learned from their son? **FCAT LA.E.2.3.1**

3. **Making Comparisons** Compare this story with one you have learned. How are they different? How are they the same? **FCAT LA.A.1.3.2**

The Republics Emerge

Guide to Reading

Main Idea

The Eurasian republics of the Caucasus and Central Asia are trying to build new economies and governments.

Terms to Know

- fault
- cash crop
- steppe
- nomad
- oasis
- elevation
- bilingual

Reading Strategy

In a chart like this, write two facts about each republic in the Caucasus and Central Asia. **FCAT** LA.A.1.3.2

Country	Facts
Armenia	
Azerbaijan	
Georgia	
Kazakhstan	
Uzbekistan	
Turkmenistan	
Kyrgyzstan	
Tajikistan	

The following are the major Sunshine State Standards covered in this section.

SS.B.2.3.8:
Knows world patterns of resource distribution and utilization

SS.B.2.3.6:
Understands the environmental consequences of people changing the physical environment in various world locations

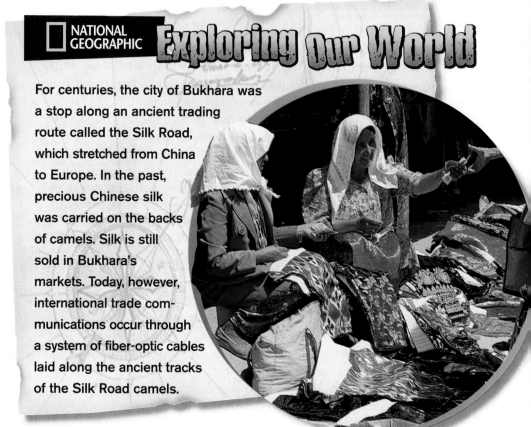

NATIONAL GEOGRAPHIC Exploring Our World

For centuries, the city of Bukhara was a stop along an ancient trading route called the Silk Road, which stretched from China to Europe. In the past, precious Chinese silk was carried on the backs of camels. Silk is still sold in Bukhara's markets. Today, however, international trade communications occur through a system of fiber-optic cables laid along the ancient tracks of the Silk Road camels.

The Eurasian republics all lie south of Russia, but in two different areas. The three republics of the **Caucasus** are located between the Black and Caspian Seas. The towering **Caucasus Mountains** give this region its name. The five republics of **Central Asia** dominate a huge area of land east of the Caspian Sea. Find these eight countries on the map on page 437.

Arabs, Turks, Persians, and Russians have ruled these countries at one time or another. Many of these people stayed, making up the different ethnic groups living in the Eurasian republics today. Disagreements among some of these groups have sparked violent conflicts.

The Eurasian republics were once part of the Soviet Union. When the Soviet Union collapsed in 1991, they became independent—some for the first time in centuries. Since then, they have struggled to move to a free market economy and democracy. What makes this struggle even more difficult is the enormous challenge of cleaning up the environment. Rapid industrialization during the Soviet era polluted the air and water. Diverting water for irrigation has drained rivers, and chemical fertilizers have badly damaged the soil.

Republics of the Caucasus

The Caucasus republics are **Armenia, Georgia,** and **Azerbaijan** (A•zuhr•by•JAHN). You may think that having the Caucasus Mountains so near would result in a cold climate. In fact, these three countries experience mostly a mild Mediterranean climate or dry steppe climate. The economic activity map below shows you that these favorable climates have resulted in much commercial farming. Farmers grow wheat, fruits, vegetables, and tea in river valleys.

Armenia   Armenia's 3.2 million people are mostly ethnic Armenians who share a unique language and culture. In A.D. 301, an Armenian king made Christianity the official religion—the first country to do so. About 94 percent of the nation's people belong to the Armenian Orthodox Church. Many Christian Armenians also live in a small territory claimed by neighboring Azerbaijan. Fighting over this land has hurt the economies of both countries.

Nearly 70 percent of Armenians live in cities. Founded in 782 B.C., **Yerevan**—the capital—is one of the world's most ancient cities.

NATIONAL GEOGRAPHIC

The Eurasian Republics: Economic Activity

Land Use
- Commercial farming
- Subsistence farming
- Ranching
- Hunting and gathering
- Manufacturing area
- Little or no activity

0 mi.   50°E   500
0 km   500
Two-Point Equidistant projection

Resources
- Coal
- Copper
- Fishing
- Gold
- Iron ore
- Lead
- Manganese
- Natural gas
- Petroleum
- Zinc

Applying Map Skills

1. What energy resources are found in the Eurasian republics?

2. What cities are manufacturing areas?

Find NGS online map resources @ www.nationalgeographic.com/maps

NATIONAL GEOGRAPHIC On Location

Kazakh Nomads

The traditional home of Kazakhs—called a yurt—can be easily taken apart and moved.

Culture Why would the Mongols and early Kazakh people need a house that could be moved? **FCAT** LA.A.2.3.1

Armenians are proud of its wide streets, attractive fountains, and colorful buildings made of volcanic stone. Although volcanoes no longer erupt here, Armenia sits uneasily on top of many **faults,** or cracks in the earth's crust. It often suffers serious earthquakes.

Azerbaijan   Azerbaijan is split in two by the country of Armenia. Most people belong to a group called Azeris and speak the Azeri language. They follow the Islamic religion.

More than half of the country's 8.2 million people live in cities. The capital, **Baku** (bah•KOO), is a port on the Caspian Sea. The center of the country's oil industry and manufacturing, Baku is known for the strong winds that blow through the city. The oil and natural gas deposits under the Caspian Sea are the most promising for the future of Azerbaijan's economy. The country has made agreements with foreign companies to develop these resources. Agriculture is important too. Farmers in dry areas use irrigation to grow cotton and tobacco as **cash crops,** or products grown for sale as exports.

Georgia   About 70 percent of Georgia's 4.7 million people are ethnic Georgians who are proud of their distinctive language, alphabet, and Christian heritage. Like Armenia, Georgia accepted Christianity in the A.D. 300s. Within the past 10 years, conflict has broken out between Georgians and the other ethnic groups in the country who want to set up their own countries.

T'bilisi (tuh•bih•LEE•see), Georgia's capital, is located near the mountains. The city has warm mineral springs heated by high temperatures inside the earth. Resorts along the mild Black Sea coast draw thousands of tourists each year. Georgia has many natural resources, such as copper, coal, manganese, and some oil. Swift rivers provide hydroelectric power for Georgia's industries. Skilled farmers produce nearly one-third of all the country's foods.

✓ Reading Check   How does Azerbaijan's religion differ from that in Armenia and Georgia?

The Central Asian Republics

The republics in Central Asia include **Kazakhstan** (kuh•ZAHK•STAHN), **Uzbekistan, Turkmenistan, Kyrgyzstan** (KIHR•gih•STAHN), and **Tajikistan.** All five countries follow the Islamic religion.

Kazakhstan   The largest of the Central Asian republics, Kazakhstan is almost four times the size of Texas. Toward the center of the country lie the Steppes. A **steppe** is a dry, treeless plain (similar to the Great

Plains in the United States). Farming is difficult in the harsh climate, but raising livestock on ranches is an important industry. Kazakhstan's mineral resources include copper, manganese, gold, zinc, and petroleum. Factories make machinery and chemicals and process foods.

About half of Kazakhstan's 14.8 million people are ethnic Kazakhs, whose ancestors were horse-riding warriors called the Mongols. Like the Mongols, the Kazakhs were mostly **nomads,** or people who move from place to place with herds of animals. Under Soviet rule, Kazakh nomads were forced to settle in one place. The Soviet government set up factories here, and Russian workers poured into the country. Today, Russians form Kazakhstan's second-largest ethnic group.

Uzbekistan   South of Kazakhstan lies Uzbekistan, which is slightly larger than California. Most of the country's 25.7 million people are Uzbeks who generally live in fertile valleys and oases. An **oasis** is a fertile or green area in a desert watered by an underground spring. **Tashkent,** the capital, is the largest city and industrial center in Central Asia. About 2,000 years ago, the oases of Tashkent, Bukhara, and Samarqand were part of the busy trade route called the Silk Road that linked China and Europe.

This country is one of the world's largest cotton producers. This boom in cotton, unfortunately, has had disastrous effects on the environment. Large farms needing irrigation have nearly drained away the rivers flowing into the **Aral Sea.** Uzbek leaders are now trying to add more variety to the economy. They want to use newly discovered deposits of oil, gas, and gold.

Turkmenistan   Turkmenistan is larger than neighboring Uzbekistan, but it has far fewer people. Why? Most of this vast country is part of a huge desert called the **Garagum** (GAHR•uh•GOOM). Look at the economic activity map on page 437. The Garagum, which means "black sand," is located in Turkmenistan's northern and central areas that have "little or no economic activity." Despite the harshness of the land, growing cotton and raising livestock are the leading economic activities. Not enough food is grown to feed everyone, however, and much food has to be imported.

Turkmenistan is important to world energy markets because it contains one of the world's largest reserves of natural gas. The country is hoping that its oil and natural gas will give it a brighter future.

Ashgabat, the capital, is Turkmenistan's largest city and leading economic and cultural center. Yet more than half of the country's 5.7 million people live in villages near oases. The Turkmen people used to be nomads who raised camels and other livestock in the desert. Like the Kazahks, the Turkmen were forced by the Soviets to settle on farms.

Kyrgyzstan   The lofty **Tian Shan** (tee•AHN SHAHN) mountain range makes up most of Kyrgyzstan. The climate here depends on an area's

The Aral Sea

This ship once moved along the waters of the Aral Sea. The sea was huge—the fourth-largest inland body of water in the world. To irrigate fields of cotton, Soviet leaders took water from the rivers that flowed into the Aral Sea. The sea shrank to one-half its former size in just 40 years. Now camels walk where fish once swam.

height above sea level, or elevation. Lower valleys and plains have warm, dry summers and chilly winters. Higher areas have cool summers and bitterly cold winters. A lack of fertile soil hinders farmers, but they manage to grow cotton, vegetables, and fruits. Many also raise sheep or cattle. Although the country has few industries, it does have valuable deposits of mercury and gold.

More than half of the people belong to the Kyrgyz ethnic group. Differences among clans, or family groups, often separate one part of the country from another. Kyrgyzstan is a bilingual country—one that has two official languages. These are Kirghiz, related to Turkish, and Russian. About 35 percent of the country's 5 million people live in cities, such as the capital, **Bishkek.**

Tajikistan Mountainous Tajikistan lies south of Kyrgyzstan. The highest mountain in Central Asia—**Ismail Samani Peak**—is located here. Mountain streams irrigate cotton, rice, and fruits grown in fertile river valleys. These streams also provide water for hydroelectric power.

The largest city is **Dushanbe** (doo•SHAM•buh), the capital. Most of Tajikistan's 6.6 million people are Tajiks, who are related to the Persians. Another 25 percent are Uzbeks, a group related to the Turks. In 1992 a bitter civil war broke out between rival clans. Many people were killed, and the economy was severely damaged. Despite a peace agreement in 1997, tensions still remain high.

✓**Reading Check** Name the five Central Asian republics.

 FCAT PRACTICE You can prepare for the FCAT-assessed standards by completing the correlated item(s) below.

Section 3 Assessment

Defining Terms
1. **Define** fault, cash crop, steppe, nomad, oasis, elevation, bilingual.

Recalling Facts
2. **Region** What common characteristics make the countries of Armenia, Azerbaijan, and Georgia a region?
3. **Economics** What is the most promising part of Azerbaijan's economy?
4. **Culture** Who were ancestors of the Kazakhs?

Critical Thinking
5. **Making Inferences** Why do most Turkmen live along the southern border of Turkmenistan?
6. **Understanding Cause and Effect** Why has the Aral Sea shrunk in size? **FCAT SC.D.2.3.2**

Graphic Organizer
7. **Organizing Information** Create a chart like the one shown below. Fill in the chart with information about Georgia and Uzbekistan that you learned in this section. **FCAT LA.A.1.3.2**

	Georgia	Uzbekistan
Ethnic group		
Natural resources		
Economic activities		

 Applying Social Studies Skills

8. **Analyzing Maps** Look at the political map on page 397 in the **Regional Atlas.** Which of the Eurasian republics do not border Russia?

TIME
PERSPECTIVES

The New Russia

Is Democracy Working?

Compiled and adapted from TIME.

In Moscow a cathedral destroyed by the Communists has been rebuilt. Older Russians are especially pleased.

A New Nation and Economy

Evaluating Media
LA.A.2.3.6

Daniel Strigin lives in Moscow, the capital of Russia. There he shares a tiny, three-room apartment with his mother, his grandmother, his wife—and the parts of a one-seat airplane. Strigin, 30, is what Russians call a *kulibini*—a part-time inventor. By day he works as a computer technician. In his free time, he works on his dream of flying a plane he built himself.

Strigin is one of tens of thousands of *kulibini* in Russia. "There is something in the Russian man's soul," he says, "that pushes him to invent."

The impulse to invent is something Russia needs badly today. Its Communist government collapsed in 1991. Since then, the country of 146 million people has been struggling to remake itself as a democracy with a **free market economy**.

Remarkable Gains

The **Russian Federation,** the official name of Russia, has made great strides:

- Russians now elect their leaders, something they had never been allowed to do before.

- Reforms have turned Russia's state-controlled economy into a free market system that grew steadily from 1999 to 2003.

Housing goes up in Provideniya, a port city west of Alaska in Russia's Far East.

WOLFGANG KAEHLER/CORBIS

- Russia has shrunk its borders. Once it had been the Soviet Union's leading power. But that union fell to pieces. Now all 15 of the former republics, including Russia, are independent nations.

Russia still has a long way to go. Its elected leaders sometimes act illegally to silence their critics. Steel and other manufacturing companies are old and controlled by a few powerful people. There aren't enough privately owned **enterprises,** or businesses. Criminal gangs and corruption thrive. And in Chechnya, part of the Russian Federation, rebels have been at war with the government since 1994.

A man votes near a statue of Vladimir Lenin, the first Communist dictator.

A man dressed as a bear advertises a new restaurant in St. Petersburg.

Billboards near St. Basil Cathedral are evidence of the new Russian economy.

From Misery to Stability

The reforms caused great hardship. Under communism the state owned all businesses. In the shift to privately owned enterprises, thousands of farms and factories failed. Millions lost their jobs, and the government had no money. In 1999, 55 million people—one out of every three Russians—scraped by on less than $6 a month.

Reforms were introduced to create a stronger free market economy. More Russians now own factories, shops and other businesses. In 1999, 61% of Russians worked for private companies, compared to only 16% in 1991. By 2003, Russia had experienced four years of relative economic and political stability.

Uncertain Change

Russia and the world are waiting to see just how permanent the reforms will be. Establishing a lasting democracy with a market economy will take a lot of work. Important steps include forming reliable government institutions and an acceptance of the rule of law by Russian society.

Russia has many strengths. It is the world's largest country, and its people are well educated. Russia's natural resources—oil, lumber, and minerals—are plentiful. And many of its privately owned factories have figured out how to make first-rate products.

"A Russian is **inventive**," says one of Daniel Strigin's *kulibini* friends, "because he has to find solutions in bad conditions."

Uncertain conditions haunt today's Russia. Time will tell whether its people will continue to have the will—and inventiveness—to overcome them. ▪

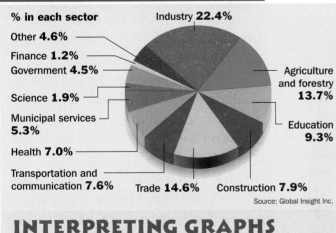

Where Russians Work

% in each sector

- Other **4.6%**
- Finance **1.2%**
- Government **4.5%**
- Science **1.9%**
- Municipal services **5.3%**
- Health **7.0%**
- Transportation and communication **7.6%**
- Trade **14.6%**
- Construction **7.9%**
- Education **9.3%**
- Agriculture and forestry **13.7%**
- Industry **22.4%**

Source: Global Insight Inc.

INTERPRETING GRAPHS

Explaining How does this graph tell you that about one in four Russians makes or sells industrial products? **FCAT MA.E.3.3.1**

443

Are Russians Better Off?

Evaluating
Media
LA.A.2.3.6

Valentina Fedotova cries when she tells her story. In 1946 she was a student nurse in the Ukrainian city of Kiev. One day the secret police arrested her. They never told her why. After a four-minute "trial," she was shipped off to Russia's brutally cold Siberia. There she spent 10 years in a labor camp, working year-round mining gold. After 10 years, she was freed. But her sentence required her to stay in Siberia for 10 more years. By the time those years were up, Fedotova

EXPLORING THE ISSUE

1. **Making Inferences** Why might younger Russians find it easier than older Russians to learn to rely on themselves?
   FCAT LA.A.1.3.2
2. **Contrasting** Elected leaders are less likely than dictators to arrest and imprison people without cause. Why do you think this is so? **FCAT** LA.A.2.3.1

was a broken woman. She never left the far east, where she now lives alone.

Millions of people who lived through the Soviet era, from 1917 to 1991, have similar stories. The Communist government headed by Joseph Stalin between 1924 and 1953 imprisoned, executed, or starved to death millions of people. Prisoners in labor camps built canals, railroads, hydroelectric stations, mines, and other industries.

A New Self-Reliance

With the freedom that followed the Soviet Union's collapse in 1991, people had to take responsibility for their lives. "In today's Russia," a businessman says, "you have to rely on yourself."

Russians are becoming more self-reliant. Thanks to reforms and private enterprise, Russia's economy is growing. Wages are rising and companies are buying materials to help them grow in the future. Growing political and economic stability, most Russians believe, make them better off today than ever. ■

▼ Many older Russians long for earlier times. This war veteran's hero is Joseph Stalin, a brutal dictator.

CHRISTOPHER MORRIS/BLACK STAR

The Road to Somewhere

Evaluating
Media
LA.A.2.3.6

As the Soviet Union was ending in 1991, protesters gathered in Moscow's Red Square. One man held a sign that said, "70 Years to Nowhere." The sign spoke of the past—the years of Communist rule that had led to a dead end.

What about the next 70 years? They should bring fairer courts, for one thing. Russian judges are used to taking the government's side. Soon juries will be deciding many cases, making courts more even-handed.

Health and Jobs

Tomorrow's Russians will probably be wealthier and healthier than today's. Now, hospital patients must supply their own food, sheets, and medicine. Life expectancy for men is only 59 years—down from 64 in 1989.

But Russia's healthcare system is getting stronger, along with the nation's economy. A stronger economy will mean more jobs and less poverty. Steady jobs should persuade Russian men to stop abusing alcohol. That drug is shortening their lives.

How quickly will these changes come? It all depends on how quickly Russians change the way they think. Russians don't yet have democracy in their hearts. They are not used to voting or taking part in community affairs, either as volunteers or as elected officials. They tend to think it is more important to help themselves than their neighbors.

▲ **Russian students hope to enjoy freedoms their parents never knew.**

Self-Serve Government

Government workers think the same way. Few see themselves as **public servants.** Many of them serve themselves first. People must pay money "under the table" to get driver's licenses, fair treatment by police, and permits to build houses.

Today "70 Years to Somewhere" could be Russia's slogan. It's just far too early to say what that somewhere will be like.

EXPLORING THE ISSUE

1. **Explaining** Why might a stronger Russian economy lead to better health? **FCAT LA.A.2.3.1**

2. **Problem Solving** What could the United States do to help Russians learn to put "democracy in their hearts"? **FCAT LA.A.2.3.1**

Helping Russia Rebuild: What Can One Person Do?

Evaluating
Media
LA.A.2.3.6

In July 2000, former hockey star Mike Gartner made boys in two Russian hockey clubs very happy. One club was in Penza, a town outside Moscow. The other club was far to the east in Novokuznetsk, a city in Siberia. Gartner gave each club something it couldn't afford—hockey equipment worth thousands of dollars.

Goals & Dreams

Gartner heads the Goals & Dreams program of the National Hockey League Players' Association (NHLPA). "We're not doing this to try to make future NHL hockey players," Gartner said. "The goal is to try to make kids better people."

That's also the goal of the head of Novokuznetsk's hockey. "We are working toward a healthier lifestyle for our youth," he said.

That's not easy in a nation as hard-pressed as Russia. The Novokuznetsk club gives its members free food and medical care. But it has no money left over to buy equipment.

Encouraging Words

You can help Russians simply by supporting efforts like the NHLPA's. You don't have to send sports equipment. You don't have to send money. Just send those groups a letter, letting them know how much you appreciate their efforts. Groups that provide assistance to others

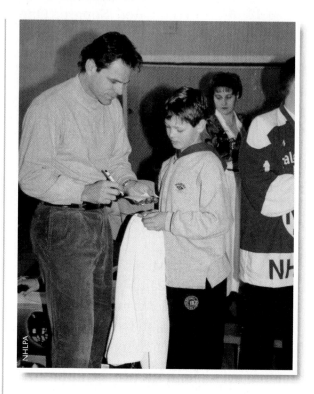

▲ Former pro hockey star Mike Gartner meets members of a Russian hockey club.

gain strength just from knowing that others care.

Many groups are helping Russia today. One is the Eurasia Foundation, based in Washington, D.C. The World Wildlife Federation is another.

And don't forget Goals & Dreams. "We have stacks of letters from kids and families thanking us," Mike Gartner said. "This is a great job—kind of like being Santa Claus." ■

REVIEW AND ASSESS

UNDERSTANDING THE ISSUE

1. Defining Key Terms
Write definitions for the following terms: *kulibini, free market economy, Russian Federation, enterprise, inventive, public servant.*

FCAT LA.A.1.3.2

2. Writing to Inform Imagine you are in a Russian middle school. Write a letter to an American friend explaining Russia's challenges. Use at least five of the key terms listed above.

FCAT LA.B.1.3.2

3. Writing to Persuade
"In today's Russia, you have to learn to rely on yourself." Write a letter to an imaginary Russian friend. Explain why self-reliance is a good thing.

FCAT LA.B.1.3.2

INTERNET RESEARCH ACTIVITY

4. Russian army units have "adopted" a few thousand of the 1 million to 2 million Russian kids who have no home. Children as young as 11 live on army bases, wear uniforms, and attend school. They are not sent to war. Elsewhere children do fight wars. To learn about them, with your teacher's help, browse the Internet for information. List ways that real child soldiers seem like, and are different from, Russian kids in uniform. Compare your list with those of your classmates.

FCAT LA.A.2.3.5

5. Since 1999, the Library of Congress has brought Russian officials to the United States to see democracy at work. Browse the Internet to find out more about this Library of Congress program. In a 250-word essay, describe the program and explain how it might benefit both Russians and Americans. Can you think of additional programs that would guide Russia?

FCAT LA.A.2.3.5, LA.B.1.3.2

The old and new reflect Russia's future. ▶

BEYOND THE CLASSROOM

6. Visit your school or local library to learn about the Soviet Union. Working in groups, find out what it was like to live under a Communist government. What basic freedoms did Russians not have? Discuss your findings with your classmates.

7. Research another nation that has exchanged one-party rule for democracy. What might Russians learn from the other nation's experience? Put your findings in a report.

FCAT LA.B.1.3.2

SERGEI GUNEYEV/TIMEPIX

RUSSIA'S 11 TIME ZONES

The earth is divided into 24 time zones, one for each hour of the day. Russia spans 11 time zones, stretching nearly halfway around the globe. We've labeled Russia's time zones from A to K. There's an hour's difference between each zone. It's always later in the East, where the sun rises, than in the West.

BUILDING MAP READING SKILLS

1. Interpreting Maps If it's 9:00 A.M. in Kaliningrad, what time is it in Moscow? What time is it in Tura, Chita, Vladivostok, and Magadan? Suppose it is 2:00 A.M., January 20, in Tomsk. What time and day is it in Samara? **FCAT MA.B.1.3.4**

2. Transferring Data Across the top of a sheet of paper, write the name of one city in each time zone, from Kaliningrad to Anadyr. Draw a clock beneath each name. Set the sixth clock at midnight. Draw the correct time on the 10 other clocks.

FOR UPDATES ON WORLD ISSUES GO TO
www.timeclassroom.com/glencoe

447

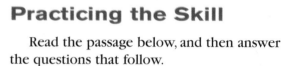

Study and Writing Skill

Using Primary and Secondary Sources

So much information comes our way in today's world. How can you analyze it to decide what is truly useful and accurate?

Learning the Skill

There are two basic types of information sources. *Primary sources* are original records of events made by the people who witnessed them. They include letters, photographs, and artifacts. *Secondary sources* are documents created after an event occurred. They report an event.

When reading sources, try to learn more about the person who wrote the information. Most people have a point of view, or bias. This bias influences the way they write about events.

To analyze information, follow these steps:

- Identify who created the document and when it was created.
- Determine whether the information is a primary or secondary source.
- Read the document. Who and what is it about? What are its purpose and main ideas?
- Determine how the author's point of view, or bias, is reflected in the work.

▼ A polluted playground in Azerbaijan

Practicing the Skill

Read the passage below, and then answer the questions that follow.

I went south to Kazakhstan and, at 4:45 A.M., stumbled off a train in Aral and went to the hospital. Beginning in the 1970s the people became ill with hepatitis, typhus, and other diseases. They drank from the rivers, as always, but now the shrunken rivers ran with sewage, industrial metals, and poisons such as DDT. "It wasn't possible to mix infant formula with that water," said a doctor. "It made goo, like soft cheese."

Dust storms often blow for days, sweeping up tons of salts and fertilizers. Doctors brace then to receive children with breathing problems. Kazakhstan, declared a Kazakh writer, was the Soviet Union's "junk heap."

Adapted from "The U.S.S.R.'s Lethal Legacy" by Mike Edwards, *National Geographic*, August 1994.

1. Is this a primary or secondary source?
2. Who is the author of this passage?
3. What is the document about?
4. Where does it take place?
5. What is the purpose of this passage? **FCAT LA.A.2.3.2**
6. What, if any, evidence of bias do you find? **FCAT LA.A.2**

Applying the Skill

Analyze one of the letters to the editor in your local newspaper. Summarize the main idea, the writer's purpose, and any primary sources the writer may refer to. **FCAT LA.A.2.3.2**

GO TO Practice key skills with **Glencoe Skillbuilder Interactive Workbook, Level 1.**

Reading Review

Section 1 | From Communism to Free Enterprise

Terms to Know

free market economy
heavy industry
light industry
nuclear energy
life expectancy

Main Idea

Russia has many resources but faces challenges in adjusting to a new economic system.

✓ **Economics** The change to a free market economy has been a challenge to many Russians as they face rising unemployment and rising prices.

✓ **Economics** Moscow, with many industries, is the economic center of Russia.

✓ **Movement** Ports in the northwest, southwest, and east carry on trade between Russia and other countries.

✓ **Location** Siberia has many resources, but the area is so cold and remote that it is difficult to tap these resources.

Section 2 | Russia's People and Culture

Terms to Know

democracy
federal republic
majority group
minority group

Main Idea

Russians have a rich cultural past and are learning to live in a democracy.

✓ **Government** Russia is a federal republic with powers divided between national and regional governments.

✓ **Culture** Russia is a huge, populous country with about 100 different ethnic groups.

✓ **Religion** Russians practice many different faiths, but most are Russian Orthodox Christians.

✓ **Culture** Russian artists, composers, and writers often used themes or traditions based on Russian history.

Section 3 | The Republics Emerge

Terms to Know

fault
cash crop
steppe
nomad
oasis
elevation
bilingual

Main Idea

The republics of the Caucasus and Central Asia are trying to build new economies and governments.

✓ **Economics** The Caucasus republics have struggled to develop their own industries and businesses but are facing many ethnic conflicts.

✓ **Environment** The Central Asian republics face enormous challenges in cleaning up their environments.

✓ **Culture** Almost all of the people in the five Central Asian republics are Muslims.

Republic Square in
Yerevan, Armenia ▶

The New Russia and Independent Republics

FCAT PRACTICE You can prepare for the FCAT-assessed standards by completing the correlated item(s) below.

Using Key Terms

Match the terms in Part A with their definitions in Part B.

A.

1. majority group
2. light industry
3. nuclear energy
4. steppe
5. bilingual
6. democracy
7. nomad
8. oasis
9. heavy industry
10. federal republic

B.

a. government in which people freely elect their leaders
b. energy from controlled atomic reactions
c. dry, treeless plain
d. group that controls the wealth and power
e. green area in a desert
f. production of consumer goods
g. person who moves from place to place
h. production of industrial goods
i. government in which national and state governments share powers
j. having two official languages

Reviewing the Main Ideas

Section 1 From Communism to Free Enterprise

11. **Economics** What type of economic system has Russia adopted?
12. **Economics** Where are Russia's most productive farmlands?
13. **Movement** What river carries almost half of Russia's river traffic?
14. **Location** Why is it difficult to tap Siberia's resources?

Section 2 Russia's People and Culture

15. **Government** What political challenges face Russians and their officials?
16. **Culture** In which city would you find the Hermitage Museum?
17. **History** What happened to religion during the Communist rule of Russia?

Section 3 The Republics Emerge

18. **Place** What is the capital of Azerbaijan?
19. **Place** What desert occupies most of Turkmenistan?
20. **Culture** What religion do the people of the Central Asian republics follow?

 NATIONAL GEOGRAPHIC

The Eurasian Republics

Place Location Activity

On a separate sheet of paper, match the letters on the map with the numbered places listed below.

1. Kazakhstan
2. Aral Sea
3. Caspian Sea
4. Turkmenistan
5. Azerbaijan
6. Armenia
7. Tajikistan
8. Baku

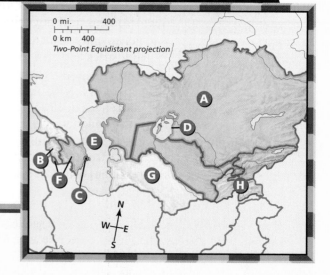

Critical Thinking

21. **Making Generalizations** How have recent changes in Russia affected its economy? **FCAT** LA.A.2.3.1

22. **Organizing Information** Create a chart like this one. Then list the similarities and differences between the economies of two Central Asian republics. **FCAT** LA.A.1.3.2

Country	Similarities	Differences

Comparing Regions Activity

23. **Culture** Look at the circle graph on page 443 titled "Where Russians Work." Create your own circle graph and title it "Where Americans Work." Find information in your textbook and on the Internet to show the jobs people in the United States hold. Do you think the Russian graph will someday look more like the U.S. graph? Why or why not? **FCAT** MA.E.1.3.1

Mental Mapping Activity

24. **Focus on the Region** Create a simple outline map of Russia and the Eurasian republics, and then label the following:

- Black Sea
- Caspian Sea
- Aral Sea
- Volga River
- Ural Mountains
- Kazakhstan
- Armenia
- Lake Baikal

Technology Skills Activity

25. **Using the Internet** Search the Internet for information on the problems facing the Aral Sea. Find out what distinctive creatures live in the Aral Sea that cannot be found anywhere else in the world. Find a map that shows what countries border the Aral Sea.

Standardized Test Practice

Directions: Study the map below, and then answer the question that follows.

1. **Which of the following statements about this map is NOT true?**

   F Chechnya lies along Russia's southern border.

   G Chechnya is situated between the Black and Caspian Seas.

   H Chechnya's landscape is mostly flat, fertile farmland.

   J Chechnya's nearest neighbor is Georgia.

Test-Taking Tip: Be careful when you see the words NOT or EXCEPT in a question. Read all the answer choices and choose the one that *does not* fit with the question. Quickly eliminate answers that are true. Make sure that your answer choice is supported by information on the map.

Unit 6

Business district at dusk, Dubai, United Arab Emirates

Man gazing out across ▶ the vast expanses of the Sahara

NATIONAL
GEOGRAPHIC

North Africa and Southwest Asia

Ancient Egyptian pyramids overlook industrial smoke-stacks. Three-thousand-year-old stone temples tower over sparkling new oil derricks. Remote mountain villages and endless desert seas of sand and gravel contrast with modern beaches overrun by tourists. All of these extremes can be found within the culture region of North Africa and Southwest Asia.

▲ Shepherd tending sheep,
Atlas Mountains, Morocco

NGS ONLINE
www.nationalgeographic.com/education

453

Focus on:

North Africa and Southwest Asia

LYING AT THE INTERSECTION of Europe, Asia, and Africa, this sprawling region has long been a meeting place for diverse peoples and cultures. Troubled by bitter conflicts and plagued by a scarcity of water, the region is also extremely rich in oil and other natural resources.

The Land

Glance at a physical map of North Africa and Southwest Asia and you will see a jumble of mountain chains. In the west, the Atlas Mountains—Africa's longest range—run through Morocco and Algeria. Slanting southeast through Turkey and Iran are the Zagros Mountains, where earthquakes often occur. Farther east in Afghanistan are the Hindu Kush—a lofty mountain range that is shared with neighboring Pakistan to the east. The Khyber Pass cuts through the Hindu Kush. The Pass has been used for centuries as a trade route linking Southwest Asia to other parts of Asia.

Seas of Sand Mountains block moist winds, helping to create vast deserts across much of the region. The Sahara, in North Africa, is the world's largest hot desert. It covers an area about the size of the continental United States. The Rub' al Khali, or Empty Quarter, covers about one-fourth of the Arabian Peninsula. The Empty Quarter has mountains of sand that reach heights of more than 1,000 feet (305 m).

Vital Waterways Through these very dry landscapes flow great rivers that bring life-giving water. The world's longest river, the Nile, runs 4,160 miles (6,693 km) through Egypt to the Mediterranean Sea. The Tigris and Euphrates Rivers flow southeast through Turkey, Syria, and Iraq. The earliest civilizations arose near these rivers.

The Climate

Water is precious in much of this region. Most areas receive a meager 10 inches (25 cm) or less of rainfall each year. In such dry lands, agriculture is only possible in limited areas. Crops grow along rivers and irrigation canals or in places where natural springs bubble to the surface to create lush but isolated oases.

In areas with a steppe climate, where enough rain falls to support grasses, people raise live-stock such as sheep, camels, and goats. Steppes cover parts of many Southwest Asian countries. A narrow band of steppe runs along the north-ern edge of the Sahara too.

Nile River flowing through
Aswan, Egypt

The areas that border the Mediterranean, Black, and Caspian Seas enjoy a milder Mediterranean climate. Although summers are hot and dry, the winter months bring enough precipitation to turn coastal lowlands into green landscapes.

The Economy

Like water, natural resources are distributed unevenly across North Africa and Southwest Asia. This helps to create great differences in living standards. The region includes some of the world's wealthiest nations—and some of the world's poorest.

An Oil-Rich Region Enormous reserves of oil and natural gas lie in certain areas, including lands in central North Africa, along the Persian Gulf, and around the Caspian Sea. Countries such as Saudi Arabia and Kuwait, which export petroleum products to fuel-hungry societies, generally enjoy high standards of living. Money

from oil exports has helped to build skyscrapers, modern freeways, schools, and hospitals.

Farming and Herding In contrast, those countries with economies based on agriculture have much lower standards of living. Only a small percentage of the region's land is suitable for growing crops. In river valleys and along the coasts, where there is water and fertile soil, farmers raise citrus fruits, grapes, dates, grains, and cotton. Nomadic herding is common across the large expanses of this region that are too dry for crops.

The People

Great pyramids, built as tombs for Egyptian rulers, rise above desert sands. They are a reminder that some of the world's oldest civilizations developed in this region. Roughly 5,000 years ago, the ancient Egyptians built a kingdom along the life-giving Nile River. The Sumerian civilization, an even older society, flourished in the fertile valley between the Tigris and Euphrates Rivers. Persians, Greeks, Romans, and Arabs all have left their mark on the cultures of North Africa and Southwest Asia.

Ancient Cities–Modern Challenges Water still dictates where people settle in this region. Most cities lie along seacoasts or rivers, or near desert oases. Among the largest cities are Cairo, Egypt; Istanbul, Turkey; and Tehran, Iran. These cities and others have been growing rapidly as

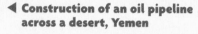

◀ **Construction of an oil pipeline across a desert, Yemen**

villagers move to them in search of a better life. As a result, governments must work to find solutions to the problems of overcrowding, poverty, and pollution.

Ethnic and Religious Rivalries

In North Africa and Southwest Asia, most of the people are Arabs. Many other ethnic groups also live in the region. This situation has sparked violent clashes. Despite the ethnic rivalries, many who live here are united by religion. Most people practice Islam, which developed in this region centuries ago. Two other major religions, Judaism and Christianity, also began here. The country of Israel is the Jewish national homeland. Differences among religions, however, have contributed to conflicts in places such as Israel and the West Bank, Lebanon, and Iraq.

Desert dwellers sharing a meal, Saudi Arabia ▼

Data Bits

Country	Automobiles per 1,000 people	Television sets per 1,000 people
Jordan	50	83
Kuwait	317	480
Lebanon	313	355
Morocco	41	165
Yemen	15	286

Population: Urban ▓ vs. Rural ▓

Country	Urban	Rural
Jordan	79%	21%
Kuwait	96%	4%
Lebanon	90%	10%
Morocco	56%	44%
Yemen	25%	75%

Sources: *World Development Indicators*, 2002; *The World Almanac*, 2004.

Exploring the Region

1. How do mountains help create deserts across much of the region?

2. What parts of the region receive the most rainfall?

3. Why do some countries in this region have high standards of living?

4. What religion do most people in the region practice?

North Africa and Southwest Asia

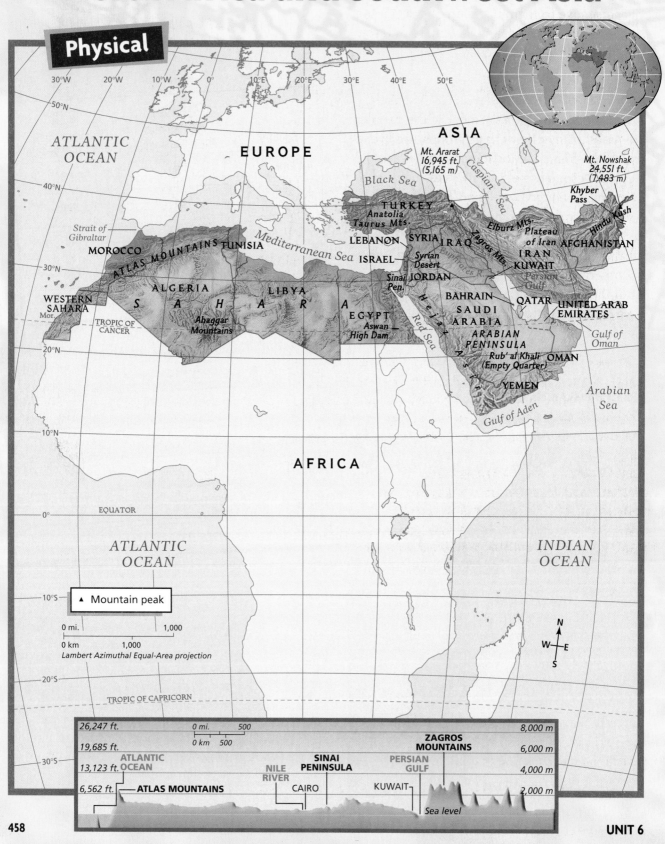

Physical

458

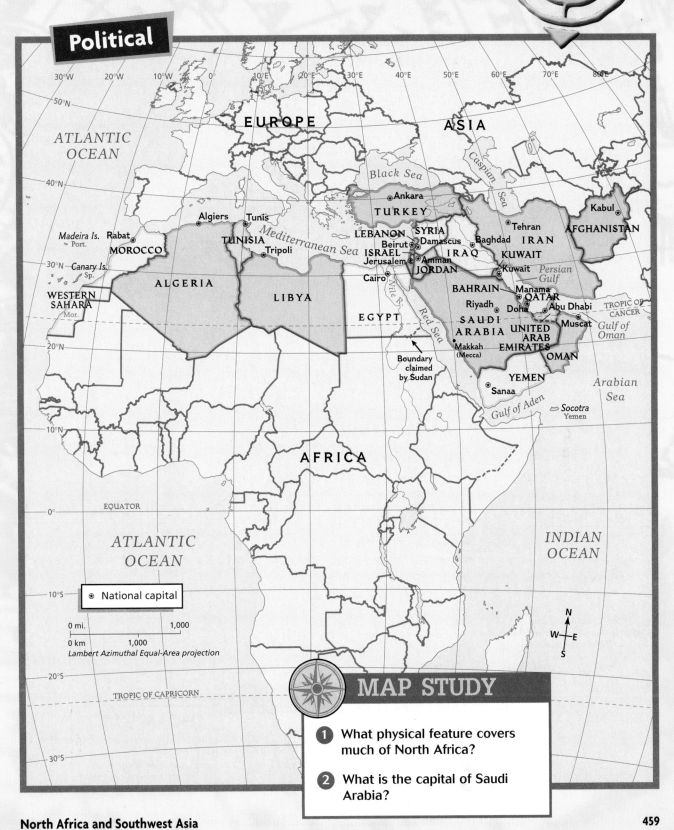

Political

EUROPE

ASIA

ATLANTIC
OCEAN

Black Sea

Caspian Sea

Ankara

TURKEY

Algiers   Tunis

Madeira Is. Rabat
Port.

Tehran

Kabul

AFGHANISTAN

LEBANON   SYRIA
Beirut   Damascus   Baghdad   IRAN

TUNISIA

Mediterranean Sea

Tripoli

ISRAEL
Jerusalem   Amman
JORDAN

IRAQ

KUWAIT

Kuwait   *Persian Gulf*

MOROCCO

Canary Is.
Sp.

ALGERIA

LIBYA

Cairo

BAHRAIN   Manama
QATAR

Riyadh   Doha   Abu Dhabi

TROPIC OF
CANCER

WESTERN
SAHARA
Mor.

EGYPT

Red Sea

SAUDI
ARABIA

UNITED
ARAB
EMIRATES

Muscat

*Gulf of
Oman*

Makkah
(Mecca)

OMAN

*Arabian
Sea*

Boundary
claimed
by Sudan

YEMEN

Sanaa

Gulf of Aden

Socotra
Yemen

AFRICA

ATLANTIC
OCEAN

INDIAN
OCEAN

EQUATOR

⊛ National capital

0 mi.   1,000

0 km   1,000
Lambert Azimuthal Equal-Area projection

N
W   E
S

TROPIC OF CAPRICORN

MAP STUDY

1 What physical feature covers much of North Africa?

2 What is the capital of Saudi Arabia?

North Africa and Southwest Asia

North Africa and Southwest Asia

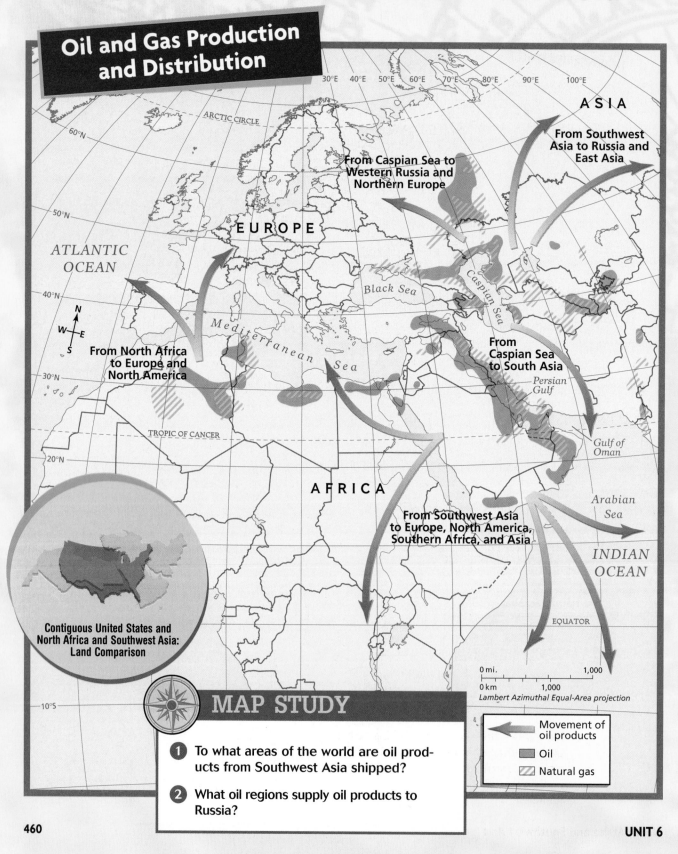

Oil and Gas Production and Distribution

From Caspian Sea to Western Russia and Northern Europe

From Southwest Asia to Russia and East Asia

ASIA

EUROPE

ATLANTIC OCEAN

Black Sea

Caspian Sea

From Caspian Sea to South Asia

From North Africa to Europe and North America

Mediterranean Sea

Persian Gulf

TROPIC OF CANCER

Gulf of Oman

AFRICA

Arabian Sea

From Southwest Asia to Europe, North America, Southern Africa, and Asia

INDIAN OCEAN

EQUATOR

0 mi. 1,000
0 km 1,000
Lambert Azimuthal Equal-Area projection

Contiguous United States and North Africa and Southwest Asia: Land Comparison

MAP STUDY

1 To what areas of the world are oil products from Southwest Asia shipped?

2 What oil regions supply oil products to Russia?

Movement of oil products

Oil

Natural gas

Geo Extremes

① **HIGHEST POINT**
Mt. Nowshak
(Afghanistan–Pakistan border)
24,551 ft. (7,483 m) high

② **LOWEST POINT**
Dead Sea
(Israel and Jordan)
1,349 ft. (411 m)
below sea level

③ **LONGEST RIVER**
Nile River
4,160 mi.
(6,693 km) long

④ **LARGEST LAKE**
Caspian Sea
143,244 sq. mi.
(371,000 sq. km)

⑤ **LARGEST DESERT**
Sahara (northern Africa)
3,475,000 sq. mi.
(9,000,208 sq. km)

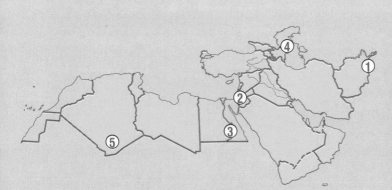

COMPARING POPULATION:
United States and Selected Countries of North Africa and Southwest Asia

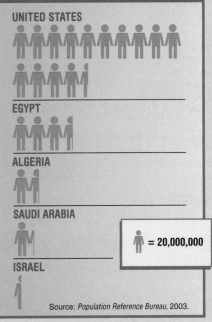

UNITED STATES

EGYPT

ALGERIA

SAUDI ARABIA

ISRAEL

= 20,000,000

Source: *Population Reference Bureau*, 2003.

URBAN POPULATIONS:
Selected Cities of North Africa and Southwest Asia

ISTANBUL, TURKEY

TEHRAN, IRAN

CAIRO, EGYPT

ALEXANDRIA, EGYPT

= 500,000

ANKARA, TURKEY

Source: *World Gazetteer*, 2003.

GRAPHIC STUDY

① The lowest point on the earth is found in this region. Where is it?

② How does the population of Cairo compare to that of Tehran? How does the population of Ankara compare to that of Cairo? **FCAT MA.E.3.3.1**

Country Profiles

  ALGERIA

POPULATION:
31,700,000
35 per sq. mi.
14 per sq. km

LANGUAGES:
Arabic, French, Berber

MAJOR EXPORT:
Petroleum

MAJOR IMPORT:
Machinery

CAPITAL:
Algiers

LANDMASS:
919,591 sq. mi.
2,381,741 sq. km

 **AFGHANISTAN**

POPULATION:
28,700,000
114 per sq. mi.
44 per sq. km

LANGUAGES:
Pashto, Dari

MAJOR EXPORTS:
Fruits and Nuts

MAJOR IMPORT:
Foods

CAPITAL:
Kabul

LANDMASS:
251,772 sq. mi.
652,090 sq. km

 BAHRAIN

POPULATION:
700,000
2,545 per sq. mi.
983 per sq. km

LANGUAGE:
Arabic

MAJOR EXPORT:
Petroleum

MAJOR IMPORT:
Machinery

CAPITAL:
Manama

LANDMASS:
266 sq. mi.
698 sq. km

 EGYPT

POPULATION:
72,100,000
186 per sq. mi.
72 per sq. km

LANGUAGE:
Arabic

MAJOR EXPORT:
Crude Oil

MAJOR IMPORT:
Machinery

CAPITAL:
Cairo

LANDMASS:
386,660 sq. mi.
1,001,449 sq. km

 IRAN

POPULATION:
66,600,000
106 per sq. mi.
41 per sq. km

LANGUAGES:
Persian, Kurdish

MAJOR EXPORT:
Petroleum

MAJOR IMPORT:
Machinery

CAPITAL:
Tehran

LANDMASS:
630,575 sq. mi.
1,633,189 sq. km

 IRAQ

POPULATION:
24,200,000
143 per sq. mi.
55 per sq. km

LANGUAGES:
Arabic, Kurdish

MAJOR EXPORT:
Crude Oil

MAJOR IMPORT:
Machinery

CAPITAL:
Baghdad

LANDMASS:
169,236 sq. mi.
438,321 sq. km

 ISRAEL

POPULATION:
6,700,000
825 per sq. mi.
319 per sq. km

LANGUAGES:
Hebrew, Arabic

MAJOR EXPORT:
Polished Diamonds

MAJOR IMPORT:
Chemicals

CAPITAL:
Jerusalem *

LANDMASS:
8,131 sq. mi.
21,059 sq. km

 JORDAN

POPULATION:
5,500,000
159 per sq. mi.
61 per sq. km

LANGUAGE:
Arabic

MAJOR EXPORT:
Phosphates

MAJOR IMPORT:
Crude Oil

CAPITAL:
Amman

LANDMASS:
34,444 sq. mi.
89,210 sq. km

* Israel has proclaimed Jerusalem as its capital, but many countries' embassies are located in Tel Aviv.

 KUWAIT

POPULATION:
2,400,000
346 per sq. mi.
134 per sq. km

LANGUAGE:
Arabic

MAJOR EXPORT:
Petroleum

MAJOR IMPORT:
Foods

CAPITAL:
Kuwait

LANDMASS:
6,880 sq. mi.
17,819 sq. km

 LEBANON

POPULATION:
4,200,000
1,045 per sq. mi.
403 per sq. km

LANGUAGES:
Arabic, French

MAJOR EXPORT:
Paper

MAJOR IMPORT:
Machinery

CAPITAL:
Beirut

LANDMASS:
4,015 sq. mi.
10,399 sq. km

 LIBYA

POPULATION:
5,500,000
8 per sq. mi.
3 per sq. km

LANGUAGE:
Arabic

MAJOR EXPORT:
Crude Oil

MAJOR IMPORT:
Machinery

CAPITAL:
Tripoli

LANDMASS:
679,359 sq. mi.
1,759,540 sq. km

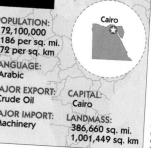 **MOROCCO** *

POPULATION:
30,700,000
178 per sq. mi.
69 per sq. km

LANGUAGES:
Arabic, French, Berber

MAJOR EXPORT:
Foods

MAJOR IMPORT:
Manufactured Goods

CAPITAL:
Rabat

LANDMASS:
269,757 sq. mi.
698,671 sq. km

* Morocco claims the Western Sahara area, but other countries do not accept this claim.

Countries and flags not drawn to scale

For more information on countries in this region, refer to the Nations of the World Data Bank in the Appendix.

OMAN
POPULATION:
2,600,000
32 per sq. mi.
12 per sq. km

LANGUAGE:
Arabic

MAJOR EXPORT:
Petroleum

CAPITAL:
Muscat

MAJOR IMPORT:
Machinery

LANDMASS:
82,031 sq. mi.
212,460 sq. km

Muscat

QATAR
POPULATION:
600,000
148 per sq. mi.
57 per sq. km

LANGUAGE:
Arabic

MAJOR EXPORT:
Petroleum

CAPITAL:
Doha

MAJOR IMPORT:
Machinery

LANDMASS:
4,247 sq. mi.
11,000 sq. km

Doha

SAUDI ARABIA
POPULATION:
24,100,000
29 per sq. mi.
11 per sq. km

LANGUAGE:
Arabic

MAJOR EXPORT:
Petroleum

CAPITAL:
Riyadh

MAJOR IMPORT:
Machinery

LANDMASS:
829,996 sq. mi.
2,149,690 sq. km

Riyadh

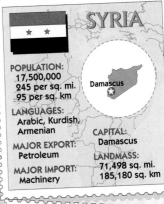

SYRIA
POPULATION:
17,500,000
245 per sq. mi.
95 per sq. km

LANGUAGES:
Arabic, Kurdish,
Armenian

MAJOR EXPORT:
Petroleum

CAPITAL:
Damascus

MAJOR IMPORT:
Machinery

LANDMASS:
71,498 sq. mi.
185,180 sq. km

Damascus

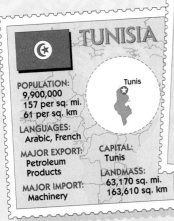

TUNISIA
POPULATION:
9,900,000
157 per sq. mi.
61 per sq. km

LANGUAGES:
Arabic, French

MAJOR EXPORT:
Petroleum
Products

CAPITAL:
Tunis

MAJOR IMPORT:
Machinery

LANDMASS:
63,170 sq. mi.
163,610 sq. km

Tunis

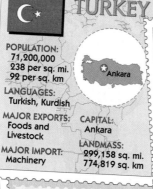

TURKEY
POPULATION:
71,200,000
238 per sq. mi.
92 per sq. km

LANGUAGES:
Turkish, Kurdish

MAJOR EXPORTS:
Foods and
Livestock

CAPITAL:
Ankara

MAJOR IMPORT:
Machinery

LANDMASS:
299,158 sq. mi.
774,819 sq. km

Ankara

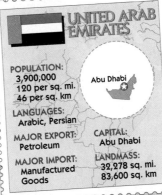

UNITED ARAB EMIRATES
POPULATION:
3,900,000
120 per sq. mi.
46 per sq. km

LANGUAGES:
Arabic, Persian

MAJOR EXPORT:
Petroleum

CAPITAL:
Abu Dhabi

MAJOR IMPORT:
Manufactured
Goods

LANDMASS:
32,278 sq. mi.
83,600 sq. km

Abu Dhabi

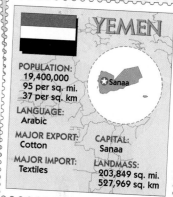

YEMEN
POPULATION:
19,400,000
95 per sq. mi.
37 per sq. km

LANGUAGE:
Arabic

MAJOR EXPORT:
Cotton

CAPITAL:
Sanaa

MAJOR IMPORT:
Textiles

LANDMASS:
203,849 sq. mi.
527,969 sq. km

Sanaa

BUILDING CITIZENSHIP

Religious Tolerance   In Southwest Asia, there are holy places of many religions, including temples, shrines, tombs, and mosques. Because Muslims are forbidden to worship statues or images, in some Islamic countries officials have destroyed ancient shrines and statues revered by Hindus or Buddhists.

1. Who owns religious properties in the United States?
2. Do you think government officials have a responsibility to protect valuable and sacred objects of all religions? **FCAT** LA.B.1.3.2

WRITE ABOUT IT

FCAT PRACTICE Completing the exercise below will help you prepare for the **FCAT Writing** test.

Write a short script that could be read by a television news broadcaster. The script should report on the destruction of a holy site by members of another religion. Present both points of view. **FCAT** LA.B.1.3.2

▲ **Destroyed Buddhist statue in Afghanistan**

Birthplace of Civilization

The World and Its People

NATIONAL GEOGRAPHIC

To learn more about the people and places of North Africa and Southwest Asia, view **The World and Its People Chapters 16** and **17** videos.

Social Studies ONLine

Chapter Overview Visit **The World and Its People** Web site at twip.glencoe.com and click on **Chapter 16–Chapter Overviews** to preview information about North Africa and Southwest Asia.

FCAT PRACTICE The activity below will help you prepare for the **FCAT Reading** test.

Compare-Contrast Make and use this foldable to help you determine how Mesopotamia and ancient Egypt were similar and different.

`FCAT LA.A.1.3.2`

Step 1 Fold a sheet of paper from side to side, leaving a 2-inch tab uncovered along the side.

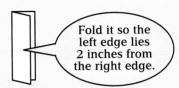

Fold it so the left edge lies 2 inches from the right edge.

Step 2 Turn the paper and fold it into thirds.

Step 3 Unfold and cut along the two inside fold lines.

Cut along the two folds on the front flap to make 3 tabs.

Step 4 Label your foldable as shown.

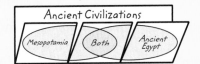

Ancient Civilizations

Mesopotamia   Both   Ancient Egypt

Reading and Writing As you read the chapter, write what you learn about these ancient civilizations under the tabs. Be sure to list similarities and differences under the appropriate tabs. `FCAT LA.A.1.3.2`

▲ **Avenue of the Sphinxes, Luxor, Egypt**

Why It Matters

Civilizations and Religions Emerge

Two of the world's first civilizations arose in Southwest Asia and North Africa about 5,000 years ago. The development of cities led to governments, laws, and trade. Organized religions emerged. These religions had the power to unite people, but also to create terrible conflict. The events that occurred centuries ago in the "birthplace of civilization" still influence our lives today.

Mesopotamia and Ancient Egypt

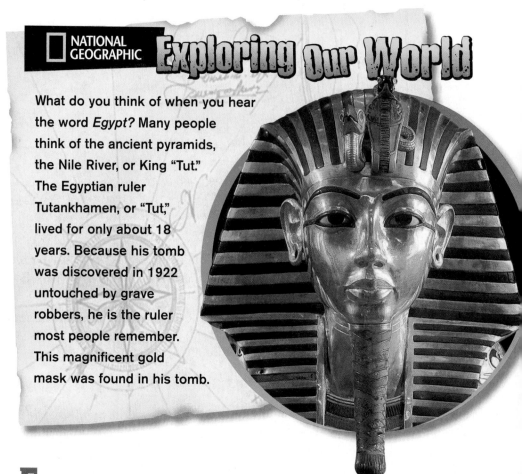

NATIONAL GEOGRAPHIC Exploring Our World

What do you think of when you hear the word *Egypt?* Many people think of the ancient pyramids, the Nile River, or King "Tut." The Egyptian ruler Tutankhamen, or "Tut," lived for only about 18 years. Because his tomb was discovered in 1922 untouched by grave robbers, he is the ruler most people remember. This magnificent gold mask was found in his tomb.

Egypt, in North Africa, and **Mesopotamia** (MEH•suh•puh•TAY•mee•uh), in Southwest Asia, were the earliest known civilizations. Historians use the term **civilization** to describe highly developed cultures. Civilizations include cities, organized governments and religions, and systems of writing. They have specialized workers, such as blacksmiths, builders, and teachers. Civilizations also use technology and metals. The time of the earliest civilizations is known as the Bronze Age, because people relied on the metal bronze, a mixture of copper and tin, to make tools and weapons.

Mesopotamia

Where were the first cities located? Where was the first school? These developments took place in Mesopotamia, a word that means "between the rivers." As the map on page 467 shows, Mesopotamia was located between the **Tigris River** and the **Euphrates River.** This region was part of the Fertile Crescent, a crescent-shaped area of rich soil that curved from the **Mediterranean Sea** to the **Persian Gulf.**

Around 4500 B.C., wandering peoples began settling along the Tigris and Euphrates Rivers. There they farmed the fertile soil left behind by yearly floods. To help control the floods, farmers built dirt walls and an irrigation system of ditches to channel the water to their fields of barley, wheat, and fruit trees. A 12-month calendar, based on phases of the moon, was developed to better predict the coming of the floodwaters. The plow was used for the first time, which made it possible to grow more food with less effort. With a steady food supply, the population grew larger.

Sumer   In time, the Mesopotamians built cities, some of which eventually held up to 40,000 people. Each city was considered a small state, or nation. The city-state of this time was made up of the city and the farmland around it. Walls made from sun-dried bricks surrounded and protected the cities.

The earliest city-states arose in an area called **Sumer,** where the Tigris and Euphrates Rivers flowed closest to each other. The Sumerians grew wealthy from trade. They exchanged dried fish, wool, barley, wheat, and metal goods for copper, tin, and timber. They invented many things, including the wheel, which helped transportation. The Sumerians also invented the sailboat, which replaced muscle power with wind power. Sumerian traders traveled by land to the Mediterranean in the west and by sea to India in the east.

Religion and Government   At the center of each city was a large, steplike tower called a ziggurat (ZIH•guh•RAT). Long stairways on the outside of the ziggurat led to a temple at the top. The temple was believed to be the home of the city's chief god or goddess. Only priests and priestesses were allowed to enter the temple.

Mesopotamia's religion was based on polytheism, or the worship of many gods and goddesses instead of just one god. At first, each city-state was a theocracy, or a government controlled by religious leaders. Mesopotamians believed that their priest-rulers received the right to rule from the gods. As the city-states grew, however, they fought one another over land and water. Military leaders became powerful and soon took the place of priests as permanent kings.

First Systems of Writing   The Sumerians were the first people to write down laws and keep lists and records. They created a form of writing known as cuneiform (kyoo•NEE•uh•FAWRM). It was made

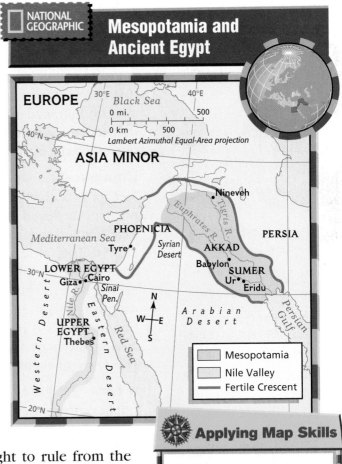

NATIONAL GEOGRAPHIC

Mesopotamia and Ancient Egypt

EUROPE

Black Sea

ASIA MINOR

Nineveh

PHOENICIA

Mediterranean Sea

Tyre

Syrian Desert

Euphrates R.

Tigris R.

AKKAD

Babylon

SUMER

Ur

Eridu

PERSIA

LOWER EGYPT

Giza

Cairo

Sinai Pen.

Arabian Desert

Persian Gulf

Western Desert

Nile R.

Eastern Desert

Red Sea

UPPER EGYPT

Thebes

Mesopotamia
Nile Valley
Fertile Crescent

0 mi.   500
0 km   500
Lambert Azimuthal Equal-Area projection

Applying Map Skills

1. What two major rivers are located in the Fertile Crescent?

2. Which is located farther north—Upper Egypt or Lower Egypt?

Find **NGS** online map resources@ www.nationalgeographic.com/maps

up of hundreds of markings shaped like wedges. The Sumerians wrote with sharp-ended reeds on moist, clay tablets. These records became permanent after the tablets were baked in the sun.

The Sumerians taught writing in schools called tablet houses. Only the wealthy could afford to send their sons—and sometimes daughters—to these schools. There, students trained to become scribes, or writers who made lists, kept records, and wrote letters for officials.

Sumerian scribes are believed to have written the world's first known story—the *Epic of Gilgamesh.* In this story, a king named Gilgamesh and his friend travel the world performing great acts of bravery. When his friend dies, Gilgamesh searches for a way to live forever. He learns that only the gods can live forever. Part of the Gilgamesh story tells of a great flood that covered the earth. The account of the flood is very much like the story of Noah's ark in the Bible.

Akkad and Babylon   About 2300 B.C., the warlike kingdom of **Akkad** conquered Sumer and several other city-states. Akkad's King Sargon created the first empire, or group of states under one ruler. Over time, the Akkadian Empire weakened. It finally fell to the kingdom of **Babylon** in about 1800 B.C.

Babylon's greatest king was Hammurabi (HA•muh•RAH•bee). A great conqueror, Hammurabi pushed the boundaries of his empire to the Mediterranean Sea. He built temples and irrigation canals. He also encouraged trade and new ideas. During this golden age, the Babylonians developed a number system based on 60. From them, we borrowed the 60-minute hour, 60-second minute, and 360-degree circle.

Hammurabi's Code   Before Hammurabi's rule, each city-state in Mesopotamia had its own codes, or collections of laws. Hammurabi took what he believed were the best laws from each code. He put these together and then issued one code that would apply to everyone in the empire. The Code of Hammurabi covered almost every aspect of daily life, including trade, debts, property, and family. Its basic idea was "an eye for an eye and a tooth for a tooth." This meant that if one person wronged another, he or she would be punished in the same way. Hammurabi had his laws carved in stone and placed where people could read them. Thus, everyone knew the rules and the punishments. The Code of Hammurabi served as a basis for future codes of law.

A New Babylon   After Hammurabi's death, his empire split into smaller territories. Centuries later, during the 500s B.C., a new Babylonian empire rose and fell. It was ruled by a warrior people called the Chaldeans. Nebuchadnezzar (NEH•buh•kuhd•NEH•zuhr), the greatest Chaldean king, rebuilt the city of Babylon and made it a center of trade and culture. Magnificent palaces and temples emerged. The royal palace was known for its "hanging gardens." These were layered beds of earth with large trees and flowering vines that seemed to hang in mid-air. According to legend, Nebuchadnezzar built the gardens to please his wife, who missed the mountains and plants of her native land.

Centers of Trade

Why did some cities develop into rich centers of trade? Since water is the easiest way to transport goods, cities located nearest rivers and seas became important trading centers. To succeed at trade, however, there must be a demand for products. The people of Mesopotamia produced extra food, but they lacked trees for construction and mineral resources to make metals. They were able to trade extra food for these raw materials.

This mummy (above right) was uncovered in the Valley of the Kings, Egypt. The coffin, or sarcophagus (above left), held a mummy and was created around 1000 B.C.

History What were the biggest tombs called?

Phoenicians As the peoples of Mesopotamia warred with neighboring states, they also traded. This helped to spread ideas and cultures. Among the most important traders were the Phoenicians, who were located mainly in what is today **Lebanon.** By about 1200 B.C., the Phoenicians had sailed as far as southern Europe and around the southern tip of Africa. They also became known for their alphabet, a set of symbols that represents the sounds of a language. To keep trade records, the Phoenicians made use of symbols, or letters, from which any number of words could be formed. The Phoenician alphabet eventually gave rise to the Hebrew, Greek, and Latin alphabets still in use today.

✓**Reading Check** Where was Mesopotamia located?

Egypt—Gift of the Nile

Like Mesopotamia, Egypt developed in a river valley. Egyptian civilization arose along the **Nile River** in northeast Africa. The Nile is the world's longest river. It flows north 4,160 miles (6,693 km) from the mountains of East Africa to the Mediterranean Sea. The last 600 miles (960 km) are in Egypt. There the river cuts a narrow, green valley through the desert. Most ancient Egyptians lived near the river and its **delta,** or a fan-shaped fertile area, near the Mediterranean. For centuries, they farmed and were protected from invaders by the desert, the sea, and the Nile's waterfalls called cataracts.

Egyptian civilization was in many ways "the gift of the Nile." Egyptians depended on the Nile for their livelihood. Every year, about the middle of July, the Nile overflowed its banks. The floodwaters went down but left behind large amounts of rich soil good for growing crops.

Web Activity Visit *The World and Its People* Web site at twip.glencoe.com and click on **Chapter 16— Student Web Activities** to learn more about the Phoenicians.

The Pharaoh   Eventually, two kingdoms formed along the Nile—**Upper Egypt** to the south and **Lower Egypt** around the delta. About 3100 B.C., a king of Upper Egypt called Narmer moved north and conquered Lower Egypt, uniting the two kingdoms.

The Egyptian ruler had the title of pharaoh (FEHR•oh), which means "great house." Like Mesopotamia, Egypt was a theocracy. Egyptians believed that their pharaoh was a god, however, as well as a ruler and priest. The pharaoh was the center of Egyptian life. He owned all the land in Egypt, and he gave gifts of land to rich Egyptians and priests. The pharaoh had dams and irrigation canals built and repaired. He chose government officials to gather taxes and carry out his orders. The pharaoh also commanded Egypt's armies.

Religion   Egyptians believed in many gods and goddesses. Each stood for some part of nature. The most important gods were the sun god Re, the river god Hapi, and the sky god Horus. Another important god was Osiris, the god of the harvest and eternal life.

The Egyptians believed in a form of life after death. They thought that the soul could not exist without the body, however. To preserve the body after death, it was embalmed. This was a process in which priests first removed certain organs from the body. Then they slowly dried the body to prevent it from decaying. Next, the embalmed body was wrapped in long strips of linen. The wrapped body was known as a mummy. The mummies of poor people were usually buried in caves or the desert sand. Those of rich people were placed in coffins, often in very elaborate tombs along with fabulous treasures.

The largest tombs belonged to the pharaohs and were called pyramids. These massive tombs were designed to protect the pharaohs' bodies from floods, wild animals, and robbers. Turn to page 472 to read about the largest pyramid—the Great Pyramid of Khufu. Great pharaohs—such as Khufu, Thutmose, and Ramses II—also were glorified with large monuments and statues. One such statue is the colossal Great Sphinx at Giza, which has the body of a lion and a human head.

Trade and Conquest   Egypt conquered many lands during its long history. It also suffered defeats. In the 1700s B.C., invaders from Asia known as the Hyksos conquered Egypt. The Hyksos ruled for about 150 years until they were overthrown. From the Hyksos, the Egyptians learned to use bronze and iron weapons and horse-drawn chariots.

With this new military and transportation technology, Egypt sought gold and gems in the African kingdom of Kush, near present-day **Sudan.** The first female pharaoh, Hatsheptsut, expanded trade even further. During her rule, Egyptian traders sailed along the coast of East Africa to the land of Punt (near present-day **Somalia**). There, they exchanged beads, metal tools, and weapons for hardwoods, incense, ivory, and other products. To the north, Egypt traded across the eastern Mediterranean with the Phoenicians and the Greeks. As they traded, the Egyptians spread ideas and accomplishments.

Egyptian Writing The ancient Egyptians wrote using hieroglyphics. This was a form of writing in which pictures were used for words or sounds. The Egyptians carved and painted hieroglyphic characters on their monuments or on papyrus (puh•PY•ruhs). Papyrus is a plant that grows along the Nile. It was used to make a form of paper, and it is the root word for *paper.* In order to write on papyrus, the Egyptians also developed ink. The dry climate of Egypt preserved some writings so well that they can still be read today.

Mathematics and Medicine The Egyptians made many other contributions to civilization. They used a number system based on ten. They also used fractions and whole numbers. They developed geometry to survey, or measure, land. The Nile's regular cycle of flooding helped the Egyptians create a calendar.

In the field of medicine, the Egyptians were the first to use splints, bandages, and compresses. They were skilled at sewing up cuts and setting broken bones. They even had remedies for hair loss and indigestion.

Decline Egypt eventually grew weak. The priests began to struggle with the pharaohs for power. In addition, much energy and money was spent trying to keep neighboring countries under Egyptian control. Egypt was eventually conquered by even greater empires—those of Greece and Rome.

✓ Reading Check How did the Egyptians view the pharaoh?

FCAT PRACTICE You can prepare for the FCAT-assessed standards by completing the correlated item(s) below.

Section 1 Assessment

Defining Terms

1. Define civilization, city-state, polytheism, theocracy, cuneiform, empire, delta, pharaoh, pyramid, hieroglyphics, papyrus.

Recalling Facts

2. History What were two early forms of writing, and where did they develop?

3. Geography Where did most Egyptians live? Why? **FCAT LA.E.2.2.1**

4. Math What mathematical contributions did Egyptians make to civilization?

Critical Thinking

5. Drawing Conclusions Why were the inventions of the wheel and the sailboat important to Sumer? **FCAT LA.A.2.3.1**

6. Understanding Cause and Effect Why was Hammurabi's code of laws an important development? **FCAT LA.A.2.3.1**

Graphic Organizer

7. Organizing Information On a diagram like this one, list ways that the Nile River influenced Egypt. **FCAT LA.A.1.3.2**

Egypt

Applying Social Studies Skills

8. Analyzing Maps Look at the map on page 467. What do the locations of the towns have in common?

ART   SCIENCE   CULTURE   TECHNOLOGY

The Egyptian Pyramids

The ancient Egyptians viewed the pharaoh, or king, as the most important person on the earth. They believed he was a god who would continue to guide them after his death. A pyramid served as a tomb for the pharaoh and provided a place where the body would safely pass into the afterlife. Rooms inside the pyramid held food, clothing, weapons, furniture, jewels, and everything else the pharaoh might need in the afterlife.

The Great Pyramid at Giza

The largest of Egypt's pyramids is the Great Pyramid of Khufu, built nearly 4,500 years ago. When the pyramid was new, it stood 482 feet (147 m) high. The square base of the pyramid covers 13 acres (about 5 ha). More than 2 million limestone and granite blocks were used in building it. These are no ordinary-sized blocks, however. The huge stones weigh an average of 2.5 tons (2.3 t) each.

Construction

For thousands of years, people have wondered how the Egyptians built the pyramids without modern tools or machinery. In the fifth century B.C., a Greek historian thought it took 100,000 people to build the Great Pyramid. Today archaeologists believe a workforce of about

FCAT PRACTICE Answering question 3 below will help you prepare for the **FCAT Writing** test.

20,000 did the job in about 20 years. Barges carried supplies and building materials for the pyramid down the Nile River. Nearby quarries supplied most of the stone. Skilled stonecutters carved the stones into the precise size and shape so that no mortar, or cementing material, was needed to hold the stones together.

Engineers think that workers built ramps and used papyrus twine to drag the huge stones to the pyramid. They formed ramps up all four sides of the pyramid and made the ramps higher and longer as the pyramid rose. They then dragged the stones up the ramps. Once finished, the ramps were cleared away. Then stonemasons smoothed and polished the stone, and the finished pyramid towered over the surrounding desert.

▶ Making the Connection

1. Why did the Egyptians build the pyramids?

2. How many workers did ancient historians and modern archaeologists each estimate it took to build the Great Pyramid?

3. **Sequencing Information** Describe the process experts think Egyptians used to build the pyramids.

FCAT LA.B.1.3.2

◀ The Great Pyramid at Giza, Egypt

Three World Religions

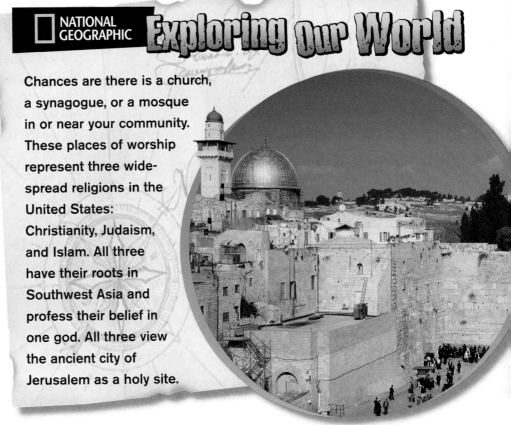

NATIONAL GEOGRAPHIC Exploring Our World

Chances are there is a church, a synagogue, or a mosque in or near your community. These places of worship represent three widespread religions in the United States: Christianity, Judaism, and Islam. All three have their roots in Southwest Asia and profess their belief in one god. All three view the ancient city of Jerusalem as a holy site.

Judaism, Christianity, and Islam have become major world faiths. All three religions are examples of monotheism, or the belief in one supreme god.

Judaism

Judaism is the oldest of these three world religions. It was first practiced by a small group of people in Southwest Asia called the Israelites. The followers of Judaism today are known as Jews. We know about the early history of the Jewish people and their religion from their holy book—the Torah.

According to Jewish belief, the Jews are descended from Abraham and Sarah, who first worshipped the one God, or Yahweh. Abraham was a herder who lived at least 3,700 years ago in what is now Iraq. The Torah states that God made a covenant, or agreement, with Abraham. If Abraham moved to the land of Canaan (Palestine), he

Jerusalem

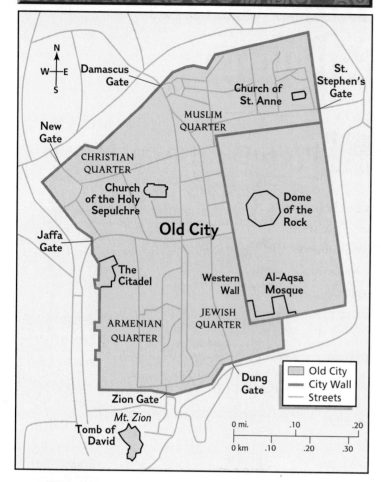

Analyzing the Map

The city of Jerusalem is divided into four quarters.

Place What quarter is located in the northeast part of the city?

would be blessed, and all nations would be blessed through him. Because of this covenant, Abraham's Israelite descendants believed that they were God's "chosen people" and would remain so as long as they followed God's laws.

The Ten Commandments The most important of these laws are the Ten Commandments. Jews believe that God revealed the Ten Commandments to a **prophet,** or messenger of God, called Moses. According to the Torah, Moses led the Israelites from slavery in Egypt. At the top of Mt. Sinai in the desert, Moses received the Ten Commandments. These rules differed from the laws of neighboring peoples because they were based on the worship of one god. The Israelites were to give their loyalty only to Yahweh. They were not to worship other gods or human-made images. Also, all people—whether rich or poor—were to be treated fairly.

The Jews About 1000 B.C., the Israelites under King David created a kingdom in the area of present-day **Israel.** The kingdom's capital was **Jerusalem.** By 922 B.C., the kingdom had split into two states—Israel and Judah. The people of Judah came to be called Jews. In later centuries, the Jews would be conquered and forced to leave their homeland many times. Eventually, the Jewish people spread to countries in many parts of the world. This scattering of the Jews was called the Diaspora. In many areas, the Jews were cruelly treated. In some areas, they were treated with tolerance and understanding. Wherever they lived, Jewish thinkers, writers, artists, and scientists increased the world's knowledge.

Judaism Today Despite hardships, the Jews have remained faithful to their religious heritage. They observe several important holy days. Every year during the festival of Passover, Jews retell the story of the exodus, or departure, of the Israelites from Egypt. Rosh Hashanah (RAHSH huh•SHAH•nuh) is New Year's Day on the Jewish calendar and is marked by prayer and solemn thoughts. Following Rosh Hashanah is Yom Kippur (YOHM kih•PUR), the holiest day in Judaism. Also called the Day of Atonement, Yom Kippur is observed by a 24-hour period of prayer and fasting.

Reading Check What are the basic laws revealed to Moses known as?

Christianity

The traditions of Judaism gave rise to the monotheistic religion known as Christianity. Christianity started in Southwest Asia among the Jews. Later, it spread to non-Jews and became one of the major influences in Western civilization.

Jesus   Centuries after the rise of Judaism, a Jew named Jesus began preaching in what today is Israel, the West Bank, and Jordan. Jesus taught that God loved all people, even those who have sinned. He told people that if they placed their trust in God, they would be forgiven.

During Jesus' lifetime, many Jews were opposed to the Romans who ruled their land. Some believed that God would send a **messiah,** or savior, to deliver them. In A.D. 30, Jesus and his **disciples,** or followers, went to Jerusalem to celebrate Passover, a Jewish holiday. Some Jews there greeted him as the messiah. This worried other Jews and Romans alike. Jesus was convicted of treason under Roman law and was crucified, or executed on a cross, outside Jerusalem. Soon afterward, the disciples proclaimed that Jesus had risen from the dead and had appeared to them. They began preaching that Jesus was the Son of God and that

FCAT PRACTICE

Completing the activity below will help you prepare for the **FCAT Reading** test.

Primary Source

COMPARING SCRIPTURE

Although there are many differences between the world's major religions, there are also many similarities. These quotes from Judaism, Christianity, and Islam illustrate the belief in good deeds.

When the holy one loves a man, He sends him a present in the shape of a poor man, so that he should perform some good deed to him, through the merit of which he may draw a cord of grace. **The Torah; Genesis 104a**

He who has two coats, let him share with him who has none: and he who has food, let him do likewise. **The Bible; Luke 3:11**

Every person's every joint must perform a charity every day the sun comes up: to act justly between two people is a charity. . . . a good word is a charity; every step you take in prayers is a charity. . . . **Saying of the Prophet Muhammad**

Analyzing Primary Sources

All three religions share the message of helping others. Why do you suppose there has been such conflict among them?

FCAT LA.A.2.3.2

anyone who believed in him and lived by his teachings would know eternal life after death. From then on, the disciples called him Christ, after the Greek word *Christos* (krees•TOS), meaning "messiah."

Spread of Christianity   The disciples spread the message of Jesus throughout the Mediterranean area and beyond. Jews and non-Jews who accepted this message became known as Christians. Stories about Jesus and early Christian writings—known as the New Testament—became part of the Christian Bible.

Until about A.D. 300, Christians faced persecution in the Roman Empire. Then the Roman emperor Constantine proclaimed that Christianity was to be a lawful religion. By A.D. 600, large areas of Southwest Asia, North Africa, and Europe were Christian. Disputes soon divided Christians into two major groups—Roman Catholics led by the pope in Italy, and Eastern Orthodox Christians who looked to the patriarch in Constantinople.

Christianity Today   Christianity has more followers than any other religion. Three major groups—Roman Catholics, Eastern Orthodox, and Protestants—make up the Christian religion today. Christians mark important events in the life of Jesus. Christmas is the celebration of his birth. In the spring, Christians remember the last days of Jesus' life on Earth. Good Friday is the day of Jesus' crucifixion. Easter, believed to be the day Jesus rose from the dead, is the most important Christian holy day.

√ Reading Check **Why was Constantine important to Christianity?**

Islam

The third monotheistic religion from Southwest Asia is Islam. It began in the A.D. 600s in the Arabian Peninsula. In the Arabic language, *Islam* means "surrender" to the will of God, or Allah. The followers of Islam are called Muslims. They believe that Muhammad is the last and greatest prophet of Islam—following Abraham, Moses, and Jesus.

Muhammad   Muhammad was born about A.D. 570 in **Makkah** (Mecca), a trading city and religious center in western Arabia. Arab pilgrims came to worship at the Kaaba, a shrine that housed a sacred black stone. According to Islamic teachings, in A.D. 610 Muhammad heard the voice of the angel Gabriel calling him to preach about God. He told the people of Makkah that there is only one God, Allah, before whom all believers are equal. He urged the rich to share with the poor. Muhammad saw life as preparation for the Day of Judgment, or the day when God would punish evildoers and reward the just.

Muhammad's message angered Makkah's rich merchants. They began to make threats against Muhammad. In A.D. 622, Muhammad and several hundred followers traveled to Yathrib (now known as Madinah), a small town north of Makkah. Muhammad's departure to Yathrib is known as the *Hijrah* (HIHJRUH), or migration.

In Madinah, Muhammad united the people politically and made them proud of their new faith. Armies from Makkah tried to capture

Madinah, but Muhammad's forces were eventually able to defeat them. Muhammad made Makkah the center of Islam and dedicated the Kaaba to the worship of Allah. By the time of Muhammad's death in A.D. 632, all of Arabia had accepted Islam. Muslim armies, merchants, and scholars began to spread Islam outside of Arabia. Over several centuries, a series of empires based on Islam ruled vast areas of Asia, North Africa, and parts of Europe.

As Islam spread, the religion branched into two main groups—Sunnis (SU•NEEZ) and Shiites (SHEE•EYETS). Most of the world's Muslims are Sunni. In the countries of Iran and Iraq, however, most people are Shiites. Sunnis and Shiites differ on which leaders should rule in the Islamic community.

The Quran At the heart of Islam is the Quran (kuh•RAN), or the Muslim holy book. Muslims believe that the Quran is the direct word of Allah as given to Muhammad. The Quran presents the **five pillars of faith,** or the five obligations all Muslims must fulfill. The first duty is the confession, or statement, of faith: "There is no god but Allah, and Muhammad is his messenger." Second, Muslims must pray five times each day, facing the holy city of Makkah. The third duty is to give charity to people in need or to institutions that are involved in education or social services. The fourth duty is to fast. This means not eating or drinking during the daylight hours of the holy month of Ramadan (RAH•muh•DAHN). This is the month, according to Muslim beliefs, in which God began to reveal the Quran to Muhammad.

The last pillar of faith is a pilgrimage. Once in each Muslim's life, he or she must, if able, journey to Makkah to pray. This journey is called the **hajj.** The reward for fulfilling all these religious duties is paradise.

✓ **Reading Check** What is the Islamic pilgrimage to Makkah called?

FCAT PRACTICE You can prepare for the FCAT-assessed standards by completing the correlated item(s) below.

Assessment

Defining Terms
1. **Define** monotheism, covenant, prophet, messiah, disciple, five pillars of faith, hajj.

Recalling Facts
2. **Religion** What are the world's three largest monotheistic religions?
3. **History** What was the Diaspora?

Critical Thinking
4. **Making Comparisons** How did the Ten Commandments differ from the religious laws of neighboring regions? **FCAT LA.A.2.2.7**
5. **Summarizing Information** What are the main holy days for each of the religions discussed in this section? **FCAT LA.A.2.3.1**

Graphic Organizer
6. **Organizing Information** Create a time line like the one below. List four key events in the foundation of Islam and their dates. **FCAT LA.A.1.3.2**

├────────────┼────────────┼────────────┤

Applying Social Studies Skills

7. **Analyzing Primary Sources** Read the quotes in the Primary Source feature on page 309. Summarize each quote in your own words. **FCAT LA.A.2.3.2**

Study and Writing Skill

FCAT PRACTICE Completing the correlated items below will help you prepare for the **FCAT Reading** test.

Using Library Resources

Your teacher has assigned a major research report, so you go to the library. As you wander the aisles surrounded by books, you wonder: Where do I start my research? Which reference tools should I use?

Learning the Skill

Libraries contain many resources. Here are brief descriptions of important ones:

- **Encyclopedia:** set of books containing short articles on many subjects arranged alphabetically
- **Biographical Dictionary:** brief biographies listed alphabetically by last names
- **Atlas:** collection of maps and charts
- **Almanac:** reference updated yearly that provides current statistics and historical information on a wide range of subjects
- **Card Catalog:** listing of every book in the library, either on cards or on a computer database; search for books by author, subject, or title
- **Periodical Guide:** set of books listing topics covered in magazines and newspaper articles

- **Computer Database:** collections of information organized for rapid search and retrieval
- **World Wide Web:** collection of information on the Internet accessed with a Web browser (*Caution: Some information may not be reliable.*)

Practicing the Skill

Suppose you are assigned a research report dealing with Islam. Read the questions below, and then decide which of the resources listed here you would use to answer each question and why. **FCAT** LA.A.2.3.5

1. During which years did Muhammad lead Muslims?
2. What is the current number of Muslims in the world today?
3. What was Muhammad's early life like? What happened to the Islamic religion after he died?

Applying the Skill

Using library resources, research the achievements of early Jews, Christians, and Muslims in the areas of architecture, math, science, and/or medicine. Present the information you find to the class. **FCAT** LA.A.2.3.5

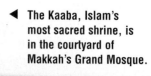

◄ The Kaaba, Islam's most sacred shrine, is in the courtyard of Makkah's Grand Mosque.

Section 1 | Mesopotamia and Ancient Egypt

Terms to Know

civilization	delta
city-state	pharaoh
polytheism	pyramid
theocracy	hieroglyphics
cuneiform	papyrus
empire	

Main Idea

The peoples of Mesopotamia and Egypt were among the first to build civilizations.

✓ **History** The first civilizations developed in Mesopotamia, which was located in the Fertile Crescent.

✓ **History** Early advancements in Mesopotamia, Sumer, and Babylon were in farming, writing, and government.

✓ **Geography** The Egyptians depended on the Nile River for their livelihood.

✓ **History** Ancient Egypt is known for pharaohs, pyramids, hieroglyphics, and mummies.

Section 2 | Three World Religions

Terms to Know

monotheism	disciple
covenant	five pillars
prophet	of faith
messiah	hajj

Main Idea

Three of the world's monotheistic religions—Judaism, Christianity, and Islam—developed in Southwest Asia.

✓ **History** Judaism is the world's oldest monotheistic religion. The Jews' belief in one God was later shared by Christianity and Islam.

✓ **Religion** Christians believe Jesus is the Messiah and the Son of God.

✓ **Religion** Muslims are followers of Islam. Muslims believe Allah is the one God, and Muhammad is the messenger.

◀ Desert areas begin where the fertile Nile River Valley ends.

Assessment and Activities

FCAT PRACTICE You can prepare for the FCAT-assessed standards by completing the correlated item(s) below.

Using Key Terms

Match the terms in Part A with their definitions in Part B.

A.

1. civilization
2. theocracy
3. cuneiform
4. pharaoh
5. polytheism
6. covenant
7. monotheism
8. hajj
9. disciple
10. city-state

B.

a. holy journey in Islam
b. follower
c. culture that has reached the level of development where people can specialize their skills
d. god-king of ancient Egypt
e. belief in many gods
f. belief in one God
g. ruled by religious leader who is also a king
h. ancient form of writing in Sumer
i. city and its surrounding countryside
j. agreement

Reviewing the Main Ideas

Section 1 Mesopotamia and Ancient Egypt

11. **History** What was a ziggurat?
12. **History** Where did the earliest city-states arise?
13. **History** What was the world's first known story?
14. **History** What concepts did we borrow from the Babylonians?
15. **Culture** For what two things are the Phoenicians known?
16. **History** Who were the Asians that invaded ancient Egypt? What technology did they share?
17. **History** Why did the Egyptians embalm their dead?

Section 2 Three World Religions

18. **Religion** What is the similarity between Yahweh and Allah? **FCAT LA.A.1.3.2**
19. **Religion** What is the role of the messiah in Jewish and Christian religious belief?
20. **Religion** Judaism, Christianity, and Islam are similar in their belief of one supreme god. List some of the differences among the three religions. **FCAT LA.A.1.3.2**

NATIONAL GEOGRAPHIC **Egypt and Southwest Asia**

Place Location Activity

On a separate sheet of paper, match the letters on the map with the numbered places listed below.

1. Persian Gulf
2. Lower Egypt
3. Euphrates River
4. Mediterranean Sea
5. Nile River
6. Israel
7. Upper Egypt
8. Saudi Arabia
9. Makkah (Mecca)
10. Jerusalem

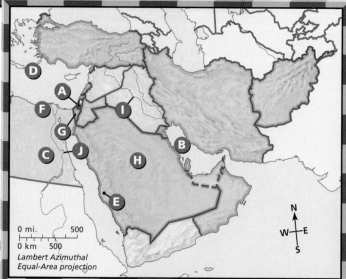

0 mi. 500
0 km 500
Lambert Azimuthal
Equal-Area projection

Critical Thinking

21. **Analyzing Information** Hammurabi wrote a code of laws to help him rule better. How would laws help a king rule? FCAT LA.E.2.2.1

22. **Categorizing Information** Create a chart like the one below. Complete the name of the holy book for each of the religions listed. FCAT LA.A.1.3.2

Religion	Holy Book
Judaism	
Christianity	
Islam	

Comparing Regions Activity

23. **Culture** As you have learned, ancient Egyptians followed a polytheistic religion. The early Greeks did as well. Use the Internet to find information on ancient Egyptian gods and goddesses and classical Greek gods and goddesses. Create a chart to compare the gods and goddesses of each. FCAT LA.A.2.3.5

Mental Mapping Activity

24. **Focusing on the Region** Create a simple outline map of Egypt and Southwest Asia. Draw in the Nile, Tigris, and Euphrates Rivers. Shade the areas where the early civilizations of ancient Egypt and Mesopotamia were located. Label the cities of Giza, Jerusalem, Babylon, and Makkah (Mecca) on your map.

Technology Skills Activity

25. **Using the Internet** Search the Internet and find several newspapers that publish online. Use at least three different sources to research recent discoveries about any ancient cultures in the region of North Africa or Southwest Asia. Use the computer to create a report on this topic. You may want to include visual materials for display. FCAT LA.A.2.3.5

Standardized Test Practice

Directions: Study the map below, and then answer the question that follows.

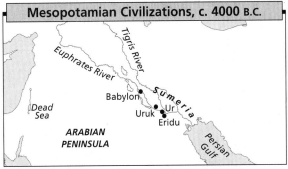

Mesopotamian Civilizations, c. 4000 B.C.

Ancient Egypt, c. 3100 B.C.

1. **What characteristic did the first Egyptian and Mesopotamian civilizations share?**

   A They were established in the same year.

   B Both civilizations began in North Africa.

   C They both developed on the banks of rivers.

   D People in both civilizations relied on hunting to obtain food.

Test-Taking Tip: When you answer a map question, do *not* rely on your memory of the map. Instead, check each answer choice against the information on the map and get rid of answer choices that are incorrect. Eliminating even one wrong choice will help you locate the correct answer.

North Africa Today

The World and Its People
NATIONAL GEOGRAPHIC

To learn more about the people and places of North Africa, view **The World and Its People Chapter 16** video.

Social Studies Online

Chapter Overview Visit **The World and Its People** Web site at twip.glencoe.com and click on **Chapter 17—Chapter Overviews** to preview information about North Africa.

FOLDABLES™
Study Organizer

FCAT PRACTICE The activity below will help you prepare for the **FCAT Reading** test.

Identifying Main Ideas Make this foldable to help you identify key facts about the people and places of North Africa. **FCAT LA.A.1.3.2**

Step 1 Fold the paper from the top right corner down so the edges line up. Cut off the leftover piece.

> Fold a triangle. Cut off the extra edge.

Step 2 Fold the triangle in half. Unfold.

> The folds will form an X that creates four equal sections.

Step 3 Cut up one fold line and stop at the middle. This forms two triangular flaps.

Step 4 Draw an X on one tab and label the other three the following: Egypt, Libya, and The Maghreb.

Step 5 Fold the X flap under the other flap and glue together.

> This makes a three-sided pyramid.

Reading and Writing As you read, write main ideas inside the foldable under each appropriate pyramid wall. **FCAT LA.A.1.3.2**

▲ Berber market at an oasis in Morocco

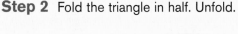
Why It Matters

Transitions

North Africa is made up of five independent countries. In past centuries, however, a series of powerful empires ruled in this part of the world. Arabs brought the religion of Islam to North Africa. In the twentieth century, the discovery of oil brought great wealth to parts of the region. Today these countries are struggling to preserve their traditions while also adapting to the modern world.

Egypt

Guide to Reading

Main Idea

Egypt's Nile River and desert landscape have shaped the lives of the Egyptian people for hundreds of years.

Terms to Know

- silt
- oasis
- phosphate
- republic
- fellahin
- bazaar
- service industries
- mosque

Reading Strategy

Draw a chart like this one. Then list five physical features of Egypt and their effects on life in Egypt.

FCAT LA.A.1.3.2

Physical Feature	Effect on Egyptians
→	
→	
→	
→	
→	

The following are the major Sunshine State Standards covered in this section.

SS.B.2.3.2:
Knows the human and physical characteristics of different places in the world and how these characteristics change over time

SS.B.2.3.5:
Understands the geographical factors that affect the cohesiveness and integration of countries

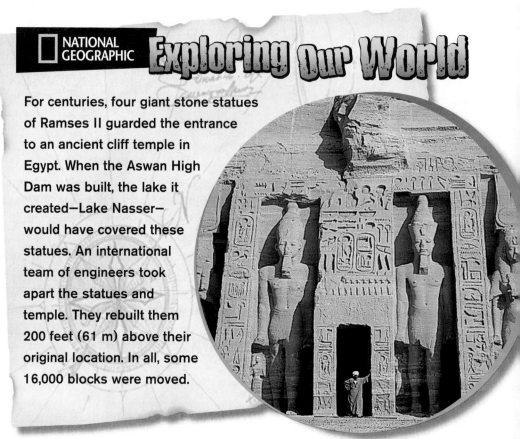

NATIONAL GEOGRAPHIC Exploring Our World

For centuries, four giant stone statues of Ramses II guarded the entrance to an ancient cliff temple in Egypt. When the Aswan High Dam was built, the lake it created—Lake Nasser—would have covered these statues. An international team of engineers took apart the statues and temple. They rebuilt them 200 feet (61 m) above their original location. In all, some 16,000 blocks were moved.

Egypt lies in Africa's northeast corner. Vast deserts sweep over most of the country. On the map on page 485, notice the **Nile River** running through Egypt. The Nile River, along with Egypt's location and deserts, has shaped life in Egypt for thousands of years.

Egypt's Land and Climate

Egypt is a large country that is about the same size as Texas and New Mexico together. Yet most of it is desert. Egypt's people crowd into less than 4 percent of the land, which is an area about twice the size of Maryland. The lifeline of Egypt is the Nile River, which supplies 85 percent of the country's water. Along the Nile's banks, you can see mud-brick villages, ancient ruins, and, once in a while, a city or town of modern buildings. The Nile River empties into the **Mediterranean Sea,** forming the Nile's delta. This fertile, low-lying land is built up from the soil carried downstream.

For centuries, the Nile's waters would rise in the spring. The swollen river carried silt, or small particles of rich soil. When it reached Egypt, the Nile flooded its banks. As the floodwaters withdrew, the silt was left behind, making the land better for farming. Today dams and channels control the river's flow for use in irrigation and in generating electric power.

Sinai Peninsula   The triangle-shaped **Sinai** (SY•NY) **Peninsula** lies southeast of the Nile delta. This area is a major crossroads between Africa and Southwest Asia. A human-made waterway called the **Suez Canal** separates the Sinai Peninsula from the rest of Egypt. Egyptians and Europeans built the canal in the mid-1860s. The Suez Canal is still one of the world's most important waterways. Ships use the canal to pass from the Mediterranean Sea to the **Red Sea.** In making this journey, they avoid traveling all the way around Africa.

Desert Areas   East of the Nile River spreads the **Eastern Desert,** also known as the Arabian Desert. West of the Nile is the much larger **Libyan** (LIH•bee•uhn) **Desert,** which covers about two-thirds of the country. Dotting both deserts are oases. An oasis is a fertile or green area in a desert. Plants grow here, giving these spots lush green growth in the midst of the hot sands.

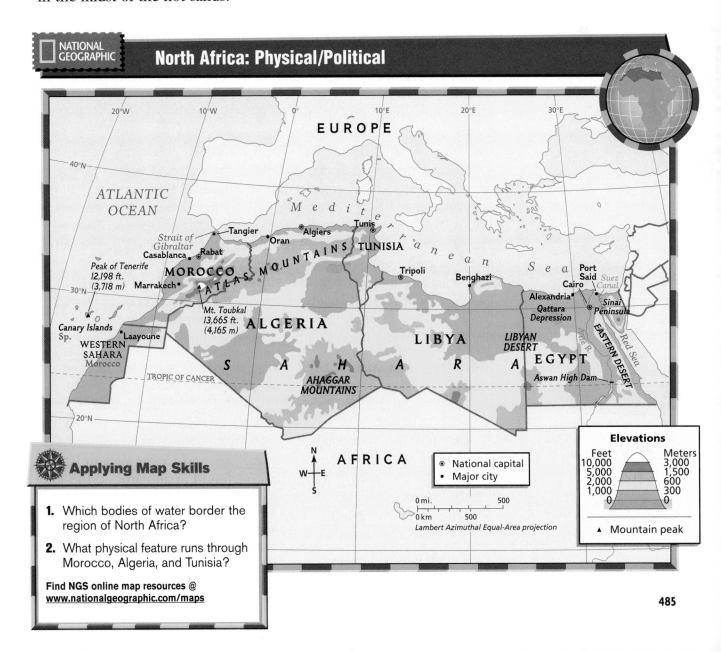

NATIONAL GEOGRAPHIC

North Africa: Physical/Political

Applying Map Skills

1. Which bodies of water border the region of North Africa?

2. What physical feature runs through Morocco, Algeria, and Tunisia?

Find NGS online map resources @ www.nationalgeographic.com/maps

485

The Eastern and Libyan Deserts are part of the **Sahara,** which is the largest desert in the world. *Sahara* comes from the Arabic word meaning "desert." The Sahara is about the size of the United States. It stretches from Egypt westward across North Africa to the Atlantic Ocean.

A Desert Climate Wherever you go in Egypt, you find a dry desert climate with hot summers and mild winters. Egypt as a whole receives little rainfall. **Cairo,** the capital, averages only about 0.4 inch (1 cm) a year. In fact, some areas receive no rain for years at a time.

Springtime in Egypt brings hot winds instead of cooling rains. These winds move west across Egypt, reaching up to 87 miles (140 km) per hour. The powerful winds can harm crops and damage houses.

✓ Reading Check Why is the Suez Canal one of the world's most important waterways?

Egypt's Economy

Egypt has a developing economy that has grown considerably in recent years. Although only about 2 percent of Egypt's land is used for farming, about 29 percent of Egypt's people work in agriculture. The best farmland lies in the fertile Nile River valley. Egypt's major crops include sugarcane, grains, vegetables, fruits, and cotton. Raw cotton, cotton yarn, and clothing are among the country's main exports.

Some farmers still work the land using the simple practices and tools of their ancestors. Many use modern methods and machinery. All, however, rely on dams to control the water needed for their fields. The largest dam is called the **Aswan High Dam.** Find it on the map on page 485. The dams give people control over the Nile's floodwaters. They can store the water for months behind the dams. Then they can release it several times during the year, rather than having just the spring floods. This control allows farmers to harvest two or three crops a year.

The dams bring challenges as well as benefits. Dams block the flow of silt, which means farmland is becoming less fertile. Farmers now rely more heavily on chemical fertilizers to grow crops. In addition, the dams prevent less freshwater from reaching the delta. So salt water from the Mediterranean Sea now flows deeper into the delta, making the land there less fertile.

Industry The Aswan High Dam provides hydroelectric power, which Egypt uses to run its growing industries. The largest industrial centers are the capital city of Cairo and the seaport of **Alexandria.** Egyptian factories make food products, textiles, and consumer goods. Tourism is another industry that is important to Egypt's economy. Visitors come to see the pyramids and majestic temples of ancient Egypt.

Egypt's main energy resource is oil, found in and around the Red Sea. Petroleum products make up almost half the value of Egypt's exports. Egypt is developing a gas export market as well. The country also has phosphates. A phosphate is a mineral salt used in fertilizer.

✓ Reading Check On what crop are many of Egypt's exports based?

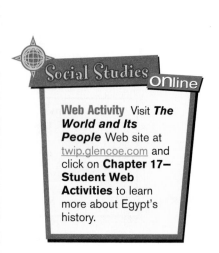

Social Studies Online

Web Activity Visit *The World and Its People* Web site at twip.glencoe.com and click on **Chapter 17— Student Web Activities** to learn more about Egypt's history.

Food

Most Egyptian meals include fava beans that have been boiled for hours to make them soft. Egypt's national dish, *ful*, includes fava beans mixed with garlic, lemon juice, olive oil, onions, and parsley. Cubes of veal or lamb meat cooked on skewers are known as kabobs. Egyptians also eat tahini—a smooth paste made of sesame seeds that is eaten as a dip or sandwich spread. *Babaganoush* is another dipping paste, but it is made with eggplant and sesame. Instead of spoons, Egyptians usually use *aysh,* or bread, to scoop up food.

Looking Closer **How does Egyptian bread differ from the bread you eat?**

The Egyptians

In Chapter 16, you learned about the ancient Egyptians. Their advanced civilization included powerful pharaohs, the building of temples and pyramids, and advances in science and technology. From 300 B.C. to A.D. 300, however, Egypt fell under the influence of Greece and Rome. You may have heard of Cleopatra, an Egyptian queen who ruled during the time of the rise of the Roman Empire.

In A.D. 641, Arabs from Southwest Asia took control of Egypt. They practiced Islam, a religion based on the belief in one God known as Allah. Most of Egypt's people began to speak the Arabic language and became Muslims, as the followers of Islam are called. Today about 94 percent of Egypt's people are Muslims.

Egypt's Modern History   By the end of the 1800s, all of Egypt, including the Suez Canal, had become part of the British Empire. Unhappy with British rule, the people of Egypt protested many times. Finally, in 1952 a group of army officers overthrew the British-supported king, and Egypt became independent. One of the army leaders, Gamal Abdel Nasser (guh•MAHL AHB•duhl NAH•suhr), was Egypt's president from 1954 to 1970. Nasser made Egypt one of the most powerful countries in the Muslim world.

Egypt is a **republic,** or a government headed by a president. A legislature makes the laws, but the president has broad powers in running the country. In the 1990s, some Islamic political and religious groups opposed the government. These groups used violence in an effort to reach their political goals. By the early 2000s, however, the government had stopped these attacks.

Rural and Urban Life   Look at the population density map in the **Geography Handbook** on page 10. Most of Egypt's 72.1 million people live within 20 miles (32 km) of the Nile River. More than half of Egypt's people live in rural areas along this narrow valley. Most are peasant farmers called fellahin (FEHL•uh•HEEN). They live in villages and farm small plots of land that they rent from landowners. Many fellahin raise only enough food to feed their families. Any food left over is sold in towns at a bazaar, or marketplace.

Life is more modern in Egypt's cities. Many city dwellers live in high-rise apartments and have jobs in manufacturing, construction, or service industries. Service industries provide services to people rather than producing goods. In bustling ports like Alexandria and Port Said (sah•EED), people engage in trade.

Cairo is a huge and rapidly growing city. Almost 8 million people are crowded into its central area, with another 7 million living in its suburbs. It is the largest city in Africa. For centuries, Cairo has been a leading center of the Muslim world. Throughout the city you see schools, universities, and mosques, or places of worship for followers of Islam.

Cairo's population is increasing at a rapid rate. Why? First, Egypt is a country with a high birthrate. Second, many fellahin have moved to Cairo to find work. The crowded city cannot provide enough houses, schools, and hospitals for all of its people. Poverty, snarled traffic, and pollution have resulted.

✓ **Reading Check** When did Egypt become fully independent?

FCAT PRACTICE You can prepare for the FCAT-assessed standards by completing the correlated item(s) below.

Section 1 Assessment

Defining Terms
1. **Define** silt, oasis, phosphate, republic, fellahin, bazaar, service industries, mosque.

Recalling Facts
2. **Human/Environment Interaction** Why is the Nile River important to Egypt?
3. **History** Who was Gamal Abdel Nasser, and what did he do for Egypt?
4. **Culture** What are the major language and religion of Egypt?

Critical Thinking
5. **Understanding Cause and Effect** How has the Aswan High Dam helped and hurt Egypt? **FCAT LA.E.2.2.1**
6. **Problem Solving** What are some ways that the Egyptian government could help solve overcrowding in Cairo? **FCAT LA.B.1.3.2**

Graphic Organizer
7. **Organizing Information** In a chart like the one below, fill in three facts about Egypt for each category. **FCAT LA.A.1.3.2**

Agriculture	Industry
1.	1.
2.	2.
3.	3.

Applying Social Studies Skills

8. **Analyzing Maps** Study the physical/political map on page 485. In what direction would you go to get from Cairo to Alexandria? **FCAT MA.B.1.3.4**

Making Connections

ART SCIENCE **CULTURE** TECHNOLOGY

An Egyptian Folktale

In many rural areas of modern Egypt, storytellers entertain the fellahin. Here is one Egyptian folktale in which a father tries to teach his son a valuable lesson.

What Will People Say?

Goha had a naughty son who would never do as he was told. When asked to do something, the boy had one ready answer. "But what will people say?" he would shake his head and say. Goha decided one day that it was time to teach his son a useful lesson, and prove to the boy that pleasing everyone was an impossible thing. This is what Goha did:

He mounted his donkey and started to the market, after ordering his son to follow him along behind on foot. In a little while they came across a group of women doing their washing at the bank of the river.

The women bawled over to Goha, "Do you have a rock instead of a heart, you merciless man? How do you have the shamelessness to ride while that poor boy of yours runs along behind?"

So, Goha got off the donkey and ordered the boy to mount, while he himself followed on foot. After some time they came across a group of old men sunning themselves at the corner of a field. One of the old men . . . yelled out in a loud and shaky voice, "I do declare! If that ain't the way to bring up an ingrate. Yes sir-ree, if you want no respect from your boy, that's the way to get it." . . .

Goha said to his son. "Have you heard? Let us both ride now."

So, father and son mounted the donkey and they continued on their way. Soon they met with some animal lovers, who called out in a

An Egyptian boy leads his donkey. ▼

FCAT PRACTICE Answering question 3 below will help you prepare for the **FCAT Reading** test.

scolding voice, . . . "How dare you ride that skinny donkey when the two of you together have flesh and bones weighing more than that poor beast?"

Goha said to his son, "I think now we had better let the donkey lead the way while we both follow on foot. . . ."

It was not long, however, before they became the prey to a crowd of jokers and jesters, who hooted and said, ". . . Either let this poor weary donkey ride on one of you, or both of you carry him. That way he shall be spared the misery of walking." . . .

From a nearby tree [Goha] cut a strong stout branch about three yards long. Next, taking some strong rope he had with him, he tied the donkey's front hoofs together, and then his hind hoofs together. He then slipped the branch between the donkey's legs so that the two ends of the branch stuck out at either end.

That done, Goha called his son, and said, "Now you put one end of this branch on your shoulder, and I will bear the other end." . . .

When finally they arrived at the market, a great crowd gathered . . . following the strange sight . . . until at last a policeman managed to break through the group. The policeman addressed Goha, saying, "You will accompany me to the police station, and from there, my fine cracked friends, you may expect to go straight to the madhouse."

Goha turned to this son, and said, "This, my son, is the result of troubling yourself over what other people will say."

From *The Black Prince and Other Egyptian Folk Tales,* told by Ahmed and Zane Zagloul. Copyright © 1971. Doubleday & Company, Inc., Garden City, NY.

► Making the Connection

1. What happens to Goha and his son at the end?

2. Who do you think should have ridden the donkey? Explain.

3. **Summarizing Information** Write the moral, or lesson, of this folktale in your own words.

FCAT LA.A.2.3.1

Libya and the Maghreb

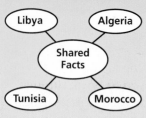

NATIONAL GEOGRAPHIC Exploring Our World

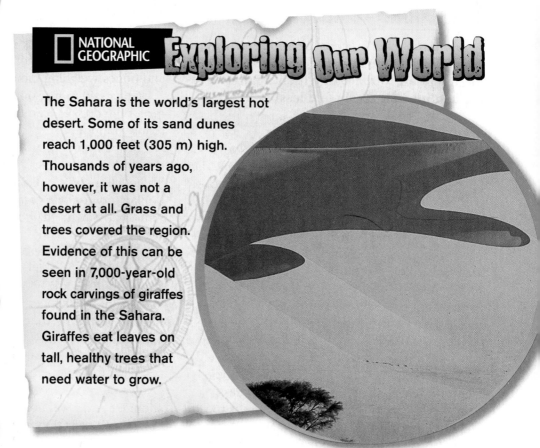

The Sahara is the world's largest hot desert. Some of its sand dunes reach 1,000 feet (305 m) high. Thousands of years ago, however, it was not a desert at all. Grass and trees covered the region. Evidence of this can be seen in 7,000-year-old rock carvings of giraffes found in the Sahara. Giraffes eat leaves on tall, healthy trees that need water to grow.

Libya, Tunisia, Algeria, and Morocco make up the rest of North Africa. Like Egypt, these countries have economies based on oil and other resources in the Sahara. Unlike Egypt, however, none of these nations enjoys the benefits of a life-giving river such as the Nile.

Libya

Libya is slightly larger than Alaska. Except for coastal lowlands, Libya is a desert area with only a few oases. In fact, the Sahara covers more than 90 percent of Libya. During the spring and fall, dust-heavy winds blow from the desert. When these fierce winds strike, temperatures in coastal areas can reach 110°F (43°C).

Libya has no permanent rivers, but aquifers lie beneath the vast desert. **Aquifers** are underground rock layers that store large amounts of water. In the 1990s, the government built pipelines to carry underground water from the desert to coastal areas.

The discovery of oil in Libya in 1959 brought the country great wealth. Libya's government uses oil money to import food, build schools and hospitals, and maintain a strong military.

Libya's People and History   Almost all of Libya's 5.5 million people have mixed Arab and Berber heritage. The Berbers were the first people known to live in North Africa. During the A.D. 600s, Arabs brought Islam and the Arabic language to North Africa. Since then, Libya has been a Muslim country, and most of its people speak Arabic.

About 86 percent of Libyans live along the Mediterranean coast. Most live in two modern cities—**Tripoli,** the capital, and Benghazi (behn•GAH•zee). Libya became independent in 1951 under a king. In 1969 a military officer named Muammar al-Qaddafi (kuh•DAH•fee) gained power and overthrew the king. Qaddafi set up a **dictatorship,** or a government under the control of one all-powerful leader.

✓Reading Check How has Libya been governed since 1969?

Tunisia

Tunisia, Algeria, and **Morocco** form a region known as the **Maghreb.** *Maghreb* means "the land farthest west" in Arabic. These three countries were given this name because they are the westernmost part of the Arabic-speaking Muslim world.

About the size of the state of Georgia, Tunisia is North Africa's smallest country. Find it on the map on page 485. Northern and central Tunisia have Mediterranean or steppe climates, which provide some rainfall. Along the fertile eastern coast, farmers grow wheat, olives, citrus fruits, and vegetables.

Tunisian factories produce food products, textiles, and oil products. In addition, tourism is a growing industry. Many visitors enjoy Tunisia's sunny shores and explore its Roman ruins and outdoor markets.

Past and Present   Tunisia's coastal location has drawn people, ideas, and trade throughout the centuries. In ancient times, Phoenician sailors founded the city of Carthage in northern Tunisia. This city was the center of a powerful trading empire and challenged Rome for control of the Mediterranean. Rome defeated and destroyed Carthage.

During the following centuries, Tunisia was part of several Muslim empires. It was a colony of France until becoming an independent republic in 1956. You can still see French influence in the cities.

Almost all of Tunisia's 9.9 million people are of mixed Arab and Berber ancestry. They speak Arabic and practice Islam. **Tunis,** with more than 1,000,000 people, is the capital and largest urban area.

✓Reading Check Why can farming take place in Tunisia?

Algeria

About one and a half times the size of Alaska, Algeria is the largest country in North Africa. Along the Mediterranean coast, you find hills, plains, and Algeria's best farmland. Inland, the land slopes up to the

Bazaar!
Taha Hammam makes pottery to sell at the bazaar. "Going to the bazaar is a lot like going to an American mall," he says. "It's a big party where everyone talks and eats and buys and sells things." Taha lives in Algiers. Although Taha wears jeans and sneakers, his parents dress in traditional clothes. His mother wears a black outer dress over a bright housedress and covers her hair with a long veil that reaches the ground. Taha's father dresses in a long robe. In school, Taha studies Arabic, religion, social studies, arithmetic, science, and art.

Morocco

Even though North Africa is mostly hot, snow can fall high in the Atlas Mountains where this Berber lives.

Human/Environment Interaction How does the environment influence the lives of the Berbers?

Atlas Mountains. Another range—the Ahaggar (uh•HAH•guhr)—lies in southern Algeria. Between these mountain ranges are areas of the Sahara known as **ergs,** or huge, shifting sand dunes.

Like neighboring Libya, Algeria must import about one-third of its food. It pays for this food by selling oil and natural gas pumped from the Sahara. These deposits have helped Algeria's industrial growth, but widespread poverty remains. Many Algerians have moved to European countries to find work.

The Algerians About 31.7 million people live in Algeria. They have mixed Arab and Berber heritage. Most of them are Muslim and speak Arabic. If you visited Algeria, you would discover centuries-old Muslim traditions blending with those of France. Why? From 1834 to 1962, Algeria was a French colony. In 1954, Algerian Arabs wanting freedom rose up against the French. A bloody **civil war,** or conflict between different groups inside a country, erupted. When the fighting ended in 1962, Algeria won independence. Many of the French fled to France.

Today Algeria is a republic, with a strong president and a legislature. In the early 1990s, Muslim political parties opposed many of the government's **secular,** or nonreligious, policies. The Muslims gained enough support to win a national election. The government, however, rejected the election results and imprisoned many Muslim opponents. An ongoing civil war has taken many lives.

Algiers, the country's capital and largest city, has nearly 2.2 million people. Many of them live in the newer sections of the city, with modern buildings and broad streets. They enjoy visiting the older sections of the city, though, which are called **casbahs.** There they walk down narrow streets, stopping to bargain with merchants in bazaars.

✓ **Reading Check** What conflict has affected Algeria since the early 1990s?

Morocco

Slightly larger than California, Morocco borders two bodies of water—the Mediterranean Sea on the north and the Atlantic Ocean on the west. The map on page 485 shows that Morocco's northern tip almost touches Europe. Here you will find the **Strait of Gibraltar.** It separates Africa and Europe by only 8 miles (13 km).

Farmers on Morocco's fertile coastal plains grow sugar beets, grains, fruits, and vegetables for sale to Europe. Many raise livestock, especially sheep. Morocco is a leading producer of phosphates, and tourism has grown as well. Visitors flock to cities like **Marrakech** and **Casablanca.** In marketplaces called souks (SOOKS), sellers in traditional hooded robes offer wares made of leather, copper, and brass.

Morocco's History and People Morocco was first settled by the Berbers thousands of years ago. Their descendants still herd and farm in the foothills of the Atlas Mountains. During the A.D. 600s, Arab invaders swept into Morocco. A century later, Arabs and Berbers together crossed the Strait of Gibraltar and conquered Spain. Their descendants, called Moors, ruled parts of Spain and developed an advanced civilization. Christian Spanish rulers drove them out in the late 1400s. Many descendants of the Moors live in Morocco today.

In the early 1900s, the Moroccan kingdom weakened, and France and Spain gained control. In 1956 Morocco became independent once again. Today the country is a **constitutional monarchy,** where a king or queen is head of state, but elected officials run the government. In Morocco, the monarch still holds many powers, however.

Beginning in the 1970s, Morocco claimed the desert region of **Western Sahara.** The discovery of minerals there sparked a costly war between Morocco and a rebel group that wanted Western Sahara to be independent. The United Nations had tried to sponsor a vote to allow the people of Western Sahara to decide their own future, but nothing has been resolved.

Morocco has about 30.7 million people. Casablanca, the largest city, is home to about 3.4 million people. **Rabat,** with 2.3 million, is the capital. Moroccan culture is based on Arab, Berber, and African traditions. Their music blends rhythms of these groups. Artists here are known for their carpets, pottery, jewelry, brassware, and woodwork.

Reading Check Who were the Moors?

FCAT PRACTICE You can prepare for the FCAT-assessed standards by completing the correlated item(s) below.

Section 2 Assessment

Defining Terms
1. **Define** aquifer, dictatorship, erg, civil war, secular, casbah, constitutional monarchy.

Recalling Facts
2. **History** Who were the Berbers?
3. **Culture** Why do many Algerians speak French?
4. **History** Why is there a dispute over control of Western Sahara?

Critical Thinking
5. **Making Generalizations** How have the physical features of North Africa affected where people live? **FCAT LA.A.1.3.2**
6. **Identifying Alternatives** How might the countries studied in this section improve their economies?

Graphic Organizer
7. **Organizing Information** Draw a diagram like the one below. Choose one country from this section and fill in each outer part of the diagram with a fact about that country.

FCAT LA.A.1.3.2

Country

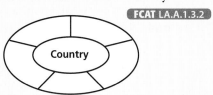

Applying Social Studies Skills

8. **Analyzing Maps** Study the map on page 485. Rabat is located on the coast of which country? Along what body of water is it located?

Technology Skill

 FCAT PRACTICE Completing the activity below will help you prepare for the **FCAT Mathematics** test.

Using a Spreadsheet

A **spreadsheet** is an electronic worksheet that can manage numbers quickly and easily. Spreadsheets are powerful tools because you can change or update information, and the spreadsheet automatically performs the calculations.

Learning the Skill

All spreadsheets follow a basic design of rows and columns. Each column is assigned a letter, and each row is assigned a number. Each point where a column and a row intersect is called a *cell.* The cell's position on the spreadsheet is labeled according to its corresponding column and row—*A1* is column A, row 1; *B2* is column B, row 2; and so on.

Spreadsheets use *formulas* to calculate numbers. To create a formula, highlight the cell you want the results in. Type an equal sign (=) and then build the formula, step-by-step. If you type the formula *=B4+B5+B6* in cell B7, the numbers in these cells are added together, and the sum shows up in cell B7.

To use division, the formula would look like this: *=A5/C2.* This divides A5 by C2. An asterisk (*) signifies multiplication: *=(B2*C3)+D1* means that you want to multiply B2 times C3, and then add D1.

Practicing the Skill

Use these steps to create a spreadsheet.

1. In cells B1, C1, and D1, type the years 1980, 1990, and 2000. In cell E1, type the word *Total.*

2. In cells A2 through A6, type the names of North Africa's countries. In cell A7, type the word *Total.*

3. In row 2, enter the number of tons of oil produced by Algeria in 1980, 1990, and 2000.

4. Repeat step 3 in rows 3 through 6 for each country. You can find the information you need for each country in a world almanac or an encyclopedia.

5. Create a formula that tells which cells to add together so the computer can calculate the number of tons of oil for each country. For example, in cell E2, you should type *=B2+C2+D2* to find the total amount of oil that Algeria produced in those years.

B2		=		
A	**B**	**C**	**D**	**E**
1	1980	1990	2000	Total
2 Algeria				
3 Egypt				
4 Libya				
5 Morocco				
6 Tunisia				
7 Total				
8				

▲ The computer highlights the cell in which you are working.

Applying the Skill

Use the spreadsheet you have created to answer these questions: Which country is the largest producer of oil? Has it always been number one? Are countries in North Africa together producing more oil or less oil today than they did 20 years ago?

FCAT MA.E.1.3.1

Section 1 — Egypt

Terms to Know
silt
oasis
phosphate
republic
fellahin
bazaar
service industries
mosque

Main Idea
Egypt's Nile River and desert landscape have shaped the lives of the Egyptian people for hundreds of years.

✓ Location Most people in Egypt live along the Nile River or in its delta.

✓ Economics About 29 percent of Egypt's people work in agriculture, but industry has grown in recent years.

✓ Culture Most people in Egypt are Muslims who follow the religion of Islam.

✓ Culture More Egyptians live in rural areas than in cities, but Cairo is the largest city in Africa.

Section 2 — Libya and the Maghreb

Terms to Know
aquifer
dictatorship
erg
civil war
secular
casbah
constitutional
  monarchy

Main Idea
The countries of Libya, Tunisia, Algeria, and Morocco share a desert environment and a mostly Arab culture.

✓ Region North Africa includes Libya and the three countries called the Maghreb—Tunisia, Algeria, and Morocco.

✓ Location These countries are all located on the Mediterranean Sea. Morocco also has a coast along the Atlantic Ocean.

✓ Region The landscape of this region is mostly desert and mountains.

✓ Economics Oil, natural gas, and phosphates are among the important resources in these countries.

✓ Culture Most of the people in these countries are Muslims and speak Arabic. Most also are of mixed Arab and Berber heritage.

◄ The pyramids at Giza, Egypt

Assessment and Activities

17

FCAT PRACTICE You can prepare for the FCAT-assessed standards by completing the correlated item(s) below.

Using Key Terms

Match the terms in Part A with their definitions in Part B.

A.

1. oasis
2. secular
3. mosque
4. casbah
5. bazaar
6. dictatorship
7. silt
8. erg
9. aquifer
10. republic

B.

a. government under an all-powerful leader
b. underground rock layer that stores water
c. old area of cities with narrow streets and small shops
d. marketplace
e. place of worship for Muslims
f. fertile or green area in a desert
g. nonreligious
h. desert region of shifting sand dunes
i. particles of soil deposited by water
j. government headed by a president

Reviewing the Main Ideas

Section 1 Egypt

11. **Place** What is the capital of Egypt?
12. **Movement** Which two bodies of water does the Suez Canal connect?
13. **Place** Describe the climate and rainfall in Egypt.
14. **Economics** Name four of Egypt's agricultural products.
15. **Government** What type of government does Egypt have today?

Section 2 Libya and the Maghreb

16. **Human/Environment Interaction** Why must Libya depend on aquifers for water?
17. **Region** What does *maghreb* mean?
18. **History** Who founded the city of Carthage in Tunisia?
19. **History** What foreign country controlled Algeria from 1834 to 1962?
20. **Economics** What energy resource is important to almost all of North Africa's countries?

 **North Africa**

Place Location Activity

On a separate sheet of paper, match the letters on the map with the numbered places listed below.

1. Red Sea
2. Morocco
3. Libya
4. Algeria
5. Atlas Mountains
6. Nile River
7. Cairo
8. Tunisia
9. Tripoli
10. Sinai Peninsula

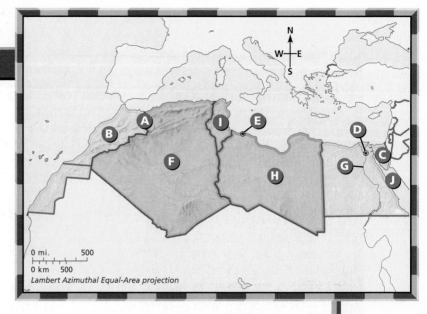

0 mi. 500
0 km 500
Lambert Azimuthal Equal-Area projection

Self-Check Quiz Visit *The World and Its People* Web site at twip.glencoe.com and click on **Chapter 17—Self-Check Quizzes** to prepare for the Chapter Test.

Critical Thinking

21. **Understanding Cause and Effect** Why are the most densely populated areas of North Africa along the Mediterranean Sea and the Nile River? **FCAT** LA.A.2.3.1

22. **Sequencing Information** On a time line like the one below, label five events or eras in Egyptian history. Include their dates.

FCAT LA.A.1.3.2

Comparing Regions Activity

23. **Geography** Turn the page to read about the severe shortages of water in the regions of North Africa and Southwest Asia. It is likely that your region does not currently face this challenge. For an entire day, notice all the different ways you use water. Write a paragraph about how your day would change if you lived in a region where water shortages were common. What might you have to do differently? **FCAT** LA.B.1.3.2

Mental Mapping Activity

24. **Focusing on the Region** Draw a simple outline map of North Africa, then label the following:

- Mediterranean Sea
- Red Sea
- Atlantic Ocean
- Nile River
- Atlas Mountains
- Egypt
- Libya
- Morocco
- Tunisia
- Algeria

Technology Skills Activity

25. **Using the Internet** Use the Internet to research life in the desert. Besides the Sahara, what other large deserts are there in the world? What kinds of life do deserts support? How do humans adapt to life in the desert? Are deserts changing in size and shape? Why? Use your research to create a bulletin board display on "Desert Life." **FCAT** LA.A.2.3.5

Standardized Test Practice

Directions: Study the graph, and then answer the question that follows. **FCAT** MA.E.3.3.1

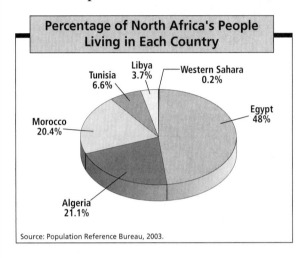

Percentage of North Africa's People Living in Each Country

Libya 3.7%
Tunisia 6.6%
Western Sahara 0.2%
Morocco 20.4%
Egypt 48%
Algeria 21.1%

Source: Population Reference Bureau, 2003.

1. **According to the graph above, which one of the following statements is true?**

   F Almost half of the people of North Africa live in Egypt.

   G Almost half of the people of North Africa live in Algeria.

   H Egypt's land area is much larger than Algeria's land area.

   J Algeria's land area is much larger than Libya's land area.

Test-Taking Tip: When analyzing circle or pie graphs, first look at the title to see what the graph shows. Next read each section of the "pie" and compare the sections to one another. Notice that no actual population figures are given on the pie graph, only percentages. All the pie sections are different sizes, but together they add up to 100 percent.

A Water Crisis

Euphrates R.
Jordan R.
Tigris R.
ALGERIA
EGYPT
SAUDI ARABIA
Nile R.

☐ Deep aquifers

Draining the Rivers The ball game is over. You are hot, sweaty, and thirsty. You press the button on the drinking fountain, but no water comes out. A crisis? Consider this: Many people in Southwest Asia and North Africa never have enough water to meet their needs.

Most of the usable water in this region comes from aquifers—underground areas that store large amounts of water—and from the Jordan, Tigris, Euphrates, and Nile Rivers. Despite these great rivers, water is scarce. The rivers flow through several countries. As each country takes its share of water, less remains for those who are downstream. A few countries have desalinization plants that turn seawater into freshwater. Desalinization is expensive, though. Water resources are further strained by many factors.

- Population growth — By 2025, about 570 million people will inhabit the region. That is too many people for the existing water supplies.

- Irrigation — About 90 percent of water supplies in Southwest Asia are used to irrigate crops.

- Pollution — River water in many places is polluted by salt, sewage, and chemicals.

Finding Solutions Faced with growing demand and decreasing supplies, countries in this region are looking for creative solutions to the water crisis.

- Some countries are recycling wastewater to use on crops.

- Advances in technology are making desalinization more affordable.

- Countries are building dams to regulate water. They are also constructing pipelines to carry water to where it is most needed.

Camels crossing Egypt's desert drink water piped from the Nile River, 300 miles (483 km) away.

Making a Difference

Wise Water Ways Scientist Sandra Postel is trying to educate others on ways to use water more wisely. In her book, *Last Oasis: Facing Water Scarcity*, Postel argues that we can no longer meet rising demands for water by building larger dams and drilling deeper wells. Instead of reaching out for more water, Postel argues, everyone needs to do more with less water. People need to conserve and recycle water and to use it more efficiently. Through her research, Postel has found that farmers, industries, and cities could cut their water use by as much as 50 percent. Water could be saved by practicing water conservation methods such as drip irrigation and water recycling. Postel hopes that governments around the world will work together to protect one of the earth's most precious resources.

Author Sandra Postel

Meeting Demand A group in Southwest Asia and North Africa is studying ways to ease water shortages in the region. The Water Demand Management Research Network (WDMRN) is made up of scientists and government representatives who are studying ways to meet the growing needs for water. The WDMRN shares information with other water researchers and holds meetings to encourage cooperation between all countries in the region.

A worker takes a drink of water at a desalinization plant in Kuwait.

What Can You Do?

Conserve Water
Saving water is as easy as turning off a faucet. Practice water conservation by taking shorter showers and by turning off the water while brushing your teeth. What other ways can you conserve water at home or at school?

Find Out More
Investigate the pathway drinking water takes in your community. Collaborate with classmates to create a bulletin board display showing how water gets from its source to a drinking fountain in your school. **FCAT** LA.A.2.3.5

Southwest Asia

The World and Its People

NATIONAL GEOGRAPHIC

To learn more about the people and places of Southwest Asia, view **The World and Its People Chapter 17** video.

Social Studies online

Chapter Overview Visit **The World and Its People** Web site at <u>twip.glencoe.com</u> and click on **Chapter 18—Chapter Overviews** to preview information about Southwest Asia.

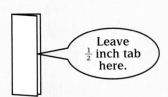

FOLDABLES™
Study Organizer

FCAT PRACTICE The activity below will help you prepare for the **FCAT Reading** test.

Categorizing Information If you ask yourself questions while reading your textbook, it will help you focus on what you are reading. Make this foldable to help you ask and answer questions about the people and places in Southwest Asia. **FCAT LA.A.1.3.2**

Step 1 Fold a sheet of paper in half from side to side, leaving a ½ inch tab along the side.

Leave ½ inch tab here.

Step 2 Turn the paper and fold it into fourths.

Fold in half, then fold in half again.

Step 3 Unfold and cut up along the three fold lines.

This will make four tabs.

Step 4 Label as shown.

Turkey, Syria, Lebanon, Jordan | Israel and the Palestinian Territories | The Arabian Peninsula | Iraq, Iran, Afghanistan

Reading and Writing As you read the chapter, ask yourself questions about these countries. Write your questions and answers under each appropriate tab. **FCAT LA.A.1.3.2**

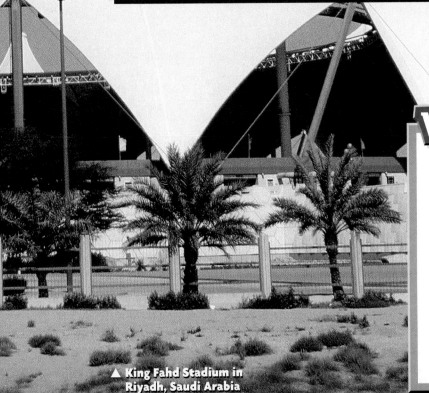

▲ **King Fahd Stadium in Riyadh, Saudi Arabia**

Why It Matters

Crossroads

Because of its location near Europe and Asia, Southwest Asia remains at the "crossroads of the world" even today. The world depends upon the oil and gas resources found here. These resources make the events that unfold in these oil-rich countries of interest to many nations. Achieving peace in this region is of global importance.

Turkey, Syria, Lebanon, Jordan

NATIONAL GEOGRAPHIC **Exploring Our World**

There is only one city in the world that lies on two continents. The Bosporus (BAHS•puhr•uhs), a strait in Turkey, separates this city—Istanbul. The Bosporus also divides Europe from Asia. It is an important seaway that links the Black Sea to the Sea of Marmara and, eventually, to the Mediterranean Sea.

A little larger than Texas, **Turkey** has a unique location—it bridges the continents of Asia and Europe. The large Asian part of Turkey occupies the peninsula known as Asia Minor. The much smaller European part lies on Europe's Balkan Peninsula. Three important waterways—the **Bosporus,** the **Sea of Marmara** (MAHR•muh•ruh), and the **Dardanelles** (DAHRD•uhn•EHLZ) separate the Asian and European parts of Turkey. Together, these waterways are called the Turkish Straits. Find these bodies of water on page RA19 of the **Reference Atlas.**

Turkey

In the center of Turkey is **Anatolia** (A•nuh•TOH•lee•uh), a plateau region rimmed by mountains. The **Pontic Mountains** border the plateau on the north. The **Taurus Mountains** tower over it on the south. Severe earthquakes often occur in northern Turkey, causing much damage and death. Lowland plains curve along Turkey's three coasts.

Turkey's climate varies throughout the country. The Anatolian plateau experiences the hot, dry summers and cold, snowy winters of the steppe climate. People living in the coastal areas enjoy a Mediterranean climate—hot, dry summers and mild, rainy winters.

Many of Turkey's people are farmers who live in the mild coastal areas. There they raise livestock and plant crops such as cotton, tobacco, fruits, and nuts for export. On the drier inland plateau, farmers grow mostly wheat and barley for use at home.

Turkey is seeking to join the European Union. The country has rich mineral resources of coal, copper, and iron. The most important industrial activities are oil refining and the making of textiles and clothing. Turkish factory workers also process foods and make cars, steel, and building materials. The country's beautiful beaches and historic sites have made tourism another growing industry.

Turkey's People Most of Turkey's 71.2 million people live in the northern part of Anatolia, on coastal plains, or in valleys. Almost 100 percent are Muslims, or followers of Islam. Turkish is the official language,

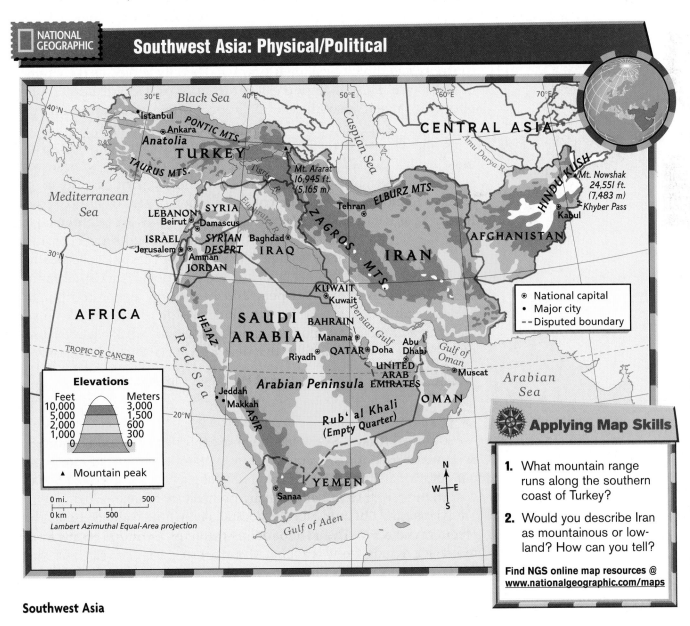

NATIONAL GEOGRAPHIC

Southwest Asia: Physical/Political

Elevations

Feet	Meters
10,000	3,000
5,000	1,500
2,000	600
1,000	300
0	0

▲ Mountain peak

0 mi. 500
0 km 500
Lambert Azimuthal Equal-Area projection

⊗ National capital
• Major city
-- Disputed boundary

Applying Map Skills

1. What mountain range runs along the southern coast of Turkey?

2. Would you describe Iran as mountainous or lowland? How can you tell?

Find NGS online map resources @ www.nationalgeographic.com/maps

Festival Time

Kudret Özal lives in Söğüt, Turkey. Every year, she and her family attend a festival that honors a warrior ancestor. She says, "At night everyone gathers to sing, dance, and tell jokes and stories." According to custom, Kudret wears clothing that covers her head, arms, shoulders, and legs.

but Kurdish and Arabic are also spoken. Kurdish is the language of the Kurds, an ethnic group who make up about 20 percent of Turkey's people. They are seeking to unite with other Kurds from Iraq, Iran, and Syria to form an independent homeland. The Turkish government has tried to turn the Kurds away from Kurdish culture and language. Tensions between the two groups have resulted in violent clashes.

Almost 70 percent of Turkey's people live in cities or towns. **Istanbul** is Turkey's largest city with nearly 9 million people. It is the only city in the world located on two continents. Istanbul is known for its beautiful palaces, museums, and mosques. Because of its location at the entrance to the **Black Sea,** Istanbul is a major trading center. Turkey's capital and second-largest city is **Ankara.**

History and Culture Istanbul began as a Greek port called Byzantium more than 2,500 years ago. Later it was renamed Constantinople after the Roman emperor Constantine the Great. For almost 1,000 years, the city was the glittering capital of the Byzantine Empire.

Many of Turkey's people today are descendants of an Asian people called Turks. These people migrated to Anatolia during the A.D. 900s. To migrate means to move from one place to another. One group of Turks—the Ottomans—conquered Constantinople in the 1400s. They, too, renamed the city, calling it Istanbul. The city served as the capital of a powerful Muslim empire called the Ottoman Empire. This empire once ruled much of southeastern Europe, North Africa, and Southwest Asia. The map on page 518 shows the extent of this empire.

World War I led to the breakup of the Ottoman Empire. During most of the 1920s and 1930s, Kemal Atatürk, a military hero, served as Turkey's first president. He introduced many political and social changes to modernize the country. Turkey soon began to consider itself European as well as Asian. Many Turkish people, however, continued to value the Islamic faith. During the 1990s, Muslim and secular, or non-religious, political groups struggled for control of Turkey's government.

Throughout the country, you can see traditional Turkish arts: colored tiles, finely woven carpets, and beautifully decorated books. Turkish culture, however, has its modern side as well. Folk music blends traditional and modern styles. Turkey also has recently produced many outstanding films that deal with social and political issues.

✔ **Reading Check** What is unusual about Turkey's largest city?

Syria

South of Turkey, **Syria** has been a center of trade for centuries. Syria was a part of many empires, but in 1946 it became an independent country. Since the 1960s, one political party has controlled Syria's government. It does not allow many political freedoms.

Syria's land includes fertile coastal plains and valleys along the Mediterranean Sea. Inland mountains running north and south keep moist sea winds from reaching the eastern part of Syria. The vast **Syrian Desert** covers this eastern region.

Agriculture is Syria's main economic activity. Farmers grow mostly cotton, wheat, and fruit. The Syrian government has built dams on the **Euphrates River,** which flows through the country. These dams provide water for irrigation as well as hydroelectric power for cities and industries. Turkey, Syria's upstream neighbor, is building a huge dam that will reduce the flow of water to Syria and Iraq. Future conflict over water from this river is a possibility.

Like many other countries of Southwest Asia, Syria has reserves of oil—the country's main export. Other industries are food processing and textiles. Syrian fabrics have been highly valued since ancient times.

The Syrians   Almost half of Syria's 17.5 million people live in rural areas. A few are bedouins—nomadic desert peoples who follow a traditional way of life. Most other Syrians live in cities. **Damascus,** the capital, is one of the oldest continuously inhabited cities in the world. It was founded as a trading center more than 4,000 years ago.

The people of Syria are mostly Arab Muslims. In many Syrian cities, you can see spectacular mosques and palaces. As in other Arab countries, hospitality is a major part of life. Group meals are a popular way of strengthening Syrian family ties and friendships. Common foods are lamb, flat bread, and bean dishes flavored with garlic and lemon.

✓ Reading Check On what river has Syria built dams?

Lebanon

Lebanon is about half the size of New Jersey. Because the country is so small, you can swim in the warm Mediterranean Sea in the west, then throw snowballs in the mountains in the east—all in the same day.

Cedar trees once covered Lebanon. Now only a few lonely groves survive in a protected area. Still, Lebanon is the most densely wooded of all the Southwest Asian countries. Pine trees thrive on the mountains.

More than 60 percent of Lebanon's people work in service industries such as banking and insurance. Manufactured products include food, cement, textiles, chemicals, and metal products. Lebanese farmers grow citrus fruits, vegetables, grains, olives, and grapes on coastal land. Shrimp are harvested from the Mediterranean Sea.

The Lebanese People   More than 88 percent of Lebanon's nearly 4.2 million people live in coastal urban areas. **Beirut** (bay•ROOT), the capital and largest city, was once a major banking and business center. European tourists called Beirut "the Paris of the East" because of its elegant shops and sidewalk cafés. Today, however, Beirut is still rebuilding after a civil war that lasted from 1975 to 1991.

Lebanon's civil war arose between Muslims and Christians. About 70 percent of the Lebanese are Arab Muslims. Most of the rest are Arab Christians. Many lives were lost in the war and many people fled as refugees. Lebanon's economy was almost destroyed. Israel invaded Lebanon during the war, finally withdrawing all its troops in 2000.

Arabic is the most widely spoken language in Lebanon. French is also an official language. Why? France ruled Lebanon before the country

Petra

One of Jordan's major tourist attractions, Petra was built during the 300s B.C. The city's temples and monuments were carved out of cliffs in the Valley of Moses in Jordan. It was a major center of the spice trade that reached as far as China, Egypt, Greece, and India. Archaeologists have found dams, rock-carved channels, and ceramic pipes that brought water to the 30,000 people who once lived here.

became independent in the 1940s. Local foods reflect a blend of Arab, Turkish, and French influences.

✓ **Reading Check** Why is Beirut in the process of rebuilding?

Jordan

A land of contrasts, **Jordan** stretches from the fertile Jordan River valley in the west to dry, rugged country in the east. Jordan lacks water resources. Irrigated farmland lies in the Jordan River valley, however. Here farmers grow wheat, fruits, and vegetables. Jordan's desert is home to tent-dwelling bedouins who raise livestock.

Jordan also lacks energy resources. Many people work in service and manufacturing industries. The leading manufactured goods are phosphate, potash, pottery, chemicals, and processed foods.

People and Government Most of Jordan's 5.5 million people are Arab Muslims. They include more than 1 million Palestinian refugees. **Amman** is the capital and largest city. On a site occupied since prehistoric times, Amman has Roman and other ancient ruins.

During the early 1900s, the Ottoman Empire ruled this area. After the Ottoman defeat in World War I, the British set up a territory that became known as Jordan. It gained independence in 1946. The country has a constitutional monarchy. Elected leaders govern, but a king is the official head of state. From 1952 to 1999, King Hussein I ruled Jordan. He worked to blend the country's traditions with modern ways. The present leader of Jordan is Hussein's son, King Abdullah II.

✓ **Reading Check** What are Jordan's leading manufactured goods?

FCAT PRACTICE You can prepare for the FCAT-assessed standards by completing the correlated item(s) below.

Section 1 Assessment

Defining Terms
1. Define migrate, bedouins.

Recalling Facts
2. **Economics** Name five of Turkey's agricultural products.
3. **Place** What landform covers eastern Syria?
4. **Place** What is the capital of Lebanon?

Critical Thinking
5. **Understanding Cause and Effect** How could a dam on the Euphrates River cause a conflict among Turkey, Syria, and Iraq? **FCAT LA.A.2.3.1**
6. **Analyzing Information** How has Istanbul's location made it a trading center? **FCAT LA.E.2.2.1**

Graphic Organizer
7. **Organizing Information** Draw a diagram like this one. Inside the large oval, list characteristics that Syria, Lebanon, and Jordan share.

FCAT LA.A.1.3.2

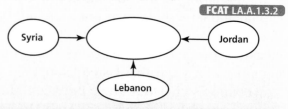

Applying Social Studies Skills

8. **Analyzing Maps** Study the map on page 503. What borders Turkey on the north? On the south?

506

Making Connections

ART   SCIENCE   CULTURE   TECHNOLOGY

FCAT PRACTICE Answering question 3 below will help you prepare for the **FCAT Reading** test.

Carpet Weaving

For thousands of years, people have been making the hand-knotted floor coverings sometimes called Persian or Turkish rugs. Valued for their rich color and intricate design, these handmade rugs are unique works of art.

History

Most experts think that the nomadic peoples of Asia were among the first to make hand-knotted carpets. They used their carpets as wall coverings, curtains, saddlebags, and coverings for the bare ground in their tents. The soft, thick rugs blocked out the cold and could also be used as a bed or blanket.

As the nomads moved from place to place, they spread the art of carpet making to new lands and peoples. Throughout the years, the greatest carpet-producing areas have included Turkey, the republics of the Caucasus, Persia (Iran), and Turkmenistan. People in other countries, including Afghanistan, Pakistan, Nepal, India, and China, also became skilled carpet weavers.

Weaving and Knotting

Early nomads wove their carpets from sheep's wool on simple wooden looms that could be rolled up for traveling. Each carpet was woven with two sets of threads. The *warp* threads run from top to bottom, and the *weft* threads are woven from side to side. Hand-tied knots form the carpet's colorful pattern. A skillful weaver can tie about 15 knots a minute. The best carpets can have more than 500 knots per square inch!

Color and Design

The beauty of woven carpets comes from the endless combination of colors and designs. Over the years, various regions developed their own

▲ Turkish carpet weavers

carpet patterns. These were passed down from generation to generation. Often the images hold special meanings. For instance, the palm and coconut often symbolize happiness and blessings.

The very first rugs were colored gray, white, brown, or black—the natural color of the wool. Then people learned to make dyes from plants and animals. The root of the madder plant, as well as certain insects, provided red and pink dye. Turmeric root and saffron supplied shades of yellow, and the indigo plant provided blue.

Making the Connection

1. How did the art of carpet weaving spread from one place to another?
2. What creates the pattern in a Turkish carpet?
3. **Drawing Conclusions** In what way do hand-knotted carpets combine art with usefulness?

FCAT LA.A.2.3.1

Israel and the Palestinian Territories

NATIONAL GEOGRAPHIC Exploring Our World

Modern and traditional cultures exist side by side throughout Israel. Israel was established as an independent country in 1948 after many years of trying to create a homeland for Jews. Since then, Jewish people from more than 100 countries have migrated to this small country. At this market in Tel Aviv-Yafo, buyers and sellers talk about current events and sports.

Israel lies at the eastern end of the Mediterranean Sea. Slightly larger than New Jersey, it is 256 miles (412 km) long from north to south and only 68 miles (109 km) wide from east to west.

Israel's Land and Climate

The mountains of Galilee lie in Israel's far north. East of these mountains is a plateau called the **Golan Heights.** South of the Golan Heights, between Israel and Jordan, is the **Dead Sea.** At 1,349 feet (411 m) below sea level, the shores of the Dead Sea are the lowest place on the earth's surface. The Dead Sea is also the earth's saltiest body of water—about nine times saltier than ocean water. The map on page 511 shows you where the Golan Heights and the Dead Sea are located.

In southern Israel, a desert called the **Negev** (NEH•GEHV) covers almost half the country. A fertile plain no more than 20 miles (32 km) wide lies along the country's Mediterranean coast. To the east, the

Jordan River cuts through the floor of a long, narrow valley before flowing into the Dead Sea.

Northern Israel has a Mediterranean climate with hot, dry summers and mild winters. About 40 inches (102 cm) of rain fall in the north each year. Southern Israel has a desert climate. Summer temperatures soar higher than 120°F (49°C), and annual rainfall is less than 1 inch (2.5 cm).

✓ Reading Check What plateau is found in northeastern Israel?

Israel's Economy

Israel's best farmland stretches along the Mediterranean coastal plain. For centuries, farmers here have grown citrus fruits, such as oranges, grapefruits, and lemons. Citrus fruits are still Israel's major agricultural export. Farther inland, you find that the desert actually blooms. This is possible because farmers add fertilizers to the soil and carefully use scarce water resources. In very dry areas, crops are grown with drip irrigation. This method uses computers to release specific amounts of water from underground tubes to the roots of plants. Israeli farmers also plant certain fruits and vegetables that do not absorb salts, such as the Negev tomatoes. As a result of technology, Israel's farmers feed not only the country's people—they even export some food to other countries.

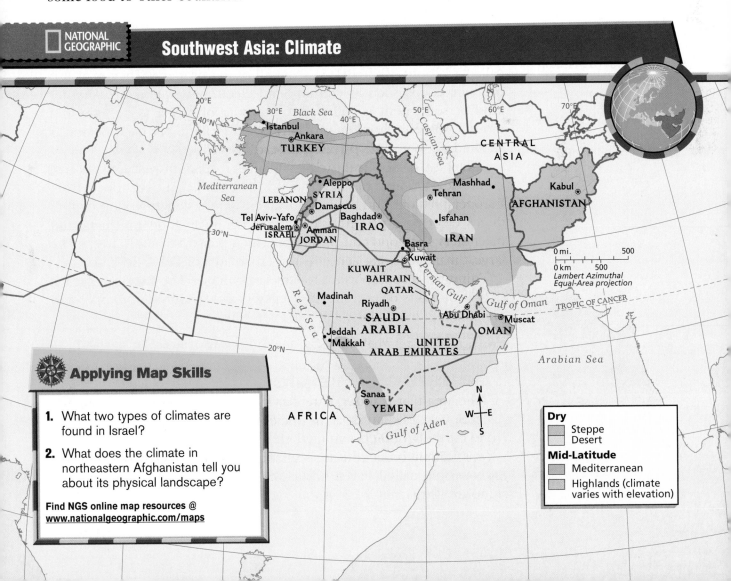

NATIONAL GEOGRAPHIC

Southwest Asia: Climate

Applying Map Skills

1. What two types of climates are found in Israel?

2. What does the climate in northeastern Afghanistan tell you about its physical landscape?

Find NGS online map resources @ www.nationalgeographic.com/maps

Dry
Steppe
Desert

Mid-Latitude
Mediterranean
Highlands (climate varies with elevation)

Israel

Cartloads of apples are transported to market from a farm settlement called a kibbutz in Metulla, Israel.

Place How do Israeli farmers make the desert bloom?

About 9 percent of Israelis live and work on farm settlements. Many join together to grow and sell crops. People in one type of settlement called a **kibbutz** (kih•BUTS) share all of the property. They may also produce goods such as clothing and electronic equipment. Another kind of settlement is called a **moshav** (moh•SHAHV). People in a moshav share in farming, production, and selling, but each person is allowed to own some private property as well.

Israel is the most industrialized country in Southwest Asia. Its economic development has been supported by large amounts of aid from European nations and the United States. Israel's skilled workforce produces electronic products, clothing, chemicals, food products, and machinery. Diamond cutting and polishing is also a major industry. The largest manufacturing center is the urban area of **Tel Aviv-Yafo.**

Mining is also important to Israel's economy. The Dead Sea area is rich in deposits of potash. The Negev is also a source of copper and phosphate, a mineral used in making fertilizer.

✓ Reading Check What city is the largest manufacturing center in Israel?

The Israeli People

The area that is today Israel has been home to different groups of people over the centuries. The ancient traditions of these groups have led to current conflicts among their descendants. About 80 percent of Israel's 6.7 million people are Jews. The other 20 percent belong to an Arab people called Palestinians. Most Palestinians are Muslims, but some are Christians.

As you learned in Chapter 16, the ancient Jews under King David created a kingdom in about 1000 B.C. Over time, the region was ruled by Greeks, Romans, Byzantines, Arabs, and Ottoman Turks. Under the Romans, the area was called Palestine. The Jews twice revolted against Roman rule but failed to win their freedom. In response, the Romans ordered all Jews out of the land.

Prejudice against the Jews caused them much hardship. In the late 1800s, some European Jews began to move back to Palestine. These settlers, known as Zionists, had planned to set up a safe homeland for Jews in their ancestral land.

The Birth of Israel   During World War I, the British won control of Palestine. They supported a Jewish homeland there. Most of the people living in Palestine, however, were Arabs who also claimed the area as their homeland. To keep peace with the local Arab population, the British began to limit the number of Jews entering Palestine.

During World War II, Germans killed millions of Europe's Jews and others. The mass imprisonment and slaughter of European Jews is known as the Holocaust. It brought worldwide attention to Jews. After World War II, many remaining Jews were left homeless. The number who wanted to migrate to Palestine increased.

In 1947 the United Nations voted to divide Palestine into a Jewish and an Arab state. The Arabs in Palestine and in neighboring countries disagreed with this division. In May 1948, the British left the area, and the Jews set up the independent country of Israel in their part of Palestine. David Ben-Gurion (BEHN•gur•YAWN) became Israel's first leader.

War soon broke out between Israel and its Arab neighbors. The war ended in 1949 with Israel's victory. Many Palestinian Arabs fled to neighboring countries and became refugees. At the same time, many Jews from Europe and other nations began moving to the new state of Israel.

Israel later fought other wars with its Arab neighbors. In one conflict, Israel won control of neighboring Arab areas, such as the **West Bank** and the **Gaza Strip.** Palestinian Arabs, now left homeless, demanded their own country. During the 1970s and 1980s, many Palestinians and Israelis died fighting one another. Steps toward peace began when Israel and Egypt signed a treaty in 1979. Agreements made between Israel and Palestinian Arab leaders in 1993 and between Israel and Jordan in 1994 also moved the region toward peace.

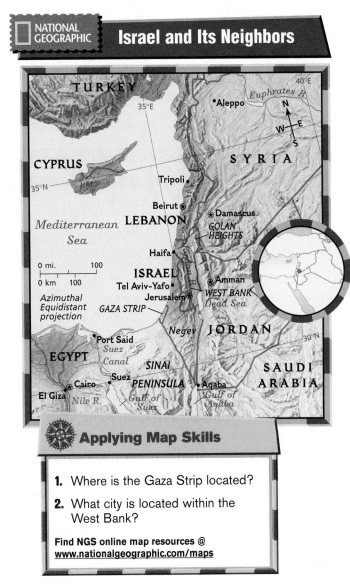

NATIONAL GEOGRAPHIC

Israel and Its Neighbors

Applying Map Skills

1. Where is the Gaza Strip located?

2. What city is located within the West Bank?

Find **NGS** online map resources @
www.nationalgeographic.com/maps

In the 1993 agreement, Israel agreed to turn over two areas to the Palestinians. The West Bank lies on the western bank of the Jordan River and surrounds **Jerusalem.** The Gaza Strip is located on the Mediterranean coast and shares a border with Egypt. Find these areas on the map on page 511. Palestinians now have limited control of some of these areas. Yet some Jews still live in these two regions, and tensions between the two groups remain. Many issues—particularly control of Jerusalem—need to be settled before Palestinians achieve independence. In addition, Palestinian Arabs have fewer freedoms and economic opportunities than their Jewish neighbors. In late 2000, violence erupted again because of the inability to resolve these issues.

Israel Today   More than 90 percent of Israel's people live in urban areas. The largest cities are Jerusalem, Tel Aviv-Yafo, and Haifa (HY•fuh). Israel proclaimed Jerusalem as its capital in 1950.

A single law—the Law of Return—increased Israel's population more than any other factor. Passed in 1950, the law states that Jews anywhere in the world can come to Israel to live. As a result, Jewish people have moved to Israel from many countries.

Israel is a democratic republic, which is a government headed by elected officials. A president represents the country at national events. A prime minister heads the government. The Israeli parliament, or Knesset, meets in a modern building in Jerusalem.

✔**Reading Check** Over what two areas do Palestinians have limited control?

FCAT PRACTICE   You can prepare for the FCAT-assessed standards by completing the correlated item(s) below.

Assessment

Defining Terms
1. Define kibbutz, moshav, Holocaust.

Recalling Facts
2. Location What is the lowest place on the earth's surface? What is its elevation?

3. History What is a Zionist?

4. Place What percentage of Israel's people live in urban areas? What percentage farm?

Critical Thinking
5. Analyzing Information What is the major disagreement between Israel and the Palestinians? **FCAT LA.A.2.3.1**

6. Drawing Conclusions Why do you think Israel has worked so hard to develop its agricultural and manufacturing industries?
FCAT LA.A.2.3.1

Graphic Organizer
7. Organizing Information On a diagram like this one, list three things that helped Israel's agricultural success. **FCAT LA.A.1.3.2**

```
┌─────────────┐
│  ─────────  │
│  ─────────  │──→ Israel's ability to feed its people
│  ─────────  │
└─────────────┘
```

Applying Social Studies Skills

8. Analyzing Maps Study the map on page 511. What country borders Israel to the north? To the northeast? To the east?

The Arabian Peninsula

Guide to Reading

Main Idea

Money from oil exports has boosted standards of living in most countries of the Arabian Peninsula.

Terms to Know

- wadi
- desalinization
- caliph

Reading Strategy

Create a diagram like this one and give four examples of how oil has benefited the Arabian Peninsula.

FCAT LA.A.1.3.2

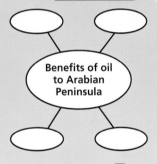

Benefits of oil to Arabian Peninsula

The following are the major Sunshine State Standards covered in this section.

SS.A.2.3.2:
Knows how major historical developments have had an impact on the development of civilizations

SS.B.2.3.8:
Knows world patterns of resource distribution and utilization

NATIONAL GEOGRAPHIC Exploring Our World

Thousands of years ago, nomads in Arabia and Africa tamed camels. They were the only animals that could make the long journey across the desert, thanks to their ability to go for days without food or water. For centuries, camels were the main source of transport, milk, and meat in the desert. Today they are also valued for their racing speed.

Find the Arabian Peninsula on the map on page 503. Notice that its highest elevations are in the south. The mostly desert land in the north borders Iraq, then it slopes toward the **Persian Gulf.**

Saudi Arabia

Saudi Arabia, the largest country in Southwest Asia, is about the size of the eastern half of the United States. Vast deserts cover this region. The largest and harshest desert is the **Rub' al Khali,** or Empty Quarter, in the southeast. The Empty Quarter has mountains of sand that reach heights of more than 1,000 feet (305 m).

Because of the generally dry, desert climate, Saudi Arabia has no rivers or permanent bodies of water. Highlands dominate the southwest, however, and rainfall there irrigates fertile croplands in the valleys. Water sometimes comes from seasonal wadis, or dry riverbeds filled by rainwater from rare downpours. The desert also holds oases.

Analyzing the Graph

Southwest Asia has more known oil than all other regions of the world combined.

Region What percentage of the world's known oil reserves does Southwest Asia hold?

 FCAT MA.E.3.3.1

 Textbook *update*

Visit twip.glencoe.com and click on **Chapter 18– Textbook Updates.**

FCAT PRACTICE

Completing the exercise above will help you prepare for the **FCAT Mathematics** test.

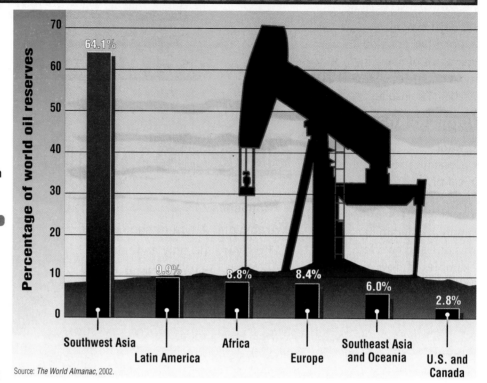

Source: *The World Almanac,* 2002.

An Oil-Based Economy Saudi Arabia holds a major share of the world's oil. This entire region is by far the world's leading producer of oil. The graph above compares the amount of oil reserves in Southwest Asia with those of other regions.

Since 1960 Saudi Arabia and some other oil producers have formed the Organization of Petroleum Exporting Countries (OPEC). Together they work to increase income from the sale of oil. Today OPEC countries supply more than 40 percent of the world's oil. By increasing or reducing supply, they are able to influence world oil prices.

Oil has helped Saudi Arabia boost its standard of living. Money earned by selling oil has built schools, hospitals, roads, and airports. Aware that someday its oil will run out, Saudi Arabia's government has been trying to broaden the economy. In recent years, it has given more emphasis to industry and agriculture. To get more water and grow more food, the government has spent much money on irrigation and desalinization. This is a process that takes salt out of seawater.

Spread of Islam In Chapter 16, you learned about Muhammad and the holy Islamic city of Makkah, which is located in western Saudi Arabia. After Muhammad died in A.D. 632, his closest followers chose a new leader known as a **caliph,** or "successor." Caliphs were both political and religious leaders.

Under the early caliphs, Arab Muslims conquered neighboring lands and created a vast empire. By A.D. 750, Islamic expansion— shown on the map on page 518—included North Africa and what is now Spain extending almost to India. As time passed, many of the conquered peoples accepted Islam and the Arabic language.

By the end of the A.D. 900s, the Arab Empire had broken up into smaller kingdoms. During the next few centuries, waves of invaders known as Mongols swept into the Muslim world from central Asia. The Ottoman Turks, as you learned in Section 1, later moved into the region. They created a Muslim empire that lasted until the early 1900s.

Between the 700s and 1300s, scholars in the Arab Empire made many contributions to mathematics, astronomy, chemistry, medicine, and the arts. They also preserved much of the learning of the ancient Greeks and Romans. When Arabic texts were translated into Latin, European scholars could study the ancient works they thought had been lost after the fall of Rome.

The People Today In 1932 a monarchy led by the Saud family unified the country's many clans. The Saud family still rules today. Most of the 24.1 million Saudis live in towns and villages either along the oil-rich Persian Gulf coast or around oases. The capital and largest city, **Riyadh** (ree•YAHD), sits amid a large oasis in central Saudi Arabia. Once a small town, Riyadh now has skyscrapers and busy highways.

As in other Muslim countries, Islam strongly influences life in Saudi Arabia. Government, business, school, and home schedules are timed to Islam's five daily prayers and two major yearly celebrations. Much government attention has been given to preparing Makkah and Madinah for the several million Muslims who visit each year. Saudi customs concerning the roles of women in public life are stricter than in most other Muslim countries. Saudi women may work outside the home but only in jobs that avoid close contact with men.

✓ Reading Check What influences almost every part of Saudi Arabian culture?

The Persian Gulf States

Kuwait (ku•WAYT), **Bahrain** (bah•RAYN), **Qatar** (KAH•tuhr), and the **United Arab Emirates** are located along the Persian Gulf. Beneath their flat deserts and offshore areas lie vast deposits of oil. The Persian Gulf states have used profits from oil exports to build prosperous economies. Political and business leaders, however, are aware that oil revenues depend on constantly changing world oil prices. As a result, they have encouraged the growth of other industries. Their goal is to build a more varied economy.

The people of the Persian Gulf states once made a living from activities such as pearl diving, fishing, and camel herding. Now they have modern jobs in the oil and natural gas industries. They also enjoy a high standard of living. Using income from oil, their governments provide free education, health care, and other services. Many workers from other countries have settled in these countries. They work in the modern cities and oil fields to benefit from the economic boom.

✓ Reading Check How have the economies of the Persian Gulf states changed since the discovery of oil?

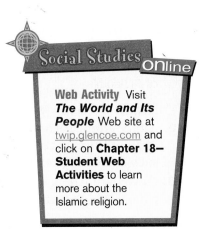

Social Studies Online

Web Activity Visit *The World and Its People* Web site at twip.glencoe.com and click on **Chapter 18—Student Web Activities** to learn more about the Islamic religion.

Oman and Yemen

At the southeastern and southern ends of the Arabian Peninsula are the countries of **Oman** and **Yemen.** Oman is largely desert, but its bare land yields oil—the basis of the country's economy. Until recently, most of the people of Oman lived in rural villages. The oil industry has drawn many of these people—and foreigners—to **Muscat,** the country's capital. Other natural resources include natural gas, copper, marble, and limestone. Agricultural products include dates, bananas, camels, and cattle.

Oman's location also has made the country important to world oil markets. The northern part of Oman guards the strategic Strait of Hormuz. Oil-bearing tankers have to go through this narrow waterway to pass from the Persian Gulf into the **Arabian Sea.**

Southwest of Oman lies Yemen, which is made up of a narrow coastal plain and inland mountains. In ancient times, Yemen was famous for its rich trade in fragrant tree resins such as myrrh (MUHR) and frankincense. Yemen's capital, the walled city of **Sanaa** (sahn•AH), was once a crossroads for camel caravans that carried goods from as far away as China.

Today Yemen is the only country of the Arabian Peninsula that does not have large deposits of oil. Most of the people are farmers or herd sheep and cattle. They live in the high fertile interior where Sanaa is located. Farther south lies Aden (AH•duhn), a major port for ships traveling between the Arabian Sea and the Red Sea.

▲ A village in Oman

✓ Reading Check **What makes Yemen different from other countries in the Arabian Peninsula?**

FCAT PRACTICE You can prepare for the FCAT-assessed standards by completing the correlated item(s) below.

Section 3 — Assessment

Defining Terms
1. **Define** wadi, desalinization, caliph.

Recalling Facts
2. **Place** What is the Empty Quarter?
3. **Government** Who rules Saudi Arabia, and what is its form of government?
4. **Culture** What is the significance of the city of Makkah?

Critical Thinking
5. **Analyzing Information** Why is the Strait of Hormuz considered to be of such strategic importance? **FCAT** LA.A.2.3.1
6. **Drawing Conclusions** How do the nations of OPEC affect your life? **FCAT** LA.A.2.3.1

Graphic Organizer
7. **Organizing Information** On a diagram like this one, list three ways that Islam influences life in Saudi Arabia. **FCAT** LA.A.1.3.2

Influences of Islam →
→
→

Applying Social Studies Skills
8. **Analyzing Graphs** Study the graph on page 514. Which region of the world has the second-largest reserves of oil? **FCAT** MA.E.3.3.1

Iraq, Iran, and Afghanistan

Guide to Reading

Main Idea

Iraq, Iran, and Afghanistan have recently fought wars and have undergone sweeping political changes.

Terms to Know

- alluvial plain
- embargo
- shah
- Islamic republic

Reading Strategy

Create a chart like this one and list one fact about the people in each country. **FCAT** LA.A.1.3.2

Country	People
Iraq	
Iran	
Afghanistan	

The following are the major Sunshine State Standards covered in this section.

SS.A.3.3.2:
Understands the historical events that have shaped the development of cultures throughout the world

SS.A.3.3.5:
Understands the differences between institutions of Eastern and Western civilizations (e.g., differences in governments, social traditions and customs, economic systems and religious institutions)

SS.B.2.3.5:
Understands the geographical factors that affect the cohesiveness and integration of countries

NATIONAL GEOGRAPHIC Exploring Our World

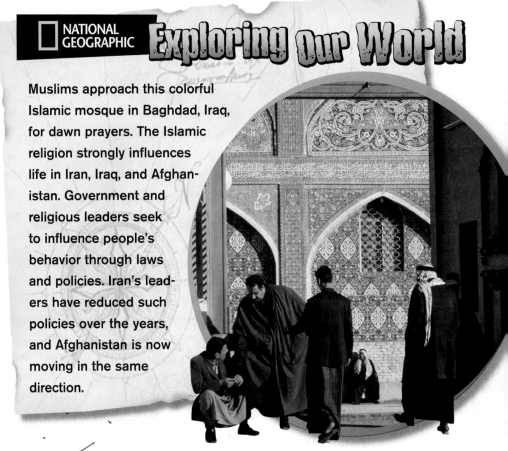

Muslims approach this colorful Islamic mosque in Baghdad, Iraq, for dawn prayers. The Islamic religion strongly influences life in Iran, Iraq, and Afghanistan. Government and religious leaders seek to influence people's behavior through laws and policies. Iran's leaders have reduced such policies over the years, and Afghanistan is now moving in the same direction.

Iraq, Iran, and Afghanistan are located in a region where some of the world's oldest civilizations developed. This region has experienced turmoil throughout history and even today.

Iraq

As you read in Chapter 16, the world's first known cities arose between the Tigris and Euphrates Rivers. These rivers are the major geographic features of **Iraq.** Between the two rivers is an alluvial plain, or an area built up by rich fertile soil left by river floods. Most farming takes place here. Farmers grow wheat, barley, dates, cotton, and rice.

Oil is the country's major export. Iraq's factories process foods and make textiles, chemicals, and construction materials.

People and Government About 70 percent of Iraq's 24.2 million people live in urban areas. **Baghdad,** the capital, is the largest city.

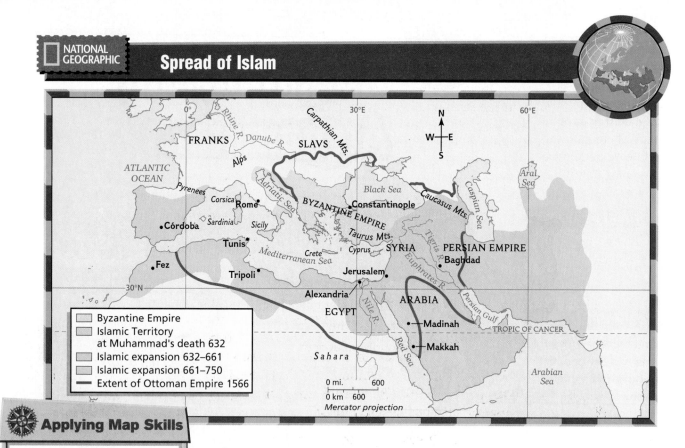

Byzantine Empire
Islamic Territory
  at Muhammad's death 632
Islamic expansion 632–661
Islamic expansion 661–750
Extent of Ottoman Empire 1566

0 mi. 600
0 km 600
Mercator projection

Applying Map Skills

1. Which period of Islamic expansion included Egypt?

2. Did Islamic territory completely encircle the Mediterranean Sea?

Find NGS online resources @
www.nationalgeographic.com/maps

From the A.D. 700s to 1200s, Baghdad was the center of a large Muslim empire that made many advances in the arts and sciences. Muslim Arabs make up the largest group in Iraq's population. The second-largest group consists of another Muslim people, the Kurds, who want to form their own country.

Modern Iraq gained its independence as a kingdom in 1932. In 1958 the last king was overthrown in a revolt. Since then, military leaders have governed Iraq as a dictatorship. Dictator Saddam Hussein ruled with an iron hand from 1979 to 2003. In the 1980s, Iraq fought a bloody war with its neighbor Iran. Then in 1990, partly because of a dispute over oil, Iraq invaded neighboring Kuwait. This action led to the Persian Gulf War in 1991. A United Nations force led by the United States pushed Iraqi troops out of Kuwait.

Saddam stayed in power despite losing the war. He refused to agree to demands from the United Nations that he give up his vast store of destructive weapons. As a result, the United Nations continued an embargo on trade with Iraq that it had introduced before the war. An **embargo** is an order that restricts trade with another country. This severely damaged Iraq's economy.

In the early 2000s, the United Nations sent experts into Iraq to search for weapons of mass destruction. The United States did not believe Saddam was fully cooperating. In March 2003, American and British forces invaded Iraq. Less than a month later, Saddam was overthrown, and plans were made to create a democratic government in Iraq. Then Saddam was captured by a U.S.-led coalition in December 2003.

✓ **Reading Check** What two rivers have influenced the history of Iraq?

Iran

Once known as Persia, **Iran** is slightly larger than Alaska. Two vast ranges—the **Elburz Mountains** and the **Zagros Mountains**—surround a central desert plateau. Iran is an oil-rich nation. The first oil wells in Southwest Asia were drilled here in 1908. Like Saudi Arabia, Iran is trying to promote other industries in order to become less dependent on oil earnings. Major Iranian industries produce textiles, metal goods, construction materials, and beautiful carpets valued worldwide. Farmers grow wheat, rice, sugar beets, and cotton. Some use ancient underground channels to bring water to their fields. Iran is also the world's largest producer of pistachio nuts.

The Iranian People Iran's 66.6 million people differ from those of other Southwest Asian countries. More than one-half are Persians, not Arabs or Turks. The Persians' ancestors migrated from Central Asia centuries ago. They speak Farsi, or Persian, the official language of Iran. Other languages include Kurdish, Arabic, and Turkish. About 65 percent of Iranians live in urban areas. **Tehran,** located in northern Iran, is the largest city and the capital. Iran is also home to about 2 million people from Iraq and Afghanistan who have fled recent wars. Nearly 98 percent of Iran's people practice some form of Islam.

Iran's Government About 2,000 years ago, Iran was the center of the powerful Persian Empire ruled by kings known as **shahs.** In 1979 religious leaders overthrew the last monarchy. Iran is now an **Islamic republic,** a government run by Muslim religious leaders. The government has introduced laws based on its understanding of the Quran. Many Western customs seen as a threat to Islam are forbidden here.

✔️ **Reading Check** How do Iranians differ in ethnic background from most other Southwest Asians?

Iran and Afghanistan

An Iranian family picnics in the hills above Tehran (below left). Under the Taliban, women in Afghanistan were rarely allowed in public (below right).

Government What form of government does Iran have? What group led Afghanistan in the 1990s?

NATIONAL GEOGRAPHIC On Location

Afghanistan

Landlocked **Afghanistan** (af•GA•nuh•STAN) is mostly covered with the rugged peaks of the **Hindu Kush** mountain range. The Khyber (KY•buhr) Pass cuts through the mountains and for centuries has been a major trade route linking Southwest Asia with other parts of Asia. The capital, **Kabul** (KAH•buhl), lies in a valley.

Afghanistan's 28.7 million people are divided into about 20 different ethnic groups. The two largest groups are the Pashtuns and the Tajiks. Almost 70 percent of the people farm, growing wheat, fruits, and nuts and herding sheep and goats.

A Country at War During the 1980s, the Afghan people fought against Soviet troops who had invaded their country. When the Soviets left Afghanistan in 1989, the Afghan people faced poverty, food shortages, and rising crime. The country collapsed into civil war. For leadership, many people turned to the Taliban, a group of fighters educated at Islamic schools in Pakistan. They set up very strict laws based on their view of Islam. For example, men had to grow beards, and women had to completely cover themselves in public and could not hold jobs or go to school. In October 2001, after the attacks on the World Trade Center and Pentagon, the United States accused the Taliban of supporting terrorists and began bombing Taliban forces. By mid-November, the Taliban government had collapsed. The United Nations then began working with local leaders to create a new government for Afghanistan.

✓ Reading Check What trade route cuts through the Hindu Kush?

FCAT PRACTICE You can prepare for the FCAT-assessed standards by completing the correlated item(s) below.

Assessment

Defining Terms
1. **Define** alluvial plain, embargo, shah, Islamic republic.

Recalling Facts
2. **Economics** What is Iraq's major export?

3. **Culture** What are the two largest ethnic groups in Iraq?

4. **Government** What type of government does Iran have?

Critical Thinking
5. **Understanding Cause and Effect** Why did American and British forces invade Iraq? **FCAT LA.A.2.3.1**

6. **Drawing Conclusions** Why do you think the Afghan people turned to the Taliban for leadership after the Soviets left? **FCAT LA.E.2.2.1**

Graphic Organizer
7. **Organizing Information** Create a chart like this one for each of the following countries: Iraq, Iran, and Afghanistan. Then write one fact about the country under each heading. **FCAT LA.A.1.3.2**

Country		
Capital	Landforms	Agriculture
People	Religion	Government

Applying Social Studies Skills

8. **Analyzing Maps** Study the map on page 503. Between what bodies of water is Iran located?

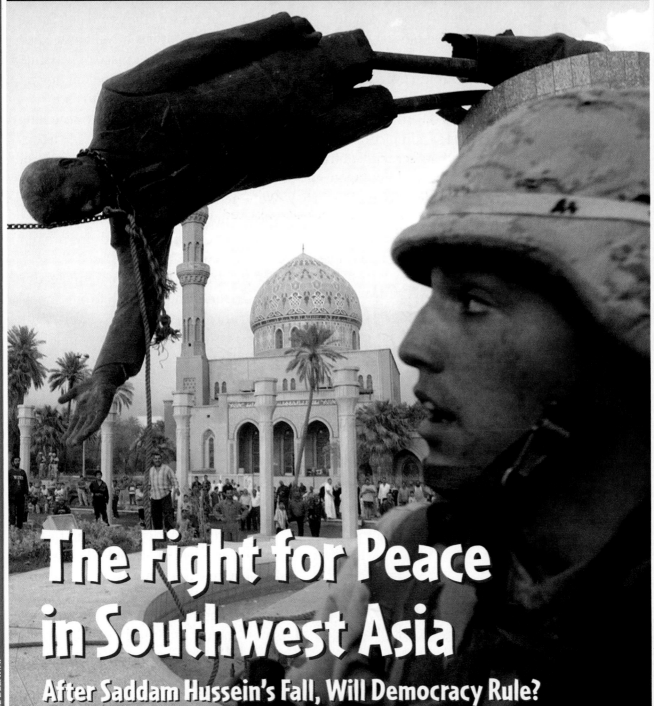

TIME
PERSPECTIVES

The Fight for Peace in Southwest Asia

After Saddam Hussein's Fall, Will Democracy Rule?

JEROME DELAY/AP

A Shi'ite confronts U.S. troops in An Najaf.

Oil is Iraq's biggest industry.

War Without End?

Evaluating
Media
LA.A.2.3.6

In early April 2003, a platoon of U.S. soldiers stood outside a mosque in the city of An Najaf, Iraq. They had been in Iraq since March 19, when troops from several nations, led by U.S. forces, invaded the country. By the end of April, the invaders accomplished their goal, ending the rule of Saddam Hussein, Iraq's cruel dictator.

But in early April, the fighting was still going on, especially in cities like An Najaf. An Najaf is one of Iraq's holiest cities. It is the burial place of Ali, the cousin and son-in-law of Muhammad,

the last and greatest prophet of Islam. Every year tens of thousands of **Shi'ite** (SHEE•EYET) **Muslims** travel to An Najaf to visit the **mosque,** or place of worship. Shi'ites (also called Shia) belong to one of the two main branches of Islam.

The American soldiers were searching for gunmen who had shot at U.S. troops from inside the mosque. Hundreds of Shi'ites blocked their way. The Shi'ites were ready to fight to protect their sacred house of worship. "In the city, okay," one man shouted in broken English. "In the mosque, no!"

Acting quickly, the platoon leader calmed them down. "Drop to one knee!" he ordered his troops. "Point your weapons at the ground. Now smile!"

The Iraqis smiled back. Some even laughed. A moment of danger had passed.

A Terrorist Act

Almost five months later, a bomb exploded outside the same mosque. It killed Ayatollah Mohammed Baqir al-Hakim, a key Shi'ite leader. Some Shi'ites hated al-Hakim. They thought he was too friendly with Americans. Small groups of **Sunni** (SOO•NEE) **Muslims** felt the same way. Sunnis are members of the second branch of Islam.

After Saddam Hussein was toppled, small bands of Sunnis continued to attack U.S. troops. These groups demanded that the U.S. and its allies leave Iraq. Fighting raged on for months. ◼

Where Iraq's Muslims Live

TURKEY

Tigris River

Euphrates River

Mosul

SYRIA

Tikrit

Zagros Mountains

IRAN

SYRIAN DESERT

IRAQ

Baghdad

An Najaf

SAUDI ARABIA

Basra

KUWAIT

Persian Gulf

IRAQ

Iraq's Muslims
(as a percent of Iraq's population)
Arab Shiites (60%)
Arab Sunnis (20%)
Sunni Kurd (17%)
Not shown: Christian and other (3%)

0 mi   100
0 km   100

N

Making Inferences Why did most attacks against Americans by Sunnis take place between Baghdad and Tikrit? Where would you expect to hear Kurdish spoken?

Members of Iraq's temporary government had the job of writing a new constitution.

A man votes to elect city officials in Bahrain.

Bahraini women voted for the first time in 2002.

Putting Iraq on Its Feet

Evaluating Media
LA.A.2.3.6

The fighting that drove Saddam Hussein from power left wreckage that had to be cleaned up. U.S. forces began tackling these problems in late April 2003, just six weeks after the war had begun. Rebuilding Iraq meant two things. First, it meant fixing just about everything. Electric power plants, water pumping stations, roads, schools, and hospitals had all been in terrible shape for years. The oil industry, once Iraq's major moneymaker, had collapsed.

The second part of rebuilding Iraq was more difficult. It required Iraqis to create a **democracy,** or government in which citizens vote for their leaders, from scratch. They had to agree on the shape of the new government. They had to draw up a **constitution,** or body of laws, that described how each part of the government worked. They had to hold free elections, appoint judges, and hire people to make the government function.

At the time, Afghanistan was struggling with similar problems. Freed from a cruel dictatorship in 2002, Afghanis were inventing their own democracy. Their constitution is a reminder of how important religion is in Southwest Asia. "No law," it says, "will be made that will oppose Islamic principles."

Fresh Air

The events in Iraq helped support moves toward more open government in the following countries.

- In 2002 voters in Bahrain elected their **parliament,** or lawmaking body, for the first time in 30 years.

- In 2003 men and women in Oman were given the right to vote in parliamentary elections.

- Qatar's new constitution, adopted in 2003, guarantees freedom of the press and women's voting rights.

- Kuwait's parliament approved a 2003 plan to let women vote and run for city offices.

These changes, small as they may seem, had a powerful impact on other nations in the area. Along with the Iraq war, they even convinced the princes who run Saudi Arabia to open the door to democracy slightly. Saudis will be able to elect some city officials in 2004.

In the fall of 2003, Jordan's King Abdullah II commented on the changes occurring in his country. "We are at the beginning of a new stage in terms of democracy and freedom," he said.

EXPLORING THE ISSUE

1. **Summarizing** What does the title of this entire feature mean? **FCAT** LA.A.2.3.1

2. **Making Generalizations** What do you think the subtitle "Fresh Air" says about this specific article? **FCAT** LA.A.1.3.2

Demand for Freedom in Iran

Evaluating Media
LA.A.2.3.6

HASAN SARBAKHSHIAN/AP

▲ **Students gathered in Tehran, Iran's capital, to demand democracy.**

In 1979 Iranians had had enough of their **shah,** or king. In their eyes, he acted more like a European than an Iranian. Shi'ite Muslim **clerics,** or religious leaders, took control of the government. They turned the nation upside down. Women who held jobs and wore what they wanted, for example, could now do neither.

One of the women who lost her right to work was Shirin Ebadi, a devout Muslim and a judge. The clerics allowed only men to be judges. So Ebadi quit and began practicing law. She spent the next 20 years defending the rights of people who had been mistreated by the government.

The government and its supporters weren't happy to be challenged. Ebadi was thrown into jail for a short time and threatened with death. But she never looked back. "The beauty of life," she said, "is to fight in a difficult situation, like it is in Iran."

Pressure for Change

During the late 1990s, millions of Iranians couldn't find jobs. Political freedoms were nonexistent. Curfews and "morality police" limited even basic activities such as when people could go shopping, where they could meet, and what clothing they could choose to wear in public. Iranians demanded a stronger economy and more freedom. Ebadi became one of their leaders.

When the government failed to respond to the demands, some Iranians looked abroad for assistance. "Tell the Americans to help us, to liberate us like they did the Iraqis and Afghanis," a government employee begged an American reporter.

Shirin Ebadi wants peaceful change, a position that won her praise from around the world. In 2003 she was awarded the Nobel Prize for Peace. "The prize does not just belong to me," she told a crowd of thousands who had come to cheer her. "It belongs to all the freedom-loving people who are working for democracy, freedom, and human rights in Iran."

EXPLORING THE ISSUE

1. **Explaining** What did Shirin Ebadi do that made the government angry with her?
   FCAT LA.A.2.3.1

2. **Cause and Effect** What led to the demands for freedom? **FCAT** LA.E.2.2.1

Road Map to Nowhere?

Evaluating Media
LA.A.2.3.6

The **Palestinians** are the grandchildren and great-grandchildren of the 600,000 Palestinians who fled their homes during an Arab-Israeli war in 1948. They believe that Israel took their land, and they want it back. A violent cycle of revenge-attack-revenge began between the two peoples.

The Israelis argue that they didn't chase the Palestinians off their land. They point out that tens of thousands of Palestinians remained, and that their offspring are now Israeli citizens. The Israelis say they are willing to help Palestinians set up their own country on land next door to Israel. But first they want the Palestinians to agree that they have no right to Israel's land.

Keeping Hope Alive

The United States has proposed a "road map for peace" between the Israelis and Palestinians. The goal was an independent Palestinian state by 2005. In early June 2003, both sides accepted the plan. But two months later the violence began again, and the road map reached a dead end.

People on both sides refused to give up hope. In October 2003, a group of Palestinians and Israelis announced that they had worked out their own road map. Members of the group didn't represent their governments. They just wanted to prove that it was possible to find a way to peace through **negotiations,** or compromise.

"We were told over and over that there was no [Palestinian] to talk to,"

RINA CASTELNUOVO/AP

▲ Palestinian and Israeli signers of a 2003 peace pact with President Bush and Jordan's king (right)

said an Israeli who helped work out the plan. "It now turns out that there is someone to talk to and something to talk about."

A Palestinian agreed. "In all previous negotiations with Israel," he said, "nobody could have hoped to have achieved this dream." Millions of Israelis and Arabs are hoping that such a dream will soon come true.

Despite hopes on both sides, the road to peace remains long and difficult. The region's cycle of violence continues and it is not easy to stop. Political disagreements in Israel, unrest in the Palestinian areas, and instability in neighboring Lebanon complicate the issue. Whether any of the proposed "roadmaps" eventually leads to peace remains to be seen. ■

EXPLORING THE ISSUE

1. **Making Predictions** How do you think the Arab-Israeli conflict will end? **FCAT** LA.A.1.3.2

2. **Problem Solving** Identify problems that keep the conflict alive. What changes would you make to solve them?

Rebuilding Iraq: What Can One Person Do?

Evaluating
Media
LA.A.2.3.6

Putting Iraq back together is a job for experts. Right? Wrong! Volunteers from all over the United States are doing what they can to help Iraqis get back on their feet. Here are some examples:

Children in Platteville, Iowa, sent school supplies to the city of Tikrit, Iraq, where there's a shortage of pencils and paper. "We hear parents teach their children to hate Americans," said Dayna Andersen, 15. "If we do something good for them, maybe they will think differently." Dayna's brother, a U.S. soldier in Iraq, distributed the supplies.

Students in middle schools throughout the United States wrote essays in support of Operation Tribute to Freedom. OTF is a U.S. Defense Department program that encourages Americans to show appreciation for U.S. soldiers in Iraq and Afghanistan. For information, contact **www.defenselink.mil/specials/tribute**

In Salem, Oregon, Allison Pollard and 14 other teenagers raised $5,000 to bring a 10-month-old Iraqi child to the United States for a life-saving heart operation.

Esra Naama, a graduate of Irvine High School in Irvine, California, is helping to raise money to set up an Internet café in Baghdad. An **Internet café** is a place where people can gather to rent computers and surf the Internet. "It'll help the Iraqi people learn about the world and how the world learns,"

▲ **Californian Esra Naama raised money to start an Internet café in Baghdad, Iraq.**

said Esra, who came to the United States from Iraq when she was 11 years old.

The United Nations has a big idea. It set up five-day soccer camps for teenagers from Iraq and three other Arab nations. Each team is made up of players from all four nations. The UN hopes that the camps will help build lasting bonds between people from each country. This sort of project is too elaborate for volunteers. But there's nothing to stop students from raising money for soccer balls and shipping them to children in Iraq. ▪

EXPLORING THE ISSUE

1. Categorizing What do these volunteer efforts have in common? **FCAT** LA.A.2.2.7

2. Making Inferences What do you think motivates volunteers like Dayna Andersen and Esra Naama? **FCAT** LA.A.1.3.2

REVIEW AND ASSESS

UNDERSTANDING THE ISSUE

1. Defining Key Terms Write definitions for the following terms: *Shi'ite Muslim, mosque, Sunni Muslim, democracy, constitution, parliament, shah, cleric, Palestinian, negotiation, Internet café.* **FCAT LA.A.1.3.2**

2. Writing to Inform In a 300-word article about Iraq, describe an emotional scene that you read about or saw on TV. Describe your reaction. **FCAT LA.B.1.3.2**

3. Writing to Persuade What is the most important thing that Americans should know about Iraq? Put your answer in a brief letter to the editor of your local newspaper. Support your letter with facts. Use at least four of the key terms above. **FCAT LA.B.1.3.2**

INTERNET RESEARCH ACTIVITY

4. Navigate to Columbia University's Middle East and Jewish Studies site at **www.columbia.edu/cu/lweb/indiv/mideast/cuvlm**. Scroll down to Middle East Resources by Subject. Click on the links until you find a site that interests you. Write two paragraphs explaining what the site taught you. **FCAT LA.A.2.3.5**

5. Navigate to **www.cpa-iraq.org**, the home page of the Coalition Provisional Authority. What is the Coalition doing to combat terrorism in Iraq? Make a list of the coalition's activities and title it, "The CPA's Job in Iraq." Share your list with your classmates. Go to **www.baghdadbulletin.com** for an Iraqi view of the rebuilding of Iraq.

BEYOND THE CLASSROOM

6. Visit your school or local library. Find out more about Islam, the world's second-largest religion. What event led to the split between the Shi'ites (or Shia) and the Sunnis? **FCAT LA.A.2.3.5**

▲ These Muslim boys study Islam at religious schools.

7. Research a country such as Iraq, Northern Ireland, or Bosnia where people have suffered from terrorist attacks. Find out how groups or individuals outside the government have tried to end the violence. Present your findings to the class.

Believers Who Share a Common Ground

Religion plays a big role in Southwest Asia and North Africa. This graph suggests why. It shows what religions are practiced in the region's 10 largest nations.

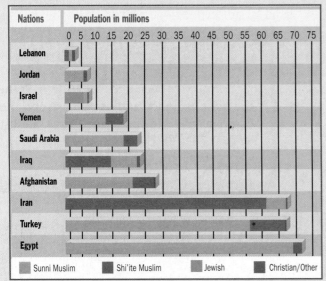

Nations	Population in millions
	0 5 10 15 20 25 30 35 40 45 50 55 60 65 70 75
Lebanon	
Jordan	
Israel	
Yemen	
Saudi Arabia	
Iraq	
Afghanistan	
Iran	
Turkey	*
Egypt	

■ Sunni Muslim ■ Shi'ite Muslim ■ Jewish ■ Christian/Other

*Alawi Muslim, a Shi'ite offshoot

BUILDING GRAPH READING SKILLS

1. Analyzing the Data In how many of these nations are Sunnis the largest Muslim group? **FCAT MA.E.3.3.1**

2. Making Inferences Under Saddam Hussein, Sunnis held most of the power in the Iraqi government. Why might Iraqi Shi'ites feel they have more of a right than Sunnis to hold top government jobs today? **FCAT LA.A.1.3.2**

3. Drawing Conclusions Where might competition between Sunnis and Shi'ites be strongest? Where might it be weakest? **FCAT LA.A.1.3.2**

FOR UPDATES ON WORLD ISSUES GO TO www.timeclassroom.com/glencoe

527

Technology Skill

Evaluating a Web Site

The Internet has become a valuable research tool. It is convenient to use, and the information contained on the Internet is plentiful. However, some Web site information is not necessarily accurate or reliable. When using the Internet as a research tool, you must distinguish between quality information and inaccurate or incomplete information. You also must consider the source of the information and whether facts or opinions are presented.

▲ **The Peace Corps Web site is government sponsored.**

Learning the Skill

There are a number of things to consider when you are evaluating a Web site. Most important is to check the accuracy of the source and content. The author and publisher or sponsor of the site should be clearly indicated. You must also determine the usefulness of the site. The information on the site should be current, and the design and organization of the site should be appealing and easy to navigate.

To evaluate a Web site, ask yourself the following questions:

- Are the facts on the site documented?
- Does the site contain a bibliography?
- Is the author clearly identified?
- Does the site explore the topic in-depth or only provide generalizations?
- Does the site contain links to other useful and up-to-date resources?
- Is the information easy to access? Is it properly labeled?

Practicing the Skill

Visit the Peace Corps Web site listed below and answer the following questions.

1. Who is the author or sponsor of the Web site?
2. What links does the site contain? Are they appropriate to the topic?
3. What sources were used for the information contained on the site?
4. Does the site explore the topic in-depth? Why or why not?
5. Is the design of the site appealing? Why or why not?

Applying the Skill

Locate two Web sites about Iran. Evaluate them for accuracy and usefulness, and then compare them to the Peace Corps site listed below. **FCAT LA.A.2.3.5**

www.peacecorps.gov/kids/index.html

Reading Review

Section 1	Turkey, Syria, Lebanon, Jordan

Terms to Know
migrate
bedouins

Main Idea
Turkey, Syria, Lebanon, and Jordan lie at the crossroads of Europe and Asia.

✓**Location** Turkey lies in both Europe and Asia.

✓**Economics** Turkey is becoming more industrialized, with textiles and clothing as major industries. Tourism is also a growing industry.

✓**Culture** Most of Turkey's people now live in cities or towns.

✓**Economics** Farming is the main economic activity in Syria.

✓**History** Lebanon is rebuilding and recovering after a civil war.

✓**Place** Water shortages in Jordan restrict the land available for farming.

Section 2	Israel and the Palestinian Territories

Terms to Know
kibbutz
moshav
Holocaust

Main Idea
After years of conflict, the Jewish nation of Israel and neighboring Arab countries still struggle to achieve peace.

✓**Culture** About 80 percent of Israel's population are Jews. They have moved to Israel from many countries.

✓**History** Israel and its Arab neighbors continue to experience violent conflict over the issues that divide them.

Section 3	The Arabian Peninsula

Terms to Know
wadi
desalinization
caliph

Main Idea
Money from oil exports has boosted standards of living in most countries of the Arabian Peninsula.

✓**Economics** Saudi Arabia is the world's leading oil producer.

✓**Culture** The Islamic religion affects almost all aspects of life in Saudi Arabia.

✓**Economics** The Persian Gulf states have strong economies based on oil.

Section 4	Iraq, Iran, and Afghanistan

Terms to Know
alluvial plain
embargo
shah
Islamic republic

Main Idea
Iraq, Iran, and Afghanistan have recently fought wars and have undergone sweeping political changes.

✓**Economics** Iraq is recovering from an international trade embargo and war.

✓**Culture** Oil-rich Iran is ruled by Muslim religious leaders.

✓**Place** Afghanistan is mountainous and relatively undeveloped.

Chapter 18

Assessment and Activities

FCAT PRACTICE You can prepare for the FCAT-assessed standards by completing the correlated item(s) below.

Using Key Terms

Match the terms in Part A with their definitions in Part B.

A.

1. migrate
2. desalinization
3. alluvial plain
4. wadi
5. caliph
6. bedouins
7. Holocaust
8. kibbutz
9. embargo
10. shah

B.

a. taking salt out of seawater
b. Iran's former monarch
c. mass slaughter of European Jews
d. nomadic, desert people
e. to move from one place to another
f. area built up from soil deposited by river floods
g. Israeli farm or settlement where people share property
h. restriction on trade
i. dry riverbed filled by rainwater from rare downpours
j. successor to Muhammad

Reviewing the Main Ideas

Section 1 Turkey, Syria, Lebanon, Jordan

11. **Place** What is Turkey's largest city?
12. **Place** What bodies of water form the Turkish Straits?
13. **Place** What makes Damascus an important city?
14. **History** Why was Beirut called "the Paris of the East"?

Section 2 Israel and the Palestinian Territories

15. **History** When was the modern nation of Israel created?
16. **Government** What is the Law of Return?

Section 3 The Arabian Peninsula

17. **Economics** What is OPEC?
18. **Place** What is the capital of Saudi Arabia?

Section 4 Iraq, Iran, and Afghanistan

19. **Economics** Where does most of the farming in Iraq take place?
20. **Culture** How do the people of Iran differ from other Southwest Asian peoples?
21. **Place** What landform makes up much of Afghanistan?

 **Southwest Asia**

Place Location Activity

On a separate sheet of paper, match the letters on the map with the numbered places listed below.

1. Persian Gulf
2. Zagros Mountains
3. Euphrates River
4. Turkey
5. Iran
6. Israel
7. Iraq
8. Saudi Arabia
9. Makkah
10. Jerusalem

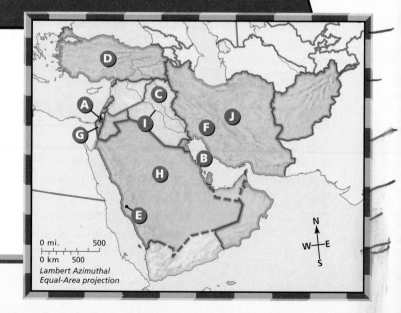

0 mi. 500
0 km 500
Lambert Azimuthal Equal-Area projection

Social Studies Online

Self-Check Quiz Visit *The World and Its People* Web site at twip.glencoe.com and click on **Chapter 18—Self-Check Quizzes** to prepare for the Chapter Test.

Critical Thinking

22. **Evaluating Information** Goods were moved from Southwest Asia to other parts of the world through several routes. How are goods brought to your community? Make a list of all the routes a product would take to get from Southwest Asia to your town.

23. **Analyzing Information** On a chart like this, list a reason for the importance of oil and water to Southwest Asia and one result of their abundance or scarcity. **FCAT LA.A.1.3.2**

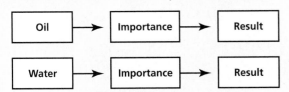

Comparing Regions Activity

24. **Culture** For one week, count the number of stories in your local newspaper about countries in Southwest Asia. Then count the number of stories about European countries. Which number is greater? Why do you think this is so?

Mental Mapping Activity

25. **Focusing on the Region** Draw a simple outline map of Southwest Asia, and then label the following:

- Turkey
- Persian Gulf
- Red Sea
- Israel
- Mediterranean Sea
- Iran
- Saudi Arabia
- Yemen
- Iraq
- Afghanistan

Technology Skills Activity

26. **Using the Internet** Search the Internet and find several newspapers that publish current events online. Research an event that took place in one of the countries of Southwest Asia. Create a poster about the event.

FCAT LA.A.2.3.5

Standardized Test Practice

Directions: Study the graph below, and then answer the question that follows.

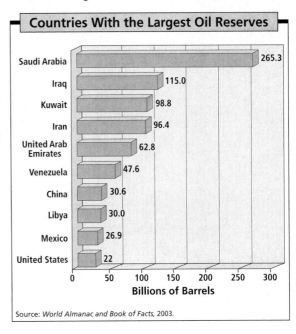

Countries With the Largest Oil Reserves

Country	Billions of Barrels
Saudi Arabia	265.3
Iraq	115.0
Kuwait	98.8
Iran	96.4
United Arab Emirates	62.8
Venezuela	47.6
China	30.6
Libya	30.0
Mexico	26.9
United States	22

Source: *World Almanac and Book of Facts*, 2003.

1. **How many of the ten countries with the largest oil reserves are located in Southwest Asia?** **FCAT MA.E.3.3.1**

   A one

   B three

   C five

   D seven

Test-Taking Tip: You need to rely on your memory as well as analyze the graph to answer this question. Look at each country, then think back to the countries you studied in Chapter 18. Which of those listed on the graph did you just learn about?

Unit 7

Waterfront of
Cape Town,
South Africa

Woman making
butter in Chad

NATIONAL
GEOGRAPHIC

Africa South of the Sahara

The region of Africa south of the Sahara is home to more than 2,000 ethnic groups. Its hot, humid forests and dry grasslands support a variety of wild animals. Both people and animals face tough challenges in this region. The people are struggling to build stable governments and economies. The animals are threatened with extinction as human activities destroy natural habitats.

NGS ONLINE
www.nationalgeographic.com/education

REGIONAL ATLAS

Focus on:

Africa South of the Sahara

STRADDLING THE EQUATOR, Africa south of the Sahara lies almost entirely within the Tropics. Famous for its remarkable wildlife, this region also has the world's fastest-growing human population. Settling ethnic rivalries and improving low standards of living are just two of the challenges facing the people in this region.

The Land

Africa south of the Sahara has the highest overall elevation of any world region. A narrow band of low plains hugs the Atlantic and Indian Ocean coastlines. Inland, the land rises from west to east in a series of steplike plateaus. Separating the plateaus are steep cliffs. The region has no long mountain ranges and few towering peaks, although Mt. Kenya and Kilimanjaro are exceptions. At 19,340 feet (5,895 m), Kilimanjaro's summit is the highest point on the African continent.

Thundering Waterways Great rivers arise in this region's interior highlands. As rivers spill from one plateau to the next, they create thundering waterfalls, such as the spectacular Victoria Falls (facing page). It is known locally as *Mosi oa Tunya*—"smoke that thunders." Although the Nile River is Africa's longest river, the Congo River is a giant in its own right, winding 2,715 miles (4,370 km) through Africa's heart, near the

Equator. Many of Africa's rivers provide hydroelectric power as well as transportation to areas that are too remote for overland travel.

Continental Rift The Great Rift Valley slices through eastern Africa like a steep-walled gash in the continent. The valley, formed by movements of the earth's crust, extends from Southwest Asia southward to the Zambezi River in Mozambique. It cradles a chain of deep lakes, some of which hold more species of fish than any other inland body of water in the world.

The Climate

Imagine that you are standing at the Equator in Africa. If you traveled north or south from there, you would pass through four major climate regions, one after the other.

Rain Forests and Savannas Tropical rain forests lie along the Equator and fill the great basin of the Congo River in central and western Africa. Heavy storms bring 80 inches (203 cm)

534

UNIT 7

Victoria Falls, on the Zambezi River ▼

◀ **Elephants roaming near Kilimanjaro, Tanzania**

535

or more of rain each year. The canopy is the primary layer of rain forests and is alive with flowers, fruits, monkeys, parrots, and snakes.

As you move away from the Equator, rain forests give way to tropical savannas. These vast grasslands are home to some of the continent's most famous large mammals, including elephants, lions, rhinoceroses, and giraffes.

Steppe and Desert Climates
As you move farther from the Equator, rainfall becomes scarce, and tropical savannas give way to drier steppes. Finally you encounter very dry areas where deserts dominate the landscape. Deserts cover more of Africa than any other continent. The largest deserts south of the Sahara are the Namib and the Kalahari.

The Economy

Africa south of the Sahara is rich in mineral resources, but these resources are not evenly distributed. Nigeria has huge reserves of oil. South Africa has fabulous deposits of gold and diamonds, making it the wealthiest country in the region. Overall, however, Africa south of the Sahara has the lowest standard of living of any world region.

Struggling to Develop
Manufacturing plays only a small role in the region's economy. In the past, colonial rulers used Africa as a source of raw materials and left the continent largely undeveloped. Today the nations south of the Sahara are struggling to industrialize.

Most people in Africa south of the Sahara still depend on small-scale farming or livestock herding for their livelihoods. They are usually able to raise only enough food to feed their families. Some farmers work on plantations that grow crops for export to other countries. Such crops include coffee, cacao, cotton, peanuts, tea, bananas, and sisal (a fiber). Drought is a constant problem for the region's farmers.

The People

Thousands of years ago, great kingdoms and empires developed in Africa south of the Sahara. In the northeast, one kingdom extended its rule into Egyptian territory. In West Africa, wealthy empires emerged by trading salt for gold.

From Kingdoms to Nations
In the 1400s and 1500s, Europeans began trading with African societies, carrying away gold, spices, ivory, and enslaved people. By the late 1800s, European nations had

◀ **Woman fertilizing crops in Zimbabwe**

claimed almost all of Africa. For profit and political advantage, they carved the continent into colonies. In the process, they ripped apart once-unified regions and threw together ethnic groups that did not get along.

Most African nations won their independence in the mid-1900s. Many countries that emerged from colonial rule were politically unstable and had crippled economies.

Varied Lifestyles
Today more than 711 million people inhabit Africa south of the Sahara. They represent some 2,000 ethnic groups and speak 800 different languages. Nearly three-fourths of the population live in rural areas. Although Africa is the least urbanized continent, its cities are growing. Lured by the promise of better living conditions, people are flocking to African cities. These are among the fastest-growing urban areas in the world.

Crowded market in Lagos, Nigeria ▼

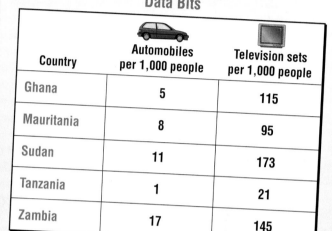

Data Bits

Country	Automobiles per 1,000 people	Television sets per 1,000 people
Ghana	5	115
Mauritania	8	95
Sudan	11	173
Tanzania	1	21
Zambia	17	145

Religions

Country	Islam	Christian	Traditional Beliefs
Ghana	16%	63%	21%
Mauritania	100%	—	—
Sudan	70%	5%	25%
Tanzania	35%	30%	35%
Zambia	24-49%	50-75%	1%

Sources: *World Development Indicators*, 2002; *World Almanac*, 2004.

Exploring the Region

1. What happens when Africa's rivers flow from one plateau to another?
2. Which climate zone is centered on the Equator?
3. What makes South Africa the region's most prosperous country?
4. How did colonial rule affect Africa south of the Sahara?

REGIONAL ATLAS

Africa South of the Sahara

Physical

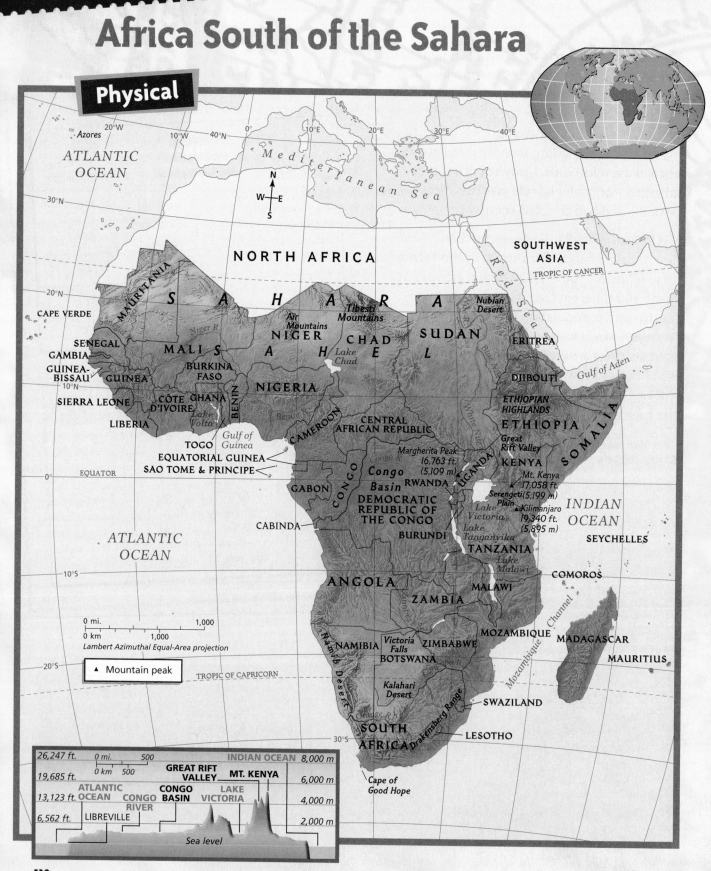

ATLANTIC OCEAN

Azores

20°W

10°W

40°N

0°

10°E

20°E

30°E

40°E

Mediterranean Sea

N
W E
S

30°N

SOUTHWEST ASIA

NORTH AFRICA

TROPIC OF CANCER

CAPE VERDE

20°N

MAURITANIA

S A H A R A

Tibesti Mountains

Air Mountains

Nubian Desert

Red Sea

SENEGAL

Niger R.

NIGER

CHAD

SUDAN

ERITREA

GAMBIA

MALI

S

A

H

E

L

GUINEA-BISSAU

10°N

BURKINA FASO

Lake Chad

DJIBOUTI

Gulf of Aden

GUINEA

SIERRA LEONE

CÔTE D'IVOIRE

GHANA

NIGERIA

Benue

CAMEROON

CENTRAL AFRICAN REPUBLIC

ETHIOPIAN HIGHLANDS

ETHIOPIA

SOMALIA

LIBERIA

Lake Volta

BENIN

White Nile

Blue Nile

TOGO

Gulf of Guinea

EQUATORIAL GUINEA

SAO TOME & PRINCIPE

EQUATOR

0°

GABON

Congo R.

CONGO

Congo Basin

DEMOCRATIC REPUBLIC OF THE CONGO

Margherita Peak 16,763 ft. (5,109 m)

RWANDA

UGANDA

Great Rift Valley

KENYA

Mt. Kenya 17,058 ft. (5,199 m)

Serengeti Plain

Kilimanjaro 19,340 ft. (5,895 m)

INDIAN OCEAN

CABINDA

BURUNDI

Lake Victoria

Lake Tanganyika

SEYCHELLES

ATLANTIC OCEAN

10°S

TANZANIA

Lake Malawi

COMOROS

ANGOLA

MALAWI

ZAMBIA

MOZAMBIQUE

MADAGASCAR

0 mi. 1,000
0 km 1,000
Lambert Azimuthal Equal-Area projection

Namib Desert

Victoria Falls

ZIMBABWE

MAURITIUS

20°S

▲ Mountain peak

TROPIC OF CAPRICORN

NAMIBIA

BOTSWANA

Mozambique Channel

Orange R.

Kalahari Desert

Drakensberg Range

SWAZILAND

30°S

SOUTH AFRICA

LESOTHO

Cape of Good Hope

26,247 ft.	0 mi. 500		INDIAN OCEAN	8,000 m
19,685 ft.	0 km 500	GREAT RIFT VALLEY	MT. KENYA	6,000 m
	ATLANTIC OCEAN	CONGO BASIN	LAKE VICTORIA	4,000 m
13,123 ft.		CONGO RIVER		
6,562 ft.	LIBREVILLE			2,000 m
			Sea level	

Political

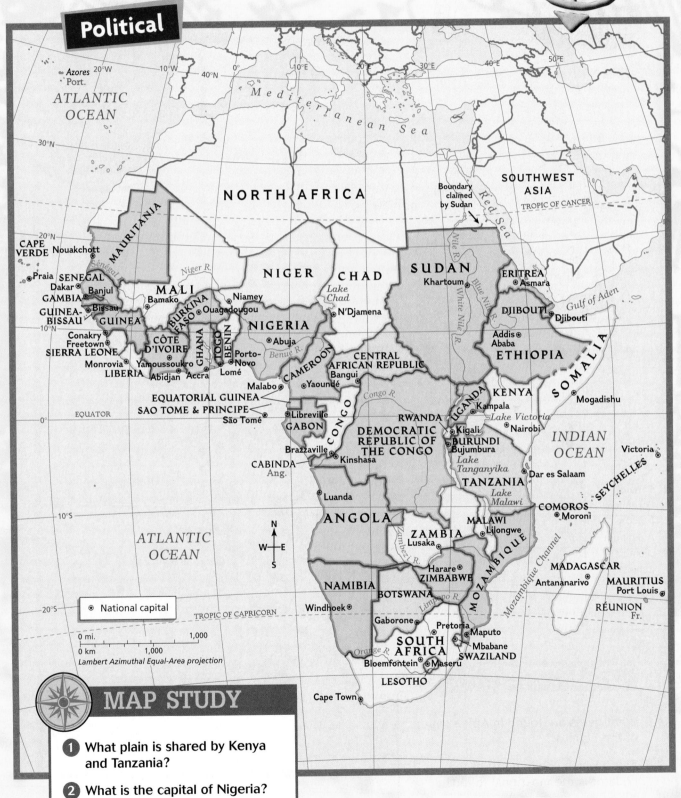

ATLANTIC OCEAN

Azores Port.

Mediterranean Sea

NORTH AFRICA

SOUTHWEST ASIA

Boundary claimed by Sudan

TROPIC OF CANCER

CAPE VERDE

Nouakchott

MAURITANIA

Praia

SENEGAL
Dakar ⊛
Banjul ⊛
GAMBIA
GUINEA-BISSAU
Bissau ⊛
GUINEA
Conakry ⊛
Freetown ⊛
SIERRA LEONE
Monrovia ⊛
LIBERIA

Senegal

Niger R.

MALI
Bamako ⊛

BURKINA FASO
Ouagadougou ⊛

NIGER
Niamey ⊛

CHAD
N'Djamena ⊛

Lake Chad

SUDAN
Khartoum ⊛

ERITREA
⊛ Asmara

Nile R.

Blue Nile R.

White Nile R.

Red Sea

Gulf of Aden

DJIBOUTI ⊛ Djibouti

CÔTE D'IVOIRE
Yamoussoukro ⊛
Abidjan ⊛

GHANA
Accra ⊛

TOGO
Lomé ⊛

BENIN
Porto-Novo ⊛

NIGERIA
⊛ Abuja

Benue R.

CAMEROON
⊛ Yaoundé

CENTRAL AFRICAN REPUBLIC
Bangui ⊛

Addis Ababa ⊛

ETHIOPIA

SOMALIA

⊛ Mogadishu

Malabo ⊛

EQUATORIAL GUINEA
SAO TOME & PRINCIPE
São Tomé ⊛

GABON
Libreville ⊛

CONGO
Brazzaville ⊛

CABINDA Ang.

Congo R.

DEMOCRATIC REPUBLIC OF THE CONGO
Kinshasa ⊛

RWANDA
Kigali ⊛

BURUNDI
Bujumbura ⊛

UGANDA
Kampala ⊛

Lake Victoria

KENYA
⊛ Nairobi

Lake Tanganyika

TANZANIA
Dar es Salaam ⊛

INDIAN OCEAN

Victoria ⊛

SEYCHELLES

EQUATOR

Luanda ⊛

ANGOLA

Lake Malawi

COMOROS
⊛ Moroni

MALAWI
Lilongwe ⊛

ZAMBIA
Lusaka ⊛

Zambezi R.

MOZAMBIQUE

Mozambique Channel

MADAGASCAR
Antananarivo ⊛

MAURITIUS
Port Louis

RÉUNION Fr.

NAMIBIA
Windhoek ⊛

BOTSWANA
Gaborone ⊛

ZIMBABWE
Harare ⊛

Limpopo R.

Orange R.

SOUTH AFRICA
Pretoria ⊛
Bloemfontein ⊛
Cape Town ⊛

Maputo ⊛
Mbabane ⊛
SWAZILAND
Maseru ⊛
LESOTHO

ATLANTIC OCEAN

N W E S

⊛ National capital

TROPIC OF CAPRICORN

0 mi. 1,000
0 km 1,000

Lambert Azimuthal Equal-Area projection

MAP STUDY

1 What plain is shared by Kenya and Tanzania?

2 What is the capital of Nigeria?

Africa South of the Sahara

Gems and Minerals

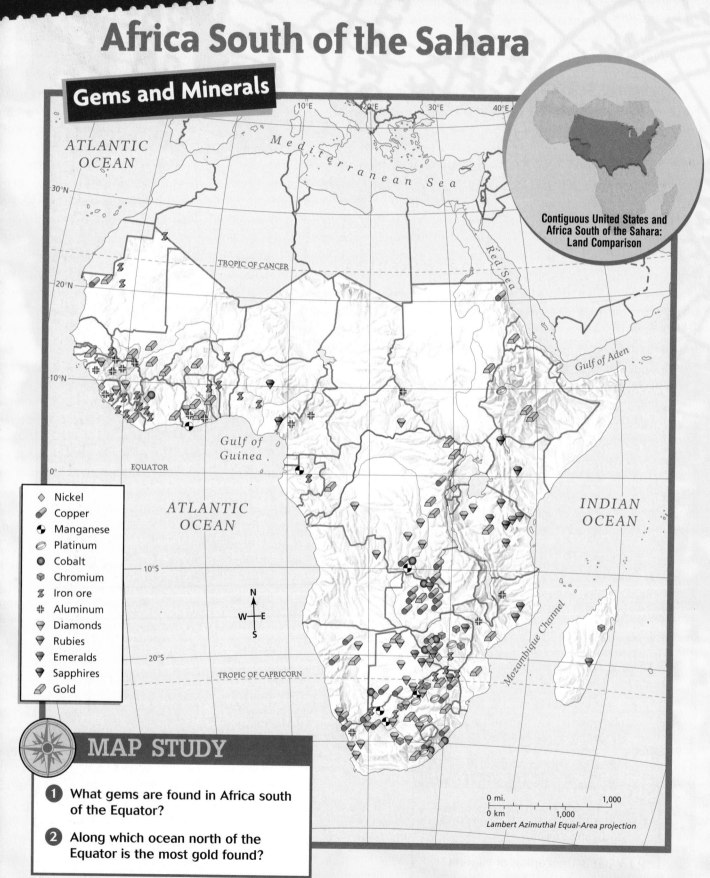

Contiguous United States and
Africa South of the Sahara:
Land Comparison

ATLANTIC
OCEAN

Mediterranean Sea

30°N

TROPIC OF CANCER

20°N

Red Sea

Gulf of Aden

10°N

Gulf of
Guinea

EQUATOR

ATLANTIC
OCEAN

INDIAN
OCEAN

10°S

N
W—E
S

Mozambique Channel

20°S

TROPIC OF CAPRICORN

◇ Nickel
🥟 Copper
◕ Manganese
⬭ Platinum
● Cobalt
⬡ Chromium
⚡ Iron ore
✛ Aluminum
▽ Diamonds
▼ Rubies
▼ Emeralds
▼ Sapphires
🥠 Gold

0 mi.   1,000
0 km   1,000
Lambert Azimuthal Equal-Area projection

MAP STUDY

1 What gems are found in Africa south
of the Equator?

2 Along which ocean north of the
Equator is the most gold found?

Geo Extremes

① **HIGHEST POINT**
Kilimanjaro (Tanzania)
19,340 ft. (5,895 m) high

② **LOWEST POINT**
Lake Assal (Djibouti)
512 ft. (156 m)
below sea level

③ **LONGEST RIVER**
Nile River
4,241 mi.
(6,825 km) long

④ **LARGEST LAKE**
Lake Victoria (Kenya,
Uganda, and Tanzania)
26,834 sq. mi.
(69,500 sq. km)

⑤ **LARGEST ISLAND**
Madagascar
226,642 sq. mi.
(587,000 sq. km)

⑥ **HOTTEST PLACE**
Dalol, Denakil Depression
(Ethiopia)
93°F (34°C) annual
average temperature

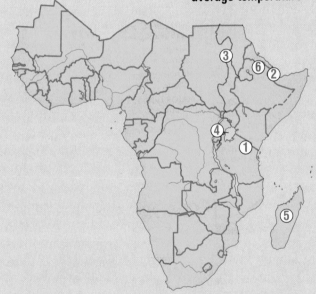

COMPARING POPULATION:
United States and Selected Countries of Africa South of the Sahara

UNITED STATES

NIGERIA

DEMOCRATIC REPUBLIC OF THE CONGO

SOUTH AFRICA

KENYA

= 30,000,000

SENEGAL

Source: *Population Reference Bureau*, 2003.

SELECTED RURAL AND URBAN POPULATIONS:
Africa South of the Sahara

	Rural	Urban
WEST AFRICA		
Niger	79%	21%
Cape Verde	36%	64%
CENTRAL AFRICA		
Angola	65%	35%
Central African Republic	58%	42%
EAST AFRICA		
Rwanda	94%	6%
Djibouti	16%	84%
SOUTHERN AFRICA		
Lesotho	71%	29%
South Africa	42%	58%

Source: *The World Almanac*, 2004.

GRAPHIC STUDY

1 What is the longest river in Africa?

2 Of the African countries shown in the chart at lower right, which is least urbanized? Which is most urbanized?

FCAT MA.E.1.3.1

REGIONAL ATLAS

Country Profiles

 ## ANGOLA

POPULATION:
13,100,000
27 per sq. mi.
10 per sq. km

LANGUAGES:
Portuguese,
Local Languages

MAJOR EXPORT:
Crude Oil

MAJOR IMPORT:
Machinery

CAPITAL:
Luanda

LANDMASS:
481,351 sq. mi.
1,246,699 sq. km

 ## BENIN

POPULATION:
7,000,000
162 per sq. mi.
63 per sq. km

LANGUAGES:
French, Fon, Yoruba

MAJOR EXPORT:
Cotton

MAJOR IMPORT:
Foods

CAPITAL:
Porto-Novo

LANDMASS:
43,483 sq. mi.
112,621 sq. km

 ## BOTSWANA

POPULATION:
1,600,000
7 per sq. mi.
3 per sq. km

LANGUAGES:
English, Setswana

MAJOR EXPORT:
Diamonds

MAJOR IMPORT:
Foods

CAPITAL:
Gaborone

LANDMASS:
224,606 sq. mi.
581,730 sq. km

 ## BURKINA FASO

POPULATION:
13,200,000
125 per sq. mi.
48 per sq. km

LANGUAGES:
French, Local
Languages

MAJOR EXPORT:
Cotton

MAJOR IMPORT:
Machinery

CAPITAL:
Ouagadougou

LANDMASS:
105,792 sq. mi.
274,001 sq. km

 ## BURUNDI

POPULATION:
6,100,000
567 per sq. mi.
219 per sq. km

LANGUAGES:
Kirundi, French

MAJOR EXPORT:
Coffee

MAJOR IMPORT:
Machinery

CAPITAL:
Bujumbura

LANDMASS:
10,745 sq. mi.
27,830 sq. km

 ## CAMEROON

POPULATION:
15,700,000
86 per sq. mi.
33 per sq. km

LANGUAGES:
French, English,
Local Languages

MAJOR EXPORT:
Crude Oil

MAJOR IMPORT:
Machinery

CAPITAL:
Yaoundé

LANDMASS:
183,568 sq. mi.
475,441 sq. km

 ## CAPE VERDE

POPULATION:
500,000
305 per sq. mi.
118 per sq. km

LANGUAGES:
Portuguese, Crioulo

MAJOR EXPORT:
Shoes

MAJOR IMPORT:
Foods

CAPITAL:
Praia

LANDMASS:
1,556 sq. mi.
4,030 sq. km

 ## CENTRAL AFRICAN REPUBLIC

POPULATION:
3,700,000
15 per sq. mi.
6 per sq. km

LANGUAGES:
French, Sango,
Arabic, Hunsa

MAJOR EXPORT:
Diamonds

MAJOR IMPORT:
Foods

CAPITAL:
Bangui

LANDMASS:
240,533 sq. mi.
622,981 sq. km

 ## CHAD

POPULATION:
9,300,000
19 per sq. mi.
7 per sq. km

LANGUAGES:
French, Arabic,
Sara, Sango

MAJOR EXPORT:
Cotton

MAJOR IMPORT:
Machinery

CAPITAL:
N'Djamena

LANDMASS:
495,753 sq. mi.
1,284,000 sq. km

 ## COMOROS

POPULATION:
600,000
735 per sq. mi.
284 per sq. km

LANGUAGES:
Arabic, French,
Comoran

MAJOR EXPORT:
Vanilla

MAJOR IMPORT:
Rice

CAPITAL:
Moroni

LANDMASS:
861 sq. mi.
2,230 sq. km

 ## CONGO

POPULATION:
3,700,000
28 per sq. mi.
11 per sq. km

LANGUAGES:
French, Lingala,
Monokutuba

MAJOR EXPORT:
Crude Oil

MAJOR IMPORT:
Machinery

CAPITAL:
Brazzaville

LANDMASS:
132,046 sq. mi.
341,999 sq. km

Countries and flags not drawn to scale

UNIT 7

For more information on countries in this region, refer to the Nations of the World Data Bank in the Appendix.

CONGO, Democratic Republic of the

POPULATION:
56,600,000
63 per sq. mi.
24 per sq. km

LANGUAGES:
French, Lingala, Kingwana

MAJOR EXPORT:
Diamonds

MAJOR IMPORT:
Manufactured Goods

CAPITAL:
Kinshasa

LANDMASS:
905,351 sq. mi.
2,344,859 sq. km

CÔTE D'IVOIRE

POPULATION:
17,000,000
136 per sq. mi.
53 per sq. km

LANGUAGES:
French, Dioula

MAJOR EXPORT:
Cocoa

MAJOR IMPORT:
Foods

CAPITALS:
Yamoussoukro, Abidjan

LANDMASS:
124,502 sq. mi.
322,460 sq. km

DJIBOUTI

POPULATION:
700,000
73 per sq. mi.
28 per sq. km

LANGUAGES:
French, Arabic

MAJOR EXPORTS:
Hides and Skins

MAJOR IMPORT:
Foods

CAPITAL:
Djibouti

LANDMASS:
8,958 sq. mi.
23,201 sq. km

EQUATORIAL GUINEA

POPULATION:
500,000
47 per sq. mi.
18 per sq. km

LANGUAGES:
Spanish, French, Fang, Bubi, Ibo

MAJOR EXPORT:
Petroleum

MAJOR IMPORT:
Machinery

CAPITAL:
Malabo

LANDMASS:
10,830 sq. mi.
28,050 sq. km

ERITREA

POPULATION:
4,400,000
96 per sq. mi.
37 per sq. km

LANGUAGES:
Afar, Amharic, Arabic, Tigre

MAJOR EXPORT:
Livestock

MAJOR IMPORT:
Processed Foods

CAPITAL:
Asmara

LANDMASS:
45,405 sq. mi.
117,599 sq. km

ETHIOPIA

POPULATION:
70,700,000
166 per sq. mi.
64 per sq. km

LANGUAGES:
Amharic, Tigrinya, Orominga

MAJOR EXPORT:
Coffee

MAJOR IMPORTS:
Foods and Livestock

CAPITAL:
Addis Ababa

LANDMASS:
426,371 sq. mi.
1,104,301 sq. km

GABON

POPULATION:
1,300,000
13 per sq. mi.
5 per sq. km

LANGUAGES:
French, Local Languages

MAJOR EXPORT:
Crude Oil

MAJOR IMPORT:
Machinery

CAPITAL:
Libreville

LANDMASS:
103,347 sq. mi.
267,669 sq. km

GAMBIA

POPULATION:
1,500,000
344 per sq. mi.
133 per sq. km

LANGUAGES:
English, Mandinka, Fula

MAJOR EXPORT:
Peanuts

MAJOR IMPORT:
Foods

CAPITAL:
Banjul

LANDMASS:
4,363 sq. mi.
11,300 sq. km

GHANA

POPULATION:
20,500,000
222 per sq. mi.
86 per sq. km

LANGUAGES:
English, Local Languages

MAJOR EXPORT:
Gold

MAJOR IMPORT:
Machinery

CAPITAL:
Accra

LANDMASS:
92,100 sq. mi.
238,539 sq. km

GUINEA

POPULATION:
9,000,000
95 per sq. mi.
37 per sq. km

LANGUAGES:
French, Local Languages

MAJOR EXPORT:
Bauxite

MAJOR IMPORT:
Petroleum Products

CAPITAL:
Conakry

LANDMASS:
94,927 sq. mi.
245,861 sq. km

GUINEA-BISSAU

POPULATION:
1,300,000
92 per sq. mi.
36 per sq. km

LANGUAGES:
Portuguese, Crioulo, Fula

MAJOR EXPORT:
Cashews

MAJOR IMPORT:
Foods

CAPITAL:
Bissau

LANDMASS:
13,946 sq. mi.
36,120 sq. km

Africa South of the Sahara

NATIONAL GEOGRAPHIC

REGIONAL ATLAS

Country Profiles

KENYA

POPULATION:
31,600,000
141 per sq. mi.
54 per sq. km

LANGUAGES:
English, Swahili

MAJOR EXPORT:
Tea

MAJOR IMPORT:
Machinery

CAPITAL:
Nairobi

LANDMASS:
224,081 sq. mi.
580,370 sq. km

LESOTHO

POPULATION:
1,800,000
153 per sq. mi.
59 per sq. km

LANGUAGES:
English, Sesotho,
Zulu, Xhosa

MAJOR EXPORT:
Clothing

MAJOR IMPORT:
Corn

CAPITAL:
Maseru

LANDMASS:
11,718 sq. mi.
30,350 sq. km

LIBERIA

POPULATION:
3,300,000
77 per sq. mi.
30 per sq. km

LANGUAGES:
English, Local
Languages

MAJOR EXPORT:
Diamonds

MAJOR IMPORT:
Natural Gas

CAPITAL:
Monrovia

LANDMASS:
43,000 sq. mi.
111,370 sq. km

MADAGASCAR

POPULATION:
17,000,000
75 per sq. mi.
29 per sq. km

LANGUAGES:
French, Malagasy

MAJOR EXPORT:
Coffee

MAJOR IMPORT:
Machinery

CAPITAL:
Antananarivo

LANDMASS:
226,656 sq. mi.
587,039 sq. km

MALAWI

POPULATION:
11,700,000
255 per sq. mi.
98 per sq. km

LANGUAGES:
Chewa, English

MAJOR EXPORT:
Tobacco

MAJOR IMPORT:
Foods

CAPITAL:
Lilongwe

LANDMASS:
45,745 sq. mi.
118,480 sq. km

MALI

POPULATION:
11,600,000
24 per sq. mi.
9 per sq. km

LANGUAGES:
French, Bambara

MAJOR EXPORT:
Cotton

MAJOR IMPORT:
Machinery

CAPITAL:
Bamako

LANDMASS:
478,838 sq. mi.
1,240,190 sq. km

MAURITANIA

POPULATION:
2,900,000
7 per sq. mi.
3 per sq. km

LANGUAGES:
Hasaniya Arabic,
Wolof

MAJOR EXPORT:
Fish

MAJOR IMPORT:
Foods

CAPITAL:
Nouakchott

LANDMASS:
395,954 sq. mi.
1,025,521 sq. km

MAURITIUS

POPULATION:
1,200,000
1,550 per sq. mi.
598 per sq. km

LANGUAGES:
English, Creole,
Bhojpuri, French

MAJOR EXPORT:
Sugar

MAJOR IMPORT:
Foods

CAPITAL:
Port Louis

LANDMASS:
788 sq. mi.
2,041 sq. km

MOZAMBIQUE

POPULATION:
17,500,000
56 per sq. mi.
22 per sq. km

LANGUAGES:
Portuguese,
Local Languages

MAJOR EXPORT:
Cashews

MAJOR IMPORT:
Foods

CAPITAL:
Maputo

LANDMASS:
309,494 sq. mi.
801,590 sq. km

NAMIBIA

POPULATION:
1,900,000
6 per sq. mi.
2 per sq. km

LANGUAGES:
English, Afrikaans, Local Languages

MAJOR EXPORT:
Diamonds

MAJOR IMPORT:
Construction
Materials

CAPITAL:
Windhoek

LANDMASS:
318,259 sq. mi.
824,291 sq. km

NIGER

POPULATION:
12,100,000
25 per sq. mi.
10 per sq. km

LANGUAGES:
French, Hausa,
Djerma

MAJOR EXPORT:
Uranium Ore

MAJOR IMPORT:
Manufactured
Goods

CAPITAL:
Niamey

LANDMASS:
489,189 sq. mi.
1,267,000 sq. km

Countries and flags not drawn to scale

For more information on countries in this region, refer to the Nations of the World Data Bank in the Appendix.

NIGERIA

POPULATION:
133,900,000
375 per sq. mi.
145 per sq. km

LANGUAGES:
English, Hausa, Yoruba, Igbo

MAJOR EXPORT:
Petroleum

MAJOR IMPORT:
Machinery

CAPITAL:
Abuja

LANDMASS:
356,668 sq. mi.
923,770 sq. km

Abuja

RWANDA

POPULATION:
8,300,000
817 per sq. mi.
315 per sq. km

LANGUAGES:
Kinyarwanda, French, English

MAJOR EXPORT:
Coffee

MAJOR IMPORT:
Foods

CAPITAL:
Kigali

LANDMASS:
10,170 sq. mi.
26,340 sq. km

Kigali

SAO TOME and PRINCIPE

POPULATION:
200,000
475 per sq. mi.
183 per sq. km

LANGUAGES:
Portuguese, Crioulo

MAJOR EXPORT:
Cocoa

MAJOR IMPORT:
Textiles

CAPITAL:
São Tomé

LANDMASS:
371 sq. mi.
961 sq. km

São Tomé

SENEGAL

POPULATION:
10,600,000
139 per sq. mi.
54 per sq. km

LANGUAGES:
French, Wolof, Pulaar, Diola

MAJOR EXPORT:
Fish

MAJOR IMPORT:
Foods

CAPITAL:
Dakar

LANDMASS:
75,954 sq. mi.
196,721 sq. km

Dakar

SEYCHELLES

POPULATION:
100,000
501 per sq. mi.
193 per sq. km

LANGUAGES:
English, French, Creole

MAJOR EXPORT:
Fish

MAJOR IMPORT:
Foods

CAPITAL:
Victoria

LANDMASS:
174 sq. mi.
451 sq. km

Victoria

SIERRA LEONE

POPULATION:
5,700,000
207 per sq. mi.
80 per sq. km

LANGUAGES:
English, Mende, Temne, Krio

MAJOR EXPORT:
Diamonds

MAJOR IMPORT:
Foods

CAPITAL:
Freetown

LANDMASS:
27,699 sq. mi.
71,740 sq. km

Freetown

SOMALIA

POPULATION:
8,000,000
33 per sq. mi.
13 per sq. km

LANGUAGES:
Somali, Arabic

MAJOR EXPORT:
Livestock

MAJOR IMPORT:
Textiles

CAPITAL:
Mogadishu

LANDMASS:
246,201 sq. mi.
637,661 sq. km

Mogadishu

SOUTH AFRICA

POPULATION:
44,000,000
93 per sq. mi.
36 per sq. km

LANGUAGES:
Afrikaans, English, Zulu

MAJOR EXPORT:
Gold

MAJOR IMPORT:
Transport Equip.

CAPITALS:
Pretoria, Cape Town, Bloemfontein

LANDMASS:
471,444 sq. mi.
1,221,038 sq. km

Pretoria
Bloemfontein
Cape Town

SUDAN

POPULATION:
38,100,000
39 per sq. mi.
15 per sq. km

LANGUAGES:
Arabic, Nubian, Ta Bedawie

MAJOR EXPORT:
Cotton

MAJOR IMPORT:
Petroleum Products

CAPITAL:
Khartoum

LANDMASS:
967,494 sq. mi.
2,505,809 sq. km

Khartoum

SWAZILAND

POPULATION:
1,200,000
173 per sq. mi.
67 per sq. km

LANGUAGES:
English, Swazi

MAJOR EXPORT:
Soft Drink Concentrates

MAJOR IMPORT:
Machinery

CAPITAL:
Mbabane

LANDMASS:
6,703 sq. mi.
17,361 sq. km

Mbabane

TANZANIA

POPULATION:
35,400,000
97 per sq. mi.
38 per sq. km

LANGUAGES:
Swahili, English

MAJOR EXPORT:
Coffee

MAJOR IMPORT:
Machinery

CAPITAL:
Dar es Salaam

LANDMASS:
364,900 sq. mi.
945,087 sq. km

Dar es Salaam

Country Profiles

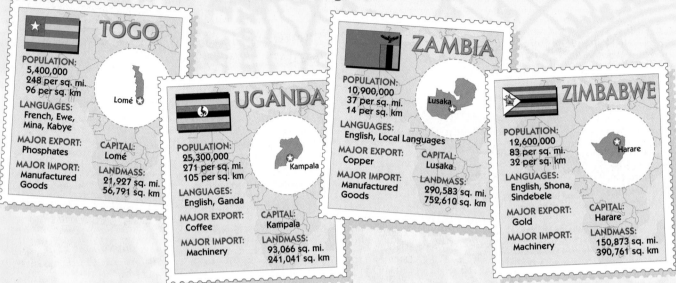

TOGO

POPULATION:
5,400,000
248 per sq. mi.
96 per sq. km

LANGUAGES:
French, Ewe,
Mina, Kabye

MAJOR EXPORT:
Phosphates

MAJOR IMPORT:
Manufactured
Goods

CAPITAL:
Lomé

LANDMASS:
21,927 sq. mi.
56,791 sq. km

Lomé

UGANDA

POPULATION:
25,300,000
271 per sq. mi.
105 per sq. km

LANGUAGES:
English, Ganda

MAJOR EXPORT:
Coffee

MAJOR IMPORT:
Machinery

CAPITAL:
Kampala

LANDMASS:
93,066 sq. mi.
241,041 sq. km

Kampala

ZAMBIA

POPULATION:
10,900,000
37 per sq. mi.
14 per sq. km

LANGUAGES:
English, Local Languages

MAJOR EXPORT:
Copper

MAJOR IMPORT:
Manufactured
Goods

CAPITAL:
Lusaka

LANDMASS:
290,583 sq. mi.
752,610 sq. km

Lusaka

ZIMBABWE

POPULATION:
12,600,000
83 per sq. mi.
32 per sq. km

LANGUAGES:
English, Shona,
Sindebele

MAJOR EXPORT:
Gold

MAJOR IMPORT:
Machinery

CAPITAL:
Harare

LANDMASS:
150,873 sq. mi.
390,761 sq. km

Harare

Countries and flags not drawn to scale

BUILDING CITIZENSHIP

Closing the Door on Racism   By 1994, South Africa's racist policy of apartheid was officially over. Nelson Mandela became the first black person to be elected president of South Africa. Just three years earlier he had been released from jail after spending 27 years there for antiapartheid activities. When he became president, he created a panel to grant pardons to both blacks and whites who had admitted to committing political crimes in the past. Mandela believed that only by "closing the door" on the past could the country move on to its future.

Why do you think Nelson Mandela was willing to pardon people?

The flags of African countries often represent the history or culture of the country. For example, the "Y" shape in the South African flag symbolizes a divided people going forward in unity. Research the flag of an African country and write a paragraph about the meaning of the flag.

FCAT LA.B.1.3.2

▼ **Women at an antiapartheid rally in South Africa**

View over terraced fields
and small settlements,
Kabale, Uganda ▼

The World and Its People | **NATIONAL GEOGRAPHIC**

To learn more about the people and places of West Africa, view **The World and Its People Chapter 19** video.

Social Studies ONLINE

Chapter Overview Visit **The World and Its People** Web site at twip.glencoe.com and click on **Chapter 19—Chapter Overviews** to preview information about West Africa.

FCAT PRACTICE The activity below will help you prepare for the **FCAT Reading** test.

Summarizing Information Make this foldable to determine what you already know, identify what you want to know, and summarize what you learn about West Africa. **FCAT LA.A.1.3.2**

Step 1 Fold a sheet of paper into thirds from top to bottom.

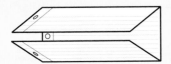

Step 2 Turn the paper horizontally, unfold, and label the three columns as shown.

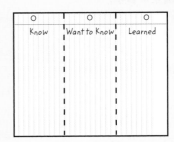

| Know | Want to Know | Learned |

Reading and Writing Before you read the chapter, write what you already know about West Africa under the "Know" tab. Write what you want to know about West Africa under the "Want to Know" tab. Then, as you read the chapter, write what you learn under the "Learned" tab. Be sure to include information you wanted to know (from the second column). **FCAT LA.A.1.3.2**

Why It Matters

Cultural Roots

Many African Americans today can trace their roots to West Africa. Enslaved peoples were carried from the "slave coast" of West Africa to the Americas in the 1600s and 1700s. Liberia was founded as a haven for returning Africans. West Africa also includes Nigeria, the continent's most populous country.

◀ **The Central Mosque of Kano, Nigeria**

Nigeria–African Giant

Guide to Reading

Main Idea

Nigeria is a large, oil-rich country that has more people than any other African nation.

Terms to Know

- mangrove
- savanna
- harmattan
- subsistence farm
- cacao
- compound
- civil war

Reading Strategy

Create a chart like the one below. Then list two facts about Nigeria in each category. **FCAT LA.A.1.3.2**

Nigeria	Fact #1	Fact #2
Land		
Economy		
People		

The following are the major Sunshine State Standards covered in this section.

SS.A.2.3.1:
Understands how language, ideas, and institutions of one culture can influence others (e.g., through trade, exploration, and immigration)

SS.B.2.3.8:
Knows world patterns of resource distribution and utilization

NATIONAL GEOGRAPHIC **Exploring Our World**

In 1991 Abuja replaced Lagos as Nigeria's capital. The new city was built in an undeveloped region in central Nigeria. Today Abuja has new buildings and a network of roads linking it with other parts of the country. It also has schools. These children prepare to pray at the Islamic Academy in Abuja.

The West African country of **Nigeria** gets its name from the **Niger River,** which flows through western and central Nigeria. One of the largest nations in Africa, Nigeria is more than twice the size of California.

From Tropics to Savannas

Nigeria has a long coastline on the **Gulf of Guinea,** an arm of the Atlantic Ocean. Along Nigeria's coast, the land is covered with mangrove swamps. A mangrove is a tropical tree with roots that extend both above and beneath the water. As you travel inland, the land becomes vast tropical rain forests. Small villages appear in only a few clearings. The forests gradually thin into savannas in central Nigeria. Savannas are tropical grasslands with only a few trees. Highlands and plateaus also make up this area. Most of the country has a tropical savanna climate with high average temperatures and seasonal rains. The grasslands of the far north have a dry steppe climate. In the winter months, a dusty wind called the **harmattan** blows south from the Sahara.

✓ **Reading Check** What kinds of vegetation are found in Nigeria?

Economic Challenges

Nigeria is one of the world's major oil-producing countries. More than 90 percent of the country's income comes from oil exports. The government has used oil profits to build highways, schools, skyscrapers, and factories. These factories make food products, textiles, chemicals, machinery, and vehicles. Still, more than one-third of Nigeria's people lack jobs and live in poverty.

Nigeria began to experience economic troubles during the 1980s. As a result of falling world oil prices, Nigeria's income dropped. At the same time, many people left their farms in search of better-paying jobs in the cities. In addition, a few years of low rainfall meant smaller harvests, so food production fell. Nigeria—which had once exported food—had to import food to feed its people.

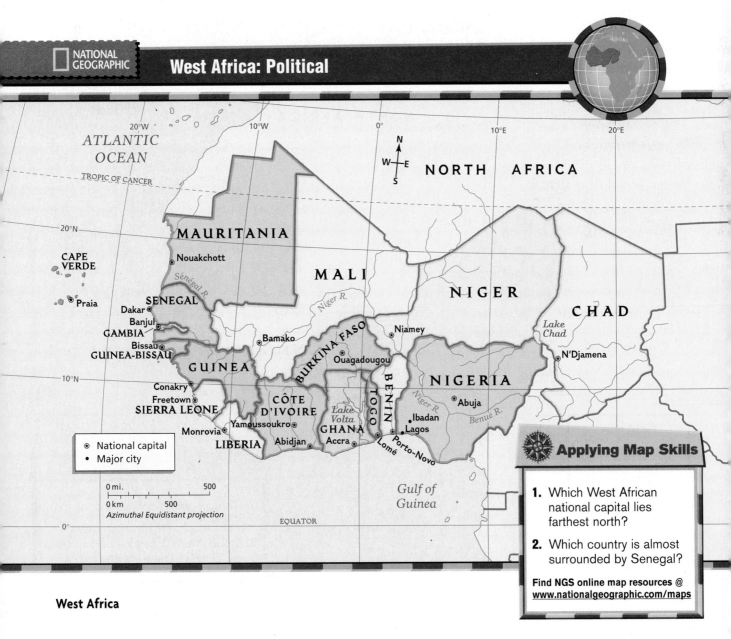

NATIONAL GEOGRAPHIC

West Africa: Political

* National capital
• Major city

0 mi. 500
0 km 500
Azimuthal Equidistant projection

Applying Map Skills

1. Which West African national capital lies farthest north?

2. Which country is almost surrounded by Senegal?

Find NGS online map resources @ www.nationalgeographic.com/maps

West Africa

Despite oil resources, Nigeria's people mainly work as farmers. Most have **subsistence farms,** or small plots where farmers grow just enough food to feed their families. Some work on larger farms that produce such cash crops as rubber, peanuts, palm oil, and cacao. The **cacao** is a tropical tree whose seeds are used to make chocolate and cocoa. Nigeria is a leading producer of cacao beans.

✓ **Reading Check** How has Nigeria's government used profits from oil sales?

Nigeria's People

About 133.9 million people live in Nigeria—more people than in any other country in Africa. The map on page 560 shows that most of the people live along the coast and around the city of **Kano** in the north.

One of the strongest bonds that Africans have is a sense of belonging to a group or a family. Nigeria has about 250 ethnic groups. The four largest are the Hausa (HOW•suh), Fulani (foo•LAH•nee), Yoruba (YAWR•uh•buh), and Ibo (EE•boh). Nigerians speak many different African languages. They use English in business and government

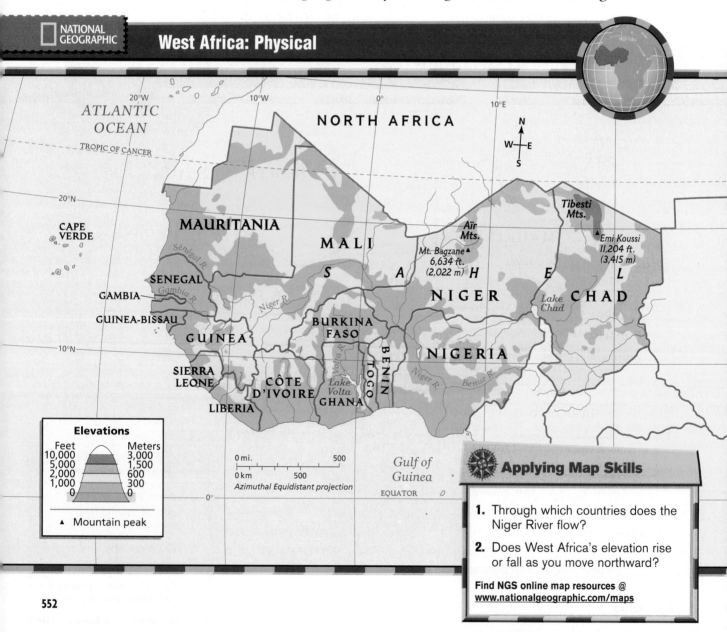

NATIONAL GEOGRAPHIC

West Africa: Physical

Elevations

Feet / Meters
10,000 / 3,000
5,000 / 1,500
2,000 / 600
1,000 / 300
0 / 0

▲ Mountain peak

0 mi. 500
0 km 500
Azimuthal Equidistant projection

Applying Map Skills

1. Through which countries does the Niger River flow?

2. Does West Africa's elevation rise or fall as you move northward?

Find NGS online map resources @ www.nationalgeographic.com/maps

Nigeria's Economy

Nigerian women canoe past an oil refinery in the Niger River delta (above left). Cacao pods are harvested in Nigeria (above).

Human/Environment Interaction What are Nigeria's important cash crops?

affairs, though. About one-half of Nigeria's people are Muslim, and another 40 percent are Christian. The remaining 10 percent practice traditional African religions.

About 60 percent of Nigerians live in rural villages. The typical family lives in a **compound,** or a group of houses surrounded by walls. Usually the village has a weekly market run by women. The women sell locally grown products such as meat, cloth, yams, nuts, and palm oil. The market also provides a chance for friends to meet.

Long-standing rural ways are changing, however. Many young men now move to the cities to find work and often send money to their families. The women stay in the villages to raise children and to farm the land. The men return home to see their families when they are able.

Nigeria's largest city is the port of **Lagos,** the former capital. Major banks, department stores, and restaurants serve the 13.5 million people who live in Lagos and its surrounding areas. **Ibadan** (EE•bah•DAHN), Kano, and Abuja (ah•BOO•jah) lie inland. **Abuja,** the present capital, is a planned city that was begun during the 1980s.

Nigerians take pride in both old and new features of their culture. Artists make elaborate wooden masks, metal sculptures, and colorful cloth. Nigerians pass on stories, sayings, and riddles by word of mouth from one generation to the next. In 1986 Nigerian writer Wole Soyinka (WAW•lay shaw•YIHNG•ka) became the first African to win the Nobel Prize in literature.

History and Government The earliest known inhabitants of the area were the Nok people. They lived between the Niger and Benue Rivers between 500 B.C. and A.D. 200. The Nok were known as skilled metalworkers and traders. Farming peoples who spoke dialects of the Bantu family of languages began to move from the Niger River region into Central and East Africa. Today Bantu-speaking peoples occupy most of Africa south of the Congo River.

Over the centuries, powerful city-states and kingdoms became centers of trade and the arts. People in what is today northern Nigeria came in contact with Muslim cultures and adopted Islam. People in the south developed cultures based on traditional African religions.

During the 1400s, Europeans arrived in Africa looking for gold and Africans to take overseas as enslaved laborers. In 1884 European leaders divided most of Africa into colonies. The borders of these colonies often sliced through ethnic lands. As a result, many ethnic groups found their members living in two or more separate territories. By the early 1900s, the British had taken control of Nigeria.

In 1960 Nigeria finally became an independent country. Ethnic, religious, and political disputes soon tore it apart, however. One ethnic group, the Ibo, tried to set up its own country. A civil war—a fight between different groups within a country—resulted. In this bloody war, starvation and conflict led to 2 million deaths. The Ibo were defeated, and their region remained part of Nigeria.

Nigeria has faced the challenge of building a stable government. Military leaders have often ruled the country. In 1999 Nigerians were able to vote for a president in free elections. Nigerians continue to work toward greater national unity, but they face enormous problems.

✓ Reading Check **What are the four largest ethnic groups in Nigeria?**

FCAT PRACTICE You can prepare for the FCAT-assessed standards by completing the correlated item(s) below.

Section 1 Assessment

Defining Terms
1. **Define** mangrove, savanna, harmattan, subsistence farm, cacao, compound, civil war.

Recalling Facts
2. **Place** Describe the changes in Nigeria's physical geography as you move from the coast inland.
3. **Place** What is the capital of Nigeria?
4. **Culture** How many ethnic groups are represented by the people of Nigeria?

Critical Thinking
5. **Understanding Cause and Effect** Why did a drop in oil prices cause economic troubles in Nigeria in the 1980s? **FCAT** LA.E.2.2.1
6. **Drawing Conclusions** Why do you think an ethnic group, such as the Ibo, would want to set up their own country?
FCAT LA.A.2.3.1

Graphic Organizer
7. **Organizing Information** On a time line like the one below, place the following events and their dates in order: Nigeria becomes independent; Nok people work in metal and trade for goods; Free elections are held; British take control of Nigeria. **FCAT** LA.A.1.3.2

Applying Social Studies Skills

8. **Analyzing Maps** Study the physical map on page 552. Into what larger body of water does the Niger River empty?

Critical Thinking Skill

Drawing Inferences and Conclusions

Suppose your teacher brought a colorful wooden mask to class, and a classmate said, "That's from Nigeria." You might infer that your classmate has an interest in African art and, therefore, recognizes the mask as coming from Nigeria.

Yoruba wood masks ▲

Learning the Skill

To *infer* means to evaluate information and arrive at a conclusion. When you make inferences, you "read between the lines," or draw conclusions that are not stated directly in the text. You must use the available facts *and* your own knowledge and experience to form a judgment or opinion about the material.

Use the following steps to help you draw inferences and make conclusions:

- Read carefully for stated facts and ideas.
- Summarize the information and list the important facts.
- Apply related information that you may already know to make inferences.
- Use your knowledge and insight to develop some conclusions about these facts.

Practicing the Skill

Read the passage below, and then answer the questions that follow.

Nigerian art forms reflect the people's beliefs in spirits and nature. Yoruba masks are carved out of wood, reflecting the forces of nature and gods. The masks are used in ceremonies to help connect with the spirit of their ancestors. The masks also appear at funerals in order to please the spirits of the dead. Of all the Yoruba masks, the helmet masks of the Epa cult are the most spectacular.

1. What topic is the writer describing?
2. What facts are presented?
3. What can you infer about the role of masks in Nigerian life? **FCAT** LA.A.1.3.2
4. What do you already know about religious ceremonies?
5. What conclusion can you make about traditional religions in Nigeria? **FCAT** LA.A.2.3.1

Applying the Skill

Study the photos of Nigerians on page 553. What can you infer about life in Nigeria from the photographs? What evidence supports this inference, or conclusion? **FCAT** LA.A.2.3.1

GO TO Practice key skills with **Glencoe Skillbuilder Interactive Workbook, Level 1.**

Guide to Reading

Main Idea

The Sahel countries face a continuing struggle to keep grasslands from turning into desert, but the coastal countries receive plenty of rainfall.

Terms to Know

- overgraze
- drought
- desertification
- bauxite
- phosphate

Reading Strategy

Create five charts like this one, filling in at least one key fact about five West African countries for each category. **FCAT** LA.A.1.3.2

Country	
Land	
Economy	
Culture	

The following are the major Sunshine State Standards covered in this section.

SS.A.3.3.5:
Understands the differences between institutions of Eastern and Western civilizations (e.g., differences in governments, social traditions and customs, economic systems and religious institutions)

SS.A.3.3.2:
Understands the historical events that have shaped the development of cultures throughout the world

Section 2
The Sahel and Coastal West Africa

NATIONAL GEOGRAPHIC Exploring Our World

Slowly but surely, the desert is creeping into grassy inland areas of West Africa north of Nigeria. Over the past 100 years, a stretch of the Sahara about 100 miles (161 km) wide has swallowed parts of countries in West Africa. This is due in part to population growth. The already limited resources are being used up faster than they can be replaced.

Five countries—**Mauritania** (MAWR•uh•TAY•nee•uh), **Mali** (MAH•lee), **Burkina Faso** (bur•KEE•nuh FAH•soh), **Niger** (NY•juhr), and **Chad**—are located in an area known as the **Sahel.** The word *Sahel* comes from an Arabic word that means "border." In addition to the Sahel countries, West Africa includes 11 coastal countries.

Land and History of the Sahel

The Sahel receives little rainfall, so only short grasses and small trees can support grazing animals. Most people have traditionally herded livestock. Their flocks, unfortunately, have overgrazed the land in some places. When animals overgraze land, they strip areas so bare that plants cannot grow back. Then bare soil is blown away by winds.

In the Sahel, dry and wet periods usually follow each other. When the seasonal rains do not fall, drought takes hold. A drought is a long period of extreme dryness and water shortage. The latest drought occurred in the 1980s. Rivers dried up, crops failed, and millions of animals died. Thousands of people died of starvation. Millions of others fled to more productive southern areas. Overgrazing and drought have led to **desertification** where grasslands have become deserts.

Empires   From the A.D. 500s to 1500s, three great African empires— Ghana, Mali, and Songhai (SAWNG•hy)—arose in the Sahel. The empire of Ghana flourished between the A.D. 700s and 1100s. The empire was located at the upper parts of the Senegal and Niger Rivers. The people of Ghana knew how to make iron weapons, which they used to conquer neighboring groups of farmers and herders. Ghana could field an army of 200,000 warriors.

Ghana also had major deposits of gold. The wealth of the king's court was legendary. Crossing the empire were trade routes that connected gold mines in West Africa with copper and salt mines in the Sahara. Ghana prospered by taxing the goods that traders moved north and south along these routes.

The empire of Mali defeated Ghana in the A.D. 1200s. It, too, built its wealth and power on the gold and salt trade. Turn to page 566 to learn more about the rich salt trade. Mali's most famous ruler, Mansa Musa, made a journey in grand style to Makkah. This is the holy city of Islam located in the Arabian Peninsula. A faithful Muslim, Mansa Musa made his capital, Tombouctou (TOH•book•TOO), a leading center of Islamic learning. People came from all over the Muslim world to study there.

In the 1400s, Songhai replaced Mali as the most powerful West African empire. A huge army and a navy that patrolled the Niger River made Songhai the largest of the three trading empires. Songhai's rulers welcomed teachers, poets, and religious leaders from Asia and Europe.

Moroccan invaders with guns defeated Songhai in the late 1500s. During the 1800s, the Sahel region came under French rule. The French created five colonies in the area. In 1960 these five colonies

Clothing

To protect themselves from the hot Saharan sun, the Tuareg people wear layers of clothing under their long flowing robes. These loose cotton clothes help slow the evaporation of sweat and conserve body moisture. As a sign of respect for their superiors, Tuareg men cover their mouths and faces with veils. Women usually wear veils only for weddings. The veils are made of blue cloth dyed from crushed indigo. The blue dye easily rubs off onto the skin, earning the men the nickname "the Blue Men of the Desert."

Looking Closer How is the clothing of the Tuareg appropriate for the land in which they live?

became the independent nations of Mauritania, Mali, Upper Volta (now Burkina Faso), Niger, and Chad.

Reading Check How has overgrazing affected the Sahel?

The People of the Sahel

The Sahel countries are large in size but have small populations. The population density map on page 560 shows that most people live in the southern areas of the Sahel. Rivers flow here, and the land can be farmed or grazed. Yet even these areas do not have enough water and fertile land to support large numbers of people.

Today most people in the Sahel live in small towns. They are subsistence farmers who grow grains, such as millet and sorghum (SAWR•guhm). For years, many people were nomads. Groups such as the Tuareg (TWAH•rehg), for example, would cross the desert with herds of camels. The Fulani herded cattle, goats, and sheep. The recent droughts forced many of them to give up their traditional way of life and move to the towns. Here they often live in crowded camps of tents.

Mauritania borders the Atlantic Ocean. Rich fishing waters lie off the coast, but ships from other countries have overfished the area. Still, Mauritania's chief exports include fish and iron ore. The other four Sahel countries suffer from their landlocked location and lack of good transportation. Mali hopes to develop its gold mining industry. Niger has reserves of uranium, a mineral used for making nuclear fuels. Chad has petroleum deposits yet lacks the money needed to build pipelines.

The people of the Sahel practice a mix of African, Arab, and European traditions. Most are Muslims and follow the Islamic religion. They speak Arabic as well as a variety of African languages. In many of the larger cities, French is also spoken.

Reading Check Why have many people in the Sahel given up nomadic ways?

West Africa's Coastal Countries

Look at the map on page 552 to locate the **Cape Verde** Islands off the Atlantic Coast. Skipping to **Senegal,** follow the countries in order around the coast: **Gambia, Guinea-Bissau, Guinea, Sierra Leone, Liberia, Côte d'Ivoire, Ghana, Togo,** and **Benin.**

Tropical Landscape Sandy beaches, thick mangrove swamps, and rain forests cover the shores of West Africa's coastal countries. Highland areas with grasses and trees lie inland. Several major rivers flow from these highlands to the coast. They include the Sénégal, Gambia, Volta, and Niger Rivers. Rapids and shallow waters prevent large ships from traveling far inland.

Because they border the ocean, the coastal countries receive plenty of rainfall. Warm currents in the **Gulf of Guinea** create a moist, tropical rain forest climate in most coastal lowlands year-round. For many years, tropical disease, thick rain forests, and river rapids kept European explorers from entering the interior.

Exploring Economics

Monoculture

The economies of some West African countries, such as Côte d'Ivoire, depend upon the production of one or two major crops. This practice is called monoculture. Although this has the advantage of being able to produce enough product to export, it also has disadvantages. If worldwide demand for the product drops, the price also drops. A major drought or epidemic could destroy harvests and wipe out the nation's only major source of income.

Deforestation is a problem along the densely settled West African coast. Forests have been cleared to make space for palm, coffee, cacao, and rubber plantations, as well as for many small farms. As people migrate in search of work, they have formed concentrated settlements around port cities such as **Abidjan** (Côte d'Ivoire), **Accra** (Ghana), and Lagos and **Port Harcourt** (Nigeria). Oil discoveries in eastern Nigeria are now attracting even more people to the West African coast.

Despite rich agricultural resources, coastal West African countries import more in industrial goods than they export in natural products. Why? Agricultural products often rise and fall in price suddenly, and their value is not equal to finished goods. To meet their countries' needs, governments have to borrow money from international organizations.

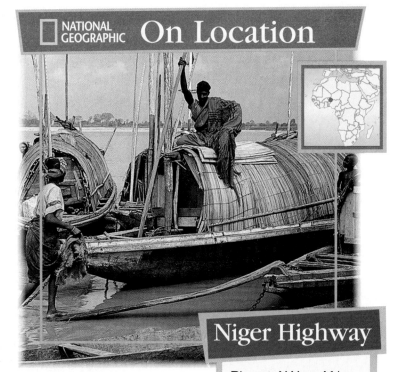

NATIONAL GEOGRAPHIC On Location

Niger Highway

Rivers of West Africa provide not only water but transportation. Here, freight boats on the Niger River deliver goods to Benin's people.

Place What prevents large ships from traveling far inland on West Africa's rivers?

History In early times, the powerful and wealthy kingdoms of Ashanti and Abomey ruled West Africa's coastal region. These kingdoms were centers of trade, learning, and the arts. Benin artists sculpted beautiful works in bronze. Intricate woodcarvings and masks represented gods, spirits, or ancestors. African dance and music also served a religious purpose. The dances were a means of communicating with the spirits. Without a written language, African dances and songs became a way to pass legends and religious traditions from generation to generation.

The Slave Trade From the late 1400s to the early 1800s, Europeans set up trading posts along the West African coast. From these posts, they traded with Africans for gold, ivory, and enslaved people. Many African states had sold people as slaves long before Europeans reached Africa. Most of these slaves were prisoners of war captured in local battles. After the development of European sailing ships, however, the slave trade became a major source of income for the kings of West African states.

Europeans enslaved millions of Africans and forced them to work on plantations and in mines in the Americas. This trade in human beings was a disaster for West Africa. The removal of so many young and skilled people devastated West African families, villages, and economies.

The French, British, and Portuguese eventually divided up the coastal region and set up colonies to obtain the region's rich resources. In 1957 Ghana became the first country in Africa to become independent. By the late 1970s, no West African country was under European rule.

✓**Reading Check** What enabled West African kings to prosper from the slave trade?

West Africa: Population Density

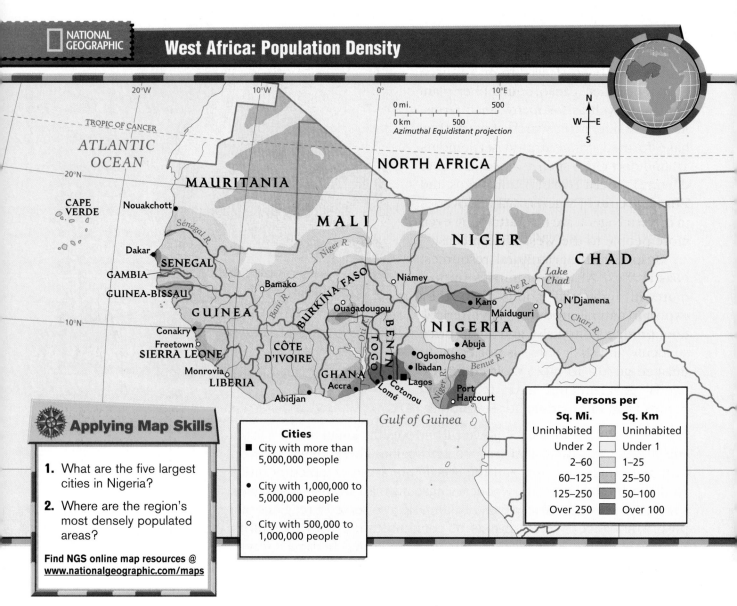

Applying Map Skills

1. What are the five largest cities in Nigeria?

2. Where are the region's most densely populated areas?

Find NGS online map resources @ www.nationalgeographic.com/maps

Cities

■ City with more than 5,000,000 people

● City with 1,000,000 to 5,000,000 people

○ City with 500,000 to 1,000,000 people

Persons per		
Sq. Mi.		**Sq. Km**
Uninhabited		Uninhabited
Under 2		Under 1
2–60		1–25
60–125		25–50
125–250		50–100
Over 250		Over 100

People of Coastal West Africa

People in coastal West Africa cherish family ties. Some practice traditional African religions, whereas others are Christian or Muslim. Local African languages are spoken in everyday conversation. Reflecting the region's colonial histories, languages such as French, English, and Portuguese are used in business and government. If you were to visit the modern coastal cities of West Africa, you would see some people dressed in Western-style business clothes and others in traditional African clothing. **Dakar** (dah•KAHR), Senegal's capital, is known for its European cafés, bustling outdoor markets, and tree-lined streets.

Most of the people in Gambia, Senegal, and Guinea work in agriculture. Guinea is also rich in bauxite and diamonds. Bauxite is a mineral used to make aluminum. Phosphate mining takes place in Senegal. Phosphate is a mineral salt used in fertilizers.

Liberia is the only West African nation that was never a colony. African Americans freed from slavery founded Liberia in 1822. **Monrovia,** the capital, was named for James Monroe—the president of the United States when Liberia was founded. From 1989 to 2003, a civil war cost many lives and destroyed much of the country's economy.

Like Liberia, Sierra Leone was founded as a home for people freed from slavery. The British ruled Sierra Leone from 1787 to 1961. Most of the land is used for farming, but the country also has mineral resources, especially diamonds. Here, too, civil war has hurt the economy.

Côte d'Ivoire has a French name that means "ivory coast." From the late 1400s to the early 1900s, a trade in elephant ivory tusks in Côte d'Ivoire brought profits to European traders. Today the ivory trade is illegal, and the country protects its few remaining elephants. The port of Abidjan is the largest urban area and economic center. It has towering office buildings and wide avenues. Most countries' embassies are in Abidjan, but **Yamoussoukro** (YAH•moo•SOO•kroh), some 137 miles (220 km) inland, is the official capital.

Ghana's people belong to about 100 ethnic groups. The Ashanti and the Fante are the largest. Many groups still keep their local kings, but these rulers have no political power. The people respect these ceremonial rulers and look to them to keep traditions alive. About 35 percent of Ghana's people live in cities. **Accra,** on the coast, is the capital and largest city. A giant dam on the Volta River provides hydroelectric power to urban areas. The dam also has created **Lake Volta,** one of the world's largest artificial lakes.

Web Activity Visit *The World and Its People* Web site at twip.glencoe.com and click on **Chapter 19— Student Web Activities** to learn more about Liberia.

✓ **Reading Check** What are the capitals of Ghana and Côte d'Ivoire?

FCAT PRACTICE You can prepare for the FCAT-assessed standards by completing the correlated item(s) below.

Section 2 Assessment

Defining Terms
1. Define overgraze, drought, desertification, bauxite, phosphate.

Recalling Facts
2. **History** What three great empires ruled in the Sahel from the A.D. 500s to 1500s?
3. **History** Which West African country was never a colony?
4. **Government** How much political power do the local kings in Ghana have?

Critical Thinking
5. **Making Predictions** What challenges do you think will arise as people move from the Sahel to more productive areas? **FCAT LA.A.2.3.1**
6. **Drawing Conclusions** Why do governments of coastal West African countries have to borrow money? **FCAT LA.A.2.3.1**

Graphic Organizer
7. **Organizing Information** On a chart like this one, write at least three different facts about the three ancient African empires of Ghana, Mali, and Songhai. **FCAT LA.A.1.3.2**

Ghana	Mali	Songhai

Applying Social Studies Skills
8. **Analyzing Maps** Study the population density map on page 560. Why would you expect the heavy population centers to be located along the coast? **FCAT MA.B.1.3.4**

Making Connections

ART   SCIENCE   CULTURE   TECHNOLOGY

Great Mosque of Djenné

In the West African city of Djenné (jeh•NAY), Mali, stands a huge structure built entirely of mud. It is the Great Mosque of Djenné, and it covers an area the size of a city block. Considered one of Africa's greatest architectural wonders, the existing Great Mosque is actually the third mosque to occupy the location.

Djenné

Located between the Sahara and the African savanna, the city of Djenné was an important crossroads on a trade route connecting northern and southern Africa. Caravans and boats carried gold, salt, and other goods through the city.

During the A.D. 1200s, the ruler of Djenné ordered the construction of the first Great Mosque. Having recently converted to Islam, he had his palace torn down to make room for the huge house of worship. The city became an important Islamic religious center. Over the years, political and religious conflicts led to a decline in the city. People abandoned the Great Mosque, and a second, much smaller one replaced it. Then in 1906, builders began to raise a new Great Mosque. Today the Great Mosque is once more an important part of the religious life of the Djenné people.

FCAT PRACTICE Answering question 3 below will help you prepare for the **FCAT Reading** test.

The Great Mosque

The Great Mosque of Djenné was built facing east toward Makkah, the holy city of Islam. It is constructed from the same sun-dried mud bricks as most of the rest of the city. The mud walls of the mosque vary in thickness between 16 and 24 inches (41 and 61 cm), providing insulation to keep the interior cool. Roof vents can be removed at night to allow cooler air inside.

With its five stories and three towers, or minarets, the mosque rises above the surrounding buildings. Inside the mosque, the main prayer hall is open to the sky. Although the mosque contains loudspeakers that are used to issue the call to prayer, there are few other modern improvements.

Maintaining the Mosque

Rain, wind, and heat can damage mud structures, and the Great Mosque would soon deteriorate without care. Each spring the people of Djenné plaster the mosque from top to bottom with fresh mud. It is a festival day, and nearly everyone volunteers. Workers climb up the sides of the mosque on wooden rods permanently mounted to the walls. They dump mud and water onto the walls, then smooth it with their bare hands. The townspeople know that, with such care, the Great Mosque will remain a place of worship for generations to come.

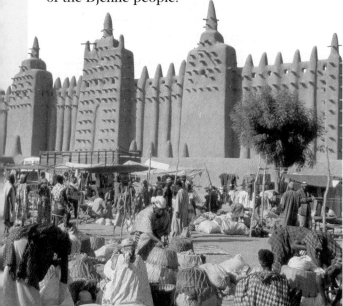

→ Making the Connection

1. When was the first Great Mosque built?
2. What elements of the Great Mosque help keep the inside cool?
3. **Making Comparisons** In what way is the Great Mosque like the other buildings in Djenné? In what way is it different? **FCAT** LA.A.2.2.7

Section 1   Nigeria—African Giant

Terms to Know

mangrove
savanna
harmattan
subsistence farm
cacao
compound
civil war

Main Idea

Nigeria is a large, oil-rich country that has more people than any other African nation.

✓ **Place** Nigeria's major landforms are coastal lowlands, savannas, highlands, plateaus, and partly dry grasslands.

✓ **Economics** More than 90 percent of Nigeria's income comes from oil exports.

✓ **Culture** Nigeria has about 250 ethnic groups. The four largest ethnic groups are the Hausa, Fulani, Yoruba, and Ibo.

Section 2   The Sahel and Coastal West Africa

Terms to Know

overgraze
drought
desertification
bauxite
phosphate

Main Idea

The Sahel countries face a continuing struggle to keep grasslands from turning into desert, but the coastal countries receive plenty of rainfall.

✓ **Region** The Sahel countries are Mauritania, Mali, Niger, Chad, and Burkina Faso.

✓ **Region** The Sahel receives little rainfall, so only short grasses and small trees can support grazing animals.

✓ **Human/Environment Interaction** Overgrazing and drought have caused many grassland areas in this region to become desert.

✓ **Region** The 11 countries that make up coastal West Africa are Senegal, Gambia, Guinea, Guinea-Bissau, Cape Verde, Liberia, Sierra Leone, Côte d'Ivoire, Ghana, Togo, and Benin.

✓ **Economics** West Africa's coastal countries import more in industrial goods than they export in natural products.

The port of Abidjan, Côte d'Ivoire ▶

Chapter 19
Assessment and Activities

FCAT PRACTICE You can prepare for the FCAT-assessed standards by completing the correlated item(s) below.

Using Key Terms

Match the terms in Part A with their definitions in Part B.

A.

1. overgraze
2. harmattan
3. drought
4. mangrove
5. compound
6. phosphate
7. desertification
8. cacao
9. subsistence farm
10. savanna

B.

a. process in which deserts expand
b. a group of houses surrounded by a wall
c. a dusty wind that blows south from the Sahara
d. mineral salt used in fertilizers
e. tropical tree whose seeds are used to make cocoa and chocolate
f. tropical grassland with scattered trees
g. produces enough to support a family's needs
h. extended period of extreme dryness
i. when animals strip the land so bare that plants cannot grow
j. tropical tree with roots above and beneath the water

Reviewing the Main Ideas

Section 1 Nigeria—African Giant

11. **Economics** What is Nigeria's major export?
12. **Economics** Name one reason Nigeria had economic troubles in the 1980s.
13. **Culture** Who was the first African to win the Nobel Prize in literature?
14. **History** Why have there been so many conflicts in Nigeria since 1960?

Section 2 The Sahel and Coastal West Africa

15. **Region** What is the meaning of the word *Sahel?*
16. **History** What was the earliest trading empire in West Africa?
17. **History** Who was Mansa Musa?
18. **Culture** What religion do most people of the Sahel follow?
19. **History** What has led to desertification in the Sahel?
20. **Movement** Why are ships unable to sail very far inland in coastal West Africa?
21. **History** What was the slave trade?
22. **Culture** What are the largest ethnic groups in Ghana?

NATIONAL GEOGRAPHIC **West Africa**

Place Location Activity

On a separate sheet of paper, match the letters on the map with the numbered places listed below.

1. Gulf of Guinea
2. Nigeria
3. Niger River
4. Liberia
5. Cape Verde
6. Lagos
7. Mali
8. Ghana
9. Chad
10. Monrovia

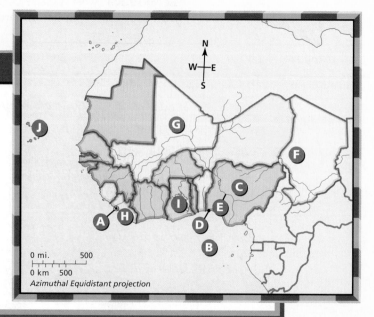

0 mi. 500
0 km 500
Azimuthal Equidistant projection

 **Social Studies**  **ONline**

Self-Check Quiz Visit *The World and Its People* Web site at <u>twip.glencoe.com</u> and click on **Chapter 19—Self-Check Quizzes** to prepare for the Chapter Test.

 ## Critical Thinking

23. **Evaluating Information** What do you feel is the major challenge facing the countries of West Africa today? Explain your answer.

24. **Sequencing Information** After reviewing this chapter, choose what you feel are five of the most important events in the history of West Africa. Place those events and their dates on a time line like this one.
FCAT LA.A.1.3.2

 ## Comparing Regions Activity

25. **Culture** West African arts have had a powerful impact on other cultures. Out of West Africa came detailed bronze work, musical rhythms, and wooden masks. The influence of African art is apparent in the work of Spanish artist Pablo Picasso. He painted geometric shapes and figures, as well as masklike faces. Research to find other ways African arts and music have influenced cultures. **FCAT** LA.A.2.3.5

 ## Mental Mapping Activity

26. **Focusing on the Region** Create a simple outline map of West Africa, and then label the following:

- Niger River
- Senegal
- Atlantic Ocean
- Côte d'Ivoire
- Gulf of Guinea
- Chad
- Tropic of Cancer
- Mali
- Nigeria
- Mauritania
- Niger
- Liberia

 ## Technology Skills Activity

27. **Using the Internet** Search on the Internet for information about one of the ancient empires of West Africa. Look for maps, pictures, and descriptions of the important places and rulers. Then write a report using the information you find. Share your report with the rest of the class. **FCAT** LA.A.2.3.5

Standardized Test Practice

Directions: Study the graph, and then answer the question that follows.

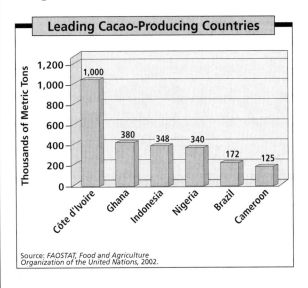

Leading Cacao-Producing Countries

Thousands of Metric Tons

Côte d'Ivoire: 1,000
Ghana: 380
Indonesia: 348
Nigeria: 340
Brazil: 172
Cameroon: 125

Source: *FAOSTAT, Food and Agriculture Organization of the United Nations, 2002.*

1. **What countries on the graph are leading cacao-producing countries from West Africa?** **FCAT** MA.E.3.3.1
   A Ghana, Indonesia, and Nigeria
   B Côte d'Ivoire, Ghana, and Indonesia
   C Côte d'Ivoire, Nigeria, and Cameroon
   D Côte d'Ivoire, Ghana, and Nigeria

Test-Taking Tip: The important words in this question are "from West Africa." You need to use information on the graph as well as information you learned in Chapter 19 to answer this question. As with any graph, read the title bar and information along the side and bottom of the graph first. Then analyze and compare the sizes of the bars to one another.

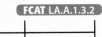

 565

People trade salt and other goods at a market on the Niger River in ancient Africa.

PLEASE PASS THE SALT: Africa's Salt Trade

Passing the salt at dinner may not be a big deal, but in parts of Africa, salt built empires. How did such a basic substance come to play such an important role in Africa?

Good as Gold

Salt is essential for life. Every person contains about 8 ounces (227 g) of salt—enough to fill several saltshakers. Salt helps muscles work, and it aids in digesting food. In hot climates, people need extra salt to replace the salt lost when they sweat. In tropical Africa, salt has always been precious.

Salt is plentiful in the Sahara and scarce in the forests south of the Sahara (in present-day countries such as Ghana and Côte d'Ivoire). These conditions gave rise to Africa's salt trade. Beginning in the A.D. 300s, Berbers drove camels carrying European glassware and weapons from Mediterranean ports into the Sahara. At the desert's great salt deposits, such as those near the ancient sites of Terhazza and Taoudenni, they traded European wares for salt.

The salt did not look like the tiny crystals in a saltshaker. It was in the form of large slabs, as hard as stone. The slabs were pried from hardened salt deposits that were left on the land long ago when landlocked seas evaporated. The salt slabs were loaded onto camels, and the animals were herded south. To people in the south, salt was literally worth its weight in gold. The slabs were cut into equal-sized blocks and exchanged for gold and other products such as ivory and kola nuts. Salt was also traded for enslaved people.

Rise and Decline

Camels arrived in Africa from Asia in A.D. 300. Before that time only a trickle of trade, mostly carried by human porters, made it across the blistering desert. In time, caravans of thousands of camels loaded with tons of salt arrived at southern markets.

Local kings along the trade routes put taxes—payable in gold—on all goods crossing their realms. The ancient empires of Mali, Ghana, and Songhai rose to great power from wealth brought by the salt trade.

Trade routes also provided avenues for spreading ideas and inventions. By the A.D. 800s, Arab traders brought to Africa a system of weights and measures, a written language, and the concept of money. They also brought a new religion—Islam.

Today trucks have replaced many of the camels. Salt no longer dominates trade in the region. However, salt is still important, and the salt trade continues in Mali and in the markets of other West African nations.

QUESTIONS

1 What goods were exchanged in the salt trade?

2 How did the salt trade affect regions south of the Sahara?

A present-day salt caravan in Niger ▶

NATIONAL GEOGRAPHIC

Salt Trade Routes

ATLANTIC OCEAN

Mediterranean Sea

SAHARA

Teghazza
Taoudenni

NIGER

NIGER

Red Sea

ASIA

N
W—E
S

Lake Chad

CÔTE D'IVOIRE   GHANA

0 mi. 1,000
0 km 1,000

Songhai   Salt deposit
Mali   --► Trade routes
Ghana   —— Present boundaries

Central and East Africa

The World and Its People NATIONAL GEOGRAPHIC

To learn more about the people and places of Central and East Africa, view *The World and Its People* **Chapters 20** and **21** videos.

Social Studies online

Chapter Overview Visit *The World and Its People* Web site at twip.glencoe.com and click on **Chapter 20—Chapter Overviews** to preview information about Central and East Africa.

FCAT PRACTICE 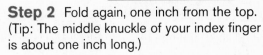 The activity below will help you prepare for the **FCAT Reading** test.

Compare-Contrast Make this foldable to compare and contrast traditional and modern cultures in Central and East Africa.

FCAT LA.A.1.3.2, LA.A.2.2.7

Step 1 Fold one sheet of paper in half from side to side.

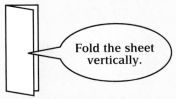

Fold the sheet vertically.

Step 2 Fold again, one inch from the top. (Tip: The middle knuckle of your index finger is about one inch long.)

Step 3 Open and label as shown.

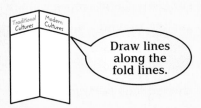

Draw lines along the fold lines.

Reading and Writing As you read this chapter, record information in the two columns of your foldable chart. Be sure to write the information you find in the appropriate column of your foldable.

FCAT LA.A.1.3.2, LA.A.2.2.7

▲ **Elephants on the Serengeti Plain in Tanzania**

Why It Matters

Rich in Heritage

Some of Africa's most important early civilizations flourished in the location that is now part of Central and East Africa. These societies grew to become large and complex as they developed the skills to master the region's difficult environment. They were successful farmers, herders, metalworkers, artisans, and merchants. Today the people of this region are facing difficult challenges just to survive.

Central Africa

Guide to Reading

Main Idea

Central Africa has rich natural resources that are largely undeveloped because of civil war and poor government decisions.

Terms to Know

- canopy
- hydroelectric power
- tsetse fly
- deforestation

Reading Strategy

Create a chart like this one. Choose two countries of Central Africa. Then list two facts about the people of each country.

FCAT LA.A.1.3.2

Country	Fact #1	Fact #2

The following are the major Sunshine State Standards covered in this section.

SS.B.2.3.5:
Understands the geographical factors that affect the cohesiveness and integration of countries

SS.B.2.3.8:
Knows world patterns of resource distribution and utilization

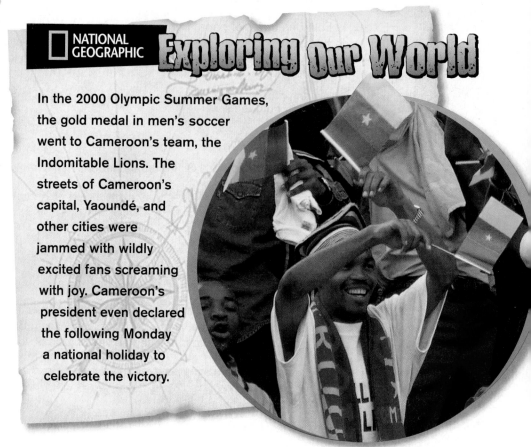

NATIONAL GEOGRAPHIC Exploring Our World

In the 2000 Olympic Summer Games, the gold medal in men's soccer went to Cameroon's team, the Indomitable Lions. The streets of Cameroon's capital, Yaoundé, and other cities were jammed with wildly excited fans screaming with joy. Cameroon's president even declared the following Monday a national holiday to celebrate the victory.

Central Africa includes seven countries. They are the **Democratic Republic of the Congo, Cameroon,** the **Central African Republic, Congo, Gabon** (ga•BOHN), **Equatorial Guinea,** and **São Tomé** (sow too•MAY) **and Príncipe** (PRIHN•sih•pee). Africa's second-longest river—the **Congo River**—flows through the center of the Democratic Republic of the Congo in the very heart of Africa.

Democratic Republic of the Congo

One-fourth the size of the United States, the Democratic Republic of the Congo has only about 23 miles (37 km) of coastline. Most of its land borders other African countries—nine in all.

High, rugged mountains rise in the eastern part of the country. Here you will find four large lakes—Lake Albert, Lake Edward, Lake Kivu, and Lake Tanganyika. **Lake Tanganyika** is the longest freshwater lake in the world. It is also the second deepest, after Russia's Lake Baikal. Savannas, or tropical grasslands with few trees, cover the highlands in the far north and south of the country. In these areas, lions and leopards stalk antelopes and zebras for food.

One of the world's largest rain forests covers the center of the Democratic Republic of the Congo. The treetops form a **canopy,** or an umbrella-like forest covering. The canopy is so thick that sunlight rarely reaches the forest floor. More than 750 different kinds of trees grow here. The rain forests are being destroyed at a rapid rate, however, as they are cleared for timber and farmland.

The mighty Congo River—about 2,800 miles (4,506 km) long—weaves its way through the country on its journey to the Atlantic Ocean. The river current is so strong that it carries freshwater about 100 miles (161 km) into the ocean. The Congo River and its tributaries, such as the Kasai River, provide **hydroelectric power,** or electricity generated by flowing water. In fact, these rivers produce more than 10 percent of all the world's hydroelectric power. The Congo River is also the country's highway for trade and travel.

Resources and Industry The Democratic Republic of the Congo has the opportunity to be a wealthy nation. The country exports gold, petroleum, diamonds, and copper. It is a main source of diamonds, as shown on the graph below. Most of these diamonds are used in strong industrial tools that cut metal. The country's factories make steel, cement, tires, shoes, textiles, processed foods, and beverages.

The Democratic Republic of the Congo has not been able to take full advantage of its rich resources, however. Why? One reason is the difficulty of transportation. Many of the minerals are found deep in the country's interior. Lack of roads and the thick rain forests make it hard to reach these areas. Another reason is political unrest. For many years, power-hungry leaders kept the nation's wealth for themselves. Then a

The Okapi
The Democratic Republic of the Congo is the only home for the okapi (oh•KAH•pee). With its long, tough tongue, the okapi pulls leaves off the branches of young trees. Its tongue is so long that the okapi can use it to clean its eyes.

NATIONAL GEOGRAPHIC
Leading Diamond-Producing Countries

Analyzing the Graph

Three of the world's top diamond-producing countries are in Africa south of the Sahara.

Economics Which two countries produce the most diamonds in Africa? FCAT MA.E.3.3.1

Visit twip.glencoe.com and click on **Chapter 20— Textbook Updates.**

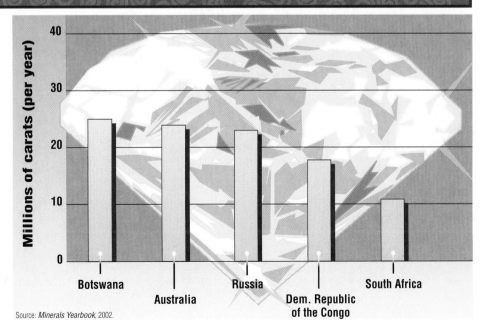

Millions of carats (per year)

Botswana   Australia   Russia   Dem. Republic of the Congo   South Africa

Source: *Minerals Yearbook,* 2002.

civil war broke out in the late 1990s. This war hurt efforts to develop the country's economy. In 2002 an agreement was signed by all remaining warring parties to end the fighting.

The Congolese People The Democratic Republic of the Congo's 56.6 million people consist of more than 200 different ethnic groups. One of these groups is the Kongo people, after whom the country is named. The country's official language is French, but many people speak local languages, such as Lingala or Kingwana. More than 75 percent of Congolese are Christians, mostly Roman Catholic.

Most Congolese people live in rural, or country, areas. Less than one-third are city dwellers. Still, **Kinshasa,** the capital, has about 6 million people. Because of civil war, life in this country is unsettled. Many people in the cities are without work.

In rural areas, people follow traditional ways of life. They plant seeds, tend fields, and harvest crops. Most of the harvest goes to feeding the

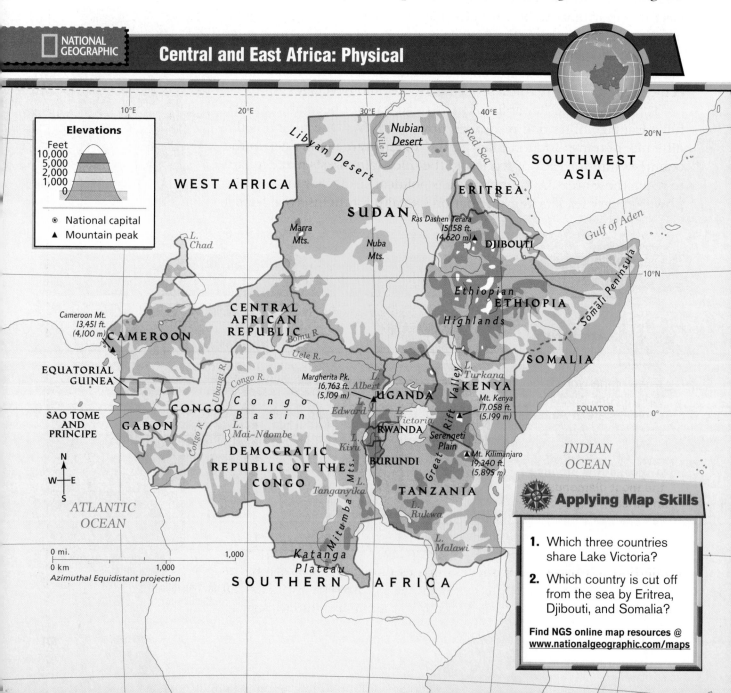

NATIONAL GEOGRAPHIC

Central and East Africa: Physical

Elevations

Feet
10,000
5,000
2,000
1,000
0

⊛ National capital
▲ Mountain peak

WEST AFRICA

Libyan Desert

Nubian Desert

Nile R.

Red Sea

SOUTHWEST ASIA

ERITREA

SUDAN

Ras Dashen Terara
15,158 ft.
(4,620 m) ▲

DJIBOUTI

Gulf of Aden

L. Chad

Marra Mts.

Nuba Mts.

Somali Peninsula

Cameroon Mt.
13,451 ft.
(4,100 m) ▲

CAMEROON

CENTRAL AFRICAN REPUBLIC

Bomu R.

Uele R.

Ethiopian Highlands

ETHIOPIA

SOMALIA

EQUATORIAL GUINEA

Congo R.
Ubangi R.

Margherita Pk.
16,763 ft.
(5,109 m) ▲

L. Albert

UGANDA

L. Turkana

KENYA

Mt. Kenya
17,058 ft.
(5,199 m) ▲

EQUATOR

SAO TOME AND PRINCIPE

CONGO

Congo Basin

GABON

Congo R.

L. Mai-Ndombe

L. Edward

L. Victoria

RWANDA

Serengeti Plain

Great Rift Valley

INDIAN OCEAN

N
W–E
S

DEMOCRATIC REPUBLIC OF THE CONGO

L. Kivu

BURUNDI

▲ Mt. Kilimanjaro
19,340 ft.
(5,895 m)

ATLANTIC OCEAN

L. Tanganyika

Mitumba Mts.

TANZANIA

L. Rukwa

0 mi. 1,000
0 km 1,000
Azimuthal Equidistant projection

Katanga Plateau

SOUTHERN AFRICA

L. Malawi

Applying Map Skills

1. Which three countries share Lake Victoria?

2. Which country is cut off from the sea by Eritrea, Djibouti, and Somalia?

Find NGS online map resources @ www.nationalgeographic.com/maps

family. Any extra goes to the local market—or to the boats moving along the rivers—to sell or trade for goods the people need.

History and Government   The Congo region was first settled about 10,000 years ago. The Bantu people—ancestors of most of the Congolese people today—moved here from Nigeria around the A.D. 600s and 700s. Several powerful kingdoms arose in the savannas south of the rain forests. The largest of these was the Kongo.

In the late 1400s, European traders arrived in Central Africa. During the next 300 years, European and African agents enslaved many people from the Congo region. Most of these Africans were transported to the Americas.

The current Democratic Republic of the Congo was once a European colony. It became independent in 1960 and was named Zaire. A harsh dictator named Mobutu Sese Seko ruled Zaire until civil wars in neighboring Rwanda and Burundi sparked a civil war in Zaire. In 1997 Mobutu's government was finally overthrown, and again the country was given a new name. Zaire became the Democratic Republic of the Congo and another dictator took power. In 2002 the country began to set up a representative government and is still working on the transition.

✓ **Reading Check**   What was the Democratic Republic of the Congo formerly called?

Market Day

This marketplace in Kinshasa, Democratic Republic of the Congo, is bustling with activity.

Culture How is this market different from where your family shops? How is it similar?

Cameroon and the Central African Republic

Find Cameroon and the Central African Republic on the map on page 572. These countries lie just north of the Equator. Most people in the Central African Republic and Cameroon farm for a living. A few large plantations raise cacao, cotton, tobacco, and rubber for export. Some people herd livestock in areas that are safe from tsetse flies. A parasite that is often transmitted by the bite of the tsetse (SEET•see) fly causes a deadly disease called sleeping sickness. Turn to page 576 to find out more about sleeping sickness.

These two countries are only beginning to industrialize, or base their economies more on manufacturing and less on farming. Cameroon has had greater success in this effort. It has coastal ports and forest products, petroleum, and bauxite. The Central African Republic can claim only diamond mining as an important industry.

Rural Living

A row of thatch houses stands in a village in rural Democratic Republic of the Congo (right). This village in Gabon (above) boasts a very different type of house.

Culture Why might house styles differ from country to country?

A colony of France from 1910 until 1960, the Central African Republic recognizes French as its official language. Yet most of its people speak Sango, the national language of the Central African Republic. This helps ease communication among the many ethnic groups. Cameroon was divided between the British and the French until 1960. As a result, it uses both English and French as its official languages.

✓ Reading Check   Why has Cameroon had greater success than the Central African Republic in industrializing?

Congo and Gabon

Congo and Gabon both won their independence from France in 1960. A plain stretches along the Atlantic coast of Congo and rises to low mountain ranges and plateaus. Here the Congo River supports most of the country's farmlands and industries. To the north, a large swampy area along the Ubangi River supports dense vine thickets and tropical trees. Both the Ubangi and Congo Rivers provide Congo with hydroelectric power. They also provide access to the Atlantic Ocean for trade and transport.

More than half of Congo's and Gabon's people farm small plots of land. Both countries' economies rely on exports of lumber. They are beginning to depend more on rich offshore oil fields, however, for their main export. Congo also exports diamonds. Gabon suffers from deforestation, or the widespread cutting of too many trees. Gabon also has valuable deposits of manganese and uranium.

Only about 1.3 million people live in Gabon—mainly along rivers or in the coastal capital, **Libreville.** Congo's 3.7 million people generally live along the Atlantic coast or near the capital, **Brazzaville.**

✓ Reading Check   What two exports are most important to Congo and Gabon?

Island Countries

Once a Spanish colony, Equatorial Guinea won its independence in 1968. Equatorial Guinea includes land on the mainland of Africa and five islands. Today the country is home to about 500,000 people. Most live on the mainland, although the capital and largest city—**Malabo** (mah•LAH•boh)—is on the country's largest island.

Farming, fishing, and forestry are the country's main economic activities. For many years, timber and cacao grown in the islands' rich volcanic soil were the main exports. Oil was recently discovered and now leads all other exports.

The island country of São Tomé and Príncipe gained its independence from Portugal in 1975. The Portuguese had first settled here about 300 years earlier. At that time, no people lived on the islands. Today about 200,000 people live here, with almost all of them living on the main island of São Tomé.

São Tomé and Príncipe are volcanic islands. As a result, the soil is rich and productive. Farmers on the islands grow various crops, including coconuts and bananas for export. The biggest export crop is cacao, which is used to make cocoa and chocolate.

✓ **Reading Check** Which of these island countries is also located on the African mainland?

 **FCAT PRACTICE** You can prepare for the FCAT-assessed standards by completing the correlated item(s) below.

Section 1 Assessment

Defining Terms
1. Define canopy, hydroelectric power, tsetse fly, deforestation.

Recalling Facts
2. **Economics** Why has the Democratic Republic of the Congo not been able to take full advantage of its resources? **FCAT LA.A.2.3.1**
3. **Place** How has Cameroon's location helped it prosper?
4. **Economics** What natural resource was recently discovered in Equatorial Guinea?

Critical Thinking
5. **Evaluating Information** Why do you think Europeans wanted to colonize parts of Africa such as the Congo?
6. **Understanding Cause and Effect** How could furniture buyers in the United States affect lumber exports in Central Africa? **FCAT LA.A.2.3.1**

Graphic Organizer
7. **Organizing Information** Complete a chart like this with one fact about each country.

FCAT LA.A.1.3.2

Country	Fact
Democratic Republic of the Congo	
Cameroon	
Central African Republic	
Congo	
Gabon	
Equatorial Guinea	
São Tomé & Príncipe	

 Applying Social Studies Skills

8. **Analyzing Maps** Study the physical map on page 572. The Ubangi River forms part of the boundaries of which countries?

Battling Sleeping Sickness

Since the 1300s, people in Africa south of the Sahara have battled a disease now commonly called sleeping sickness. Yet it was not until the early 1900s that scientists began to understand the disease and that it was transmitted through the bite of an infected tsetse fly.

The Tsetse Fly

Found only in parts of Africa, the tsetse fly is the common name for any of about 21 species of flies that can transmit sleeping sickness. The flies are larger than the houseflies common to the United States. Tsetse flies thrive in forests and in areas of thick shrubbery and trees near lakes, ponds, and rivers.

Although the bite of a tsetse fly is painful, the bite itself is not necessarily harmful. What gives the tsetse fly its dreadful reputation is the disease-causing parasite it may carry.

FCAT PRACTICE Answering question 3 below will help you prepare for the **FCAT Reading** test.

Sleeping Sickness

The World Health Organization (WHO) estimates that more than 60 million people in Africa are at risk of being infected with sleeping sickness. As many as 500,000 people carry the disease. If left untreated, the disease leads to a slow breakdown of bodily functions and, eventually, death. Sleeping sickness is not always fatal. When the disease is treated in its early stages, most people recover. Treatment is expensive, however, and many of those infected lack medical care. Even if they are cured, they may become infected again.

Governments Work Together

Preventing the spread of sleeping sickness requires a united action on the part of the governments of the many African nations affected by the disease. Thirty-seven African countries lie within the African tsetse belt. This belt covers a total of more than 6 million square miles (10 million sq. km) in an area stretching from Senegal to South Africa. African leaders have met in conferences and passed a resolution to get rid of tsetse flies from the continent. Perhaps working together to fight a common enemy will encourage the governments to consult on other regional issues as well.

▶ Making the Connection

1. Where do tsetse flies live?

2. What causes sleeping sickness?

3. **Drawing Conclusions** Why is treatment of infected humans only part of the solution to eliminating sleeping sickness? **FCAT LA.A.2.3.1**

◀ **Children in Central Africa have learned to report bites of the tsetse fly.**

People of Kenya and Tanzania

Guide to Reading

Main Idea

Kenya and Tanzania are countries in East Africa with diverse landscapes and peoples.

Terms to Know

- coral reef
- poaching
- free enterprise system
- cassava
- sisal
- habitat
- ecotourist

Reading Strategy

Create a chart like this one. Then list facts about the land, economy, and people of Kenya and Tanzania.

FCAT LA.A.1.3.2

Fact	Kenya	Tanzania
Land		
Economy		
People		

The following are the major Sunshine State Standards covered in this section.

SS.A.3.3.1:
Understands ways in which cultural characteristics have been transmitted from one society to another (e.g., through art, architecture, language, other artifacts, traditions, beliefs, values, and behaviors)

SS.A.3.3.5:
Understands the differences between institutions of Eastern and Western civilizations (e.g., differences in governments, social traditions and customs, economic systems and religious institutions)

NATIONAL GEOGRAPHIC Exploring Our World

The Masai (mah•SY) are one of Kenya's many ethnic groups. Rituals have shaped their lives for hundreds of years. Young men take part in an important four-day ceremony. When it ends, they become elders and help make group decisions. In the ceremony, elders tell them, "Drop your weapons and use your head and wisdom instead."

Both traditional and modern cultures meet in the East African country of **Kenya.** The Masai follow ways of life similar to their ancestors, whereas city dwellers live in apartments and work in offices.

Kenya

Kenya is about two times the size of Nevada. The country's Indian Ocean coastline has stretches of white beaches lined with palm trees. Offshore lies a **coral reef,** a natural formation at or near the water's surface that is made of the skeletons of small sea animals. In the central part of the country, lions, elephants, rhinoceroses, and other wildlife roam an upland plain. Millions of acres are set aside by the government to protect plants and wildlife. Still, in recent years there has been heavy **poaching,** or the illegal hunting of protected animals.

In the western part of the country are highlands and the **Great Rift Valley.** This valley is really a fault—a crack in the earth's crust.

(See the photo on page 40.) The Great Rift Valley begins in southeastern Africa and stretches about 3,000 miles (4,825 km) north to the Red Sea. Lakes have formed in many places, and volcanoes also dot the area. One of them—**Mt. Kenya**—rises 17,058 feet (5,199 m) high. It is in the Great Rift Valley that fossils of early human ancestors have been found. These fossils date back about 4 million years.

Kenya's Economy Kenya has a developing economy based on a **free enterprise system.** This means that people can start and run businesses with limited government involvement. Kenya's capital, **Nairobi** (ny•ROH•bee), has become a center of business for all of East Africa. The city's good transportation and communications systems have encouraged foreign companies to set up regional headquarters here.

Many Kenyans remain poor, however. Farmers raise corn, bananas, cassava, and sweet potatoes. **Cassava** is a plant whose roots are ground to make porridge. Some larger farms raise coffee and tea for export. In recent years, corrupt practices of government officials have hurt the economy.

One of the fastest-growing industries in Kenya is tourism. Thousands of tourists visit each year. Visitors often take tours called safaris in

FCAT
PRACTICE

Completing the exercise below will help you prepare for the **FCAT Reading** test.

Literature

A CHANGING KENYA

As developing countries modernize, traditional ways of life often change. In the following poem, Kenyan poet and playwright Micere Githae Mugo expresses the challenge of living in a changing world.

WHERE ARE THOSE SONGS?
by Micere Githae Mugo

Where are those songs
my mother and yours
always sang
fitting rhythms
to the whole
vast span of life?
. . . .
I have forgotten
my mother's song
my children
will never know.

This I remember:
Mother always said
sing child sing
make a song
and sing
beat out your own rhythms
the rhythms of your life
but make the song soulful
and make life
sing
. . . .

From "Where are those Songs" by Micere G. Mugo. Reprinted by permission of the author.

Analyzing Literature

What do you think the poet's mother meant when she said to "beat out your own rhythms"? **FCAT** LA.A.2.3.2

jeeps and buses to see the country's wildlife in its natural surroundings.

History and Government In the A.D. 700s, Arab traders from Southwest Asia settled along the East African coast. As Arab culture blended with African, the Swahili language eventually emerged. The name *Swahili* comes from an Arabic word meaning "of the coast." The language has features of several African languages, as well as Arabic. Today Kenya's two official languages are Swahili and English.

The British made Kenya a colony in 1920 after World War I. They took land from the Africans and set up farms to grow coffee and tea for export. By the 1940s, Kenya's African groups, such as the Mau Mau, fought in violent civil wars to end British rule. Kenya finally won its independence in 1963 and became a republic. The country's first president, Jomo Kenyatta (JOH•moh kehn•YAHT•uh), won respect as an early leader in Africa's movement for freedom. Under Kenyatta, Kenya enjoyed economic prosperity and had a stable government. In recent years, the economy has weakened. In response, many Kenyans have demanded democratic changes.

Kenya Today Kenya's roughly 31 million people are divided among 40 different ethnic groups. The Kikuyu (kee•KOO•yoo) people are Kenya's main group, making up almost one-fourth of the population. Most Kenyans live in rural areas where they struggle to grow crops. Many people have moved to cities in search of a better life.

The people of Kenya believe in *harambee,* which means "pulling together." The spirit of *harambee* has led the different ethnic groups to build schools and clinics in their communities. They have raised money to send good students to universities.

About one-third of Kenya's people live in cities. Nairobi is the largest city, with about 2.3 million people. **Mombasa** (mohm•BAH•sah) is Kenya's chief port on the Indian Ocean. This city has the best harbor in East Africa, making it an ideal site for oceangoing trade.

✓ Reading Check What city is Kenya's chief port?

Tanzania

Tourists flock to Tanzania's **Serengeti** (SEHR•uhn•GEH•tee) **Plain.** It is famous for its wildlife preserve, huge grasslands, and patches of trees and shrubs. To the north, near the Kenyan border, a snowcapped

NATIONAL GEOGRAPHIC **On Location**

Nairobi, Kenya

Like most cities, Kenya's capital has crowded markets, high-rise office buildings, and elegant mansions. Many city workers maintain close ties to relatives in the countryside.

Place About how many people live in Nairobi?

Central and East Africa: Political

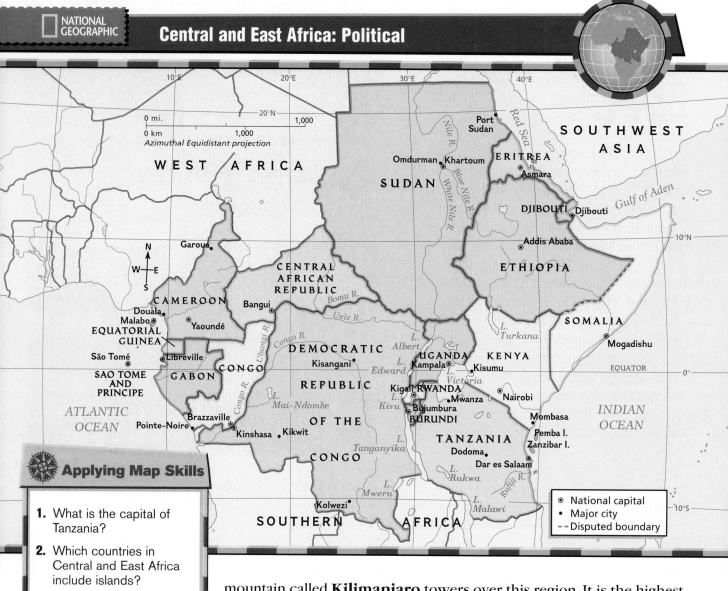

Azimuthal Equidistant projection

National capital
Major city
-- Disputed boundary

Applying Map Skills

1. What is the capital of Tanzania?

2. Which countries in Central and East Africa include islands?

Find NGS online map resources @ www.nationalgeographic.com/maps

mountain called **Kilimanjaro** towers over this region. It is the highest point in Africa. The Great Rift Valley cuts two gashes through Tanzania, one in the center of the country and the other along the western border. Unusual fish swim in the deep, dark waters of Lake Tanganyika (TAN•guhn•YEE•kuh). Lake Victoria, also in Tanzania, is Africa's largest lake and one of the sources of the Nile River.

Tanzania's Economy   More than 80 percent of all Tanzanians work in farming or herding. Important export crops are coffee and sisal, a plant fiber used to make rope and twine. Do you enjoy eating baked ham? If so, you might have tasted the spice called cloves, often used to flavor ham. The islands of Zanzibar and Pemba, off the coast of Tanzania, produce more cloves than any other place in the world.

Tourism is a fast-growing industry in Tanzania. The government has set aside several national parks to protect the habitats of the country's wildlife. A habitat is the type of environment in which a particular animal species lives. Serengeti National Park covers about 5,600 square miles (14,504 sq. km). Lions and wild dogs hunt among thousands of zebras, wildebeests, and antelopes. The park attracts many ecotourists, or people who travel to another country to view its natural wonders.

Tanzania's leaders are also taking steps to preserve farmland. In recent years, many trees have been cut down. Without trees, the land cannot hold soil or rainwater in place. As a result, the land dries out, and soil blows away. To prevent the land from becoming desert, the government of Tanzania has announced a new policy. For every tree that is cut down, five new trees should be planted.

History and Government In 1964 the island country of Zanzibar united with the former German colony of Tanganyika to form Tanzania. Since then, Tanzania has been one of Africa's more politically stable republics. During the 1960s, Tanzania's socialist government controlled the economy. By the 1990s, however, it had moved toward a free enterprise system. In taking this step, Tanzania's leaders hoped to improve the economy and reduce poverty. Meanwhile, the government also moved toward more democratic elections with more than one political party.

Culture Tanzania's 35.4 million people include more than 120 different ethnic groups. Each group has its own language, but most people also speak Swahili. The two main religions are Christianity and Islam. Tanzanian music and dance dominate much of East Africa's culture. In **Dar es Salaam,** Tanzania's capital, you can hear strong rhythms and Swahili lyrics performed by local dance bands.

✓ Reading Check What is Tanzania doing to preserve farmland?

I Am a Samburu
Nimfa Lekuuk is a member of the Samburu of northern Kenya. The word *Samburu* means "the people with the white goats." Nimfa wears the traditional clothes of Samburu women. She is in standard 7 now. "Standard" is the Kenyans' term for *grade.* She studies language, math, history, geography, science, arts and crafts, and religions.

FCAT PRACTICE You can prepare for the FCAT-assessed standards by completing the correlated item(s) below.

Section 2 Assessment

Defining Terms

1. Define coral reef, poaching, free enterprise system, cassava, sisal, habitat, ecotourist.

Recalling Facts

2. Place Describe the Great Rift Valley.

3. Culture What are Kenya's official languages?

4. Culture What are the two major religions of Tanzania?

Critical Thinking

5. Making Inferences Why might two countries such as Tanganyika and Zanzibar unite? FCAT LA.A.1.3.2

6. Drawing Conclusions Why would the government of Tanzania put so much effort into preserving its national parks?

FCAT LA.A.2.3.1

Graphic Organizer

7. Organizing Information Review the information about the history and government of Kenya. Then, on a time line like the one below, label four important events and their dates in Kenya's history. FCAT LA.A.1.3.2

Applying Social Studies Skills

8. Analyzing Maps Study the political map on page 580. Name the four bodies of water that border Tanzania. On which body of water is Dar es Salaam located?

Uganda, Rwanda, and Burundi

NATIONAL GEOGRAPHIC Exploring Our World

If you walk through the mountain rain forests of Rwanda, you might feel you are being watched. Who's watching you? It could be one of the world's 600 remaining gorillas—the rarest and largest of the great apes. Every day these gorillas face the threat of death from poachers, loss of their habitat, disease, and civil war.

West of Kenya and Tanzania lie **Uganda, Rwanda,** and **Burundi.** All three are landlocked—they have no land touching a sea or an ocean. Instead, they use three large lakes for transportation and trade.

Uganda

Once called "the pearl of Africa," Uganda is a fertile, green land of mountains, lakes, and wild animals. About the size of Oregon, the country consists mainly of a central plateau. South of the plateau is **Lake Victoria.** Although Uganda lies on the Equator, temperatures are mild because of the country's high elevation.

Uganda's rich soil and plentiful rain make the land good for farming. About 80 percent of Uganda's workers are employed in agriculture. The map on page 583 shows that most farmers work on subsistence farms. They grow **plantains**—a kind of banana—cassava, potatoes, corn, and grains. Some plantations grow coffee, cotton, and tea for export. Coffee makes up nearly three-fourths of Uganda's exports. Uganda's few factories make cement, soap, sugar, metal, and shoes.

The Ugandans Uganda's 25.3 million people live mainly in rural villages in the southern part of the country. **Kampala,** the capital, lies on the shores of Lake Victoria, making it a port city for local trade.

About two-thirds of Ugandans are Christians. The remaining one-third practice Islam or traditional African religions. At one time there were large numbers of Hindus and Sikhs from South Asia living in the country. A dictator, Idi Amin, drove them out in 1972. Recently, the Ugandan government has invited them back, and many have returned.

Ugandans belong to more than 40 different ethnic groups. They have a rich cultural heritage of songs, folktales, and poems. In the past, these were passed only by word of mouth from one generation to the next. Today this heritage is also preserved in books. Traditions are also reflected in the Ugandans' diet. Meals often include beans, beef, goat, mutton, cornmeal, and a variety of tropical fruits.

History and Government For much of the 1900s, the British ruled Uganda. After Uganda won its freedom in 1962, fighting broke out among ethnic groups. Under their kings, these ethnic groups had enjoyed autonomy, or self-government, in their local territories. These kings lost power in 1967, and the ethnic regions were tightly bound to the central government. The dictator Idi Amin's cruel rule

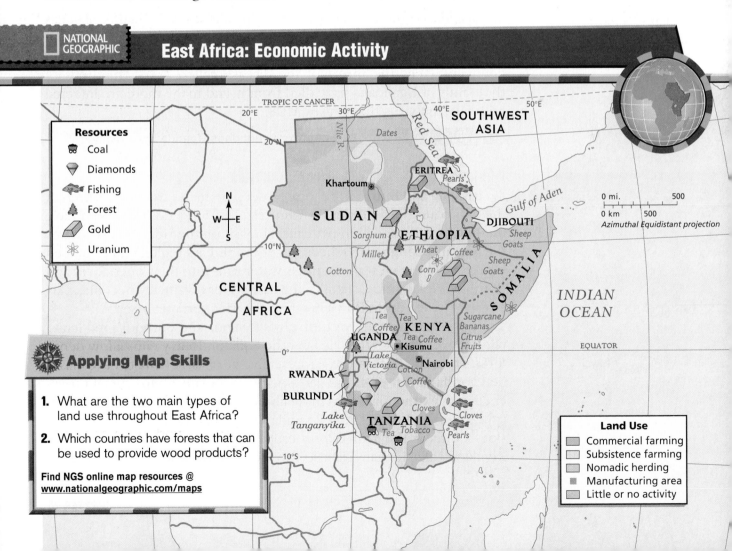

NATIONAL GEOGRAPHIC

East Africa: Economic Activity

Applying Map Skills

1. What are the two main types of land use throughout East Africa?

2. Which countries have forests that can be used to provide wood products?

Find NGS online map resources @ www.nationalgeographic.com/maps

Kampala, Uganda

Public transportation in Kampala includes passenger boats on Lake Victoria.

Region Which countries border Lake Victoria?

hurt Uganda throughout much of the 1970s. Since the mid-1990s, the national government has allowed ethnic groups to once again have kings, but only as local ceremonial leaders.

Uganda's economy has recently seen solid growth. Uganda also has a stable government. It is a republic with an elected president and legislature. Still, the future is clouded. Uganda, along with other African countries, faces the threat of the disease called AIDS. Hundreds of thousands of Ugandans have died from it, and many more are infected with HIV, the virus that causes AIDS.

✓ **Reading Check** What kind of government does Uganda have today?

Rwanda and Burundi

Rwanda and Burundi are located deep in inland East Africa. Each of the two countries is about the same size as Maryland. They both have mountains, hills, and high plateaus. They sit on the ridge that separates the Nile and Congo watersheds. A **watershed** is a region that is drained by a river. To the west of the ridge, water runs into the Congo River and flows to the Atlantic Ocean. To the east, water eventually becomes part of the Nile River and flows north to the Mediterranean Sea.

As in Uganda, high elevation gives Rwanda and Burundi a moderate climate even though they lie near the Equator. Heavy rains allow dense forests to grow. Within these forests live gorillas. Scientists have classified gorillas as an **endangered species**—a plant or an animal threatened with extinction. Learn more about protecting gorillas on page 76.

Farmers in Burundi and Rwanda work small plots that dot the hillsides. Coffee is the main export crop. The people who live along Lake Kivu and Lake Tanganyika also fish. Because Burundi and Rwanda are landlocked, they have trouble getting their goods to foreign buyers. Few paved roads and no railroads exist. Most goods must be transported by road to Lake Tanganyika, where boats take them to Tanzania or the Democratic Republic of the Congo. Another route is by dirt road to Tanzania and then by rail to Dar es Salaam.

Ethnic Conflict   Rwanda and Burundi have large populations and small areas. As a result, they are among the most densely populated countries in Africa. Rwanda, for example, has an average of 817 people per square mile (315 per sq. km). Yet only 5 percent of the people live in cities.

Two ethnic groups—the Hutu and the Tutsi—form most of the population of Rwanda and Burundi. The Hutu make up 80 percent or more of the population in both countries, but the Tutsi traditionally controlled the governments and economies. A constant power struggle between these two groups erupted into a full-scale civil war and genocide in the 1990s. **Genocide** is the deliberate murder of a group of people because of their race or culture. A Hutu-led government in Rwanda killed hundreds of thousands of Tutsi people. Two million more became **refugees,** or people who flee to another country to escape persecution or disaster. The fighting between the Hutu and Tutsi has lessened, but both countries face many challenges as they try to rebuild with the help and cooperation of the international community.

✓ Reading Check   **Which ethnic group makes up the majority of the population in Rwanda and Burundi?**

FCAT PRACTICE   You can prepare for the FCAT-assessed standards by completing the correlated item(s) below.

Assessment

Defining Terms

1. **Define** plantains, autonomy, watershed, endangered species, genocide, refugee.

Recalling Facts

2. **Location** Explain the factors that affect Uganda's climate.

3. **Place** What is the capital of Uganda?

4. **Region** What endangered species lives in the forests of Rwanda and Burundi?

Critical Thinking

5. **Understanding Cause and Effect** How could a deadly epidemic, such as AIDS, affect a country's economy? **FCAT LA.A.2.3.1**

6. **Analyzing Information** How have ethnic differences created problems for Uganda, Rwanda, and Burundi? **FCAT LA.A.2.3.1**

Graphic Organizer

7. **Organizing Information** Draw a diagram like the one below. Then write two facts about Uganda under each of the category headings in the outer ovals. **FCAT LA.A.1.3.2**

People — Uganda — Economy
History

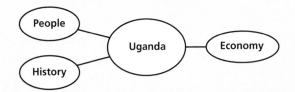

Applying Social Studies Skills

8. **Analyzing Maps** Study the economic activity map on page 583. Which countries in East Africa have gold resources?

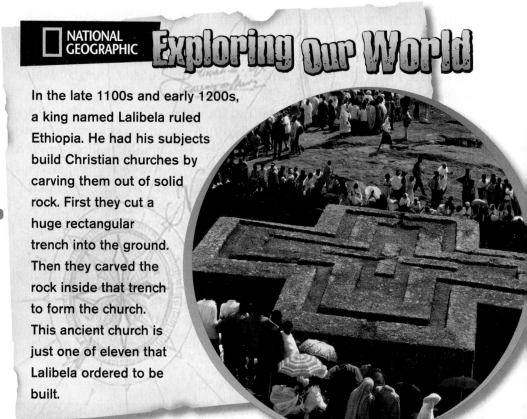

NATIONAL GEOGRAPHIC Exploring Our World

In the late 1100s and early 1200s, a king named Lalibela ruled Ethiopia. He had his subjects build Christian churches by carving them out of solid rock. First they cut a huge rectangular trench into the ground. Then they carved the rock inside that trench to form the church. This ancient church is just one of eleven that Lalibela ordered to be built.

The northern part of East Africa is a region called the Horn of Africa. This region got its name because it is shaped like a horn that juts out into the Indian Ocean. The countries here are **Sudan, Ethiopia, Eritrea** (EHR•uh•TREE•uh), **Djibouti** (jih•BOO•tee), and **Somalia.**

Sudan

Sudan is the largest country in Africa—about one-third the size of the continental United States. The northern part is covered by the sand dunes of the Sahara and Nubian Desert. Nomads raise camels and goats here. The most fertile part of the country is the central region. In this area of grassy plains, the two main tributaries of the Nile River—the **Blue Nile River** and the **White Nile River**—join together at **Khartoum** (kahr•TOOM), Sudan's capital. The southern part of Sudan receives plenty of rain and has some fertile soil. It also holds one of the world's largest swamps, which drains into the White Nile.

Most of Sudan's people live along the Nile River or one of its tributaries. They use water from the Nile to irrigate their fields. Farmers grow sugarcane, grains, nuts, dates, and cotton—the country's leading export. Sheep and gold are other important exports. Recently discovered oil fields in the south offer another possibility of income.

Sudan's Past and Present   In ancient times, Sudan was the center of a powerful civilization called Kush. The people of Kush had close cultural and trade ties with the Egyptians to the north. Kushites traded metal tools for cotton and other goods from India, Arabia, and China. They built a great capital at Meroë (MAR•oh•EE). It had huge temples, stone palaces, and small pyramids. Kush began to lose power around A.D. 350.

During the A.D. 500s, missionaries from Egypt brought Christianity to the region. About 900 years later, Muslim Arabs entered northern Sudan and converted its people to Islam. From the late 1800s to the 1950s, the British and the Egyptians together ruled the country. Sudan became an independent nation in 1956. Since then, military leaders have generally taken over.

In the 1980s, the government began a "reign of terror" against the southern Christian peoples. The fighting has disrupted the economy and caused widespread hunger, especially in the south. A recent drought—a long period of extreme dryness and water shortages—made the situation

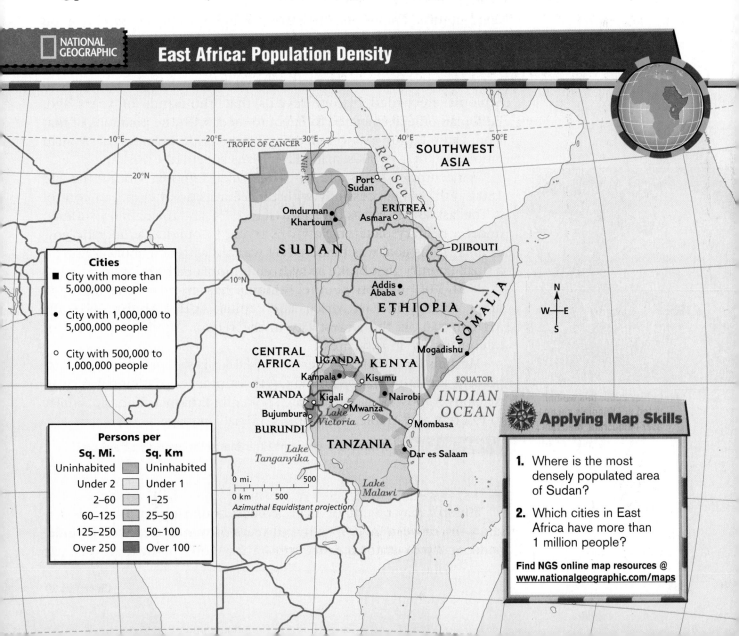

East Africa: Population Density

NATIONAL GEOGRAPHIC

Cities

■ City with more than 5,000,000 people

● City with 1,000,000 to 5,000,000 people

○ City with 500,000 to 1,000,000 people

Persons per

Sq. Mi.		Sq. Km
Uninhabited		Uninhabited
Under 2		Under 1
2–60		1–25
60–125		25–50
125–250		50–100
Over 250		Over 100

0 mi. 500
0 km 500
Azimuthal Equidistant projection

Applying Map Skills

1. Where is the most densely populated area of Sudan?

2. Which cities in East Africa have more than 1 million people?

Find NGS online map resources @ www.nationalgeographic.com/maps

worse. Millions have starved to death, and major outbreaks of diseases have swept through the country. The war continues despite occasional peace talks aimed at granting the south greater independence. The **TIME Reports** feature on pages 591–597 looks at Sudanese refugees.

✓ Reading Check What is the main export of Sudan?

Ethiopia

Landlocked Ethiopia is almost twice the size of Texas. Ethiopia's landscape varies from hot lowlands to rugged mountains. The central part of Ethiopia is a highland plateau sliced through by the Great Rift Valley. The valley forms deep river gorges and sparkling waterfalls. Mild temperatures and good soil make the highlands Ethiopia's best farming region. Farmers raise grains, sugarcane, potatoes, and coffee. Coffee is a major export crop. The southern highlands are believed to be the world's original home of coffee.

Rain is not consistent in many parts of Ethiopia. Low rainfall can lead to drought, and then Ethiopia's people suffer. In the 1980s, a drought caused famine, which attracted the world's attention. At that time, a drought turned fields once rich in crops into seas of dust. Despite food aid, more than 1 million Ethiopians died from starvation and disease.

Ethiopia's History and People Scientists have found what they believe to be the remains of the oldest known human ancestors in Ethiopia. Recorded history reveals that, thousands of years ago, Ethiopian officials traveled to Egypt to meet with the pharaohs of that land. Later, Ethiopia developed important trade links to the Roman Empire. In the A.D. 300s, many Ethiopians accepted Christianity.

For centuries, kings and emperors ruled Ethiopia. During the late 1800s, Ethiopia successfully withstood European attempts to control it. The last emperor was overthrown in 1974, and the country suffered under a military dictator. Now it is trying to build a democratic government. This goal was hindered by warfare with neighboring Eritrea, a small country that broke away from Ethiopia in 1993.

With 70.7 million people, Ethiopia has more people than any other country in East Africa. The capital, **Addis Ababa** (AH•dihs AH•bah•BAH), is the largest city in the region. About 85 percent of Ethiopians live in rural areas.

Muslims form about 45 percent of Ethiopia's population. About 40 percent are Ethiopian Orthodox. Others practice traditional African religions. Almost 80 languages are spoken in Ethiopia. Amharic, similar to Hebrew and Arabic, is Ethiopia's official language.

✓ Reading Check What crisis brought Ethiopia to the world's attention?

▲ In May 2000, this woman voted in Ethiopia's second-ever democratic election.

Eritrea

Ethiopia may be one of Africa's oldest countries, but Eritrea is certainly the newest. In 1993, after 30 years of war, Eritrea won its independence from Ethiopia. Eritrea sits on the shores of the Red Sea. It has

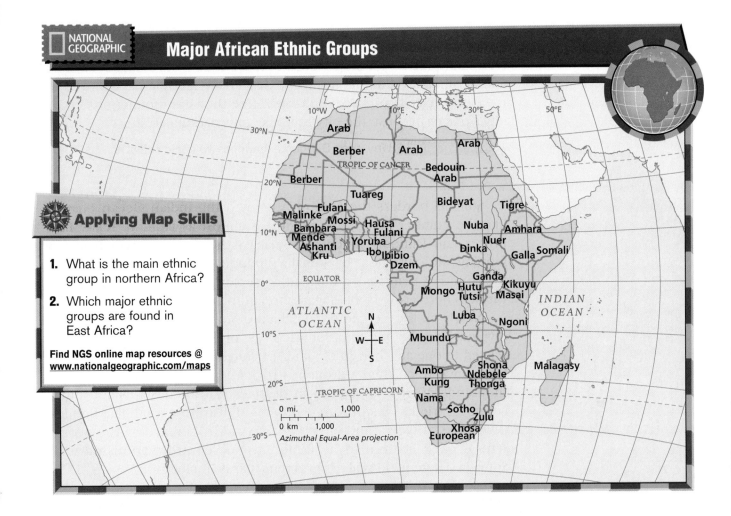

Applying Map Skills

1. What is the main ethnic group in northern Africa?

2. Which major ethnic groups are found in East Africa?

Find NGS online map resources @ www.nationalgeographic.com/maps

a narrow plain that stretches about 600 miles (966 km) along the coast. When Eritrea became a country, Ethiopia became landlocked.

Most of Eritrea's 4.4 million people farm. Farming here is uncertain work because the climate is dry. The long war with Ethiopia also hurt farming. The war did have a positive effect on some of Eritrea's people, however. Women formed about one-third of the army that won the war. After the war ended, the new government passed laws that gave women more rights than they ever had before.

✓ **Reading Check** When and from what country did Eritrea win independence?

Djibouti

Evidence that the earth is undergoing change can be seen in Djibouti. This country lies at the northern tip of the Great Rift Valley, where three of the earth's plates join. **Plates** are huge slabs of rock that make up the earth's crust. In Djibouti, two of these plates are pulling away from each other. As they separate, fiery hot rock rises to the earth's surface, causing volcanic activity.

Djibouti wraps around a natural harbor at the point where the Red Sea meets the Gulf of Aden. This tiny country is one of the hottest, driest places on the earth. Its landscape is covered by rocky desert. Here and there, you will find the desert interrupted by salt lakes and rare patches of grassland.

Djibouti's 700,000 people are mostly Muslims. In the past, they lived a nomadic life of herding. Because of Djibouti's dry climate, farming and herding are difficult. In recent years, many people have moved to the capital city, also called **Djibouti.** Here they have found jobs in the city's docks, because the city is a busy international seaport.

✓ **Reading Check** Why does Djibouti experience volcanic activity?

Somalia

Somalia borders the Gulf of Aden and the Indian Ocean. Shaped like the number seven, the country is almost as large as Texas. Like Eritrea and Djibouti, much of Somalia is hot and dry, which makes farming difficult. Most of Somalia's people are nomadic herders on the country's plateaus. In the south, rivers provide water for irrigation. Farmers here grow fruits, sugarcane, and bananas.

Nearly all the people of Somalia are Muslims, but they are deeply divided. They belong to different clans, or groups of people who are related to one another. In the late 1980s, disputes between these clans led to civil war. When a drought struck a few years later, hundreds of thousands of people starved to death. The United States and other countries tried to restore some order and distribute food. The fighting continued, however, and often kept the aid from reaching the people who needed it. Even today, armed groups control various parts of Somalia. There is no real government that is in charge.

✓ **Reading Check** What kind of conflict led to civil war in Somalia?

FCAT PRACTICE You can prepare for the FCAT-assessed standards by completing the correlated item(s) below.

Assessment

Defining Terms

1. **Define** plate, clan.

Recalling Facts

2. **Place** What is the capital of Ethiopia?

3. **History** What is the only country of East Africa that was never colonized by Europeans?

4. **Government** Describe the current political situation in Somalia. **FCAT LA.B.1.3.2**

Critical Thinking

5. **Making Inferences** What factors do you think might have led to the settlement of Khartoum, Sudan's capital? **FCAT LA.A.1.3.2**

6. **Understanding Cause and Effect** How did a war bring increased rights to women in Eritrea? **FCAT LA.E.2.2.1**

Graphic Organizer

7. **Organizing Information** On a diagram like the one below, list the major religions practiced in countries of the Horn of Africa. Write the religions under each country's name. **FCAT LA.A.1.3.2**

Sudan — Religions — Ethiopia

Djibouti — Religions — Somalia

Applying Social Studies Skills

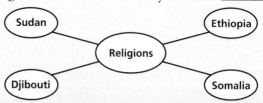

8. **Analyzing Maps** Study the ethnic groups map on page 589. What major ethnic groups are found in the Horn of Africa?

TIME PERSPECTIVES

EXPLORING WORLD ISSUES

Refugees On the Move

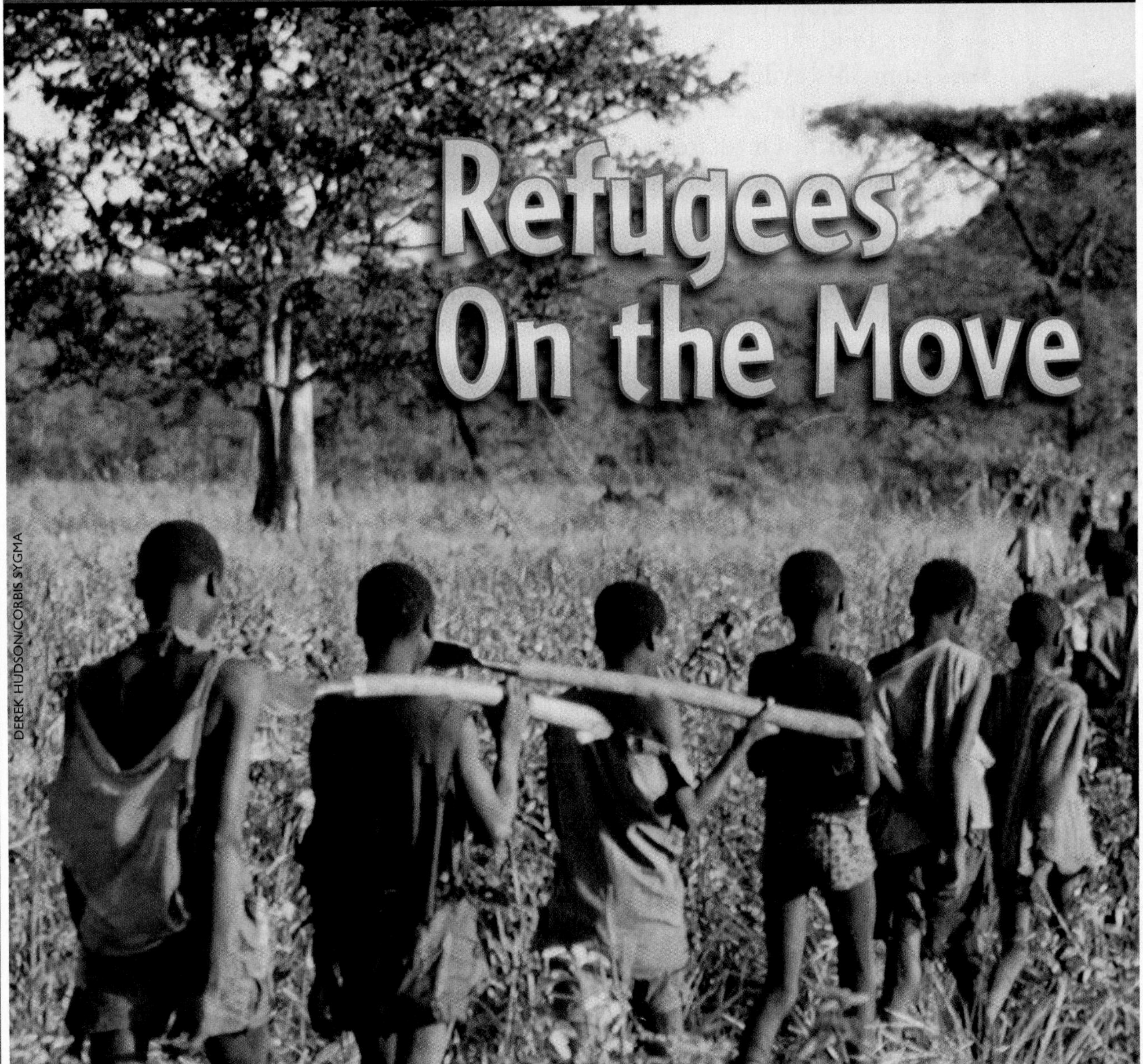

DEREK HUDSON/CORBIS SYGMA

The Lost Boys of Sudan

Compiled and adapted from TIME.

EXPLORING WORLD ISSUES

At a refugee camp, boys collected sticks and reeds to make huts, then cooked a rare meal of beans.

The Lost Boys of Sudan

Evaluating Media
LA.A.2.3.6

In November 1987, William Deng was tending cattle several miles from his village in southern Sudan. Two brothers and some cousins were with him. One afternoon they heard distant gunfire but ignored it. "The next morning," William said, "we saw the smoke. I climbed a tree and saw that my whole village was burned."

They raced to the village. There they learned that government troops had swept through. "Nobody was left standing," William said. "Some were wounded; some were killed. My father was dead. So we just ran away. I was 5."

The boys headed toward Ethiopia. Crossing marshlands and desert, they joined thousands of other Sudanese, mostly boys. They walked for two months. They ate berries, dried leaves, birds, and mice—anything they could find. Thousands died. "You think that maybe later that will be you," said one boy.

Into Ethiopia

The survivors finally reached a refugee camp in Ethiopia. **Refugees** are people forced by fear to find refuge, or shelter, outside their countries.

In 1991 Ethiopia closed its camps. Soldiers forced all of the "Lost Boys of Sudan," as they came to be called, back to their homeland.

After a year in Sudan, 10,000 of the boys fled to a refugee camp in Kenya. And there they stayed—some for as long as 10 years.

All Too Common

Sadly, William's experience is not unique. Throughout Africa south of the Sahara, millions of people have had to flee their homes. Most live in crowded camps set up by groups such as the United Nations. There they wait—until it is safe to go home, or until another country lets them stay.

Africans on the Move

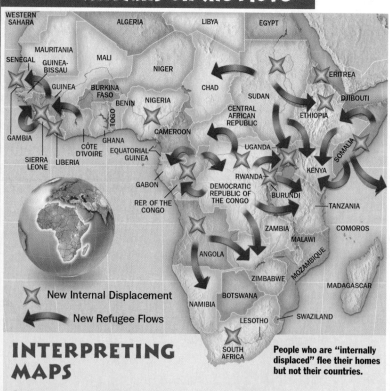

✡ New Internal Displacement

← New Refugee Flows

People who are "internally displaced" flee their homes but not their countries.

INTERPRETING MAPS

Comparing and Contrasting What do Nigeria, Eritrea, and South Africa have in common?

Older boys "adopted" younger ones.

Some drew on clay.

The youngest wore the faces of suffering.

TOP PHOTOS: DEREK HUDSON/CORBIS SYGMA

The Lost Boys are victims of a Sudanese civil war that began in 1983. U.S. president George W. Bush explained in 2001, "Some 2 million Sudanese have lost their lives; 4 million more have lost their homes." The Sudan, he concluded, is a "disaster area for human rights."

Human rights include the right to safety, to food, and to shelter, among other things. In democracies, they also include the rights of citizens to choose their own leaders and to express opinions that are different from the government's.

Defining Refugees' Rights

In 1951, members of the United Nations agreed to guarantee basic human rights to refugees. They signed a **convention,** or special document, that gives refugees a unique legal status, or position. That status gives them the right to **asylum,** or safety, in foreign countries. It also gives them the right to be treated like any other foreign resident of their host country.

The convention defines refugees as people who leave their countries to flee **persecution.** Persecution is unfair treatment based on such characteristics as race, religion, or ethnic background. Recently the United Nations expanded this definition. Today people whose governments can't protect them from the dangers of war are also entitled to refugee status, the UN says.

The boys made huts to protect themselves from rain and wild animals.

DEREK HUDSON/CORBIS SYGMA

EXPLORING THE ISSUE

1. **Drawing Conclusions** Why do you think thousands of the Lost Boys traveled together instead of alone?
   FCAT LA.A.1.3.2
2. **Making Predictions** How might your life change if you no longer had the basic human rights listed here?
   FCAT LA.A.2.3.1

Environmental Refugees

People who flee natural disasters, such as floods and famines, aren't refugees. They are "displaced persons" or "environmental refugees." Immigrants aren't refugees, either. Immigrants may leave their countries to get an education or find a better job. Refugees like the Lost Boys of Sudan have little choice. They flee their countries to find safety. ■

Africa's Troubled Past

Evaluating
Media
LA.A.2.3.6

Refugees have existed in many places, not only countries in Africa. Yet rarely has the flow of refugees been as widespread as it is today. Worldwide, about 35 million people were on the move in 2002. Nearly 22 million of them were **internally displaced persons (IDPs)**—people who flee to safety inside their own countries. About 13 million more were refugees seeking freedom from war and persecution outside their countries. During 2002, Africa alone held more than 3 million refugees and at least 11 million IDPs.

The Impact of Violence

The presence of these uprooted people is reshaping Africa. Away from their villages, refugees no longer grow crops, worsening food shortages. The crush of refugees drains the resources of the already poor countries that host them. And refugees sometimes spread AIDS, a disease that by 2001 had killed the parents of 12 million African children.

Many experts trace Africa's refugee problem back to the late 1800s. That's when European nations began to carve the continent into colonies. Africa's

▲ War chased thousands of terrified Burundians into the Congo in 1995.

ELIZABETH L. GILBERT/CORBIS SYGMA

2,000 ethnic groups speak around one thousand languages. But European colonizers failed to respect those differences. They set up boundaries that split individual ethnic groups into many pieces. Other borders forced traditional enemies such as Rwanda's Hutu and Tutsi to share the same space.

How America Is Different

Colonists living in Britain's 13 colonies didn't face such problems in 1776. When the U.S. was born, most Americans spoke English and shared similar values. They were ready to rule themselves as a democracy.

Africa's colonies became independent nearly two centuries later. But they contained groups that had little interest in working together. That made it hard for democracy to take root. In many nations, armed groups muscled their way to power. Such struggles for control turned millions of Africans into refugees. ■

EXPLORING THE ISSUE

1. **Making Inferences** In what ways might Africa's refugee problem hurt all Africans? **FCAT** LA.A.1.3.2

2. **Analyzing Information** How might the refugee problem keep governments from building roads and providing services such as education and health care?
FCAT LA.A.2.3.1

Struggling to Survive

When refugees enter another country, they may face dangers. In 1997, for example, soldiers rounded up refugees who had lived many years in Tanzania. They forced the refugees into camps. "I never thought the Tanzanian government would do this to us," said a woman who fled Burundi in 1971. "I am now held in a refugee camp, but my children are still outside. They have no money to come here."

Even refugees allowed to stay in private homes face risks. "We are frequently arrested by the police," said an Ethiopian who fled to Kenya. "They require bribes before they will release us."

Refugee Children

For children, refugee life brings special problems. Those separated from their parents must fend for themselves. Some girls and boys are forced to become soldiers. Others must work for little or no pay. Abby, 14, fled the war in Sierra Leone. Now she lives in a refugee camp in Guinea. "In the morning," she said, "I fetch water, sweep, and pray. Then I go find a job for the day. I usually pound rice. I get no food, only [a tiny amount of money]. I will be in the sun until evening. I feel pain all over my body. I don't go to school. I live with my grandmother, and she is very old. I need to take care of her."

Many of the overcrowded camps are dirty and unhealthy. But until their countries become safe again, the refugees have few choices. Either they stay in the camps, or they return home to the horrors they fled. ▨

AFP PHOTO/NEWSCOM

▲
A Hutu woman and child walk to a refugee camp near the Rwanda-Tanzania border.

EXPLORING THE ISSUE

1. Drawing Conclusions What do you think makes many refugee camps so difficult to live in?
`FCAT LA.A.2.3.1`

2. Problem Solving Gather information from the text to identify problems faced by refugees in camps. Consider changes that might be made to the camps to improve life there. `FCAT LA.A.2.3.1`

Helping Refugees: What Can One Person Do?

Evaluating Media
LA.A.2.3.6

Countries that offer asylum to refugees are known as **host countries.** Starting life over in a host country can be hard for refugees and their families. William Deng and Joseph Maker are among more than 3,000 Lost Boys of Sudan who have found refuge in the United States. William lives in Grand Rapids, Michigan. Joseph lives in Houston, Texas, as do 170 other Lost Boys. In both places, local people taught them how to take buses, shop, and even use faucets and refrigerators. Many of those helpers were volunteers.

Eventually, many refugees who get such help grow to love their adopted country. They come to love it as much as or even more than people born there. ▨

◀ These Michigan second graders are learning English at school.

Strangers in a New Land

Joseph Maker and fellow Lost Boys felt they had landed on another planet when they reached Houston, their new home. They had to be taught to use electricity, running water, air conditioners, flush toilets, stoves, and telephones.

Packaged foods baffled them. At the refugee camp in Kenya, they had eaten the same meal—beans and lentils—every day for nine years. In Houston they discovered junk food—and the fear of getting fat. "I've heard in America, people can become big," said Joseph's friend James Thon Aleer.

The newcomers also had to learn new ways to act. In Sudan, it's disrespectful to look into the eyes of the person you're speaking to. In America, it's impolite to look away. Joseph and his friends adopted the American way, something they think helped all of them get jobs.

One thing they picked up quickly was American humor. The tag on James Thon Aleer's key chain says "Don't Mess with Texas."

▲ Joseph Maker found a warm welcome in Houston, Texas.

EXPLORING THE ISSUE

1. **Categorizing** If you were an African refugee in your community, what things might confuse you the most? **FCAT LA.A.2.3.1**

2. **Problem Solving** How might volunteers help refugees adapt to life in your community?

REVIEW AND ASSESS

UNDERSTANDING THE ISSUE

1. Defining Key Terms
Write definitions for the following terms: *refugee, human rights, convention, asylum, persecution, internally displaced person,* and *host country.* **FCAT LA.A.1.3.2**

2. Writing to Inform Write a 250-word article about the refugee issue. Use the key terms listed above. **FCAT LA.B.1.3.2**

3. Writing to Persuade
"There is no greater sorrow on Earth than the loss of one's native land." A Greek thinker wrote those words about 2,500 years ago. Is his statement as true today? Write a short essay to explain. **FCAT LA.B.1.3.2**

INTERNET RESEARCH ACTIVITIES

4. With your teacher's help, use Internet resources to find information on issues involving refugees in the world, particu-larly in Africa today. Write a brief report on current "refugee hot spots" in Africa south of the Sahara. Be prepared to report on these problems in class. **FCAT LA.A.2.3.5**

5. With your teacher's help, choose two nations in Africa south of the Sahara. Then use Internet resources to learn more about these countries. Concentrate your research on refugee problems in your chosen nations and report your findings to the class. **FCAT LA.A.2.3.5**

BEYOND THE CLASSROOM

6. Visit your school or local library to find books in which young refugees share their experiences. (Enter the key words "refugee children" on the **Amazon.com** Web site, and you can find some titles to start with.) Bring those books to class to share with your classmates.

▲ **This Hmong boy from Laos now lives in Wisconsin.**

STEVE LISS

7. Research a refugee problem outside Africa.
List ways that it is like—and different from—refugee problems in Africa. Report your findings to your classmates.

8. Work in groups
to come up with ways young people could make it easier for newcomers to your community. Put your suggestions on a poster. Include phone numbers of groups that provide services for refugees. Display the poster for all students to see.

Where the World's Refugees Come From

(Top Sources of Refugees as of January 1, 2003)

Afghanistan	3,500,000
Palestinians	3,000,000
Burma	510,000
Sudan	475,000
Angola	410,000
Congo-Kinshasa	410,000
Burundi	400,000
Vietnam	302,000
Somalia	300,000
Iraq	294,000
Eritrea	290,000
Liberia	280,000
Croatia	251,000
El Salvador	203,000
China	178,000
Total	**10,803,000**

Around the world in 2002, some 13 million people lived as refugees. This table lists the 15 nations that most of them fled. Besides refugees, nearly 22 million others are internally displaced persons (IDPs). IDPs seek safety inside their nations' borders but far from their homes.

Source: U.S. Committee for Refugees

BUILDING SKILLS FOR READING TABLES

1. Categorizing Use your text to categorize the 15 nations listed here under one of five regions: Africa, Central America, Eastern Europe, Southeast Asia, and Southwest Asia.

2. Analyzing Data Which of the above regions have the greatest and smallest number of refugees?

3. Transferring Data Create a bar graph based on the country data in this table. **FCAT MA.E.1.3.1**

FOR UPDATES ON WORLD ISSUES GO TO www.timeclassroom.com/glencoe

Critical Thinking Skill

Making Predictions

Predicting consequences is sometimes difficult and risky. The more information you have, however, the more accurate your predictions will be.

Learning the Skill

Follow these steps to learn how to better predict consequences:

- Gather information about the decision or action that you are considering.
- Use your knowledge of history and human behavior to identify what consequences could result.
- Analyze each of the consequences by asking yourself: How likely is it that this will occur?

Practicing the Skill

Study the graph below, and then answer these questions:

1. What is measured on this graph? Over what time period?

2. In what year did the fewest tourists visit Kenya?
3. What trend does the graph show?
4. Do you think that this trend is likely to continue? **FCAT** MA.E.3.3.1
5. On what do you base this prediction?
6. List three possible consequences of this trend. **FCAT** MA.D.1.3.2

Applying the Skill

Analyze three articles in your local newspaper. Predict three consequences of the actions in each of the articles. On what do you base your predictions? **FCAT** LA.A.2.3.5

GO TO Practice key skills with **Glencoe Skillbuilder Interactive Workbook, Level 1.**

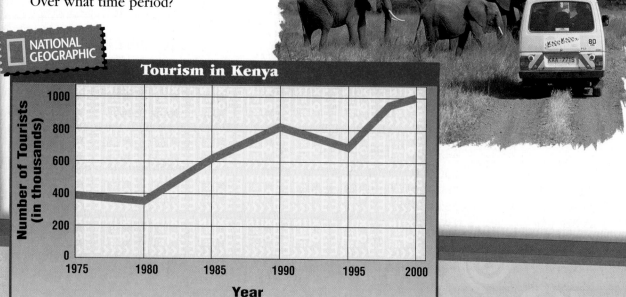

NATIONAL GEOGRAPHIC

Tourism in Kenya

Number of Tourists (in thousands) / Year

Source: *Europa Year Book; Yearbook of Tourism Statistics, 1978–1999.*

Chapter 20 Reading Review

Section 1 — Central Africa

Terms to Know
canopy
hydroelectric power
tsetse fly
deforestation

Main Idea
Central Africa has rich natural resources that are largely undeveloped because of civil war and poor government decisions.
✓Movement The Congo River—the second-largest river in Africa—provides transportation and hydroelectric power.
✓Economics The Democratic Republic of the Congo has many resources but has not been able to take full advantage of them.
✓Culture Sango is the national language of the Central African Republic. It eases communication among the many ethnic groups.
✓Economics The economies of Congo and Gabon rely on exports of lumber.

Section 2 — People of Kenya and Tanzania

Terms to Know
coral reef
poaching
free enterprise
  system
cassava
sisal
habitat
ecotourist

Main Idea
Kenya and Tanzania are countries in East Africa with diverse landscapes and peoples.
✓Place Western Kenya is marked by highlands and the Great Rift Valley.
✓Economics Many people in Kenya are farmers. Coffee and tea are grown for export. Tourism is also a major industry in Kenya.
✓Culture Kenya's people speak Swahili and English.
✓Economics Farming and tourism are Tanzania's main economic activities.
✓Government Tanzania's government has been stable and democratic.

Section 3 — Uganda, Rwanda, and Burundi

Terms to Know
plantains
autonomy
watershed
endangered species
genocide
refugee

Main Idea
Uganda, Rwanda, and Burundi have suffered much conflict in recent years.
✓Place Uganda, Rwanda, and Burundi are landlocked countries with high elevation and rainy, moderate climates.
✓Economics Most people in all three countries practice subsistence farming.
✓History Rwanda and Burundi suffered a brutal civil war in the 1990s between the Hutu and the Tutsi ethnic groups.

Section 4 — The Horn of Africa

Terms to Know
plate
clan

Main Idea
The countries of the Horn of Africa have all been scarred by conflict in recent years.
✓History Sudan has been torn by a civil war between the northern Muslim Arabs and the southern African peoples.
✓Place Ethiopia has good farmland, but scarce rainfall can cause drought.
✓Government Eritrea recently won its independence from Ethiopia.
✓History Civil war and drought have caused suffering in Somalia.

Assessment and Activities

FCAT PRACTICE You can prepare for the FCAT-assessed standards by completing the correlated item(s) below.

Using Key Terms

Match the terms in Part A with their definitions in Part B.

A.

1. canopy
2. tsetse fly
3. poaching
4. endangered species
5. habitat
6. genocide
7. hydroelectric power
8. clan
9. refugee
10. ecotourist

B.

a. electricity created by flowing water
b. family, or group of related people
c. deliberate murder of a group of people because of race or culture
d. person who flees to another country for safety
e. hunting and killing animals illegally
f. topmost layer of a rain forest
g. person who travels to view natural wonders
h. environment where an animal species lives
i. insect whose bite can cause sleeping sickness
j. plant or animal in danger of dying out

Reviewing the Main Ideas

Section 1 Central Africa

11. **Economy** How has transportation affected the economy of the Democratic Republic of the Congo?
12. **Culture** What is the official language of the Central African Republic? Why?
13. **History** Who originally settled São Tomé and Príncipe?

Section 2 People of Kenya and Tanzania

14. **Culture** What does the term *harambee* mean to Kenyans?
15. **Economics** In which part of Tanzania are cloves produced?
16. **Region** Name some of the animals that live on the Serengeti Plain.

Section 3 Uganda, Rwanda, and Burundi

17. **Economics** What is Uganda's main export?
18. **Movement** How do Burundi and Rwanda get their goods to foreign buyers?
19. **Culture** What two ethnic groups fought in Rwanda and Burundi?

Section 4 The Horn of Africa

20. **Place** What is the largest country in Africa?
21. **Place** What is Africa's newest country?

**NATIONAL GEOGRAPHIC** **Central and East Africa**

Place Location Activity

On a separate sheet of paper, match the letters on the map with the numbered places listed below.

1. Congo River
2. Cameroon
3. Kenya
4. Central African Republic
5. Sudan
6. Tanzania
7. Democratic Republic of the Congo
8. Somalia
9. Rwanda
10. Gabon

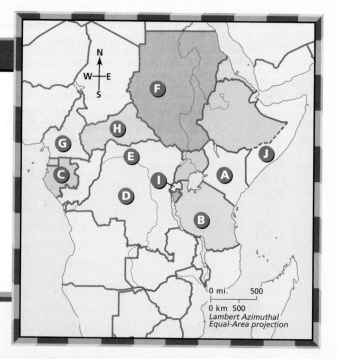

0 mi. 500
0 km 500
Lambert Azimuthal Equal-Area projection

Critical Thinking

22. **Drawing Conclusions** Central and East Africa depend on agriculture as a main economic activity. Why is a good transportation system important to an agricultural society?

23. **Sequencing Information** In a diagram like the one below, describe and put in order the steps that can lead to the creation of a desert. **FCAT** LA.A.1.3.2

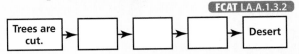

Trees are cut. → ☐ → ☐ → ☐ → Desert

─Comparing Regions Activity─

24. **Geography** Did you know that a plant originally from the plateaus of central Ethiopia is used to make one of the most sought after products in the world? Your teachers or other adults may drink this product every day. It is coffee! Ethiopia is the country that produces the most coffee in Africa. What other countries in the world produce coffee? List ten coffee-producing countries. Compare the countries' geographies to the geography of central and east Africa. How are they similar and different? **FCAT** LA.A.2.3.1

Mental Mapping Activity

25. **Focusing on the Region** Create a simple outline map of Africa, and then label the following:

- Sudan
- Cameroon
- Kenya
- Tanzania
- Democratic Republic of the Congo
- Lake Victoria
- Uganda
- Congo River
- Nile River

Technology Skills Activity

26. **Developing a Multimedia Presentation** Choose one of Africa's endangered animals and create a multimedia presentation about it. Include pictures or video clips of the animal, maps of its habitat area, and the steps being taken to protect this animal. **FCAT** LA.A.2.3.5

Standardized Test Practice

Directions: Study the map below, and then answer the question that follows.

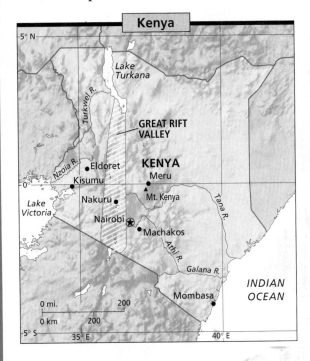

1. **About how many miles is it from Nairobi to Mombasa?**

   F 100 miles

   G 200 miles

   H 300 miles

   J 400 miles

Test-Taking Tip: Look carefully at the map key to understand its *scale,* or distance from one point to another. If you find it difficult to judge distances visually, use a small piece of scrap paper to measure the units described in the key.

601

21

Southern Africa— A Varied Region

To learn more about the people and places of southern Africa, view **The World and Its People Chapter 22** video.

Chapter Overview Visit **The World and Its People** Web site at twip.glencoe.com and click on **Chapter 21—Chapter Overviews** to preview information about southern Africa.

Why It Matters

Challenges

Even though many countries in southern Africa are rich in resources, challenges still exist. They are working to develop their economies or deal with other social and political changes. For example, South Africa was virtually isolated from the world community because of its racist policies. Today, after decades of struggling for justice and equality, South Africa faces new challenges. Poverty and the spread of AIDS plague the lives of many people.

FOLDABLES™ Study Organizer

FCAT PRACTICE The activity below will help you prepare for the **FCAT Reading** test.

Categorizing Information Make the following foldable to help you organize data about historic and modern events that have occurred in the countries of southern Africa. **FCAT LA.A.1.3.2**

Step 1 Fold a sheet of paper from side to side, leaving a 2-inch tab uncovered along the side.

Fold it so the left edge lies 2 inches from the right edge.

Step 2 Turn the paper and fold it into thirds.

Step 3 Unfold the paper and cut along the two inside fold lines.

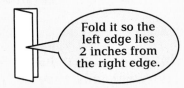

Cut along the two folds on the front flap to make 3 tabs.

Step 4 Label the foldable as shown.

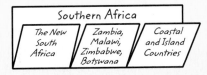

Southern Africa

| The New South Africa | Zambia, Malawi, Zimbabwe, Botswana | Coastal and Island Countries |

Reading and Writing As you read the chapter, write information under each appropriate tab of your foldable to record past and present events that have affected the countries and cultures of southern Africa. **FCAT LA.A.1.3.2**

NATIONAL GEOGRAPHIC Exploring Our World

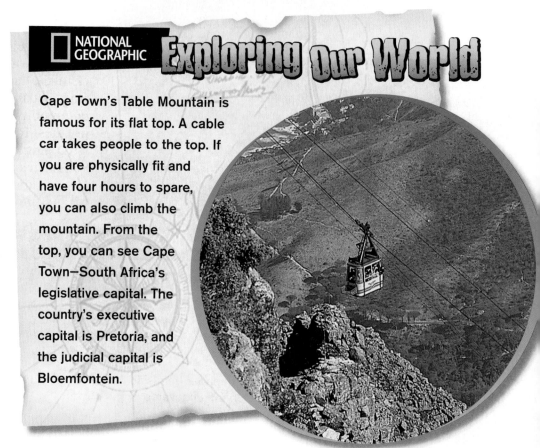

Cape Town's Table Mountain is famous for its flat top. A cable car takes people to the top. If you are physically fit and have four hours to spare, you can also climb the mountain. From the top, you can see Cape Town—South Africa's legislative capital. The country's executive capital is Pretoria, and the judicial capital is Bloemfontein.

South Africa (officially called the Republic of South Africa) is a land of beautiful scenery and great mineral wealth. Here you will find Africa's biggest mammal—the African elephant. You will also find the smallest mammal—the miniature shrew. To protect these creatures, the government has set aside land as national parks.

A Land Rich in Resources

South Africa, located at the southern tip of Africa, touches the Atlantic and Indian Oceans. The **Namib Desert** is in the northwest. The **Cape of Good Hope** is the southernmost point of Africa.

South Africa is the most industrialized country in Africa. An **industrialized country** is one in which a great deal of manufacturing occurs. Not all South Africans benefit from this prosperous economy, however. In rural areas, many people live in poverty and continue to depend on subsistence farming.

In terms of mineral resources, South Africa is one of the richest countries in the world. It is the world's largest producer and exporter of gold. It has large deposits of diamonds, chromite, platinum, and coal as well. The country also exports machinery, chemicals, clothing, and processed foods. Crops cultivated on irrigated, high-technology farms include corn, wheat, fruits, cotton, sugarcane, and potatoes. Ranchers on the central plains raise sheep, cattle for beef, and dairy cows.

✓ **Reading Check** How have South Africa's resources helped its economy?

South Africa's History and People

About 44 million people live in South Africa. Black African ethnic groups make up about 78 percent of the population. Most trace their ancestry to Bantu-speaking peoples who settled throughout Africa between A.D. 100 and 1000. The largest ethnic groups in South Africa today are the Sotho (SOO•too), Zulu, and Xhosa (KOH•suh).

In the 1600s, the Dutch settled in South Africa. They were known as the **Boers,** a Dutch word for farmers. German, Belgian, and French settlers joined them. Together these groups were known as Afrikaners

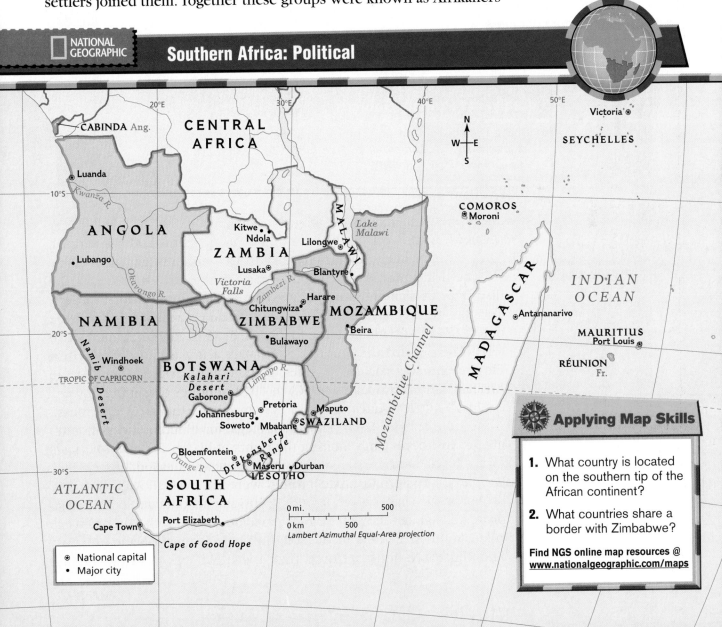

NATIONAL GEOGRAPHIC

Southern Africa: Political

Applying Map Skills

1. What country is located on the southern tip of the African continent?

2. What countries share a border with Zimbabwe?

Find NGS online map resources @ www.nationalgeographic.com/maps

Primary Source

NELSON MANDELA
(1918–)

As a young man, Nelson Mandela spoke out against apartheid and was arrested. He spent a total of 27 years in jail before being released in 1990.

"It was during those long and lonely years [in prison] that my hunger for the freedom of my own people became a hunger for the freedom of all people, white and black. I knew as well as I knew anything that the oppressor must be liberated just as surely as the oppressed. A man who takes away another man's freedom is a prisoner of hatred, he is locked behind the bars of prejudice and narrow-mindedness. When I walked out of prison, that was my mission, to liberate the oppressed and the oppressor both. . . . We have not taken the final step of our journey, but the first step on a longer and even more difficult road. For to be free is not merely to cast off one's chains, but to live in a way that respects and enhances the freedom of others."

From *The Long Walk to Freedom: The Autobiography of Nelson Mandela* by Nelson Mandela.

Analyzing Primary Sources

What do you think Mandela is referring to in the title of his autobiography, *The Long Walk to Freedom*? What is the walk a symbol for? **FCAT LA.A.2.3.2**

FCAT PRACTICE

Completing the exercise above will help you prepare for the **FCAT Reading** test.

and spoke their own language—Afrikaans (A•frih•KAHNS). They pushed Africans off the best land and set up farms and plantations. They brought many laborers from India to work on sugar plantations.

The British first came to South Africa in the early 1800s. Later, the discovery of diamonds and gold attracted many more British settlers. Tensions between the British and the Afrikaners resulted in the 1902 defeat of the Afrikaners in the Boer War. In 1910 Afrikaner and British territories became the Union of South Africa. It was part of the British Empire and was ruled by whites. Black South Africans founded the African National Congress (ANC) in 1912 in hopes of gaining power.

In 1948 the whites set up a system of apartheid, or "apartness." **Apartheid** (uh•PAHR•TAYT) made it illegal for different races and ethnic groups to mix, thus limiting the rights of blacks. For example, laws forced black South Africans to live in separate areas, called "homelands." People of non-European background were not even allowed to vote.

For more than 40 years, people inside and outside South Africa protested against the practice of apartheid. Many black Africans were jailed for their actions in the long struggle for justice and equality. The United Nations declared that apartheid was "a crime against humanity." Many countries cut off trade with South Africa. Finally, in 1991 apartheid ended. South Africa held its first democratic election in April 1994. Voters elected Nelson Mandela as the country's first black president.

The People South Africa has 11 official languages, including Afrikaans, English, Zulu, and Xhosa. About two-thirds of South Africans are Christians, whereas the rest practice traditional African religions.

One of the challenges facing South Africa today is to develop a better standard of living for its poorer people. Most European South Africans live in modern homes and enjoy a high standard of living. Most black, Asian, and mixed-group South Africans live in rural areas and crowded townships, or neighborhoods outside cities. The government has introduced measures to improve education and basic services.

Another challenge facing South Africa is the AIDS epidemic. Millions of people throughout Africa have been infected with HIV, the virus that causes AIDS. South Africa is one of the countries hit hardest.

Lesotho and Swaziland Within South Africa lie two other African nations—**Lesotho** (luh•SOO•too) and **Swaziland.** These tiny kingdoms are enclaves—small countries located inside a larger country. Both are poor countries that depend heavily on South Africa. Lesotho's only natural resource is water, some of which it sells to South Africa. Many of Lesotho's and Swaziland's people are engaged in subsistence farming. Others work in mines in South Africa.

▲ Although altitude and poor soil make farming difficult in Lesotho, most people are subsistence farmers.

 **Reading Check** How do Lesotho and Swaziland earn money from South Africa?

FCAT PRACTICE You can prepare for the FCAT-assessed standards by completing the correlated item(s) below.

Section 1 Assessment

Defining Terms
1. **Define** industrialized country, Boer, apartheid, township, enclave.

Recalling Facts
2. **Place** Name the largest mammal and the smallest mammal in Africa.
3. **Government** Who is Nelson Mandela?
4. **Culture** What challenges face South Africa?

Critical Thinking
5. **Drawing Conclusions** How did the rest of the world view apartheid? **FCAT LA.A.2.3.1**
6. **Analyzing Information** Why do you think workers in Lesotho and Swaziland travel to South Africa to work in mines? **FCAT LA.A.2.3.1**

Graphic Organizer
7. **Organizing Information** In a chart like the one below, write the resources and products of South Africa in the two boxes. **FCAT LA.A.1.3.2**

South Africa	
Resources	Products

 Applying Social Studies Skills

8. **Analyzing Maps** Study the political map on page 605. What are the three national capitals of the Republic of South Africa?

Making Connections

ART   SCIENCE   CULTURE   TECHNOLOGY

Mining and Cutting Diamonds

FCAT PRACTICE Answering question 3 below will help you prepare for the **FCAT Reading** test.

A diamond is a mineral made entirely of carbon. It is the hardest known substance on the earth and the most popular gemstone. Most diamonds formed billions of years ago deep inside the earth's mantle. There, intense pressure and heat transformed carbon into diamond crystal.

Mining

There are two major techniques used for mining diamonds: open pit and underground mining. In open pit mining, the earth is dug out in layers, creating a series of roads that circle down into a pit. After drills and explosives loosen the rock containing diamonds, workers use shovels and trucks to remove it. When the pit becomes too deep to reach easily, underground mining may begin.

Underground mining requires sinking a shaft into the ground and tunneling to the rock. Explosives blast the rock loose, and the resulting rubble is crushed and carried to the surface for further processing.

To remove the diamonds, the crushed rock is mixed with water and placed in a washing pan. Heavier minerals, such as diamonds, settle to the bottom, while lighter material rises to the top and overflows. Next, the heavier mixture travels to a grease table. Diamonds cling to the grease while other wetted minerals flow past. Workers continue the sorting and separating by hand.

Cutting

The newly mined diamond resembles a piece of glass, not a sparkling jewel. To enhance their brilliance and sparkle, gem-quality diamonds are precisely cut and polished. The cutter uses high-speed diamond-tipped tools to cut facets, or small flat surfaces, into the stone. One of the most popular diamond cuts is the brilliant cut, which has 58 facets. The job of the cutter requires extreme skill, because the diamond's beauty depends on how the angles of the facets are cut.

→ Making the Connection

1. What are diamonds made of?

2. Why are gemstone diamonds cut and polished?

3. **Making Comparisons** How are open pit and underground diamond mining techniques alike? How are they different? **FCAT LA.A.2.2.7**

NATIONAL GEOGRAPHIC

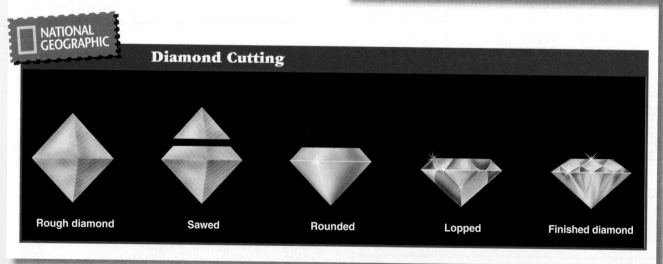

Diamond Cutting

Rough diamond   Sawed   Rounded   Lopped   Finished diamond

Zambia, Malawi, Zimbabwe, Botswana

Guide to Reading

Main Idea

Most of inland southern Africa is rich in resources and home to a wide variety of ethnic groups.

Terms to Know

• copper belt
• sorghum

Reading Strategy

Create a chart like this one. Then list the main economic activities of each country. FCAT LA.A.1.3.2

Country	Economic Activities
Zambia	
Malawi	
Zimbabwe	
Botswana	

The following are the major Sunshine State Standards covered in this section.

SS.A.3.3.5:
Understands the differences between institutions of Eastern and Western civilizations (e.g., differences in governments, social traditions and customs, economic systems and religious institutions)

SS.C.2.3.7:
Understands the current issues involving rights that affect local, national, or international political, social, and economic systems

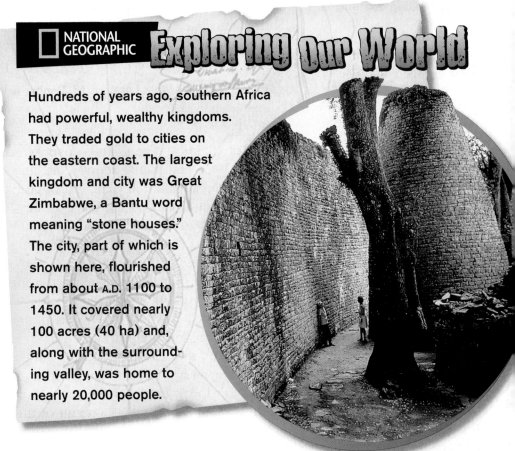

NATIONAL GEOGRAPHIC **Exploring Our World**

Hundreds of years ago, southern Africa had powerful, wealthy kingdoms. They traded gold to cities on the eastern coast. The largest kingdom and city was Great Zimbabwe, a Bantu word meaning "stone houses." The city, part of which is shown here, flourished from about A.D. 1100 to 1450. It covered nearly 100 acres (40 ha) and, along with the surrounding valley, was home to nearly 20,000 people.

The four countries of inland southern Africa include **Zambia, Malawi** (mah•LAH•wee), **Zimbabwe,** and **Botswana** (baht•SWAH•nah). Find these four countries on the map on page 605. They have several things in common. First, they all are landlocked. A high plateau dominates much of their landscape and gives them a mild climate. Second, about 70 percent of the people practice subsistence farming in rural villages. Thousands move to cities each year to look for work.

Zambia

Zambia is slightly larger than Texas. The **Zambezi** (zam•BEE•zee) **River**—one of southern Africa's longest rivers—crosses the country. The Kariba Dam spans the river and creates a large amount of hydroelectricity. Also along the Zambezi River are the spectacular Victoria Falls, named in honor of British Queen Victoria, who ruled in the 1800s. The falls are known locally as *Mosi oa Tunya,* or "smoke that thunders."

What's for Dinner?

Kabemba Mwape hurries home from the market in Chavuma, Zambia. He carries a live pig on the back of his bike. Although Kabemba's family will enjoy the pig for dinner, they usually eat porridge. Kabemba's family is relatively wealthy. They can afford to pay for meat, bicycles, and the high price of school uniforms and books for Kabemba's education. He knows English, but he speaks his native language of Lozi while he is at the market.

A large area of copper mines, known as a copper belt, stretches across northern Zambia. One of the world's major producers of copper, Zambia relies on it for more than 80 percent of its income. As a result, when world copper prices go down, Zambia's income goes down too. As copper reserves dwindle, the government has encouraged city dwellers to return to farming. Zambia must import much of its food.

Once a British colony, Zambia gained its independence in 1964. The country's 10.9 million people belong to more than 70 ethnic groups and speak many languages. English is the official language. Those who live in urban areas such as **Lusaka,** the capital, work in mining and service industries. Villagers grow corn, rice, and other crops to support their families. Most people eat porridge made from corn.

✓ **Reading Check** What happens to Zambia when copper prices go down?

Malawi

Green plains and grasslands cover western areas of narrow Malawi. Vast herds of elephants, zebras, and antelope roam animal reserves here. The Great Rift Valley runs through eastern Malawi. In the middle of it lies beautiful **Lake Malawi.** This lake holds about 500 fish species, more than any other inland body of water in the world. Malawi is also famous for its more than 400 orchid species.

Malawi is one of the world's least developed countries. The economy relies on agriculture. Malawi exports tobacco, tea, and sugar. Farmers also grow sorghum, a tall grass whose seeds are used as grain and to make syrup. Malawi depends on economic assistance.

Bantu-speaking people arrived in the area about 2,000 years ago, bringing with them knowledge of iron-working. During the mid-1800s, Scottish missionary David Livingstone came to Malawi. He was the most famous European explorer to reach Malawi. Today most people here are Protestant Christians as a result of the teachings of missionaries.

In 1964 the British colony became independent. Malawi has recently returned to democratic government after a long period of rule by a dictator. As a result of years of harsh government, modern Malawi writers emphasize themes such as human rights and abuse of power.

Malawi is one of the most densely populated countries in Africa. It has about 255 people per square mile (98 people per sq. km). Jobs are scarce, so thousands seek work in South Africa and Zambia.

✓ **Reading Check** What types of landforms cover western Malawi?

Zimbabwe

Crossing Zimbabwe, you might think you were in the western United States. The vast plateau is studded with large outcrops of rock. The **Limpopo River** winds through southern lowlands. The Zambezi River crosses the north.

Mining gold, copper, iron ore, and asbestos provides most of the country's income. Some large plantations grow coffee, cotton, and tobacco. Europeans own many of the large plantations, whereas most

Sculpture

Since the 1950s, Shona artists in Zimbabwe have carved attractive stone figures that are highly valued throughout the world. Mostly self-taught, Shona sculptors use sand and beeswax to polish the stone and heat it with fire to bring out the stone's color. They rarely begin carving with a specific subject in mind. Instead, the artists allow the qualities of the stone to determine the figure they will create. Many artists believe that the spirit in the stone speaks to them.

Looking Closer An example of Shona work is this sculpture of an African bird (below right). What other figures from their environment do you think Shona artists sculpt?

Africans own only small plots. Since the 1980s, the government has tried to redistribute land to Africans, but recently this has caused chaos and violence. This has, in turn, hurt the economy and caused widespread shortages of basic goods. Recently, President Robert Mugabe has been criticized, and in 2003 groups of people launched strikes to pressure him to retire early.

Nearly 34 percent of Zimbabwe's adult population has AIDS. This negatively affects the economy. People who have the disease often cannot work to support their families. The government lacks the means to deal with the AIDS crisis effectively.

Zimbabwe takes its name from an ancient African city and trading center—Great Zimbabwe. This remarkable stone fortress was built by an ethnic group called the Shona in the A.D. 1100s to 1400s. The Shona and the Ndebele (ehn•duh•BEH•leh) ruled large stretches of south-central Africa until the late 1800s. In the 1890s, the British controlled the area and called it Rhodesia. They named it after Cecil Rhodes, a British businessman who expanded British rule in Africa.

Africans eventually organized into political groups and fought European rule. In 1980 free elections brought an independent African government to power. The country was renamed Zimbabwe. Today Zimbabwe has about 12.6 million people. About one-fourth of the population is Christian. Others practice traditional African religions. The largest city is **Harare** (hah•RAH•ray), the capital.

Art and music in Zimbabwe come in many forms. Some artists, as shown above, work with stone. Others carve beautiful wood sculptures and make pottery. Musicians play instruments such as a talking drum, which when played sounds like it is "talking."

Reading Check How has AIDS affected Zimbabwe's economy?

Social Studies Online

Web Activity Visit *The World and Its People* Web site at twip.glencoe.com and click on **Chapter 21—Student Web Activities** to learn more about Zimbabwe.

Exploring GOVERNMENT

Stable Democracy

AIDS is a serious problem in many African countries. The governments of some countries, such as Zimbabwe, do not have the resources to deal with the disease. Other countries, such as Botswana, are working with the international community to combat the spread of AIDS. Because of Botswana's stable, democratic government, clinics have been established, roads are well maintained, and medical supplies can be quickly distributed.

Botswana

Botswana lies in the center of southern Africa. The vast **Kalahari Desert** spreads over southwestern Botswana. This hot, dry area has rolling, red sands and low, thorny shrubs. The **Okavango River** in the northwest forms one of the largest swamp areas in the world. This area of shifting streams is home to an abundance of wildlife.

Botswana's national emblem (as well as its basic monetary unit) is a one-word motto—*Pula*—meaning "rain." In Botswana, there is never much of it. From May to October, the sun bakes the land. Droughts occur often, and many years can pass before the rains fall again.

Botswana is rich in mineral resources. Diamonds account for more than 75 percent of the country's export income. Thousands of tourists visit Botswana's game preserves every year. Farming is difficult, and the country grows only about 50 percent of the food it needs. It must import the rest. To earn a living, many people work in South Africa for several months a year.

After nearly 80 years of British colonial rule, Botswana became independent in 1966. Today it has one of Africa's strongest democracies. Many of Botswana's people are Christians, although a large number practice traditional African religions. The official language is English, but 90 percent of the population speak an African language called Setswana. **Gaborone** is the capital and largest city. Here, and in other large cities in Africa, Western lifestyles and clothing are common.

✓ Reading Check **What is Botswana's biggest source of export income?**

FCAT PRACTICE You can prepare for the FCAT-assessed standards by completing the correlated item(s) below.

Section 2 Assessment

Defining Terms
1. **Define** copper belt, sorghum.

Recalling Facts
2. **Economics** What is Zambia's most important export?
3. **Place** What makes Lake Malawi unique?
4. **Culture** Where did Zimbabwe get its name?

Graphic Organizer
5. **Organizing Information** Choose two of the countries in this section. Write the name and three facts about each country in the outer ovals. Where the ovals overlap, write facts that are true of both countries. **FCAT LA.A.1.3.2**

Country 1   Country 2

Critical Thinking
6. **Synthesizing Information** Imagine that someone from Great Zimbabwe traveled to Zimbabwe today. What do you think he or she would describe as the greatest difference between then and now? **FCAT LA.A.2.3.1**
7. **Analyzing Information** Why do you think the people of Botswana chose *Pula*, or "rain," as their motto? **FCAT LA.A.1.3.2**

Applying Social Studies Skills

8. **Analyzing Maps** Study the political map on page 605. What five African nations does the Tropic of Capricorn cross?

Social Studies Skill

FCAT PRACTICE Completing the correlated items below will help you prepare for the **FCAT Mathematics** test.

Reading a Time Zones Map

The earth rotates 360° in 24 hours. The earth's surface has been divided into 24 time zones. Each time zone represents 15° longitude, or the distance that the earth rotates in 1 hour.

Learning the Skill

The Prime Meridian, or 0° longitude, is the starting point for figuring out time around the world. Traveling west from 0° longitude, it becomes 1 hour earlier for each time zone crossed. Traveling east, it becomes 1 hour later for each time zone crossed. The international date line is set at the 180° line of longitude. Traveling west across this imaginary line, you add a day. Traveling east, you subtract a day. To read a time zones map:

- Choose a place for which you already know the time and locate it on the map.
- Locate another place and determine if it is east or west of the first place.
- Count the time zones between the two.
- Calculate the time by either adding (going east) or subtracting (going west) an hour for each time zone.
- Determine whether you have crossed the date line, and identify the day of the week.

Practicing the Skill

1. On the map below, if it is 4 P.M. in Miami, what time is it in Cape Town? **FCAT MA.B.1.3.4**
2. If it is 10:00 A.M. in Tokyo on Tuesday, what day and time is it in Moscow? **FCAT MA.B.1.3.4**

Applying the Skill

Imagine you have a friend living in Rome, Italy. What time (your time) would you call if you wanted to talk to your friend after 7:00 P.M.?
FCAT MA.B.1.3.4

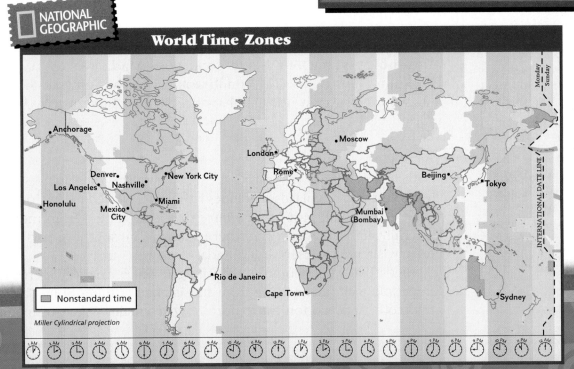

World Time Zones

NATIONAL GEOGRAPHIC

Nonstandard time

Miller Cylindrical projection

Coastal and Island Countries

Guide to Reading

Main Idea

Africa's coastal and island countries are struggling to develop their economies.

Terms to Know

- exclave
- slash-and-burn farming
- cyclone

Reading Strategy

Create a chart like the one below. Then fill in two key facts about each of southern Africa's coastal and island countries.

FCAT LA.A.1.3.2

Country	Fact #1	Fact #2
Angola		
Namibia		
Mozambique		
Madagascar		
Comoros		
Seychelles		
Mauritius		

The following are the major Sunshine State Standards covered in this section.

SS.A.3.3.5:
Understands the differences between institutions of Eastern and Western civilizations (e.g., differences in governments, social traditions and customs, economic systems and religious institutions)

SS.B.2.3.5:
Understands the geographical factors that affect the cohesiveness and integration of countries

NATIONAL GEOGRAPHIC Exploring Our World

Ostriches, lions, and elephants have found a way of surviving in the Namib Desert located along Namibia's Atlantic Ocean coast. Most nights a damp fog forms over the ocean. This fog floats inland, carrying moisture as far as 60 miles (97 km). Some of the hardy animals here survive by eating moistened tree leaves or finding small water holes.

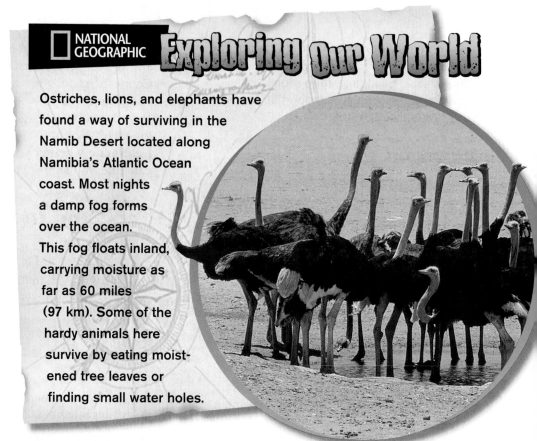

Angola and **Namibia** have long coastlines on the Atlantic Ocean. **Mozambique** and four island countries—**Madagascar** (MA•duh•GAS•kuhr), **Comoros** (KAH•muh•ROHZ), **Seychelles** (say•SHEHL), and **Mauritius** (maw•RIH•shuhs)—are located in southern Africa's Indian Ocean region.

Angola

Angola is almost twice the size of Texas. The map on page 605 shows you that Angola also includes a tiny exclave called **Cabinda.** An exclave is a small part of a country that is separated from the main part. Hilly grasslands cover northern Angola. The southern part of the country is a rocky desert. In Cabinda, rain forests thrive.

Angola's main economic activity is agriculture. About 85 percent of the people make their living from subsistence farming. Some farmers grow coffee and cotton for export. Angola's main source of income, however, is oil. Oil deposits off the coast of Cabinda account for 90 percent of Angola's export earnings. Other important industries include diamond mining, fish processing, and textiles. Still, Angola is not a wealthy country. Different groups have struggled for control of the country, which has hurt the economy.

Most of Angola's people trace their ancestry to the Bantu-speaking peoples who spread across much of Africa many centuries ago. In the 1400s, the Kongo kingdom ruled a large part of northern Angola.

From the 1500s until its independence in 1975, Angola was a colony of Portugal. Portugal is still an important trading partner, and Portuguese is the official language. Bantu and other African languages are also widely spoken. Almost 50 percent of Angolans practice the Roman Catholic faith brought to Angola by the Portuguese.

After Angola gained its independence, civil war broke out among different political and ethnic groups. The fighting has lasted more than 25 years and continues to bring great suffering to the people.

✓ Reading Check With so many resources, why is Angola's economy weak?

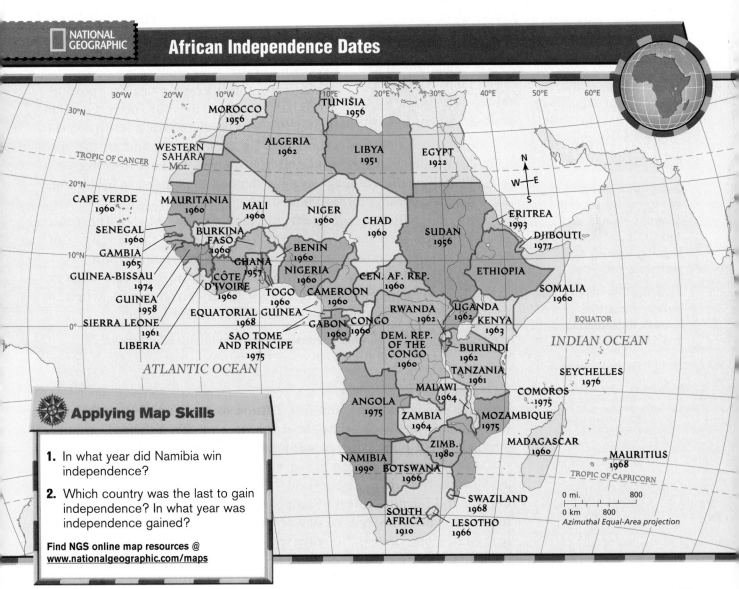

NATIONAL GEOGRAPHIC

African Independence Dates

Applying Map Skills

1. In what year did Namibia win independence?

2. Which country was the last to gain independence? In what year was independence gained?

Find NGS online map resources @ www.nationalgeographic.com/maps

Maputo, Mozambique

A high-rise building is being constructed in Maputo. Hotels and industrial projects are helping the city's economy grow.

Economics What slowed industrial growth in Maputo in the 1980s and 1990s?

Namibia

Namibia is one of Africa's newest countries. Namibia became independent in 1990 after 75 years of rule by the Republic of South Africa. Before that, it was a colony of Germany.

A large plateau runs through the center of the country. This area of patchy grassland is the most populous section of Namibia. The rest is made up of deserts. The **Namib Desert,** located along Namibia's Atlantic coast, is a narrow ribbon of towering dunes and rocks. Tourists come from all over the world to "sand-board" down these dunes. The Kalahari Desert stretches across the southeastern part of the country. As you might guess, most of Namibia has a hot, dry climate.

Namibia has rich deposits of diamonds, copper, gold, zinc, silver, and lead. It is a leading producer of uranium, a substance used to make nuclear fuels. The economy depends on the mining, processing, and exporting of these minerals.

Despite this mineral wealth, most of Namibia's people live in poverty. The income from mineral exports goes to a small group of Namibia's people and to the foreign companies that have invested in Namibia's mineral resources. As a result, half of the country's people depend on subsistence farming, herding, and working in food industries.

Only 1.9 million people live in Namibia. It is one of the most sparsely populated countries in Africa. In fact, in the language of Namibia's Nama ethnic group, *namib* means "the land without people." Most Namibians belong to African ethnic groups. A small number are of European ancestry. Namibians speak African languages, whereas most of the white population speaks Afrikaans and English.

✓ Reading Check When did Namibia become an independent country?

Mozambique

Sand dunes, swamps, and fine natural harbors line Mozambique's long Indian Ocean coastline. In the center of this Y-shaped country stretches a flat plain covered with grasses and tropical forests.

Most people in Mozambique are farmers. Some practice slash-and-burn farming—a method of clearing land for planting by cutting and burning forests. Slash-and-burn farming, along with commercial logging, has caused deforestation. Deforestation can, in turn, lead to flooding during the rainy season. Such floods drove more than one million people from their homes in early 2000. Mozambique also experiences deadly cyclones. A **cyclone** is an intense storm system with heavy rain and high circular winds.

Mozambique's major crops are cashews, cotton, sugarcane, tea, coconuts, and tropical fruits. The main source of income, however, comes from its seaports. South Africa, Zimbabwe, Swaziland, and Malawi all pay to use the docks at **Maputo,** the capital, and other ports.

During the 1980s and early 1990s, a fierce civil war slowed industrial growth. In recent years, however, foreign companies have begun to invest in metal production, natural gas, fishing, and transportation services.

Most of Mozambique's 17.5 million people belong to one of 16 major African ethnic groups. A former colony of Portugal, Mozambique's official language is Portuguese, but most people speak African languages. About half of the people practice traditional African religions. Most of the rest are Muslim or Christian.

Reading Check What is a negative result of slash-and-burn farming?

Madagascar

The island of Madagascar broke away from the African mainland about 160 million years ago. As a result, it has many plants and animals that are not found elsewhere. Its economy relies on agriculture, including fishing and forestry. It produces most of the world's vanilla beans. The main cash crop is coffee, and rice is also grown. About 80 percent of the island has been slashed and burned. The government has taken steps to save the remaining forests and to reduce poverty.

Only about 22 percent of Madagascar's people are city dwellers. **Antananarivo** (AHN•tah•NAH•nah•REE•voh), the capital, lies in the central plateau. Called "Tana" for short, this city is known for its colorful street markets, where craftspeople sell a variety of products.

Music revolves around dance rhythms that reflect Madagascar's Southeast Asian and African heritage. The people are known for their rhythmic style of singing accompanied only by hand clapping.

Reading Check Why does Madagascar have wildlife that appears nowhere else on the earth?

▲ This ring-tailed lemur lives on the island of Madagascar.

Small Island Countries

Far from Africa in the Indian Ocean are three other island republics—Comoros, Seychelles, and Mauritius. The people of these countries have many different backgrounds.

Comoros The three islands of Comoros were formed by volcanoes thousands of years ago. Dense tropical forests cover the islands today. Most of the approximately 600,000 people are farmers. The main crops are rice, vanilla, cloves, coconuts, and bananas. Even though agriculture employs 80 percent of the workforce, Comoros cannot grow enough food for its growing population. The government is trying to encourage industry, including tourism.

The people of Comoros are a mixture of Arabs, Africans, and people from Madagascar. They speak Arabic, French, and Comoran. Most practice Islam. Once ruled by France, the people of Comoros declared their independence in 1975. Since then, they have suffered from fighting among political groups for control of the government.

Seychelles The country of Seychelles is a group of 86 islands. About half of the islands are granite with high green peaks. The rest are small, flat coral islands with few people. Nearly 90 percent of the country's roughly 100,000 people live on Mahé, the largest island.

Seychelles was not inhabited until the 1700s. It has been under French and then British rule, but it finally became independent in 1976. Most of the country's people are of mixed African, European, and Asian descent. Coconuts and cinnamon are the chief cash crops. Fishing and tourism are important industries as well.

Mauritius Like Comoros, the islands of Mauritius were formed by volcanoes. Palm-dotted white beaches line the coasts. Sugar is the main agricultural export. Major industries are located in **Port Louis,** the capital. Clothing and textiles account for about half of the country's export earnings. Tourism is an important industry too.

Mauritians come from many different backgrounds. About 70 percent are descendants of settlers from India. The rest are of African, European, or Chinese ancestry. Because of this varied ethnic heritage, the foods of Mauritius have quite a mix of ingredients. You can sample Indian chicken curry, Chinese pork, African-made roast beef, and French-style vegetables.

✓ Reading Check What created the islands of Comoros and Mauritius?

FCAT PRACTICE You can prepare for the FCAT-assessed standards by completing the correlated item(s) below.

Section 3 Assessment

Defining Terms

1. **Define** exclave, slash-and-burn farming, cyclone.

Recalling Facts

2. **Economics** What is Angola's main source of income?

3. **Place** Which two deserts are in Namibia?

4. **Location** Where are most of the world's vanilla beans grown?

Critical Thinking

5. **Understanding Cause and Effect** Why is Namibia one of the most sparsely populated countries in Africa? **FCAT LA.E.2.2.1**

6. **Evaluating Information** How do the foods of Mauritius show its heritage? **FCAT LA.E.2.2.1**

Graphic Organizer

7. **Organizing Information** Create a diagram like the one below. Then write facts about Madagascar that fit the category heading in each of the outer ovals. **FCAT LA.A.1.3.2**

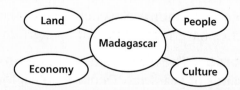

Applying Social Studies Skills

8. **Analyzing Maps** Study the map of African independence dates on page 615. Which southern African country first achieved independence?

Reading Review

Section 1 | The New South Africa

Terms to Know
industrialized country
Boer
apartheid
township
enclave

Main Idea

South Africa has great mineral wealth and has recently seen major social and political changes.

✓ **Economics** Because of its abundant mineral resources, South Africa has the most industrialized economy in Africa.

✓ **Government** In 1994 South Africa held its first democratic election in which people from all ethnic groups could vote.

✓ **Government** South Africa is working to improve the lives of its poorer citizens.

Section 2 | Zambia, Malawi, Zimbabwe, Botswana

Terms to Know
copper belt
sorghum

Main Idea

Most of inland southern Africa is rich in resources and home to a wide variety of ethnic groups.

✓ **Economics** Zambia is one of the world's largest producers of copper.

✓ **Economics** Zimbabwe has many mineral resources and good farmland.

✓ **Economics** Mining and tourism earn money for Botswana, but many of its people work in South Africa for several months each year.

Section 3 | Coastal and Island Countries

Terms to Know
exclave
slash-and-burn farming
cyclone

Main Idea

Africa's coastal and island countries are struggling to develop their economies.

✓ **Economics** Angola's main source of income is oil.

✓ **Culture** Few Namibians benefit from the country's rich mineral wealth. Most live in poverty.

✓ **Human/Environment Interaction** Slash-and-burn farming in Mozambique has led to deforestation and flooding. Neighboring countries pay fees for the use of Mozambique's ports.

✓ **Location** Madagascar's island location has resulted in many plants and animals found nowhere else in the world.

✓ **Economics** Comoros continues to be a mainly agricultural economy, but Mauritius has succeeded in developing a variety of industries.

✓ **Economics** Eighty-six islands form the country of Seychelles.

▲ A supermarket in Gabarone, Botswana, provides shoppers with a variety of food products.

Chapter 21 Assessment and Activities

FCAT PRACTICE You can prepare for the FCAT-assessed standards by completing the correlated item(s) below.

Using Key Terms

Match the terms in Part A with their definitions in Part B.

A.

1. copper belt
2. cyclone
3. exclave
4. slash-and-burn farming
5. township
6. apartheid
7. Boer
8. industrialized country
9. sorghum
10. enclave

B.

a. separating racial and ethnic groups
b. storm with high circular winds
c. country that relies on manufacturing
d. small nation located inside a larger country
e. large area of copper mines
f. small part of a nation separated from the main part of the country
g. areas of forest are cleared by burning
h. tall grass used as grain and to make syrup
i. settlement outside cities in South Africa
j. Dutch farmer in South Africa

Reviewing the Main Ideas

Section 1 The New South Africa

11. **Location** What is the southernmost point of Africa?
12. **History** When was South Africa's first election allowing all people to vote?
13. **Economics** What is Lesotho's only important natural resource?

Section 2 Zambia, Malawi, Zimbabwe, Botswana

14. **Place** What river crosses Zambia?
15. **Economics** Where is the copper belt?
16. **Economics** How are the people of Malawi supported?
17. **History** What was Great Zimbabwe?
18. **History** Who ruled Botswana for nearly 80 years?

Section 3 Coastal and Island Countries

19. **History** What European country colonized Angola?
20. **Culture** What does *namib* mean?
21. **Culture** What is the official language of Mozambique?
22. **Economics** What is Madagascar's main cash crop?

 **NATIONAL GEOGRAPHIC** **Southern Africa**

Place Location Activity

On a separate sheet of paper, match the letters on the map with the numbered places listed below.

1. Madagascar
2. Lake Malawi
3. Zambezi River
4. Kalahari Desert
5. Angola
6. Zimbabwe
7. Pretoria
8. Mozambique
9. South Africa
10. Namibia

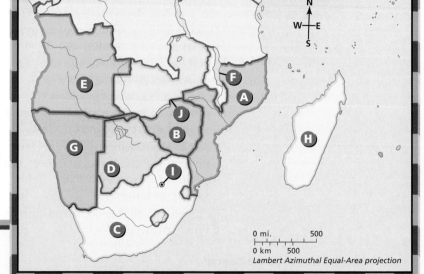

0 mi. 500
0 km 500
Lambert Azimuthal Equal-Area projection

 Critical Thinking

23. **Supporting Generalizations** What facts support the statement "South Africa has the most industrialized economy in Africa"?
FCAT LA.A.1.3.2

24. **Evaluating Information** Many countries of southern Africa are hoping to build and improve their industries. On a chart like the one below, list the positive and negative aspects of industrialization under the correct headings. **FCAT** LA.A.1.3.2

Industrialization	
Positives	Negatives

 Comparing Regions Activity

25. **History** Use the map on page 615 to create a time line that shows when each African country gained independence. In a different color, add dates that are important to the history of the United States civil rights movement. Do you see any overlap of the two sets of dates? Think about possible links between these two regions and their activities.

 Mental Mapping Activity

26. **Focusing on the Region** Create a simple outline map of southern Africa, and then label the following:

- Atlantic Ocean
- Lesotho
- Madagascar
- Angola
- South Africa
- Cape Town
- Namib Desert
- Mozambique
- Indian Ocean
- Botswana

 Technology Skills Activity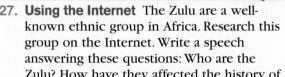

27. **Using the Internet** The Zulu are a well-known ethnic group in Africa. Research this group on the Internet. Write a speech answering these questions: Who are the Zulu? How have they affected the history of southern Africa? Where do they live today?
FCAT LA.A.2.3.5

Standardized Test Practice

Directions: Study the map below, and then answer the question that follows.

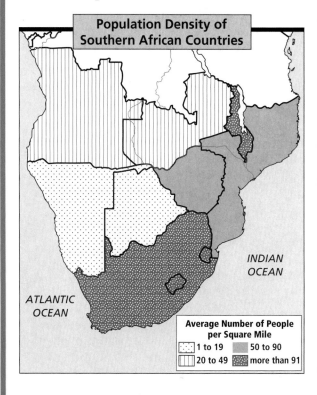

Population Density of Southern African Countries

INDIAN OCEAN

ATLANTIC OCEAN

Average Number of People per Square Mile
- 1 to 19
- 20 to 49
- 50 to 90
- more than 91

1. **Of the following, which country has the fewest people per square mile?**

   A Lesotho

   B Malawi

   C South Africa

   D Namibia

Test-Taking Tip: This question involves recalling where countries are located as well as using the legend. Start with the answer choices. Think about what you learned about each country. You may be able to get rid of wrong answer choices simply by recalling these facts.

Taj Mahal,
Agra, India

Macaques in a hot
spring, Japan

NATIONAL GEOGRAPHIC

Asia

For many people in the Western Hemisphere, the region of Asia—in the Eastern Hemisphere—brings to mind exotic images. Ancient temples stand in dense rain forests. Farmers work in flooded rice fields. Pandas nibble bamboo shoots. Yet bustling cities, gleaming skyscrapers, and high-technology industries can also be found here. Turn the page to learn more about this region and its more than 3 billion people.

▲ **Monks wrapping statue of Buddha in yellow cloth, Thailand**

623

Focus on:
Asia

THE REGION OF ASIA is made up of surprisingly diverse landscapes. It includes a large chunk of the Asian continent, together with island groups that fringe its southern and eastern shores. Some of the world's oldest civilizations and religions had their beginnings in Asia. Now more than 3 billion people call this region home.

The Land

Covering roughly 7.8 million square miles (20.2 sq. km), the Asian region stretches from the mountains of western Pakistan to the eastern shores of Japan. It reaches from the highlands of northeastern China to the tropical islands of Indonesia. The region's long, winding coastlines are washed by two major oceans—the Indian and the Pacific—as well as many seas.

Lofty Landscape Several mountain ranges slice through central Asia. Most famous are the towering Himalaya. The earth's tallest peak—Mount Everest—is located here. North of the Himalaya lies the vast Plateau of Tibet, so high it has been called the Roof of the World. Beyond the plateau are two immense deserts: the Taklimakan and the Gobi.

Ring of Fire Other mountain ranges cut across northeastern China, run down the Korean Peninsula, and sweep through the peninsulas of Southeast Asia. Japan, Indonesia, and other mountainous islands lie offshore along the Ring of Fire. This is an area where adjoining plates of the earth's crust slip and buckle, setting off earthquakes and volcanic eruptions.

Mighty Rivers Great rivers begin in Asia's lofty center. On their journey to the sea, they flow through fertile plains in several countries. The most important rivers include the Indus in Pakistan, the Ganges and Brahmaputra in India and Bangladesh, the Yangtze and Yellow in China, and the Mekong in Southeast Asia.

The Climate

A person traveling across Asia would need clothes to suit almost every possible climate. The snowcapped mountains and high, windswept plateaus of northern and central Asia can be bitterly cold. The deserts can shimmer with heat by day, yet be frosty at night. Lowlands and coastal plains enjoy milder climates. The peninsulas of Southeast Asia and the islands straddling

Terraced rice fields,
Bali, Indonesia

◄ Street flooded by monsoon
rain, Tamil Nadu, India

the Equator have mostly tropical climates. They are cloaked in dense rain forests. Seasonal winds called monsoons blow across much of Asia, bringing dry weather in winter and drenching rains in summer.

The Economy

Agriculture is the major economic activity across most of Asia. The region's rugged mountains and vast deserts mean that only a small amount of the land is suitable for growing crops, however. For example, only about 10 percent of China's land can be used for agriculture. To feed the region's huge population, Asian farmers must make the most of every possible bit of farmland. Terraces allow farmers to grow rice on steep hillsides. Rice, which grows well in places with warm temperatures and plenty of water, is the most important food crop in Asia. China, India, Indonesia, and Bangladesh are the leading rice producers in the world.

Most of Asia's manufacturing takes place in Japan, South Korea, Taiwan, China, and India.

China and India are rich in coal, iron ore, and other natural resources. Japan, however, has few mineral resources and must import fuel and nearly all the raw materials it uses. Still, Japan has become one of the world's leading manufacturers of cars, electronic products, and other goods. In some of the region's other countries, such as Laos, Vietnam, and Bhutan, industry is less developed.

The People

Nestled in fertile river valleys, some of the world's oldest civilizations arose in Asia thousands of years ago. Until the 1500s, Asia was more advanced than Europe in culture and technology. East Asians founded cities, set up states, and carved out trade routes.

Religious Traditions Ancient religions also took root in Asia. Both Hinduism and Buddhism, for example, originated in India. Hindus remain concentrated in India, but over time Buddhism spread throughout the region. The region's most widespread faith—Islam—began in Southwest Asia.

Europeans arrived in the region around 1500, bringing Christianity to some of the people. By the early 1800s, many Asian countries had fallen under European control. Many became European colonies and Western ideas spread throughout the region.

Modern Times In the early 1900s, Japan became Asia's leading power. World War II resulted in Japan's defeat, but it also ended Europe's hold on Asia. Nearly all of the Asian lands ruled by foreigners became independent by the mid-1900s.

◀ **Robot welding car bodies in a factory, Japan**

In many cases, however, independence in Asia was followed by political turmoil and conflict. Much of the region was caught up in the global struggle between communist and non-communist countries. Many countries were torn apart by civil wars between communists and other groups.

Today China, Vietnam, and North Korea have Communist governments. Nepal and Bhutan are ruled by traditional monarchs. Military leaders control Myanmar. Japan, India, and the Philippines are democracies.

About 3.6 billion people live in Asia. China, Indonesia, Bangladesh, and Japan are among the world's most heavily populated countries. Asia's population, however, is very unevenly distributed. Most Asians make their homes in river or mountain valleys or near seacoasts. As a result, some parts of Asia are among the most crowded places in the world. They include Bangladesh, eastern China, northern India, southern Japan, and the island of Java in Indonesia.

Jodhpur, India ▼

China

Data Bits

🚗	Automobiles per 1,000 people	3
📺	Television sets per 1,000 people	291
VOTE	Democratic elections	No

Ethnic Makeup

Other 8%

Han Chinese 92%

World Ranking

GNP per capita in US $

Life expectancy

1st

50th

100th — 125th $860

80th 70 years

150th

Population: Urban ▦ vs. Rural ▦

37% | 63%

Sources: *World Desk Reference*, 2000; *World Development Indicators*; *The World Factbook*, 2003; *The World Almanac*, 2004.

Exploring the Region

1. Why is the Plateau of Tibet called the Roof of the World?

2. How do monsoons affect the region?

3. What is the most important food crop in Asia?

4. Name two religions that originated in the region.

Asia

Physical

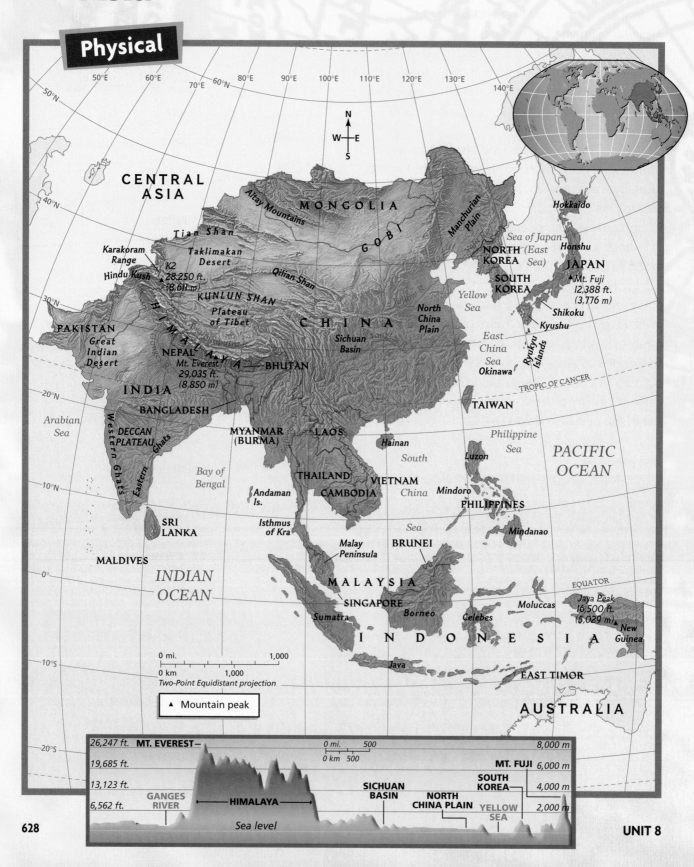

- ▲ Mountain peak

Two-Point Equidistant projection

0 mi. 1,000
0 km 1,000

CENTRAL ASIA

Altay Mountains

MONGOLIA

GOBI

Manchurian Plain

Hokkaido

Tian Shan

Karakoram Range

Taklimakan Desert

K2 28,250 ft. (8,611 m)

Hindu Kush

Qilian Shan

NORTH KOREA

Sea of Japan (East Sea)

Honshu

JAPAN

▲ Mt. Fuji 12,388 ft. (3,776 m)

SOUTH KOREA

Yellow Sea

Shikoku

KUNLUN SHAN

Plateau of Tibet

CHINA

North China Plain

Kyushu

HIMALAYA

PAKISTAN

Great Indian Desert

NEPAL

Mt. Everest 29,035 ft. (8,850 m)

BHUTAN

Sichuan Basin

East China Sea

Ryukyu Islands

Okinawa

TROPIC OF CANCER

INDIA

BANGLADESH

DECCAN PLATEAU

TAIWAN

Arabian Sea

Western Ghats

Eastern Ghats

MYANMAR (BURMA)

LAOS

Hainan

Philippine Sea

PACIFIC OCEAN

Bay of Bengal

THAILAND

CAMBODIA

VIETNAM

South China Sea

Luzon

Mindoro

PHILIPPINES

Andaman Is.

SRI LANKA

Isthmus of Kra

Mindanao

MALDIVES

Malay Peninsula

BRUNEI

MALAYSIA

INDIAN OCEAN

SINGAPORE

Sumatra

Borneo

Celebes

Moluccas

EQUATOR

Java Peak 16,500 ft. (5,029 m)

New Guinea

I N D O N E S I A

Java

EAST TIMOR

AUSTRALIA

26,247 ft. **MT. EVEREST** — 8,000 m

19,685 ft. 6,000 m MT. FUJI

13,123 ft. SOUTH KOREA 4,000 m

GANGES RIVER **HIMALAYA** SICHUAN BASIN NORTH CHINA PLAIN YELLOW SEA

6,562 ft. 2,000 m

Sea level

0 mi. 500
0 km 500

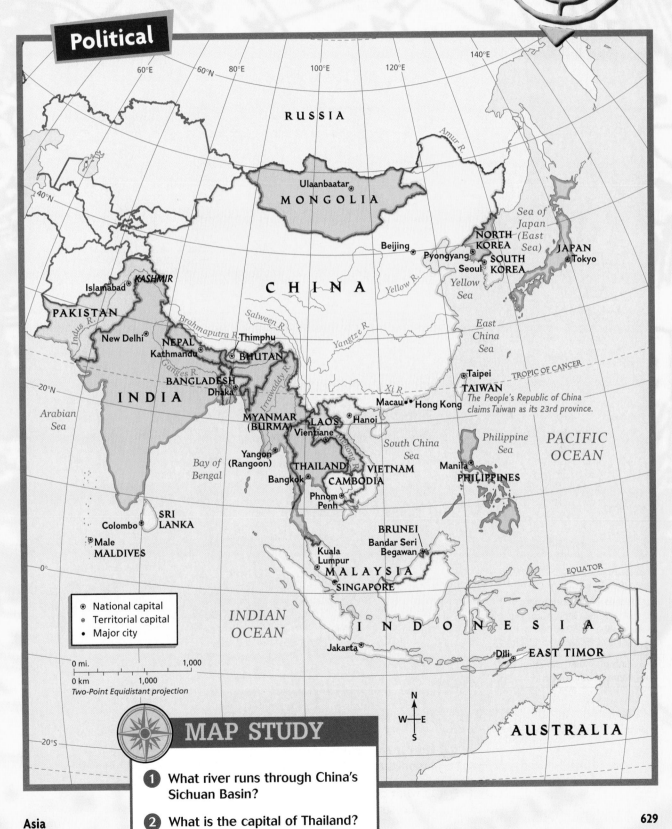

Political

140°E

60°E 60°N 80°E 100°E 120°E

40°N

RUSSIA

Ulaanbaatar ⊛

MONGOLIA

Amur R.

NORTH KOREA
Beijing ⊛
Pyongyang ⊛
Seoul ⊛ SOUTH KOREA

Sea of Japan (East Sea)

JAPAN
⊛ Tokyo

CHINA

KASHMIR

Islamabad ⊛

Yellow R.

Yellow Sea

East China Sea

PAKISTAN

New Delhi ⊛

Salween R.

Brahmaputra R.

Thimphu ⊛
NEPAL
Kathmandu ⊛ BHUTAN

Yangtze R.

Indus R.

20°N

Ganges R.

BANGLADESH
Dhaka ⊛

⊛ Taipei
TAIWAN

TROPIC OF CANCER

Xi R.

Macau • • Hong Kong

The People's Republic of China claims Taiwan as its 23rd province.

INDIA

Arabian Sea

MYANMAR (BURMA)

Irrawaddy R.

LAOS
Vientiane ⊛ • Hanoi

Yangon (Rangoon)

Mekong R.

South China Sea

Philippine Sea

PACIFIC OCEAN

Bay of Bengal

THAILAND
Bangkok ⊛ CAMBODIA
VIETNAM

Manila ⊛
PHILIPPINES

Phnom Penh ⊛

Colombo ⊛ SRI LANKA

BRUNEI
Bandar Seri Begawan ⊛

⊛ Male
MALDIVES

Kuala Lumpur ⊛
MALAYSIA
⊛ SINGAPORE

0°

- ⊛ National capital
- ⊙ Territorial capital
- • Major city

INDIAN OCEAN

I N D O N E S I A

EQUATOR

0 mi.   1,000
0 km   1,000
Two-Point Equidistant projection

Jakarta ⊛

Dili ⊙ EAST TIMOR

N
W ⊕ E
S

20°S

AUSTRALIA

MAP STUDY

1 What river runs through China's Sichuan Basin?

2 What is the capital of Thailand?

Asia

Monsoons

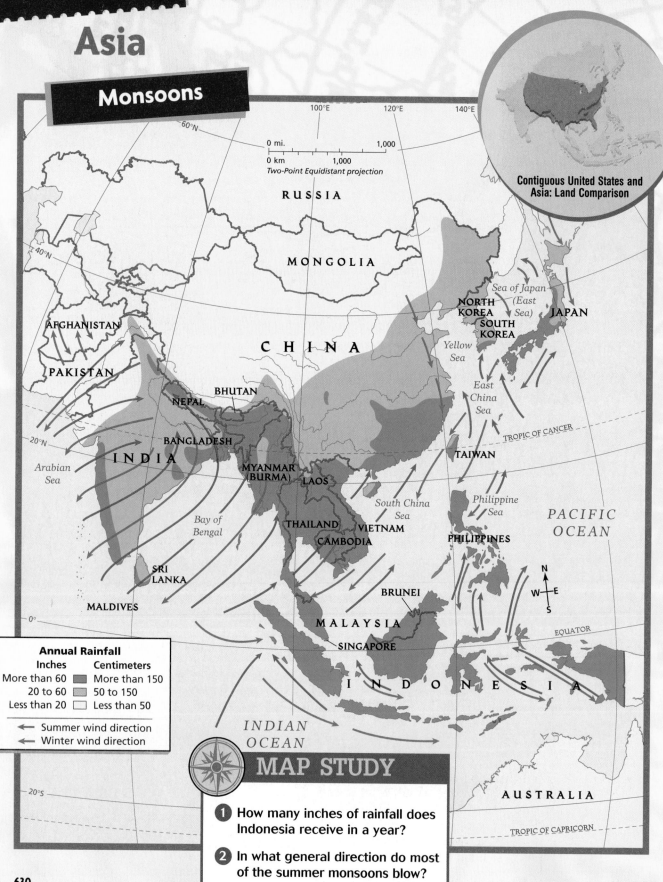

Contiguous United States and
Asia: Land Comparison

RUSSIA

Two-Point Equidistant projection

0 mi.   1,000
0 km   1,000

100°E   120°E   140°E

60°N

40°N

20°N

0°

20°S

MONGOLIA

AFGHANISTAN

PAKISTAN

CHINA

NEPAL

BHUTAN

BANGLADESH

INDIA

Arabian
Sea

MYANMAR
(BURMA)

LAOS

THAILAND

CAMBODIA

VIETNAM

Bay of
Bengal

SRI
LANKA

MALDIVES

MALAYSIA

SINGAPORE

NORTH
KOREA

SOUTH
KOREA

Sea of Japan
(East
Sea)

JAPAN

Yellow
Sea

East
China
Sea

TAIWAN

TROPIC OF CANCER

South China
Sea

Philippine
Sea

PHILIPPINES

PACIFIC
OCEAN

BRUNEI

N
W   E
S

EQUATOR

I N D O N E S I A

INDIAN
OCEAN

AUSTRALIA

TROPIC OF CAPRICORN

Annual Rainfall

Inches	Centimeters
More than 60	More than 150
20 to 60	50 to 150
Less than 20	Less than 50

← Summer wind direction
← Winter wind direction

MAP STUDY

1 How many inches of rainfall does
Indonesia receive in a year?

2 In what general direction do most
of the summer monsoons blow?

UNIT 8

Geo Extremes

① **HIGHEST POINT**
Mt. Everest
(Nepal and Tibet)
29,035 ft. (8,850 m) high

② **LOWEST POINT**
Turpan Depression (China)
505 ft. (154 m)
below sea level

③ **LONGEST RIVER**
Yangtze (China)
3,964 mi.
(6,380 km) long

④ **LARGEST DESERT**
Gobi (Mongolia and China)
500,000 sq. mi.
(1,295,000 sq. km)

⑤ **HIGHEST WATERFALL**
Mawsmai (India)
1,148 ft. (350 m) high

⑥ **LARGEST ISLAND**
New Guinea (Indonesia
and Papua New Guinea)
306,000 sq. mi.
(792,536 sq. km)

⑦ **WETTEST PLACE**
Mawsynram (India)
467 in. (1,186 cm)
average annual rainfall

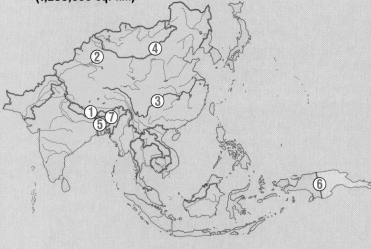

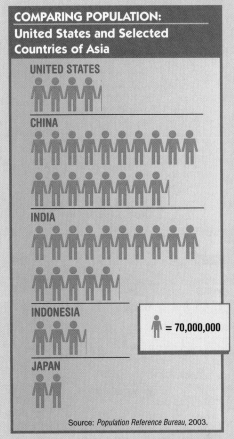

COMPARING POPULATION:
United States and Selected
Countries of Asia

UNITED STATES

CHINA

INDIA

INDONESIA

JAPAN

= 70,000,000

Source: *Population Reference Bureau*, 2003.

WORLD POPULATION:
Asia's Share of the World's People

Rest of World 39.3%

China 20.4%

India 16.9%

Indonesia 3.5%

Pakistan 2.4%

Japan 2.1%

Bangladesh 2.3%

Rest of Asia 13.1%

Source: *Population Reference Bureau*, 2003.

GRAPHIC STUDY

❶ The highest point in Asia is also the
highest point in the world. What is it?

❷ What percentage of the world's population lives in Asia? **FCAT** MA.E.3.3.1

Asia

Country Profiles

BANGLADESH

POPULATION:
146,700,000
2,639 per sq. mi.
1,019 per sq. km

LANGUAGE:
Bengali

MAJOR EXPORT:
Clothing

CAPITAL:
Dhaka

MAJOR IMPORT:
Machinery

LANDMASS:
55,598 sq. mi.
143,999 sq. km

 Dhaka

BHUTAN

POPULATION:
900,000
52 per sq. mi.
20 per sq. km

LANGUAGES:
Dzonkha, Local
Languages

MAJOR EXPORT:
Cardamom

CAPITAL:
Thimphu

MAJOR IMPORT:
Fuels

LANDMASS:
18,147 sq. mi.
47,001 sq. km

Thimphu

BRUNEI

POPULATION:
400,000
162 per sq. mi.
63 per sq. km

LANGUAGES:
Malay, English,
Chinese

MAJOR EXPORT:
Crude Oil

CAPITAL:
Bandar Seri
Begawan

MAJOR IMPORT:
Machinery

LANDMASS:
2,228 sq. mi.
5,771 sq. km

 Bandar Seri Begawan

CAMBODIA

POPULATION:
12,600,000
180 per sq. mi.
69 per sq. km

LANGUAGES:
Khmer, French

MAJOR EXPORT:
Timber

CAPITAL:
Phnom Penh

MAJOR IMPORT:
Construction
Materials

LANDMASS:
69,900 sq. mi.
181,041 sq. km

 Phnom Penh

CHINA

POPULATION:
1,289,000,000
349 per sq. mi.
135 per sq. km

LANGUAGE:
Mandarin Chinese

MAJOR EXPORT:
Machinery

CAPITAL:
Beijing

MAJOR IMPORT:
Machinery

LANDMASS:
3,696,100 sq. mi.
9,572,899 sq. km

 Beijing

EAST TIMOR

POPULATION:
800,000
136 per sq. mi.
53 per sq. km

LANGUAGES:
Tetun, Javanese,
Portuguese

MAJOR EXPORT:
Coconut Products

CAPITAL:
Dili

MAJOR IMPORT:
Manufactured
Goods

LANDMASS:
5,741 sq. mi.
14,869 sq. km

 Dili

INDIA

POPULATION:
1,069,000,000
842 per sq. mi.
325 per sq. km

LANGUAGES:
Hindi, English,
Local Languages

MAJOR EXPORTS:
Gems and
Jewelry

CAPITAL:
New Delhi

MAJOR IMPORT:
Crude Oil

LANDMASS:
1,269,340 sq. mi.
3,287,591 sq. km

 New Delhi

INDONESIA

POPULATION:
220,500,000
300 per sq. mi.
116 per sq. km

LANGUAGES:
Bahasa Indonesia,
Javanese

MAJOR EXPORT:
Crude Oil

CAPITAL:
Jakarta

MAJOR IMPORT:
Manufactured
Goods

LANDMASS:
735,355 sq. mi.
1,904,569 sq. km

 Jakarta

JAPAN

POPULATION:
127,500,000
874 per sq. mi.
337 per sq. km

LANGUAGE:
Japanese

MAJOR EXPORT:
Machinery

CAPITAL:
Tokyo

MAJOR IMPORT:
Manufactured
Goods

LANDMASS:
145,869 sq. mi.
377,801 sq. km

 Tokyo

LAOS

POPULATION:
5,600,000
61 per sq. mi.
24 per sq. km

LANGUAGES:
Lao, French

MAJOR EXPORT:
Wood Products

CAPITAL:
Vientiane

MAJOR IMPORT:
Machinery

LANDMASS:
91,429 sq. mi.
236,801 sq. km

 Vientiane

Countries and flags not drawn to scale

For more information on countries in this region, refer to the Nations of the World Data Bank in the Appendix.

MALAYSIA

POPULATION:
25,100,000
197 per sq. mi.
76 per sq. km

LANGUAGES:
Malay, English, Chinese

MAJOR EXPORT:
Electronic Equipment

CAPITAL:
Kuala Lumpur

MAJOR IMPORT:
Machinery

LANDMASS:
127,317 sq. mi.
329,751 sq. km

Kuala Lumpur

MALDIVES

POPULATION:
300,000
2,461 per sq. mi.
950 per sq. km

LANGUAGES:
Maldivian Divehi, English

MAJOR EXPORT:
Fish

CAPITAL:
Male

MAJOR IMPORT:
Machinery

LANDMASS:
116 sq. mi.
300 sq. km

Male

MONGOLIA

POPULATION:
2,500,000
4 per sq. mi.
2 per sq. km

LANGUAGE:
Khalkha Mongol

MAJOR EXPORT:
Copper

CAPITAL:
Ulaanbaatar

MAJOR IMPORT:
Fuels

LANDMASS:
604,826 sq. mi.
1,566,499 sq. km

Ulaanbaatar

MYANMAR

POPULATION:
49,500,000
189 per sq. mi.
73 per sq. km

LANGUAGES:
Burmese, Local Languages

MAJOR EXPORT:
Beans

CAPITAL:
Yangon (Rangoon)

MAJOR IMPORT:
Machinery

LANDMASS:
261,228 sq. mi.
676,581 sq. km

Yangon (Rangoon)

NEPAL

POPULATION:
25,200,000
443 per sq. mi.
171 per sq. km

LANGUAGE:
Nepali

MAJOR EXPORT:
Clothing

CAPITAL:
Kathmandu

MAJOR IMPORT:
Petroleum Products

LANDMASS:
56,826 sq. mi.
147,179 sq. km

Kathmandu

NORTH KOREA

POPULATION:
22,700,000
487 per sq. mi.
188 per sq. km

LANGUAGE:
Korean

MAJOR EXPORT:
Minerals

CAPITAL:
Pyongyang

MAJOR IMPORT:
Petroleum

LANDMASS:
46,541 sq. mi.
120,541 sq. km

Pyongyang

PAKISTAN

POPULATION:
149,100,000
485 per sq. mi.
187 per sq. km

LANGUAGES:
Urdu, English, Punjabi, Sindhi

MAJOR EXPORT:
Cotton

CAPITAL:
Islamabad

MAJOR IMPORT:
Petroleum

LANDMASS:
307,375 sq. mi.
796,101 sq. km

Islamabad

PHILIPPINES

POPULATION:
81,600,000
704 per sq. mi.
272 per sq. km

LANGUAGES:
Tagalog, English

MAJOR EXPORT:
Electronic Equipment

CAPITAL:
Manila

MAJOR IMPORT:
Raw Materials

LANDMASS:
115,830 sq. mi.
300,000 sq. km

Manila

SINGAPORE

POPULATION:
4,200,000
17,528 per sq. mi.
6,768 per sq. km

LANGUAGES:
Chinese, Malay, Tamil, English

MAJOR EXPORT:
Computer Equipment

CAPITAL:
Singapore

MAJOR IMPORT:
Aircraft

LANDMASS:
239 sq. mi.
619 sq. km

Singapore

REGIONAL ATLAS

Country Profiles

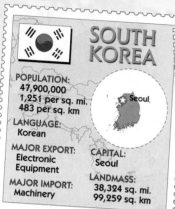

SOUTH KOREA

POPULATION:
47,900,000
1,251 per sq. mi.
483 per sq. km

LANGUAGE:
Korean

MAJOR EXPORT:
Electronic
Equipment

CAPITAL:
Seoul

MAJOR IMPORT:
Machinery

LANDMASS:
38,324 sq. mi.
99,259 sq. km

SRI LANKA

POPULATION:
19,300,000
761 per sq. mi.
294 per sq. km

LANGUAGES:
Sinhalese, Tamil,
English

MAJOR EXPORT:
Textiles

CAPITAL:
Colombo

MAJOR IMPORT:
Machinery

LANDMASS:
25,332 sq. mi.
65,610 sq. km

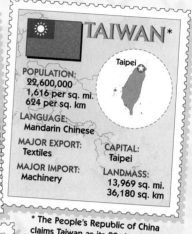

TAIWAN*

POPULATION:
22,600,000
1,616 per sq. mi.
624 per sq. km

LANGUAGE:
Mandarin Chinese

MAJOR EXPORT:
Textiles

CAPITAL:
Taipei

MAJOR IMPORT:
Machinery

LANDMASS:
13,969 sq. mi.
36,180 sq. km

* The People's Republic of China
claims Taiwan as its 23rd province.

THAILAND

POPULATION:
63,100,000
318 per sq. mi.
123 per sq. km

LANGUAGES:
Thai, Local Languages

MAJOR EXPORT:
Manufactured
Goods

CAPITAL:
Bangkok

MAJOR IMPORT:
Machinery

LANDMASS:
198,116 sq. mi.
513,120 sq. km

VIETNAM

POPULATION:
80,800,000
631 per sq. mi.
244 per sq. km

LANGUAGES:
Vietnamese,
Local Languages

MAJOR EXPORT:
Crude Oil

CAPITAL:
Hanoi

MAJOR IMPORT:
Machinery

LANDMASS:
128,066 sq. mi.
331,691 sq. km

Countries and flags not drawn to scale

BUILDING CITIZENSHIP

Women's Rights Not all countries have the same laws for men and women. In some countries, women are not allowed to own property, vote, go to school, or work. Part of the reason for this is that women's contributions to society in the area of raising children and running a household are not as valued as men's contributions.

Why is it important in the United States that men and women have equal rights and that those rights are protected by the law?

FCAT LA.A.2.3.2

WRITE ABOUT IT **FCAT PRACTICE** Completing the activity below will help you prepare for the **FCAT Writing** test.

Imagine that you are a sixth grade exchange student from an Asian country. Write a letter to your sister at home describing some activities that girls in your American school take part in on an equal basis with boys. **FCAT** LA.B.1.3.2

Vietnamese mother and baby ▶

▲ Three generations of a
Chinese family

The World and Its People NATIONAL GEOGRAPHIC

To learn more about the people and places of South Asia, view **The World and Its People Chapter 23** video.

Social Studies Online

Chapter Overview Visit **The World and Its People** Web site at twip.glencoe.com and click on **Chapter 22–Chapter Overviews** to preview information about South Asia.

FOLDABLES™
Study Organizer

Categorizing Information Make this foldable to organize information from the chapter to help you learn more about the land, economy, government, history, and religions of seven South Asian countries.

FCAT LA.A.1.3.2

Step 1 Collect four sheets of paper and place them about ½ inch apart.

Keep the edges straight.

Step 2 Fold up the bottom edges of the paper to form eight tabs.

This makes all tabs the same size.

Step 3 When all the tabs are the same size, crease the paper to hold the tabs in place and staple the sheets together. Turn the paper and label each tab as shown.

SOUTH ASIA
Maldives
Bangladesh
Sri Lanka
Bhutan
Nepal
Pakistan
India

Staple together along the fold.

Reading and Writing As you read, use your foldable to write down the main ideas about each South Asian country. Record the main ideas under each appropriate tab of your foldable. **FCAT** LA.A.1.3.2

◀ **A temple in Bhaktapur, Nepal**

Why It Matters

Working Toward Stability

Many countries in South Asia have roots in ancient civilizations but have become independent relatively recently. Because of this, there are political and religious differences within this region that threaten its stability. The governments of South Asia are working to overcome these differences. Today, countries in the region are trying to develop closer economic ties and free trade agreements.

India-Past and Present

Guide to Reading

Main Idea

India is trying to develop its resources to meet the needs of its rapidly growing population.

Terms to Know

- subcontinent
- monsoon
- green revolution
- jute
- cottage industry
- pesticide
- caste
- reincarnation

Reading Strategy

Create a chart like this one. Then fill in at least two key facts about India under each category. **FCAT LA.A.1.3.2**

India	
Land	Economy
History	Religion

The following are the major Sunshine State Standards covered in this section.

SS.A.3.3.5:
Understands the differences between institutions of Eastern and Western civilizations (e.g., differences in governments, social traditions and customs, economic systems and religious institutions)

SS.A.3.3.4:
Knows significant historical leaders who have influenced the course of events in Eastern and Western civilizations since the Renaissance

Exploring Our World

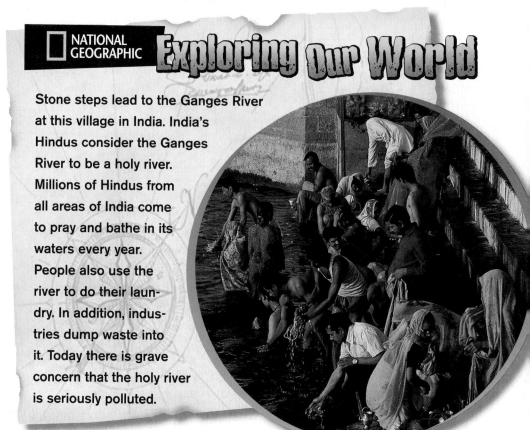

Stone steps lead to the Ganges River at this village in India. India's Hindus consider the Ganges River to be a holy river. Millions of Hindus from all areas of India come to pray and bathe in its waters every year. People also use the river to do their laundry. In addition, industries dump waste into it. Today there is grave concern that the holy river is seriously polluted.

India and several other countries—Pakistan, Bangladesh (BAHNG•gluh•DEHSH), Nepal, Bhutan, Sri Lanka, and the Maldives—make up the South Asian subcontinent. A subcontinent is a large landmass that is part of another continent but distinct from it.

India's Land and Economy

Two huge walls of mountains—the **Karakoram** (KAH•rah•KOHR•ahm) **Range** and the **Himalaya** (HIH•muh•LAY•uh)—form India's northern border and separate South Asia from the rest of Asia. (See the map on page 645.) The tallest mountains in the world, the Himalaya's snowcapped peaks average more than 5 miles (8 km) in height. Edging India's southern coasts are the **Eastern Ghats** and the **Western Ghats.** In central India, the **Satpura Range** divides the country.

North of the Satpura lies the vast **Ganges Plain.** It boasts some of the most fertile soil in the country and holds about 40 percent of India's people. The **Ganges River** flows through the Ganges Plain to the **Bay of Bengal.** South of the Satpura Range lies the **Deccan Plateau.** Forests, farmland, and rich deposits of minerals make it a valuable region.

Most of India is warm or hot all year. The Himalaya block cold northern air from sweeping south into the country. Monsoons, or seasonal winds that blow steadily from the same direction for months, also influence the climate. During the rainy season (June through September), southern monsoon winds bring moist air from the Indian Ocean. The map on page 630 shows monsoon patterns for summer and winter.

The Green Revolution   Today India produces most of the food it needs. In the past, it was very different. The world's worst recorded food disaster, known as the Bengal Famine, occurred in 1943 when the United Kingdom ruled India. An estimated 4 million people died of starvation that year alone. When India won its independence in 1947, government officials turned their attention to improving India's farm output. The green revolution was an effort to use modern techniques and science to increase production of food.

The government built dams to collect monsoon rains. The dams stored the water and spread it out through irrigation ditches during the dry season. Farmers could then plant more than one crop each year. New, stronger strains of wheat, rice, and corn were also developed that could withstand diseases and droughts and produce more grains.

India's farmers today raise a variety of crops, including rice, wheat, cotton, tea, sugarcane, and jute. Jute is a plant fiber used for making rope, burlap bags, and carpet backing. India is the world's second-largest rice producer, after China.

Industry   Huge factories in India's cities turn out cotton textiles and produce iron and steel. Oil and sugar refineries loom over many urban skylines. Recently, many American computer companies have opened offices in India. Mining is another major industry. India has rich deposits of coal, iron ore, manganese, and bauxite. Its major exports are gems and jewelry.

Many Indian products are manufactured in cottage industries. A cottage industry is a home- or village-based industry in which family members, including children, supply their own equipment to make goods. Items produced in cottage industries include cotton cloth, silk cloth, rugs, leather products, and metalware.

NATIONAL GEOGRAPHIC **On Location**

Two Views of India

The growing middle class lives comfortably in India's suburbs (above), but the poor in India's cities must struggle to survive (above left).

Human/Environment Interaction How would the green revolution benefit India's people?

Environmental Challenges India's economic growth has created challenges to its environment. Thousands of acres of forests have been cleared for farming. Both water and land have been polluted from industrial wastes and **pesticides**, or chemicals used to kill insects that destroy crops. Burning coal is also harmful. The Ganges River is considered by many experts to be one of the world's most polluted rivers.

All of these developments have played a part in destroying animal habitats. India's elephants, lions, tigers, leopards, monkeys, and panthers have been greatly reduced in number. The government has set up more than 350 national parks and preserves to save these animals.

✓ Reading Check How has economic growth hurt India's environment?

India's History and People

About 4,000 years ago, the first Indian civilization built well-planned cities along the **Indus River** valley in present-day Pakistan. In the 1500s B.C., warriors known as Aryans (AR•ee•uhns) entered the subcontinent from Central Asia. They set up kingdoms in northern India. Aryan beliefs gradually blended with the practices of the local people to form the religion of Hinduism.

Over time, Hinduism organized India's society into groups called castes. A **caste** is a social class based on a person's ancestry. Under such a system, people are born into a particular caste, which determines the jobs they can hold and whom they can marry. The caste system still influences Indian life, although laws now forbid unfair treatment of "lower" castes.

About 80 percent of India's people today are Hindus. Hindus honor many gods and goddesses, including Brahma the Creator, Vishnu the Preserver, and Siva the Destroyer. Hinduism teaches that after the body dies, the soul is reborn, often in an animal or human form. This process, called **reincarnation**, is repeated until the soul

▲ This statue represents Siva, one of Hinduism's many deities.

EXPLORING CULTURE

Clothing

What is more comfortable than a pair of well-worn blue jeans? Denim—the strong blue cotton fabric—is part of modern life. Blue-dyed textiles (fabrics) are nothing new, however. They were being produced in India as long ago as 2700 B.C. Ancient Indians were among the first in the world to master techniques for dyeing cotton and other types of fabric. Using more than 300 different plants, Indian textile makers created brilliant fabric dyes. They also discovered how to make dyes permanent, so they would not wash out.

Looking Closer **Look at the Country Profiles on pages 632–634. Which countries' main export is cotton, textiles, or clothing?**

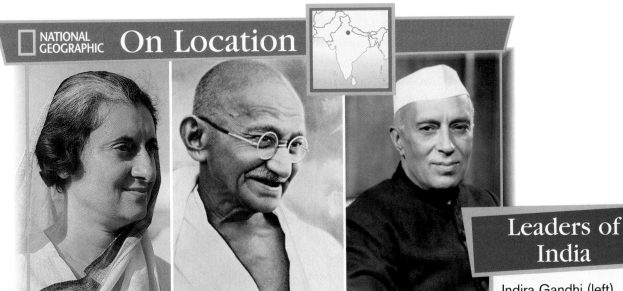

Leaders of India

Indira Gandhi (left) Mohandas Gandhi (center), and Jawaharlal Nehru (right) were instrumental in bringing democracy to India.

History Which country ruled India before it won its independence?

reaches perfection. For this reason, many Hindus believe it is wrong to kill any living creature. Cows are viewed as sacred and roam freely.

Buddhism started in India about 500 B.C. but largely declined there by 300 B.C. The religion of Islam has had much more influence on India's history. In the A.D. 700s, Muslims from Southwest Asia brought Islam to India. In the 1500s, they founded the Mogul Empire and ruled India for 200 years.

Today India's 140 million followers of Islam form one of the world's largest Muslim populations. Other religions include Christianity, Sikhism (SEE•KIH•zuhm), Buddhism, and Jainism (JY•NIH•zuhm). Conflict sometimes occurs among members of India's different religious groups. The Sikhs, who practice Sikhism, believe in one God as Christians and Muslims do, yet Sikhs also have other beliefs similar to Hindus. Many Sikhs would like to form their own country.

Religion has influenced the arts of India. Ancient Hindu builders constructed temples with hundreds of statues. Hindu writers composed stories about deities. Among Muslim achievements are large mosques, palaces, and forts. One of the finest Muslim buildings in India is the Taj Mahal. Turn to page 643 to learn more about this building.

Independence The British were the last of India's conquerors, ruling from the 1700s to the mid-1900s. They built roads, railroads, and seaports. They also made large profits from the plantations, mines, and factories they set up. An Indian leader named Mohandas Gandhi led a nonviolent movement to free India from Britain's rule. His efforts brought India independence from the United Kingdom in 1947.

Before independence, the British government had decided to divide India into two countries—one Hindu (India) and one Muslim (East and West Pakistan). After independence, millions of Hindus fled toward India. Muslims migrated toward Pakistan. Violence resulted from these mass migrations, and more than a million people were killed.

Government India has 25 states and 7 territories. **New Delhi** was built specifically to be the country's capital. India is a representative democracy. The head of state is a president, whose duties are mainly ceremonial. The real power lies with the prime minister. The first prime minister of India was Jawaharlal Nehru, who was elected in 1947. His daughter, Indira Gandhi, was also prime minister. She led India almost continually from 1966 until her assassination in 1984.

Daily Life More than 1 billion people call India their home. The country has 18 official languages, of which Hindi is the most widely used. English is often spoken in business and government, however. About 70 percent of the people live in rural villages. The government has been working to provide villagers with electricity, drinking water, better schools, and paved roads. Still, many villagers move to cities to find jobs and a better standard of living.

India's cities are very crowded. Bicycles, carts, animals, and people fill the streets. **Mumbai** (formerly Bombay), **Delhi, Calcutta,** and **Chennai** each have more than 5 million people and are growing rapidly. Modern high-rise buildings tower over slum areas where many live in deep poverty. In 1979 the well-known missionary Mother Teresa won the Nobel Peace Prize for her efforts to help the poor in Calcutta.

One of the most popular holidays is Diwali (dee•VAH•lee), the Festival of Lights. It is a Hindu celebration marking the coming of winter and the victory of good over evil. Indians also like watching movies. India's movie industry turns out more films than Hollywood.

√ Reading Check **What percentage of India's people live in rural villages?**

FCAT PRACTICE You can prepare for the FCAT-assessed standards by completing the correlated item(s) below.

Section 1 Assessment

Defining Terms
1. **Define** subcontinent, monsoon, green revolution, jute, cottage industry, pesticide, caste, reincarnation.

Recalling Facts
2. **Location** What two mountain ranges form India's northern border?

3. **Culture** What is the most widely followed religion in India?

4. **History** Which Indian leader led a movement that brought India its independence in 1947?

Critical Thinking
5. **Understanding Cause and Effect** How do monsoon winds affect India's climate?
 FCAT LA.E.2.2.1

6. **Drawing Conclusions** What challenges do you think the caste system caused?
 FCAT LA.A.2.3.1

Graphic Organizer
7. **Organizing Information** India is becoming a more modern country but still has many traditional ways. Create a chart like this one. Then list both modern and traditional aspects of India. **FCAT LA.A.1.3.2**

Modern Aspects	Traditional Aspects

Applying Social Studies Skills

8. **Analyzing Maps** Look at the population density map on page 653. Where are the most densely populated areas of India?

Making Connections

ART   SCIENCE   CULTURE   TECHNOLOGY

The Taj Mahal

Considered one of the world's most beautiful buildings, the Taj Mahal was built by the Muslim emperor Shah Jahan of India. He had it built to house the grave of his beloved wife, Mumtaz Mahal. She died in 1631 shortly after giving birth to their fourteenth child.

▲ The Taj Mahal, Agra, India

Background

While they were married, Mumtaz Mahal and Shah Jahan were constant companions. The empress went everywhere with her husband, even on military expeditions. She encouraged her husband to perform great acts of charity toward the poor. This earned her the love and admiration of the Indian people.

After his wife's death, Shah Jahan ordered the construction of the finest monument ever built. A team of architects, sculptors, calligraphers, and master builders participated in the design. More than 20,000 laborers and skilled craft workers

FCAT PRACTICE Answering question 3 below will help you prepare for the **FCAT Reading** test.

from India, Persia, the Ottoman Empire, and Europe worked together to build the monument. For 22 years they worked to complete the Taj Mahal, which holds a tomb, mosque, rest house, elaborate garden, and arched gateway.

The Mausoleum

The central part of the Taj Mahal is the domed marble mausoleum, or tomb, built on a square marble platform. The central dome is 213 feet (65 m) tall, and four smaller domed chambers surround it. A high minaret, or tower, marks each corner of the platform.

Inside the central chamber, delicately carved marble screens enclose the caskets of Mumtaz Mahal and Shah Jahan. He was buried next to his wife after his death in 1666. Following Islamic tradition, the caskets face east toward Makkah, the holy city of Islam.

The white marble from which the mausoleum is built seems to change color throughout the day as it reflects light from the sun and moon. Detailed flower patterns are carved into the marble walls and inlaid with colorful gemstones. Verses from Islamic religious writings are etched in calligraphy into the stone archways.

Making the Connection

1. Who is buried in the Taj Mahal?

2. Who built the Taj Mahal and how long did it take?

3. **Understanding Cause and Effect** How did Shah Jahan's feelings for his wife affect the grave site he built for her? **FCAT LA.A.2.3.1**

Pakistan and Bangladesh

Guide to Reading

Main Idea

Once a single nation, Pakistan and Bangladesh today are separate countries that border India on the west and east.

Terms to Know

- tributary
- delta
- cyclone

Reading Strategy

Draw a diagram like this one. In the outer ovals, write statements that are true of each country under the headings. Where the ovals overlap, write statements that are true of both countries. **FCAT** LA.A.1.3.2

Pakistan ⬭⬭ Bangladesh

The following are the major Sunshine State Standards covered in this section.

SS.A.3.3.3:
Knows how physical and human geographic factors have influenced major historical events and movements

SS.B.2.3.9:
Understands ways the interaction between physical and human systems affects current conditions on Earth

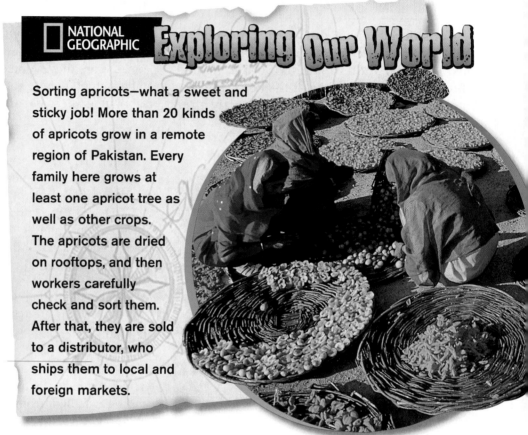

NATIONAL GEOGRAPHIC Exploring Our World

Sorting apricots—what a sweet and sticky job! More than 20 kinds of apricots grow in a remote region of Pakistan. Every family here grows at least one apricot tree as well as other crops. The apricots are dried on rooftops, and then workers carefully check and sort them. After that, they are sold to a distributor, who ships them to local and foreign markets.

Two countries in South Asia—**Pakistan** and **Bangladesh**—are largely Muslim. Although they share the same religion, the two countries have very different cultures and languages.

For many centuries, Pakistan and Bangladesh were part of India. In 1947 they separated from largely Hindu India and together formed one Muslim country called Pakistan. The western area was called West Pakistan, and the eastern area, East Pakistan. Cultural and political differences between the two led to a violent conflict in 1971. When the war ended, West Pakistan kept the name of Pakistan. East Pakistan became a separate new country called Bangladesh.

Pakistan

Pakistan is about twice the size of California. The country also claims **Kashmir,** a mostly Muslim territory on the northern border of India and Pakistan. Kashmir is currently divided between Pakistan and

India. Both countries want to control the entire region, mainly for its vast water resources. This dispute over Kashmir has sparked three wars between Pakistan and India. In fact, the conflict threatens the rest of the world because both Pakistan and India have nuclear weapons.

Towering mountains occupy most of northern and western Pakistan. The world's second-highest peak, **K2,** rises 28,250 feet (8,611 m) in the Karakoram Range. Another range, the **Hindu Kush,** lies in the far north. Several passes cut through its rugged peaks. The best known is the **Khyber Pass.** For centuries, it has been used by people traveling through South Asia from the north.

Plains in eastern Pakistan are rich in fertile soil deposited by rivers. The major river system running through these plains is the **Indus River** and its tributaries. A **tributary** is a small river that flows into a larger one. West of the Indus River valley, the land rises to form a mostly dry plateau. Another vast barren area—the **Great Indian Desert**—lies east of the Indus River valley and reaches into India.

Pakistan's Economy   Pakistan has fertile land and enough energy resources to meet its needs. About half of the people are farmers. A

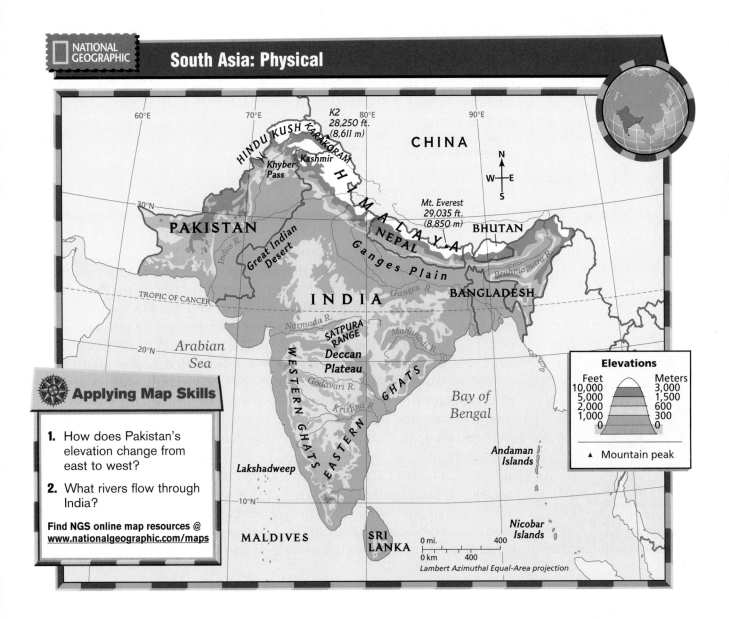

NATIONAL GEOGRAPHIC

South Asia: Physical

Applying Map Skills

1. How does Pakistan's elevation change from east to west?

2. What rivers flow through India?

Find **NGS** online map resources @ www.nationalgeographic.com/maps

Elevations

Feet	Meters
10,000	3,000
5,000	1,500
2,000	600
1,000	300
0	0

▲ Mountain peak

0 mi. 400
0 km 400
Lambert Azimuthal Equal-Area projection

large irrigation system helps them grow crops such as sugarcane, wheat, rice, and cotton. Cotton and textiles are the country's main exports. Other important industries include cement, fertilizer, food processing, and chemicals. Many people make metalware, pottery, and carpets in cottage industries. Pakistan's economy is struggling, however, because of frequent changes of government.

The Pakistanis   Since independence, Pakistan has had many changes of government. Some of these governments and officials were elected, including a female prime minister, Benazir Bhutto. In other cases, the army seized power from an elected government. The most recent army takeover occurred in 1999, and military leaders still control the country.

About 97 percent of Pakistanis are Muslims. The influence of Islam is seen in large, domed mosques and people bowed in prayer at certain times of the day. Among the major languages are Punjabi and Sindhi. The official language, Urdu, is the first language of only 9 percent of the people. English is widely spoken in government.

Almost 70 percent of Pakistan's people live in rural villages. Most follow traditional customs and live in small homes of clay or sun-dried mud. Pakistanis live in large cities as well. **Karachi,** a seaport on the Arabian Sea, is a sprawling urban area. It has traditional outdoor markets, modern shops, and hotels. In the far north lies **Islamabad,** the capital. The government built this well-planned, modern city to draw people inland from crowded coastal areas. Most people in Pakistan's cities are factory workers, shopkeepers, and craft workers who live in crowded neighborhoods. Wealthier city dwellers live in modern homes.

✓Reading Check What are Pakistan's main exports?

Bangladesh

Bangladesh, about the size of Wisconsin, is nearly surrounded by India. Although Bangladesh is a Muslim country like Pakistan, it shares many cultural features with eastern India.

If you saw Bangladesh for the first time, one word might come to mind—water. Two major rivers—the **Brahmaputra** (BRAHM•uh•POO•truh) and the **Ganges**—flow through the lush, low plains that cover most of Bangladesh. These two rivers unite with a third, smaller river before entering the Bay of Bengal. The combined rivers form the world's largest delta. A delta is a soil deposit located at the mouth of a river. In Bangladesh's delta area, the rivers constantly shift course, creating many thin fingers of land. The people depend on the rivers for transportation and for farming.

Bangladesh has tropical and subtropical climates. As in India, the monsoons affect Bangladesh. Raging floods often drown Bangladesh's low, flat land. Water also runs down from deforested slopes upriver in northern India. Together, these violent flows of water cause thousands of deaths and leave millions of people without homes. When the monsoons end, cyclones may strike Bangladesh. A cyclone is an intense tropical storm system with high winds and heavy rains. Cyclones, in

turn, can be followed by deadly tidal waves that surge from the Bay of Bengal. As deadly as the monsoons and cyclones can be, problems also occur if the rains come too late. When this happens, crops often fail and there is widespread hunger.

A Farming Economy   Most people of Bangladesh earn their living by farming. Rice is the most important crop. The fertile soil and plentiful water make it possible for rice to be grown and harvested three times a year. Other crops include sugarcane, jute, and wheat. Cash crops of tea grow in hilly regions in the east. Despite good growing conditions, Bangladesh cannot grow enough food for its people. Its farmers have few modern tools and use outdated farming methods. In addition, the disastrous floods can drown crops and cause food shortages.

Bangladesh has an important clothing industry. It exports large amounts of manufactured clothing to other countries. You may even be wearing clothes that were made in Bangladesh.

The People   With about 146.7 million people, Bangladesh is one of the most densely populated countries in the world. It is also one of the poorest countries. About 75 percent of the people live in rural areas. Because of floods, people in rural Bangladesh have to build their houses on platforms. Many people have moved to crowded urban areas to find work in factories. Their most common choice is **Dhaka** (DA•kuh), Bangladesh's capital and major port.

Most of Bangladesh's people speak Bengali. About 83 percent of the people are Muslim, and most of the rest are Hindus. Muslim influences are strong in the country's art, literature, and music.

✓ Reading Check   **What is an important industry in Bangladesh?**

FCAT PRACTICE   You can prepare for the FCAT-assessed standards by completing the correlated item(s) below.

Section 2 **Assessment**

Defining Terms
1. **Define** tributary, delta, cyclone.

Recalling Facts
2. **Region**   What region has been the source of conflict between Pakistan and India?
3. **History**   Why has the Khyber Pass been important?
4. **Movement**   Why was Islamabad built inland?

Critical Thinking
5. **Analyzing Information**   Why can rice be grown three times a year in Bangladesh?
6. **Drawing Conclusions**   Why are Pakistan's and Bangladesh's economies struggling?
   FCAT LA.A.2.3.1

Graphic Organizer
7. **Organizing Information**   Draw a diagram like this one. At the ends of the arrows, list three effects on Bangladesh caused by summer monsoon rains.   **FCAT** LA.A.1.3.2

Monsoons

Applying Social Studies Skills

8. **Analyzing Maps**   Look at the physical map on page 645. Which rivers have deltas in Bangladesh?

Social Studies Skill

Reading a Circle Graph

Have you ever watched someone serve pieces of pie? When the pie is cut evenly, everybody gets the same size slice. If one slice is cut a little larger, however, someone else gets a smaller piece.

Learning the Skill

A **circle graph** is like a sliced pie. Often it is even called a pie chart. In a circle graph, the complete circle represents a whole group—or 100 percent. The circle is divided into "slices," or wedge-shaped sections representing parts of the whole.

To read a circle graph, follow these steps:

- Read the title of the circle graph to find out what the subject is.
- Study the labels or the key to see what each "slice" represents.
- Compare the sizes of the circle slices.

 FCAT PRACTICE Completing the correlated items below will help you prepare for the **FCAT Mathematics** test.

Practicing the Skill

Look at the graph below to answer the following questions.

1. What is the subject of the circle graph?
2. Which religion in South Asia has the most followers? **FCAT MA.E.3.3.1**
3. What percentage practice Islam? **FCAT MA.E.3.3.1**
4. What is the combined percentage of Buddhist and Christian followers? **FCAT MA.E.3.3.1**

Applying the Skill

Quiz at least 10 friends about the capitals of India, Pakistan, and Bangladesh. Create a circle graph showing what percentage knew (a) all three capitals, (b) two capitals, (c) one capital, or (d) no capitals. **FCAT MA.E.1.3.1**

GO TO Practice key skills with **Glencoe Skillbuilder Interactive Workbook, Level 1.**

NATIONAL GEOGRAPHIC

Religions of South Asia

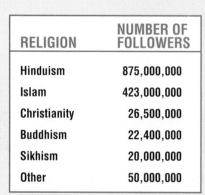

RELIGION	NUMBER OF FOLLOWERS
Hinduism	875,000,000
Islam	423,000,000
Christianity	26,500,000
Buddhism	22,400,000
Sikhism	20,000,000
Other	50,000,000

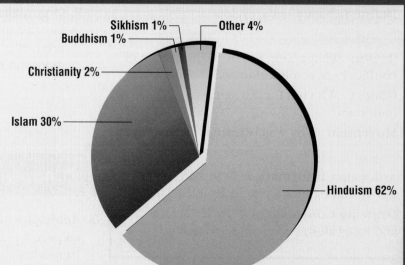

Sikhism 1%
Buddhism 1%
Other 4%
Christianity 2%
Islam 30%
Hinduism 62%

Source: *The World Factbook*, 2003.

Guide to Reading

Main Idea

The other countries of South Asia include mountainous Nepal and Bhutan and the island countries of Sri Lanka and the Maldives.

Terms to Know

- *dzong*
- atoll
- lagoon

Reading Strategy

Create a chart like this one. Then write the main economic activities of these countries in South Asia. **FCAT** LA.A.1.3.2

Country	Economic Activities
Nepal	
Bhutan	
Sri Lanka	
Maldives	

The following are the major Sunshine State Standards covered in this section.

SS.A.3.3.5:
Understands the differences between institutions of Eastern and Western civilizations (e.g., differences in governments, social traditions and customs, economic systems and religious institutions)

SS.B.2.3.8:
Knows world patterns of resource distribution and utilization

Section 3

Mountain Kingdoms, Island Republics

NATIONAL GEOGRAPHIC Exploring Our World

Perched on poles planted into the ocean floor, Sri Lankan fishers await their next catch. Although Sri Lanka is trying to build a modern economy, traditional work still goes on. Some people gave up fishing when Sri Lanka seemed ready to become a major tourist destination. However, years of ethnic warfare have kept tourists away and slowed the economy.

Of the four other countries of South Asia, two are landlocked kingdoms and two are island republics. **Nepal** and **Bhutan** both lie among the towering peaks of the Himalaya. The island countries of **Sri Lanka** and the **Maldives** lie south of India in the Indian Ocean.

Mountainous Nepal

Nepal—about the size of Arkansas—forms a steep stairway to the world's highest mountain range. The Himalaya, dominating about 80 percent of Nepal's land area, are actually three mountain ranges running side by side. Nepal is home to 8 of the 10 highest mountains in the world. **Mount Everest,** the highest, soars 29,035 feet (8,850 m).

Swift rivers cut through the lower ranges in the south, shaping fertile valleys. A flat, fertile river plain runs along Nepal's southern border with India. The plain includes farmland, swamps, and rain forests. Tigers, elephants, and other wild animals roam these forests.

Nepal has a humid subtropical climate in the south and a highland climate in the north. Monsoon rains often flood the southern plains area.

Nepal's economy depends almost entirely on farming. Farmers grow rice, sugarcane, wheat, corn, and potatoes to feed their families. Most fields are located on the southern plains or on terraced plots among the lower mountain slopes.

As the population increases, farmers move higher up the slopes. There they clear forests for new fields and use the cut trees for fuel. Stripped of trees, however, the slopes erode very easily. Valleys are often flooded, fields destroyed, and rivers filled with mud.

Nepal was not linked to other countries for centuries. Today, there are roads and air service to India and Pakistan, so trade is not as limited. Herbs, jute, rice, and wheat are exported to India. In return, Nepal imports gasoline, fertilizer, and machinery. Clothing and carpets now make up the country's most valuable exports. Nepal's rugged mountains attract thousands of climbers and hikers each year, creating a growing tourist industry.

Nepal's People   Nepal has 25.2 million people. Most are related to peoples in northern India and Tibet. One group—the Sherpa—is known for its skill in guiding mountain climbers. About 85 percent of Nepal's people live in rural villages. A growing number live in **Kathmandu,** Nepal's capital and largest city. Nepal is a parliamentary democracy ruled by a prime minister, who is appointed by Nepal's king.

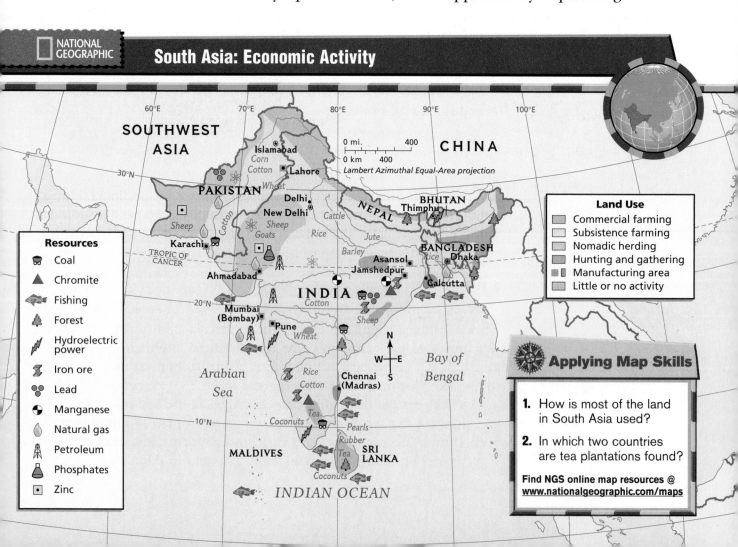

NATIONAL GEOGRAPHIC

South Asia: Economic Activity

Land Use
- Commercial farming
- Subsistence farming
- Nomadic herding
- Hunting and gathering
- Manufacturing area
- Little or no activity

Resources
- Coal
- Chromite
- Fishing
- Forest
- Hydroelectric power
- Iron ore
- Lead
- Manganese
- Natural gas
- Petroleum
- Phosphates
- Zinc

Applying Map Skills

1. How is most of the land in South Asia used?

2. In which two countries are tea plantations found?

Find NGS online map resources @ www.nationalgeographic.com/maps

The founder of Buddhism, Siddartha Gautama (sihd•DAHR•tuh GAU•tuh•muh), was born in the Kathmandu region about 563 B.C. Raised as a prince, Gautama gave up his wealth and became a holy man in India. Known as the Buddha, or "Enlightened One," he taught that people could find peace from life's troubles by living simply, doing good deeds, and meditating. Buddhism later spread to other parts of Asia.

Today Hinduism is Nepal's official religion, but Buddhism is practiced as well. If you visit Nepal, you will find temples and monuments of both religions scattered throughout the country.

✓ **Reading Check** What has helped Nepal trade with other countries?

Bhutan—Land of the Thunder Dragon

East of Nepal lies an even smaller kingdom—Bhutan. Bhutan is about half the size of Indiana. The map on page 650 shows you that a small part of India separates Bhutan from Nepal.

As in Nepal, the Himalaya are the major landform of Bhutan. Violent mountain storms are common and are the basis of Bhutan's name, which means "land of the thunder dragon." In the foothills of the Himalaya, the climate is mild. Thick forests cover much of this area. To the south—along Bhutan's border with India—lies an area of subtropical plains and river valleys.

More than 90 percent of Bhutan's people are subsistence farmers. They live in the fertile mountain valleys and grow the spice cardamom, oranges, rice, corn, and potatoes. People also herd cattle and yaks, which are a type of oxen. Bhutan is trying to develop its economy, but the very high mountains slow progress. Building roads is difficult, and there are no railroads. However, Bhutan has built hydroelectric plants to create electricity from rushing mountain waters. It now exports electricity to India. Tourism is a new industry, but the government limits the number of tourists to protect Bhutan's cultural traditions.

Bhutan's People Bhutan has about 900,000 people. Most speak the Dzonkha dialect and live in rural villages that dot southern valleys and plains. **Thimphu,** the capital, is located in the southern area.

Bhutan was once called the Hidden Holy Land because of its isolation and its Buddhist religion. In the 1960s, new roads and other connections opened Bhutan to the outside world. Most people remain deeply loyal to Buddhism. In Bhutan, Buddhist centers of prayer and study are called *dzongs.* They have shaped the country's art and culture.

NATIONAL GEOGRAPHIC **On Location**

Bhutan

This woman makes her living by herding yaks in one of Bhutan's mountain valleys.

Economics What is slowing Bhutan's economic progress?

Analyzing the Graph

Mount Everest is the tallest mountain on the earth.

Place What is the tallest mountain in North America?

FCAT MA.E.3.3.1

FCAT
PRACTICE

Completing the exercise above will help you prepare for the **FCAT Mathematics** test.

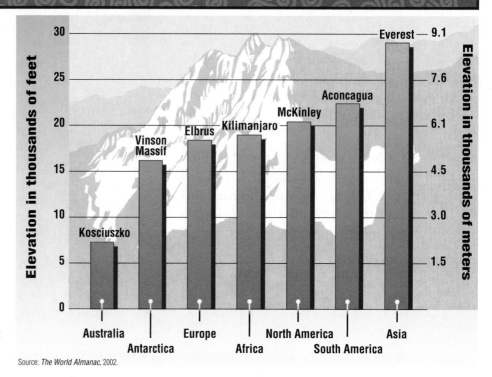

Source: *The World Almanac*, 2002.

For many years, Bhutan was ruled by strong kings. In 1998 the country began to move toward democracy. At that time, the ruling king agreed to share his power with an elected legislature.

✓**Reading Check** What is the main religion in Bhutan?

Sri Lanka—Brilliant Island

Pear-shaped Sri Lanka lies about 20 miles (32 km) off the southeastern coast of India. A little larger than West Virginia, Sri Lanka is a land of white beaches, dense forests, and abundant wildlife. Much of the country along the coast is rolling lowlands. Highlands cover the center. Rivers flow from the highlands, providing irrigation for crops.

The country has tropical climates with wet and dry seasons. Monsoon winds and heavy rains combine with the island's warm temperatures and fertile soil to make Sri Lanka a good place to farm.

Sri Lanka has long been known for its agricultural economy. Many farmers grow rice and other food crops in lowland areas. In the higher elevations, tea, rubber, and coconuts grow on large plantations. The country is one of the world's leading producers of tea and rubber.

The country is also famous for its sapphires, rubies, and other gemstones. Forests contain valuable woods, such as ebony and satinwood, as well as a variety of birds and animals. To protect the wildlife, the government has set aside land for national parks.

In the past 20 years, Sri Lanka's economy has become more industrialized. Factories produce textiles, fertilizers, cement, leather products, and wood products for export. New and growing industries include telecommunications, insurance, and banking. **Colombo,** the capital, is a bustling port on the country's western coast.

Sri Lanka's People   For centuries, Sri Lanka prospered because of its location on an important ocean route between Africa and Asia. It was a natural stopping place for seagoing traders. Beginning in the 1500s, Sri Lanka—then known as Ceylon—came under the control of European countries. The British ruled the island from 1802 to 1948, when it became independent. In 1972 Ceylon took the name of Sri Lanka, an ancient term meaning "brilliant land." Today Sri Lanka is a republic with a president who carries out ceremonial duties. Real power is held by a prime minister, who is the head of government.

About 19.3 million people live here. They belong to two major ethnic groups: the Sinhalese (SIHN•huh•LEEZ) and the Tamils (TA•muhlz). Forming about 74 percent of the population, the Sinhalese live in the southern and western parts of the island. They speak Sinhalese and are mostly Buddhist. The Tamils make up about 18 percent of the population. They live in the north and east, speak Tamil, and are Hindus.

Since 1983 the Tamils and the Sinhalese have fought a violent civil war. The minority Tamils claim they have not been treated justly by the

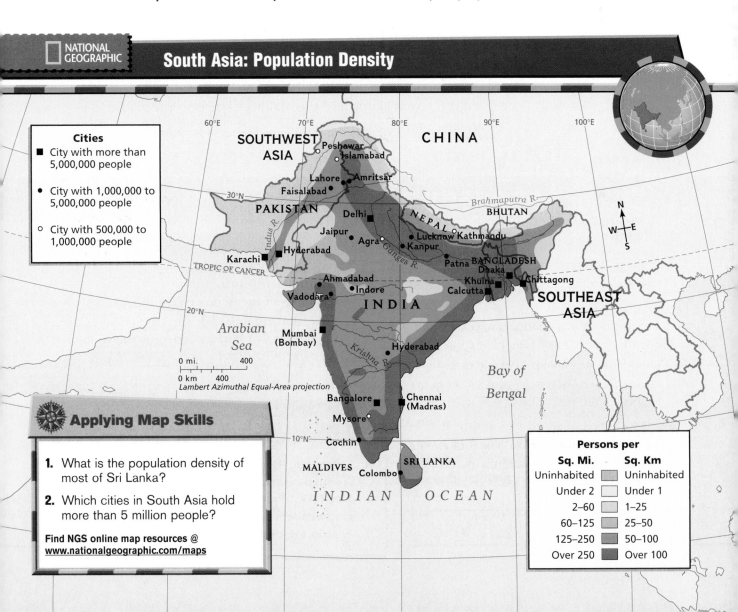

NATIONAL GEOGRAPHIC

South Asia: Population Density

Cities

■ City with more than 5,000,000 people

• City with 1,000,000 to 5,000,000 people

○ City with 500,000 to 1,000,000 people

Applying Map Skills

1. What is the population density of most of Sri Lanka?

2. Which cities in South Asia hold more than 5 million people?

Find NGS online map resources @ www.nationalgeographic.com/maps

Persons per	
Sq. Mi.	**Sq. Km**
Uninhabited	Uninhabited
Under 2	Under 1
2–60	1–25
60–125	25–50
125–250	50–100
Over 250	Over 100

0 mi. 400
0 km 400
Lambert Azimuthal Equal-Area projection

majority Sinhalese. They want to set up a separate Tamil nation in northern Sri Lanka. Thousands have lost their lives in the fighting. A cease-fire began in 2001 after nearly two decades of fighting.

Reading Check What are the two main ethnic groups in Sri Lanka?

The Maldives

About 370 miles (595 km) south of India lie the Maldives, made up of about 1,200 coral islands. Many of the islands are atolls. An **atoll** is a low-lying, ring-shaped island that surrounds a lagoon. A **lagoon** is a shallow pool of water near a larger body of water. Only 200 of the islands are inhabited. The climate of the Maldives is warm and humid throughout the year. Monsoons bring plenty of rain.

Most of the Maldives have poor, sandy soil. Only a limited number of crops can grow, including sweet potatoes, grains, and watermelon. In recent years, the Maldives's palm-lined sandy beaches and coral formations have attracted many tourists. As a result, tourism is now the largest industry. Fishing is the second-largest industry.

The first people to arrive in the Maldives came from southern India and Ceylon (Sri Lanka) several thousand years ago. Over the years, the islands' position near major sea routes brought traders from many other places. Today about 300,000 people live in the Maldives. Some 60,000 of them make their home in **Male** (MAH•lay), the capital. Most are Muslims. The islands, which came under British rule during the late 1890s, became independent in 1965. The local traditional ruler lost his throne three years later, and the Maldives became a republic.

Reading Check What is the main industry in the Maldives?

 FCAT PRACTICE You can prepare for the FCAT-assessed standards by completing the correlated item(s) below.

Section 3 Assessment

Defining Terms
1. Define *dzong,* atoll, lagoon.

Recalling Facts
2. **Economics** What products have recently become Nepal's most valuable exports?
3. **Place** How do Bhutan's people earn a living?
4. **Economics** How has Sri Lanka's economy changed in the past 20 years?

Graphic Organizer
5. **Organizing Information** List four events from Sri Lanka's history and their dates on a time line like this one. **FCAT LA.A.1.3.2**

Critical Thinking
6. **Summarizing Information** What were the teachings of the Buddha? **FCAT LA.A.2.3.1**
7. **Formulating an Opinion** Do you agree with the decision of Bhutan's government to limit tourism? Why or why not? **FCAT LA.A.2.3.8**

 Applying Social Studies Skills

8. **Analyzing Maps** Look at the population density map on page 653 and the physical map on page 645. What is the population density of the southern part of Nepal? The northern part? Explain the difference. **FCAT MA.B.1.3.4**

Section 1 | India—Past and Present

Terms to Know
subcontinent
monsoon
green revolution
jute
cottage industry
pesticide
caste
reincarnation

Main Idea
India is trying to develop its resources to meet the needs of its rapidly growing population.

✓ **Place** India is the largest country in South Asia in size and population.

✓ **Place** The Himalaya and the monsoons affect India's climate.

✓ **Economics** India's economy is based on farming and industry.

✓ **Culture** India has many languages and religions, but the majority of Indians are Hindus.

✓ **Government** India is a representative democracy.

Section 2 | Pakistan and Bangladesh

Terms to Know
tributary
delta
cyclone

Main Idea
Once a single nation, Pakistan and Bangladesh today are separate countries that border India on the west and east.

✓ **History** Cultural and political differences between Pakistan and Bangladesh led to war and separation in 1971.

✓ **Economics** Pakistan has fertile land and energy resources, but its economy is not well developed because of a history of unstable governments.

✓ **Location** The Ganges and Brahmaputra Rivers form deltas in Bangladesh.

✓ **Place** Bangladesh is a densely populated and poor country.

Section 3 | Mountain Kingdoms, Island Republics

Terms to Know
dzong
atoll
lagoon

Main Idea
The other countries of South Asia include mountainous Nepal and Bhutan and the island countries of Sri Lanka and the Maldives.

✓ **Region** The Himalaya are the major landform of Nepal and Bhutan.

✓ **Economics** Most people in Nepal are farmers, but the production of clothing and carpets has gained importance in recent years.

✓ **Culture** The Buddhist religion has shaped the art and culture of Bhutan.

✓ **Economics** Sri Lanka has industrialized, but agriculture is still important.

✓ **Economics** Tourism is the biggest industry in the Maldives.

◄ A teacher and his students have class outdoors on a pleasant day in Bhutan.

chapter 22

Assessment and Activities

FCAT PRACTICE You can prepare for the FCAT-assessed standards by completing the correlated item(s) below.

Using Key Terms

Match the terms in Part A with their definitions in Part B.

A.

1. monsoon
2. cyclone
3. green revolution
4. jute
5. subcontinent
6. reincarnation
7. pesticide
8. caste
9. *dzong*
10. cottage industry

B.

a. social class based on a person's ancestry
b. seasonal wind
c. family members supply their own equipment to make goods
d. large landmass that is part of another continent but distinct from it
e. Buddhist center for prayer and study
f. chemical used to kill insects
g. intense storm system with high winds
h. a government effort to use modern farming methods
i. the belief that after the body dies, the soul is reborn
j. plant fiber used for making rope, burlap bags, and carpet backing

Reviewing the Main Ideas

Section 1 India—Past and Present

11. **Place** What forms a barrier between South Asia and the rest of Asia?
12. **Place** How do the Himalaya affect India's climate?
13. **Economics** What kinds of goods are produced by India's cottage industries?
14. **History** What did Hinduism organize India's society into?

Section 2 Pakistan and Bangladesh

15. **Place** What river flows through Pakistan?
16. **Human/Environment Interaction** What often happens when the rains come too late in Bangladesh?
17. **Economics** What do most of the people of Bangladesh do for a living?

Section 3 Mountain Kingdoms, Island Republics

18. **Place** What is Nepal's capital?
19. **History** Why was Bhutan once called the Hidden Holy Land?
20. **History** What is the basis of the civil war in Sri Lanka?
21. **Location** How did Sri Lanka's location allow it to prosper for many centuries?

NATIONAL GEOGRAPHIC **South Asia**

Place Location Activity

On a separate sheet of paper, match the letters on the map with the numbered places listed below.

1. Ganges River
2. New Delhi
3. Brahmaputra River
4. Indus River
5. Sri Lanka
6. Himalaya
7. Bangladesh
8. Mumbai
9. Western Ghats
10. Deccan Plateau

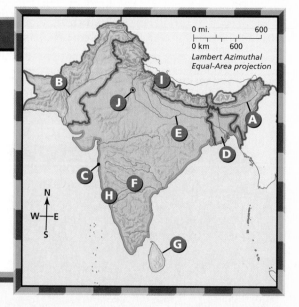

0 mi. 600
0 km 600
Lambert Azimuthal Equal-Area projection

Self-Check Quiz Visit *The World and Its People* Web site at twip.glencoe.com and click on **Chapter 22—Self-Check Quizzes** to prepare for the Chapter Test.

Critical Thinking

22. **Identifying Alternatives** In this chapter you read about South Asia, a region with much poverty. What problems do you think a country faces when it has so many poor people? What are some solutions to this poverty? **FCAT LA.A.2.3.1**

23. **Understanding Cause and Effect** Create a diagram like this one. List a physical feature of South Asia in the left-hand box. In the right-hand box, explain how that feature affects people's lives. **FCAT LA.A.2.3.1**

Comparing Regions Activity

24. **Culture** The Taj Mahal in India is one of the world's most impressive structures. Also impressive are the pyramids in Egypt. Use the information in your textbook to write a paragraph describing each. Include why each was built and compare the reasons. **FCAT LA.B.1.3.2**

Mental Mapping Activity

25. **Focusing on the Region** Create a simple outline map of South Asia, and then label the following:

- Ganges River
- Sri Lanka
- Kashmir
- Pakistan
- Nepal
- Indian Ocean
- Bhutan
- Bangladesh
- Ganges Plain
- New Delhi

Technology Skills Activity

26. **Using the Internet** Use the Internet to research tourism in one of the following countries: Nepal, India, or Sri Lanka. Create a travel brochure about a trip to the country, featuring information on the equipment and clothing that is needed, the availability of guides, costs, and so on. **FCAT LA.A.2.3.5**

Standardized Test Practice

Directions: Study the graph below, and then answer the questions that follow.

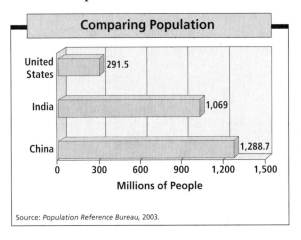

Comparing Population

United States — 291.5
India — 1,069
China — 1,288.7

Millions of People

Source: *Population Reference Bureau, 2003.*

1. **How many people live in India?**
   A 1,069   **FCAT MA.E.3.3.1**
   B 1,000,069
   C 1,069,000,000
   D 1,069,000,000,000

2. **About how many more people live in India than in the United States?**
   F 2.5 times as many   **FCAT MA.E.3.3.1**
   G 3.6 times as many
   H 4.5 times as many
   J 5.6 times as many

Test-Taking Tip: You often need to use math skills in order to understand graphs. Look at the information along the sides and bottom of the graph to find out what the bars on the graph mean. Notice that on the graph above, the numbers represent millions of people. Therefore, you need to multiply the number on each bar by 1,000,000 to get the correct answer.

23

China and Its Neighbors

The World and Its People

NATIONAL GEOGRAPHIC

To learn more about the people and places of China, view *The World and Its People* **Chapter 24** video.

Social Studies online

Chapter Overview Visit *The World and Its People* Web site at twip.glencoe.com and click on **Chapter 23—Chapter Overviews** to preview information about China.

FOLDABLES™
Study Organizer

The activity below will help you prepare for the **FCAT Reading** test.

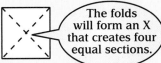

Identifying Main Ideas Make this foldable to help you identify key facts about the people and places of China and its neighbors. **FCAT LA.A.1.3.2**

Step 1 Fold the paper from the top right corner down so the edges line up. Cut off the leftover piece.

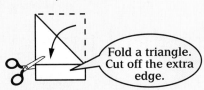

Fold a triangle. Cut off the extra edge.

Step 2 Fold the triangle in half. Unfold.

The folds will form an X that creates four equal sections.

Step 3 Cut up one fold line and stop at the middle. This forms two triangular flaps.

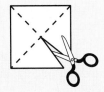

Step 4 Draw an X on one tab and label the other three the following: Mongolia; China; Taiwan.

Step 5 Fold the X flap under the other flap and glue together.

This makes a three-sided pyramid.

Reading and Writing As you read the chapter, write main ideas inside the foldable under each appropriate pyramid wall. **FCAT LA.A.1.3.2**

◀ *Part of the Great Wall of China*

Why It Matters

Opening Doors

Built to keep out foreigners, the Great Wall of China is the country's best-known structure. For centuries, China has worked to protect its culture from outside influences. Recently however, the need to develop its economy has motivated China to begin opening its doors to trade with other countries. In addition, Beijing—the capital of China—was chosen in 2001 to host the 2008 Summer Olympics.

China's Land and New Economy

Guide to Reading

Main Idea

China—the third-largest country in the world—has very diverse landforms. China's rapidly growing economy has changed in recent years.

Terms to Know

- dike
- fault
- communist state
- consumer goods

Reading Strategy

Create a diagram like this one. Then list two facts under each heading in the outer ovals. **FCAT LA.A.1.3.2**

The following are the major Sunshine State Standards covered in this section.

SS.D.2.3.1:
Understands ways production and distribution decisions are determined in the United States economy and how these decisions compare to those made in market, tradition-based, command, and mixed economic systems

SS.B.2.3.9:
Understands ways the interaction between physical and human systems affects current conditions on Earth

NATIONAL GEOGRAPHIC **Exploring Our World**

Giant pandas look cute and cuddly, but actually they are somewhat hot-tempered. You would be hot-tempered as well, if your habitat were dwindling in size. Fewer than 1,000 pandas live in the wild, and about 140 live in zoos. The wild pandas make their home on the eastern edge of the Plateau of Tibet. They eat mainly bamboo stems and leaves.

China (officially called the People's Republic of China) lies in the central part of eastern Asia. It is the third-largest country in area, after Russia and Canada. China is just slightly larger than the United States.

China's Landscape

The map on the next page shows the many landforms that are within China's vast area. Rugged mountains cover about one-third of the country. Find the **Himalaya, Kunlun Shan, Tian Shan,** and **Altay Mountains** on the map.

Also located in China is the world's largest plateau. This high, flat land, commonly called the "Roof of the World," is really the **Plateau of Tibet.** Its height averages about 14,800 feet (4,500 m) above sea level. Scattered shrubs and grasses cover the plateau's harsh landscape. Pandas, golden monkeys, and other rare animals roam the thick forests found at the eastern end of this plateau.

In addition to very high elevations, western China has some extremely low areas. The Turpan Depression, east of the Tian Shan, lies about 505 feet (154 m) *below* sea level. It is partly filled with salt lakes. It also is the hottest area of China. Daytime temperatures can reach as high as 122°F (50°C).

In northwestern China, mountain ranges circle desert areas. One of these areas is the **Taklimakan Desert**—an isolated region with very high temperatures. Sandstorms here can last for days and create huge, drifting sand dunes. Farther east lies another desert, the **Gobi.** About twice the size of Texas, the Gobi has rocks and stones instead of sand.

The map below shows that eastern China has plains along the Yellow, East China, and South China Seas. About 90 percent of China's people live on these fertile plains. Rich in minerals, eastern China is the site of the largest urban manufacturing areas, including **Beijing** and **Shanghai.** In hilly areas, farmers grow crops on terraced fields. Northern China holds many natural resources as well. China is a world leader in mining coal and iron ore. Tourists visit southeastern China to see its scenic waterfalls and steep gorges.

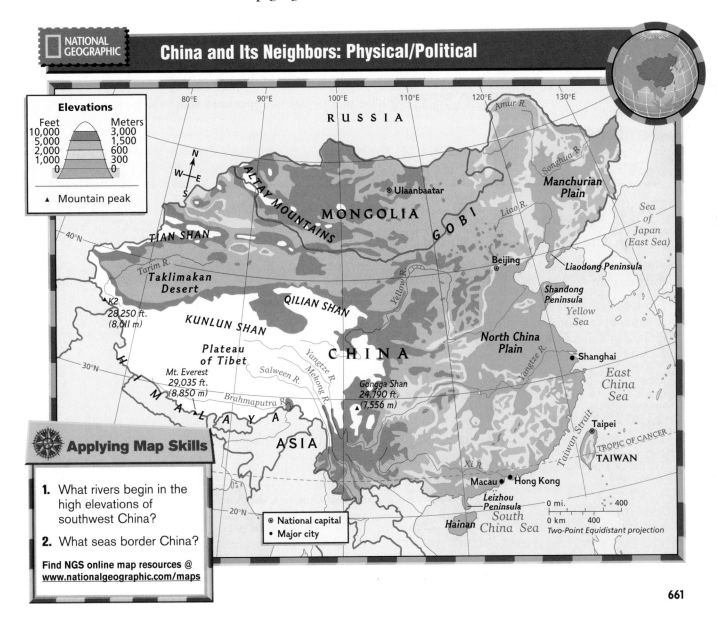

NATIONAL GEOGRAPHIC

China and Its Neighbors: Physical/Political

Elevations

Feet	Meters
10,000	3,000
5,000	1,500
2,000	600
1,000	300
0	0

▲ Mountain peak

Applying Map Skills

1. What rivers begin in the high elevations of southwest China?

2. What seas border China?

Find NGS online map resources @ www.nationalgeographic.com/maps

⊛ National capital
• Major city

Two-Point Equidistant projection

Web Activity Visit *The World and Its People* Web site at twip.glencoe.com and click on **Chapter 23– Student Web Activities** to learn more about China's rivers.

Rivers Three of China's major waterways—the **Yangtze** (YANG•SEE), **Yellow,** and **Xi** (SHEE) **Rivers**—flow through the plains and southern highlands. They serve as important transportation routes and also as a source of soil. How? For centuries, these rivers have flooded their banks in the spring. The floodwaters have deposited rich soil to form flat river basins that can be farmed. China's most productive farmland is found in valleys formed by these major rivers.

Despite their benefits, the rivers of China have also brought much suffering. The Chinese call the Yellow River "China's sorrow." In the past, its flooding cost hundreds of thousands of lives and caused much damage. Floods in July and August 1998 killed at least 3,000 and caused an estimated $20 billion in damage. To help control floods, the Chinese have built dams and dikes, or high banks of soil, along the rivers. Turn to page 665 to learn more about the Three Gorges Dam, a project that is underway on the Yangtze River.

An Unsteady Land In addition to floods, people in eastern China face another danger—earthquakes. Their part of the country stretches along the Ring of Fire, a name that describes Pacific coastal areas with volcanoes and frequent earthquakes. Eastern China lies along a fault, or crack in the earth's crust. As a result, earthquakes in this region are common—and can be very violent. Because so many people live in eastern China, these earthquakes can be disastrous.

✓ **Reading Check** What problem does China have with its large rivers?

Completing the exercise below will help you prepare for the **FCAT Mathematics** test.

Leading Rice-Producing Countries

Analyzing the Graph

The most important food crop in Asia is rice.

Economics How many millions of tons of rice does China produce in a year? **FCAT MA.E.3.3.1**

Visit twip.glencoe.com and click on **Chapter 23– Textbook Updates.**

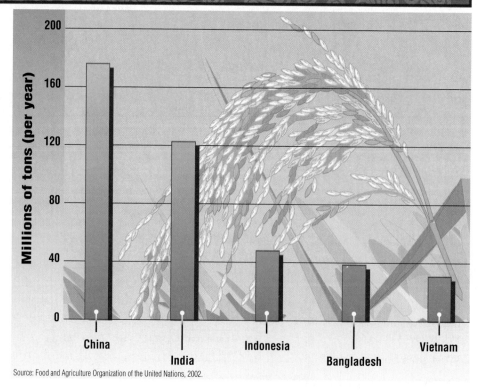

Source: Food and Agriculture Organization of the United Nations, 2002.

A New Economy

Since 1949, China has been a **communist state** in which the government has strong control over the economy and society as a whole. This means that government officials—not individuals or businesses—decide what crops to grow, what products to make, and what prices to charge. China discovered that the communist system created many problems. China fell behind other countries in technology, and manufactured goods were of poor quality.

In recent years, China's leaders have begun many changes to make the economy stronger. Without completely giving up communism, the government has allowed many features of a free enterprise system to take hold. Under this system, the government allows individuals to choose what jobs they want and where to start their own businesses. Workers can keep the profits they make. Farmers can grow and sell what they wish.

As a result of these and other changes, China's economy has boomed. Factories produce textiles, chemicals, electronic equipment, airplanes, ships, and machinery. Many of the items you own were probably made in China. Farm output has also risen rapidly. Because of mountains and deserts, only 10 percent of China's land is able to be farmed. Yet China is now a world leader in producing various agricultural products, including rice, tea, wheat, and potatoes.

Foreign Trade Eager to learn about new business methods, China has asked other countries to invest in, or put money into, Chinese businesses. Many companies in China are now jointly owned by Chinese and foreign businesspeople. Foreign companies expect two benefits from investing in China. First, they can pay Chinese workers less than they pay workers in their own countries. Second, companies in China have hundreds of millions of possible customers for their goods.

Results of Growth Because of economic growth, more of China's people are able to get jobs in manufacturing and service industries. Wages have increased, and more goods are available to buy. Some Chinese now enjoy a higher standard of living. They can afford **consumer goods,** or products people buy for themselves, such as

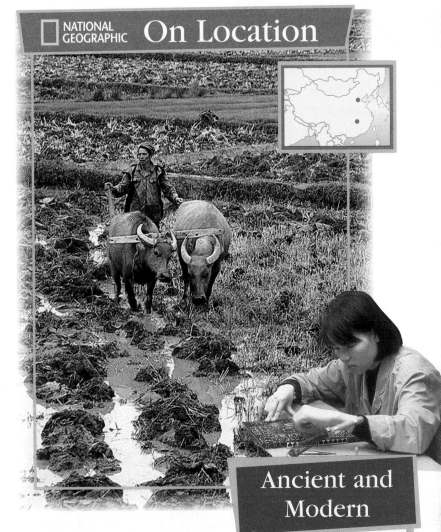

NATIONAL GEOGRAPHIC **On Location**

Ancient and Modern

In China's rural areas, ancient farming methods are still used (above left). However, in industrialized cities, high technology is being developed (above).

Government How has the government affected the economy in China?

Labor Costs

There's a good chance your clothes and shoes were manufactured in China. Some American companies can manufacture their products at much lower costs in China because the wages paid to workers there are low by U.S. standards. These companies pay more and offer better working conditions than Chinese employers. Still, some Americans are concerned about exploiting Chinese workers to make higher profits for U.S. companies.

televisions, cars, and motorcycles. Not everyone has adjusted well to the new economy, however. Many Chinese find that prices have risen faster than their incomes. Some Chinese have become very rich, while others remain poor.

China's economic growth has also harmed the environment. Many factories dump poisonous chemicals into rivers. Others burn coal, which gives off smoke that pollutes the air. This pollution leads to lung disease, which is the number one cause of death in China.

Hong Kong and Macau The cities of **Hong Kong** and **Macau** (muh•KOW) are an important part of the economic changes taking place in China. Both of these cities were once controlled by European countries—Hong Kong by the United Kingdom, and Macau by Portugal. China regained control of Hong Kong in 1997 and of Macau in 1999. Both are centers of manufacturing, trade, and finance. Chinese leaders hope that the successful businesses in these cities will help spur economic growth in the rest of the country.

At the same time, foreign companies that are considering investing in these cities must ask themselves whether China will stand by its "one country, two systems" pledge. The pledge refers to China's promise to allow Western freedoms and capitalism to exist side by side with Chinese communism. The **Time Reports: Focus on World Issues** on pages 671–677 takes a look at the economies and political freedoms of China and other countries in East Asia.

✓ Reading Check **To what does "one country, two systems" refer?**

FCAT PRACTICE You can prepare for the FCAT-assessed standards by completing the correlated item(s) below.

Section 1 Assessment

Defining Terms

1. **Define** dike, fault, communist state, consumer goods.

Recalling Facts

2. **Place** Name China's two large deserts.

3. **Region** What two very important functions do China's rivers perform?

4. **Economics** What has caused China's economy to boom?

Critical Thinking

5. **Summarizing Information** How are China's rivers both a blessing and a disaster?

6. **Making Comparisons** How is a communist economic system different from a free enterprise system? **FCAT LA.A.2.2.7**

7. **Analyzing Information** What benefits does China receive from foreign investments?

Graphic Organizer

8. **Organizing Information** Create a diagram like this one. In the proper places on the oval, fill in the physical features you would encounter if you traveled completely around China. **FCAT LA.A.1.3.2**

China

Applying Social Studies Skills

9. **Analyzing Maps** Look at the map on page 661. What is the capital of China?

Making Connections

ART   SCIENCE   CULTURE   TECHNOLOGY

The Three Gorges Dam

Since 1919, Chinese officials have dreamed of building a dam across the Yangtze, the third-longest river in the world. Curving through the heart of China, the river provides an important highway for moving people and products from town to town. Yet the Yangtze is unpredictable. For thousands of years, floods have harmed the millions of people who live along its banks. Now construction is under way to build the dam.

The Dam

In 1994 the Chinese government began a 17-year-long project to build the Three Gorges Dam. It will eventually be 1.5 miles (2.4 km) wide and more than 600 feet (183 m) high. The dam is being built about halfway between the cities of Chongqing and Wuhan. (See the map on page 668.) The dam will benefit China in several ways. First, it will control water flow and stop floods. Second, its system of locks will allow large ships to travel inland. This will reduce trade and transportation costs for the millions of people who live inland. Third, the dam will create electricity using turbines, or water-driven engines.

FCAT PRACTICE Answering questions 2 and 3 below will help you prepare for the **FCAT Mathematics** and **Reading** tests.

Controversy

Even with all the proposed benefits, many people within China and elsewhere have questioned the wisdom of building the dam. When completed, the dam will create a deep reservoir nearly 400 miles (644 km) long. This reservoir will flood more than 100 towns and force nearly 1.2 million people to move. Many of these people must leave the farms that their families have worked for centuries. Historians point out that the reservoir will also wash away more than 1,000 important historical sites, including the homeland of the first people to settle the region about 4,000 years ago.

Environmentalists caution that the dam may create pollution and health risks. Industrial sites, once they lie underwater, may leak hazardous chemicals. Sewage from communities surrounding the dam could flow directly into the reservoir and into the Yangtze River. In the past, this problem was less serious because the fast-moving waters of the Yangtze carried waste quickly out to sea.

Making the Connection

1. How have the unpredictable waters of the Yangtze River affected the Chinese?

2. Create a physical map of China showing the major rivers. Mark where the Three Gorges Dam is being built. **FCAT MA.B.1.3.4**

3. **Interpreting Points of View** List three reasons in support of constructing the Three Gorges Dam and three reasons against it. **FCAT LA.A.2.3.8**

◀ This is the city of Fengdu today (top) and as it will look when the dam and reservoir are completed (bottom).

Dynasties to Communism

Guide to Reading

Main Idea

The arts and ideas of ancient times still influence China today.

Terms to Know

- dynasty
- human rights
- exile
- calligraphy
- pagoda

Reading Strategy

Create a chart like this one. Then list two key facts in the right column for each item in the left column.

FCAT LA.A.1.3.2

China	
History	
Government	
Urban and Rural Life	
Arts	

The following are the major Sunshine State Standards covered in this section.

SS.A.3.3.4:
Knows significant leaders who have influenced the course of events in Eastern and Western civilizations since the Renaissance

SS.A.3.3.2:
Understands the historical events that have shaped the development of cultures throughout the world

NATIONAL GEOGRAPHIC — Exploring Our World

How do you celebrate the coming of a new year? This costumed figure lives in Tibet. He is a Buddhist monk, or holy man, performing an important ritual celebrating the Tibetan New Year. The mask and colorful robes show that he plays a special role in rituals designed to defeat the forces of evil.

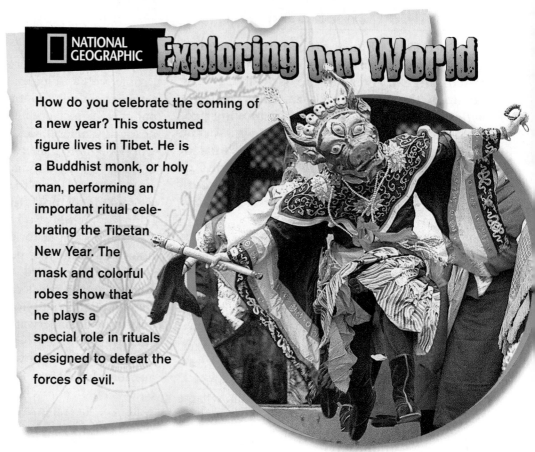

China's population of 1.29 billion is about one-fifth of the world's people. About 92 percent of these people belong to the ethnic group called Han Chinese. They have a distinctive culture. The remaining 8 percent belong to 55 other ethnic groups. Most of these groups, such as the Tibetans, live in the western part of China. They have struggled to protect their traditions from Han Chinese influences.

China's History

China's civilization is more than 4,000 years old. For many centuries until the early 1900s, rulers known as emperors or empresses governed China. Many lived in the Imperial Palace, located in the heart of **Beijing,** China's capital. A **dynasty,** or line of rulers from a single family, would hold power until it was overthrown. Then a new leader would start a new dynasty. Under the dynasties, China built a highly developed culture and conquered neighboring lands.

As their civilization developed, the Chinese tried to keep out foreign invaders. In many ways, this was easy. On most of China's borders, natural barriers such as seas, mountains, and deserts already provided protection. Still, invaders threatened from the north. To defend this area, the Chinese began building the Great Wall of China about 2,200 years ago. Over the centuries, the wall was continually rebuilt and lengthened. In time, it snaked more than 4,000 miles (6,437 km) from the Yellow Sea in the east to the deserts of the west. It still stands today.

Beliefs and Inventions   Chinese thinkers believed that learning was a key to good behavior. About 500 B.C., a thinker named Kongfuzi (KOONG•FOO•DZUH), or Confucius, taught that people should be polite, honest, brave, and wise. Children were to obey their parents, and every person was to respect the elderly and obey the country's rulers. Kongfuzi's teachings shaped China's government and society until the early 1900s.

During Kongfuzi's time, another thinker named Laozi (LOW•DZUH) arose. His teachings, called Daoism (DOW•IH•zuhm), stated that people should live simply and in harmony with nature. While Kongfuzi's ideas appealed to government leaders, Laozi's beliefs attracted artists and writers.

Buddhism came to China from Central Asia about A.D. 100. This religion taught that meditation, wisdom, and morality could help people find relief from life's problems. Over time, the Chinese mixed Buddhism, Daoism, and the ideas of Kongfuzi. This mixed spiritual heritage still influences many Chinese people today.

The early Chinese were inventors as well as thinkers. Did you know that they were using paper and ink before people in other parts of the world? Other Chinese inventions include silk, the magnetic compass, printed books, gunpowder, and fireworks. For hundreds of years, China was the most advanced civilization in the world.

Communist China   Foreign influences increasingly entered China during the 1700s and 1800s. Europeans especially wanted to get fine Chinese goods such as silk, tea, and pottery. The United Kingdom and other countries used military power to force China to trade.

In 1911 a Chinese uprising under the Western-educated Dr. Sun Yat-sen overthrew the last emperor. China became a republic, or a country governed by elected leaders. Disorder followed until the Nationalist political party took over. The Communist Party gained power as well. After World War II, the Nationalists and the Communists fought for control of China. General Chiang Kai-shek (jee•AHNG KY•SHEHK) led the Nationalists. Mao Zedong (MOW DZUH•DOONG) led the Communists.

In 1949 the Communists won and set up the People's Republic of China under Mao Zedong and Zhou Enlai (JOH ehn•LY). The Nationalists fled to the offshore island of Taiwan. There they set up a rival government.

Reading Check Why was the Great Wall of China built?

Believe It or Not!

Clay Warriors
One of the most fascinating archaeological finds in China was the clay army buried to guard the tomb of China's first emperor. The huge vault, covering 20 square miles (52 sq. km), was discovered in 1974. The clay warriors stand in four separate underground pits. In pit one are 6,000 life-size figures in military formation. Pit two contains 1,400 chariots and men. The third pit has an elite command force, and the fourth pit is empty, possibly abandoned before the work was completed. Each of the nearly 7,500 foot soldiers, horsemen, archers, and chariot riders were individually crafted more than 2,200 years ago.

China's Government and Society

After 1949 the Communists completely changed the mainland of China. All land and factories were taken over by the government. Farmers were organized onto large government farms, and women joined the industrial workforce. Dams and improved agricultural methods brought some economic benefits. Yet many government plans went wrong, and individual freedoms were lost. Many people were killed because they opposed communism.

After Mao Zedong died in 1976, a new Communist leader, Deng Xiaoping (DUHNG SYOW•PING), decided to take a new direction. He wanted to make China a more open country. One way to do this was to give people more economic freedom. The government kept tight control over all political activities, however. It continued to deny individual freedoms and acted harshly against any Chinese who criticized its actions. In 1989 about 100,000 students and workers gathered in Beijing's Tiananmen (TEE•EHN•AHN•MEHN) Square. The students and workers called for democracy and demanded political reforms in China. The government answered by sending tanks and troops. These government forces killed or injured thousands of protesters and arrested thousands more.

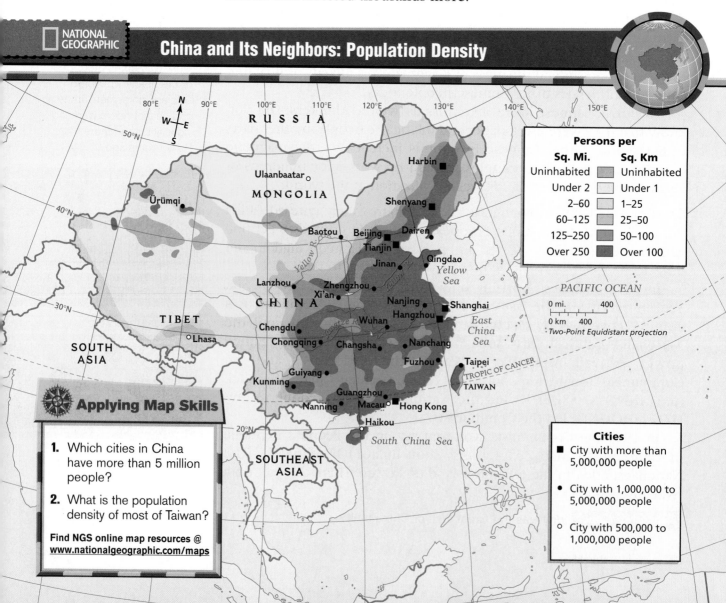

China and Its Neighbors: Population Density

NATIONAL GEOGRAPHIC

Persons per

Sq. Mi.	Sq. Km
Uninhabited	Uninhabited
Under 2	Under 1
2–60	1–25
60–125	25–50
125–250	50–100
Over 250	Over 100

0 mi. 400
0 km 400
Two-Point Equidistant projection

Cities
- ■ City with more than 5,000,000 people
- ● City with 1,000,000 to 5,000,000 people
- ○ City with 500,000 to 1,000,000 people

Applying Map Skills

1. Which cities in China have more than 5 million people?

2. What is the population density of most of Taiwan?

Find NGS online map resources @ www.nationalgeographic.com/maps

Countries around the world have protested the Chinese government's continued harsh treatment of people who criticize it. They say that Chinese leaders have no respect for **human rights.** These are the basic freedoms and rights, such as freedom of speech, that all people should enjoy. Because of China's actions, some people say that other countries should not trade with China.

China's leaders have also been criticized for their actions in Tibet. Tibet was once a separate Buddhist kingdom. China took control of the area in 1950 and crushed a rebellion there about nine years later. The Tibetan people have demanded independence since then. The Dalai Lama (DAH•ly LAH•muh), the Buddhist leader of Tibet, now lives in exile in India. Someone in **exile** is unable to live in his or her own country because of political beliefs. The Dalai Lama travels around the world trying to win support for his people.

NATIONAL GEOGRAPHIC **On Location**

Urban Life

Hundreds of thousands of people use bicycles—not cars—to get around Beijing and other cities.

Place About how many people live in China's cities?

Rural Life About 63 percent of China's people live in rural areas. The map on page 668 shows that most Chinese are crowded into the fertile river valleys of eastern China. Families work hard in their fields. They often use hand tools because mechanical equipment is too expensive.

Village life has improved in recent years. Most rural families now live in three- or four-room houses. They have enough food and some modern appliances. Many villages have community centers. People gather there to watch movies and play table tennis and basketball.

Urban Life More than 503 million Chinese people live in cities. China's cities are growing rapidly as people leave farms hoping to find better-paying jobs. Living conditions in the cities are crowded, but most homes and apartments have heat, electricity, and running water. Many people now earn enough money to buy extra clothes and televisions. They also have more leisure time to attend concerts or Chinese operas, walk in parks, or visit zoos.

✓ **Reading Check** Why have people in other countries criticized China's government?

China's Culture

China is famous for its traditional arts. Chinese craft workers make bronze bowls, jade jewelry, decorated silk, glazed pottery, and fine porcelain. The Chinese are also known for their painting, sculpture, and architecture.

China and Its Neighbors

▲ **Bronze vessel from the Shang dynasty**

▲ **Porcelain bowl from the Ming dynasty**

The Chinese love of nature has influenced painting and poetry. Chinese artists paint on long panels of paper or silk. Artwork often shows scenes of mountains, rivers, and forests. Artists attempt to portray the harmony between people and nature.

Many Chinese paintings include a poem written in **calligraphy,** which is the art of beautiful writing. Chinese writing is different from the print you are reading right now. It uses characters that represent words or ideas instead of letters that represent sounds. There are more than 50,000 Chinese characters, but the average person recognizes only about 4,000 to 5,000.

The Chinese developed bronze casting and the first porcelain centuries ago. Porcelain is made from coal dust and fine, white clay. Painted porcelain vases from early China are considered to be priceless today.

Most buildings in China's cities are modern. Yet traditional buildings still stand. Some have large, tiled roofs with edges that curve gracefully upward. Others are Buddhist temples with many-storied towers called **pagodas.** These buildings hold large statues of the Buddha.

Foods Cooking differs greatly from region to region in China. In coastal areas, people enjoy fish, crab, and shrimp dishes. Central China is famous for its spicy dishes made with hot peppers. A typical Chinese meal includes vegetables with bits of meat or seafood, soup, and rice or noodles. Often the meat and vegetables are cooked quickly in a small amount of oil over very high heat. This method—called stir-frying—allows the vegetables to stay crunchy.

✓ Reading Check **Where would you find statues of Buddha in China?**

FCAT PRACTICE You can prepare for the FCAT-assessed standards by completing the correlated item(s) below.

Section 2 Assessment

Defining Terms

1. Define dynasty, human rights, exile, calligraphy, pagoda.

Recalling Facts

2. History Name two thinkers who influenced life in China.

3. History Who led the Nationalists after World War II? Who led the Communists after World War II? Who won control of China?

4. Culture What scenes are commonly found in Chinese paintings?

Critical Thinking

5. Making Predictions How might the teachings of Kongfuzi prevent rebellions in China? **FCAT LA.A.1.3.2**

6. Summarizing Information Why did Europeans want to force China to trade with them? **FCAT LA.A.2.3.1**

Graphic Organizer

7. Organizing Information Create a time line like this one. Then list at least five dates and their events in China's history. **FCAT LA.A.1.3.2**

Applying Social Studies Skills

8. Analyzing Maps Look at the population density map on page 668. How does the population density in western China differ from eastern China?

TIME PERSPECTIVES

East Asia:
Report Card on Democracy
Who's Free, Who Isn't?

A South Korean Running for Office

GLADE MICHAEL/CORBIS SYGMA

A Chinese Soldier Unable to Vote

RENE BURRI/MAGNUM PHOTOS

Compiled and adapted from TIME.

North Koreans at Pyongyang, their nation's capital.
North Korean generals dedicate a new statue.

Escape From Horror

Evaluating
Media
LA.A.2.3.6

Kang Kil-Ok made a terrifying journey in 1997. In the dead of night, she fled from North Korea to China over the frozen Tumen River. North Korean border guards shot at her and missed. "Somehow," Kang said later, "we made it to the other side."

In recent years more than 300,000 brave North Koreans have escaped to China. These people felt they had no choice. North Korea is one of the world's most brutal dictatorships. Its citizens have very few rights. The nation's Communist government assigns citizens jobs and places to live. It tells those who run farms and factories what and how much to produce. It jails and even executes people who refuse to follow orders. The result is a nation whose people must face many hardships. There are shortages of just about everything: fuel, fertilizer, electricity, food, and medicine.

During the 1990s, a severe food shortage left as many as two million North Koreans dead. The United States and other nations sent millions of dollars of food aid into the country. The government, however, distributed most of it to North Korea's 1.2 million soldiers and the families of top officials.

Kang left North Korea after her mother died. Kang's brother had already gone to China. When he disappeared, police beat their mother to get her to tell them where he went. "My mother's knees were so badly bruised, she couldn't even stand up," Kang said. "They kicked her with boots and whacked her with sticks. It made me realize I had to leave North Korea, too." Her mother died three months later.

Most of those who flee North Korea have a common goal. They hope to stay in China long enough to find a way to South Korea, one of Asia's most modern, democratic nations.

North Korea's Freedom House Score:
Not Free. *Political Rights: 7.
Civil Liberties: 7.*

Who's Free, Who's Not in East Asia

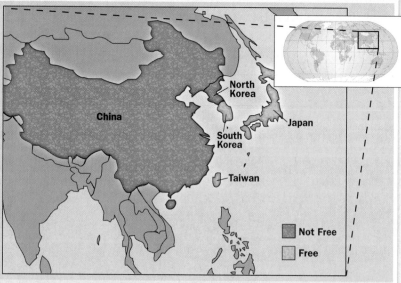

China

North Korea

Japan

South Korea

Taiwan

Not Free

Free

Making Comparisons

How many countries are there in East Asia? How many are not free? Which country borders China? Is it free or not free?

A busy street in Beijing, China's capital

Shanghai, China, is home to many new businesses.

Chinese shoppers in a Shanghai department store

China: A Nation on the Move

In China, Kang lived in constant fear. The Chinese send **escapees** they capture back to North Korea. Those sent home are tossed into jail, tortured, and sometimes executed.

Like North Korea, China is not a free country. Citizens can't vote to choose

What Is a Democracy?

A **democracy** is a government in which the final authority rests with the nation's people. Voters elect representatives who carry out the people's wishes.

Democracies are not all the same. All grant their people **political rights.** They hold free elections and allow political parties to compete for votes. Stronger democracies also protect the **civil liberties,** or freedoms, of every citizen.

The U.S. government is the second type. An organization called Freedom House gives it top grades for its defense of liberty and political rights. Freedom House is a private, not-for-profit organization based in Washington, D.C. It has promoted democratic values around the world since the 1940s.

Every year Freedom House decides how well the world's nations are defending the rights and freedoms of their citizens. Then it gives each nation two grades: one for political rights, one for civil liberties. The scores range from 1 (best) to 7 (worst). You will find the 2003 scores for East Asian nations at the end of each article in this report.

their leaders. They have few basic rights. Communist Party leaders make all the important decisions. Thousands of people are in jail today simply because they dared to criticize the government.

In one important way, China is freer than North Korea. It lets people run their own businesses. For 30 years, the government ran all the nation's enterprises, from farms to restaurants. But the farms barely produced enough to feed the nation of 1.3 billion people. China's factories at that time produced poorly-made goods.

During the late 1970s, the government let its citizens own businesses and farm their own plots of land. The chance to earn good pay in private business has given the Chinese a reason to work harder. Today only the United States produces more goods and services than China.

After four years in China, Kang found out that her brother was in South Korea. He sent her the money to pay people to smuggle her out of China. In June 2001, she landed at the airport outside Seoul, South Korea's capital.

China's Freedom House Score: Not Free. *Political Rights:* 7. *Civil Liberties:* 6. ▪

EXPLORING THE ISSUE

1. **Cause and Effect** Why did Kang leave North Korea? **FCAT LA.E.2.2.1**

2. **Making Inferences** China has 1.3 billion citizens. How might this have helped Kang stay there for four years? **FCAT LA.A.1.3.2**

South Korea: The Feel of Freedom

For Kang, South Korea seemed like another planet. Only eleven nations produce more goods and services than South Korea. One of those nations is China, whose population is 27 times larger than South Korea's.

▲ Seoul, South Korea's capital, pulses with life. It is an exciting symbol of the nation's success.

On average, each South Korean produces 20 times more than each North Korean. South Korea boasts the largest automobile factory in the world. The same factory builds trains that cruise at 180 miles an hour (300 km/h). Seoul is a dazzling mix of skyscrapers and neon—signs of the nation's success.

Politically, South Korea is far different from North Korea and China. Its five major political parties and several smaller ones battle for votes in fair elections. About 70 percent of the nation's eligible voters take part. In the United States, that figure is closer to 50 percent.

Getting used to a society that allows so much competition is hard for North Koreans. "We are so used to living with what we are given," said Byung, who escaped from North Korea with his wife, mother, and two small sons. Byung won't reveal his last name. He is afraid that the North Korean government will punish those of his relatives who remain behind. "We don't understand that it is up to us to find and hold a job. The biggest surprise is that everyone is free here to say what they want."

Kang agrees. "I know what freedom feels like here," she said.

South Korea isn't a perfect democracy, though. Its officials sometimes accept money in exchange for making decisions that benefit individuals or businesses. The government often arrests people suspected of being Communists. But overall, South Korea is one of Asia's strongest democracies.

South Korea's Freedom House Score:
Free. *Political Rights:* 1.
Civil Liberties: 2. ▪

EXPLORING THE ISSUE

1. **Explaining** How is South Korea different from North Korea and China politically?
   FCAT LA.A.2.3.1
2. **Analyzing** What does Kang mean when she says she knows what freedom feels like? **FCAT LA.A.2.3.2**

PHOTODISC/PUNCHSTOCK

Taiwan: Young Tiger

Taiwan is an island province of China. Its citizens like to view it as a separate country, however, because it has been on its own since 1949. Politically, Taiwan boasts four major parties and many smaller ones. Citizens vote for their leaders in open elections. Some politicians have been arrested for "buying" votes.

Like South Korea, Taiwan is called an "Asian Tiger" because of its powerful economy. Private businesses drive the economy. Money earned from exports and imports fuels it.

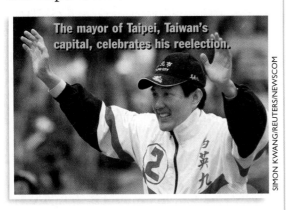

The mayor of Taipei, Taiwan's capital, celebrates his reelection.

SIMON KWANG/REUTERS/NEWSCOM

Independent courts protect the rights of the Taiwanese. However, women and minorities often face discrimination on the job. Journalists must be careful about what they say. Many observers are impressed that the Taiwanese enjoy so many freedoms. This is because Taiwan didn't hold its first free presidential election until 1996.

Taiwan's Freedom House Score: Free. *Political Rights:* 2. *Civil Liberties:* 2. ▪

Japan: Shining Democracy

Japan is one of the world's greatest success stories. Its economy is the world's third strongest, after those of the United States and China.

Business people like these keep Japan's economy strong.

PHOTODISC/PUNCHSTOCK

Japan's experiment with democracy began in 1947, soon after its defeat in World War II. At the time, Japan's emperor held most of the power. In 1947 a new **constitution** transferred that power to the people. The emperor became a **figurehead,** a ceremonial leader without much power.

As in Taiwan, women and minority group members often feel like second-class citizens. But Japan's courts do all they can to protect citizens' rights.

Japan's Freedom House Score: Free. *Political Rights:* 1. *Civil Liberties:* 2. ▪

EXPLORING THE ISSUE

1. **Evaluating Information** How can you tell that Taiwan and Japan are ruled by law?
   FCAT LA.A.1.3.2
2. **Analyzing Information** What makes Taiwan's and Japan's democracies alike?
   FCAT LA.A.2.2.7

Promoting Democracy: What Can One Person Do?

Evaluating Media
LA.A.2.3.6

According to Freedom House, there are more democracies today than at any time in history. Still, more than 2 billion people don't live in democratic nations. They are denied the right to vote and to enjoy the sort of freedoms that Americans take for granted.

This is an issue that concerns people everywhere. In 2002 representatives of more than 100 democracies met in Seoul, South Korea. They discussed ways to spread democracy. One solution they came up with had to do with schools. They agreed to try to persuade developing nations to teach **civics,** or courses about democracy.

This approach has been successful before. After World War II, schools in Germany and Japan, the two defeated powers, began to teach civics courses. Today those two nations enjoy the many benefits of freedom.

What can you do to help promote civics courses abroad? You can write to your representative in Congress. Explain why you think the U.S. government should help other nations develop such courses. Send the letter to your local newspaper, too.

Another way you can help spread democracy is to work with groups such as Amnesty International. Dozens of such groups are trying to make democracy catch on throughout the world. When they discover a government

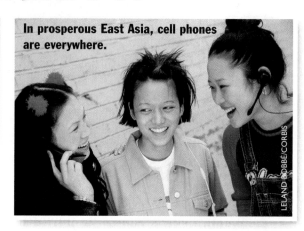

In prosperous East Asia, cell phones are everywhere.

LELAND BOBBÉ/CORBIS

abusing its citizens' rights, these groups say so. Amnesty International gets its thousands of supporters to write letters to the government's top leader. One letter won't change the world. But thousands of them remind leaders who act irresponsibly that the world is watching. To see how such campaigns work, go to Amnesty International's Web page, **www.amnestyusa.org**. Click on "Act Now!"

"What you do may seem terribly insignificant," Mohandas Gandhi said, "but it is terribly important that you do it anyway." Gandhi knew what he was talking about. He led the campaign that won India its independence in 1947.

EXPLORING THE ISSUE

1. **Finding the Main Idea** Come up with a title that will tell readers what this article is about. **FCAT LA.A.2.3.1**

2. **Compare and Contrast** This article suggests two ways to spread democracy. How are they alike? How are they different? **FCAT LA.A.2.3.1**

REVIEW AND ASSESS

UNDERSTANDING THE ISSUE

1. Defining Key Terms Write the definitions for the following terms: *democracy, political rights, civil liberties, escapee, constitution, figurehead, civics.* **FCAT LA.A.1.3.2**

2. Writing to Inform Imagine you are a North Korean and have just escaped to China. Write a letter to a friend and explain why you left North Korea. **FCAT LA.B.1.3.2**

3. Writing to Persuade In a brief essay, explain what the Chinese people would gain if their country were a democracy. **FCAT LA.B.1.3.2**

INTERNET RESEARCH ACTIVITY

4. The Internet is changing politics throughout Asia. In South Korea, online newspapers like *OhmyNews* can sway elections. *OhmyNews* posts hundreds of stories every day. Ordinary citizens write most of them. Go to **www.ohmynews.com**. Click around and study the pictures. What do the pictures suggest about the subjects South Koreans seem most interested in? Make a list and compare it with those of your classmates.

5. In China, millions of people have access to the Internet. China's courts have jailed people who use the Internet to criticize the government. Type in the key words "China" and "Internet" on an Internet search engine to find out why China's government both likes and fears the Internet. Write a short essay with your answers. **FCAT LA.A.2.3.5**

BEYOND THE CLASSROOM

6. Visit your school or local library to learn more about

CHRIS STEELE PERKINS/MAGNUM PHOTOS

▲ **In Tokyo, teens like to wear "street clothes."**

democracy in East Asia. Working in three groups, learn what it was like to live in Taiwan, South Korea, or Japan before these lands became democratic. Discuss your findings with your classmates.

7. Research a former Communist nation in Europe. What problems did that nation face while reinventing itself as a democracy? Write your findings in a short report. **FCAT LA.B.1.3.2**

Taiwan: From Dictatorship to Democracy

How one "Asian Tiger" went from military rule to free elections

1949 1950	1960	1970	1980	1990	2000

1950
The army controls Taiwan, allowing only one political party.

1949
Communists take over China. Two million non-Communist Chinese flock to the island of Taiwan.

1950s
Land is sold to small farmers.

1960s
Businesses make TVs, textiles, and other goods for export.

1970s
The government requires schooling for everyone. The economy grows rapidly.

1980s
The economy is the second strongest in Asia.

1986
New political parties are allowed.

1987
Military rule is lifted.

2000
Taiwan has its first peaceful transfer of power from the Nationalist to the Democratic Progressive Party.

BUILDING TIME LINE SKILLS

1. Analyzing Data How many years does this time line cover? What major changes took place during that time?

2. Making Inferences Which came first in Taiwan, economic growth or democracy? Why wasn't it the other way around? **FCAT LA.A.2.3.1**

FOR UPDATES ON WORLD ISSUES GO TO
www.timeclassroom.com/glencoe

China's Neighbors

NATIONAL GEOGRAPHIC

Exploring Our World

In the remote, harsh land of western Mongolia, a centuries-old tradition continues. Hunters train eagles to bring their kill back to the human hunter. The people say that female eagles make the best hunters. Because they weigh more than males, they can capture larger prey. Like all eagles, they have superb vision—eight times better than a human's.

Taiwan is an island close to China's mainland, and Mongolia borders China on the north. Throughout their histories, Taiwan and Mongolia have had close ties to their larger neighbor.

Taiwan

About 100 miles (161 km) off the southeastern coast of China lies the island country of **Taiwan.** It is slightly smaller than the states of Connecticut and Massachusetts put together. Through Taiwan's center runs a ridge of steep, forested mountains. On the east, the mountains descend to a rocky coastline. On the west, they fall away to a narrow, fertile plain. This flat area is home to the majority of the island's people. Like southeastern China, Taiwan has mild winters and hot, rainy summers.

Taiwan's Economy Taiwan has one of the world's most prosperous economies. Taiwan's wealth comes largely from high-technology industries, manufacturing, and trade with other countries. **High-technology industries** produce computers and other kinds of electronic equipment. Workers in Taiwan's factories make many different products, including computers, calculators, radios, televisions, and telephones. You have probably seen goods from Taiwan sold in stores in your community.

Taiwan has a growing economic influence on its Asian neighbors. Many powerful companies based in Taiwan have recently built factories in the People's Republic of China and Thailand. Despite their political differences, Taiwan and mainland China have strengthened their economic ties since the 1990s.

Agriculture also contributes to Taiwan's economy. The island's mountainous landscape limits the amount of land that can be farmed. Still, some farmers have built terraces on mountainsides to grow rice. Other major crops include sugarcane, citrus fruits, sweet potatoes, pineapples, tea, and soybeans. In fact, Taiwan's farmers produce enough food to feed their own people and also enough to export.

Taiwan's History and People   For centuries, Taiwan was part of China's empire. Then in 1895, Japan took the island after defeating China in war. The Japanese developed the economy of Taiwan but treated the people very harshly. After Japan's loss in World War II, Taiwan was returned to China.

In 1949 the Nationalists under Chiang Kai-shek arrived in Taiwan from the Chinese mainland. Along with them came more than 1.5 million refugees fleeing Communist rule. Fearing a Communist invasion, the Nationalists kept a large army in the hope of someday retaking the mainland. They also blocked other political groups from sharing in the government.

By the early 1990s, local Taiwanese were allowed more opportunities in government. The one-party system ended, and Taiwan became a democracy. Taiwan is still officially part of China, but many people would like to declare Taiwan independent. China claims Taiwan as its twenty-third province and believes that it should be under China's control. China has threatened to use force against Taiwan if the island declares its independence.

NATIONAL GEOGRAPHIC **On Location**

Taiwan

Many electronic industries have headquarters in Taiwan.

Place What kinds of products do high-technology factories in Taiwan produce?

About 75 percent of Taiwan's 22.6 million people live in urban areas. The most populous city—with 2.6 million people—is the capital, **Taipei.** This bustling center of trade and commerce has tall skyscrapers and modern stores. If you stroll through the city, however, you will see Chinese traditions. Buddhist temples, for example, still reflect traditional Chinese architecture.

Reading Check Why is Taiwan's economy one of the world's strongest?

Ulaanbaatar

Ulaanbaatar in Mongolia began as a Buddhist community in the early 1600s. Today it is a modern cultural and industrial center.

Place Why is Mongolia known as the Land of the Blue Sky?

Mongolia

Landlocked **Mongolia** is a country about the size of Alaska. Rugged mountains and high plateaus rise in the west and central regions. The bleak landscape of the Gobi spreads over the southeast. The rest of the country is covered by steppes, which are dry treeless plains often found on the edges of a desert.

Known as the Land of the Blue Sky, Mongolia boasts more than 260 days of sunshine per year. Yet its climate has extremes. Rainfall is scarce, and fierce dust storms sometimes sweep across the landscape. It is very hot in the summer. In the winter, temperatures fall below freezing at night.

For centuries, most of Mongolia's people were nomads. Nomads are people who move from place to place with herds of animals. Even today, many Mongolians tend sheep, goats, cattle, or camels on the country's vast steppes. Important industries in Mongolia use products from these animals. Some factories use wool to make textiles and clothing. Others use the hides of cattle to make leather and shoes. Some farmers grow wheat and other grains. Mongolia also has deposits of copper and gold.

Mongolia's History and People Mongolia's people are famous for their skills in raising and riding horses. In the past, they also were known as fierce fighters. In the 1200s, many groups of Mongols joined together under one leader, Genghis Khan (JEHNG•guhs KAHN). He led Mongol armies on a series of conquests. The Mongols eventually carved out the largest land empire in history, ruling 80 percent of Eurasia by A.D. 1300. An empire is a collection of different territories under one ruler. The Mongol Empire stretched from China all the way to eastern Europe.

During the 1300s, the Mongol Empire weakened and fell apart. China ruled the area that is now Mongolia from the 1700s to the early 1900s. In 1924 Mongolia gained independence and created a strict Communist government under the guidance of the Soviet Union. The country finally became a democracy in 1990. Since then, the Mongolian economy has moved slowly from government control to a free enterprise system.

About 85 percent of Mongolia's 2.5 million people are Mongols. They speak the Mongol language. About 60 percent of the people live in urban areas. The largest city is the capital, **Ulaanbaatar** (OO•LAHN•BAH•TAWR). Mongolians in the countryside live on farms. A few still follow the nomadic life of their ancestors. These herder-nomads live in yurts, large circle-shaped structures made of animal skins that can be packed up and moved from place to place.

Mongolians still enjoy the sports and foods of their nomadic ancestors. The favorite meal is boiled sheep's meat with rice, washed down with tea. The biggest event of the year is the Naadam Festival, held all over the country in mid-summer. It consists of a number of sporting events, including wrestling, archery, and horse racing.

Since before the days of the Mongol Empire, most people in Mongolia have been Buddhists. Buddhism has long influenced Mongolian art, music, and literature. Traditional music has a wide range of instruments and singing styles. In one style of Mongolian singing, male performers produce harmonic sounds from deep in the throat, releasing several notes at once.

For centuries, Buddhist temples and other holy places dotted the country. Under communism, religious worship was discouraged. Many of these historic buildings were either destroyed or left to decay. Today people are once again able to practice their religion. They have restored or rebuilt many of their holy buildings.

✓ Reading Check **What religion do most Mongolians practice?**

FCAT PRACTICE You can prepare for the FCAT-assessed standards by completing the correlated item(s) below.

Section 3 Assessment

Defining Terms
1. **Define** high-technology industry, steppe, nomad, empire, yurt.

Recalling Facts
2. **Economics** What kinds of products are made in Taiwan?
3. **Government** Why has Taiwan not claimed independence from China?
4. **History** Which Mongol warrior conquered much of Eurasia by A.D. 1300?

Critical Thinking
5. **Understanding Cause and Effect** Why did many people flee to Taiwan from China in 1949? **FCAT LA.A.2.3.1**
6. **Drawing Conclusions** Why do you think Communist leaders discouraged religious worship in Mongolia? **FCAT LA.A.2.3.1**

Graphic Organizer
7. **Organizing Information** Create a diagram like this one. Then write either Taiwan or Mongolia in the center oval. Write at least one fact about the country under the headings in each of the outer ovals. **FCAT LA.A.1.3.2**

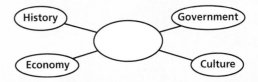

Applying Social Studies Skills
8. **Analyzing Maps** Look at the map on page 661. What mountains rise in western Mongolia? What desert is found in southern and southeastern Mongolia?

Critical Thinking Skill

FCAT PRACTICE Completing the correlated items below will help you prepare for the **FCAT Reading** test.

Distinguishing Fact From Opinion

Distinguishing fact from opinion can help you make reasonable judgments about what others say and write. Facts can be proved by evidence such as records, documents, or historical sources. Opinions are based on people's differing values and beliefs.

Learning the Skill

The following steps will help you identify facts and opinions:

- Read or listen to the information carefully. Identify the facts. Ask: Can these statements be proved? Where would I find information to prove them?
- If a statement can be proved, it is factual. Check the sources for the facts. Often statistics sound impressive, but they may come from an unreliable source.
- Identify opinions by looking for statements of feelings or beliefs. The statements may contain words like *should, would, could, best, greatest, all, every,* or *always.*

Practicing the Skill

Read the paragraph below, and then answer the questions that follow.

Anyone who thinks the Internet is not used in China has been asleep at the mouse. China's government-owned factories and political system may seem old-fashioned. When it comes to cyberspace, however, China is moving at Net speed. Internet use is growing explosively. In 1997 only 640,000 Chinese were using the Internet. By 2000, the number had increased to 12.3 million. The Phillips Group estimates that by 2005, the online population should hit 85 million.

1. Identify facts. Can you prove that Chinese Internet use is increasing?
   FCAT LA.A.2.3.8
2. Note opinions. What phrases alert you that these are opinions? **FCAT** LA.A.2.3.8

3. What is the purpose of this paragraph?
   FCAT LA.A.2.3.8

Applying the Skill

Watch a television commercial. List one fact and one opinion that are stated. Does the fact seem reliable? How can you prove the fact? **FCAT** LA.A.2.3.8

GO TO Practice key skills with **Glencoe Skillbuilder Interactive Workbook, Level 1.**

◀ Chinese students attend an Internet exhibit in Beijing.

Reading Review

Section 1   China's Land and New Economy

Terms to Know
dike
fault
communist state
consumer goods

Main Idea
China—the third-largest country in the world—has very diverse land-forms. China's rapidly growing economy has changed in recent years.

✓ **Place** Rugged mountains and harsh deserts cover western and northern China.

✓ **Culture** About 90 percent of China's people live in the lowlands of eastern China.

✓ **Place** China's rivers bring fertile soil along with the danger of flooding to the eastern plains.

✓ **Economics** China's leaders have changed the economy to give the people more economic freedom. The economy has grown rapidly as a result.

✓ **Economics** Many companies in China are now jointly owned by Chinese and foreign businesspeople. This is because foreign companies can pay workers less than they pay workers in their own countries, and they have millions of possible customers in the Chinese people.

Section 2   Dynasties to Communism

Terms to Know
dynasty
human rights
exile
calligraphy
pagoda

Main Idea
The arts and ideas of ancient times still influence China today.

✓ **History** The ancient teachings of Kongfuzi, Daoism, and Buddhism still influence the people of China.

✓ **History** For thousands of years, dynasties of emperors ruled China. Today Communist leaders keep tight control over all areas of political life.

✓ **Culture** China is famous for the skill of its craft workers and for its distinctive painting and architecture.

Section 3   China's Neighbors

Terms to Know
high-technology
  industry
steppe
nomad
empire
yurt

Main Idea
Taiwan and Mongolia have been influenced by Chinese ways and traditions.

✓ **Government** Taiwan is an island off southeast China. The government of China does not recognize Taiwan as a separate country.

✓ **Economics** Taiwan's prosperous economy has influenced other Asian economies.

✓ **Place** Mongolia has rugged terrain and a harsh landscape.

✓ **Culture** Some people in Mongolia still follow a traditional nomadic lifestyle, and herding remains an important economic activity.

FCAT PRACTICE You can prepare for the FCAT-assessed standards by completing the correlated item(s) below.

Using Key Terms

Match the terms in Part A with their definitions in Part B.

A.

1. fault
2. dynasty
3. exile
4. high-technology industry
5. dike
6. communist state
7. pagoda
8. calligraphy
9. human rights
10. yurt

B.

a. a building with many-storied towers
b. country whose government has strong control over the economy and society
c. high bank of soil along a river to prevent flooding
d. basic freedoms and rights
e. crack in the earth's crust
f. the art of beautiful writing
g. nomadic tent made of animal skins
h. state of being unable to live in one's own country because of political beliefs
i. line of rulers from the same family
j. industry that produces electronic equipment

Reviewing the Main Ideas

Section 1 China's Land and New Economy

11. **Place** Where do most of China's people live?
12. **Place** What major rivers flow through the plains and southern highlands of China?
13. **Human/Environment Interaction** How has the new economy contributed to air pollution in China? **FCAT SC.D.2.3.2**
14. **Economics** Give three reasons why China's economy has boomed.

Section 2 Dynasties to Communism

15. **Culture** What are the ideas of Kongfuzi? Of Laozi?
16. **History** Name three Chinese inventions.
17. **Government** What kind of government did China have between 1911 and 1949?

Section 3 China's Neighbors

18. **Economics** Why is Taiwan's economy important in Asia?
19. **Place** How does Mongolia's landscape prevent much farming?
20. **Economics** How are Mongolia's main industries related to herding?

NATIONAL GEOGRAPHIC China & Neighbors

Place Location Activity

On a separate sheet of paper, match the letters on the map with the numbered places listed below.

1. Plateau of Tibet
2. Yellow River
3. Yangtze River
4. Hong Kong
5. Gobi
6. Beijing
7. Mongolia
8. Shanghai
9. Taklimakan Desert
10. Himalaya

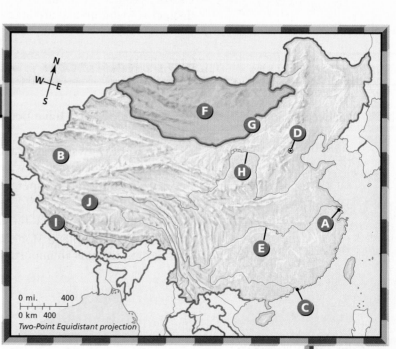

0 mi. 400
0 km 400
Two-Point Equidistant projection

Self-Check Quiz Visit *The World and Its People* Web site at twip.glencoe.com and click on **Chapter 23—Self-Check Quizzes** to prepare for the Chapter Test.

Critical Thinking

21. **Drawing Conclusions** Why do you think China wanted to be isolated from European countries in the 1700s and 1800s? **FCAT LA.A.2.3.1**

22. **Organizing Information** Create a chart like the one below. Under each heading, write at least two facts about China. **FCAT LA.A.1.3.2**

Land	Economy	History	Government	People

Comparing Regions Activity

23. **Culture** Research to find information on Chinese art and architecture. Then choose a country in eastern Europe, such as Ukraine, and research its art traditions. How are the art forms similar and different? Include illustrations and photos of what you find.

FCAT LA.A.2.3.5

Mental Mapping Activity

24. **Focusing on the Region** Create a simple outline map of China and its neighbors, and then label the following:

- Himalaya
- Yellow River
- Taiwan
- Beijing
- Gobi
- Ulaanbaatar
- Yangtze River
- Hong Kong

Technology Skills Activity

25. **Developing a Multimedia Presentation** Using the Internet, research one of the arts of China. You might choose painting, architecture, literature, music, or a craft such as casting bronze or making silk. Create a museum exhibit that presents your findings. Include photographs that show examples of works from different periods in Chinese history.

FCAT LA.A.2.3.5

Standardized Test Practice

Directions: Study the map below, and then answer the questions that follow.

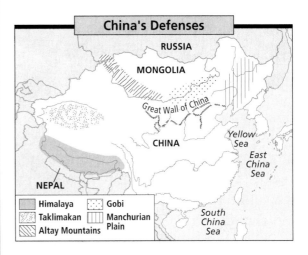

China's Defenses

Key: Himalaya, Taklimakan, Altay Mountains, Gobi, Manchurian Plain

1. **Where is the Gobi?**

   A Near China's Russian border

   B In the southwestern part of China

   C In the Himalaya

   D Along China's border with Mongolia

2. **Which of the following is a human-made defense?**

   F The Great Wall of China

   G The Gobi

   H The Taklimakan

   J The Himalaya

Test-Taking Tip: Look for key words that will help you find the correct answer. An example is *human-made* in question 2. In this case, all of the answer choices are *natural* defenses of China except for the correct answer. Look at the map closely, using its title, the key, and the information shown on the map to find the correct answer choice.

Soft and sleek, silk is a valuable textile.

The Silk Road

Was there really a road made of silk? Well, not exactly. Silk, however, was one of the main products carried along the Silk Road—a system of trade routes that linked ancient China and the empires of the West. When Chinese silk became fashionable in Rome, the precious cloth traveled the Silk Road.

A Risky Route

The road itself was anything but soft and smooth. Traveling from China, camels laden with silk and other cargo trudged through deserts, including the Taklimakan, a name meaning "go in and you won't come out." Sandstorms and intense heat made passage difficult. Farther along the route, the Pamir mountain range thrust an ice- and snow-covered barrier in the way. The road was dangerous as well. Bandits attacked often, stealing valuable goods.

Few traveled the entire 4,000-mile (6,437-km) series of routes. Instead, merchants bought goods in trading posts and oases along the way and sold them at other markets farther along, much as relay runners pass a baton.

Chinese Secret Agent

Zhang Qian, an agent on a secret mission for Chinese Emperor Wudi, may have started the silk trade. In 139 B.C. invaders swept into China, despite China's Great Wall. Zhang Qian was sent far into Central Asia to find allies to help fight the invaders. He found no allies. Instead, he brought back strong horses for the military, which he had bought with bolts of silk.

Soon the Chinese were trading silk with the Parthian Empire, which is present-day Iran. It is said that Rome wanted silk after its soldiers spotted silk banners fluttering above Parthian troops. By the A.D. 100s, China and Rome were trading a variety of goods. From the East came such exotic items as silk, spices, and fruits. Rome paid in glass, wool, and ivory, but mostly in gold.

Ideas also traveled the Silk Road. From India, the religion of Buddhism reached China. Christianity and Islam spread eastward as well. Chinese techniques for making paper and explosives traveled west. Western methods of cloth manufacturing and better gun design went to China. The process for making silk, however, traveled nowhere until much later. The Chinese successfully guarded their secret—that silk was made from the strands of a silkworm's cocoon.

For centuries, goods and ideas traveled between East and West. In the 1300s, however, the Silk Road began to decline as sea routes proved safer than land routes. Nevertheless, even today, parts of the Silk Road are busy with trade—and tourism. In addition to camels, tour buses now travel the caravan routes.

QUESTIONS

1 How is the Silk Road "made of silk"?

2 What were some obstacles along the Silk Road?

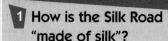
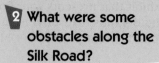

A man and his camel travel the Silk Road in China. ▶

NATIONAL GEOGRAPHIC

Silk Road Routes

— Silk Road

RUSSIA

Velikiy Novgorod

Moscow

Caspian Sea

MONGOLIA

Istanbul (Constantinople)

Aral Sea

Pamirs

Black Sea

Taklimakan Desert

Anxi

Xi'an

Mediterranean Sea

Antioch

IRAN

Samarqand

CHINA

Baghdad

IRAQ

INDIA

AFRICA

Arabian Sea

Bay of Bengal

South China Sea

N
W E
S

0 mi.   1,000
0 km   1,000
Miller projection

Chapter 24

Japan and the Koreas

The World and Its People NATIONAL GEOGRAPHIC

To learn more about the people and places of Japan and the Koreas, view **The World and Its People Chapter 25** video.

Social Studies online

Chapter Overview Visit **The World and Its People** Web site at twip.glencoe.com and click on **Chapter 24—Chapter Overviews** to preview information about Japan and the Koreas.

 FCAT PRACTICE The activity below will help you prepare for the **FCAT Reading** test.

Compare-Contrast Make this foldable to help you compare and contrast the people and places of Japan and the Koreas. **FCAT LA.A.2.3.1**

Step 1 Fold one sheet of paper in half from top to bottom.

Step 2 Fold it in half again, from side to side.

Step 3 Unfold the paper once. Sketch an outline of the Koreas and Japan across both tabs and label them as shown.

Step 4 Cut up the fold of the top flap only.

This cut will make two tabs.

Reading and Writing As you read the chapter, write what you learn about these countries under the appropriate tab. Use your notes to determine how these countries are alike and different. **FCAT LA.A.2.3.1**

Why It Matters

Rebuilding

A little more than 50 years ago, Japan and Korea were nations largely destroyed by war. Japan and South Korea recovered to become important centers of technology with prosperous economies. North Korea, under a communist system of government, faces very poor economic conditions. Challenges exist today as these nations learn to relate to one another.

◄ **A bullet train races past Mount Fuji, the national symbol of Japan.**

Japan–Past and Present

NATIONAL GEOGRAPHIC **Exploring Our World**

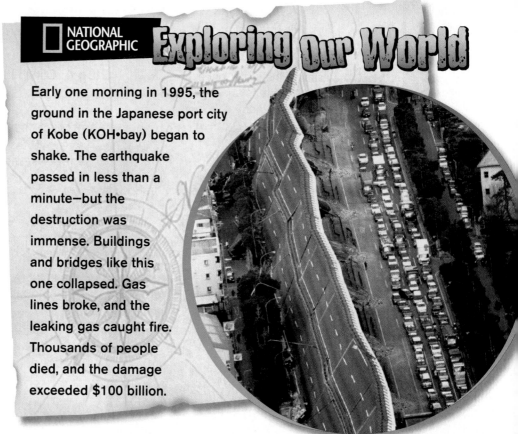

Early one morning in 1995, the ground in the Japanese port city of Kobe (KOH•bay) began to shake. The earthquake passed in less than a minute—but the destruction was immense. Buildings and bridges like this one collapsed. Gas lines broke, and the leaking gas caught fire. Thousands of people died, and the damage exceeded $100 billion.

The city of Kobe suffered an earthquake because Japan lies on the Ring of Fire. This name refers to an area surrounding the Pacific Ocean where the earth's crust often shifts. Japan experiences thousands of earthquakes each year. People in Japan also have to deal with tsunamis (tsu•NAH•mees). These huge sea waves caused by undersea earthquakes are very destructive along Japan's Pacific coast.

Japan's Mountainous Islands

Japan is an archipelago (AHR•kuh•PEH•luh•GOH), or a group of islands, off the coast of eastern Asia between the Sea of Japan and the Pacific Ocean. Four main islands and thousands of smaller ones make up Japan's land area. The largest islands are **Hokkaido** (hoh•KY•doh), **Honshu, Shikoku** (shee•KOH•koo), and **Kyushu** (KYOO•SHOO).

These islands are actually the peaks of mountains that rise from the floor of the Pacific Ocean. The mountains are volcanic, but many are no longer active. The most famous peak is **Mount Fuji,** Japan's highest mountain and national symbol. Rugged mountains and steep, forested hills dominate most of Japan. Narrowly squeezed between the seacoast and the mountains are plains. The **Kanto Plain** in eastern Honshu is Japan's largest plain. **Tokyo,** the capital, and **Yokohama,** one of Asia's major port cities, are located here. You will find most of Japan's cities, farms, and industries on the coastal plains.

No part of Japan is more than 70 miles (113 km) from the sea. In bay areas along the jagged coasts lie many fine harbors and ports. The northern islands receive cold Arctic Ocean winds and currents. The Pacific Ocean, in contrast, sends warm ocean currents to the southern part of Japan.

✓ **Reading Check** What are the two major landforms in Japan?

NATIONAL GEOGRAPHIC

Japan and the Koreas: Physical/Political

Applying Map Skills

1. What bodies of water lie between Japan and the Koreas?

2. What is Japan's highest peak? How high is it?

Find NGS online map resources @ www.nationalgeographic.com/maps

Japan's Economy

Japan's industries have benefited from having highly skilled workers. The people of Japan value hard work, cooperation, and education. After high school graduation, many Japanese students go on to a local university.

Industry Japan has few mineral resources, so it must import raw materials, such as iron ore, coal, and oil. However, Japan is an industrial giant known around the world for the variety and quality of its manufactured goods. Japan's modern factories use new technology and robots to make their products quickly and carefully. These products include automobiles and other vehicles. The graph on page 12 in the **Geography Handbook** shows you that Japan leads the world in automobile production. Japan's factories also produce consumer goods such as electronic equipment, watches, small appliances, and calculators. Other factories produce industrial goods such as steel, cement, fertilizer, plastics, and fabrics.

FCAT
PRACTICE

Completing the exercise below will help you prepare for the **FCAT Reading** test.

Literature

SADAKO AND THE THOUSAND PAPER CRANES
by Eleanor Coerr

This book tells the true story of a young Japanese girl living in the aftermath of World War II. Radiation from the atomic bomb dropped on Hiroshima caused Sadako to get leukemia. Sadako turned to the ancient art of origami (folding paper to make objects) for strength and courage.

While Sadako closed her eyes, Chizuko put some pieces of paper and scissors on the bed . . . "I've figured out a way for you to get well," she said proudly. "Watch!" She cut a piece of gold paper into a large square. In a short time she had folded it over and over into a beautiful crane. Sadako was puzzled. "But how can that paper bird make me well?" "Don't you remember that old story about the crane?" Chizuko asked. "It's supposed to live for a thousand years. If a sick person folds one thousand paper cranes, the gods will grant her wish and make her healthy again." . . . With the golden crane nearby she felt safe and lucky. Why, in a few weeks she would be able to finish the thousand. Then she would be strong enough to go home.

Source: *Sadako and the Thousand Paper Cranes* by Eleanor Coerr. Copyright 1977. The Putnam Publishing Group.

Analyzing Literature

Sadako died before she finished making the one thousand paper cranes, but she became a national heroine in Japan. What was it about Sadako that made other Japanese people feel connected to her and proud of her? **FCAT LA.E.2.3.1**

Agriculture Farmland in Japan is very limited. Yet farmers use fertilizers and modern machinery to produce high crop yields. They also practice **intensive cultivation,** which means they grow crops on every available piece of land. Crops grow on terraces cut in hillsides and even between buildings and highways. In warmer areas, farmers harvest two or three crops a year. The chief crop is rice, a basic part of the Japanese diet. Other important crops include sugar beets, potatoes, fruits, and tea. Seafood is an important part of the people's diet as well. Japan's fishing fleet is one of the world's largest and provides nearly 15 percent of the world's fish.

Past and Present

Past and present come together in Japan. Here, a priest of the ancient Shinto religion blesses a family's shiny new car.

Place Where was this car probably made? Why?

Economic Challenges Japan is one of the world's leading exporters. Because of trade restrictions, the country imports few finished goods from other countries, however. This has led to disagreements with trading partners who want to export more goods to Japan.

Another challenge facing Japan is preserving the environment. Air pollution from power plants has produced acid rain. Because of overfishing, supplies of seafood have dropped. The government has passed laws to limit the amount of fish that can be caught each year.

✓ Reading Check What are some products made by Japanese manufacturers?

Japan's History and Government

Japan's history reaches back many centuries. The Japanese trace their ancestry to various **clans,** or groups of related families. These clans originally came from the mainland of Asia and lived on the islands as early as the late A.D. 400s.

The Japanese developed close ties with China on the Asian mainland. Ruled by emperors, Japan modeled its society on the Chinese way of life. The Japanese also borrowed the Chinese system of writing and accepted the Buddhist religion brought by Chinese missionaries. Today most Japanese practice Buddhism along with Shinto, Japan's own traditional religion.

In the 790s, the power of emperors began to decline. From the late 1100s to the 1860s, Japan was ruled by **shoguns,** or military leaders, and powerful land-owning warriors known as the **samurai.**

teen Scene

Hard Hats to School?

Okajima Yukiko and Sataka Aya walk along ash-covered sidewalks to Kurokami Junior High School. Why are they wearing hard hats? Their city is near Japan's Mount Oyama Volcano, which has just erupted. Yukiko and Aya have grown up facing the dangers of volcanic eruptions, earthquakes, and tsunamis. At school their first class starts at 8:30 A.M., and their last class ends at 3:40 P.M. Yukiko and Aya must go to school every second Saturday of the month too.

Like China, Japan did not want to trade with foreign countries. In 1853 the United States government sent a fleet headed by Commodore Matthew Perry to Japan to demand trading privileges. In response to this action and other outside pressures, the Japanese started trading with other countries.

In the late 1800s, Japanese leaders began to use Western ideas to modernize the country, improve education, and set up industries. By the early 1900s, Japan was the leading military power in Asia.

In the 1930s, Japan needed more resources for its growing population. It took land in China and spread its influence to Southeast Asia. In 1941 Japanese forces attacked the American naval base at Pearl Harbor in Hawaii. This attack caused the United States to enter World War II. After four years of fighting, Japan surrendered when the United States dropped atomic bombs on the cities of **Hiroshima** and **Nagasaki.** By that time, many of Japan's cities lay in ruins and the economy had collapsed. With help from the United States, Japan became a democracy and quickly rebuilt its ruined economy.

Government Japan's democracy is in the form of a constitutional monarchy. The emperor is the official head of state, but elected officials run the government. Voters elect representatives to the national legislature. The political party with the most members chooses a prime minister to lead the government.

Japan has great influence as a world economic power. In addition, it gives large amounts of money to poorer countries. Japan is not a military power, though. Because of the suffering that World War II caused, the Japanese have chosen to keep Japan's military small.

The government of Japan has improved health care and education for its people. Japan has the lowest infant death rate in the world, and its literacy rate is 100 percent. The crime rate in Japan is very low.

✓ Reading Check What kind of government does Japan have?

Japan's People and Culture

About the size of California, Japan has 127.5 million people—nearly one-half the population of the United States. Most of Japan's people belong to the same Japanese ethnic background. Look at the map on page 700 to see where most of Japan's people live. About 80 percent are crowded into urban areas on the coastal plains. The four large cities of Tokyo, Yokohama, Nagoya, and Osaka form a megalopolis, or a huge urban area made up of several large cities and communities near them.

Japan's cities have tall office buildings and busy streets. Homes and apartments are small and close to one another. Many city workers crowd into subway trains to get to work. Men work long hours and arrive home very late. Women often quit their jobs to raise children and return to work outside the home when the children are grown.

You still see signs of traditional life, even in the cities. Parks and gardens give people a chance to take a break from the busy day. It is common to see a person dressed in a traditional garment called a kimono walking with another person wearing a T-shirt and jeans.

Only 21 percent of Japan's people live in rural areas. In both rural and urban Japan, the family traditionally has been the center of one's life. Each family member had to obey certain rules. Grandparents, parents, and children all lived in one house. Many family groups today consist only of parents and children.

Religion Many Japanese practice two religions—Shinto and Buddhism. Shinto began in Japan many centuries ago. It teaches respect for nature, love of simple things, and concern for cleanliness and good manners. Shinto is different from other religions. First, there is no person who founded or started the religion. Shinto did not spread to many other areas of the world, but stayed mostly in Japan. Second, there is no collection of writings that make up scripture, such as the Bible or the Quran. In addition to Shinto, Buddhism teaches respect for nature and the need to achieve inner peace.

Traditional Arts Japan's religions have influenced the country's arts. Many paintings portray the beauty of nature, often with a few simple brush strokes. Some even include verses of poetry. Haiku (HY•koo) is a well-known type of Japanese poetry that is written according to a specific formula. Turn to page 697 to learn more about haiku.

Japanese artists became famous for a style of painting (borrowed from the Chinese) known as wood-block printing. It involved carving a picture into a block of wood, applying ink to the raised surface of the carved block, and printing the picture on paper or some other surface. Japanese

▲ *Evening Snow, Mt. Fuji*, by Toyokuni II is a wood-block print from the 1830s.

Customs

Japanese people greet each other by bowing. The person who has a lower social status usually bows first, the lowest, and the longest. The lower you bow, the more you honor and respect the other person. The most common bow lasts for one or two seconds. A very low bow is used for a superior or for a formal occasion, such as a first meeting, and may be held for about three seconds. Bows are also a nonverbal way to say thank you, good-bye, and to apologize. Many times, especially when saying good-bye, both people bow several times.

Looking Closer **Which man in this photo is of lower status? How can you tell?**

wood-block prints enjoyed a golden age in the 1800s. They eventually made their way to Europe, influencing the French Impressionists.

The Japanese also have a rich heritage of literature and drama. Many scholars believe that the world's first novel came from Japan. The novel is called *The Tale of Genji* and was written by a noblewoman about A.D. 1000. Since the 1600s, Japanese theatergoers have attended the historical plays of the Kabuki theater. In Kabuki plays, actors wearing brilliantly colored costumes perform on colorful stages.

Many of Japan's sports have their origins in the past. A popular sport is sumo, an ancient Japanese form of wrestling. In sumo, two players each try to force the other to touch the ground with any part of their body other than their feet. Participants in sumo typically weigh at least 300 pounds (136 kg). Two ancient martial arts—judo and karate—also developed in this area. Today martial arts are practiced both for self-defense and for exercise.

Modern Pastimes   Along with traditional arts, the people of Japan enjoy modern pastimes. Many Japanese are enthusiastic about baseball, a sport borrowed from American culture. There are professional baseball leagues in Japan, and several Japanese players have become stars in the major leagues of the United States. Despite Japan's strong emphasis on education, life is not all work for Japanese young people. They enjoy rock music, modern fashions, television, and movies. Japanese cartoons and video games are popular around the world.

✓ Reading Check **What two main religions are practiced in Japan?**

FCAT PRACTICE   You can prepare for the FCAT-assessed standards by completing the correlated item(s) below.

Assessment

Defining Terms
1. **Define** tsunami, archipelago, intensive cultivation, clan, shogun, samurai, constitutional monarchy, megalopolis.

Recalling Facts
2. **Location** Why does Japan experience earthquakes?
3. **History** Who were the samurai?
4. **Culture** How have Japan's religions influenced the country's arts?

Critical Thinking
5. **Summarizing Information** Why do the Japanese not want a large military?
6. **Synthesizing Information** Name three values of the Japanese people that enable them to be such skilled workers.
   FCAT LA.A.2.3.1

Graphic Organizer
7. **Organizing Information** Create a diagram like this one. List Japan's economic successes in the large oval and its economic challenges in each of the smaller ovals. **FCAT LA.A.1.3.2**

Economic Successes
Challenge   Challenge   Challenge

Applying Social Studies Skills

8. **Analyzing Maps** Look at the physical/political map on page 691. What physical features are located near Tokyo, Japan?

Making Connections

ART   SCIENCE   CULTURE   TECHNOLOGY

Haiku

FCAT PRACTICE Completing the correlated items below will help you prepare for the **FCAT Reading** test.

Haiku is a type of poetry that first became popular in Japan during the 1600s. A haiku is a three-line poem, usually about nature and human emotions. The traditional haiku requires 17 syllables—5 in the first line, 7 in the second line, and 5 in the third line. All of the haiku below, written by famous Japanese poets, concern the subject of New Year's Day.*

For this New Year's Day,
The sight we gaze upon shall be
Mount Fuji.
Sôkan

That is good, this too is good,—
New Year's Day
In my old age.
Rôyto

New Year's Day;
Whosoever's face we see,
It is care-free.
Shigyoku

New Year's Day:
My hovel,
The same as ever.
Issa

New Year's Day:
What luck! What luck!
A pale blue sky!
Issa

The dawn of New Year's Day;
Yesterday,
How far off!
Ichiku

▲ This Japanese wood-block print shows two girls playing a New Year's game.

The first dream of the year;
I kept it a secret,
And smiled to myself.
Shô-u

*Translation may have affected the number of syllables.
Excerpts from *Haiku, Volume II.* Copyright © 1952 by R.H. Blyth. Reprinted by permission of Hokuseido Press.

Making the Connection

1. How does the poet Shigyoku think most people react to New Year's Day? **FCAT LA.A.2.3.2**

2. From his poem, how can you tell that Ichiku sees the New Year as a new beginning? **FCAT LA.A.2.3.2**

3. **Making Comparisons** Compare the two poems by Issa. How does his mood change from one to the other? **FCAT LA.A.1.3.2**

Guide to Reading

Main Idea

South Korea and North Korea share the same peninsula and history, but they have very different political and economic systems.

Terms to Know

- parallel
- famine

Reading Strategy

Create a time line like this one to record four important dates and their events in Korean history. **FCAT** LA.A.1.3.2

├──────┼──────┼──────┤

The following are the major Sunshine State Standards covered in this section.

SS.A.2.3.1:
Understands how language, ideas, and institutions of one culture can influence others (e.g., through trade, exploration, and immigration)

SS.B.2.3.9:
Understands ways the interaction between physical and human systems affects current conditions on Earth

The Two Koreas

Section 2

NATIONAL GEOGRAPHIC Exploring Our World

One of Korea's most sacred places is the shrine at Sokkuram. Built in the A.D. 700s, the shrine has 40 statues, including this 11-foot (3.4-m) statue of the Buddha. The original builders created a complex system of stone passages that let air circulate in the shrine. Today air conditioning keeps the statues in good condition.

The **Korean Peninsula** juts out from northern China, between the Sea of Japan (East Sea) and the Yellow Sea. For centuries, this peninsula held a unified country. Today the peninsula is divided into two nations—Communist **North Korea** and non-Communist **South Korea.**

A Divided Country

The history of human activity on the Korean Peninsula can be traced back thousands of years. From the 100s B.C. until the early A.D. 300s, neighboring China ruled Korea. When Chinese control ended, separate Korean kingdoms arose throughout the peninsula.

From A.D. 668 to 935, a single kingdom called Silla (SHIH•luh) united much of the peninsula. During this time, Korea made many cultural and scientific advances. For example, Silla rulers built one of the world's earliest astronomical observatories in the A.D. 600s. Other dynasties, or ruling families, followed the Silla.

In the 1400s, scholars invented a new way to write the Korean language. This new system—called *hangul* (HAHN•GOOL)—used fewer than 30 symbols. This is far fewer than the thousands of characters needed to write Chinese. This means the Korean system is much easier to learn. One of the great achievements of early Koreans was pottery. Korean potters still make bowls and dishes that are admired worldwide.

The Korean Peninsula was a stepping stone between Japan and mainland Asia. Trade and ideas went back and forth. In 1910 the Japanese conquered Korea and made it part of their empire. They governed the peninsula until the end of World War II in 1945.

Division and War   Troops from the Communist Soviet Union soon took over the northern half of Korea. American troops occupied the southern half. Korea eventually divided along the 38th **parallel**, or line of latitude. A Communist state arose in what came to be called North Korea. A non-Communist government controlled South Korea.

In 1950 the armies of North Korea attacked South Korea. They hoped to unite all of Korea under Communist rule. United Nations countries, led by the United States, rushed to support South Korea. China's Communist leaders eventually sent troops across the **Yalu River** to help North Korea. The Korean War finally ended in 1953—without a peace treaty or a victory for either side. By the 1960s, two separate countries had developed on the Korean Peninsula.

After years of bitterness, the two Koreas developed closer relations in the 1990s. In the year 2000, the leaders of North Korea and South Korea held a meeting for the first time since the division.

√ Reading Check Why is the Korean Peninsula divided?

South Korea

Much of South Korea is covered by mountains. Most South Koreans live in coastal areas where they are affected by monsoons. During the summer, a monsoon from the south brings hot, humid weather. In the

Korean Border

More than 50 years after the fighting stopped in Korea, troops still patrol the border between North and South Korea (below left). Seoul, South Korea's modern capital (below right), is less than 25 miles (40 km) from the border.

Location Where was the line of division drawn between the two countries?

NATIONAL GEOGRAPHIC On Location

Japan and the Koreas: Population Density

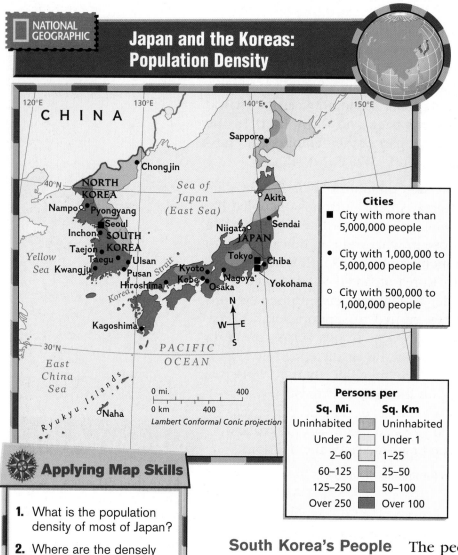

Cities

- ■ City with more than 5,000,000 people
- ● City with 1,000,000 to 5,000,000 people
- ○ City with 500,000 to 1,000,000 people

0 mi. 400
0 km 400
Lambert Conformal Conic projection

Persons per

Sq. Mi.		Sq. Km
Uninhabited		Uninhabited
Under 2		Under 1
2–60		1–25
60–125		25–50
125–250		50–100
Over 250		Over 100

Applying Map Skills

1. What is the population density of most of Japan?

2. Where are the densely populated areas of the Koreas?

Find NGS online map resources @ www.nationalgeographic.com/maps

winter, a monsoon blows in from the north, bringing cold, dry weather.

South Korea is one of east Asia's economic powers, despite an economic crisis in the 1990s. Manufacturing and trade dominate South Korea's economy. The country is a leading exporter of ships, cars, textiles, computers, and electronic appliances.

South Korean farmers own their land, although most of their farms are very small. The major crops are rice, barley, onions, potatoes, cabbage, apples, and tangerines. Rice is the country's basic food item. One of the most popular Korean dishes is *kimchi,* a highly spiced blend of vegetables mixed with chili, garlic, and ginger. Many farmers also raise livestock, especially chickens. Some add to their income by fishing.

South Korea's People   The people of the two Koreas belong to the same Korean ethnic group. South Korea has nearly 48 million people. About 80 percent live in cities and towns in the coastal plains. South Korea's capital, **Seoul,** is the largest city.

Most city dwellers live in tall apartment buildings. Many own cars, but they also use buses, subways, and trains to travel to and from work. In rural areas, people live in small, one-story homes made of brick or concrete blocks. A large number of South Koreans have emigrated to the United States since the end of the Korean War.

Buddhism, Confucianism, and Christianity are South Korea's major religions. The Koreans have developed their own culture, but Chinese religion and culture influenced the traditional arts of Korea. In Seoul, ancient palaces are modeled after the Imperial Palace in Beijing, China. Historic Buddhist temples dot the hills and valleys of the countryside.

Like Japan, Korea has a tradition of martial arts. Have you heard of tae kwon do? This martial art originated in Korea. Those who study it learn mental discipline as well as self-defense.

✓ **Reading Check**   What are the major religions in South Korea?

North Korea

Separated from China by the Yalu River, North Korea is slightly larger than South Korea. Like South Korea, monsoons affect the climate here, but the central mountains block some of the winter monsoon.

The North Korean government owns and runs factories and farms. It spends much money on the military. Unlike prosperous South Korea, North Korea is economically poor. Coal and iron ore are plentiful, but industries suffer from old equipment and power outages.

Most of North Korea is hills and mountains separated by deep, narrow valleys. Although there is little land to farm, more than 30 percent of North Koreans are farmers. They work on large, government-run farms. These farms do not grow enough food to feed the country. A lack of fertilizer recently produced **famines**, or severe food shortages. North Korea relies heavily on international food aid.

North Korea's People   North Korea has about 22.7 million people. About 60 percent live in urban areas along the coasts and river valleys. **Pyongyang** is the capital and largest city. Largely rebuilt since the Korean War, Pyongyang has many modern buildings and monuments to Communist leaders. Most of these monuments honor Kim Il Sung, who became North Korea's first ruler in the late 1940s. After Kim's death in 1994, his son Kim Jong Il became the ruler.

The government places the needs of the communist system over the needs of citizens. In 2002 North Korea stated it would make nuclear weapons. This has increased tensions with the United States and other countries who want North Korea to end their nuclear weapons program. Talks in 2003 failed to resolve the issue.

Social Studies ONLine

Web Activity Visit *The World and Its People* Web site at twip.glencoe.com and click on **Chapter 24– Student Web Activities** to learn more about South Korea.

✓ Reading Check **Who controls the economy of North Korea?**

FCAT PRACTICE   You can prepare for the FCAT-assessed standards by completing the correlated item(s) below.

Section 2 Assessment

Defining Terms
1. Define parallel, famine.

Recalling Facts
2. **Location** Where is the Korean Peninsula?
3. **History** Who were the Silla?
4. **Economics** What products are made in South Korea?

Critical Thinking
5. **Making Comparisons** How does the standard of living in South Korea differ from that in North Korea? **FCAT LA.A.2.3.1**
6. **Summarizing Information** What country has had the greatest influence on the culture and arts of South Korea? Explain. **FCAT LA.A.2.3.1**

Graphic Organizer
7. **Organizing Information** Create a diagram like this one. Write facts about each country's economy, government, and natural resources in the outer ovals. Where the ovals overlap, write facts that are common to both countries. **FCAT LA.A.1.3.2**

South Korea   North Korea

Applying Social Studies Skills
8. **Analyzing Maps** Turn to the population density map on page 700. What is the most populous city on the Korean Peninsula? In which country is it located?

Critical Thinking Skill

Making Comparisons

When you make comparisons, you determine similarities and differences among ideas, objects, or events. By comparing maps and graphs, you can learn more about a region.

Learning the Skill

Follow these steps to make comparisons:

- Identify or decide what will be compared.
- Determine a common area or areas in which comparisons can be drawn.
- Look for similarities and differences within these areas.

Practicing the Skill

Use the map and graph below to make comparisons and answer these questions:

1. What is the title of the map? The graph?
2. How are the map and graph related?
3. Which country has the most exports and imports? **FCAT MA.E.3.3.1**
4. Does a country's size have any effect on the amount it exports? Explain. **FCAT MA.D.1.3.2**
5. What generalizations can you make about this map and graph? **FCAT MA.D.1.3.2**

Applying the Skill

Survey your classmates about an issue in the news. Summarize the opinions and write a paragraph comparing the different opinions. **FCAT LA.A.2.3.5**

GO TO Practice key skills with **Glencoe Skillbuilder Interactive Workbook, Level 1.**

NATIONAL GEOGRAPHIC

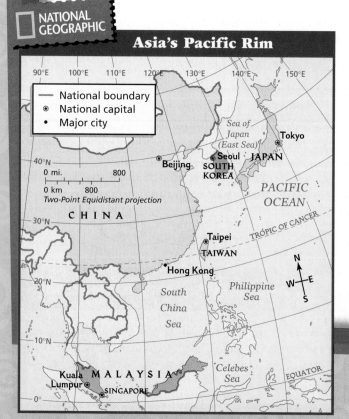

Asia's Pacific Rim

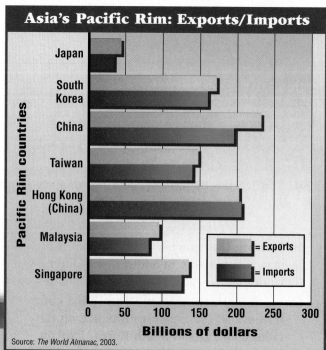

Asia's Pacific Rim: Exports/Imports

Source: *The World Almanac,* 2003.

Chapter 24 Reading Review

Section 1 — Japan—Past and Present

Terms to Know

tsunami
archipelago
intensive cultivation
clan
shogun
samurai
constitutional monarchy
megalopolis

Main Idea

Although Japan's people have few mineral resources, they have built a prosperous country.

✓ **Location** Japan is an archipelago along the Ring of Fire in the western Pacific Ocean. Volcanoes, earthquakes, and tsunamis may strike these islands.

✓ **Economics** Japan is mountainous, but with intensive cultivation its limited farmland is very productive.

✓ **Economics** Japan has few resources. Through trade, the use of advanced technology, and highly skilled workers, Japan has built a strong industrial economy.

✓ **History** The Japanese people have been strongly influenced by China and also by Western countries.

✓ **Culture** Most people in Japan live in crowded cities.

✓ **Culture** Japanese religion has encouraged a love of nature and simplicity.

Section 2 — The Two Koreas

Terms to Know

parallel
famine

Main Idea

South Korea and North Korea share the same peninsula and history, but they have very different political and economic systems.

✓ **Culture** The Korean Peninsula lies just south of northern China, and China has had a strong influence on Korean life and culture.

✓ **Government** After World War II, the peninsula became divided into two countries—Communist North Korea and non-Communist South Korea.

✓ **Economics** South Korea has a strong industrial economy.

✓ **Culture** Most South Koreans live in cities, enjoying a mix of modern and traditional life.

✓ **Government** North Korea's Communist government does not allow its people many freedoms and spends a great deal of money on the military. North Korea is economically poor.

Because of its beautiful forest-covered mountains, Korea was once known as the "Land of the Morning Calm." ▶

Assessment and Activities

FCAT PRACTICE You can prepare for the FCAT-assessed standards by completing the correlated item(s) below.

Using Key Terms

Match the terms in Part A with their definitions in Part B.

A.

1. samurai
2. tsunami
3. intensive cultivation
4. shogun
5. archipelago
6. parallel
7. constitutional monarchy
8. clan
9. famine
10. megalopolis

B.

a. group of related families
b. military leader in early Japan
c. chain of islands
d. emperor is the official head of state, but elected officials run the government
e. powerful land-owning warriors in Japan
f. huge wave caused by an undersea earthquake
g. severe food shortage
h. huge urban area made up of several large cities
i. line of latitude
j. growing crops on every available piece of land

Reviewing the Main Ideas

Section 1 Japan—Past and Present

11. **Human/Environment Interaction** How do Japan's farmers achieve high crop yields?
12. **Economics** What consumer goods and industrial goods are made in Japan?
13. **History** How did Japan change in the late 1800s?
14. **Location** What four cities make up Japan's megalopolis?
15. **Culture** Name three of Japan's traditional arts.

Section 2 The Two Koreas

16. **Location** What large Asian nation lies north of the Korean Peninsula?
17. **History** Why did Korea become divided in 1945?
18. **Movement** How do summer and winter monsoons differ in Korea?
19. **Economics** What are the main economic activities in South Korea?
20. **Human/Environment Interaction** Why has North Korea suffered from famine in recent years?

 **NATIONAL GEOGRAPHIC** Japan and the Koreas

Place Location Activity

On a separate sheet of paper, match the letters on the map with the numbered places listed below.

1. Mount Fuji
2. Sea of Japan (East Sea)
3. North Korea
4. South Korea
5. Tokyo
6. Honshu
7. Yalu River
8. Seoul
9. Pyongyang
10. Hokkaido

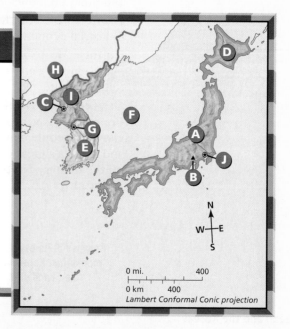

0 mi.   400
0 km   400
Lambert Conformal Conic projection

Self-Check Quiz Visit *The World and Its People* Web site at <u>twip.glencoe.com</u> and click on **Chapter 24—Self-Check Quizzes** to prepare for the Chapter Test.

Critical Thinking

21. **Drawing Conclusions** Why might North Korea find it difficult to change from a communist system to a noncommunist system? Keep in mind the country's location.

22. **Organizing Information** Create a chart like this one. In each column, write two main ideas about Japan, South Korea, and North Korea as they relate to the topics in the first column. **FCAT LA.A.1.3.2**

Topic	Japan	South Korea	North Korea
Land			
Economy			
History			
People			

Comparing Regions Activity

23. **Geography** Compare the geography of the Korean Peninsula with the geography of Baja California. What are the similarities and/or differences? Write a paragraph describing them. **FCAT LA.B.1.3.2**

Mental Mapping Activity

24. **Focusing on the Region** Create a map of Japan and the Koreas, and add these labels:

- Honshu
- North Korea
- Korean Peninsula
- Yalu River
- Pacific Ocean
- Tokyo
- Seoul
- Hiroshima

Technology Skills Activity

25. **Using the Internet** Use the Internet to research traditional Japanese culture. You might look at Japanese gardens, Buddhism, literature, or painting. Create a bulletin board display with pictures and write captions that explain what the images show.

FCAT LA.A.2.3.5

Standardized Test Practice

Directions: Read the paragraph below, and then answer the questions that follow.

In A.D. 1185 Japan's emperor gave political and military power to a shogun, or general. The shogun system proved to be quite strong. Even though the Mongol warrior Kublai Khan tried twice to invade Japan, he did not succeed. On the first invasion in 1274, Japanese warriors and the threat of a storm forced the Mongols to leave. On the second invasion in 1281, about 150,000 Mongol warriors came by ship, but a typhoon arose and destroyed the fleet. The Japanese thought of the storm as the kamikaze, or "divine wind." They believed that their islands were indeed sacred.

1. **In what century did shoguns gain political power in Japan?**

   A tenth century

   B eleventh century

   C twelfth century

   D thirteenth century

2. **In what century did the Mongol warrior Kublai Khan try to invade Japan?**

   F tenth century

   G eleventh century

   H twelfth century

   J thirteenth century

Test-Taking Tip: Century names are a common source of error. Remember, in Western societies, a baby's first year begins at birth and ends at age one. Therefore, if you are now 14 years old, you are in your fifteenth year. Using the same type of thinking, what century began in 1201?

Southeast Asia

The World and Its People

NATIONAL GEOGRAPHIC

To learn more about the people and places of Southeast Asia, view **The World and Its People Chapter 26** video.

Social Studies online

Chapter Overview Visit **The World and Its People** Web site at twip.glencoe.com and click on **Chapter 25–Chapter Overviews** to preview information about Southeast Asia.

FOLDABLES™
Study Organizer

FCAT PRACTICE The activity below will help you prepare for the **FCAT Reading** test.

Identifying Main Ideas Make this foldable to help you identify key facts about the people and places of Southeast Asia. **FCAT** LA.A.1.3.2

Step 1 Fold the paper from the top right corner down so the edges line up. Cut off the leftover piece.

Fold a triangle. Cut off the extra edge.

Step 2 Fold the triangle in half. Unfold.

The folds will form an X that creates four equal sections.

Step 3 Cut up one fold line and stop at the middle. This forms two triangular flaps.

Step 4 Draw an X on one tab and label the other three the following: Mainland Countries, Indonesia, and Other Island Countries.

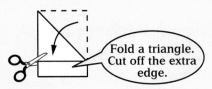

Step 5 Fold the X flap under the other flap and glue together.

This makes a three-sided pyramid.

Reading and Writing As you read, write main ideas inside the foldable under each appropriate pyramid wall. **FCAT** LA.A.1.3.2

Why It Matters

A High Price for Prosperity

Some Southeast Asian countries—such as Indonesia, Malaysia, and Singapore—have become major economic centers. They manufacture goods and export natural resources. One possible negative impact of this economic prosperity might be the destruction of the region's beautiful landscapes.

▲ **Outdoor restaurants are popular in Singapore.**

Life on the Mainland

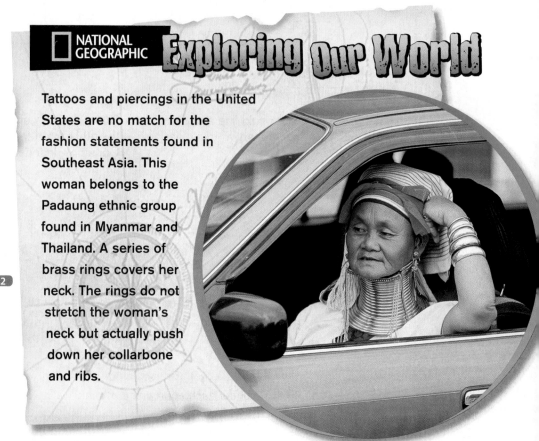

NATIONAL GEOGRAPHIC

Exploring Our World

Tattoos and piercings in the United States are no match for the fashion statements found in Southeast Asia. This woman belongs to the Padaung ethnic group found in Myanmar and Thailand. A series of brass rings covers her neck. The rings do not stretch the woman's neck but actually push down her collarbone and ribs.

South of China and east of India lies Southeast Asia. This region includes thousands of islands and a long arm of land called the **Malay Peninsula.** Several countries lie entirely on the mainland of Southeast Asia. They are Myanmar, Thailand, Laos, Cambodia, and Vietnam.

Myanmar

Myanmar, also called Burma, is about the size of Texas. Rugged, steep mountains sweep through its western and eastern borders. Two wide rivers—the **Irrawaddy** (IHR•ah•WAH•dee) and the **Salween**—flow through vast lowland plains between these mountain ranges. Monsoons, or seasonal winds that blow over a continent for months at a time, cause wet summers and dry winters in Myanmar.

About two-thirds of the country's people farm. The main crops are rice, sugarcane, beans, and peanuts. Some farmers work their fields with tractors, but most rely on plows pulled by water buffalo.

Myanmar exports wood products, gas, and foods such as beans and rice. The country provides about 75 percent of the world's teakwood. Myanmar's prized forests are decreasing, however, because of deforestation. This is the widespread cutting of trees. Fortunately, the country also exports precious gems. Precious gems are valuable stones such as rubies, sapphires, and jade.

Almost 75 percent of Myanmar's 49.5 million people live in rural areas. The most densely populated part of the country is the fertile Irrawaddy River valley. Many rural dwellers build their homes on poles above the ground for protection from floods and wild animals.

The capital and largest city, **Yangon** (formerly called Rangoon), is famous for its modern university and its gold-covered Buddhist temples. Buddhism is the main religion in Myanmar. Most people are of Burman heritage, and Burmese is the main language.

Myanmar was part of British India for many years. It became an independent republic in 1948. Since then, military leaders have turned Myanmar into a socialist country. Socialism is an economic system in which most businesses are owned and run by the government. Some

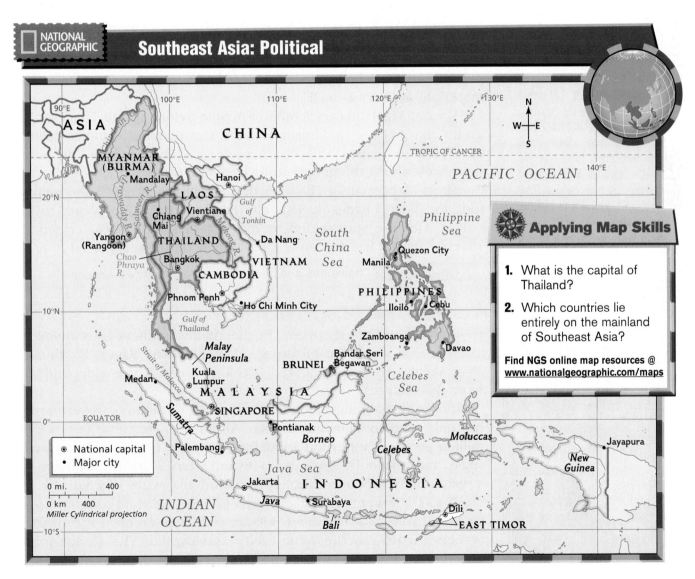

NATIONAL GEOGRAPHIC

Southeast Asia: Political

Applying Map Skills

1. What is the capital of Thailand?

2. Which countries lie entirely on the mainland of Southeast Asia?

Find NGS online map resources @ www.nationalgeographic.com/maps

⊛ National capital
• Major city

0 mi.   400
0 km   400
Miller Cylindrical projection

people have tried to build a democracy in Myanmar. A woman named Aung San Suu Kyi (AWNG SAN SOO CHEE) has become a leader in this struggle. In 1991 she was awarded the Nobel Peace Prize for her efforts but still faces opposition from the government today.

Reading Check Where is Myanmar's most densely populated area?

Thailand

The map on page 709 shows you that **Thailand** looks like a flower on a stem. The "flower" is the northern part, located on the mainland. The "stem" is a narrow strip on the Malay Peninsula. The country's main waterway—the **Chao Phraya** (chow PRY•uh) **River**—flows through a central plain. Like Myanmar, Thailand has wet summer monsoons and dry winter monsoons.

Once called Siam, *Thailand* means "land of the free." It is the only Southeast Asian country that has never been a European colony. The Thai people trace their independence as a kingdom back to the A.D. 1200s. Thailand is a constitutional monarchy with a king.

One of Thailand's agricultural products is rubber. The government has taken steps to limit deforestation to protect this industry. Thailand is also one of the world's leading producers of tin and tungsten. Most manufacturing is located near **Bangkok,** the capital. Workers make cement, textiles, computers, and electrical appliances. Tourism is an important industry as well.

Most of Thailand's 63.1 million people belong to the Thai ethnic group and practice Buddhism. Hundreds of Buddhist temples called *wats* dot the cities and countryside. Buddhist monks, or holy men, walk among the people to receive food offerings.

About 80 percent of Thais live in rural villages, although thousands look for jobs in Bangkok. This city has beautiful temples and royal palaces that are surrounded by modern skyscrapers and crowded streets. Bangkok has so many cars that daily traffic jams last for hours.

Reading Check Thailand is a leading producer of what two elements?

Laos and Cambodia

Landlocked **Laos** is covered by mountains. Southern Laos includes a fertile area along the **Mekong** (MAY•KAWNG) **River,** Southeast Asia's longest river. Once a French colony, Laos became independent more than fifty years ago.

Laos is an economically poor country. Its Communist government has only recently allowed tourism. About 80 percent of Laos's 5.6 million people live in rural areas. Farmers grow rice, sweet potatoes, sugarcane, and corn along the Mekong's fertile banks. Industry is largely undeveloped because of isolation and years of civil war. A **civil war** is a fight among different groups within a country. Laos lacks railroads and has electricity in only a few cities. **Vientiane** (vyehn•TYAHN) is the largest city and capital. The Communist government discourages religion, but most Laotians remain Buddhists.

Life as a Monk

After his grandfather died, Nattawud Daoruang became a novice Buddhist monk. "You see," he says, "Thai Buddhists believe they can get to paradise by holding on to a monk's robe. So I became a monk for a month to help my grandfather get to paradise. The novice monks had to get up at 5:00 A.M. and meditate. After that, we had free time so we read comics and played games on the monks' Play Station™. In the afternoons, we walked around the village with the monks to get food and drink."

Architecture

The temple of Angkor Wat in northwestern Cambodia was built during the 1100s. Dedicated to the Hindu god Vishnu, much of the temple is covered with elaborately carved characters from Hindu legends. The Khmer people designed Angkor Wat to represent the Hindu view of the universe. The moat surrounding the temple stood for the oceans. The tall central tower symbolized Mount Meru, center of the universe and home of the various forms of the Hindu supreme being.

Looking Closer How does the design of Angkor Wat reflect the beliefs of the builders?

Cambodia　For many years, **Cambodia** was a rich farming country that exported rice and rubber. By the 1980s, its economy was in ruins because of years of civil war and harsh Communist rule. Cambodia's few factories produce items such as wood products, textiles, and rubber.

Most of Cambodia's 12.6 million people belong to the Khmer (kuh•MEHR) ethnic group. About 82 percent live in rural villages. The rest live in cities such as the capital, **Phnom Penh** (puh•NAWM PEHN). Buddhism is Cambodia's main religion. About 1,000 years ago, Cambodia was the center of the vast Khmer Empire. During Khmer rule, huge temple complexes like Angkor Wat were built.

In modern times, Cambodia was under French rule, becoming independent in 1953. Since the 1960s, there has been almost constant warfare among rival political groups. A Communist government led by the dictator Pol Pot took control in the mid-1970s. Pol Pot forced many city dwellers to move to rural areas and work as farmers. More than 1 million Cambodians died. Some fled to other countries. In 1993 Cambodia brought back its king, but rivalry among political groups continues.

✔ Reading Check Why is Cambodia's economy in ruins?

Vietnam

Vietnam's long eastern coastline borders the **Gulf of Tonkin,** the **South China Sea,** and the **Gulf of Thailand.** In the north lies the fertile delta of the Red River. A delta is an area of land formed by soil deposits at the mouth of a river. In the south you find the wide, swampy delta of the Mekong River. Monsoons bring wet and dry seasons.

Farmers grow large amounts of rice, sugarcane, cassava, sweet potatoes, corn, bananas, and coffee in river deltas. Vietnam's mountain forests provide wood, and the South China Sea yields large catches of fish.

With almost 80.8 million people, Vietnam has the largest population in mainland Southeast Asia. About 75 percent live in rural villages. The largest urban area is **Ho Chi Minh** (HOH CHEE MIHN) **City,** named for the country's first Communist leader. Located in the south, it used to be called Saigon (sy•GAHN). Vietnam's capital, **Hanoi,** is located in the north. Most people are Buddhists and belong to the Vietnamese ethnic group. The rest are Chinese, Cambodians, and other Asian ethnic groups. Vietnamese is the major language, but Chinese, English, and French are also spoken.

The ancestors of Vietnam's people came from China more than 2,000 years ago. From the late 1800s to the mid-1950s, Vietnam was under French rule. Vietnamese Communists drove out the French in 1954. The Communist government controlled northern Vietnam, while an American-supported government ruled the south. In the 1960s, fighting between these two groups led to the Vietnam War. During this extended conflict, more than 2.5 million Americans helped fight against the Communists. The United States eventually withdrew its forces in 1973. Within two years, the Communists had captured the south. Many thousands of people fled Vietnam, settling in the United States and other countries.

In recent years, Vietnam's Communist leaders have opened the country to Western ideas, businesses, and tourists. They have also loosened government controls on the economy. In these two ways, the Communist leaders hope to raise Vietnam's standard of living.

✓ **Reading Check** What is the largest urban area in Vietnam?

FCAT PRACTICE You can prepare for the FCAT-assessed standards by completing the correlated item(s) below.

Section 1 Assessment

Defining Terms

1. Define precious gems, deforestation, socialism, civil war.

Recalling Facts

2. **Economics** What does Myanmar export?

3. **History** What led to the Vietnam War?

4. **Economics** What has slowed the economies of Laos and Cambodia?

Graphic Organizer

5. **Organizing Information** Create a time line like this one. Then list four events and their dates in Vietnam's history. **FCAT LA.A.1.3.2**

Critical Thinking

6. **Summarizing Information** What makes Thailand unique among the countries of Southeast Asia? **FCAT LA.A.2.3.1**

7. **Making Predictions** In recent years, the Communist leaders in Vietnam have tried to improve the country's standard of living. How do they hope to do this? Do you think these actions will help? Why or why not?

FCAT LA.A.2.3.1

 Applying Social Studies Skills

8. **Analyzing Maps** Look at the political map on page 709. What city is located at 21°N, 106°E?

Social Studies Skill

Reading a Contour Map

A trail map would show the paths you could follow if you went hiking in the mountains. How would you know if the trail follows an easy, flat route, though, or if it cuts steeply up a mountain? To find out, you need a **contour map.**

Learning the Skill

Contour maps use lines to outline the shape—or contour—of the landscape. Each contour line connects all points that are at the same elevation. This means that if you walked along one contour line, you would always be at the same height above sea level.

Where the contour lines are far apart, the land rises gradually. Where the lines are close together, the land rises steeply. For example, one contour line may be labeled 1,000 meters (3,281 ft.). Another contour line very close to the first one may be labeled 2,000 meters (6,562 ft.). This means that the land rises 1,000 meters (3,281 ft.) in just a short distance.

To read a contour map, follow these steps:

- Identify the area shown on the map.
- Read the numbers on the contour lines to determine how much the elevation increases or decreases with each line.
- Locate the highest and lowest numbers, which indicate the highest and lowest elevations.
- Notice the amount of space between the lines, which tells you whether the land is steep or flat.

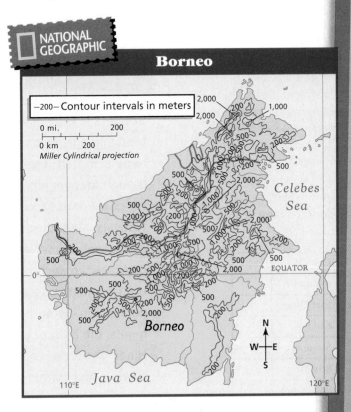

NATIONAL GEOGRAPHIC

Borneo

—200— Contour intervals in meters

0 mi. 200
0 km 200
Miller Cylindrical projection

Practicing the Skill

Study the contour map above, and then answer the following questions.

1. What area is shown on the map?
2. What is the lowest elevation on the map?
3. What is the highest elevation on the map?
4. Where is the landscape flattest? How can you tell?
5. How would you describe the physical geography of this island?

Applying the Skill

Turn to page 10 in the **Geography Handbook.** Use the contour map of Sri Lanka to answer the five questions above.

Diverse Island Cultures

NATIONAL GEOGRAPHIC **Exploring Our World**

Villagers in Bali, Indonesia, carry food and gifts to a local Hindu temple. In Bali, it seems as though there is an unending chain of religious festivals. More than 60 festivals a year are dedicated to such events and items as percussion instruments, the birth of a Hindu goddess, woodcarving, and learning.

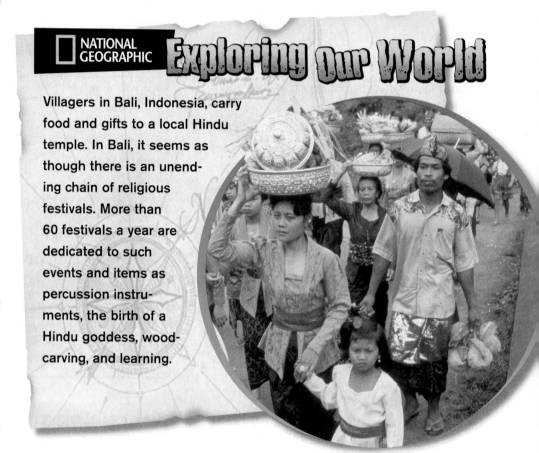

The island countries of Southeast Asia are Indonesia, East Timor, Malaysia, Singapore, Brunei (bru•NY), and the Philippines. **Indonesia** is Southeast Asia's largest country. It is an archipelago of more than 13,600 islands.

Indonesia and East Timor

The map on page 709 shows you the major islands of Indonesia—**Sumatra, Java,** and **Celebes** (SEH•luh•BEEZ). Indonesia also shares two large islands with other countries. Most of the island of **Borneo** belongs to Indonesia. In addition, Indonesia controls the western half of the island of Timor. Another country—**East Timor**—lies on the eastern half.

Indonesia lies where two of the earth's tectonic plates meet. Tectonic **plates** are huge slabs of rock that make up the earth's crust. Indonesia's location on top of these plates causes it to experience earthquakes.

The volcanoes that formed Indonesia have left a rich covering of ash that makes the soil good for farming. Because Indonesia lies on the Equator, its climate is tropical. Monsoons bring a wet season and a dry season. The tropical climate, combined with fertile soil, has allowed dense rain forests to spread.

Economic Activities   Foreign companies build factories on the island of Java because labor is inexpensive. Agriculture provides work for nearly half of the people of Indonesia. Farmers grow rice, coffee, cassava, tea, and peanuts. The country of East Timor also has agricultural products such as coffee, mangoes, and vanilla.

Indonesia has large reserves of oil and natural gas. Its mines yield tin, silver, nickel, copper, bauxite, and gold. Dense rain forests provide teak and other valuable woods. Some companies that own large tracts of land are cutting down the trees very quickly. The environment suffers from this deforestation. When the trees are cut down, rich soil runs off into the sea during heavy rains.

People of Indonesia and East Timor   Indonesia has about 220.5 million people—the fourth-largest population in the world. It is also one of the world's most densely populated countries. On Java you will find **Jakarta** (juh•KAHR•tuh), Indonesia's capital and largest city. It has modern buildings and streets crowded with cars and bicycles.

Forty-five percent of Indonesians belong to the Javanese ethnic group. The official language, Bahasa Indonesia, is taught in schools. Indonesia has more followers of Islam than any other country. Other religions, such as Christianity and Buddhism, are also practiced. On the beautiful island of **Bali,** Hindu beliefs are held by most of the people.

Thousands of years ago, Hindus and Buddhists from India settled the islands that are today Indonesia. Their descendants set up kingdoms. These kingdoms grew wealthy by controlling the trade that passed through the waterways between the Indian and Pacific Oceans. In the A.D. 1100s, traders from Southwest Asia brought Islam to the region. Four hundred years later, Europeans arrived to acquire the valuable spices grown here. They brought Christianity to the islands. The Dutch eventually controlled most of the islands as a colony. Independence finally came to Indonesia in 1949.

In the late 1990s, severe economic problems led to unrest. Indonesia's people forced their dictator to resign. Today the country has a democratic government. With so many different ethnic groups, many small political parties arise. As a result, Indonesia's leaders find it difficult to form a government that is strong enough to deal with challenges.

Most recently, the people of East Timor, who are largely Roman Catholic and were once ruled by Portugal, voted for independence from Indonesia. In 2002 East Timor was internationally recognized as independent and the world's newest democracy. About 800,000 people live here.

✓ Reading Check When did East Timor win its independence?

Exchange of Knowledge

Malacca, in Malaysia, was the richest seaport in the world in the 1500s. Merchants from India, China, and Japan met Portuguese, British, and Dutch traders. These merchants and traders were responsible for the exchange of knowledge as well as goods. Today, thanks to its geographic location, Singapore has replaced Malacca as the chief center of trade.

East Timor's Challenges

East Timor's road to freedom—finally won on May 20, 2002—was long and difficult. Independence has also brought challenges. One of Asia's poorest countries, East Timor suffers from the effects of war and drought. The possibility of wealth from untapped offshore oil and gas fields, however, may brighten East Timor's future.

Malaysia

A Malaysian worker taps a rubber tree to get the milky liquid called latex.

Economics What other products does Malaysia export?

Malaysia

Malaysia is located on the southern end of the Malay Peninsula and also on the island of Borneo. Dense rain forests and rugged mountains make up the landscape. The **Strait of Malacca** lies to the west of the Malay Peninsula. A strait is a narrow body of water between two pieces of land. The Strait of Malacca is an important waterway for trade between the Indian Ocean and the Java Sea.

Malaysia is a world leader in exporting rubber and palm oil. The country also exports petroleum and natural gas. Malaysia is rich in tin, iron ore, copper, and bauxite. Consumer and high-technology goods, including microchips, are produced here. Malaysia's ports are important centers of trade as well. **Kuala Lumpur** (KWAH•luh LUM•PUR) is the capital and largest city. The Petronas Towers—among the world's tallest buildings—soar above this city. In contrast, many rural villagers live in thatched-roof homes built on posts a few feet off the ground.

Most of Malaysia's 25.1 million people belong to the Malay ethnic group. Their ancestors came from southern China thousands of years ago. In the 1800s, the British—who then ruled Malaysia—brought in Chinese and South Asian workers to mine tin and to work on rubber plantations. As a result, in marketplaces today you can hear Malay, Chinese, Tamil, and English spoken. Most Malaysians are Muslims, but there are also large numbers of Buddhists, Christians, and Hindus.

✓ Reading Check Where are the Petronas Towers located?

Singapore, Brunei, and the Philippines

Singapore lies off the southern tip of the Malay Peninsula. It is made up of Singapore Island and 58 smaller islands. Singapore is one of the world's smallest countries, yet it has one of the world's most productive economies. The city of **Singapore** is the capital and takes up much of Singapore Island. Once covered by rain forests, Singapore Island now holds highways, factories, office buildings, and docks.

The city of Singapore has one of the world's busiest harbors. It is a free port. This is a place where goods can be unloaded, stored, and shipped again without payment of import taxes. Huge amounts of goods pass through this port. Singapore's many factories make high-tech goods, machinery, chemicals, and paper products. Because of their productive trade economy, the people of Singapore enjoy a high standard of living.

Founded by the British in the early 1800s, Singapore became an independent republic in 1965. Most of the country's 4.2 million people are Chinese, but Malaysians and Indians make up about 25 percent of the population.

Brunei On the northern coast of Borneo lies another small nation—**Brunei.** Oil and natural gas exports provide about half of the country's income. Brunei's citizens receive free education and medical care, as well as low-cost housing, fuel, and food. Today the government is investing in new industries to avoid reliance on income from fuels. All political and economic decisions are made by Brunei's sultan, or ruler.

The Philippines The **Philippines** includes about 7,000 islands in the South China Sea. Volcanic mountains and forests dominate the landscape. About 40 percent of the people farm. They have built terraces on the steep mountain slopes. Terraced fields are strips of land cut out of a hillside like stair steps.

Cities in the Philippines are busy and modern. **Manila,** the country's capital, is a great commercial center. Factory workers here produce high-tech goods, food products, chemicals, clothing, and shoes.

Named after King Philip II of Spain, the Philippines spent more than 300 years as a Spanish colony. As a result of the Spanish-American War, the United States controlled the islands from 1898 until World War II. In 1946 the Philippines became an independent democratic republic.

The Philippines is the only Christian country in Southeast Asia. About 90 percent of Filipinos follow the Roman Catholic religion, brought to the islands by Spanish missionaries. The culture today blends Malay, Spanish, and American influences.

Social Studies Online

Web Activity Visit *The World and Its People* Web site at twip.glencoe.com and click on **Chapter 25—Student Web Activities** to learn more about the Philippines.

✓Reading Check For whom was the Philippines named and why?

FCAT PRACTICE You can prepare for the FCAT-assessed standards by completing the correlated item(s) below.

Section 2 Assessment

Defining Terms

1. Define plate, strait, free port, terraced field.

Recalling Facts

2. Location Which five islands are Indonesia's largest?

3. Economics Why do the people of Singapore enjoy a high standard of living? **FCAT LA.E.2.2.1**

4. Culture What religion do most Filipinos practice?

Critical Thinking

5. Making Inferences How does Brunei's government use its fuel income?

6. Drawing Conclusions Why is it difficult for government officials to rule Indonesia? **FCAT LA.A.2.3.1**

Graphic Organizer

7. Organizing Information Create a diagram like this one. In the center, list similarities of the countries listed. In the outer ovals, write two ways that the country differs from the others. **FCAT LA.A.1.3.2**

Malaysia — Singapore — Similarities — Brunei — Philippines

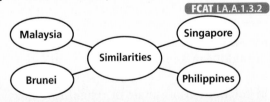

Applying Social Studies Skills

8. Analyzing Maps Look at the map on page 709. What countries share the island of Borneo?

Making Connections

ART SCIENCE CULTURE TECHNOLOGY

Shadow Puppets

FCAT PRACTICE Answering question 3 below will help you prepare for the **FCAT Reading** test.

Late at night, long after dark has fallen on a small stage in Java, a shadow puppet show is about to begin. The glow of a lamp shines behind a wide linen screen. Puppets stand hidden from direct view. The "good" characters are on the right. The "bad" ones are placed on the left. The audience waits anxiously on the other side of the screen. Once the story begins, the performance will continue until dawn.

▲ The *dalang* and his orchestra

The Performance

Wayang kulit, the ancient Indonesian shadow puppet theater, dates back at least 1,000 years. Today there are several thousand puppeteers. This makes shadow puppets the strongest theater tradition in Southeast Asia.

Shadow puppets are flat leather puppets. Many have movable limbs and mouths that are operated by sticks. During the show, the puppets cast their shadows onto the screen. The *dalang,* or puppeteer, sits behind the screen and manipulates the figures. He brings each to life in one of the more than 200 traditional puppet stories.

The Stories

Although Islam is now the major religion of Indonesia, much of the traditional shadow puppet theater is based on stories from two ancient Hindu epics from India. At one time, the principal purpose of shadow puppetry was to provide moral and religious instruction in Hinduism. Now the stories combine Hindu themes with elements of Buddhism and Islam, as well as Indonesian history and folklore. Often the performance is given in celebration of public or religious holidays or to honor a wedding or birth.

The Puppeteer

The skill of the *dalang* is critical to the show's success. The *dalang* operates all the puppets, narrates the story, provides sound effects, and directs the gong, drum, and flute orchestra that accompanies the puppet show. The puppeteer changes his voice to create an individual sound for each character. The *dalang* performs without a script or notes, adding jokes and making small changes to suit the crowd and the occasion. Because a shadow puppet show can last as long as nine hours, the *dalang* must have both a tremendous memory and great endurance.

Many *dalangs* carve their own puppets, having learned this art from earlier generations. Each figure must appear in a specific size, body build, and costume. Even the shape of the eyes tells about the figure's character and mood.

Making the Connection

1. How do shadow puppets move?
2. What kinds of stories do shadow puppet shows present?
3. **Drawing Conclusions** In what way is the *dalang* a master of many different art forms? **FCAT LA.A.2.3.1**

Reading Review

Section 1 — Life on the Mainland

Terms to Know
precious gems
deforestation
socialism
civil war

Main Idea
The countries of mainland Southeast Asia rely on agriculture as a major source of wealth.

✓ **Region** Mainland Southeast Asia includes the countries of Myanmar, Thailand, Laos, Cambodia, and Vietnam.

✓ **Place** These countries have highland areas and lowland river valleys with fertile soil. Monsoons bring heavy rains in the summer.

✓ **History** Thailand is the only country in Southeast Asia that is free of the influence of colonial rule.

✓ **Economics** Conflict has hurt the economies of Laos, Cambodia, and Vietnam.

Section 2 — Diverse Island Cultures

Terms to Know
plate
strait
free port
terraced field

Main Idea
The island countries of Southeast Asia have a variety of cultures and economic activities.

✓ **Region** The island countries of Southeast Asia include Indonesia, East Timor, Malaysia, Singapore, Brunei, and the Philippines.

✓ **Place** Indonesia—with the world's fourth-largest population—is an archipelago formed by volcanoes.

✓ **Economics** Indonesia has rich supplies of oil, natural gas, and minerals.

✓ **Government** Indonesia's leaders face the challenge of creating a nation out of a land with many different groups and political parties.

✓ **Economics** Malaysia produces palm oil and rubber, among other goods. Its capital, Kuala Lumpur, is a commercial center.

✓ **Economics** The port of Singapore is one of the world's busiest trading centers.

✓ **Culture** The Philippines shows the influence of Malaysian, Spanish, and American culture.

People in Bangkok, Thailand, face traffic snarls and pollution that are among the worst in the world. ▶

FCAT PRACTICE You can prepare for the FCAT-assessed standards by completing the correlated item(s) below.

Using Key Terms

Match the terms in Part A with their definitions in Part B.

A.

1. free port
2. deforestation
3. plate
4. strait
5. terraced field
6. civil war
7. socialism
8. precious gems

B.

a. the widespread cutting of trees
b. war fought between groups within a country
c. strip of land cut out of a hillside
d. economic system in which the government owns many businesses
e. stones such as rubies, sapphires, and jade
f. place where shipped goods are not taxed
g. slab of rock that makes up the earth's crust
h. narrow body of water that runs between two land areas

Reviewing the Main Ideas

Section 1 Life on the Mainland

9. **Economics** What products do workers in Thailand make?
10. **Culture** What are *wats*?
11. **Economics** What countries have poor economies because of recent conflict?
12. **Economics** How is Vietnam trying to improve its economy?

Section 2 Diverse Island Cultures

13. **Economics** How do nearly half of the people of Indonesia make a living?
14. **Location** How does location make Indonesia a center of trade?
15. **Government** Why does Indonesia have many political parties?
16. **Location** Why is the Strait of Malacca important?
17. **Economics** What economic activities are important in Singapore in addition to its harbor industry?
18. **Economics** What resources have made Brunei wealthy?
19. **Culture** How does religion show Spanish influence in the Philippines?

 **Southeast Asia**

Place Location Activity

On a separate sheet of paper, match the letters on the map with the numbered places listed below.

1. Mekong River
2. South China Sea
3. Gulf of Tonkin
4. Hanoi
5. Indonesia
6. Singapore
7. Thailand
8. Vietnam
9. Indian Ocean
10. Philippines

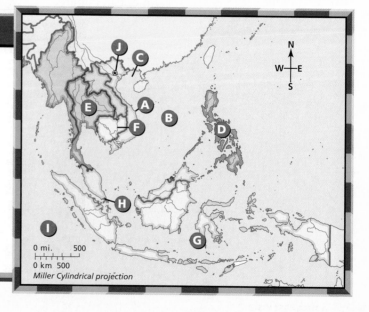

0 mi.   500
0 km 500
Miller Cylindrical projection

Critical Thinking

20. Predicting Outcomes Experts believe that Brunei has enough oil reserves to last until 2018. What might happen to the country's economy and standard of living at that time?

21. Organizing Information Create a chart like this one. List three countries—Indonesia, a country from mainland Southeast Asia, and another from island Southeast Asia. Under the other columns, write two facts about each country you listed. **FCAT LA.A.1.3.2**

Country	Land	Economy	People

Comparing Regions Activity

22. Geography Compare the island countries of Southeast Asia to the island countries in the Caribbean. What landforms are similar and different? How does geography affect the economies of these island countries? Write a paragraph using the information you find. **FCAT LA.B.1.3.2**

Mental Mapping Activity

23. Focusing on the Region Draw a map of Southeast Asia, and then label the following:

- Borneo
- Irrawaddy River
- Java
- Malay Peninsula
- Philippines
- South China Sea
- Strait of Malacca
- Thailand

Technology Skills Activity

24. Using the Internet Use the Internet to learn about the foods in a Southeast Asian country. Find recipes and pictures. Prepare a display that shows a typical meal, or cook the meal yourself and share it with the class. **FCAT LA.A.2.3.5**

Standardized Test Practice

Directions: Study the graph below, and then answer the questions that follow.

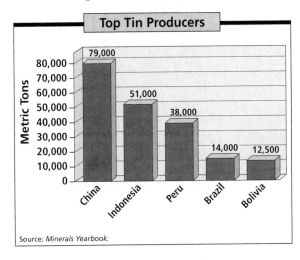

Top Tin Producers

Source: *Minerals Yearbook.*

1. About how much tin does Indonesia produce each year? **FCAT MA.E.3.3.1**

A 51,000,000 metric tons

B 51,000 metric tons

C 51.00 million metric tons

D 51.00 billion metric tons

2. About how much tin does Bolivia produce each year? **FCAT MA.E.3.3.1**

F 12,500 metric tons

G 12,500,000 metric tons

H 12.5 million metric tons

J 12.5 billion metric tons

Test-Taking Tip: In order to understand any type of graph, look carefully around the graph for keys that show how it is organized. On this bar graph, the numbers along the left side represent the exact number shown. You do not have to multiply by millions or billions to find the number of metric tons.

Fur seal on the beach, Antarctica

Boy selling fish, Samoa

Australia, Oceania, and Antarctica

Australia, Oceania, and Antarctica are grouped together more because of their nearness to one another than because of any similarities among their peoples. These lands lie mostly in the Southern Hemisphere. Australia is a dry continent that is home to unusual wildlife. Oceania's 25,000 tropical islands spread out across the Pacific Ocean. Frozen Antarctica covers the earth at the South Pole.

◄ **Lone tree in the outback, Australia**

Focus on:

Australia, Oceania, and Antarctica

LYING ALMOST ENTIRELY in the Southern Hemisphere, this region includes two continents and thousands of islands scattered across the Pacific Ocean. Covering a huge portion of the globe from the Equator to the South Pole, the region includes landscapes ranging from polar to tropical.

The Land

Both a continent and a single country, Australia is a vast expanse of mostly flat land. A chain of hills and mountains known as the Great Dividing Range runs down the continent's eastern edge. Between this range of mountains and the Pacific Ocean lies a narrow strip of coastal land. West of the Great Dividing Range lies Australia's large—and very dry—interior. Here in the Australian "outback" are seemingly endless miles of scrubland, as well as three huge deserts.

Along Australia's northeastern coast lies the Great Barrier Reef. This famous natural wonder is the world's largest coral reef, home to brilliantly colored tropical fish and underwater creatures.

Across the Tasman Sea from Australia lies New Zealand, made up of two main islands— North Island and South Island—and many smaller ones. Both North Island and South Island have sandy beaches, emerald hillsides, and snow-tipped mountains. Plateaus and hills dominate the rest of New Zealand's landscape.

Oceania North and east of New Zealand is Oceania. Its roughly 25,000 islands lie scattered across the Pacific Ocean on both sides of the Equator. Some of these islands are volcanic. Others are huge formations of rock that have risen from the ocean floor. Still others are low-lying coral islands surrounded by reefs.

Antarctica The frozen continent, Antarctica covers and surrounds the South Pole. It is almost completely buried under an enormous sheet of ice. The ice is as much as 2 miles (3.2 km) thick in places and holds 70 percent of the world's freshwater.

The Climate

Australia is one of the driest continents in the world. Its eastern coast does receive rainfall from the Pacific Ocean. Mountains block this moisture from reaching inland areas, however. Much of Australia's outback has a desert climate.

No place in New Zealand is more than 80 miles (129 km) from the sea. This country has only one climate region: marine west coast.

▼ Sheep grazing near Mount Egmont, New Zealand

◄ Emperor penguins, Antarctica

This means that New Zealand has mild temperatures and plentiful rainfall throughout the year.

The islands of Oceania have mostly tropical climates, with warm temperatures and distinct wet and dry seasons. Rain forests cover many of the islands.

Antarctica is one of the coldest and windiest places on the earth, as well as one of the driest. It receives so little precipitation that it is considered a desert—the world's largest cold desert.

The Economy

Mines dot the Australian landscape. Its ancient rocks and soils are rich in minerals such as uranium, bauxite, iron ore, copper, nickel, and gold. Little of Australia's land is good for growing crops. Instead, vast cattle and sheep ranches—or stations, as the Australians call them—spread across much of the country. The worst drought in almost 100 years occurred in 2002–2003, which had a negative impact on the economy.

Sheep far outnumber people in New Zealand, where pastures are lush and green almost year-round. New Zealand is one of the world's leading producers of lamb and wool. New Zealand's main crops include wheat, barley, potatoes, fruits, and vegetables.

The people of Oceania depend primarily on fishing and farming. Across much of Oceania, the soil and climate are not favorable for widespread agriculture. Islanders generally raise only enough food for themselves. Yet some larger islands have rich volcanic soil. In such places, cash crops of fruits, sugar, coffee, and coconut products are grown for export.

Antarctica is believed to be rich in mineral resources. To preserve Antarctica for research and exploration, however, many nations have agreed not to mine this mineral wealth. In fact, 43 nations signed the Antarctic Treaty in 1959 to commit to peace and science. They even agreed to share their scientific observations and results.

The People

The first settlers in this region probably came from Asia thousands of years ago. Australia's first inhabitants, the ancestors of today's Aborigines, may have arrived more than 40,000 years ago. Not until about A.D. 1000, however, did seafaring peoples reach the farthest islands of Oceania.

The British colonized Australia and New Zealand in the 1700s and 1800s. These two countries gained their independence in the early 1900s. Many South Pacific islands were not freed from colonial rule until after World War II. Today Australia and Oceania are a blend of European, traditional Pacific, and Asian cultures.

◀ **Girl selling fruit, French Polynesia**

Despite its vast size, this is the least populous of all the world's regions. It is home to only about 32 million people. More than half of these live in Australia, where they are found mostly in coastal cities such as Sydney and Melbourne. Roughly 4 million people live in New Zealand, which also has large urban populations along its coasts. Oceania is less urbanized. Antarctica has no permanent human inhabitants at all. Groups of scientists live and work on the frozen continent for brief periods to carry out their research.

▼ **The city of Melbourne, along the southeastern coast of Australia**

Australia

Data Bits

🚗	Automobiles per 1,000 people	485
📺	Television sets per 1,000 people	716
VOTE	Democratic elections	Yes

Ethnic Makeup

Aboriginal and Other 1%
Asian 7%
Caucasian 92%

World Ranking

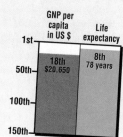

GNP per capita in US $
1st
18th $20,650
50th
100th
150th

Life expectancy
8th 78 years

Population: Urban ▓ vs. Rural ▓

91%   9%

Sources: *World Desk Reference*, 2000;
World Development Indicators; *The World Almanac*, 2004.

Exploring the Region

1. Which two continents lie in this region?
2. Why is Antarctica considered a desert?
3. Why is so little of Australia's land good for farming?
4. Where do most of the region's people live?

REGIONAL ATLAS

Australia, Oceania, and Antarctica

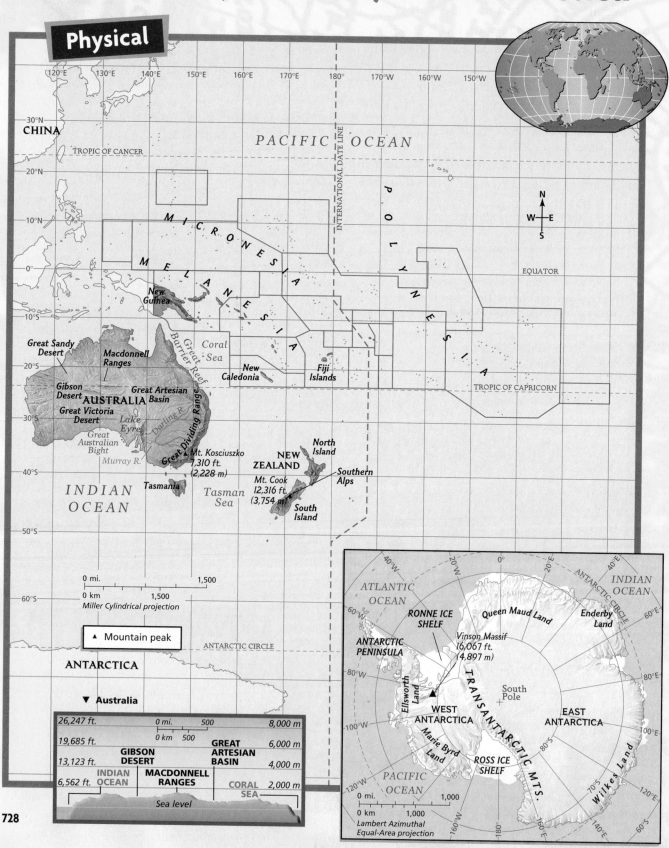

Physical

120°E 130°E 140°E 150°E 160°E 170°E 180° 170°W 160°W 150°W

30°N
CHINA
TROPIC OF CANCER
PACIFIC OCEAN
INTERNATIONAL DATE LINE
20°N
10°N
MICRONESIA
POLYNESIA
0°
MELANESIA
EQUATOR
New Guinea
10°S
Great Sandy Desert
Macdonnell Ranges
Coral Sea
New Caledonia
Fiji Islands
20°S
Great Barrier Reef
Gibson Desert
Great Artesian Basin
AUSTRALIA
TROPIC OF CAPRICORN
Great Victoria Desert
Lake Eyre
Darling R.
30°S
Great Australian Bight
Great Dividing Range
Murray R.
North Island
NEW ZEALAND
Mt. Kosciuszko 7,310 ft. (2,228 m)
40°S
Southern Alps
INDIAN OCEAN
Tasmania
Tasman Sea
Mt. Cook 12,316 ft. (3,754 m)
South Island
50°S

N
W   E
S

0 mi. 1,500
0 km 1,500
Miller Cylindrical projection

60°S
ANTARCTIC CIRCLE

▲ Mountain peak

ANTARCTICA

▼ **Australia**

26,247 ft.	0 mi. 500	8,000 m
19,685 ft.	0 km 500	6,000 m
	GIBSON DESERT	GREAT ARTESIAN BASIN
13,123 ft.		4,000 m
INDIAN OCEAN	MACDONNELL RANGES	
6,562 ft.		2,000 m
		CORAL SEA 2,000 m
Sea level		

40°W 20°W 0° 20°E 40°E
ATLANTIC OCEAN
ANTARCTIC CIRCLE
INDIAN OCEAN
60°W
RONNE ICE SHELF
Queen Maud Land
Enderby Land
60°E
ANTARCTIC PENINSULA
Vinson Massif 16,067 ft. (4,897 m)
80°W
Ellsworth Land
WEST ANTARCTICA
TRANSANTARCTIC MTS.
South Pole
EAST ANTARCTICA
80°E
100°W
Marie Byrd Land
ROSS ICE SHELF
PACIFIC OCEAN
120°W
0 mi. 1,000
0 km 1,000
Lambert Azimuthal Equal-Area projection
Wilkes Land
70°E
100°E

728

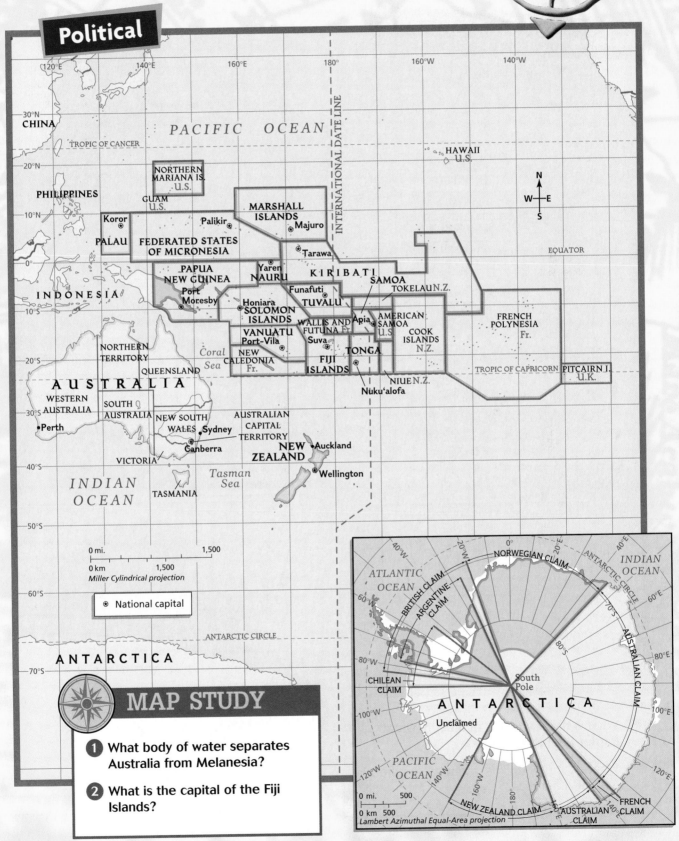

Political

PACIFIC OCEAN

30°N
CHINA
TROPIC OF CANCER

20°N
PHILIPPINES

NORTHERN
MARIANA IS.
U.S.

GUAM
U.S.

Koror
PALAU

Palikir
FEDERATED STATES
OF MICRONESIA

10°N

MARSHALL
ISLANDS
Majuro

Tarawa

INTERNATIONAL DATE LINE

HAWAII
U.S.

EQUATOR

N
W E
S

INDONESIA

PAPUA
NEW GUINEA
Port
Moresby

Yaren
NAURU

Funafuti
TUVALU

Honiara
SOLOMON
ISLANDS

KIRIBATI

SAMOA

Apia
WALLIS AND
FUTUNA Fr.
Suva

TOKELAU N.Z.

AMERICAN
SAMOA
U.S.

FRENCH
POLYNESIA
Fr.

10°S

VANUATU
Port-Vila

NEW
CALEDONIA
Fr.

Coral
Sea

FIJI
ISLANDS

TONGA

COOK
ISLANDS
N.Z.

NORTHERN
TERRITORY

QUEENSLAND

Nuku'alofa

NIUE N.Z.

TROPIC OF CAPRICORN

PITCAIRN I.
U.K.

20°S

AUSTRALIA

WESTERN
AUSTRALIA

SOUTH
AUSTRALIA

NEW SOUTH
WALES Sydney

Perth

30°S

AUSTRALIAN
CAPITAL
TERRITORY

Canberra

VICTORIA

NEW
ZEALAND

Auckland

INDIAN
OCEAN

TASMANIA

Tasman
Sea

Wellington

40°S

50°S

0 mi.   1,500

0 km   1,500
Miller Cylindrical projection

60°S

⊛ National capital

ANTARCTIC CIRCLE

ANTARCTICA

70°S

MAP STUDY

1 What body of water separates Australia from Melanesia?

2 What is the capital of the Fiji Islands?

ATLANTIC
OCEAN

NORWEGIAN CLAIM

INDIAN
OCEAN

ANTARCTIC CIRCLE

BRITISH CLAIM

ARGENTINE
CLAIM

AUSTRALIAN CLAIM

CHILEAN
CLAIM

South
Pole

ANTARCTICA

Unclaimed

PACIFIC
OCEAN

NEW ZEALAND CLAIM

AUSTRALIAN
CLAIM

FRENCH
CLAIM

0 mi.   500

0 km   500
Lambert Azimuthal Equal-Area projection

REGIONAL ATLAS

Australia, Oceania, and Antarctica

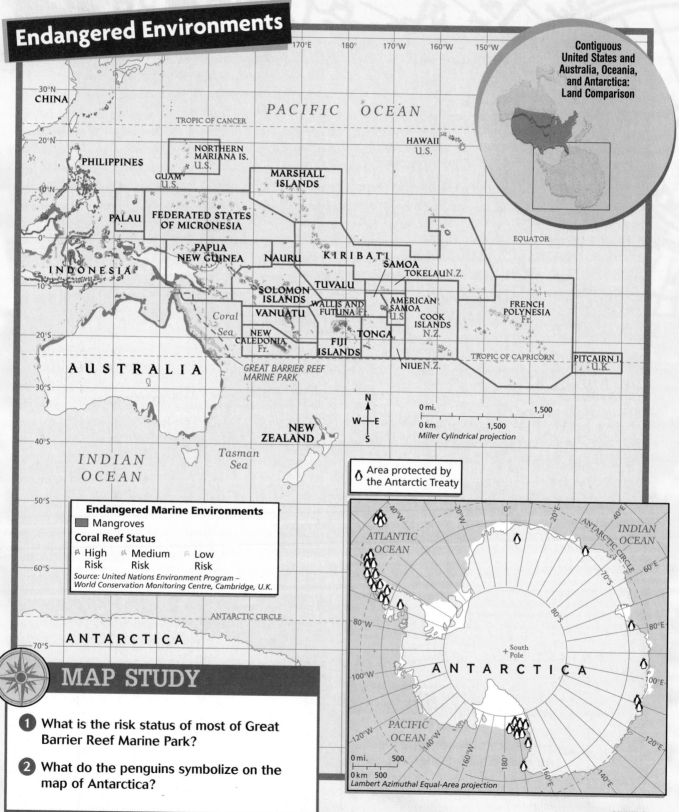

Endangered Environments

Contiguous
United States and
Australia, Oceania,
and Antarctica:
Land Comparison

Endangered Marine Environments

Mangroves

Coral Reef Status

High Risk   Medium Risk   Low Risk

Source: United Nations Environment Program –
World Conservation Monitoring Centre, Cambridge, U.K.

Area protected by
the Antarctic Treaty

Miller Cylindrical projection

Lambert Azimuthal Equal-Area projection

MAP STUDY

① What is the risk status of most of Great
Barrier Reef Marine Park?

② What do the penguins symbolize on the
map of Antarctica?

Geo Extremes

① **HIGHEST POINT**
Vinson Massif (Antarctica)
16,067 ft. (4,897 m) high

② **LOWEST POINT**
Bently Subglacial Trench
(Antarctica)
8,366 ft. (2,550 m)
below sea level

③ **LONGEST RIVER**
Murray-Darling (Australia)
2,310 mi. (3,718 km) long

④ **LARGEST LAKE**
Lake Eyre (Australia)
3,600 sq. mi.
(9,324 sq. km)

⑤ **LARGEST HOT DESERT**
Great Victoria (Australia)
134,650 sq. mi.
(348,742 sq. km)

⑥ **LARGEST COLD DESERT**
Antarctica
5,100,000 sq. mi.
(13,209,000 sq. km)

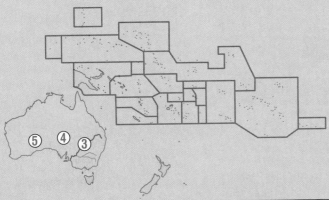

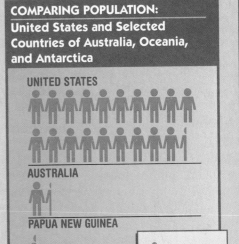

COMPARING POPULATION:
United States and Selected
Countries of Australia, Oceania,
and Antarctica

UNITED STATES

AUSTRALIA

PAPUA NEW GUINEA

🧍 = 15,000,000

NEW ZEALAND

Source: *Population Reference Bureau*, 2003.

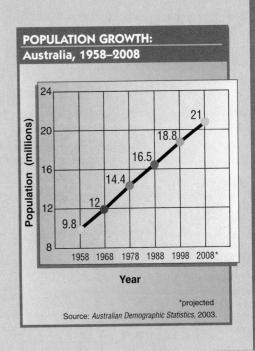

POPULATION GROWTH:
Australia, 1958–2008

*projected
Source: *Australian Demographic Statistics*, 2003.

GRAPHIC STUDY

① The largest cold desert in this region is also
the largest desert in the *world*. What is it?

② By how much is Australia's population
expected to have grown between 1958
and 2008? **FCAT** MA.E.3.3.1

Australia, Oceania, and Antarctica

REGIONAL ATLAS

Country Profiles

AUSTRALIA

POPULATION:
19,900,000
7 per sq. mi.
3 per sq. km

LANGUAGE:
English

MAJOR EXPORT:
Coal

MAJOR IMPORT:
Machinery

CAPITAL:
Canberra

LANDMASS:
2,988,888 sq. mi.
7,741,220 sq. km

Canberra

FEDERATED STATES of MICRONESIA

POPULATION:
100,000
426 per sq. mi.
164 per sq. km

LANGUAGES:
English, Local
Languages

MAJOR EXPORT:
Fish

MAJOR IMPORT:
Foods

CAPITAL:
Palikir

LANDMASS:
270 sq. mi.
699 sq. km

Palikir

KIRIBATI

POPULATION:
100,000
348 per sq. mi.
134 per sq. km

LANGUAGES:
English, Gilbertese

MAJOR EXPORT:
Coconut Products

MAJOR IMPORT:
Foods

CAPITAL:
Tarawa

LANDMASS:
282 sq. mi.
730 sq. km

Tarawa

FIJI ISLANDS

POPULATION:
900,000
123 per sq. mi.
47 per sq. km

LANGUAGES:
English, Fijian,
Hindi

MAJOR EXPORT:
Sugar

MAJOR IMPORT:
Machinery

CAPITAL:
Suva

LANDMASS:
7,054 sq. mi.
18,270 sq. km

Suva

MARSHALL ISLANDS

POPULATION:
100,000
791 per sq. mi.
305 per sq. km

LANGUAGES:
English, Local
Languages

MAJOR EXPORT:
Coconut Products

MAJOR IMPORT:
Foods

CAPITAL:
Majuro

LANDMASS:
69 sq. mi.
179 sq. km

Majuro

NAURU

POPULATION:
10,000
1,412 per sq. mi.
545 per sq. km

LANGUAGES:
Nauruan, English

MAJOR EXPORT:
Phosphates

MAJOR IMPORT:
Foods

CAPITAL:
Yaren

LANDMASS:
9 sq. mi.
23 sq. km

Yaren

NEW ZEALAND

POPULATION:
4,000,000
38 per sq. mi.
15 per sq. km

LANGUAGE:
English

MAJOR EXPORT:
Wool

MAJOR IMPORT:
Machinery

CAPITAL:
Wellington

LANDMASS:
104,452 sq. mi.
270,531 sq. km

Wellington

PALAU

POPULATION:
20,000
113 per sq. mi.
44 per sq. km

LANGUAGES:
English, Palauan

MAJOR EXPORT:
Fish

MAJOR IMPORT:
Machinery

CAPITAL:
Koror

LANDMASS:
178 sq. mi.
461 sq. km

Koror

PAPUA NEW GUINEA

POPULATION:
5,500,000
31 per sq. mi.
12 per sq. km

LANGUAGES:
English, Local
Languages

MAJOR EXPORT:
Gold

MAJOR IMPORT:
Machinery

CAPITAL:
Port Moresby

LANDMASS:
178,703 sq. mi.
462,841 sq. km

Port Moresby

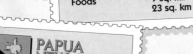

SAMOA

POPULATION:
200,000
157 per sq. mi.
61 per sq. km

LANGUAGES:
Samoan, English

MAJOR EXPORT:
Coconut Products

MAJOR IMPORT:
Foods

CAPITAL:
Apia

LANDMASS:
1,097 sq. mi.
2,841 sq. km

Apia

SOLOMON ISLANDS

POPULATION:
500,000
44 per sq. mi.
17 per sq. km

LANGUAGES:
English, Local
Languages

MAJOR EXPORT:
Cocoa

MAJOR IMPORT:
Machinery

CAPITAL:
Honiara

LANDMASS:
11,158 sq. mi.
28,899 sq. km

Honiara

Countries and flags not drawn to scale

For more information on countries in this region, refer to the Nations of the World Data Bank in the Appendix.

TONGA

POPULATION:
100,000
370 per sq. mi.
143 per sq. km

LANGUAGES:
Tongan, English

MAJOR EXPORT:
Squash

MAJOR IMPORT:
Foods

CAPITAL:
Nuku'alofa

LANDMASS:
290 sq. mi.
751 sq. km

Nuku'alofa

TUVALU

POPULATION:
10,000
1,000 per sq. mi.
385 per sq. km

LANGUAGES:
Tuvalu, English

MAJOR EXPORT:
Coconut Products

MAJOR IMPORT:
Foods

CAPITAL:
Funafuti

LANDMASS:
10 sq. mi.
26 sq. km

Funafuti

VANUATU

POPULATION:
200,000
45 per sq. mi.
17 per sq. km

LANGUAGES:
Bislama, English, French

MAJOR EXPORT:
Coconut Products

MAJOR IMPORT:
Machinery

CAPITAL:
Port-Vila

LANDMASS:
4,707 sq. mi.
12,191 sq. km

Port-Vila

BUILDING CITIZENSHIP

Voting Nearly all eligible voters participate in elections in Australia. All citizens over 18 years old are required to vote in all local, state, and national elections. If they don't vote, they can be fined up to 50 Australian dollars. To make it easier, elections are held on Saturdays and voting is done at schools, churches, and other convenient locations. In the United States, only about half of eligible people vote in the presidential elections.

Why do so many people in the United States not exercise their right to vote?

This woman is exercising her right to vote. ▼

FCAT PRACTICE Completing the activity below will help you prepare for the **FCAT Reading** Test.

Voting and participating in political activities are important parts of belonging to a democratic society. Yet in the United States, most people do not vote. Imagine you are the head of elections for your city and it is your responsibility to encourage people to vote in upcoming elections for mayor and the city council. Design a flyer that will be mailed to all households to encourage people to vote.

FCAT LA.B.1.3.2

Chapter 26

Australia and New Zealand

The World and Its People · NATIONAL GEOGRAPHIC

To learn more about the people and places of Australia and New Zealand, view *The World and Its People* **Chapter 27** video.

Social Studies online

Chapter Overview Visit *The World and Its People* Web site at twip.glencoe.com and click on **Chapter 26—Chapter Overviews** to preview information about Australia and New Zealand.

Why It Matters

An Isolated Region

Australia and New Zealand have been called "the last places on Earth" because they are so far from other lands. Within Australia, some farmers in the remote outback region often have to drive several hours on unpaved roads to reach a distant rural town. Yet despite its isolation and distance from other countries, Australia has a prosperous economy that ties it very closely to the rest of the world.

◀ **Ayers Rock in central Australia**

FOLDABLES™
Study Organizer

Making Predictions Make this foldable to record information about Australia and New Zealand. You will then use it to make predictions about the future of the countries. **FCAT LA.A.2.3.1**

Step 1 Fold one sheet of paper in half from top to bottom.

Step 2 Fold it in half again, from side to side.

Step 3 Unfold the paper once. Sketch an outline of Australia and New Zealand across the front tabs and label your foldable as shown.

Step 4 Cut along the fold of the top flap only.

This cut will make two tabs.

Reading and Writing As you read the chapter, write what you learn about these countries under the appropriate tabs of your foldable. Then use that information to make predictions about the future economic growth and development of these countries.

FCAT LA.A.2.3.1

Australia–Land Down Under

Guide to Reading

Main Idea

Both a continent and a country, Australia has many natural resources but relatively few people.

Terms to Know

- coral reef
- outback
- station
- marsupial
- boomerang
- bush

Reading Strategy

Create a chart like this one. Then fill in two facts about Australia for each category.

FCAT LA.A.1.3.2

Land	History
Climate	Government
Economy	People

The following are the major Sunshine State Standards covered in this section.

SS.B.2.3.3:
Understands ways cultures differ in their use of similar environments and resources

SS.B.2.3.8:
Knows world patterns of resource distribution and utilization

NATIONAL GEOGRAPHIC Exploring Our World

Signs along Australia's lonely outback warn drivers that they may meet camels, wombats, or kangaroos. This road stretches for 800 miles (1,287 km) between Western and South Australia. With only 11 rest stops along the way, perhaps meeting a kangaroo would be a good thing. It might make the drive seem less lonely.

Australia, the sixth-largest country in the world, is also a continent. It is sometimes referred to as the "Land Down Under" because it is located in the Southern Hemisphere.

Australia's Landscape

Plateaus and plains spread across most of Australia. The map on page 742 shows you that the country has low mountain ranges as well, including the **Great Dividing Range.** The island of **Tasmania** is also part of Australia. The **Great Barrier Reef** lies off the country's northeastern coast. Here, coral formations have piled up for millions of years to create a colorful chain that stretches 1,250 miles (2,012 km). A **coral reef** is a structure formed by the skeletons of small sea animals.

Narrow plains run along the south and southeast of Australia. These fertile flatlands hold the best farmland and most of the country's people. Two major rivers, the **Murray** and the **Darling,** drain this region.

Australians use the name outback for the inland regions of their country. Mining camps and cattle and sheep ranches called stations dot this region. One cattle station is almost twice as large as Delaware.

Water is scarce in Australia. In the **Great Artesian Basin,** however, water lies in deep, underground pools. Ranchers drill wells and bring the underground water to the surface for their cattle. Australia's western plateau is even drier. Most people who cross the deserts and ranges on this vast plateau do so by airplane.

Unusual Animals About 200 million years ago, the tectonic plate upon which Australia sits separated from the other continents. As a result, Australia's native plants and animals are not found elsewhere in the world. Two well-known Australian animals are kangaroos and koalas. Both are marsupials, or mammals that carry their young in a pouch. Turn to page 740 to read more about some of Australia's animals.

✔️Reading Check **Where do most of Australia's people live?**

Australia's Economy

Australia has a strong, prosperous economy. The country is a treasure chest overflowing with mineral resources. These riches include iron ore, zinc, bauxite, gold, silver, opals, diamonds, and pearls. Australia

Social Studies Online

Web Activity Visit *The World and Its People* Web site at twip.glencoe.com and click on **Chapter 26— Student Web Activities** to learn more about the Great Barrier Reef.

FCAT
PRACTICE

Completing the exercise below will help you prepare for the **FCAT Reading** test.

Literature

GREAT MOTHER SNAKE
Aboriginal Legend

Aboriginal bark painting ▶

Most cultures developed stories to help explain their beginnings. In this Aboriginal legend, the Great Mother Snake is credited with creating Australia as well as all of its human and animal inhabitants.

❝ *. . . Then finally She awoke and brought from the womb on the Earth itself, man and woman. And they learned from the Mother Snake how to live in peace and harmony with all these creatures who were their spiritual cousins. . . . And man and woman were now the caretakers of this land. And the Great Snake then entered a large water hole where she guards the fish and other water creatures, so that when the Aboriginal people fish they know to take only as much as they can eat, because if someone should take more than they need through greed or kills for pleasure, they know that one dark night, the Great Mother Snake will come . . . and punish the one who broke this tribal law.*❞

Source: *Great Mother Snake*, an Aboriginal legend.

Analyzing Literature

Why would it be important for people in this culture to take from the earth only as much as they needed? **FCAT LA.A.2.3.2**

Architecture

The Sydney Opera House—one of the most famous buildings in the world—stands on a peninsula jutting out into the harbor of Sydney, Australia. The soaring, shell-like roof and walls are made of reinforced concrete covered with gleaming white ceramic tiles. Inside are an opera house, concert hall, theater, and other entertainment facilities. Completed in 1973, the Sydney Opera House is regarded as a masterpiece of modern architecture.

Looking Closer **What do you think this building resembles?**

also has energy resources, including coal, oil, and natural gas. Mineral and energy resources make up more than one-third of Australia's exports.

Australia's dry climate limits farming. With irrigation, however, farmers grow grains, sugarcane, cotton, fruits, and vegetables. The main agricultural activity is raising livestock, especially cattle and sheep. Australia is the world's top producer and exporter of wool. Ranchers also ship beef and cattle hides.

Manufacturing includes processed foods, transportation equipment, metals, cloth, and chemicals. High-technology industries, service industries, and tourism also play a large role in the economy. Ocean shipping enables Australia to export goods to distant markets. More than half go to Asia. The United States is also an important market for exports.

Despite its huge area, Australia has only 19.9 million people. The country has long needed more skilled workers to develop its resources and build its economy. Thus, the government has encouraged immigration. More than 5 million immigrants have arrived in recent decades.

✓ **Reading Check** What is Australia's main agricultural activity?

Australia's History and People

Australia's Aborigines (A•buh•RIHJ•neez) are the descendants of the first immigrants who came from Asia at least 40,000 years ago. For centuries, the nomadic Aborigines hunted, gathered plants, and searched for water. They developed a weapon called a boomerang. It is a flat, bent, wooden tool that hunters throw to stun prey. If the boomerang misses, it curves and sails back to the hunter.

The Dutch were the first Europeans to travel to Australia in the late 1600s. In 1770 Captain James Cook reached Australia and claimed it for Great Britain. At first the British government used Australia as a place

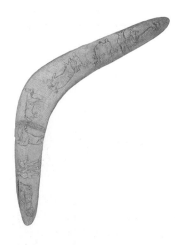

▲ Aboriginal boomerang

to send prisoners. Then the British set up colonies, especially after gold was discovered in the outback in 1851. Land was taken from the Aborigines, and many died of European diseases. Today nearly 300,000 Aborigines live in Australia. Many are moving to cities to find jobs. In 1967 the Australian government recognized the Aborigines as citizens.

The Government   In 1901 the colonies united to form the Commonwealth of Australia. Today Australia has a British-style parliamentary democracy. A prime minister is the head of government. Australians still accept the British monarch as a ceremonial leader. Many Australians, however, would like their country to become a republic with an Australian president.

Like the United States, Australia has a federal system of government. This means that political power is divided between a national government and state governments. The country has six states and two territories, the **Northern Territory** and the **Australian Capital Territory.**

City and Rural Life   About 90 percent of Australians live in cities. **Sydney** and **Melbourne** are the largest cities. **Canberra,** the capital, was a planned city located inland to draw people into the outback. About 10 percent of Australians live in rural areas known as the bush. Many rural people also live and work on the stations that dot the outback.

Australians speak English, but "Aussies," as they call themselves, have some different words. For example, Australians say "G'Day" as a form of hello and cook beef on a "barbie," or barbeque grill.

✓ **Reading Check** What kind of government does Australia have?

FCAT PRACTICE   You can prepare for the FCAT-assessed standards by completing the correlated item(s) below.

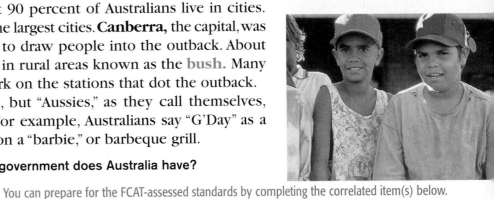

Section 1 Assessment

Defining Terms

1. **Define** coral reef, outback, station, marsupial, boomerang, bush.

Recalling Facts

2. **History** Why does Australia have animals that are not found on other continents?

3. **Economics** What are four mineral resources found in Australia?

4. **History** Who are the Aborigines?

Critical Thinking

5. **Understanding Cause and Effect** How does climate affect agriculture in Australia?

6. **Drawing Conclusions** How does life in Australia show that the country was once a colony of the United Kingdom?   **FCAT LA.A.2.3.1**

Graphic Organizer

7. **Organizing Information** Create a time line like this one with at least four dates in Australia's history. Write the dates on one side of the line and the corresponding event on the opposite side.   **FCAT LA.A.1.3.2**

├──────────┼──────────┼──────────┤

Applying Social Studies Skills

8. **Analyzing Maps** Look at the physical/political map on page 742. What mountain peak represents the highest elevation in Australia? What mountain range is it part of?

Australia and New Zealand

Making Connections

ART   SCIENCE   CULTURE   TECHNOLOGY

Australia's Amazing Animals

FCAT PRACTICE

Answering question 3 will help you prepare for the **FCAT Science** and **Reading** tests.

Australia is home to some fascinating and unusual animals. In fact, many of Australia's animal species are found nowhere else in the world.

Kangaroos

Ask people what comes to mind when they think of Australian animals, and they will probably say the kangaroo. Kangaroos are marsupials—mammals whose young mature inside a pouch on the mother's belly. The young kangaroo, called a joey, stays there for months, eating and growing. Australia is home to more than 50 species of kangaroo, ranging in size from the 6-foot (2-m) red kangaroo to the 9-inch (23-cm) musky rat-kangaroo. No matter what their size, all kangaroos have one thing in common—big hind feet. Kangaroos bound along at about 20 miles (32 km) per hour. In a single jump, a kangaroo can hop 10 feet (3 m) high and cover a distance of 45 feet (14 m).

Koalas

Because of their round face, big black nose, large fluffy ears, and soft fur, people sometimes call these animals koala bears. Yet they are not bears at all. The koala is a marsupial. The female's pouch opens at the bottom. Strong muscles keep the pouch shut and the young koalas, also called joeys, safe inside. The koala is a fussy eater who feeds only on leaves of eucalyptus trees. Although there are over 600 species of eucalyptus that grow in Australia, koalas eat only a few types. The leaves also provide the animals with all the moisture they need. Quiet, calm, and sleepy, koalas spend most of their time in the trees.

▲ Koala and joey

Platypus and Emu

The odd-looking platypus is one of the world's few egg-laying mammals. Sometimes called a duck-billed platypus, the animal has a soft, sensitive, skin-covered snout. The platypus is a good swimmer who lives in burrows along the streams and riverbanks of southern and eastern Australia. It uses its bill to stir the river bottom in search of food.

After the ostrich, the Australian emu is the world's second-largest bird. Although the emu cannot fly, its long legs enable it to run at speeds of up to 30 miles (48 km) per hour. Another interesting characteristic of the emu is its nesting behavior. Although the female lays the eggs, the male emu sits on them until they are ready to hatch.

◄ Kangaroo and joey

Emu ▼

Making the Connection

1. What are marsupials?

2. How far can a kangaroo hop in a single jump?

3. **Making Comparisons** Compare two different animals that live in Australia. How are they alike? How are they different? **FCAT SC.G.1.3.2, LA.A.2.3.1**

New Zealand

Guide to Reading

Main Idea

New Zealand is a small country with a growing economy based on trade.

Terms to Know

- geyser
- *manuka*
- fjord
- geothermal energy
- hydroelectric power

Reading Strategy

Create a time line like this one with at least four dates in New Zealand's history. Write the dates on one side of the line and the corresponding event on the opposite side.

FCAT LA.A.1.3.2

The following are the major Sunshine State Standards covered in this section.

SS.B.2.3.8:
Knows world patterns of resource distribution and utilization

SS.A.3.3.2:
Understands the historical events that have shaped the development of cultures throughout the world

NATIONAL GEOGRAPHIC Exploring Our World

Have you ever tasted a ripe green kiwifruit (KEE•wee•FROOT)? If so, it might have been grown on a New Zealand farm like the one shown here. After all, New Zealand is one of the world's leading producers of this tasty fruit. The kiwifruit, once known as the Chinese gooseberry, is now named for the kiwi bird—New Zealand's national symbol.

New Zealand lies in the Pacific Ocean about 1,200 miles (1,931 km) southeast of its nearest neighbor, Australia. In contrast to Australia's flat, dry land, New Zealand is mountainous and very green. Its climate is mild and wet. Both New Zealand and Australia are located in the Southern Hemisphere, so their summer starts in December and their winter starts in June.

New Zealand's Land

New Zealand is about the size of Colorado. It includes two main islands—**North Island** and **South Island**—as well as many smaller islands. The **Cook Strait** separates the two main islands.

North Island   A large plateau forms the center of North Island. Three active volcanoes and the inactive Mount Egmont are located here. You also find **geysers,** or hot springs that spout steam and water through a crack in the earth.

Small shrubs called *manuka* grow well in the plateau's fertile volcanic soil. Fertile lowlands, forested hills, and sandy beaches surround

741

North Island's central plateau. On the plateau's slopes, sheep and cattle graze. Fruits and vegetables are grown on the coastal lowlands.

South Island   The **Southern Alps** run along South Island's western coast. Snowcapped **Mount Cook,** the highest peak in New Zealand, soars 12,316 feet (3,754 m). Glaciers lie on mountain slopes above green forests and sparkling blue lakes. Long ago, these glaciers cut deep fjords (fee•AWRDS), or steep-sided valleys, into the mountains. The sea has filled these fjords with crystal-blue waters.

To the east of the Southern Alps stretch the Canterbury Plains. They form New Zealand's largest area of flat or nearly flat land. Farmers grow grains and ranchers raise sheep here.

Plants and Animals   New Zealanders take pride in their unique wildlife. Their national symbol is a flightless bird called the kiwi. Giant kauri (KOWR•ee) trees once dominated all of North Island. About 100 years ago, European settlers cut down many of these trees, using the wood to build homes and ships. Today the government protects kauri trees. One of them is more than 2,000 years old.

✓ Reading Check   Which island of New Zealand has glaciers and fjords?

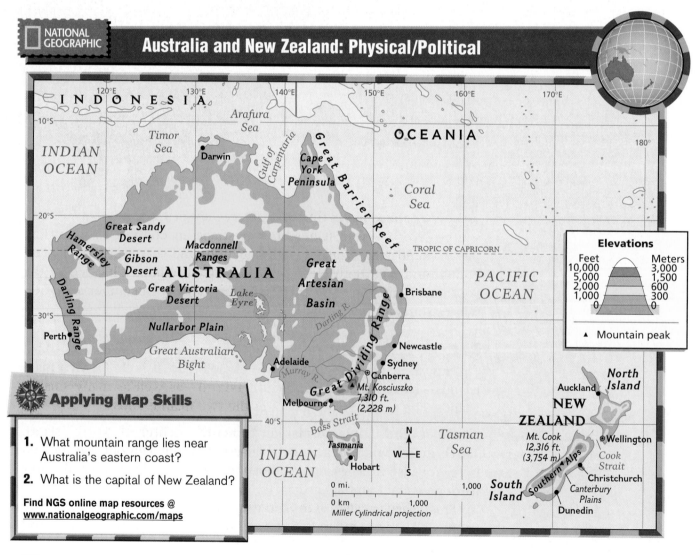

NATIONAL GEOGRAPHIC

Australia and New Zealand: Physical/Political

Applying Map Skills

1. What mountain range lies near Australia's eastern coast?

2. What is the capital of New Zealand?

Find NGS online map resources @ www.nationalgeographic.com/maps

New Zealand's Economy

New Zealand has a thriving agricultural economy. Sheep are an important agricultural resource. New Zealand is the second-leading wool producer in the world. Lamb meat is another important export. Apples, barley, wheat, and corn are the main crops.

Trade with other countries is an important part of New Zealand's economy. Its main trading partners are Australia, Japan, the United States, and the United Kingdom. There are benefits and dangers due to New Zealand's dependence on trade. If the economies of other countries are growing quickly, demand for goods from New Zealand will rise. If their economies slow, however, these countries will buy fewer products. This can cause hardship in New Zealand. In recent years, trade has increased, and New Zealanders enjoy a high standard of living.

Mining and Manufacturing New Zealand sits on top of the molten rock that forms volcanoes. As a result, it is rich in **geothermal energy,** or electricity produced from steam. The major source of energy, however, is **hydroelectric power**—electricity generated by flowing water. New Zealand also has coal, oil, iron ore, silver, and gold.

The country is rapidly industrializing. The main manufactured items are wood products, fertilizer, wool products, and shoes. Service industries and tourism also play large roles in the economy.

√ **Reading Check** How does its dependence on trade with other countries present both benefits and dangers to New Zealand?

Maori

In recent years, the Maori culture has experienced a revival in New Zealand. Some Maoris dress in traditional costumes for special celebrations.

History How did the Maoris arrive in New Zealand?

New Zealand's History and People

People called the Maoris (MOWR•eez) are believed to have arrived in New Zealand between A.D. 950 and 1150. They probably crossed the Pacific Ocean in canoes from islands far to the northeast. Undisturbed for hundreds of years, the Maoris developed skills in farming, weaving, fishing, bird hunting, and woodcarving.

The first European explorers came to the islands in the mid-1600s. Almost 200 years passed before settlers—most of them

British—arrived. In 1840 British officials signed a treaty with Maori leaders. In this treaty, the Maoris agreed to accept British rule in return for the right to keep their land. More British settlers eventually moved onto Maori land. War broke out in the 1860s—a war that the Maoris lost.

In 1893 the colony became the first land to give women the right to vote. New Zealand was also among the first places in which the government gave help to people who were elderly, sick, or out of work.

New Zealand became independent in 1907. The country is a parliamentary democracy in which elected representatives choose a prime minister to head the government. Five seats in the parliament can be held only by Maoris. Today about 10 percent of New Zealand's 4 million people are Maoris. The rest are mostly descendants of British settlers. Asians and Pacific Islanders, attracted by the growing economy, have increased the diversity of New Zealand's society.

About 86 percent of the people live in urban areas. The largest cities are **Auckland,** an important port, and **Wellington,** the capital. Both are on North Island, where about 75 percent of the people live.

New Zealanders take advantage of the country's mild climate and beautiful landscapes. They enjoy camping, hiking, hunting, boating, and mountain climbing in any season. They also play cricket and rugby, sports that originated in Great Britain.

✓ Reading Check **What group settled New Zealand about 1,000 years ago?**

FCAT PRACTICE You can prepare for the FCAT-assessed standards by completing the correlated item(s) below.

Section 2 Assessment

Defining Terms
1. **Define** geyser, *manuka*, fjord, geothermal energy, hydroelectric power.

Recalling Facts
2. **Region** How do New Zealand's land and climate compare to Australia's?

3. **Economics** What two animal products are important exports for New Zealand?

4. **History** Most of New Zealand's people are descendants of settlers from what European country?

Critical Thinking
5. **Analyzing Information** Why do you think New Zealand's government guarantees the Maoris a certain number of seats in the parliament? **FCAT** LA.A.1.3.2

6. **Making Predictions** With so many different peoples settling in New Zealand, how do you think the country's culture might change? **FCAT** LA.A.1.3.2

Graphic Organizer
7. **Organizing Information** Imagine that you are moving to New Zealand. Write a question you would ask for each topic in the chart below. **FCAT** LA.A.1.3.2

Physical features	Economy	Recreation
Climate	Government	Culture

Applying Social Studies Skills

8. **Analyzing Maps** Look at the map on page 742. Which New Zealand island has higher mountains? How can you tell?

TIME PERSPECTIVES

Closing the Gap

Symbol of Unity: New Zealand's National Rugby Team

Compiled and adapted from TIME.

DAVE E. HOUSER/ CORBIS

In their ancestors' clothes, Maoris do a fierce dance. Land is sacred to Australia's Aborigines (right).

The New World Down Under

Evaluating Media
LA.A.2.3.6

When Ngataua Omahuru was five years old, he made a big mistake. Ngataua (en•gah•TOW•ah) was a **Maori,** a native New Zealander. He and his family lived in the forest beneath Mount Taranaki, a volcano on New Zealand's North Island.

One day in 1869, Ngataua made the mistake of wandering away from his parents. A band of British soldiers kidnapped him.

New Zealand was a British colony then. Europeans had been settling there in great numbers for more than 40 years. They had moved onto Maori land, paying nothing or very little for it. Maoris who tried to protect their land were often forced off it at gunpoint.

Ngataua ended up in the home of William Fox, the head of the colony's government. Fox and his wife changed Ngataua's name to William Fox. They sent him to English schools. They cut all his links to the Maori world.

A Rich Culture

Through their religion, the Maoris felt close to their ancestors and to nature. They expressed themselves through song, poetry, weaving, woodcarving, and even tattooing. They were brave and clever warriors.

About 200 years ago, New Zealand was home to dozens of iwi, or tribes. This map shows where 10 of them were located.

The British, called **Pakehas** (pa•KAY•haws) by the Maoris, did not value the Maori culture. The Pakehas were **ethnocentric,** or convinced that no way

Maori Iwi Lands

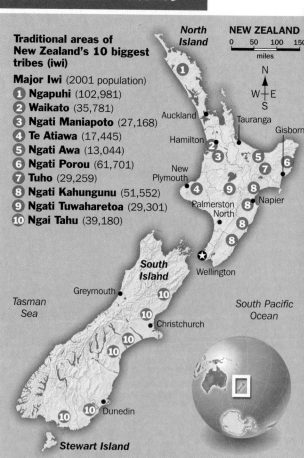

Traditional areas of New Zealand's 10 biggest tribes (iwi)

Major Iwi (2001 population)
1. **Ngapuhi** (102,981)
2. **Waikato** (35,781)
3. **Ngati Maniapoto** (27,168)
4. **Te Atiawa** (17,445)
5. **Ngati Awa** (13,044)
6. **Ngati Porou** (61,701)
7. **Tuho** (29,259)
8. **Ngati Kahungunu** (51,552)
9. **Ngati Tuwaharetoa** (29,301)
10. **Ngai Tahu** (39,180)

NEW ZEALAND
0   50   100   150
miles

North Island

Auckland
Tauranga
Gisborn
Hamilton
New Plymouth
Napier
Palmerston North
Wellington
South Island
Greymouth
Christchurch
Tasman Sea
South Pacific Ocean
Dunedin
Stewart Island

INTERPRETING MAPS

Making Inferences Suppose you were a Ngapuhi living 200 years ago. About how far would you have had to travel to reach the Ngai Tahu? What might have made this trip difficult and dangerous?

Maori and Pakeha children play together. The gap between the two groups is closing.

Women in traditional dress perform Maori dances.

Aborigine Cathy Freeman lights the Olympic flame in 2000.

of life was better than their own. They believed the Maoris would be better off leaving their ways behind.

That decision guided Pakeha thinking for a century. The Maoris were taught they had nothing in their culture to be proud of. Cut loose from their traditions but not fully accepted by whites, the Maoris fell on hard times.

They are still trying to recover. Compared with Pakehas, Maoris today learn less and earn less. They die more readily from cancer, diabetes, and heart disease.

New Zealanders are trying to close the gaps between the two groups. They are doing it both to be fair and to keep their nation strong. In 50 years, the Maoris will make up almost one-fourth of the country's population.

Australia's Ghosts

A similar issue haunts Australia, 1,200 miles (1,931 km) west of New Zealand. Australia's native people, the **Aborigines,** make up about 1 percent of the population. For tens of thousands of years, all of Australia was theirs.

In 1788 British settlers arrived. They began almost immediately to separate the Aborigines from their culture. They drove the Aborigines off land that they greatly respected, or considered **sacred.** The British killed many who resisted.

The Australian settlers repeated the New Zealand settlers' mistakes. They tried to make the first Australians more like them.

Some of their methods were especially harsh. The government decided that Aborigine children would be better off in the hands of white families. So from 1910 to 1971, as many as 100,000 Aborigine children were removed from their parents. White families adopted most of them. Few of the children ever saw their birth mothers again.

Fighting for Maori Rights

Ngataua Omahuru got to see his mother again. As a young lawyer, he returned to his homeland on business. His real family recognized him, and he saw how badly they had been treated. He devoted the rest of his life to helping the Maoris fight for their **rights,** or benefits guaranteed by law.

It would take the Maoris almost a century to get a fair hearing. By then, Maori foods, words, art, and songs had become part of New Zealand's culture. New Zealanders today realize just how much they would lose if the Maori way of life ever disappeared. ◼

EXPLORING THE ISSUES

1. **Making Inferences** Why do you think British settlers believed their way of life was best?

   FCAT LA.A.1.3.2

2. **Problem Solving** If you could, what two things would you change to improve the Maoris' lives?

Broken Promises

Around noon on February 6, 1840, about 75 people stood under a tent in the coastal hamlet of Waitangi, New Zealand. The gathering included Maori chiefs, British settlers, missionaries, and military men.

They were there to sign a treaty. The treaty gave Great Britain the right to rule New Zealand. It gave the Maoris Great Britain's promise to protect them and their land.

The deal made sense to the Maoris. Shady businessmen had begun grabbing Maori land. The chiefs felt that Britain's military muscle was the only thing that could stop the thefts.

Founding Charter

The **Treaty of Waitangi** became New Zealand's founding document. It is as important to New Zealanders as the U.S. Constitution is to Americans. It granted British citizenship to the Maoris. It also described how Maoris and European settlers would share responsibility for New Zealand.

But an agreement is only as strong as the will to enforce it. Greedy settlers took control of New Zealand's government. They used small conflicts as excuses to take over huge pieces of Maori land.

BETTMANN/CORBIS

▲ **Maori children in traditional dress**

The Maoris tried to embarrass the Pakehas into living up to the treaty. They plowed up the lawns of rich settlers who lived on stolen land. They met Pakeha troops with singing children who offered the soldiers bread.

But in the end nothing, not even the support of many white settlers, could keep the Maoris from losing more land. **Waitangi Day** is a national holiday in New Zealand. Many Maoris refuse to celebrate it, and few people wonder why. ▨

EXPLORING THE ISSUES

1. **Explaining** What does the sentence "An agreement is only as strong as the will to enforce it" mean? **FCAT LA.A.2.3.1**

2. **Making Inferences** Why might it have been hard for Great Britain's government to live up to its side of the agreement? **FCAT LA.A.1.3.2**

Closing the Gap

How do you fix a problem that began some 200 years ago? New Zealanders have three answers. They hope to keep the Maori culture alive. They want Maoris to have the skills they need to succeed. And they want to pay the **iwi,** or tribes, for land their ancestors lost to the British colonists.

Maoritanga, the Maori way of life, is in trouble. Few people speak the Maori language. To help more people learn it, schools have begun to teach it. They also teach Maori traditions, along with Maori arts and crafts, music, and dance. Maoris now have an "all-Maori" TV channel too.

Prescription for Success

Equipping Maoris to succeed is another challenge. The government calls its solution "closing the gap"—in skills, wages, housing, and health care. Maoris are being encouraged to stay in school longer, so that they can find and keep good jobs.

The land issue is difficult. The government can't return land to the Maoris that it doesn't own without hurting the people who live on it now. The Maoris will be paid for lost land and other lost "treasures," such as fishing rights.

By 2001, the Waitangi Tribunal had awarded several iwi a total of $300 million. The tribunal, or claims court, won't finish its work until around 2012.

"The process [of sorting through Maori claims] is about more than money," one panel member said. "It is

▲ This is New Zealand's Prime Minister Helen Clark in 2001. New Zealand was the first land to let all women vote.

about renewing a relationship that was intended to be based on trust."

That was the spirit of the Treaty of Waitangi. This time, New Zealanders are determined to make it work. ▣

EXPLORING THE ISSUE

1. **Explaining** What does the title of this article mean? Where is the gap, and why do you think it exists? **FCAT LA.A.2.3.1**

2. **Drawing Conclusions** Why might some Maoris be unhappy with the Waitangi Tribunal's decisions? **FCAT LA.A.2.3.1**

Bridging the Gaps at Home: What Can One Person Do?

Evaluating
Media
LA.A.2.3.6

Ngataua Omahuru, the Maori who was raised in the Pakeha world, did a lot to help his people. He was successful in part because he knew both worlds well.

Americans are fortunate to live in a country that has many cultures. But

▲ Auckland, with 400,000 people, is New Zealand's largest city.

how many of us take the time to really understand another culture? If we did, we could help bridge the gaps that often keep Americans apart.

Here's one way to start. First, choose an immigrant group that you would like to learn more about. You'll have a lot of choices, because all Americans have immigrant roots. And that includes Native Americans, whose ancestors came from Asia thousands of years ago.

Detective Work

Second, get together with a couple of your classmates who share your interest

in this group. As a team, find out all you can about it. One person could research when members of the group came to the United States in large numbers. Another team member could look into whether a particular event prompted them to leave their homeland at that time. Here are more questions for your team to consider: How did Americans view the newcomers? How have those views changed? How do members of this group see themselves today—as members of an ethnic group, as Americans, or as both? How has this group changed the way Americans define themselves?

Share your findings with the rest of the class. Write an article that summarizes your findings for a school newspaper or a Web page. Create a poster that depicts what you learned about this immigrant group. Display the poster at your school or local library. By doing so, you will help others appreciate the glittering mosaic of American life. ■

EXPLORING THE ISSUE

1. **Making Generalizations** In 2001, one of every 10 Americans had been born in another country. Why do you think the United States looks attractive to people from other countries?

2. **Cause and Effect** Write a new title for this *TIME Reports* feature. Share it with your classmates. Explain why you think your title fits the story. **FCAT** LA.A.2.3.1

REVIEW AND ASSESS

UNDERSTANDING THE ISSUE

1. Defining Key Terms Write definitions for the following terms: *Maori, Pakeha, ethnocentric, Aborigine, sacred, rights, Treaty of Waitangi, Waitangi Day, iwi, Maoritanga.* `FCAT LA.A.1.3.2`

2. Writing to Inform Write a short article describing the history of the Treaty of Waitangi. Use at least five of the terms listed above. `FCAT LA.B.1.3.2`

3. Writing to Persuade Why is it important to respect other cultures? Write a short article to support your view, using the experiences of New Zealand and Australia as examples. `FCAT LA.B.1.3.2`

INTERNET RESEARCH ACTIVITY

4. With your teacher's help, use Internet resources to learn more about New Zealand. Read about the history of the Maori language. Read about the Maori Language Commission, and what it does. How important is language to a culture's survival? Write a short essay answering that question, using facts you find in your search. `FCAT LA.B.1.3.2`

5. With your teacher's help, use Internet resources to find information on Maori food. Try to find specific sites that list Maori recipes in particular. Browse through the traditional recipes. Then write a 250-word article explaining how those recipes provide clues to where the Maoris live, how they cook, and what foods their great-grandparents ate. `FCAT LA.A.2.3.5`

BEYOND THE CLASSROOM

6. Compare the map on page 746 with the physical/political map of New Zealand on page 742. What does the physical/political map tell you about the land the iwi occupied? In a short essay, describe in general

BETTINA A. STAMMEN

▲ **A banana leaf serves as a plate for traditional Maori food.**

terms what one iwi's traditional land may have looked like. `FCAT LA.B.1.3.2`

7. Visit your school or local library to find books on the Maoris or Aborigines. (A good but long one is Peter Walker's *The Fox Boy*, which tells Ngataua Omahuru's story.) Prepare an oral book report to deliver in class. Make sure to note the author's point of view. `FCAT LA.A.2.3.1`

The Making of a Multicultural Society

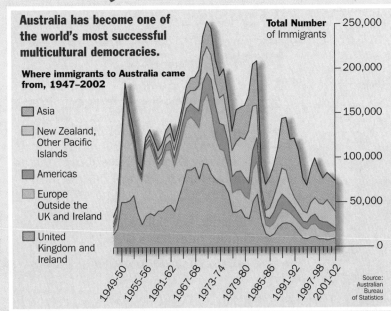

Australia has become one of the world's most successful multicultural democracies.

Where immigrants to Australia came from, 1947–2002

- ☐ Asia
- ☐ New Zealand, Other Pacific Islands
- ☐ Americas
- ☐ Europe Outside the UK and Ireland
- ☐ United Kingdom and Ireland

Total Number of Immigrants

— 250,000
— 200,000
— 150,000
— 100,000
— 50,000
— 0

1949-50 1955-56 1961-62 1967-68 1973-74 1979-80 1985-86 1991-92 1997-98 2001-02

Source: Australian Bureau of Statistics

BUILDING GRAPH READING SKILLS

1. Analyzing the Data In 2002 there were about 89,000 immigrants. Which two places did most immigrants come from? `FCAT MA.E.3.3.1`

2. Making Inferences What might make people want to leave their homelands and settle in Australia? `FCAT LA.A.1.3.2`

FOR UPDATES ON WORLD ISSUES GO TO www.timeclassroom.com/glencoe

Study and Writing Skill

 FCAT PRACTICE Completing the correlated items below will help you prepare for the **FCAT Reading** test.

Outlining

Outlining may be used as a starting point for writing. The writer begins with the rough shape of the material and gradually fills in the details in a logical manner. You may also use outlining as a method of note taking and organizing information as you read.

Learning the Skill

There are two types of outlines—formal and informal. An informal outline is similar to taking notes—you write words and phrases needed to remember main ideas. In contrast, a formal outline has a standard format. Follow these steps to formally outline information:

- Read the text to identify the main ideas. Label these with Roman numerals.
- Write subtopics under each main idea. Label these with capital letters.
- Write supporting details for each subtopic. Label these with Arabic numerals.
- Each level should have at least two entries that are indented from the level above.
- All entries should use the same grammatical form, whether they are phrases or complete sentences.

▼ **A huge sheep herd pours down a ravine on New Zealand's North Island.**

Practicing the Skill

On a separate sheet of paper, copy the following outline for Section 2 of this chapter. Then use your textbook to fill in the missing subtopics and details. **FCAT LA.A.1.3.2**

> I. New Zealand's Land
>   A. North Island
>   1. Central plateau surrounded by fertile lowlands
>   2. Active volcanoes and geysers
>   B. _____
>   1. Southern Alps on western coast
>   2. _____
>   C. Plants and Animals
>   1. _____
>   2. _____
> II. New Zealand's Economy
>   A. Agriculture
>   1. _____
>   2. _____
>   B. Trading Partners
>   1. _____
>   2. _____
>   3. _____
>   4. _____
>   C. _____
>   1. _____
>   2. Wood products, fertilizer, wool products, and shoes
> III. New Zealand's History and People
>   A. _____
>   B. _____

Applying the Skill

Following the guidelines above, prepare an outline for Section 1 of this chapter.

FCAT LA.A.1.3.2

GO TO Practice key skills with **Glencoe Skillbuilder Interactive Workbook, Level 1.**

Section 1 — Australia—Land Down Under

Terms to Know
coral reef
outback
station
marsupial
boomerang
bush

Main Idea
Both a continent and a country, Australia has many natural resources but relatively few people.

✓ **Place** Dry plateaus and lowland plains spread across most of Australia.

✓ **History** Because Australia has been separated from other continents for millions of years, unusual plants and animals developed here.

✓ **Economics** Most of Australia's wealth comes from minerals and the products of its ranches. It is the world's leading producer and exporter of wool.

✓ **Culture** Australia has relatively few people, most of whom live along the coasts.

Australian ranchers in the outback ▶

Section 2 — New Zealand

Terms to Know
geyser
manuka
fjord
geothermal energy
hydroelectric power

Main Idea
New Zealand is a small country with a growing economy based on trade.

✓ **Place** New Zealand has volcanic mountains, high glaciers, deep-cut fjords, fertile hills, and coastal plains. The climate is mild and wet.

✓ **Economics** New Zealand's economy is built on trade. Sheepherding is an important activity, and wool and lamb meat are major exports.

✓ **History** The people called the Maoris first came to New Zealand about 1,000 years ago.

✓ **Culture** Most people live on North Island, where the country's two main cities can be found.

✓ **History** New Zealand was the first land to allow women to vote.

Assessment and Activities

FCAT PRACTICE You can prepare for the FCAT-assessed standards by completing the correlated item(s) below.

Using Key Terms

Match the terms in Part A with their definitions in Part B.

A.

1. boomerang
2. bush
3. station
4. geothermal energy
5. outback
6. *manuka*
7. marsupial
8. hydroelectric power
9. coral reef
10. geyser

B.

a. electricity produced from steam
b. flat, bent, wooden weapon that stuns prey or returns to the thrower
c. mammal that carries its young in a pouch
d. hot spring that shoots hot water into the air
e. rural area in Australia
f. structure formed by the skeletons of small sea animals
g. name for entire inland region of Australia
h. cattle or sheep ranch in Australia
i. electricity generated by flowing water
j. small shrub found in New Zealand

Reviewing the Main Ideas

Section 1 Australia—Land Down Under

11. **Location** Why is Australia called the "Land Down Under"?
12. **Place** For what is the outback used?
13. **Economics** What does Australia lead the world in producing and exporting?
14. **History** What country colonized Australia?
15. **Culture** What percentage of people live in Australia's cities?
16. **Location** Why was Canberra located inland?

Section 2 New Zealand

17. **Location** On which island do most New Zealanders live?
18. **History** When did New Zealand gain its independence from Britain?
19. **Economics** What are two sources of electric power in New Zealand?
20. **Culture** How many New Zealanders have Maori heritage?
21. **Human/Environment Interaction** What leisure activities do New Zealanders enjoy that are made possible by the country's climate?

 **NATIONAL GEOGRAPHIC** **Australia and New Zealand**

Place Location Activity

On a separate sheet of paper, match the letters on the map with the numbered places listed below.

1. Auckland
2. Sydney
3. Tasmania
4. Great Barrier Reef
5. Great Dividing Range
6. Southern Alps
7. Great Artesian Basin
8. Wellington
9. Canberra
10. Melbourne

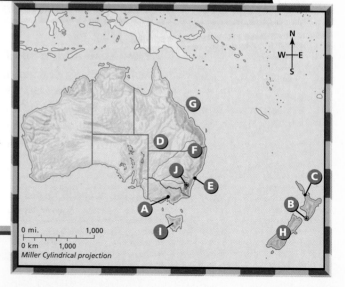

0 mi. 1,000
0 km 1,000
Miller Cylindrical projection

Critical Thinking

22. **Understanding Cause and Effect** Why do most Australians and New Zealanders live in coastal areas? **FCAT LA.E.2.2.1**

23. **Organizing Information** Create two ovals like these. In the outer ovals, write four facts about each country under its heading. Where the ovals overlap, write three facts that are true of both countries. **FCAT LA.A.1.3.2**

Australia   New Zealand

Comparing Regions Activity

24. **Geography** Choose one of the physical features found in Australia or New Zealand. You might choose the Great Barrier Reef or the geysers or glaciers of New Zealand. Then choose a physical feature in the United States, such as Death Valley or the Grand Canyon. Create a poster that includes a map, photographs, and facts about each feature. What conclusions can you draw about similarities or differences between the two features?

Mental Mapping Activity

25. **Focusing on the Region** Create a simple outline map of Australia and New Zealand, and then label the following:

- North Island
- South Island
- Auckland
- Tasman Sea
- Wellington
- Darling River
- Great Artesian Basin
- Cook Strait

Technology Skills Activity

26. **Using the Internet** Use the Internet to find out more about one of Australia's or New Zealand's cities. Prepare a travel brochure for a tourist who might visit the city. Describe the city's main attractions. **FCAT LA.A.2.3.5**

Standardized Test Practice

Directions: Study the graph below, and then answer the question that follows.

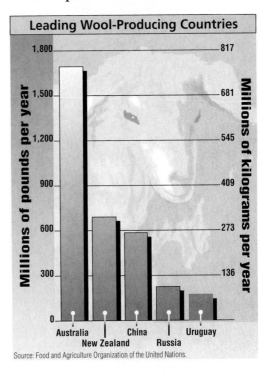

Leading Wool-Producing Countries

Millions of pounds per year — 1,800; 1,500; 1,200; 900; 600; 300; 0

Millions of kilograms per year — 817; 681; 545; 409; 273; 136

Australia   New Zealand   China   Russia   Uruguay

Source: Food and Agriculture Organization of the United Nations.

1. **How much wool does Australia produce per year?** **FCAT MA.E.3.3.1**

   A 1,800 pounds

   B 1,800,000 pounds

   C about 1,700 pounds

   D about 1,700,000,000 pounds

Test-Taking Tip: Remember to read the information along the sides of the graph to understand what the bars represent. In addition, eliminate answers that you know are wrong.

Chapter 27

Oceania and Antarctica

The World and Its People 📀📼 **NATIONAL GEOGRAPHIC**

To learn more about the people and places of Oceania and Antarctica, view *The World and Its People* **Chapter 28** video.

Social Studies Online

Chapter Overview Visit *The World and Its People* Web site at <u>twip.glencoe.com</u> and click on **Chapter 27–Chapter Overviews** to preview information about Oceania and Antarctica.

FCAT PRACTICE The activity below will help you prepare for the **FCAT Reading** test.

Summarizing Information Make this foldable and use it to help you summarize what you learn about Oceania and Antarctica. **FCAT LA.A.2.3.1**

Step 1 Stack four sheets of paper, one on top of the other. On the top sheet of paper, trace a large circle.

Step 2 With the papers still stacked, cut out all four circles at the same time.

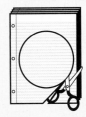

Step 3 Staple the paper circles together at one point around the edge.

Staple here.

This makes a circular booklet.

Step 4 Label the front circle **Oceania** and take notes on the pages that open to the right. Flip the book over and label the back **Antarctica**. Take notes on the pages that open to the right.

Oceania

Reading and Writing As you read the chapter, write facts about the people and geography of Oceania and Antarctica in the appropriate places of your circular foldable booklet.

FCAT LA.A.2.3.1

▲ Houses on stilts in Moorea Lagoon, Tahiti

Why It Matters

A World of Water

The water world of the Pacific Ocean covers one-third of the earth. It is larger than all the world's land areas combined. Tens of thousands of islands lie in this remote part of the globe. As technology shrinks the world, many societies of this region are struggling to maintain their cultural identities.

Pacific Island Cultures and Economies

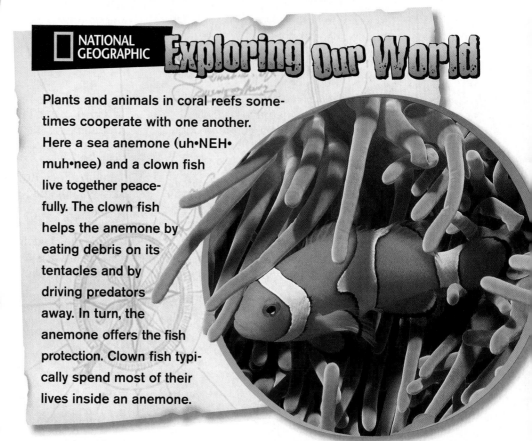

NATIONAL GEOGRAPHIC Exploring Our World

Plants and animals in coral reefs sometimes cooperate with one another. Here a sea anemone (uh•NEH•muh•nee) and a clown fish live together peacefully. The clown fish helps the anemone by eating debris on its tentacles and by driving predators away. In turn, the anemone offers the fish protection. Clown fish typically spend most of their lives inside an anemone.

Oceania is a culture region that includes about 25,000 islands in the Pacific Ocean. Geographers group Oceania into three main island regions—**Melanesia, Micronesia,** and **Polynesia.**

Melanesia

The islands of Melanesia lie across the **Coral Sea** from Australia. The largest country is **Papua New Guinea** (PA•pyu•wuh noo GIH•nee). Slightly larger than California, the country's 5.5 million people also make it Oceania's most populous island. Southeast of Papua New Guinea are three other independent island countries: the **Solomon Islands,** the **Fiji** (FEE•jee) **Islands,** and **Vanuatu** (VAN•WAH•TOO). Near these countries is **New Caledonia,** a group of islands ruled by France.

Rugged mountains and dense rain forests cover Melanesia's islands. Narrow, fertile plains hug the coastlines. Most of Melanesia has a tropical climate with temperatures between 70°F (21°C) and 80°F (27°C).

Most Melanesians work on subsistence farms. Others work on farms that produce coffee, palm oil, and cacao for export. **Cacao** is a tropical tree whose seeds are used to make chocolate. Sugarcane is exported as sugar and molasses. Coconut oil from **copra,** or dried coconut meat, is used to make margarine, soap, and other products.

Some Melanesian islands hold rich mineral resources such as gold, oil, copper, and nickel. Several islands export timber and fish. Melanesia is also becoming a popular tourist destination.

Melanesia's People Almost all Melanesians are ethnic Pacific Islanders. Two island groups hold exceptions. About one-third of New Caledonia's people are Europeans. In the Fiji Islands, almost half of the people are of Indian descent. The ancestors of these Indians were brought from British India in the late 1800s and early 1900s to work on sugarcane plantations. Today ethnic Indians control much of the

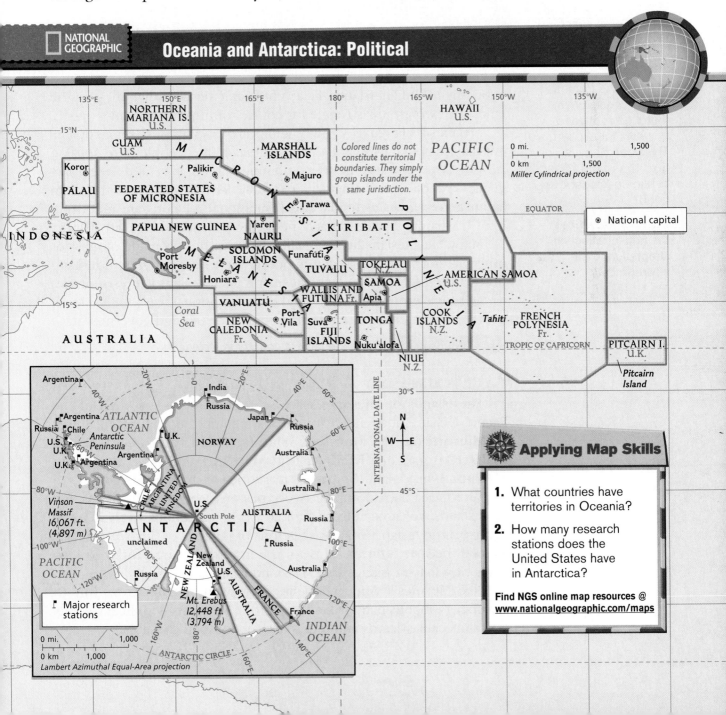

NATIONAL GEOGRAPHIC

Oceania and Antarctica: Political

Colored lines do not constitute territorial boundaries. They simply group islands under the same jurisdiction.

⊛ National capital

Applying Map Skills

1. What countries have territories in Oceania?

2. How many research stations does the United States have in Antarctica?

Find **NGS** online map resources @ **www.nationalgeographic.com/maps**

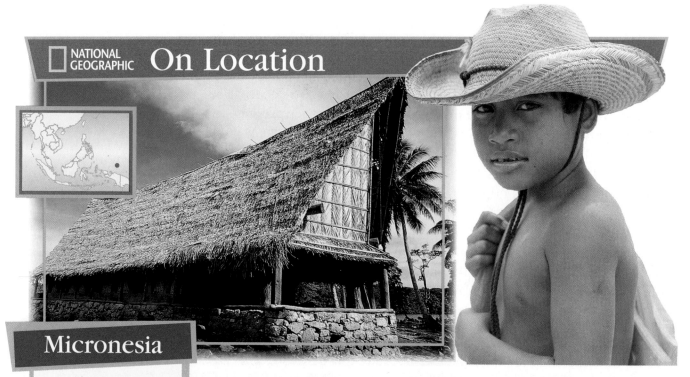

Micronesia

Many of the homes in Micronesia have thatched roofs and no walls (above left). This young boy is from the island of Yap in Micronesia (above right).

Culture How does the house reflect an adaptation to the environment?

economy of the Fiji Islands. Fijians of Pacific descent own most of the land. The two groups struggle for control of the government.

Melanesia's languages and religions are diverse. More than 700 languages are spoken in Papua New Guinea alone. People here speak a **pidgin language** formed by combining parts of several different languages. People speak English in the Fiji Islands. French is the main language of New Caledonia. Local traditional religions are practiced, but Christianity is widespread. The Indian population is mostly Hindu.

Many Melanesians live in small villages in houses made of grass or other natural materials. Recently, people have built concrete houses to protect themselves from tropical storms. Melanesians keep strong ties to their local group and often hold on to traditional ways. Only a small number live in cities, often working in businesses and government.

✓**Reading Check** What is the largest country in Melanesia?

Micronesia

The islands of Micronesia are scattered over a vast area of the Pacific Ocean. Independent countries include the **Federated States of Micronesia,** the **Marshall Islands, Palau** (puh•LOW), **Nauru** (nah•OO•roo), and **Kiribati** (KIHR•uh•BAH•tee). The **Northern Mariana Islands** and **Guam** are territories of the United States.

Micronesia is made up of two types of islands—high islands and low islands. Volcanic activity formed the mountainous **high islands** many centuries ago. Coral, or skeletons of millions of tiny sea animals, formed the **low islands.** Most of the low islands are **atolls,** or low-lying, ring-shaped islands that surround lagoons.

Like Melanesia, Micronesia has a tropical climate. From July to October, typhoons may strike. These tropical storms with heavy winds and rains cause deaths and much destruction in the islands.

On Micronesia's high islands, the volcanic soil is rich. Most people are subsistence farmers who grow cassava, sweet potatoes, bananas, and coconuts. Some high island farmers also raise livestock. People in the low islands rely on fishing.

Several Micronesian islands have phosphate, a mineral salt that is used to make fertilizer. Phosphate supplies are now gone on Kiribati, and they have almost run out on Nauru. The Federated States of Micronesia and the Marshall Islands have phosphate but lack the money to mine this resource.

Challenges in Micronesia include unemployment, overfishing, and overdependence on aid. Micronesia receives financial aid from the United States, the European Union, and Australia. With this money, the Micronesians have built roads, ports, airfields, and small factories. Clothing is made on the Northern Mariana Islands. Beautiful beaches draw tourists here.

Micronesia's People Southeast Asians first settled Micronesia about 4,000 years ago. Explorers, traders, and missionaries from European countries came in the 1700s and early 1800s. By the early 1900s, many European countries, the United States, and Japan held colonies here.

During World War II, the United States and Japan fought a number of bloody battles on Micronesian islands. After World War II, most of Micronesia was turned over to the United States as trust territories. Trust territories are areas temporarily placed under control of another nation. Some of these islands served as sites for hydrogen bomb testing. Since the 1970s, most have become independent.

Many of Micronesia's people are Pacific Islanders. They speak local languages, although English is spoken on Nauru, the Marshall Islands, and throughout the rest of Micronesia. Christianity, brought by Western missionaries, is the most widely practiced religion. Micronesians generally live in villages headed by local chiefs. In recent years, many young people have left the villages to find jobs in towns.

✓ Reading Check In what two ways were Micronesia's islands formed?

Polynesia

Polynesia includes three independent countries—**Samoa, Tonga,** and **Tuvalu.** A vast group of islands is under French rule and is known as **French Polynesia. Tahiti,** Polynesia's largest island, is part of this French-ruled area. **American Samoa,** a United States territory, is also part of this region.

Most Polynesian islands are high volcanic islands, some with tall, rugged mountains. Other islands are low atolls. With little soil, the only vegetation is scattered coconut palms. Because Polynesia lies in the Tropics, the climate is hot and humid.

Polynesians fish or grow crops for their food. Some farmers export coconuts and tropical fruits. The main manufacturing activity is food processing. American Samoa supplies about one-third of the tuna brought into the United States. Tonga exports squash and vanilla.

Exploring Economics

The Fate of Nauru

Micronesia's most famous phosphate island is Nauru, an 8-square-mile coral atoll. The name *Nauru* means "nowhere." Over the last 90 years, Nauru's citizens have chosen to "consume" their island by mining the coral as phosphate and selling it as fertilizer. The government of Nauru is now working to develop other industries, such as fishing and tourism, in preparation for the day when the phosphate is gone.

Tourism is one of the fastest growing industries of Polynesia. Tourists come by air or sea to the emerald green mountains and white palm-lined beaches. New hotels, shops, and restaurants have been built to accommodate the needs of these tourists.

Polynesia's People   Very little is known about the origins of the Polynesians. Historians believe that their ancestors used canoes to cross the Pacific Ocean from Asia hundreds of years before the birth of Christ. They also believe that the Polynesians must have been gifted navigators.

When the Polynesian people traveled from island to island, they carried everything they would need with them, including pigs, hens, and dogs. As soon as the Polynesians arrived at an island, they planted young banana and breadfruit trees. The influence of these early Polynesians can be seen today in the vegetation, languages, music, and dances of the southern Pacific islands.

During the late 1800s, several European nations divided Polynesia among themselves. They built military bases on the islands and later added airfields. The islands served as excellent refueling stops for long voyages across the Pacific. Beginning in the 1960s, several Polynesian territories chose independence, while others remained territories.

About 600,000 people live in Polynesia. Most Polynesians live in rural villages, but an increasing number of people are moving to towns and cities. **Papeete** (PAH•pay•AY•tay), located on Tahiti, is the capital of French Polynesia and the largest city in the region.

✓ Reading Check   What is the largest island in Polynesia?

FCAT PRACTICE   You can prepare for the FCAT-assessed standards by completing the correlated item(s) below.

Section 1 Assessment

Defining Terms

1. **Define** cacao, copra, pidgin language, high island, low island, atoll, phosphate, trust territory.

Recalling Facts

2. **Region** What three regions make up Oceania?
3. **Economics** What two kinds of economic activities are most important in these regions?
4. **History** What groups first settled the lands of Micronesia?

Critical Thinking

5. **Analyzing Information** How might over-dependence on aid be a challenge for Micronesia?
6. **Drawing Conclusions** Why do many people in Melanesia speak a pidgin language?
   FCAT LA.A.2.3.1

Graphic Organizer

7. **Organizing Information** Create a chart like this one. List all the island groups of Oceania under their specific region. Then note whether they are independent countries or territories.
   FCAT LA.A.1.3.2

Melanesia	Micronesia	Polynesia	Country/Territory of ?

Applying Social Studies Skills

8. **Analyzing Maps** Look at the political map on page 759. Which territories are colonies of France?

Study and Writing Skill

FCAT PRACTICE Completing the correlated items below will help you prepare for the **FCAT Reading** and **Writing** tests.

Writing a Report

Writing skills allow you to organize your ideas in a logical manner. The writing process involves using skills you have already learned, such as taking notes, outlining, and sequencing information.

Learning the Skill

Use the following guidelines to help you apply the writing process:

- Select an interesting topic. Do preliminary research to determine whether your topic is too broad or too narrow.
- Write one or two sentences that state what you want to prove, discover, or explain in your writing. This will be the focus of your entire paper.
- Research your topic and make a list of main ideas. List facts and source information for each main idea on note cards.

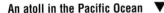

An atoll in the Pacific Ocean ▼

- Your report should have an introduction, a body, and a conclusion that summarizes and restates your findings.
- Each paragraph should express one main idea in a topic sentence. Additional sentences should support or explain the main idea by using details and facts.

Practicing the Skill

Read the following paragraph, and then answer the questions that follow.

> Most of Micronesia's low islands are atolls—low-lying, ring-shaped islands that surround lagoons. An atoll begins as a ring of coral that forms around the edge of a volcanic island. Over time, wind and water erode the volcano, wearing it down to sea level. Eventually, only the atoll remains above the surface. The calm, shallow seawater inside the atoll is called a lagoon.

1. What is the main idea of this paragraph?
2. What are the supporting sentences?
3. What might be the topic of an additional paragraph that follows this one?

FCAT LA.A.2.3.1

Applying the Skill

Suppose you are writing a report on Oceania. Answer the following questions about the writing process. **FCAT LA.B.1.3.2**

1. How could you narrow this topic?
2. What are three main ideas?
3. Name three possible sources of information.

The Frozen Continent

Guide to Reading

Main Idea

Antarctica is a harsh land of rock and ice. The world's nations have agreed to leave the frozen continent open to scientific study.

Terms to Know

- crevasse
- ice shelf
- iceberg
- krill
- ozone

Reading Strategy

Create a chart like the one below. Under each heading, fill in at least one fact about Antarctica. **FCAT** LA.A.1.3.2

Antarctica	
Land	Climate
Resources	People

The following are the major Sunshine State Standards covered in this section.

SS.B.2.3.8:
Knows world patterns of resource distribution and utilization

SS.B.1.3.6:
Understands ways in which regional systems are inter-connected

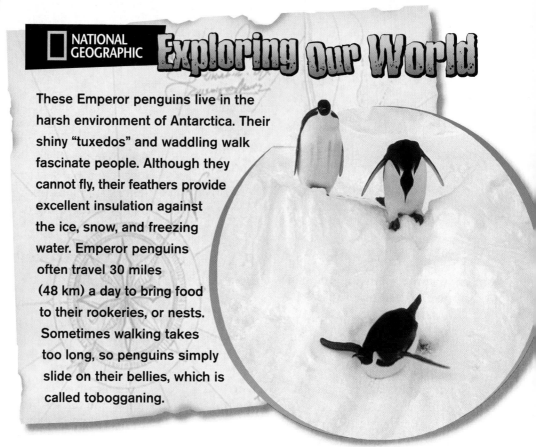

NATIONAL GEOGRAPHIC Exploring Our World

These Emperor penguins live in the harsh environment of Antarctica. Their shiny "tuxedos" and waddling walk fascinate people. Although they cannot fly, their feathers provide excellent insulation against the ice, snow, and freezing water. Emperor penguins often travel 30 miles (48 km) a day to bring food to their rookeries, or nests. Sometimes walking takes too long, so penguins simply slide on their bellies, which is called tobogganing.

Antarctica sits at the southern end of the earth. Icy ocean water surrounds it. Freezing ice covers it. Cold winds blow over it. The least explored of all the continents, this frigid mysterious land is larger than either Europe or Australia.

Unique Antarctica

Picture Antarctica as a rich, green land covered by forests and lush plants. Does this description match your mental image of the continent? Fossils discovered here reveal that millions of years ago, Antarctica was inhabited by dinosaurs and small mammals.

Today, however, a huge ice cap buries nearly 98 percent of Antarctica's land area. In some spots, this ice cap is 2 miles (3.2 km) thick—about the height of 10 tall skyscrapers stacked upon one another. This massive "sea" of ice holds about 70 percent of all the freshwater in the world.

The Antarctic ice cap is heavy and strong, and it also moves. In some areas, the ice cap forms crevasses, or cracks, that plunge more than 100 feet (30 m). At the Antarctic coast, the ice cap spreads past the land into the ocean. This layer of ice above the water is called an **ice shelf.** Huge chunks of ice sometimes break off, forming **icebergs,** which float freely in the icy waters.

Highlands, Mountains, and Valleys Beneath most of the ice cap, however, Antarctica has highlands, mountains, and valleys—the same landforms you find on other continents. A long mountain range called the **Transantarctic Mountains** crosses the continent. The highest peak in Antarctica, the **Vinson Massif,** rises 16,067 feet (4,897 m). The Transantarctic Mountains sweep along the Antarctic Peninsula, which reaches within 600 miles (966 km) of South America's Cape Horn. East of the mountains is a high, flat plateau where you find the **South Pole,** the southernmost point of the earth. On an island called **Ross Island,** off Antarctica's coast, rises **Mount Erebus** (EHR•uh•buhs). It is Antarctica's most active volcano.

Climate Now that you have a mental picture of Antarctica's ice cap, think about this: Antarctica receives so little precipitation that it is the world's largest, coldest desert. Inland Antarctica receives no rain and hardly any new snow each year. Antarctica has a polar ice cap climate. Imagine summer in a place where temperatures may fall as low as −30°F (−35°C) and climb to only 32°F (0°C). Antarctic summers last from December through February. Winter temperatures along the coasts fall to −40°F (−40°C), and in inland areas to a low of −100°F (−73°C).

✓ Reading Check What landforms are found under Antarctica's ice cap?

Antarctica

Elephant seals lounge on the coast of Elephant Island off the Antarctic Peninsula (below). Mount Erebus, on the opposite side of Antarctica (below left), has a lava lake that is often studied by scientists.

Environment How might an eruption of Mount Erebus affect Antarctica?

NATIONAL GEOGRAPHIC On Location

Resources of Antarctica

Antarctica has a harsh environment, but it can still support life. Most of the plants and animals that live here are small, however. The largest inland animal is an insect that reaches only one-tenth of an inch in length. Penguins, fish, whales, and many kinds of flying birds live in or near the seas surrounding Antarctica. Many eat a tiny, shrimplike creature called **krill.**

Scientists believe that the ice of Antarctica hides a treasure chest of minerals. They have found major deposits of coal and smaller amounts of copper, gold, iron ore, manganese, and zinc. Petroleum might lie offshore.

These mineral resources have not yet been tapped. To do so would be very difficult and costly. Also, some people feel that removing these resources would damage Antarctica's fragile environment. Another reason is that different nations would disagree over who has the right to these resources. Forty-three nations have signed the Antarctic Treaty, which prohibits any nation from taking resources from the continent. It also bans weapons testing in Antarctica.

✓ Reading Check **What is the Antarctic Treaty?**

A Vast Scientific Laboratory

The Antarctic Treaty says that Antarctica should only be used for peaceful, scientific purposes. Many countries have scientific research stations here, but no single nation controls the vast continent. In January—summer in Antarctica—about 10,000 scientists come to study the land, plants, animals, and ice of this frozen land. Some 1,000 hardy scientists even stay during the harsh polar winter.

Much of the research focuses on ozone. Ozone is a type of oxygen that forms a layer in the atmosphere. The ozone layer protects all living things on the earth from certain harmful rays of the sun. In the 1980s, scientists discovered a weakening, or "hole," in this layer above Antarctica. If such weakening continues, the sun's harmful rays may cause skin cancer in humans and destroy plants. Turn to page 772 to learn more about the earth's ozone layer.

This frozen world attracts more than just scientists, though. Each year, a few thousand tourists come to Antarctica. Because it has such a harsh environment, however, Antarctica is the only continent in the world that has no permanent population.

✓ Reading Check **Why are scientists studying the ozone layer?**

Villa Las Estrellas

Humans can adapt to life under the most difficult of conditions. One example of this is the Villa Las Estrellas, or Village of the Stars. Located in Chile's Antarctic Territory, the "town" has a school, hospital, supermarket, post office, bank, telephone, television, and Internet service. There is even a gym and a sauna. Village residents include members of Chile's air force and their families, as well as scientists from various countries. In all, about 240 people can live in Villa Las Estrellas. Many stay for two years at a time.

Like Penguins   Daily dress in Villa Las Estrellas consists of thermal underclothes, warm boots, and dark sunglasses to protect the eyes against the sun's strong ultraviolet rays. Villagers must survive extreme temperatures down to −13°F (−25°C) with an even more bone-chilling wind factor. They do not stay inside all day, however. Adults walk from house to house to visit their neighbors. The children seem to enjoy the experience more than anyone else. One resident described outdoor playtime: "The children go crazy over the snow and enjoy sledding or just tobogganing downhill on their stomachs. They look like penguins!"

Global Village   The countries of Russia, China, Korea, Brazil, Poland, Argentina, and Uruguay have military or scientific bases close to the village. In Antarctica, normal tensions between countries do not seem to matter. Every Wednesday afternoon, the different bases send soccer teams to the Chilean gymnasium for a game of indoor soccer. Once a year, a "winter Olympics" is held in volleyball and basketball. Visitors to the different bases mix freely with the people who live in them. Villa Las Estrellas may be as close to a real global village as the earth has ever seen.

Social Studies Online

Web Activity Visit *The World and Its People* Web site at twip.glencoe.com and click on **Chapter 27– Student Web Activities** to learn more about Antarctica.

✓ **Reading Check**   What is one way that humans have adapted to the harsh Antarctic environment?

FCAT PRACTICE   You can prepare for the FCAT-assessed standards by completing the correlated item(s) below.

Section 2 Assessment

Defining Terms
1. Define crevasse, ice shelf, iceberg, krill, ozone.

Recalling Facts
2. Place What covers nearly 98 percent of Antarctica?

3. Location Where in Antarctica would you find the most living things?

4. Human/Environment Interaction Why do scientists come to Antarctica?

Critical Thinking
5. Summarizing Information Why have countries agreed not to use the resources of Antarctica? **FCAT LA.A.2.3.1**

6. Writing Questions Imagine that you are planning a trip to Antarctica. What questions would you ask scientists working there?
FCAT LA.A.2.3.5

Graphic Organizer
7. Organizing Information Create a chart like the one below, and then look at the political map on page 759. In your chart, list the various national claims made in Antarctica by the world's countries. Then give the number of research stations for each country. **FCAT LA.A.1.3.2**

Countries With Claims in Antarctica	Number of Research Stations

Applying Social Studies Skills

8. Analyzing Maps Look at the physical map on page 728. What mountain range cuts across Antarctica?

Making Connections

Antarctica's Environmental Stations

For nearly 200 years, adventurers, explorers, geographers, and scientists have been drawn to the icy wilderness of Antarctica. Scientific research is the major human activity on this remarkable continent.

Polar Science

In the 1950s, countries began to talk of preserving Antarctica as an international laboratory for scientific research. Today a formal treaty guarantees free access and research rights for scientists of many countries. Antarctica now holds more than 40 research stations.

Types of Research

Geologists, biologists, climatologists, and astronomers are some of the many scientists who come to Antarctica to study. Understanding the earth's environment is a major focus. The Antarctic ice cap contains 90 percent of the world's ice and 70 percent of its freshwater. Changes here can affect the world's oceans and climates.

Scientists in Antarctica were the first to discover the holes in the ozone layer. Such holes can expose life on the earth to too much ultraviolet radiation.

Researchers in Antarctica also study the earth's history. Locked in the continent's ice crystals and air bubbles are clues to the earth's past. Fossils show how landmasses existed before the formation of today's continents.

The harsh living conditions of Antarctica provide another subject for study. The National Aeronautics and Space Administration (NASA) sends engineers and scientists to Antarctica to learn how to survive in extreme conditions, such as those humans might someday encounter on visits to other planets.

Research station at the South Pole ▶

Life at the Edge

Living and working in Antarctica's polar wilderness demands special equipment, well-trained people, and a sizable dose of caution. Freeze-dried food, layers of warm, quick-drying clothes, insulated boots, and specially designed pyramid tents keep researchers well-fed, warm, and dry. Researchers quickly learn the importance of staying inside during whiteout conditions, when snow and fog create a total lack of visibility.

The Antarctic environment is a fragile one, and researchers take care to protect it. All trash and wastes are removed from the continent. Mining of mineral resources is banned, and laws protect native plants and animals. Such care ensures that Antarctica will continue to hold exciting discoveries for years to come.

▶ Making the Connection

1. What do researchers study in Antarctica?
2. What discovery did researchers make about the ozone layer?
3. **Summarizing Information** What items do researchers in Antarctica use to stay warm and dry?

FCAT LA.A.2.3.1

Reading Review

Section 1   Pacific Island Cultures and Economies

Terms to Know

cacao
copra
pidgin language
high island
low island
atoll
phosphate
trust territory

Main Idea

Oceania is made up of thousands of Pacific Ocean islands organized into countries and territories.

✓ **Region** Oceania is a huge area of vast open ocean and about 25,000 islands.

✓ **Region** Geographers divide Oceania into three regions: Melanesia, Micronesia, and Polynesia.

✓ **Place** High islands were formed by volcanoes. Low islands were made from coral.

✓ **Place** Papua New Guinea, in Melanesia, is the largest and most populous country of Oceania.

✓ **Economics** The main economic activities in Oceania are farming and tourism. Some islands have important minerals or other resources.

✓ **History** Most people of Oceania are descendants of people who left Southeast Asia on canoes thousands of years ago.

Fijian schoolgirls buy ▶
snacks from an Indian
merchant in Suva.

Section 2   The Frozen Continent

Terms to Know

crevasse
ice shelf
iceberg
krill
ozone

Main Idea

Antarctica is a harsh land of rock and ice. The world's nations have agreed to leave the frozen continent open to scientific study.

✓ **Location** Antarctica lies at the southern end of the earth.

✓ **Place** Most of the continent, which has mountain ranges and a plateau, is covered by a huge, thick ice cap.

✓ **Place** Most plants and animals that live in Antarctica are small. Larger animals thrive in the waters off the coast.

✓ **Economics** Antarctica has many minerals, but many nations have signed a treaty agreeing not to remove these resources.

✓ **Culture** Antarctica is a major center of scientific research, but it is the only continent with no permanent human population.

Assessment and Activities

Using Key Terms

Match the terms in Part A with their definitions in Part B.

A.

1. pidgin language
2. copra
3. trust territory
4. ice shelf
5. phosphate
6. ozone
7. low island
8. iceberg
9. high island
10. krill

B.

a. mineral salt used to make fertilizer
b. tiny, shrimplike animal
c. Pacific island formed by volcanic activity
d. combines elements of several languages
e. chunk of a glacier that floats free
f. dried coconut meat
g. layer of ice above water in Antarctica
h. area temporarily placed under control of another nation
i. Pacific island formed of coral
j. layer in the atmosphere that blocks certain harmful rays of the sun

Reviewing the Main Ideas

Section 1 Pacific Island Cultures and Economies

11. **History** Why are there South Asians on the Fiji Islands?
12. **Human/Environment Interaction** Which is likely to have better farmland—a high island or a low island? Why?
13. **Government** New Caledonia is ruled by which European country?
14. **Economics** What attracts tourists to Oceania?
15. **History** From where did the people who first settled Oceania originally come?

Section 2 The Frozen Continent

16. **Place** What is significant about Mount Erebus?
17. **Location** What marine birds feed in the seas near Antarctica?
18. **Economics** What resources have been found in Antarctica?
19. **Government** What agreement bans the use of Antarctica's resources?
20. **Human/Environment Interaction** Why do scientists study the ozone layer in Antarctica?

Oceania and Antarctica

Place Location Activity

On a separate sheet of paper, match the letters on the map with the numbered places listed below.

1. Antarctic Peninsula
2. South Pole
3. Vinson Massif
4. Marshall Islands
5. Papua New Guinea
6. Fiji Islands
7. French Polynesia
8. Coral Sea
9. Solomon Islands

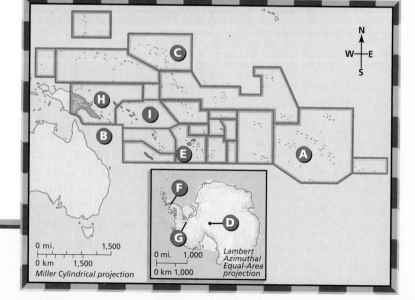

Self-Check Quiz Visit *The World and Its People* Web site at twip.glencoe.com and click on **Chapter 27—Self-Check Quizzes** to prepare for the Chapter Test.

Critical Thinking

21. **Making Generalizations** You have read about two areas with very different climates. Write a generalization about how climate affects the way people live in each area.

22. **Organizing Information** Make a chart like this one. Under each heading, write a fact about each of the four regions you studied in this chapter: Melanesia, Micronesia, Polynesia, and Antarctica. **FCAT** LA.A.1.3.2

Landforms	Climate	Economy or Resources	People

Comparing Regions Activity

23. **Geography** The region of northern Siberia in Russia has one of the coldest climates in the world. Research to find what plants and animals live here. Compare this information to what lives on the continent of Antarctica. What similarities and differences do you see? **FCAT** LA.A.2.3.5

Mental Mapping Activity

24. **Focusing on the Region** Create an outline map of Antarctica. Refer to the map on page 728, and then label the following:

   - Antarctic Circle
   - Vinson Massif
   - Antarctic Peninsula
   - Pacific Ocean
   - Atlantic Ocean
   - South Pole

Technology Skills Activity

25. **Building a Database** Research three animals of Oceania. Create a database of the information you find. Include separate fields for the following items: name of species, location, type of habitat, diet, natural predators, and population status. Then use the database information to create a map showing the location of each species.

Standardized Test Practice

Directions: Read the paragraph below, and then answer the question that follows.

Because of the abundance of marine life in the clear Pacific waters, fresh fish is the primary traditional food of Oceania's people. This is especially true in the low coral islands, where there is little land suitable for farming. The rich volcanic soil of the high islands allows pineapples, coconuts, bananas, and sweet potatoes to grow. In Papua New Guinea, pork is a favorite food. Great feasts of pork, greens, and yams are social gatherings for whole villages. At these feasts, pigs are cooked for about eight hours over hot stones set in an "earth oven"—or large hole in the ground.

1. **Which of the following statements *best* summarizes the paragraph above?** **FCAT** LA.A.2.3.1

   F People in the high islands are able to grow and eat pineapples, bananas, and sweet potatoes.

   G In the low islands, the coral prevents much farming.

   H The Pacific Ocean is the source of the fish that most people eat.

   J Physical geography influences the traditional foods of Oceania's people.

Test-Taking Tip: When a question uses the word *best*, it means that more than one answer might be correct. Your job is to pick the *best* answer. This question also asks for a summary of the passage. Read through all of the answer choices before choosing the one that provides a more general restatement of the information.

OZONE
Earth's Natural Sunscreen

The Ozone Hole If you spend lots of time outdoors, you probably know that "SPF 30" is a rating for sunscreen. The higher a sunscreen's Sun Protection Factor (SPF), the longer you can be exposed to sunlight before your skin begins to burn. Earth has a sunscreen too. It is called ozone. Ozone is a kind of gas. A thin band of ozone high above the earth shields the planet from the sun's most harmful ultraviolet (UV) rays. This ozone is being depleted, however. The satellite images (above right) show an expanding ozone hole above Antarctica. For several decades, the ozone layer has been in trouble.

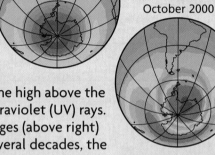

October 1980

October 1990

October 2000

Thicker Ozone   Thinner Ozone

Source: Ozone Processing Team, NASA, GSFC.

 Human-made chemicals, particularly chlorofluorocarbons (CFCs), destroy ozone and thin the ozone layer. CFCs were used for years in refrigerators, air conditioners, foam-insulated cups, aerosol sprays, and in some cleaning products.

 Ozone losses of about 10 percent have occurred over Europe, Canada, and other parts of the Northern Hemisphere too.

When ozone is destroyed, more UV rays strike the earth. Exposure to harmful rays can cause skin cancer in humans, destroy plants, and kill ocean plankton.

Reversing the Damage The good news is that ozone destruction can be reversed. Officials around the world are taking action.

 In 1992 an international treaty called for a global ban of CFCs by 1996. Today there are fewer CFCs in the atmosphere.

 Some scientists predict full recovery of the ozone layer by 2050.

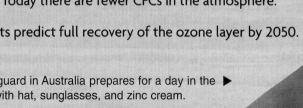

A lifeguard in Australia prepares for a day in the ▶ sun with hat, sunglasses, and zinc cream.

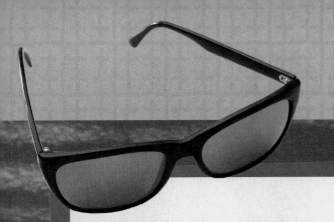

Making a Difference

Ozone Prizewinners Three scientists shared the 1995 Nobel Prize in chemistry for their research on ozone. Americans Mario Molina (right) and F. Sherwood Rowland and Dutch citizen Paul Crutzen shared the honor after describing the chemical processes by which ozone is formed and destroyed in the atmosphere. Before they explored the issue, little was known about how human-made chemicals affect ozone. The three scientists were able to show that the release of CFCs into the air damages the ozone layer. Their important research led governments around the world to ban the use of CFCs.

Mario Molina

Keeping Watch Antarctica has long been seen as a barometer of Earth's health. Scientists from all over the world live and work in research stations scattered throughout Antarctica. In 1985 scientists reported that the ozone layer over Antarctica had decreased dramatically. Since then, they have been closely watching the ozone layer, collecting data from special instruments that record ozone levels. Governments and environmental groups use this information to determine what can be done to correct the problem.

What Can You Do?

Get Involved
Organize a "Sun Alert" campaign to warn younger students about the dangers of overexposure to the sun.

Find Out More
On the Trail of the Missing Ozone, an online book, tells why we need the ozone layer and how to prevent ozone depletion. You can read it at www.epa.gov/ozone/science/missoz/index.html. Share what you learn with the class. **FCAT** LA.A.2.3.5

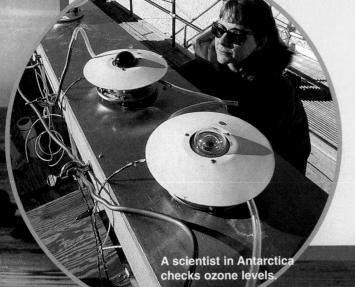

A scientist in Antarctica checks ozone levels.

Appendix

Contents

What Is an Appendix? 775

Nations of the World Data Bank.............................776

Standardized Test Skills Handbook..................786

Honoring America...............798

Gazetteer 799

Glossary..................................807

Spanish Glossary 814

Index 823

Acknowledgments..............841

What Is an Appendix?

An appendix is the additional material you often find at the end of books. The information below will help you learn how to use the Appendix in *The World and Its People*.

NATIONS OF THE WORLD DATA BANK

The **Nations of the World Data Bank** that begins on page 776 lists all of the world's countries and various categories of information for each. For example, each country's type of government, form of currency, and literacy rate—among other topics—are listed in the data bank.

SKILLS HANDBOOK

The **Standardized Test Skills Handbook** requires you to learn and apply many key skills that you will use throughout the study of geography as well as other subject areas.

GAZETTEER

A **gazetteer** is a geographical dictionary. It lists many important geographic features, most of the world's countries, and many cities of the world. Each entry also includes latitude and longitude and a page number where each entry can be found on a map in your textbook.

GLOSSARY AND SPANISH GLOSSARY

A **glossary** is a list of important or difficult terms found in a textbook. The glossary gives a definition of each term as it is used in the book. Since words sometimes have other meanings, you may wish to consult a dictionary to find other uses for the term. The glossary also includes page numbers telling you where in the textbook the term is used. The **Spanish glossary** is the English glossary translated into Spanish.

INDEX

An **index** is an alphabetical listing at the end of a book that includes the subjects of that book and the page numbers where those subjects can be found. The index in this book also lets you know that certain pages contain maps, graphs, photos, or paintings about the subject.

ACKNOWLEDGMENTS

This section lists photo credits and/or literary credits for the book. You can look at this section to find out where the publisher obtained the permission to use photographs or to use excerpts from other books.

Test Yourself!

Do you think you can use an appendix quickly and easily? Try it. Find the answers to these questions by using the Appendix on the following pages.

1. What does *canopy* mean?
2. Where did you find what the word *canopy* means?
3. What is the Spanish word for *cassava*?
4. What kind of currency does Spain use?
5. What are the latitude and longitude of Moscow?
6. On what pages can you find information about Cuba?

Appendix User Tip

When using an appendix, be sure to notice and use the guide words at the top of the page. These guide words indicate the alphabetically first and last entries on that page.

Nations of the World
DATA BANK

Today we are learning to understand the connected world in which we live. As technology makes communication easier, we interact globally more than ever. Each country has its own unique identity, however. Using this chart will help you compare and contrast information about government, economy, and culture.

COUNTRY Capital	GOVERNMENT		ECONOMICS			SOCIAL & CULTURAL		
	Type of Government	Date Founded	*GNP Ranking	GNP Per Capita	Currency	Literacy	**Infant Mortality	Primary Religion(s)
Afghanistan Kabul	Republic	2001	101st	$270	Afghani	36%	143	Muslim
Albania Tirana	Republic	1991	131st	$760	Lek	87%	37	Muslim, Eastern Orthodox, Catholic
Algeria Algiers	Republic	1962	52nd	$1,500	Algerian Dinar	70%	38	Muslim
Andorra Andorra la Vella	Parliamentary Democracy	1993	155th	$15,600	Euro	100%	4	Catholic
Angola Luanda	Republic	1975	126th	$260	Kwanza	42%	194	Indigenous, Catholic, Protestant
Antigua and Barbuda St. John's	Parliamentary Democracy	1981	166th	$7,380	E. Car. Dollar	89%	21	Protestant, Catholic
Argentina Buenos Aires	Republic	1816	17th	$8,950	Argentine Peso	97%	16	Catholic
Armenia Yerevan	Republic	1991	137th	$560	Dram	99%	41	Eastern Orthodox
Australia Canberra	Parliamentary Democracy	1901	14th	$20,650	Australian Dollar	100%	5	Protestant, Catholic
Austria Vienna	Federal Republic	1918	22nd	$27,920	Euro	98%	4	Catholic
Azerbaijan Baku	Republic	1991	118th	$510	Manat	97%	82	Muslim
Bahamas Nassau	Parliamentary Democracy	1973	124th	$11,940	Bahamian Dollar	96%	26	Protestant, Catholic

*Gross National Product   **deaths/1,000 live births

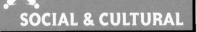

COUNTRY Capital	Type of Government	Date Founded	*GNP Ranking	GNP Per Capita	Currency	Literacy	**Infant Mortality	Primary Religion(s)
Bahrain Manama	Monarchy	1971	104th	$7,800	Bahrain Dinar	89%	19	Muslim
Bangladesh Dhaka	Republic	1971	51st	$360	Taka	43%	66	Muslim, Hindu
Barbados Bridgetown	Parliamentary Democracy	1966	145th	$6,560	Barbados Dollar	97%	13	Protestant
Belarus Minsk	Republic	1991	61st	$2,150	Belarus Ruble	100%	14	Eastern Orthodox
Belgium Brussels	Constitutional Monarchy	1830	19th	$26,730	Euro	98%	5	Catholic, Protestant
Belize Belmopan	Parliamentary Democracy	1981	162nd	$2,670	Belizean Dollar	94%	27	Catholic, Protestant
Benin Porto-Novo	Republic	1960	133rd	$380	CFA Franc	41%	87	Indigenous, Christian, Muslim
Bhutan Thimphu	Constitutional Monarchy	1907	172nd	$430	Ngultrum	42%	105	Buddhist, Hindu
Bolivia La Paz, Sucre	Republic	1825	91st	$970	Boliviano	87%	56	Catholic
Bosnia and Herzegovina Sarajevo	Republic	1992	160th	$288	Marka	93%	23	Muslim, Eastern Orthodox, Catholic
Botswana Gaborone	Republic	1966	105th	$3,310	Pula	80%	67	Indigenous, Christian
Brazil Brasília	Federal Republic	1889	8th	$4,790	Real	86%	32	Catholic
Brunei Bandar Seri Begawan	Constitutional Monarchy	1984	116th	$14,240	Brunei Dollar	92%	14	Muslim, Buddhist, Christian
Bulgaria Sofia	Republic	1991	82nd	$1,170	Lev	99%	14	Eastern Orthodox, Muslim
Burkina Faso Ouagadougou	Republic	1960	130th	$250	CFA Franc	27%	100	Muslim, Indigenous
Burundi Bujumbura	Republic	1966	157th	$140	Burundi Franc	52%	72	Christian, Indigenous
Cambodia Phnom Penh	Constitutional Monarchy	1953	125th	$300	Riel	70%	76	Buddhist
Cameroon Yaoundé	Republic	1960	86th	$620	CFA Franc	79%	70	Indigenous, Christian, Muslim
Canada Ottawa	Parliamentary Democracy	1867	9th	$19,640	Canadian Dollar	97%	5	Catholic, Protestant
Cape Verde Praia	Republic	1975	169th	$1,090	Escudo	77%	51	Catholic, Protestant
Central African Republic Bangui	Republic	1960	152nd	$320	CFA Franc	51%	93	Indigenous, Protestant, Catholic, Muslim

*Gross National Product   **deaths/1,000 live births

Nations of the World **DATABANK**

COUNTRY Capital	Type of Government	Date Founded	*GNP Ranking	GNP Per Capita	Currency	Literacy	**Infant Mortality	Primary Religion(s)
Chad N'Djamena	Republic	1960	147th	$230	CFA Franc	48%	96	Muslim, Christian
Chile Santiago	Republic	1823	43rd	$4,820	Chilean Peso	96%	9	Catholic, Protestant
China Beijing	Communist State	1949	7th	$860	Yuan	82%	25	Atheist, Buddhist, Daoist, Confucian
Colombia Bogotá	Republic	1819	39th	$2,180	Colombian Peso	93%	23	Catholic
Comoros Moroni	Republic	1975	181st	$400	Comoran Franc	57%	80	Muslim
Congo, Democratic Republic of the Kinshasa	Dictatorship	1960	103rd	$110	Congolese Franc	66%	97	Catholic, Protestant
Congo, Republic of the Brazzaville	Republic	1960	144th	$670	CFA Franc	84%	95	Christian, Indigenous
Costa Rica San José	Republic	1838	85th	$2,680	Colón	96%	11	Catholic
Côte d'Ivoire Yamoussoukro, Abidjan	Republic	1960	81st	$710	CFA Franc	51%	98	Muslim, Indigenous, Christian
Croatia Zagreb	Republic	1991	69th	$4,060	Kuna	99%	7	Catholic
Cuba Havana	Communist State	1959	72nd	$1,650	Cuban Peso	97%	7	Catholic
Cyprus Nicosia	Republic	1960	92nd	$9,400	Cyprus Pound	98%	8	Eastern Orthodox, Muslim
Czech Republic Prague	Republic	1993	48th	$5,240	Koruna	100%	5	Atheist, Catholic
Denmark Copenhagen	Constitutional Monarchy	1849	25th	$38,890	Krone	100%	5	Protestant
Djibouti Djibouti	Republic	1977	167th	$750	Djibouti Franc	68%	107	Muslim
Dominica Roseau	Republic	1978	179th	$3,040	E. Car. Dollar	94%	15	Catholic, Protestant
Dominican Republic Santo Domingo	Republic	1865	76th	$1,750	Dom. Rep. Peso	85%	34	Catholic
East Timor Dili	Republic	2002	—	—	U.S. Dollar	48%	50	Catholic
Ecuador Quito	Republic	1830	71st	$1,570	Sucre	93%	32	Catholic
Egypt Cairo	Republic	1953	42nd	$1,200	Egyptian Pound	58%	35	Muslim
El Salvador San Salvador	Republic	1841	78th	$1,810	Colón	80%	27	Catholic

*Gross National Product   **deaths/1,000 live births

GOVERNMENT

ECONOMICS

SOCIAL & CULTURAL

COUNTRY Capital	Type of Government	Date Founded	*GNP Ranking	GNP Per Capita	Currency	Literacy	**Infant Mortality	Primary Religion(s)
Equatorial Guinea Malabo	Republic	1968	168th	$1,060	CFA Franc	86%	89	Catholic
Eritrea Asmara	Republic	1993	158th	$230	Nakfa	59%	76	Muslim, Christian
Estonia Tallinn	Republic	1991	107th	$3,360	Kroon	100%	12	Protestant
Ethiopia Addis Ababa	Federal Republic	1995	99th	$110	Birr	43%	103	Muslim, Eastern Orthodox, Indigenous
Fiji Islands Suva	Republic	1987	139th	$2,460	Fiji Dollar	94%	13	Christian, Hindu
Finland Helsinki	Republic	1917	31st	$24,790	Euro	100%	4	Protestant
France Paris	Republic	1958	4th	$26,300	Euro	99%	4	Catholic
Gabon Libreville	Republic	1960	110th	$4,120	CFA Franc	63%	55	Christian
Gambia Banjul	Republic	1970	170th	$340	Dalasi	40%	75	Muslim
Georgia T'bilisi	Republic	1991	111th	$860	Lari	99%	51	Eastern Orthodox, Muslim
Germany Berlin	Federal Republic	1949	3rd	$28,280	Euro	99%	4	Protestant, Catholic
Ghana Accra	Republic	1960	95th	$390	Cedi	75%	53	Christian, Indigenous, Muslim
Greece Athens	Republic	1975	32nd	$11,640	Euro	98%	6	Eastern Orthodox
Grenada St. George's	Parliamentary Democracy	1974	174th	$3,140	E. Car. Dollar	98%	17	Catholic, Protestant
Guatemala Guatemala City	Republic	1838	74th	$1,580	Quetzal	71%	38	Catholic, Protestant
Guinea Conakry	Republic	1958	119th	$550	Guinean Franc	36%	93	Muslim
Guinea-Bissau Bissau	Republic	1974	176th	$230	Guinea Peso	42%	110	Indigenous, Muslim
Guyana Georgetown	Republic	1970	162nd	$800	Guy. Dollar	99%	38	Christian, Hindu
Haiti Port-au-Prince	Republic	1804	128th	$380	Gourde	53%	76	Catholic, Protestant
Honduras Tegucigalpa	Republic	1838	113th	$740	Lempira	76%	30	Catholic
Hungary Budapest	Republic	1989	50th	$4,510	Forint	99%	9	Catholic, Protestant

*Gross National Product   **deaths/1,000 live births

GOVERNMENT

ECONOMICS

SOCIAL & CULTURAL

COUNTRY Capital	Type of Government	Date Founded	*GNP Ranking	GNP Per Capita	Currency	Literacy	**Infant Mortality	Primary Religion(s)
Iceland Reykjavík	Republic	1944	94th	$26,580	Icelandic Króna	100%	4	Protestant
India New Delhi	Federal Republic	1950	15th	$370	Indian Rupee	60%	60	Hindu, Muslim
Indonesia Jakarta	Republic	1949	23rd	$1,110	Rupiah	89%	38	Muslim
Iran Tehran	Islamic Republic	1979	34th	$1,780	Iranian Rial	79%	44	Muslim
Iraq Baghdad	Transitional Government	1958	65th	$950	Iraqi Dinar	40%	55	Muslim
Ireland Dublin	Republic	1949	44th	$17,790	Euro	98%	5	Catholic
Israel Jerusalem[1]	Republic	1948	37th	$16,180	Shekel	95%	7	Jewish, Muslim
Italy Rome	Republic	1946	6th	$20,170	Euro	99%	6	Catholic
Jamaica Kingston	Parliamentary Democracy	1962	117th	$1,550	Jamaican Dollar	88%	13	Protestant
Japan Tokyo	Constitutional Monarchy	1947	2nd	$38,160	Yen	99%	3	Shinto, Buddhist
Jordan Amman	Constitutional Monarchy	1946	96th	$1,520	Jordanian Dinar	91%	19	Muslim
Kazakhstan Astana	Republic	1991	62nd	$1,350	Tenge	98%	59	Muslim, Eastern Orthodox
Kenya Nairobi	Republic	1964	83rd	$340	Kenyan Shilling	85%	63	Protestant, Catholic, Indigenous
Kiribati Tarawa	Republic	1979	188th	$910	Australian Dollar	98%	51	Catholic, Protestant
Korea, North Pyongyang	Communist State	1948	64th	$1,390	Won	99%	26	Atheist, Buddhist, Confucian
Korea, South Seoul	Republic	1948	11th	$10,550	Won	98%	7	Christian, Buddhist
Kuwait Kuwait	Constitutional Monarchy	1961	58th	$17,390	Kuwaiti Dinar	84%	11	Muslim
Kyrgyzstan Bishkek	Republic	1991	134th	$480	Som	97%	75	Muslim, Eastern Orthodox
Laos Vientiane	Communist State	1975	142nd	$400	Kip	53%	89	Buddhist
Latvia Rīga	Republic	1991	100th	$2,430	Lat	100%	15	Protestant, Catholic, Eastern Orthodox
Lebanon Beirut	Republic	1944	77th	$3,350	Lebanese Pound	87%	26	Muslim, Christian

[1] Most countries maintain embassies in Tel Aviv.   *Gross National Product   **deaths/1,000 live births

GOVERNMENT

ECONOMICS

SOCIAL & CULTURAL

COUNTRY Capital	Type of Government	Date Founded	*GNP Ranking	GNP Per Capita	Currency	Literacy	**Infant Mortality	Primary Religion(s)
Lesotho Maseru	Constitutional Monarchy	1966	150th	$680	Loti	85%	86	Christian, Indigenous
Liberia Monrovia	Republic	1847	154th	$330	Liberian Dollar	58%	132	Indigenous, Christian, Muslim
Libya Tripoli	Military Dictatorship	1969	57th	$5,220	Libyan Dinar	83%	27	Muslim
Liechtenstein Vaduz	Constitutional Monarchy	1719	151st	$40,000	Swiss Franc	100%	5	Catholic
Lithuania Vilnius	Republic	1991	88th	$2,260	Litas	100%	14	Catholic
Luxembourg Luxembourg	Constitutional Monarchy	1868	70th	$45,360	Euro	100%	5	Catholic
Macedonia, Former Yugoslav Republic of Skopje	Republic	1991	135th	$1,100	Macedonia Denar	94%	12	Eastern Orthodox, Muslim
Madagascar Antananarivo	Republic	1960	120th	$250	Ariary	69%	80	Indigenous, Christian
Malawi Lilongwe	Republic	1966	136th	$210	Kwacha	63%	105	Protestant, Catholic, Muslim
Malaysia Kuala Lumpur	Constitutional Monarchy	1963	36th	$4,530	Ringgit	89%	19	Muslim, Buddhist, Daoist, Confucian
Maldives Male	Republic	1965	173rd	$1,180	Rufiyaa	97%	60	Muslim
Mali Bamako	Republic	1960	129th	$260	CFA Franc	46%	119	Muslim
Malta Valletta	Republic	1974	122nd	$9,330	Maltese Lira	93%	6	Catholic
Marshall Islands Majuro	Republic	1986	185th	$1,610	U.S. Dollar	94%	32	Protestant
Mauritania Nouakchott	Islamic Republic	1960	153rd	$440	Ouguiya	42%	74	Muslim
Mauritius Port Louis	Republic	1992	112th	$3,870	Mauritian Rupee	86%	16	Hindu, Catholic, Muslim
Mexico Mexico City	Federal Republic	1823	16th	$3,700	Mexican Peso	93%	24	Catholic
Micronesia, Federated States of Palikir	Republic	1986	180th	$1,920	U.S. Dollar	89%	32	Catholic, Protestant
Moldova Chişinău	Republic	1991	140th	$460	Leu	99%	42	Eastern Orthodox
Monaco Monaco	Constitutional Monarchy	1911	106th	$11,000	Euro	99%	6	Catholic

*Gross National Product   **deaths/1,000 live births

GOVERNMENT

ECONOMICS

SOCIAL & CULTURAL

COUNTRY Capital	Type of Government	Date Founded	*GNP Ranking	GNP Per Capita	Currency	Literacy	**Infant Mortality	Primary Religion(s)
Mongolia Ulaanbaatar	Republic	1992	156th	$390	Tugrik	99%	57	Buddhism
Morocco Rabat	Constitutional Monarchy	1956	54th	$1,260	Dirham	52%	45	Muslim
Mozambique Maputo	Republic	1975	132nd	$140	Metical	48%	199	Indigenous, Christian, Muslim
Myanmar Yangon	Military Dictatorship	1948	41st	$1,500	Kyat	83%	70	Buddhist
Namibia Windhoek	Republic	1990	123rd	$2,110	Namibian Dollar	84%	68	Christian, Indigenous
Nauru Yaren	Republic	1968	187th	$7,270	Australian Dollar	95%	10	Protestant, Catholic
Nepal Kathmandu	Constitutional Monarchy	1990	108th	$220	Nepalese Rupee	45%	71	Hindu
Netherlands Amsterdam	Constitutional Monarchy	1815	12th	$25,830	Euro	99%	4	Catholic, Protestant
New Zealand Wellington	Parliamentary Democracy	1907	47th	$15,820	N. Zealand Dollar	99%	6	Protestant, Catholic
Nicaragua Managua	Republic	1838	143rd	$410	Gold Cordoba	68%	31	Catholic
Niger Niamey	Republic	1960	141st	$200	CFA Franc	18%	124	Muslim
Nigeria Abuja	Federal Republic	1963	55th	$280	Naira	68%	71	Muslim, Christian, Indigenous
Norway Oslo	Constitutional Monarchy	1905	27th	$36,100	Norwegian Krone	100%	4	Protestant
Oman Muscat	Traditional Monarchy	1970	79th	$4,820	Omani Rial	76%	21	Muslim
Pakistan Islamabad	Federal Republic	1956	45th	$500	Pakistani Rupee	46%	77	Muslim
Palau Koror	Republic	1994	186th	$5,000	U.S. Dollar	92%	16	Christian, Indigenous
Panama Panama City	Republic	1903	92nd	$2,670	Balboa	93%	21	Catholic, Protestant
Papua New Guinea Port Moresby	Parliamentary Democracy	1975	115th	$930	Kina	66%	55	Indigenous, Catholic, Protestant
Paraguay Asunción	Republic	1811	80th	$200	Guaraní	94%	28	Catholic
Peru Lima	Republic	1824	46th	$2,610	Nuevo Sol	91%	37	Catholic
Philippines Manila	Republic	1946	38th	$1,200	Philippine Peso	96%	25	Catholic

*Gross National Product   **deaths/1,000 live births

GOVERNMENT

ECONOMICS

SOCIAL & CULTURAL

COUNTRY Capital	Type of Government	Date Founded	*GNP Ranking	GNP Per Capita	Currency	Literacy	**Infant Mortality	Primary Religion(s)
Poland Warsaw	Republic	1990	29th	$3,590	Zloty	100%	9	Catholic
Portugal Lisbon	Republic	1910	33rd	$11,010	Euro	93%	6	Catholic
Qatar Doha	Traditional Monarchy	1971	93rd	$11,600	Qatari Riyal	83%	20	Muslim
Romania Bucharest	Republic	1991	56th	$1,410	Leu	99%	18	Eastern Orthodox
Russia Moscow	Federal Republic	1991	13th	$2,680	Ruble	99%	20	Eastern Orthodox
Rwanda Kigali	Republic	1962	146th	$210	Rwandan Franc	70%	103	Catholic, Protestant
St. Kitts and Nevis Basseterre	Parliamentary Democracy	1983	177th	$6,260	E. Car. Dollar	97%	15	Protestant, Catholic
St. Lucia Castries	Parliamentary Democracy	1979	163rd	$3,510	E. Car. Dollar	67%	14	Catholic, Protestant
St. Vincent and the Grenadines Kingstown	Parliamentary Democracy	1979	175th	$2,420	E. Car. Dollar	96%	15	Protestant, Catholic
Samoa Apia	Constitutional Monarchy	1962	182nd	$1,140	Tala	100%	30	Christian
San Marino San Marino	Republic	1600	183rd	$7,830	Euro	96%	6	Catholic
Sao Tome and Principe São Tomé	Republic	1975	189th	$290	Dobra	79%	46	Catholic, Protestant
Saudi Arabia Riyadh	Traditional Monarchy	1932	187th	$7,150	Saudi Riyal	79%	48	Muslim
Senegal Dakar	Republic	1960	109th	$540	CFA Franc	40%	58	Muslim
Serbia and Montenegro Belgrade	Republic	2002	84th	$900	Dinar, Euro	93%	17	Eastern Orthodox, Muslim
Seychelles Victoria	Republic	1976	165th	$6,910	S. Rupee	58%	16	Catholic
Sierra Leone Freetown	Republic	1971	161st	$160	Leone	31%	147	Muslim, Indigenous, Christian
Singapore Singapore	Republic	1965	35th	$32,810	Singapore Dollar	93%	4	Buddhism, Muslim
Slovakia Bratislava	Republic	1993	66th	$3,680	Koruna	100%	9	Catholic, Protestant
Slovenia Ljubljana	Republic	1991	67th	$9,840	Tolar	100%	4	Catholic

*Gross National Product   **deaths/1,000 live births

Nations of the World DATABANK

GOVERNMENT

ECONOMICS

SOCIAL & CULTURAL

COUNTRY Capital	Type of Government	Date Founded	*GNP Ranking	GNP Per Capita	Currency	Literacy	**Infant Mortality	Primary Religion(s)
Solomon Islands Honiara	Parliamentary Democracy	1978	171st	$870	Solomon Is. Dollar	54%	23	Protestant, Catholic
Somalia Mogadishu	Transitional Government	1960	159th	$100	Somali Shilling	38%	120	Muslim
South Africa Bloemfontein, Cape Town, Pretoria	Republic	1961	30th	$3,210	Rand	86%	61	Christian, Indigenous
Spain Madrid	Constitutional Monarchy	1978	10th	$14,490	Euro	98%	5	Catholic
Sri Lanka Colombo	Republic	1972	75th	$800	Sri Lankan Rupee	92%	15	Buddhist, Hindu
Sudan Khartoum	Republic	1956	90th	$290	Sudanese Dinar	61%	66	Muslim, Indigenous
Suriname Paramaribo	Republic	1975	164th	$1,320	Guilder	93%	25	Hindu, Protestant, Catholic, Muslim
Swaziland Mbabane	Monarchy	1968	149th	$1,520	Lilangeni	82%	67	Christian, Indigenous
Sweden Stockholm	Constitutional Monarchy	1809	21st	$26,210	Swedish Krona	99%	3	Protestant
Switzerland Bern	Federal Republic	1848	18th	$26,210	Swiss Franc	99%	4	Catholic, Protestant
Syria Damascus	Republic	1946	73rd	$1,120	Syrian Pound	77%	32	Muslim
Taiwan Taipei	Republic	1949	20th	$10,320	Taiwanese Dollar	86%	7	Buddhist, Confucian, Daoist
Tajikistan Dushanbe	Republic	1991	138th	$330	Somoni	99%	113	Muslim
Tanzania Dar es Salaam	Republic	1964	97th	$210	Tanzanian Shilling	78%	104	Muslim, Indigenous, Christian
Thailand Bangkok	Constitutional Monarchy	1932	26th	$2,740	Baht	96%	22	Buddhism
Togo Lomé	Republic	1960	148th	$340	CFA Franc	61%	69	Indigenous, Christian, Muslim
Tonga Nuku'alofa	Constitutional Monarchy	1970	184th	$1,810	Pa'anga	99%	13	Christian
Trinidad and Tobago Port-of-Spain	Republic	1976	102nd	$4,250	T&T Dollar	99%	25	Catholic, Hindu, Protestant
Tunisia Tunis	Republic	1956	68th	$2,110	Tunisian Dinar	74%	27	Muslim
Turkey Ankara	Republic	1923	24th	$3,130	Turkish Lira	87%	44	Muslim
Turkmenistan Ashgabat	Republic	1991	127th	$640	Manat	98%	73	Muslim

*Gross National Product   **deaths/1,000 live births

GOVERNMENT

ECONOMICS

SOCIAL & CULTURAL

COUNTRY Capital	Type of Government	Date Founded	*GNP Ranking	GNP Per Capita	Currency	Literacy	**Infant Mortality	Primary Religion(s)
Tuvalu Funafuti	Parliamentary Democracy	1978	190th	$330	Australian Dollar	55%	21	Protestant
Uganda Kampala	Republic	1963	98th	$330	Ugandan Shilling	70%	88	Catholic, Protestant, Indigenous, Muslim
Ukraine Kiev	Republic	1991	49th	$1,335	Hryvnia	100%	21	Eastern Orthodox
United Arab Emirates Abu Dhabi	Federal Monarchy	1971	53rd	$17,400	U.A.E. Dirhem	78%	16	Muslim
United Kingdom London	Constitutional Monarchy	1707	5th	$20,870	Pound Sterling	99%	5	Protestant, Catholic
United States Washington, D.C.	Federal Republic	1776	1st	$29,080	U.S. Dollar	97%	7	Protestant, Catholic
Uruguay Montevideo	Republic	1828	63rd	$6,130	Uruguay Peso	98%	14	Catholic
Uzbekistan Tashkent	Republic	1991	59th	$1,020	Sum	99%	72	Muslim
Vanuatu Port-Vila	Republic	1980	178th	$1,340	Vatu	53%	58	Protestant, Catholic
Vatican City —	Sovereign State under the Pope	1929	—	—	Euro	100%	—	Catholic
Venezuela Caracas	Federal Republic	1821	40th	$3,480	Bolivar	93%	24	Catholic
Vietnam Hanoi	Communist State	1954	60th	$310	Dong	94%	31	Buddhist
Yemen Sanaa	Republic	1990	114th	$270	Rial	50%	65	Muslim
Zambia Lusaka	Republic	1964	121st	$370	Zambian Kwacha	81%	99	Christian, Muslim, Hindu
Zimbabwe Harare	Republic	1980	89th	$720	Zimbabwe Dollar	91%	66	Christian, Indigenous

*Gross National Product   **deaths/1,000 live births

Standardized Test

Skills Handbook

Standardized tests are one way educators measure what you have learned. This handbook is designed to help you practice for standardized test questions. On the pages that follow, you will find a review of the major critical thinking skills that you will need to master to be successful when taking tests.

Contents

Interpreting a Map 787

Interpreting a Political Map 788

Interpreting Charts 789

Making Comparisons 790

Interpreting Primary Sources 791

Interpreting a Political Cartoon 792

Interpreting a Circle Graph 793

Drawing Inferences and
    Conclusions 794

Comparing Data 795

Categorizing and Analyzing
    Information 796

Sequencing Events 797

Interpreting a Map

Before 1492, people living in Europe in the Eastern Hemisphere had no idea that the continents of North America and South America in the Western Hemisphere existed. That was the year Christopher Columbus first reached the Americas. His voyage of exploration paved the way for other European voyages to the Western Hemisphere. The voyages of the early explorers brought together two worlds. Previously these parts of the globe had no contact with each other. Trade between the hemispheres changed life for people on both sides of the Atlantic Ocean. The trade between the peoples of the Eastern Hemisphere and the Western Hemisphere is referred to as the Columbian Exchange.

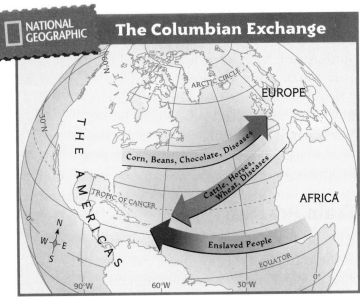

The Columbian Exchange

Skills Practice

Although globes are the best, most accurate way to show places on the round earth, people can more easily use maps to represent places. A map is made by taking data from a round globe and placing it on a flat surface. To read a map, first read the title to determine the subject of the map. Then read the map key or the labels on the map to find out what the colors and symbols on the map mean. Use the compass rose to identify the four cardinal directions of north, south, east, and west. Study the map of the Columbian Exchange and answer the questions that follow on a separate sheet of paper.

1. What is the subject of the map?

2. What do the arrows represent?

3. What continents are shown on the map?

4. What foods did Europeans acquire from the Americas?

5. What did the Americas acquire from Europe?

6. What people were brought from Africa to the Americas?

7. In what direction is Europe from the Americas?

DIRECTIONS: Use the map and your knowledge of social studies to answer the following question on a separate sheet of paper.

1. Which of the following statements about the Columbian Exchange is true? **FCAT LA.A.2.3.1**

   A Food products were traded only between Africa and the Americas.

   B Europeans acquired cattle from the Americas.

   C Europeans introduced corn, tomatoes, and beans to Native Americans.

   D Enslaved Africans were brought to the Americas.

Interpreting a Political Map

By 1750, or the middle of the eighteenth century, there were 13 British colonies in North America. A colony is a group of people living in one place who are governed by rulers in another place. The British colonists in America were ruled by the monarchy and Parliament of Great Britain. That meant that rulers living 3,000 miles away made laws for the American colonists.

Skills Practice

Political maps illustrate divisions between territories such as nations, states, colonies, or other political units. These divisions are called boundaries. Lines represent the boundaries between political areas. To interpret a political map, read the map title to determine what geographic area and time period it covers. Identify the colonies or other political units on the map. Look at the map key for additional information. Study the map on this page and answer the questions that follow on a separate sheet of paper.

1. List the New England Colonies.

2. Which were the Middle Colonies?

3. Which Middle Colony bordered Pennsylvania to the north?

4. Which was the southernmost early British colony?

5. Name the body of water that formed the eastern border of the colonies.

6. Where was Charles Town located?

NATIONAL GEOGRAPHIC

The Thirteen Colonies, 1750

Lake Ontario
ME. (part of Mass.)
Lake Erie
N.H.
Salem
N.Y. Boston● ●Plymouth
Hartford● ●
New Haven● MASS.
R.I.
CONN.
PA. ●New York City
Philadelphia● ●N.J.
40°N
0   200 miles
0   200 kilometers
Lambert Equal-Area projection
DEL.
St. Mary's● ●MD.
VA.
Jamestown●
ATLANTIC OCEAN
N.C.
N
W   E
S
70°W
S.C.
Charles Town●
GA.
Savannah●
60°W   30°N

● Town or City
New England Colonies
Middle Colonies
Southern Colonies

FCAT PRACTICE

DIRECTIONS: Use the map and your knowledge of social studies to answer the following questions on a separate sheet of paper.

1. The New England Colony that covered the largest land area was FCAT MA.B.1.3.4

  A Virginia.

  B Pennsylvania.

  C Massachusetts.

  D New Hampshire.

2. The northernmost Middle Colony is the present-day state of FCAT MA.B.1.3.4

  F Maryland.

  G New York.

  H Massachusetts.

  J Pennsylvania.

3. The settlement of Plymouth was located

  A near Jamestown. FCAT MA.B.1.3.4

  B in Massachusetts.

  C in the Southern Colonies.

  D in Virginia.

Interpreting Charts

Government is a necessary part of every nation. It gives citizens stability and provides services that many of us take for granted. However, governments can sometimes have too much power.

The United States was founded on the principle of limited government. Limited governments require all people to follow the laws. Even the rulers must obey rules set for the society. A democracy is a form of limited government. Not all forms of government have limits. In unlimited governments, power belongs to the ruler. No laws exist to limit what the ruler may do. A dictatorship is an example of an unlimited government.

Skills Practice

Charts are visual graphics that categorize information. When reading a chart, be sure to look at all the headings and labels. Study the charts on this page and answer the questions that follow on a separate sheet of paper.

1. What do the charts compare?

2. Which political systems are forms of limited government?

3. Which form of government often uses military rule?

4. In which political system does the king or queen have complete power?

Limited Governments

Representative Democracy	Constitutional Monarchy
People elect leaders to rule	King or queen's power is limited
Individual rights important	Individual rights important
More than one political party	More than one political party
People give consent to be governed	People elect governing body

Unlimited Governments

Dictatorship	Absolute Monarchy
One person or small group rules	King or queen inherits power
Few personal freedoms	Usually some freedoms
Rule by force, often military	Officials are appointed by king or queen
Ruler does not have to obey rules	Monarch has complete authority

FCAT PRACTICE

DIRECTIONS: Use the charts and your knowledge of social studies to answer the following questions on a separate sheet of paper.

1. Information found in the charts shows that the most restrictive form of government is a

    A dictatorship.   **FCAT MA.E.3.3.1**

    B representative democracy.

    C absolute monarchy.

    D constitutional monarchy.

2. Under which type of government do citizens have the most power? **FCAT MA.E.3.3.1**

    F unlimited government

    G limited government

    H absolute monarchy

    J dictatorship

3. An example of an unlimited government is

    A the United States in the 1960s. **FCAT LA.A.2.3.1**

    B Libya in the 1970s.

    C the United Kingdom in the 1980s.

    D Mexico in the 1990s.

Making Comparisons

The roots of representative democracy in the United States can be traced back to colonial times. In 1607 English settlers founded the colony of Jamestown in present-day Virginia. As the colony developed, problems arose. Later, colonists formed the House of Burgesses to deal with these problems. Citizens of Virginia were chosen as representatives to the House of Burgesses. This became the first legislature, or lawmaking body, in America.

Today citizens of the United States elect representatives to Congress. The major function of Congress is to make laws for the nation. There are two houses, or chambers, of the U.S. Congress. Legislative bodies with two houses are said to be bicameral. The bicameral Congress of the United States includes the Senate and the House of Representatives. Article I of the U.S. Constitution describes how each house will be organized and how its members will be chosen.

Skills Practice

When you make a comparison, you identify and examine two or more groups, situations, events, or documents. Then you identify any similarities and differences between the items. Study the information presented on the chart on this page and answer the questions that follow on a separate sheet of paper. **FCAT LA.A.2.3.1**

1. What two things does the chart compare?

2. How are the qualifications for each house of the U.S. Congress similar?

The U.S. Congress

House of Representatives	Senate
Qualifications: • Must be 25 years old • Must be U.S. citizen for 7+ years • Must live in the state they represent	**Qualifications:** • Must be 30 years old • Must be U.S. citizen for 9+ years • Must live in the state they represent
Number of Representatives: • 435 total representatives; number of representatives per state is based on state population	**Number of Representatives:** • 100 total senators; two senators elected from each state regardless of state population
Terms of Office: • Two-year terms	**Terms of Office:** • Six-year terms

DIRECTIONS: Use the chart and your knowledge of social studies to answer the following questions on a separate sheet of paper.

1. Which of the following statements best reflects information shown in the chart? **FCAT MA.E.3.3.1**

   A The Senate has more members than the House of Representatives.

   B Representatives to the House are elected to two-year terms.

   C House members must be residents of their states for at least 9 years.

   D A state's population determines its number of senators.

2. One inference that can be made from information shown on the chart is that **FCAT LA.A.1.3.2**

   F Texas elects more senators than Rhode Island.

   G Texas elects more House members than Rhode Island.

   H Texas elects fewer senators than Rhode Island.

   J Texas elects fewer House members than Rhode Island.

Interpreting Primary Sources

When Thomas Jefferson wrote the Declaration of Independence, he used the term "unalienable rights." Jefferson was referring to the natural rights that belong to humans. He and the other Founders of our nation believed that government could not take away the rights of the people.

Skills Practice

Primary sources are records of events made by the people who witnessed them. A historical document such as the Declaration of Independence is an example of a primary source. Read the passage below and answer the questions that follow on a separate sheet of paper. **FCAT LA.A.2.3.1**

> "We hold these truths to be self-evident, that all men are created equal, that they are endowed by their Creator with certain unalienable Rights, that among these are Life, Liberty, and the pursuit of Happiness . . ."
>
> —Declaration of Independence, July 4, 1776

1. What does the document say about the equality of men?

2. List the three natural, or unalienable, rights to which the document refers.

After gaining independence, American leaders wrote the U.S. Constitution in 1787. The Bill of Rights includes the first 10 amendments, or additions, to the Constitution. The First Amendment protects five basic rights of all American citizens. Study the chart on this page and answer the questions that follow. **FCAT LA.A.2.3.1**

1. Which right allows Americans to express themselves without fear of punishment by the government?

2. Which right allows people to worship as they please?

3. Which right allows citizens to publish a pamphlet that is critical of the president?

4. What is the Bill of Rights?

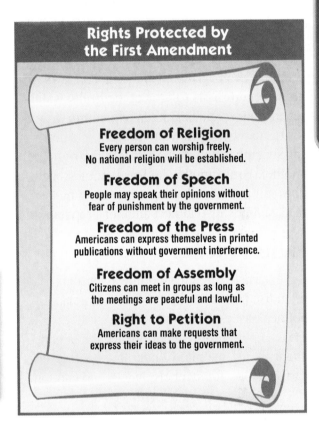

Rights Protected by the First Amendment

Freedom of Religion
Every person can worship freely.
No national religion will be established.

Freedom of Speech
People may speak their opinions without fear of punishment by the government.

Freedom of the Press
Americans can express themselves in printed publications without government interference.

Freedom of Assembly
Citizens can meet in groups as long as the meetings are peaceful and lawful.

Right to Petition
Americans can make requests that express their ideas to the government.

FCAT PRACTICE

DIRECTIONS: Use the chart and your knowledge of social studies to answer the following question on a separate sheet of paper.

1. Which First Amendment right protects citizens who are staging a protest outside a government building? **FCAT LA.A.2.3.1**

A freedom of speech

B freedom of the press

C freedom of assembly

D freedom of religion

Interpreting a Political Cartoon

Just as the government of the United States is limited in its powers, freedoms extended to Americans also have limits. The First Amendment was not intended to allow Americans to do whatever they please without regard to others. Limits on freedoms are necessary to keep order in a society of so many people. The government can establish laws to limit certain rights to protect the health, safety, security, or moral standards of a community. Rights can be restricted to prevent one person's rights from interfering with the rights of another. For example, the freedom of speech does not include allowing a person to make false statements that hurt another's reputation.

Skills Practice

The artists who create political cartoons often use humor to express their opinions on political issues. Sometimes these cartoonists are trying to inform and influence the public about a certain topic. To interpret a political cartoon, look for symbols, labels, and captions that provide clues about the message of the cartoonist. Analyze these elements and draw some conclusions. Study the political cartoon on this page and answer the questions that follow on a separate sheet of paper. **FCAT LA.A.2.3.2**

1. What is the subject of the cartoon?

2. What words provide clues as to the meaning of the cartoon?

3. Whom does the person in the cartoon represent?

4. What is the person doing?

5. What do the subject's thoughts suggest about the task faced by those involved in planning the new nation's government?

6. What limits are placed on First Amendment rights? Why are these rights limited?

LET'S SEE NOW...WE'LL GIVE THEM FREEDOM, BUT NOT TOO MUCH FREEDOM; LIBERTY, BUT NOT TOO MUCH LIBERTY; RIGHTS, BUT NOT TOO MANY RIGHTS...

P. harris

FCAT PRACTICE

DIRECTIONS: Use the political cartoon and your knowledge of social studies to answer the following questions on a separate sheet of paper.

1. The most appropriate title for the cartoon is

   FCAT LA.A.2.3.1

   A Limits on Government.

   B Parliament at Work.

   C Limiting Rights.

   D Unlimited Government.

2. The sources of our rights as citizens of the United States come from which of the following?

   FCAT LA.A.1.3.2

   F the Declaration of Independence and the U.S. Constitution

   G the will of the president

   H unwritten customs and traditions

   J the United Nations charter

Interpreting a Circle Graph

"E pluribus unum" is a Latin phrase found on United States coins. It means "Out of many, one." The United States is sometimes called a "nation of immigrants." Unless you are a Native American, your ancestors came to America within the last 500 years.

Groups of people who share a common culture, language, or history are referred to as ethnic groups. American neighborhoods include many different ethnic groups. The circle graph on this page shows the major ethnic groups in the United States.

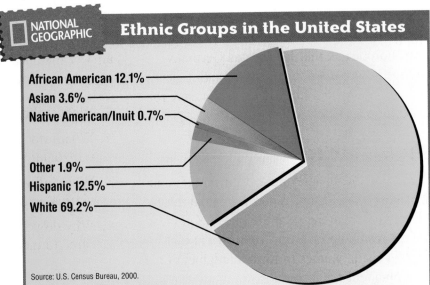

NATIONAL GEOGRAPHIC

Ethnic Groups in the United States

African American 12.1%
Asian 3.6%
Native American/Inuit 0.7%
Other 1.9%
Hispanic 12.5%
White 69.2%

Source: U.S. Census Bureau, 2000.

Skills Practice

A circle graph shows percentages of a total quantity. Each part, or slice, of the graph represents a part of the total quantity. To read a circle graph, first read the title. Then study the labels to find out what each part represents. Compare the sizes of the circle slices. Study the circle graph and answer the questions that follow on a separate sheet of paper. **FCAT MA.E.3.3.1**

1. What information does this circle graph present?

2. Which ethnic group includes the largest percentage of Americans?

3. Which groups represent less than 1 percent of the people in the United States?

4. What percentage of the United States population is represented by African Americans?

5. The smallest ethnic group has lived in the United States the longest. What is this ethnic group?

FCAT PRACTICE

DIRECTIONS: Use the graph and your knowledge of social studies to answer the following questions on a separate sheet of paper.

1. Which group's population is about three times greater than the number of Asians? **FCAT MA.E.3.3.1**

   A African American

   B White

   C Native American/Inuit

   D Other

2. How does the Hispanic population compare to the African American population of the United States? **FCAT MA.E.3.3.1**

   F It is greater than the African American population.

   G It is the smallest segment of the United States population.

   H It is less than half the size of the African American population.

   J It is slightly less than the African American population.

Drawing Inferences and Conclusions

During the mid-nineteenth century, immigration to the United States increased. People from European countries such as Germany and Ireland traveled to America seeking new opportunities. Life, however, was not easy for these immigrants.

Skills Practice

To infer means to evaluate information and arrive at a conclusion. When you make inferences, you "read between the lines." You must use the available facts and your own knowledge of social studies to form a judgment or opinion about the material.

Line graphs are a way of showing numbers visually. They are often used to compare changes over time. Sometimes a graph has more than one line. The lines show different quantities of a related topic. To analyze a line graph read the title and the information on the horizontal and vertical

axes. Use this information to draw conclusions. Study the graph on this page and answer the questions that follow on a separate sheet of paper. **FCAT** MA.E.3.3.1

1. What is the subject of the line graph?

2. What information is shown on the horizontal axis?

3. What information is shown on the vertical axis?

4. Why do you think these immigrants came to the United States?

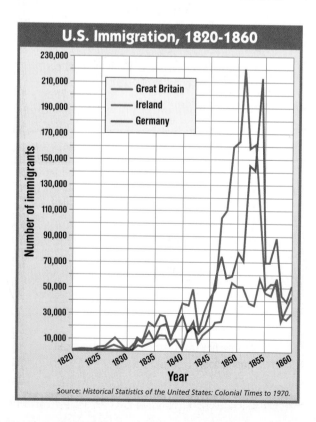

U.S. Immigration, 1820–1860

Great Britain
Ireland
Germany

Number of immigrants: 230,000 / 210,000 / 190,000 / 170,000 / 150,000 / 130,000 / 110,000 / 90,000 / 70,000 / 50,000 / 30,000 / 10,000

Year: 1820 / 1825 / 1830 / 1835 / 1840 / 1845 / 1850 / 1855 / 1860

Source: *Historical Statistics of the United States: Colonial Times to 1970.*

FCAT PRACTICE

DIRECTIONS: Use the line graph and your knowledge of social studies to answer the following questions on a separate sheet of paper.

1. The country that provided the most immigrants to the United States between the years 1820 and 1860 was **FCAT** MA.E.3.3.1

  A Great Britain.

  B Ireland.

  C Germany.

  D France.

2. In about what year did the number of German immigrants to the United States reach a peak?

  F 1845   **FCAT** MA.E.3.3.1

  G 1852

  H 1855

  J 1860

3. Irish migration to the United States increased in the mid-1800s because of **FCAT** MA.E.3.3.1

  A a terrible potato famine in Ireland.

  B the failure of a German revolution in 1848.

  C the nativist movement.

  D the availability of low-paying factory jobs.

Comparing Data

The world's earliest civilizations developed more than 6,000 years ago. The discovery of farming led to the rise of ancient cities in Mesopotamia and the Nile River valley. These early cities shared one important characteristic—they each arose near waterways. Since water was the easiest way to transport goods, the settlements became centers of trade.

Since then cities have grown all over the world. Every 10 years, the United States Census Bureau collects data to determine the population of the United States. (A census is an official count of people living in an area.) The first census was conducted in 1790. At that time, there were 3.9 million people in the 13 original states. The most recent census occurred in 2000. The results of that census showed that more than 280 million people reside in the 50 states that make up our nation.

POPULATION OF FIVE LARGEST U.S. CITIES, 1790

City	Number of People
New York City	33,131
Philadelphia	28,522
Boston	18,320
Charleston	16,359
Baltimore	13,503

POPULATION OF FIVE LARGEST U.S. CITIES, 2000*

City	Number of People
New York City	8,008,278
Los Angeles	3,694,820
Chicago	2,896,016
Houston	1,953,631
Philadelphia	1,517,550

*Numbers do not include metropolitan areas.

Skills Practice

The charts on this page show populations of the five most populous cities in the United States during different time periods. When comparing information on charts be sure to read the titles and headings to define the data being compared. Study the charts and answer the questions below on a separate sheet of paper. **FCAT MA.E.3.3.1**

1. Which U.S. city had the greatest population in 1790?

2. Which U.S. city had the greatest population in 2000?

3. What was the population of Philadelphia in 1790?

4. What was Philadelphia's population in 2000?

5. Which city had the third-largest population in 1790?

6. Which cities are on both lists?

FCAT PRACTICE

DIRECTIONS: Use the charts and your knowledge of social studies to answer the following questions on a separate sheet of paper.

1. One inference that can be made from the charts is that the most populous cities in the United States **FCAT MA.E.3.3.1**

   A have good weather.

   B were founded early in our nation's history.

   C are port cities.

   D are in the eastern United States.

2. In 1790 the major cities of the United States were all **FCAT MA.E.3.3.1**

   F larger than 20,000 people.

   G located in the East.

   H Northern cities.

   J founded for religious reasons.

Categorizing and Analyzing Information

Economic systems describe the ways in which societies produce and distribute goods and services. Early societies, such as Mesopotamia, used bartering as their system of trade. In the seventeenth and eighteenth centuries, European countries practiced mercantilism in which colonies provided wealth to their parent countries. Great Britain used this idea to gain wealth from its North American colonies. The economy of the United States is based on the principle of free enterprise. Americans have the freedom to own businesses with limited interference from the government.

Because Americans are employed in a variety of industries, our economy is the largest and among the most diverse in the world. The U.S. economy includes the following parts:

- Manufacturing and mining make up 18 percent of the economy.
- Agriculture makes up 2 percent of the economy.
- Service and information industries make up 80 percent of the economy.

Skills Practice

Grouping information into categories is one way of making the information easier to understand. The economic systems of today's world can be classified into four basic groups. Study the chart on this page and answer the questions that follow on a separate sheet of paper. **FCAT MA.E.3.3.1, MA.E.1.3.1**

1. Under which economic system does the government have the most control?

2. Under which system would people be most likely to have the same job as their parents?

3. Use the information about the U.S. economy on this page to create a circle graph. Then answer this question: Industries related to farming represent what percentage of the U.S. economy?

WORLD ECONOMIC SYSTEMS

Traditional	Command	Market	Mixed
Based on customs	Government controls production, prices, and wages	Individuals control production, prices, and wages	Individuals control some aspects of economy
Trades are passed down through generations	Communism; Government owns businesses	Free enterprise; Individuals own businesses	Government regulates selected industries and restricts others

FCAT PRACTICE

DIRECTIONS: Use the chart and your knowledge of social studies to answer the following questions on a separate sheet of paper.

1. Which economic system provides individuals with the most economic freedom? **FCAT LA.A.2.2.7**

A traditional

B command

C market

D mixed

2. The United States has this type of economic system. **FCAT LA.A.2.3.1**

F traditional

G command

H market

J mixed

Sequencing Events

The free enterprise economic system of the United States has encouraged Americans to invent and produce new technology throughout the history of our nation. Using its rich natural and human resources, Americans are continually advancing the economy through technology. The tremendous economic growth of the United States at certain times in history, such as after the Civil War, resulted from foundations laid early in the nation's history and affects the growth of the United States economy today.

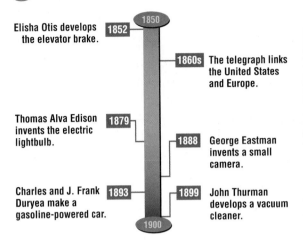

Skills Practice

Sequencing information involves placing facts in the order in which they occurred. Listed below are technological advances that occurred at different times in history, transforming the world economy. Find the date of each invention by studying the time line on page 98 of your textbook. On a separate sheet of paper, take notes by writing the date beside each invention. Then sequence the inventions by rewriting them in the order in which they were invented.

- Telephone
- Cellular phone
- Steamboat
- Space shuttle
- Radio
- Airplane
- Automobile
- Steam locomotive
- Internet
- Television

In the late 1800s, innovations in technology and new business combinations helped the United States grow into an industrial power. By the year 1900, the United States's industrial production was the greatest around the world.

Read the time line on this page. Determine the subject of the time line and summarize it in a few words. Then write a title for the time line on a separate sheet of paper. **FCAT LA.A.2.3.1**

DIRECTIONS: Use the events you have sequenced and your knowledge of social studies to answer the following questions on a separate sheet of paper.

1. Which of the following inventions occurred last? **FCAT LA.A.2.3.1**

   A steam locomotive

   B telephone

   C airplane

   D steamboat

2. During the late 1700s, 1800s, and early 1900s, new inventions and developments in the area of transportation, such as the steamboat, steam locomotive, and airplane, resulted in **FCAT LA.A.2.3.1**

   F increased poverty among urban Americans.

   G an end to westward migration.

   H the creation of new markets for trade.

   J rural growth.

3. In the early 1800s, steamboats dramatically improved the transport of goods and passengers **FCAT LA.A.1.3.2**

   A along major roads.

   B along major inland rivers.

   C between the Americas and Africa.

   D in the West.

Honoring America

For Americans, the flag has always had a special meaning. It is a symbol of our nation's freedom and democracy.

Flag Etiquette

Over the years, Americans have developed rules and customs concerning the use and display of the flag. One of the most important things every American should remember is to treat the flag with respect.

- The flag should be raised and lowered by hand and displayed only from sunrise to sunset. On special occasions, the flag may be displayed at night, but it should be illuminated.

- The flag may be displayed on all days, weather permitting, particularly on national and state holidays and on historic and special occasions.

- No flag may be flown above the American flag or to the right of it at the same height.

- The flag should never touch the ground or floor beneath it.

- The flag may be flown at half-staff by order of the president, usually to mourn the death of a public official.

- The flag may be flown upside down only to signal distress.

- When the flag becomes old and tattered, it should be destroyed by burning. According to an approved custom, the Union (stars on blue field) is first cut from the flag; then the two pieces, which no longer form a flag, are burned.

★ ★ ★ ★ ★ ★ ★ ★

The Star-Spangled Banner

O! say can you see, by the dawn's early light,
What so proudly we hail'd at the twilight's last gleaming,
Whose broad stripes and bright stars through the perilous fight,
O'er the ramparts we watched, were so gallantly streaming?
And the Rockets' red glare, the Bombs bursting in air,
Gave proof through the night that our Flag was still there;
O! say, does that star-spangled banner yet wave
O'er the Land of the free and the home of the brave!

The Pledge of Allegiance

I pledge allegiance to the Flag of the United States of America and to the Republic for which it stands, one Nation under God, indivisible, with liberty and justice for all.

GAZETTEER

Gazetteer

A gazetteer (GA•zuh•TIHR) is a geographic index or dictionary. It shows latitude and longitude for cities and certain other places. Latitude and longitude are shown in this way: 48°N 2°E, or 48 degrees north latitude and two degrees east longitude. This Gazetteer lists many important geographic features and most of the world's largest independent countries and their capitals. The page numbers tell where each entry can be found on a map in this book. As an aid to pronunciation, most entries are spelled phonetically.

Abidjan [AH•bee•JAHN] Capital of Côte d'Ivoire. 5°N 4°W (p. 539)

Abu Dhabi [AH•boo DAH•bee] Capital of the United Arab Emirates. 24°N 54°E (p. 459)

Abuja [ah•BOO•jah] Capital of Nigeria. 8°N 9°E (p. 539)

Accra [ah•KRUH] Capital of Ghana. 6°N 0° longitude (p. 539)

Addis Ababa [AHD•dihs AH•bah•BAH] Capital of Ethiopia. 9°N 39°E (p. 539)

Adriatic [AY•dree•A•tihk] **Sea** Arm of the Mediterranean Sea between the Balkan Peninsula and Italy. 44°N 14°E (p. 284)

Afghanistan [af•GA•nuh•STAN] Central Asian country west of Pakistan. 33°N 63°E (p. 459)

Albania [al•BAY•nee•uh] Country on the Adriatic Sea, south of Serbia and Montenegro. 42°N 20°E (p. 285)

Algeria [al•JIHR•ee•uh] North African country east of Morocco. 29°N 1°E (p. 459)

Algiers [al•JIHRZ] Capital of Algeria. 37°N 3°E (p. 459)

Alps [ALPS] Mountain ranges extending through central Europe. 46°N 9°E (p. 284)

Amazon [A•muh•ZAHN] **River** Largest river in the world by volume and second-largest in length. 2°S 53°W (p. 180)

Amman [a•MAHN] Capital of Jordan. 32°N 36°E (p. 459)

Amsterdam [AHM•stuhr•DAHM] Capital of the Netherlands. 52°N 5°E (p. 285)

Andes [AN•DEEZ] Mountain system extending north and south along the western side of South America. 13°S 75°W (p. 180)

Andorra [an•DAWR•uh] Small country in southern Europe between France and Spain. 43°N 2°E (p. 285)

Angola [ang•GOH•luh] Southern African country north of Namibia. 14°S 16°E (p. 539)

Ankara [AHNG•kuh•ruh] Capital of Turkey. 40°N 33°E (p. 459)

Antananarivo [AHN•tah•NAH•nah•REE•voh] Capital of Madagascar. 19°S 48°E (p. 539)

Arabian [uh•RAY•bee•uhn] **Peninsula** Large peninsula extending into the Arabian Sea. 28°N 40°E (p. 458)

Argentina [AHR•juhn•TEE•nuh] South American country east of Chile. 36°S 67°W (p. 181)

Armenia [ahr•MEE•nee•uh] European-Asian country between the Black and Caspian Seas. 40°N 45°E (p. 397)

Ashgabat [AHSH•gah•BAHT] Capital of Turkmenistan. 38°N 58°E (p. 397)

Asmara [az•MAHR•uh] Capital of Eritrea. 16°N 39°E (p. 539)

Astana Capital of Kazakhstan. 51°N 72°E (p. 397)

Asunción [ah•SOON•see•OHN] Capital of Paraguay. 25°S 58°W (p. 181)

Athens Capital of Greece. 38°N 24°E (p. 285)

Atlas [AT•luhs] **Mountains** Mountain range on the northern edge of the Sahara. 31°N 5°W (p. 458)

Australia [aw•STRAYL•yuh] Country and continent in Southern Hemisphere. 25°S 135°W (p. 729)

Austria [AWS•tree•uh] Western European country east of Switzerland and south of Germany and the Czech Republic. 47°N 12°E (p. 285)

Azerbaijan [A•zuhr•BY•JAHN] European-Asian country on the Caspian Sea. 40°N 47°E (p. 397)

Baghdad Capital of Iraq. 33°N 44°E (p. 459)

Bahamas [buh•HAH•muhz] Country made up of many islands between Cuba and the United States. 23°N 74°W (p. 180)

Bahrain [bah•RAYN] Country located on the Persian Gulf. 26°N 51°E (p. 459)

Baku [bah•KOO] Capital of Azerbaijan. 40°N 50°E (p. 397)

Balkan [BAWL•kuhn] **Peninsula** Peninsula in southeastern Europe. 42°N 20°E (p. 284)

Baltic [BAWL•tihk] **Sea** Sea in northern Europe that is connected to the North Sea. 55°N 17°E (p. 284)

Bamako [BAH•mah•KOH] Capital of Mali. 13°N 8°W (p. 539)

Bangkok [BANG•KAHK] Capital of Thailand. 14°N 100°E (p. 629)

Bangladesh [BAHNG•gluh•DEHSH] South Asian country bordered by India and Myanmar. 24°N 90°E (p. 629)

Bangui [BAHNG•GEE] Capital of the Central African Republic. 4°N 19°E (p. 539)

Banjul [BAHN•JOOL] Capital of Gambia. 13°N 17°W (p. 539)

Barbados [bahr•BAY•duhs] Island country between the Atlantic Ocean and the Caribbean Sea. 14°N 59°W (p. 181)

Beijing [BAY•JIHNG] Capital of China. 40°N 116°E (p. 629)

Beirut [bay•ROOT] Capital of Lebanon. 34°N 36°E (p. 459)

Belarus [BEE•luh•ROOS] Eastern European country west of Russia. 54°N 28°E (p. 285)

Belgium [BEHL•juhm] Western European country south of the Netherlands. 51°N 3°E (p. 285)

Belgrade [BEHL•GRAYD] Capital of Serbia and Montenegro. 45°N 21°E (p. 285)

Belize [buh•LEEZ] Central American country east of Guatemala. 18°N 89°W (p. 181)

Belmopan [BEHL•moh•PAHN] Capital of Belize. 17°N 89°W (p. 181)

Benin [buh•NEEN] West African country west of Nigeria. 8°N 2°E (p. 539)

Berlin [behr•LEEN] Capital of Germany. 53°N 13°E (p. 285)

Bern Capital of Switzerland. 47°N 7°E (p. 285)

Bhutan [boo•TAHN] South Asian country northeast of India. 27°N 91°E (p. 629)

Bishkek [bihsh•KEHK] Capital of Kyrgyzstan. 43°N 75°E (p. 397)

Bissau [bihs•SOW] Capital of Guinea-Bissau. 12°N 16°W (p. 539)

Black Sea Large sea between Europe and Asia. 43°N 32°E (p. 285)

Bloemfontein [BLOOM•FAHN•TAYN] Judicial capital of South Africa. 26°E 29°S (p. 539)

Bogotá [BOH•goh•TAH] Capital of Colombia. 5°N 74°W (p. 181)

Bolivia [buh•LIHV•ee•uh] Country in the central part of South America, north of Argentina. 17°S 64°W (p. 181)

Bosnia and Herzegovina [BAHZ•nee•uh HEHRT•seh•GAW•vee•nuh] Southeastern European country between Croatia and Serbia and Montenegro. 44°N 18°E (p. 285)

Botswana [bawt•SWAH•nah] Southern African country north of the Republic of South Africa. 22°S 23°E (p. 539)

Brasília [brah•ZEEL•yuh] Capital of Brazil. 16°S 48°W (p. 181)

Bratislava [BRAH•tih•SLAH•vuh] Capital of Slovakia. 48°N 17°E (p. 285)

Brazil [bruh•ZIHL] Largest country in South America. 9°S 53°W (p. 181)

Brazzaville [BRAH•zuh•VEEL] Capital of Congo. 4°S 15°E (p. 539)

Brunei [bru•NY] Southeast Asian country on northern coast of the island of Borneo. 5°N 114°E (p. 628)

Brussels [BRUH•suhlz] Capital of Belgium. 51°N 4°E (p. 285)

Bucharest [BOO•kuh•REHST] Capital of Romania. 44°N 26°E (p. 285)

Budapest [BOO•duh•PEHST] Capital of Hungary. 48°N 19°E (p. 285)

Buenos Aires [BWAY•nuhs AR•eez] Capital of Argentina. 34°S 58°W (p. 181)

Bujumbura [BOO•juhm•BUR•uh] Capital of Burundi. 3°S 29°E (p. 539)

Bulgaria [BUHL•GAR•ee•uh] Southeastern European country south of Romania. 42°N 24°E (p. 285)

Burkina Faso [bur•KEE•nuh FAH•soh] West African country south of Mali. 12°N 3°E (p. 539)

Burundi [bu•ROON•dee] East African country at the northern end of Lake Tanganyika. 3°S 30°E (p. 539)

Cairo [KY•ROH] Capital of Egypt. 31°N 32°E (p. 459)

Cambodia [kam•BOH•dee•uh] Southeast Asian country south of Thailand and Laos. 12°N 104°E (p. 629)

Cameroon [KA•muh•ROON] Central African country on the northeast shore of the Gulf of Guinea. 6°N 11°E (p. 539)

Canada [KA•nuh•duh] Northernmost country in North America. 50°N 100°W (p. 119)

Canberra [KAN•BEHR•uh] Capital of Australia. 35°S 149°E (p. 729)

Cape Town Legislative capital of the Republic of South Africa. 34°S 18°E (p. 539)

Cape Verde [VUHRD] Island country off the coast of western Africa in the Atlantic Ocean. 15°N 24°W (p. 539)

Caracas [kah•RAH•kahs] Capital of Venezuela. 11°N 67°W (p. 181)

Caribbean [KAR•uh•BEE•uhn] **Islands** Islands in the Caribbean Sea between North America and South America, also known as West Indies. 19°N 79°W (p. 180)

Caribbean Sea Part of the Atlantic Ocean bordered by the West Indies, South America, and Central America. 15°N 76°W (p. 180)

Caspian [KAS•pee•uhn] **Sea** Salt lake between Europe and Asia that is the world's largest inland body of water. 40°N 52°E (p. 396)

Caucasus [KAW•kuh•suhs] **Mountains** Mountain range between the Black and Caspian Seas. 43°N 42°E (p. 396)

Central African Republic Central African country south of Chad. 8°N 21°E (p. 539)

Chad [CHAD] Country west of Sudan in the African Sahel. 18°N 19°E (p. 539)

Chile [CHEE•lay] South American country west of Argentina. 35°S 72°W (p. 181)

China [CHY•nuh] Country in eastern and central Asia, known officially as the People's Republic of China. 37°N 93°E (p. 629)

Chişinău [KEE•shee•NOW] Capital of Moldova. 47°N 29°E (p. 285)

Colombia [kuh•LUHM•bee•uh] South American country west of Venezuela. 4°N 73°W (p. 181)

Colombo [kuh•LUHM•boh] Capital of Sri Lanka. 7°N 80°E (p. 629)

Comoros [KAH•muh•ROHZ] Small island country in Indian Ocean between the island of Madagascar and the southeast African mainland. 13°S 43°E (p. 539)

Conakry [KAH•nuh•kree] Capital of Guinea. 10°N 14°W (p. 539)

Congo [KAHNG•goh] Central African country east of the Democratic Republic of the Congo. 3°S 14°E (p. 539)

Congo, Democratic Republic of the Central African country north of Zambia and Angola. 1°S 22°E (p. 539)

Copenhagen [KOH•puhn•HAY•guhn] Capital of Denmark. 56°N 12°E (p. 285)

Costa Rica [KAWS•tah REE•kah] Central American country south of Nicaragua. 11°N 85°W (p. 181)

Côte d'Ivoire [KOHT dee•VWAHR] West African country south of Mali. 8°N 7°W (p. 539)

Croatia [kroh•AY•shuh] Southeastern European country on the Adriatic Sea. 46°N 16°E (p. 285)

Cuba [KYOO•buh] Island country in the Caribbean Sea. 22°N 79°W (p. 180)

Cyprus [SY•pruhs] Island country in the eastern Mediterranean Sea, south of Turkey. 35°N 31°E (p. 285)

Czech [CHEHK] **Republic** Eastern European country north of Austria. 50°N 15°E (p. 285)

Dakar [dah•KAHR] Capital of Senegal. 15°N 17°W (p. 539)

Damascus [duh•MAS•kuhs] Capital of Syria. 34°N 36°E (p. 459)

Dar es Salaam (DAHR EHS sah•LAHM] Capital of Tanzania. 7°S 39°E (p. 539)

Denmark [DEHN•MAHRK] Northern European country between the Baltic and North Seas. 56°N 9°E (p. 285)

Dhaka [DA•kuh] Capital of Bangladesh. 24°N 90°E (p. 629)

Djibouti [jih•BOO•tee] East African country on the Gulf of Aden. 12°N 43°E (p. 539)

Doha [DOH•huh] Capital of Qatar. 25°N 51°E (p. 459)

Dominican [duh•MIH•nih•kuhn] **Republic** Country in the Caribbean Sea on the eastern part of the island of Hispaniola. 19°N 71°W (p. 181)

Dublin [DUH•blihn] Capital of Ireland. 53°N 6°W (p. 285)

Dushanbe [doo•SHAM•buh] Capital of Tajikistan. 39°N 69°E (p. 397)

East Timor [TEE•MOHR] Previous province of Indonesia, now under UN administration. 10°S 127°E (p. 629)

Ecuador [EH•kwuh•DAWR] South American country southwest of Colombia. 0° latitude 79°W (p. 181)

Egypt [EE•jihpt] North African country on the Mediterranean Sea. 27°N 27°E (p. 459)

El Salvador [ehl SAL•vuh•DAWR] Central American country southwest of Honduras. 14°N 89°W (p. 181)

Equatorial Guinea [EE•kwuh•TOHR•ee•uhl GIH•nee] Central African country south of Cameroon. 2°N 8°E (p. 539)

Eritrea [EHR•uh•TREE•uh] East African country north of Ethiopia. 17°N 39°E (p. 539)

Estonia [eh•STOH•nee•uh] Eastern European country on the Baltic Sea. 59°N 25°E (p. 285)

Ethiopia [EE•thee•OH•pee•uh] East African country north of Somalia and Kenya. 8°N 38°E (p. 539)

Euphrates [yu•FRAY•TEEZ] **River** River in southwestern Asia that flows through Syria and Iraq and joins the Tigris River. 36°N 40°E (p. 458)

Fiji [FEE•jee] **Islands** Country comprised of an island group in the southwest Pacific Ocean. 19°S 175°E (p. 729)

Finland [FIHN•luhnd] Northern European country east of Sweden. 63°N 26°E (p. 285)

France [FRANS] Western European country south of the United Kingdom. 47°N 1°E (p. 285)

Freetown [FREE•TOWN] Capital of Sierra Leone. 9°N 13°W (p. 539)

French Guiana [gee•A•nuh] French-owned territory in northern South America. 5°N 53°W (p. 181)

Gabon [ga•BOHN] Central African country on the Atlantic Ocean. 0° latitude 12°E (p. 539)

Gaborone [GAH•boh•ROH•NAY] Capital of Botswana. 24°S 26°E (p. 539)

Gambia [GAM•bee•uh] West African country along the Gambia River. 13°N 16°W (p. 539)

Georgetown [JAWRJ•TOWN] Capital of Guyana. 8°N 58°W (p. 181)

Georgia [JAWR•juh] European-Asian country bordering the Black Sea south of Russia. 42°N 43°E (p. 397)

Germany [JUHR•muh•nee] Western European country south of Denmark, officially called the Federal Republic of Germany. 52°N 10°E (p. 285)

Ghana [GAH•nuh] West African country on the Gulf of Guinea. 8°N 2°W (p. 539)

Great Plains The continental slope extending through the United States and Canada. 45°N 104°W (p. 118)

Greece [GREES] Southern European country on the Balkan Peninsula. 39°N 22°E (p. 285)

Greenland [GREEN•luhnd] Island in northwestern Atlantic Ocean and the largest island in the world. 74°N 40°W (p. 119)

Guatemala [GWAH•tay•MAH•lah] Central American country south of Mexico. 16°N 92°W (p. 181)

Guatemala City Capital of Guatemala. 15°N 91°W (p. 181)

Guinea [GIH•nee] West African country on the Atlantic coast. 11°N 12°W (p. 539)

Guinea-Bissau [GIH•nee bih•SOW] West African country on the Atlantic coast. 12°N 20°W (p. 539)

Gulf of Mexico Gulf on part of the southern coast of North America. 25°N 94°W (p. 118)

Guyana [gy•AH•nuh] South American country between Venezuela and Suriname. 8°N 59°W (p. 181)

Haiti [HAY•tee] Country in the Caribbean Sea on the western part of the island of Hispaniola. 19°N 72°W (p. 181)

Hanoi [ha•NOY] Capital of Vietnam. 21°N 106°E (p. 629)

Harare [hah•RAH•RAY] Capital of Zimbabwe. 18°S 31°E (p. 539)

Havana [huh•VA•nuh] Capital of Cuba. 23°N 82°W (p. 181)

Helsinki [HEHL•SIHNG•kee] Capital of Finland. 60°N 24°E (p. 285)

Himalaya [HI•muh•LAY•uh] Mountain ranges in southern Asia, bordering the Indian subcontinent on the north. 30°N 85°E (p. 628)

Honduras [hahn•DUR•uhs] Central American country on the Caribbean Sea. 15°N 88°W (p. 181)

Hong Kong [HAWNG KAWNG] Port and industrial center in southern China. 22°N 115°E (p. 629)

Hungary [HUHNG•guh•ree] Eastern European country south of Slovakia. 47°N 18°E (p. 285)

Iberian [eye•BIHR•ee•uhn] **Peninsula** Peninsula in southwest Europe, occupied by Spain and Portugal. 41°N 1°W (p. 284)

Iceland Island country between the North Atlantic and Arctic Oceans, 65°N 20°W (p. 285)

India [IHN•dee•uh] South Asian country south of China and Nepal. 23°N 78°E (p. 629)

Indonesia [IHN•duh•NEE•zhuh] Southeast Asian island country known as the Republic of Indonesia. 5°S 119°E (p. 629)

Indus [IHN•duhs] **River** River in Asia that begins in Tibet and flows through Pakistan to the Arabian Sea. 27°N 68°E (p. 628)

Iran [ih•RAN] Southwest Asian country that was formerly named Persia. 31°N 54°E (p. 459)

Iraq [ih•RAHK] Southwest Asian country west of Iran. 32°N 43°E (p. 459)

Ireland [EYER•luhnd] Island west of Great Britain occupied by the Republic of Ireland and Northern Ireland. 54°N 8°W (p. 285)

Islamabad [ihs•LAH•muh•BAHD] Capital of Pakistan. 34°N 73°E (p. 629)

Israel [IHZ•ree•uhl] Southwest Asian country south of Lebanon. 33°N 34°E (p. 459)

Italy [IHT•uhl•ee] Southern European country south of Switzerland and east of France. 44°N 11°E (p. 285)

Jakarta [juh•KAHR•tuh] Capital of Indonesia. 6°S 107°E (p. 629)

Jamaica [juh•MAY•kuh] Island country in the Caribbean Sea. 18°N 78°W (p. 181)

Japan [juh•PAN] East Asian country consisting of the four large islands of Hokkaido, Honshu, Shikoku, and Kyushu, plus thousands of small islands. 37°N 134°E (p. 628)

Jerusalem [juh•ROO•suh•luhm] Capital of Israel and a holy city for Christians, Jews, and Muslims. 32°N 35°E (p. 459)

Jordan [JAWRD•uhn] Southwest Asian country south of Syria. 30°N 38°E (p. 459)

Kabul [KAH•buhl] Capital of Afghanistan. 35°N 69°E (p. 459)

Kampala [kahm•PAH•lah] Capital of Uganda. 0° latitude 32°E (p. 539)

Kathmandu [KAT•MAN•DOO] Capital of Nepal. 28°N 85°E (p. 629)

Kazakhstan [kuh•ZAHK•STAHN] Large Asian country south of Russia and bordering the Caspian Sea. 48°N 59°E (p. 397)

Kenya [KEHN•yuh] East African country south of Ethiopia. 1°N 37°E (p. 539)

Khartoum [kahr•TOOM] Capital of Sudan. 16°N 33°E (p. 539)

Kiev [KEE•ihf] Capital of Ukraine. 50°N 31°E (p. 285)

Kigali [kee•GAH•lee] Capital of Rwanda. 2°S 30°E (p. 539)

Kingston [KIHNG•stuhn] Capital of Jamaica. 18°N 77°W (p. 181)

Kinshasa [kihn•SHAH•suh] Capital of the Democratic Republic of the Congo. 4°S 15°E (p. 539)

Kuala Lumpur [KWAH•luh LUM•PUR] Capital of Malaysia. 3°N 102°E (p. 629)

Kuwait [ku•WAYT] Country on the Persian Gulf between Saudi Arabia and Iraq. 29°N 48°E (p. 459)

Kyrgyzstan [KIHR•gih•STAN] Central Asian country on China's western border. 41°N 75°E (p. 397)

Laos [LOWS] Southeast Asian country south of China and west of Vietnam. 20°N 102°E (p. 629)

La Paz [lah PAHS] Administrative capital of Bolivia, and the highest capital in the world. 17°S 68°W (p. 181)

Latvia [LAT•vee•uh] Eastern European country west of Russia on the Baltic Sea. 57°N 25°E (p. 285)

GAZETTEER

Lebanon [LEH•buh•nuhn] Country south of Syria on the Mediterranean Sea. 34°N 34°E (p. 459)

Lesotho [luh•SOH•TOH] Southern African country within the borders of the Republic of South Africa. 30°S 28°E (p. 539)

Liberia [ly•BIHR•ee•uh] West African country south of Guinea. 7°N 10°W (p. 539)

Libreville [LEE•bruh•VIHL] Capital of Gabon. 1°N 9°E (p. 539)

Libya [LIH•bee•uh] North African country west of Egypt on the Mediterranean Sea. 28°N 15°E (p. 459)

Liechtenstein [LIHKT•uhn•SHTYN] Small country in central Europe between Switzerland and Austria. 47°N 10°E (p. 285)

Lilongwe [lih•LAWNG•GWAY] Capital of Malawi. 14°S 34°E (p. 539)

Lima [LEE•mah] Capital of Peru. 12°S 77°W (p. 181)

Lisbon [LIHZ•buhn] Capital of Portugal. 39°N 9°W (p. 285)

Lithuania [LIH•thuh•WAY•nee•uh] Eastern European country northwest of Belarus on the Baltic Sea. 56°N 24°E (p. 285)

Ljubljana [lee•oo•blee•AH•nuh] Capital of Slovenia. 46°N 14°E (p. 285)

Lomé [loh•MAY] Capital of Togo. 6°N 1°E (p. 539)

London [LUHN•duhn] Capital of the United Kingdom, on the Thames River. 52°N 0° longitude (p. 285)

Luanda [lu•AHN•duh] Capital of Angola. 9°S 13°E (p. 539)

Lusaka [loo•SAH•kah] Capital of Zambia. 15°S 28°E (p. 539)

Luxembourg [LUHK•suhm•BUHRG] Small European country between France, Belgium, and Germany. 50°N 7°E (p. 285)

Macau [muh•KOW] Port in southern China. 22°N 113°E (p. 629)

Macedonia [MA•suh•DOH•nee•uh] Southeastern European country north of Greece. 42°N 22°E (p. 285). Macedonia also refers to a geographic region covering northern Greece, the country Macedonia, and part of Bulgaria.

Madagascar [MA•duh•GAS•kuhr] Island in the Indian Ocean off the southeastern coast of Africa. 18°S 43°E (p. 539)

Madrid [muh•DRIHD] Capital of Spain. 41°N 4°W (p. 285)

Malabo [mah•LAH•boh] Capital of Equatorial Guinea. 4°N 9°E (p. 539)

Malawi [mah•LAH•wee] Southern African country south of Tanzania and east of Zambia. 11°S 34°E (p. 539)

Malaysia [muh•LAY•zhuh] Southeast Asian country with land on the Malay Peninsula and on the island of Borneo. 4°N 101°E (p. 628)

Maldives [MAWL•DEEVZ] Island country southwest of India in the Indian Ocean. 5°N 42°E (p. 629)

Mali [MAH•lee] West African country east of Mauritania. 16°N 0° longitude (p. 539)

Managua [mah•NAH•gwah] Capital of Nicaragua. 12°N 86°W (p. 181)

Manila [muh•NIH•luh] Capital of the Philippines. 15°N 121°E (p. 629)

Maputo [mah•POO•toh] Capital of Mozambique. 26°S 33°E (p. 539)

Maseru [MA•zuh•ROO] Capital of Lesotho. 29°S 27°E (p. 539)

Mauritania [MAWR•uh•TAY•nee•uh] West African country north of Senegal. 20°N 14°W (p. 539)

Mauritius [maw•RIH•shuhs] Island country in the Indian Ocean east of Madagascar. 21°S 58°E (p. 539)

Mbabane [uhm•bah•BAH•nay] Capital of Swaziland. 26°S 31°E (p. 539)

Mediterranean [MEH•duh•tuh•RAY•nee•uhn] **Sea** Large inland sea surrounded by Europe, Asia, and Africa. 36°N 13°E (p. 284)

Mekong [MAY•KAWNG] **River** River in southeastern Asia that begins in Tibet and empties into the South China Sea. 18°N 104°E (p. 628)

Mexico [MEHK•sih•KOH] North American country south of the United States. 24°N 104°W (p. 180)

Mexico City Capital of Mexico. 19°N 99°W (p. 181)

Minsk [MIHNSK] Capital of Belarus. 54°N 28°E (p. 285)

Mississippi [MIH•suh•SIH•pee] **River** Large river system in the central United States that flows southward into the Gulf of Mexico. 32°N 92°W (p. 118)

Mogadishu [MOH•guh•DEE•SHOO] Capital of Somalia. 2°N 45°E (p. 539)

Moldova [mawl•DAW•vuh] Small European country between Ukraine and Romania. 48°N 28°E (p. 285)

Monaco [MAH•nuh•KOH] Small country in southern Europe on the French Mediterranean coast. 44°N 8°E (p. 285)

Mongolia [mahn•GOHL•yuh] Country in Asia between Russia and China. 46°N 100°E (p. 629)

Monrovia [muhn•ROH•vee•uh] Capital of Liberia. 6°N 11°W (p. 539)

Montevideo [MAHN•tuh•vuh•DAY•OH] Capital of Uruguay. 35°S 56°W (p. 181)

Morocco [muh•RAH•KOH] North African country on the Mediterranean Sea and the Atlantic Ocean. 32°N 7°W (p. 459)

Moscow [MAHS•KOW] Capital of Russia. 56°N 38°E (p. 397)

Mount Everest [EHV•ruhst] Highest mountain in the world, in the Himalaya between Nepal and Tibet. 28°N 87°E (p. 628)

Mozambique [MOH•zahm•BEEK] Southern African country south of Tanzania. 20°S 34°E (p. 539)

Muscat [MUHS•KAHT] Capital of Oman. 23°N 59°E (p. 459)

Myanmar [MYAHN•MAHR] Southeast Asian country south of China and India, formerly called Burma. 21°N 95°E (p. 629)

Nairobi [ny•ROH•bee] Capital of Kenya. 1°S 37°E (p. 539)

GAZETTEER

Namibia [nuh•MIH•bee•uh] Southern African country south of Angola on the Atlantic Ocean. 20°S 16°E (p. 539)

Nassau [NA•SAW] Capital of the Bahamas. 25°N 77°W (p. 181)

N'Djamena [uhn•jah•MAY•nah] Capital of Chad. 12°N 15°E (p. 539)

Nepal [NAY•PAHL] Mountain country between India and China. 29°N 83°E (p. 629)

Netherlands [NEH•thuhr•lundz] Western European country north of Belgium. 53°N 4°E (p. 285)

New Delhi [NOO DEH•lee] Capital of India. 29°N 77°E (p. 629)

New Zealand [NOO ZEE•luhnd] Major island country southeast of Australia in the South Pacific. 42°S 175°E (p. 729)

Niamey [nee•AHM•ay] Capital of Niger. 14°N 2°E (p. 539)

Nicaragua [NIH•kuh•RAH•gwuh] Central American country south of Honduras. 13°N 86°W (p. 181)

Nicosia [NIH•kuh•SEE•uh] Capital of Cyprus. 35°N 33°E (p. 285)

Niger [NY•juhr] West African country north of Nigeria. 18°N 9°E (p. 539)

Nigeria [ny•JIHR•ee•uh] West African country along the Gulf of Guinea. 9°N 7°E (p. 539)

Nile [NYL] **River** Longest river in the world, flowing north through eastern Africa. 19°N 33°E (p. 458)

North Korea [kuh•REE•uh] East Asian country in the northernmost part of the Korean Peninsula. 40°N 127°E (p. 629)

Norway [NAWR•WAY] Northern European country on the Scandinavian peninsula. 64°N 11°E (p. 285)

Nouakchott [nu•AHK•SHAHT] Capital of Mauritania. 18°N 16°W (p. 539)

Oman [oh•MAHN] Country on the Arabian Sea and the Gulf of Oman. 20°N 58°E (p. 459)

Oslo [AHZ•loh] Capital of Norway. 60°N 11°E (p. 285)

Ottawa [AH•tuh•wuh] Capital of Canada. 45°N 76°W (p. 119)

Ouagadougou [WAH•gah•DOO•goo] Capital of Burkina Faso. 12°N 2°W (p. 539)

Pakistan [PA•kih•STAN] South Asian country northwest of India on the Arabian Sea. 28°N 68°E (p. 629)

Palau [puh•LOW] Island country in the Pacific Ocean. 7°N 135°E (p. 729)

Panama [PA•nuh•MAH] Central American country on the Isthmus of Panama. 9°N 81°W (p. 180)

Panama City Capital of Panama. 9°N 79°W (p. 181)

Papua New Guinea [PA•pyu•wuh NOO GIH•nee] Island country in the Pacific Ocean north of Australia. 7°S 142°E (p. 729)

Paraguay [PAR•uh•GWY] South American country northeast of Argentina. 24°S 57°W (p. 181)

Paramaribo [PAH•rah•MAH•ree•boh] Capital of Suriname. 6°N 55°W (p. 181)

Paris [PAR•uhs] Capital of France. 49°N 2°E (p. 285)

Persian [PUHR•zhuhn] **Gulf** Arm of the Arabian Sea between Iran and Saudi Arabia. 28°N 51°E (p. 458)

Peru [puh•ROO] South American country south of Ecuador and Colombia. 10°S 75°W (p. 181)

Philippines [FIH•luh•PEENZ] Island country in the Pacific Ocean southeast of China. 14°N 125°E (p. 629)

Phnom Penh [puh•NAWM PEHN] Capital of Cambodia. 12°N 106°E (p. 629)

Poland [POH•luhnd] Eastern European country on the Baltic Sea. 52°N 18°E (p. 285)

Port-au-Prince [POHRT•oh•PRIHNS] Capital of Haiti. 19°N 72°W (p. 181)

Port Moresby [MOHRZ•bee] Capital of Papua New Guinea. 10°S 147°E (p. 729)

Port-of-Spain [SPAYN] Capital of Trinidad and Tobago. 11°N 62°W (p. 181)

Porto-Novo [POHR•toh•NOH•voh] Capital of Benin. 7°N 3°E (p. 539)

Portugal [POHR•chih•guhl] Country west of Spain on the Iberian Peninsula. 39°N 8°W (p. 285)

Prague [PRAHG] Capital of the Czech Republic. 51°N 15°E (p. 285)

Pretoria [prih•TOHR•ee•uh] Executive capital of South Africa. 26°S 28°E (p. 539)

Puerto Rico [PWEHR•toh REE•koh] Island in the Caribbean Sea; U.S. Commonwealth. 19°N 67°W (p. 181)

Pyongyang [pee•AWNG•YAHNG] Capital of North Korea. 39°N 126°E (p. 629)

Qatar [KAH•tuhr] Country on the southwestern shore of the Persian Gulf. 25°N 53°E (p. 459)

Quito [KEE•toh] Capital of Ecuador. 0° latitude 79°W (p. 181)

Rabat [ruh•BAHT] Capital of Morocco. 34°N 7°W (p. 459)

Reykjavík [RAY•kyah•VEEK] Capital of Iceland. 64°N 22°W (p. 285)

Rhine [RYN] **River** River in western Europe that flows into the North Sea. 51°N 7°E (p. 284)

Riga [REE•guh] Capital of Latvia. 57°N 24°E (p. 285)

Rio Grande [REE•oh GRAND] River that forms part of the boundary between the United States and Mexico. 30°N 103°W (p. 119)

Riyadh [ree•YAHD] Capital of Saudi Arabia. 25°N 47°E (p. 459)

Rocky Mountains Mountain system in western North America. 50°N 114°W (p. 118)

Romania (ru•MAY•nee•uh] Eastern European country east of Hungary. 46°N 23°E (p. 285)

Rome [ROHM] Capital of Italy. 42°N 13°E (p. 285)

Russia [RUH•shuh] Largest country in the world, covering parts of Europe and Asia. 60°N 90°E (p. 397)

Rwanda [ruh•WAHN•duh] East African country south of Uganda. 2°S 30°E (p. 539)

Sahara [suh•HAR•uh] Desert region in northern Africa that is the largest hot desert in the world. 24°N 2°W (p. 458)

Saint Lawrence [LAWR•uhns] **River** River that flows from Lake Ontario to the Atlantic Ocean and forms part of the boundary between the United States and Canada. 48°N 70°W (p. 119)

Sanaa [sahn•AH] Capital of Yemen. 15°N 44°E (p. 459)

San José [SAN hoh•ZAY] Capital of Costa Rica. 10°N 84°W (p. 181)

San Marino [SAN muh•REE•noh] Small European country located in the Italian peninsula. 44°N 13°E (p. 285)

San Salvador [san SAL•vuh•DAWR] Capital of El Salvador. 14°N 89°W (p. 181)

Santiago [SAN•tee•AH•goh] Capital of Chile. 33°S 71°W (p. 181)

Santo Domingo [SAN•toh duh•MIHNG•goh] Capital of the Dominican Republic. 19°N 70°W (p. 181)

Sao Tome and Principe [SOW•too•MAY PREEN•see•pee] Small island country in the Gulf of Guinea off the coast of central Africa. 1°N 7°E (p. 539)

Sarajevo [SAR•uh•YAY•voh] Capital of Bosnia and Herzegovina. 43°N 18°E (p. 285)

Saudi Arabia [SOW•dee uh•RAY•bee•uh] Country on the Arabian Peninsula. 23°N 46°E (p. 459)

Senegal [SEH•nih•GAWL] West African country on the Atlantic coast. 15°N 14°W (p. 539)

Seoul [SOHL] Capital of South Korea. 38°N 127°E (p. 629)

Serbia and Montenegro [SUHR•bee•uh MAHN•tuh•NEE•groh] Eastern European country south of Hungary. 44°N 21°E (p. 285)

Seychelles [say•SHEHL] Small island country in the Indian Ocean off eastern Africa. 6°S 56°E (p. 539)

Sierra Leone [see•EHR•uh lee•OHN] West African country south of Guinea. 8°N 12°W (p. 539)

Singapore [SIHNG•uh•POHR] Southeast Asian island country near tip of Malay Peninsula. 2°N 104°E (p. 629)

Skopje [SKAW•PYAY] Capital of the country of Macedonia. 42°N 21°E (p. 285)

Slovakia [sloh•VAH•kee•uh] Eastern European country south of Poland. 49°N 19°E (p. 285)

Slovenia [sloh•VEE•nee•uh] Southeastern European country south of Austria on the Adriatic Sea. 46°N 15°E (p. 285)

Sofia [SOH•fee•uh] Capital of Bulgaria. 43°N 23°E (p. 285)

Solomon [SAH•luh•muhn] **Islands** Island country in the Pacific Ocean northeast of Australia. 7°S 160°E (p. 729)

Somalia [soh•MAH•lee•uh] East African country on the Gulf of Aden and the Indian Ocean. 3°N 45°E (p. 539)

South Africa [A•frih•kuh] Country at the southern tip of Africa, officially the Republic of South Africa. 28°S 25°E (p. 539)

South Korea [kuh•REE•uh] East Asian country on the Korean Peninsula between the Yellow Sea and the Sea of Japan. 36°N 128°E (p. 629)

Spain [SPAYN] Southern European country on the Iberian Peninsula. 40°N 4°W (p. 285)

Sri Lanka [SREE•LAHNG•kuh] Country in the Indian Ocean south of India, formerly called Ceylon. 9°N 83°E (p. 629)

Stockholm [STAHK•HOHLM] Capital of Sweden. 59°N 18°E (p. 285)

Sucre [SOO•kray] Constitutional capital of Bolivia. 19°S 65°W (p. 181)

Sudan [soo•DAN] East African country south of Egypt. 14°N 28°E (p. 539)

Suriname [SUR•uh•NAH•muh] South American country between Guyana and French Guiana. 4°N 56°W (p. 181)

Suva [SOO•vah] Capital of the Fiji Islands. 18°S 177°E (p. 729)

Swaziland [SWAH•zee•LAND] Southern African country west of Mozambique, almost entirely within the Republic of South Africa. 27°S 32°E (p. 539)

Sweden [SWEED•uhn] Northern European country on the eastern side of the Scandinavian peninsula. 60°N 14°E (p. 285)

Switzerland [SWIHT•suhr•luhnd] European country in the Alps south of Germany. 47°N 8°E (p. 285)

Syria [SIHR•ee•uh] Southwest Asian country on the east side of the Mediterranean Sea. 35°N 37°E (p. 459)

Taipei [TY•PAY] Capital of Taiwan. 25°N 122°E (p. 629)

Taiwan [TY•WAHN] Island country off the southeast coast of China; the seat of the Chinese Nationalist government. 24°N 122°E (p. 629)

Tajikistan [tah•JIH•kih•STAN] Central Asian country east of Turkmenistan. 39°N 70°E (p. 397)

Tallinn [TA•luhn] Capital of Estonia. 59°N 25°E (p. 285)

Tanzania [TAN•zuh•NEE•uh] East African country south of Kenya. 7°S 34°E (p. 539)

Tashkent [tash•KEHNT] Capital of Uzbekistan. 41°N 69°E (p. 397)

T'bilisi [tuh•bih•LEE•see] Capital of the Republic of Georgia. 42°N 45°E (p. 397)

Tegucigalpa [tay•GOO•see•GAHL•pah] Capital of Honduras. 14°N 87°W (p. 181)

Tehran [TAY•uh•RAN] Capital of Iran. 36°N 52°E (p. 459)

Thailand [TY•LAND] Southeast Asian country east of Myanmar. 17°N 101°E (p. 629)

Thimphu [thihm•POO] Capital of Bhutan. 28°N 90°E (p. 629)

Tigris [TY•gruhs] **River** River in southeastern Turkey and Iraq that merges with the Euphrates River. 35°N 44°E (p. 458)

Tirana [tih•RAH•nuh] Capital of Albania. 42°N 20°E (p. 285)

Togo [TOH•goh] West African country between Benin and Ghana on the Gulf of Guinea. 8°N 1°E (p. 539)

Tokyo [TOH•kee•OH] Capital of Japan. 36°N 140°E (p. 629)

Trinidad and Tobago [TRIH•nuh•DAD tuh•BAY•goh] Island country near Venezuela between the Atlantic Ocean and the Caribbean Sea. 11°N 61°W (p. 181)

Tripoli [TRIH•puh•lee] Capital of Libya. 33°N 13°E (p. 459)

Tunis [TOO•nuhs] Capital of Tunisia. 37°N 10°E (p. 459)

Tunisia [too•NEE•zhuh] North African country on the Mediterranean Sea between Libya and Algeria. 35°N 10°E (p. 459)

Turkey [TUHR•kee] Country in southeastern Europe and western Asia. 39°N 32°E (p. 459)

Turkmenistan [tuhrk•MEH•nuh•STAN] Central Asian country on the Caspian Sea. 41°N 56°E (p. 397)

Uganda [yoo•GAHN•dah] East African country south of Sudan. 2°N 32°E (p. 539)

Ukraine [yoo•KRAYN] Eastern European country west of Russia on the Black Sea. 49°N 30°E (p. 285)

Ulaanbaatar [OO•LAHN•BAH•TAWR] Capital of Mongolia. 48°N 107°E (p. 629)

United Arab Emirates [EH•muh•ruhts] Country made up of seven states on the eastern side of the Arabian Peninsula. 24°N 54°E (p. 459)

United Kingdom Western European island country made up of England, Scotland, Wales, and Northern Ireland. 57°N 2°W (p. 285)

United States of America Country in North America made up of 50 states, mostly between Canada and Mexico. 38°N 110°W (p. 119)

Uruguay [YUR•uh•GWAY] South American country south of Brazil on the Atlantic Ocean. 33°S 56°W (p. 181)

Uzbekistan [UZ•BEH•kih•STAN] Central Asian country south of Kazakhstan. 42°N 60°E (p. 397)

Vanuatu [VAN•WAH•TOO] Country made up of islands in the Pacific Ocean east of Australia. 17°S 170°W (p. 729)

Vatican [VA•tih•kuhn] **City** Headquarters of the Roman Catholic Church, located in the city of Rome in Italy. 42°N 13°E (p. 285)

Venezuela [VEH•nuh•ZWAY•luh] South American country on the Caribbean Sea between Colombia and Guyana. 8°N 65°W (p. 181)

Vienna [vee•EH•nuh] Capital of Austria. 48°N 16°E (p. 285)

Vientiane [vyehn•TYAHN] Capital of Laos. 18°N 103°E (p. 629)

Vietnam [vee•EHT•NAHM] Southeast Asian country east of Laos and Cambodia. 18°N 107°E (p. 629)

Vilnius [VIL•nee•uhs] Capital of Lithuania. 55°N 25°E (p. 285)

Warsaw [WAWR•SAW] Capital of Poland. 52°N 21°E (p. 285)

Washington, D.C. Capital of the United States, in the District of Columbia. 39°N 77°W (p. 119)

Wellington [WEH•lihng•tuhn] Capital of New Zealand. 41°S 175°E (p. 729)

West Indies [IHN•deez] Caribbean islands between North America and South America. 19°N 79°W (p. 180)

Windhoek [VIHNT•HUK] Capital of Namibia. 22°S 17°E (p. 539)

Yamoussoukro [YAH•moo•SOO•kroh] Second capital of Côte d'Ivoire. 7°N 6°W (p. 539)

Yangon [YAHNG•GOHN] Capital of Myanmar, formerly called Rangoon. 17°N 96°E (p. 629)

Yangtze [YANG•SEE] **River** Principal river of China that begins in Tibet and flows into the East China Sea near Shanghai, also known as the Chang Jiang [CHAHNG jee•AHNG]. 31°N 117°E (p. 628)

Yaoundé [yown•DAY] Capital of Cameroon. 4°N 12°E (p. 539)

Yellow River River in northern and eastern China, also known as the Huang He [HWAHNG HUH]. 35°N 114°E (p. 628)

Yemen [YEH•muhn] Country south of Saudi Arabia on the Arabian Peninsula. 15°N 46°E (p. 459)

Yerevan [YEHR•uh•VAHN] Capital of Armenia. 40°N 44°E (p. 397)

Zagreb [ZAH•GREHB] Capital of Croatia. 46°N 16°E (p. 285)

Zambia [ZAM•bee•uh] Southern African country north of Zimbabwe. 14°S 24°E (p. 539)

Zimbabwe [zihm•BAH•bway] Southern African country northeast of Botswana. 18°S 30°E (p. 539)

A

absolute location   exact position of a place on the earth's surface (p. 5)

acid rain   rain containing high amounts of chemical pollutants (pp. 70, 135, 370)

adobe   sun-dried clay bricks (p. 202)

airlift   system of carrying supplies by aircraft (p. 322)

alluvial plain   area that is built up by rich fertile soil left by river floods (p. 517)

altiplano   large highland plateau (p. 271)

altitude   height above sea level (pp. 193, 243)

apartheid   system of laws that separated racial and ethnic groups and limited the rights of blacks in South Africa (p. 606)

aquifer   underground rock layer that water flows through (pp. 50, 490)

archipelago   group of islands (pp. 219, 690)

artifact   object made by early people (p. 27)

atmosphere   layer of air surrounding the earth (p. 30)

atoll   low-lying, ring-shaped island that surrounds a lagoon (pp. 654, 760)

autobahn   superhighway (p. 351)

autonomy   self-government (pp. 168, 583)

axis   imaginary line that runs through the earth's center between the North and South poles (p. 31); *also* horizontal (bottom) or vertical (side) line of measurement on a graph (p. 11)

B

bar graph   graph in which vertical or horizontal bars represent quantities (p. 11)

basin   low area surrounded by higher land (p. 232)

bauxite   mineral used to make aluminum (pp. 220, 560)

bazaar   marketplace (p. 488)

bedouins   nomadic desert peoples of Southwest Asia (p. 505)

bilingual   referring to a country that has two official languages (pp. 167, 440)

birthrate   number of children born each year for every 1,000 people (p. 88)

blockade   to forcibly prevent entry to an area (p. 321)

Boers   name for the Dutch who were the first European settlers in South Africa (p. 605)

bog   low swampy land (pp. 342, 368)

boomerang   Australian weapon that is flat, bent, and made of wood that either strikes a target or curves and sails back to the person who threw it (p. 738)

bush   rural areas of Australia (p. 739)

C

cacao   tropical tree whose seeds are used to make chocolate and cocoa (pp. 552, 759)

caliph   successor to Muhammad (p. 514)

calligraphy   art of beautiful writing (p. 670)

campesino   Colombian farmer (p. 257)

canopy   umbrella-like covering formed by the tops of trees in a rain forest (pp. 214, 571)

cardinal directions   basic directions on the earth: north, south, east, west (p. 8)

cartographer   person who makes maps (p. 6)

casbah   older section of Algerian cities (p. 492)

cash crop   product grown to be sold for export (pp. 256, 438)

cassava   plant with roots that can be ground into flour to make bread or porridge (p. 578)

caste   social class based on a person's ancestry (p. 640)

caudillo   military ruler (p. 243)

channel   body of water wider than a strait between two pieces of land (p. 42)

chart   graphic way of presenting information clearly (p. 12)

charter   written agreement guaranteeing privileges and freedoms (p. 302)

circle graph   round or pie-shaped graph showing how a whole is divided (p. 12)

city-state   city and its surrounding countryside (p. 467)

civilizations   highly developed cultures (pp. 84, 466)

civil war   fight among different groups within a country (pp. 492, 554, 710)

clan   group of people related to one another (pp. 590, 693)

Classical   relating to the ancient Greek and Roman world (p. 294)

climate   usual, predictable pattern of weather in an area over a long period of time (p. 52)

climograph   combination bar and line graph giving information about temperature and precipitation (p. 13)

coalition government   government in which two or more political parties work together to run a country (p. 360)

Cold War   period between the late 1940s and late 1980s when the United States and the Soviet Union competed for world influence without actually fighting each other (pp. 319, 414)

collection   process in the water cycle during which streams and rivers carry water back to the oceans (p. 49)

colony   overseas territory or settlement tied to a parent country (p. 146)

common law   unwritten set of laws based on local customs (p. 300)

GLOSSARY

commonwealth   partly self-governing territory (p. 223)

communism   economic, social, and political system based on the teachings of Karl Marx, which advocated the elimination of private property (p. 316)

communist state   country whose government has strong control over the economy and society as a whole (pp. 221, 369, 413, 663)

compound   group of houses surrounded by walls (p. 553)

condensation   process in which air rises and cools, which makes the water vapor it holds change back into a liquid (p. 49)

conservation   careful use of resources so they are not wasted (p. 71)

constitutional monarchy   government in which a king or queen is the official head of state, but elected officials run the government (pp. 342, 493, 694)

consul   elected chief official of the Roman Republic (p. 296)

consumer goods   household products, clothing, and other goods people buy to use for themselves (pp. 378, 663)

contiguous   areas that are joined together inside a common boundary (p. 126)

continent   massive land area (p. 35)

continental divide   mountainous area from which rivers flow in different directions (p. 352)

continental shelf   plateau off each coast of a continent that lies under the ocean and stretches for several miles (p. 40)

cooperative   farm owned and operated by the government (p. 222)

copper belt   large area of copper mines in northern Zambia (p. 610)

copra   dried coconut meat, which is used to make margarine, soap, and other products (p. 759)

coral reef   structure at or near the water's surface formed by the skeletons of small sea animals (pp. 129, 577, 736)

cordillera   group of mountain ranges that run side by side (pp. 160, 254)

core   center of the earth, formed of hot iron mixed with other metals (p. 35)

cottage industry   home- or village-based industry in which family members supply their own equipment to make goods (pp. 315, 639)

covenant   agreement (p. 473)

crevasse   deep crack in the Antarctic ice cap (p. 764)

crop rotation   varying what is planted in a field to avoid using up all the minerals in the soil (p. 70)

crust   uppermost layer of the earth (p. 35)

cultural diffusion   the process of spreading new knowledge and skills to other cultures (p. 84)

culture   way of life of a group of people who share similar beliefs and customs (p. 80)

culture region   different countries that have cultural traits in common (p. 85)

cuneiform   Sumerian writing system using wedge-shaped symbols pressed into clay tablets (p. 467)

current   moving streams of water in the world's oceans (p. 56)

cyclone   intense storm system with heavy rain and high winds (pp. 617, 646)

czar   name for emperor in Russia's past (p. 411)

death rate   number of people out of every 1,000 who die in a year (p. 87)

deforestation   widespread cutting of forests (pp. 70, 235, 574, 709)

delta   area formed from a soil deposit located at the mouth of a river (pp. 42, 469, 646)

democracy   government in which leaders rule with consent of the citizens (pp. 83, 294, 429)

desalinization   process used to make seawater drinkable (p. 514)

desertification   process by which grasslands change to desert (p. 557)

deterrence   maintenance of military power for the purpose of discouraging an attack (p. 320)

developed country   country in which a great deal of manufacturing is carried out (p. 96)

developing country   country that is working toward industrialization (p. 96)

dialect   local form of a language that differs from the main language in pronunciation or the meaning of words (p. 81)

dictatorship   government under the control of one all-powerful leader (pp. 83, 491)

dike   high banks of soil built along rivers to control floods (p. 662)

disciple   follower of a specific teacher (p. 475)

divine right of kings   belief that royalty ruled by the will of God (p. 306)

dominion   self-governing nation that accepts the British monarch as head of state (p. 166)

drought   long period of extreme dryness (pp. 55, 556)

dry farming   method in which the land is left unplanted every few years so that it can store moisture (p. 358)

dynasty   line of rulers from the same family (p. 666)

dzong   Buddhist center of prayer and study in Bhutan (p. 651)

earthquake   violent and sudden movement of the earth's crust (p. 36)

economic system   system that sets rules for how people decide what goods and services to produce and how they are exchanged (p. 93)

ecosystem   place where the plants and animals are dependent upon one another and their surroundings for survival (p. 72)

ecotourist   person who travels to another country to view its natural wonders (pp. 215, 581)

elevation height above sea level (pp. 9, 40, 440)

elevation profile cutaway diagram showing changes in elevation of land (p. 13)

El Niño combination of temperature, wind, and water effects in the Pacific Ocean that causes heavy rains in some areas and drought in others (p. 55)

embargo order that restricts or prohibits trade with another country (pp. 222, 518)

emigrate to move to another country (p. 91)

emperor absolute ruler of an empire (p. 296)

empire group of lands under one ruler (pp. 267, 468, 680)

enclave small territory entirely surrounded by a larger territory (p. 607)

endangered species plant or animal under the threat of completely dying out (p. 584)

environment natural surroundings (p. 24)

equinox day when day and night are of equal length in both hemispheres (p. 32)

erg huge area of shifting sand dunes in the Sahara (p. 492)

erosion process of wearing away or moving weathered material on the earth's surface (p. 38)

escarpment steep cliff between higher and lower land (p. 233)

estancia ranch (p. 240)

ethnic cleansing forcing people from a different ethnic group to leave their homes (p. 379)

ethnic group people who share a common history, language, religion, and physical characteristics (p. 81)

euro common currency adopted by countries in the European Union (p. 325)

evaporation process in which the sun's heat turns liquid water into water vapor (p. 48)

exclave small part of a country that is separated from the main part (p. 614)

exile inability to live in one's own country because of political beliefs (p. 669)

export to trade goods to other countries (p. 95)

famine lack of food (pp. 88, 701)

fault crack in the earth's crust (pp. 37, 438, 662)

favela slum area (p. 234)

federal republic government divided between national and state powers (pp. 147, 204, 351, 429)

fellahin farmers in Egypt who live in villages and work on small plots of land that they rent from landowners (p. 488)

feudalism political and social system in which a lord gave land to a noble to work, govern, and defend, in return for the noble's loyalty (p. 301)

five pillars of faith basic religious obligations of Islam (p. 477)

fjord steep-sided valley cut into mountains by the action of glaciers (pp. 354, 742)

foothill low hill at the base of a mountain range (p. 267)

fossil preserved remains or impressions of early humans, animals, or plants (p. 27)

fossil fuel coal, oil, or natural gas (p. 135)

free enterprise system economic system in which people start and run businesses with limited government intervention (pp. 131, 415, 578)

free market economy see *free enterprise system* (p. 424)

free port place where goods can be unloaded, stored, and shipped again without needing to pay any import taxes (p. 716)

free trade removing trade barriers so that goods flow freely among countries (pp. 96, 136)

free trade zone area where people can buy goods from other countries without paying extra taxes (p. 223)

gaucho cowhand (p. 240)

genocide mass murder of a people because of their race, religion, ethnicity, politics, or culture (pp. 317, 585)

geographic information systems (GIS) special software that helps geographers gather and use information about a place (pp. 6, 25)

geography the study of the earth in all its variety (p. 22)

geothermal energy electricity produced by natural underground sources of steam (pp. 357, 743)

geyser spring of water heated by molten rock inside the earth so that, from time to time, it shoots hot water into the air (pp. 357, 741)

glacier giant slow-moving sheets of ice (pp. 38, 49, 159)

glasnost Russian policy of "openness" (p. 415)

globalization development of a world culture and an interdependent world economy (p. 100)

Global Positioning System (GPS) group of satellites that travels around the earth which can be used to tell exact locations on the earth (pp. 6, 25)

great circle route ship or airplane route following a great circle; the shortest distance between two points on the earth (p. 6)

greenhouse effect buildup of certain gases in the atmosphere that, like a greenhouse, hold more of the sun's warmth (p. 58)

green revolution great increase in food grains production due to the use of improved seeds, pesticides, and efficient farming techniques (p. 639)

groundwater water that fills tiny cracks and holes in the rock layers below the earth's surface (p. 50)

guild medieval workers' organization (p. 302)

habitat type of environment in which a particular animal species lives (p. 580)

GLOSSARY

GLOSSARY

hacienda large ranch (p. 199)

hajj religious journey to Makkah that Muslims are expected to make at least once during their lifetime if they are able to do so (p. 477)

harmattan dry, dusty wind that blows south from the Sahara (p. 551)

heavy industry manufactured goods such as machinery, mining equipment, and steel (pp. 356, 426)

hemisphere one-half of the globe; the Equator divides the earth into Northern and Southern Hemispheres; the Prime Meridian divides it into Eastern and Western Hemispheres (p. 4)

hieroglyphics form of writing that uses signs and symbols (pp. 198, 471)

high island Pacific island formed by volcanic activity (p. 760)

high-technology industry industry that produces computers and other kinds of electronic equipment (p. 678)

Holocaust systematic murder of more than 6 million European Jews and 6 million others by Adolf Hitler and the Nazis during World War II (pp. 317, 511)

human resources supply of people who can produce goods (p. 314)

human rights basic freedoms and rights that all people should enjoy (p. 669)

humid continental climate weather pattern characterized by long, cold, snowy winters and short, hot summers (p. 64)

humid subtropical climate weather pattern characterized by hot, humid, rainy summers and short, mild winters (p. 65)

hurricane violent tropical storm with high winds and heavy rains (p. 193)

hydroelectric power electricity generated by flowing water (pp. 242, 571, 743)

iceberg chunk of a glacier that has broken away and floats free in the ocean (p. 765)

ice shelf layer of ice above water in Antarctica (p. 765)

immigrant person who moves to a new country to make a permanent home (p. 148)

imperialism system of building foreign empires for military and trade advantages (p. 316)

import to buy goods from another country (p. 95)

indulgences pardons for sins, given or sold by the Catholic Church (p. 305)

industrialize to change an economy to rely more on manufacturing and less on farming (pp. 195, 412)

industrialized country country in which a great deal of manufacturing occurs (p. 604)

intensive cultivation growing crops on every available piece of land (p. 693)

interdependence dependence of countries on one another for goods, raw materials to make goods, and markets in which to sell goods (p. 100)

irrigation farming practice followed in dry areas to collect water and bring it to crops (p. 71)

Islamic republic government run by Muslim religious leaders (p. 519)

island body of land smaller than a continent and surrounded by water (p. 40)

isthmus narrow piece of land that connects two larger pieces of land (pp. 40, 212)

jade shiny, usually green gemstone (p. 197)

jute plant fiber used for making rope, burlap bags, and carpet backing (p. 639)

kibbutz settlement in Israel where the people share property and produce goods (p. 510)

krill tiny, shrimplike animal that lives in waters off Antarctica and is food for many other creatures (p. 766)

lagoon shallow pool of water surrounded by reefs, sandbars, or atolls (p. 654)

land bridge narrow strip of land that joins two larger landmasses (p. 190)

landfill area where trash companies dump the waste they collect (p. 136)

landform individual features of the land (p. 23)

landlocked country with no land bordering a sea or an ocean (pp. 271, 372)

La Niña pattern of unusual weather in the Pacific Ocean that has opposite effects of El Niño (p. 56)

latitude location north or south of the Equator, measured by imaginary lines (parallels) that are numbered in degrees north or south (pp. 5, 192)

leap year year that has an extra day; occurs every fourth year (p. 31)

life expectancy the number of years that an average person is expected to live (p. 428)

light industry making of such goods as clothing, shoes, furniture, and household products (p. 426)

line graph graph in which one or more lines represent changing quantities over time (p. 11)

literacy rate percentage of people who can read and write (p. 215)

llanos grassy plains (p. 242)

local wind pattern of wind caused by landforms in a particular area (p. 56)

longitude location east or west of the Prime Meridian, measured by imaginary lines (meridians) numbered in degrees east or west (p. 5)

low island Pacific island formed of coral and having little vegetation (p. 760)

magma   hot, melted rock that sometimes flows to the earth's surface in a volcanic eruption (p. 35)

maize   Native American name for corn (p. 198)

majority group   group in society that controls most of the wealth and power, though not always the largest group in numbers (p. 430)

mangrove   tropical tree with roots that extend both above and beneath the water (p. 550)

manor   feudal estate made up of a manor house or castle and land (p. 301)

mantle   rock layer about 1,800 miles (2,897 km) thick between the earth's core and the crust (p. 35)

manuka   small shrub of New Zealand (p. 741)

map key   code that explains the lines, symbols, and colors used on a map (p. 8)

maquiladora   factory that assembles parts made in other countries (p. 194)

marine west coast climate   weather pattern characterized by rainy and mild winters and cool summers (p. 63)

marsupial   mammal that carries its young in a pouch (p. 737)

Mediterranean climate   weather pattern characterized by mild, rainy winters and hot, dry summers (p. 64)

megalopolis   pattern of heavy urban settlement over a large area (pp. 127, 694)

meridian   see *longitude* (p. 5)

messiah   in Judaism and Christianity, a savior sent by God (p. 475)

mestizo   person with mixed Spanish and Native American background (p. 256)

migrant worker   person who travels from place to place when extra help is needed to plant or harvest crops (p. 205)

migrate   to move from one place to another (p. 504)

minority group   group of people who are different in some characteristic from the group with the most power and wealth in a region (p. 430)

missionary   person who spreads religious views (p. 300)

monarchy   form of government in which a king or queen inherits the right to rule (p. 83)

monotheism   belief in one God (p. 473)

monsoon   seasonal wind that blows over a continent for months at a time (p. 639)

moor   treeless, windy highland area with damp ground (p. 340)

moshav   settlement in Israel where people share property but also own some private property (p. 510)

mosque   place of worship for followers of Islam (pp. 380, 488)

multilingual   able to speak several languages (p. 348)

multinational company   firm that does business in several countries (p. 348)

mural   wall painting (p. 198)

national debt   money owed by a nation's government (p. 206)

natural resource   product of the earth that people use to meet their needs (p. 92)

navigable   body of water wide and deep enough to allow the passage of ships (pp. 134, 266, 345)

neutrality   refusal to take sides in disagreements and wars between countries (p. 352)

newsprint   type of paper used for printing newspapers (p. 163)

nomads   people who move from place to place with herds of animals (pp. 373, 439, 680)

nonrenewable resource   natural resource such as minerals that cannot be replaced (p. 93)

nuclear energy   power made by creating a controlled atomic reaction (p. 428)

nuclear weapon   weapon whose destructive power comes from a nuclear reaction (p. 319)

oasis   a fertile or green area in a desert (pp. 439, 485)

obsidian   hard, black glass created by the cooled molten lava of a volcano (p. 198)

orbit   path that a body in the solar system travels around the sun (p. 29)

outback   inland regions of Australia (p. 737)

overgraze   to allow livestock to strip areas so bare that plants cannot grow back (p. 556)

ozone   type of oxygen that forms a layer in the atmosphere and protects all living things on the earth from certain harmful rays of the sun (p. 766)

pagoda   many-storied Buddhist temple (p. 670)

pampas   vast treeless, grass-covered plains of South America (p. 240)

papyrus   Egyptian paper (p. 471)

parallel   see *latitude* (pp. 5, 699)

parliamentary democracy   government in which voters elect representatives to a lawmaking body which chooses a prime minister to head the government (pp. 166, 216, 341)

peat   plants partly decayed in water that can be dried and used for fuel (p. 342)

peninsula   piece of land with water on three sides (pp. 40, 191)

perestroika   Soviet policy that loosened government controls and permitted its economy to move towards free enterprise (p. 415)

permafrost   permanently frozen lower layers of soil in the tundra and subarctic regions (p. 406)

pesticides   powerful chemicals that kill crop-destroying insects (pp. 71, 640)

pharaoh   ruler of ancient Egypt (p. 470)

GLOSSARY

GLOSSARY

phosphate　mineral salt used in fertilizers (pp. 486, 560, 761)

pictograph　graph in which small symbols represent quantities (p. 12)

pidgin language　language formed by combining elements of several different languages (p. 760)

plain　low-lying stretch of flat or gently rolling land (p. 40)

plantain　kind of banana (p. 582)

plantation　large farm that grows a single crop for sale (p. 194)

plate　huge slab of rock that makes up the earth's crust (pp. 589, 714)

plateau　flat land with higher elevation than a plain (p. 40)

plate tectonics　theory that the earth's crust is not an unbroken shell but consists of plates, or huge slabs of rock, that move (p. 35)

plaza　public square (p. 202)

poaching　illegal hunting of protected animals (p. 577)

polder　area of land reclaimed from the sea (p. 347)

polis　Greek term for "city-state" (p. 294)

polytheism　belief in more than one god (p. 467)

pope　head of the Roman Catholic Church (pp. 299, 371)

population density　average number of people living in a square mile or square kilometer (p. 89)

potash　type of mineral salt that is often used in fertilizers (p. 385)

prairie　rolling, inland grassy area with very fertile soil (p. 160)

precious gems　valuable gemstones, such as rubies, sapphires, and jade (p. 709)

precipitation　water that falls back to the earth as rain, snow, sleet, or hail (p. 49)

prime minister　official who heads the government in a parliamentary democracy (p. 167)

privatize　to transfer the ownership of factories from the government to individual citizens (p. 375)

productivity　measurement of the amount of work accomplished in a given time (p. 314)

projection　in mapmaking, a way of drawing the round Earth on a flat surface (p. 7)

prophet　messenger of God (p. 474)

province　regional political division similar to states (p. 158)

pyramid　huge stone structure that served as an elaborate tomb or monument (p. 470)

quota　number limit on how many items of a particular product can be imported from a particular country (p. 95)

rain forest　dense forest that receives high amounts of rain each year (p. 59)

rain shadow　dry area on the inland side of coastal mountains (p. 58)

recycling　reusing materials instead of throwing them out (p. 136)

refugee　person who flees to another country to escape persecution or disaster (pp. 91, 379, 585)

reincarnation　rebirth of a soul in a new body (p. 640)

relief　differences in height in a landscape; how flat or rugged the surface is (p. 9)

renewable resource　natural resource that cannot be used up or can be replaced naturally or grown again (p. 92)

representative democracy　government in which the people are represented by elected leaders (p. 146)

republic　strong national government headed by elected leaders (pp. 216, 296, 487)

responsibilities　duties owed by citizens to their government and other citizens (p. 99)

reunification　bringing together the two parts of Germany under one government (p. 351)

revolution　one complete orbit around the sun (p. 31); a great and often violent change (p. 306)

rights　benefits and protections guaranteed by law (p. 99)

rural　area in the countryside (p. 150)

samurai　powerful land-owning warriors in Japan (p. 693)

satellite nation　nation politically and economically dominated or controlled by another, more powerful country (p. 321)

sauna　wooden room heated by water sizzling on hot stones (p. 356)

savanna　broad grassland in the Tropics with few trees (pp. 62, 550)

scale bar　on a map, a divided line showing the map scale, usually in miles or kilometers (p. 8)

secede　to withdraw from a national government (p. 147)

secular　nonreligious (p. 492)

selva　tropical rain forests in Brazil (p. 232)

serf　farm laborer who could be bought and sold along with the land (pp. 301, 412)

service industry　business that provides services to people instead of producing goods (pp. 132, 195, 488)

shah　title given to kings who ruled Iran (p. 519)

shogun　military leader in early Japan (p. 693)

silt　small particles of rich soil (p. 484)

sirocco　hot, dry winds that blow across Italy from North Africa (p. 360)

sisal　plant fiber used to make rope and twine (p. 580)

slash-and-burn farming　method of clearing land for planting by cutting and burning forests (p. 616)

smog　thick haze of fog and chemicals (p. 206)

socialism   economic system in which most businesses are owned and run by the government (p. 709)

sodium nitrate   chemical used in fertilizer and explosives (p. 274)

solar system   Earth, eight other planets, and thousands of smaller bodies that all revolve around the sun (p. 29)

sorghum   tall grass with seeds that are used as grain and to make syrup (p. 610)

spa   resort that has hot mineral springs that people bathe in to regain their health (p. 374)

station   cattle or sheep ranch in Australia (p. 737)

steppe   partly dry grassland often found on the edges of a desert (pp. 67, 383, 406, 438, 680)

strait   narrow body of water between two pieces of land (pp. 42, 716)

strike   refusal to work, usually by a labor organization, until demands are met (p. 315)

subarctic   weather pattern characterized by severely cold, bitter winters and short, cool summers (p. 65)

subcontinent   large landmass that is part of another continent but distinct from it (p. 638)

subsistence farm   small plot where a farmer grows only enough food to feed his own family (pp. 194, 552)

suburb   smaller community that surrounds a city (p. 150)

summer solstice   day with the most hours of sunlight and the fewest hours of darkness (p. 32)

taiga   huge forests of evergreen trees that grow in subarctic regions (p. 406)

tariff   tax added to the value of goods that are imported (p. 95)

terraced field   strips of land cut out of a hillside like stair steps so the land can hold water and be used for farming (p. 717)

textiles   woven cloth (p. 315)

theocracy   form of government in which one individual ruled as both religious leader and king (p. 467)

townships   crowded neighborhoods outside cities in South Africa where most nonwhites live (p. 607)

trench   valley in the ocean floor (p. 41)

tributary   small river that flows into a larger river (p. 645)

Tropics   low-latitude region between the Tropic of Cancer and the Tropic of Capricorn (p. 53)

trust territory   area temporarily placed under control of another nation (p. 761)

tsetse fly   insect whose bite can kill cattle or humans with a deadly disease called sleeping sickness (p. 573)

tsunami   huge sea wave caused by an earthquake on the ocean floor (pp. 36, 690)

tundra   vast rolling treeless plain in high latitude climates in which only the top few inches of ground thaw in summer (pp. 66, 159, 406)

union   labor organization that negotiates for improved worker conditions and pay (p. 315)

urban   area in the city (p. 150)

urbanization   movement to cities (p. 90)

vaquero   cowhand (p. 193)

vassal   noble in medieval society who swore loyalty to a lord in return for land (p. 301)

wadi   dry riverbed filled by rainwater from rare downpours (p. 513)

water cycle   process in which water moves from the oceans to the air to the ground and finally back to the oceans (p. 48)

watershed   region drained by a river (p. 584)

water vapor   water in the form of gas (p. 48)

weather   unpredictable changes in air that take place over a short period of time (p. 52)

weathering   natural process that breaks surface rocks into boulders, gravel, sand, and soil (p. 37)

welfare state   country that uses tax money to support people who are sick, needy, jobless, or retired (p. 355)

winter solstice   day with the fewest hours of sunlight (p. 32)

yurt   large circle-shaped tent made of animal skins that can be packed up and moved from place to place (p. 681)

GLOSSARY

absolute location/ubicación absoluta posición exacta de en lugar en la superficie de la Tierra (pág. 5)

acid rain/lluvia ácida lluvia que contiene grandes cantidades de contaminantes químicos (págs. 70, 135, 370)

adobe/adobe ladrillos secados al Sol (pág. 202)

airlift/puente áereo sistema de transportar suministros por avión (pág. 322)

alluvial plain/llanura aluvial área creada por el suelo fértil que se acumula después de las inundaciones causadas por los ríos (pág. 517)

altiplano/altiplano meseta grande y muy elevada; también se llama altiplanicie (pág. 271)

altitude/altitud altura sobre el nivel del mar (págs. 193, 243)

apartheid/apartheid sistema de leyes que separaba los grupos raciales y étnicos y limitaba los derechos de la población negra (pág. 606)

aquifer/manto acuífero capa de rocas subterránea por la cual corre el agua (págs. 50, 490)

archipelago/archipiélago grupo de islas (págs. 219, 690)

artifact/artefacto objeto construido por pueblos antiguos (pág. 27)

atmosphere/atmósfera capa de aire que rodea la Tierra (pág. 30)

atoll/atolón isla de muy poca elevación que se forma alrededor de una laguna en la forma de un anillo (págs. 654, 760)

autobahn/autobahn autopista muy rápida (pág. 351)

autonomy/autonomía gobernarse por sí mismo (págs. 168, 583)

axis/eje terrestre línea imaginaria que atraviesa el centro de la Tierra entre el Polo Norte y el Polo Sur (pág. 31); también la línea vertical (del lado) u horizontal (de abajo) de una gráfica que se usa para medir (pág. 11)

bar graph/gráfica de barras gráfica en que franjas verticales u horizontales representan cantidades (pág. 11)

basin/cuenca área baja rodeada de tierras más elevadas (pág. 232)

bauxite/bauxita mineral que se usa para hacer aluminio (págs. 220, 560)

bazaar/bazar mercado (pág. 488)

bedouins/beduinos gente nomádica del desierto del sudoeste de Asia (pág. 505)

bilingual/bilingüe se refiere a un país que tiene dos idiomas oficiales (págs. 167, 440)

birthrate/índice de natalidad número de niños que nace cada año por cada mil personas (pág. 88)

blockade/bloquear impedir por la fuerza la entrada a un área (pág. 321)

Boers/bóers los holandeses que fueron los primeros colonos en Sudáfrica (pág. 605)

bog/ciénaga tierra baja y pantanosa (págs. 342, 368)

boomerang/bumerán arma australiana que es plana, curvado y de madera que se lanza para que golpee un objetivo o de la vuelta de la persona que la lanzó (pág. 738)

bush/campo áreas rurales de Australia (pág. 739)

cacao/cacao árbol tropical cuyas semillas se usan para hacer chocolate y cocoa (págs. 552, 759)

caliph/califa sucesor de Mahoma (pág. 514)

calligraphy/caligrafía el arte de escribir con letra muy bella (pág. 670)

campesino/campesino agricultor (pág. 257)

canopy/bóveda techo formado por las copas de los árboles en los bosques húmedos (págs. 214, 571)

cardinal directions/puntos cardinales cuatro direcciones básicas en la Tierra: norte, sur, este, oeste (pág. 8)

cartographer/cartógrafo persona que hace mapas (pág. 6)

casbah/casbah la sección antigua de las ciudades de Argelia; también se llama *alcazaba* (pág. 492)

cash crop/cultivo comercial producto que se cultiva para exportación (págs. 256, 438)

cassava/yuca planta con raíces que se pueden convertir en harina para hacer pan o gachas (pág. 578)

caste/casta clase social basada en la ascendencia de una persona (pág. 640)

caudillo/caudillo gobernante militar (pág. 243)

channel/canal una masa de agua entre dos tierras que tiene más anchura que un estrecho (pág. 42)

chart/cuadro manera gráfica de presentar información con claridad (pág. 12)

charter/cédula acuerdo escrito garantizando privilegios y libertades (pág. 302)

circle graph/gráfica de círculo gráfica redonda que muestra como un todo es dividido (pág. 12)

city-state/ciudad estado ciudad junto con las tierras que la rodean (pág. 467)

civilizations/civilizaciones culturas altamente desarrolladas (págs. 84, 466)

civil war/guerra civil pelea entre distintos grupos dentro de un país (págs. 492, 554, 710)

clan/clan grupo de personas que están emparentadas (págs. 590, 693)

SPANISH GLOSSARY

Classical/Clásico   relacionado a la antigua Roma y Grecia (pág. 294)

climate/clima   el patrón que sigue el estado del tiempo en un área durante muchos años (pág. 52)

climograph/gráfica de clima   gráfica que combina barras y líneas para dar información sobre la temperatura y la precipitación (pág. 13)

coalition government/gobierno por coalición gobierno en que dos o más partidos trabajan juntos para dirigir un país (pág. 360)

Cold War/Guerra Fría   período entre los fines de los 1940 y los fines de los 1980 en que los Estados Unidos y la Unión Soviética compitieron por tener influencia mundial sin pelear uno contra el otro (págs. 319, 414)

collection/drenaje   proceso durante el ciclo hidrológico en que los ríos llevan el agua de regreso a los océanos (pág. 49)

colony/colonia   territorio o poblado con lazos a un país extranjero (pág. 146)

common law/derecho común   grupo de leyes no escritas basadas en costumbres locales (pág. 300)

commonwealth/estado libre asociado   territorio que en parte se gobierna por sí solo (pág. 223)

communism/comunismo   sistema económico social y político basado en las enseñanzas de Karl Marx, el cual abogaba por la eliminación de propiedades privadas (pág. 316)

communist state/estado comunista   país cuyo gobierno mantiene mucho control sobre la economía y la sociedad en su totalidad (págs. 221, 369, 413, 663)

compound/complejo residencial   grupo de viviendas rodeada por una muralla (pág. 553)

condensation/condensación   proceso en que el aire sube y se enfría, lo cual hace que el vapor de agua que contiene se convierta de nuevo en líquido (pág. 49)

conservation/conservación   uso juicioso de los recursos para no malgastarlos (pág. 71)

constitutional monarchy/monarquía constitucional   gobierno en que un rey o reina es el jefe de estado oficial pero los gobernantes son elegidos (págs. 342, 493, 694)

consul/cónsul   oficial en jefe electo en la república romana (pág. 296)

consumer goods/bienes de consumo   productos para la casa, ropa y otras cosas que la gente compra para su uso personal (págs. 378, 663)

contiguous/contiguas   áreas adyacentes dentro de la misma frontera (pág. 126)

continent/continente   masa de tierra inmensa (pág. 35)

continental divide/línea divisoria continental área montañosa de la cual los ríos desciendan en diferentes direcciones (pág. 352)

continental shelf/plataforma continental   meseta formada por parte de un continente que se extiende por varias millas debajo del mar (pág. 40)

cooperative/cooperativa   granja que es propiedad y es operada por el gobierno (pág. 222)

copper belt/cinturón de cobre   área extensa de minas de cobre en el norte de Zambia (pág. 610)

copra/copra   pulpa seca del coco que se usa para hacer margarina, jabón y otros productos (pág. 759)

coral reef/arrecife coralino   estructura formada al nivel del mar o cerca de éste por los esqueletos de pequeños animales marinos (págs. 129, 577, 736)

cordillera/cordillera   grupo de cadenas paralelas de montañas (págs. 160, 254)

core/núcleo   centro de la Tierra, que está formado de hierro caliente y otros metales (pág. 35)

cottage industry/industria familiar   industria basada en una casa o aldea en que los miembros de la familia usan sus propias herramientas para hacer productos (págs. 315, 639)

covenant/alianza   pacto entre Dios y los hebreos (pág. 473)

crevasse/grieta   rajadura profunda en el casquete de hielo de la Antártida (pág. 764)

crop rotation/rotación de cultivos   variar lo que se siembra en un terreno para no agotar todos los minerales que tiene el suelo (pág. 70)

crust/corteza   capa de afuera de la Tierra (pág. 35)

cultural diffusion/difusión cultural   el proceso de esparcir nuevos conocimientos y habilidades a otras culturas (pág. 84)

culture/cultura   modo de vida de un grupo de personas que comparten creencias y costumbres similares (pág. 80)

culture region/región cultural   países que tienen los mismos rasgos culturales (pág. 85)

cuneiform/cuneiforme   sistema de escritura Sumeria que usa símbolos en forma de cuñas hundidas en tabletas de arcilla (pág. 467)

current/corriente   movimiento de las aguas del mar (pág. 56)

cyclone/ciclón   tormenta violenta con vientos muy fuertes y mucha lluvia (págs. 617, 646)

czar/zar   título de los antiguos emperadores rusos (pág. 411)

death rate/índice de mortalidad   número de personas de cada mil que mueren en un año (pág. 87)

deforestation/deforestación   la extensa destrucción de los bosques (págs. 70, 235, 574, 709)

delta/delta   área formada por el suelo que deposita un río en su desembocadura (págs. 42, 469, 646)

democracy/democracia   gobierno en el cual los líderes gobiernan con el consentimiento de los ciudadanos (págs. 83, 294, 429)

desalinization/desalinización   proceso de hacer el agua de mar potable (pág. 514)

desertification/desertización   proceso por el cual los pastos se convierten en desiertos (pág. 557)

deterrence/disuasión   el mantener el poder militar con el propósito de desalentar un ataque (pág. 320)

developed country/país desarrollado   país donde hay mucha manufactura de productos (pág. 96)

developing country/país en vías de desarrollo   país que está industrializándose (pág. 96)

dialect/dialecto   forma local de un idioma que se diferencia del idioma normal por su pronunciación o por el sentido de algunas palabras (pág. 81)

dictatorship/dictadura   gobierno bajo el control de un líder que tiene todo el poder (págs. 83, 491)

dike/dique   muros de tierra muy altos construidos a lo largo de los ríos para controlar las inundaciones (pág. 662)

disciple/discípulo   partidario de un maestro específico (pág. 475)

divine right of kings/derecho divino de los reyes   la creencia de que los reyes governaban por la voluntad de Dios (pág. 306)

dominion/dominio   naciones que se gobiernan por sí solas que aceptan al monarca británico como jefe de estado (pág. 166)

drought/sequía   largos períodos de sequedad (págs. 55, 556)

dry farming/agricultura en seco   método de cultivar en que la tierra se deja sin sembrar cada varios años para que almacene humedad (pág. 358)

dynasty/dinastía   serie de gobernantes de la misma familia (pág. 666)

dzong/dzong   centro budista en Bután para rezar y estudiar (pág. 651)

earthquake/terremoto   movimiento violento e inesperado de la corteza de la Tierra (pág. 36)

economic system/sistema económico   sistema que establece reglas que determinan cómo las personas deciden cuáles bienes y servicios van a producir y cómo los van a intercambiar (pág. 93)

ecosystem/ecosistema   lugar en el cual las plantas y animales dependen unos de otros y de sus alrededores para sobrevivir (pág. 72)

ecotourist/ecoturista   persona que viaja a otro país para ver sus bellezas naturales (págs. 215, 581)

elevation/elevación   altura por encima del nivel del mar (págs. 9, 40, 440)

elevation profile/perfil de elevaciones   diagrama que muestra los cambios en la elevación de la tierra como si se hubiera hecho un corte vertical del área (pág. 13)

El Niño/El Niño   combinación de la temperatura, los vientos y los efectos del agua en el océano Pacífico que causa lluvias fuertes en algunas áreas y sequía en otras (pág. 55)

embargo/embargo   orden que limita o prohibe el comercio con otro país (págs. 222, 518)

emigrate/emigrar   mudarse a otro país (pág. 91)

emperor/emperador   gobernante absoluto de un imperio (pág. 296)

empire/imperio   grupo de países bajo un gobernante (págs. 267, 468, 680)

enclave/enclave   territorio pequeño totalmente rodeado por un territorio más grande (pág. 607)

endangered species/especie en vías de extinción   planta o animal que está en peligro de desaparecer completamente (pág. 584)

environment/medio ambiente   alrededores naturales (pág. 24)

equinox/equinoccio   día en que el día y la noche tienen la misa duración en los dos hemisferios (pág. 32)

erg/ergio   inmensas áreas en el Sahara en que se mueven las dunas de arena (pág. 492)

erosion/erosión   proceso de mover los materiales desgastados en la superficie de la Tierra (pág. 38)

escarpment/escarpa   acantilado empinado entre una área baja y una alta (pág. 233)

*estancia/*estancia   rancho (pág. 240)

ethnic cleansing/limpieza étnica   forzar a personas de un grupo étnico distinto a abandonar el lugar donde viven (pág. 379)

ethnic group/grupo étnico   personas que tienen el mismo idioma, historia, religión y los mismos rasgos físicos (pág. 81)

euro/eurodólar   moneda común adoptada por los países de la Unión Europea (pág. 325)

evaporation/evaporación   proceso mediante el cual el calor del sol convierte el agua líquida en vapor de agua (pág. 48)

exclave/territorio externo   parte pequeña de un país que está separada de la parte principal (pág. 614)

exile/exilio   tener que vivir fuera de su país nativo por causa de sus creencias políticas (pág. 669)

export/exportar   comerciar y mandar bienes a otros países (pág. 95)

famine/hambruna   falta de alimentos (págs. 88, 701)

fault/falla   fractura en la corteza de la Tierra (págs. 37, 438, 662)

favela/favela   barrio pobre y deteriorado (pág. 234)

federal republic/república federal   nación en que el poder está dividido entre el gobierno nacional y el de los estados (págs. 147, 204, 351, 429)

fellahin/felás   granjeros en Egipto que viven en aldeas y cultivan pequeños terrenos que arriendan de un hacendado (pág. 488)

feudalism/feudalismo   sistema político y social en el cual un lord cedía tierra a un noble para que la trabajara, gobernara y defendiera, obligándose éste rendirle fidelidad (pág. 301)

five pillars of faith/cinco pilares de fé   obligaciones religiosas básicas del Islam (pág. 477)

fjord/fiordo   valle creado por el movimiento de glaciares en las montañas que deja laderas sumamente empinadas (págs. 354, 742)

foothill/estribaciones   colinas bajas al pie de una cadena de montañas (pág. 267)

fossil/fósil   las huellas o restos preservados de seres humanos, animales o plantas antiguos (pág. 27)

fossil fuel/combustibles fósiles   carbón, petróleo o gas natural (pág. 135)

free enterprise system/sistema de libre empresa   sistema económico en que la gente empieza y administra negocios con poca intervención del gobierno (págs. 131, 415, 578)

free market economy/economía del libre comercio   *véase* free enterprise system (pág. 424)

free port/puerto libre   lugar donde las mercancías se pueden descargar, almacenar y embarcar de nuevo sin tener que pagar derechos de importación (pág. 716)

free trade/libre comercio   eliminar las barreras al comercio para que se puedan mover productos libremente entre países (págs. 96, 136)

free trade zone/zona de cambio libre   área donde la gente puede comprar bienes de otros países sin pagar impuestos adicionales (pág. 233)

gaucho/gaucho   vaquero (pág. 240)

genocide/genocidio   asesinato en masa de personas a causa de su raza, religión, etnicidad, política o cultura (págs. 317, 585)

geographic information systems (GIS)/sistemas de información geográfica (SIG)   programas de computadoras especiales que ayudan a los geógrafos a obtener y usar la información geográfica sobre un lugar (págs. 6, 25)

geography/geografía   el estudio de la Tierra y de toda su variedad (pág. 22)

geothermal energy/energía geotérmica   electricidad producida por fuentes de vapor subterráneas naturales (págs. 357, 743)

geyser/géiser   manantial de agua calentado por rocas fundidas dentro de la Tierra que, de vez en cuando, arroja agua caliente al aire (págs. 357, 741)

glacier/glaciar   capa de hielo inmensa que se mueve muy lentamente (págs. 38, 49, 159)

glasnost/glasnost   política rusa de "franqueza" (pág. 415)

globalization/globalización   desarrollo de una cultura y economía interdependiente mundiales (pág. 100)

Global Positioning System (GPS)/Sistema global de posición (GPS)   grupo de satélites que le dan la vuelta a la Tierra y se usan para localizar lugares exactos en la Tierra (págs. 6, 25)

great circle route/línea de rumbo   ruta que sigue un círculo máximo; usada por aviones y barcos porque es la distancia más corta entre dos puntos en la Tierra (pág. 6)

greenhouse effect/efecto invernadero   la acumulación de ciertos gases en la atmósfera que mantienen más del calor del Sol, como hace un invernadero (pág. 58)

green revolution/revolución verde   gran aumento en la producción de granos debido al uso de semillas, pesticidas y técnicas agrícolas perfeccionadas (pág. 639)

groundwater/agua subterránea   agua que llena las rajaduras y hoyos en las capas de roca debajo de la superficie de la Tierra (pág. 50)

guild/gremio   organización de trabajadores en la época medieval (pág. 302)

habitat/hábitat   tipo de ambiente en que vive una especie animal en particular (pág. 580)

hacienda/hacienda   un rancho grande (pág. 199)

hajj/*hajj*   viaje religioso a La Meca que todo musulmán debe hacer por lo menos una vez en la vida si puede (pág. 477)

harmattan/harmattan   viento seco y lleno de polvo que sopla hacia el sur desde el Sahara (pág. 551)

heavy industry/industria pesada   manufactura de productos como maquinaria, equipo de minería y acero (págs. 356, 426)

hemisphere/hemisferio   una mitad del globo terráqueo; el ecuador divide la Tierra en los hemisferios norte y sur; el primer meridiano la divide en hemisferios este y oeste (pág. 4)

hieroglyphics/jeroglíficos   forma de escribir que usa signos y símbolos (págs. 198, 471)

high island/isla oceánica   isla del Pacífico formada por actividad volcánica (pág. 760)

high-technology industry/industria de alta tecnología   industria que produce computadoras y otras clases de equipo electrónico (pág. 678)

Holocaust/Holocausto   matanza sistemática de más de 6 millones de judíos europeos y 6 millones de personas más por Adolfo Hitler y los nazis durante la Segunda Guerra Mundial (págs. 317, 511)

human resources/recursos humanos   suministro de personas quienes pueden producir bienes de consumo (pág. 314)

human rights/derechos humanos   libertades y derechos básicos que todas las personas deben disfrutar (pág. 669)

humid continental climate/clima húmedo continental   patrón del estado del tiempo con inviernos largos, fríos y con mucha nieve y veranos cortos y calurosos (pág. 64)

humid subtropical climate/clima húmedo subtropical   patrón del estado del tiempo con veranos calurosos, húmedos y lluviosos e inviernos cortos y templados (pág. 65)

hurricane/huracán   tormenta tropical violenta con vientos y lluvias fuertes (pág. 193)

SPANISH GLOSSARY

hydroelectric power/energía hidroeléctrica
electricidad generada por una corriente de agua
(págs. 242, 571, 743)

iceberg/iceberg   pedazo de un glaciar que se ha
desprendido y flota libremente en los océanos
(pág. 765)

ice shelf/plataforma de hielo   capa de hielo sobre
el mar en la Antártida (pág. 765)

immigrant/inmigrante   persona que se muda
permanentemente a un país nuevo (pág. 148)

imperialism/imperialismo   el sistema de
desarrollar imperios extranjeros para ventaja militar
y comercial (pág. 316)

import/importar   comprar productos de otro país
(pág. 95)

indulgences/indulgencias   perdón por los pecados
concedido o vendido por la Iglesia Católica (pág. 305)

industrialize/industrializar   cambiar una economía
de manera que dependa más de la manufactura que
de la agricultura (págs. 195, 412, 604)

industrialized country/país industrializado   país
en el cual ocurre mucha manufactura (pág. 604)

intensive cultivation/cultivo intensivo   labrar
toda la tierra posible (pág. 693)

interdependence/interdependencia   países que
dependen unos de otros para bienes, materia prima
para producir bienes y mercados en los cuales
vendan sus productos (pág. 100)

irrigation/irrigación   práctica agrícola en áreas
secas de colectar agua y llevarla a los cultivos
(pág. 71)

Islamic republic/república islámica   gobierno
dirigido por líderes musulmanes (pág. 519)

island/isla   masa de tierra más pequeña que un
continente, rodeada de agua (pág. 40)

isthmus/istmo   lengua de tierra que conecta a dos
masas de tierra más grandes (págs. 40, 212)

jade/jade   piedra preciosa reluciente, usualmente
de color verde (pág. 197)

jute/yute   fibras de una planta que se usan para
hacer soga, sacos y el revés de alfombras (pág. 639)

kibbutz/kibutz   poblado en Israel donde las
personas comparten la propiedad y producen bienes
(pág. 510)

krill/krill   animales diminutos parecidos a los
camarones que viven en las aguas alrededor de la
Antártida y sirven de alimento para muchos otros
animales (pág. 766)

lagoon/laguna   masa de agua poco profunda
rodeada por arrecifes, bancos de arena o un atolón
(pág. 654)

land bridge/puente de tierra   franja de tierra que
une a dos masas de tierra mayores (pág. 190)

landfill/vertedero de basura   lugar donde las
compañías que recogen la basura botan los residuos
que colectan (pág. 136)

landform/accidente geográfico   característica
particular de la tierra (pág. 23)

landlocked/rodeado de tierra   país que no tiene
tierras bordeadas por un mar u océano (págs. 271,
372)

La Niña/La Niña   patrón infrecuente en el estado
del tiempo del océano Pacífico que tiene los efectos
contrarios a los de El Niño (pág. 56)

latitude/latitud   posición al norte o al sur del
ecuador, medida por medio de líneas imaginarias
(paralelos) que son numeradas con grados norte o
sur (págs. 5, 192)

leap year/año bisiesto   año que tiene un día
adicional; cada cuarto año (pág. 31)

life expectancy/expectativas de vida   el número
de años que se espera que viva la persona promedio
(pág. 428)

light industry/industria ligera   fabricación de
productos como muebles, ropa, zapatos y artículos
para el hogar (pág. 426)

line graph/gráfica lineal   gráfica en que una o
varias líneas representan cambios de cantidad a
través del tiempo (pág. 11)

literacy rate/índice de alfabetización   porcentaje
de personas que saben leer y escribir (pág. 215)

llanos/llanos   planicie cubierta de hierba
(pág. 242)

local wind/vientos locales   patrones en los
vientos causados por los accidentes geográficos de
un área en particular (pág. 56)

longitude/longitud   posición al este o el oeste del
primer meridiano, medida por medio de líneas
imaginarias (meridianos) numeradas con grados este
u oeste (pág. 5)

low island/isla coralina   isla del Pacífico formada
por coral que tiene poca vegetación (pág. 760)

magma/magma   roca caliente y fundida que a
veces fluye hasta la superficie de la Tierra en
erupciones volcánicas (pág. 35)

maize/maíz   nombre Native Americano del elote
(pág. 198)

majority group/grupo mayoritario   grupo en una
sociedad que controla la mayoría de la riqueza y el
poder, el cual no siempre es el grupo más numeroso
(pág. 430)

SPANISH GLOSSARY

mangrove/mangle   árbol tropical con raíces que se extienden por encima y por debajo del agua (pág. 550)

manor/feudo   estado feudal compuesto de una casa solariega o castillo y tierra (pág. 301)

mantle/manto   capa de rocas de 1,800 millas (2,897 km.) de grueso entre el núcleo y la corteza de la Tierra (pág. 35)

manuka/manuka   pequeño arbusto de Nueva Zelanda (pág. 741)

map key/leyenda   explicación de las líneas, símbolos y colores usados en un mapa; también se llama clave del mapa (pág. 8)

maquiladora/maquiladora   fábrica donde se ensamblan piezas hechas en otros países (pág. 194)

marine west coast climate/clima húmedo marítimo   patrón del estado del tiempo con inviernos lluviosos y templados y veranos frescos (pág. 63)

marsupial/marsupial   mamífero que lleva a sus crías en una bolsa (pág. 737)

Mediterranean climate/clima húmedo mediterráneo   patrón del estado del tiempo con inviernos lluviosos y templados y veranos calurosos y secos (pág. 64)

megalopolis/megalópolis   área extensa de mucha urbanización (págs. 127, 694)

meridian/meridiano   *véase* longitude (pág. 5)

messiah/Mesías   en judaísmo y cristianismo, el salvador enviado por Dios (pág. 475)

mestizo/mestizo   persona cuya ascendencia incluye indios americanos y españoles (pág. 256)

migrant worker/trabajador itinerante   persona que viaja a distintos lugares donde hacen falta trabajadores para sembrar y cosechar cultivos (pág. 205)

migrate/migrar   mudarse de un lugar a otro (pág. 504)

minority group/grupo minoritario   grupo de gente quien es diferente en alguna característica del grupo con mayor poder y riqueza en una región (pág. 430)

missionary/misionero   persona que difunde ideas religiosas (pág. 300)

monarchy/monarquía   tipo de gobierno en que un rey o reina hereda el derecho de gobernar (pág. 83)

monotheism/monoteísmo   creencia en un solo Dios (pág. 473)

monsoon/monzón   vientos que soplan en un continente por varios meses seguidos en ciertas estaciones del año (pág. 639)

moor/páramo   área elevada y sin árboles pero con mucho viento y tierra húmeda (pág. 340)

moshav/*moshav*   poblados en Israel en que la gente comparte alguna propiedad pero también tiene propiedad privada (pág. 510)

mosque/mezquita   edificio de devoción islámico (págs. 380, 488)

multilingual/multilingüe   que puede hablar varios idiomas (pág. 348)

multinational company/multinacional compañía   compañía que hace negocios en varios países (pág. 348)

mural/mural   pintura hecha sobre una pared (pág. 198)

national debt/deuda pública   dinero debido por el gobierno de una nación (pág. 206)

natural resource/recurso natural   producto de la Tierra que la gente usa para satisfacer sus necesidades (pág. 92)

navigable/navegable   masa de agua ancha y profunda suficiente para que los barcos puedan viajar por ella (págs. 134, 266, 345)

neutrality/neutralidad   negarse a ponerse a favor de uno de los adversarios en un desacuerdo o una guerra entre países (pág. 352)

newsprint/papel de periódico   tipo de papel en que se imprimen los periódicos (pág. 163)

nomads/nómadas   gente que se muda de un lugar a otro con sus manadas o rebaños de animales (págs. 373, 439, 680)

nonrenewable resource/recurso no renovable   recurso natural, como minerales, que no puede reemplazarse (pág. 93)

nuclear energy/energía nuclear   energía producida por medio de una reacción atómica controlada (pág. 428)

nuclear weapon/arma nuclear   arma cuya fuerza destructiva viene de una reacción nuclear (pág. 319)

oasis/oasis   área fértil o verde en un desierto (págs. 439, 485)

obsidian/obsidiana   piedra vítrea de color negro formada por el enfriamiento de la lava líquida de un volcán (pág. 198)

orbit/órbita   trayectoria que los cuerpos en el sistema solar siguen alrededor del Sol (pág. 29)

outback/tierra adentro   el interior de Australia (pág. 737)

overgraze/pastar excesivamente   cuando el ganado despoja los pastos hasta tal punto que las plantas no pueden crecer de nuevo (pág. 556)

ozone/ozono   tipo de oxígeno que forma una capa en la atmósfera que protege a todas las cosas vivas de ciertos rayos del Sol que son peligrosos (pág. 766)

pagoda/pagoda   templo budista de muchos pisos (pág. 670)

SPANISH GLOSSARY

pampas/pampa   llanura de gran extensión en América del Sur sin árboles y cubierta de hierba (pág. 240)

papyrus/papiro   papel egipcio (pág. 471)

parallel/paralelos   *véase* latitude (págs. 5, 699)

parliamentary democracy/democracia parlamentaria   gobierno en que los votantes eligen a representantes a un cuerpo que hace las leyes y que selecciona a un primer ministro para que sea el jefe del gobierno (págs. 166, 216, 341)

peat/turba   plantas parcialmente descompuestas en agua que se pueden secar y usar como combustible (pág. 342)

peninsula/península   masa de tierra con agua alrededor de tres lados (págs. 40, 191)

perestroika/perestroika   política soviética que relajó los controles gubernamentales y permitió que la economía se moviera hacia de libre empresa (pág. 415)

permafrost/permafrost   capa de suelo congelada en la tundra y las regiones subárticas; también se llama permagel (pág. 406)

pesticides/pesticidas   sustancias químicas poderosas que matan a los insectos que destruyen los cultivos (págs. 71, 640)

pharaoh/faraón   soberano del antiguo Egipto (pág. 470)

phosphate/fosfato   sal mineral que se usa en los abonos (págs. 486, 560, 761)

pictograph/pictograma   gráfica en que pequeños símbolos representan cantidades (pág. 12)

pidgin language/lengua franca   lenguaje formado al combinar elementos de varios idiomas distintos (pág. 760)

plain/llanura   extensión de tierra plana u ondulante a elevaciones bajas (pág. 40)

plantain/plátano de cocinar   tipo de banano (pág. 582)

plantation/plantación   granja grande en que se siembra un solo cultivo para venderse (pág. 194)

plate/placa   plancha de roca inmensa que forma parte de la corteza de la tierra (págs. 589, 714)

plateau/meseta   planicie a elevaciones más altas que las llanuras (pág. 40)

plate tectonics/tectónica de placas   teoría que dice que la corteza de la Tierra no es una envoltura enteriza, sino que está formada por placas, o planchas de roca inmensas, que se mueven (pág. 35)

plaza/plaza   sitio donde se reúne el público (pág. 202)

poaching/caza furtiva   cacería ilegal de animales protegidos (pág. 577)

polder/pólder   área de tierra ganada del mar (pág. 347)

polis/polis   término griego para "cuidad estado" (pág. 294)

polytheism/politeísmo   que cree en más de un dios (pág. 467)

pope/papa   líder de la Iglesia Católica Apostólica Romana (págs. 299, 371)

population density/densidad de población   promedio de personas que viven en una milla cuadrada o kilómetro cuadrado (pág. 89)

potash/potasa   tipo de sal mineral que a menudo se usa en los abonos (pág. 385)

prairie/pradera   área de pastos ondulantes en el interior con suelo muy fértil (pág. 160)

precious gems/piedras preciosas   valiosas piedras preciosas, como el rubí, el zafiro y el jade (pág. 709)

precipitation/precipitación   agua que regresa a la Tierra en la forma de lluvia, nieve, aguanieve o granizo (pág. 49)

prime minister/primer ministro   líder del gobierno en una democracia parlamentaria (pág. 167)

privatize/privatizar   transferir la propiedad de fábricas de las manos del gobierno a las de individuos (pág. 375)

productivity/productividad   la medida de la cantidad de trabajo ejecutado en un tiempo dado (pág. 314)

projection/proyección   una de las maneras de dibujar la Tierra redonda en una superficie plana para hacer un mapa (pág. 7)

prophet/profeta   mensajero de Dios (pág. 474)

province/provincia   división política regional, parecida a un estado (pág. 158)

pyramid/pirámide   estructura de piedra gigantesca que sirvió como tumba o monumento elaborado (pág. 470)

quota/cuota   límite en la cantidad de un producto que se puede importar de un país en particular (pág. 95)

rain forest/bosque húmedo   bosque denso que recibe grandes cantidades de lluvia todos los años (pág. 59)

rain shadow/sombra pluviométrica   área seca en el lado interior de montañas costeras (pág. 58)

recycling/reciclaje   usar materiales de nuevo en vez de botarlos (pág. 136)

refugee/refugiado   persona que huye de un país a otro para evitar la persecución o un desastre (págs. 91, 379, 585)

reincarnation/reencarnación   renacimiento del alma en un cuerpo nuevo (pág. 640)

relief/relieve   las diferencias en altitud de una zona; lo plana o accidentada que es una superficie (pág. 9)

renewable resource/recurso renovable   recurso natural que no se puede gastar, que la naturaleza puede reemplazar o que se puede cultivar de nuevo (pág. 92)

representative democracy/democracia representativa   gobierno en que las personas están representadas por dirigentes elegidos (pág. 146)

republic/república   gobierno nacional fuerte encabezado por líderes elegidos (págs. 216, 296, 487)

responsibilities/responsabilidades   deberes que la genta debe a su gobierno (pág. 99)

reunification/reunificación   juntar de nuevo las dos partes de Alemania bajo un mismo gobierno (pág. 351)

revolution/revolución   una órbita completa alrededor del Sol (pág. 31); un gran cambio, a menudo violento (pág. 306)

rights/derechos   beneficios y protecciones que están garantizados por ley (pág. 99)

rural/rural   área en el campo (pág. 150)

samurai/samurai   propietarios y guerreros poderosos del Japón (pág. 693)

satellite nation/nación satélite   nación dominada o controlada política y económicamente por otro país más poderoso (pág. 321)

sauna/sauna   cuarto de madera calentado por agua que hierve sobre piedras calientes (pág. 356)

savanna/sabana   pastos extensos en los Trópicos con pocos árboles (págs. 62, 550)

scale bar/barra de medir la escala   en un mapa, línea con divisiones que muestra la escala del mapa, generalmente en millas o kilómetros (pág. 8)

secede/secesión   separarse de un gobierno nacional (pág. 147)

secular/secular   no religioso (pág. 492)

selva/**selva**   bosque húmedo tropical, como el de Brasil (pág. 232)

serf/siervo   labrador que podía ser comprado y vendido con la tierra (págs. 301, 412)

service industry/industria de servicio   negocio que proporciona servicios a la gente en vez de producir productos (págs. 132, 195, 488)

shah/sha   título de los reyes que gobernaban Irán (pág. 519)

shogun/shogun   líder militar en Japón antiguo (pág. 693)

silt/cieno   pequeñas partículas de suelo fértil (pág. 484)

sirocco/siroco   vientos calurosos y secos que soplan a través de Italia desde el norte de África (pág. 360)

sisal/sisal   fibra de una planta que se usa para hacer soga y cordel (pág. 580)

slash-and-burn farming/agricultura por tala y quema   método de limpiar la tierra para el cultivo en que se cortan y se queman los bosques (pág. 616)

smog/smog   neblina espesa compuesta de niebla y sustancias químicas (pág. 206)

socialism/socialismo   sistema económico en que la mayoría de negocios son propiedad y están dirigidos por el gobierno (pág. 709)

sodium nitrate/nitrato de sodio   sustancia química usada en abonos y explosivos (pág. 274)

solar system/sistema solar   la Tierra, ocho planetas adicionales y miles de astros más pequeños que giran alrededor del Sol (pág. 29)

sorghum/sorgo   cereal de tallo alto cuyas semillas sirven de alimento y del cual se hace un jarabe para endulzar (pág. 610)

spa/termas   balneario con manantiales de agua mineral caliente en que la gente se baña para recobrar su salud (pág. 374)

station/estación   rancho donde se crían ganado vacuno u ovejas en Australia (pág. 737)

steppe/estepa   pastos parcialmente secos que a menudo se encuentran en los bordes de un desierto (págs. 67, 383, 406, 438, 680)

strait/estrecho   masa de agua delgada entre dos masas de tierra (págs. 42, 716)

strike/huelga   una negativa a trabajar, usualmente por una organización de trabajo, hasta que las demandas sean solucionadas (pág. 315)

subarctic/subártico   patrón del estado del tiempo con inviernos extremadamente fríos y veranos cortos y frescos (pág. 65)

subcontinent/subcontinente   masa de tierra grande que forma parte de un continente pero se puede diferenciar de él (pág. 638)

subsistence farm/granja de subsistencia   terreno pequeño en el cual un granjero cultiva sólo lo suficiente para alimentar a su propia familia (págs. 194, 552)

suburb/suburbio   comunidad pequeña en los alrededores de una ciudad (pág. 150)

summer solstice/solsticio de verano   día con más horas de sol y menos horas de oscuridad (pág. 32)

taiga/taiga   bosques enormes de árboles de hoja perenne en regiones subárticas (pág. 406)

tariff/arancel   impuesto sobre el valor de bienes importados (pág. 95)

terraced field/terrazas   franjas, parecidas a escalones, que se cortan en la ladera de una colina para que el suelo aguante el agua y se pueda usar para la agricultura (pág. 717)

textiles/textiles   tela tejida (pág. 315)

theocracy/teocracia   forma de gobierno en la cual un individuo gobernaba como líder religioso tanto como rey (pág. 467)

townships/municipios   barrios abarrotados de gente en las afueras de las ciudades de Sudáfrica donde viven la mayoría de las personas que no son blancas (pág. 607)

trench/fosa marina   valle en el fondo del mar (pág. 41)

SPANISH GLOSSARY

tributary/afluente río pequeño que desagua en un río más grande (pág. 645)

Tropics/Trópicos región entre el Trópico de Cáncer y el Trópico de Capricornio (pág. 53)

trust territory/territorio en fideicomiso área que está bajo el control temporario de otra nación (pág. 761)

tsetse fly/mosca tsetsé insecto cuya picada puede matar al ganado o a los seres humanos por medio de la enfermedad del sueño (pág. 573)

tsunami/tsunami ola inmensa causada por un terremoto en el fondo del mar (págs. 36, 690)

tundra/tundra inmensas planicies ondulantes y sin árboles en latitudes altas con climas en que sólo varias pulgadas del suelo de la superficie se deshielan (págs. 66, 159, 406)

union/sindicato organización laboral que negocia para mejorar las condiciones y pago de los trabajadores (pág. 315)

urban/urbano parte de una ciudad (pág. 150)

urbanization/urbanización movimiento hacia las ciudades (pág. 90)

vaquero/vaquero pastor de ganado vacuno (pág. 193)

vassal/vasallo noble en la sociedad medieval quien juraba lealtad a un lord en cambio de tierra (pág. 301)

wadi/uadi lecho de un río seco que llenan los aguaceros poco frecuentes (pág. 513)

water cycle/ciclo hidrológico proceso mediante el cual el agua se mueve de los océanos al aire, del aire a la tierra y de la tierra a los océanos una vez más (pág. 48)

watershed/cuenca fluvial región drenada por un río (pág. 584)

water vapor/vapor de agua agua en forma de gas (pág. 48)

weather/estado del tiempo cambios en la atmósfera que son difíciles de pronosticar y tienen lugar durante un período de tiempo corto (pág. 52)

weathering/desgaste proceso natural que rompe la superficie rocosa en peñas, grava, arena y suelo (pág. 37)

welfare state/estado de bienestar social estado que usa el dinero recaudado por los impuestos para mantener a personas que están enfermas, pobres, sin trabajo o retiradas (pág. 355)

winter solstice/solsticio de invierno día con menos horas de sol (pág. 32)

yurt/*yurt* tienda de campaña grande y circular hecha de pieles de animales que se puede desmantelar y llevar de un lugar a otro (pág. 681)

SPANISH GLOSSARY

INDEX

c=chart	m=map
d=diagram	p=photo
g=graph	ptg=painting

A.D. (anno Domini), 298
Abdullah II, 506
Abidjan, Côte d'Ivoire, 559, 561
Abomey, 559
Aborigines, 726, *ptg737,*
    738–739, *p739,* 747
absolute location, 5, *d5*
absolute monarchies, 83
Abuja, Nigeria, *p550,* 553
Acapulco, Mexico, 194
Accra, Ghana, 559, 561
acid rain, 37, 70, 135, 351, 370
Aconcagua, 183, 239, *g652*
addicts, 263
Addis Ababa, Ethiopia, 588
adobe, 202
Adriatic Sea, 381
Afghanistan, 89, 454, 462, *p519,*
    520, 523
Africa: ethnic groups of, *m589;*
    plate tectonics and, 35; popula-
    tion growth in, 76. *See also*
    Africa, south of the Sahara;
    Central and East Africa; North
    Africa and Southwest Asia;
    Southern Africa; West Africa.
Africa, south of the Sahara,
    533–567; climate of, 534;
    country profiles of, *c542–546;*
    economy of, 536; extreme points
    of, 541; gems and minerals of,
    m540; landforms of, 534; people
    of, 536–537; physical geography
    of, *m538;* political geography of,
    m539; population comparisons of,
    c541. See also Central and East
    Africa; Southern Africa; West
    Africa.
African Americans, 152
African National Congress
    (ANC), 606
Afrikaners, 605–606
Age of Exploration, 305
Age of Revolution, 306–307
Agricultural Revolution, 84
agriculture: in Angola, 614; in
    Asia, 626; in Australia, 738; in
    Canada, 116; in Chile, 274; in
    Colombia, 256; in Comoros, 617;
    in Ecuador, 268–269; in Egypt,
    486; in France, 345; in Indonesia,
    715; in Israel, 509, *p510;* in
    Japan, 693; in Latin America, 178;
    in Madagascar, 617; in Mexico,
    194; in Netherlands, *p347;* of
    New Zealand, 743; in Sri Lanka,
    652; in Taiwan, 679; in United
    States, 116. *See also* farming.

AIDS: in Africa, 594; in Botswana,
    612; in Central and East Africa,
    594; in South Africa, 607; in
    Uganda, 584; in Zimbabwe, 611
airlift, *p322*
air pollution, 37, 69, *p70,* 135,
    428, 664, 693
Akkad, 468
Alaska (U.S.), 114, 121, 129
Albania, 288, 380, 381, *p381*
Alberta, Canada, 163
Alexander I, 420
Alexander II, 412–413
Alexander the Great, 295
Alexandria, Egypt, 295, 486
Algeria, 454, 462, 491–492
Algiers, Algeria, 492
Allah, 477. *See also* Islam.
alliances, 316
Allies, 317
alluvial plain, 517
alphabet, 469. *See also* languages.
alpine vegetation, *p68,* 349
Alps, *p281,* 350
Altay Mountains, 660
altiplano: in Bolivia, 271; in Chile,
    274
altitude, 193, *d193,* 243. *See also*
    elevation.
Amazon Basin, 232, 235, 267
Amazon rain forest, 25,
    p230–231
Amazon River, 176, 183,
    p230–231, 232, *p232*
amendments, constitutional, 146
"Americanization," 103
American Revolution, 307
American Samoa, 761
Amharic language, 588
Amman, Jordan, 506
Amnesty International, 676
Amur River, 392
Anatolia, Turkey, 502–503
Andersen, Hans Christian, 357
Andes Mountains, 24, *p177,* 232,
    p253, m260, 266
Andorra, 288, 358
Angel Falls, 183, *p243*
Angkor Wat, *p711*
Angola, 542, 614–615
Ankara, Turkey, 504
***Anna Karenina* (Tolstoy),** 435
Annan, Kofi, 99
Antananarivo, Madagascar, 617
Antarctica, 24, *p29,* 66, *p97,* 176,
    p722, 722–733, *p725,* 731,
    p764, p 765, 764–768, *p773;* cli-
    mate of, 724–726; economy of,
    726; endangered environments
    of, *m730;* extreme points of, 731;
    landforms of, 724; people of,

    726–727; physical geography of,
    m728; political geography of,
    m729, m759; population
    comparisons of, *c727, c731*
Antarctic Treaty of 1959, 726,
    766
anthropologists, 26
Antigua, 184
apartheid, 546, *p546,* 606
Appalachian Mountains, 114,
    p115, 128, 159
apprentices, 302
apricots, *p644*
aqueducts, 297
aquifers, 490, 498
Arab Empire, 514–515
Arabian Desert, 485
Arabian Peninsula, 454
Arabian Sea, 516
Arabs, 456, 491–493, 504
Aral Sea, 439, *p439*
archaeologists, 26, *p505, p667*
archipelago, 219, 690
architecture: in Cambodia, *p711;*
    earthquakes and, *p37;* Leaning
    Tower of Pisa (Italy), *p361;* in
    Micronesia, *p760;* Sydney Opera
    House (Australia), *p738*
Arctic, *p115,* 159
Arctic Circle, 354
Arctic Ocean, 50, 114, 392, 405
Argentina, 176, 183–184,
    239–241
Armenia, 392, 400, 437–438
Arnesen, Liv, *p97*
arrowheads, *p26*
artifacts, *ptg26,* 27
arts, 82, *ptg203,* 282, 303, 395,
    p429, p433
Aryans, 640
Ashanti, 559, 561
Ashgabat, Turkmenistan, 439
Asia, 622–634; climate of,
    624–626; country profiles of,
    c632–634; economy of, 626;
    extreme points in, 631; landforms
    of, 624; monsoons in, *m630;* peo-
    ple of, 626–627; physical geogra-
    phy of, *m628;* political geography
    of, *m629;* population comparisons
    in, *c631. See also* Central Asia;
    China; Eurasian republics; Japan;
    Mongolia; North Africa and
    Southwest Asia; North Korea;
    South Asia; Southeast Asia; South
    Korea; Taiwan.
Asia Minor, 502
Assembly of First Nations, 170
Asunción, Paraguay, 242
Aswan High Dam, *p484,* 486
asylum, 593, 596

INDEX

Atacama Desert, 176, 183, 273
Atatürk, Kemal, 504
Athens, Greece, p294, 294–295, 362
Atlanta, Georgia (U.S.), p131
Atlantic Coastal Plain, 127
Atlantic Ocean, 50, 280
Atlas Mountains, p452–453, 454, 492, p492
atmosphere, 30, 69–70
atoll islands, 654, 760–761, p763
atomic bombs, 317, 692
Auckland, New Zealand, 744, p750
Aung San Suu Kyi, 710
Australia, p39, p722–723, 722–733, p727, 731, p734–736, 734–740, p772; Aborigines of, 747; animals of, 737, 740; climate of, 724–726; country profile of, c732; economy of, 726, 737–738; endangered environments of, m730; extreme points of, 731; government of, 739; history of, 738–739; landforms of, 724, 736–737; people of, 726–727, 738–739; physical geography of, m728; political geography of, m729; population comparisons of, c727, c731; voting in, p733
Australian Capital Territory (Australia), 739
Austria, 288, 353
authority, in European Union, 329
autonomy, 168
Autosub, 51, p51
autumnal equinox, 32
axis, of planets, 31, d31
Axis Powers, 317
Ayers Rock, p734–735
Azerbaijan, 392, 400, 438
Azores, p34
Aztec, 178, 199, 201, p201

B.C. (before Christ), 298
Babylon, 468
Bach, Johann Sebastian, 352
Baghdad, Iraq, 517, p517
Bahamas, 184, 219, 221, 228
Bahrain, 462, 515–516, p523
Baja California, 191
Baku, Azerbaijan, 438
Bali, Indonesia, p625, 715
Balkan Peninsula, 361, 377
ballet, in Russia, p434
Baltic republics, 371
Baltic Sea, 371
Bancroft, Ann, p97
Banff National Park, Canada, p158, 160
Bangkok, Thailand, 710, p719
Bangladesh, p52, 632, 646–647

Bantu, 553–554, 573, p609, 610, 615
Barbados, 184, 221
Barbuda, 184
Barcelona, Spain, 359
barriers to trade, 95
base map, 28
Basque, 359
bauxite, 220, 560, 715
Bavaria, p350
Bay of Bengal, 639, 646
Bay of Fundy, 121
bazaars, 488, p491
bears, polar, p115
bedouins, 505
Beethoven, Ludwig von, 352
Beijing, China, 666, p669, p673
Beirut, Lebanon, 505
Belarus, 288, 385–386
Belgium, 288, 347
Belgrade, Serbia, 380
Belize, 184, 212, 216–217
Benelux countries, 320–321, 347–348
Bengal Famine, 639
Benghazi, Libya, 491
Ben-Gurion, David, 511
Benin, 542, 558, p559
Bently Subglacial Trench, 731
Benue River, 553
Berbers, p482–483, 491–493, p492, 566
Bergen, Norway, p355
Berlin, Germany, p87, p319, 321–322
Berlin airlift, p322
Bern, Switzerland, 352
Bhaktapur, Nepal, p636–637
Bhutan, 632, p651, 651–652
Bhutto, Benazir, 646
Bible, 468
bilingual country, 167–168, 440
biodiversity, 72
biosphere, 69, 72
birth rate, 88
Bishkek, Kyrgyzstan, 440
bishops of Rome, 299
Black Forest, 351, p351
black market, 291
Black Sea, 280, 407, 456, p502, 504
blizzards, p53
blockade, 321
Blue Nile River, 586
Boers, 605
Boer War, 606
Bogatá, Colombia, 255
Bohemia, 374
bolero, 360
Bolívar, Simón, 243, 256, 272
Bolivia, 183, 184, p271, 271–273
Bonaparte, Napoleon, 307, 412, 420, ptg420, 434
boomerang, 738
border patrols, in Korea, p699
Borneo, 714

Bosnia and Herzegovina, 288, 323, m369, 380
Bosporus, 502, p502
Botswana, 542, 612
Brahma deity (Hinduism), 640
Brahmaputra River, 624, 646
Brasilia, Brazil, 236, p238
Bratislava, Slovakia, 375, p414
Brazil, 179, p179, 184, p230–231, 230–237; Amazon River in, 176; cities of, 236; coffee growing in, 95; culture of, 235–237; economic system of, 233–235; government of, 237; history of, 235–236; landforms of, 232–233; manufacturing in, 178; rain forest in, 187, p187
Brazzaville, Congo, 574
British Columbia (Canada), p156–157, 161–163
British Isles, 340. See also United Kingdom.
Brunei, 632, 717
Brussels, Belgium, 347
Bucharest, Romania, 378
Budapest, Hungary, 373, p373
Buddhism, p622–623, 626, 641, p666, 667, 681, 686, 693, 695, 700, 710, p710, 712
Buenos Aires, Argentina, 91, 240, p247
Bukhara, Uzbekistan, p436
Bulgaria, 288, 378
Burkina Faso, 542, 556, 558
Burundi, 542, 584–585, 595
Bush, George W., 140, p261, 263, p331, 593
bush (pAustralia), 739
Byzantine Empire, 297, 299, m301, 504

Cabinda, 614
cacao, p553
Caesar Augustus, 296–297
Cairo, Egypt, 456, 486, 488
Calcutta, India, 642
calendars: in ancient Egypt, 471; Aztec, 201, p201
California (U.S.), p134
caliph, 514
calligraphy, 670
Calvin, John, 305
Cambodia, 632
camels, p513, p687
Cameroon, 542, p570, 573–574
campesinos, 257
Canada, 114–123, 156–173; bilingual nature of, 167–168; climate of, 114–116; country profile of, c122; economic regions of, 161–163; economy of, 116; ethnic diversity of, 168–169; extreme points of, c121, m121; food production of, m120; history of, 165–167; landforms of, 114,

158–161; native peoples of, 170; North American Free Trade Agreement (NAFTA) and, 136; Nunavut Territory of, 168; people of, 116–117; physical geography of, *m118*; polar bears in, *p115*; political geography of, *m119*; provinces of, *c123*; waterways of, 114

Canadian Shield, 159
Canberra, Australia, 739
Cancún, Mexico, 194
canopy, of forest, 62
Canterbury Plains, 742
Cape Horn, 273
Cape of Good Hope, 305, 604
Cape Town, South Africa, *p532, p602–603, p604*
Cape Verde Islands, 542, 558
capitalism, 94, 424
Captiva Island, Florida (U.S.), *p133*
capybaras, *p242*
cardinal directions, 8, 33
Caribbean islands, 219–223
Caribbean Sea, 191, 213
Carnival: in Brazil, *p236,* 237; in Central America, 217
Carpathian Mountains, 280, 368, 373, 377, 383
carpets, Persian, 507
Carthage, Tunisia (ancient), 491
Casablanca, Morocco, 492–493
casbahs, 492
Cascade Range, 129
cash crops, 256, 438
Caspian Sea, 392, 399, 407, 436, 456, 461
caste system, 640
Castro, Fidel, 222
cataracts, 469
categorizing information, 238, 328
Cathedral of Monterrey, Monterrey, Mexico, *p188–189*
Cather, Willa, 151
Catherine the Great, 411
Catholicism. *See* Roman Catholicism.
Caucasus Mountains, 392, 406, 436–438
caudillos, 243
cause and effect, 416
cave paintings, *ptg26*
Cayenne, French Guiana, 245
Celebes, Indonesia, 714
cell phones, *p676*
Celts, 343
census, 108, *p108*
Central African Republic, 542, 573–574
Central America, 176, 212–217; economic regions and systems, *m213*; economic systems of, 213–215; history of, 215–217; landforms of, 212–213; political geography of, *m213. See also*

Latin America; *and specific countries of Central America.*
Central and East Africa, 568–601; AIDS in, 594; Burundi, 584–585; Cameroon, 573–574; Central African Republic, 573–574; Congo, 574; Democratic Republic of the Congo, 570–573; Djibouti, 589–590; economic activity of, *m583;* Equatorial Guinea, 575; Eritrea, 588–589; Ethiopia, 588; Gabon, 574; Kenya, 577–579; physical geography of, *m572;* political geography of, *m580;* population density of, *m587;* refugees in, 591–596; Rwanda, 584–585; São Tomé and Principe, 575; sleeping sickness in, 576; Somalia, 590; Sudan, 586–588, 592–593; Tanzania, 579–581; Uganda, 582–584
Central Asia, 436, 438–440. *See also* Russian and Eurasian republics; South Asia.
Central Highlands, 212
Central Lowland, 128
Central Mosque, Kano, Nigeria, *p548–549*
Ceylon (Sri Lanka), 653
Chad, *p532,* 542, 556, 558
Chaldeans, 468
chancellor, of Germany, 351
channel, 42
Chao Phraya River, 710
chaparral, 64
Charlemagne, 300
charters, 302
Chaucer, Geoffrey, 304
Chávez, Hugo, 244
Chavuma, Zambia, *p610*
Chechnya, Russia, 430
Cheetah Conservation Fund, 77
cheetahs, *p76,* 76–77
Chennai, India, 642
Chernobyl Nuclear Power Plant, Ukraine, *p383*
Chiang Kai-shek, 667, 679
Chiapas (Mexico), 205
Chicago, Illinois (U.S.), *p128*
Chihuahuan Desert, *p48*
child labor, *p105, p315*
Children's Environmental Trust Foundation, 251
Chile, 176, 178, 183–184, *p272,* 273–274
Chile Antarctic Territory, 766–767
China, 84, 631, 632, *p658–659,* 658–673; culture of, 669–670; economy of, 663–664; government of, 668–669, 673; history of, 666–667; Korea and, 698; landforms of, 660–662; North Korean refugees in, 672; people of, 669; physical geography of, *m661;* Silk Road and, 686; Three Gorges Dam in, 665; trade and, 105

Chinese gooseberry, *p741*
Chipaya, *p271*
Chişinău, Moldova, 386
chlorofluorocarbons, 772–773
chocolate, *p352, p553*
Christianity, 293, 299–300, 457, 475–476, *p475;* ancient Rome and, 297; in Asia, 626; in China, 686; in Ethiopia, *p586;* in India, 641; in Lebanon, 505; in Melanesia, 760; in South Korea, 700; in Uganda, 583. *See also* Eastern Orthodox Christianity; Roman Catholicism; Russian Orthodox Christianity.
Chunnel, 325
Church of the Resurrection, St. Petersburg, Russia, *p395*
Cinco de Mayo, 203
circle graphs, 12, *g12,* 648, *g648*
Cisneros, Sandra, 151
cities: of Brazil, 236; growth of, 302; of India, *p639;* of Mexico, 202; of Russia, *p431*
city-states, Greek, 295
Ciudad Juárez, Mexico, 194
civic participation, 99
civics, 676
civilizations, early, *m86. See also* Egypt; Greece; Mesopotamia.
civil liberties, 673
civil wars, 492, 710
Civil War (U.S.), 147
Clark, Helen, *p749*
Classical Europe, 294
Classical Greece, 282
Cleopatra, 487
climate, 47, 52–59; of Africa, south of the Sahara, 534–536; of Andean countries, *m273;* of Antarctica, 765; of Asia, 624–626; of Australia, Oceania, and Antarctica, 724–726; of Canada, 114–116; of Caribbean islands, 220; dry, 67; of Egypt, 486; of Europe, 280–282; highland, 68; high latitude, 65–66; of Indonesia, 715; of Israel, 508–509; landforms and, 56–58; of Latin America, 176; of Melanesia, 758–759; of Mexico, 192–193; of Micronesia, 760; mid-latitude, 63–65; of Nepal, 650; of Nigeria, 550–551; of North Africa and Southwest Asia, 454–456; ocean currents and, 56; people and, 41; people's impact on, 58–59; of Polynesia, 761; regions of, *m63;* of Russia, 404–405, *m405,* 420–421; of Saudi Arabia, 513; of Southwest Asia, *m509;* of Sri Lanka, 652; stability of, 51; sun and, 53–54; tropical, 62; of Turkey, 503; of United States, 114–116, 130; vegetation zones and, 61–68; weather and, 52–53; of West

INDEX

Africa coastal countries, 558; wind and, 54–56
clothing, *p640*; of ancient soldiers, *p297*; of Inuit, *p166*; in Mexico, *p194*; in West Africa, *p557*
coalition governments, in Italy, 360
coal mining, in Poland, *p370*
coastal plains, 127
Coast Mountains, 160
cocaine, 253, 256, 259–264, *m260*
coca leaves, 256
Code of Hammurabi, 468
Coerr, Eleanor, 692
coffee production: in Brazil, *g234*; in Colombia, *p256*
Cold War, 319–323, 413–415, 428
Colombia, 176, 184, 216, 254–265; economic resources of, 255–256; history and people of, 256–257; illegal drugs and, 259–264; landforms of, 254–255
"Colombian Gold," 253
Colombo, Sri Lanka, 653
colonies, 166
Columbian Exchange, 220, 228, *m229*, 305
Columbus, Christopher, 220, 228, 254, 305
COMECON. *See* Council for Mutual Economic Assistance (COMECON).
command economies, 93, 321, 413
commercial farming, 94
common law, 300
Common Market, 321, 324, 330
commonwealth, 223
communication, 98, *c98*
communism, 221, 283, 291, 316, 320, 324, 331, 367, 369, 378, 386, 394, 401, 424–426, 663, 667, 679, 680, 699; in Cambodia, 711; in Laos, 710; in Vietnam, 712
Comoros, 542, 617–618
comparisons, making, 702
compass rose, 33
computers, 85
concentration camps (World War II), *p318*
conclusions, drawing, 555
condensation, 49
Confucianism, 667, 700
Congo, 542–543, 574
Congo River, 534, 571, 574
coniferous trees, 64, 349
conservation, 71, 499
Constantine the Great (Constantine I), 297, 299, 476, 504
Constantinople, 297, 299, 504
constitution: of Iraq, 523; of Japan, 675; of United Kingdom,

307; of United States, 125, 146, 329
Constitutional Convention (U.S.), 147
constitutional monarchies, 83; of Japan, 694; of Morocco, 493; of Spain, 359; of Sweden, 355; of United Kingdom, 342
consuls, 296
consumer goods, 378
contiguous states, 126
Continental Congress, 147
continental divide, 129, 352
continental drift, 35–36, *m45*
continental rift, 534
continental shelf, 40–41
continents, 22, *m41*, *g652*
contour maps, 713
convention documents, 593
convents, 300
Cook, James, 738
Cook Strait, 741
Coon Come, Matthew, 170, *p170*
Copán, Honduras, 216
Copenhagen, Denmark, 356–357, *p357*
copper belt, 610
coral reefs, 129, *p758*, 760
cordillera, 160, 254. *See also* mountains.
core, of earth, 34, *d35*
Corpus Christi, *p244*
Cortés, Hernán, 199
Costa Rica, 184, 212–215, *m213*, *p215*, 216–217
Côte d'Ivoire, 543, 558, 561
cottage industry, 315, 639
Council for Mutual Economic Assistance (COMECON), 321
covenant, 473. *See also* Judaism.
Cree, 170
Crete, 361
Crimean Peninsula, 383
critical thinking, 238, 416, 555, 598, 682, 702
Croatia, 288, 323, *m369*, 379
crop rotation, 70
crops: cash, 438; genetically altered, 332; monoculture, 558. *See also* agriculture; farming.
crucifixion, 475
Crusades, 300
crust, of earth, 34–37, *d35*
Crutzen, Paul, 773
Cuba, 184, 219, 221–222
culture, 78–85, *m84*; of ancient Greece, 295; in architecture, *p37*; of Brazil, 235–237; of Canada, 116–117; of Caribbean islands, 220–222; change in, 84–85; of Chile, 274; of China, 669–670; "clash" of, 103; of Colombia, 257; definition of, 80–83; of Egypt, *p487*; of Japan, 695–696; learning about, 106; of Mexico, 203–204; minority, 430; of Morocco, 493; of Pacific Ocean

islands, *p756–757*; of Peru, 267; of Portugal, 359; of Russia, 433–434; of Spain, 359; of Tanzania, 581; of Turkey, 504; of United States, 116–117, *p150*, 150–152; of Zimbabwe, *p611*
cuneiform writing, 467–468
currents, ocean, 56, *m57*
customs, Japanese, *p695*
customs dogs, 262
Cuzco, Peru, 267
cyclones, 617, 646–647
Cyprus, 288, 361
Cyrillic alphabet, 378–379, 386, 432
czars, 411–412
Czechoslovakia, *p414*
Czech Republic, 288, *p366–367*, *p372*, 374, *p374*, *p376*

da Gama, Vasco, 305
Dakar, Senegal, 560
Dalai Lama, 669
dalang, 718, *p718*
Dallas, Texas (U.S.), *p152*
Dalol, Denakil Depression, 541
Damascus, Syria, 505
Danube River, 280, 287, 350, 372, *p373*, 377
Daoism, 667
Dardanelles, 502
Dar es Salaam, Tanzania, 581
Darwin, Charles, 270
databases, using, 258
***David* (Michelangelo),** *p303*
da Vinci, Leonardo, 282, 304, 308
***da Vinci, Leonardo, self-portrait* (da Vinci),** *ptg308*
Day of the Dead, 204
Dayton Peace Accords, 380
Dead Sea, 461, 508
death rate, 87
Death Valley, California (U.S.), 121
debt, foreign, Mexican, 205–206
Deccan Plateau, 639
de Cervantes, Miguel, 304
deciduous trees, 64, 349
Declaration of First Nations (Native Americans), 167
Declaration of Independence (U.S.), 147, 167
deforestation, 70, 235, 616
Delhi, India, 642
Delphi, Greece, *p278*
delta, of rivers, 42, 469, 484, 711
Delta Plan Project, 347
demand, supply and, 93
democracy, 294, 673, 675–676; in Asia, 627; in East Timor, 715; in Indonesia, 715; in Iraq, 523; in modern Russia, 429, 441–446; representative, 146

INDEX

democratic republic government, 512, 717
Democratic Republic of the Congo, 543, 570–573, *p574*
Deng Xiaoping, 668
Denmark, 288, 356–357
Department of Homeland Security, 140, 149
desalinization, 498
desert climate, *p67,* 130; of Antarctica, 726, 765; of Australia, 724
deserts: in Africa, *p23*; Atacama Desert, 176, 183, 273; Chihuahuan Desert, *p48*; of Egypt, 485–486; Garagum Desert, 439; Gobi, 624, 631, 661, 680; Great Indian Desert, 645; Great Victoria Desert, 731; Kalahari Desert, 536, 612; Namib Desert, 536, 604, 616; Negev Desert, 508; Nubian Desert, 586; Rub' al Khali Desert, 513; Sahara, *p452,* 454, 461, 486, *p490, p556,* 566; Syrian Desert, 504; Taklimakan Desert, 624, 661, 686
desertification, 557
deterrence, 320
development, 96, 105
Dhaka, Bangladesh, *p52,* 647
dialects, 81. *See also* languages.
diamond production, *m571,* 605, 612
Dias, Bartholomeu, 305
Diaspora, 474
dictatorships, 83, 148, 491, 518, 672, 711
directions, 33
displaced persons, 593–594
divine right of kings, 306
Diwali, 642
Djibouti, 541, 543, 589–590
Djibouti, Djibouti, 590
Dnieper River, 383
Dominica, 185
Dominican Republic, 185, 220–223
Don River, 406
Dostoyevsky, Fyodor, 434
drought, 55, 556, 587, 612
drugs, illegal, 253, 256, 259–264, *m260*
Drug Treatment Court, 263
dry climates, 67
dry desert climate, 486, 513
dry farming, 358
dry steppe climate, 130, 437
Dubai, United Arab Emirates, *p452*
Dublin, Ireland, 343
Dushanbe, Tajikistan, 440
Dutch. *See* Netherlands.
dynasties, 666, 698
dzongs, 651
Dzonkha, 651

eagles, *p678*
Eakins, Thomas, 151
Earth: forces shaping, 34–38; layers of, *d35*; as planet, 29–32
earthquakes, 22, 190, 192, 407, 454, 502, *p690, p694,* 714; in Central America, 212; in China, 662; plate tectonics and, 36–37; in Ring of Fire, 624
East Africa. *See* Central and East Africa.
East Berlin, Germany, *p319*
Easter eggs, 382, *p382*
Eastern Desert, 485–486
eastern Europe. *See* Europe, eastern.
Eastern Ghats, 638
Eastern Orthodox Christianity, 299, 378–379, 385, 476
Eastern Roman Empire, 297
East Germany, 321
East Timor, 632, 714, 715
eclipses, *p30,* 344
economic regions and systems, 83, 93–94, *c94, m95*; of Africa, south of the Sahara, 536–537; of Argentina, 240; of Asia, 626; of Australia, 737–738; of Australia, Oceania, and Antarctica, 726; of Bolivia, 272; of Brazil, 233–235; of Canada, 116, *c117, m161,* 161–163; of Caribbean islands, 220; of Central America, 213–215; of Central and East Africa, *m583*; of Chile, 274; of China, 663–664; of Colombia, 255–256; command economy as, 413; of Egypt, 486; of Eurasian republics, *m437*; of Europe, 282; of Hungary, 373; of India, 638–640, *p640*; of Indonesia, 715; of Israel, 509–510; of Japan, 692–693; in Kenya, 578–579; of Latin America, 178, *c179*; of Mexico, 193–195; of modern Russia, *p424, m425,* 426–428; of New Zealand, 743; of Nigeria, 551–552, *p553*; of North Africa and Southwest Asia, 456; of Pakistan, 645–646; of Poland, 369; of Portugal, 359; of Russia and Eurasian republics, 394; of Slovakia, 375; of South America, *m240*; in South Asia, *m650*; of Spain, 359; specialization in, 95; of Taiwan, 678–679; of Tanzania, 580–581; of United Kingdom, 341; of United States, 116, *c117,* 131–135, *m132*; of Venezuela, 243
ecosystems, 72
ecotourist, 215, 581
Ecuador, 185, *p253,* 266, 268–269
education, *p646*

Egypt, *p19,* 84, 462, *p464–465, p484,* 484–489; ancient, *m467,* 469–471; climate of, 486; desert areas of, 485–486; economy of, 486; folktales of, 489; modern history of, 487; people of, 487–488; Sinai peninsula and, 485
Eiffel Tower, Paris, France, *p338–339*
Elburz Mountains, 519
elections, *p588,* 733
electrical generation, *p92*
electronic databases, 258
elephants, 536, *p535, p568–569, p598*
Elephant seals, *p765*
elevation, 40, 57, 224, *c224,* 440
***El Gaucho Martín Fierro* (Hernández),** 246
Elizabeth I, 304
ellipses, orbits as, 29
El Niño, 55–56, *d56*
El Salvador, 185, 212, 216
embalming, in ancient Egypt, *p469,* 470
embargo, 222, 518
emeralds, *p254*
emigrants, 91
Emperor penguins, *p725, p764*
emperors, Roman, 296
Empty Quarter, 513
emus, 740, *p740*
endangered spaces, 76
energy resources, 134. *See also* hydroelectric power.
Engels, Friedrich, *ptg416*
England, 304, *p312–313,* 340, *p340. See also* Great Britain; United Kingdom.
enterprises, 442
entertainment industry, 135
environment, 24; balance in, 69–72; of China, 664; climate in, 47; endangered in Australia, Oceania, and Antarctica, *m730*; of India, 640; in Indonesia, 715; of Japan, 693; modern European, 326; of modern Russia, 428
environmental refugees, 593
environmental stations, 768, *p768*
Equator, 4, 5, 32, 53, 59–60, 61–62, 176, 192, 243, 266, 534, 573, 715
Equatorial Guinea, 543, 575
equinoxes, 32, *p197*
Eriksson, Lief, 354
Eritrea, 543, 588–589
erosion, 23, 38, 70, 235, 428, 650
escapees, 673
estancias: in Argentina, 240; in Colombia, 256
Estonia, 288, 371
Ethiopia, 541, 543, 588, 592, 595

ethnic cleansing, 379
ethnic groups, 81; of Africa,
  m589; of Australia, 726; of
  Cambodia, 711; of Canada, *c121,*
  168–169; of China, 666; of
  Ghana, 561; of Indonesia, 715; of
  Kenya, 579, *p581*; of Latin
  America, *c183*; of modern Russia,
  430; of New Zealand, *p743*; of
  Nigeria, 552; of Russia, 394–395,
  g395; of Rwanda and Burundi,
  585; of South Africa, 605; of Sri
  Lanka, 653–654; of United States,
  c121, p145, 149–150; of
  Zimbabwe, 611
ethnocentrism, 746
EU. *See* European Union (EU).
Euphrates River, 454, 456, 466,
  505, 517
Eurasia, 404, 680
Eurasia Foundation, 446
Eurasian republics, 436–446;
  economic activity of, *m437*
euro, 325, *p325,* 329, *p329*
Europe, 278–291, *m328*;
  Classical, 294–297, *m295*; climate of, 280–282; Cold War and,
  319–320, *m320*; country profiles
  of, *c288–291*; economic systems
  of, 282; environmental issues
  and, 326; European union and,
  320–321, 324–326, 328–332;
  extreme points of, 287; influence
  of, 283; landforms of, 280; languages of, *m286, c385*; Medieval,
  299–302; modern era of,
  314–318; people of, 282–283;
  physical geography of, *m284*;
  political geography of, *m285*;
  Protestant Reformation in,
  304–305; Renaissance in,
  303–304; revolutions in, 283;
  World War I in, 316; World
  War II in, 317, 318. *See also*
  specific countries of Europe.
Europe, eastern, 321–323, *p324,*
  366–389; Albania, 381; Baltic
  republics, 371; Belarus, 385–386;
  Bosnia and Herzegovina, 380;
  Bulgaria, 378; Croatia, 379;
  Czech Republic, 374; Hungary,
  372–373; Macedonia, 380;
  Moldova, 386; Poland, 368–371;
  population density of, *m384*;
  Romania, 377–378; Serbia and
  Montenegro, 380; Slovakia, 375;
  Slovenia, 379; Ukraine, 382–385
Europe, western, 338–365;
  Andorra, 358; Austria, 353;
  Belgium, 347; Denmark,
  356–357; Finland, 356; France,
  345–347; Germany, 350–352;
  Greece, 361–362; Iceland, 357;
  Italy, 360–361; Luxembourg,
  348; Netherlands, 347–348;
  Norway, 354–355; Portugal,
  358–360; Republic of Ireland,
  342–343; Spain, 358–360;
  Stonehenge, 344; Sweden,
  355–356; Switzerland, 352–353;
  United Kingdom, 340–342
**European Atomic Energy
  Community (EURATOM),** 325
**European Commission to the
  United States,** 332
European Economic Community,
  321
European Russia, 405–406
European Union (EU), 96, 283,
  320–321, 324–326, 328–332,
  355,356, 359, 362
evaporation, 48
Everglades, Florida (U.S.), *p134*

Fabergé, Carl, *p433,* 434
facts *versus* opinions, 682
fado, 360
Falkland Islands, 241
Fante, 561
Farley, Chris, 260–261, *p260*
farming, 647, 650; in Argentina,
  240; in Caribbean islands, 220;
  commercial, 94; cotton, *p152*;
  dry, 358; genetically altered crops
  and, 332; intensive cultivation in,
  693; monoculture, 558; in
  Myanmar, 708; in North Africa
  and Southwest Asia, 456; slash-
  and-burn, 616; subsistence, 96,
  194, 214, 267, 558, 582, 607,
  p607, 614, 616, 651, 761. *See
  also* agriculture.
Farsi language, 519
Faulkner, William, 151
faults, in earth's crust, 37, 438
favelas, 234
federal government, 146, 204,
  351, 429, 739
Federated States of Micronesia,
  732, 760
fellahin, 488–489
Ferdinand and Isabella, of Spain,
  304
Fertile Crescent, *m86,* 467,
  m467
fertilizers, 70
feudalism, 301
fiestas, 203, *p204*
figurehead, emperor as, 675
Fiji Islands, 732, *p769*
Filipovic, Zlata, 380
"Final Solution," 318
Finland, 289, 356
fishing, 162
five pillars of faith, 477
fjords, 354, 742
flamenco, 360
Flemish language, 347
flexible structures, *p37*
Florida (U.S.), *p20–21, p133,*
  p134
food: Canadian production of,
  m120; in Egypt, *p487*; United
  States production of, *m120. See
  also* agriculture; farming.
foothills, 267
foreign debt, Mexican, 205–206
foreign trade, 663
**Former Yugoslav Republic of
  Macedonia (F.Y.R.O.M.),** 290,
  380
Fossey, Dian, 77
fossil fuels, 93, 135
fossils, 27, 764
Fox, Vicente, 204
France, *p279,* 287, 289, *p299,*
  300, *p316,* 326, *p338–339,*
  p345, 345–347; Cambodia and,
  711; Caribbean islands and, 221;
  Comoros and, 618; mountains of,
  p23; New Caledonia and, 758;
  Seychelles and, 618; vegetation
  map of, *m349*
Frank, Anne, 348
Franklin, Shirley, *p131*
Freedom House, 672–676
Freedom Tower, 141, *d141*
free enterprise, 94, 116, 131,
  161; in China, 663; in Kenya,
  578; in Mongolia, 680
free market system, 424; in
  Russia, 394; in Slovakia, 375
free ports, 716
free trade, 96, 136, 157, 223,
  271, 329–330
French Guiana, 185, 239, 245
French language, 165–166, 572
French Polynesia, *p726,* 761–762
French Revolution, 307
freshwater, 41, 49–50
Fuentes, Carlos, 203
Fulani, 552, 558
fur seal, *p722*

Gabon, 543, 574, *p574*
Gaborone, Botswana, 612
Gaelic language, 340
Gagarin, Yuri, 409
Galápagos Islands, *m255,* 268,
  270; tortoise of, 270, *p270*
Gambia, 543, 558
Gandhi, Indira, *p641,* 642
Gandhi, Mohandas, 641, *p641,*
  676
Ganges Plain, 638
Ganges River, 624, *p638,* 639,
  646
Garagum Desert, 439
Gartner, Mike, 446
gauchos, 240, 246, *p246*
Gautama, Siddartha, 651
Gaza Strip, 511–512, *m511*
Gdańsk, Poland, 370
gems, *g571*; in Africa, *m540*
genetically altered crops, 332
Geneva, Switzerland, 352
Genghis Khan, 680

INDEX

genocide, 317
geographic information systems (GIS), 6, 25, 28
geography, 1; defined, 22; five themes of, 2; handbook for, 1–15; human, 3, 24; physical, 2, 22–23, *p23*; six essential elements of, 2–3; terms of, 14–15; tools of, 6, 24–25; uses of, 3, 26
Georgetown, Guyana, 244
Georgia, 392, *c400,* 438
geothermal energy, 357, 743
Germany, 289, 300, 316, *p319,* 326, *p350,* 350–352
geysers, 357, 741
Ghana, 543, 558
Ghana Empire, 557, 566
Giant pandas, *p660*
giant sequoia, *p61*
Gibraltar, 493
giraffes, *p532–533,* 536
GIS. *See* geographic information systems (GIS).
glaciers, 38; of Canada, 159; in Chile, 273
glasnost, 415
Glenn, John, 409
globalization, 99, 101–106, *m102, p103*
Global Positioning System (GPS), 6, 25
global warming, 58–59, 70, 332
Gobi, 624, 631, 661, 680
Golan Heights, 508, *m511*
Goode's Interrupted Equal-Area projection, 7, *m7*
Gorbachev, Mikhail, 323, 415, *p415*
gorillas, 76–77, *p77, p582*
Gothic cathedrals, 282
government, 83, *c83;* of Algeria, 492; of Asia, 627; of Australia, 739; of Bahrain, *p523;* of Brazil, 237; of Canada, 166–167; of China, 668–669, 673; of Czech Republic, 374; of Democratic Republic of the Congo, 573; of Egypt, 487; of Germany, 351; of Greece, 362; of Iraq, *p523;* of Israel, 512; of Italy, 360; of Japan, 693; of the Maldives, 654; of Mesopotamia, 467; of Mexico, 204; of modern Russia, 429; of Morocco, 493; of Nepal, 650; of Nigeria, 554; of Norway, 355; of Pakistan, 646; pollution laws and, 428; of Portugal, 359; of Slovakia, 375; of Spain, 359; of Sweden, 355; of Tanzania, 581; of Uganda, 583–584; of United Kingdom, 341; of United States, *d148;* of Venezuela, 243–244
GPS. *See* Global Positioning System (GPS).
Granada, Nicaragua, *p216*
Gran Chaco, 242
Grand Banks, 162
Grand Canyon, *p40,* 121, 135

Grandfather and His Little Grandson, The (Tolstoy), 435
Grand Mosque, Makkah, Saudi Arabia, *p478*
Grand Teton National Park, *p46–47*
graphs, *g11,* 11–12, *g12;* bar, 11, *g11, g13;* circle/pie, 12, *g12,* 648, *g648;* climo-, 13, *g13;* line, 11, *g11, g13;* picto-, 12, *g12*
grasslands, 64
Great Artesian Basin, 737
Great Barrier Reef, *p39,* 724, 736
Great Britain, 287, 314. *See also* England; United Kingdom.
Great Depression, 317
Great Dividing Range, 724, 736
Greater Antilles, 219
Great Indian Desert, 645
Great Lakes, 114, 128, 134, 160
Great Mosque of Djenné, Djenné, Mali, 562
Great Mother Snake, 737
Great Plains, 128, *p128,* 160
Great Pyramid of Khufu, Egypt, 470, 472, *p495*
Great Rift Valley, *p40,* 534, 577, 580, 588, 589, 610
Great Sphinx at Giza, Egypt, 470
Great Victoria Desert, 731
Great Wall of China, *p658–659,* 667
Great War (World War I), 316
Great Zimbabwe, *p609,* 611
Greece, *p278,* 289, *p294,* 361–362, *p362;* classical, 282; empire of, *m295;* Golden Age of, 294–295
Greek Orthodox Christians, 362
Greek theater, *p295*
greenhouse effect, 30, 58–59
Greenland, 51, 66, 356
green revolution, 639
Grenada, 185, 221
groundwater, 50
Guadalajara, Mexico, 194
Guadeloupe, Lesser Antilles, *p210–211,* 221
Guam, 760
Guaraní, 242
Guatemala, *p174,* 185, 212–213, 215–217
Guatemala City, Guatemala, 217
Guayaquil, Ecuador, 269
Guianas, 244–245
guilds, 302, *ptg302*
Guinea, 543, 558
Guinea-Bissau, 543, 558
Gulf Coastal Plain, 127
Gulf of Guinea, 550, 558
Gulf of Mexico, 114, 191
Gulf of Thailand, 711
Gulf of Tonkin, 711
GUM state department store, *p431*
Gutenberg, Johannes, 304
Guyana, 185, 239, 244

habitats, endangered, 76, 640
haciendas, 199
Haifa, Israel, 512
haiku, 695, 697
Haiti, 185, 220–222, 222
Halifax, Nova Scotia (Canada), 162
Hammurabi's Code, 468
Han Chinese, 666
hangul language, 698–699
Hanoi, Vietnam, 712
harambee, 579
Harare, Zimbabwe, 611
Hatsheptsut, 470
Hausa, 552
Hawaii (U.S.), 129
Hawthorne, Nathaniel, 151
heat islands, 58
heavy industry, 356, 426
Helsinki, Finland, 356
hemispheres, 4, *d4*
Henry VII, of England, 304
Hermitage Museum, St. Petersburg, Russia, *p427,* 434
Hernández, José, 246
heroin, 261, *p261*
Herzegovina. *See* Bosnia and Herzegovina.
Hidalgo, Miguel, 200
Hidden Holy Land (Bhutan), 651
hieroglyphics: Egyptian, 470–471; Mayan, 198
highland climate, 68, *p68,* 650
high latitude climates, 65–66
high-technology industry, 678, *p679,* 716, 738
hijackings, 138
Hijrah, 476
Hijuelos, Oscar, 151
Himalaya, 36, 39, 624, 638, 649, 651, 660
Hinduism, 626, *p638,* 640, *p640,* 651, 715, 760
Hindu Kush, 454, 520, 645
Hiroshima, Japan, 692, 694
Hispaniola, 219, 222
historians, 26
history, 82; of Argentina, 240–241; of Australia, 738–739; of Brazil, 235–236; of Canada, 165–167; of Caribbean islands, 220–222; of Central America, 215–217; of Colombia, 256–257; of Democratic Republic of the Congo, 573; of Europe, 292–308, 312–333; of India, 640–641; of Israel, 511–512; of Japan, 693–694; of Kenya, 579; of Libya, 491; of modern Egypt, 487 (*See also* Egypt, ancient); of Mongolia, 680–681; of Morocco, 493; of New Zealand, 743–744; of Nigeria, 553–554; of Sahel countries (West Africa), 556–557; of South Africa, 605–607; of Taiwan, 679;

of Tanzania, 581; of Tunisia, 491; of Turkey, 504; of Uganda, 583–584; of United States, 145–149; of Venezuela, 243–244; of Vietnam, 712; of West Africa coastal countries, 559

Hitler, Adolf, *p317,* 317–318, 420

HIV, 584. *See also* AIDS.

Ho Chi Minh City, Vietnam, 712

hockey, *p168*

Hokkaido Island, Japan, 690

Holland. *See* Netherlands.

Holocaust, 317–318, 511

Holy Roman Empire, 300

Homer, Winslow, 151

Honduras, 185, 212, 215, *p215,* 216

Hong Kong, China, *p18,* 664

Honshu Island, Japan, 690

Horn of Africa, 586

Horseshoe Falls, *p171*

host countries, for refugees, 596

Hudson Bay, 159

Hughes, Langston, 151, 152

Hugo, Victor, 347

Huguenots, 305

human geography, 3, 23–24

humanism, 303–304

human resources, 314

human rights, 593, 634

humid continental climate, 64, *p65,* 130, 404

humidity, 48

humid subtropical climate, 65, *p65,* 130, 650

Hungarian Plain, 372

Hungary, *p278,* 289, 331, 372–373

Hurricane Mitch, *p215*

hurricanes, 55, 193, 213, 220

Hussein, Saddam, 518, 522

Hussein I, 506

Hutu, 585

hydroelectric power, 92, 170, 242, 486, 505, 561, 571, 609, 743

hydrosphere, 69, 71

Hyksos, 470

Ibadan, Nigeria, 553

Iberian Peninsula, 358–360

Ibo, Nigeria, 552

ice, 38

ice cap climate, 66, *p66*

Iceland, 289, 357

ice shelves, 51

Idaho (U.S.), 61

Idi Amin, 583

Ilo, Peru, 271

immigrants, 91, 148, 593

imperialism, 316

Inca, 178, 228, *p266,* 267

independence: in Africa, *m615;* in Argentina, *p247;* in Asia, 627; in Australia, 726; of Caribbean

islands, 221; in Central America, 216; in Colombia, 256; in Mexico, 200; in Thailand, 710

Independence Day, Mexican, 203, *p204*

India, *p79,* 84, *p622, p625, p627,* 631, 632, 638–643; economy of, 639–640; Guyana and, 244; history of, 640–641; Kashmir, *p93;* landforms of, 638–639; Myanmar and, 709; people of, 641; Taj Mahal in, 643, *p643*

Indian Ocean, 50

Indonesia, *p625,* 631, 632, 714–715, 718

Indonesian puppet theater, 718

indulgences, 304–305, *ptg305*

Indus River, 640, 645

Industrial Revolution, 147, 282, 314, *p314, p315,* 341

industry, 85, 105; in Argentina, 240; in Asia, 626, *p626;* in Australia, 738; in Caribbean islands, 220; in Central America, 215; in Chile, 274; in China, *p663;* of Egypt, 486; entertainment, 132; heavy, 356, 426; in India, 639; in Indonesia, 715; in Japan, 692–693; light, 426; in Malaysia, 716; in Mexico, *p194,* 195; in Myanmar, 709; in New Zealand, 743; in Singapore, 716; in Taiwan, 678, *p679;* textile, 315; in Thailand, 710; in United States, *p116,* 135, *p135*

inferences, making, 328, 380, 555

Information Revolution, 85

initiative, 401

insulation, 51

"intelligent" buildings, *p37*

intensive cultivation, 693

interdependence, 100

interior plains, 128, *p128*

intermediate directions, 33

internally displaced persons (IDPs), 594

International Space Station, 409

Internet, 98, *c98,* 526, 528, *p528,* 682, *p682;* access to, *c107;* conservation and, 77; culture and, 84, 106; global economy and, *p101,* 104, *p104,* 106; World Wide Web on, 106

Internet café, 526

Inuit, 159, *p166,* 168

inventiveness, 443

investments, 663

Iran, 462, 519, 524

Iraq, 84, 462, 517–518, 521–523, *p521–523,* 526

Ireland, Republic of, *p283,* 289, 342–343

"iron curtain," 414

Irrawaddy River, 708

irrigation, 71, 498

Islam, 359, 457, 477, *p478, m518, p527;* in Bangladesh, 647;

in China, 686; dating system of, 298; in Egypt, 487; in India, 641, 643; in Indonesia, 715; in Iraq, *p517, m522;* in Israel, 510; in Jordan, 506; in Malaysia, 716; in the Maldives, 654; in Pakistan, 646; in Saudi Arabia, 515; in Tunisia, 491; in Turkey, 503

Islamabad, Pakistan, 646

Islamic republic, 519

islands, 40

Ismail Samani Peak, 440

Israel, 457, 462, *p473,* 474, *p508,* 508–512; Arab conflict with, 525; climate of, 509; economy of, 509–510; history of, 511–512; landforms of, 508–509; neighbors of, *m511;* people of, 510–512

Istanbul, Turkey, 456, *p502,* 504

isthmus, 40, 212

Isthmus of Panama, 215

Itaipu Dam, Paraguay, 242

Italy, 287, *c289,* 296, *p360,* 360–361, *p361*

Ivan the Great (Ivan III), 411, *ptg411*

Ivan the Terrible (Ivan IV), *ptg411*

iwi, 749

jade, 197

Jainism, 641

Jakarta, Indonesia, 715

Jamaica, 185, 219–221, *c224*

Japan, *p622, p626,* 632, *p675,* 675, *p688–689,* 690–697; after World War I, 316; culture of, 695–696; economy of, 692–693; government of, 693; haiku of, 697; history of, 693–694; landforms of, 690–691; people of, 694–695; physical geography of, *m691;* political geography of, *m691;* population density of, *m700*

Jasper National Park, Canada, 160

Java, Indonesia, 714, 718

Jefferson, Thomas, *p147*

Jerusalem, Israel, *p473,* 474, *m474,* 512

Jesus of Nazareth, 297, 475

jet stream, *d56*

Jews, 473–474. *See also* Israel; Judaism.

Jodhpur, India, *p627*

Jordan, 462, *p505,* 506

Jordan River, 509

Joyce, James, 343

Judaism, 300, 370, 457, 473–474. *See also* Israel.

judo, 696

Julius Caesar, 296

Jupiter, 29

Jutland Peninsula, 356

Kaaba, 477, *p478*
Kabale, Uganda, *p547*
Kabuki theater, 696
Kabul, Afghanistan, 520
Kahlo, Frida, 203
Kalahari Desert, 536, 612
Kaliningrad, Russia, 426
Kamchatka Peninsula, 407
Kampala, Uganda, 583, *p584*
kangaroos, 737, 740, *p740*
Kano, Nigeria, *p548–549,* 552, 553
Kanto Plain, 691
Karachi, Pakistan, 646, *p647*
Karakoram Range, 638
karate, 696
Kasai River, 571
Kashmir, *p93,* 644
Kathmandu, Nepal, 650
kauri trees, 742
Kayapo Indians, 235
Kazakh nomads, *p438,* 439
Kazakhstan, 392, 400, 438–439
Kennedy, John F., *p330*
Kenya, *p532,* 541, 544, 577–579, 595; refugees in, 592
Kenyatta, Jomo, 579
Key West, Florida (U.S.), *p20–21*
Khmer, 711, *p711*
Khyber Pass, 454, 520, 645
kibbutz, 510, *p510*
Kiev, Ukraine, 384–385, 410
Kievan Rus, 410
Kikuyu, 579
Kilimanjaro, 534, *p535,* 541, 580, *g652*
Kim Il Sung, 701
Kim Jong Il, 701
kimonos, 695
King Fahd Stadium, *p500–501*
King, Martin Luther, Jr., 148
kings, divine right of, 306
Kingwana language, 572
Kinshasa, Democratic Republic of the Congo, 572, *p573*
Kiribati, 732, 760
kiwi (bird), 742
kiwifruit, *p741*
Knesset, 512
koalas, 737, 740, *p740*
Kobe, Japan, *p690*
Kongfuzi (Confucius), 667
Kongo kingdom, 573
Korea, 698–699, *p703;* division of, 698–699, *p699* (*See also* North Korea; South Korea); landforms of, *m691*
Korean Peninsula, 624, 698–699
Kosciuszko, *g652*
Kosovo, Serbia, *p90,* 380
Kuala Lumpur, Malaysia, 716
Kukulcan, *p197,* 198
kulibini, 442
Kunlun Shan, 660

Kurdish language, 504
Kurokami, Japan, *p694*
Kush, 470
Kush civilization, 587
Kuwait, 456, 462, 515–516, 518, 523
Kyrgyzstan, 392, 400, 439–440
Kyushu Island, Japan, 690

labor: child, *p105, p315;* cost of, 664; globalization and, 102–103
Labrador, Canada, 162
lagoons, 654, 760
Lagos, Nigeria, *p537,* 553, 559
Lake Albert, 570
Lake Assal, 541
Lake Baikal, 392, 399, 407–408, *p417*
Lake Balaton, 372
Lake Edward, 570
Lake Eyre, 731
Lake Kivu, 570
Lake Malawi, 610
Lake Maracaibo, 183, 242
Lake Nasser, *p484*
Lake Nicaragua, *p216*
Lake Superior, 121
Lake Tanganyika, 570
Lake Titicaca, 183, 266
Lake Vänern, 287
Lake Victoria, 541, 580, 582–583
Lake Volta, 561
Lalibela, 586
land bridges, 190–192
landfills, 136
landforms, 23; of Africa, south of the Sahara, 534; of Antarctica, 764–765; of Asia, 624; of Australia, 736–737; of Australia, Oceania, and Antarctica, 724; of Brazil, 232–233; of Canada, 114, 158–161; of Central America, 212–213; of China, 660–662; climate and, 56–58; of Colombia, 254–255; erosion and, 38; of Europe, 280; of India, 638–639; of Israel, 508–509; of Japan, 690–691; of New Zealand, 741–742; of North Africa and Southwest Asia, 454; of Pakistan, 644–645; of Sahel countries (West Africa), 556–557; types of, 39–41; of United States, 114, 126–129; water and, 42; weathering and, 37
Land of the Blue Sky, 680
Landsat images, 24
land use planners, 25
languages, 80–81; Afrikaans, 606; Amharic, 588; Arabic, 504; Bantu, 553–554; Basque, 359; Dzonkha, 651; of Europe, *m286, c385;* Farsi, 519; Flemish, 347; French, 165–166, 572; Gaelic, 340; hangul, 698–699;

Kingwana, 572; Kurdish, 504; Lingala, 572; pidgin, 760; Portuguese, 179, 235; Quechua, 268; Setswana, 612; Spanish, *p150,* 179; Swahili, 579, 581; in United States, 150, *p150;* Vietnamese, *p150;* Welsh, 340
La Niña, 55–56
Laos, 632
Laozi, 667
La Paz, Bolivia, 272
Latin America, *p174–175,* 174–187; climates of, 176; country profiles of, *c184–187;* economic systems of, 178, *c179;* ethnic groups in, *c183;* extreme points of, *c183;* modern, 179; mountains of, 176; people of, 178; physical geography of, *m180;* plains of, 176; political geography of, *m181;* population of, *c183;* populations, *c179;* urban population of, *m182. See also specific Latin American countries.*
latitude, 5, *d5,* 53, 60, *m60,* 192
Latvia, 289, 371, *p371*
Laurentian Highlands, 160
Law of Return, 512
Leaning Tower of Pisa, Italy, *p361*
learning, lifetime, 106
Lebanon, 462, 505–506
leeward side, 58
lemurs, ring-tailed, *p617*
Lena River, 392
Lenin, Vladimir, *p402–403,* 413, *ptg416*
Lesotho, 544, 607, *p607*
Lesser Antilles, *p210–211,* 219
leukemia, 692
Liberia, 544, 549, 558
liberties, 138, *d138,* 140. *See also* rights.
library resources, 478
Libreville, Gabon, 574
Libya, 462, 490–491
Libyan Desert, 485–486
lichens, 66
Liechtenstein, 289, 350, 352
lifetime learning, 106
Lighthouse of Commerce, Monterrey, Mexico, *p188–189*
light industry, 426
Lima, Peru, 267
Limpopo River, 610
line graph, 11, *g11, g13*
Lingala language, 572
lions, 536
Lisbon, Portugal, 359
lithosphere, 69–70
Lithuania, 289, 371
Little Mermaid, Copenhagen, Denmark, *p357*
Livingstone, David, 610
llanos, 176, 242, 254
Locke, John, 306
logging, 76, *p76*

INDEX

Loire River, 326, 345
London, England, *p312–313,*
p340, 342, *p342*
longitude, 5, *d5,* 60, *m60,* 613
Los Angeles, California (U.S.),
135
Lost Boys of Sudan, 592–593,
p592–593
Louvre Museum, Paris, France,
p279
Lower Egypt, *m467,* 470
Loyalists, in Northern Ireland,
343
Ludwig II, 350
Lusaka, Zambia, 610
Luther, Martin, 305, *ptg305,* 351
Luxembourg, 289, 348
Luxor, Egypt, *p464–465*

macaques, *p622*
Macau, China, 664
Macedonia, Former Yugoslav
Republic of (F.Y.R.O.M.), 290,
380
Machu Picchu, *p266,* 267
Madagascar, 42, 541, 544, 617
Madeira Islands, *p71*
Madinah, Saudi Arabia, 476–477
Madison, James, *p147*
Madrid, Spain, 359
Magdalena River, 176
Maghreb, 491
magma, 35. *See also* volcanoes.
Magyars, 372
Mahal, Mumtaz, 643
Maine (U.S.), *p126*
majority group, 81, 430
Makkah, Saudi Arabia, 476–477,
p478, 514–515, 557, 562, 643
Malabo, Equatorial Guinea, 575
Malacca, Malaysia, 716
malaria, 218
Malawi, 544
Malay, 716
Malay Peninsula, 708, 716
Malaysia, 633, 716, *p716*
Maldives, 633, 654
Male, Maldives, 654
Mali, 544, 556, 557–558
Mali Empire, 557, 566
Malta, *p281,* 290
Malvinas Islands, 241
Mandela, Nelson, 546, 606–607
mangrove swamps, 550
Manitoba, Canada, *p112,*
162–163
manors, 300–301
mantle, of earth, 34–35
manufacturing, *p116. See also*
industry.
manuka, 741
Maori, 743, *p743, m746,*
p746–747, 746–750, *p748*
maoritanga, 749

Mao Zedong, 667
maps, 6, 7, 8, *p22,* 24–25, *m28;*
contour, 10, *m10,* 713; keys to, 8,
33; mental, 144; physical, 9, *m9,*
196; political, 9, *m9;* population,
334; projections, 7, *m7;* thematic,
10, *m10,* 86; vegetation, *m229,*
349, *m349. See also* physical
geography; political geography.
Maputo, Mozambique, *p616,* 617
maquiladoras, 194, *p194*
Mardalsfossen, Norway, 287
Mariana Trench, 41
marijuana, 262
marine west coast climate,
63–64, *p65,* 130, 273; in New
Zealand, 724
Maritime Provinces, Canada,
159, 162
market economy, 93–94, 369.
See also free enterprise.
Marrakech, Morocco, 492
Mars, 29
Marshall Islands, 732, 760
Marshall Plan, 319
marsupials, 737, 740, *p740*
martial arts, 696, 700
Martinique, 221
Marx, Karl, 316, *ptg416*
Masai, 577, *p577*
mathematics, in ancient Egypt, 471
Mau Mau, 579
Mauritania, 544, 556, 558
Mauritius, 544, 618
Mawsmai waterfall, 631
Mawsynram, India, 631
Maya, *p175,* 178, 198, 205,
215–216
May Day, 433
McDonald, Andy, 264
McKinley, *g652*
Mecca. *See* Makkah, Saudi Arabia.
medicine, in ancient Egypt, 471
Medieval Europe, 299–302, *m301*
Mediterranean climate, 64, *p65,*
273, 437, 456, 509; in United
States, 130
Mediterranean Sea, 280, 360,
407, 454, 467, *p502*
megalopolis, 127, 694
Mekong River, 624, 710
Melanesia, 758–760
Melbourne, Australia, *p727,* 739
mental mapping, 144
Mercator projection, 7, *m7*
Mercury, 29
meridians, 5, *d5,* 60, *m60. See also*
longitude.
Mesopotamia, 466–469, *m467*
mestizos, 256, 269, 274
Mexico, *p175, p178,* 186,
p188–189, 188–209, *p190;* altitude zones of, *c193;* cities and
villages of, 202; climates of,
192–193; culture of, 203–204;
economic regions of, 193–195;
foreign debt of, 205–206; govern-

ment of, 204; as land bridge,
190–192; manufacturing in, 178;
Native American civilizations of,
197–199, 201; North American
Free Trade Agreement (NAFTA)
and, 136; physical geography of,
196, *m196;* political geography
of, *p191;* pollution in, 206; population growth in, 204–205; revolutions in, 200; Spain and, 199
Mexico City, Mexico, 91, 179,
192, *p192,* 194, 199
Mexico Through the Centuries
(Rivera), *ptg203*
Michelangelo, 282, *p303,* 304
Micronesia, *p760,* 760–761, 301
Middle Ages, 293, 299
mid-latitude climates, 63–65
Midwest United States, 133–134
migrant workers, 205
migration, 476, 504
Milan, Italy, *p360*
military control of government,
627
minerals, 76; in Africa, *m540;* in
Antarctica, 766; in Canada, 116;
in United States, 116, 132, 134.
See also economic regions and
systems.
minority group, 81, 430. *See also*
ethnic groups.
Minsk, Belarus, 386
missionaries, 300
Mississippi River, 114, 121, 128
mixed economies, 94
mobility of population, 150
Mogul Empire, 641
Moldova, 290, 386
Molina, Mario, 773, *p773*
Mombasa, Kenya, 579
Monaco, 290
Mona Lisa (da Vinci), *ptg308*
monarchies, 83, 147, 515, 627.
See also constitutional monarchies.
monasteries, 300
Monet, Claude, 347
Mongol Empire, 680
Mongolia, 631, 633, 678, *p678,*
680–681, *p681*
Mongols, 410–411, *p438,* 439
Monnet, Jean, 330, *p330*
monoculture, 558
Monroe, James, 560–561
Monroe Doctrine, 211
Monrovia, Liberia, 560–561
monsoons, 55, *p625,* 626, *m630,*
639, 646, 654, 701, 708, 715
Mont Blanc, 287
Montenegro, 380. *See also* Serbia
and Montenegro.
Monterrey, Mexico, *p188–189,*
194
Montevideo, Uruguay, 241–242
Montreal, Canada, 162
moon, 30
Moorea Lagoon, Tahiti, *p756–757*

Morocco, *p452–453,* 454, 462, *p482–483, p492,* 492–493
Morrison, Toni, 151
Moscow, Russia, *p390, p402–403, p422–423,* 426, 430
moshav, 510
Mosi oa Tunya, **(Victoria Falls),** 534, *p535,* 609
mosques, 522; in Bosnia and Herzegovina, 380
Mother Teresa, 381, 642
mountain gorillas, 76–77, *p77*
mountains, *g652;* of Antarctica, 765; Caribbean islands as, 219–220; climate of, 68; as continental divide, 129, 352; cordillera, 160, 254; highest, *g652;* in France, *p23;* as landforms, 39; of Latin America, 176; rainfall and, 57–58; *See also specific peaks and ranges.*
Mount Cook, 742
Mount Egmont, *p725,* 741
Mount Elbrus, 399, *g652*
Mount Erebus, 765, *p765*
Mount Etna, 22
Mount Everest, *p25,* 39, 624, 631, 649, *g652*
Mount Fuji, *p688–689,* 691
Mount Kenya, 534, 578
Mount McKinley, 121, 129, *p129, g652*
Mount Meru, 711
Mount Nowshak, 461
Mount Oyama Volcano, *p694*
Mount Pinatubo, *p55*
Mount Sinai, 474
mouth, of rivers, 42
movable type, 304
Mozambique, 534, 544, 616–617
Mozambique Channel, 42
Muhammad, 298, 477, 514. *See also Islam.*
Muiden, Netherlands, *p292–293*
Muiderslot Castle, Muiden, Netherlands, *p292–293*
multilingual people, 348
multimedia presentations, 164
multinational companies, 348
Mumbai (Bombay), India, 642
Munich, Germany, 352
murals, Mayan, 198
Murmansk, Russia, 426
Murray-Darling River, 731, 736
Musa, Mansa, 557
Muscat, Oman, 516
Muscovy, 411
Muslims, 300, 477, *p527;* in Albania, 381; in Bangladesh, 647; in Bosnia and Herzegovina, 380; in Bulgaria, 378; in China, 686; in Egypt, 487; in India, 641, 643; in Indonesia, 715; in Iran, 519; in Iraq, *p517, m522;* in Israel, 510; in Jordan, 506; in Lebanon, 505; in Malaysia, 716; in the Maldives, 654; in Pakistan, 646;

in Russia, 432; in Saudi Arabia, 515; in Serbia and Montenegro, 380; in Turkey, 503. *See also Islam.*
Myanmar, 633, *p708,* 708–710

Naadam Festival, 681
Naama, Esra, 526
NAFTA. *See* North American Free Trade Agreement (NAFTA).
Nagasaki, Japan, 694
Nairobi, Kenya, 578–579
Namib Desert, 536, 604, *p614,* 616
Namibia, *p614,* 616
Nasser, Gamal Abdel, 487
National Aeronautics and Space Administration (NASA), 768
national debt, of Mexico, 206
National Hockey League Players' Association (NHLPA), 446
Nationalist political party (China), 667
Nationalists, in Northern Ireland, 343
National Socialist German Workers' Party, 317
Native Americans, *p117,* 167; of Amazon Basin, 235; of Bolivia, 273; of Canada, 170; of Caribbean islands, 220; of Central America, 215–216; of Latin America, 178; of Mexico, 197–199, *m198,* 201; of Paraguay, 242; of Peru, 267; of United States, 145–146, 152, *p152*
NATO. *See* North Atlantic Treaty Organization (NATO).
natural resources, 92–93; availability of, 41; in Canada, 116; in United States, 116, 132, 134
Nauru, 732, 760–761
navigable lakes, 266
navigable rivers, 134, 345
Nazis, 291, 317, 413
Ndebele, 611
Nebuchadnezzar, 468
Negev Desert, 508
negotiations, 525
Nehru, Jawaharlal, *p641,* 642
Nepal, 89, 631, 633, *p636–637,* 649–651
Neptune, 29
Netherlands, *p282,* 287, 290, *p292–293, p347,* 347–348; Australia and, 738; Guyana and, 244; Indonesia and, 715; Suriname and, 245
neutrality, of Switzerland, 352
Neva River, 426, *p427*
New Caledonia, 758
Newcomen, Thomas, 315
New Delhi, India, 642
Newfoundland, Canada, 162

New Guinea, *p18,* 631
New York City, New York (U.S.), *p112,* 133, *p145*
New Zealand, 724, *p725,* 732, *p741,* 741–744; economy of, 743; history and people of, 743–744; landforms of, 741–742; Maori of, 746–750
Niagara Falls, *p171*
Nicaragua, 186, 212, 215, 216, *p216*
Nicholas II, 413
Nieuwerkerk aan den Ijssel, Netherlands, 287
Niger, 544, 556, 558
Nigeria, 536, *p537,* 545, *p548–549,* 549, 550–554, 559; climate of, 550–551; economy of, 551–552, *p553;* government of, 554; history of, 553–554; people of, 552–553
Niger River, 550, 553, *p559*
Nile River, 454, *p455,* 461, 469, *p479,* 484, 486, 488, 534, 541, 580
nitrogen, 30
Noah's ark, 468
Nobel Peace Prize, 642, 710
Nobel Prize, 553, 773
Nok, 553
nomads, 84; Aborigines, 738; Berbers, 566; Fulani, 558; of Hungary, 373; of Kazakhstan, 439; of Mongolia, 680; of Syria, 505; Tuareg, 558
nonrenewable resources, 93
Nordic countries, 354–357
North Africa and Southwest Asia, 452–463; climate of, 454–456; country profiles of, *c462–463;* economic regions and systems of, 456; extreme points of, 461; landforms of, 454; oil and gas production of, *m460;* people of, 456–457; physical geography of, *m458, m503;* political geography of, *m459, m503;* today, 483, 484–488, 490–493, 501, 502–527; water crisis in, 498–499, *m498, p498, p499. See also* Christianity; Egypt, ancient; Islam; Judaism; Mesopotamia; *specific countries of North Africa.*
North American Free Trade Agreement (NAFTA), 96, 102, 136, 163, 195
North Atlantic Current, 280
North Atlantic Treaty Organization (NATO), 320, 325–326
northeast United States, 133
Northern Hemisphere, 32
Northern Ireland, 341–343, *p343*
Northern Mariana Islands, 760
Northern Territory (Australia), 739

INDEX

North European Plain, 40, 280, 345, 368, 392, *p393*, 405–406

North Island, New Zealand, 741–742, *m742*

North Korea, 633, 698–699, 701; physical geography of, *m691*; political geography of, *m691*; population density of, *m700*; refugees from, 672

Northwest Territories (Canada), 159

Norway, 287, 290, 354–355, *p355*

note taking, 376

Notre Dame Cathedral, Paris, France, *p346*

Novokuznetsk, Siberia (Russia), 446

Nubian Desert, 586

nuclear energy, 93, 428

Nunavut Territory (Canada), 159, 168

oases, 454, 456, *p482–483,* 485

Ob-Irtysh River, 392, 399

obsidian, 198

Oceania, 722–733, 758–762; climate of, 724–726; country profiles of, *c732–733*; economy of, 726; endangered environments of, *m730*; extreme points of, 731; landforms of, 724; people of, 726–727; physical geography of, *m728*; political geography of, *m729, m759*; population comparisons of, *c727, c731*. *See also specific countries.*

oceans, 40–41, *m41*, 50; climate and, 56; currents of, *m57*; earthquakes in, 36; exploring, 51; temperature of, *d56. See also* Arctic Ocean; Atlantic Ocean; Indian Ocean; Pacific Ocean; water.

oil and gas production, 456, *p456, m460, g514,* 514–516, 519, *p522,* 551, *p553,* 615, 738; in Argentina, 240; in Brunei, 717; in Indonesia, 715; in Venezuela, 243–244

oil reserves, *g514*

okapi, *p571*

Okavango River, 612

O'Keeffe, Georgia, 151

Olmec, *p80,* 178, 197–198, 215

Omahuru, Ngataua, 746, 750

Oman, 463, 516, *p516,* 523

"one country, two systems" pledge, 664

Ontario (Canada), 162

OPEC. *See* Organization of Petroleum Exporting Countries (OPEC).

Operation Tribute to Freedom, 526

opinions *versus* **facts,** 682

orbits, of planets, 29

Orczy, Baroness, 306

Organization of Petroleum Exporting Countries (OPEC), 514

origami, 692, *p692*

Orinoco River, 176, 243

Orozco, José Clemente, 203

Ortiz, Simon J., 152

Oslo, Norway, 355

ostriches, *p614*

Ottawa, Ontario (Canada), 162

Ottoman Empire, 297, 504, 506

outback, 724, 737, 739

outlining, 752

oxygen, 30, 231

ozone layer, 70, 766, 768, 772–773, *p773*

Pacific coast, 129, 135

Pacific Ocean, 50, *p756–757, p763*

Pacific Rim, *m702, g702*

Padaung, *p708*

paella, 359

pagodas, 670

Pakehas, 746

Pakistan, *p105,* 454, 633, 640, 641, *p644,* 644–646

Palau, 732, 760

Palestinians, 473, 510–511, 525. *See also* Israel.

Pamir Mountains, 392

pampas, 176, 240, 246

Pamplona, Spain, *p358*

Panama, *p177,* 186, 212, 216

Panama Canal, 215, 218, *d218, p225*

pandas, giant, *p660*

Pangaea, 35, *d45*

Papeete, Tahiti, 762

Papua New Guinea, 732, 758

papyrus, 471

Paraguay, 186, 239, *p239,* 241–242

parallels, 5, *d5,* 60, *m60. See also* latitude.

Paramaribo, Suriname, 245

paramilitary forces, in Colombia, 261

Paricutín, 190, *p190*

Paris, France, *p279, p338–339,* 346–347, *p346*

Parliament, British, 306–307

parliamentary democracy, 166–167; in Australia, 739; in Belize, 216; in Caribbean islands, 221; in Czech Republic, 374; in Nepal, 650; in New Zealand, 744; in Norway, 355; in United Kingdom, 341

parliamentary republic: in Bahrain, 523; in Greece, 362; in Portugal, 359

Parthenon, Athens, Greece, *p294,* 362

Parthian Empire, 686

participation, civic, 99, 291

Partnership for a Drug-Free America, 264

Party of Institutional Revolution (PRI), 204

Pashtuns, 520

Patagonia, Argentina, 239–240

Patriot Act, *See* USA Patriot Act.

Paul, 297

Pax Romana, 296, 297

Paz, Octavio, 203

Pearl Harbor, Hawaii (U.S.), 694

Peloponnesian War, 295

Pemba, 580

penguins, *p725, p764*

peninsulas, 40; Arabian Peninsula, 454; Baja California, 191; Balkan Peninsula, 361, 377; Crimean Peninsula, 383; Europe as, 280; Iberian Peninsula, 358–360; Italian Peninsula, 296, 360; Jutland Peninsula, 356; Kamchatka Peninsula, 407; Korean Peninsula, 698; Malay Peninsula, 708; Sinai Peninsula, 485; Yucatán Peninsula, 191, *m196,* 197, 198

Pentagon (U.S.), 138, 520

Penza, Russia, 446

people: of Africa, south of the Sahara, 536–537; of Algeria, 492; of Argentina, 241; of Asia, 626–627; of Australia, 738–739; of Australia, Oceania, and Antarctica, 726–727; Basque, 359; of Bhutan, 651–652; of Bolivia, 272–273; of Bulgaria, 378; of Canada, 116–117; of China, *p635,* 669; climate and, 58–59; of Colombia, 256–257; of Czech Republic, 374; of Democratic Republic of the Congo, 572–573; of Ecuador, 269; of Egypt, 487–488; of Europe, 282–283; of France, 346–347; of Germany, 351–352; of Greece, 362; of Hungary, 373; of India, 640–641; of Indonesia, 715; of Israel, 510–512; of Italy, 361; of Japan, 694–696; of Jordan, 506; landforms and, 41; of Latin America, 178; of Lebanon, 505–506; of Melanesia, 759–760; of Micronesia, 761; of modern Russia, 431–433; of Mongolia, 680–681; of Morocco, 493; of Nepal, 650–651; of New Zealand, 743–744; of Nigeria, 552–553; of North Africa and Southwest Asia, 456–457; of Pakistan, 646; of Poland, 370–371; of Polynesia, 762; of Republic of Ireland, 343; of Russia and Eurasian republics, 394–395; of Sahel countries (West Africa), 558; of Saudi Arabia, 515; of South Africa,

605–607, *p607*; of South Korea, 700; of Sri Lanka, 653–654; of Syria, 505; of Taiwan, 679; of Turkey, 503–504; of Ukraine, 384–385; of United Kingdom, 342; of United States, 116–117; of Venezuela, 244; of Vietnam, 712; of West Africa coastal countries, 560–561

People's Republic of China. *See* China.

perestroika, 415

permafrost, 66, 392

Péron, Juan, 241

Perry, Matthew, 694

persecution, 593

Persian Gulf, 467

Persian rugs, 507

Persian Wars, 295

Peru, *p101, p174,* 183, 186, 266–268, *p275*

Peru Current, 266, 273

Peter, 297

Peter the Great, 410, *ptg410,* 411, 426

Petra, Jordan, *p505*

Petronas Towers, Kuala Lumpur, Malaysia, 716

pharaohs, 469–470

Philip II of Macedonia, 295

Philippines, 633

philosophy, 294–295

Phnom Penh, Cambodia, 711

Phoenicians, 104, 469, 491

Phoenix, Arizona (U.S.), *p263*

phosphate, 486, 560, 761

physical geography, 22–23; of Africa, south of the Sahara, *m538*; of Asia, *m628*; of Australia, Oceania, and Antarctica, *m728*; of Brazil, *m233*; of Canada, *m118*; of Central and East Africa, *m572*; of China, *m661*; of Europe, *m284*; of Japan, *m691*; of Koreas, *m691*; of Latin America, *m180*; of Mexico, 196, *m196*; of North Africa, *m485*; of North Africa and Southwest Asia, *m458*; of Russia and Eurasian republics, *m396*; of South Asia, *m645*; of Southwest Asia, 503; of United States, *m118, m127*; of West Africa, *m552*

pictograph, 12, *g12*

pidgin language, 760

Piedmont, 128

pipelines, water, 498

pirarucu, *p232*

Pisa, Italy, *p361*

plains, of Latin America, 176. *See also* pampas.

plantations: in Central America, 213; in Mexico, 194

Plateau of Mexico, 192

Plateau of Tibet, 40, 624, 660

plateaus, 40, 129

plate tectonics, 35–37, *d36,* 39; in Indonesia, 714

platypus, 740

plazas, in Mexico, 202

Pluto, 29

Poland, 290, *p368,* 368–371, *p370*

polar bears, *p115*

polar ice cap climate, 765

polar science, 768

polders, 347

polis, 294

political geography: of Africa, south of the Sahara, *m539*; of Andean countries, *m255*; of Asia, *m629*; of Australia, Oceania, and Antarctica, *m729*; of Brazil, *m233*; of Canada, *m119*; of Central America, *m213*; of Central and East Africa, *m580*; eastern Europe, *m369*; of Europe, *m285*; of Europe, 1950, *m320*; of Japan, *m691*; of Latin America, *m181*; of Mexico, *p191*; of North Africa and Southwest Asia, *m459*; of North Korea, *m691*; of Oceania and Antarctica, *m759*; of Russia and Eurasian republics, *m397*; of Southeast Asia, 709; of Southern Africa, *m605*; of South Korea, *m691*; of Southwest Asia, 503; of United States, *m119*; of West Africa, *m551*; of western Europe, *m341*

political rights, 673

pollution, 326, 428; air, 37, 69, *p70,* 135, 351, 664, 693; in Mexico, 206; in Russia, 394; water, 71, 498, *p638*

Pol Pot, 711

Polynesia, 761–762

polytheism, 467

Pontic Mountains, 502

popes, 299

Popocatepetl, 192, *p192*

population: of Africa, *c537*; of Africa, south of the Sahara, *c541*; of Asia, *c627*; of Australia, Oceania, and Antarctica, *c727, c731*; of Canada, *c117, c121*; density of, *m89, m149, m205, 334, m384,* 487–488, *m560, m653, m700*; of Europe, *c283, c287*; growth of, 76, 87–88, *c88*; of Latin America, *c179, m182, c183*; locations of, 88–90; of Mexico, 204–205; mobility of, 150; movement of, 90–91; of North Africa and Southwest Asia, *c457, c461*; rural, 150, 432, 487–488, *c627, p662*; of Russian and Eurasian republics, *c395, c399*; suburban, 150; trends in, 26; of United States, *c117, c121*; urban, 150, 487–488, *c627*; of Vietnam, 712

population density, 89

porcelain, 670

Port-au-Prince, Haiti, 222

Port Harcourt, Nigeria, 559

Port Louis, Mauritius, 618

ports, free, 716

Portugal, 290, 358–360; Angola and, 615; Brazil and, 236–237; East Timor and, 715; Macau and, 664; population density of, *m334*

Portuguese language, 179, 235

Postel, Sandra, 499

pottery, *p491*

Prague, Czech Republic, *p366–367, p372,* 374, *p376*

Prairie Provinces (Canada), 159, *p162,* 162–163

precipitation, 49. *See also* rainfall.

predictions, making, 598

prefects, 245

prehistory, 27

presentations, multimedia, 164

prevailing winds, *m54*

primary sources, 448, 606

Prime Meridian, 4, 5, 60, 613

prime ministers, 167

printing press, 304

privacy, 139

privatization, 375

productivity, 314

pronunciation, 81. *See also* languages.

Protestantism, 221

Protestant Reformation, 304–305

provinces, 158

public servants, 445

Puerto Rico, 186, 219, 220, 221–223

Puerto Vallarta, Mexico, 194

Punt, 470

Puritans, 305

Putin, Vladimir, 430

Pyongyang, North Korea, *p672,* 701

pyramids: Aztec, 199; Egyptian, 456, 470, 472, *p495*

Pyrenees Mountains, 280, 358–359

pysanky, 382, *p382*

Qaddhafi, Muammar, 491

Qatar, 463, 515, 523

Quebec (Canada), 162, 167

Quebec City, Quebec (Canada), 162, *p165*

Quechua, 268. *See also* Inca.

quipu, 267. *See also* Inca.

Quito, Ecuador, *p253,* 269

quotas, trade, 95

Quran, 477, 519. *See also* Islam.

Rabat, Morocco, 493

racism, 546

radar, 24

radiation, atomic bombs and, 692

INDEX

rainfall: in Amazon Basin, 232; in Botswana, 612; in Egypt, 486; in Israel, 509; in Mexico, 193; mountains and, 57–58. *See also* acid rain.
rain forests, 59, 62, 176; in Africa, 534; Amazon, 25, *p230–231*; in Asia, 626; in Brazil, 187, *p187,* 232–233; in Central America, *p212,* 213–215; in Democratic Republic of the Congo, 571; in Melanesia, 758; in Panama, *p177*; in Rwanda, *p582*; vanishing, 250, *p250*
rain shadow, 58, *d58*
Ramses II, *p484*
recycling, 136, 498
Red Sea, 485
Red Square, Moscow, Russia, *p422–423*
refugees, *p90,* 91, 379, 506; in Africa, *m592*; in Central and East Africa, 591–596; in Ethiopia, 592; host countries for, 596, *p596*; in Taiwan, 679; in Tanzania, *p595*
region, 2, 24
Reims, France, *p299*
reincarnation, 640–641
religion, 80, 82, *c82,* 304–305; in Africa, *c537*; in ancient Egypt, 470; ancient Mexican, *p197*; in Asia, 626; in China, 667; of Europe, *c287*; in India, 640–641; in Japan, 693, *p693,* 695; in Latin America, *p178*; in Mesopotamia, 467; in Russia, 432; tolerance of, 463; in Uganda, 583; in United States, 150. *See also specific religions.*
Rembrandt van Rijn, 348
Renaissance, 282, *p303,* 303–304
renewable resources, 92–93
Renoir, Pierre-Auguste, 347
Repin Institute, Russia, *p429*
report writing, 763
representative democracy, 146
representative government, 83
Republic of South Africa. *See* South Africa.
republic, federal, 146
republic government, 296; of Algeria, 492; of Egypt, 487; of the Maldives, 654
Republic of Ireland, 342–343
resources. *See* natural resources.
reunification, of Germany, 351
revolutions: American, 307; in Europe, 283, 306–307; in Mexico, 200; of planets, 31; Russian, 413
Reykjavik, Iceland, 357
Rhine River, 280, 326, 350
rhinoceroses, 536
Rhodes, Cecil, 611
Rhodesia, 611
Rhodope Mountains, 378
rice production, *g662*
Ridge, Tom, 140, 142

Rīga, Latvia, *p371*
rights, 139, 747; human, 593, 634; political, 673; unalienable, 167; women's, 634
Rimsky-Korsakov, Nikolay, 434
Ring of Fire, 407, 624, 662
ring-tailed lemurs, *p617*
Rio de Janeiro, Brazil, 179, *p179,* 234, *p236*
Rio de la Plata, 176
Rio Grande, 176, 206
Rivera, Diego, 203, *ptg203*
rivers, 42; continental divide and, 352; navigable, 134, 345
Riyadh, Saudi Arabia, *p500–501,* 515
Robinson projection, 7, *m7*
Rocky Mountains, *p112–113,* 114, 129, 160
Roman Catholicism, 299; in Argentina, 241; in Brazil, 236; in Caribbean islands, 221; in Central America, 217; in Chile, 274; in Colombia, 256; in Croatia, 379; in East Timor, 715; in Italy, 361; in Latin America, 176, *p178,* 179; in Philippines, 717; in Poland, 371; in Russia, 432; in Slovakia, 375; in Spain and Portugal, 359; spread of, 476; in Uruguay, 242; in Venezuela, 244. *See also* Christianity.
Romania, 290, *p377,* 377–378
Roman law, 296
Rome, ancient, 282, 296–297; Colosseum of, *p296*; empire of, *m295,* 296
Rome, Italy, 360
Rosetta Stone, *p470*
rotation, of planets, 29, 31
Rotterdam, Netherlands, *p282*
Rousseau, Jean Jacques, 306
Rowland, F. Sherwood, 773
Royal Danish Ballet, *p356*
Rub' al Khali Desert, 454, 513
rubber trees, *p716*
Ruhr Valley, 351
rural population, 150, *c283,* *p431,* 432, 487–488, *c627, p663*
Russia, 386, *p390–391, p393,* 400, *p402–403,* 402–434, 441–447, *p422–423*; climate of, 392–394, 404–405, 420–421; communism, fall in, 424–426; culture of, 433–434; democracy in, 429, 441–446; early, 410–413; east of Ural Mountains, 406–407; economic regions of, *m425,* 426–428; environmental issues in, 428; ethnic challenges in, 430; European, 405–406; expansion of, *m412*; inland waters of, 407–408; landforms of, 392; modern, 422–451; people of, 431–433; political challenges in, 429–430; Soviet era of, 413–415; in space race, 409; winter temperatures in, *m421*

Russia and Eurasian republics, 390–401; country profiles of, *c400–401*; economy of, 394; extreme points in, 399; people of, 394–395; physical geography of, *m396*; political geography of, *m397*; snow cover in, *m398*
Russian Federation, 442
Russian Orthodox Christianity, 432
Russian Revolution, 412
Rwanda, 545, 584–585

sacred lands (Australia), 747
***Sadako and the Thousand Paper Cranes* (Coerr),** 692
safety checks, *d138,* 139, *p139,* *p140*
saffron, 93, *p93*
Sahara, *p452,* 454, 461, *p479,* 486, *p490,* 493, *p556,* 566
Sahel countries, 556–558
Saint Kitts, 221
Sakhalin, Russia, 399
salt trade of Africa, 566, *p567, m567*
salt water, 50. *See also* desalinization.
Salween River, 708
Samburu, *p581*
Samoa, *p722,* 732, 761
samurai, 693
Sanaa, Yemen, 516
San Andreas Fault, 37
sand, 454
San Francisco, California (U.S.), *p92*
San José, Costa Rica, *p215,* 217
San Juan, Puerto Rico, 223
San Marino, 290, 360
San Martín, José de, 240
San Salvador, Bahamas, 220
Santiago, Chile, *p272,* 273
Santo Domingo, Dominican Republic, 220
San Xavier del Bac, Arizona (U.S.), *p146*
São Francisco River, 176
São Paulo, Brazil, 179, 234
São Tomé and Principe, 545, 575
Sarajevo, Bosnia and Herzegovina, 380
Saskatchewan, Canada, *p162,* 163
satellite nations of Soviet Union, 321, 414
Satpura Range, 638
Saturn, 29
Saudi Arabia, 456, *p457,* 463, *p478, p500–501,* 513–515
saunas, 356
savanna climate, 220
savannas, 550, 570
Scandinavia, 282
***Scarlet Pimpernel, The* (Orczy),** 306

"scorched earth policy," 420
Scotland, 340
scribes, 468
Scriptures, 475
scuba diving, *p219*
sea anemone, *p758*
seals, *p765*
Sea of Marmara, 502, *p502*
seasons, *d31,* 31–32
secession, 147
secondary sources, 448
secular policies, 492
security, in U.S., 137–143, *d138,*
  p139, p140, 148–149
Seine River, 326, 345
Seko, Mobutu Sese, 573
selvas, 232
Senate (Rome), 296
Senegal, 545, 558
Seoul, South Korea, *p674, p699,*
  700
September 11, 2001, 138, *p138,*
  139, 148–149, 520
sequencing information, 238
Sequieros, David Alfero, 203
sequoia, *p61*
Serbia and Montenegro, 290,
  323, *m369,* 380
Serengeti Plain, *p568–569,*
  579–580
serfs, 301, 412
service industries, 132, 195, 743
Setswana language, 612
Seychelles, 545, 618
Shackleton, Ernest, *p766*
Shah Jahan, 643
shahs, 519
Shakespeare, William, 304, 342
Shanghai, China, 661, *p673*
Shaw, George Bernard, 343
Shepard, Alan, 409
Sherpas, 650
Shi'ite Muslims, 477, 522
Shikoku Island, Japan, 690
Shinto religion, 693, *p693,* 695
shoguns, 693
Shona, 611, *p611*
Siberia (Russia), *p390–391, p400,*
  406, *p406, p407,* 413, *p417,*
  427, 446
Siberian tigers, *p390–391, p404*
Sicily, 360
Siddartha Gautama, 651
Sierra Leone, 545, 558, 561, 595
Sierra Madre Mountains, 176,
  191–192
Sikhism, 641
silk, *p436, p686*
Silk Road, 439, 686, *m687*
Silla kingdom, 698
Sinai Peninsula, 485
Singapore, 633, *p706–707,* 716
Sinhalese, 653–654
sirocco winds, 360
Siva deity (Hinduism), 640, *p640*
Skopje, Macedonia, 380
skydiving, *p20–21*

slash-and-burn farming, 616
slave trade, 147, 559
Slavs, 370, 374, 384, 394, 430
sleeping sickness, 573, 576
Sloan, John, 151
sloth, three-toed, *p177*
Slovakia, 290, *p374,* 375
Slovenia, 291, 323, *m369,* 379
smugglers, drug, 260, 262
snow cover, in Russia, *m398.* See
  also climate.
soccer, *p268, p329*
social groups, 80–81
socialist government, of Tanzania,
  581
social scientists, 80
sodium nitrate, 274
Sofia, Bulgaria, 378
Sögüt, Turkey, 504
Sokkuram shrine (Korea), *p698*
solar eclipses, *p30*
solar energy, 93
solar system, 29–31, *d30*
Solidarity (Poland), 370
Solomon Islands, 732, 758
solstices, 32, 344
Solzhenitsyn, Alexander, 432,
  434
Somalia, 470, 545, 590
Songhai Empire, 557, 566
Sotho, 605
souks, 492
source of rivers, 42
sources, primary and secondary,
  448
South Africa, *p532,* 536, 545,
  p602–603, p604, 604–607;
  Namibia and, 616
South America: plate tectonics
  and, 35. *See also* Latin America;
  *and specific Latin American
  countries.*
South Asia, 636–657; Bangladesh,
  646–647; Bhutan, 651–652; economic regions and systems of,
  m650; India, 638–643; Maldives,
  654; Nepal, 649–651; Pakistan,
  644–646; physical geography of,
  m645; population density of,
  m653; Sri Lanka, 652–654
South China Sea, 711
Southeast Asia, 706–721; Brunei,
  717; Cambodia, 711; Indonesia,
  714–715, 718; Laos, 710;
  Malaysia, 716; Myanmar,
  708–710; political geography of,
  709; Singapore, 716–717;
  Thailand, 710; Vietnam, 711–712
Southern Africa, 602–621;
  Angola, 614–615; Botswana, 612;
  Comoros, 617–618; diamond
  mining in, 608; Madagascar, 617;
  Malawi, 610; Mauritius, 618;
  Mozambique, 616–617; Namibia,
  616; political geography of,
  m605; Seychelles, 618; South

Africa, 604–607; Zambia,
  609–610; Zimbabwe, 610–611
Southern Alps, 742
Southern Hemisphere, 32
South Island, New Zealand, 742,
  m742
South Korea, 634, 674, 698–700;
  physical geography of, *m691;*
  political geography of, *m691;*
  population density of, *m700*
south United States, 133
Southwest Asia: climate of, *m509.*
  See also North Africa and
  Southwest Asia.
Soviet Union, 321, 394, 413–415,
  436. *See also* Russia.
Soyinka, Wole, 553
space race, 409
Spaceship Earth, 21
space shuttle, 22
Space Station, International, 409
Spain, 291, *p358,* 358–360;
  Central America and, 216; Mexico
  and, 199; Philippines and, 717;
  population density of, *m334*
Spanish-American War, 223, 717
Spanish language, *p150,* 179
Sparta, Greece, 295
specialization, economic, 95
species, endangered, 76, *m76*
spin, of planets, 29
spreadsheets, 494
Sri Lanka, 634, *p649,* 652–654
St. Basil's Cathedral, Moscow,
  Russia, *p390*
St. Kitts and Nevis, 186, 221
St. Lawrence River, 160, 166
St. Lawrence Seaway, 114, 134,
  d159
St. Lucia, 186
St. Petersburg, Russia, *p393,*
  p395, 406, 420, 426–427, *p427,*
  434
St. Vincent and the
  Grenadines, 186
Stalin, Joseph, 384, 413, 420,
  444, *p444*
stations, 737
Statue of Liberty, New York
  (U.S.), *p124–125*
steppe climate, 67, *p67,* 273,
  454
steppes, 438, 536, 680; in Russia,
  394, 406, *p407;* in Ukraine, 383
Stockholm, Sweden, 356
Stoker, Bram, 378
Stonehenge, United
  Kingdom, 344, *p344*
storms, 55
Strait of Gibraltar, 492
Strait of Hormuz, 516
Strait of Magellan, 42, 273
Strait of Malacca, 716
straits, 42
Stravinsky, Igor, 434
subarctic climate, 65–66, *p66,*
  130

subcontinent, 638
subsistence farming, 96, 759; in Angola, 614; in Bhutan, 651; in Central America, 214; in Lesotho and Swaziland, 607, *p607*; in Mexico, 194; in Micronesia, 761; in Namibia, 616; in Peru, 267; in Uganda, 582; in West Africa, 558
suburban populations, 150
suburbs, 432; of India, *p639*
Sucre, Bolivia, 272
Sudan, 470, 545, 586–588, 592–593
Suez Canal, 485, 487
sultans, 717
Sumatra, Indonesia, 714
Sumer, 456, 467
summer solstice, 32
sumo wrestling, 696
sun, 30–32; Earth's climate and, 53–54
Sunni Muslims, 477, 522
sunscreen ratings, 772, *p772*
Sun Yat-sen, 667
supply and demand, 93; for illegal drugs, 263
Suriname, 186, 239, 245
Suva, Fiji Islands, *p769*
Swahili language, 579, 581
swamps, mangrove, 550
Swaziland, 545, 607
Sweden, 287, 291, *p354*, 355–356
Switzerland, *p281*, 291, *p352*, 352–353
Sydney, Australia, 727, *p738*, 739
Sydney Opera House, Sydney, Australia, *p738*
Syria, *c463*, 504–505
Syrian Desert, 504

Table Mountain, *p602–603*, 604, *p604*
tabulating machines, 108
tae kwon do, 700
Tahiti, 761–762
taiga, 66, 394, 406, *p407*
Taíno, 220
Taipei, Taiwan, 679
Taiwan, *p70*, 634, 667, 675, 678–679
Tajikistan, 392, 401, 440
Tajiks, 520
Taj Mahal, Agra, India, *p622*, 641, 643, *p643*
Taklimakan Desert, 624, 661, 686
Tale of Genji, The, 696
Taliban, *p519*, 520
Tamil Nadu, India, *p625*
Tamils, 653–654
Tan, Amy, 151
Tanganyika, 581

Tanzania, 541, 545, *p568–569*, 579–581; refugees in, 595, *p595*
Taoudenni, 566
tariffs, 95
Tashkent, Uzbekistan, 439
Tasmania, Australia, 736
Tasman Sea, 724
Taurus Mountains, 502
Taxco, Mexico, *p202*
T'bilisi, Georgia, 438
Tchaikovsky, Peter, 395, 412, 434
technology, 97–98, *c98*, *p116*, *p135*, 136, 678–679
tectonics. *See* plate tectonics.
Tehran, Iran, 456, 519, *p519*, *p524*
Tel Aviv-Yafo, Israel, *p508*, 510, 512
telenovelas, 237
temperate climates, 63
temperatures: latitude effects on, 192; ocean, *d56*; winter, *m421*
tenants, 301
Ten Commandments, 474
Tenochtitlán, 199
Teotihuacán, *p199*
Terhazza, 566
terracing, 70, *p71*
terrorism, *p138*, 148–149, 326; defense against, 137–143
Texas (U.S.), *p116*, *p128*, *p152*, 200
textiles, 315
Thailand, *p622–623*, 634, *p708*
thematic maps, 10, *m10*, 86, *m86*
theocracy, 470
Theodosius I, 297
thinking, critical, 416, 598, 702
"Third World," 96
Three Gorges Dam, China, 662, 665
three-toed sloth, *p177*
thunderstorms, 55
Tiananmen Square, Beijing, China, 668
Tian Shan, 392, 439, 660
Tibet, 631, 666, *p666*, 669
tierra caliente altitude, 193
Tierra del Fuego (Chile), *p272*, 273
tierra fria altitude, 193
tierra templada altitude, 193
Tigris River, 454, 456, 466, 517
Tijuana, Mexico, 194
Tikal, Guatemala, 216
timberline, 68
time zones, *m447*, 613, *m613*
Timor, 714
Tirana, Albania, 381
Togo, *c546*, 558
Tokyo, Japan, 691
tolerance, religious, 463
Tolstoy, Leo, 434, 435, *ptg435*
Tombouctou, Mali, 557
Tonga, 733, 761
topsoil, 70

Torah, 473
tornadoes, 55
Toronto, Canada, 160, *p160*, 162, *p168*
tourism: in Antarctica, 766; in Argentina, 239; in Australia, 738; in Botswana, 612; in Brazil, 234; in Bulgaria, 378; in Canada, *p158*; in Caribbean islands, *p219*, 220; in Central America, 215; in China, 661; in Egypt, 486; in France, *p316*, *p345–346*, 345–347; in Georgia, 438; in Greece, 362; in Jordan, *p505*; in Kenya, *p598*, *g598*; in Laos, 710; in the Maldives, 654; in Melanesia, 759; in Mexico, 194; in Micronesia, 761; in Morocco, 492; in New Zealand, 743; in Norway, 354; in Polynesia, 762; in Portugal, 359; in Puerto Rico, 223; in Russia, 408; in Spain, 359; in Tanzania, 579–580; in United States, *p134*, 135
Toussaint-Louverture, Francois-Dominique, 222
trade: ancient routes of, 104; free, 96, 136, 157, 223, 271, 329–330; restrictions on, 693; slave, 147; water transport and, 468; world, 94–96, 136
traditional economic systems, 93
traits, 80
Transantarctic Mountains, 765
Transdanubia region (Hungary), 372
transportation, 98, *c98*
Transportation Security Administration (TSA), 139
Trans-Siberian Railroad, 413, *p417*
Transylvania, *p378*
Treaty of Waitangi, 748–749
trees: coniferous, 64; deciduous, 64; rubber, *p716*; in vegetation map, 349
trenches, in oceans, 41
Trinidad and Tobago, 186, 220, 221
Tripoli, Libya, 491
tropical climate, 62, 130, 176, 243, 558, 626, 652, 715, 724, 758–761
tropical rain forest climate, 62, *p62*, 534
tropical savanna climate, 62, *p62*, 536, 550
Tropic of Cancer, 32, 53, 192, 255
Tropic of Capricorn, 32, 53, 255
Truman Doctrine, 320
tsetse flies, 573, 576
tsunamis, 36, 690
Tuareg, *p557*, 558
Tucson, Arizona (U.S.), *p146*
tundra, 116, 159, *p400*; in Russia, 392, 406, *p407*; in Scandinavia, 282; in United States, 130

tundra climate, 66, *p66*
Tunis, Tunisia, 491
Tunisia, 463, 491
Turkey, 454, 463, 502–504, 507
Turkish Straits, 502
Turkmenistan, 392, 401, 439
Turpan Depression, 631, 661
Tutankhamen, *p466*
Tutsi, 585
Tuvalu, 733, 761
Twain, Mark, 151
Twelve Tables (Roman law), 296
typhoons, 55, 760

Ubangi River, 574
Uganda, 541, *c546, p547,* 582–584
Ukraine, 291, 382–385, *p383,* 410
Ukrainian Easter eggs, 382, *p382*
Ulaanbaatar, Mongolia, *p680,* 681
unalienable rights, 167
undersea earthquakes, 36
Union of South Africa, 606
Union of Soviet Socialist Republics (USSR), 413. *See also* Russia; Russia and Eurasian republics.
unions, 315
United Arab Emirates, *p452,* 463, 515
United Kingdom, 61, 287, 291, 340–342; Australia and, 726, 739; Botswana and, 612; in Egypt, 487; Guyana and, 244; Hong Kong and, 664; India and, 639, 641; Israel and, 511; Jordan and, 506; Kenya and, 579; Maldives and, 654; Myanmar and, 709; New Zealand and, 744; Parliament of, 306–307; Seychelles and, 618; Singapore and, 717; South Africa and, 605–606; Sri Lanka and, 653; Suriname and, 245; Uganda and, 583; Zambia and, 610. *See also* England; Great Britain.
United Nations, 99, 493, 511, 518, 526, 592, 606–607, 699
United Nations Educational, Scientific, and Cultural Organization (UNESCO), 269
United States (U.S.), 24, 114–155; after World War I, 316; American Revolution in, 307; American Samoa and, 761; Caribbean islands and, 221, 223; climate of, 114–116, 130; culture of, 150–152; economic leadership of, 131–132; economy of, 116, 133–135; ethnic groups of, 149–150; extreme points of, *c121, m121;* flag, *p143;* food production of, *m120;* Grand Teton

National Park, Wyoming, *p46–47;* history of, 145–149; landforms of, 114, 126–129; in Mexican history, 200; Micronesia and, 760; North American Free Trade Agreement (NAFTA) and, 136; people of, 116–117; Philippines and, 717; physical geography of, *m118, m127;* political geography of, *m119;* population density of, *m149;* states of, *c122–123;* terrorism and, 137–142; Vietnam and, 712; waterways of, 114
Upper Egypt, *m467,* 470
Upper Volta, 558
Ural Mountains, 394, 404–407, 427
Uranus, 29
urbanization, 90
urban population, 150, *c283, p431,* 487–488, *c627*
urban sprawl, 91
Uruguay, 187, 239, 241–242
U.S. Census Bureau, 108, *p108*
U.S. Coast Guard, 262
U.S. Constitution, 125, 146, 329
U.S. Customs Service, 262, *p262*
U.S. Declaration of Independence, 167
U.S. Department of Defense, 526
U.S. Postal Service, 108
USA Patriot Act, 139
Uzbekistan, 392, 401, 439

Vaidés Peninsula, 183
Vancouver, British Columbia (Canada), *p156–157,* 163
van Gogh, Vincent, 348
vanilla beans, 617
Vanuatu, 733, 758
vaqueros, 193
vassals, 301
Vatican City, 291, 360–361
vegetation, 61–68; in dry climates, 67; in highland climates, 68; in high latitude climates, 65–66, *p66;* in mid-latitude climates, 63–65; regions of, *m64;* spread of, *m229;* in tropical climates, 62
Venezuela, 183, 187, 239, 242–244
Venice, Italy, 360, *p360*
Venus, 29
Verdun, France, *p316*
vernal equinox, 32
Victoria Falls, 534, *p535,* 609
Vienna, Austria, 353, *p353*
Vientiane, Laos, 710
Vietnam, 634, *p634*
Vietnamese language, *p150*
Vikings, 354
Villa, Francisco "Pancho," 200
Villa Las Estrellas, Chile Antarctic Territory, 766–767

Vinson Massif, *g652,* 731, 765
Virgin Islands, 187, 221
Vishnu deity (Hinduism), 640
Vladivostok, Russia, 413, 427
volcanoes, 575, 589, 617, 624, 662, 690–691, *p694,* 715; in Antarctica, 765; in Azores, *p34;* in Caribbean, 219; in Central America, 212; in Chile, 273; in Iceland, 357; in Italy, 360; in Latin America, 176; magma of, 35; in Micronesia, 760; mountains from, 39; Mount Etna, 22; Mt. Pinatubo, *p55;* in New Zealand, 741, 743; in Oceania, 724; Paricutín, *p190;* in Polynesia, 761; Popocatepetl, 192, *p192;* in Russia, 407
Volga River, 392, 406, 408, 427
Volgograd, Russia, *p390,* 406
voting, 733, 744

Waitangi Day, 748
Wales, 340
Walesa, Lech, 370
Walloons, 347
War and Peace **(Tolstoy),** 434, 435
Warsaw, Poland, 370
Warsaw Pact, 321
Washington, D.C. (U.S.), *m33, p53,* 133
Washington (U.S.), 61
Washington, George, *p147*
water: bodies of, 42; in Canada, 114; crisis in North Africa, 498–499, *p498–499;* cycle of, 48–49, *d49;* fresh, 41; management of, 71; in North Africa and Southwest Asia, 454; pollution of, 428; resources of, 49–50; in Russia, 407–408; trade and, 468; in United States, 114; in weathering, 37–38. *See also* oceans.
Water Demand Management Research Network (WDMRN), 499
Watt, James, 315
Wayang kulit, 718
weather, climate and, 52–53
weathering, 37
weaving, 507
Web sites, 528
Weiler, Kaelin, 264
welfare state (Sweden), 355
Wellington, New Zealand, 744
Welsh language, 340
West Africa: coastal countries of, 558–561; Great Mosque of Djenné of, 562; Nigeria, 550–554; physical geography of, *m552;* political geography of, *m551;* population density of,

m560; Sahel countries of, 556–558; salt trade of, 566
West Bank, 511–512, *m511*
western Europe. *See* Europe, western.
Western Ghats, 638
Western Sahara (Morocco), 493
western United States, 134–135
West Indies, 219
West Virginia (U.S.), *p115*
White Nile River, 586
Wieliczka, Poland, *p368*
Wilder, Laura Ingalls, 151
Williams, Serena, *p265*
Williams, Venus, *p265*
windmills, *p92*
winds, 38; climate and, 54–56; electricity from, *p92*; landforms and, 56–57; prevailing, *m54*; sirocco, 360
windward side, 57
Winkel Tripel projection, 7, *m7*
winter solstice, 32
Wojtyla, Karol (Pope John Paul II), 371
women's rights, 634
wood-block printing, *p695*
World Health Organization (WHO), 576
world trade, 94–96, 136
World Trade Center, New York (U.S.), 138, 141, 520; memorial on site of, 141, *d141, d143*

World War I, 148, 316, 504
World War II, 148, 317, 370, *p421*, 511, 676, 692, 694, 761
World Wide Web, 106
World Wildlife Federation, 446
writing reports, 763
Wudi (Chinese Emperor), 686
Wyoming (U.S.), *p46–47*

Xhosa, 605
Xi River, 662

Yagua, *p104*
yaks, *p651*
Yalu River, 699, 701
Yamoussoukro, Côte d'Ivoire, 561
Yangon, Myanmar, 709
Yangtze River, 624, 631, 662
Yap Island, Micronesia, *p760*
Yeats, William Butler, 343
yellow fever, 218
Yellow River, 624, 662
Yellowstone National Park, 135
Yeltsin, Boris, 430, *p430*
Yemen, *p456, 463, 516*
Yenisey River, 394
Yerevan, Armenia, 437

Yokohama, Japan, 691
Yoruba, 552; wooden masks of, *p555*
Yucatán Peninsula, 191, *p197*, 198
Yugoslavia, *p90*, 323, 379
yurts, *p438,* 681

Zagreb, Croatia, 379
Zagros Mountains, 454, 519
Zaire (Democratic Republic of the Congo), 573
Zambezi River, 534, 609, 610
Zambia, *c546, p610*
Zanzibar, 580–581
Zapata, Emiliano, 200
Zealand Island, Denmark, 356
Zhang Qian, 686
Zhou Enlai, 667
ziggurat, 467
Zimbabwe, *c546,* 610–611
Zionists, 511
Zlata's Diary (Filipovic), 380
Zulu, 605
Zurich, Switzerland, 352
Zvezda space station module, 409

INDEX

Text

99 From **Millennium Report, April 3, 2000** by Kofi Annan, secretary-general of the United Nations. United Nations Press Release SG/SM/7343 GA/9705, April 3, 2000. Copyright 2001 by United Nations; **152 Survival This Way** by Simon J. Ortiz. Reprinted by permission of the author. **I, Too** in *Collected Poems* by Langston Hughes. Copyright 1994 by the Estate of Langston Hughes. Reprinted by permission of Alfred A. Knopf, a Division of Random House, Inc; **167 A Declaration of First Nations.** Copyright 2001 by Assembly of First Nations National Indian Brotherhood. (http://www.afn.ca/About%AFN/a_declaration_of_first_nations.htm) **235** From **Botoque, Bringer of Fire** in *Folklore, Myths, and Legends, a World Perspective,* edited by Donna Rosenberg. Copyright 1977. NTC Publishing; **246** From **The Gaucho Martín Fierro** adapted from the Spanish and rendered into English verse by Walter Owen. Copyright 1936 by Farrar & Rinehart. Reprinted by permission of Henry Holt and Company, LLC; **306** From **The Scarlet Pimpernel** by Baroness Orzy. Copyright 1961 Doubleday and Company, Inc; **380** From **Zlata's Diary: A Child's Life in Sarajevo** translated with notes by Christina Pribichevich-Zoric. Translation copyright by Fixot et editions Robert Laffont, 1994 Viking, published by the Penguin Group, Penguin Books USA Inc. NY; **432** From **Nobel Lecture, 1972** by Alexander Isayevich Solzhenitsyn in *Bartlett's Familiar Quotations.* Copyright 1992 by Little, Brown and Company Inc, Boston; **435 The Grandfather and His Little Grandson** by Leo Tolstoy in *A Harvest of Russian Children's Literature,* edited by Miriam Morton. Copyright 1967 by Miriam Morton. University of California Press, Berkeley and Los Angeles, CA; **489** From **The Black Prince and Other Egyptian Folk Tales** told by Ahmed and Zane Zagloul. Copyright 1971 by Doubleday & Company, Inc., Garden City, NY; **578** From **Where are those Songs** by Micere G. Mugo. Reprinted by permission of the author; **606** From **Long Walk to Freedom: The Autobiography of Nelson Mandela** by Nelson Mandela. Copyright 1994 by Nelson Rolihlahla Mandela. Little, Brown and Company; **692** From **Sadako and the Thousand Paper Cranes** by Eleanor Coerr. Copyright 1977. The Putnam Publishing Group; **697** From **Haiku, Volume II.** Copyright 1952 by R.H. Blyth. Reprinted by permission of Hokuseido Press; **737** From **Great Mother Snake** an Aboriginal legend. Glencoe would like to acknowledge the artists and agencies who participated in illustrating this program: Ortelius Design, Inc.

Photographs

Cover (top to bottom) AI Interactive, CORBIS, Grant Faint/Getty Images, Getty Images, Pacific Stock, *Pablo Corral Vega/CORBIS, CORBIS, (bkgd) AI Interactive; **1** (t)Dallas & John Heaton/CORBIS, Jamie Herron/CORBIS, Owen Franken/CORBIS; **2, 3, 16–17** Getty Images; **18** (t)CORBIS, (b)Robert Landau/CORBIS; **18–19** S. Purdy Matthews/Getty Images; **20–21** Norman Kent Productions/oi2.com; **22** NASA/National Geographic Image Collection; **23** (t)Richard T. Nowitz/National Geographic Image Collection, (b)Yann Arthus-Bertrand/CORBIS; **25** Galen Rowell/CORBIS; **26** (l)Shelly Grossman/Woodfin Camp, (tr)Christie's Images/CORBIS, (br)Getty Images; **28** file photo; **29** Maria Stenzel/National Geographic Image Collection; **30** Timothy G. Laman/National Geographic Image Collection; **34** Natalie Fobes/National Geographic Image Collection; **37** Michael K. Nichols/National Geographic Image Collection; **39** David Doubilet/National Geographic Image Collection; **40** Michael K. Nichols/National Geographic Image Collection, (inset)Wolfgang Kaehler/CORBIS; **46–47** Digital Vision/Getty Images; **48** George Grall/National Geographic Image Collection; **51** Southampton Oceanography Centre; **52** J. Blair/National Geographic Image Collection; **53** Medford Taylor/National Geographic Image Collection; **55** CORBIS; **61** Phil Schermeister/National Geographic Image Collection; **62** (l)Michael K. Nichols/National Geographic Image Collection, (r)Beverly Joubert/National Geographic Image Collection; **65** (l)James P. Blair/National Geographic Image Collection, (tr)Annie Griffiths Belt/National Geographic Image Collection, (c)Jodi Cobb/National Geographic Image Collection, (br)Raymond K. Gehman/National Geographic Image Collection; **66** (t)Natalie Fobes/National Geographic Image Collection, (c)George F. Mobley/National Geographic Image Collection, (b)Raymond Gehman/CORBIS; **67** (l)James L. Stanfield/National Geographic Image Collection, (r)Phil Schemeister/National Geographic Image Collection; **68** Pat Jerrold Papilio/CORBIS; **69** Bryan & Cherry Alexander; **70** Jodi Cobb/National Geographic Image Collection; **71** Robert Harding/CORBIS; **76** (l)Gerry Ellis/ENP Images, (r)Jose Azel/Aurora/PictureQuest; **77** (t c)Lisa Hoffner/Wildeye Photography, (b)Art Wolfe/Getty Images; **78–79** Anthony Cassidy/Getty Images; **80** Kenneth Garrett/National Geographic Image Collection; **87** Gerd Ludwig/National Geographic Image Collection; **90** AFP/CORBIS; **92** Jim Sugar Photography/CORBIS; **93** Steve McCurry/National Geographic Image Collection; **97** AP/Wide World Photo; **98** (t)Private Collection/The Bridgeman Art Library, (tc bc)Glencoe file, (b)NASA; **99** AFP/CORBIS; **108** Bettmann/CORBIS; **112** (l)Steve McCurry, (r)Michael Lewis; **112–113** David R. Stoecklein; **115** Susie Post, (inset)Norbert Rosing; **116** Richard Nowitz/Phototake/PictureQuest; **117** Eugene Fisher and Barbara Brundege; **124–125** Mitchell Funk/Getty Images; **126** David Hiser/National Geographic Image Collection; **128** (l)Steven L. Raymer/National Geographic Image Collection, (r)Vincent Musl/National Geographic Image Collection; **129** Roy Corral/Getty Images; **131** AP/Wide World Photos; **133** Gregory Scott Doramus/Omnigraphix; **134** (l)Getty Images, (r)Marvin E. Newman/Getty Images; **135** Joel Satore/National Geographic Image Collection; **145** CORBIS; **146** Ira Block/National Geographic Image Collection; **147** The White House Historical Association; **150** Mary Kate Denny/PhotoEdit; **152** CORBIS; **156–157** SuperStock; **158** Raymond K. Gehman/National Geographic Image Collection; **160** Diaphor Agency/Index Stock; **162** David A. Harvey/National Geographic Image Collection; **164** (l)Daniel J. Wiener/National Geographic Image Collection, (r)Aaron Haupt; **165** Marie-Louise Brimberg/National Geographic Image Collection; **166** Michael Evan Sewell/Visual Pursuit; **167** Index Stock Imagery/PictureQuest; **168** Marie-Louise Brimberg/National Geographic Image Collection; **170** Reuters NewMedia/CORBIS; **171** Richard T. Nowitz/National Geographic Image Collection; **174** (l)David Levy/Getty Images, (r)Oliver Benn/Getty Images; **174–175** Kenneth Garrett/National Geographic Society Image Collection; **177** Norbert Wu/Getty Images, (inset)William J. Hebert/Getty Images; **178** Sisse Brimberg; **179** Chad Ehlers/Getty Images; **187** Michael K. Nichols/National Geographic Image Collection; **188–189** Randy Faris/CORBIS; **190** Bettmann/CORBIS; **192** Albert Moldvay/National Geographic Image Collection; **194** Joel Satore/National Geographic Image Collection; **197** Tomasz Tomaszewski/National Geographic Image Collection; **199** Vladimir Pcholkin/Getty Images; **201** James L. Amos/National Geographic Image Collection; **202** David A. Harvey/National Geographic Image Collection; **203** Peter Menzel/Stock Boston; **204** Tomas Tomaszewski/National Geographic Image Collection; **210–211** Sylvain Grandadam/Getty Images; **212** Art Wolfe; **215** (t)Jan Butchofsky-Houser/CORBIS, (b)Vincent Musl/National Geographic Image Collection; **216** Michael S. Yamashita/CORBIS; **219** Jonathan Blair/National Geographic Image Collection; **221** (l)Tony Arruza/CORBIS, (r)Michael K. Nichols/National Geographic Image Collection; **222** Robert A. Tyrrell; **225** George Mobley/National Geographic Image Collection; **228** (l)Getty Images, (r)Giraudon/Art Resource, NY; **229** Loren McIntyre; **230–231** Layne Kennedy/CORBIS; **232** Alex Webb/Magnum; **235** Kennan Ward/CORBIS Stock Market; **236** (l)Jim Zuckerman/CORBIS, (r)Yann Arthus-Bertrand/CORBIS; **238** Jeremy Horner/CORBIS; **239** Louis O. Mazzatenta/National Geographic Image Collection; **242** Robert Caputo/Aurora; **243** Pablo Corral V/CORBIS; **244** Jacques Jangoux/Getty Images; **246** Kit Houghton Photography/CORBIS; **247** Winfield I. Parks, Jr./National Geographic Image Collection; **250** (t bl)Michael & Patricia Fogden, (br)William Albert Allard; **250–251** Stuart Franklin; **251** (t)Marc Van Roosmalen/Conservation International, (b)Michael Doolittle; **252–253** Paul Harris/Getty Images; **256** Richard S. Durrance/National Geographic Image Collection; **266** Frank & Helen Schreider/National Geographic Image Collection; **268** Michael J. Doolittle/The Image Works; **270** Art Wolfe; **271** Maria Stenzel/National Geographic Image Collection; **272** (l)Richard T. Nowitz/National Geographic Image Collection, (r)James L. Stanfield/National Geographic Image Collection; **275** William A. Allard/National Geographic Image Collection; **278** (t)IFA-Bilderteam-Travel/Bruce Coleman Inc., (b)Robert Everts/Getty Images; **278–279** SuperStock; **281** D.C. Lowe/Getty Images, (inset)Chris Haigh/Getty Images; **282** Bert Blokhuis/Getty Images; **283** Ron Sanford/Getty Images; **291** Mary Kate Denny/PhotoEdit; **292–293** Christian Sarramon/CORBIS; **294** Ira Block/National Geographic Image Collection; **295** Vanni Archive/CORBIS; **296** Richard T. Nowitz/National Geographic Image Collection; **297** Museo della Civilta Romana, Rome/Art Resource, NY; **299** Richard List/CORBIS; **302** Archivo Iconografico, SA/CORBIS; **303** David Lees/CORBIS; **304** Sistine Chapel, Vatican, Rome/Fratelli Alinari/SuperStock; **305** The Art Archive; **306** Matt Meadows; **308** (l)Bettmann/CORBIS, (r)Gianni Dagli Orti/CORBIS; **312–313** Philippa Lewis/CORBIS; **314** The Art Archive/Dagli Orti/Musee National d'Art Moderne, Paris; **315** Culver Pictures, Inc.; **316** (l)CORBIS, (r)Craig Aurness/CORBIS; **317** Hulton-Deutsch Collection/CORBIS; **318** V. Yudin/Sovfoto/Eastfoto/PictureQuest; **319** Owen Franken/CORBIS; **322** (l)Culver Pictures/PictureQuest, (r)Bettmann/CORBIS; **324** James Stanfield/National Geographic Image

ACKNOWLEDGMENTS

Collection; **325** AFP/CORBIS; **338–339** Photowood, Inc./CORBIS Stock Market; **340** London Aerial Photo Library/CORBIS; **342** Stephen Beer/Getty Images; **343** Tim Thompson/CORBIS; **344** Adam Woolfitt/CORBIS; **345** James L. Stanfield/National Geographic Image Collection; **346** (t)Brand X/Getty Images, (r)Jonathan P. Blair/National Geographic Image Collection; **347** Michael John Kielty/CORBIS; **350** Ric Ergenbright/CORBIS; **351** Owen Franken/CORBIS; **352** Sisse Brimberg/National Geographic Image Collection; **353** AFP/CORBIS; **354** Tomasz Tomaszewski/National Geographic Image Collection; **355** (l)Buddy May/CORBIS, (r)Richard S. Durrance/National Geographic Image Collection; **356** Sisse Brimberg/National Geographic Image Collection; **357** SuperStock; **358** David Cumming, Eye Ubiquitous/CORBIS; **359** Gerard Degeorge/CORBIS; **360** (t)Getty Images, (b)Vittoriano Rastelli/CORBIS; **361** Louis O. Mazzatenta/National Geographic Image Collection; **362** A. Ramey/PhotoEdit; **366** Brand X/Getty Images; **366–367** Foto World/Getty Images; **368** Tomasz Tomaszewski/National Geographic Image Collection; **370** James L. Stanfield/National Geographic Image Collection; **371** Steven L. Raymer/National Geographic Image Collection; **372** Peter Blakely/CORBIS Saba; **373** Dean Conger/CORBIS; **374** Stephanie Heimann/Sovfoto; **376** James Stanfield/National Geographic Image Collection; **377** Steve Raymer/CORBIS; **378** Peter Wilson/CORBIS; **379** Francoise de Mulder/CORBIS; **380** Aaron Haupt; **381** Catherine Karnow/CORBIS; **382** (l)Kelly-Mooney Photography/CORBIS, (r)Craig Aurness/CORBIS; **383** Gerd Ludwig/National Geographic Image Collection; **390** (l)Bruce Dale, (r)Alain Le Garsmeur/Getty Images; **390–391** Marc Moritsch/National Geographic Society Image Collection; **393** Simeone Huber/Getty Images, (inset)Jay Dickman; **394** B. Klipinitsen, M. Moshkov/Sovfoto/Eastfoto/PictureQuest; **395** Michael Nichols/National Geographic Image Collection; **400** Paul Harris/Getty Images; **401** KS Studios; **402–403** John Lamb/Getty Images; **404** Tom Brakefield/CORBIS; **406** Bryan & Cherry Alexander; **407** (l)Andre Gallant/Getty Images, (c)Wolfgang Kaehler/CORBIS, (r)A. Solomonov/Sovfoto/Easfoto/PictureQuest; **409** NASA; **410** Giraudon/Art Resource, NY; **411** Stock Montage; **414** Marc Garanger/CORBIS; **415** David & Peter Turnley/CORBIS; **416** Farrell Grehan/CORBIS; **417** Wolfgang Kaehler/CORBIS; **420** Giraudon/Art Resource, NY; **421** Sovfoto/Eastfoto/PictureQuest; **422–423** David & Peter Turnley/CORBIS; **424** Gerd Ludwig/National Geographic Image Collection; **427** Steve Kokker/Lonely Planet Images; **429** Sisse Brimberg/National Geographic Image Collection; **430** Shone/Sipa Press; **431** (l)Marc Garanger/CORBIS, (r)David Turnley/CORBIS; **432** Richard Howard/Black Star Publishing/PictureQuest; **433** Kremlin Museums–Moscow–Russia/Bridgeman Art Library; **434** Bob Krist/CORBIS; **435** Roger-Viollet/Musee du Petit Palais, Paris/Bridgeman Art Library, London/New York; **436** Wolfgang Kaehler; **438** Index Stock Imagery/PictureQuest; **439** Gerd Ludwig/National Geographic Image Collection; **448** Gerd Ludwig/National Geographic Image Collection; **449** Michael S. Yamashita/CORBIS; **452** (t)Hugh Sitton/Getty Images, (b)David Coulson; **452–453** X. Richer/Hoaqui, Photo Researchers; **455** James Strachan/Getty Images; **456** Getty Images; **457** Wayne Eastep/Getty Images; **463** AP/Wide World Photo; **464–465** Wolfgang Kaehler; **466** Kenneth Garrett/National Geographic Image Collection; **469** (l)Gianni Dagli Orti/CORBIS, (r)Charles & Josette Lenars/CORBIS; **470** Wolfgang Kaehler; **472** Steve Vidler/SuperStock; **473** Gary Cralle/Getty Images; **475** (t)CMCD/Photodisc, (c)C Squared Studios/Photodisc, (b)Robert Harding/CORBIS; **478** AP/Wide World Photos; **479** Kenneth Garrett/National Geographic Image Collection; **482–483** W.N. Westermann/CORBIS; **484** Stephen Studd/Getty Images; **487** AP/Wide World; **489** Owen Franken/CORBIS; **490** George Steinmetz/National Geographic Image Collection; **491–492** K.M. Westermann/CORBIS; **495** Reza/National Geographic Image Collection; **498** Ed Kashi; **498–499** James L. Stanfield; **499** (l)Ed Kashi, (r)Courtesy of Sandra Postel; **500–501** Wolfgang Kaehler/CORBIS; **502** Patrick Ward/CORBIS; **504** James L. Stanfield/National Geographic Image Collection; **505** Annie Griffiths Belt/National Geographic Image Collection; **507** Arthur Thevenart/CORBIS; **508** I. Talby/Index Stock; **510** Richard T. Nowitz/CORBIS; **513** James L. Stanfield/National Geographic Image Collection; **516** J. Stanfield/National Geographic Image Collection; **517** Charles & Josette Lenars/CORBIS; **519** (l)Alexandra Avakian/National Geographic Image Collection, (r)Jon Spaull/CORBIS; **522** (l)AP/Wide World Photos, (c)Ali Fraidoon/AP, (r)Langeuin Jacques/CORBIS Sygma; **523** (l)Suhaib Salam/Reuters/Newscom, (r)Murad Sezer/AP; **524** Hasan Sarbakhshian/AP; **525** Rina Castelnuovo/AP; **526** Douglas Graham/Roll Call Photos/Newscom; **528** Doug Martin; **532** (l)Hugh Sitton/Getty Images, (r)Jacques Jangoux/Getty Images; **532–533** Manoj Shah/Getty Images; **535** Ian Murphy/Getty Images, (inset)Renee Lynn/Getty Images; **536** Ian Murphy/Getty Images; **537** Will Curtis/Getty Images; **546** David & Peter Turnley/CORBIS; **547** Nicholas Parfitt/Getty Images; **548–549** Paul Almasy/CORBIS; **550** AP/Wide World Photos; **553** (l)AP/Wide World Photos, (r)Robert W. Moore/National Geographic Image Collection; **555** (l)Bowers Museum of Cultural Art/CORBIS, (r)Davis Factor/CORBIS; **556** Steve McCurry/Magnum Photos, Inc.; **557** Carol Beckwith & Angela Fisher/Robert Estall Photo Agency; **559** Robert W. Moore/National Geographic Image Collection; **562** Nik Wheeler/CORBIS; **563** AP/Wide World Photos; **566** Michael A. Hampshire; **567** James L. Stanfield; **568–569** W. Perry Conway/CORBIS; **570** AP/Wide World Photos; **571** Michael K. Nichols/National Geographic Image Collection; **573** Daniel Laine/CORBIS; **574** (l)Ann and Carl Purcell/Words & Pictures/PictureQuest, (r)James A. Sugar/Black Star Publishing/PictureQuest; **576** David Turnley/CORBIS; **577–578** Carol Beckwith & Angela Fisher/Robert Estall Photo Agency; **579** The Purcell Team/CORBIS; **581** Frank Lane Picture Agency/CORBIS; **582** Art Wolfe; **584** Chinch Gryniewicz/Ecoscene/CORBIS; **586** Dave Bartruff/CORBIS; **588** AP/Wide World Photos; **595** AFP Photo/Newscom; **598** Darrell Gulin/CORBIS; **602–603** Pictor; **604** Wolfgang Kaehler; **606** Turnley Collection/CORBIS; **607** Nik Wheeler/CORBIS; **609** Walter Edwards/National Geographic Image Collection; **610** Chris Johns/National Geographic Image Collection; **611** Robert Holmes/CORBIS; **614** Des & Jen Bartlett/National Geographic Image Collection; **616** AP/Wide World Photos; **617** Art Wolfe/Getty Images; **619** National Geographic Society Image Collection; **622** (l)Tim Davis/Getty Images, (r)David Sutherland/Getty Images; **622–623** Waranun Chutchawan-Tipakorn; **625** Hilarie Kavanagh/Getty Images, (inset)Martin Puddy/Getty Images; **626** Paul Chesley/Getty Images; **627** Steve McCurry/National Geographic Image Collection; **634** Steve Raymer/CORBIS; **635** Keren Su/Getty Images; **636–637** Tibor Bognar/CORBIS Stock Market; **638** George F. Mobley/National Geographic Image Collection; **639** Steve McCurry/National Geographic Image Collection; **640** (t)Oriental Museum, Durham University, UK/The Bridgeman Art Library, London/New York, (b)Lindsay Hebberd/CORBIS; **641** (l)SuperStock, (c)Bettmann/CORBIS, (r)Hulton/Archive; **643** Brian Vikander/CORBIS; **644** Jonathan Blair/National Geographic Image Collection; **646** Brian Vikander/CORBIS; **647** Ed Kashi/National Geographic Image Collection; **649** Steve McCurry/National Geographic Image Collection; **651** Paul Chesley/Getty Images; **655** Robert Holmes/CORBIS; **658–659** Christopher Arnesen/Getty Images; **660** Keren Su/CORBIS; **663** (t)Michele Burgess/CORBIS, (b)Kevin R. Morris/CORBIS; **665** Bob Sacha; **666** AFP/CORBIS; **667** The Telegraph Colour Library/FPG; **669** Joseph Sohm/ChromoSohm Inc./CORBIS; **670** (t)Freer Gallery of Art, Washington, DC, (b)Bonhams, London, UK/Bridgeman Art Library; **678** How-Man Wong/CORBIS; **679** Marc Garanger/CORBIS; **680** Nik Wheeler/CORBIS; **681** James L. Stanfield/National Geographic Image Collection; **682** AFP/CORBIS; **686** Cary Wolinsky/Stock Boston; **687** Keren Su/CORBIS; **688–689** Dallas and John Heaton/CORBIS; **690** Reuters NewMedia Inc./CORBIS; **692** Steve Cole/Photodisc; **693** Karen Kasmauski/Matrix; **694** Roger Ressmeyer/CORBIS; **695** (t)Christie's Images/CORBIS, (b)Will & Deni McIntyre/Getty Images; **697** Asian Art & Archaeology, Inc./CORBIS; **698** Carmen Redondo/CORBIS; **699** (l)Nathan Benn/CORBIS, (r)Wolfgang Kaehler/CORBIS; **703** Neil Beer/CORBIS; **706–707** Bob Krist/Getty Images; **708–710** Paul Chesley/National Geographic Image Collection; **711** Kevin R. Morris/CORBIS; **714** Roger Ressmeyer/CORBIS; **716** Earl & Nazima Kowall/CORBIS; **718** David Hanson/Getty Images; **719** AP/Wide World Photos; **722** (l)David Madison/Getty Images, (r)David Hiser/Getty Images; **722–723** Oliver Strewe/Getty Images; **725** Oliver Strewe/Getty Images, (inset)Johnny Johnson/Getty Images; **726** Nicholas DeVore/Getty Images; **727** Glen Allison/Getty Images; **733** Elaine Shay; **734–735** Larry Williams/CORBIS Stock Market; **736** R. Ian Productions P Lloyd/National Geographic Image Collection; **737** Penny Tweedie/CORBIS; **738** (t)Australian Picture Library/CORBIS, (b)Horniman Museum, London, UK/Heini Schneebeli/Bridgeman Art Library; **739** (t)Paul A. Souders/CORBIS, (bl)Earl & Nazima Kowall/CORBIS, (br)Charles Philip Cangialosi/CORBIS; **740** (t)Australian Picture Library/CORBIS, (b)Earl & Nazima Kowall/CORBIS, Charles Philip Cangialosi/CORBIS; **741** Kevin Fleming/CORBIS; **743** Neil Rabinowitz/CORBIS; **752** Kevin Fleming/CORBIS; **753** Larry Mulvehill/Image Works; **756–757** Dana Edmunds/FPG; **758** Hal Beral/CORBIS; **760** (l)Ben Simmons/CORBIS Stock Market, (r)SuperStock; **763** David Doublet/National Geographic Image Collection; **764** Wolfgang Kaehler/CORBIS; **765** (l)SuperStock, (r)David Madison/Getty Images; **766** Underwood & Underwood/CORBIS; **768** Galen Rowell/CORBIS; **769** AP/Wide World Photos; **772** Christine Osborne/CORBIS; **772–773** Penny Tweedie/CORBIS; **773** (t)PhotoDisc, (c)Bettmann/CORBIS, (b)George F. Mobley; **774** Getty Images.